RELIABLE COMPUTER SYSTEMS

RELIABLE COMPUTER SYSTEMS

DESIGN AND EVALUATION

THIRD EDITION

Daniel P. Siewiorek

Carnegie Mellon University
Pittsburgh, Pennsylvania

Robert S. Swarz

Worcester Polytechnic Institute
Worcester, Massachusetts

CRC Press
Taylor & Francis Group
Boca Raton London New York

CRC Press is an imprint of the
Taylor & Francis Group, an **informa** business

AN A K PETERS BOOK

First published 1998 by A K Peters, Ltd.

Published 2018 by CRC Press
Taylor & Francis Group
6000 Broken Sound Parkway NW, Suite 300
Boca Raton, FL 33487-2742

First issued in paperback 2019

No claim to original U.S. Government works

ISBN 13: 978-0-367-44764-9 (pbk)
ISBN 13: 978-1-56881-092-8 (hbk)

Visit the Taylor & Francis Web site at
http://www.taylorandfrancis.com

and the CRC Press Web site at
http://www.crcpress.com

Trademark products mentioned in the book are listed on page 890.

Library of Congress Cataloging-in-Publication Data
Siewiorek, Daniel P.
    Reliable computer systems : design and evaluation / Daniel P.
Siewiorek, Robert S. Swarz. – 3rd ed.
      p. cm.
    First ed. published under title: The theory and practice of
reliable system design.
    Includes bibliographical references and index.
    ISBN 1-56881-092-X
    1. Electronic digital computers – Reliability. 2. Fault-tolerant
computing. I. Swarz, Robert S. II. Siewiorek, Daniel P. Theory
and practice of reliablesystem design. III. Title.
    QA76.5.S537 1998   98-202237
    004-dc21   CIP

CREDITS

Figure 1-3: Eugene Foley, "The Effects of Microelectronics Revolution on Systems and Board Test," *Computers,* Vol. 12, No. 10 (October 1979). Copyright © 1979 IEEE. Reprinted by permission.

Figure 1-6: S. Russell Craig, "Incoming Inspection and Test Programs," *Electronics Test* (October 1980). Reprinted by permission.

Credits are continued on pages 885-890, which are considered a
continuation of the copyright page.

To Karon and Lonnie

A Special Remembrance:

During the development of this book, a friend, colleague, and fault-tolerant pioneer passed away. Dr. Wing N. Toy documented his 37 years of experience in designing several generations of fault-tolerant computers for the Bell System electronic switching systems described in Chapter 8. We dedicate this book to Dr. Toy in the confidence that his writings will continue to influence designs produced by those who learn from these pages.

CONTENTS

PREFACE

System reliability has been a major concern since the beginning of the electronic digital computer age. The earliest computers were constructed of components such as relays and vacuum tubes that would fail to operate correctly as often as once every hundred thousand or million cycles. This error rate was far too large to ensure correct completion of even modest calculations requiring tens of millions of operating cycles. The Bell relay computer (c. 1944) performed a computation twice and compared results; it also employed error-detecting codes. The first commercial computer, the UNIVAC I (c. 1951), utilized extensive parity checking and two arithmetic logic units (ALUs) in a match-and-compare mode. Today, interest in reliability pervades the computer industry—from large mainframe manufacturers to semiconductor fabricators who produce not only reliability-specific chips (such as for error-correcting codes) but also entire systems.

Computer designers have to be students of reliability, and so do computer system users. Our dependence on computing systems has grown so great that it is becoming difficult or impossible to return to less sophisticated mechanisms. When an airline seat selection computer "crashes," for example, the airline can no longer revert to assigning seats from a manual checklist; since the addition of round-trip check-in service, there is no way of telling which seats have been assigned to passengers who have not yet checked in without consulting the computer. The last resort is a free-for-all rush for seats. The computer system user must be able to understand the advantages and limitations of the state-of-the-art in reliability design; determine the impact of those advantages and limitations upon the application or computation at hand; and specify the requirements for the system's reliability so that the application or computation can be successfully completed.

The literature on reliability has been slow to evolve. During the 1950s reliability was the domain of industry, and the quality of the design often depended on the cleverness of an individual engineer. Notable exceptions are the work of Shannon [1948] and Hamming [1950] on communication through noisy (hence error-inducing) channels, and of Moore and Shannon [1956] and von Neumann [1956] on redundancy that survives component failures. Shannon and Hamming inaugurated the field of coding theory, a cornerstone in contemporary systems design. Moore, Shannon, and von Neumann laid the foundation for development and mathematical evaluation of redundancy techniques.

During the 1960s the design of reliable systems received systematic treatment in industry. Bell Telephone Laboratories designed and built an Electronic Switching System (ESS), with a goal of only two hours' downtime in 40 years [Downing, Nowak, and Tuomenoksa, 1964]. The IBM System/360 computer family had extensive serviceability features [Carter et al., 1964]. Reliable design also found increasing use in the aerospace industry, and a triplicated computer helped man land on the moon [Cooper and Chow,

1976; Dickinson, Jackson, and Randa, 1964]. The volume of literature also increased. In 1962 a Symposium on Redundancy Techniques held in Washington, D.C., led to the first comprehensive book on the topic [Wilcox and Mann, 1962]. Later, Pierce [1965] published a book generalizing and analyzing the Quadded Redundancy technique proposed by Tryon and reported in Wilcox and Mann [1962]. A community of reliability theoreticians and practitioners was developing.

During the 1970s interest in system reliability expanded explosively. Companies were formed whose major product was a reliable system (such as Tandem). Due to the effort of Algirdas Avizienis and other pioneers, a Technical Committee on Fault Tolerant Computing (TCFTC) was formulated within the Institute of Electrical and Electronic Engineers (IEEE). Every year since 1971, the TCFTC has held an International Symposium on Fault-Tolerant Computing.

In 1982, when the first edition of *The Theory and Practice of Reliable System Design* was published, the time was ripe for a book on the design of reliable computing structures. The book was divided into two parts—the first being devoted to the fundamental concepts and theory and the second being populated with a dozen chapters that represented detailed case studies. The second edition follows the same basic structure, but is divided into three parts. Part I deals with the theory and Parts II and III with the practice of reliable design. The appendices provide detailed information on coding theory, design for testability, and the MIL-HDBK-217 component reliability model.

In recent years, the number of reliability and redundancy techniques has continued to expand, along with renewed emphasis on software techniques, application of older techniques to newer areas, and in-depth analytical evaluation to compare and contrast many techniques. In Part I, Chapters 3 and 5 have been expanded to include these new results. More case studies have been developed on the frequency and manifestation of hardware and software system failures. Chapter 2 has been updated to include summaries of this new material. Likewise, Chapter 4 has been enlarged to cover testing techniques commencing with prototypes through manufacturing, field installation, and field repair. The new additions to Part I have resulted in over a 50 percent increase in the number of references cited in the second edition over the first edition.

Part II of the second edition has undergone an even more dramatic change. In the first edition, Part II surveyed twelve different computer systems, ranging from one-of-a-kind research vehicles to mass-produced general-purpose commercial systems. The commercial systems focused on error detection and retry and represented three of the case studies. Four case studies represented one-of-a-kind research systems. Three other systems sought limited deployment in aerospace and message-switching applications. Only two of the case studies represented wider-spread deployment of fault-tolerant systems numbering in the thousands. Furthermore, each case study represented almost a unique architecture with little agreement as to the dominant approach for building fault-tolerant systems.

In the intervening years between the first and second editions, fault tolerance has established itself as a major segment of the computing market. The number of deployed fault-tolerant systems is measured in the tens of thousands. Manufacturers are developing the third- and fourth-generation systems so that we can look back at the evolutionary trajectory of these "fault-tolerant computer families." There has also been a convergence with respect to the system architecture of preference. While the commercial systems still depend upon error detection and retry, the high-reliability systems rely upon triplication and voting, and the high-availability systems depend upon duplication and matching. The case studies have been reduced to nine in order for more space to be devoted to technical details as well as evolutionary family growth. Two case studies represent general-purpose commercial systems, three represent research and aerospace systems, and four represent high-availability systems. The approaches used in each of these three application areas can be compared and contrasted. Of special interest are the subtle variations upon duplication and matching used by all four high-availability architectures. In total, almost 50 percent of the material in the second edition is new with respect to the first edition.

This book has three audiences. The first is the advanced undergraduate student interested in reliable design; as prerequisites, this student should have had courses in introductory programming, computer organization, digital design, and probability. In 1983, the IEEE Computer Society developed a model program in computer science and engineering. This program consisted of nine core modules, four laboratory modules, and fifteen advanced subject areas. One of those advanced subject areas was "fault-tolerant computing." Table P–1 illustrates how this book can be used in support of the module on fault-tolerant computing.

TABLE P–1

Mapping of the book to modules in Subject Area 20: Fault-Tolerant Computing, of the 1983 IEEE Computer Society Model Undergraduate Program in Computer Science and Engineering

Module	Appropriate Chapter
1. Need for Fault-Tolerant Systems: Applications, fault avoidance, fault tolerance, levels of implementation elements	Ch. 1, Fundamental Concepts Ch. 3, Reliability Techniques
2. Faults and Their Manifestations: Sources, characteristics, effects, modeling	Ch. 2, Faults and Their Manifestations
3. Error Detection: Duplication, timeouts, parity checks	Ch. 3, Reliability Techniques
4. Protective Redundancy: Functional replication, information redundancy, temporal methods	Ch. 3, Reliability Techniques
5. Fault-Tolerant Software: N-version programming, recovery blocks, specification validation, proof, mutation	Ch. 3, Reliability Techniques
6. Measures of Fault Tolerance: Reliability models, coverage, availability, maintainability	Ch. 5, Evaluaton Criteria Ch. 6, Financial Considerations
7. Case Studies	Introduction to Part II and further examples from Chapters 7 to 11 as time permits

The second audience is the graduate student seeking a second course in reliable design, perhaps as a prelude to engaging in research. The more advanced portions of Part I and the system examples of Part II should be augmented by other books and current research literature as suggested in Table P–2. A project, such as design of a dual system with a mean-time-to-failure that is an order of magnitude greater than nonredundant systems while minimizing life-cycle costs, would help to crystallize the material for students. An extensive bibliography provides access to the literature.

The third audience is the practicing engineer. A major goal of this book is to provide enough concepts to enable the practicing engineer to incorporate comprehensive reliability techniques into his or her next design. Part I provides a taxonomy of reliability techniques and the mathematical models to evaluate them. Design techniques are illustrated through the series of articles in Part II, which describe actual implementations of reliable computers. These articles were written by the system designers. The final chapter provides a methodology for reliable system design and illustrates how this methodology can be applied in an actual design situation (the DEC VAXft 310).

Acknowledgments. The authors wish to express deep gratitude to many colleagues in the fault-tolerant computing community. Without their contributions and assistance this book could not have been written. We are especially grateful to the authors of the papers who shared their design insights with us.

Special thanks go to Joel Bartlett (DEC-Western), Wendy Bartlett (Tandem), Thomas Bissett (DEC), Doug Bossen (IBM), William Bruckert (DEC), Richard Carr (Tandem), Kate Connolly (IBM), Stanley Dickstein (IBM), Dave Garcia (Tandem), Jim Gray (Tandem), Jeffrey P. Hansen (CMU), Robert Horst (Tandem), M.Y. Hsiao (IBM), Robert Jardine (Tandem), Doug Jewett (Tandem), Robert W. Kocsis (Jet Propulsion Lab.), Dan Lenoski (Tandem), Dix McGuire (Tandem), Bob Meeker (IBM), Dick Merrall (IBM), Larry Miller (IBM), Louise Nielsen (IBM), Les Parker (IBM), Frank Sera (IBM), Mandakumar Tendolkar (IBM), Liane Toy (AT&T), Wing Toy (AT&T), and Steven Webber (Stratus).

Jim Franck and John Shebell of Digital provided material and insight for Chapters 4 and 6 respectively. Jim Gray provided data on Tandem system failures that have been included in Chapter 2.

Jeff Hansen, David Lee, and Michael Schuette provide material on mathematical modeling, computer aids, and techniques. Comments from several reviewers and students were particularly helpful.

Special thanks are due to colleagues at both Carnegie-Mellon University and Digital Equipment Corporation (DEC) for providing an environment conducive to generating and testing ideas, especially Steve Director, Dean of the Engineering College, and Nico Habermann, Dean of the School of Computer Science. The entire staff of Digital Press provided excellent support for a timely production.

The professionalism of the staff at Technical Texts is deeply appreciated as they provided invaluable assistance throughout the production of the book. A special acknowledgment is also due Sylvia Dovner whose countless suggestions and attention to details contributed towards her goal of a "user friendly" book. The manuscript

TABLE P–2
Proposed structure for graduate course

Chapters	Augmentation
Ch. 1, Fundamental Concepts	
Ch. 2, Faults and Their Manifestations	Ross [1972] and/or Shooman [1968] for random variables, statistical parameter estimation ARINC [1964] for data collection and analysis
Ch. 3, Reliability and Availability Techniques	Appendix A, Peterson and Weldon [1972] for coding theory; Sellers, Hsiao, and Bearnson [1968b] for error-detection techniques *Proceedings of Annual IEEE International Symposium on Fault-Tolerant Computing* Special issues of the IEEE *Transactions on Computers* on Fault-Tolerant Computing (e.g., November 1971, March 1973, July 1974, May 1975, June 1976, June 1980, July 1982, 1986, April 1990) Special issues of *Computer* on Fault-Tolerant Computing (e.g., March 1980, July 1984, July 1990)
Ch. 4, Maintainability and Testing Techniques	Breuer and Friedman [1976] for testing; *Proceedings of Cherry Hill Test Conference* Special issues of *Computer* on Testing (e.g., October 1979) ARINC [1964] for maintenance analysis
Ch. 5, Evaluation Criteria	Ross [1972], Howard [1971], Shooman [1968], Craig [1964] for Markov models and their solutions
Ch. 6, Financial Considerations	Phister [1979]
Part II	October 1978 special issue of the *Proceedings of the IEEE*

provided many unforeseen "challenges," and Sylvia's perseverance was the glue that held the project together. That the book exists today is due in no small part to Sylvia's efforts.

This book would not have been possible without the patience and diligence of Mrs. Laura Forsyth, who typed, retyped, and mailed the many drafts of the manuscript. Her activities as a "traffic controller" were vital to the project.

Finally, the support and understanding of our families is the central ingredient that made this book possible. From the occupation of the dining room table for weeks at a time for reorganizing text or double-checking page proofs to missing social events or soccer games, their patience and sacrifice over the last five years enabled the project to draw to a successful conclusion.

REFERENCES* ARINC [1964]; Breuer and Friedman [1976]; Carter et al. [1964]; Cooper and Chow [1976]; Craig [1964]; Dickinson, Jackson, and Randa [1964]; Downing, Nowak, and Toumenoksa [1964]; Hamming [1950]; Howard [1971]; Moore and Shannon [1956]; Peterson and Weldon [1972]; Phister [1979]; Pierce [1965]; Ross [1972]; Sellers, Hsiao, and Bearnson [1968b]; Shannon [1948]; Shooman [1968]; von Neumann [1956]; Wilcox and Mann [1962].

* For full citations of the shortened references at the end of each chapter, see References at the back of the book.

I | THE THEORY OF RELIABLE SYSTEM DESIGN

Part I of this book presents the many disciplines required to construct a reliable computing system. Chapter 1 explains the motivation for reliable systems and provides the theoretical framework for their design, fabrication, and maintenance. It presents the hierarchy of physical levels into which a computer system is customarily partitioned and introduces the stages into which the life of a computer system is divided. Chapter 1 also provides a detailed discussion of two stages in a system's life: manufacturing and operation. Lastly, the chapter identifies several of the costs of ownership for a computer system and specifies some of the parameters that the designer can control to increase customer satisfaction.

Chapter 2 discusses errors and fault manifestations in a computer system. A review of applicable probability theory is presented as an aid to understanding the mathematics of the various fault distributions. Common techniques for matching empirical data to fault distributions, such as the maximum likelihood estimator, linear regression, and the chi-square goodness-of-fit test, are discussed. Chapter 2 also introduces methods for estimating permanent failure rates, including the MIL-HDBK-217 procedure, a widely used mathematical model of permanent faults in electronic equipment, and the life-cycle testing and data analysis approaches. It addresses the problem of finding an appropriate distribution for intermittent and transient errors by analyzing field data from computer systems of diverse manufacturers.

Chapter 3 deals with reliability techniques, or ways to improve the mean time to failure. It presents a comprehensive taxonomy of reliability and availability techniques. There is also a catalog of techniques, along with evaluation criteria for both hardware and software.

Chapter 4 deals with maintainability techniques, or ways to improve the mean time to repair of a failed computer system. It provides a taxonomy of testing and maintenance techniques, and describes ways to detect and correct sources of errors at each stage of a computer's life cycle. Specific strategies for testing during the manufacturing phase are discussed. The chapter explains several logic-level acceptance tests, such as exclusive-OR testing, signature analysis, Boolean difference, path sensitization, and the *D*-algorithm. It also introduces a discipline, called design for testability, which attempts to define properties of easy-to-test systems. The chapter concludes with a discussion of symptom directed diagnosis which utilizes operational life data to predict and diagnose failures.

How can a reliable or maintainable design be mathematically evaluated? That is, if a system is supposed to be down no more than two hours in 40 years, how can one avoid waiting that long to confirm success? Chapter 5 defines a host of evaluation criteria, establishes the underlying mathematics, and presents deterministic models and simulation techniques. Simple series-parallel models are introduced as a method for evaluating the reliability of nonredundant systems and systems with standby sparing. Next, several types of combinatorial (failure-to-exhaustion) models are described. The chapter also introduces ways of reducing nonseries, nonparallel models to more tractable forms.

Chapter 5 continues with Markov models, which define various system states and express the probability of going from one state to another. In these models, the probability depends only on the present state and is independent of how the present state was reached. After describing several other simulation and modeling techniques, the chapter concludes with a case study of an effort to make a more reliable version of a SUN workstation using the techniques defined in Chapter 3.

Finally, Chapter 6 is concerned with the financial considerations inherent in the design, purchase, and operation of a computer system. The discussion adopts two major viewpoints: that of the maintenance provider and that of the system's owner/operator. An explanation of the various sources of maintenance costs, such as labor and materials, is followed by an overview of the field service business. Several maintenance cost models are suggested, along with a method for assessing the value of maintainability features. The chapter describes two of the many ways of modeling the life-cycle costs of owning and operating a computer system; these cost models are essential to the system designer in understanding the financial motivations of the customer.

1 FUNDAMENTAL CONCEPTS

Historically, reliable computers have been limited to military, industrial, aerospace, and communications applications in which the consequence of computer failure is significant economic impact and/or loss of life. Reliability is of critical importance wherever a computer malfunction could have catastrophic results, as in the space shuttle, aircraft flight-control systems, hospital patient monitors, and power system control.

Reliability techniques have become of increasing interest to general-purpose computer systems because of several recent trends, four of which are presented here.

1. *Harsher Environments:* With the advent of microprocessors, computer systems have been moved from the clean environments of computer rooms into industrial environments. The cooling air contains more particulate matter; temperature and humidity vary widely and are frequently subject to spontaneous changes; the primary power supply fluctuates; and there is electromagnetic interference.

2. *Novice Users:* As computers proliferate, the typical user knows less about proper operation of the system. Consequently, the system has to be able to tolerate more inadvertent user abuse.

3. *Increasing Repair Costs:* As hardware costs continue to decline and labor costs escalate, a user cannot afford frequent calls for field service. Figure 1–1 depicts the relation between cost of ownership and the addition of reliability and maintainability features. Note that as hardware costs increase, service costs decrease because of fewer and shorter field service calls.

4. *Larger Systems:* As systems become larger, there are more components that can fail. Because the overall failure rate of a system is directly related to the sum of the failure rates of its individual components, designs that tolerate faults resulting from component failure can keep the system failure rate at an acceptable level.

As the need for reliability has increased in the industrial world, so has the interest in fault tolerance. Manufacturers of large mainframe computers, such as IBM, Unisys, and Amdahl, now use fault-tolerant techniques both to improve reliability and to assist field service personnel in fault isolation. Minicomputer manufacturers incorporate fault-tolerant features in their designs, and some companies, such as Tandem, have been formed solely to market fault-tolerant computers.

Fault-tolerant computing is the correct execution of a specified algorithm in the presence of defects. The effect of defects can be overcome by the use of redundancy.

FIGURE 1–1
Cost of ownership as a function of reliability and maintainability

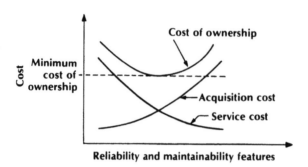

This redundance can be either temporal (repeated executions) or physical (replicated hardware or software). At the highest level, fault-tolerant systems are categorized as either highly available or highly reliable.

- **Availability:** The availability of a system as a function of time, $A(t)$, is the probability that the system is operational at the instant of time, t. If the limit of this function exists as t goes to infinity, it expresses the expected fraction of time that the system is available to perform useful computations. Activities such as preventive maintenance and repair reduce the time that the system is available to the user. Availability is typically used as a figure of merit in systems in which service can be delayed or denied for short periods without serious consequences.
- **Reliability:** The reliability of a system as a function of time, $R(t)$, is the conditional probability that the system has survived the interval $[0,t]$, given that the system was operational at time $t = 0$. Reliability is used to describe systems in which repair cannot take place (as in satellite computers), systems in which the computer is serving a critical function and cannot be lost even for the duration of a repair (as in flight computers on aircraft), or systems in which the repair is prohibitively expensive. In general, it is more difficult to build a highly reliable computing system than a highly available system because of the more stringent requirements imposed by the reliability definition. An even more stringent definition than $R(t)$, sometimes used in aerospace applications, is the maximum number of failures anywhere in the system that the system can tolerate and still function correctly.

This chapter describes the basic concepts in a three-dimensional reliability framework. This framework allows the various constraints, techniques, and decisions in the design of reliable systems to be mapped. The first dimension in the framework is the physical hierarchy, which ranges from primitive components to complex systems. The second dimension is the time in the system's life, which includes various stages from concept through manufacturing and operation. The third dimension is the cost of the system relative to customer satisfaction and physical resources. This framework is the foundation for all techniques and approaches to reliable systems that are covered in subsequent chapters of this book.

PHYSICAL LEVELS IN A DIGITAL SYSTEM*

The first dimension in the reliability framework pertains to the physical levels in a digital system. Digital computer systems are enormously complex, and some hierarchical concept must be used to manage this complexity. In the hierarchy, each level contains only information important to its level and suppresses unnecessary information about lower levels. System designers frequently utilize a hierarchy in which the levels coincide with the system's physical boundaries, as listed in Table 1–1.

• **Circuit Level:** The circuit level consists of such components as resistors, capacitors, inductors, and power sources. The metrics of system behavior include voltage, current, flux, and charge. The circuit level is not the lowest possible level at which to describe a digital system. Various electromagnetic and quantum mechanical phenomena underlie circuit theory, and the operation of electromechanical system devices (such as disks) requires more than circuit theory to model their operation.

• **Logic Level:** The logic level is unique to digital systems. The *switching-circuit* sublevel is composed of such things as gates and data operators built out of gates. This sublevel is further subdivided into sequential and combinatorial logic circuits, with the fundamental difference being the absence of memory elements in combinatorial circuits. The *register transfer* sublevel, the next higher level, deals with registers

TABLE 1–1 *Hierarchical levels for digital computers*

Level/Sublevel	Components	Level/Sublevel	Components

PMS (highest level)	Processors
	Memories
	Switches
	Controllers
	Transducers
	Data operators
	Links
		Logic
		  Switching circuit
			Sequential
			  Flip-flops; latches; delays
			Combinatorial
			  Gates; encoders/decoders;
			  data operators

Program
  ISP
	Memory state
	Processor state
	Effective address
	  calculation
	Instruction decode
	Instruction execution
		Register transfer	Data
			  Registers; operators; data paths
			Control
			  Hardwired
			    Sequential logic machines
			  Microprogramming
			    Microsequencer; microstore

High-level language	Software	Circuit (lowest level)	Resistors Capacitors Inductors Power sources Diodes Transistors

* This discussion is adapted from Siewiorek, Bell, and Newell, 1982.

and functional transfers of information among registers. This sublevel is frequently further subdivided into a data part and a control part. The data part is composed of registers, operators, and data paths. The control part provides the time-dependent stimuli that cause transfers between registers to take place. In some computers, the control part is implemented as a hard-wired state-machine. With the availability of low-cost read-only memories (ROMs), microprogramming is now a more popular way to implement the control function.

• **Program Level:** The program level is unique to digital computers. At this level, a sequence of instructions in the device is interpreted, and it causes action upon a data structure. This is the *instruction set processor* (ISP) sublevel. The ISP description is used in turn to create software components that are easily manipulated by programmers—the *high-level-language* sublevel. The result is software, such as operating systems, run-time systems, application programs, and application systems.

• **PMS (Processor, Memory, Switch) Level:** Finally, the various elements—input/output devices, memories, mass storage, communications, and processors—are interconnected to form a complete system.

TEMPORAL STAGES OF A DIGITAL SYSTEM

The second dimension in the reliability framework is that of time. The point at which a technique or methodology is applied during the life cycle of a system may be more important than the physical level.

From a user's viewpoint, a digital system can be treated as a "black box" that produces outputs in response to input stimuli. Table 1–2 lists the numerous stages in the life of the box as it progresses from concept to final implementation. These stages include specification of input/output relationships, logic design, prototype debugging, manufacturing, installation, and field operation. Deviations from intended behavior, or errors, can occur at any stage as a result of incomplete specifications, incorrect

TABLE 1–2
Stages in the life of a system

Stage	Error Sources	Error Detection Techniques
Specification and design	Algorithm design Formal specifications	Simulation Consistency checks
Prototype	Algorithm design Wiring and assembly Timing Component failure	Stimulus/response testing
Manufacture	Wiring and assembly Component failure	System testing Diagnostics
Installation	Assembly Component failure	System testing Diagnostics
Operational life	Component failure Operator errors Environmental fluctuations	Diagnostics

implementation of a specification into a logic design, and assembly mistakes during prototyping or manufacturing.

During the system's operational life, errors can result from change in the physical state or damage to hardware. Physical changes may be triggered by environmental factors such as fluctuations in temperature or power supply voltage, static discharge, and even α-particle emissions. Inconsistent states can also be caused by both operator errors and design errors in hardware or software. Operational causes of outage are relatively evenly distributed among hardware, software, maintenance actions, operations, and environment. Table 1–3 depicts the distribution of outages from seven different studies. As illustrated by the table, substantial gains in reliability will result only when all sources of outage are addressed. For example, complete elimination of hardware caused outages will only increase time between errors by about 25 percent.

Design errors, whether in hardware or software, are those caused by improper translation of a concept into an operational realization. Closely tied to the human creative process, design errors are difficult to predict. Gathering statistical information about the phenomenon is difficult because each design error occurs only once per system. The rapid rate of development in hardware technology constantly changes the set of design trade-offs, further complicating the study of hardware design errors. In the last decade, there has been some progress in the use of redundancy—using additional resources beyond the minimum required to perform the task successfully—to control software design errors.

Any source of error can appear at any stage; however, it is usually assumed that certain sources of error predominate at particular stages. Furthermore, error-detection

TABLE 1–3 *Probability of operational outage caused by various sources*

Source of Outage	AT&T Switching Systems [Toy, 1978][a]	Bellcore [Ali, 1986][a]	Japanese Commercial Users	Tandem [Gray, 1985]	Tandem [Gray, 1987]	Northern Telecom	Mainframe Users
Hardware	0.20	0.26[c]	0.75[f]	0.18	0.19	0.19	0.45
Software	0.15	0.30[d]	0.75[f]	0.26	0.43	0.19	0.20
Maintenance	—	—	0.75[f]	0.25	0.13	—	0.05
Operations	0.65[b]	0.44[e]	0.11	0.17	0.13	0.33	0.15
Environment	—	—	0.13	0.14	0.12	0.28[g]	0.15

Note: Dashes indicate that no separate value was reported for that category in the cited study.

[a] Data shows the fraction of downtime attributed to each source. Downtime is defined as any service disruption that exceeds 30 seconds duration. The Bellcore data represented a 3.5 minute downtime per year per system.

[b] Total is split between procedural errors (0.30) and recovery deficiencies (0.35).

[c] 47 percent of the hardware failures occurred because the second unit failed before the first unit could be replaced.

[d] Data applies to recovery software.

[e] Total is split between procedural errors (0.42) and operational software (0.02).

[f] Study only reported probability of vendor-related outage (i.e., 0.75 is split between vendor hardware, software, and maintenance).

[g] Of the total amount, 0.15 is attributed to power.

techniques can be tailored to the manifestation of fault sources. Thus, at each stage of system life there is a primary methodology for detecting errors.

Two important stages in the life of a system—the manufacturing stage and the operational life stage—are discussed in the following subsections. A third important stage, design, is the subject of the remaining chapters in Part I.

The Manufacturing Stage

A careless manufacturing process can make even the most careful design useless. The manufacturing stage begins with the final portion of the prototype stage in a process called *design maturity testing*.

Design Maturity Testing. A design maturity test (DMT) estimates the mean time to failure (MTTF) for a new product before the product is committed to volume manufacturing. The DMT is conducted to isolate and correct repetitive systemic problems that, if left in the design, would result in higher service costs and customer dissatisfaction.

The DMT is accomplished by operating a set of sample devices for a prolonged time (typically 6 to 8 units for 2 to 4 months) to simulate actual field operation. In cases in which the duty cycle of the equipment is less than 100 percent, the duty cycle under test may be increased to 100 percent to accelerate testing. As failures are observed and recorded, they are classified according to such factors as failure mode, time, or environmental cause. Similar failures are then ranked in groups by decreasing frequency of occurrence.

This procedure establishes priorities for eliminating the causes. After the fundamental cause of the failure is found and corrective design action is taken, the operation of the modified or repaired test samples provides a closed-loop evaluation of the efficacy of the change. Repeating the procedure improves the design of the test samples until their estimated MTTF meets the specifications with a certain statistical confidence.

The progress of the test can be monitored with a chart prepared in advance for

FIGURE 1–2
Reliability demon-stration chart for monitoring the progress of a de-sign maturity test [From data in von Alven, 1964]

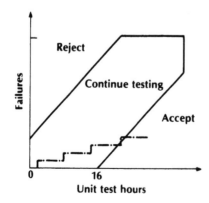

the product under test, as shown in Figure 1–2. It provides an objective criterion for judging the MTTF of a product with a predetermined statistical risk. The chart, which is based on four parameters relating to the upper bound of the MTTF, the minimum acceptable MTTF, and the risks to both consumer and producer, is divided into three areas: accept, reject, or continue testing. When the performance line crosses into the accept region, the test samples' MTTF is at least equal to the minimum acceptable MTTF (with the predetermined risk of error), and the design should be accepted. If the performance line crosses into the reject region, the MTTF of the design is probably lower than the acceptable minimum with its corresponding probability of error; testing should be suspended until the design has been sufficiently improved and it can reasonably be expected to pass the test.

The DMT is a time consuming, costly process as illustrated in Chapter 4. Many manufacturers are replacing it by a reliability growth test as described in Chapter 4.

Incoming Inspection. Incoming inspection is an attempt to cull weak or defective components prior to assembly or fabrication into subsystems, as shown in Figure 1–3. All semiconductor processes yield a certain number of defective devices. Even after the semiconductor manufacturer has detected and removed these defective devices, failures will continue to occur for a time known as the *infant mortality period*. This period is typically 20 weeks or fewer during which the rate of failures continues to decline. At the end of this period, failures tend to stabilize at a constant rate for a long time, sometimes 25 years or more. Ultimately the failure rate begins to rise again, in a period known as the *wear-out period*. This variation in failure rate as a function of time is illustrated by the bathtub-shaped curve shown in Figure 1–4.

As shown in Figure 1–5, the failure rate can be considered to be the sum of three factors: (1) *infant mortality*, which decreases with time, (2) *steady-state stress*, which is constant with time, and (3) *wear-out*, which increases with time. Chapter 2 describes the Weibull model for estimating the impact of infant mortality failures during early product life.

The cost of component failure depends upon the level at which the failure is detected: The higher the level, the more expensive the repair. Fault detection at the semiconductor component level minimizes cost. Fault detection at the next highest level, the board, has been estimated at $5; at the system test level, $50; and at the field service level, $500 [Russell, 1980]. The level at which a computer manufacturer detects initial and infant mortality failures is a function of the incoming test program chosen.

Example. Even relatively low semiconductor failure rates can cause substantial board yield problems, which are aggravated by the density of the board. Consider a board with 40 semiconductor devices that have an initial failure rate of 1 percent:

Probability board not defective = $(0.99)^{40}$ = 0.669

The benefits of an incoming inspection program can be easily quantified. The value of culling bad semiconductor components before they are inserted into the

FIGURE 1–3
*Typical steps in the
manufacture of a
digital system.
[From Foley, 1979;
© 1979 IEEE]*

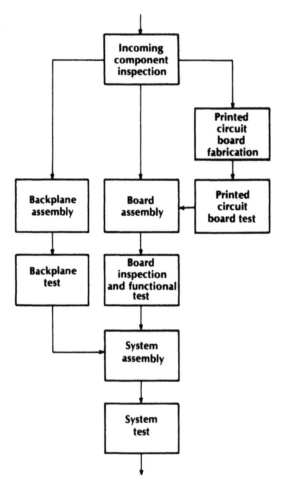

board is the most easily measured benefit. Board/system test savings, inventory reduction, and service personnel savings depend on the particular strategy used. To calculate the value of removing defective components at incoming inspection, multiply the number of bad parts found by the cost of detecting, isolating, and repairing failures at higher levels of integration. The following formula estimates the total savings:

$$D = 5B + 50S + 500F$$

where D = dollar savings
 B = number of failures at board test level
 S = number of failures at system test level
 F = number of failures in the field

FIGURE 1–4
Bathtub-shaped curve depicting component failure rate as a function of time

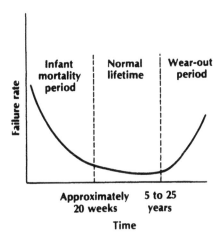

This formula can be translated into annual savings by considering total component volume and mean failure rate data:

Potential annual savings = annual component volume
    × [(% initial failures)(% failures detected at board level ×$5
    + % failures detected at system level × $50)]
    + [(% infancy failures)(% failures detected at system level × $50
    + % failures detected in the field × $500)]

FIGURE 1–5
Factors that contribute to the failure rate of a component over time

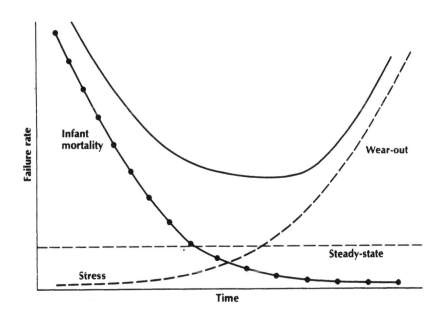

Typical savings for 100 percent incoming inspection can be estimated and compared with the cost of the automatic test equipment required to carry out such testing. Figure 1–6 shows the potential annual savings as a function of annual component volumes. A family of curves is shown for overall failure rates of 0.8, 1.2, 2.0, and 4.0 percent.

Process Maturity Testing. The term *process* includes all manufacturing steps to acquire parts, assemble, fabricate, inspect, and test a product during volume production. The rationale for process maturity testing (PMT) is that newly manufactured products contain some latent defects built in by the process that produced them.

A large number of units, usually the first 120 off the production line, are operated for 96 hours, often in lot sizes convenient to the particular production process. They are operated (burned in) in a manner that simulates the normal production process environment as closely as possible. If the burn-in and production process environments differ significantly, appropriate test results must be adjusted accordingly. Infant mortality characteristics may fluctuate significantly throughout the test lot. The composite of these individual failure characteristics is considered the normal infancy for the device. The end of the burn-in period for production equipment is determined by the normal infancy curve thus derived from the PMT. The objective is to ship products of consistently good quality and acceptable MTTF after a minimum burn-in period. Typical production burn-in times are 20 to 40 hours.

PMT is used to identify several classes of failures. Infancy failures are problems generally caused by parts that were defective from the time they were received. In largely solid-state devices, component problems will remain in this category until they are identified and controlled by either incoming inspection or changes implemented by the component vendor. Manufacturing/inspection failures are generally failures repaired by readjustments or retouching. Examples include parts damaged by the assembly process or defects that bypassed the normal incoming test procedures.

FIGURE 1–6

Potential annual savings from screening and testing as a function of annual component volumes [From Craig, 1980]

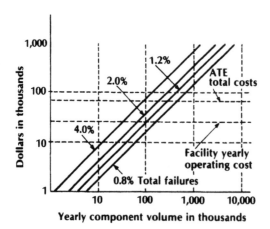

Engineering failures are recurrent problems in the design that have not yet been corrected or new problems that have not yet been resolved because of lack of experience. Residual failures are problems that have not yet recurred and for which there is no corrective action except to repair them when they occur. These are the truly random failures.

Experience has shown that the three major recurring problems usually account for 75 percent of all failures. It is reasonable to expect that the correction of the top four to six recurring problems will yield a tenfold improvement in MTTF. The current trend is to have the manufacturing line produce the DMT units, so that the data derived during DMT can be used to identify and remove process-related defects. In this case PMT is redundant and unnecessary.

The Operational Life Stage

Over the years, with the accumulation of experience in the manufacture of semiconductor components, the failure rate per logic device has steadily declined. Figure 1–7 depicts the number of failures per million hours for bipolar technology as a function of the number of gates on a chip. The Mil Model 217A curves were derived from 1965 data. The curves for Mil Models 217B, 217C, 217D, and 217E (see Appendix E) were generated from 1974, 1979, 1982, and 1986 reliability prediction models, respectively. Actual failure data are also plotted to calibrate the Mil models. The curve field data was derived from a year-long reliability study of a sample of video terminals [Harrahy, 1977]. The curve life cycle data was derived from elevated temperature testing of chips, followed by the application of a mathematical model that translated the failure rates to ambient temperatures [Siewiorek et al., 1978b]. Finally, the improvement in the 3000-gate Motorola MC 6800 is plotted [Queyssac, 1979]. In general, the Mil Model 217 is conservative, especially with respect to large-scale integration (LSI) and random-access memory (RAM) chips. See Chapter 2 for a more detailed discussion.

Two trends are noteworthy. First, there is more than an order of magnitude decrease in failure rate per gate. Plots of failure per bit of bipolar random access memory indicate that the failure rates per gate and per bit are comparable for comparable levels of integration. Obviously, the chip failure rate is a function of chip complexity and is not a constant. Failure rate per function (gate or bit) decreases by one order of magnitude over two orders of magnitude of gate complexity and by two to three orders of magnitude of memory complexity. The failure rate decreases in direct proportion to increases in complexity.

The second trend is that the Mil model predicted failure rate decreases with time. Each model predicts an increase in failure rate per function beyond a particular complexity, presumably because of the immaturity of the fabrication process at that scale of integration at that time.*

---

* The switch from a polynomial to an exponential function in number of gates occurs at 100 in 217B and 1000 in 217C, reflecting the improvements in the fabrication process over time.

14

I. THE THEORY OF RELIABLE SYSTEM DESIGN

FIGURE 1–7

Failure rate per gate as a function of chip complexity for bipolar technology

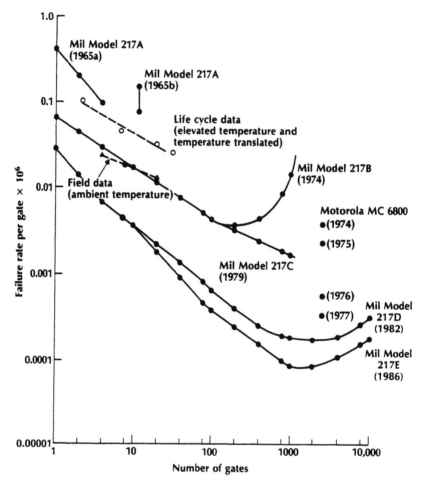

Example. Consider a system composed of a constant number of semiconductor chips. Because the chips double in density every one to two years, the number of functions, f, in the system is proportional to changes in time, Δt:

$$f \propto 2^{\Delta t}$$

where t is time in years. The failure rate per function, from Figure 1–6, is proportional to the squre root of the number of functions per chip:*

$$r \propto f^{1/2}$$

---

* Shooman [1989] used this equation to propose models for 1965, 1975, 1985 by passing straight lines through the Mil Models 217A, 217C, and 217E curves. He found proportionality constants of 0.32, 0.04, and 0.004, respectively, which represent almost an order of magnitude improvement each decade.

Hence,

$$r \propto 2^{\Delta t/2}$$

and the mean time to failure is

$$\text{MTTF} \propto \frac{1}{r} \propto \frac{1}{2^{(\Delta t/2)}}$$

This result implies that over a 10-year period, a system with the same number of semiconductor chips has increased its logic complexity by a factor of 1024 and decreased its MTTF by a factor of 32. Hence, system reliability has not kept pace with system complexity.

Without sufficient attention to reliability, complex, high-performance machines can be on the verge of becoming virtually unusable. For example, when the Los Alamos Scientific Laboratory evaluated the reliability of its CRAY-1 over a 6-month period, the mean time to failure was found to be 4 hours [Keller, 1976]. The average repair time was only about 25 minutes because of the skilled on-site maintenance crew. Even so, this represented the loss of about 100 billion potential machine operations [Avizienis, 1978]. Gains in system reliability cannot be attained from improved component reliability alone. Redundancy must be introduced. Redundancy techniques are the subject of Chapter 3.

When reliability is a primary design goal, however, system reliability per unit functionality can actually improve over time. Figure 1–8 plots the hard failures per year per MIPS (million instructions per second) of several generations of IBM processors by year of processor introduction. The year of introduction fixes the basic technology. The data on processor mean time to failure was compiled from a year's worth of operational data (March 1987 to March 1988) from the subscribers to UCC9/Reliability Plus, a service provided by University Computing Corporation and Reliability Research to IBM mainframe users. UCC9/Reliability Plus collects data about system errors from the on-line system error log, calculates failure statistics such as operational hours between hard failures, and ranks the installation with respect to other subscribers. The performance of IBM mainframes was taken from Datapro Research Corporation's annual "Hardware Roundup" article. From Figure 1–8 we see that IBM mainframes have improved their time between failures per unit functionality by a factor of 30 in 15 years, or a 20 percent improvement per year compounded. These improvements have been achieved both by improvement in basic component reliability and by the use of redundancy. Chapter 7 gives a detailed description of the techniques used in the IBM 3090 series.

Maintenance and repair during the field operational stage are the customer's primary contacts with system reliability. In the early days of computers, repairing a downed system was an art. Diagnostics that were halted or trapped when certain instructions were executed gave clues to the location of the failure, but did not pinpoint the failing field replaceable unit (FRU). To identify the failing FRU, technicians swapped circuit boards one by one with "known good boards" in the hope of eventually

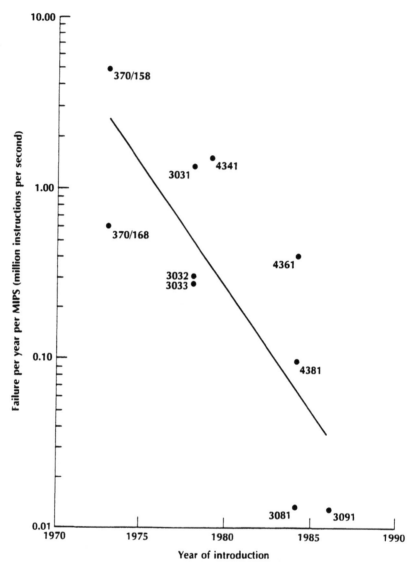

FIGURE 1–8
Improvement in hard failure rate for IBM mainframes

restoring the system to proper operation. In time, diagnostic techniques were developed that were better able to identify the specific failed FRU before any boards were swapped; then, the failed board could rapidly be replaced with a good one. Today, symptom directed diagnosis has replaced the traditional diagnostic program.

Unfortunately, as on-site repair time is decreased by better diagnosis, travel time to the site becomes a limiting factor. At today's labor and transportation rates, the cost of travel time frequently exceeds the cost of the actual repair. Return trips, which occur because the failed FRU was identified but the field service engineer had no replacement along, are very cost inefficient. Alternative service strategies have been developed in response to these factors, and include customer carry-in service for small computers and service vans that carry enough sets of spare parts to permit long absences from the branch field service office.

A good example of a current field service approach is Digital Equipment Corporation's Digital Diagnosis Center (DDC). An overview of the Remote Diagnosis Network is shown in Figure 1–9. When customers detect or suspect a computer malfunction, they call a special telephone response line that is attended 24 hours a day, 7 days a week. The heart of the DDC is a VAX8800 configuration with auto-dial equipment. Once attached to the customer's failing computer (typically within 15 minutes), the DDC host system directs the diagnosis process based on results produced by the system under test. A configuration file is kept on each system supported.

An expert system analyzes the system error log to identify the "signature" of the failure. The signature is then mapped to a suspected FRU. When the analysis is complete, the problem is described to the local field service branch office, which then dispatches the right person with the right part to the site. The on-site field engineer replaces the predetermined failed part and verifies the resolution of the problem. Final results of the corrective action are transmitted to the DDC to update the system's maintenance log. Information about problem areas in various computer systems is passed on to the engineering development groups to assist them in making improvements in the future.

The ultimate goal of no down time due to maintenance is achieved by Stratus

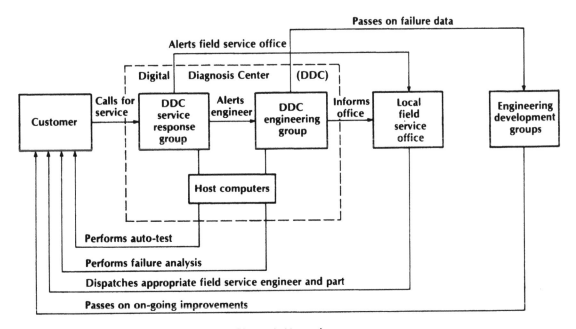

FIGURE 1–9 *DEC's Remote Diagnosis Network*

(Chapter 8) through a combination of fault tolerance, an on-line Customer Assistance Center (CAC), and an overnight courier service. The Stratus architecture contains on-line duplicates for every component. In addition, every component is enhanced with hardware error detectors. When an error is discovered, a red light on the component is illuminated, a maintenance interrupt is generated, the board removes itself from service, and the duplicate component continues processing without any loss of data. The operating system runs diagnostics and employs an incident of failure algorithm to determine if the fault was transient or permanent. If the fault is transient, the component is returned to service. If the fault is permanent, the CAC is called. The computer in the CAC reconfirms the diagnosis, selects a replacement board of the same revision level, prints board installation instructions, and ships the board to the customer via overnight courier. The first time the customer realizes there is a problem is when the replacement board arrives. Without powering down the system or crashing the software, the customer removes the old board and replaces it with the new board. The new board is automatically synchronized to the operation of the system and the full fault-tolerant capability of the system is restored.

Even though the Stratus approach drives up the initial purchase cost of the system, it reduces the cost of service from an industrial average of 9 percent of life-cycle cost (LCC) per year to 6 percent of LCC per year. More and more users are turning to LCC, rather than just initial purchase cost, as the appropriate cost metric for evaluating alternative systems.

COST OF A DIGITAL SYSTEM

The third dimension of the reliability framework, in addition to physical level and temporal stage, is cost. The cost of ownership of a computer system is not limited to initial purchase; significant costs recur during the life of a system. As a result, computer owners frequently develop mathematical models that enable them to make optimal decisions, minimizing the total cost of ownership.* Some of the significant costs of ownership are described here.

• *Purchase Price:* The purchase price of a computer, though significant, can represent less than half the cost of ownership, computed on the basis of net present value. The purchase price usually includes system hardware, documentation, software license fees, training, and installation. The potential owner of a computer always has renting and leasing alternatives to consider; these can sometimes be advantageous in terms of cash flow or net present value.

• *Site Preparation:* Many computers require special operating environments. This may include special air conditioning, with closely controlled temperature, humidity, and airborne particulate matter size and density. A large computer may also require a raised floor for cabling. The main power supply may require a separate transformer with three-phase service and radio frequency interference filters. In some installations, an uninterruptible power supply is essential either to increase system availability or to

---

* These financial considerations are discussed in detail in Chapter 6.

prevent loss of data. The major cause of unexplained system crashes is a marginal power distribution network.

• *Maintenance:* All computers require some degree of preventive and corrective maintenance. The user usually has the option of purchasing a field service contract at a fixed price or paying for field service on a time-and-materials basis. The maintenance can come from the computer manufacturer, the original equipment manufacturer, a third party, or it may be performed by the customer. The trade-offs inherent in decisions about when and how often to perform preventive maintenance also affect cost of ownership.

• *Supplies:* A computer system requires paper for the printers, disks and tapes for the mass storage devices, and other periodically replaced material. Very significant, too, is the power required to run a computer. With ever-escalating energy costs, supplying power to a computer for its operational lifetime can be one of the most significant expenses associated with ownership.

• *Cost of Downtime:* Depending on the application of the system, the cost of downtime can be either trivial or crucial. In a system that acquires revenue, for example, the cost of downtime can far exceed the actual purchase price. This parameter requires careful evaluation by the potential customer.

Example. Consider a system that has only an initial cost, I, and a failure rate, λ. The cost, C, of owning this system for n years can be expressed as

$$C = I + \sum_{i=1}^{n} \frac{S_i P_i}{(1 + D)^i}$$

where S_i = the cost of one corrective maintenance call in year i
P_i = the expected number of failures during year i
D = the discount rate

The discount rate expresses the value of money in terms of time. For example, if you need $100 in 2 years and can get 10 percent annual interest in a savings account, you need to put away only $100/1.1^2 = \$82.65$ today. Here, 10 percent represents the discount rate.

Assume that the failure rate is constant over the period in question. Then,

$$C = I + P \sum_{i=1}^{n} \frac{S_i}{(1 + D)^i}$$

Further assume that the system has a 5-year life, that a service call costs $300, and that the discount rate is 20 percent. Expressing λ in failures per million hours and noting the fact that there are 8760 hours in a year results in

$$C = I + (300) \frac{8760\lambda}{10^6} \sum_{i=1}^{5} \frac{1}{(1.2)^i} = I + 7.86\lambda$$

Example. Consider a system that costs $21,000 and has a failure rate of 6500 per million hours (equivalent to a mean time to failure of 154 hours). Its cost of ownership, using the preceding assumptions, is $72,090. Now consider another system that costs more to purchase, $27,500, but is more reliable. Its failure rate is 4400, or an MTTF of 227 hours, and its cost of ownership is $62,084. Although the second system is 31 percent more expensive to purchase, its 47 percent increase in reliability results in a 14 percent reduction in 5 year cost of ownership.

Customer Satisfaction

Customer satisfaction is a complex function of system cost, performance, reliability, and maintainability. Figure 1–10 depicts the major activities in the design and marketing of a computer system. The goal of all these activities is to produce a system that fulfills its intended use, thereby satisfying the customer.

Once the need for a reliable system is established, a design is determined. Enhanced reliability usually involves some degree of hardware redundancy, and maintainability improvements usually involve the addition of self-testing circuits, both of which increase the design effort and ultimately the product cost. Following the design decisions, a product development plan is established. The development plan determines the marketing, maintenance, and business plans, all of which are affected by the hardware cost. Reliability (mean time to failure [MTTF]) and maintainability (mean time to repair [MTTR]) are also factors in both the maintenance plan and the business plan, which determines the manufacturing, marketing, and field service strategies. The marketing plan generates sales forecasts, which are a function of product cost. Sales forecasts also influence the business plan and the maintenance plan, which produces the cost of field service, which further affects the marketing plan.

Thus, all the components of product development, marketing, and maintenance interact with and influence one another, and each has a model that can be used for predictive and evaluation purposes. Taken together, these factors also combine to form the basis for customer satisfaction as it relates to performance and the cost of ownership.

The Designable Parameters

The reliability, availability, and maintainability features of a computer system can be related to designable parameters that translate into various measures of customer satisfaction:

Designable Parameter	Measure of Customer Satisfaction
Increased mean time to failure	Decrease number of times computer is unavailable for operation
Decreased mean time to repair	Decrease amount of time computer is unavailable when a failure occurs
Increased mean time to crash	Decrease the probability that data is lost

FIGURE 1–10
Major activities in the design and marketing of a computer system

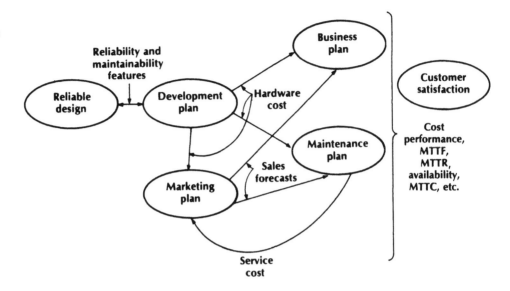

In addition, the use of fault tolerance in hardware has the following advantages, which also result in higher levels of customer satisfaction:

Simplifies recovery for software and user applications.
Saves time.
Provides transparency to the user.
Increases probability of successful recovery, given early detection.
Simplifies software recovery and reduces dependence on implementation.
Isolates design errors through error detection logic so that future implementations are even more reliable.

SUMMARY

This chapter has introduced a three-dimensional framework for reliability in computer systems. Two of the dimensions relate to the hierarchical physical levels in digital systems and to the various stages in the systems' life span. The dimension of cost relates to the levels of customer satisfaction in terms of the total costs of ownership, including the initial product cost, the cost of failures, and the cost of designing the system for reliability. In subsequent chapters, the student of systems reliability should keep in mind the question, Where in the reliability framework does the technique or methodology being presented apply?

REFERENCES

Ali, 1986; Avizienis, 1978; Craig, 1980; Foley, 1979; Gray, 1985, 1987; Harrahy, 1977; Keller, 1976; Queyssac, 1979; Russell, 1980; Shooman, 1989; Siewiorek et al., 1978b; Siewiorek, Bell, and Newell, 1982; Toy, 1978; von Alven, 1964.

2 FAULTS AND THEIR MANIFESTATIONS

Designing a reliable system requires finding a way to prevent errors caused by the logical faults arising from physical failures. Figure 2–1 depicts the possible sources of such errors and service failures. Service can be viewed from the hierarchical physical levels within the system, such as service delivered by a chip or by the designer, or service may be viewed from the system level by the user. In either case, the following terms [Laprie, 1985; Avizienis, 1982] are used:

- *Failure* occurs when the delivered service deviates from the specified service; failures are caused by errors.
- *Error* is the manifestation of a fault within a program or data structure; errors can occur some distance from the fault sites.
- *Fault* is an incorrect state of hardware or software resulting from failures of components, physical interference from the environment, operator error, or incorrect design.
- *Permanent* describes a failure or fault that is continuous and stable; in hardware, permanent failures reflect an irreversible physical change. (The word *hard* is used interchangeably with *permanent*.)
- *Intermittent* describes a fault that is only occasionally present due to unstable hardware or varying hardware or software states (for example, as a function of load or activity).
- *Transient* describes a fault resulting from temporary environmental conditions. (The word *soft* is used interchangeably with *transient*.)

A permanent fault can be caused by a physical defect or an inadequacy in the design of the system. Intermittent faults can be caused by unstable or marginally stable hardware or an inadequacy in design. Environmental conditions as well as some design errors can lead to transient faults. All these faults can cause errors. Incorrect designs and operator mistakes can lead directly to errors.

The distinction between *intermittent* and *transient* faults is not always made in the literature [Kamal, 1975; Tasar and Tasar, 1977]. The dividing line is the applicability of repair [Breuer, 1973; Kamal and Page, 1974; Losq, 1978; Savir, 1978]. Intermittent faults resulting from physical conditions of the hardware, incorrect hardware or software design, or even from unstable but repeated environmental conditions are potentially detectable and repairable by replacement or redesign; faults due to temporary environmental conditions, however, are incapable of repair because the hardware is physically undamaged. It is this attribute of transient faults that magnifies their importance.

FIGURE 2–1
*Sources of errors
and service failures*

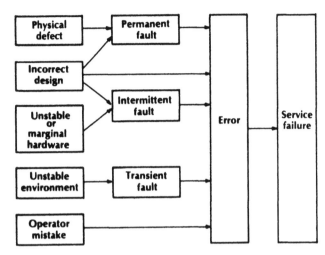

Even in the absence of all physical defects, including those manifested as intermittent faults, errors will still occur.

Avizienis [1985] presented classes of faults based on their origin. These fault classes are similar to the classification of faults presented by Toy [1978] for the Bell Electronic Switching Systems. Two basic fault classes and their description are as follows:

- **Physical faults:** These stem from physical phenomena internal to the system, such as threshold changes, shorts, opens, etc., or external changes, such as environmental, electromagnetic, vibration, etc.
- **Human faults:** These may be either *design faults*, which are committed during system design, modification, or establishment of operating procedures, or they may be *interaction faults*, which are violations of operating or maintenance procedures.

According to this classification, physical faults can be introduced or occur either during the manufacturing stage or during operation life. Physical faults during the useful operational life of the system are caused by physical processes that occur through normal and abnormal use. Design faults are caused by improper translation of an idea or concept into an operational realization. Interaction faults are caused by ambiguous documentation or human inattention to detail.

What are the sources of errors? What is the relative frequency of errors? How do faults manifest themselves as errors? Do the arrival times of faults (or errors) fit a probability distribution? If so, what are the parameters of that distribution? This chapter attempts to answer these questions and introduces a variety of fault models for the design and evaluation of fault-tolerant systems. The following section discusses the origin and frequency of errors by type of fault causing the errors. The remainder of the chapter focuses on fault manifestations within systems according to the hierarchical physical levels given in Chapter 1. It also presents the mathematical distributions that describe the probability of fault occurrence.

SYSTEM ERRORS   *Origin of Errors by Type of Fault*

Transient and intermittent faults have been seen as a major source of errors in systems in several studies. For example, an early study for the U.S. Air Force [Roth et al., 1967a] showed that 80 percent of the electronic failures in computers are due to intermittent faults. Another study by IBM [Ball and Hardie, 1967] indicated that "intermittents comprised over 90% of field failures." Transient faults, which have been observed in microprocessor chips [Brodsky, 1980], will become a more frequent problem in the future with shrinking device dimensions, lower energy levels for indicating logical values, and higher-speed operation.*

Table 2–1 gives the ratios of measured mean time between errors (MTBE) (due to all three fault types) to mean time to failure (MTTF) (due to permanent faults) for several systems. The last row of this table is the estimate of permanent and transient failure rates for a 1-megaword, 37-bit memory composed of 4K MOS RAMs [Geilhufe, 1979; Ohm, 1979]. In this case, transient errors are caused by α-particles emitted by the decay of trace radioactive particles in the semiconductor packaging materials. As they pass through the semiconductor material, α-particles create sufficient hole-electron pairs to add charge to or remove charge from bit cells. By exposing MOS RAMs

TABLE 2–1

Ratios of all errors to permanent errors

System/Technology	Error Detection Mechanism	System MTBE for all Fault Types (hrs)	System MTTF for Permanent Faults (hrs)	MTBE/MTTF
CMUA PDP-10, ECL	Parity	44	800–1600	0.03–0.06
CM* LSI-11, NMOS	Diagnostics	128	4200	0.03
C.vmp TMR LSI-11	Crash	97–328	4900	0.02–0.07
Telettra, TTL	Mismatch	80–170	1300	0.06–0.13
SUN-2, TTL, MOS	Crash	689	6552	0.11
IM × 37 RAM, MOS	Parity	106	1450	0.07

Source: Data from Siewiorek et al., 1978a; Morganti, 1978; McConnel, Siewiorek, and Tsao, 1979; Geilhufe, 1979; Ohm, 1979; Lin and Siewiorek, 1990.

* The same semiconductor evolution that has led to increased reliability per gate or bit has also introduced new failure modes. The smaller dimensions of semiconductor devices have decreased the amount of energy required to change the state of a memory bit. The loss of memory information caused by the decay of radioactive trace elements in packaging material has been documented. Studies show that even in sheltered environments such as well-conditioned computer rooms, transient/intermittent errors are 20 to 50 times more prevalent than hard failures. Transient/intermittent errors also exhibit clustering (a high probability that, once one error has occurred, another will occur soon), workload dependence (the heavier the system workload, the more likely an error), and common failure modes (more than one system, or portion of a system, affected simultaneously).

FIGURE 2–2

*Operational life er-
ror rate as function
of RAM densities
[From Geilhufe,
1979; ©1979 IEEE]*

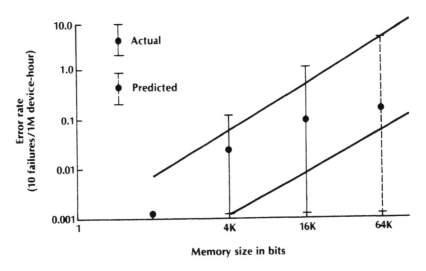

Memory size in bits

to artificial α-particle sources, the operational life error rate can be determined as a function of RAM density (Figure 2–2), voltage, and cycle time.

The Sun-2 data shown in Table 2–1 is derived from a study that observed 13 SUN-2 workstations on the Carnegie Mellon University Andrew network [Lin and Siewiorek, 1990]. Each workstation was composed of a Motorola 68010 processor with a 10-MHz clock and up to 4 Fujitsu Eagle-470 Mbyte disk drives. These workstations were used as a distributed file server system. Sampling techniques indicated that their workload was essentially constant.

Over 21 workstation-years of data from the Sun-2 file server system accumulated and is summarized as follows:

Source of Error	Number of Occurrences	Mean Time to Occurrence (hrs)
Permanent fault	29	6552
Intermittent fault	610	58
Transient fault	446	354
System crash	298	689

Permanent faults were determined through interviews with field service personnel and analysis of system maintenance logs. The most severe manifestation of an error is a system crash wherein the system software has to be reloaded and restarted. System crashes were determined from an on-line, distributed diagnostics system. All errors in the system log prior to a permanent fault were examined and allocated to either transient or intermittent.* If an error occurred indicating the same physical device

* It was assumed that a permanent failure resulted in only one system crash after which the system was totally inoperable.

within less than a week of the previous error, the error was deemed to be caused by an intermittent fault. Since the mean time to a transient fault was over two weeks, it was felt that there was little probability of inadvertently mixing intermittent and transient faults.

A number of interesting observations can be made from the Sun-2 data. The permanent faults represented approximately 10 percent of the system crashes. Thus, if permanent faults were eliminated, the system crash rate would only be improved by about 10 percent. The ratio of intermittent faults to permanent faults is about 20. Thus, the first intermittent symptom appears over 1200 (20 × 58 hours between intermittent occurrences) hours prior to the repair activity. This data represents a large window of vulnerability and provides ample opportunity for trend analysis to help isolate the source of failure (for example, see Symptom-Directed Diagnosis in Chapter 4). If we subtract the number of permanent faults from the system crashes and divide by the total number of faults we see that on average only 1 out of every 4 faults causes a system crash.*

In summary, since the only information available on errors is collected by relevant error-detecting mechanisms, it is very difficult in practice to detect all errors or determine their exact source. Very few studies have systematically attempted to determine the cause of errors. The existing evidence is that the vast majority are due to nonpermanent (i.e., intermittent or transient) faults.

Frequency of Errors by Type of Fault

The ultimate goal of any fault-tolerant system is not only to produce few errors but suffer as little down time as possible. Hardware modules are constantly improving their reliability and soon will reach in excess of 100,000 hours mean time between failure per module. However, transient and intermittent faults are 20–100 times more prevalent than hard failures, and these faults can lead to a system outage. Even after vendor and user quality assurance, thousands of bugs remain in system software. Most software failures are transient leading to a dump and restart of the system.

For example, typical sources of failure for a mainframe computing system as well as the typical mean time between failure (MTBF) and mean time to repair (MTTR) are given in the following table [Gray, 1990]:

Source of Failure	MTBF	MTTR
Power	2000 hrs	1 hr
Phone lines		
Soft	0.1 hr	0.1 sec
Hard	4000 hrs	10 hrs
Hardware modules	10,000 hrs	10 hrs
Software	1 bug/1,000 lines of code	

---

* Interestingly enough, 14 of the 29 permanent faults had 3 or fewer error log entries, and of those 14, 8 had no error log entries prior to repair, all of which indicates that there is substantial room for improvement in error-detecting mechanisms.

Since the outage of telephone lines due to soft failures is frequent and recovery is very quick, phone line outages tend to be scattered, impacting individual terminals but not the complete system. However, some form of redundancy, such as providing alternative paths, is clearly required to reduce the frequency of telephone line failures.

Among the several other studies providing data on how often computers fail is a survey of Japanese computer users [Watanabe, 1986], which included 1383 institutions over the period from June 1984 to July 1985. These users reported 7517 outages* with an average MTBF of 10 weeks and an average outage duration of 90 minutes. The sources of outage, the probability that the outage was due to the source, and the MTBF are given in the following table [Gray (Watanabe, translator), 1986]:

Source of Outage	Probability	MTBF (months)
Vendor hardware, software, and maintenance	0.420	5
Application software	0.250	9
Communication lines	0.120	18
Environment	0.112	24
Operations	0.093	24

In 1985 and 1987, Gray [1990] surveyed the Early Warning Reports (EWR) from Tandem's customer's systems. From June 1985 until June 1987, 1,300 customers were surveyed. Over 6,000 systems composed of 16,000 processors and 97,000 disks were included. The data represented 12,000 system years, 32,000 CPU years, 97,000 disk years of experience. Reports of 490 system failures were provided by 205 customers. The following table lists the sources of outage, the probability that an outage was due to the source, and the MTBF for the source [Gray, 1990]:

Sources of Outage	Probability	MTBF (yrs)
Hardware	0.29	140
Software	0.36	63
Operations	0.13	211
Maintenance	0.11	200
Environment	0.10	235

Resultant mean time between failures for a system was approximately 27 years.

Example. It is interesting to compare the theoretically predicted and actually measured probability of a disk pair failing. As will be shown in Chapter 5, the MTBF for a duplex system with failure rate λ and repair rate μ is given by Eq. 1.

$$\text{MTBF} \sim \frac{\mu}{2\lambda^2} \tag{1}$$

---

* The author did not define the meaning of outage; we may consider an outage to be a failure to provide service.

TABLE 2–2
Outage data for the Tandem two-year study

Source of Outage	Probability	Source of Outage	Probability
Hardware		Operations	
Disks	0.49	Procedures	0.42
Communications	0.24	Configuration	0.39
Processors	0.18	Move	0.13
Wiring	0.09	Overflow	0.04
Spares	0.01	Upgrade	0.01
Maintenance			
Disks	0.67		
Communications	0.20		
Processors	0.13		

Source: Gray, 1987.

For a 50,000 hour MTBF disk (failure rate = 1/50,000) with a 5-hour MTTR (repair rate = 1/5), Eq. 1 predicts a 28,000-year MTBF:

$$MTBF = \frac{(1/5)}{2(1/50,000)(1/50,000)} = 2.5 \times 10^8 \text{ hours} = 28,539 \text{ years}$$

Thirty-five double disk failures were reported in the 48,000 disk-pair years yielding a MTBF of 1371 years. The actually measured reliability was a factor of 20 less than theoretical, but it is a factor of 200 better than nonredundant disks. The MTBF of a CPU pair was measured at 877 years.

Table 2–2 further subdivides into constituent parts the sources of outage reported by Tandem customers. Both in hardware and in maintenance, disks and communications are the most probable sources of outage. In operations, procedural and configuration problems represent the major source of outage.

In another study [Gray, 1987], a large Tandem customer was examined in detail. The customer, a manufacturer, had 13 sites, with 10 sites in the United States, 1 in Canada, 1 in Mexico, and 1 in England. The customer had 14 nodes composed of 54 processors and 120 disks and made 18 system-years of data available for the study, including reports of 199 outages, yielding a 4-week MTBF. Of the 199 outages, 52 were due to power, yielding an MTBF of 4 months for power and an average outage duration of 1 hour; 22 were due to communication lines, yielding an average MTBF of 10 months for communications and an average outage duration of 11 hours; 47 were due to scheduled reorganizations of transfer files; 27 outages were due to installation of software; and the remaining 51 outages were distributed as indicated in Table 2–3. Table 2–3 lists the source of outages and the probability that the outages were due to the source. The table also gives the sources and probabilities for 99 unscheduled outages. As we can see, power is the largest single contributor to unscheduled outage. Figure 2–3 gives a distribution of the duration of power outage as a function of frequency for this Tandem study. By way of comparison, Figure 2–4 depicts the cumulative distribution of power outage durations for 350 Bell Canada locations studied

TABLE 2–3
Outage data for Tandem manufacturing customer

	Total Outages (n = 199)		Unscheduled Outages (n = 99)	
	Source	Probability	Source	Probability
	Power	0.261	Power	0.525
	Reorganization of transfer files	0.236	Communication lines	0.222
	Installation of software	0.136	Application software	0.101
	Communication lines	0.111	Max files	0.081
	Reconfiguration	0.091	Hardware	0.051
	Application software	0.050	Corrupted files	0.020
	Testing	0.040		
	Max files	0.040		
	Hardware	0.025		
	Corrupted files	0.010		

Source: Gray, 1987.

during a period of 8376 months [BNR, 1984]. During that time, 1420 outages were recorded, producing over 3600 hours of down time. The average outage lasted 2.54 hours. The graph in Figure 2–4 represents the percentage of outages that exceeded the duration marked on the horizontal axis. For example, about 24 percent of the outages exceeded 3 hours. Thus, if batteries that produce 3 hours of reserve power had been available at all locations, an average 24 percent of the locations would have insufficient power to maintain operation.

By way of contrast, 50 percent of the Tandem power outages exceeded 3 hours. Figure 2–5 depicts the number of Tandem customers reporting the specified number of outages during the two-year study. Over three-fourths of the customers had no outage in the two-year period. However, some customers had a large number of

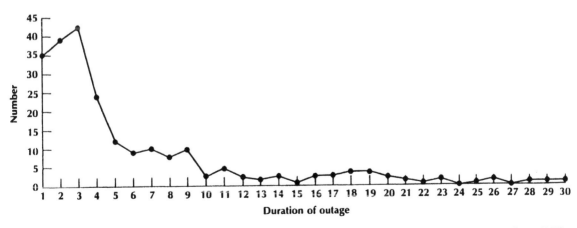

FIGURE 2–3 *Duration of power outages for Tandem manufacturing customer [From Gray, 1987]*

FIGURE 2–4
*Cumulative distri-
bution of power
outage durations
for Bell Canada
Study [From BNR,
1984]*

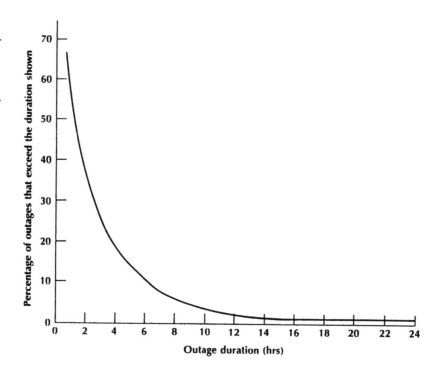

Outage duration (hrs)

problems that seemed to be independent of the size of the system. All large customers had some outages; hence, a customer with 140 CPUs and 20 systems should expect approximately one outage per year.

In summary, systems fail for many reasons, including hardware failure, incorrect design of hardware or software, improper operation or maintenance, and unstable environments. The probability of error is distributed over this entire spectrum with no single cause dominating. Hardware is rarely responsible for failures, and the frequency rate can often be measured in years rather than weeks or hours.

FIGURE 2–5
*Number of Tan-
dem customers re-
porting n outages
in two-year study
[From Gray, 1987]*

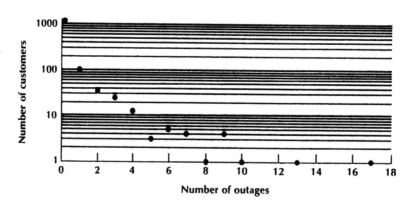

Number of outages

FAULT MANIFESTATIONS

Another essential ingredient for designing fault tolerant systems is to know how faults manifest into errors. What is the appearance of a fault to the next highest physical level of the design hierarchy? What is the relative probability of each manifestation? This section attempts to answer these questions by providing models of fault manifestations (i.e., fault models) and their relative probability for various levels of abstraction. Table 2–4 summarizes the fault models. This section discusses circuit-level, logic-level, and systems-level (i.e., program and PMS) fault manifestations and their relative probabilities.

Circuit-Level Fault Models

Circuit-level defects are the lowest level in the hierarchy of failures. There are numerous ways in which a semiconductor chip can fail. Some failures result from defects in the manufacturing process; others are caused by stress during normal operation.

The following are examples of MOS device failures [Czeck, Siewiorek, Segall, 1988; Fantini, 1984; Mangir, 1984; Middendorf and Hausken, 1988]:

1. Thin oxide breakdown is a primary mechanism which is caused by large electric fields in the insulator, usually in the gate oxide.
2. Electromigration, the drifting of metal atoms toward the cathode, is a common wear-out mechanism influenced by high current densities in the conductor.

TABLE 2–4 *Fault models for hierarchical physical levels of a digital system*

Level	Fault Model	Basis	Limitation
PMS	Communication lost, delayed, or unordered; lost nodes	Abstraction of behavior	Unknown and complex failure modes
Program	Data change; message or process lost; data inconsistent; time outs	Abstraction of behavior	Unknown and complex failure modes
Logic			
Register transfer Switching circuit	Data change; wrong assertion, source, or destination	Abstraction of behavior	Based on RT models, not implementation
Sequential	Complement or dual function truth table modification	Ad hoc observation	Many realizations and fault modes
Combinatorial	Gate output stuck at 0 or 1; Single stuck line	TTL and PC board behavior	Technology outdated
Circuit	New and missing devices; shorts and breaks (opens); transistors stuck on/off	Processing defects	Simulation overhead; difficult to observe and fault insert

Source: Czeck, 1991.

3. "Hot electron" trapping in the gate oxide is caused by high temperature and high electric fields in the channel of a MOS transistor.
4. Soft or transient errors are produced by α-particles and cosmic radiation, which create several electron-hole pairs affecting stored charges.
5. Electric overstress caused by improper environmental conditions such as electrostatic discharge, may cause multiple physical failures.
6. Other life failures are caused by an array of sources, including design deficiencies, production techniques, mechanical stress, and corrosion.

Little has been published on the distribution of field failures caused by the variation introduced by the manufacturing and operation environment. Additionally, knowledge regarding the effects of field failures on circuit behavior is limited, but several sources give isolated information. Lloyd and Knight [1984] empirically support the classification into a single failure model of shorts and opens caused by electromigration, but give no information on the resulting behavior. Timoc et al. [1983] attempted to map physical failures to logical models; several failures resulted in "stuck-at"* behavior, while others resulted in parametric faults.

It is interesting to contrast faults originating in manufacturing and field operation. In field operation, the frequency of failures is highest for gate oxide and next highest for opens and shorts in metal runs [Czeck, 1991]:

	Manufacturing	Field
Oxide	<10%	25%–75%
Metal	30%–40%	4%–17%

Oxide failures result in transistors stuck off (for both oxide breakdown and electron trapping). Metal failures result in open and shorted metal lines, breaks, and bridges (for electromigration). During manufacturing on the other hand, Ferguson [1987] reports less than 10 percent of mask defects cause oxide problems and 30 percent to 40 percent cause extra or missing metal, with an insignificant percentage of faults causing transistor stuck-off faults.

The Reliability Analysis Center (RAC) of the Rome Air Development Center (RADC) collects reliability data from government and industry on all phases of component development, assembly, testing, and field operation. The data are summarized in publications dealing with digital integrated circuits (ICs), hybrid circuits, linear/interface devices, memory/LSI, discrete transistors/diodes, and nonelectronic parts.

Summary data are provided on device fall-out rates (the percentage that fail initial screening), accelerated life testing (performed at high temperatures), and field operation. Analysis indicates the effect of package type, logic family, complexity, temper-

---

* Rather than respond to changing inputs, transistors may fail so that they always produce one output value. The transistor is referred to as "stuck at" that single value.

ature, environment, and screening class on failure rates. Detailed information gathered in each individual test of a device includes the following:

Device function

Test purpose: life, environmental/screening

Technology: bipolar; MOS; MOS, silicon gate; CMOS

Device complexity

Manufacturer/part number

Package material/type: ceramic, ceramic-metal, epoxy, silicone, phenolic, CAN, DIP, flat-pack

Number of pins

Screening class: MIL-STD-883 class B, MIL-STD-883 class C, selected screening, previously subjected to burn-in, previously subjected to environmental test, commercial off-the-shilf

Rated operational temperature

Ending date of test

Source of data: part-level environmental test, equipment-level reliability demonstration test, equipment-level checkout and burn-in, part-level burn-in, part-level life test

Test type: accelerated life (operating), autoclave, bond strength, burn-in, constant acceleration, electrical parameter measurement, leak, electrical measurement (functional), high pressure, humidity life (nonoperating), intermittent life, lead fatigue, mechanical shock, moisture resistance, dynamic operation life, operating life (equipment-level), power cycle, reverse bias life, humidity life with reverse bias, salt atmosphere, solderability, electrical measurement (static parameters), storage life, temperature-vibration-power cycle, temperature cycle, thermal shock, varied frequency vibration, visual inspection, wearout life test, X-ray

Stress level: ambient temperature, number of cycles, minimum and maximum stresses

Number of devices tested

Total number of device hours

Number of failed devices

Description of failures

Table 2–5 classifies the IC failures observed in the RAC data. Table 2–6 and Figure 2–6 summarize the data as a function of technology. Many of the defects relate to manufacture and assembly; others develop as a result of aging. To eliminate as many of these defects as possible before board insertion, various screening tests are employed to stress devices and promote early failure. The majority of the test types listed in the RAC data are electrical, mechanical, or environmental screens. Table 2–7 illustrates screening tests that can be used to uncover multiple defect types. Because screening consumes time, money, and resources, the amount of screening used is a major decision. The optimum amount is a function of screening costs, device costs, fall-out rate, and cost of device failure in an assembled system.

TABLE 2–5 *Integrated circuit failure classifications*

Failure Classification	Source	Failure Classification	Source
Surface	Contamination	Metalization defects	Open
	Foreign material/stray particles		Short
	Inversion/channeling		Pitted/corroded
	Surface leakage		Smeared/scratched
Bulk defects	Crystal imperfections		Electromigration
	Cracked, chipped die	Bond defects	Misplaced
Oxide defects	Gate oxide pinholes		Multiple band
	Field oxide pinholes		Smeared/overbanded
	Oxide fault		Lifted
	Oxide short/breakdown		Broken wire
	Glassivation defect		Intermetallic compound
Diffusion defects	Diffusion anomaly	Die defects	Cracked/chipped
	Diffusion spike	Input/output circuit defects	Excessive leakage
	Isolation defect		Circuit short
	Mask fault		

Logic-Level Fault Models

To determine the effect of failures on logic functions, circuit-level fault must be used to generate logic-level fault classes, which in turn are used to formulate system-level fault classes, and so on, since the hierarchical abstraction process prevents proliferation of details.

Most logic-level fault models are based on manufacturing defects, which is only a concern during a fraction of the system's lifetime [Abraham and Fuchs, 1986]. Logic-level faults have two other important properties: extent and value. The extent of a fault may be an independent occurrence (local) affecting a single logical variable, or it may be correlated with other simultaneous occurrences (related) because of the density of logic elements or the failure of a common element. The fault value may be deter-

TABLE 2–6
Summary of observed defects in RAC data: SSI, MSI, LSI

General Defect Classification	CMOS		Standard TTL	
	No. Malfunctions	Relative Percent	No. Malfunctions	Relative Percent
Surface	65	38%	66	16%
Bulk	12	7	29	7
Oxide	54	32	59	14
Diffusion	10	6	32	8
Metalization	14	8	213	51
Input/output circuit	15	9	17	4

Source: Data from Rickers, 1976, and Klein, 1976.

FIGURE 2–6
IC defects observed in RAC study (data from Table 2–6)

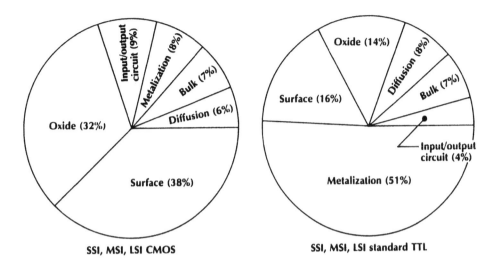

SSI, MSI, LSI CMOS   SSI, MSI, LSI standard TTL

minate (such as stuck-at-1) or indeterminate (for example, it varies between logical 0 and 1).

Switching-Circuit Fault Models. The way circuit level faults are manifested at the switching circuit level is a function of the way the basic circuit components operate. There are two general types of transistors used in digital circuits: metal oxide semiconductors (MOS) and transistor-transistor logic (TTL). MOS transistors behave like a bidirectional switch letting current flow in either direction. TTL transistors either block the current or allow current to flow in only one direction.

Switch-level fault models [Bryant, 1984] are used for MOS devices where unidirectional logic gate models do not adequately detail the bidirectional behavior of such devices under certain fault types (e.g., bridging and stuck open and closed transistors). Switch-level models contain nodes connected by bidirectional transistors (switches); faults are nodes stuck high or low, transistors stuck open or closed, and extra or missing transistors. Low-level simulations and models are required because the modes of devices, especially CMOS [Galiay, Crouzet, and Vergniault, 1980], cannot be modeled at the gate or higher levels. Furthermore, there is limited generation and test coverage assessment, but the simulation cannot be used for large systems because modeling and simulation time become prohibitive.

Gate-level fault models assume that inputs and outputs of gates are stuck at high or low logic values, but that the gate functions correctly. The faults are based on printed circuit (PC) boards, TTL, and pre-TTL logic (circa 1960). The following gate-level fault models have been used successfully as abstractions of the physical defect mechanisms:

• *Stuck-at:* Logical values in lines, gates, pins, and the like are permanently constrained to a value of stuck-at-1 (s-a-1) or 0 (s-a-0).

TABLE 2–7
Tests to detect manufacturing defects in ICs

Screening Test	Substrate Bonding Defects	Substrate Thin Film Defects	Bulk Silicon Defects	Silicon Surface Defects	Contamination or Corrosion	Wire Bonding Defects	Die Metalization Defects	Electrical Stability	Resistor and Chip Defects	Hermetic Seal Defects	Package Defects	External Lead Defects	Cracked Die or Substrates
Wafer probe		x	x			x	x	x					
Wafer inspection				x	x		x						x
Precap inspection	x	x		x	x	x	x						x
Stabilization bake			x	x	x	x	x	x					
Thermal cycling	x	x		x		x	x		x	x	x		x
Thermal shock	x	x		x		x	x		x	x	x		x
Hermeticity										x	x		
Centrifuge	x			x	x						x		
Mechanical shock	x			x	x						x		x
Vibration	x			x	x						x		
Burn-in		x	x	x	x	x	x	x					
Radiographic	x			x	x					x			x
External visual										x	x	x	
Scanning electron microscope		x		x	x		x						x

Source: Data from Rickers, 1976, and Klein, 1976.

- *Bridging:* Two or more adjacent signal lines are physically shorted together, introducing in some logic families an additional "wired-AND" or "wired-OR" function.
- *Short* or *Open:* These faults correspond to missing (open) or additional (short) connections.
- *Unidirectional:* Multiple signal lines are in error in the same logical direction when some single failure occurs, due to the geometric nature of circuits. (For example, an open circuit in a memory-select line may cause a word to be incorrectly read as all 1s—that is, correct 0s have been transformed into incorrect 1s.)

The gate-level fault model is not applicable to MOS implementations because failure modes are possible that transform a combinational MOS circuit into a sequential circuit [Wadsack, 1978]*, and complex MOS circuit implementations do not map gate

---

* Results from [Ferguson, 1987] show that the occurrence of these types of faults from manufacturing defects is less than 2 percent of all faults that occur.

lines to circuit nodes. Beh et al. [1982] emphasized that fault models should be consistent with manufacturing defects, and developed a methodology relating TTL processing defects to their logic behavior. Beh's work was limited to the demonstration of which defects can be modeled by gate-level stuck-at faults and did not attempt to develop new fault models.

Ferguson [1987] and Shen, Maly, and Ferguson [1985] developed fault models based on processing mask defects and mapped the defects to gate-level fault models, illustrating that only 50 percent of the faults are representable by a gate-level single stuck line fault. The following gives the manufacturing fault manifestations and probability of occurrence for a representative circuit [Shen, Maly, and Ferguson, 1985]:

Fault Type	Number	Probability
Line stuck-at	132	0.28
Transistor stuck-at	70	0.15
Floating line	101	0.21
Bridging	144	0.30
Miscellaneous	29	0.06

Note that these fault manifestations, predicted by seeding mask layers with defects from manufacturing-derived distributions, circuit extraction, and simulation, are not equally likely. Furthermore, only 28 percent are specifically stuck-at line faults. At best, only 64 percent of the faults can be modeled as single or multiple stuck-at faults. Indeed, bridging faults represent the largest single category. Marchal [1985] challenged the stuck-at models used in functional testing with simulations of faulted microprocessor internal buses. Results show that fault models should be realization- and technology-dependent, with models updated as technology advances. These approaches require realization details and do not further abstract faults to higher levels.

Register Transfer-Level Fault Models.* As integration levels increase further, testing based on implementation faults becomes prohibitive, and functional testing approaches, either implementation-dependent or -independent, must be used [Hayes, 1985; Su and Lin, 1984]. Thatte and Abraham [1978, 1979, 1980] presented the ground work for functional testing, with fault models based on possible scenarios of failures occurring within the control section, data section, or data storage of a generalized microprocessor. These models were implementation-independent; hence, they did not embody a complete fault library, but they were used to generate test procedures for microprocessors. Silberman and Spillinger [1986] presented a formalized methodology to define the functional level fault model, given the implementation of a circuit, its related defects, and the input vector. The resultant functional fault model was then used in simulations to acquire a better estimate of implementation fault coverage, thus saving the overhead of low-level simulation.

Instruction set processor testing has been proposed and implemented [Davidson, 1984; Davidson and Lewandowski, 1986], with fault models mostly ad hoc. Stuck-at faults of input and output nets and mutation operation in the microprocessor (Thatte

* This section is adapted from Czeck et al., 1989.

and Abraham model) and in control resources (instruction fetch and decode units) have been included in this architectural-level fault model. The evaluation of these models was based on test coverage results from simulations at the architectural and gate levels, with results of the architectural simulations, at best, tracking the coverage of the test programs and showing which fault models are appropriate.

Throughout the referenced papers, the goal was to substantiate or formalize the fault models used at the higher levels based on known failure modes* or lower level fault models. There are still some limitations in predicting higher (component) level fault behavior, even with fault models based on manufacturing defect distributions. Using a gate-level emulation of an avionic processor, an 87 percent coverage of all gate-level faults and a 98 percent coverage for all component† (pin) level faults were demonstrated [McGough and Swern, 1981, 1983; McGough, Swern, and Bavuso, 1983]. These studies concentrated on logic value faults and did not consider parametric or other faults.

Some results from software testing support the concept of functional testing based on abstract fault models. One interesting result is the comparison between "black-box" testing, which is similar to the functional level in hardware, and structural testing, which is similar to the component level. In "black-box" testing the internal structure of the module is unknown. The test input generation proceeds from specifications given to the module, with an emphasis on boundary values of both the input and output vectors. In structural or "white-box" testing, the internal structure of the program is known, and the test generation typically attempts to exercise *all paths*. Howden [1980] showed that "black-box" testing was significantly more effective in error detection than structural testing because of subtleties in the data selection. Data for "white-box" testing are geared to exercise each path once for some data, but data for "black-box" testing are geared to exercise the program for the range of valid data. Lai [1979, 1981] and Lai and Siewiorek [1983] showed the merits of functional testing of hardware without the details of hardware implementation.

System-Level Fault Models

The manifestations of intermittent and transient faults and of incorrect hardware and software design are much harder to determine than permanent faults. The permanent fault models often can be applied to intermittent faults; however, because the fault is present only temporarily and because most contemporary computer systems do not have substantial on-line error detection, the normal manifestations of an intermittent fault are at the system level (such as system crash or I/O channel retry). Transient faults and incorrect designs do not have a well-defined, bounded, basic fault model. Transient faults are a combination of local phenomena (such as ground loops, static electricity discharges, power lines, and thermal distributions) and universal phenomena (such as cosmic rays, α-particles, power supply characteristics, and mechanical design).

---

* Most of the failure modes considered were during the manufacturing phase.
† A component, as used in this study, is defined as a single SSI, MSI, or LSI chip.

Even if models could be developed for transient faults and incorrect designs, they would quickly become obsolete because of the rapid changes in technology.

Design Faults. The design and operation of a computer is a system-level activity composed of many elements such as the human organization in which the activity is embedded, software manuals, and the computer-aided design or operations software. While a design fault may be localized to a component on one particular level of abstraction, the fault is a result of a complex design system. Furthermore, most computer systems do not have enough instrumentation to trace the propagation of a fault from its origin to its manifestation. Thus, design faults are most often propagated to the program or PMS level before an error is detected. Very often, naturally occurring faults are also propagated to the systems level. One way to determine how well a system is designed to tolerate errors is to experimentally inject a known fault. This section discusses design faults and system behavior with naturally occurring and artificially injected faults.

Errors that occur during the early stages of system life are the most difficult to collect data on and to generalize. While there are several studies on the detection and correction of bugs in software, there are very few published studies on hardware design faults. In the design of the IBM 3081, it was estimated that one error was encountered for every 4000 circuits in data path (regular) design, and one error was encountered for every 1000 circuits on control (random) design [Monachino, 1982]. Another study was conducted by International Computers Limited (ICL) during the construction of a mid-range mainframe built from Schottky TTL [Faulkner, Bartlett, and Small, 1982]. Errors were attributed to specification (incorrect specifications, ambiguities, and omissions), environment (technology rule violations such as timing and loading, noise, and design automation software mistakes), and realization (logic design errors, concurrency problems, initializations, error management fault, compatibility, testability/maintainability, initialization, and clock distribution).

The design phase was divided into individual subsystem debugging (before system integration) and integration of the subsystems to form a whole system, as well as integration with previously existing products (after system integration). The following table summarizes the number of printed circuit boards (PCBs) in the main region of the (ICL) computer as well as the number of faults discovered before and after system integration [Faulkner, Bartlett, and Small, 1982]:

	Faults per PCB Before System Integration	Faults per PCB After System Integration	Number of PCBs
Processor	12.0	1.5	43
Memory	5.5	2.5	41
I/O	6.0	1.75	29

Table 2–8 lists the sources and distribution of faults during the design integration phases. As expected, logical faults represent the majority of the problems prior to the hardware integration. After integration of the boards into a system, logical faults still

TABLE 2–8

Fault data for ICL hardware design

Source	Percent Before System Integration	Percent After System Integration
Logic error	52	21
Testability/maintainability	17	12
Compatibility	15	4
Technology rules violated	6	25
Clock fault	6	2
Specification	4	19
Error management	–	10
Noise	–	4
Design automation errors	–	2
Performance	–	1

Source: Data from Faulkner, Bartlett, and Small, 1982; © 1982 IEEE.

remain, but occur roughly equally with specification and physical faults (violation of physical design rules).

A series of studies to validate the behavior of FTMP, a prototype fault-tolerant multi-processor, indicated the following types of design faults [Clune, 1984; Feather, 1985; and Czeck, 1986]:

• Many of the exception interrupts did not have proper interrupt handlers. These exceptions included arithmetic overflow, write protection violation, illegal opcode, stack overflow, privileged instruction violation, and privileged mode call. Generation of these exceptions in user mode caused a halt instruction to be executed. Furthermore, the interrupt vector for the divide exception was not implemented. A division by zero in user mode crashed the machine. To avoid stalling the system because of exceptions, all application software was executed in privileged mode, in which interrupts are ignored.

• All tasks were specified to execute within a 40-millisecond frame. The frame boundaries were considered to be hard deadlines, and tasks were not to be allowed to execute beyond a frame boundary. The task dispatcher required 15, 66, and 40 milliseconds to schedule three consecutive tasks. This repeatable scheduling pattern was never satisfactorily explained. As a result, application tasks (including the dispatcher time) required 40, 110, and 90 milliseconds to execute. Again the sequence was repetitive.

• In order to provide adequate time for a task to complete, a "frame stretching" mechanism was provided whereby a task could ask for more time. Repeated use of the frame stretching mechanism allowed a task to monopolize a processor and lock out all other tasks.

• Arranging for the first task in the dispatcher table to point to itself as the next task also caused an infinite loop in which the single task monopolized the processor.

Lee [1989] studied the design faults from a commercial pipelined CPU implementing a virtual memory 32-bit architecture.* During the CPU development project, a design log entry was recorded for *every* problem the design team encountered. The faults are summarized in Table 2–9, which shows the design log entries classified into categories and organized in a descending order of percentage of the total design log entries. According to the different phases of the project, these faults are divided into three columns: Phase 1 spans the time period from the conception of the project to the time the register transfer level (RTL) design is available, Phase 2 spans up to when the detailed gate-level logic design is complete in the design database, and Phase 3 starts from the time the first prototype machine was ready for debug use. The percentages shown in the phase columns are the percentage of the total faults in that time phase. The last column reflects the relative percent over all faults in all phases.

This design log reflects the state of the art in the mid–1980s. One interesting point worth noting is the very low number of design tool faults (only 0.13%). This low figure reflects not only the robustness of the tools, but also their relative simplicity, which leaves many design activities to human engineering efforts (otherwise, the total number of errors would be much smaller). All faults are possible at every stage in a product's life cycle. The only difference is the frequency of faults. Naturally, realization faults did not appear in the earlier phases because the design had not yet been reduced to physical devices.

The majority of faults in this log fall into the category of logic design faults. These faults could be subclassifed as follows:

Simple logic fault, such as missing term in logic equation or incorrect signal destination, incorrect logic equation, incorrect signal polarity, and missed signal latching

Concurrency/interlock logic fault, such as correct signal read during wrong cycle or interlock signal asserted at wrong cycle

Logic not conforming to specifications, such as design not meeting the specification's requirement

Logic design faults dominate all three time periods. Automatic tools for the translation from the RTL design to the gate-level design should eliminate a majority of these human-induced logic design faults.

Microcode verification methods [Joyner and Carter, 1976] are maturing rapidly and can be applied to the microcode portion of the design. However, verification methods are not expected to remove all microcode problems in a real design. Proving microcode is similar to proving the correctness of software. This problem could be included with the general design verification problem. Console code faults fall into the domain of software. Software engineering techniques should be able to assist in correcting this area. Timing analysis tools were extensively utilized during the whole course of this

---

* The remainder of this section is adapted from Lee, 1989.

TABLE 2–9
Design log entries for CPU study

Fault Category	Phase 1	Phase 2	Phase 3	Total of All Faults, All Phases
Logic design faults	20.88%	45.28%	19.68%	33.10%
Microcode faults	18.68%	11.05%	12.20%	12.43%
Timing design faults	0	9.16%	16.93%	10.75%
Console code faults	0	0	14.17%	5.02%
RTL coding faults	25.27%	3.50%	0	5.02%
RTL model faults	3.29%	7.28%	1.96%	4.88%
Physical design faults	0	7.81%	4.88%	4.88%
Simulation process problems	13.18%	4.04%	2.36%	4.61%
Specification misinterpretation	1.09%	1.08%	6.30%	2.93%
AVP* process problems	4.39%	1.35%	2.36%	2.09%
AVP internal problems	7.69%	0.54%	1.96%	1.95%
Misc.	3.29%	1.61%	1.96%	1.95%
Incorrect signal names	2.19%	0.81%	2.75%	1.67%
Fabrication process faults	0	0.81%	3.15%	1.53%
Bad components	0	0.27%	3.54%	1.39%
Component specification faults	0	1.89%	1.18%	1.39%
Mechanical design faults	0	1.08%	1.57%	1.11%
Gate level model faults	0	0.80%	1.57%	0.97%
Console disk problems	0	0	1.57%	0.56%
Documentation faults	0	0.80%	0	0.42%
Incorrect rework orders	0	0	1.18%	0.42%
Release control problems	0	0.27%	0.78%	0.42%
Design tool fault	0	0.27%	0	0.13%
Power system problem	0	0	0.39%	0.13%
Total faults	100%	100%	100%	100%
Related with pipelines	6.6%	2.96%	1.18%	2.79%

*Architectural verification program.
Source: Data from Lee, 1989.

CPU project, and thus contributed to the detection of almost 45 percent of all timing faults even before the first prototype machine was constructed. The reason it did not detect all timing faults during the second phase is that the number of timing paths was too large to completely analyze during this phase.

RTL coding faults in Table 2–9 refer to incorrectness in the implementation of the RTL model when the concept in the designer's mind was correct. In a sense, this fault class is similar to the simple logic design fault. On the other hand, the RTL model fault is a conceptual design fault; that is, the designer's concept about the RTL model was incorrect from the start. This class of faults is more significant because while other fault classes could benefit from the available automatic tools, the human thought process is not supported by many tools. The design faults (including microcode faults and RTL model faults) constitute about 17.45 percent of the total faults. The percentage of design faults associated with the pipeline concurrent/interlock design is 16.13. Thus, 2.79 percent of the total faults are related to the pipelining. Physical design faults, such as an unroutable wire or missing pull-down resistors, could largely be eliminated using automatic tools. Problems with the simulation process are mainly associated with the actual simulation and the interface between different files. Strict project management should eliminate all these problems as well as release control problems.

The architectural verification program used in this project generates random sequences of macro instruction that are executed on the RTL models, gate-level models, and the real hardware prototype. The result from the machine under development is then compared with another known "good" implementation of the target architecture. There is no guarantee that the result from the "good" implementation is correct whenever there is a discrepancy between these two executions. Human intervention and interpretation of the target architecture are then necessary to resolve the problem. All other fault categories should be resolved or reduced through more rigid documentation from the engineering group, better communication between different organizations, higher component specification standards, and stricter component screening procedures.

Naturally Occurring Faults.* Consider now the types of system-level manifestations that might be expected from intermittent faults, transient faults, and incorrect design. The experience reported next, which is derived from an extensive study of system crashes on C.mmp, a multiprocessor in which 16 processors converse with 16 memories through a crosspoint switch, indicate that system-level fault behavior is complex. There is a large gap between logic-level fault models and system-level manifestations. Much work remains to be done before an acceptable system-level model can be developed.

In C.mmp memory parity faults were the most common, accounting for 50 to 100 percent of the system crashes. Most were transient. Often the memory failure rate determined the mean time to crash.

It was difficult to locate the source of the transient faults, since there are few trace points in most data paths on C.mmp. The fact that powerful debugging aids were not included in the logical design continuously hampered development. Little could be done for the standard processors, but aids could have been incorporated in all the custom-built logic. A similar weakness was apparent in the software: Often information about a failure was lost by the operating system, making recording of the conditions for transients unreliable.

A particularly difficult transient fault was the problem of false NXMs. The processor reported a nonexistent memory (NXM) exception, but subsequent analysis showed that the memory was responding, and the instructions, registers, and index words were well formed. No exception should have resulted. Timing problems were suspected, but there was insufficient information available to isolate the fault.

Another difficult transient fault was associated with stack operation. These prob-

* This section is excerpted and adapted from Siewiorek et al., 1978a.

lems usually appeared as incorrect execution of subroutine call/return instructions or interrupt entry/exit mistakes. The most common form of the error was one too many (or one too few) words pushed (or popped) from the stack. This transient fault was relatively rare, and no method of recovering from it was developed.

A pleasant surprise was the reliability of the crosspoint switch; however, an early problem required considerable effort to fix. Certain conditions, characterized by a memory access not completed by the UNIBUS master, could cause the switch to deadlock because of the lack of a time-out circuit in the memory port control logic. Any other processor attempting to access the deadlocked memory port would block until it was manually cleared. This situation was often caused by poorly designed I/O controllers that recovered from errors by simply aborting the current access, with no regard for proper termination of UNIBUS or crosspoint switch protocols. While the known cases that caused deadlocked memory ports were isolated and individually remedied, the most important result was an appreciation of the design principle of *mutual suspicion*. The crosspoint switch should never trust that an operation started will necessarily be completed; it must be prepared to time-out, clear itself, and report a fault condition to the requesting processor.

The interprocessor bus was as unreliable as the crosspoint switch was trustworthy. The reliability was so poor that, if a cheap and highly effective method of software recovery had not been found, the bus would have been unusable. The mode of failure was transient loss of interprocessor interrupts and changing interrupt level.

The data shown in Figure 2–7 were culled from the crash reports produced by the C.mmp operating system's suspect/monitor crash logging system. These dumps were manually analyzed to determine the reason for the crash. Sometimes the reason could not be found; the analysis was always error-prone because the crash records were never intended as a precise reliability measure. Rather, they were programmers' and engineers' tools to isolate trouble spots in the system. With this caveat in mind, the data may be discussed.

A fault causing a crash may be the result of either hardware or software. Of the five crash symptoms plotted in Figure 2–7, only parity faults were necessarily caused by hardware. All the other crashes are brought about by either hardware or software, and analysis is required to determine the actual cause. The source of most faults can be determined, but a substantial number of crashes of unknown origin remain. The frequency of software-related faults is strongly correlated to the introduction of new features. Being new and relatively untested, these features are likely to have previously undetected faults. Once the feature is installed, any errors caused by it were found and corrected very quickly. Therefore, the trend was bursts of errors, with any particular error becoming less frequent as time passes. In Figure 2–7, the four months with high software crash counts all follow this trend, even though new faults kept the counts high for several consecutive months.

Artificially Injected Faults. In order to bridge the gap between observed system behavior and logic-level fault models, carefully designed experiments must be conducted. Table 2–10 depicts the results of injecting transient stuck-at-one (zero) faults of various

FIGURE 2–7
*Summary of
C.mmp crash data
[From Siewiorek
et al., 1978a; ©1978
IEEE]*

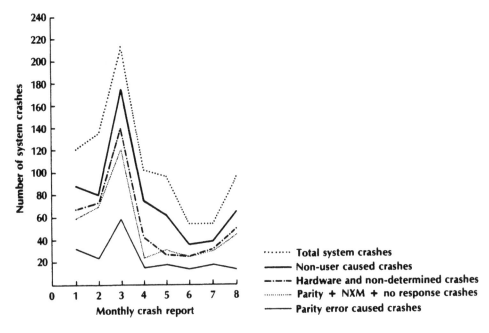

durations into different lines of the processor-memory bus of a Motorola 68000 [Schuette et al., 1986]. Longer duration faults are more likely to be detected, although the fault latency (time from fault injection until detection) was approximately constant. Faults in the fetch cycle were much more likely to be detected than data faults since the Motorola 68000 detects illegal operation codes. Thus, a high percentage of even simple, incorrect stuck-at-one (zero) faults have either a long error-detection latency or go completely undetected. The table also illustrates that the probability of error detection and the detection latency is highly dependent upon the function of the bus line. In particular, certain address line faults and control line faults are difficult to detect and have high error-detection latencies.

Table 2–11 lists the distribution of injected faults by the mechanisms that detected them. A little over 47 percent of the faults were detected by built-in error-detection mechanisms in the Motorola 68000 (e.g., odd address, illegal address, etc.). A further 8 percent of the faults caused a permanent change in the processor state yet did not alter the output of the benchmark. Next, the same faults were injected into one copy of three identical computations that used software voting to tolerate faults. Approximately 9 percent more of the faults were not only tolerated but also did not produce disagreement among the voted outputs. A further 33 percent were detected, with 31 percent of these being corrected by the voter. A little less than 2 percent of the faults were not correctible even by voting.

Arlat, Crouzet, and Laprie [1989] injected 529 hardware faults into the memory of a Motorola 68000 system. A coverage of 55 percent was observed for hardware mech-

TABLE 2–10 *Injected faults in the Motorola 68000 processor study*

	Number of Instances	Number Detected	Percentage	Average Latency (μs)	Standard Deviation (μs)	Tolerated Instances with Permanent Changes
Fault duration						
1 cycle	493	202	41	13,000	85,000	43
2 cycles	484	298	61	12,000	70,000	56
4 cycles	460	313	68	14,000	91,000	52
Bus type						
Instruction	1,053	724	69	4,100	42,000	122
Data	384	89	23	82,000	200,000	29
Line faulted						
D0	131	79	60	4,300	23,000	19
D7	131	78	60	1,200	9,000	9
D8	131	63	48	1,600	10,000	11
D15	130	81	62	210	550	17
A1	131	72	55	450	960	16
A4	131	67	51	24,000	110,000	15
A8	129	76	59	1,600	10,000	13
A12	131	94	72	81,000	210,000	58
LDS	131	97	73	98	520	8
UDS	130	92	71	51	200	8
DTACK	131	14	11	43,000	100,000	5
Total/Average	1,437	813	58	13,000	82,000	179

Source: Schuette et al., 1986; ©1986 IEEE.

anisms and 92 percent was observed for software diagnostics. A total of 5760 faults were injected into the total system of which software detected 32 percent, hardware detected 2 percent, and both detected 19 percent for a total coverage of 53.6 percent.

Fault injection can be used to validate the fault handling mechanisms of systems as well as to produce a model for system-level manifestations of faults. A fault injection-based automated testbed (FIAT) [Segall et al., 1988] provides for the automatic seeding of faults selected from fault classes into a user-provided workload. Experiments are automatically conducted and statistics analyzed. Two types of error detection coverage were identified:

1. Latent/active faults detection coverage (LAC): the ratio of detected faults to latent (nondetected) faults.*

---

* Experimental evidence suggests that there is a strong linear dependency of LAC on the amount of unrefreshable data associated with the workload.

TABLE 2–11
Distribution of injected faults in the Motorola 68000 study

Fault Detection Mechanism	Probability
Built-in detection	
Detected	0.473
Tolerated with permanent changes	0.081
Software voting	
No voted data error	0.093
Tolerated with permanent changes	0.003
Voted data error	
Corrected	0.311
Tolerated with permanent changes	0.021
Unrecoverable errors*	0.018

*Unmaskable errors in data or inability to completely execute benchmarks.
Source: Schuette et al., 1986; ©1986 IEEE.

2. Error detection coverage (EDC): the ratio of application and operating system detected errors divided by all detected errors.*

Two workloads—matrix multiplication and selection sort—were studied. The code size varied from 1300 to 1500 bytes, with data varying between 300 and 1000 bytes. Three fault instances were exhaustively injected:

- *Two-bit compensating faults:* Two bits of a 32-bit word were inverted to represent faults that would not be detected by simple parity in the memory, bus, or data register.
- *Zero-a-byte:* Contiguous 8-bit segments of a 32-bit word were zeroed to emulate a chip-select failure, a race condition, or bus transceiver package failure.
- *Set-a-byte:* Contiguous 8-bit segments of a 32-bit word were set to emulate faults similar to those in zero-a-byte.

The following table [Segall et al., 1988] indicates LAC percentage as a function of the workload and fault instance:

Latent/Active Fault Detection Coverage

Workload	Fault Instance (%)			
	2-Bit	Zero	Set	Total
3 × 3 matrix multiplication	62.1	53.6	61.9	59.2
4 × 4 matrix multiplication	62.7	52.7	62.7	59.4
6 × 6 matrix multiplication	56.7	43.2	55.7	51.9
Selection sort	59.4	—	59.3	59.3

It is interesting to note that the LAC percentage is very similar to that achieved by transient fault injection transient errors on the Motorola 68000 bus (58 percent)

* Faults injected into data regions that are initialized prior to use will have no effect upon the computation. To eliminate these null faults, three means of error detection were utilized: the operating system, the application software, and a comparison of the injected workload to a fault-free controlled workload. The EDC is thus 1 − (comparator detected errors/all detected errors).

[Schuette et al., 1986]. The EDC percentage [Segall et al., 1988] as a function of the workload and fault instance is as follows:

Error Detection Coverage

Workload	Fault Instance (%)			
	2-Bit	Zero	Set	Total
3 × 3 matrix multiplication	65.9	60.4	58.0	61.4
4 × 4 matrix multiplication	66.5	59.8	58.8	61.7
6 × 6 matrix multiplication	69.1	62.6	59.7	63.8
Selection sort	68.0	N/A	61.4	64.7

The EDC is slightly larger than the LAC.

It is interesting to observe that only five system-level manifestations of errors resulted from these fault-injection experiments. These manifestations included the following:

- *Tasks Stop:* When the operating system detected an illegal instruction, illegal data, illegal address, or some other miscellaneous condition, it aborted the task abnormally.
- *Invalid Output:* In this case both of the computation tasks sent results to the comparitor, but the comparitor detected a discrepancy between the two output strings.
- *Response Too Late:* In this case the faulty computation task neither sent results to the comparitor nor exhibited any signs of abnormal termination; consequently, the comparitor waited until its time-out and then displayed an error message.
- *Machine Crash:* When a fault injection caused the machine to reboot, this was considered a machine crash.
- *Machine Hang:* On rare occasions, a fault injection caused a processor stop condition in the machine.

While a probability of error detection is important, the time to respond to an error is almost as significant, especially in real-time systems. The first component in error handling time is error latency. *Error latency* is defined as the time that lapses between the injection of a fault and its detection by the system. The following table [Segall et al., 1988] gives the mean error latency as a function of the system manifestation that first detected the error:

Mean Error Latency (in seconds)

Workload	System-Level Manifestation of Error		
	Response Too Late	Invalid Output	Task Stop
3 × 3 matrix multiplication	5.09	2.43	5.10
4 × 4 matrix multiplication	5.18	2.46	5.17
6 × 6 matrix multiplication	5.16	2.58	5.19
Selection sort	6.14	3.26	5.98

Note that the latency is measured in seconds, indicating that a large amount of system activity can occur between the injection of an error and its detection. These results were obtained through over 130,000 individual fault injection experiments.

FIAT has also been used to compare alternative fault-tolerant strategies. For example, consider two computational engines, a primary and a secondary engine. At the start of its computation, the primary informs the secondary of the task, as well as the time frame for the next interaction. The primary then executes the request and the secondary waits for the next interaction. If the time between interactions exceeds the time frame (i.e., primary failure), the secondary then initiates a recovery action and becomes the primary. If the primary detects that no secondary exists (i.e., secondary failure), it creates a secondary. Two-bit compensating faults were injected, resulting in an EDC of 74 percent and an average error detection latency of 4.2 seconds. Next, the primary/secondary system was augmented by adding check summing to each computational engine. A check sum is appended to code and data blocks during compilation. The code is regenerated when reading the blocks from memory during run time and is compared with the predetermined code to detect errors. This scheme detected 94.5 percent of the injected faults with an average detection time of 3.1 seconds. Thus, automated systems such as FIAT represent one way of performing complex system design trade-offs.

**FAULT
DISTRIBUTIONS**

Thus far, this chapter has summarized observed behavior by probabilities and averages. In order to predict the behavior of complete systems, these probabilities must be determined as a function of time. This section provides the necessary background to determine what time varying mathematical distributions fit the observed data. The section starts with a review of basic probability, then introduces the probability distributions most often encountered in reliability modeling. The section concludes with techniques used to decide which probability distribution is the best approximation to observed data. The theory introduced in this section will be applied to modeling permanent, intermittent, and transient fault data in the remainder of the chapter.

Probability Review

Central to the study of probability is the notion of *randomness*. A phenomenon is considered random if its future behavior is not exactly predictable. Tossing a pair of dice or measuring the time between α-particle emissions by a radioactive sample are examples of experiments that involve random phenomena. In many cases, it is more interesting to know the value of a number associated with the experiment under observation rather than the actual outcome. Thus, there must be a function that associates a number with every possible outcome of an experiment. Such a function is called a *random variable*. The time between any two failures of an electronic component, the number of jobs processed by a computer center in one day, or the time to the next crash of a time-sharing system are examples of random variables.

For each random variable, X, its *cumulative distribution function* (CDF), denoted $F(x)$, is defined as

$$F(x) = P(X \leq x) \tag{2}$$

That is, $F(x)$ is the probability P that the event X is less than or equal to the value of x. If X is a discrete random variable, all its possible values $(x_1, x_2, x_3, \ldots)$ can be put into one-to-one correspondence with the positive integers. The *probability mass function* (PMF), denoted $f(x)$, is then defined as

$$f(x) = P(X = x) \tag{3}$$

If X is a continuous random variable, its *probability density function* (PDF), denoted $f(x)$, is defined as

$$f(x) = \frac{dF}{dx} \tag{4}$$

such that, in general

$$P(a \leq x \leq b) = \int_a^b f(x)\, dx \tag{5}$$

The two most important parameters used to describe or summarize the properties of a random variable X are the *mean* or *expected value* $E[X]$ and the variance σ_X^2. If X is discrete,

$$E[X] = \sum_{x_i} x_i f(x_i) = x_1 f(x_1) + x_2 f(x_2) + \cdots \tag{6}$$

while if X is continuous,

$$E[X] = \int_{-\infty}^{\infty} x f(x)\, dx \tag{7}$$

The *variance* is defined as

$$\sigma_X^2 = E[(x - E[x])^2] \tag{8}$$

The mean acts as a kind of summary of what we expect from a random variable, and the variance measures the deviations of a random variable from its mean. The *standard deviation* σX (the square root of the variance) is also used to measure the variability of a random variable about its mean.

Two more functions are of particular interest in reliability theory. If the random variable under study is the time T to the next failure of a system or component the *reliability function* $R(t)$ is defined as

$$R(t) = 1 - F(t) \tag{9}$$

$$= P[T > t] \tag{10}$$

$R(t)$ is thus the probability of not observing any failure before time t.

Finally, the *hazard function* $z(t)$ is defined as

$$z(t) = \frac{f(t)}{1 - F(t)} \tag{11}$$

With renewal processes techniques, it can be shown that $z(t - \tau)\Delta t$ is the conditional probability that the nth failure occurs in the infinitesimal interval $(t, t + \Delta t)$ given that the $(n - 1)$st point occurs at time τ [Snyder, 1975]. Hence, failures/unit time are the units of $z(t)$, and $z(t)$ provides a description of how the instantaneous probability of failure evolves in time.

Fault Distribution Models

Exponential Distribution. The exponential distribution is the one most commonly encountered in reliability models. The probability density function (PDF), cumulative distribution function (CDF), reliability function, and hazard (failure rate) function are

$$\text{PDF} = f(t) = \lambda e^{-\lambda t} \tag{12}$$

$$\text{CDF} = F(t) = 1 - e^{-\lambda t} \tag{13}$$

$$\text{Reliability function} = R(t) = e^{-\lambda t} \tag{14}$$

$$\text{Hazard function} = z(t) = \lambda \tag{15}$$

The parameter λ is sometimes referred to as the *failure rate* because (in reliability theory) it describes the rate at which failures occur in time. The value e is the base of the natural logarithm (approximately 2.718).

The failure rate λ is usually assumed to be a constant greater than zero. In reality, λ is usually a function of time as depicted in the bathtub-shaped curve in Figure 1–4. During early life there is a higher failure rate, called infant mortality, due to the failure of weaker components. Often these infant mortalities result from a defect or stress introduced in the manufacturing process. Once the infant mortalities are eliminated, the system settles into operational life, in which the failure rate is approximately constant. The system then approaches wear-out in which time and use (such as mechanical stress due to temperature cycling, or ion or metal migration) cause the failure rate to increase. For most cases we will assume a constant failure rate. For the exponential distribution, the mean is $1/\lambda$ and the standard deviation is $1/\lambda$.

Weibull Distribution. The Weibull distribution has two parameters: α (the shape parameter) and λ (the scale parameter). The probability density function, cumulative distribution function, reliability function, and hazard (failure rate) function of the Weibull distribution are shown in Eqs. 16 through 19 (for $\alpha > 0$, $\lambda > 0$):

$$\text{PDF} = f(t) = \alpha\lambda(\lambda t)^{\alpha-1}e^{-(\lambda t)^{\alpha}} \tag{16}$$

$$\text{CDF} = F(t) = 1 - e^{-(\lambda t)^{\alpha}} \tag{17}$$

$$\text{Reliability function} = R(t) = e^{-(\lambda t)^{\alpha}} \tag{18}$$

$$\text{Hazard function} = z(t) = \alpha\lambda(\lambda t)^{\alpha-1} \tag{19}$$

Note that the values of all these functions depend on time only through the product of the scale factor and time, λt.

Because the failure rate is given by $(\lambda t)^{\alpha}$, the shape parameter directly influences the failure rate:

- If $\alpha < 1$, the failure rate is decreasing with time.
- If $\alpha = 1$, the failure rate is constant with time, resulting in an exponential distribution.
- If $\alpha > 1$, the failure rate is increasing with time. ($\alpha = 2$ is the special case of a linearly increasing failure rate, known as the Rayleigh distribution.)

For the Weibull distribution, the mean (denoted by μ, where $\mu = E[x]$) and standard deviation (denoted by σ, where $\sigma = \sigma_x$) are defined as follows in terms of α and λ:

$$\mu = \frac{\Gamma(\alpha + 1)/\alpha}{\lambda} \tag{20}$$

$$\sigma = \sqrt{\frac{\Gamma(\alpha + 2)}{\alpha} - \frac{\Gamma^2(\alpha + 1)}{\alpha}} \tag{21}$$

where the gamma function, $\Gamma(\omega)$, is given by

$$\int_0^{\infty} \rho^{\omega-1} e^{-\rho} d\rho.$$

The influence of the Weibull parameters on the mean of the distribution is illustrated in Figure 2–8. Since the Weibull is a function of two parameters, several combinations of λ, α yield the same mean. Actual observed errors are plotted in Figure 2–8 to illustrate typical values for λ and α. With only the mean and standard deviation available, the Weibull failure rate can be determined to be decreasing, constant, or increasing as follows:

- If $\mu < \sigma$, the failure rate is decreasing.
- If $\mu = \sigma$, the failure rate is constant.
- If $\mu > \sigma$, the failure rate is increasing.

Geometric Distribution. If t takes only the discrete times 0, 1, 2, . . . , then replacing $e^{-\lambda}$ by the discrete probability q and replacing t by n obtains the discrete time geometric distribution corresponding to the continuous time exponential distribution. The probability mass function, cumulative distribution function, and reliability function of the geometric distribution are shown in Eqs. 22 through 24 (for $0 < q < 1$):

$$PMF = f(n) = q^n - q^{(n+1)} = q^n(1 - q) \tag{22}$$

$$CDF = F(n) = 1 - q^n \tag{23}$$

$$\text{Reliability function} = R(n) = q^n \tag{24}$$

The mean μ and standard deviation σ of the geometric distribution are defined as follows in terms of q:

$$\mu = \frac{1}{1 - q} \tag{25}$$

FIGURE 2–8
Means of Weibull distributions [From McConnel, Siewiorek, and Tsao, 1979]

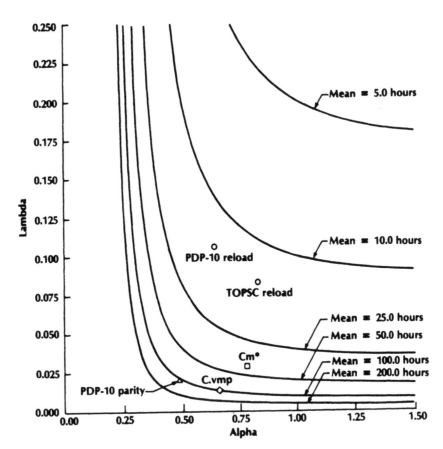

$$\sigma = \frac{q^{1/2}}{1 - q} \tag{26}$$

Discrete Weibull Distribution. Like the geometric distribution deriving from the exponential distribution, the discrete Weibull distribution is obtained from the Weibull distribution by substituting q for $e^{-\lambda^\alpha}$ and n for t [Nakagawa and Osaki, 1975]. The probability mass function, cumulative distribution function, reliability function, and hazard function of the discrete Weibull distribution are shown in Eqs. 27 through 30 (for $0 < q < 1$):

$$\text{PMF} = f(n) = q^{n^\alpha}(1 - q^{(n+1)^\alpha - n^\alpha}) \tag{27}$$

$$\text{CDF} = F(n) = 1 - q^{n^\alpha} \tag{28}$$

$$\text{Reliability function} = R(n) = q^{n^\alpha} \tag{29}$$

$$\text{Hazard function} = z(n) = 1 - q^{(n+1)^\alpha - n^\alpha} \tag{30}$$

The mean, μ, of the discrete Weibull function is given by

$$\sum_{k=0}^{\infty} q^{k^{\alpha}} \tag{31}$$

It is very difficult to derive a closed-form formula for this sum for any q and α. In this book, the geometric distribution and the discrete Weibull distribution are used only to approximate the exponential and Weibull distributions, respectively.

Techniques for Matching Sampled Data to Distribution Models

Maximum Likelihood Estimators. After the decision to characterize the failures of a given system or component with a particular distribution, the problem is to determine (estimate) the values of the parameters of the distribution from experimental data. One of the simplest methods of estimation is that of maximum likelihood [Melsa and Cohen, 1978]. Let $\bar{x}_n$ be a vector of observed data and let $\bar{\theta}$ be a vector of unknown parameters. If $P(\bar{x}_n|\bar{\theta})$ is the probability of observing x_n given the parameters of $\bar{\theta}$, the *maximum likelihood* (ML) estimation of $\bar{\theta}$, denoted $\bar{\theta}_{ML}$, is the value of $\bar{\theta}$ for which $P(\bar{x}_n|\bar{\theta})$ is maximum; that is,

$$P(\bar{x}_n|\bar{\theta}_{ML}) \geq P(\bar{x}_n|\bar{\theta}) \tag{32}$$

for any value of $\bar{\theta}$.

Assume, for example, that the time to failure is described by an exponential distribution. The vector $\bar{\tau} = (\tau_1, \tau_2, \ldots, \tau_N)$ is a collection of observed times to failure and is needed to compute the maximum likelihood value of λ in the exponential distribution. The function $P(\bar{\tau}|\lambda)$ is given by

$$P(\bar{\tau}|\lambda) = (\lambda e^{-\lambda \tau_1})(\lambda e^{-\lambda \tau_2}) \cdots (\lambda e^{\lambda \tau_N}) \tag{33}$$

$$P(\bar{\tau}|\lambda) = e^{-\lambda \sum_{i=1}^{N} \tau_i + N \ln \lambda} \tag{34}$$

The function in Eq. 34 will be at a maximum for $\lambda = \lambda_{ML}$. Maximizing the preceding function is equivalent to minimizing the function

$$f(\lambda) = \lambda \sum_{i=1}^{N} \tau_i - N \ln \lambda$$

Differentiating with respect to λ and setting the derivative equal to zero obtains the following value of λ:

$$\lambda_{ML} = \frac{N}{\sum_{i=1}^{N} \tau_i}$$

which is equal to the inverse of the sample mean time to failure.

Maximum Likelihood Estimation of Weibull Parameters. The maximum likelihood estimators (MLE), denoted α_{ML} and λ_{ML}, for the Weibull distribution satisfy the following equations [Thoman, Bain, and Antle, 1969]:

$$\frac{N}{\alpha_{ML}} + \sum_{j=1}^{N} \ln X_{ML} = N \frac{\sum_{j=1}^{N} X_j^{\alpha_{ML}} \ln X_j}{\sum_{j=1}^{N} X_j^{\alpha_{ML}}} \qquad (35)$$

$$(\lambda_{ML})^{\alpha_{ML}} = \frac{N}{\sum_{j=1}^{N} X_j^{\alpha_{ML}}} \qquad (36)$$

Once the value of the shape parameter is known, Eq. 36 can be used to calculate the scale parameter λ_{ML}. Equation 35 can be used to derive a difference equation in the form

$$\alpha_{ML_{i+1}} = \text{Function } (\alpha_{ML_i}, \bar{X}_N)$$

A quickly converging solution can be found by using the Newton-Raphson method [Thoman, Bain, and Antle, 1969]. The linear estimate of α_{ML} found by the linear regression analysis described next is useful as an initial value for the iterative solution process.

Linear Regression Analysis. Graphical linear regression analysis of the cumulative distribution function is often used to fit data to the Weibull function because of the computational complexity of obtaining the MLE values [Berger and Lawrence, 1974]. This technique is based on the transformation of the Weibull cumulative distribution function (Eq. 17) into a linear function of $\ln(t)$:

$$\ln \left[\ln \frac{1}{1 - F(t)} \right] = \alpha \ln t + \alpha \ln \lambda \qquad (37)$$

If the data are from a Weibull distribution, the plot should approximate a straight line. The line is fitted to the data by applying the method of least squares to the transformed points [Miller and Freund, 1965]. The slope of the straight line is an estimate of α, and the Y-intercept divided by the slope is an estimate of $\ln(\lambda)$. The value of the function $F(t)$ is estimated by

$$F(t_j) = \frac{j - 0.5}{N} \qquad (38)$$

If nothing else, the results of linear regression analysis are useful as an indication of the desirability of performing the more involved analyses.

Confidence Intervals. Point estimates such as those obtained by linear regression or maximum likelihood estimation are only approximations and rarely match the values they are intended to estimate. Because of this, interval estimates are often desirable. These are intervals that can be asserted with some certainty to contain the actual value of the parameter under consideration. The most common application of this idea is expressed in *confidence intervals*. For $0 < p, < 1$, a p-level confidence interval is a range within which the actual value of the estimated parameter would fall with probability p, if the experiment were repeated many times. That is, to say that a certain range of values is a 0.90 confidence interval for a parameter means that in repeated sampling, 90 percent of the confidence intervals so constructed would contain the actual parameter values [Miller and Freund, 1965].

Goodness-of-Fit Tests. After a distribution has been chosen to describe the probabilistic behavior of failures of some system and its parameters have been estimated, a goodness-of-fit test can give quantitative information about the likelihood that the system is actually following that distribution.

In a chi-square goodness-of-fit test, each observed value of a random variable is assigned to one of k categories, $C_1, \ldots, C_k$. Given the total number of observed values, the expected number of observations in each category is computed according to the hypothetical distribution. Let O_i and E_i be the number of observed and expected observations, respectively, in category i. The χ^2 (chi-square) statistic is given by

$$\chi^2 = \sum_{i=1}^{k} \frac{(O_i - E_i)^2}{E_i}$$

The number of degrees of freedom of this χ^2 statistic is $m = k - n - 1$, where n is the number of parameters that have been estimated from the same experimental data that are being used in the test. A level of significance, α, must be chosen such that the probability that a chi-square random variable with m degrees of freedom will exceed χ_α^2 is α. (The values of χ_α^2 can be found in such tables as Pear, 1954.) If $\chi^2 \geq \chi_\alpha^2$, the hypothesis that the failures are properly characterized by the hypothetical distribution must be rejected. Otherwise, the hypothesis is accepted. Finally, it should be noted that all the E_i must be equal to at least 5. To make each $E_i \geq 5$, it may be necessary to pool categories. A reasonable level of confidence is 0.05.

Example 1. Data are collected from the file system of a time-sharing system about the transient faults in 8 disk drives in an effort to discover whether the time between transient errors follows an exponential distribution. The estimated value of λ is 0.1344 (time in minutes) corresponding to a MTBF of about 7 minutes. The total number of observed errors is 877 in a 5-day interval. Table 2–12a shows the observed errors by division into time categories and the expected number of errors in each time category according to an exponential distribution. For instance, the first row in the table means that 548 errors were observed with times between errors of 0 to 5 minutes, while an exponential distribution with $\lambda = 0.1344$ gives the expected number of errors in that range as 429.20 (given that the total number of failures is 877). The remaining categories have to be pooled until no E_i is smaller than 5. The result of this operation is shown in Table 2–12b. The number of degrees of freedom is $m = 8 - 1 - 1 = 6$ because there are eight different categories, and one parameter (λ) has been estimated from the data. For 6 degrees of freedom, $\chi_{0.05}^2 = 12.592$. Since $\chi^2 > \chi_{0.05}^2$, the hypothesis that the time between errors has an exponential distribution must be rejected.

TABLE 2–12 *Data on transient faults for the time-sharing file system (Example 1)*

a. Collected Data						b. Pooled Categories			
Time Category (mins)	Observed Errors, O_i	Expected Errors E_i	Time Category (mins)	Observed Errors O_i	Expected Errors, E_i	Time Category (mins)	O_i	E_i	$(O_i - E_i)^2/E_i$
0–5	548	429.20	55–60	2	0.2639	0–5	548	429.20	32.88
5–10	148	219.15	60–65	1	0.1347	5–10	148	219.15	23.10
10–15	63	111.89	65–70	1	0.06881	10–15	63	111.89	21.36
15–20	35	57.13	70–75	1	0.03514	15–20	35	57.13	8.57
20–25	28	29.17	75–80	1	0.01794	20–25	28	29.17	0.04
25–30	18	14.89	80–85	1	0.009160	25–30	18	14.89	0.64
30–35	12	7.60	85–90	1	0.004690	30–35	12	7.60	2.53
35–40	6	3.88	90–95	1	0.002395	35–∞	25	7.93	36.74
40–45	3	1.98	95–100	1	0.001215			Total χ^2 =	125.86
45–50	1	1.01	100–105	1	0.000627				
50–55	3	0.5178							

Example 2. The times between crashes of a time-sharing system (see Table 2–13) have been recorded for one month of system operation. The goal is to find out whether the distribution of time between crashes follows a Weibull distribution. The maximum likelihood estimates of the Weibull parameters are $\lambda = 0.0888$, and $\alpha = 0.98$ (time units in hours) corresponding to a time between crashes of about 11 hours. Table 2–13a gives the observed counts in several ranges of time between crashes. After pooling categories so that no E_i is smaller than 5, Table 2–13b is obtained. The number of degrees of freedom is $m = 9 - 2 - 1 = 6$. For a χ^2 random variable with 6 degrees of freedom, $\chi^2_{0.05} = 12.592$. Because $\chi^2 < \chi^2_{0.05}$, the hypothesis that the distribution of the time to crash is a Weibull is accepted.

Another goodness-of-fit statistical test is the Kolmogorov-Smirnov test. The Kolmogorov-Smirnov test has been developed for known parameters or for the exponential distribution [Lilliefors, 1969]. If the parameters of the distribution are estimated from the experimental data or the distribution is not exponential, the Kolmogorov-Smirnov test may give extremely conservative results.

DISTRIBUTION MODELS FOR PERMANENT FAULTS: THE MIL-HDBK-217 MODEL

The Reliability Analysis Center has extensively studied statistics on electronic component failures. The data have led to the development of a widely used reliability model of chip failures, the MIL-HDBK-217,* which is periodically updated, starting with 217A in 1965 and progressing to model 217E of 1986. The component failure data presented in this section is compared to the model that was current at the time of the data collection.

* A more detailed explanation of the model is found in Appendix D.

TABLE 2–13 *Data on time between crashes in one month for time-sharing file system (Example 2)*

a. Collected Data				b. Pooled Categories			
Time Category (hrs)	Observed Errors, O_i	Time Category (hrs)	Observed Errors, O_i	Time Category (hrs)	O_i	E_i	$(O_i - E_i)^2/E_i$
0–1	6	11–12	1	0–2	9	9.97	0.09
1–2	3	12–14	2	2–4	7	8.17	0.16
2–3	5	14–15	2	4–6	12	6.79	3.97
3–4	2	15–16	1	6–8	2	5.67	2.37
4–5	7	16–17	1	8–11	9	6.80	0.70
5–6	5	17–18	3	11–15	5	6.66	0.41
6–7	1	18–21	1	15–20	5	5.61	0.06
7–8	1	21–24	4	20–28	6	5.14	0.14
8–9	3	24–29	1	28–∞	5	5.13	0.003
9–10	4	29–38	3				
10–11	2	38–75	2			Total χ^2 = 7.95	

For MIL-HDBK-217E, reliability is assumed to be an exponential distribution with the failure rate for a single chip taking the form

$$\lambda = \pi_L \pi_Q (C_1 \pi_T \pi_V + C_2 \pi_E)$$

where π_L = *learning factor,* based on the maturity of the fabrication process (assumes a value of 1 or 10)

π_Q = *quality factor,* based on incoming screening of components (values range from 0.25 to 20)

π_T = *temperature factor,* based on the ambient operating temperature and the type of semiconductor process (values range from 0.1 to 1000)

π_E = *environmental factor,* based on the operating environment (values range from 0.38 to 220)

π_V = *voltage stress derating factor for CMOS devices* (values range from 1 to over 10 as a function of supply voltage and temperature; value is 1 for other technologies)

C_1, C_2 = *complexity factors,* based on the number of gates (for random logic) or bits (for memory) in the component and the number of pins

Since new component types are continually being introduced and because the learning curve for any component type changes as field experience accumulates, there is some question of the accuracy of this MIL-HDBK-217 model, particularly with regard to rapidly changing technologies such as MOS RAMs and ROMs.

Typical component failure rates are in the range of 0.01–1.0 per million hours. Thus, tens of millions of component hours are required to gain statistically significant results. Two separate approaches can be used to gather sufficient data for comparison with the MIL-HDBK-217 model: life-cycle testing of components and analysis of field data on failure rates.

Life-Cycle Testing

Life-cycle testing involves a small number of components in a controlled environment. Frequently, temperature is elevated to accelerate failure mechanisms. An acceleration factor is then used to equate 1 hour at elevated temperature to a number of hours at ambient temperature. The acceleration factor is usually derived from the Arrhenius equation:

$$R = Ae^{-E_a/kT}$$

where R = reaction rate constant
   A = a constant
   E_a = activation energy in electron-volts
   k = Boltzmann's constant
   T = absolute temperature

Example. A life-cycle test is designed whereby components will be heated to 125°C. We want to know how many hours at 25°C ambient will be represented by each hour at 125°C. Let $R(125)$ be the reaction rate at 125°C and $R(25)$ be the reaction rate at 25°C. The temperature acceleration factor is thus

$$\frac{R(125)}{R(25)}$$

To convert from °C to °K, we add 273. Using the Arrhenius equation for R, we get

$$\frac{R(125)}{R(25)} = \frac{Ae^{-E_a/398k}}{Ae^{-E_a/298k}} = e^{-(E_a/k)[(1/398)-(1/298)]}$$

In MIL-HDBK-217B, E_a is assumed to be 0.7 eV for MOS devices. Boltzmann's constant is 0.8625×10^{-4} eV/°K. Thus,

$$\frac{R(125)}{R(25)} = e^{(-0.7/0.8625)10^{-4}[(1/398) - (1/298)]} = e^{6.843} = 937$$

Hence 1 hour at 125°C is equivalent to 937 hours at 25°C.

Because of the exponential in the Arrhenius equation, accelerating factors can become quite large. They can, however, be plotted as a graph for easy look-up. Figure 2–9 depicts acceleration factors for various activation energies. For the life-cycle test example, curve 3 applies. The acceleration factor for any two temperatures is found by taking the ratio of the two acceleration factors with respect to 25°C. For example, 1 hour at 125°C for an activation energy of 0.41 eV is equal to about 10 hours at 85°C (900/90 = 10).

Consider conversion of time at 125°C to time at 50°C. MIL-HDBK-217B for bipolar devices assumes an activation energy of 0.41 eV (curve 2 in Figure 2–9). The acceleration

FIGURE 2–9

Graph of failure rate acceleration factors [From Thielman, 1975; reprinted by permission of Signetics]

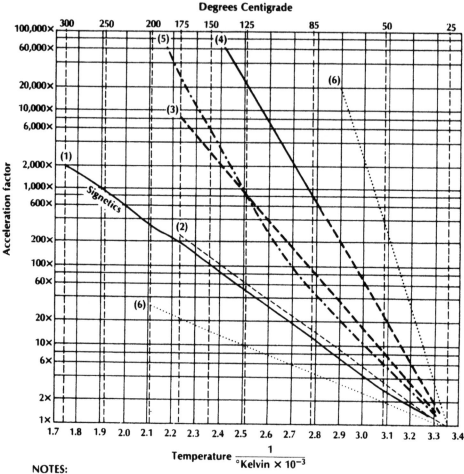

NOTES:

1. Calculated from the Signetics Failure Rate vs. Temperature Graph in [Signetics, 1975]. Signetics uses acceleration factors of 15 (for +85°C), 100 (for +150°C), 200 (for +175°C), 350 (for +200°C), 970 (for +250°C), and 2100 (for +300°C) to relate to +25°C equivalent ambient temperature. The graph equates to an "activation energy" $E_a = 0.41$ eV.

2. Calculated from MIL-HDBK-217B, 20 September, 1974. The graph equates to an "activation energy" $E_a = 0.41$ eV and is applicable to all bipolar digital (except ECL) in the normal mode of operation.

3. Calculated from MIL-HDBK-217B, 20 September, 1974. The graph equates to an "activation

energy" $E_a = 0.70$ eV and is applicable to all MOS, all linear, and bipolar ECL devices in the normal modes of operation.

4. Calculated from MIL-STD-883A, 15 November, 1974. The graph equates to an "activation energy" $E_a = 1.02$ eV.

5. The curved graph is the result of plotting the "rule of thumb" that failure rates (hence acceleration factors) double for every + Δ10°C.

6. All competitor data (available to Signetics) produced graphs falling within these two boundaries. The two boundaries equate to "activation energies" $E_a = 0.23$ eV (for lower bound) and $E_a = 1.92$ eV (for the upper bound).

factor at 125°C is approximately 60, while at 50°C it is about 4 (relative to 25°C). Thus, the effective acceleration is 60/4 or 15. For MIL-STD-883A (used to qualify components for procurement) an activation energy of 1.02 eV is assumed (curve 4 in Figure 2–9). The effective acceleration factor is (20,000/20 = 1000). The accelerating factors differ by over a factor of 60.

The Arrhenius equation assumes only one activation energy, and the reaction rate is assumed to be a uniform function of temperature. Assuming a straight line (on a semilog scale) can result in substantial errors. Figure 2–10 illustrates the nonlinear behavior. Consider the three test points, 150°C, 125°C, and 85°C. Drawing a best-fit straight line through these points in Figure 2–10 on the 1970 curve yields a failure rate of about 0.0002 at 25°C, whereas the 25°C observed point is 0.0013, too low by a factor of 7. The same three points on the 1975 curve suggest a failure rate of 0.06 instead of 0.0017, which is too high by a factor of 35.

In summary, data from accelerated life-cycle testing must be reviewed carefully,

FIGURE 2–10

Nonlinear plots of failure rate acceleration factors [From Thielman, 1975; reprinted by permission of Signetics]

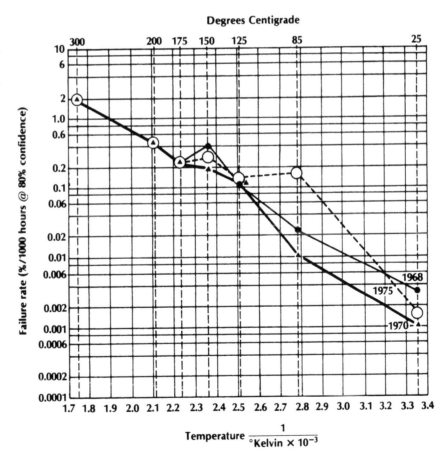

especially if it is being used to extrapolate to operational life failure rates. Life-cycle testing stresses the temperature related failure modes. The environmental effects of aging and mechanical stress are not measured, even though they may constitute from 10 percent (at high temperature) to 70 percent (at low temperature) of the failure rate.

Failure Rate Field Data

The Reliability Analysis Center collects field failure rate data. Figure 2–11 depicts 50 collections of field data representing SSI and MSI complexity devices from various screening classes and operating in various environments. Altogether, 0.921×10^9 device operating hours and 328 failures are represented. For most of the data collections, no

FIGURE 2–11
Comparison of SSI and MSI device field data and MIL-HDBK-217C predicted failure rates [From Nicholls, 1979]

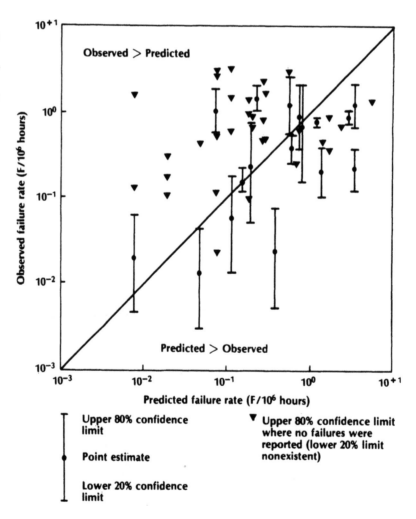

failures were observed; hence, only an upper 80 percent confidence limit can be plotted. For those data sets with observed failures, both the upper 80 percent and the lower 20 percent confidence limits were calculated. The MIL-HDBK-217B–calculated values in general made assumptions leading to optimistic predictions; for example, data from multiple sources operating in the 26–50°C junction temperature range were treated as one source operating at 26°C. Hence, the region where the predicted failure rate is greater than the observed failure rate has been exaggerated.

Of the 50 data collections, 17 (34 percent) have predicted failure rates greater than those observed, 7 (14 percent) have predicted failure rates equal to those observed, and 26 (52 percent) have predicted failure rates less than those observed. Of the 17 data collections with observed failures, 8 (47 percent) had a predicted failure rate greater than that observed, and 2 (12 percent) a predicted failure rate less than that observed. Even given the difficulty in gathering enough data to generate statistically meaningful comparisons, the MIL-HDBK-217B model for older technologies, such as TTL, SSI, and MSI, appears relatively accurate in absolute terms (i.e., within a factor of two of observed data). For comparisons between designs, then, the MIL model is more than adequate for established technologies.

Figure 2–12 compares 32 collections of field data on RAM failures with the failure rate predicted by the MIL-HDBK-217C model [Klein, 1976]. Of the 23 data collections with observed failures, 17 (74 percent) have a predicted failure rate greater than observed, 5 (22 percent) have predicted failure rates equal to observed, and only 1 (4 percent) has a predicted failure rate less than observed. In all, 13 (57 percent) of the data collections have observed failure rates more than a factor of 10 less than predicted, and 11 of these 13 data sets were for 1K and 4K MOS RAMs. The 217B/217C models were extremely pessimistic on predicting LSI—especially MOS LSI—failure rates.

Automated Failure Rate Calculation. A computer program, *Lambda*, has been written [Elkind, 1980a] that simplifies the procedure of computing a system's failure rate. A system may be described to the program in the form of a list of chips and/or subsystems that can be recursively nested. Parameters such as the various MIL-HDBK-217 factors can be modified to obtain a sensitivity analysis. The format of this file is

[Module name

Body]

where Body is a listing of all the component chips and submodules. A chip is identified either by an integer specifying the number of chips of this type used or by an integer followed by an F, specifying the number of functions (such as NAND gates) of this chip type that were used. This is then followed by a comma and the name of the chip. Submodules are constructed on the same format as modules.

Table 2–14 shows the data for the SUN-2/50 produced by *Lambda* for MIL-HDBK-217E parameters. The failure rates for the SUN and the submodules are shown with the percentage of the failure rate for each module that is attributed to each submodule.

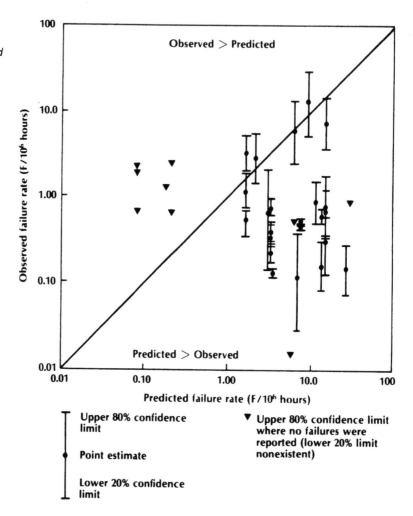

FIGURE 2–12
Comparison of RAM field data and MIL-HDBK-217C predicted failure rates [From Klein, 1976]

In the case of partially used chips, *Lambda* prorates the chip failure rate by the fraction of the total number of functions used.

The parameters of the MIL-HDBK-217 model can be varied by subsystem or even chip type, so that variations in ambient temperature (such as a board near a power supply) or technology (such as a new chip for which all parameters are not known) can be modeled. At the chip level, it is also possible to modify the number of devices on a chip to gauge the effect of the size of the new chip type on the design. Furthermore, individual chip type or entire chip class (RAM, MOS, LSI) can be arbitrarily assigned any complexity derating factors in order to test the sensitivity of the system failure rate as a function of the unknown parameter.

TABLE 2–14 *Output from Lambda for the SUN-2/50 study (with failure rate in failures per million hours)*

(Quantity)Module	Lambda (Single Module)	Lambda (All Module Copies)	(Quantity)Module	Lambda (Single Module)	Lambda (All Module Copies)
SUN	138.7355	100.000	(1) MEMORY	82.4447	59.426
(1) PROCESSOR	4.8390	3.488	(1) MM.CONTROL	39.9107	48.409
(1) PROC.SUPPORT	5.4206	3.907	(1) MMC.SSI.MSI	1.1491	2.879
(1) PROC.PALS	2.1841	40.292	(1) MMC.RAM	38.7615	97.121
(1) PROC.SSI.MSI	2.7943	51.550	(1) MAIN.MEMORY	40.9333	49.649
(1) PROC.RC	0.4422	8.157	(1) MM.SSI.MSI	1.6743	4.090
(1) BOOT.STRAP	9.8182	7.077	(1) MM.RC	7.6148	18.603
(1) BOOT.ROM	6.6852	68.090	(1) MM.RAM	31.6442	77.307
(1) BOOT.SSI.MSI	1.3474	13.724	(1) DVMA	1.6007	1.942
(1) BOOT.PALS	1.7856	18.186	(1) DVMA.SSI.MSI	0.2830	17.677
(1) CLOCK.CKTS	2.1691	1.563	(1) DVMA.PALS	1.3177	82.323
(1) VIDEO.LOGIC	16.2676	11.726	(1) SERIAL.IO	8.1328	5.862
(1) ADDR.DECODER	8.4429	51.900	(2) SIO.CTRL	3.6153	88.907
(1) VIDEO.RAM	4.8517	57.465	(1) SIO.SSI.MSI	0.5234	6.436
(1) VBI.SSI.MSI	3.5912	42.535	(1) SIO.RC	0.3787	4.657
(1) VMEM.CTRL	5.2704	32.398	(1) ETHERNET	2.8325	2.042
(1) VMC.PALS	3.1402	59.582	(1) ETHERNET.CTRL	0.3796	13.400
(1) VMC.SSI.MSI	1.2260	23.262	(1) ENET.SSI.MSI	1.9832	70.017
(1) VMC.RC	0.9042	17.156	(1) ETHERNET.RC	0.4697	16.583
(1) V.SHIFT.LOGIC	0.4555	2.800	(1) VME	4.5865	3.306
(1) V.BUS.IFACE	2.0988	12.902	(1) VME.SSI.MSI	3.1130	67.874
(1) VBI.PALS	1.3177	62.785	(1) VME.PALS	1.2995	28.334
(1) VBI.SSI.MSI	0.7811	37.215	(1) VME.RC	0.1739	3.792
			(1) INTERRUPTS	2.2245	1.603

DISTRIBUTION MODELS FOR INTERMITTENT AND TRANSIENT FAULTS

While there have been various attempts at modeling intermittent and transient faults, there is no widely accepted model that uses parameters of a design to predict these faults. Instead, this section presents some data collected from actual systems and fits a probability distribution to the data.

Data Collection

Andrew File Servers. The Andrew file servers used at Carnegie Mellon University are a collection of 13 SUN workstations, each connected to 4 Fujitsu Eagle M2351 disk drives. The Vice file servers are used for mass storage of files for a network of approximately 5000 nodes. The file servers run under Berkeley UNIX with enhancements in the error logging mechanism for the purposes of this research. Load on the file servers was assumed to be constant due to the large number of independent nodes issuing requests for data. Thus, it was assumed that the transient error rates are constant and do not fluctuate as a function of time of day.

The published MTTF for the disk drives is 20,000 hours. Thus, a file server should be expected to fail every 5000 hours because of a disk failure. In the study, it was found that the actual MTTF for the disk drives was 86,900 hours, which is much better than the published value. The study collected information on a total of 29 repair activities, 7 disk failures, 7 CPU failures, 7 memory failures, and 8 controller failures.

Tandem TNS II. The main source of data for this study [Hansen, 1988] is a set of 5 Tandem TNS II systems operated by Pittsburgh Plate Glass Industries. The Tandem system is a fault-tolerant multiprocessor system, with 3 of the machines in the study having 3 processors and the other 2 having 4 and 8 processors, respectively.

A common event log is maintained for the whole system. Entries in the log include reports about events such as memory errors, I/O errors, and processor or bus failures, as well as housekeeping entries such as disk mounts or dismounts. Each entry in the log consists of a time stamp, an error code, a processor number, and other information specific to the event.

VAX-11/780. In addition to the Andrew and Tandem event logs, event logs from thirteen VAX-11/780s running the VMS (Virtual Memory System) operating system were also studied [Hansen, 1988]. The VMS logs contain on the average of 300 entries per day. About half of these are housekeeping entries such as time-stamps and tape/disk mounts and dismounts.

Distribution of Intermittent Faults

Data on intermittent faults for the Andrew file servers was obtained from the system event log by first marking the occurrence of device repairs. Then for each repair action, all entries in the event log pertaining to that device were extracted as potential intermittent faults. The time lines of 15 of the 29 repair actions and their corresponding intermittent errors are given in Lin [1988]. Parity error messages having addresses from different memory boards and system software error messages have been found to signal faulty CPUs, disk controllers, and memory boards. These "ambiguous" errors are mapped into the CPU, disk controller, or memory time line whose last error is closest in time to the occurrence of the "ambiguous" error. If the "ambiguous" parity error is not within a specified window for any time line, it is treated as a transient and discarded. The window selected was 354 hours, the mean interarrival time of transient errors (see Lin, 1988).

For example, a parity error is mapped onto a CPU intermittent time line if the interarrival time to the next CPU error is less than 354 hours. On the other hand, a software error is not mapped into a disk controller time line if the interarrival time to the next error on that time line is greater than 354 hours. The time line of a disk on file server 12 is shown in Figure 2–13. Periods of increasing error rate, which appear as either clusters of errors or decreasing interarrival times between errors (suggesting a Weibull failure distribution with $\alpha > 1$), are obvious. Most of these clustering patterns can be identified in an observation window typically spanning less than 200 hours, and

FIGURE 2–13
Time line of intermittent errors leading to corresponding disk repair actions on Vice file server 12 [From Lin, 1988]

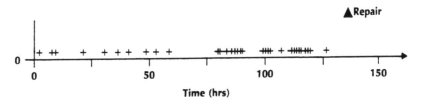

the majority of the failures were preceded by error log indications over 1000 hours prior to repair.

The result of matching the data to distribution models, including the estimates of the Weibull and exponential parameters and the chi-square goodness-of-fit test results for several repair actions, is summarized in Table 2–15. Each of the 12 repair actions is identified as to which file server it repaired. The FRU (field replaceable unit) column shows the repaired device, the errors column lists the number of intermittent error events before repair, and the Mean column shows the average of the interarrival times between intermittent errors. The next columns list the parameters of the Weibull function fit: The α and λ linear columns give the linear regression estimates; the α and λ MLE columns give maximum likelihood estimates; the number of categories and χ^2 columns show the number of categories and the result of the chi-square test. The last two columns list the λ MLE parameter of an exponential fit and its χ^2 statistic.

TABLE 2–15 *Intermittent fault data for Vice file system study*

Repair Action	File Server	FRU	Errors	Mean Time (hrs)	Weibull α Linear	λ Linear	α MLE	λ MLE	No. of Categories	χ^2	Exponential λ MLE	No. of Categories	χ^2
1	Vice 2	xy0-2	48	19	0.6419	0.0455	1.5356	0.0116	2	0.07	0.0501	2	0.01
2		xy0-1	1	—	—	—	—	—	—	—	—	—	—
3		mem	11	102	0.7809	0.0097	0.9210	0.0092	2	1.33	0.0098	2	1.53
4	Vice 3	con	13	118	0.8474	0.0097	0.7631	0.0098	2	2.25	0.0084	2	2.57
5	Vice 4	cpu	7	174	1.2728	0.0084	1.1737	0.0054	1	0.00	0.0057	1	0.00
6	Vice 5	cpu(A+B)	14	275	0.2251	0.0342	0.4647	0.0078	2	1.62	0.0036	2	2.46
		[b]cpu-A	7	12	0.7568	0.0803	1.3164	0.0637	1	0.00	0.0814	1	0.00
		[b]mem-B	7	618	1.5862	0.0013	0.6390	0.0017	1	0.00	0.0016	1	0.00
7, 8[a]		xy2&con	13	21	0.6671	0.1599	0.6848	0.0381	2	0.19	0.0476	2	0.10
9	Vice 6	xy2-1	40	10	0.1677	9.8432	0.5213	0.0303	2	9.23	0.0930	2	6.98
10		xy2-2	18	39	0.1683	3.5546	0.4781	0.0225	1	0.00	0.0255	1	0.00
11	Vice 7	cpu	5	106	1.3338	0.0191	1.0784	0.0091	1	0.00	0.0094	1	0.00
12	Vice 8	cpu	18	210	1.2794	0.0080	0.9116	0.0047	3	1.57	0.0047	3	2.09

[a]Repair actions 7 and 8 occurred within a short period of time. The disk controller was replaced due to a string of disk errors. However, xy2 disk was lost at power up. Therefore data points were accounted for both repairs.
[b]Repair actions are listed as unsuccessful repairs leading to successful repairs (Vice5 cpu(A+B)).
Source: Lin, 1988.

Although nearly all the faults fail the chi-square test because of lack of data (at least four categories are needed for a Weibull fit and three for an exponential fit), several interesting findings are noted. First, on the average, 21 (610 errors/29 repairs) intermittent errors were observed per repair activity and the mean of the interarrival times is 58 hours, indicating that the first symptom might occur as early as 50 days (21 × 58 = 1218 hours) prior to the attempted repair. Second, the average number of intermittent errors*, is smaller than the minimum 25 data points required for an accurate estimate of the statistical parameters, implying that the faulty behavior is usually repaired before enough data is collected for traditional statistical techniques to be conclusive. Third, although the estimates of parameters are inconclusive, among the 17 parameters (excluding the unnumbered entries, which are subsets of the previous numbered entries), 6 α ML values are greater than 1, 3 are close to 1 (between 0.76 and 1), and 8 are less than one, suggesting no strong relationship between intermittents and the Weilbull-shaped parameter.

Distribution of Transient Faults

Transient faults were extracted from the Andrew system event log by subtracting known hard-failure–induced intermittent faults; that is, the intermittent faults listed in the previous section. The data exhibited three types of the most commonly seen transient errors: system software errors (event type SOFT), parity errors (event type MEM), and unscheduled system reboots (e.g., watchdog resets). The total number of crashes caused by transient faults is 269, which accounts for 90 percent of total system crashes; that is, 269/(269 + 29). Note that other published data also indicates that hard failures cause less than 10 percent of system crashes [Malaiya, 1979]. The MTTC is calculated as 504 hours for each server and 53 hours for the file system.[†]

Modeling of transient faults also begins with the analysis of their interarrival time. The interarrival times are calculated using the time stamp information from the system event log. The hazard function is formulated and analyzed to identify its associated reliability function. In total, 446 transient errors are plotted in Figure 2–14. The x-axis divides the interarrival times into 20-hour bins, while the y-axis shows the number of occurrences in each bin. The obvious skew toward the low end for all the data indicates that the Weibull distribution is a likely candidate for the reliability function. Table 2–16 shows the shape, scale parameters, and chi-square test results of the Weibull and exponential fittings of transient faults for the 13 file servers. The table is similar to Table 2–15. The data in boldface represents file servers whose number of categories is insufficient to perform the chi-square goodness-of-fit tests, implying their estimates of the parameters are inconclusive. Even so, only one out of the four rows has an α greater than 1. The α MLE values for all the other servers are less than 1. Furthermore,

---

* Fourteen of the 29 repair actions had four or fewer error log entries prior to a repair action.
† The assumption of near constant load on the file system was tested by sampling the load (CPU utilization, I/O access frequency) every 53 hours (the system mean time to crash). The system usage was found to be uniform, thus verifying the assumption that system load could be factored out as a variable in this study.

FIGURE 2–14
Hazard functions of the Vice file system transient errors [From Lin, 1988]

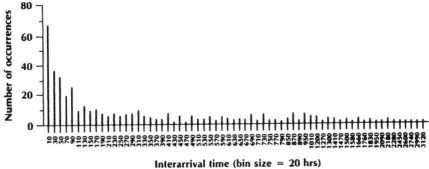

Interarrival time (bin size = 20 hrs)

the Weibull χ^2 value is less than the exponential χ^2 value, suggesting the Weibull with a decreasing error rate is a better fit to the data than the exponential. In fitting the data to the Weibull function, Vice 2 is the only server that failed the chi-square test. Vice 2 passed the chi-square test at a confidence level of 0.1. It is believed that some extraneous data from testing might have been captured because of the experimental nature of Vice 2 in its early stage of operation (i.e., it was the first file server). Therefore, transient faults follow the Weibull distribution with a decreasing failure rate.

Each file server has an average of 34 transient errors, and the average interarrival time is 354 hours. As indicated previously, this average was used to determine whether an "ambiguous" error was part of an intermittent string of errors or whether it was

TABLE 2–16 *Distributions for transient faults for Vice file system study*

File Server	Time (hrs)	Errors	Mean Time (hrs)	Weibull α Linear	Weibull λ Linear	Weibull α MLE	Weibull λ MLE	No. of Categories	χ^2	Exponential λ MLE	Exponential No. of Categories	χ^2
Vice 2	16770	41	386	0.5223	0.0035	0.5666	0.0023	5	6.28	0.0026	4	**8.59**
Vice 3	16770	54	262	0.7991	0.0045	0.8047	0.0041	10	8.10	0.0038	9	12.64
Vice 4	16770	27	561	0.4427	0.0022	0.6569	0.0022	5	5.59	0.0018	5	11.01
Vice 5	15360	31	291	0.8148	0.0031	0.6471	0.0037	5	5.32	0.0034	4	**8.78**
Vice 6	15360	87	167	0.3387	0.0096	0.7161	0.0059	14	11.28	0.0059	14	17.23
Vice 7	13584	25	407	0.9137	0.0024	0.8886	0.0025	5	3.28	0.0025	4	5.89
Vice 8	12936	25	370	1.0931	0.0039	0.7818	0.0030	5	3.34	0.0027	5	5.67
Vice 9	**12936**	**18**	**515**	**0.4065**	**0.0048**	**0.4013**	**0.0018**	**1**	**0.00**	**0.0019**	**1**	**0.00**
Vice 10	12936	62	154	0.3276	0.0131	0.6407	0.0065	9	5.89	0.0065	9	10.12
Vice 11	**12936**	**11**	**668**	**1.3767**	**0.0022**	**1.0686**	**0.0015**	**2**	**0.67**	**0.0015**	**2**	**0.44**
Vice 12	12672	20	435	0.3883	0.0049	0.5855	0.0028	3	4.27	0.0023	3	5.14
Vice 13	**12672**	**12**	**733**	**1.0093**	**0.0015**	**0.5817**	**0.0020**	**2**	**2.01**	**0.0014**	**2**	**2.56**
Vice 14	12672	33	351	0.5998	0.0031	0.4686	0.0034	4	4.35	0.0028	5	6.69

Note: Bold indicates file server data with insufficient categories for χ^2 test.
Source: Lin, 1988.

due to a random transient error. Note the smallest mean of the interarrival times for transient errors is 154 hours in Vice 10, and a minimum of 25 error points spanning up to 18 months are required to gain an accurate estimate in this system analysis. Moreover, most of the repair actions were performed before system statistical trends developed, indicating that users do not tolerate that large a number of errors. Thus, a new method should be sought for fault prediction. The dispersion frame technique, which was developed to perform failure prediction based on the observation that there exists a period of increasing error rate before most hardware failures, is described in Chapter 4. The dispersion frame technique uses a maximum of 5 error points for fault prediction.

Preliminary study on the validity of the process to factor out the intermittent from the transient errors in the file server logs was performed by simulating the mixing of two Weibull processes: intermittent with $\alpha_i > 1$ and transient with $\alpha_t < t$. The resultant mixed process is fitted to a Weibull function where both the ratios of α_i/α_t and the number of the events from each process are compared to those observed. The methodology and results of the simulation process are detailed in Lin [1988], illustrating that the assumption of a single transient and a single intermittent source at any given time is an adequate first order approximation.

Graphical Analysis Techniques

Data on interarrival time can be plotted as a histogram to form an approximation of the probability density function (PDF) for transient errors. This technique is useful in initially deciding on which distributions to study. System restarts on the VMS systems and Tandem processors, and transient disk errors on the Andrew file servers, are selected for the analysis here. In order to get a good fit, all of the available data from each of the three different systems is used. The obvious skew toward the low end for all the data collected indicates that the Weibull distribution should be used.

The PDF of the interarrival times is plotted with the PDF for the ML approximation in Figure 2–15. The Weibull parameters can also be estimated graphically by transforming the data in the graph. Using Eq. 37, the data can be transformed into a linear graph as shown in Figure 2–16a. The parameters α and λ can be estimated by doing linear regression on the transformed curve. Transformed curves for the VMS systems and Tandem processors are shown in Figures 2–16b and 2–16c, respectively. For all three systems, the data fit a straight line from which the Weibull parameters can be estimated. These estimated Weibull parameters are presented in the following table, along with the maximum likelihood estimations [Hansen, 1988]:

	Time (hrs)	Inter- arrivals	Mean	Standard Deviation	α Linear	α MLE	λ Linear	λ MLE
Andrew	183,374	446	411.2	259.7	0.611	0.708	0.00484	0.00383
VMS	22,339	145	154.0	301.3	0.406	0.427	0.0154	0.0160
Tandem	42,561	97	438.8	877.2	0.208	0.300	0.0128	0.0155

FIGURE 2–15
Distribution of An-
drew disk errors
[From Hansen,
1988]

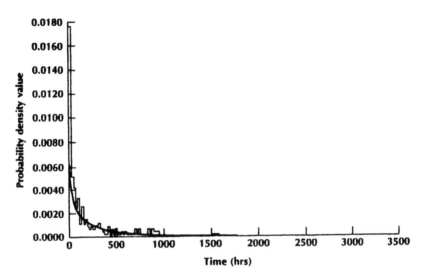

Multiple Reporting

In larger systems such as the VMS and Tandem machines, it is often difficult to recognize faults from the error log. A single fault will often generate a large number of error reports. One of the first studies of this problem was done by Tsao [1983]. Tsao found that specific fault events in a system will in general produce multiple entries in the event log. Groups of related events caused by the same fault are called *tuples*. Tandem and VMS system analysis used a time-based heuristic to determine if events are related and should be grouped into a tuple.

The main heuristic used to group events is based on the interarrival times between tuples. If the interarrival time between two errors is less than some clustering time ϵ, then the errors are included in the same tuple. This process continues until an inter-arrival time exceeding the clustering time occurs, at which point a new tuple is started. In addition to this simple heuristic, more complex heuristics are sometimes used. If certain similarities exist between the current error and the tuple that is being formed, then a larger clustering time might be used for that particular error.

As an example, consider Figure 2–17. In this scenario, 9 errors (represented by the vertical lines) were condensed into 3 tuples (represented by the horizontal bars). The first 2 tuples were formed by only applying a time-based rule with a clustering time of ϵ_1. The errors h and i were found to be related to previous errors by some hypothetical criteria and so the longer clustering time ϵ_2 is used for those errors.

Each of the tuples formed by this process represents a particular type of fault in the system. The fault analysis techniques used in diagnosing the Andrew file servers can then be applied to the tuples. The major drawback of the tupling technique is the possibility of recording tuples that do not really represent a single fault. It is possible that a fault may occur before the effects of the previous fault have dissipated. When

FIGURE 2–16
Graphical analysis of transformed Weilbull parameters [From Hansen, 1988]

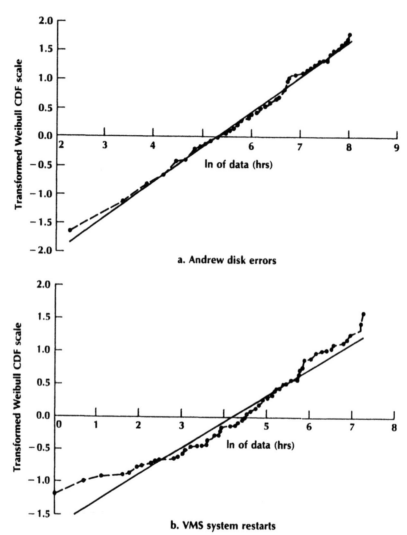

a. Andrew disk errors

b. VMS system restarts

this occurs, a collision results. The collision rate is dependent on the clustering time ϵ and has been studied by Hansen [1988].

Machine Similarities. Another interesting finding from the Hansen [1988] study was the observation that machines of the same manufacturer exhibited similar error log characteristics. The relative arrival rates of various tuple types were examined on a number of VAX and Tandem systems. For each of the machine types, only a small number of different behaviors were noted. The differences were measured by creating a vector of tuple arrival rates for each machine and computing the correlation between these vectors. In the VMS analysis, all but one of the 13 systems analyzed fell into one of

FIGURE 2–16
(continued)

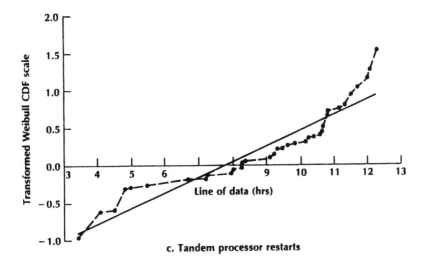

c. Tandem processor restarts

two types of behavior. The Tandem analysis was a little more complicated than the VMS analysis since the Tandem systems are multi-processor machines. The Tandem logs showed a similar clustering behavior when individual processors were compared, but not when whole systems were compared.

SOFTWARE FAULT MODELS

While individual case studies of the occurrence and extermination rate of "bugs" in a software project have appeared in the literature, there have been few rigorously controlled and carefully documented experiments on how errors occur in software. Many of the software reliability models are aimed at the latter stages of the software development cycle and are not applicable to either the early design phases or the operational phase. Furthermore, these models are based upon simplistic assumptions such as constant error rates and independence of events. The problem of data collection is further aggravated by the fact that the apparent reliability of a piece of software is correlated to how frequently design errors are exercised as opposed to the number of design errors present. The NAA Langley Research Center has undertaken a series of software reliability studies to gather software failure data and to develop models

FIGURE 2–17
Tuple clustering algorithm [From Tsao, 1983]

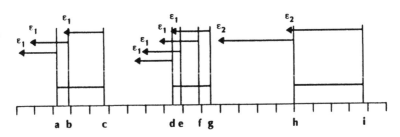

for software reliability [Finelli, 1988]. Nagel and Skrivan [1982], Dunham [1986], and Dunham and Lauterbach [1988] conducted controlled experiments with multiple programmers to determine the rate of software error manifestation. New programs were written to existing specifications. The programs were subjected to a set of experimental inputs and output of the program was compared to an existing program that had been in use over a long period of time and was considered to be correct. When an error was found, the fault that produced the error was identified and corrected. The number of executions of the program since the last error had occurred was recorded; this represented the rate of error occurrence. Each corrected fault represented a "stage" in the development of the program. Thus, the stage tells how many faults have been corrected. A run of a program refers to length of time between failures resulting from the successive detection and correction of faults.

Many software reliability growth models assume that faults contribute equally to the rate at which a program generates errors. That is, all faults are considered equally likely to produce an error on any execution of the program. This implies that the program failure rate is constant until a fault is removed, and that the failure rate decreases by equal amounts as each successive fault is fixed. Both NASA studies observed widely varying error rates for the faults identified. Dunham [1986] produced over 15,250,000 program executions. Three versions of a launch interceptor condition were generated and 11 faults were discovered in program one, 1 in program two, and 19 in program three. The number of program executions was recorded from the beginning of a program run until the detection of an error. For each fault, the time intervals between errors were summed over all runs and divided into the number of runs on which that fault produced an error. Data for the first and third programs are reproduced in Table 2–17. The error rate for individual faults varies over several orders of magnitude. The error rate per stage can be plotted on semi-log paper as shown in Figure 2–18. A log-linear error rate is observed with respect to the number of faults that have been corrected.

The NASA studies also found an interaction between faults that at sometimes masked and at other times amplified the probability of error. The following table [Dunham, 1986] shows the results of interactions between two different faults:

Fault 7 Present	Fault 8 Present	Faults 7 and 8 Present	Number of Cases
S	S	S	1,714,177
S	S	F	4,990
S	F	S	349
S	F	F	19
F	S	S	473
F	S	F	0
F	F	S	1,122
F	F	F	12

TABLE 2–17
Individual error rates for faults in two programs

Program 1			Program 3		
Fault Number	Number of Runs Found	Error Rate	Fault Number	Number of Runs Found	Error Rate
1	100	0.914	1	100	0.794
2	100	0.544	2	78	0.000352
3	100	0.030	5	100	0.0126
4	100	0.00259	6	100	0.0213
5	100	0.0155	8	100	0.0126
6	100	0.00922	9	100	0.0213
7	100	0.00486	10	100	0.0213
8	95	0.000314	11	100	0.0213
9	9	0.00000940	12	100	0.0503
10	1	0.00000101	13	100	0.0126
11	2	0.00000202	14	100	0.0213
			15	100	0.0213
			16	100	0.0198
			17	96	0.000383
			18	100	0.000935
			19	5	0.00000511

Source: Dunham, 1986; ©1986 IEEE.

FIGURE 2–18
Log-linear trend of program error rate for the data in Table 2–17 [From Dunham, 1986; ©1986 IEEE]

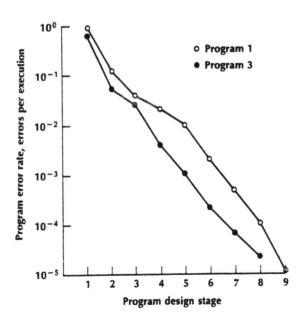

The first column shows success (S) or failure (F) for a program with only fault 7 present. The second and third columns show the success or failure behavior when only fault 8 or both faults 7 and 8 are present, respectively. The last column shows the number of parallel executions of the three versions of the program in which the various combinations of successes and failures occurred. The correct version of the program was used to determine success or failure of the individual runs. Note that there are cases in which the presence of two faults masks the presence of a fault (the third, fifth, and seventh lines of the table) or cause errors that the faults individually did not cause (such as line two in the table). Similar behavior has been observed in hardware faults.

A subsequent study found that not only do faults interact but they also tend to produce errors that are grouped together. In many cases, a set of contiguous input data values tended to cause the same fault to produce errors [Ammann and Knight, 1987]. Figure 2–19 shows a two-dimensional cut through a multi-dimensional input space wherein the input parameters and all other dimensions are held constant. An X represents an input value that caused a single fault to produce an erroneous output, while the dots represent inputs that produced good outputs. These regions, called *error crystals* by Finelli [1988], are a particular concern in real-time applications where the input variables may be slowly varying and thus triggering multiple errors because of a single fault.

SUMMARY

Sources of errors were traced to their origins in hardware, software, environment, design, and human mistakes. The predominance of transient and intermittent faults was demonstrated. Fault manifestations were discussed at both the component and system levels. The mathematics governing the two major statistical fault distributions (exponential and Weibull) were introduced, along with maximum likelihood, regression, confidence interval, and goodness-of-fit tests.

Permanent faults were shown to follow an exponential distribution with the failure rate parameter, λ, predictable by the MIL-HBDK-217 model. Some pitfalls in accelerated temperature testing were illustrated. Transient and system-level error manifestations (observed over 248,000 hours) follow a Weibull distribution across a wide range of system size and redundancy.

The mathematical techniques introduced in the analysis of permanent and transient faults can be used to confirm fault distributions and/or estimate parameters of the fault distributions for more accurate reliability evaluation.

REFERENCES

Abraham and Fuchs, 1986; Ammann and Knight, 1987; Arlat, Crouzet, and Laprie, 1989; Avizienis, 1982, 1985; Ball and Hardie, 1967; Beh et al., 1982; Bellis, 1978; Berger and Lawrence, 1974; BNR, 1984; Breuer, 1973; Brodsky, 1980; Bryant, 1984; Clune, 1984; Czeck, 1989; Czeck, Siewiorek, and Segall, 1988; Davidson, 1984; Davidson and Lewandowski, 1986; Dunham, 1986; Dunham and Lauterbach, 1988; Elkind, 1980a; Fantini, 1984; Faulkner, Bartlett, and Small, 1982; Feather, 1985; Ferguson, 1987; Finelli, 1988.

FIGURE 2–19

Error crystal due to one fault [From Finelli, 1988]

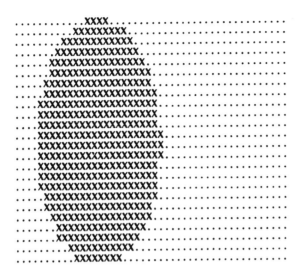

Galiay, Crouzet, and Vergniault, 1980; Geilhufe, 1979; Gray, 1987, 1990; Hansen, 1988; Hayes, 1985; Howden, 1980; Joyner and Carter, 1976; Kamal, 1975; Kamal and Page, 1974; Klein, 1976; Lai, 1979, 1981; Lai and Siewiorek, 1983; Laprie, 1985; Lee, 1989; Lilliefors, 1969; Lin, 1988; Lin and Siewiorek, 1990; Lloyd and Knight, 1984; Losq, 1978; Malayia, 1979; Mangir, 1984; Marchal, 1985; McConnel, 1980; McConnel, Siewiorek, and Tsao, 1979; McGough and Swern, 1981, 1983; McGough, Swern, and Bavuso, 1983; Melsa and Cohen, 1978; Middendorf and Hausken, 1988; Miller and Freund, 1965; Monachino, 1982; Morganti, 1978; Morganti, Coppadoro, and Ceru, 1978.

Nagel and Skrivan, 1982; Nakagawa and Osaki, 1975; Nicholls, 1979; Ohm, 1979; Pear, 1954; Rickers, 1976; Roth et al. 1967a; Savir, 1978; Schuette et al., 1986; Segall et al., 1988; Shen, Maly, and Ferguson, 1985; Siewiorek, Canepa, and Clark, 1977; Siewiorek et al., 1978a; Signetics, 1975; Silberman and Spillinger, 1986; Snyder, 1975; Sturges, 1926; Su and Lin, 1984; Swan, Fuller, and Siewiorek, 1977; Tasar and Tasar, 1977; Thatte and Abraham, 1978, 1979, 1980; Thielman, 1975; Thoman, Bain, and Antle, 1969; Timoc et al., 1983; Toy, 1978; Tsao, 1983; Wadsack, 1978; Watanabe, 1986.

PROBLEMS

1. The reliability function $R(t)$ describes the probability of not observing any failure before time t. Another reliability metric sometimes used to compare the reliabilities of two alternate designs is mission time improvement (MTI). It is the ratio of the times at which the two system reliability functions decay below some specific value, say 0.9. Compute the MTI (λ_a, λ_b) for (a) an exponential distribution and (b) a Weibull distribution with a constant shape parameter.

2. Using the data in Table 2–8, make the transformation suggested in Eq. 36 and estimate the Weibull parameters, λ and α, by making a least-squares fit to the transformed data. Test the hypothesis that the data follow this distribution. Assume that failures occur at the end point of each interval.

3. Consider a MOS RAM, with $\pi_L = 1$, $\pi_Q = 16$, $\pi_T = 25$, and $\pi_E = 1$. Plot the failure rate, λ, as a function of number of bits according to MIL-HDBK-217E. (See Appendix D.)

4. Consider two computers A and B.
   a. Assuming an exponential distribution, what is the probability that at least one will survive 10,000 hours if their failure rate is 1 failure per million hours?
   b. Assuming a Weibull distribution with shape parameter of 0.6, what is the probability that at least one will survive 10,000 hours if their scale parameter is 1 per million hours? What is the reliability difference between the exponential and Weibull at this point?
   c. Repeat parts (a) and (b) assuming the exponential failure rate is 100 per million hours and the Weibull scale parameter is 100 per million hours. What is the reliability difference of the exponential and Weibull at this point?

3 RELIABILITY TECHNIQUES

Steven A. Elkind and Daniel P. Siewiorek

This chapter presents a spectrum of techniques available to the designer of reliable digital systems. The spectrum spans the range of techniques derived to deal with the problem of building computers from unreliable components. Although the emphasis is on techniques that deal with hard (component) failures, most of the techniques are also effective against transient and intermittent faults.

The techniques that lead to increased reliability can be divided into two basic approaches: fault* intolerance (fault avoidance) and fault tolerance. *Fault intolerance* results from conservative design practices such as the use of high-reliability components. The goal of fault intolerance or avoidance is to reduce the possibility of a failure. Even with the most careful fault avoidance, however, failures will eventually occur and result in system failure (hence, fault intolerance). *Fault tolerance* uses redundancy to provide the information needed to negate the effects of failures. The redundancy is manifested in one of two ways: extra time or extra components. Time redundancy, which is usually provided by software, involves such techniques as extra executions of the same calculation, which may be accomplished by different methods. However, component redundancy entails the use of extra gates, memory cells, bus lines, functional modules, and the like to supply the extra information needed to guard against the effect of failures.

A summary of the reliability techniques covered in this chapter is shown in Table 3–1. The reliability techniques spectrum for both hardware and software is broken up into four major classes: fault avoidance, fault detection, masking redundancy, and dynamic redundancy. These classes are not exact. Some basic techniques have properties pertaining to more than one class, and others, which are considered basic techniques, do require concurrent use of other techniques. Further, while the reliability techniques are shown categorized according to their most common application area, software techniques can be used in hardware design situations and vice versa.

The discussion of reliability techniques in this chapter treats each technique as a basic entity. Whenever possible, a measure of the technique's effectiveness is pro-

* In the reliability and fault tolerance literature, the terms *fault* and *failure* are sometimes used interchangeably. In coding theory literature, *failure* and *error* are used interchangeably. These practices are followed in parts of this chapter in deference to common usage. In addition, we use the term *reliability* in its broadest sense throughout this chapter. The techniques in this chapter can be used to enhance a broad range of abilities, such as availability, maintainability, repairability, and so forth.

TABLE 3–1 *Classification of reliable techniques*

Hardware Techniques		Software Techniques	
Class	Technique	Class	Technique
Fault avoidance	Environment modification	Fault avoidance	Modularity
	Quality changes	(software	Object-oriented programming
	Component integration level	engineering)	Capability-based programming
Fault detection	Duplication		Formal proofs
	Error detection codes	Fault detection	Program monitoring
	M-of-N codes, parity, checksums,	Masking	Algorithm construction
	arithmetic codes, cyclic codes	redundancy	Diverse programming
	Self-checking and fail-safe logic	Dynamic	Forward error recovery
	Watch-dog timers and timeouts	redundancy	Backward error recovery
	Consistency and capability checks		Retry, checkpointing,
	Processor monitoring		journaling, recovery blocks
Masking	NMR/voting		
redundancy	Error correcting codes		
	Hamming SEC/DED,[1] other codes		
	Masking logic		
	Interwoven logic, coded-state machines		
Dynamic	Reconfigurable duplication		
redundancy	Reconfigurable NMR[2]		
	Backup sparing		
	Graceful degradation		
	Reconfiguration		
	Recovery		

[1] Single-error correction/double-error detection
[2] N-modular redundancy

vided, and the application of the technique to different areas of digital design is illustrated, often with brief examples from specific systems. Although most of the major techniques now in use are covered in this chapter, the particular technique under discussion may be only representative of a class of similar techniques; in these cases, references are given for other techniques in the same class.

An overview of the system-failure response stages is given in the next section to provide a time frame for utilization of the techniques discussed in the remainder of the chapter. The next section also proposes a taxonomy of the techniques that takes these stages into account.

**SYSTEM-FAILURE
RESPONSE
STAGES**

A redundant system may go through as many as eight stages in response to the occurrence of a failure. Designing a reliable system involves the selection of a coordinated failure response that combines several reliability techniques. The ordering of these stages in the following paragraphs corresponds roughly to the normal chronology of a fault occurrence, although the actual timing may be different in some instances.

• **Fault confinement:** This stage limits the spread of fault effects to one area of the system, thereby preventing contamination of other areas. Fault confinement can be achieved through liberal use of fault-detection circuits, consistency checks before performing a function ("mutual suspicion"), and multiple requests/confirmations before performing a function. These techniques may be applied in both hardware and software.

• **Fault detection:** This stage recognizes that something unexpected has occurred in the system. Many techniques are available to detect faults, but an arbitrary period of time, called *fault latency*, may pass before detection occurs. Fault-detection techniques are divided into two major classes: off-line detection and on-line detection. With *off-line detection*, the device is not able to perform useful work while under test. Diagnostic programs, for example, run in a stand-alone fashion even if they are executed on idle devices or multiplexed with the operations software. Thus, off-line detection assures integrity before and possibly at intervals during operation, but not during the entire time of operation. *On-line detection*, on the other hand, provides a real-time detection capability that is performed concurrently with useful work. On-line techniques include parity and duplication.

• **Diagnosis:** This stage is necessary if the fault detection technique does not provide information about the failure location and/or properties.

• **Reconfiguration:** This stage occurs when a fault is detected and a permanent failure is located. The system may be able to reconfigure its components either to replace the failed component or to isolate it from the rest of the system. The component may be replaced by backup spares. Alternatively, it may simply be switched off and the system capability degraded in a process called *graceful degradation*.

• **Recovery:** This stage utilizes techniques to eliminate the effects of faults. Two basic approaches to recovery are based on the techniques of fault masking and retry. *Fault-masking* techniques hide the effects of failures by allowing redundant information to outweigh the incorrect information. In *retry*, a second attempt at an operation is made and is often successful because many faults are transient in nature, doing no physical damage. One form of recovery, often called *rollback*, makes use of the fact that the system operation is backed up to some point in its processing prior to fault detection and operation recommences from this point. Fault latency becomes an important issue because the rollback must go far enough back to avoid the effects of undetected errors that occurred before the detected one.

• **Restart:** This stage occurs after the recovery of undamaged information. A "hot" restart, which is a resumption of all operations from the point of fault detection, is possible only if no damage has occurred. A "warm" restart implies that only some of the processes can be resumed without loss. A "cold" restart corresponds to a complete reload of the system, with no processes surviving.

• **Repair:** In this stage, a component diagnosed as having failed is replaced. As with detection, repair can be either on-line or off-line. In off-line repair, either the system will continue if the failed component is not necessary for operation, or the system must be brought down to perform the repair. In on-line repair, the component may be replaced immediately by a backup spare in a procedure equivalent to reconfiguration, or operation may continue without the component, as is the case with masking redundancy or graceful degradation. In either case of on-line repair, the failed component may be physically replaced or repaired without interrupting system operation.

• **Reintegration:** In this stage the repaired module must be reintegrated into the system. For on-line repair, reintegration must be accomplished without interrupting system operation.

The first stage, fault confinement, attempts to limit the effect of faults by localizing the damage and accelerating its detection. On fault detection, the system is brought down, diagnosed, and manually reconfigured to allow a restart. Before operation recommences, the software process must first be rolled back to a point before the errors occurred and then restarted. Finally, after the failed module is repaired and put back on line, the system is halted temporarily to allow the module to be reintegrated into the system. Figure 3–1 depicts a time line of the stages in fault handling once detection has occurred. The figure also illustrates some of the reliability measurement concepts discussed in Chapter 2: the mean time between failure (MTBF), mean time to detection (MTTD, sometimes called error latency), mean time to repair (MTTR), and availability.

Figure 3–2 proposes a taxonomy of system-failure response strategies that starts with the two basic categories of nonredundant and redundant systems. The only approach available to nonredundant systems is the use of fault-intolerance techniques, which require human intervention on all eight stages of fault handling. Redundant systems have historically used the three major design approaches of fault detection,

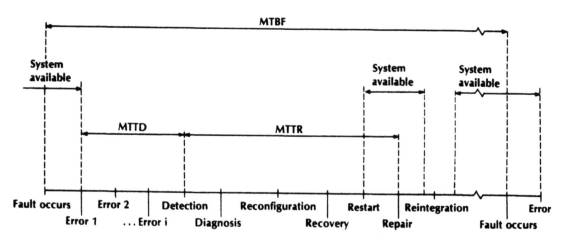

FIGURE 3–1 *Scenario for on-line detection and off-line repair. The measures MTBF, MTTD, and MTTR are the average times between failures, to detection, and to repair.*

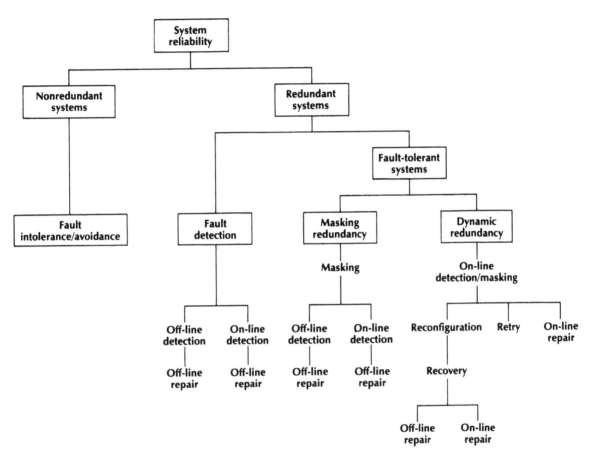

FIGURE 3–2 *Taxonomy of system-failure response strategies*

masking redundancy, and dynamic redundancy to automate one or several of the eight stages of fault handling. Fault detection provides no tolerance to faults, but gives warning when they occur. It is used in small systems such as micro- and minicomputers, some of which may incorporate simple on-line detection mechanisms. This branch does not represent fault tolerance in the strictest sense; even though faults are detected, they cannot be tolerated (except for retry upon transient faults).

Masking redundancy, also called *static redundancy*, tolerates failures, but gives no warning of them. It is used in such systems as computers with error-correcting code memories or with majority-voted ·redundancy in a fixed configuration (that is, the logical connections between circuit elements remain constant).

Dynamic redundancy covers those systems whose configuration can be dynamically changed in response to a fault, or in which masking redundancy, supplemented by on-line fault detection, allows on-line repair. Examples include multiprocessor

FIGURE 3–3
Cost range of redundancy techniques (in terms of the redundancy required)

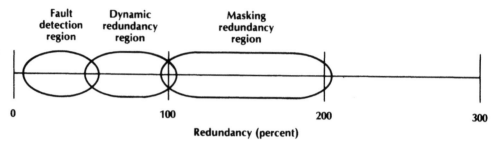

systems that can degrade gracefully in response to processing element failures and triplicated systems that are designed for on-line repair.

The range in cost of fault-tolerant techniques is almost a continuum in terms of percentage of redundancy. Figure 3–3 depicts three regions of hardware redundancy, each corresponding to one of the three major areas of the fault-tolerance technique spectrum. Even though most techniques in each area fit within these regions, individual techniques may fall well outside them.

The fault intolerance branch of Figure 3–2 relies on the fault-avoidance class of techniques. Because it is mainly a straightforward application of conservative design practices, fault avoidance is only covered briefly in this chapter. However, it is important to note that most successful designs use a balanced combination of both fault avoidance and fault tolerance. The final design is the result of trade-offs among cost, performance, and reliability. Cost, performance, and reliability goals are usually incompatible to some degree, and their relative importance depends on the ultimate application of the final product. For example, some fault-tolerant techniques may find little application in cost-sensitive commercial computing systems, but may be required for long-term space missions.

HARDWARE FAULT- AVOIDANCE TECHNIQUES

The fault-avoidance approach to increasing computer reliability lessens the possibility of failures. If fault avoidance alone cannot economically meet system design goals, fault-detection and/or fault-tolerance techniques must be used. Some fault-avoidance techniques are intended to decrease the possibility of transient faults. For example, the signal-to-noise ratio can effectively be increased by such techniques as careful signal routing, shielding, cabinet grounding, and input-line static filters.

Other fault-avoidance techniques are useful against both hard and transient faults. A design rule that limits the fanout of gates to a small number, for example, decreases power dissipation (decreasing thermal effects, and thus hard failures). Fanout limitation also increases the effective noise margin at the inputs of subsequent gates and thus decreases the possibility of a transient fault. The possibilities for human errors can be reduced through such measures as labeling and documentation. In addition, the possibility of assembly errors can be minimized, for example, by the use of printed circuit boards and connectors that are shaped in such a way that they cannot be plugged in backward or into the wrong slots.

This section presents three techniques for avoiding hard failures. The goal is to obtain a smaller integrated circuit failure rate as determined by the MIL-HDBK-217E model given in Chapter 2, according to the following formula:

Failure Rate Formula

$$\lambda = \pi_L \pi_Q (C_1 \pi_T \pi_V + C_2 \pi_E)$$

where λ = failure rate, failures per million hours (fpmh)

π_L = learning curve factor

π_Q = quality factor

C_1, C_2 = complexity factors

π_T = temperature factor

π_V = voltage stress factor

π_E = environment factor

Fault avoidance can be obtained by manipulating factors that affect the failure rate. The following subsections cover possible changes in environment, quality, and complexity factors.

Environment Modification

Two of the parameters in the failure rate formula are related to the operating environment. The first is π_E, which is specified for general classes of environmental conditions. Table 3–2 gives some examples of the MIL-HDBK-217E environment factors. Ground benign environment implies air-conditioned computer rooms; ground fixed environment implies office or factory floor installations. Conditions (and π_E values) between the extremes provided by Mil model 217E can be estimated. (For more of the standard π_E values, see Appendix D.) Usually the operating environment is beyond the designer's control and thus is not a means of affecting system reliability.

The other parameter affected by the environment is π_T, which is a function of junction temperature. The junction temperature is a result of several factors: ambient air temperature, heat transfer from chip to package and package to air, and the heat created by the power consumed on the chip. Junction temperature can be modified by changing power dissipation, heat sinking of boards and chips, and controlling air temperature and air flow. Power dissipation is controllable to some extent by fanout limitation. In gate array and master slice technologies, power dissipation can be controlled during chip design. Heat sinking may be necessary for selected devices, and it is sometimes even used for all ICs in a given design.

While complex, expensive fluid cooling systems (such as freon cooling) have occasionally found use in systems that require high power dissipation ECL logic and high component densities [Russel, 1978], a cabinet ventilation system is sufficient in most cases. Fans can be installed to increase air flow through the cabinet and to lower cabinet air temperature. Fans can also be used to increase air flow across the circuit boards, improving heat transfer from the component packages to the air.

Careful design of the cabinet itself is also important in improving air flow and heat

TABLE 3–2
Examples of environment factors

Environment Condition	π_E Factor	Description
Ground benign	0.38	Nearly zero environmental stress, with optimum engineering operation and maintenance
Space, flight	0.9	Earth orbital . . . [no] access for maintenance
Ground fixed	2.5	Conditions less than ideal to include installation in permanent racks, with adequate cooling air, maintenance by military personnel, and possible installation in unheated buildings
Airborne inhabited (cargo)	2.5	Typical cargo compartment conditions without environmental extremes of pressure, temperature, and vibration
Missile, launch	13.0	Severe conditions . . . related to missile launch and . . . space vehicle boost into orbit . . . reentry and landing

Source: MIL-HDBK-217E, U.S. Department of Defense, 1986.

transfer. The VAX 8600 provides a good example of cabinet design for improved cooling (Figure 3–4). The blower system provides filtered air from outside the cabinet. To minimize the air temperature near the circuit boards, the power supplies are placed downstream; thus, the cooling air flows through the logic card cage before picking up the heat of the modular power supplies (MPS units). The air is routed through the logic card cage in such a way that it provides maximum flow across the logic boards. Finally, the air flows through a muffler system to decrease the amount of noise introduced into the computer room.

Hot spots, which often occur on circuit boards when heat-producing components reside on the lee side (or airflow shadow) of other components, can be designed out of a system. For example, the Texas Instrument ASC (Advanced Scientific Computer) uses air cooling, unlike most high-performance machines. In its original design, empty spaces were left on the PC board when no chips were required. A careful study of the air flow revealed that the empty spaces caused turbulent air flow, which resulted in nonuniform heat transits. Designers carefully studied the properties of cooling air flow and found that empty spaces on the PC board increased board-level air turbulence. The turbulence caused nonuniform heat transfer, and hot spots resulted. The solution was the addition of dummy packages in spaces where no actual ICs were used.

The air-cooled IBM 4381 utilizes some of the packaging technology developed for the 3081 water-cooled thermal conduction modules (TCM). (See Chapter 7 for a more detailed description of TCM technology.) Impingement cooling is used in the IBM 4381 packaging (Figure 3–5). Heat from the dies is conducted through a thermal paste to the package cap, which has integrated air channels. Air is forced in through the top of the package and exits through slots in the side. The top of the package is in an air chamber separate from the sides, so there is no interference between the cool air entering and the warm air exiting.

FIGURE 3–4
*Air flow path in
VAX 8600
[Courtesy of Digi-
tal Equipment Cor-
poration]*

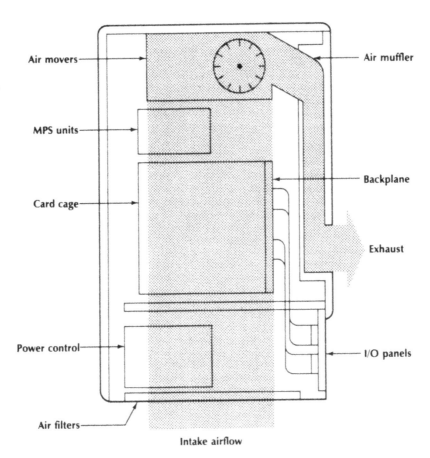

Air movers — Air muffler

MPS units

Backplane

Card cage

Exhaust

Power control

I/O panels

Air filters

Intake airflow

FIGURE 3–5
*A cross-section of
the IBM 4381 mod-
ule [Oktay, Des-
sauer, and Hor-
vath, 1983;
Reprinted by per-
mission from Inter-
national Business
Machines Corpora-
tion]*

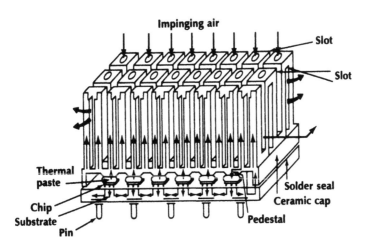

Impinging air   Slot

Slot

Thermal
paste

Solder seal
Ceramic cap

Chip

Substrate

Pin   Pedestal

TABLE 3–3

Results of Lambda analysis of SUN-2/50 workstation with no cooling (in-cabinet temperature of 45°C)

(Quantity)/Module	Lambda (Single Module)	% Lambda (All Module Copies)
(1) SUN	468.2215	100.000
(1) PROCESSOR	7.7938	1.665
(1) PROC.SUPPORT	19.2214	4.105
(1) BOOT.STRAP	39.7850	8.497
(1) CLOCK.CKTS	3.0414	0.650
(1) VIDEO.LOGIC	24.1636	5.161
(1) ADDR.DECODER	15.4244	63.833
(1) VMEM.CTRL	5.3824	22.275
(1) V.SHIFT.LOGIC	0.7525	3.114
(1) V.BUS.IFACE	2.6042	10.778
(1) MEMORY	342.7228	73.197
(1) MM.CONTROL	271.8397	79.318
(1) MAIN.MEMORY	69.0727	20.154
(1) DVMA	1.8103	0.528
(1) SERIAL.IO	11.9515	2.553
(1) ETHERNET	7.2050	1.539
(1) VME	6.4335	1.374
(1) INTERRUPTS	5.9035	1.261

MTTF: 2135.7 hrs   Est. number parts: 904.0   Est. number pins: 7374

Sortkey Summary Statistics

Key	Components	Net Lambda	% System Lambda
IC:SSI	77.0	29.9294	6.39
IC:MSI	100.0	25.3862	5.42
IC:LSI	4.0	19.1194	4.08
IC:ROM	4.0	34.7528	7.42
IC:RAM	166.0	338.9111	72.38
IC:NMOS	18.0	330.6420	70.62
TRANS:BIP	1.0	0.0033	0.00

Example. A SUN-2/50 workstation provides an example of the range of improvement available through temperature modification. Table 3–3 shows the results of a Lambda [Elkind, 1983] failure rate analysis of the SUN 2/50 design assuming an expected ambient (package) temperature of 45°C. This assumption is reasonable with normal room temperatures and no ventilation other than convection currents within the cabinet. The system failure rate is 468 failures per million hours (FPMH), which is equivalent to a mean time to failure (MTTF) of 2136 hours.

Table 3–4 shows the effect of placing a few small fans in the cabinet. If the increased circulation can lower the cabinet temperature by 5 degrees, the failure rate drops to 353 FPMH, a decrease of 25 percent. The MTTF increases to 2832 hours, an increase of 33 percent. Table 3–5 shows the effect of using a better

TABLE 3–4
Results of Lambda analysis of SUN-2/50 workstation with fans installed in cabinet (in-cabinet temperature of 40°C)

(Quantity)/Module	Lambda (Single Module)	% Lambda (All Module Copies)
(1) SUN	353.1150	100.000
(1) PROCESSOR	6.2527	1.771
(1) PROC.SUPPORT	13.3933	3.793
(1) BOOT.STRAP	28.8613	8.173
(1) CLOCK.CKTS	2.6501	0.751
(1) VIDEO.LOGIC	19.6265	5.558
(1) ADDR.DECODER	12.3892	63.125
(1) VMEM.CTRL	4.4875	22.864
(1) V.SHIFT.LOGIC	0.6337	3.229
(1) V.BUS.IFACE	2.1161	10.782
(1) MEMORY	258.3175	73.154
(1) MM.CONTROL	200.6863	77.690
(1) MAIN.MEMORY	56.1600	21.741
(1) DVMA	1.4713	0.570
(1) SERIAL.IO	8.9759	2.542
(1) ETHERNET	5.2954	1.500
(1) VME	5.2102	1.475
(1) INTERRUPTS	4.5321	1.283

MTTF: 2831.9 hrs   Est. number parts: 904.0   Est. number pins: 7374

Sortkey Summary Statistics

Key	Components	Net Lambda	% System Lambda
IC:SSI	77.0	21.6896	6.14
IC:MSI	100.0	20.2197	5.73
IC:LSI	4.0	14.6445	4.15
IC:ROM	4.0	24.9164	7.06
IC:RAM	166.0	254.3017	72.02
IC:NMOS	18.0	243.6777	69.01
TRANS:BIP	1.0	0.0031	0.00

ventilating system, perhaps including ducting, blowers, and filters, which is capable of a 10° reduction in temperature. This modification almost doubles the MTTF of the system.* The failure rate analyses have ignored the cooling system (fan) failure rates because there are usually multiple fans, and the failure of only one fan will not cause immediate system failure.

It is thus possible to obtain reliability improvement through an effective ventilation system and changes in cabinet design. However, other considerations may override good engineering design practice. For example, marketing considerations may pre-

* Note that this example does not quite fit the old rule of thumb that a 10° temperature drop increases the MTTF factor of 2.

Table 3-5
Results of Lambda analysis of SUN-2/50 workstation with cabinet ventilation system (in-cabinet temperature of 35°C)

(Quantity)/Module	Lambda (Single Module)	% Lambda (All Module Copies)
(1) SUN	266.1182	100.000
(1) PROCESSOR	5.0000	1.879
(1) PROC.SUPPORT	9.3421	3.511
(1) BOOT.STRAP	20.8132	7.821
(1) CLOCK.CKTS	2.3442	0.881
(1) VIDEO.LOGIC	16.0142	6.018
(1) ADDR.DECODER	9.9732	62.278
(1) VMEM.CTRL	3.7711	23.549
(1) V.SHIFT.LOGIC	0.5370	3.353
(1) V.BUS.IFACE	1.7328	10.820
(1) MEMORY	194.1004	72.938
(1) MM.CONTROL	146.9865	75.727
(1) MAIN.MEMORY	45.9176	23.657
(1) DVMA	1.1962	0.616
(1) SERIAL.IO	6.7438	2.534
(1) ETHERNET	3.9797	1.495
(1) VME	4.2716	1.605
(1) INTERRUPTS	3.5091	1.319

MTTF: 3757.7 hrs   Est. number parts: 904.0   Est. number pins: 7374

Softkey Summary Statistics

Key	Components	Net Lambda	% System Lambda
IC:SSI	77.0	15.9375	5.99
IC:MSI	100.0	16.2862	6.12
IC:LSI	4.0	11.1998	4.21
IC:ROM	4.0	17.7163	6.66
IC:RAM	166.0	189.8515	71.34
IC:NMOS	18.0	178.2292	66.97
TRANS:BIP	1.0	0.0029	0.00

clude the use of noisy fans in certain environments such as offices. A quieter system is possible but cooling is then left to convection, and the loss in MTTF is absorbed in exchange for a more saleable product.

Quality Changes

The use of higher quality components is reflected in the parameter π_Q (quality factor) of the failure rate formula. Table 3-6 lists some of the standard quality levels for integrated circuits, as used in the Mil model 217E. (A more complete list is found in Appendix D.) The quality level is affected by several factors, including the manufacturing process, packaging, and screening. The major factor for determining the quality level is screening done during and after each manufacturing step.

TABLE 3–6
Examples of quality-level factors

Component Class	π_Q Factor	Description
B	1	Procured in full accordance with MIL-M-38510, Class B requirements [Parts falling in this or higher classifications are commonly referred to as "mil-spec" or "hi-rel" components.]
D	10	Commercial (or non-mil standard) part, hermetically sealed, with no screening beyond the manufacturer's regular quality assurance practices
D-1	20	Commercial (or nonmil standard) part, packaged or sealed with organic materials (e.g., epoxy, silicone, or phenolic)

Source: MIL-HDBK-217E, U.S. Department of Defense, 1986.

The final value of π_Q is determined by the types and frequency of testing and processing. Tests can be performed with different degrees of thoroughness: They can be done for each component, for sample components from each manufacturing lot, or for periodic samples every few lots. Additional tests may be performed if higher quality components are needed for special applications. Lower quality components (i.e., higher π_Q) are either the result of less stringent testing and processing or are components that failed testing for higher standards but still meet lower quality grade specifications.

The use of higher quality components is an obvious strategy for improving reliability. The simplest implementation is to buy high-reliability ("hi-rel") components directly from the manufacturer. However, such components may be expensive (usually twice as much as commercial grade), and not all the properties required of military grade components make sense in a commercial environment. There are two possible solutions to these problems. The first is in-house screening/burn-in whereby only the relevant tests for the components' anticipated application are applied. The second is specification of hi-rel components for only those areas of a design in which they are most economically effective.

Component users who do their own screening avoid some of the harsher military environmental tests that the component manufacturer must perform (and charge for) on Mil-rated devices. Figure 3–6, for example, diagrams the Texas Instruments Class C qualification process for integrated circuits [Texas Instruments, 1976]. (See Table 2–13 for a more complete listing of screening tests.)

Component burn-in tests can also be used to eliminate weak components. The process is accomplished by continual simulated operation of all the components, possibly at higher than normal temperatures. Slight overvoltages are sometimes applied at signal and power inputs. In addition, entire assemblies or systems can be burned in by the manufacturer before shipment. This last procedure has the advantage of eliminating incompatibilities between components that have passed testing, but whose parameters combine to result in poor or improper operation (often a cause of intermittent faults).

FIGURE 3–6

Texas Instruments MACH-IV qualification process for class C components [From Texas Instruments, 1976]

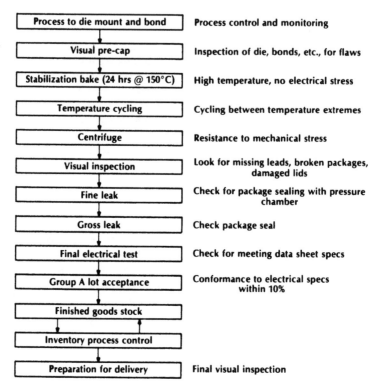

Process to die mount and bond	Process control and monitoring
Visual pre-cap	Inspection of die, bonds, etc., for flaws
Stabilization bake (24 hrs @ 150°C)	High temperature, no electrical stress
Temperature cycling	Cycling between temperature extremes
Centrifuge	Resistance to mechanical stress
Visual inspection	Look for missing leads, broken packages, damaged lids
Fine leak	Check for package sealing with pressure chamber
Gross leak	Check package seal
Final electrical test	Check for meeting data sheet specs
Group A lot acceptance	Conformance to electrical specs within 10%
Finished goods stock	
Inventory process control	
Preparation for delivery	Final visual inspection

Improving the quality of components by screening/burn-in tests not only increases reliability but also can lead to a reduction of manufacturing and warranty costs. The cost of replacing a defective component increases by about an order of magnitude for each manufacturing step. Craig [1980] reports that the typical cost for screening out a bad IC is 50¢. Repair of the board resulting from a bad chip costs about $5 on the plant floor; diagnosis and repair of the same failure in an assembled system costs $50. During the warranty period, when the system is in the field and where sophisticated, special test set-ups are not available, the same repair costs the manufacturer $500 (and might cost the customer $5000 in lost revenue and time). If only 0.5 percent (a typical value) of the components used are bad or weak, a system with 1,000 components has a $(1-0.995^{1000})$ or 99.3 percent chance that repair will be necessary during the assembly process (so-called rework) or the warranty period because of a component that could have been screened out. Alternatively, an average of five such repair incidents could be expected for each system in addition to incidents resulting from normal failures (those caused by components that would survive screening), since the expected number of defective components in a system is 1000×0.005.

Examples. Reconsider the SUN-2/50 analysis in Table 3–4, in which the quality factor for all components is 20. The Lambda analysis shows that the memory chips

TABLE 3–7
Results of Lambda analysis of SUN-2/50 workstation (in-cabinet temperature of 40°C and hermetically sealed memory chips)

(Quantity)/Module	Lambda (Single Module)	% Lambda (All Module Copies)
(1) SUN	141.2887	100.000
(1) PROCESSOR	19.1210	13.533
(1) PROC.SUPPORT	13.3933	9.479
(1) BOOT.STRAP	8.8357	6.254
(1) CLOCK.CKTS	2.6501	1.876
(1) VIDEO.LOGIC	15.1487	10.722
(1) ADDR.DECODER	7.9115	52.225
(1) VMEM.CTRL	4.4875	29.623
(1) V.SHIFT.LOGIC	0.6337	4.183
(1) V.BUS.IFACE	2.1161	13.969
(1) MEMORY	58.5194	41.418
(1) MM.CONTROL	26.8758	45.926
(1) MAIN.MEMORY	30.1724	51.560
(1) DVMA	1.4713	2.514
(1) SERIAL.IO	9.0152	6.381
(1) ETHERNET	5.2954	3.748
(1) VME	4.9939	3.535
(1) INTERRUPTS	4.3159	3.055

MTTF: 7077.7 hrs   Est. number parts: 904.0   Est. number pins: 7374

Sortkey Summary Statistics

Key	Components	Net Lambda	% System Lambda
IC:SSI	77.0	21.6896	15.35
IC:MSI	100.0	20.2590	14.34
IC:LSI	4.0	27.5128	19.47
IC:ROM	4.0	4.4582	3.16
IC:RAM	166.0	50.0259	35.41
IC:NMOS	18.0	62.2775	44.08
TRANS:BIP	1.0	0.0031	0.00

(RAM and ROM), used extensively in the design, have a total failure rate of 279 FPMH, accounting for 79 percent of the system failure rate. (For example, 73 percent of the SUN-2/50 failure rate is in the memory, and 99 percent of that is due to the RAM chips.) An improvement in the quality of memory chips alone should result in a major increase in overall reliability. If all memory chips with a π_Q of 20 can be obtained (MIL-STD quality class D, hermetically sealed), either by purchase or by in-house screening and burn in, the system failure rate drops to 141 FPMH, a 60 percent improvement in the system's failure rate and a 150 percent increase in MTTF. Table 3–7 shows the Lambda analysis of this modified design.

As another example, consider the possibility of burning in all SUN-2/50 systems before shipment. The burn-in time is made long enough to improve the quality

TABLE 3–8
Results of Lambda analysis of SUN-2/50 workstation (in-cabinet temperature of 40°C and all chips hermetically sealed)

(Quantity)/Module	Lambda (Single Module)	% Lambda (All Module Copies)
(1) SUN	88.1062	100.000
(1) PROCESSOR	3.1263	3.548
(1) PROC.SUPPORT	3.2997	3.745
(1) BOOT.STRAP	6.2143	7.053
(1) CLOCK.CKTS	1.6304	1.851
(1) VIDEO.LOGIC	10.1421	11.511
(1) ADDR.DECODER	5.3216	52.470
(1) VMEM.CTRL	3.1531	31.089
(1) V.SHIFT.LOGIC	0.2788	2.748
(1) V.BUS.IFACE	1.3887	13.692
(1) MEMORY	55.8445	63.383
(1) MM.CONTROL	26.0464	46.641
(1) MAIN.MEMORY	28.7241	51.436
(1) DVMA	1.0740	1.923
(1) SERIAL.IO	1.8850	2.140
(1) ETHERNET	1.8042	2.048
(1) VME	2.8201	3.201
(1) INTERRUPTS	1.3396	1.520

MTTF: 11349.9 hrs   Est. number parts: 904.0   Est. number pins: 7374

Sortkey Summary Statistics

Key	Components	Net Lambda	% System Lambda
IC:SSI	77.0	5.4148	6.15
IC:MSI	100.0	7.7619	8.81
IC:LSI	4.0	4.5429	5.16
IC:ROM	4.0	4.4582	5.06
IC:RAM	166.0	50.0259	56.78
IC:NMOS	18.0	35.2220	39.98
TRANS:BIP	1.0	0.0031	0.00

factor of all components by, say, 10 points ($\Delta \pi_Q = 10$). The π_Q of the hi-rel RAMs is assumed not to be affected, since additional burn in of these will have little effect. As shown by the Lambda analysis in Table 3–8, the system failure rate drops to 88 FPMH, a net improvement in system failure rate of 75 percent and in MTTF of 300 percent over the design of Table 3–4 (for which $\pi_Q = 20$ for all components, including the RAM chips).

Complexity Factors

The two complexity factors in the failure rate formula are related to the level of component integration. The first, C_1, deals with the complexity of the integrated circuit,

TABLE 3–9
Results of Lambda analysis of a 10,000-gate system constructed from chips with an identical gate count

Number of Gates per Chip	Number of Chips	Failure Rate per Chip	Total Failure Rate
4	2500	0.0364	91.0
20	500	0.0364	18.2
100	100	0.0367	3.67
400	25	0.0526	1.32
2000	5	0.1107	0.55
10000	1	1.0112	1.01

Note: Power dissipation was assumed linear with the number of gates on a chip accounting for the increase in failure rate as chip density increases.

while C_2 deals with the complexity of the package. Historically, LSI component technology has been used for several reasons other than improving reliability. The cost of a single chip is usually less than that of the set of standard SSI/MSI components needed to implement the same function. Fewer chips means fewer solder joints, less board space, and thus lower costs in board manufacture and assembly. Normally, power consumption is lower and performance benefits from shorter signal paths. In sum, more functionality can fit into less space, consume less power, operate at least as fast, and cost little or no more.

Designers frequently overlook the fact that higher integration levels also improve reliability. In the Mil model 217E, however, the failure rate of a component does not increase linearly with its complexity (measured in gates or bits on the chip). This relationship is reflected in Figure 1–7, which plots the failure rate as a function of gates. The individual gate failure rate decreases as the gate count per package goes up. As a result, the total system failure rate decreases as the level of integration increases. Thus, reliability becomes an additional factor in the decision to use LSI components where possible. Table 3–9 demonstrates the effect of larger scale integration by using chips of different complexity to build a 10,000-gate system. Changes in integration level from 4 to 10,000 gates per package result in system failure rates ranging from 91 FPMH to 0.55 FPMH, or a range of 165 to 1.

Standard LSI circuits are often not available in the exact functionality a design requires. Alternative solutions include adapting the design to fit the available components or fabricating a custom LSI chip. An increasing number of systems manufacturers are developing in-house LSI circuit design and production capabilities, and large volume requirements may make outside design and manufacture worthwhile. Conversely, if only a small volume of custom ICs is required, the manufacturing process may not have the opportunity to stabilize and traverse the learning curve. The result is that the custom chip may be more unreliable than the equivalent SSI/MSI circuit (that is, the learning curve factor π_L in the failure rate formula is greater for a custom chip than it is for mature components according to MIL-HDBK-217E). The learning curve problem is avoided in the gate array and transistor array approaches to customized LSI circuits. These and other technologies are programmable either in manufacture

TABLE 3–10 *Summary of SUN-2/50 fault-avoidance designs*

Analysis Table	Temperature (°C)	RAM π_Q	π_Q	λ(FPMH)	MTTF (hrs)	Notes
3–3	45	20	20	468.22	2136	Base design, no cooling
3–4	40	20	20	353.12	2832	Fans installed
3–5	35	20	20	266.11	3758	Cabinet ventilation system
N/A	45	20	20	195.06	5127	Hermetic chips
N/A	40	20	20	182.87	5469	Fans installed, hermetic memory chips
N/A	45	20	10	300.04	3333	Hi-rel memory chips
N/A	45	10	10	253.5	3945	All chips hi-rel
3–7	40	20	10	141.29	7078	Fans, hi-rel and hermetic memory chips
N/A	40	10	10	191.68	5217	Fans, all chips hi-rel
3–8	40	10	10	88.11	11350	Fans, all chips hi-rel and hermetic
N/A	35	10	10	73.06	13687	Cabinet ventilation, all chips hi-rel and hermetic

(such as by a final metalization step) or in the field (such as in electrically alterable ROMs and field programmable logic arrays).

Summary of Results of SUN-2/50 Analyses

Table 3–10 summarizes all of the SUN-2/50 examples used in the discussion of fault-avoidance techniques, showing the effects of the various approaches (temperature, quality, and integration). The table also includes a few designs not discussed that demonstrate the combination of more than one approach. Note that a 6.4 to 1 MTTF improvement is attained solely through fault-intolerant techniques.

HARDWARE FAULT-DETECTION TECHNIQUES

While fault-avoidance techniques attempt to decrease the possibility of failures, fault-detection techniques deal with the inevitability of failures. The key to these techniques is redundancy—that is, extra information or resources beyond those needed during normal system operation. Most of this section is devoted to techniques useful in detecting failures, or more exactly, in detecting the faults and errors that are caused by failures.

Reliability functions, $R(t)$, and the measures derived from them are not very useful in considerations of the effectiveness of failure-detection. Redundant hardware, in fact, actually contributes to a reduced $R(t)$ when corrective action does not follow detection. The concept of coverage, however, provides the view of reliability required when discussing detection techniques. This section uses two measurements of *coverage*.* The first, called *general coverage*, is more qualitative. Usually, general coverage

* The issues involving coverage measurement are discussed in detail in Chapter 5.

specifies the classes of failures that are detectable and may include failure-detection percentages for different classes of failures.

The second form of coverage, called *explicit coverage*, is the probability that a failure (any failure) is detected. It is denoted by C and can be determined from the general coverage specifications by using the average of the coverages for all possible classes of failures, weighted by the probability of occurrence of each failure class. Thus, C is more difficult to obtain, since the relative probabilities are implementation-dependent and indeed may not be known. In many instances, simplifying assumptions are employed for the possible failure modes and probabilities. For these reasons, the techniques discussed in this section will always have the general coverage measure and, when possible, the explicit coverage C.

Cost and performance effects of fault-detection techniques are also important. Dollar costs are impossible to give here. Even explicit costs in numbers of chips will often be hard to predict without knowing details of specific implementations, and the same is true of performance effects. Diagnosability is yet another important issue when considering fault-detection techniques. Diagnosability is usually considered in terms of diagnostic resolution—that is, the size of the region to which the fault can be isolated. In many systems diagnostic resolution to the field-replaceable unit (FRU) is considered necessary. Since diagnostic resolution is a function of implementation, it is difficult to determine accurately without specific details. Thus, the information on cost, performance, and diagnosability is necessarily vague in the following discussions of fault-detection techniques.

Duplication

Conceptually, duplication is the simplest fault-detection technique. Two identical copies are employed. When a failure occurs, the two copies are no longer identical, and a simple comparison detects the fault. The simplicity, low cost, and low-performance impact of the comparison technique are particularly attractive. Duplication is applicable to all areas and levels of computer design and thus is widely used.

Duplication successfully detects all single faults except that of the comparison element. In some cases, particularly for memories or multiple line output circuits, failures in both copies are detected as long as at least one failure results in a nonoverlapping failure. An example of a nonoverlapping failure is a duplicated 8-bit word. If the first copy has a failure in bit position 0 and the second copy has failures in bit positions 0 and 5, the failures in bit position 0 will not be detected if they result in identical errors. The bit position 5 failure, however, is nonoverlapping and will be detected. Identical faults from the identical modules are not detectable because both copies are in agreement. Thus, in many cases, physical division and/or separation of the modules is a necessity.

There are many variants on duplication. Some combine duplication with other techniques, resulting in increased coverage of some classes of failures or in fault tolerance (such as reconfiguration and error correction, some of which are covered in the section on dynamic redundancy).

Duplication Studies. One method for increasing coverage is the swap-and-compare technique used on the C.mmp multiprocessor [Siewiorek et al., 1978a]. Initially used for important data structures in memory, the technique can also be applied to other areas of a computer. Figure 3–7 illustrates the concept. There are two copies of a word, but one copy has its two bytes reversed. Error checking involves swapping the bytes of one copy prior to comparison. In addition to covering all single, nonoverlapping failures, swap-and-compare provides coverage of most identical failures affecting both copies (such as bit-plane failure).

In duplication, both copies may be subject to identical failures (common-mode failures), particularly if both have an identical design error or if both reside on the same IC chip. Sedmak and Liebergot [1980] propose the use of complementary functions to solve this problem for VLSI IC chips (Figures 3–8 and 3–9). This approach is similar in concept to dual-diversity reception of radio signals, in which the same signal is received by two different antennae and receivers. One copy of the logic is the logical dual of the other copy. Common failure modes would probably cause different error effects, resulting in detection and thus coverage of these modes. A similar solution is to use both "on-set" and "off-set" realizations for the two copies [Tohma and Aoyagi, 1971]. The on-set is the set of input and state variables that result in logical one outputs. The off-set results in logical zero outputs.

Duplicate information may already be present in a circuit so that the amount of additional redundancy needed may be small. An example is a possible internal modification to the Advanced Micro Devices AM2901 bit-slice ALU chip. In the chip are functional units that compute $A + B$, AB, and $A \oplus B$ (the last one is part of the adder). Because $A \oplus B = (A + B) \oplus (AB)$, the two sets of signals can be used to check each other. In this case, the only additional elements needed to utilize the duplicate information would be two XOR gates (one to form one of the duplicate signals and the other to compare the two signals).

Real-Time Duplication Examples. Duplication can also be carried out at the bus level. The Sperry Univac 1100/60, for example, uses comparison at the bus level for its instruction processors [Boone, Liebergot, and Sedmak, 1980]. The processor is split into two 36-bit subprocessors. Each subprocessor is duplicated, and only one of the two duplicates drives the master data bus during any one microcycle. The other drives the duplicate data bus (Figure 3–10). Both copies operate in the same way on the same

FIGURE 3–7
Swap-and-compare check scheme for critical data structures in C.mmp

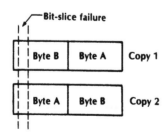

FIGURE 3–8
Proposed use of duplicate circuits on generalized VLSI chip, in which complementary implementations improve resistance to common failure modes [From Sed- mak and Liebergot, 1980; © 1980 IEEE]

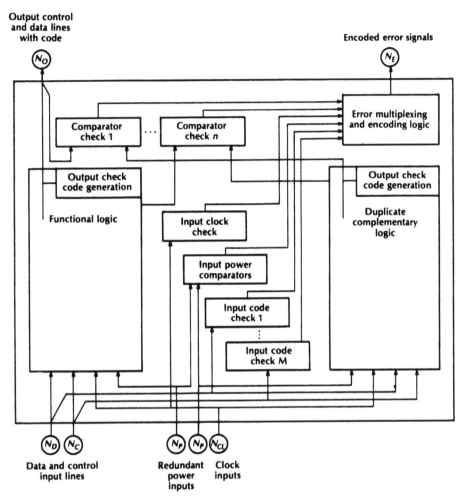

data. At the end of the microcycle the results are compared. A disagreement causes interruption of operations. Univac's implementation of this scheme produced a per- formance increase as a result of splitting driven loads between the two subprocessors.

Comparing module outputs is not the only way to apply duplication. The AT&T No. 1 processor demonstrates duplication at the system level, but comparison is performed at the register-transfer level [Toy, 1978]. Certain key values within each of the dual central control units (CCs) are compared by matchers residing within each CC. Only one CC is on line at a time; the other is running in microcycle lockstep. The oscillator in the on-line CC drives the clock circuits in both. The matcher immediately detects any divergence in operation. This level of duplication decreases error latency, increases coverage, and has the side effect of making system diagnosis easier and quicker. Each of the matching circuits compares 24 bits from each CC during the 5.5

FIGURE 3–9

Functional versus duplicate complementary circuits for the VLSI chip in Figure 3–8 [From Sedmak and Liebergot, 1980; © 1980 IEEE]

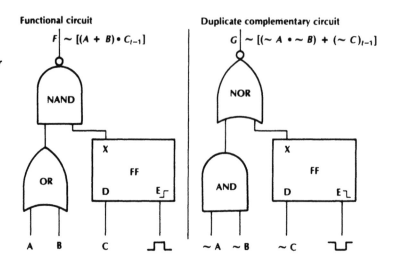

Truth Table

Inputs			Outputs	
A_t	B_t	C_t	F_t	G_t
L	L	L	H	L
L	L	H	H	L
L	H	L	H	L
L	H	H	L	H
H	L	L	H	L
H	L	H	L	H
H	H	L	H	L
H	H	H	L	H

Key

Symbol	Meaning
~	NOT
•	LOGICAL AND
+	LOGICAL INCLUSIVE OR
subscript t	Time period t
subscript $t - 1$	Time period $t - 1$
$E_\int$	Enable on low to high transition of clock
$E_\daleth$	Enable on high to low transition of clock

FIGURE 3–10

Duplication at bus level in Sperry/Univac 1100/60 [From Boone, Liebergot, and Sedmak, 1980; © 1980 IEEE]

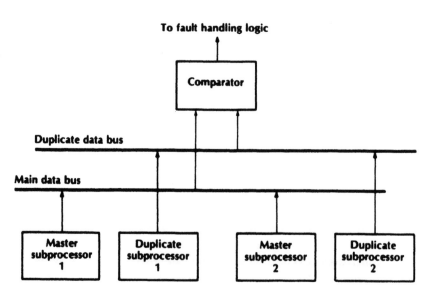

μsec machine cycle. Each CC has two matchers, and each matcher has access to six 24-bit sets of internal nodes (Figure 3–11). The processing performed during the machine cycle determines which set is checked, and a mismatch generates an interrupt. A diagnostic program is run to locate the faulty CC, which is then removed from service for repair.

The Stratus XA2000 series of fault-tolerant multiprocessors uses a pair of Motorola 68000 family processors running in parallel on each processor board for detection of faults on the off-the-shelf processor chips. This approach requires the application of external logic to perform the checking and error reporting. Two reduced instruction set microprocessor chips illustrate direct support for duplication-based checking. The AMD AM29000 [Johnson, 1987] has a master/slave ability determined by a "test" pin. The outputs of the slave copy are disabled, although it sees the same input stream as the master. The chip checks to see if the values at the input to its (disabled) output drivers are the same as the values on the external pins (driven by the master). The Motorola 88000 provides a similar capability [McLeod, 1988].

Duplication Costs. The cost of duplication is twice that of an equivalent simplex system, plus the cost of the comparison element. Performance degradation can result from at least two sources. The first is lack of synchronization between the compared signals, which could be remedied by either a common clock or a delay period before comparison. Some delay would result in any event from the inevitable variance in propagation times and other parameters in the circuits of both copies. The other source of degradation is the propagation and decision time required by the comparison element. Normally, the performance loss due to these factors is small enough not to detract from the benefits of duplication.

At a cost in performance, expenses can be halved by using the same hardware to perform duplicate operations, one following the other in time. This time redundancy at least doubles execution time. It also is more susceptible to nondetection of faults because the same hardware, with the same problem, is used for both operations. Transient faults would not be a problem, but hard failures would be. Hard-failure coverage could be increased somewhat by carrying out the operation with a different ordering or algorithm, using as many different resources as possible. Although a single failed ALU would probably give bad results both times, the results would differ for most failures and still result in a mismatch and failure detection. For example, a string of additions could be performed twice in different order, or could be done the second time by forming and adding the two's complements and negating the result.

Duplication Disadvantages. One frequently perceived problem of duplication (and some other redundancy techniques) is incomplete use of resources. A duplicated computer, for example, is actually two processors performing the same task in parallel, with a loss of half the available computing power. As a result, in some designs only part of the processing is done in parallel by both copies, and checking is performed for only the portion of processing still performed in duplicate. All other processing is performed on only one processor or the other. In this case, duplication is usually at the task level

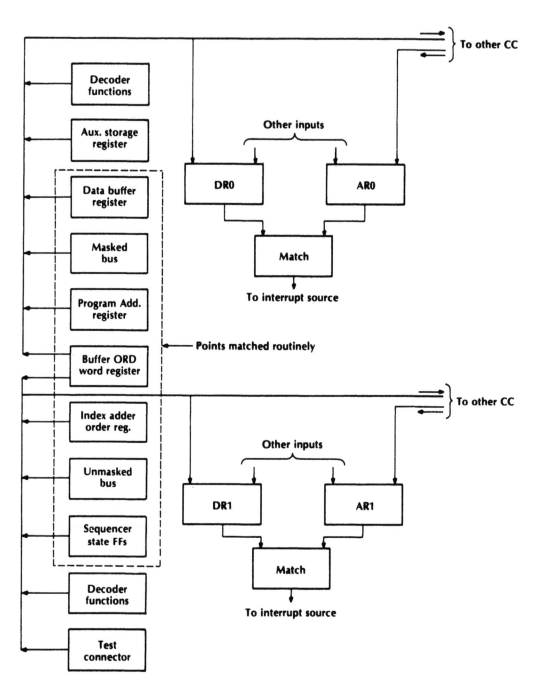

FIGURE 3–11 *Bell ESS-1 CC match access [From Toy, 1978; © 1978 IEEE]*

and the comparison is performed between the intermediate and/or final results of the two task instantiations. The yield is increased utilization of the hardware; the disadvantages are decreased coverage and increased error latency. Careful design, however, can minimize these disadvantages, and in many instances the remaining coverage is more than sufficient.

Another source of performance degradation with processors duplicated in this fashion is the bus bandwidth consumed by interprocess communication. While this is an expected overhead in multiprocessing architectures, the problem is increased by the bandwidth needed for duplication. One possible solution can be found in the Tandem computer.* The Tandem design attacks this problem with its Dynabus, a high-speed interprocessor bus used solely for interprocessor communication. All I/O and memory accesses are handled through a more conventional bus.

Duplication, like all other reliability techniques, involves the classic dilemma of "Who shall watch over the guardians?" In the case of duplication, failure in the matching equipment results either in no error detection or in an occasional or permanent false indication of error. This problem can be alleviated with additional cost, complexity, and/or performance degradation, as the matching circuit is made more reliable using some of the techniques in the following sections. The problem, however, can never be completely solved. There are decreasing returns to adding more and more redundancy. Eventually, the redundancy becomes a liability too large to accept in cost, performance, or even reduced net system reliability. This point is demonstrated in Chapter 5, which contains an extensive example of a Motorola 6809 single-board computer redesign.

Error-Detection Codes

Error-detection codes are systematic applications of redundancy to information. As shown in Figure 3–12a, the concept of codes is simple: For the *set of all possible words* only a subset of them represents valid information, which is the *set of code words*. In essence, many redundancy techniques can be considered coding techniques. Duplication, for example, can be considered a code whose valid elements are words consisting of two identical symbols. Error detection with codes consists of determining whether an input is a valid code word. Most of the codes of concern to a computer system designer are binary codes, in which the code words are made from a combination of 1's and 0's.

Code Properties. There are many different ways to compare the effectiveness of two different codes. One metric is the relative encoding efficiency, which can be determined as the ratio of the number of valid code words to the total number of possible symbols. A second metric is known as *Hamming distance*—that is, the number of bit positions on which two code words differ. The minimum distance, d, of a code is

---

* The Tandem computer does not use duplication as a means of error detection. However, the Dynabus design could prove useful in a system where duplication is used.

defined as the minimum Hamming distance, d, found between any two code words. The minimum distance represents the number of independent, single-bit errors that the code can detect. Since some common failure modes corrupt more than one bit at a time, a third metric is general coverage—that is, a qualitative listing of errors that the code can detect. These three metrics form some of the so-called properties of a code.

• *Hamming Distance*: Figure 3–12b shows the space of the 3-bit words. Each edge of the cube represents a distance-1 transition between adjacent words in the space. Consider a code taken from this space, in which all code words have an odd number of 1's. These are the boxed words in the figure. The minimum distance between code words is 2, and any distance-1 transition results in a noncode word. The distance-1 transitions from code words represent single-bit errors. Thus, for this code (odd parity), any single error is detectable. The nonboxed points of this set form another code (even parity) with the same coverage of single failures. For both codes, any distance-2 transition (double error) results in another code word, and is thus a nondetectable error.

• *General Coverage*: Another code is formed by joining a 2-bit value with its complement. This code is called the CD code because the second half is the complemented duplicate of the first half. The set of valid code words is $D = \{0011, 0110, 1001, 1100\}$. This code has a minimum distance of 2. Detection for this code consists of a check to see whether the 4-bit input is an element of D, or equivalently, not an element of D'.

Figure 3–12c illustrates the 4-bit word space containing this code. The CD code words are marked by &. Each arc in the figure is a distance-1 transition—that is, a single-bit flip. Between 1100 and 1001, at least two bit flips (errors) must occur. Between 1100 and 0011, four bit flips must occur to produce the wrong code word. Some of the intermediate paths consist entirely of noncode words. Thus, the code will detect any single-bit error, but some double errors will go undetected because they result in another code word (the wrong one). Herein lies a key to code performance: The use of a code with a minimum distance, d, allows detection of any t errors, where $t < d$. Duplication can be considered a code with $d = 2$, triplication (three copies) a code with $d = 3$, and, in general, replication with n copies a code with $d = n$. (Note that the CD code of Figure 3–12c is a variation on duplication in which the extra copy is the complement of the original. This design gives protection against all multiple adjacent unidirectional faults. For example, if the code is used for a register that resides on one IC chip, a failure of the chip that results in the grounding of some or all outputs could be detected.)

• *Coding Efficiency Ratio*: Two other distance-2 codes are shown in Figure 3–12c. The first, called the 2/4 (2-of-4) code, consists of all the words (marked by @) containing exactly two 1's. This code requires slightly less redundancy than the CD code because it allows six codes out of the code space instead of the CD code's four. Although the 2/4 code detects all adjacent unidirectional errors, it detects fewer distance-2 errors than the CD code. The other code is an even-parity code (boxed words). This code

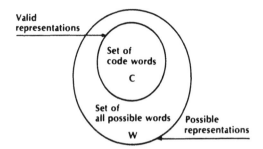

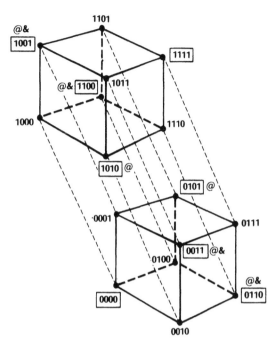

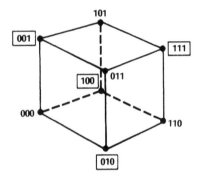

a. Example code space where the set of invalid representations (noncode words) is W – C

c. Expanded word space cube with 1 bit added to the word size

b. 3-bit word space

Key: Boxed words = even parity; @ = a code word in a 2/4 *m-of-n* code; & = code words from complemented duplication code; unmarked words = odd parity.

FIGURE 3–12 *Error-detection coding*

has the least redundancy, for it allows eight code words out of the code space. However, it has no coverage of distance-2 errors and will detect only some multiple adjacent unidirectional errors. In particular, it will not detect a unidirectional failure affecting all bits. The odd-parity code (all the unmarked points in Figure 3–12c) has the same drawbacks as even parity, except that it will detect both the all-0's failure mode and the all-1's failure mode.

Table 3–11 summarizes the three properties of the four codes in Figure 3–12c. Other properties of codes include the difficulty of error detection and decoding. To detect errors, actual values must be encoded, or transformed into valid code words that, upon receipt, must be checked for validity, Nonseparable codes must also be decoded, or transformed back into original form before use. Decoding is eased with

TABLE 3–11
Three properties of the codes shown in Figure 3–12c

Code	Coding Efficiency Ratio		Hamming Distance	General Coverage
	Bits in Word	Code Words		
CD	4	4	2	Any single-bit error; 66% of double-bit errors; any multiple adjacent unidirectional error
2/4	4	6	2	Any single-bit error; 33% of double-bit errors; any multiple adjacent unidirectional error
Even parity	4	8	2	Any single-bit error; no double-bit error; not all multiple adjacent unidirectional errors; not all-0's or all-1's errors
Odd parity	4	8	2	Any single-bit error; no double-bit errors; not all multiple adjacent unidirectional errors; all-0's and all-1's errors

sparable codes consisting of only two parts (the original value and the appended code bits). In linear separable codes, each check bit is calculated as a linear combination of some of the data bits. Parity-check codes are linear separable codes for which each check bit can be calculated as the parity bit (sum modulo-2) of some subset of the data bits. Parity-check codes can be encoded and decoded using parity generation and parity-check matrices (for details, see Tang and Chien [1969]). Some codes can be decoded efficiently in a serial fashion, bit by bit in a shift register, but may be difficult to decode in a parallel fashion. These serial-decodable codes are used in applications that employ serial data streams.

Yet another property of codes is whether they are invariant or closed with respect to data operations. In the simple addition of code words, the result may or may not be another code word, or it may not be the correct code word. Conversely, there are codes that are invariant with respect to some set of operations, or for which there exist simple algorithms for generating the code word that should result from the operation (short of the process of decode, operate, encode).

The four codes shown in Figure 3–12c constitute the spectrum of code choices for a 4-bit code word. While other error-detection codes might not be as simple as these four, they are generally better in some respects. Most require less redundancy to achieve the minimum distance property. In some cases, codes can be modified, extended, or combined with other codes or redundancy techniques to increase the general coverage property. For example, a distance-d code can be modified by a further restriction on the valid code words, such as using a subset of code words that contains a high percentage with a minimum distance greater than d. Often, however, increased effectiveness may not be reflected in the minimum distance, as in the examples of

Figure 3–12c, where the CD code is a subset of the 2/4 code, and the 2/4 code is in turn a subset of the even-parity code.

If some fault classes are more probable than others, the code choice is affected. The CD code example of Figure 3–12c detects not only single faults but also all adjacent unidirectional faults up to and including the entire word. The following subsections present a representative sample of the more common error-detection codes. The references [Tang and Chien, 1969; Peterson and Weldon, 1972; Rao, 1974; MacWilliams and Sloane, 1978] provide more additonal coverage of error-detection codes.

M-of-N Codes. An *m-of-n* code (*m/n* code) consists of *n*-bit code words in which *m* (and only *m*) bits are 1's. Thus, there are $_nC_m$ code words.* For example, the 2/4 code has $_4C_2$, or six possible code words. The set of code words for the 2/4 code is {1100, 1010, 1001, 0101, 0011, 0110}. This code detects all single and unidirectional faults. The basic concept for the *m-of-n* codes is simple, but they have several disadvantages. One is that circuitry for parallel detection and decoding is complex, whereas a serial decoder can be made by simply using a counter for the 1-bits.

Another problem is that they often require a large amount of redundancy. For example, in the case of *k* data bits with 2^k values possible, then at least *k* extra coding bits are needed if the code is to be separable, as in the example of Figure 3–13a (that is, detection is necessary, decoding is not). Less redundancy can be used at the cost of adding a decoder and encoder. For example, if there are four data bits (*k* = 4) a 3/6 code could be used in place of a separable 4/8 code, since only 16 code words are needed. The 3/6 code has 20 code words and less redundancy than a 4/8 code, which has 70 code words. If there are $_nC_m$ code words and only $q < {_nC_m}$ of them are to be allowed, there is less coverage of multiple faults unless the erroneous code words are also detected. In the 3/6 code example there are four unused code words that could pass undetected as errors, and in the 4/8 code there would be 54 undetectable unused code words.

One common use of *m/n* is in control circuitry. To produce a separable *m/n* coding, extra lines are used in addition to the output control lines. The redundancy lies in extra logic for encoding (determining the value of the extra lines) and in the detection logic. In some cases, extra lines are not needed or can be reduced in number. For instance, the number of set lines may be less than or equal to some maximum number. Consider a control module with four output lines whose possible output states are shown in Figure 3–13a. Either two or three lines are set at any one time, and the addition of a single line can produce a 3/5 separably coded output. Figures 3–13b and c show the implementation of this scheme, including a TTL error detector. Because the control line states (0110, 0101) are not valid, the demultiplexer (demux) outputs for 5 and 6 are not included in the circuit even though such a code word is a valid 3/5 code word. The logic that generates the redundant signal provides fault detection only for signals from which it is independent. Thus, the logic for the fifth line would

---

* $_nC_m$ is a shorthand expression for the number of unique combinations of *n* things taken *m* at a time. A verbal shorthand for this term is "*n* choose *m*."

FIGURE 3–13

Example control module and 3/5 code checker

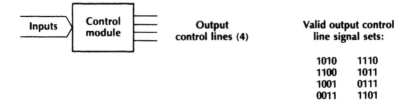

a. Four-output control module and valid output line states

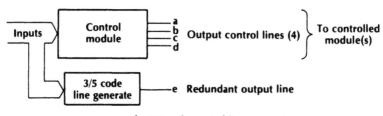

b. 3/5 code control line generation

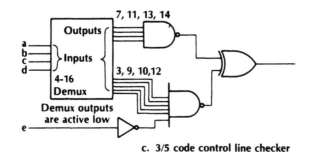

c. 3/5 code control line checker

normally not use the other four module outputs as its inputs. Otherwise, the only coverage afforded is over corruption of the signals on the wires, not over the logic that generates them.

The AT&T No. 3A processor uses an *m*-of-*n* code in its microstore. The TO and FROM control fields in the microword are each encoded in a 4/8 code and are interlaced with the address field (Figure 3–14). This arrangement gives coverage of multiple adjacent unidirectional errors and all even numbers of bit failures in the address field as well. This would not be the case if the address were kept separated, for it is covered only by a single-parity bit. More complete details of the scheme, including decoding/detection implementation, are given in Toy [1978]. In a paper written about the microstore alone, Cook et al. [1973] present a detailed examination of its design.

Parity Codes. If a given group of bits has an even number of 1's, it is defined as having even parity. If the number of 1's is odd, the group has odd parity. Parity codes involve

FIGURE 3–14
4/8 coding in AT&T's No. 3A Processor microstore [From Toy, 1978; © 1978 IEEE]

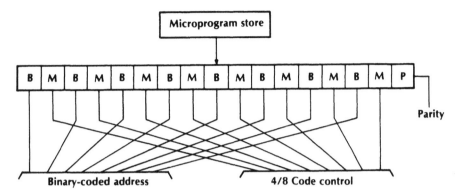

the addition of an extra bit to each group of bits so that the resulting word has even parity or odd parity, depending on the implementation. Parity codes are linear separable codes and give on-line detection of errors.

For a b-bit group of bits, the (even) parity can be generated by using a b-input XOR gate. Because large XOR gates are not available as standard logic functions, the parity can be generated using a b-input tree of 2-input XOR gates or one of the standard parity-generation chips (such as the 74190, which encodes an 8-bit input, decodes a 9-bit input, and can be used in a modular fashion for longer words). Parity codes are suitable for serial detection and encoding, needing only a single memory cell and a single XOR gate to perform the modulo-2 addition of the bits in the word.

The choice between even and odd parity depends upon the prevalent failure mode. Even parity gives detection of the all-1's failure mode if the parity group (data bits and parity bit) is an odd number of bits long, but not for an even number of bits. Even parity also does not detect the all-0's failure mode. Odd parity detects the all-0's failure mode for parity groups of all lengths, and the all-1's failure mode for parity groups an even number of bits long.

Figure 3–15 illustrates the following variants of parity encoding, and Table 3–12 summarizes the properties of these five basic techniques.

• **Bit-per-Word Parity:** In this technique one parity bit is appended to the entire data word. It is one of the least expensive forms of error detection, because it requires a minimum of redundancy in terms of information transferred, and one parity tree can be used for both encoding and detection if information is both transmitted and received. In addition to the extra bits and parity tree, other hardware is needed for such uses as setting parity error-detection status bits and allowing wrong parity to be written for maintenance (testing) purposes. Bit-per-word parity codes detect all single-bit errors and all errors that involve an odd number of bits. The all-1's and all-0's failure coverage is as discussed previously, with the entire code word becoming the parity group. The costs of bit-per-word parity for a b-bit word are $1/b$ redundancy in data, a b-bit parity tree encoder, a $(b + 1)$-bit parity tree decoder (in some cases a single

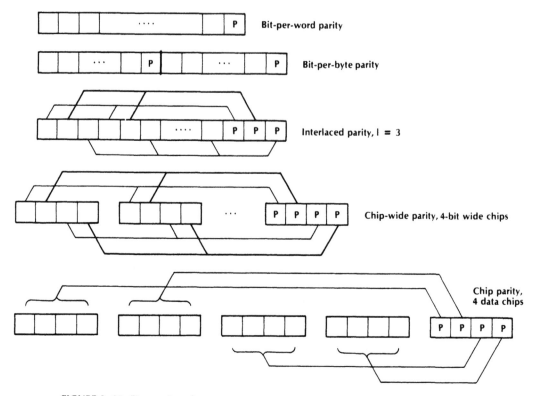

FIGURE 3–15 *Five parity schemes*

encoder/decoder tree is possible), and a logic delay of approximately $\lceil \log_2(b + 1) \rceil$* gate levels in the encoding and detection operations.

• **Bit-per-Byte Parity:** An extra bit is added to each byte of data in this technique. Alternating even and odd parity in the bytes of the data word gives improved coverage, since both wordwide stuck-at-1 and wordwide stuck-at-0 failure modes are covered. The wordwide failure mode is a common result of timing and select-line errors. Also, the bit-per-byte code detects all single- or odd-number errors in each byte. Thus, as long as at least one byte contains an odd number of failures, many more kinds of multiple errors in a word are detectable. The diagnostic resolution is also improved over bit-per-word parity, because fewer data bits are covered by each parity bit. Encoding and detection are faster because the parity trees have fewer inputs and thus fewer gate levels of delay. The extra costs are more parity trees and a redundancy of $1/m$ where there are m bits per byte. The C.mmp multiprocessor used this technique for its shared memory [Siewiorek et al., 1978a].

* The ceiling symbol $\lceil \ \rceil$, means round the value up to the next highest integer.

TABLE 3–12 *Properties of the basic parity techniques*

Technique	Bit Redun- dancy	Parity Trees			General Coverage
		Number	Size	Delay	
Bit-per- word	$1/b$	1	$a = b + 1$	$\lceil \log_2 a \rceil$	All single-bit errors; all odd-bit errors
Bit-per- byte	$1/m$	b/m	$a = m + 1$	$\lceil \log_2 a \rceil$	All single-bit errors; all errors with an odd number in at least one byte
Interlaced	i/b	i	$a = \lceil b/i \rceil + 1$	$\lceil \log_2 a \rceil$	All single-bit errors; all errors with an odd number in at least one parity group; large number of adjacent multiple unidirectional errors
Chip-wide	w/b	w	$a = \lceil b/w \rceil + 1$	$\lceil \log_2 a \rceil$	All single-bit errors; all errors with an odd number in at least one parity group; large number of adjacent multiple unidirectional errors; any single-chip failure
Chip	$1/w$	$\lceil b/w \rceil$	$a = w + 1$	$\lceil \log_2 a \rceil$	All single-bit errors; all errors with an odd number on at least one chip; 50% of single-chip failures; points to failed chip for single errors

• **Interlaced parity:** In this technique, i parity bits are appended to the data word. Each parity bit is associated with a group of (b/i) bits, and is generated by forming the parity over every ith bit, starting in a different bit position for each parity bit. The encoded word thus has i separate parity groups. Interlaced parity covers single-bit errors in each group, as well as all multiple errors in which at least one group has an odd number of errors. If the parity sense (odd/even) is alternated from group to group, the code covers a large number of unidirectional failures. Thus, interlaced parity would be particularly useful for buses, where the shorting-together of signal lines is a common failure mode, as well as for whole-chip failures of memory and bus transceiver chips. These failures are sure to be detected relatively quickly. The diagnostic resolution of interlaced parity is to the parity group in error. As for bit-per-byte parity, the speed of detection and encoding is increased as a result of the smaller parity tree sizes. The costs are an i/b redundancy, and i parity trees of $\lceil b/i \rceil + 1$ bits for detection.

• **Chip-Wide parity:** Proposed for memories in which each word is spread over $(\lceil b/w \rceil)w$-bit-wide chips [McKevitt, 1972], this technique is actually a special case of interlaced parity. There are w parity bits appended to each data word, and they reside on their own w-bit-wide memory chip. Each parity bit is the parity over the same bit position on all the other chips. When single-bit-wide chips are used, chip-wide parity is the same as duplication. The coverage is the same as for interlaced parity, with the additional property that any single/chip failure is detectable (as long as at least one bit is in error). This technique is also applicable to many other areas of digital system design in which blocks of signals (control, data) are to be protected.

• **Chip Parity:** Another way of detecting single-chip failures is to use a parity bit for each chip. The chip parity bits are stored separately from the chips they cover. The advantage of this technique, which is called chip parity, is that a parity error detection immediately locates the failed chip. Chip parity thus has a more useful diagnostic resolution than chip-wide parity. However, if data bit values are uniformly distributed and the 0-to-1 and 1-to-0 failure modes are equally likely, chip parity has only a 0.5 probability of detecting failure of an entire chip (for a given data word). This is because there is a 0.5 probability that the parity bit is the correct one for the erroneous data on the chip. Chip-wide parity, on the other hand, has a $(1 - (0.5)^w)$ probability of detection in the same situation, given w-bit-wide chips. The cost of chip parity is b/w extra bits per word and $(\lceil b/w \rceil)(w + 1)$-bit parity trees.

Parity Code Applications and Studies. Parity can be used to detect addressing faults in a memory by storing the parity of the address and data with the memory word. On access, the stored parity is compared with that of the data and address used. If the parity is wrong, then the word retrieved is incorrect, the word retrieved was stored in the wrong place, or the wrong word was retrieved. In this way, all single-bit addressing errors as well as data errors are detected.

In some applications of parity, the redundancy needed may already be partially or wholly present. An example is a host-to-microprocessor network in which the network allows direct host communication with the individual microprocessors. The bus for the network has a data field and a 3-bit opcode field:

Wire	Function	
Bus<1:8>	Data	
Bus<9:11>	Function	
	000	Write address
	001	Write network CSR
	010	Write data
	011	Unused
	100	Read device characteristics (polling)
	101	Read CSR
	110	Read data
	111	Unused
Bus<12>	Strobe	
Bus<13>	Acknowledge	

There are two unusued opcodes (011 and 111). If an opcode starting in 01 is used for data writes and one starting in 11 is used for data reads, the third bit could carry the parity of the data field. Given a prediction that 90 percent of the bus transactions will be data reads and writes, this scheme would give bit-per-word parity protection on 90 percent of the bus activity without any extra bus wires.

In a design analysis for the use of parity on a processor-memory bus, three alternatives were used. The first was simple (17,16) parity. The second was the same (17,16) parity with a modification that performs a cumulative parity check of the entire two-way bus transaction. The address sent to the memory has an appended parity bit. The parity appended to the returned data word is formed as the modulo-2 sum of the received address parity bit, the computed parity of the received address, and the parity of the memory word itself. This scheme provides detection of a failure in the memory parity checker. The third alternative was an interlaced (18,16) parity ($i = 2$) with alternated parity senses, modified as before to provide a cumulative parity check on the bus transaction. Table 3–13 shows the coverage of several different failure classes for this scheme. From the table it can be determined that the cumulative (17,16) parity is better than the simple (17,16) parity because it detects a large number of memory unit parity generate/check errors and the (18,16) cumulative parity provides the best coverage of the three.

The standard LSI chips used in systems design are not usually designed for the external application of error-detection codes to check for proper chip operation. Data

TABLE 3–13
Percentage of coverage of processor-memory bus failures

Error Type	Coverage		
	(17,16) Parity (%)	(17,16) Cumulative (%)	(18,16) Cumulative (%)
Hard failure:			
Bus all 1	50	50	100
Bus all 0	50	50	100
Bus half 1	0	0	Near 100
Bus half 0	0	0	Near 100
Wire-or:			
2 wires	100	100	100
3 wires	0	0	88
4 wires	0	0	100
5 wires	0	0	0
Single bit*	100	100	100
Double bit			
Adjacent	0	0	100
Random	0	0	Near 100
Triple bit	100	100	100
Quadruple bit			
Two pairs adjacent	0	0	0
Two adjacent	0	0	Near 100
Three adjacent	0	0	100
Four adjacent	0	0	50
Random	0	0	0
Parity generate and check			
Stuck-at-ok	0	100	100
Stuck-at-1	50	50	Near 100
Stuck-at-0	50	50	Near 100

* One bit value, not a failed wire

transformations occur internally for which codes are not invariant. In some cases, however, partial checking can be accomplished without resorting to duplication, as in the DEC-system 2020 processor. A parity code is used on the bus that feeds an AM2901 bit-sliced ALU. As the data are gated into the 2901, the bus monitor checks them for proper parity.

If the data are merely being read into the 2901 register file, their parity bit is simultaneously stored in an external register (Figure 3–16). The external register has 2 bits associated with each register in the 2901: the parity bit and a "parity-valid" bit, which remains set as long as no data transformations are performed on the contents of the corresponding internal register. The parity-valid bit value is determined by the control signals for the 2901. When the data are brought out to the bus from the 2901, their parity is generated before they are placed on the bus. If the parity-valid bit is still set, the stored parity is used to verify that the data have no errors. This scheme provides fault detection for the 2901 register file, internal data paths, and the parts of the ALU used to move data internally without transformation.

Even though parity (and other) codes are not invariant with respect to data transformations, it is possible to use parity as a check on the data operation, if, given the inputs to the operation, the parity of the result of the transformation can be predicted. One study in this area by Chinal [1977] proposed a high-speed parity prediction circuit for binary adders. In another study, Khodadad-Mostashiry [1979] presented a general method for predicting the parity of any transformation, and in particular, bit-sliced functional circuits. The resulting prediction circuit, however, is often much more complex than the circuit it checks. Fujiwara and Matsuoka [1985] developed an extended and generalized version of parity prediction checkers.

FIGURE 3–16

Use of parity to detect errors during nontransformation operations in LSI ALU chips in the DEC 2020

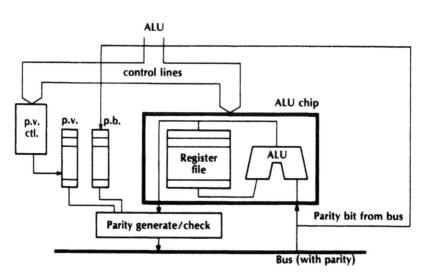

Checksums. One of the least expensive methods of fault detection is *checksumming*. The checksum for a block of s words is formed by adding together all of the words in the block modulo-n, where n is arbitrary. The block of s words and its checksum together constitute a code word in a linear separable code. The number of bits in the sum is usually limited. This quantity is then compared with the checksum formed and stored when the block was last transmitted. In memories, the checksum must be stored along with the data block. If any word within the block is modified, the checksum must also be modified at the same time. The stored checksum is normally kept physically separate from the data block to limit the effect of catastrophic failure on the fault-detecting capability.

Although checksumming is inexpensive in terms of excess information, it has three disadvantages. First, it is best suited to applications in which data are handled in large, contiguous blocks, such as buses that carry data in blocks, sequential storage, and block-transfer peripherals.

Second, checksumming in memories takes a long time to detect faults even when reading a single word, for s words must be read and added, and then the sum compared with the stored value. Thus, checksumming is not suited to on-line checking when reading from memories. If the technique is used in a writable store, the checksum must be updated on each write by reading the old data and checksum, subtracting the old data, adding the new data, and finally storing both the data and the updated checksum.

The cumbersome procedure, however, may not be a problem when writing is infrequent or when updating is performed in parallel with subsequent system operations not involving the memory. The memory checksum (and checksum update on writes) may be performed by dedicated hardware without interference to the rest of the system, as shown in Figure 3–17. The checksum can also be performed by the ALU or other system component, which will cause a degradation of the system's throughput. If it takes t_c seconds to perform a checksum for one block, and on the average a block of memory is checked every T_c seconds, the system performance is degraded by t_c/T_c. The additional degradation caused by a checksum update time of t_w when writes are performed every T_w seconds is, on the average, t_w/T_w.

The third disadvantage of checksumming is low diagnostic resolution. In memories, the detected fault could be in the block of s words, the stored checksum, or the checking circuitry. In data transmission, the fault could be in the data source, the transmission medium, or the checking circuitry.

Although cumbersome for random access writable stores, checksumming is very applicable to read-only memory, which can be checked by a background process. The Pluribus system uses checksum error detection on both shared-code storage and local-code storage [Ornstein et al., 1975]. Another application would be microstore checks performed by dedicated hardware or console processors. Finally, critical data structures and program codes could occasionally be verified through software-implemented checksumming.

Four checksumming techniques are presented in the following paragraphs. The first is a single-precision checksum; the second is an extended-precision (extended-

FIGURE 3–17
Memory with checksum error detection

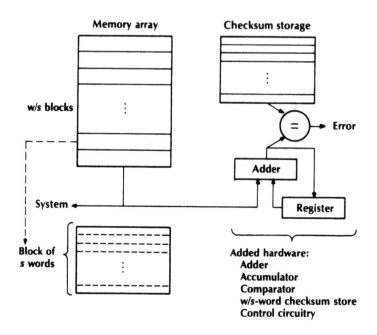

word-length) checksum; and the third, the Honeywell checksum, is a modified double-precision technique.* The fourth technique, low-cost residue code, gives better coverage than the single-precision checksum for about the same cost.

• **Single-Precision Checksum:** In this technique, the memory is divided into blocks of s words, each having b bits. The checksum is a b-bit word that is the modulo-(2^b) sum of the s words in the block. The memory redundancy for this system is $1/(s + 1)$. Errors in any one column will cause either the corresponding checksum bit or the carry to the adjacent column to be in error. Thus, for the most significant column, the error coverage afforded by the information contained in the carry is lost. The bit positions nearby pose the same problem in lesser degrees, depending on their distance from the most significant bit. Thus, error coverage varies for each bit position, with the best coverage available for errors in the least significant bit. As the size of the block that the checksum guards increases, coverage decreases. Thus, coverage is a function of block size and column(s) in error. (See Jack et al. [1975] or Siewiorek and Swarz [1982] for the formulas for coverage.)

• **Extended Precision Checksum:** In this technique, if the checksum being formed is A bits longer than the memory word length, the coverage is greater than that afforded by the single-precision checksum. In particular, if $s < 2^A$, then the coverage for all columns is the same as for the lowest order column in the single-precision checksum,

---

* More complete information on these can be found in Jack et al. [1975], from which much of the discussion here was abstracted.

because there can be no overflow and thus no loss of information in the carry bits from the higher order columns. The probability of detecting any type of error is thus 100 percent.

• **Honeywell Checksum:** This technique is a modified double-precision checksum technique in which successive pairs of memory words in a block are concatenated. The checksum is formed by combining double-length quantities to form a double-length word. Thus, any single-column error in memory will affect two columns in the checksum being formed. Overflow can still cause loss of carry-bit information.

• **Low-Cost Residue Code:** This technique is a modification of the single-precison checksum, with an end-around carry adder. The end-around carry retains the information normally lost with the most significant carry bit; it results in modulo-m addition where $m = 2^b - 1$ for a b-bit adder. This technique [Usas, 1978] provides about the same single-word coverage as the single-precision checksum. The coverage for double-bit errors is slightly better, and is much better for unidirectional errors in one column or two adjacent columns. The number of possible undetectable 2- and 3-bit errors is

$$U_2 = sb(s - 1) \qquad \text{for } b > 2$$
$$U_3 = s^2 b(s - 1) \qquad \text{for } b > 3$$

where s is the block length.

When one column or two adjacent columns have unidirectional errors, the total number of possible undetectable errors is

$$U_{1\text{col}} = bU$$

$$U_{2\text{col}} = (b - 1)(2N - 2U)$$

where
$$U = 2 \sum_{1 \leqslant k \leqslant P} {}_s C_{[k(2b-1)]}$$
$$N = \sum_{1 \leqslant i \leqslant Q} \sum_{0 \leqslant k \leqslant R_i} (-1)^k {}_s C_k \, {}_{T_i} C_{s-1}$$
$$T_i = i(2^b - 1) + s - 4i - 1$$
$$P = s/(2^b - 1)$$
$$Q = 3s/(2^b - 1)$$
$$R_i = i(2^b - 1)/4$$

With these formulas, Usas showed the low-cost residue code to be superior to the single-precision checksum.

Arithmetic Codes. An arithmetic code, A, has the property that $A(b * c) = A(b) * A(c)$ where b and c are noncoded operands, $*$ is one of a set of arithmetic operations (such as addition and multiplication), and $A(x)$ is the arithmetic code word for x. Thus, the set of code words in A is closed with respect to a specific set of arithmetic operations. Such a code can be used to detect or correct errors and to check the results of arithmetic operations.* Some operations (such as logical operations), however, cannot be checked by arithmetic codes and must be performed on unencoded operands.

This section provides an introduction to three classes of arithmetic codes: AN, residue-*m*, and inverse residue-*m* arithmetic codes. Appendix B, a paper by Avizienis [1971], examines the three classes in detail, and other sources of information are Rao [1974]; Sellers, Hsiao, and Bearnson [1968b]; and Avizienis [1973].

The simplest arithmetic codes are the *AN codes*. These codes are formed by multiplying the data word by a number that is not a power of the radix of the representation (such as 2 for binary). The redundancy is determined by the multiplier chosen, called the *modulus*. AN codes are invariant with respect to unsigned arithmetic. If the code chosen has $A = 2^a - 1$ and a length that is a multiple of *a* bits, it is also invariant (using one's-complement algorithms) with respect to the operations of addition and left and right arithmetic shifting. Additionally, complementation and sign detection are the same [Avizienis, 1973].

An example of a single-error-detecting AN code is the 3N code. An *n*-bit word is encoded simply by multiplying by 3. This adds at most 2 bits of redundancy and can be encoded quickly and inexpensively in parallel with an $(n + 1)$-bit adder (Figure 3–18). Error checking is performed by confirming that the received word is evenly divisible by 3, and can be accomplished with a relatively simple combinational logic decoder. Although there is one more bit than in bit-per-word parity for roughly the same coverage, the operation of other system functions (such as ALU and address calculations) can be checked. The hardware cost is a $(2/n) \times 100$ percent memory element increase, an $(n + 1)$-bit adder for encoding, a combinational decoding circuit, and extra control circuitry. The delay on reads results from a small number of gate delays, and on writes from the delay of the adder. Avizienis [1973] presents algorithms for operations involving AN codes, and discusses in detail the design of a 15N code arithmetic processing unit used in an early version of the JPL–STAR computer (see Avizienis et al. [1971].

Residue codes are a class of separable arithmetic codes. In the *residue-m code*, the residue of a data word *N* is defined as $R(N) = N \bmod m$. The code word is formed by concatenating *N* with $R(N)$ to produce *N*|*R* (the vertical bar denotes concatenation). The received word *N'*|*R'* is checked by comparing $R(N')$ with *R'*. If they are equal, no error has occurred. Figure 3–19 is a block diagram of a residue-*m* code arithmetic unit.

A variant of the residue-*m* code is the *inverse residue-m code*. The separate check quantity, *Q*, is formed as $Q = m - (N \bmod m)$. The inverse residue code has greater coverage of repeated-use faults than does the residue code. A repeated-use fault occurs when a chain of operations is performed sequentially on the same faulty hardware before checking is performed. For example, iterative operations such as multiplication and division are subject to repeated-use faults. Both the residue-*m* and inverse residue-

---

* Other codes are not invariant with respect to arithmetic operations. For some separable linear codes other than arithmetic codes, the check symbol portion of the result can be produced by a prediction circuit. Usually such circuits are complex. Wakerly [1978] details check symbol prediction for parity-check codes and checksum codes.

FIGURE 3–18

Simple encoder for 3N single-error-detecting arithmetic code

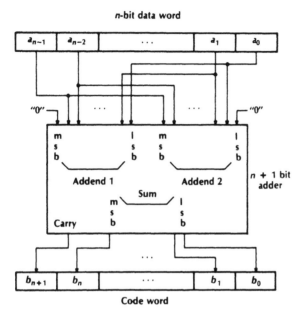

Code word

m codes can be used with either one's-complement or two's-complement arithmetic. The JPL–STAR computer [Avizienis et al., 1971] uses an inverse residue-15 code. Elsewhere, Avizienis [1973] describes the adaptation of 2's-complement arithmetic for use with an inverse residue code.

In both the AN and residue codes, the detection operations can be complex, except when the check moduli (A for AN codes, m for residue-m codes) are of the form $2^a - 1$. The check operation in this case can be performed using an a-bit adder with end-around carry, serially adding a-bit bytes of the data word (or code word for AN codes) [Avizienis, 1971, 1973]. In effect, this operation performs the division of the word by the check modulus. The operation can also be implemented in a faster, parallel fashion. Arithmetic codes with check moduli of this form are called *low-cost arithmetic codes*.

FIGURE 3–19

Block diagram of an arithmetic unit using residue-m code

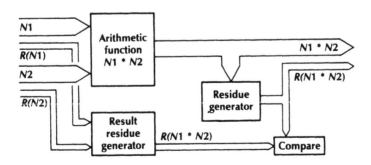

Cyclic Codes. In cyclic codes, any cyclic (end-around) shift of a code word produces another code word. Cyclic codes are easily implemented using linear-feedback shift registers, which are made from XOR gates and memory elements. These codes find frequent (though not exclusive) use in serial applications such as sequential-access devices (tapes, bubble memories, and disks) as well as data links. Sometimes encoding is performed independently and in parallel over several serial-bit streams, as in a multiple-wire bus. The bits of each byte are transmitted simultaneously. The cyclic redundancy check (CRC) check bits for each bit stream are generated for the duration of the block transmission and are appended to the end of the block.

In discussion of cyclic codes, the term (n,k) code is often used. In this expression, n is the number of bits in the entire code word, while k is the number of data bits. Thus, in an (n,k) separable code there are $(n - k)$ bits concatenated with the data bits to form the code words. The (n,k) cyclic codes can detect all single errors in a code word, all burst errors (multiple adjacent faults) of length $b \leq (n - k)$, and many other patterns of errors, depending on the particular code. A cyclic code is uniquely and completely characterized by its generator polynomial $G(X)$, a polynomial of degree $(n - k)$ or greater, with the coefficients either 0 or 1 for a binary code. This section introduces some of these codes, and a complete discussion of these and other polynomial-based codes can be found in Tang and Chien [1969] and Peterson and Weldon [1972].

CRC Codes. Given the check polynomial $G(X)$ for an $(n - k)$ separable code, a linear-feedback shift register encoder/decoder for the CRC codes can be easily derived.* The block check register (BCR) contains the check bits at the end of the encoding process, during which the data bits have been simultaneously transmitted and fed to the input of the BCR. The BCR is an r-bit shift register, where $r = (n - k)$, the degree of $G(x)$. In Figure 3–20, the register shifts to the right, and its memory cells are labeled $(r - 1)$, $(r - 2)$, . . . , 1, 0, from left to right. The shift register is broken to the right of each cell i, where $i = (r - j)$ and j is the degree of a nonzero term in $G(X)$. At each of these points, an XOR gate is inserted, and the gate output is connected to the input of the cell on the right side of the break. The output of the gate to the right of cell 0 is connected to the input of the leftmost memory cell (cell $r - 1$) and to one of the inputs of each of the other gates. The remaining input of each gate is connected to the output of the memory cell to the left. The second input of the rightmost gate is connected to the serial data input. The result is a feedback path, whose value is the XOR of BCR bit 0 and the current data bit. Figure 3–20 thus shows the BCR for a cyclic code with

$$G(X) = X^{12} + X^{11} + X^3 + X^2 + X + 1$$

This CRC-12 code is often used with 6-bit bytes of data because the check bits fit evenly into two 6-bit bytes. The XOR gates are placed to the right of the five shift

---

* The following discussion is based in part on the CRC chapter in McNamara [1977].

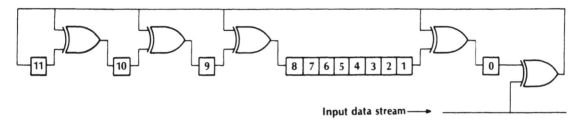

FIGURE 3–20 *Block check register for CRC-12 cyclic code*

register cells, {(12 − 12), (12 − 11), (12 − 3), (12 − 2), (12 − 1)} or {0, 1, 9, 10, 11}. The output of the rightmost XOR gate is fed back into the register via the other XOR gates.

In operation, the BCR is preloaded with an initial value (normally all 0's). The data are simultaneously transmitted and fed to the data input of the BCR. When the output of the data-input XOR gate has stabilized, the shift register is clocked. Once the last data bit has been transmitted, the BCR contains the check bits of the code word. The contents of the BCR are then transmitted starting with the rightmost bit, but without feedback.

The following listing shows a CRC-12 BCR operation with a 12-bit data word:

Shift Clock	BCR Contents	Input Data Bit	Feedback (input XOR bit 0)
0	0000 0000000 0	1	1
1	1111 0000000 1	0	1
2	1000 1000000 1	0	1
3	1011 0100000 1	1	0
4	0101 1010000 0	0	0
5	0010 1101000 0	0	0
6	0001 0110100 0	0	0
7	0000 1011010 0	0	0
8	0000 0101101 0	0	0
9	0000 0010110 1	0	1
10	1111 0001011 1	0	1
11	1000 1000101 0	1	1
12	1011 0100010 0		

The transmitted data bits are 100000001001 (right-most bit first), and the transmitted check bits are 101101000100 (right-most bit first). The same BCR is used at the receiving end. The input stream is fed to the BCR input in the same way, with the data bits going to both the BCR and the destination. The BCR is preloaded with the same value as that used in the transmitting BCR. The received check bits are input to the BCR following the data bits. When preloading involves all 0's, the result in the receiver should be 0.

CRC-12 is a (12 + k, k) code that provides error detection of all burst errors of length 12 or less. The data length is arbitrary. Thus, redundancy and coverage probability change with the data length. CRC-16 is a $(16 + k, k)$ code based on the generator polynomial

$$G(X) = X^{16} + X^{15} + X^2 + 1$$

CRC-CCITT is another $(16 + k, k)$ code, with

$$G(X) = X^{16} + X^{12} + X^5 + 1$$

Both CRC-16 and CRC-CCITT provide detection for all burst errors 16 bits long or less, and 99 percent of bursts greater than 16 bits. CRC-16 is used by the DDCMP and Bisync protocols, while CRC-CCITT is used by the ANSI X.25, HDLC, and SDLC protocols. These $(16 + k, k)$ codes are normally used when the data are in 8-bit bytes because the check bits consume exactly 2 bytes; however, k can be any arbitrary length. Figure 3–21 shows a BCR for CRC-CCITT.

CRC Code Applications. IBM's synchronous data link control data communications protocol uses the CRC-CCITT cyclic code with a small variation: The BCR is preloaded with all 1's instead of all 0's. At the end of the data transmission the BCR contents are complemented (logical complement) before being transmitted. This scheme allows detection of extra or missing 0's at the beginning and end of the data fields, which are of variable length. At the receiver, the BCR result must equal $F0B8_{16}$.

CRC encoders/decoders are available as integrated circuit chips. An example is the Fairchild F6856 Synchronous Protocol Communications Controller chip, which provides communications protocol handling for microprocessor systems [Kole, 1980]. Embedded on the chip is a CRC encoder/decoder. The chip is designed to handle CRC-12, CRC-16, CRC-CCITT, and several other CRC codes. In addition, the internal BCR can be preset optionally with all 0's or all 1's. Another available integrated circuit is the Signetics 2653 intelligent bus monitor, analyzed in depth in Weissberger [1980]. In addition to its other functions, the circuit provides CRC checking and generation.

CRC checks are performed in software to detect errors in critical data structures and programs. An algorithm, shown in Figure 3–22, is essentially a software implementation of a linear feedback shift register. A processor register is used as a shift

FIGURE 3–21
Block check register for CRC-CCITT cyclic code

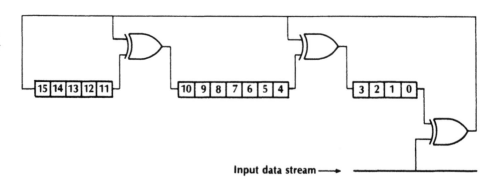

Input data stream →

register, and the XOR feedback gates are replaced by a CRC constant, which is XORed with the register. The CRC constant is formed by finding the numbers, i, for which $i = [(r - 1) - j]$, where j is the degree of a nonzero term in $G(X)$ (except for the X' term). The bits i of the CRC constant are 1's, and the rest are 0's. The bits are labeled $(r - 1)$ for the leftmost (most significant) bit, to 0 for the least significant bit. The constant for CRC-CCITT is 8408_{16}, and is $0F01_{16}$ for CRC-12. This algorithm would be useful, for example, when a separate maintenance or console processor performs occasional checking for microstore corruption via a CRC.

The Interdata 8/32 uses the algorithm of Figure 3–22 in its microcoded CRC instruction [Interdata, 1975]. The VAX-11/780 has a CRC instruction that performs cyclic redundancy checking or encoding for up to 64K 8-bit bytes in memory. $G(X)$ can be any check generator polynomial of degree 32 or less [DEC, 1977]. The VAX uses the algorithm and constants as described previously.

Cyclic codes can also be encoded and decoded in parallel for nonserial applications. Like other linear codes, they can be processed with matrix techniques. An example of parity-check matrices can be found in the section on Hamming codes. For more details on forming the parity-check and parity-generation matrices for cyclic codes, see Tang and Chien [1969].

```
register temp <(r-1):0> ;                  !r^th degree G(X) ;
variable bcr <(r-1):0> ;                   !will hold block check character ;
variable flag <0> ;
variable input <(b-1):0> ;                 !input data byte ;
integer variable counter ;
logical variable new.code.word ;
constant bcr.preload <(r-1):0>=00..0_16 ;  !would be FFFF_16 for SDLC ;

constant crc.constant <(r-1):0> = XX..XX_16 ; ! 8408_16 for CRC-CCITT

                                             0F01_16 for CRC-12 ;


                                           ! this algorithm updates the block check character
begin                                      for a new data byte. new.code.word is TRUE only if
                                           a new CRC computation is to be commenced, i.e., if
                                           this is the first byte in a CRC code word. ;


    if new.code.word then bcr ← bcr.preload ;
    temp ← 0 ;
    temp <(b-1):0> ← input ;
    temp ← temp XOR bcr ;
    for counter ← 0 to (r-1) do
            begin
                    flag ← temp <0> ;
                    shift.right (temp) ;        ! shift temp right one, shifting 0 into temp <r-1> ;
                    if (flag = 1) then temp ← temp XOR crc.constant ;
            end ;

    bcr ← temp ;                           ! bcr now contains current check characters ;
end ;
```

FIGURE 3–22 *An algorithm for computation of CRC bits using processor registers*

Self-Checking and Fail-Safe Logic

Although duplication and codes are general solutions to fault detection, both techniques are vulnerable to single-point failures in the comparison element (duplication) or the decoder/detector element (codes). These single points of failure can be eliminated through self-checking and fail-safe logic design. These logic design techniques can be used for general-purpose logic design as well as for comparators and checkers. Due to space limitations, the following subsections can only serve to introduce the topics of self-checking and fail-safe logic. Self-checking logic is treated in depth in a comprehensive text by Waverly [1978], and both topics have been the focus of numerous studies, some of which are listed in Table 3–14.

Totally Self-Checking (TSC) Circuits. Self-checking circuit design is based on the premise that the circuit inputs are already encoded in some code and that the circuit outputs are also to be encoded. The inputs and outputs are not necessarily in the same code. The following definitions from Anderson [1971] and Anderson and Metze [1973] are based on this premise:

• *Self-Testing:* A circuit is self-testing if, for every fault from a prescribed set, the circuit produces a noncode output for at least one code input.

• *Totally Self-Checking* (TSC): A circuit is totally self-checking not only if it is self-testing but also if it is fault secure—that is, if, for every fault from a prescribed set, the circuit never produces an incorrect output for code inputs.

Thus, to be self-testing, the circuit must experience a set of inputs during normal operation that tests for all faults in the prescribed set. If such a set of inputs is not assured, the circuit is self-testing only for the faults that are tested. This same restriction applies to TSC circuits.

These definitions are illustrated by a TSC comparison element (derived from the TSC comparison element in Wakerly [1978]). A dual-rail signal is a coded signal whose two bits are always complementary. This is equivalent to the 1/2 code. The comparison element checks for the equality of the two dual-rail signals at its inputs, and it outputs a dual-rail signal (01 or 10) only if the inputs are both equal and properly encoded; otherwise, it outputs a noncode word, either 00 or 11. In addition, the comparison element is self-testing for any internal single fault and is thus TSC as long as all four possible sets of code inputs appear during normal operation. Figure 3–23 shows the logic circuit for the comparison element, while Table 3–15 shows an analysis of the possible single stuck-at-faults and the inputs that test for them. An input signal tests a fault in the circuit if the output is a noncode word. To test for all faults in the set (*m*, *n*, *o*, *p*: stuck-at-1), all four possible input signal sets must appear. As a result, all four signal sets must appear at the circuit input during normal operation. Conversely, it can be seen that there is no stuck-at fault that is not tested by at least one of these signals. Thus, the comparator is self-testing (given a guarantee of all four signal sets appearing). Finally, further examination of Table 3–15 shows that under stuck-at faults at *a*, *b*, *c*, or *d*, the outputs are either noncode words or the correct code word (i.e., the code

TABLE 3–14
Studies on self-checking and fail-safe logic

Technique/Focus of Study	Reference
Self-Checking	
Combinational Circuits	
m-n codes	Anderson and Metze [1973]; Marouf and Friedman [1977]; Piestrak [1983]; Efstathiou and Halatsis [1983]; Nanya and Tohma [1983]; Tao, Lala, and Hartmann [1987]
Berger codes	Marouf and Friedman [1978]
Separable codes	Ashjaee and Reddy [1976]
Equality checker	Hughes, McCluskey, and Lu [1983]
Sequential Circuits	
General Theory	Carter and Schneider [1968]; Osman and Weiss [1973]; Diaz, Geffroy, and Courvoisier [1974]; Ozgunner [1977]; Pradhan [1978a, 1978b]
Applications	
PLA	Khakbaz and McCluskey [1982]; Mak, Abraham, and Davidson [1982]; Fuchs and Abraham [1984]
AT&T No. 3A Processor	Toy [1978]; Cook et al. [1973]
1750A Processor	Halbert and Base [1984]
4-bit Microprocessor	Crouzet and Landrault [1980]
General	Fujiwara and Matsuoka [1985]
Fail-Safe	
General Theory	Mine and Koga [1967]; Tokura, Kasami, and Hashimoto [1971]; Diaz, Azema, and Ayache [1979]
Sequential Circuits	Sawin [1975]; Diaz, Geffroy, and Courvoisier [1974]; Patterson and Metze [1974]; Tohma [1974]; Mukai and Tohma [1974]

word that would appear in normal operation). Since these stuck-at faults produce a condition equivalent to having noncode inputs, the circuit is shown to be fault secure as well. The circuit is thus TSC because it is both fault secure and self-testing. Note that since stuck-at faults of signals *a*, *b*, *c*, and *d* are equivalent to faults in the input signals, these conditions show the response of a nonfaulty comparator to faulty (noncode) inputs.

FIGURE 3–23
Logic circuit of basic TSC comparison element

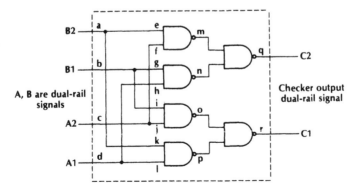

TABLE 3–15 *TSC dual-rail comparator responses to stuck-at-faults*

Inputs		Normal	Outputs C2C1 Resulting from Single Stuck-at-1 Faults																	
B2B1	A2A1	Output	a	b	c	d	e	f	g	h	i	j	k	l	m	n	o	p	q	r
01	01	10	11	10	11	10	10	10	10	10	10	11	11	10	10	00	10	10	10	11
01	10	01	11	01	01	11	11	01	01	11	01	01	01	01	01	01	00	01	11	01
10	01	01	01	11	11	01	01	11	11	01	01	01	01	01	01	01	01	00	11	01
10	10	10	10	11	10	11	10	10	10	10	11	10	10	11	00	10	10	10	10	11

Inputs		Normal	Outputs C2C1 Resulting from Single Stuck-at-0 Faults																	
B2B1	A2A1	Output	a	b	c	d	e	f	g	h	i	j	k	l	m	n	o	p	q	r
01	01	10	10	00	10	00	10	10	00	00	10	10	10	10	10	10	11	11	00	10
01	10	01	01	00	00	01	01	01	01	01	00	00	01	01	11	11	01	01	01	00
10	01	01	00	01	01	00	01	01	01	01	01	01	00	00	11	11	01	01	01	00
10	**10**	10	00	10	00	10	00	00	10	10	10	10	10	10	10	10	11	11	00	10

Some operations are not amenable to the use of codes, and full duplication is the least redundant form of checking that can be used. To check the logical operations AND and OR, for example, duplication can be used with a TSC comparator. Wakerly [1974] has proposed partially self-checking logic as a less expensive alternative.

Partially Self-Checking (PSC) Circuits. A circuit is partially self-checking if it is self-testing for a set N of normal inputs and a set F_t of faults, and is fault-secure for a set I (a nonnull subset of N) and a set F_s. In the normal operation of a PSC circuit, all faults from F_t are tested. In addition, for a subset I of the normal inputs, no incorrect code output can be produced by a fault in the set F_s. Thus, PSC logic provides eventual detection of a fault at the cost of introducing fault latency (undetected faults produced prior to fault detection). The benefit is a redundancy cost lower than that of duplication.

Self-Checking Models and Examples. Figure 3–24 shows a general model for a TSC network proposed by Anderson [1971], consisting of both a TSC functional circuit and a TSC checker. The advantage of this network over the TSC functional circuit alone is that a correct checker output from the network guarantees that the network functional output is correct.

Conceptually, the simplest form of a TSC functional circuit is duplication, in which two copies of the function are used. Together, their total inputs and outputs are coded (duplication). As stated before, for some functions duplication may be the least redundant coding alternative for achieving TSC. The only other component of a duplication-based TSC network is the TSC comparator, which performs the checking of the functional outputs. The most economical form of checker complements one set of the functional unit outputs before routing it to the comparison element [Anderson, 1971].

FIGURE 3–24
A TSC network made from TSC elements

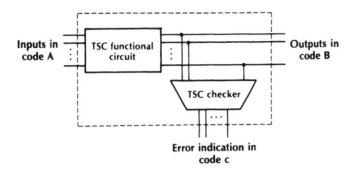

In this case, a checker for an arbitrary number of inputs can use the two-signal input dual-rail comparator of Figure 3–23 as the basic element. These elements are assembled in tree fashion, using $\log_2 n$ two-input dual-rail signal comparators. Figure 3–25 shows the entire TSC duplication network scheme. To qualify for the self-testing property each checker basic module must receive the four input signals mentioned previously. It is not necessary, however, to apply all possible combinations of dual-rail signals to the entire checker to test it completely. Anderson [1971] has shown that for every size comparator built as a tree of the basic dual-rail checker modules, at least one set of four tree input signals will ensure complete self-testing for any single fault in the checker. If the four signal sets are assured of appearing during normal operation, the network is TSC.

The same comparison checker can be used to make a TSC separable-code error detector [Ashjaee and Reddy, 1976; Wakerly, 1978]. The inputs to the checker are the received check character and a locally generated check character, as shown in Figure 3–26. Wakerly [1978] provides the proof of the TSC property for this detector. As in

FIGURE 3–25
TSC network based on duplication as a code

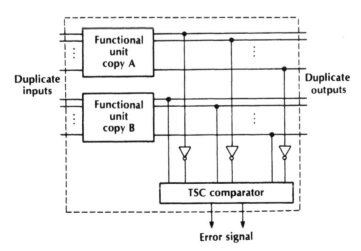

FIGURE 3–26
TSC detector for separable codes, based on a TSC comparator

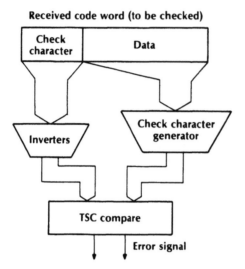

the duplication scheme, the self-test property of the comparison checker must be assured by having the check characters that appear include a set of four characters that tests for all possible faults in the checker. For (n, k) codes in which all $2^{(n-k)}$ possible combinations of the check bits appear, this is no problem. Other codes, however, may present more difficulty. The residue-3 arithmetic code check character, for example, has only three possible values (00, 01, and 10); thus, all four signals necessary for self-testing do not appear and the checker cannot be TSC.

Wakerly [1974] has proposed models for three types of PSC networks, shown in Figure 3–27. All three have two modes of operation: secure or insecure. In the secure mode, which is used during operation with code inputs that map into code outputs, the network is TSC. The insecure mode, which is invoked by fixing the error outputs to a nonerror indication, is used when a noncode output from the functional circuit is the correct function of the inputs. An example would be the AND and OR functions of an ALU operating on residue-m-coded inputs. In the insecure mode, the PSC network is neither self-testing nor fault secure.

The Type 1 PSC network is the simplest. Its disadvantage is that the outputs are necessarily noncode outputs in the insecure operating mode. The Type 2 PSC network solves this problem by reencoding outputs during insecure operation; thus, all outputs are coded outputs unless there are faults in the encoder. However, there is no guarantee that the code outputs are the correct outputs during insecure operation. A Type 3 PSC network causes less delay than a Type 2 network on secure mode outputs by using a bus switch for the check character. During secure operations, the Type 2 network does not output the check character until it has been regenerated locally; the Type 3 network immediately gates the check symbol from the functional circuit. Both Types 2 and 3 have the same delay during insecure operations. One drawback of the Type 3 scheme is that a faulty output during the secure mode may be used before the error is detected by the checker.

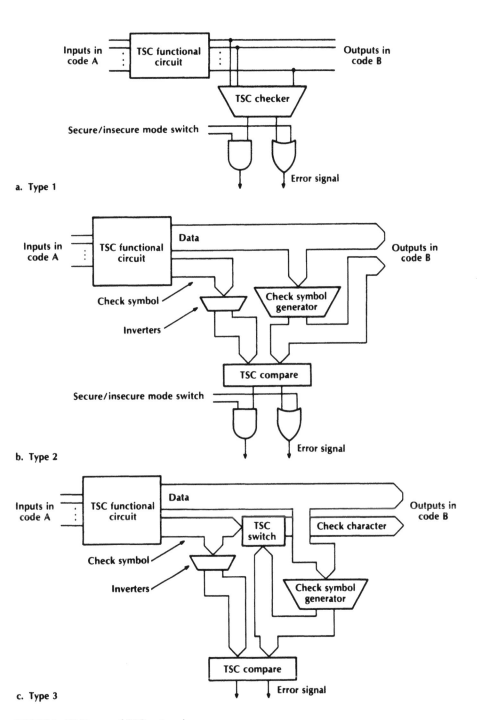

FIGURE 3–27 *Types of PSC networks*

Wakerly [1974] produced a PSC ALU made with 4-bit 74181 adder chips, and with inputs coded in the distance-2 residue-15 code. A single stuck-at fault in one of the 74181s produced a detectable error during addition or subtraction. Hence, this ALU network is fault-secure for the operations of addition and subtraction for all single stuck-at faults. In addition, the circuit is fault-secure for the other circuit functions for which the residue-15 code is invariant: A, B, A', B', 0, and 1. The 74181 can be shown to be self-testing for all single faults provided all of the following operations occur during normal use:

Addition and subtraction (tests carry logic)

The set of operations A XOR B and (A XOR B)' or the set A, B, A', B', or some other combination of operations that tests for all possible single faults in the logic function circuitry

At least one arithmetic and one logic function, to test the carry enable logic

If all these operations are assured to occur, the ALU network is TSC for one's-complement addition and subtraction, A, B, A', B', 0, and 1. If the other 74181 functions are used, the network is operating in an insecure mode and is only partially self-checking. This ALU is a Type 2 PSC network; the necessary re-encoder for outputs during the insecure mode of operation is already present in the TSC checker.

Another application of self-checking techniques is the programmed logic array (PLA), which is a common structure in current VLSI designs. These circuits often make up a significant portion of on-chip control logic. Much work has been done on developing methods of on-line detection of PLA faults. One common approach makes use of a common fault model for PLAs: All single faults will result in a unidirectional change in part of the PLA. Most of the approaches also require that no more than one product term be active at a time. A self-checking PLA results from the application of self-checking checkers, unidirectional, and 1-of-n codes.

Fail-Safe Circuits. A circuit is fail-safe if, for every fault from a prescribed set, any input produces a "safe" output—that is, one of a preferred set of erroneous outputs. Fail-safe techniques are thus not concerned with the detection of faults per se, and they can result in lower redundancy costs than self-checking techniques. A traffic light with a fail-safe output of stuck-at-red on all sides is a good example of a fail-safe system [Mine and Koga, 1967]. Stuck-at-red is the most desirable failed state because all drivers approaching the intersection must stop, and they may proceed only after realizing the light is broken. This state causes the least possible harm, for any driver will enter the intersection with extreme caution and at a low speed.

Watch-Dog Timers and Timeouts

Watch-Dog Timers. Watch-dog timers are a simple and inexpensive means of keeping track of proper process function. In this procedure, a timer is maintained as a process separate from the process it checks. If the timer is not reset before it expires, the corresponding process has probably failed in some way; the assumption is that any failure or corruption of the checked process will cause it to miss resetting its watch-dog. However, coverage is limited because data and results are not checked. All the timer provides is an indication of possible process failure. The process may be only partially failed and produce errors, and yet still be able to reset its timer. The coverage may be improved if the checked process has to exercise a large proportion of its internal components in order to reset its watch-dog.

The watch-dog timer concept can be implemented in either software or hardware, and the process it guards can be either a software or a hardware process. In fact, the computing process and the timer could be running on the same hardware. In this and most other cases, at least one other process monitors the timer, or is interruptible by it, to handle possible failure situations.

Watch-dog timers are used extensively in many systems. In a typical supermini-computer system, there are software watch-dog timers at all levels of network proto-cols, on I/O operations, and on synchronization primitives (e.g., spinlocks). There are hardware watch-dog timers on buses, I/O adapters, and keep-alive timers.

Pluribus [Ornstein et al., 1975], a reliable multiprocessor designed primarily for use as a switching node for the ARPANET, makes extensive use of both hardware and software watch-dog timers. These timers have time spans of from 5 microseconds to 2 minutes. Subsystems that are monitored by timers go through a cycle of a known length. Part of each cycle is a complete self-consistency check. Failure to reset the timer is seen as an indication that the subsystem has failed in such a way that it cannot recover by itself. Message buffers, for example, have 2-minute watch-dog timers that are reset each time the buffer is returned to the free list of unused buffers. If the timer runs out, the buffer is forced back to the free list by the process that the timer alerts upon expiring. Another timer in each processor interrupts the processor every 1/15 second if not reset. This timer prevents subsystems from waiting forever for a resource that is erroneously allocated and thus will not be released. A final example of the timer is the bus arbiter. If there is no bus activity for 1 second, the bus arbiter resets all the processors. This is useful, for example, when all processors execute a spurious halt command that somehow gets planted in the common program store. In this case, the 60-hertz processor timers cannot help because a halted processor will not respond to interrupts. Pluribus also has several other timers not mentioned here.

The VAX-11/780 (Chapter 7) is a more commercially oriented system that makes use of a watch-dog timer. The console processor monitors the micromachine activity. If the micromachine does not strobe an interrupt line to the LSI-11 console processor at least every 200 microseconds, the console processor will try to determine the reason for the failure.

Bus Timeouts. Bus timeouts are also based on the principle that some operations should take no more than a certain maximum time to complete. Time limits are set for certain responses required by the bus protocol. Thus, when one device (e.g., master) requires a response from another device (e.g., slave), a failure to respond in time indicates a possible failure. Timeouts are different from watch-dog timers in that they provide a finer check of control flow.

Timeout detection is provided on the buses of most computers, including the PDP-11 Unibus. During the interrupt request/bus grant sequence, a timeout is generated if the requesting device does not respond to the bus grant signal in 5 to 10 microseconds. Similarly, during data transfers, a 10- to 20-microsecond timeout detection occurs if the slave device does not respond to the bus master's synchronization signal. The Unibus bus specifications [DEC, 1979] do not specify the exact response to these timeout detections; the response depends on the particular PDP-11 model. Generally, however, the processor response is a trap to a bus timeout handling routine.

Consistency and Capability Checking

Consistency Checking. A simple fault-detection technique that often requires minimal hardware redundancy, consistency checking verifies that the intermediate or final results are reasonable, either on an absolute basis (fixed text) or as a simple function of the inputs used to derive the result. One form of consistency checking is a range check, which confirms that a computed value is in a valid range. For example, a computed probability must lie between 0 and 1. The range can be narrowed further if a priori probabilities are known. Weekly paychecks should have positive denominations and should not exceed some maximum value (such as a function of normal and overtime pay rates and the 168 hours in the week). Similarly, commercial aircraft altitude sensors should indicate elevations between Death Valley and 45,000 feet.

Most computers use some form of consistency checking. Address checking, opcode checking, and arithmetic operation checking are the most common forms of consistency checking. In its usual form, address checking consists of verifying that the address to be accessed exists. DEC PDP-11s provide a nonexistent memory (NXM) trap for this purpose. Further coverage may be provided by making sure that the address for a write is actually a RAM and not a ROM location, and that an I/O address is consistent with the operation to be performed. Checking for a valid opcode occurs before instruction execution commences. Without this check it is possible to perform undefined and (usually) undesirable operation sequences in the CPU. For example, programmers of some microprocessors occasionally utilize undocumented opcodes with unique actions. This use of undefined processor features is undesirable because of possible unknown side-effects. Underflow and overflow checking of binary arithmetic, a form of range checking, is provided in most computers, either in hardware or in program run-time systems.

Another form of consistency checking is to utilize a memory in which the parity bit on any word can be arbitrarily set for either parity sense (odd or even). In practice, data words would use odd parity and instruction words even parity. In addition to parity errors, addressing errors and programming errors are likely to be discovered. Examples are data words accidentally accessed during instruction fetch and program code erroneously overwritten with data. When an addressing and a parity error occur simultaneously, however, there is a chance that they will complement each other, and result in no error detection.

Capability Checking. This form of fault detection is usually part of the operating system, although it may be realized as a hardware mechanism. In this concept, access to objects is limited to users with the proper authorization. Objects include memory segments and I/O devices; users might be processes or even independent physical processors in a system. Further functionality is provided by allowing multiple levels of access privileges for different user/object combinations, such as execute only, read only, and read/write privilege levels in a disk system. One common means of checking access privileges is through the memory-mapping mechanism of virtual address machines. An example is the virtual address generation mechanism for Cm*, shown in Figure 3–28 [Swan, Fuller, and Siewiorek, 1977]. A *capability* in Cm* consists of a 3-bit field specifying access rights and a 16-bit field containing the segment name. During the address translation, the access rights are checked against the operation to be performed. If the operation is not permitted, an error trap is forced.

Capability checking provides more than fault detection, it also provides some fault isolation by locking out corrupted users. For example, it should prevent a bad process from erroneously overwriting portions of memory to which it has no legal access. More information on capability checking can be found in texts on operating systems design.

Another method of capability checking is the use of passwords. The Pluribus system incorporates password protection. A processor that does not reset its watchdog timer will be restarted by an outside process. To prevent spurious resets, the process must give the proper password before it can initiate a reset. A Boeing duplicated processor system used password protection for a similar purpose in its reconfiguration hardware; the goal was to prevent spurious reconfiguration of the system [Wachter, 1975].

FIGURE 3–28
Virtual address calculation with capability checking in Cm*

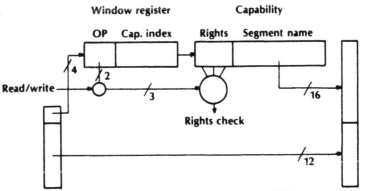

Processor Monitoring

Error detection is often designed into processor data paths alone, since checking the random logic of control parts is not as easy (or as cost-effective). Another problem is that designers must often use off-the-shelf microprocessor chips that have little or no checking built into them. One solution mentioned before is to duplicate such elements. There is another class of more efficient methods that may be applicable to the system being designed—a set of techniques that can be grouped under the term *processor monitoring*. These techniques have less overhead than duplication, and can be used to detect control logic failures and check standard microprocessors. Figure 3–29 depicts the canonical arrangement of a monitor with respect to the processor and memory. Techniques can be classified by the information monitored: control-flow and assertion checking.

Control-Flow Monitoring. Control-flow monitoring techniques detect sequence errors. A sequence error causes a processor to jump to an incorrect next instruction. A special form of a sequence error is the branch decision resulting from a processor selecting a branch destination different from what should be selected, given the current condition code values. Implemented completely in software, it is able to detect all sequence errors that result in a jump to a location outside the current loop-free interval.

One of the first control-flow monitoring techniques [Yau and Chen, 1980] checked the sequence of execution of loop-free intervals. Implemented completely in software, it is able to detect all sequence errors that result in a jump to a location outside the current loop-free interval.

Structural integrity checking (SIC) [Lu, 1982] focuses on the sequencing of high-level language constructs. It detects all sequence errors resulting in a jump to a location outside the current high-level language construct.

Macroinstruction control-flow monitoring has been the focus of several investigators. In each of these techniques, the application program is divided into blocks. Sequencing within each block is checked instruction by instruction. Checking at the macroinstruction level rather than at the block level significantly improves the detection of sequence errors. The concept was introduced by Namjoo [1982], using a technique called path signature analysis (PSA), and by Sridhar and Thatte [1982].

One macroinstruction control-flow monitoring technique, termed signature instruction stream (SIS) [Shen and Schuette, 1983], is depicted in Figure 3–30. In this

FIGURE 3–29
Typical processor-monitor organization [From Wilken and Shen, 1988; © 1988 IEEE]

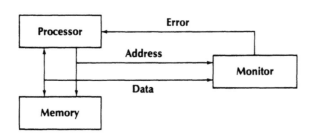

FIGURE 3–30
*Basic embedded
signaturing for
macroinstruction
control-flow mon-
itoring technique
[From Shen and
Schuette, 1983;
© 1983 IEEE]*

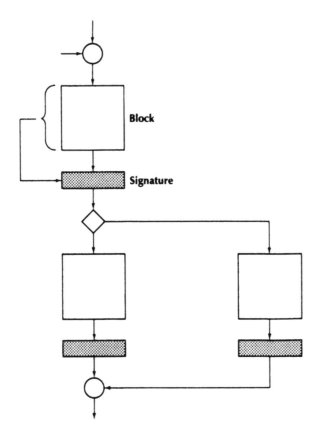

technique, the instruction stream has a known characteristic signature—that is, the CRC checksum of the instruction stream. At each branch point, the CRC is embedded in the code by storing it in the location following the branch. The monitor reads the instruction stream as it goes by to the processor, and forms the CRC When it sees a branch opcode in the instruction stream, it forces a read of the following memory location retrieving the stored CRC (and sends a no operation (NOP) message to the processor in its place). The monitor compares the stored value against its computed value, and signals an error if there is a mismatch. Thus, errors in program flow caused by internal control errors, memory errors, or data errors will be detected.

The compiler that generates the program is modified to calculate and embed the stored signatures. Given a typical between-branch code segment length of 4 to 10 instructions, the memory overhead for this method is 10 to 25 percent this also impacts performance (extra memory cycles). The monitor is typically much simpler than the processor it monitors. One other drawback of this technique is error latency—the average time for detection is several processor instruction executions

One variant of this technique is branch-address hashing [Schuette and Shen, 1987], in which the CRC is not explicitly stored, but instead XORed with the branch destination, producing a "hashed" branch address. The monitor forms CRCs of the instruction stream as before. However, when it sees a branch instruction, it intercepts the hashed destination address and XORs it with the calculated signature. If the CRC is correct, the resultant value will be the correct branch address. If the on-line CRC is incorrect because of an incorrect instruction flow, the unhashed address will also be wrong—and a gross sequence error is induced. The intent is that this gross error will cause branches to data locations, which will cause the processor's own architectural checks (such as illegal opcode and nonexistent memory) to detect the problem. This technique reduces the memory and performance overhead of the basic SIS method, at the cost of increased latency and slightly lower coverage.

The effectiveness of the SIS technique was verified through the construction of a hardware fault inserter for an MC68000 system. Results of the experiments [Schuette and Shen, 1987; Schuette et al., 1986] were given in Chapter 2. In summary, 2891 faults were inserted in the system with and without the SIS technique in operation. Without SIS, the system was able to detect 57 percent of the faults inserted. With SIS, the coverage was raised to 82 percent. The coverage of faults resulting in sequence errors was 98 percent.

The preceding SIS methods use vertical signatures—that is, the signature is checked at the end of a vertical path. Continuous signature monitoring (CSM) [Wilken and Shen, 1988] uses horizontal signatures; the intermediate signatures are stored (and checked) at each memory location. This eliminates latency, but costs a significant amount of extra memory. A lower cost method is to XOR one bit of the intermediate signature with the parity bit for each memory location (no extra bits). The loss of detection coverage is made up by also using a vertical signature check. Table 3–16 summarizes the overhead in program storage and performance for several monitoring techniques.

Assertion Checking. Techniques commonly referred to as assertion checking attempt to make use of properties of program data by periodically checking for invariant properties [Leveson and Harvey, 1983; Mahmood, McCluskey, and Lu, 1983; Mahmood, Ersoz, and McCluskey, 1985; Saib, 1977]. Assertion checking requires the user to identify invariant properties of program data and devise code that will check for these properties. Examples of invariant properties include cases in which a variable's value is bound to within a particular range, the output values of a function are related to the input values by the inverse of the function, and variable values in a set increase (decrease) monotonically. Research has focused on developing systematic procedures for identifying invariant properties [Leveson and Harvey, 1983; Mahmood, McCluskey, and Lu, 1983]; however, success is still dependent upon the existence of invariants in the application. Error coverage of the assertions varies significantly.

There have also been attempts to introduce invariant properties into program data through the use of encoding techniques [Huang and Abraham, 1984; Taylor, Morgan, and Black, 1980]. An example of a technique that uses encoding to create invariants in matrices is algorithm-based fault tolerance (ABFT) [Huang and Abraham, 1984]. In ABFT,

TABLE 3–16 *Program storage costs and error-detection coverage of several control-flow monitoring techniques*

Reference/Technique	Program Storage Overhead (%)	Monitor Required	Performance Penalty (%)	Error Coverage
Yau and Chen [1980]	90–135	No	35–140	All sequence errors resulting in jump outside current loop-free interval; all branch decision errors
Lu [1982]/SIC	N/A	Yes	N/A	All sequence errors resulting in jump outside current high-level language construction
Sridhar and Thatte [1983]	15	Yes	10	All sequence errors resulting in jump outside current loop-free interval
Namjoo [1982]/PSA	12–21	Yes	6–15	99.5–99.9 percent of sequence errors, except branch decision errors
Shen and Schuette [1983]/SIS	6–15	Yes	6–14	96 percent of sequence errors, except branch decision errors
Wilken and Shen [1988]/CSM	3–7	Yes	0.6–1.5	99.99 percent of sequence errors, except branch decision errors

Source: Schuette, 1989.

a checksum is calculated for each row and column of a matrix, representing the sum of all elements in the row or column. The checksums are appended to the appropriate row or column, creating an encoded matrix. The programs that manipulate matrices are altered to produce an encoded matrix as output when presented with encoded matrices as input. The checksums are recalculated upon completion of each matrix operation to determine consistency.

Extensions of Basic Monitoring Techniques. Monitoring techniques can often be combined with other redundancy techniques to reduce cost. For example, the tags for capability checking can be overlapped with the error-correction code (ECC) bits in memory [Gumpertz, 1981]. With the widespread availability of general-purpose multiprocessors, approaches have also been developed to employ unutilized processors as monitors. Fabre et al. [1988] assume a dynamically changing set of tasks, with each task being executed as N-redundant copies. Unutilized processors execute additional copies of each task, thereby increasing redundancy without affecting the task scheduling.

Processor-monitoring concepts can be applied to microengines or strengthened by special instructions in a new processor design [Sridhar and Thatte, 1982; Iyengar and Kinney, 1982, 1985]. Abstractions of processor behavior other than instruction-flow CRC can be used (see, for insance, Schmid et al. [1982]; Namjoo [1983]). Mahmood and McCluskey [1988] provide a comprehensive survey of this class of techniques.

Designing Fault Detection into Systems

Fault detection is useful not only for data integrity and as the first step to fault tolerance; it is also a critical element in maintaining the system. Intermittent faults are the source of a major proportion of system problems, and test-based approaches such as diagnostic programs and built-in tests are unlikely to detect and isolate intermittent problems. Thus, on-line fault detection is the best means of isolating intermittent faults.

Fault-detection design for data integrity and recovery may not be adequate to implicate the failing component or module, which makes repair difficult. The solution is a systematic approach to the design of fault detection in the system. The IBM error detection/fault isolation methodology is one such approach [Cordi, 1984; Tendolkar and Swann, 1982], and it has been applied to all IBM processor designs (see Chapter 7). The basic approach is to build a simple probability model of fault isolation in the system, including such factors as circuit element failure probabilities, fault-detection probabilities, fault detector placement, and physical partitioning. The resulting model is used both to guide the design process and to develop repair strategies for the machine.

HARDWARE MASKING REDUNDANCY TECHNIQUES

Fault-detection techniques supply warnings of faulty results, but do not provide actual tolerance of faults. Fault masking, however, employs redundancy that provides fault tolerance by either isolating or correcting fault effects before they reach module outputs. Fault masking is a "static" form of redundancy [Short, 1968; Avizienis, 1977]; the logical interconnection of the circuit elements remains fixed, and no intervention occurs from elements outside the module. Thus, when the masking redundancy is exhausted by faults in the module, any further faults will cause errors at the output.

Notification of fault occurrence is implicit in fault detection, but in the pure form of fault masking, the effects of faults are automatically neutralized without notification of their occurrence. Pure fault masking thus gives no warning of a deteriorating hardware state until enough faults have accumulated to cause an error. As a result, most fault-masking techniques are extended to provide fault detection as well. The additional redundancy needed for this purpose is usually minor. In the case of a few fault-masking techniques, however, fault detection is either impossible or too costly.

The following presentations of fault-masking techniques discuss fault-detection extensions where applicable. Because fault masking provides fault tolerance, the reliability function becomes a meaningful measurement of technique effectiveness. This section provides simple reliability models for the techniques it presents. Models that are more detailed are usually possible and provide more accurate information. More detailed reliability models are the subject of Chapter 5.

N-Modular Redundancy with Voting

Duplication with output comparison was considered as a fault-detection technique in the earlier section on duplication. If a third copy of the functional circuit is added, enough redundant information is available to allow fault masking of a failure in any one of the three copies. This masking is accomplished by means of a majority (two-out-of-three) vote on the circuit outputs. The groundwork for the triple modular redundancy (TMR) technique was first laid by von Neumann [1956]. He proposed a configuration employing independently computed copies of a signal, with "restoring organs" placed between logical operations.

Figure 3–31a illustrates the basic concept of TMR. The concept can be extended to include N copies with majority voting at the outputs. The resulting technique is called N-modular redundancy, or NMR. Normally N is made an odd number to avoid the uncertain state in which the output vote is a tie. The cost of N-modular redundancy is N times the basic hardware cost, plus the cost of the voter. The voter causes a delay in signal propagation, leading to a decrease in performance. Additional performance–cost overhead results from the necessity to synchronize the multiple copies (this problem is discussed later in this section).

The reliability formulas for TMR and NMR, which are given in Chapter 5, are somewhat pessimisic in that they assume a failed copy's output is always incorrect. However, some failures in two or more copies may occur in such a way that an error is avoided. Such failures are called *compensating failures*. For example, consider a module output failed stuck-at-1 in a TMR network. If the same line fails on another copy, there is no error caused if it fails stuck-at-0. In this case, whichever value the remaining nonfaulty line takes on, it has another to match it and the correct voted output results. Another possibility is nonoverlapping failures, such as a failure in memory location 123 on one memory module and a failure in memory location 67 on another. Although these failures are on two different copies, they do not act together in the voting process to cause an error. Models of TMR systems that take compensating failures into account are discussed in detail in Chapter 5.

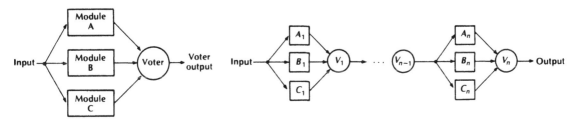

a. Basic TMR configuration   b. Cascading of TMR modules

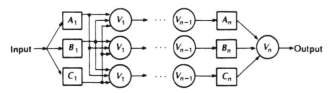

c. Triplicated voters for the cascading TMR modules

FIGURE 3–31 *Triple modular redundancy*

A complex system can be partitioned into smaller subsystems, each of which can be transformed into an NMR configuration. Figure 3–31b shows a system transformed into a cascaded series of TMR modules. The advantage of partitioning is that the resulting design can withstand more failures than the equivalent configuration with only one large triplicated module. However, subdivision cannot be extended to arbitrarily small modules, because voter unreliability ultimately overrides any potential reliability gains.

The TMR configurations shown so far have single points of failure: the voters. In the circuit of Figure 3–31a, the only solution is to make the voter more reliable through a fault-avoidance and/or fault-tolerance technique. In the circuit of Figure 3–31b, however, all but one of the single points of failure can be removed by triplicating the voters themselves, as illustrated in Figure 3–31c. If a triplicated output is desired, all single points of failure are removed. If functional considerations allow, the circuitry can be broken into modules, and voters can be located so as to maximize reliability. Gurzi [1965] has shown that for nonredundant voter configurations (Figure 3–31b), reliability is maximized when the functional modules have identical reliabilities, R. If all the voters have reliability, R_v, the maximum system reliability is attained when the functional breakdown is such that

$$R_v = \frac{1}{(3 - 2R)R^\alpha} \qquad (1)$$

with

$$\alpha = \frac{2R}{3 - 2R}$$

The upper limit of reliability gain in this case is

$$\frac{\text{TMR network reliability}}{\text{Nonredundant network reliability}} = \frac{(3R^2 - 2R^3)^n R_v^n}{R^n} \leq (9/8)^n R_v^n$$

where n is the number of partitions.

Figure 3–32a can be used to arrive at the optimum partitions graphically. If R_v and R fall within the parabola, the TMR network is more reliable than the equivalent nonredundant network. The solid line is the optimum decision curve of Eq. 1.

Figure 3–32b shows the decision boundaries for configurations similar to Figure 3–31c with triplicated voters. In this case, $R_{m_i} = R (i = 2, 3, \ldots, n)$, and $R_{m_1} = R \cdot R_v$. The two solid lines indicate a trade-off between R and R_v. The optimum falls between the two lines. In this case, the maximum reliability improvement is also

$$\frac{R_{\text{TMR}}}{R_{\text{nonredundant}}} \leq (9/8)^n R_v^n$$

Finally, the nonredundant voter scheme is better than the TMR voter scheme if

$$R < \frac{3}{2(1 + R_v)}$$

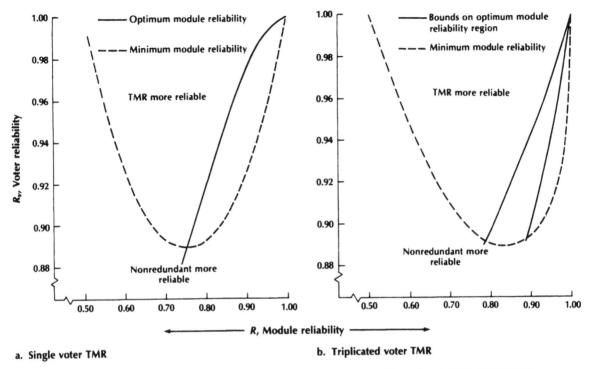

FIGURE 3–32 *Decision regions for TMR configurations [From Gurzi, 1965; © 1965 IEEE]*

More complex TMR networks are possible. Figure 3–33, for example, shows a nonredundant network and a TMR equivalent. The reliability evaluation of such complex TMR structures is also discussed in Chapter 5.

Voter Design. In digital systems, majority voting is normally performed on a bit-by-bit basis. The majority function for a single-bit line can be performed by a 1-bit adder. The triplicated outputs are fed into the adder data and carry-in inputs; the carry-out output is the majority-voted result (see Figure 3–34). For a module with *n* output lines, the TMR implementation has three modules and *n* single-bit voters. Threshold logic [Hampel and Winder, 1971] has also been used for voting. In threshold logic, the output is 1 only if at least a minimum number (the threshold) of inputs are 1.

Voting on analog signals is a particularly important topic to designers of control and data collection systems that require ultrareliable sensors. Using multiple analog-to-digital converters and performing bit-by-bit voting on their digital outputs is not satisfactory, because the least significant bits are almost certain not to agree even when everything is working properly. The normal approach is to perform "voting" in the analog domain instead. One possibility is to take the mean instantaneous value (average the three signals); averaging is the method used for the redundant sensor inputs

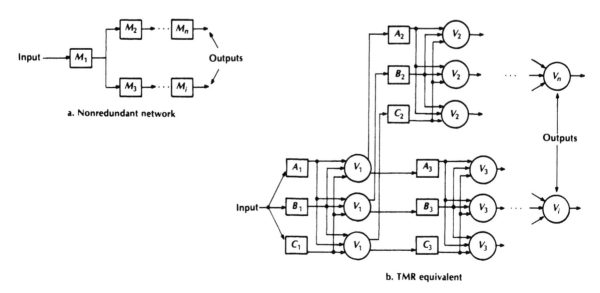

a. Nonredundant network

b. TMR equivalent

FIGURE 3–33 *TMR applied to more complex networks*

FIGURE 3–34
*Logic signal voting
with a 1-bit adder*

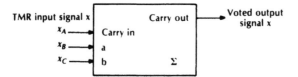

in the NASA Airborne Advanced Reconfigurable Computer Systems [McCluskey and Ogus, 1977]. The average could also be weighted by a priori probabilities of sensor reliability and accuracy. Another possibility is to take the mean of the two most similar signals [Klaassen and Van Peppen, 1977a]. Figure 3–35 illustrates yet another scheme, called *pseudo voting* [Dennis, 1974], which chooses the median of the three signals. Thus, if at a given instant, the three sensors had outputs of 1.0, 2.5, and 2.8 volts, respectively, the median value of 2.5 volts would be used. This approach has the advantage of being simple to implement. More complete treatment of analog voting, including methods and accuracy analysis, can be found in Dennis [1974], and Klaassen and Van Peppen [1977a, 1977b].

Voting Applications at Various System Levels. Voting has been used extensively in prototype and production systems. Table 3–17 lists examples of studies on the use of voting at various levels in the digital system hierarchy. While majority voting at the gate level has been proposed, voting has only been used at the module level and above, due to the cost of the voting unit.

FIGURE 3–35
*Pseudo voting by
selection of a me-
dian analog signal
[From Dennis,
1974]*

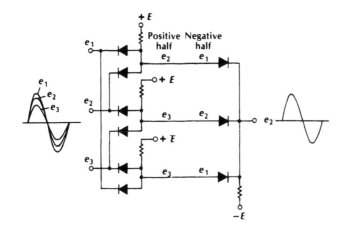

TABLE 3–17 *Studies on voting at various levels in the digital system hierarchy*

Level of Voting Application	Reference	Comments
Gate level	Brown, Tierney, and Wasserman [1961]	Partitions too small for practicality
Module level	Cooper and Chow [1976]; Dickinson, Jackson, and Randa [1964]	Saturn IB and Saturn V on-board launch vehicle computers; seven modules with approximately ten outputs each
	Avizienis et al. [1971]	JPL–STAR computer test and repair processor (TARP); voted outputs distributed
	Stiffler [1976]; Avizienis [1978]	Fault-tolerant spaceborne computer (FTSC); configuration and control unit outputs voted on at each destination
Bus level	Siewiorek, Canepa, and Clark [1977a]	C.vmp (computer-voted multiprocessor); bus divided in half by bidirectional voter
	Smith and Hopkins [1978]; Hopkins, Smith, and Lala [1978]	FTMP (fault-tolerant multiprocessor); voting on serial buses between processor and memory triads.
Software level	Chen and Avizienis [1978]	*N*-version programming; different implementations of a program to the same specification executed concurrently; voting on results with hard, transient, and design errors tolerated
	Wensley et al. [1978]	SIFT (software implemented fault tolerance); *N* copies of identical software concurrently executed and outputs voted.

Synchronization. As with duplication, synchronization of the multiple copies in *N*-modular redundancy is necessary to prevent false outputs. Figure 3–36 illustrates one of the problems that can result without proper synchronization. The signal line in question carries pulses of fixed duration and is used in a master-slave protocol. The first set of pulses occurs soon enough for the simple voter of Figure 3–34 to provide a valid signal. The second set of signals causes a voted output that may be too short for proper operation of the slave logic. The slave may never respond, resulting in a time-out at the master. If the slave device is triplicated, the different copies may respond differently to the runt pulse, resulting in divergent slave behavior, and ultimately, loss of slave synchronization. In the third set of pulses, even though the voted master request pulse is valid, the lagging master may not be ready to receive the reply when it is transmitted. In this case the operation of the lagging processor may diverge from that of the other two, leading to a loss of master synchronization.

The problem of synchronization is often solved by using a common clock. Unless the clock is fault tolerant, however, a single point of failure exists. Another solution is the synchronizing voter shown in Figure 3–37a. Incoming request pulses are latched. If pulses are received from two lines, the voter waits for a period for the lagging master to catch up. If the third pulse comes before the waiting period is over, the voted pulse is sent out immediately, minimizing delay. The one shot at the output ensures a voted pulse signal of the proper duration. The problems and solutions of synchronization in C.vmp are discussed at length in Chapter 10. More detailed consideration of the problems of synchronization and voting can be found in Davies and Wakerly [1978] and McConnel and Siewiorek [1981]. Davies and Wakerly also discuss the design of a fully synchronized TMR clock, in which synchronization is achieved by inserting a voter into the feedback path of each of the three crystal oscillators (Figure 3–37b).

Other Issues in Majority Voted Systems. Fault detection in *N*-modular redundancy can be provided by a disagreement detector that usually operates in parallel with the voter. The disagreement detector is an important element in NMR systems that are reconfigurable. Even in nonreconfigurable systems they act as an aid in diagnosis and can be used to warn of a deteriorating hardware state as the redundancy is exhausted. Some of the systems that use disagreement detectors include C.vmp, JPL–STAR, and FTMP.

In the earlier consideration of software triplication, it was mentioned that using three different implementations of the same process provides protection from software

FIGURE 3–36
Triplicated request line using a pulse signaling convention

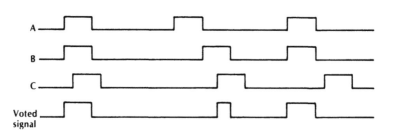

FIGURE 3–37
*Synchronizing con-
figurations [(a)
From McConnel
and Siewiorek,
1981; © 1981 IEEE.
(b) From Davies
and Wakerly, 1978;
© 1978 IEEE]*

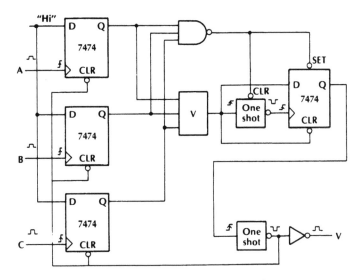

a. **Synchronized voter for pulse signals**

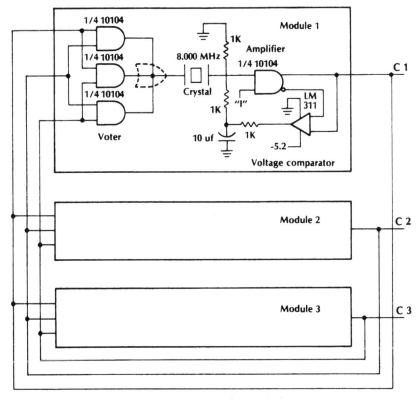

b. **Fully synchronized TMR clock**

design errors as well as from hard failures. A scheme based on a similar principle has been proposed for protection against both hardware design errors and inadequacies in component screening [Platteter, 1980]. Because only a tiny fraction of a microprocessor's possible states can be tested in the few seconds normally allowed in electrical screening tests, complete confidence in a complex LSI chip is almost impossible. Three microprocessors are employed in a TMR configuration; each is from a different source, but implements the same architecture (such as 8080As from three different manufacturers). All three share the same clock and inputs, and thus operate synchronously in lockstep. When employed with a disagreement detector to report faults in any of the chips, this strategy can also be used for more thorough testing of components over a long test period.

As mentioned in the section on duplication, when a computing element is replicated for voting, only a fraction of the available computing power is utilized because all copies are performing the same task. As with duplication, the solution is to use the multiple processors for independent tasks and invoke the voting mode only when necessary. Voting might occur periodically for critical tasks to ensure that all processors are running properly and/or when there is some indication of a possible malfunction (such as power supply flicker, processor self-test warning, or memory parity error). System performance benefits from such a scheme, at the cost of increased susceptibility to uncorrected (and undetected) errors during operation in independent mode. C.vmp and SIFT are examples of TMR systems that can trade off performance for reliability. C.vmp and SIFT can switch between voting and independent modes under program control, permitting use as a three-processor multiple processor in independent mode.

One final problem with triplication is the occasional occurrence of common-mode transient faults. A possible solution is to deliberately skew the synchronization of the programs running in the three processors, but the data on common-mode phenomena are incomplete.

Error-Correcting Codes

Error-correcting codes (ECC codes) are the most commonly used means of masking redundancy. In particular, a large proportion of current primary memory designs use Hamming single-error-correcting (SEC) codes. There are several reasons for the popularity of SEC coded memories. First, they are inexpensive in terms of both cost and performance overhead. The redundancy of SEC codes is only 10 to 40 percent, depending on the design. Decoding and encoding delays are relatively miniscule. Second, the increasing dense RAM chips in use are more prone to soft (transient) faults, such as memory-cell charge loss caused by α-particles and cosmic rays. Third, random access memories constitute an increasingly large part of digital systems and currently contribute as much as 60 to 70 percent of system failure rates. Finally, LSI SEC code correction/detection chips have become available, reducing both the dollar and performance costs of employing SEC codes.

Other error-correction codes with different characteristics are available. Some provide multiple-error correction, but may prove economical only in special applications because the redundancy and decoding delay of multiple-error-correcting codes increase dramatically with error-correcting ability. Some error codes are well suited for specific applications in which the code properties can be used to advantage and the code limitations make little or no difference. Serial decoding, for example, is usually much less expensive than parallel decoding. Serial decoding can be used when data are transmitted serially or when performance is not as critical. In such an application an efficient multiple-error-correcting code can be employed that requires less redundancy but whose complexity would be prohibitive in a parallel decoder. In other situations, limitations on possible failure modes may be used to advantage. For example, in many applications multiple errors will almost always appear closely grouped in space or time (burst errors). In these cases, special codes called *burst-error correction codes* may be employed. Finally, there are error-correcting codes that are invariant with respect to certain arithmetic operations, and hence are suitable for use in checking arithmetic processors. Some of these codes are an extension of arithmetic error-detection codes mentioned previously.

Code Distance. The concepts introduced in the section on error-detection codes also apply to error-correction codes. The minimum distance of a code determines its error-correction/detection abilities. For example, the code C = (0010, 0101) is contained in the space of 4-bit words illustrated in Figure 3–12c and has a minimum distance of 3. This code can detect any single or double error. It can also be used to correct any single error, since a word with a single error will be closer to the code word from which it is derived than it is to the other code word. In general, a code with distance d can correct any pattern of up to t errors, where $(2t + 1) \le d$.* All ECCs can be used to provide error detection, error correction, or both correction and detection. There is, however, a trade-off between detection and correction capabilities. In general, a distance-d code can correct up to t errors and detect an additional p errors, where $(2t + p + 1) \le d$.

The most important class of error-correcting codes is the linear error-correction codes. Linear error-correction codes can be described in terms of their parity check matrices (PCMs). The PCM for an (n,k) linear code is an $(n - k)$ by n matrix whose elements are 0's and 1's (for binary codes). Each column corresponds to a bit in the code word, and each row corresponds to a check bit. If the n-element column vector **r** represents the received code word, and the parity-check matrix is **H**, the decoding operation is represented by the matrix operation

$$\mathbf{H} \cdot \mathbf{r} = \mathbf{s}$$

where **s** is an $(n - k)$-element row vector called the *syndrome*. Most codes are formed by n-element column vectors with 0 syndromes, or expressed more rigorously, the code is the null space of **H**. Note that the all-0's word is always a code word when the null space of the PCM forms the code. Codes that are formed by the null space of a

* *N*-modular redundancy can be considered an application of an (*N*, 1) distance-*N* code.

PCM are often called parity-check codes. If the PCM is binary, the syndrome can be calculated using $(n - k)$ binary trees. Each tree corresponds to a different row of the PCM, with its inputs specified by the bit positions in the row that are 1's.

Now consider the set of n column vectors e_i $(i = 1, 2, \ldots, n)$, where the vector has a single 1 located in position i. If f is the code word transmitted, a received word with a single error in position i can be represented by

$$r = f + e_i$$

If m errors are present in the bit locations specified by the set E, the received word can be represented by

$$r = f + \sum_{i \in E} e_i$$

The decoding operation for r is thus

$$H \cdot r = H \cdot f + H \cdot \left(\sum_{i \in E} e_i \right) = H \cdot \left(\sum_{i \in E} e_i \right) = s'$$

Note that

$$\sum_{i \in E} e_i$$

is the same as the all-0's code word with m errors. For t-error-correcting codes, the syndrome s' is unique for each pattern of t or fewer errors, and can thus be used to correct the errors present if $m \le t$. If $t < m < d$ (for a distance-d code), the syndrome indicates that an uncorrectable error has occurred. The actual correction operation based on s varies for different codes, particularly if the code is used for special error classes (such as b-bit burst errors, where $b \le (n - k)/2$). Thus, the explanation of the correction operation is best left to the references cited later. The correction operations for the Hamming SEC codes and the orthogonal Latin square codes, however, are relatively simple and are explained here.

Erasure Codes. As for error-detection codes, distance is not the only consideration in the properties of error-correction codes. In many applications, tolerance of special classes of failures is often important, and codes have been derived to tolerate unidirectional errors, burst errors, and multiple adjacent unidirectional errors. In addition, the properties of the error sources in a given situation may be used to advantage. For example, in most communication channels, errors occur in a completely random fashion. In digital circuits, however, once a bit value is in error, there is a high probability that errors will continue to occur in that bit (such as hard or intermittent failures of memory cells, sense amps, and bus lines). This form of error (sometimes called an *erasure*) can be put to use if a history of error locations is kept [Ingle and Siewiorek, 1973a].

Consider a bus with a single-parity bit in which a particular bit line is known to be failed. If the possibility of additional failures and transient faults can be ignored, any parity error that occurs must be caused by the bad bit line. Thus, the error location is known and the error can be corrected. In memories a history may be unnecessary, because erasures caused by failed bits in a memory word can be found by writing and reading an arbitrary word and its complement into the memory location. XORing of the two retrieved values determines the position of stuck-at-failures.

An algorithm that allows correction of up to $(d - 2)$ errors using a distance-d code is given in Figure 3–38a [Ingle and Siewiorek, 1973a]. This algorithm assumes that only one new error can occur before it is discovered (that is, for a received word with a errors in it, $a - 1$ of them are in already known erasure positions), and that at most $(d - 2)$ erasures exist. The algorithm uses the code itself to correct only single errors at a time. During a given iteration, the algorithm changes the bit values in locations specified by some subset of the known erasures, forms a new single-error-correction syndrome, and then performs the single-bit correction specified by the syndrome. Next, it forms a new syndrome from the corrected word to determine if the correction just performed (the combination of erasure positions and single-error correction) was valid. Thus, if a $(d - 1)$st error occurs during use of this algorithm, it is mistakenly corrected to a code word that is at a distance d from the correct word and only distance-1 from the received word. Figure 3–38b shows a table-lookup implementation of this scheme. Note that the erasure-correction algorithm of Figure 3–38a can be greatly simplified when used with a distance-3 (single-error correcting) or distance-4 (single-error-correcting/double-error-detecting) code.

Presumably, the $(d - 1)$st error can be corrected if, when there are $(d - 2)$ erasures, it is assumed at the beginning of the correction process that at least one error exists

```
k = number of known failures (<d-2) ;
i = 0 ;
r = received word ;
s = syndrome ;
for i = 0 to k do
    begin
        for j = 1 to kCi do
            begin
                pick a new permutation of i of the known failure locations
                    and change the corresponding bits of r ;
                form s ;
                if s ≠ 0 then
                    begin
                        temp = r corrected using s (change only one bit location);
                        reform s using temp ;
                        if s = 0 then ; ! errors corrected successfully ;
                            begin
                                update history of failed bit locations if there is
                                    a new failure location indicated ;
                                EXIT ;
                            end ;
                    end ;
            end ;
    end;
signal (uncorrectable error) ; ! a nonzero s could not be found using the
                                 known failure locations ;
```

a. Proposed algorithm

b. Proposed table look-up implementation algorithm

FIGURE 3–38 *Correcting up to d − 2 errors in a distance-d code, using knowledge of erasures present [(a) From Ingle and Siewiorek, 1973a; © 1976 IEEE]*

in an erasure position. The algorithm of Figure 3–38a is changed by incrementing i from 1 instead of 0 when $k = d - 1$. This modification means, however, that a single error occurring in a nonerasure position will cause an error if $d - 1$ erasures are known, even if it is the only bit in error. Stiffler [1978] proposed a corrector design based on an algorithm similar to Figure 3–38a. The design can be varied to correct up to any e errors, $e < d$, and detect an additional p errors, $e < (e + p) < d$.

An erasure correction technique similar to that of Figure 3–38a is used in a prototype memory described by Carter and McCarthy [1976]. This design uses a subset of Hamming SEC/DED distance-4 codes called *maintenance codes,* in which the data word W and its bit-wise complement W' have identical check bits. The memory also utilizes the fact that hard stuck-at-α failures can be discovered by writing and reading back both a word and its complement, then XORing the results to learn the location of the failures (pointed to by set bits in the result). Stuck-at-α means a bit is stuck at either 1 or 0. As shown before, this information can be used to correct up to $d - 2$ errors in a word, or in this casse, two errors. The memory can detect permanent triple faults and recover from all permanent double faults. Black, Sundberg, and Walker [1977] describe a spacecraft computer memory that can correct single errors and erasures.

With the addition of erasure correction, consideration must include the possibility of transient and soft errors and the ways in which they affect the validity of the schemes just presented. If an error history is being maintained, there is the problem of ensuring that the recorded erasure locations are caused by hard failures instead of transient errors; otherwise, the storage space may quickly become saturated with spurious erasure locations. Chapter 7 describes how IBM uses erasure correction to tolerate a mixture of permanent and soft errors.

The following subsections present samples of several kinds of ECCs. Except for the Hamming codes, this coverage is neither detailed nor complete. Peterson and Weldon [1972], Berlekamp [1968], MacWilliams and Sloan [1978], Blahut [1984], Hill [1986], and Lin [1970] are excellent general references on coding theory as it applies to digital systems. A paper by Tang and Chien [1969] provides a good introduction to coding theory. An article by Pradhan and Stiffler [1980] is a general discussion of error codes: their properties, applications, limitations, and possible ways to overcome these limitations. The article also contains an extensive bibliography on codes and code applications. A book by Rao [1974] is a complete treatment of arithmetic error codes. Finally, new codes, modifications of old ones, and more efficient ways of employing codes are constantly being introduced. The *IEEE Transactions on Computers,* the *IBM Journal of Research and Development,* and the proceedings of the annual Fault-Tolerant Computing Symposiums (published by the IEEE) are good sources for papers on coding theory and applications.

Hamming SEC Codes. As mentioned before, Hamming SEC codes are the most commonly encountered codes in computer systems. For k data bits, an (n,k) Hamming code requires c additional check bits, where

$$2^c \geq c + k + 1$$

$$
\begin{array}{cccc}
\text{Data bits} & & \text{Check bits} \\
d_1 \; d_2 \; d_3 \; d_4 & c_1 \; c_2 \; c_3 \\
\begin{bmatrix}
1 & 1 & 1 & 0 & 1 & 0 & 0 \\
1 & 0 & 1 & 1 & 0 & 1 & 0 \\
0 & 1 & 1 & 1 & 0 & 0 & 1
\end{bmatrix}
\end{array}
\cdot
\begin{bmatrix}
d_1 \\ d_2 \\ d_3 \\ d_4 \\ c_1 \\ c_2 \\ c_3
\end{bmatrix}
$$

Syndrome $= [S_1 S_2 S_3]$

Received data word

$S_1 = d_1 \oplus d_2 \oplus d_3 \oplus c_1$
$S_2 = d_1 \oplus d_3 \oplus d_4 \oplus c_2$
$S_3 = d_2 \oplus d_3 \oplus d_4 \oplus c_3$

a. Parity-check matrix and syndrome formation for a (7,4) Hamming SEC code

	Data bits				Check bits			Syndrome			
Code word (no error)	1	1	1	0		1	0	0	0 0 0	(Zero syndrome implies no error)
One error (box)	1	1	1	[1]		1	0	0	0 1 1	(Matches d_4 column)
Two errors (boxes)	1	[0]	1	0		1	[1]	0	1 1 1	(Matches d_3 column—results in erroneous correction)

b. Received code words and their syndromes for 0, 1, and 2 errors

$$
\begin{array}{ccccccc}
c_1 & c_2 & d_1 & c_3 & d_2 & d_3 & d_4 \\
\begin{bmatrix}
1 & 0 & 1 & 0 & 1 & 0 & 1 \\
0 & 1 & 1 & 0 & 0 & 1 & 1 \\
0 & 0 & 0 & 1 & 1 & 1 & 1
\end{bmatrix}
\end{array}
$$

c. Parity-check matrix for (7,4) Hamming code for which syndrome is the binary-coded position of the bit in error

FIGURE 3–39 *Hamming SEC code examples*

Thus, $n = c + k$. These codes are separable. They are best described in terms of their parity-check matrices. Figure 3–39a shows the parity-check matrix for a (7,4) Hamming SEC code. A received code word is decoded by forming the dot product of the matrix and the code word column vector as shown, using modulo-2 addition. The result is a c-bit vector called the *syndrome*. If the syndrome is all 0's, no correctable error is present. If a single error occurs, the syndrome matches the column in the check matrix corresponding to the bit in error. A multiple error results in a false syndrome that is indistinguishable from the syndrome for one or no errors; thus, Hamming SEC codes have a minimum distance of 3. Figure 3–39b shows a code word and its syndrome for 0, 1, and 2 errors.

As stated previously, a syndrome generator for this code can be made using c parity trees, with the inputs for each tree being the code-word bits with 1's in the row corresponding to the syndrome bit. Encoding for this code uses the same set of parity trees, with the check-bit inputs corresponding to the check bit being generated held at 0. This matrix is not unique for a (7,4) Hamming SEC code; any 4 by 7 matrix will work as long as no two columns are alike, none is all 0's, and, for easier encoding, the columns corresponding to the c check bits contain only a single 1 in each.

The "classic" form of parity-check matrix is of the form shown in Figure 3–39c, originally proposed by Hamming [1950]. Each column of this matrix includes the binary-coded representation of the column number containing it (columns are numbered starting with 1). The check bits are located in bit positions $2^i(i = 0, 1, 2, \ldots, (n - k - 1))$. Thus, in the event of an error, the syndrome is actually the binary-coded number of the bit position in error. This may allow a simpler design for the circuitry that uses the syndrome to perform the correction.

Because a nonzero syndrome is an indication of an error, a small amount of extra circuitry will provide a means of error notification, and thus, error detection. In addition, a small increase in the size of the code word can result in improved error-detection capabilities. Most implementations of the Hamming codes use an extra check bit, which allows detection of all double errors. In the "classic" Hamming code, this check bit is the parity of all the other check and data bits in the code word (even-parity sense). The check matrix is changed by adding both an extra check-bit column with a single 1 and a row of all 1's that corresponds to the extra overall parity bit. A PCM for an (8,4) Hamming SEC/DED (single-error-correcting/double-error-detecting) code is shown in Figure 3–40a. A nonzero syndrome not matching any column indicates a double (or greater) error. In the case of this (8,4) code, the last three syndrome bits point to the column number in error (numbered starting with 0) as long as the first bit is 1. If the first bit is a 0 and any of the others nonzero, a double or greater error has occurred. If all the bits are 0, there is no error. This is demonstrated in Figure 3–40b, which shows the syndromes for a received word with 0, 1, and 2 errors.

The following method illustrates one way of understanding how the SEC codes work. Remember that the process of decoding the code word is expressed by the formula

$$\mathbf{H} \cdot \mathbf{c} = \mathbf{s} = 0$$

where $\mathbf{s}$ is the $(n - k)$-bit syndrome, $\mathbf{H}$ is the check matrix, and $\mathbf{c}$ is the code word. If $\mathbf{r}$ is the received word, with errors, it can be expressed as

$$\mathbf{r} = \mathbf{c} + \mathbf{e}$$

where $\mathbf{e}$ is a bit vector with 1's in the locations corresponding to the bits in error, and "+" is a bit-wise XOR. Because of the linear property of these types of codes, the syndrome for $\mathbf{r}$ will be

$$\mathbf{H} \cdot \mathbf{r} = \mathbf{H} \cdot (\mathbf{c} + \mathbf{e}) = \mathbf{H} \cdot \mathbf{c} + \mathbf{H} \cdot \mathbf{e} = \mathbf{H} \cdot \mathbf{e}$$

since $\mathbf{H} \cdot \mathbf{r} = 0$. In the second example of Figure 3–40b, $\mathbf{c}$ is 11100100, and $\mathbf{e}$ is 01000000. The product of $\mathbf{e}$ and the matrix of Figure 3–40a is 1101—the same as shown in the figure.

Based on this concept, it can be shown why single-error correction works. An $\mathbf{e}$ with a single bit will always produce the column of the matrix corresponding to that

FIGURE 3–40
*Hamming SEC/DED
code examples*

$$
\begin{array}{cccccccc}
d_1 & d_2 & d_3 & d_4 & c_1 & c_2 & c_3 & c_4 \\
\end{array}
\begin{bmatrix}
1 & 1 & 1 & 1 & 1 & 1 & 1 & 1 \\
1 & 1 & 1 & 0 & 0 & 1 & 0 & 0 \\
1 & 0 & 1 & 1 & 0 & 0 & 1 & 0 \\
0 & 1 & 1 & 1 & 0 & 0 & 0 & 1 \\
\end{bmatrix}
\cdot
\begin{bmatrix}
d_1 \\ d_2 \\ d_3 \\ d_4 \\ c_1 \\ c_2 \\ c_3 \\ c_4 \\
\end{bmatrix}
= [S_1 S_2 S_3 S_4]
$$

a. Parity-check matrix for (8,4) Hamming SEC/DED code

Number of errors	Received data bits				Received check bits				Syndrome			
	d_1	d_2	d_3	d_4	c_1	c_2	c_3	c_4	S_1	S_2	S_3	S_4
Zero	1	1	1	0	0	1	0	0	0	0	0	0
One	1	0	1	0	0	1	0	0	1	1	0	1
Two	1	0	1	0	0	1	1	0	0	1	1	1

b. Received words and their syndromes

bit. This concept can also be used to understand how the double-error-detection property of SEC/DED codes works. A double error is represented by an **e** vector with two 1's. The product of this **e** and **H** is the sum of two columns of the matrix. In order for this kind of error to be distinguishable from a correctable single error, the sum of any two columns must not equal any column in the matrix. This is why extra redundancy is required (that is, the preceding extra check bit beyond that required solely for an SEC code). The basic Hamming code can be modified to detect/correct multiple adjacent errors, detect an all zero error, concatenate code words to reduce required redundancy, decrease decoding cost/delay, and to diagnose rather than correct errors. Examples of these modifications are given below. Note that similar modifications can be made to any code.

Multiple Adjacent Bit Errors. Increasingly, system designs require the use of 4-bit-wide and 8-bit-wide RAM chips. In this case, SEC codes will not provide protection from failures affecting entire chips or individual words on a single chip (4 or 8 bits); in fact, they will not guarantee detection of all such errors. These errors are known as *b*-adjacent errors ($b = 4$, $b = 8$ in the preceding examples). Fortunately, there are ECCs that provide for detection and/or correction of *b*-adjacent errors, and are suitable for use in memories. These are SEC/DED/SBC (single-byte correction) and SBC/DBD (single-byte correction, double-byte detection) codes.

A variation of the Hamming SEC/DED code can be used to correct any single-byte error and detect any double-byte error. This is accomplished (assuming 8-bit bytes) by using eight Hamming codes in parallel in the same fashion as for interlaced parity (described in the previous section on parity codes).* Thus, for a 64-bit data word with 8-bit bytes, each Hamming syndrome is formed using every eighth bit. In essence, eight 13-bit Hamming code words are being evaluated in parallel. The redundancy is 63 percent. If 16-bit bytes are used, the number of parallel code words is four (22 bits each), with a 38 percent redundancy. Even though this scheme is easy to implement using readily available standard-support ICs (discussed later), other codes also to be discussed later provide similar fault-masking capability but require lower redundancy.

As was seen earlier, for SEC/DED codes the sum of any two columns of the parity-check matrix is not equal to any column in the matrix. To get byte error detection, the sum of any number of columns within a byte is not equal to any column in the matrix. The trick is to derive matrices that satisfy this property. The following matrix [Chen, 1984] is an example of a (40,32) SEC/DED/SBD code ($b = 4$):

```
1111  0000  1111  0000  1000  1000  1000  1000  1000  0000
0000  1111  0000  1111  0100  0100  0100  0100  0100  0000
1111  1111  0000  0000  0010  0010  0010  0010  0010  0000
0000  0000  1111  1111  0001  0001  0001  0001  0001  0000
1000  1000  1000  1000  1111  1111  0000  0000  0000  1000
0100  0100  0100  0100  0000  0000  1111  1111  0000  0100
0010  0010  0010  0010  1111  0000  1111  0000  0000  0010
0001  0001  0001  0001  0000  1111  0000  1111  0000  0001
```

Any error pattern of up to 4 bits, confined to a single 4-bit byte, will be detected as an uncorrectable error. For single- and double-bit errors, the code works in the same way as an ordinary SEC/DED code. Note that the matrix is formatted to show the correspondence of the matrix columns to the 4-bit wide bytes.

Chen [1983], Reddy [1978], and Kaneda [1984] provide methods of generating matrices for SEC/DED/SBD codes. Chen [1986a] and Chen [1986b] provide methods of generating matrices for SBC/DBD codes. Among other codes that will work are Reed-Solomon and BCH codes. Chen [1984] provides a good survey of error-correction codes for memories built with semiconductor RAM chips.

Table 3–18 summarizes the required redundancy for a variety of error-correction codes as a function of the bit width of memory chips for the codes described in Appendix A.

Detecting an All-0's Error. The codes in Table 3–18 do not detect the all-0's failure mode, for the all-0's word is a code word. In the many hardware designs prone to an all-0's failure mode (such as through a power failure in a memory array or a failure in a select circuit), this problem can be overcome by a modified Hamming code. The code of Figure 3–40, for example, could be modified by using the odd instead of even parity sense for the overall parity-check bit. Pradhan and Stiffler [1980] give an example

---

* In fact, assuming b-bit bytes, this scheme can correct any pattern of errors spanning at most b adjacent bits, even if the pattern transcends a byte boundary. Such a pattern is known as a b-bit burst error.

TABLE 3–18
Redundancy for a spectrum of error-correction codes

Data Bits	SEC/DED Bits/Byte	SEC/DED/SBD Bits/Byte		SBC/DBD			DEC/TED
		4	8	2	4	8	
8	5	6	9	–	–	–	9
16	6	6	10	8	12	24	11
32	7	7	10	10	12	24	13
64	8	8	10	10	12	24	15
128	9	9	11	12	12	24	17

of a modified Hamming code that detects multiple unidirectional failures short of the all-1's or all-0's failure.

Concatenating Code Words to Reduce Redundancy. It is possible to obtain a Hamming code with a lower amount of redundancy by concatenating several data words and coding the resultant longer word. The (8,4) code previously used for a 4-bit data word has 100 percent redundancy. If 8 data words are concatenated, the resulting 32 bits of data can be protected by using a (39,32) Hamming SEC/DED code with only 22 percent redundancy. There is a greater possibility of a fatal error because the single-bit-correction ability is now distributed over five times as many bits. Also, the parity trees needed for decoding have more gate levels and thus a longer delay. Finally, with a RAM, on writes, the old code word must be retrieved, the old data byte replaced by the new one, and the new code word formed and stored. These increases, however, are often balanced by the much lower redundancy (and cost) needed.

Decreasing Decoding Delays. When k data bits are needed, there is often no (n,k) code with the desired properties. Thus, many of the codes used are shortened, such as an (n,k') code shortened to an $(n - i, k' - i)$ code, where $k' = k + i$. This can be accomplished by assuming that i of the data bits are always 0. The resultant PCM is that of the (n,k') code, with the i columns corresponding to the always-0 data bits deleted. Often the columns to be deleted can be chosen to minimize the decoder complexity. Most implementations of Hamming codes are examples of shortened codes. Consider a (21,16) Hamming SEC code. According to the criteria for Hamming codes, the 5 check bits will provide SEC protection for up to 26 data bits. Thus, any (21,16) Hamming code is actually a shortened (31,26) Hamming code.

Some shortened Hamming codes have useful special properties. Hsiao [1970] describes a set of SEC/DED codes that are equivalent to conventional Hamming codes, in that they require the same number of check bits. These codes, known as optimal odd-weight column codes, use a parity-check matrix in which the number of 1's is minimal. Each column has an odd number of 1's, and the number of 1's in each row is as close to the average number per row as possible. The result is a minimum number of inputs to the syndrome generation parity trees, which means the syndrome generator has fewer components and fewer gate-level delays. The conventional Hamming SEC/DED codes, in contrast, require an n-input tree for the overall parity check. Thus, the codes described by Hsiao result in better cost, reliability, and performance.

There are other possibilities for improving the implementation of Hamming SEC/DED codes. Carter, Duke, and Jessep [1973] propose an efficient method of decoding called *lookaside correction*. In this scheme, the SEC/DED code word is translated to a byte-parity encoded word. The code employed is a special subset of SEC/DED codes called *rotational codes*. These codes also have a minimum number of 1's in the check matrix. Carter, Duke, and Jessep show that a received code word with a correctable error translates to a byte-parity encoded word with a detectable parity error. Thus, detection of byte-parity errors indicates that error correction is necessary with the received code word; otherwise, the data is ready for transmission on a byte-parity encoded bus. With no error present, the translation-and-check operation is faster than the decoding and recoding (into byte-parity code) operation required in a conventional Hamming code implementation.

Error Diagnosis. The same single-chip failure coverage and diagnostic resolution that chip parity provides can be obtained with less redundancy by using a variant of the Hamming single-error correcting (SEC) codes. Assume there are m w-bit-wide chips for a data word, and that c_i ($i = 1, 2, \ldots, m$) is the parity of the ith chip. The addition of n parity bits, where

$$2^n > m + n$$

can be used to give detection of any single-chip failure and diagnostic resolution to the failed chip or parity bit. The parity check bits are formed similarly to the Hamming SEC code bits. The difference is that the check bits are formed from the c_i's (chip parities) instead of from individual data bits as in the SEC code. The full technique will not be given here; an example will be used instead. This example is a 32-bit-wide microstore made from four 8-bit-wide chips. Three parity bits are used, and are computed as

$$P_1 = c_1 + c_2 + c_4$$
$$P_2 = c_1 + c_3 + c_4$$
$$P_3 = c_2 + c_3 + c_4$$

After a microword has been read, the parity check bits are computed and XORed with the stored parity bits. If any of the resultant bits are nonzero, the three bits ($p_3 p_2 p_1$) form a syndrome that is uniquely associated with a particular chip or parity bit in error. The cost for this scheme is n extra bits per word, n parity trees with $\lceil \log_2(m + n) \rceil$ inputs, and m parity trees with w inputs if w-bit-wide chips are used. The coding/decoding circuitry is greater than for chip parity, but the decrease in redundant bits can be significant, especially for large memories. On the other hand, coverage of multiple chip failures is much lower, and in the case of multiple chip failures, the syndrome may point to a nonfaulty chip if it is nonzero.

If a Hamming code is employed purely for masking purposes (that is, there is no error notification if the error is correctable), deterioration of the hardware may be present but unknown to the system maintainer. Furthermore, it is desirable to be able to test the encoding/decoding hardware. Thus, most implementations of Hamming-coded memory systems include the ability to write noncode words and to read memory words without the correction being performed. This provision aids in the diagnosis of memory problems. Reliability and performance modeling of Hamming (and other) SEC codes is deferred to Chapter 5, where the topic is covered in depth.

ECC Applications. A great many commercial computers, over a large range of sizes and performance, use Hamming SEC codes for main memory. Among these are several models of the IBM 360/370/308X/309X series, the VAX-11/780/750/8600/8700, the Univac 1100 series numerous engineering workstations, and the AT&T ESS-1. In addition, many manufacturers of plug-compatible aftermarket memories offer SEC add-on memory for various computers. Hamming SEC codes see usage in other areas of computer design, particularly buses.

ECC is increasingly important in processor design today. Almost all computer systems today use some form of cache memory. Until recently, most caches have been write-through caches—data written into the cache is also sent to main memory at the same time. For these caches, then, all of the contents of the cache are duplicated in main memory. Using parity to detect errors is adequate for recovery, as the data can always be retrieved from the copy in main memory. However, processor-memory bandwidth is even more critical as processor speeds increase faster than memory system bandwidths; shared bus multiprocessor techniques aggravate the bottleneck. Write-back caches alleviate this problem. Data written into the cache is not immediately written through to main memory; thus, memory write traffic is cut significantly. The drawback is that there is no backup copy of this "dirty" cache data in main memory, and parity alone is no longer sufficient for recovery. The increasingly common solution to this problem is the application of error-correction codes.

The VAX 8600, for example, uses an SEC/DED code for its write-back cache (Chapter 7 contains a detailed description of the VAX 8600 design). In many cases, a write-back cache design will need to employ 4-bit-wide or 8-bit-wide static RAM chips. Single-bit failures are the dominant failure mode for such chips, while subarray row/column failures are much less dominant. Both failure modes will affect only one bit of data per address; hence, SEC/DED codes will protect against them. Failures affecting the entire chip or multiple bits in a word are much less likely, but still possible. If the system requires a higher level of data integrity or reliability, an SEC/DED/SBD or SBC/DBD code will be needed.

Several semiconductor manufacturers are now supplying LSI support chips for SEC code memories. Among these are the Advanced Micro Devices AM2960 and AMZ8160, the Motorola MC68540, and the Fujitsu MB1412A. Most of these chips use modified Hamming SEC/DED codes. The MB1412A, for example, is an 8-bit (data) slice that can also be stacked for data words of 2, 4, or 8 bytes. The AM2960 and AMZ8160 are 16 bits wide but can be used for data words of 2, 4, or 8 bytes. The MC68540 is a

16-bit wide unit to be used for data words of 1, 2, or 4 bytes that also detects the all-0's and all-1's failure mode.

Of course, ECC implementations may not work correctly if there are failures in the decoding logic that implements them. Gaitanis [1988] presents a technique for designing totally self-checking (TSC) correction/detection logic for SEC/DED codes.

Other Error-Correction Codes. Although Hamming SEC/DED codes are the most commonly used codes in computers, there are several others, many of which are effective against particular classes of errors. For example, Tang and Chien [1969] discuss classes of cyclic codes for correcting single errors, burst errors, multiple independent errors, and multiple-character (i.e., byte) errors. This section briefly presents a few other codes as an indication of the abundant possibilities that codes offer.

Burst-Error Correction Codes. Burst-error correction codes are uniquely suited to some applications in digital systems. A b-bit burst error is an error pattern that spans b bits in a word. Another form of multiple error is a b-adjacent error, in which the errors occur within specific b-bit boundaries, such as byte boundaries. The b-adjacent error-correction code is particularly useful in designs organized as several parallel byte-wide modules. In such designs, a single failure can affect an entire block of signal lines. In a memory of $(h \times b)$-bit words organized as h b-bit-wide memory chips, for example, a failure of the addressing logic in one chip would cause the simultaneous failure of b adjacent bits.

The interlaced multiple Hamming code can correct b-adjacent errors. Other codes provide similar protection with less redundancy, such as those formed from binary-coded characters instead of individual bits. Thus, for characters of b bits, there are 2^b possible characters. The PCM elements are b-bit characters instead of 0's and 1's and the parity check summations are performed over the characters in the code word modulo-(2^b). Thus, the error-detection/correction characteristics are in terms of b-bit characters, and the codes are effective against b-adjacent errors. Since b-adjacent errors are a subset of b-bit burst errors, burst-error codes are also effective. The following are examples of studies on this class of codes:

Type of Code	Reference
Reed–Solomon cyclic codes	Peterson and Weldon [1972]
	Tang and Chien [1969]
b-adjacent error-correction codes	Bossen [1970]
	Reddy [1978]
	Srinivasan [1971b]
	Bhatt and Kinney [1978]
	Hong and Patel [1972]
	Fujiwara and Kawakami [1971]
	Carter and Wadia [1980]
	Kaneda and Fujiwara [1980]

Unidirectional Error Code. Unidirectional errors are a common hazard in digital systems. In this type of error, the signal lines in error have all made the same transition, that is, 0-to-1 or 1-to-0, but not both. These errors may or may not be adjacent. On an open collector bus, for example, a gating circuit failed in the on state can cause multiple signals to be gated onto the bus. The signal lines affected will carry the wire-or of the desired and spurious signals, resulting in unidirectional 0-to-1 errors. Other possible causes of unidirectional failures are power failures, shorts, and loss of charge in memory cells. The all-0's and all-1's failure modes mentioned previously are a case of multiple adjacent unidirectional failures. If multiple unidirectional errors are likely to occur in an application requiring an error-correcting code, the best code to use is one that at least detects such failures. Pradhan [1980] has developed a class of separable random-error-correcting codes that also detect any number of unidirectional errors.

Latin Square Codes. Hsiao, Bossen, and Chien [1970] state that usually, the less redundancy a code has relative to its error-correction ability, the greater are the complexity, delay, and cost of the decoder. From this principle, they derive a class of codes in which a systematic addition of redundancy adds error-correction ability. In particular, their orthogonal Latin square codes are $(m^2 + 2tm, m^2)$ codes that can correct any t errors ($t \leq (m + 1)/2$). Thus, the code length grows linearly with t for a given data length. These codes are quickly decodable in parallel using simple majority logic decoding [Peterson and Weldon, 1972; Tang and Chien, 1969]. The parity-check matrices are easy to construct. The high redundancies produce parity-check matrices with few 1's, resulting in simple (minimal) decoding circuitry. Finally, the systematic nature of the matrix allows modular additions to the decoder for increased error-correction ability. Needed for each bit are t modules, each containing $2m$-bit parity trees, and a $(2t + 1)$-bit majority voter. Figure 3–41 shows the PCMs and one of the bit-correction slices for the (15,9) and (21,9) single- and double-error correcting Latin square codes. Decoding is performed by a majority vote among the received value of a data bit and two values calculated for it from the other received bits. For nine data bits, double-error correction is the maximum attainable with this class of codes.

Product Codes. Product codes are the result of the simultaneous applications of two codes in a particular fashion. (Tang and Chien [1969] refer to these codes as N-dimensional codes.) Figure 3–42a illustrates the concept, in which the check bits in the lower right-hand corner may be formed either as row checks on the column check bits or vice versa. If the two codes used have minimum distance d_1 and d_2, respectively, the product code formed by them has weight $d_1 d_2$. This concept can be extended to N dimensions (N codes applied simultaneously). One product code, often used on tapes and other serial devices, is the result of using single-bit parity along both the horizontal and vertical axes. Because parity is a distance-2 code, the result is a distance-4 code. In practice, a single error produces a parity error detected by both vertical and horizontal parity. The intersection of these two parity errors points to the bit in error (see Figure 3–42b).

Furthermore, it can be seen that any double error is detectable. The parity product

FIGURE 3–41

*Latin square code
parity-check matrix
with one bit-slice
of decoder for
nine data bits
[From Hsiao, Bos-
sen, and Chien,
1970; Reprinted by
permission from
International Busi-
ness Machines
Corporation]*

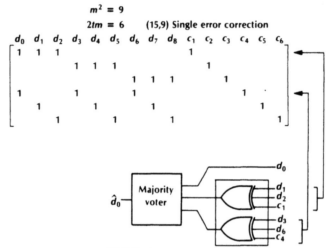

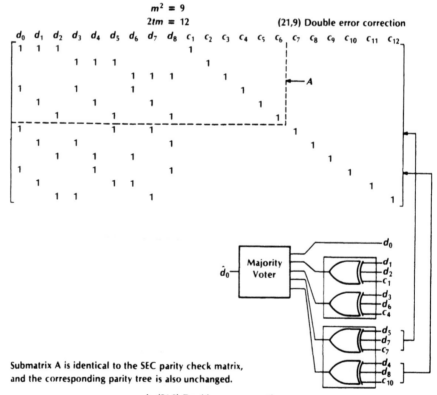

Submatrix A is identical to the SEC parity check matrix,
and the corresponding parity tree is also unchanged.

b. (21,9) Double-error correction

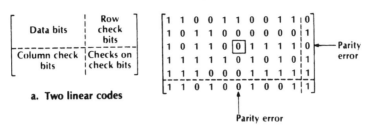

FIGURE 3–42
Product codes

a. Two linear codes

b. Two even-parity codes

code is applicable to random-access memories as well as to serial application, and can result in less redundancy than a comparable Hamming SEC/DED code. The section on single-error-correcting memory models in Chapter 5 examines the use of the code in detail and compares its reliability, cost, and performance with the Hamming SEC/DED code.

Arithmetic Error-Correction Codes. AN arithmetic error-detection codes were discussed earlier. With a sufficiently large modulus A, an AN code is capable of error correction. Table 3–19, from Kautz [1962], lists the check modulus, maximum data length, and code word length for a number of possible single-error-correcting AN codes. In practice, these codes are decoded like the error-detection AN codes, with division by the check modulus. If the remainder of the division (the residue) is 0, there is no error. A single-bit error in the rth bit position results in a residue of ($\pm 2^r$ modulo A); Kautz suggests that the correction be performed by table look-up using the residue. Because none of the AN codes of Table 3–19 are low-cost check moduli (see the previous section on arithmetic codes), the division operation to obtain the residue is complex.

Rao [1972] presents a modification of AN codes that allows for more efficient decoding. Other studies on arithmetic error-correcting codes focus on the residue-number-system (RNS) codes (Watson and Hasting [1966], Mandelbaum [1972a], Barsi and Maestrini [1973, 1974]); the biresidue class of separable codes (Rao [1970]); and the application of ECCs to byte-sliced processors (Neumann and Rao [1975]).

Masking Logic

Discussion of the two previous masking techniques did not include fault masking at the gate level of digital design. N-modular redundancy with voting is used almost exclusively for modules or for functional partitions of designs. Coding is normally applied when some regular structure is present, as in memories or buses. Thus, in both NMR and coding applications a single restoring organ (voter, decoder/corrector) normally protects a set of hardware that is much more complex and error prone than the restoring organ itself. In fact, the increased regularity of control logic obtained through the use of PLAs and microcode techniques means that error-coding techniques can have an important impact on system reliability. However, some random logic always

TABLE 3–19
Single-error-correcting AN codes

Check Modulus A	Maximum Data Length k	Code Word Length n
13	2	6
19	4	9
23	6	11
29	9	14
37	12	18
47	17	23
53	20	26
59	23	29
61	24	30
67	26	33
71	28	35
79	32	39
83	34	41
101	42	50
103	43	51

Source: From Kautz, 1962.

remains that cannot be protected through the straightforward application of error codes.

This section discusses techniques other than module replication that have been devised for random logic. These techniques perform restoration at the gate level or, for sequential machines, at the state level, usually with a massive use of redundant gates. Because of their high cost, few of the techniques have seen actual use. The discussion is divided into two parts: the first concerns gate-level masking; the second deals with the applications of error codes to the states of finite-state machines.

Interwoven Logic. Several techniques have been proposed for gate-level fault masking. All employ redundant inputs to each gate. Among these are von Neumann's original work on circuits with interspersed restoring organs, quadded logic [Tryon, 1962; Jensen, 1963], and radial logic [Klaschka, 1969]. Pierce [1965] combined these variant schemes into a general theory of what he termed *interwoven logic*. Some of the basic precepts of interwoven logic are briefly presented here, based largely upon Pierce [1965].

Faults in logic circuitry are considered to be limited to stuck-at-α (where $\alpha = 0, 1$) faults on gate outputs, gate inputs, or input lines to the network. The effect on the logic depends on the value of the fault and the type of gate whose inputs are affected. Consider a NAND gate. If one of its inputs is stuck-at-0, its output is forced to be 1 regardless of the gate's other inputs. On the other hand, a stuck-at-1 input does not force the output to 0 unless the other inputs are also 1. Thus, two types of faults exist: critical faults, which by themselves force a certain gate output, and subcritical faults, which alone will not cause a gate output error. The following table lists some common gates and their critical and subcritical input faults:

Gate Type	Critical Faults	Subcritical Faults
AND	$1 \rightarrow 0$	$0 \rightarrow 1$
OR	$0 \rightarrow 1$	$1 \rightarrow 0$
NOT	$0 \rightarrow 1, 1 \rightarrow 0$	None
NAND	$1 \rightarrow 0$	$0 \rightarrow 1$
Majority	None	$0 \rightarrow 1, 1 \rightarrow 0$

In a network of AND gates a critical fault is propagated through the network—a critical input fault on a gate in one layer forces an output error that is critical to the subsequent layers of AND gates. If, however, the network is composed of alternating layers of AND and OR gates, a critical fault may be stopped within two layers—a critical input fault to one layer results in an output error that is a subcritical input fault in the following layer. Similarly, an all-NAND (or all-NOR) gate network may stop a critical fault within two layers. Finally, majority-logic faults may be stopped after only one layer because there are no possible critical faults.

Interwoven logic makes use of the properties of subcritical and critical faults by assuring that the effects of up to t faults in any layer are masked by subsequent layers; t is design-dependent, and the circuit so designed is called t-fault tolerant. Fault tolerance is accomplished by using redundant gates with redundant inputs. The interconnections between logic layers are *interwoven* so that critical faults at one stage are masked out in subsequent stages through the mixing of faulty and good replicated signals. Figure 3–43 illustrates this masking action as well as a necessary condition— the interweaving pattern must vary from layer to layer. Without this variation, the fault will propagate.*

Using the principles of critical and subcritical faults, interweaving, and weave-pattern variation, Pierce developed a general theory of implementing interwoven logic. To correct any t critical errors, the redundancy in gates must be $R = (t + 1)^2 = B^2$, and each gate must have B times the inputs needed for the corresponding gate in the nonredundant realization. At least three different interweaving patterns are needed if the circuit has feedback (such as flip-flops or loops). A pattern consists of B groupings. If the redundant copies of a gate are numbered from 1 to R, each of the B groupings contains a unique set of B different numbers; there are no overlaps between groups.

Finally, each group in a pattern must have elements drawn from at least B different groups in any of the other patterns, as Table 3–20 shows for $t = 1, 2$, and 3. In the table, a grouping, such as (a, b, c) for $t = 2$, implies that the output from a gate, a, is connected to an input on each of the gates a, b, and c in the next layer; the same applies for the outputs of gates b and c. In Figure 3–43, the grouping g_2 of the single-fault-tolerant groupings was used for the X inputs, while the grouping g_1 was used for

---

* The inputs to the interwoven logic circuit must also be independently replicated if the circuit is to tolerate input faults.

FIGURE 3–43
Fault tolerance via interwoven logic

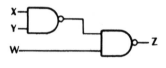

a. Nonredundant circuit

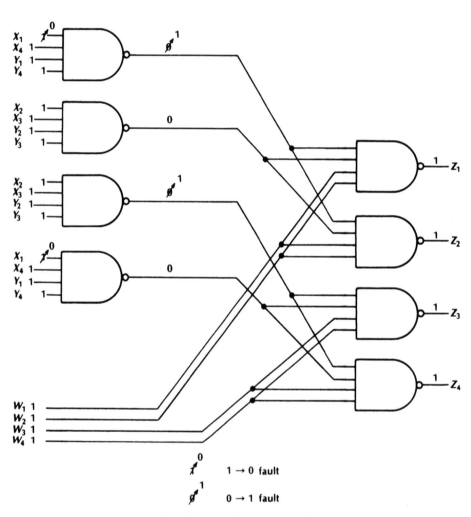

b. Fault-tolerant interwoven circuit

TABLE 3–20
Groupings (g_i) for interweaving patterns for t = 1, 2, and 3

	Single-Fault Tolerant $t = 1, B = 2, R = 4$	Double-Fault Tolerant $t = 2, B = 3, R = 9$	Triple-Fault Tolerant $t = 3, B = 4, R = 16$
	$g_1 = (1,2)(3,4)$	$g_1 = (1,2,3)(4,5,6)(7,8,9)$	$g_1 = (1,2,3,4)(5,6,7,8)(9,10,11,12)(13,14,15,16)$
	$g_2 = (1,4)(2,3)$	$g_2 = (1,4,7)(2,5,8)(3,6,9)$	$g_2 = (1,5,9,13)(2,6,10,14)(3,7,11,15)(4,8,12,16)$
	$g_3 = (1,3)(2,4)$	$g_3 = (1,6,8)(5,7,3)(9,2,4)$	$g_3 = (1,6,12,15)(2,5,11,16)(3,8,9,14)(4,7,10,12)$

Source: From Pierce, 1965.

the inputs to the second level of gates. A critical 0-to-1 input fault to one layer is masked out by the next layer; thus, the input fault in signal X does not cause an error in output Z. If the same interweaving pattern had been used in both layers, the fault would have been propagated.

The need for a shorthand notation of interwoven logic is demonstrated in Figure 3–43, in which a simple nonredundant two-gate logic function is transformed into a complex tangle of gates and interconnections. Figure 3–44 illustrates the notation to be used. A symbol for replicated gates is formed by using a double line for the gate symbol edge. The term g_i inside the symbol indicates the weaving pattern that is to be used to connect the replicated gates to the previous layer.

The gate in Figure 3–44 is a gate used in *quadded logic*, where $t = 1$, $B = 2$, and $R = 4$; however, the notation can also be generalized to higher redundancy. Quadded logic was first introduced by Tryon [1962] for use with AND, OR, and NOT logic. There are two problems with the use of this family of logic gates if two-level correction is to be assured at all times. First, the AND and OR logic levels must be strictly alternated. Second, because the NOT gate (inverter) has only one input and no subcritical faults, it does not provide any fault masking. Also, when a NOT is placed between AND and

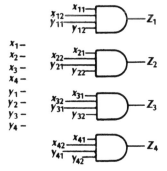

a. Symbol for quadded gate, with inputs woven with pattern g_i

b. Expansion of quadded gate into four physical gates, with inputs x_{jk} and y_{jk}

jk \ g_i	g_1	g_2	g_3
11	1	1	1
12	2	4	3
21	1	2	2
22	2	3	4
31	3	2	1
32	4	3	3
41	3	1	2
42	4	4	4

c. Table of interweaving patterns g_i, and the relation for each pattern between the inputs to gate j(x_{jk} and y_{jk}) and the output gate number (k) of the previous stage

FIGURE 3–44 *Weaving notation*

OR layers, the effect is to make the two layers it joins identical, since what would normally be a subcritical output fault is inverted into a critical input error.

The two difficulties can be overcome in part by rearrangement of the logic function and, in part, by the insertion of identity-AND or -OR gates (one leg fixed at 1 and 0, respectively) where appropriate (see Figure 3–46b). Requiring alternating AND/OR gate levels is not a problem when NOR gates [Jensen, 1963] or NAND gates are used in implementing quadded logic. Figures 3–45a and 3–46b show NAND and quadded NAND gate realizations of the same circuit. Finally, the principles of two-layer masking also apply to single-layer fault-correcting technologies such as majority gate logic.

Radial logic [Klaschka, 1969] is a variation of interwoven logic that offers single-fault tolerance with a gate redundancy factor of only two. This is possible if the gates used fail in a nonsymmetric (fail-safe) manner. In particular, for radial logic based on NOR gates, the gates used must be unlikely to experience 0-to-1 failures at their outputs. In other words, it is assumed that critical input faults cannot occur. If this is the case, the fault is corrected at the next duplicated stage. Klaschka gave RTL implementations of NOR gates that are unlikely to have 0-to-1 output failures.

Freeman and Metze [1972] proposed a form of interwoven logic called *dotted logic*, derived from the use of dotted outputs of NAND and/or NOR gates (such as utilizing the wire-or that results from connecting the outputs of TTL open-collector gates). Although gates are implicit at the dotted connections, the actual gate count as well as the number of interconnections is greatly reduced.

Finally, Pradhan and Reddy [1974a] proposed a design method using two-level AND and OR logic that can tolerate subcritical faults both on its inputs and caused by internal failures. As in radial logic, gates with asymmetric failure modes are required. In this scheme, the inputs that result in a logical-one output are coded in a distance-*d* code. At most, then, duplication of the inputs is required. Further reductions in

FIGURE 3–45

Implementations of the logic function $f = d(\overline{ab} + \overline{c})$

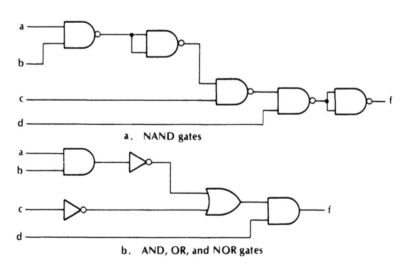

a. NAND gates

b. AND, OR, and NOR gates

FIGURE 3–46
*Quadded imple-
mentations of the
circuit of Figure
3–45*

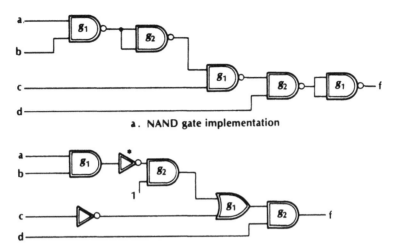

a. NAND gate implementation

b. AND, OR, NOR gates implementation (note the extra inverter, marked
by an asterisk)

complexity can be achieved through the use of don't-care output conditions for some
input combinations. The resulting' design tolerates up to $(d - 1)$ internal subcritical
faults, given a distance-d coded input. Alternatively, a total of t faults (combined
internal and external) can be tolerated, where $(2t + 1 \le d)$.

Reliability modeling of interwoven logic can be extremely complex, and no models
will be given here. Pierce [1965] developed a complex method of obtaining a lower
limit on the reliability. Jensen [1963] developed a cut-set model for quadded logic
(Chapter 5 discussed reliability modeling with the use of cut sets). Abraham [1975]
developed a combinatorial procedure for modeling interwoven logic, as well as an
easily calculable formula for providing a tight lower limit on the network reliability.

In addition to reliability, there is another factor to be considered in the employment of interwoven logic. By the very nature of internal fault masking, the logic
network that results is difficult or impossible to diagnose. When a fault occurs, no
notice is given unless the outputs are in error. Even with outputs in error, diagnosis is
difficult without probing the internal signals. Tryon [1962] suggested a possible solution: removing the power from some of the redundant gates, thereby forcing their
outputs to values that effectively eliminate them from the network. At the same time,
some of the redundant inputs must be neutralized.

Coded State Machines. The interwoven logic techniques can be used to implement
sequential (synchronous or asynchronous) logic. However, there are other techniques
that could result in lower redundancy and simpler designs. The basic concept, first
proposed by Armstrong [1961], is that the state of the machine, represented by its

state variables, can be encoded in an error-correction code. Thus, any fault can be masked if it causes a correctable error in the state of the machine.*

Figure 3–47a shows a generic form for a finite state machine. If input errors are ignored, there are two sources of error in the machine: the combinational logic and the memory elements. Figure 3–47b demonstrates Armstrong's solution to faults in the combinational logic. The logic network is split into k independent units, each devoted to producing a subset of p of the output signals. An additional $(n - k)$ subunits produce independently generated sets of error-code check bits for the k functional outputs. Thus, the net output of this circuit is p parallel (n,k) coded signals. If $p = 1$, the result is a single set of output signals that forms an (n,k) code word. Conceptually, the check-bit units are not difficult to design, for the check-bit functions can be derived as the XOR of the appropriate output-bit functions.

Combinational logic of the type illustrated in Figure 3–47a is used to provide both coded output signals and coded feedback (next-state) signals for the machine. The decoder/corrector for the state signals is placed between the memory elements and the current state inputs to the combinational logic. In this way, faults in both the combinational logic and the memory elements can be tolerated. In a companion paper to Armstrong's, Ray-Chaudhuri [1961] developed a class of minimally redundant codes tailored to this application.

Armstrong showed that, when coupled with maintenance (faulty component replacement), a state machine implemented in this fashion has a greatly improved reliability over that of the equivalent nonredundant version. He also stated that for some large systems this technique yields a redundancy at least as great as for triplication, but that for others it may be considerably less. The actual redundancy can be determined only by a detailed design.

Others have worked on this concept since Armstrong's paper. Frank and Yau [1966] proposed designing sequential machines using error-code state assignments. Mandelbaum [1972b] suggested a scheme in which, given a sequential machine M, a simpler machine M' is derived into which the states of M can be mapped. M' is operated independently of M, but uses the same inputs, and it supplies the check bits for the state encoding. Meyer [1971] discussed state assignment and design realization for tolerance of memory-cell faults. Russo [1965] proposed fault-tolerant counters with distance-3 coded states. Reed and Chiang [1970] discussed error-coded state counters and also offered a synthesis procedure for fault-tolerant sequential circuits.

Larsen and Reed [1972] presented a synthesis procedure for fault-tolerant sequential machines. Using an analysis based on this procedure, they demonstrated that for a given ability to tolerate faults, replication is more reliable as well as simpler to implement. Conversely, they found that for a fixed complexity (gate count, cost), schemes that use orthogonal (majority-logic decodable) codes are more reliable. Os-

---

* The following discussion primarily concerns synchronous machines. In asynchronous machines, state assignment problems occur because of the possibility of races, hazards, and the like. However, Pradhan and Reddy [1974b] have extended these principles to asynchronous machines, and Pradhan [1978b] described a method of realizing fault-tolerant asynchronous coded-state machines using read-only memories.

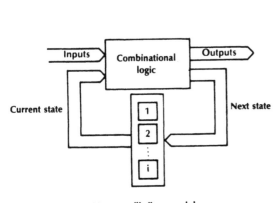

a. Generic design for a sequential circuit (In asynchronous circuits the memory elements are replaced by delays.)

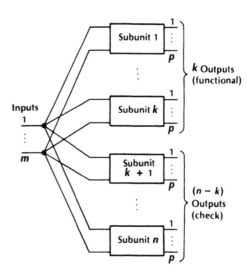

b. Division of logic network into subunits for outputs in k independent sets

FIGURE 3–47 *Error detection in coded state machines [(b) From Armstrong, 1961; © 1961 AT&T]*

man and Weiss [1973] developed a technique that can be used to reduce the redundancy in fault-tolerant logic. In Figure 3–47a it can be seen that considerable redundancy is incurred by separate generation of the outputs; their technique allows some of the circuitry to be shared between modules generating the output functions. If this sharing is performed properly, the reliability is not affected and there are considerable savings. Osman and Weiss applied this technique to both triplication and parity-check codes.

HARDWARE DYNAMIC REDUNDANCY TECHNIQUES

Another approach to increased reliability utilizes redundancy in a dynamic way. Dynamic redundancy techniques involve the *reconfiguration* of system components in response to failures. The reconfiguration prevents failures from contributing their effects to the system operation. In many instances, reconfiguration amounts to disconnecting the damaged units from the system. If fault masking is used as part of the dynamic redundancy scheme, the removal of failed components may be postponed until enough failures have accumulated to threaten an impending nonmaskable failure.

Reconfiguration is triggered either by internal detection of faults in the damaged subunit or by detection of errors in its output.* Thus, fault-detection techniques (with

---

* Reconfiguration can be performed either automatically by the system itself (on-line repair) or manually by operations or maintenance personnel (off-line repair). In the first case, the system experiences a temporary pause before operation continues; in the second, the halt is longer and may require complete reinitialization. Hence, on-line repair improves both reliability and availability, whereas off-line repair usually only increases availability. The emphasis in this section is upon on-line repair.

or without masking) form the basis of dynamic redundancy. A system's chance of a successful reconfiguration is greatly dependent on its fault-detection ability. Three issues are involved in the employment of fault detection in a reconfigurable system. The first is the confinement of fault effects before unrecoverable damage occurs; the second is fault detection; and the third is correct diagnosis of the failure location, so that the faulty unit—and only the faulty unit—is marked for remedial action (removal and/or replacement). Thus, the two fault-detection criteria of coverage and diagnosability (see the earlier section on fault-detection techniques) are important factors in the choice of a detection technique. Detection coverage in particular is commonly used in deriving the reliability formula of a dynamically redundant system. In modeling dynamically redundant systems, coverage is often generalized to mean the probability of a successful reconfiguration; successful fault detection then becomes only one of the factors in determining coverage, along with the probabilities of successful error confinement and resource switching.

The following subsections present several dynamic redundancy techniques that utilize a combination of fault detection, fault masking, and reconfiguration. The first subsection discusses methods that use duplication for detection as well as for fault tolerance; the second treats N-modular redundancy-based designs. Duplication and N-modular redundancy-based reconfiguration require massive amounts of redundancy solely for error detection (and/or correction). Other, less-redundant forms of fault detection (correction) can also provide a basis for dynamic redundancy. The more hardware-efficient detection techniques (such as parity, ECCs, and timers) can be used to monitor the health of individual modules. Such detectors can be located either inside or outside the modules they monitor. They can exist either in hardware or software. The subsections on backup sparing, graceful degradation, and reconfiguration present reconfiguration techniques that are usually based on the less redundant detection methods. Backup sparing is the provision of spare units that remain unused until an active unit fails. In graceful degradation, the functionality and/or performance is allowed to degrade as parts of the system fail and are removed without replacement. The subsection on reconfiguration presents miscellaneous dynamic redundancy techniques that do not fit into the categories provided by the other sections.

The effect of transient errors on the various reconfiguration techniques is not discussed here. If there is no specific mechanism for determining that an error is caused by a transient, perfectly good modules may be switched out when a transient occurs. Fortunately, a technique exists that is common to most of the reconfiguration methods discussed here. This technique, called *retry*, returns the module initially diagnosed as failed to the system for another chance. Detection of an error immediately after the module is returned to service is a good indication that the module is in fact defective.

The final subsection on dynamic redundancy discusses recovery, the actions taken after reconfiguration to erase failure effects and restore the state of the system and the process(es) it was executing before the failure. Recovery is usually performed by special software, but often requires some support by hardware mechanisms.

Reconfigurable Duplication

Fault detection by duplication and comparison was discussed earlier in this chapter. In a static configuration, a duplicated system does not provide fault tolerance, for only disagreement can be determined in the presence of a fault. Two enhancements to the duplicated system can, however, produce fault tolerance.* The first enhancement needed is the ability to determine which of the two modules is faulty if a disagreement is detected. The second enhancement is the ability to disconnect the faulty module and at the same time disable the comparison element. Thus, upon fault detection (mismatch), diagnosis determines the faulty copy, which is then removed from service. The resulting simplex system continues to function.

Figure 3–48a illustrates the concept of reconfigurable duplication. In the figure, only one of the duplicated units (the active unit) is connected to the system outputs. The other (standby) unit is functioning in parallel with the active unit, but is not connected to the outputs. In practice, the duplicate modules are often resident on

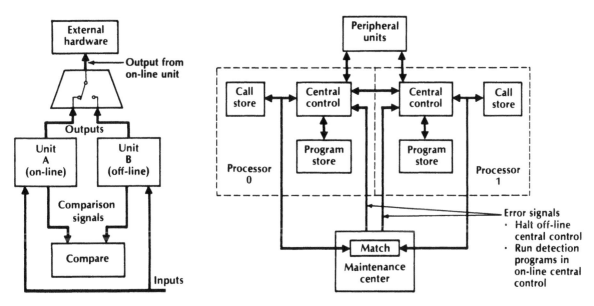

a. Generic design, where a detected mismatch during comparison of characteristic signals triggers reconfiguration

b. AT&T ESS-2, where two processors run synchronously and comparison of the call store input registers is performed constantly

FIGURE 3–48 *Reconfigurable duplication*

* In this discussion, duplication is considered only as the basis for fault detection. This form of duplication should not be confused with "duplication," in which an extra copy is presented as a standby spare, and is not used for fault detection by comparison. The latter form is discussed in subsequent subsections.

the same bus (or buses), and the switching function is performed by the bus interface unit in each module.

Fault Determination. When a fault is detected by a mismatch, there are several means of determining the faulty copy and switching it out. Four methods are discussed here. The first is to run a diagnostic program. In the AT&T ESS-2 (Chapter 8), for example, the active processor runs a self-diagnostic program. If the diagnostic is failed, control is passed to the standby processor. The faulty processor is taken off line to run maintenance programs that facilitate its rapid repair. Figure 3–48b shows a block diagram of the ESS-2 organization.

Another means of identifying the faulty copy is to include self-checking capabilities in each module. The joint occurrence of an internally detected fault and a mismatch provides immediate determination of the faulty copy. The use of comparison in addition to self-checking provides more coverage than self-checking alone. The UDET 7116 telephone switching system control [Morganti, Coppadoro, and Ceru, 1978], for example, uses a set of internal hardware checkers (such as parity or timers) to automatically switch a faulty CPU out of service. The primary detection mechanism in the UDET 7116, however, is duplication. When a mismatch occurs with no internal alarm indication, both CPUs are taken off line and forced to run diagnostics. The first to successfully complete its self-diagnosis becomes the active CPU. The AT&T ESS-1, -1A, and -2 processors also use internal self-checking in conjunction with duplication. Finally, the internal detection mechanisms can also be used in conjunction with diagnostic software.

The AT&T 3B20D [Becker, 1983; Wallace and Barnes, 1984], the latest in the line of ESS processors, also utilizes dual CPUs. However, these units have extensive self-checking, and the duplicate processor is used as a standby. The standby's memory is kept consistent via a memory update link. See Chapter 8 for more details.

As mentioned earlier, the Stratus XA2000 series of fault-tolerant multiprocessors uses a pair of 68000 family processors running in parallel on each processor board for fault detection. The fault tolerance is obtained by using a second processor board. One board is the active unit, and the other serves as a standby. When a mismatch is detected on the primary processor board, the standby processor pair takes its place. See Chapter 8 for more information.

A third approach to determining the faulty processor is to use a watch-dog timer. In the AT&T ESS-2, for example, the active processor must reset a timer periodically. If it fails to do so, the timer automatically invokes a change of control to the standby processor. Thus, the timer protects the system when the active processor becomes stuck while attempting to perform the diagnostic after a mismatch has occurred. Timers are used in another fashion in the AT&T ESS-1A. When the current configuration does not function, a set of timers is used to force a sequence of reconfigurations until a working configuration is found.

The last method of fault determination is the use of an outside arbiter to control the configuration. In the COMTRAC railroad traffic control computer [Ihara et al., 1978], a mismatch forces both processors to run identical test programs. The test program exercises the entire processor in the course of calculating a single constant. If a failure is present, there is a high probability that the calculation will result in a wrong answer. The results from the two processors are compared with a stored constant by a special controller (called the dual system controller, or DSC), as shown in Figure 3–49a. Based on the results of the test, the DSC performs the proper configuration action as illustrated in Figure 3–49b. Designers at Boeing Aerospace used a similar concept in a duplication-based design of a prototype aerospace computer [Wachter, 1975]. In the Boeing design, the reconfiguration control logic can be assessed only by a "good" machine, that is, one that can successfully construct two levels of key words. The key construction process is designed to make successful key construction by a faulty processor unlikely.

Use of Synchronization. The problems of synchronization with replicated processes has been discussed previously (see the subsections on duplication and N-modular redundancy with voting). Three examples of different synchronization methods that can be applied to reconfigurable duplication systems are presented here. In the first, the duplicated modules perform in lockstep to a common clock, which is synchronized at the microcycle level. This method is used on the AT&T ESS-1, -1A, and -2 processors, as well as the UDET 7116. Comparisons in these telephone-switching control processors are performed at the end of each clock period.

The AXE telephone-switching control [Ossfeldt and Jonsson, 1980] uses a different method of synchronization. Each of its two processors is formed of asynchronous functional units (e.g., microinstruction generator, ALU) that communicate via a central processor bus (CPB), as shown in Figure 3–50. One of these units is the update and match unit (UPM), which performs the detection function. On most microinstructions, data from the active processor CPB is input to a buffer in the standby processor's UPM. The data are held in the buffer to await comparison with the data on the standby processor's CPB. Synchronization of the two processors is performed by the UPMs, which keep a count of the bus cycles. The UPM on the faster side periodically brings its processor back into synchronization by simulating a busy signal on the control lines of its own CPB.

A third method of synchronization is used by the COMTRAC system. Synchronization is maintained at the program task level. The dual system controller (DSC) is used to ensure that both processors are performing the same calculations. When both computers have finished the calculation, the DSC compares the two results. If a mismatch occurs, the DSC then invokes the diagnosis mode discussed earlier. Figure 3–49b illustrates the procedure.

A simple reliability model for a reconfigurable duplication system with individual module reliability R_m is

$$R_{sys} = [R_m^2 + 2CR_m(1 - R_m)]R_k \tag{2}$$

In Eq. 2, R_k is the reliability of the control, switching, and matching circuitry. C is the coverage factor, and represents the combined probability of successful fault detection and reconfiguration. A system with reconfigurable duplication can achieve increased

FIGURE 3–49
*Synchronization,
matching, and re-
configuration in
the COMTRAC
computer, with
synchronization
and matching per-
formed at the task
level [From Ihara et
al., 1978; © 1978
IEEE]*

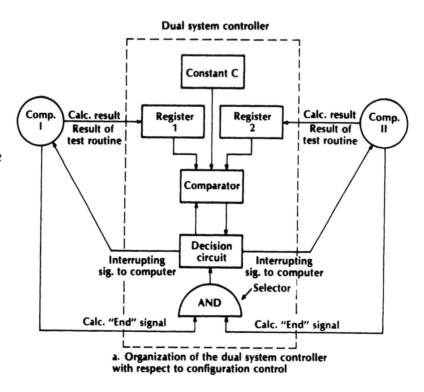

**a. Organization of the dual system controller
with respect to configuration control**

reliability and availability if a faulty module can be repaired while the rest of the system remains on line. In such a case, the model of Eq. 2 is pessimistic. The more complex modeling techniques of Chapter 5 (such as Markov modeling) are needed to properly evaluate a system with repair.

Reconfigurable NMR

One of the drawbacks of *N*-modular redundancy with voting (NMR) is that fault-masking ability deteriorates as more copies fail. The faulty modules eventually outvote the good modules. However, an NMR system could continue to function if the known bad modules could be discounted in the vote. Two methods of reconfiguration based on NMR realize this potential. The first, hybrid redundancy, replaces failed modules with previously unused spares. The second modifies the voting process dynamically as the system deteriorates. The latter method actually encompasses a variety of techniques, which can be loosely classified under the term *adaptive voting*. Both hybrid redundancy and adaptive voting depend upon detection of disagreements and the ability to determine the identity of the module(s) not agreeing with the majority.

Hybrid Redundancy. This technique obtains its name from the fact that it is the wedding of two redundancy techniques: *N*-modular redundancy with voting (discussed earlier)

FIGURE 3–49
Continued

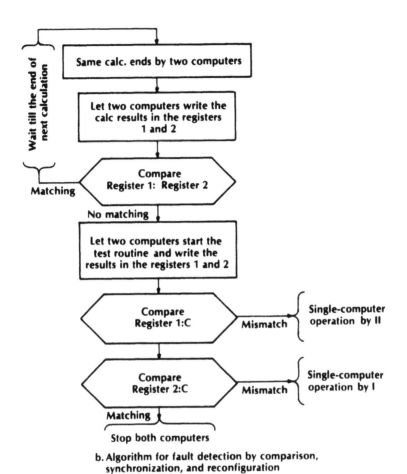

b. Algorithm for fault detection by comparison,
synchronization, and reconfiguration

and backup sparing (discussed later). Figure 3–51 illustrates the basic concept. A "core" of N identical modules is in use at any one time, with their outputs voted upon to produce the system output. When a disagreement is detected, the module or modules in the minority are considered to be failed and are replaced by the equivalent number of spare modules. Initially, the system contains a total of $(N + S)$ modules. As long as there are never more than $t = \lfloor N/2 \rfloor$ failed modules in the core before reconfiguration can take place, the system can tolerate the failure of $P = (t + S)$ of its modules. Thus, assuming the reliability of the modules on standby is the same as for those on-line, the system reliability is:

$$R_{sys} = R_{vsd} \sum_{i=0}^{P} {_{n+s}C_i}\, R_m^{(N+S-i)}(1 - R_m)^i \tag{3}$$

R_m is the individual module reliability, and R_{vsd} is the reliability of the unit composed of the voter, switch, and disagreement detector (VSD unit). Eq. 3 is a simple model. It

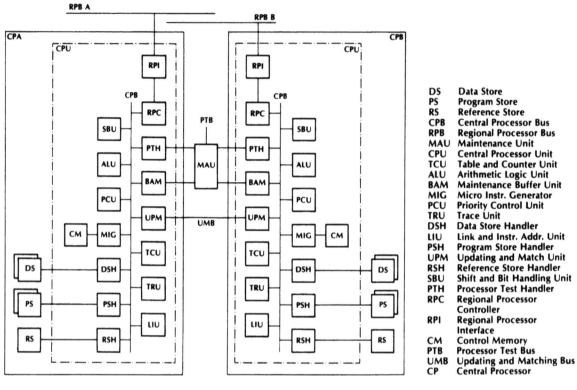

DS	Data Store
PS	Program Store
RS	Reference Store
CPB	Central Processor Bus
RPB	Regional Processor Bus
MAU	Maintenance Unit
CPU	Central Processor Unit
TCU	Table and Counter Unit
ALU	Arithmetic Logic Unit
BAM	Maintenance Buffer Unit
MIG	Micro Instr. Generator
PCU	Priority Control Unit
TRU	Trace Unit
DSH	Data Store Handler
LIU	Link and Instr. Addr. Unit
PSH	Program Store Handler
UPM	Updating and Match Unit
RSH	Reference Store Handler
SBU	Shift and Bit Handling Unit
PTH	Processor Test Handler
RPC	Regional Processor Controller
RPI	Regional Processor Interface
CM	Control Memory
PTB	Processor Test Bus
UMB	Updating and Matching Bus
CP	Central Processor

FIGURE 3–50 *Organization of the duplicated processor in the AXE telephone-switching control processor [From Ossfeldt and Jonsson, 1980; © 1980 IEEE]*

FIGURE 3–51
Basic organization of a hybrid-redundant system

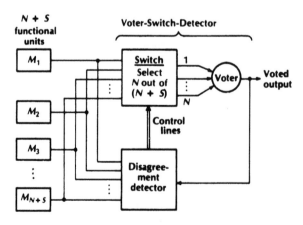

assumes that as long as there are spares remaining, reconfiguration occurs before there are enough failed modules in the core to outvote the good modules. The model also does not take compensating failures into account. One final factor not considered is that the standby units may be unpowered until they are switched in. A module in an unpowered state will probably have a lower failure rate; if so, Eq. 3 will provide a pessimistic estimation of the system reliability.

Mathur and Avizienis [1970] derived a reliability model for hybrid redundant systems that takes the standby failure rates into account. They then used the model to examine the trade-offs between N, S, and R_m. The VSD unit is assumed to be perfect ($R_{vsd} = 1$). Figure 3–52 demonstrates the use of the model for a hybrid TMR system with up to six spare modules. In Figure 3–52a, the standby failure rate is assumed to be equal to the on-line failure rate, with the result being that a system with one spare is more reliable than a simplex system if $R_m > 0.23$. Figure 3–52b assumes that the standby failure rate is only 10 percent of the on-line rate. The crossover point has shifted, and a system with one spare is more reliable than the simplex system if $R_m > 0.17$. Another result of the model is that for a system with one spare, a TMR system ($N = 3$) is more reliable than an NMR system ($N > 3$) if $R_m < 0.55$. For a system with two spares, a TMR system is better than an NMR system if $R_m < 0.62$.

Examination of Equation 3 shows that hybrid system reliability is greatly dependent on the switch complexity. If every spare can be connected with every voter (total assignment), it can be seen that as the core size (N) and the number of spares (S) grow, the switch complexity grows even more rapidly. Eventually, the switch unreliability dominates the reliability of the system, and the hybrid system becomes less reliable than a simplex system. Siewiorek and McCluskey [1973a] demonstrated that total assignment is not necessary. Assuming a perfect switch, the same reliability is achieved even if only ($\lceil N/2 \rceil + 1$) of the voter inputs can be connected to every spare module. (Note that for $N = 3$, this is the same as total assignment.) Because no switch can in practice be perfect, such a partial connection strategy tends to be more reliable

FIGURE 3–52

Plots of hybrid TMR system reliability (R_s) vs. individual module reliability (R_m). S is the number of spares. [From Mathur and Avizienis, 1970; reprinted by permission of AFIPS]

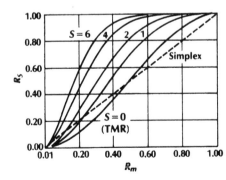

a. System with standby failure rate equal to on-line failure rate

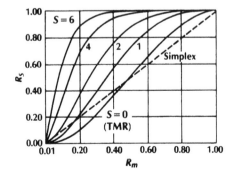

b. System with standby failure rate 10% of on-line failure rate

than the total assignment strategy; the switch for partial connection is less complex and thus more reliable.

In a companion paper, Siewiorek and McCluskey [1973b] presented a design for a low-complexity switch. Figure 3–53 shows the iterative cell array switch for a TMR core. The switch works in the following fashion. A clock pulse causes the outputs of the modules to appear, and the outputs of the N core modules are gated to the voter inputs. The same clock pulse, suitably delayed in accordance with the VSD unit propagation delays, loads disagreement signals into the condition flip-flops. Based on the condition of its corresponding module (agree/disagree with the voted output) and the condition of the iterative cells to its left (0, 1, 2, or [3 or more] good modules present), each iterative cell decides whether to connect its module to the voter, and if so, to which voter input. Table 3–21 contains the cell state and output tables for the iterative cells used in the design of Figure 3–53.

One of the problems with an iterative cell switch of the form of Figure 3–53 is the propagation delay through the chain of iterative cells, particularly for large N and S. Siewiorek and McCluskey proposed three different solutions to the problem: carry bypass, carry lookahead, and redesign of the cell. The first two solutions are similar to those found in fast adders. The last solution, cell redesign, was shown to be the fastest for $(N + S) < 12$, while the carry bypass method was shown to be the least complex. Finally, the iterative cell switch (or any other hybrid redundancy switch) was shown to be simpler if a threshold voter with $(N + S)$ inputs is used. The threshold is set at $\lceil (N + 1)/2 \rceil$, and the switching function is realized merely by using AND gates to connect modules to the voter inputs.

Siewiorek and McCluskey [1973b] modeled the cost and complexity of several different approaches to the design of switches for hybrid redundancy, and found the iterative cell switch to be generally superior. Ingle and Siewiorek [1973b, 1976] proposed reliability models for various switch designs. Assuming that switch complexity grows linearly with N and S (the iterative cell method approaches this growth), they found that there is a certain number of spares for which reliability is maximized; beyond that number, the reliability decreases. In addition, they found that maximum reliability for most hybrid TMR systems is reached with one or two spares. Finally, they determined that hybrid TMR systems may have lower mission times than simple TMR systems. Ogus [1973, 1974] obtained similar results in another analysis of iterative cell switch reliability.*

Adaptive Voting. Adaptive voting is a technique in which, for modules i, the voter inputs n_i are weighted by the factors a_i. In the pure form of adaptive voting, the decision is based on the sum $\Sigma a_i n_i$, using a threshold detector. The a_i are modified over time by the accumulated history of disagreements and fault detection. In practical digital systems, the a_i are usually zero or one, and the voting may or may not be performed by a threshold voter. Thus, hybrid redundancy can be considered a form of adaptive

---

* A derivation of complexity and reliability models for hybrid redundancy is presented in Chapter 5.

FIGURE 3–53
An iterative cell switch for a TMR core and two standby spares [From Siewiorek and McCluskey, 1973; © 1973 IEEE]

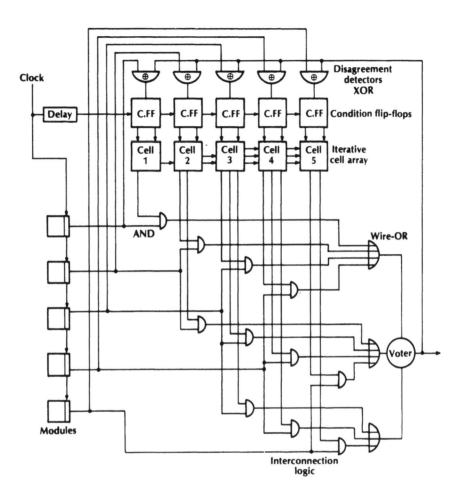

TABLE 3–21
Cell state and output tables for the iterative cell switch network of Figure 3–53

| | Cell State Table | | | Output Table | |
| | C_i Failed | C_i Functional | | C_i Failed | C_i Functional |
Current State	0	1	Current State	0	1
A (0)*	A	B	A (0)*	000	100
B (1)	B	C	B (1)	000	010
C (2)	C	D	C (2)	000	001
D (3+)	D	D	D (3+)	000	000
	Next state			$V_1^i V_2^i V_3^i$	

V_j^i: Connect module i to voter input j.

* Number of previous cells functional.
Source: From Siewiorek and McCluskey, 1973b; © 1973 IEEE.

voting, with the a_i determined by the switch. Two other proposed forms of adaptive voting techniques are discussed here: NMR/simplex and self-purging redundancy.

NMR/Simplex. In NMR/simplex systems [Mathur, 1971a; Mathur and DeSousa, 1975], the initial configuration is conventional NMR. When one module fails, it and one other module are removed from the system, leaving an $(N - 2)$ modular redundancy system. The removal of two modules preserves the property that all votes are unambiguous; no tie is possible. Eventually, the system deteriorates to a simplex system. C.vmp (see Chapter 10) or any other TMR system capable of independent (nonvoting) mode operation has the potential of being a TMR/simplex system with only minor modifications. Upon detection of a failure, a TMR/simplex version of C.vmp would go into independent mode operation, with the on-line processor selected from the two remaining processors. The NMR/simplex concept can be extended to allow the intermediate step of duplicate operation (detection with a standby spare) before the final step of simplex operation is necessary.

Self-Purging. Figure 3–54 illustrates self-purging redundancy [Losq, 1976].* A comparison of Figures 3–53 and 3–54 shows a similarity between self-purging redundancy and hybrid redundancy implemented with an iterative cell switch. This is particularly true if the hybrid redundant design incorporates the threshold voter simplifications mentioned previously. In self-purging redundancy, all P modules are initially connected to the voter, and are removed only when they disagree with the voted output. The delayed clock line avoids spurious resets caused by delay in the voter. Module retry (in case of transient errors) and system initialization are accomplished via the retry line. For hybrid redundancy with a TMR core, the iterative cell switch for each module requires eight gates and a flip-flop, including the AND gate for gating the module output to the voter input. (This is for a threshold voter only. The majority voter iterative cell switch requires even more gates.) The self-purging switch, on the other hand, requires only three gates and a flip-flop for each module, regardless of the number of redundant modules in the system. The decreased complexity of the self-purging redundancy switch is one reason for its being more reliable than the hybrid redundancy switch. The other factor is that a single failure in the self-purging redundancy switch element attached to one module will not affect the other switch elements and modules. In contrast, a failure in an iterative cell may cause an error that will propagate to other switch cells via the carry lines.

The threshold for a P-module self-purging system voter can be as low as 1 if 0-to-1 errors cannot occur, and as high as $(P - 1)$ if 1-to-0 failures are impossible. If 0-to-1 errors do occur, the threshold must be higher than 1. This is particularly true if stuck-at-1 failures can occur in a switch output. Losq found that in general, the optimum threshold for a self-purging system is equivalent to half the number of remaining good

---

* The switching circuitry in Figure 3–54 is altered from Losq's design by the addition of the delayed clock line and the attached AND gates. This is necessary to avoid spurious flip-flop resets caused by the propagation delay of the voter. The AND gates can be eliminated if clocked SR flip-flops are used.

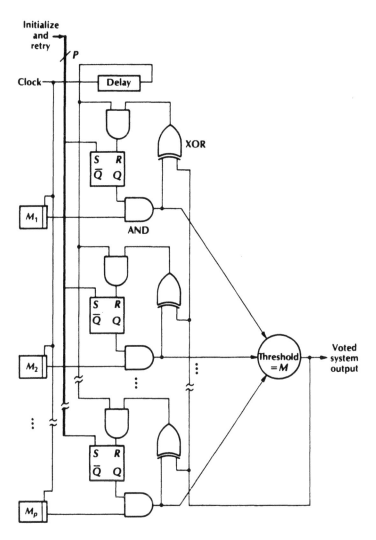

modules. The variable threshold can be obtained by using a threshold voter with *P* weight-2 inputs and *P* weight-1 inputs (or a threshold voter with 3*P* weight-1 inputs). The weights of the inputs are the weights used when summing inputs to determine whether the threshold is reached (weighted sum); thus, a weight-2 input counts twice as much as a weight-1 input. The $\overline{Q}$ output of each condition flip-flop, shown uncon- nected in Figure 3–54, is connected to a weight-1 input; the gated module output is connected to a weight-2 input (or two weight-1 inputs).

After deriving an accurate and simple reliability model for self-purging redundancy, Losq demonstrated that if the standby failure rate is equal to the active failure rate, the self-purging design is potentially more reliable than the equivalent hybrid redundant design. Unfortunately, threshold gates are analog circuit elements; large threshold gates are not available as standard integrated circuits. As a result, threshold voters must be implemented either from discrete components or from standard logic gates and they become prohibitively complex for even moderate numbers of inputs. Although it was not considered in the preceding analysis, this practical limitation on threshold voters must be taken into account when considering the use of self-purging redundancy or any other technique that includes a threshold voter. For a large number (P) of redundant modules, a self-purging system requires a complex (thus, less reliable) and expensive threshold voter. In a hybrid system with the same number of redundant modules, however, the threshold voter complexity is limited because it has only N inputs, not the $(N + S) = P$ inputs required for the self-purging system; the hybrid system may thus be more reliable and less complex than the self-purging system.

Distributed Voting. *Sift-out redundancy* [DeSousa and Mathur, 1978] is proposed as an alternative to hybrid and self-purging redundancy techniques. With N-redundant modules in the initial configuration, sift-out redundancy can tolerate up to $(N - 2)$ module failures. This is comparable to the fault tolerance of hybrid redundancy with a TMR core and to self-purging redundancy (voter threshold = 2). The major difference in sift-out redundancy is that there is no actual voting element; the bad module outputs are eliminated by distributed pairwise comparison. As a result, the restoring organ for sift-out redundancy is potentially simpler than that for hybrid and self-purging redundancies.

Figure 3–55 shows the basic configuration for a system with sift-out redundancy.

FIGURE 3–55
Basic configuration for sift-out redundancy [From Mathur and DeSousa, 1978; © 1978 IEEE]

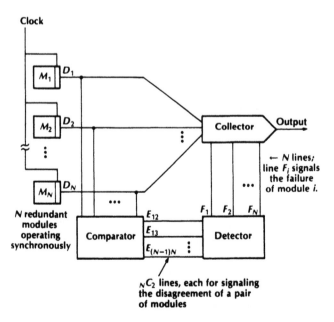

The comparator, used to detect disagreements between all possible pairs of the functional modules, contains $_NC_2$ XOR gates. Using $_NC_2$ signal lines, the comparator signals the detector about which pairs are not in agreement. The detector uses these signals to identify the faulty module. Included in the detector are N memory cells; the ith cell is set when it is determined that the ith module has failed. The detector contains N flip-flops and $(_NC_2 + N)$ NOR gates. Finally, the collector uses the N detector outputs, each one signaling the state of a single module (failed/nonfailed), to determine which module outputs to ignore, and which to sift out. The collector requires $(N + 1)$ NOR gates. Figure 3–56 shows the design of a sift-out restoring organ, with $N = 4$. If XOR gate implementation requires X elemental (e.g., NOR) gates, the total complexity of the sift-out restoring organ is

$$(X + 1)_NC_2 + 2N + 1$$

NOR gates and N flip-flops. if $X = 1$, as assumed previously when comparing iterative

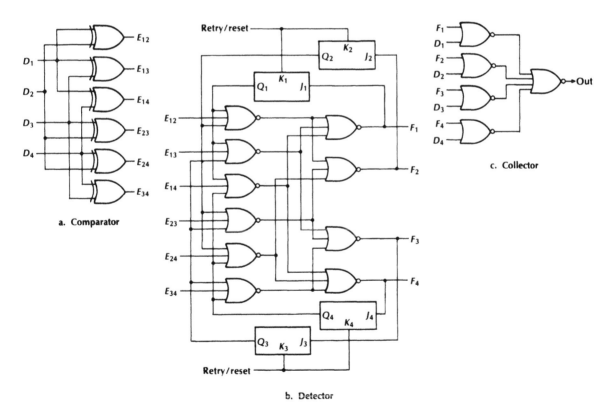

a. Comparator

b. Detector

c. Collector

FIGURE 3–56 *Design of restoring organ elements for sift-out redundancy scheme (Figure 3–55) using four redundant modules, with a fault tolerance of two module failures [From Mathur and DeSousa, 1978; © 1978 IEEE]*

TABLE 3–22 *Comparison of restoring organ complexity for hybrid TMR, self-purging, and sift-out redundancy techniques*

	Hybrid				Self-Purging				Sift-out	
N	Gates	T.V.* Gates	Total Gates	Flip-Flops	Gates	T.V.* Gates	Total Gates	Flip-Flops	Total Gates	Flip-Flops
4	36	10	46	4	12	10	22	4	21	4
5	45	16	59	5	15	16	31	5	31	5
6	54	23	83	6	18	23	41	6	43	6

*Approximate number of gates needed to implement N-input threshold voter with threshold of 2.
Assumptions:
Iterative cell hybrid redundancy, TMR core: $9N$ gates, N flip-flops, N-input threshold gate (threshold = 2)
Self-purging redundancy: $2N$ gates, N flip-flops, N-input threshold gate (threshold = 2)
Sift-out redundancy: $N^2 + N + 1$ gates, N flip-flops (threshold = 2)

cell-switch hybrid redundancy with self-purging redundancy, the total number of gates required is

$$N^2 + N + 1$$

Table 3–22 compares the restoring organ complexities for self-purging redundancy (voter threshold = 2), hybrid TMR redundancy (with a threshold gate voter), and sift-out redundancy for several amounts of redundancy. All the designs are able to tolerate up to $(N - 2)$ module failures. If the complexity of the threshold voters (the number of standard logic gates needed to implement one) is taken into account, it can be seen that sift-out redundancy requires less total restoring organ complexity than does hybrid redundancy for the range of N considered. Furthermore, sift-out redundancy and self-purging redundancy are roughly equal in terms of restoring organ complexity;* the major difference between the two techniques is that the self-purging redundancy scheme is vulnerable to some multiple stuck-at-1 failures, while the collector for sift-out redundancy (as shown in Figure 3–56) is vulnerable to some multiple stuck-at-0 failures. Unlike the self-purging restoring organ, however, the collector for sift-out redundancy can be designed (with little change in complexity) to be vulnerable to the form of stuck-at failures that are less likely to occur; that is, if stuck-at-0 failures are less likely than stuck-at-1 failures for the modules being used, then the collector design shown in Figure 3–56 should be used. The two possible collector designs are logical duals of each other.

Example Applications of NMR. Four examples of actual systems employing reconfigurable N-modular redundancy techniques are the JPL–STAR, the Space Shuttle computer, FTMP, and SIFT. Only the SIFT computer will be described in detail in later chapters. The test and repair process (TARP) in the JPL–STAR spacecraft computer [Avizienis

* Note that if each XOR gate requires four simpler gates to implement, sift-out redundancy is much less attractive because of its heavy use of XOR gates in the comparator.

et al., 1971] is hybrid redundant. The TARP must be ultrareliable, because it forms the "hard core"—the part of the system that must be functioning to enable the system to be reconfigured. The TARP design uses hybrid TMR with a threshold voter.

The Space Shuttle computer [Sklaroff, 1976; AWST, 1981] uses four of its five computers as a redundant set during critical mission phases, in a fashion similar to NMR/simplex; the fifth performs noncritical tasks in simplex mode and acts as a simplex backup for the primary system. The control outputs of the four primary computers are voted on at the control actuators. In addition, each computer listens to the outputs of the three other computers and compares those signals with its own via special software. If a computer detects a disagreement, it signals the disagreeing computer. The received disagreement detection signals are voted on in the redundancy management circuitry of each computer; if the vote is positive, the redundancy management unit removes its computer from service. Up to two computer failures can be tolerated in voting mode operation. After the second failure, the system converts to a duplex system that can survive one additional computer failure by using comparison and self-test methods. The fifth computer contains a backup flight software package written by Rockwell International, while the package running on the primary computer was written by IBM. This was done in case program bugs are encountered in the primary software during flight.

The FTMP computer [Hopkins, Smith, and Lala, 1978] is implemented from a set of processor/cache, memory, and I/O modules, all interconnected by redundant common serial buses (Figure 3–57a). Computations are performed by triads: three processor/caches* and three memories performing the same operation in voting mode and synchronized at the clock level. Voting is performed in each memory and in each processor/cache at its interface to the bus. Thus, because most processing utilizes the cache, voting is not necessarily performed at every clock cycle, but whenever data is transferred over the bus. Multiple triads can operate at the same time, thereby affording multiprocessing capabilities. Configuration is controlled by a redundant "bus guardian" in each module that controls access to the bus. Upon detection of a module failure, once the affected triad has completed its current operation, another triad forces reconfiguration of the affected triad. If sufficient spares are available, the failed module is replaced. Otherwise, the triad is broken up and the good modules are added to the pool of spares.

The SIFT computer (Chapter 10), on the other hand, is implemented from a set of self-contained computers and redundant buses (Figure 3–57b).[†] Each computer broadcasts its results, and software voting is performed in each computer at intermediate points in each NMR task. Synchronization and reconfiguration are also performed by software. Reconfiguration occurs by ignoring the broadcasts of known bad computers

---

* The term *cache* used in this context is misleading, for the memory unit attached to the processor does not perform quite the same function that a cache in a high-performance computer does. A better term would be *local* or *scratchpad* memory.

[†] The bus shown in Figure 3–57b is consistent with the SIFT design in Chapter 10. The current implementation of SIFT, however, does not use redundant buses. Instead, a totally connected scheme is used, in which a pair of unidirectional serial links connects each pair of computers (one link in each direction).

FIGURE 3–57
Block diagrams of the FTMP and SIFT flight control computers [From Rennels, 1980; © 1980 IEEE]

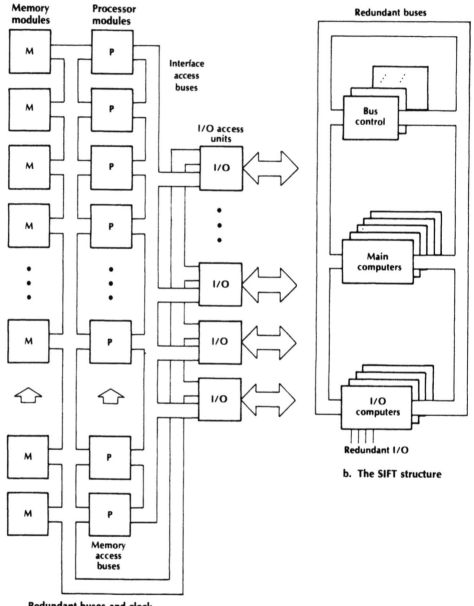

a. The FTMP structure

b. The SIFT structure

and reallocating tasks to nonfaulty computers. Critical tasks are performed in an NMR fashion (the redundancy N is variable, depending on the criticality); noncritical tasks can be executed by single computers.

Backup Sparing

In hybrid redundancy there is a core of N modules operating in parallel, with a voter determining the system output. In addition, there is initially a set, S, of backup spare modules that can be switched in to replace failed modules in the core. The concept of backup spares can also be combined with redundancy techniques other than N-modular redundancy.

In general, some means of failure detection is used to trigger the replacement of a failed on-line unit with a spare. The detection means can be internal (either through self-test or the use of self-checking circuitry), external (such as timer, parity check, reasonability check), or some combination of internal and external checks. As with hybrid redundancy, the switch complexity is an important factor. Another concern is the effectiveness of the failure-detection techniques used.

One widely used application of spares switching is in systems that are bit- or byte-sliced. Possibilities include memories physically assembled from a set of bit planes and ALUs made from ALU byte slices. Figure 3–58 shows a possible implementation of a byte-sliced system containing a single spare slice (M4). Initially, all the input multiplexers (MUX) are set to connect their right leg inputs to the modules, and the output MUXes are set to connect their left leg inputs to the system outputs. The MUXes could be replaced by pairs of open-collector AND gates with outputs tied together. When a slice fails, the MUXes are reset so that a bad slice is bypassed in both input and output data paths. If, for example, module M2 has failed, M2 can be bypassed and M4 switched in by resetting input MUX 2 to connect its left leg input to M3, while output MUXes 2 and 3 are reset to select their right leg inputs. Figure 3–58 shows the states of the MUX control lines both during normal operation and when module M2 is failed. The addition of more spares to the circuit of Figure 3–58 requires more complex arrangements. For example, the addition of a second spare requires replacement of the two-to-one MUXes by three-to-one MUXes, as well as more interconnections.

In addition to the inclusion of more spares, other concerns may affect the design of a spares switch. The arrangement in Figure 3–58, for example, will not work for memories in which the information stored in the nonfailed modules must remain in the same relational order both before and after the spare is switched in. In the example of a failure of module M2, bytes 0 and 1 are in their correct locations, but byte slice 3 now contains the byte slice 2 data, and byte slice 2 is blank. The recovery procedure for this situation involves restoring the contents of *two* byte slices. For this reason, an order-preserving switch would be better because it allows a reconfiguration that preserves the logical order of the entire system except for the placement of the failed module and its replacement. Order-preserving switches, however, are more complex than nonorder-preserving switches. For more complex arrangements (such as order-preserving switches with a large number of spares), an iterative cell-switching network

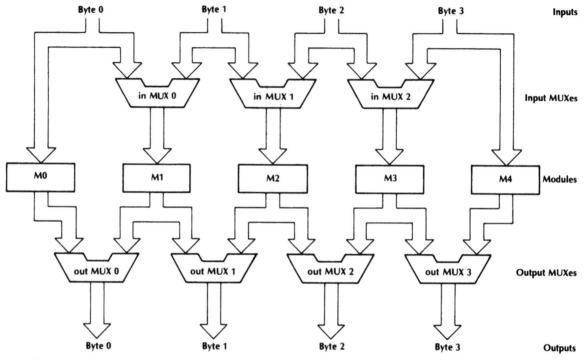

Control input to MUX: 0 (left leg), 1 (right leg)
Normal control line state: (in MUX 0, in MUX 1, in MUX 2) = (1,1,1)
                             (out MUX 0, out MUX 1, out MUX 2, out MUX 3) = (0,0,0,0)
Control line state if M2 failed: in MUX = (1,X,O)   out MUX = (0,0,1,1)   X = don't care

FIGURE 3–58 *Possible implementation of a system made from four byte-slice modules, with a fifth module added as a spare*

such as that proposed in Levitt, Green, and Goldberg [1968] could be used. The following section on reconfiguration includes a brief discussion of these switching networks as well as methods of making the networks themselves fault tolerant.

Bit-slice spares switching is often used for memories. The data and program stores in the AXE telephone exchange control computer [Ossfeldt and Jonsson, 1980], for example, incorporate both a spare-bit plane and a parity bit. Other designs have combined spares switching with error-correcting codes. For example, a design by Carter and McCarthy [1976] combines a (22,16) single-error-correcting (SEC/DED) code, erasure correction, and a spare-bit plane. A Boeing aerospace computer [Wachter, 1975], designed for extended missions without maintenance, uses a (35,28) SEC code and four spare-bit planes, with two of the spares hot and two cold. The DEC MF20 memory (for the DECSYSTEM-20) uses a (44,36) SEC/DED code. In addition, the memory has a single spare bit for each 8K words of memory. The spare bit can be switched in to replace any bit in the 8K words that the system software has determined contains a hard failure.

The Saturn V launch vehicle computer [Dickinson, Jackson, and Randa, 1964], which uses TMR for its functional modules, uses a backup sparing technique for its memory. The Saturn V memory operates in a duplex mode. The duplicate copy, however, is not used for error detection. Error detection is accomplished by the parity bit in each memory word and by the monitoring of memory-access-line drive current. If an error is detected in the on-line memory, operation is transferred to the standby memory without interruption of service or loss of data.

Arulpragasm and Swarz [1980] proposed another spare-switching memory architecture that is able to preserve data through a failure occurrence. The concept, illustrated in Figure 3–59, is an extension of the principle of product codes (discussed earlier). The spare memory box (called the *shadow box*) is identical to the other *m* memory boxes. However, a word stored at address *i* in the shadow box is actually the XOR of the words stored in the locations *i* in the on-line memory boxes. The contents of the shadow box must be updated every time a word is written into memory. In other words, if $M_s[i]$ denotes the contents of location *i* of the shadow box, $M_j[i]$ the current contents of the same location in box *j*, and $M_j'[i]$ the new contents, then at every write into location *i* in memory box *j*, the following operation is simultaneously executed in the shadow box:

$$M_s[i] = M_j[i] \oplus M_j'[i] \oplus M_s[i]$$

The details of the similar update action required in a block-code memory are discussed in Chapter 5. If one of the active memory boxes fails, the shadow box replaces it. The contents of the lost box can be resurrected by XORing the contents of the remaining memory boxes with those of the shadow box. In other words, if memory box *k* fails, the following operation is performed:

$$M_s[i] = M_s[i] \oplus \sum_{j=0}^{k-1} M_j[i] \oplus \sum_{j=k+1}^{m-1} M_j[i].$$

In its simplest form, the shadow box method requires a parity bit in each memory word for failure detection. Arulpragasm and Swarz also examined the extension of the shadow box concept with the use of error-correction codes and multiple spares. Finally, they projected the effects of the shadow box on system performance and cost, and found them to be relatively small.

The shadow box technique can be extended to secondary storage systems. Arrays

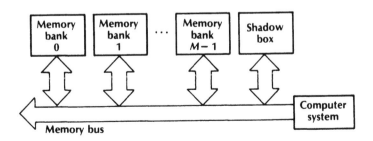

FIGURE 3–59

Shadow box memory backup technique [From Arulpragasm and Swarz, 1980; © 1980 IEEE]

of disks include spares that contain the exclusive–OR of the information on the other disks. Updates can be made on a word or page basis. Various architectures for redundant disk arrays [Ng, 1988; Patterson, Gibson, and Katz, 1988] and data reconstruction algorithms [Muntz and Lui, 1990; Stonebraker and Schloss, 1990] have been proposed. Performance [Bitton and Gray, 1988; Chen et al., 1990; Kim, 1986; Reddy and Banerjee, 1989] and reliability [Gibson et al., 1989; Schulze et al., 1989] of the proposed architectures have also been analyzed.

In other applications, the JPL–STAR [Avizienis et al., 1971] uses backup sparing extensively; the configuration is controlled by the hybrid-redundant TARP (test and repair processor). The MECRA computer [Maison, 1971] uses backup spares for its counters and registers. MECRA has eight Hamming-coded registers and four spare registers. Any of the spares can easily be used to replace any of the active registers, since both the active and spare registers are connected to the same internal bus. The spares switching for the MECRA counters are implemented in the same manner.

In another application of standby sparing, Lewis [1979] proposed a design for a fault-tolerant clock for a TMR system, shown in Figure 3–60. There are two oscillators, one of which is in standby mode. When on-line oscillator failure is detected, the spare replaces it. In addition to the use of standby sparing for the oscillator, the additional clock circuitry (such as failure detection, control, and shaping) is triplicated, with each copy of the clock circuitry residing in one functional module. The unique feature of the clock system is that careful consideration is given to the avoidance of glitches, runt pulses, pulse width variation, and missing clock pulses during the switchover (see Figure 3–36). The goal is to prevent any anomaly in the clock output that might cause desynchronization of the TMR system using the clock.

In the final reference, Losq [1975a] proposed a model for spare-switching systems using Markov chain techniques (see Chapter 5) and examined the effects of fault-detection coverage on system reliability. He found that for short mission times, a single spare results in the best reliability; for longer mission times, the optimum number of spares increases with mission time. The addition of spares beyond the optimum number decreases the chances of mission success (mission reliability). Losq also derived a method of determining the optimum number of spares.

Graceful Degradation

The dynamic redundancy techniques discussed so far have one thing in common: Redundant units are used for error detection, correction, and/or replacement of failed units. They can perform no useful work until they have replaced a failed on-line unit. Graceful degradation techniques, on the other hand, use the redundant hardware as part of the system's normal resources at all times.

There are two similar but distinct graceful degradation perspectives. In the first, system resources needed to attain a specified performance are designed so that continued (although degraded) operation is possible in the event of failures: Degraded operation is preferable to no operation at all. In the second, extra resources are added to a system to ensure that, with a high probability of success, a minimum performance

FIGURE 3–60
*Fault-tolerant clock
for TMR system us-
ing standby spar-
ing [From Lewis,
1979; © 1979 IEEE]*

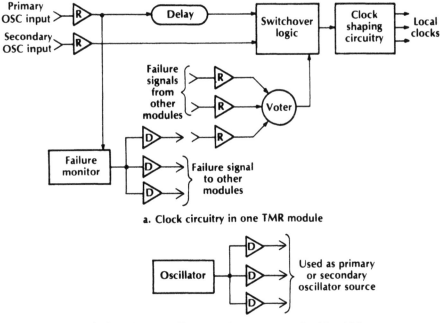

a. Clock circuitry in one TMR module

b. One of two oscillators, with a separate output for driving
clock circuitry on each TMR module

level can be maintained in the presence of failures. The extra resources are also used
to boost performance above the minimum requirements; the augmented performance
continues as long as the extra hardware is not used in overcoming failure effects.

The major purpose of both perspectives is to allow system performance to degrade
gracefully while compensating for failures. The distinction between the two perspectives usually lies in their motivations for including fault tolerance. The motivation for
the first perspective is the priority of a certain cost/performance goal, along with some
ability to continue operation in the presence of failures without regard to performance.
A computer intended primarily for time sharing is an example of such a system. With
the second perspective, the motivation is that any performance below a certain level
is not acceptable; the latter is exemplified by real-time control processors for critical
applications (such as aircraft control). In many gracefully degrading designs, it may be
impossible to classify the design goals according to one or the other perspective.

Designed-In Resources. The first form of graceful degradation occurs in a wide variety
of commercial uniprocessor systems.* In many computers, portions of memory can

* Many commercial systems contain only some of the aspects of graceful degradation. The chief missing factor
is the ability to tolerate failures; although the systems can operate in a degraded fashion, they must be manually
reconfigured (that is, the operating system is reinitialized after throwing a few switches) after the failure causes
a system crash.

be removed from the address space if they contain failures. This is often accomplished through virtual address-mapping facilities in the hardware and/or operating system software. In many disk memory subsystems, portions of individual disks can be de-allocated if they contain permanent errors. The Univac 1100 operating systems, for example, make a record of bad tracks on a disk as soon as they are discovered and avoid using bad tracks when writing files onto disk. The DEC VAX performs a similar function on its disk memory (Chapter 7). In systems with multiple disk drives, the loss of one, two, or more drives can be tolerated as long as the data lost are not essential to system operation.

Cache memories added to a system to improve performance can be bypassed in the event of failure. In the VAX-11/780, set-associative-two mapping in the cache allows the disabling of one set of the cache when a cache failure is detected (effectively turning off one-half of the cache and using the other half as a directly mapped cache). Because the cache is a write-through cache, there is no data loss involved in turning off half the cache. The VAX-11/750 has a set-associative-one cache; thus, it must shut down its entire cache if a cache failure occurs, and the performance degradation is greater than for the VAX-11/780. The Univac 1100/60 also has the ability to shut down portions of its cache.

The Cm* and C.mmp multiprocessor systems [Siewiorek et al., 1978a, 1978b] are systems for which it is not possible to specify which of the graceful degradation perspectives is relevant. Both Cm* and C.mmp were designed to exploit the high performance possible with multiprocessors. Both machines, however, were also designed to benefit from the high reliability that results when a multiprocessor system is capable of degrading gracefully with failures. Cm* and C.mmp are both capable of withstanding multiple processor and memory failures, and tasks can be reassigned to other modules. The key to the performance/reliability properties in multiprocessors like Cm* and C.mmp lies more in the systems and application software than in the hardware. In other words, the software must be written to take advantage of the "hooks" that exist in the hardware to provide graceful degradation possibilities.

Added-On Resources. The Pluribus multiprocessor [Katsuki et al., 1978], designed as a modularly expandable interface message processor (IMP) for the ARPANET, utilizes the second perspective of graceful degradation. Redundant Pluribus systems contain only one extra processor, which is used to provide extra throughput. If any processor fails, only the excess capacity is lost; although the Pluribus system throughput is degraded, the system can still supply the required performance. Likewise, the SIFT, Stratus, and Tandem computers (discussed in Chapters 10 and 8) are initially capable of exceeding performance requirements, but will allow graceful degradation of capacity as portions of the system fail. All these systems have a high probability of maintaining at least a minimum level of functionality until the end of a mission (SIFT) or until repairs can be effected (Stratus, Tandem).

Models and Evaluation Studies. Borgerson and Freitas [1975] developed a reliability model for systems using both backup spares and graceful degradation. The model is based on four different fault classes: solitary faults, space domain faults (e.g., simultaneous failure of multiple pieces of hardware), time domain faults (e.g., a second fault occurring before the first is recovered from), and resource exhaustion (running out of extra modules). In using the model to analyze the PRIME gracefully degrading computer system [Baskin, Borgerson, and Roberts, 1971], it was found that solitary and space domain multiple faults were much more of a factor in system reliability than were time domain multiple faults or resource exhaustion.

The evaluation of systems with graceful degradation involves more factors than does the evaluation of systems using other redundancy techniques. In gracefully degrading systems, performance varies widely over time as failures are accumulated but the systems continue to operate. Thus, the total amount of work done (computation performed) over a time interval is as important as a go/no-go reliability determination. Measures of combined performance and reliability properties are therefore attracting increasing attention. Proposed measures include probability distributions of capacity at time T, mean computation before failure, and the probability of a successful completion of a task started at time T. Computing resource availability is not the only factor in such measures; consideration must be given to additional degradation resulting from recovery and/or restart of processes executing when a failure occurs. Performance-related reliability measures are discussed in Chapter 5. Additional work on performance/reliability modeling is reported in papers by Losq [1977], Troy [1977], Beaudry [1978], Meyer [1978], Gay and Ketelson [1979], Mine and Hatayama [1979], and Castillo and Siewiorek [1980]. In another paper, Meyer, Furchgott, and Wu [1980] evaluated the performance and reliability of the SIFT computer in the air transport application for which it is designed.

Other Reconfiguration Techniques

Many other dynamic redundancy schemes do not fit neatly into the four categories discussed in the previous subsections. This section presents some of these other techniques, organized according to whether they apply to memory (order preserving reconfiguration) or interconnect structures (nonorder preserving reconfiguration).

Memory Reconfiguration. One memory reconfiguration approach is proposed by Hsiao and Bossen [1975]. Assume a bit-sliced memory using an SEC/DED code. In the usual straightforward design, the memory can tolerate any single-bit failure in a given memory word, but fails if any word contains two or more bit failures. If, however, the memory cell addressing function can be performed independently on each bit slice, reconfiguration of the memory is possible without using a spare bit slice. This is accomplished by skewing the address mapping when a double failure is detected, so that the new configuration contains at most a single failure in any word. In other words, the address mapping is changed so that the same address now maps into a different bit location on each module. Table 3–23 illustrates this concept. To get the maximum reconfiguration ability possible with this approach, the properties of orthogonal Latin squares are utilized.* However, if there are 2^k memory words (with k

large), using orthogonal Latin squares of order 2^k requires considerable complexity. Latin squares of a smaller size can be used instead, with the address skewing performed on blocks of memory cells in the bit plane. When using order-m Latin squares, the skewing is performed using only ($\log_2 m$) bits of the address. Thus, using order-4 Latin squares as in Table 3–23 and skewing by the two most significant bits in an address results in addresses skewed in contiguous blocks of $2^{(k-2)}$ words.

Hsiao and Bossen suggested a simple implementation based on linear feedback shift registers that allows the use of identical modules for each bit plane. Each module contains a memory bit slice and its associated addressing circuitry. The overall design of the Latin squares memory is less complex and costly than a memory with a spare bit plane. Finally, Hsiao and Bossen demonstrated the power of the technique by simulating an 8-megabyte memory using order-8 Latin squares for address skewing. In a population of 1000 memories, 500 failures were assumed to occur over a period of five years. The simulation found that a successful reconfiguration was possible for 66 percent of the failures that caused multiple errors.

Another memory reconfiguration approach arranges the memory chips in a self-healing network. The technique requires that an integral switch be built into each memory chip [Goldberg, Levitt, and Wensley, 1974].

Through the use of physical fault location information, the Univac 1100/60 is able to tolerate single-bit stuck-at-α failures in its microstore by inverting the microstore output. When a parity error is detected in the microstore, the system maintenance processor attempts to correct the error by rewriting the microstore. If the error is caused by a failure, the rewriting will not correct the problem, and the maintenance processor makes one final attempt at repair. It writes the logical complement of the microstore contents into the microstore and sets a special designator to indicate that microwords must be inverted before use. Complementing the microstore contents allows toleration of multiple failures as long as all failures cause a bit to be stuck at its inverted value.

The microstore inversion method could be extended so that each microstore location has an extra bit indicating whether the word is inverted before use. Such an extension would speed up reconfiguration because only a failed word would have to be rewritten. The fault tolerance is also increased, because the chance that multiple failed bits in a microstore would all be stuck at the same value is small.

The microstore remapping technique uses an extra bit in each word to denote that the contents are bad. A few blank microstore locations are included at the end of

---

* Definition [Hsiao and Bossen, 1975]: "A Latin square of order (size) m is an $m \times m$ square array of the digits $0, 1, \ldots, (m - 1)$, with each row and column a permutation of the [m digits]. Two Latin squares are orthogonal if, when [one] is superimposed on the other, every ordered pair of elements appears only once." The four matrices in Table 3–23 are the four possible orthogonal Latin squares of order 4. The result of superimposing the first two Latin squares in the table is as follows:

```
0, 0   0, 1   0, 2   0, 3
1, 1   1, 0   1, 3   1, 2
2, 2   2, 3   2, 0   2, 1
3, 3   3, 2   3, 1   3, 0
```

TABLE 3–23
Orthogonal Latin squares–based memory address skewing used to reconfigure a bit-sliced SEC code memory

Configuration/ External Address	Bit Planes/Internal Address				Comments
	0	1	2	3	
Initial configuration					
0	0	0	0	0	Two single-bit failures (boxes) and a third
1	1	1	①	1̄	failure (circle) cause a double
2	2	2	2	2	(noncorrectable) error.
3	3	3	3	3̄	
Second configuration					
0	0	①	2	3̄	With three tolerable single-bit failures, a
1	1	0	3	2	fourth, noncorrectable failure occurs (circle).
2	2	3	0	1̄	
3	3	2	1̄	0	
Third configuration					
0	0	2	3	1̄	The fourth failure is no longer aligned with
1	1	3	2	0	any other failure; however, another
2	2	0	1̄	3̄	configuration is needed because two old
3	3	①	0	2	failures are aligned.
Fourth configuration					
0	0	3	1̄	2	No double failures exist, but any additional
1	1	2	0	3̄	failure is unrecoverable.
2	2	1̄	3	0	
3	3	0	2	1̄	

Source: From Hsiao and Bossen, 1975.

the memory, and each word in the main part of the microstore maps into one (and only one) of the locations using a fixed mapping. When a word fails, the "remapped" indicator bit is set and a new copy of the affected word is written into its backup location (provided it is not already occupied). If the microstore is not writable, ROM could be used for all of the microstore except the indicator bits and the backup locations.

The MECRA computer [Maison, 1971] uses its main store for microstore as well. A special bit in each memory word denotes whether the location is being used for microcode. Recovery from failure in the microstore consists of simply rewriting the microcode in another part of memory. This approach is similar to the graceful degradation of main memory by memory block deallocation, which was discussed in the previous subsection.

Interconnect Reconfiguration. Interconnection networks between component modules are needed by many spare-switching and gracefully degrading systems. The complexity of the switching network can cause reliability problems. Levitt, Green, and Goldberg [1968] have proposed some methods for realizing fault-tolerant switching networks.

FIGURE 3–61
Totally connected design, in which any processor can be connected to any memory (shown with each processor i connected to memory i)

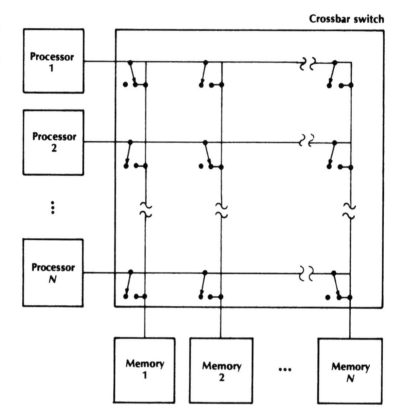

Consider the situation depicted in Figure 3–61, in which there are two types of elements—processors and memories.* The system can be made gracefully degradable because each processor can be connected to any memory through the crossbar switch. Thus, the network is totally connected; that is, any of the N inputs can be connected to any of the N outputs (one at a time). The network also allows all processors and memories to be utilized simultaneously, without waiting for a signal path to become free. Networks of this type are termed CPCU(N) [Complete Permutation–Complete Utilization ($N \times N$)] networks. CPCU(N) networks can be realized with a crossbar switch, as shown in Figure 3–61. However, the complexity of the network increases as N^2. For large N, the design complexity of the network is tremendous, especially when it also takes into account control and fan-out problems.

Fortunately, a switching network such as that in Figure 3–61 can be implemented economically from basic 2×2 crossbar switching cells, in a fashion which trades

---

* The fault-tolerant switching networks discussed here are equally employable in other applications needing crossbar or other types of switching networks, such as multiprocessors and telephone systems. For example, the C.mmp multiprocessor system [Siewiorek et al., 1978a, 1978b] uses a 16 × 16 crossbar switch to interconnect processor and memories.

FIGURE 3–62

Basic two-input-to-two-output switching cell for implementing complex switches [From Levitt, Green, and Goldberg, 1968; reprinted by permission of AFIPS]

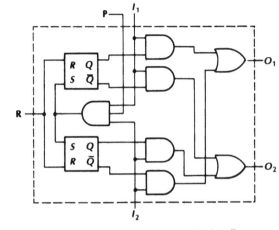

a. Crossing mode   b. Bending mode   c. Redundant implementation of basic cell

FIGURE 3–63

CPCU(8) switching network implemented from basic cells of Figure 3–62 [From Levitt, Green, and Goldberg, 1968; reprinted by permission of AFIPS]

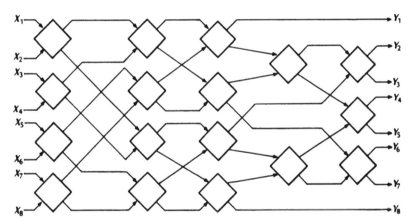

increased complexity for decreased performance. Each of the cell's two inputs (I_1, I_2) can be connected to each of the two outputs (Q_1, Q_2). The cell thus has two operating modes: crossing and bending (Figure 3–62). Figure 3–63 demonstrates the use of the basic cell in a CPCU(8) network. The most efficient procedure for implementing CPCU(N) networks, based on an iterative implementation of the network, requires

$$N\lceil \log_2 N \rceil - 2^{\log N} + 1$$

cells. The methods of employing the two-mode cells for economical and/or high-performance realization of switching networks are discussed in Levitt, Green, and Goldberg [1968], Kautz, Levitt, and Waksman [1968], and Waksman [1968]; many other references are available, in part because switching networks are important in telephone systems.

Figure 3–62 shows a possible implementation of the basic cell in which the crossing mode is attained by pulsing control input *R* high with control input *P* kept low, thereby resetting the flip-flops. The bending mode is invoked by pulsing *P* high, with inputs I_1 and I_2 kept high and *R* low. The cell of Figure 3–62c could be built with fewer components, but the circuit shown has one of the following two fail-safe responses to a single gate or flip-flop failure:

1. *Stuck-Functions*. The cell is stuck either in bending mode or crossing mode, with the outputs valid for that mode.
2. *Bad-Output*. One and only one of the output lines may contain faulty data.

These fail-safe responses can be used to make fault-tolerant networks. A CPCU(N) network that can compensate for any single stuck-at fault can be implemented from two *cascaded networks*, as shown in Figure 3–64a. For example, both subnetworks could be CPCU(N) networks. A fault in one subnetwork could be compensated for in the other network, with the good network performing the entire switching function. In this case, the faulty network is basically performing a null function; all its gates except the faulty one are being wasted.

FIGURE 3–64

Stuck-at-fault fail-safe response configuration [From Levitt, Green, Goldberg, 1968; reprinted by permission of AFIPS]

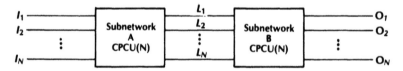

a. Cascaded network, in which damage in one subnetwork can be compensated for by the other subnetwork

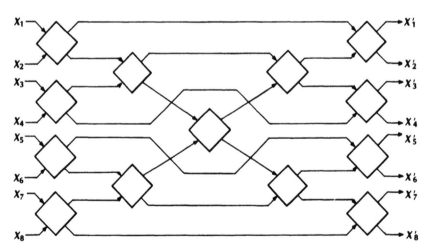

b. Compensation network used as subnetwork A

There are more efficient methods of making a single fault-tolerant network. The same overall structure of two cascaded networks is used as shown in Figure 3–64a; however, in place of the CPCU(N) network for subnetwork A, a less complex subnetwork suffices. A stuck-at fault in subnetwork B results in an interchange of the signals on two of the output leads. It is possible to compensate for it by designing subnetwork A to be capable of interchanging the signals on any two input leads; such a network is less complex than a CPCU(N) network. Figure 3–64b shows a compensation network that performs this function for $N = 8$. The structure, which can be generalized to different N, is called a "double tree" (TDT(N)) network. A TDT(N) network in general requires (3N/2) switch cells. Note that a stuck-at fault in subnetwork A can be compensated for by subnetwork B, because it is CPCU(N).*

Levitt, Green, and Goldberg [1968] examined several more techniques for making switching networks fault tolerant. Among these are single stuck-at fault-tolerant CPCU(N) networks, which are slightly more efficient (in terms of the number of gates needed) than a combination of nonredundant CPCU(N) and TDT(N) networks. They also described networks that can tolerate bad-output faults, and fault-tolerant networks of the following types (in addition to CPCU(N) networks):

Complete permutation-incomplete utilization
Incomplete permutation-order preserving
Incomplete permutation-nonorder preserving
"Shorting" [connecting outputs of stage i to inputs of stage $(i + 1)$, or bypassing (shorting around) stage $(i + 1)$]

Shen and Hayes [1980] examined the fault tolerance of other types of networks that can be implemented by means of the same basic 2 × 2 *crossbar cells* depicted in Figure 3–62. Adams, Agrawal, and Siegel [1987] provide a survey of fault tolerance in cascaded or multistage interconnection networks.

Negrini, Sani, and Stefanelli [1986] give an overview of fault-tolerance techniques for attached VLSI or WSI (wafer-scale integration) array processor structures for supercomputers. The paper addresses the use of the techniques both for on-line fault tolerance and for the configuration of elements to increase yield. This latter approach is crucial in obtaining usable yields for wafer-scale integration. In addition to scattered (random) faults, one common defect mode seen at yield time is clusters of faults that may affect several processing elements and their interconnection in the affected area. The authors discuss a variety of reconfiguration algorithms and a set of standard structures that supports them. The techniques use either structural or time redundancy, and can handle the fault types of interest.

---

* Note that only data paths have been discussed here. The issues of error detection and configuration control logic have been totally ignored. The circuitry for performing such functions can be quite complex, especially if the paths in use at the time of reconfiguration must be left untouched. Telephone exchanges, though admittedly more complex than computer interconnection networks, require computers to control the switching configuration (such as AT&T ESS-1a).

Recovery

Recovery techniques can restore enough of the system state to allow process execution to recommence without a complete restart, and with little or no loss of acquired information. Recovery techniques are usually implemented in software, but may have some hardware basis as well. The techniques considered here are all backward error recovery techniques [Randell, 1975], in which process execution is restarted at (rolled back to) some point before the occurrence of the error. Forward error recovery techniques, in contrast, attempt to continue operation with the system state at hand, even though it may be faulty. Forward error recovery is discussed in the software section of this chapter.

All forms of backward error recovery require some redundant process-state information to be recorded as the protected process executes. The information is used to roll back an interrupted process to a point for which correct state information is known. Three forms of backward error recovery are considered, ordered by the length of rollback required: retry techniques, checkpointing techniques, and journaling techniques. Retry techniques are considered in this section; checkpointing and journaling techniques are covered in the appropriate software section later in this chapter.

Retry. Retry techniques are the fastest form of error recovery, and conceptually the simplest. They depend upon detection of an error as soon as it occurs. Immediately after the error is detected, the necessary repairs are effected. If the error is transient, repair consists in pausing long enough for the transient to die away. If there is a hard failure, the system is reconfigured. The operation affected by the error is then retried, which necessitates knowing what the system state was immediately before the operation was first attempted. If the interrupted operation had already irrevocably modified some data, the retry will be unsuccessful, especially if the failure itself caused a spurious (and undiscovered) modification. Retry techniques are most commonly employed as a means of tolerating transient errors.

Applications and Examples. One retry application common to many commercial computers is I/O operation retry. Disk-read errors, for example, are common occurrences and are usually caused by transients. Without disk-read retry capabilities, system and/or job failures would occur with distressing frequency. In most modern disk drives, retry on disk-read error detection is built into the disk controller itself, removing the burden of the retry operation from the host system. Other common retry applications are retry on memory read errors and bus transaction retry (for both data and protocol errors).

The Univac 1100/60 provides retry for macroinstructions after a failure. Whenever an error is detected, the machine pauses until a special timer expires. During the pause, any transient phenomenon (such as static discharge or power fluctuation) that may have caused the error should die out without further interference, because the machine is not operating. The timer is variable for periods of up to 5 seconds, allowing for adjustment to a variety of computing environments. After the pause, a microroutine is invoked that examines the fault effects and determines whether the instruction is retryable. If a retry is possible, the retry microroutine restores the contents of the operand and addressing registers from a special retry memory provided for the purpose (the retry memory is updated every time a register is read). The macroinstruction is then refetched and its execution attempted. If the retry is not possible or if it fails, the microroutine attempts to transplant the process on another processor (assuming a multiprocessor configuration is being used). The IBM System/360 (Chapter 7) also provides extensive retry capability, performing retries for both CPU and I/O operations.

Alternate-data retry (ADR), proposed by Shedletsky [1978a], is a variation of the retry approach that offers tolerance of both hard failures and transients. The hardware is designed to be able to perform the same function using different data representations. Upon error detection, the same operation is retried using an alternate data representation; the use of a different form for the data is an attempt to ensure that the same error will not recur even if there is a hard failure. In particular, Shedletsky explored the use of C-morphic representations, in which there are two possible data representations. Each representation is the bitwise complement of the other. The design of C-morphic systems that are capable of ADR combines the elements of error-detection codes, complemented duplication, and self-checking circuitry. Shedletsky also applied ADR principles to the design of a simplified processor. The net hardware cost was slightly over that of a duplex processor system with only normal retry capability.

SOFTWARE RELIABILITY TECHNIQUES

There is a significant difference in the way that software fails versus the way that hardware fails. Since software evolves through the first two stages of system development depicted in Table 1–2 (e.g., specification and design, and prototyping) it is subject only to design errors.* That is, the programmer has made an error in the interpretation or implementation of the specification. If this error has not been discovered and corrected during validation tests, it may eventually be discovered by the user. The *observation* of errors occurs as a random process. Unlike physical failures, once they are discovered and corrected, design errors will not recur. However, an unknown number of new errors may be created in the process of correcting a known programming error.

This section explores the taxonomy of software reliability techniques summarized in Table 3–1. Since data on design errors is scarce, there is no uniformly accepted evaluation model (see Chapter 5) equivalent to Mil 217. The taxonomy of software techniques is consequently less populated than the taxonomy of hardware techniques depicted in Table 3–1.

---

* The "manufacturing" process for software merely involves replication. It is debatable whether the replication process should be considered as part of software errors. However, copying errors occur infrequently, and well-known techniques, such as checksumming, are very effective at detecting these errors.

Fault Avoidance

The advent of the stored-program digital computer created a new artifact called *software*. During the first decade, scientists and engineers experimented with the capabilities and limitations of this new media. As software systems grew in complexity at a faster rate than hardware, the focus was on developing techniques to design error-free software. This fault-avoidance approach to design was formulated in the 1960s and called *software engineering*. The software engineering concept was refined and extended during the 1970s and was in common use by the 1980s. A number of tools and methodologies evolved to support software engineering. During the 1970s these methodologies focused on "programming-in-the-small," wherein programs were characterized by simple input/output specifications with a small state space. New algorithms and abstractions such as data types were formulated.

During the 1980s, software engineering shifted to "programming-in-the-large." Systems had complex specifications with emphasis on interfaces, management, and system structures. Data bases supporting these programs were evolved and had a long life. Research produced a variety of tools, including document production, version control and configuration management, intelligent editors, and programming environments. Many of these tools focused on improving the productivity of the software developer.

Despite the gains in programming languages (e.g., Ada), programming environments (e.g., computer-aided software engineering or CASE tools), and testing procedures, the effective utilization of fault-avoidance techniques remains as much an art as a science. Systems fail because it is not possible to write specifications in a formal way—most specifications are still written in English prose—and not practical to verify formally that the implementation follows the specification. Thus, the design, coding, and testing of systems is done according to the style, experience, and best judgment of the human being to whom the task is assigned.

Figure 3–65a depicts the increasing relative cost of software from the computing budget [Shaw, 1986]. Figure 3–65b illustrates the fraction of cost going to design, programming, and integration and testing during the software development cycle [Shaw, 1986]. Other estimates of the development costs placed design at up to one-half with programming or coding being as little as one-sixth [Brookes, 1975]. However, the major portion of software cost over the life of a software system goes to maintenance, as illustrated in Figure 3–65c [Shaw, 1986]. The dominant cost of maintenance arises from not only the long life of software systems but also the constant enhancements and upgrading that result in enhanced functionality. Thus, many of the initial software engineering techniques focused on abstractions as a means of managing complexity. Abstractions have evolved from modules, to objects, to the segregation of capabilities to manipulate objects.

Modularity. Perhaps the first fault-avoidance technique to gain widespread adoption was modularity. Conceptually, the system design is broken into a number of modules that provide a concise interface to a function [Parnas, 1972]. The developer of the module

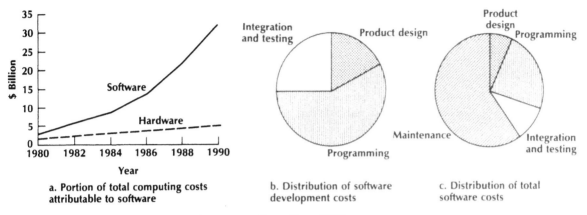

FIGURE 3-65 *Software costs [From Shaw, 1986]*

would employ "information hiding" and "defensive programming" techniques. The concise interface was all that users of the module needed to know. If the module were replaced by one that had an error corrected or had higher performance, the rest of the modules in the system would not have to be redesigned. Furthermore, the module would perform sanity checks on the parameters passed to it in order to verify that it was asked to perform an operation within its scope. This defensive programming is analogous to defensive driving in that the module should anticipate errors, instead of waiting for them to occur.

Object-Oriented Programming. A logical outgrowth of modularity was object-oriented programming. An object is an encapsulation of a data structure and some functions that can manipulate it. These export functions represent the only mechanisms for other objects to manipulate the internal data structure. As in modularity, a redesign of the internal data structures and access mechanisms would not impact the rest of the system.

As an example, consider an object called a "queue." This object could be used to synchronize other objects. For the sake of the example, let us assume we have a producer object and a consumer object. The producer object would place data into the queue by use of the "enqueue" function. Likewise, the consumer could remove data from the queue through the use of the "dequeue" function. Neither the producer nor the consumer know how the queue is implemented. In fact, the queue could be implemented in any number of ways inside the object. It could be represented as a linked list or as an array. The notion of object has been formalized in extensions to conventional programming languages. For example, Objective C and C++ are front ends to a C compiler that support user-defined objects.

One of the objections to modular and object-oriented programming is the extra overhead required in making subroutine calls and returns every time a module boundary is crossed. Although the hierarchical structure is important for handling the complexity of the design process, it introduces substantial overhead. A preprocessor can remove a major portion of this overhead by "flattening" the hierarchy into a smaller number of levels. Thus, object-oriented programs need not be substantially slower at run time than more classical programming styles.

Capability-Based Programming. In object-oriented programming, any module has equal accessibility to any other module. However, there are many cases in which it is appropriate to restrict the access rights to a module. Cabability-based programming places the protection on the access path [Jones, 1975]. (See the subsection on consistency and capability checking earlier in this chapter.) Thus, in our previous example of a queue, requests to the consumer module could only result in "queue reads," while requests through the producer process could only result in "queue writes." A request through the consumer process for a "queue read" would be terminated as an error.

Modularity, object-oriented programming, and capabilities all require "architectural discipline." Since software is malleable, there is a temptation to alter the boundaries of the modules. However, once specified, these boundaries have to be as rigid as any hardware boundary (e.g., chip, board, or backplane). Just as in hardware it is difficult to migrate functionality after the system has been implemented, so too it is difficult to modify the software boundaries. Otherwise, a minor change to a specification in one module may require modifications in a large number of modules. Indeed, it is a difficult task to even determine which modules might be affected, let alone correctly modify all those modules plus any other modules that depend upon them.

Formal Proofs. While abstractions provided useful tools for programmers to deal with complexity, there was no way to measure their effectiveness in reducing design errors. Thus, formal proofs have been proposed as a mechanism to eliminate design errors. Formal proofs attempt to demonstrate code correctness by restructuring the code as a mathematical proof. There are two basic approaches to formal proofs. The first approach creates a logical representation of the code and proceeds to prove theorems upon this secondary representation. One must ensure that the translation process from the code to the logical representation does not itself introduce errors. The second approach integrates the logical representation with the code. While proving the equivalence between two algorithms (such as a higher level specification and a lower level implementation) has been demonstrated, the proof of correctness of an arbitrary piece of code requires substantially more research. Perhaps the most aggressive attempt at proving software correct involved the operating system for the software implemented fault-tolerant (SIFT) computer. The operating system was composed of about 1,000 lines of Pascal code (Chapter 10).

There have been several attempts to use formal proofs to verify that an implementation conforms to an architecture. The most promising results come from microcode correctness verification methods.

• **Microprogram Certification System (MCS):** This interactive system, presented by Joyner, Carter, and Leeman [1976] and Carter, Joyner, and Brand [1978] is designed to aid in proving the equality between programs. The specifications for architecture and implementation are formally described, with the microcode supplied as data to the low-level description. A correspondence between these two descriptions is then formalized and the MCS is used to prove mathematically that the correspondence holds.

• **State Delta:** Proposed by Crocker [1977], this scheme is intended to prove that a system performs as specified. A state delta consists of a precondition, a postcondition, an environmental list, and a modification list. This work is extended by the state delta verification system (SDVS) at the Aerospace Corporation [Marcus, Crocker, and Landauer, 1984; Levy, 1984] to prove the correctness of microcode. The method proves the correctness of microcode, but does not detect all the logic errors that could possibly occur. To eliminate ambiguity and lack of precision, formal languages are used to describe system specifications in SDVS. The correctness criterion is a mathematical theorem stated in a formal language. The theorem states that the properties of the system specification are preserved by the implementation. The proof of the correctness criterion theorem constitutes a verification of the implementation and is performed by an automatic theorem prover. This approach depends heavily on the user to supply the state mapping between the specification and the implementation. The state mappings are used in the proof process. The SDVS system checks what the implementation is specified to do, not what the implementation *really* performs.

Additional Fault-Avoidance Techniques. Other techniques [Glasser, 1975] include the following:

• **Error Reporting:** This technique is based on tracking the number of bugs to predict the software error rate.

• **Regression Testing:** In this automated procedure, test values and test structures are systematically selected from a list of alternatives and then applied. While regression testing does not generate new situations, it can ensure that the software will not fail in situations in which it previously performed correctly.

• **Reviews:** This technique has several different levels. First, the originating programmer can systematically review software through a procedure called *desk checking*. Then, other programmers may examine the code in a *peer review*. Later, a larger audience of designers and programmers can critique these specifications and code in a *design review*. Software is further improved via a test driver and interactive debugging. When the module is deemed complete, a formal acceptance check developed by an independent testing organization attempts to validate the module. When modifications to the architecture are deemed necessary, the alteration must be approved by an independent *change review*.

• **Top-Down Design:** This technique involves hierarchically structuring a problem and successfully refining each node in the hierarchy so that a divide-and-conquer approach results. Hierarchical input-process-output (HIPO) provides a structure for defining the system. At the highest level, a program design language may be employed to specify the high-level requirements.

Redundancy Techniques

Due to the large cost of developing software (Figure 3–65a), most of the software dependability effort has focused on fault-avoidance techniques. Thus, the taxonomy of software dependability techniques based upon redundancy is sparse and dominated predominantly by research on experimental systems. However, as requirements for system dependability become more stringent, the impact of design errors must be minimized.

Algorithm Construction. In this technique, a set of high-level faults are identified, and algorithms are designed that tolerate those faults. Most of the work on algorithm construction has focused on distributed systems. In a distributed system, multiple isolated processing nodes are operating concurrently on shared information. Information is exchanged between the processors from time to time. The goal is to design the sending and receiving software in such a way that the possibility of corrupting or losing information is minimized. Many distributed systems are built upon the client/server model. In this situation, one node (the client) can request some service of another (the server). For example, a client node might request the formatting and queueing up of a document on a print server. In order to achieve a level of fault tolerance, it is obviously necessary for the server to acknowledge receipt of the request.

Commencing with Lamport [1977], theorists have studied the problem of reaching agreement among a pool of processors in the presence of failures. A large variety of algorithms have been developed to ensure agreement, assuming one of a small set of failure models.

Failure Models

- *Failed-Notified*: The failure causes the processor to stop all execution, and the other processors are immediately notified of the failure.
- *Failed-Stop*: The failure causes the processor to stop all execution, but the other processors are not notified of the failure.
- *Message Omission*: A scheduled message is not sent, not transmitted, or not received.
- *Timing*: Messages are arbitrarily delayed and/or arrive out of order.
- *Byzantine Failure*: The faulty processor continues execution and maliciously lies when asked for information. This is the worse case model since the faulty processor can generate misleading information causing a maximum of confusion.

In distributed systems, multiple copies of databases are used to tolerate failures of the communication media, nodes, or the message passing software. In order to ensure consistency between the multiple copies, one must guarantee that either all nodes successfully complete the transaction or all nodes refuse the transaction (i.e., the state of each node is the same as if no transaction had been attempted). This "indivisible" quality of a transaction is known as *atomicity*. A popular solution to atomicity is a "two-phase commit protocol" employed in commercial transaction processing systems designed by Tandem and Stratus (Chapter 8).

In the first phase of the two-phase commit protocol, all the nodes of a system are queried as to whether they can COMMIT to a transaction. Those that can enter the PREPARE state; those that cannot issue an ABORT message. Several ways exist to decide whether or not the second phase can commence. For example, the second phase might be entered if and only if all of the nodes commit to the transaction. If it is decided that the second phase can commence, a commit coordinator is selected. In phase two, the commit coordinator records the database update to ensure the ability to recover from failure. Then, all other nodes are notified to commit the transaction. The commit coordinator periodically polls each of the other nodes until all have acknowledged the update. Then and only then is the transaction considered complete.

While the two-phase commit protocol tolerates many of the failure models, it does not tolerate Byzantine failure [Lamport, Shostak, and Pease, 1982]. In order to guarantee agreement in the face of Byzantine failures, all nonfaulty receivers must agree on the value that the transmitter sent, and if the transmitter was not faulty, the value that was agreed upon must be the one that was sent. It has been shown that in order to guarantee the achievement of Byzantine agreement for at most t faults, there must be greater than $3t$ nodes in the system.

Depending on the degree of severity (the list of failure models is arranged in order from the most benign to the most malicious failure), the algorithms have increasing overhead. In the most malicious case, the algorithms require multiple transmissions of the data. The first generation of these algorithms required an exponentially increasing number of transmissions as a function of the number of processors involved. This overhead was so substantial that commercial fault-tolerant systems have decided to go with simpler, less robust algorithms.

Diverse Programming. In the diverse programming, or design diversity, redundancy technique, independently developed versions of software are concurrently executed. The technique consists of independent design teams utilizing different design methodologies, algorithms, compilers, run-time systems, and hardware components. The advantage is that the entire system is potentially more reliable than any single copy. The disadvantages are the added cost of scarce design resources, the cost of concurrent execution, and the potential sources of correlated (i.e., single point) errors, such as the original specification or the software driver for comparing results generated by the concurrent copies.

The software driver controls the execution, comparison, and voting process of the software versions. This software driver presents its own set of unique problems [Avizienis, 1985]:

- The driver is not replicated and, therefore, represents a weak link. Its specification and design must be extraordinarily simple and verifiable. The hardware analogy to this problem is the need to triplicate the voters to remove the voter as a single point of failure in TMR circuits.

- The driver must assure that the input data vector to each of the versions is identical (a nontrivial problem).
- The driver must receive data from each version in identical formats (or make efficient conversions) and check the data for equivalence in a timely manner. In some applications, the amount of data transferred and processed could be considerable.
- The driver must implement some sort of communication protocol to wait until all versions have completed their processing and then pass on the correct results to the main process. Avizienis and Chen [1977] have proposed the WAIT and SEND primitives.
- A watch-dog timer must be used to account for versions that do not complete their processing in a regular fashion.

Another problem in the practical implementation of this technique lies in the voting itself. Because of differences in compilers, numerical techniques, and format conversions, insignificant differences might be expected from version to version. The voting must ignore these minor differences.

Studies and Experimental Evaluations. Experiments in diverse programming have been conducted in universities on relatively small programs (usually less than 5000 lines of code). The following list summarizes several of these studies, in which the programs were derived primarily from English specifications ranging from 10 to 100 pages in length.

1. Chen and Avizienis [1978] conducted an initial feasibility study to determine whether *N*-version programming led to a net improvement in reliability.

Program: Text editor
Specification language: English
Programs written: 27
Programs used: 6, divided into two voting groups
Results: In group 1, only 1 version had a program error, which was masked by the other two versions. In group 2, the versions had 6, 6, and 8 errors, respectively, of which all but two were tolerated by voting.

2. A second experiment by Chen and Avizienis [1978] used partial differential equations (three different algorithms) to solve region approximation and temperature evaluation.

Program: RATE
Specification language: English
Programs written: 16
Programs used: 7, with 3 programs used for one algorithm and 2 programs used for each of the other two algorithms to yield 12 different combinations
Text cases: 32 on each of the 12 combinations for a total of 384 test runs
Results: 290 of the test runs had no failures, and 94 of the test runs had one to

three errors, with 35 of the 94 test cases having errors that were not tolerated.

Remarks: The dominant source of similar errors was the coincident omission of code to handle specific cases.

3. An extensive experiment by Kelly and Avizienis [1983] used an airport scheduler system to explore various specification techniques in an attempt to minimize the specification as a single source of error.

Program: Airport Scheduler

Specification languages: OBJ [Goguen and Tardo, 1979], English, and PDL

Programs written: 18, 11 of which aborted on input, preventing other (correct) versions from executing

Programs used: 18 (7 OBJ, 6 English, and 5 PDL), with a preprocessor module appended to each to reject invalid input

Test cases: 100 airport scheduling transactions, with the results of each recorded for each program according to one of three results: "good" (the result was as expected or contained correct data but in a bad format), "detected" (the program failed the invalid input test that was added to recover from potential abort conditions), and "undetected" (the acceptance test was passed but the data was not as expected). Using these three categories of results, 14 possible combinations of good/detected/undetected were identified and subjected to 81,600 computations.

Results:

Specification Language	Good	Detected	Undetected
OBJ	77.9%	16.8%	5.4%
English	78.6%	16.4%	5.0%
PDL	85.8%	11.3%	2.9%

Summary: The format errors were caused by disregarding the specification or by "personalizing" the output format (nonstandard output complicated the task of the voter). Undetected errors, which were similar between program versions, were caused by a mistake in the specification, a misinterpretation or misunderstanding of the specification, or an implementation error. Often, errors in one version that could be masked by two other good versions conspired with other different single errors to defeat the voting mechanism.

4. In what might be called a second-generation study, Dunham [1986] conducted an extensive experiment to test individual reliability of different programs.

Program: Launch Interpreter Condition

Specification language: English

Programs written: 3

Programs used: 3

Test cases: 1 million

Results: 1316 errors were uncovered in single versions, 60 similar errors were found in two versions, and no cases were found in which all three programs suffered similar errors.

Remarks: The individual programs had a probability of error of 0.9985, 0.992, and 0.9999, respectively.

5. Knight and Leveson [1986] studied *N*-version programming extensively.

Program: Launch Interpreter Condition
Specification language: English
Programs written: 27
Programs used: 27
Test cases: 1 million
Results: A three-version system was 19 times less likely to fail (e.g., probability of failure on a test case of 0.000037) than a single version of the program (e.g., 0.000698). Brilliant, Knight, and Levenson [1990] analyzed program errors correlated with regions of the input space.

6. A study of Shimeall and Leveson [1988] compared the effectiveness of voting in *N*-version programming and fault-avoidance techniques.

Program: Combat Simulator
Specification language: English
Programs written: 13
Programs used: 8, each of which was subjected to a short version acceptance test to ensure that the major functionality in the specification had been met
Fault-avoidance tests: (1) code reading (employing step-wise abstraction [Linger, Mills, and Witt, 1979]), (2) static data reference analysis, (3) functional testing (employing abstract function techniques [Howden, 1980]), and (4) assertion checking.
Results: 275 errors were encountered, 134 were detected by the four testing techniques alone, 107 were masked by voting alone, and 34 were detected by a combination of the four testing techniques and voting. The probability of correct execution for individual programs ranged from 0.4 to 0.92, with an average of 0.744 and a standard deviation of 0.186. When combined into triples, the probability of correct *N*-version executions ranged from 0.58 to 0.95, with a mean of 0.811 and a standard deviation of 0.094. In this experiment, there was a higher than random chance that the versions failed on the same input case.
Remarks: Voting and the four fault-avoidance testing techniques tended to detect different classes of errors. Table 3–24 depicts the number of errors in each version of the program and the techniques that detected them. As shown in Table 3–25, different classes of design errors were also detected.

7. Avizienis, Lyu, and Schutz [1988] explored the impact of programming language on design errors using an automatic (i.e., computer-controlled) landing program for commercial airliners specified by the Sperry Commercial Flight Systems division of Honeywell, Inc.

TABLE 3–24
Number of errors detected by various fault-avoidance testing techniques and N-version voting

Detection Method	Program Version								Total
	1	2	3	4	5	6	7	8	
A. Code reading only	0	2	4	2	0	1	0	16	25
B. Static analysis only	0	0	2	0	0	1	0	0	3
C. Functional test only	3	10	15	3	15	4	12	0	62
D. Assertions only	4	1	0	4	4	0	3	2	18
E. Vote detection only	7	12	18	13	15	11	16	15	107
F. Other detection only	4	2	0	1	1	1	0	3	12
Both A and C	0	1	0	0	0	0	1	0	2
Both A and D	2	0	0	1	1	0	0	0	4
Both A and E	0	0	2	0	0	0	0	1	3
Both B and C	0	0	0	0	0	0	1	0	1
Both B and E	0	0	0	0	0	0	1	0	1
Both D and C	3	0	1	1	2	0	0	0	7
Both D and E	0	0	2	0	1	1	1	1	6
Both E and C	3	0	1	3	3	6	3	0	19
A, E, C	0	3	0	0	1	0	0	1	5

Source: Shimeall and Leveson, 1988; © 1988 IEEE.

TABLE 3–25
Design fault classes detected by fault-avoidance techniques and N-version voting

Design Fault Class	Detection Method				
	Code Reading	Static Analysis	Functional Testing	Assertion Checking	Voting
Initialization code	X				
Missing error check	X				
Missing logic	X		X		X
Uninitialized variables	X	X			
Calculation errors			X		
Invalid inputs			X		
Abnormal end to program execution			X	X	X
Misaligned parameters				X	X
Incorrect subscripts				X	X

Source: Shimeall and Leveson, 1988; © 1988 IEEE.

Program: Commercial Airliner Controlled Landing
Specification language: English
Programs written: 6
Programs used: 6, each in a different language
Test cases: Over 1000 simulated landings

Results:

	Faults Detected	
Language	During Development	After 1000+ Simulations
Ada	6	0
C	13	5
Modula-2	4	1
Pascal	12	0
Prolog	26	3
LISP dialect	21	2

Remarks: Of the 82 faults that occurred during development testing, only one incidence of an identical fault occurred, caused by the misreading of a comma in the specification (65,536) as a decimal point (65.536). After over 1,000 simulated landings, four disagreements were discovered, but because they were not identical, the operation was correct. Seven other faults—none of which was related to each other or to any previously uncovered fault—were detected by an independent code inspection.

Real-Time Examples. N-version programming and the more general technique of using more than one design (design diversity) has been implemented in real-time control where safety is a major design criteria. Two-version systems have been used in both Airbus and Boeing Aircraft. Two sets of software requirements were used to design the slat and flap controls for the Airbus Industrie A310 [Martin, 1982; Hills, 1985]. The two design teams used different instruction sets and host computers. Of the errors encountered, 45 percent were caused by requirement errors or omissions, while only 15 percent were caused by coding errors. Sperry Corporation Flight Systems used a single system specification to design a two-version digital autopilot flight director for the Boeing 737-300 [Yount, 1984]. Diverse hardware and software were developed for the two versions.

Other examples involve nuclear reactor protection systems. In the Bessey pilot implementation project, three independent teams working from the same specification created the programs in different languages and tested versions that another team had created [Geiger et al., 1979; Gmeiner and Voges, 1979]. The project on diverse software produced a three-version system, using two specifications and two programming languages [Bishop et al., 1985].

Issues in the Use of Programming Diversity. In order to effectively use diverse programming, a number of issues have to be resolved. When multiple versions produce different results, how do we determine whether they are equivalent? Boolean/integer-results are usually required to be identical, whereas character strings can have minor variations, such as spacing and capitalization. Variations in real number results may be due to design errors or the inherent accuracy of the underlying algorithm or hardware. Complex data structures, such as linked lists that have many equivalent implementations for a single logical list, require special consideration. For example, consider an output whose correct results should be the list (A,B). If three versions produce (A,B), (A,X), and (Y,B), a component-by-component vote will yield a correct list, whereas treating the list as a single entity produces three separate nonagreeing results.

The use of diverse programming places added significance upon the design specification. In a sense, the use of diverse implementations pushes the source of common mode errors up one level to the specification. Specifications need to be clearly and unambiguously rewritten to minimize misinterpretations while at the same time controlling the volume of the specification document. Computer families are a primary example of a single specification (i.e., the instruction set architecture) generating diverse implementation (i.e., the various members of a computer family). The economic incentive to produce upward compatible members of the computer family that can execute the same binary images of programs is substantial. The specification language of choice is English and has led to large volumes (e.g., IBM's *Principles of Operations* and Digital Equipment Corporation's *Systems Reference Manual*) controlled by a corporation-wide architectural definition committee. Even with such tight monitoring, subtle variations inevitably surface. Standards produced by professional bodies such as the Institute of Electrical and Electronic Engineers (IEEE) also produce specifications for systems designed by diverse manufacturers. However, these standards activities require years of preparation and careful reading prior to adoption.

Software Dynamic Redundancy Techniques

Software dynamic redundancy techniques fall into two major approaches: forward and backward error recovery. Forward error recovery attempts to continue operation with the current system state even though it may be faulty. Backward error recovery uses previously saved correct state information as the starting point after a failure.

Forward Error Recovery. Forward error recovery is usually highly application-dependent, as in the case of a real-time control system in which an occasional missed response to a sensor input is tolerable. Because loss of sensor information due to a failure is not critical, the system can recover by skipping its response to the lost sensor input sample. After reconfiguration, the process proceeds immediately to deal with the following sensor input samples. Forward error recovery is not discussed further here; Randell, Lee, and Treleaven [1978] consider the topic briefly.

Backward Error Recovery. Of the four forms of backward error recovery—retry, checkpointing, journaling, and recovery blocks—only checkpointing, journaling, and recovery blocks are implemented in software and require little or no extra hardware. (Retry techniques, which usually require substantial dedicated hardware, are discussed in the hardware section of this chapter.) Retry techniques require immediate error detection to be successful, but checkpoint, journaling, and recovery block techniques allow some error latency.

Checkpointing. In checkpointing, some subset of the system state is saved at specific points (the checkpoints) during process execution. The information to be stored is the subset of the system state (data, programs, machine state) that is necessary to the continued successful execution and completion of the process past the checkpoint, and that is not backed up by other means. Rollback is part of the actual recovery process and occurs after the repair (e.g., by reconfiguration) of the physical damage that caused the detected error (or after the transient causing the error dies out). The rollback consists of resetting the system and process state to the state stored at the latest checkpoint. Hence, the only loss is the computation time between the checkpoint and the rollback, plus any data received during that interval that cannot be recreated.

Figure 3–66 graphically illustrates checkpointing. First, consider lines B and B'. Line B shows the progress process B would make if no errors occurred. Line B' shows the actual progress of process B as a result of the error occurrence scenario shown. During process B execution, checkpoints are reached at regular intervals in terms of amount of computation, not time. Point X on line B' corresponds to an error event. The vertical line segment XY is the rollback performed upon error detection. Point Y is the point in the process immediately following the checkpoint, at which execution

FIGURE 3–66
Scenario of two processes, identical except for checkpoint frequency

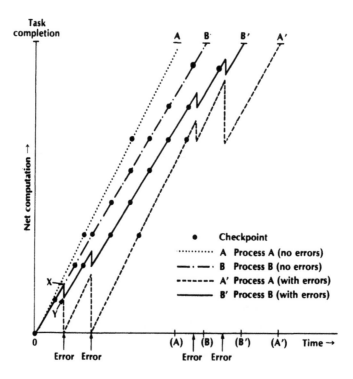

FIGURE 3-67
*Cooperating
checkpointing
processes [From
Randell, 1975;
© 1975 IEEE]*

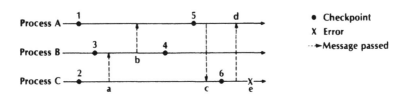

restarts. Although the actual process execution time at (B') is longer than the ideal time (B), the process does not have to start from the beginning four times, as it must without checkpointing.

Line A in Figure 3-66 represents the progress of process A in the absence of errors. Process A is identical to process B except that in order to achieve faster execution, only one-third the number of checkpoints are used. The use of fewer checkpoints lowers the overhead required for saving system states and allows process A to run around 20 percent faster than process B. The actual performance of process A is lower, however, as shown by line A'. The reason is that the rollbacks were longer for process A than for process B, and the computation time lost for this error scenario thus outweighed process A's speed advantage. Thus, it is clear that the correct choice of checkpoint locations is important. If the checkpoints are too infrequent for the error rate encountered, much computation time can be lost to rollbacks. On the other hand, too frequent checkpointing results in an unnecessary increase in computation time due to the overhead of saving-system states.

A number of issues arise from the basic checkpointing design:

1. Selecting checkpoints to minimize the amount of state information that must be saved at each checkpoint.
2. Deciding which information must be backed up for proper assurance of successful rollback.
3. Restraining multiple rollbacks that arise when multiple concurrent processes communicate with each other. That is, if one process is rolled back, any other process receiving data from it since the checkpoint must also be rolled back at least that far, which can give rise to a "domino effect," as illustrated in Figure 3-67.*
4. Avoiding error latency situations in which the validity of the state saved at the checkpoint is jeopardized by the possibility of a previous, undetected error.

Checkpointing Studies and Applications. Studies on checkpointing include the following:

1. Chandy and Ramamoorthy [1972] proposed checkpointing strategies that dynamically insert checkpoints when the expected loss of computation reaches a certain value.

---

* In Figure 3-67, a failure at point e forces process C to roll back to checkpoint 6. Because of a message sent by process C, process A must then be rolled back to checkpoint 5. Rolling back of the processes in this fashion eventually requires all three processes to be rolled back to their initial checkpoints.

2. Troy [1978] proposed a model for interacting processes operating concurrently; based on Petri net-like representations, the model allows determination of needed rollback actions when an error occurs in one of the processes.
3. Shedletsky [1978b], in a study of the problem of error latency when imperfect error detection is present, presented a method for determining rollback length and demonstrated the procedure by analyzing an imperfectly self-checking ALU.

In real-time situations, checkpointing has had a number of applications. For example, Tandem (see Chapter 8) uses checkpointing extensively. User processes can be replicated for backup purposes. The operating system has a checkpointing facility through which an active process can checkpoint its state to a backup process. The Fault-Tolerant Spaceborne Computer also employs a checkpointing scheme in which the only information needed to roll back a process is the program counter contents that were stored at its last checkpoint [DeAngelis and Lauro, 1976; O'Brien, 1976; Stiffler, 1976]. The COPRA computer uses checkpoints automatically inserted by its assembler; rollback is microprogrammed and automatically invoked by detection of an error [Meraud, Browaeys, and Germain, 1976; Meraud et al., 1979]. The JPL–STAR Operating System also employs checkpointing [Avizienis et al., 1971].

Journaling. Of the three software backward error recovery techniques, journaling is the simplest and least efficient; it requires the longest time to recover the state attained before an error. In journaling, a copy of the initial data (database, disk, file) is stored as the process begins. As the process executes, it makes a record of all transactions that affect the data. Thus, if the process fails, its effect can be recreated by running a copy of the backup data through the transactions a second time (after any failures have been repaired). The recovery takes the same amount of time as the initial attempt.

Journaling is better than completely restarting because it eliminates the loss of information involved in a restart. Many text editors use journaling to recover an editing session during which an error causes the computer to crash [Lampson, 1979]. A special program is run when the system is restarted and can be stopped at any point (up to the point where the error occurred) to recreate any intermediate states of the edited file. Typically, a three-hour editing session takes substantially less time to recreate because there are no human delays involved the second time.

Recovery Blocks. This backward error recovery technique uses blocks that are similar in nature to the blocks in modern block-structured languages. Recovery blocks [Randell, 1975] combine elements of checkpointing and backup alternatives to provide tolerance of software design faults as well as recovery from hard failures and transient errors in complex systems. The method minimizes the amount of state information backed up and releases the programmer from determining which variables should be checkpointed, and when.

Each recovery block contains variables global to that block that will be automatically checkpointed to a recovery cache if they are altered within the block. Upon entry to the recovery block, the primary alternate is executed and subjected to an acceptance test to detect any errors in the result. If the test is passed, the block is exited. If the test is failed, or if the primary alternative fails to execute, the contents of the recovery cache pertaining to this recovery block are reinstated, and the second alternate is initiated. This cycle of execution, test, rollback, and initiation of the next alternative continues until either an alternate is successful or no more alternates exist. If the block runs out of alternates, an error is signaled to the context containing the recovery block. Usually, the first alternate is the most desirable (more efficient, more powerful) and the desirability of the subsequent alternates decreases at each level.

A graphical representation of this approach to recovery blocks is shown in Figure 3–68a. Figure 3–68b shows that it is possible to nest the recovery blocks, in which case failure by exhaustion of alternates in a lower level recovery block causes the recovery block containing it to invoke the next alternate. Figure 3–68c shows the extension of recovery blocks to parallel processes, with some restrictions on the times at which messages can be passed between processes. Recovery blocks can be used at different levels of abstraction in a hierarchical system (in the same way that there can be a physical computer as well as multiple levels of virtual machines) as long as proper care is taken when designing the interfaces between the levels.

The success of the recovery block technique depends upon the ability of the acceptance test to successfully detect errors. If the alternative or back-up software provides less functionality than the primary, the acceptance test must only examine the functionality common to all the alternatives. Alternatively, Shrivastava and Akinpelu [1978] proposed a method that uses assertion statements in the recovery block. Anderson and Lee [1979] considered adding extra levels of abstraction to improve the fault tolerance of hardware/software interfaces and make them more recoverable. Russell and Tiedeman [1979] examined message passing among multiple processes within the same recovery block (a "conversation"), and its requirements on the degree of coupling between cooperating processes.

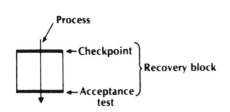

a. Graphic notation for a recovery block

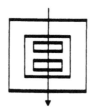

b. Nesting of recovery blocks

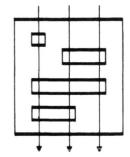

c. Multiprocess recovery blocks

FIGURE 3–68 *Use of Randell's graphical notation to demonstrate extensions beyond the simple recovery block [From Randell, 1975; © 1975 IEEE]*

Evaluations and Studies. In order to test the effectiveness of the recovery block technique, Anderson et al. [1985] used an 8000-line command-and-control system written by professional programmers to normal commercial standards. The experiment was conducted in three phases. During the first phase, one version of the software had its fault-tolerant features enabled and the second version had them disabled. The intent was to measure the effectiveness of the fault-tolerant mechanisms. During the second phase, the original command-and-control system software was utilized, but errors in the recovery software were fixed. In the third phase, several modules of the original software were rewritten by inexperienced programmers in an attempt to stress the recovery mechanisms. The following table lists the percentage of events affecting reliability in these three phases [Anderson et al., 1985]:

	Action of Recovery Mechanism			
	Failure Averted (Improved Reliability)	Equivalent Behavior (Same Reliability)	Failure Created (Less Reliability)	Uncategorizable Events
Phase 1	61.5%	26.2%	6.2%	6.2%
Phase 2	50.0	42.6	5.9	1.5
Phase 3	77.8	21.4	0	0.8
Total	66.0	28.4	3.2	2.4

Note that the equivalent behavior column includes unnecessary recovery, recovery followed by failure, defective recovery, and failure with no recovery.

The coverage (i.e., the fraction of failures occurring in a nonfault-tolerant system that are averted by the means of tolerance) for the three phases was 0.75, 0.60, and 0.81, respectively. If events that were successfully recovered from but originated in the fault-tolerant mechanisms are discounted, the coverage falls to 0.68, 0.53, and 0.81, respectively.

In another evaluation study, Shrivastava and Akinpelu [1978] evaluated the performance of a recovery cache scheme and found that the overhead involved was not high. In evaluating an experimental design of an add-on recovery cache for a PDP-11 that divides the Unibus between the processor and memory, Lee, Ghani, and Heron [1980] found no modifications to the system were required other than cutting the bus. The performance degradation for the PDP-11 recovery cache system, which is about as complex as a C.vmp-type configuration, was projected to be similar to that of C.vmp (see Chapter 10). Unlike C.vmp, the recovery cache PDP-11 will not survive hard processor failures; however, with full use of recovery blocks, it can survive transient errors and most software design errors.

Issues in the Use of Recovery Blocks. While the recovery block technique is potentially more economical in its use of run-time resources (i.e., only executing alternative copies when there are errors) than *N*-version programming (i.e., all copies must execute prior to a decision), several questions remain. What is the best way to assure that acceptance tests exhibit a high probability of detecting errors, yet require low execution overhead? What methodologies should be used to generate alternative copies? Should diverse programming be used for these alternatives? How can the rollback and restart software be made error-free? These and other questions are the topic of on-going research.

SUMMARY

The presentation of reliability techniques in this chapter followed the organization of Table 3–1, which provides a logical progression from the simplest methods of fault avoidance to the most complex methods of dynamic redundancy. Fault-detection techniques provide a means of flagging the presence of errors and offers an increase in system availability through more rapid failure diagnosis. However, because it does not provide fault tolerance, fault detection alone does not improve system reliability (at least not in terms of the reliability function). Fault-masking redundancy techniques improve system reliability by allowing the system to operate correctly in the presence of faults. Minor amounts of extra redundancy in the form of fault detection adds the benefits of error flagging and rapid diagnosis to a fault-masking design. Fault masking is limited by its static configuration—that is, a system employing a fault-masking technique cannot heal itself, but only hide its failures. Eventually, the accumulation of failures is large enough to saturate the fault-masking ability, and the entire system fails. Increased system reliability further requires the use of dynamic redundancy techniques combined with repair. Here, fault detection is combined with reconfiguration of system components to compensate for the failure and thus restore the system health. Fault masking may be considered a dynamic redundancy technique if fault masking is used to postpone reconfiguration until masked faults have accumulated sufficiently to cause system failure.

The chapter provides descriptions and examples of a multitude of individual techniques. It also provides a comprehensive review of the literature on experimental studies, and it reviews evaluation criteria and methodologies for various techniques. Finally, while the chapter does not emphasize strategies for combining two or more reliability improvement techniques, a few examples of such combinations have been mentioned, especially if vastly improved protection is provided by the combination.

REFERENCES

Abraham, 1975; Adams, Agrawal, and Siegel, 1987; Anderson, 1971; Anderson, 1975; Anderson et al., 1985; Anderson and Lee, 1979; Anderson and Lee, 1981; Anderson, Lee, and Shrivastava, 1979; Anderson and Knight, 1983; Anderson and Metze, 1973; Armstrong, 1961; Arulpragasm and Swarz, 1980; Ashjaee and Reddy, 1976; Avizienis, 1971, 1973, 1977, 1978, 1985; Avizienis and Chen, 1977; Avizienis et al., 1971, Avizienis et al. 1985; Avizienis and Kelly, 1984; Avizienis, Lyu, and Schutz, 1988; AWST, 1981.

Barsi and Maestrini, 1973, 1974; Baskin, Borgerson, and Roberts, 1971, 1972; Beaudry, 1978; Becker, 1983; Berlekamp, 1968; Bhargava, 1987; Bhatt and Kinney, 1978; Bishop et al., 1985; Bishop et al., 1986; Bitton and Gray, 1988; Black, Sundberg, and Walker, 1977; Blahut, 1984; Boone, Liebergot, and Sedmak, 1980; Borgerson and Freitas, 1975; Bossen, 1970; Bossen and Hsiao, 1982; Bouricius et al., 1971; Brilliant, Knight, and Leveson, 1989, 1990; Brookes, 1975; Brown, Tierney, and Wasserman, 1961.

Carter, 1983; Carter, Duke, and Jessup, 1973; Carter, Joyner, and Brand, 1978; Carter and McCarthy, 1976; Carter and Schneider, 1968; Carter and Wadia, 1980;

Castillo and Siewiorek, 1980; Chandy and Ramamoorthy, 1972; Chen, 1983; Chen, 1984; Chen, 1986a, 1986b; Chen and Avizienis, 1978; Chen and Hsiao, 1984; Chen et al., 1990; Chinal, 1977; Cook et al., 1973; Cooper and Chow, 1976; Codri, 1984; Craig, 1980; Cristian, 1982; Crocker, 1977; Crouzet and Landrault, 1980.

Davies and Wakerly, 1978; DeAngelis and Lauro, 1976; Dennis, 1974; DeSousa and Mathur, 1978; Diaz, Azema, and Ayache, 1979; Diaz, Geffroy, and Courvoisier, 1974; Dickinson, Jackson, and Randa, 1964; DEC, 1975, 1977, 1979; Dunham, 1986.

Eckhardt and Lee, 1985; Efstathiou and Halatsis, 1983; Elkind, 1983; Elmendorf, 1972; Fabre et al., 1988; Frank and Yau, 1966; Freeman and Metze, 1972, 1979; Fuchs and Abraham, 1984; Fujiwara and Kawakami, 1977; Fujiwara and Matsuoka, 1985.

Gaitanis, 1988; Gay and Ketelson, 1979; Geiger et al., 1979; Gibson et al., 1989; Glasser, 1975; Gmeiner and Voges, 1979; Goguen and Tardo, 1979; Goldberg, Levitt, and Wensley, 1974; Gumpertz, 1981; Gurzi, 1965.

Halbert and Bose, 1984; Hamming, 1950; Hampel and Winder, 1971; Hecht, 1976; Hill, 1986; Hills, 1985; Hong and Patel, 1972; Hopkins, Smith, and Lala, 1978; Horning et al., 1974; Howden, 1980; Hsiao, 1970; Hsaio and Bossen, 1975; Hsiao, Bossen, and Chien, 1970; Huang and Abraham, 1984; Hughes, McCluskey, and Lu, 1983.

Ihara et al., 1978; Ingle and Siewiorek, 1973a, 1973b, 1976; Interdata, 1975; Iyengar and Kinney, 1982, 1985; Jack et al., 1975; Jensen, 1963; Johnson, 1987; Jones, 1975; Joyner, Carter, and Leeman, 1976.

Kaneda, 1984; Kaneda and Fujiwara, 1980; Katsuki et al, 1978; Kautz, 1962; Kautz, Levitt, and Waksman, 1968; Kelly, 1982; Kelly and Avizienis, 1983; Kelly et al., 1988; Khakbaz and McCluskey, 1982; Khodadad-Mostashiry, 1979; Kim, 1984, 1986; Klaassen and Van Peppen, 1977a, 1977b; Klaschka, 1969; Knight and Leveson, 1985, 1986a, 1986b; Kole, 1980; Kopetz, 1976.

Lamport, 1977; Lamport, Shostak, and Pease, 1982; Lampson, 1979; Laprie, 1984; Larsen and Reed, 1972; Lee, Ghani, and Heron, 1980; Leveson and Harvey, 1983; Levitt, Green, and Goldberg, 1968; Levy, 1984; Lewis, 1979; Lin, 1970; Linger, Mills, and Levi, 1979; Littlewood, 1987; Littlewood and Miller,1987; Losq, 1975a, 1975b, 1976, 1977, 1978; Lu, 1982.

MacWilliams and Sloane, 1978; Mahmood, Ersoz, and McCluskey, 1985; Mahmood and McCluskey, 1988; Mahmood, McCluskey, and Lu, 1983; Maison, 1971; Mak, Abraham, and Davidson, 1982; Mandelbaum, 1972a, 1972b; Marcus, Crocker, and Landauer, 1984; Marouf and Friedman, 1977, 1978; Martin, 1982; Mathur, 1971a; Mathur and Avizienis, 1970; Mathur and DeSousa, 1975; McCluskey, 1985a, 1985b; McCluskey and Ogus, 1977; McConnel and Siewiorek, 1981; McDonald, 1976; McDonald and Mc-Cracken, 1977; McKevitt, 1972; McLeod, 1988; McNamara, 1977; Meraud, Browaeys, and Germain, 1976; Meraud et al., 1979; Meyer, 1971, 1978; Meyer, Furchgott, and Wu, 1980; Mine and Hatayama, 1979; Mine and Koga, 1967; Morganti, Coppadoro, and Ceru, 1978; Mukai and Thoma, 1974; Muntz and Lei, 1990; Musa, Iannino, and Okomoto, 1976.

Nagel and Skrivan, 1982; Namjoo, 1982, 1983; Nanya and Tohma, 1983; Negrini, Sani, and Stefanelli, 1986; Neumann and Rao, 1975; Ng, 1988; O'Brien, 1976; Ogus,

1973, 1974; Oktay, Dessauer, and Horvath, 1983; Ornstein et al., 1975; Osman and Weiss, 1973; Ossfeldt and Jonsson, 1980; Ozgunner, 1977.

Parnas, 1972; Patterson, Gibson, and Katz, 1988; Patterson and Metze, 1974; Peterson and Weldon, 1972; Pierce, 1965; Piestrak, 1983; Platteter, 1980; Pradhan, 1978a, 1978b, 1980; Pradhan and Reddy, 1974a, 1974b, 1978; Pradhan and Stiffler, 1980.

Ramamoorthy et al., 1981; Ramarao and Adams, 1988; Randell, 1975; Randell, Lee, and Treleaven, 1978; Rao, 1970, 1972, 1974; Ray-Chaudhuri, 1961; Reddy, 1978; Reddy and Banerjee, 1989; Reed and Chiang, 1970; Rennels, 1980; Russel, 1978; Russell and Tiedeman, 1979; Russo, 1965.

Saglietti and Ehrenberger, 1986; Saib, 1977; Sawin, 1975; Schmid et al., 1982; Schriefer, Voges, and Weber, 1983; Schuette and Shen, 1987; Schuette et al., 1986; Schulze et al., 1989; Sedmak and Liebergot, 1980; Sellers, Hsiao, and Bearnson, 1968b; Shaw, 1986; Shedletsky, 1978a, 1978b; Shen and Hayes, 1980; Shen and Schuette, 1983; Shimeall and Leveson, 1988; Short, 1968; Shrivastava and Akinpelu, 1978; Siewiorek, Bell, and Newell, 1982; Siewiorek, Canepa, and Clark, 1977a; Siewiorek and Mc-Cluskey, 1973a, 1973b; Siewiorek et al., 1978a, 1978b; Sklaroff, 1976; Smith and Hopkins, 1978; Smith and Metze, 1978; Sridhar and Thatte, 1982; Srinivason, 1971b; Stiffler, 1976, 1978; Stonebraker and Schloss, 1990; Swan, Fuller, and Siewiorek, 1977.

Tamir, Tremblay, and Rennels, 1978; Tang and Chien, 1969; Tao, Lala, and Hartmann, 1987; Taylor, Morgan, and Black, 1980; Tendolkar and Swann, 1982; Texas Instruments, 1976; Tohma, 1974; Tohma and Aoyagi, 1971; Tokura, Kasami, and Hashimoto, 1971; Torng, 1972; Toy, 1978; Troy, 1977, 1978; Tryon, 1962; Tso and Avizienis, 1987.

US, 1986; Usas, 1978. Voges, 1985; Voges, Fetsch, and Gmeiner, 1982; von Neumann, 1956; Vouk et al., 1986; Wachter, 1975; Wakerly, 1974, 1978; Waksman, 1968; Wallace and Barnes, 1984; Watson and Hastings, 1966; Weissberger, 1980; Wensley et al., 1978; Wilken and Shen, 1987, 1988; Yau and Chen, 1980; Yount, 1984.

PROBLEMS

1. There are 32 data lines on a bus protected by four interlaced parity bits. Parity bits 1 and 3 are odd parity and parity bits 2 and 4 are even parity.
   a. Sketch the data bus and indicate which lines are covered by which parity bits.
   b. List all fault sets that are detected in one bus transfer. Illustrate one fault from each set on your diagram.

2. Assuming that only transient errors lasting exactly one operation cycle of the system can occur, the triple modular redundancy is equivalent to which of the following (choose one):
   a. A Hamming single-error-correcting, double-error-detecting code
   b. A simple parity code (odd parity)
   c. A repetition code with a complete decoding algorithm
   d. A repetition code with an incomplete decoding algorithm

3. The following is a parity-check matrix for a (7,4) Hamming code:

	c_1	c_2	d_1	c_3	d_2	d_3	d_4
c_1	1	0	1	0	1	1	0
c_2	0	1	1	0	0	1	1
c_3	0	0	0	1	1	0	1

a. Write the equations for calculating the values of the check bits.
b. If $d_1 d_2 d_3 d_4$ = 1101, calculate the corresponding code word.
c. Assuming byte- (rather than bit-) wide symbols, if

$d_1 d_2 d_3 d_4$ = 23, 128, 169, 92

calculate the corresponding code word.
d. The following code word was received:

7, 41, 45, 22, 255, 96, 156

Assuming byte-wide symbols, are there any errors? If so, which byte is in error and what is its correct value? If not, why not?
e. The following code word was received: 0 0 0 0 1 0 1. Assuming bit-wide symbols, are there any errors? If so, which bit is in error and what is its correct value? If not, why not?

4. A Hamming single-error-correcting code has the following parity-check matrix:

$$H = \begin{bmatrix} 0 & 0 & 1 & 1 & 1 & 0 & 1 \\ 0 & 1 & 0 & 0 & 1 & 1 & 1 \\ 1 & 0 & 0 & 1 & 1 & 1 & 0 \end{bmatrix}$$

The word [0111011] was received; which of the following is the word sent?
a. [0110011]   b. [0111001]   c. [0111010]   d. [0001011]

5. The following is a parity matrix for a Hamming code:

	d_1	c_1	d_2	c_2	d_3	c_3	d_4
c_1	0	1	1	1	0	1	0
c_2	1	0	0	1	0	1	1
c_3	1	1	0	0	1	1	0

a. Write the parity equations for the three check bits.
b. Using these parity equations, encode the following data word: $d_1 d_2 d_3 d_4$ = 0110
c. The encoded word 1100001 ($d_1 c_1 d_2 c_2 d_3 c_3 d_4$) has a single bit-error. Which bit is in error?
d. Assuming that bit failures are independent and the probability of failure is p, what is the probability that the encoded data is not decoded correctly?
e. If the receiver and support electronics have a reliability of $k(1 - p)$, where k is a constant, what value of p maximizes the reliability of the system?

6. A binary transmission channel is said to be an erasure channel if a received bit may be neither a one nor a zero. Such an error is called an *erasure*. To correct up to e erasures, what is the minimum distance between any two code words?
a. e b. $e + 1$ c. $2e$ d. $2e + 1$

7. Which of the following cannot be a code word in a linear single-error-correcting Hamming code?
a. 0010110   b. 1101100   c. 1110110   d. 0110000   e. 1010111

8. A 3-of-6 code was modified by adding two check bits that indicated how many ones the six information bits have. What number of all possible erroneous words go undetected?
a. 20   b. 22   3. 32   d. 42   e. 41

9. What is the arithmetic distance between the two code words [100001] and [010011]?
   a. 1   b. 2   c. 3   d. 4
10. In a 25 N + 15 single-error-correcting arithmetic code, if a word [10010011] is received from the ALU, what is the corrected output of the ALU?
    a. 0001011   b. 1011011   c. 0111011   d. 1001100   e. 1110011
11. A biresidue code forms residues modulo-3 and modulo-7. An erroneous word is given as follows: ([01111], 2, 0). Assuming that the check bits are correct, what are the corrected information bits?
    a. [10000]   b. [10001]   c. [01110]   d. [01101]
12. In a computing system, memory is one of the chief sources of failures. When a high degree of data integrity is desired, the overhead for encoding and decoding may be tolerated. To correct a single-bit error (Hamming error) in an 8-bit byte, speed is to be sacrificed in favor of minimizing the total storage required for a task. The problem is thus to maximize the number of code words. Find a single-error-correcting code of block length eight with a maximum number of code words. (Hint: A linear code of block length eight has 16 code words. A code that is made up of a number of cyclic spaces has 20 code words but is not the code that maximizes the number of code words.)
13. For the double-error-correcting code with the parity-check matrix

$$H = \begin{bmatrix} 0 & 0 & 1 & 1 & 1 & 0 & 1 \\ 0 & 1 & 0 & 0 & 1 & 1 & 1 \\ 1 & 0 & 0 & 1 & 1 & 1 & 0 \\ 0 & 0 & 1 & 1 & 0 & 1 & 1 \\ 0 & 1 & 0 & 1 & 1 & 0 & 1 \\ 1 & 1 & 1 & 0 & 0 & 0 & 1 \end{bmatrix}$$

the syndrome formed was [101110]. What is the implication (choose one)?
    a. No error   b. Single error   c. Double error   d. More than two errors
14. With the same parity-check matrix, if the bits are numbered 1 through 7 from left to right, what does the syndrome [100111] imply (choose one)?
    a. A single error in position 3   b. Two bit errors in positions 1 and 4
    c. Two bit errors in positions 1 and 5   d. More than two bit errors
15. For a double-error-correcting code of block length 32, what is the least upper bound on the number of information bits (choose one)?
    a. 24   b. 25   c. 26   d. 27   e. 28
16. Given the polynomials $h(x) = x^2 + 1$ and $g(x) = x^4 + x + 1$ and the circuit in Figure P3–1 (with proper initial conditions), what output can be obtained from the incoming polynomial $f(x)$?

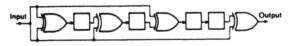

FIGURE P3–1

    a. f/gh b. fh/g c. fg/h d. fgh e. $f(g + h)$

17. With the input polynomial $x^7 + 1$ and the circuit in Figure P3–2, what is the output polynomial?

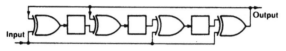

FIGURE P3–2

a. $x + 1$ b. $x^2 + 1$ c. $x^{14} + 1$ d. $x^7 + x^6 + x^5 + x^4 + x + 1$

18. A new disk storage unit is to be added to a computer system. Because the performance of the system deteriorates considerably as the result of disk failures, the new disk should be as reliable as possible. The field was narrowed to two disks, DSKRAW and DSKCRC. Both store up to 600 million bytes (8-bit wide) and run at a rate of 3600 rpm with a byte transfer frequency of 4 MHz. Both cost approximately the same. The difference lies in redundancy techniques. DSKRAW uses a read-after-write (RAW) to detect (and correct) errors in transfer, while DSKCRC uses a cyclic redundancy check. The CRC generates a 16-bit check word using a generator polynomial, $x^{16} + x^{12} + x^5 + 1$, on an information frame of any size. Carry out a reliability analysis on the two disks and make recommendations.

19. The 80486 microprocessor chip has approximately 400,000 gates.
    a. Calculate the failure rates of this architecture assuming SSI, MSI, and LSI implementation (40°C ambient).
    b. What is the effect of changing π_q for the three preceding implementations? Changing the ambient temperature from 40°C to 30°C? Compare these effects over the three different implementations.
    c. Assume that SSI chips cost 20 cents, MSI chips 50 cents, and LSI chips $10 and that screening weeds out all but 0.2 percent of the weak components. Also assume that the average diagnosis and repair cost of a bad chip is $5, plus the chip cost through the warranty period. Compare the expected repair costs for the SSI, MSI, and LSI implementations of the 80486 architecture.

20. In a memory made with 1M-bit by 4-bit-wide chips, there are 16 data bits and 2M words. The 0- and 1-bit values are equally likely. Assume chip failure modes are single-bit cell (50 percent), single-row all-0's (20 percent), single-column all-0's (20 percent), and whole-chip all-0's (10 percent).
    a. Calculate single-error-detection coverage for this scheme when the following detection techniques are used: interlaced parity ($i = 4$); chip parity, chip-wide parity, duplication, single-precision checksum (assume checksum is stored separately, one sum for the entire memory); and low-cost residue code (checksum stored separately).
    b. Estimate costs (chip counts) for the preceding memories, including check circuitry. Comment on relative performance overheads.

21. What is the CRC constant for the CRC code used by AUTODIN II, with $G(x) = x^{32} + x^{26} + x^{23} + x^{16} + x^{12} + x^{11} + x^{10} + x^8 + x^7 + x^5 + x^4 + x^2 + x + 1$? Design a BCR for this code.

22. In the multiplexer for parity-coded operands shown in Figure P3–3 [Wakerly, 1978], $\langle S_1 S_0 \rangle = \langle 01 \rangle$ transfers bus A to bus T, while $\langle 10 \rangle$ transfers bus B to bus T.
    a. Demonstrate that this circuit is totally self-checking.
    b. Design a totally self-checking multiplexer network around this TSC multiplexer; that is, the network serves as a multiplexer with a TSC error-detection indicator.

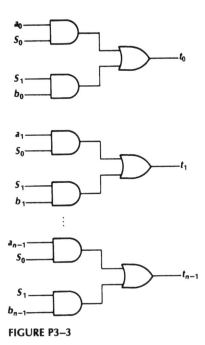

FIGURE P3–3

23. Use the next-state and output-function in the following table:

	Input			
State	01	11	10	00
a	a/1	c/0	h/0	e/1
b	c/1	a/1	d/1	f/0
c	b/1	g/0	e/1	f/1
d	g/0	c/0	d/1	e/1
e	a/1	b/0	c/0	e/0
f	b/0	b/1	g/1	h/0
g	h/0	h/1	b/0	g/1
h	e/1	c/1	d/1	a/1

next state/output

a. Design a single-error-correcting coded-state machine. Compare its cost and reliability with a TMR implementation of the same machine. The machine is synchronous, with an external clock signal.

b. Implement the next-state function in quadded logic. Compare the cost with a TMR implementation. Compare maximum clocking speeds.

24. a. Design restoring organs for a redundant module with two output lines and a redundancy factor of 5 (five identical modules) using the following techniques: NMR/simplex ($N = 5$); hybrid TMR; duplication with spares switching (assume an external diagnostic circuit can correctly determine which of the two modules is faulty with probability 0.95, and

takes 10 ms to do so); self-purging redundancy; and sift-out redundancy. Use standard TTL logic (designs down to pin number detail are not necessary).

b. Assume that new data are produced synchronously every 500 ns, that gate complexities for the function modules are 2,000 gates each, and that the duplication diagnostic circuit uses 300 gates. Compare the five designs for complexity, cost, performance, and reliability.

25. Discuss the issues involved in making a multiprocessor system gracefully degradable (cost, extra circuitry, performance, computation overhead, detection and diagnostic capability). Assume that no modification can be made to the hardware and that simple alterations can be made to the hardware.

26. For the SEC/DED/SBD code on page 154, select four columns from the matrix corresponding to a 4-bit byte. Demonstrate that any pattern of errors in that byte will generate a syndrome that will not match any other column, and is thus detectable.

27. Derive a method of applying signature checking to a finite state machine.

28. Consider the following three code words:

$x = 1\ 1\ 1\ 0\ 1\ 0$

$y = 1\ 0\ 1\ 1\ 1\ 0$

$z = 1\ 1\ 0\ 0\ 0\ 0$

a. What is the minimum Hamming distance for this code? Between which code words does this occur? Show all calculations.

b. What is the minimum arithmetic distance for this code? Between which code words does this occur? Show all calculations.

29. Select a computer system for which processor and operating system documentation is available to you. Analyze the fault-tolerance, fault-detection, and recovery techniques and abilities of the hardware/software system. Propose some low-cost improvements that might be made.

30. a. Pick a technique from each of the subsections in Chapter 3 dealing with error detection, fault masking, and dynamic redundancy. Use each independently in the design of the same (logically) microstore. Rank the designs in terms of cost, performance, and reliability.

b. Combine the techniques chosen previously in groups of two (using each technique in only one pair) and apply them to the same microstore. Rank the designs in terms of cost, performance, and reliability.

c. Select four of the previously mentioned techniques to make the best possible mocrostore design. Evaluate the cost, performance, and reliability of this design.

31. a. A digital system block diagram is shown in Figure P3–4. Discuss which fault-detection techniques can be used to prevent undetected errors in this system.

b. Discuss the application of TMR with voting to this system. Consider replication at various architectural levels.

c. Discuss the application of error-correcting codes to this system in at least five different segments of the design.

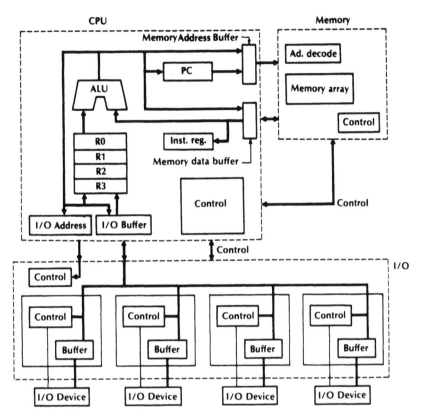

FIGURE P3-4

4 MAINTAINABILITY AND TESTING TECHNIQUES

A significant proportion of maintenance procedures involve some form of diagnosis, not only to isolate the failed component but also to ensure that the repair operation is successful. Generally speaking, diagnosis can be either retrospective or predictive (see the discussion in Maxion and Siewiorek, 1985). *Retrospective diagnosis* seeks to determine what caused a system failure—the "What happened?" question. It can increase system availability by facilitating the quick revival of fallen systems. *Predictive diagnosis* seeks to determine when a failure will occur—the "What if?" question. Predictive diagnosis (failure prediction) can turn corrective maintenance into preventive maintenance, thereby increasing perceived system reliability. Retrospective diagnosis enables operators and maintainers to assess problems immediately and restore service quickly, while predictive diagnosis can be used to guide preventive and preemptive maintenance. In each case, system downtime is reduced.

Diagnosis is often associated with device troubleshooting and is sometimes confused with testing. It is important to understand the distinction between diagnosis and testing. *Testing* is a measurement procedure whose goal is to provide information sufficient for determining whether or not a unit under test responds to a stimulus in accordance with a prespecified standard. *Diagnosis* is a constrained search procedure whose goal is to guide the administration of tests. Results of testing are often used diagnostically to provide additional symptomatic evidence for deciding which further tests to perform. In practice, the two processes—testing and diagnosis—are often mixed indistinguishably.

The two basic approaches to the diagnosis of system failure are the specification-based and symptom-based approaches [Maxion and Siewiorek, 1985]. In a specification-based approach, system design specifications provide information for determining the expected behavior of a system under particular conditions. Diagnostic tests based on this projected behavior are then developed. Traditional diagnostic programs, of the sort employed to help isolate a fault after evidence of failure has surfaced, are exemplary of the specification-based approach. These programs "diagnose" by returning good or bad results from prespecified tests. Such programs are limited in important ways, particularly in their ability to isolate unanticipated faults.

Symptoms-based diagnosis is the identification of a (fault) condition based on its symptoms. This type of diagnosis uses the information captured in system event logs (sometimes called error logs) and real-time monitoring data to diagnose faults.* Much

---

* Event logs are records of system events as documented by the operating system. An event log could

as an automobile's history tells a story to a mechanic, past sequences of events can be reconstructed from system event logs, often revealing the circumstances under which an error or other significant event occurred. Symptom-based diagnosis bases its diagnostic judgments on evaluations of system behavior. The symptoms on which the approach is based are frequently more accurate indicators of the actual state of a system than are the indicators in a specification-based approach. Moreover, it is a common observation that standard diagnostic programs cannot stress a system in the same way that an actual system workload can, and hence they are often incapable of replicating a failure.

This chapter examines maintainability from the perspective of both specification-based and symptom-based diagnosis.

SPECIFICATION-BASED DIAGNOSIS

The core of specification-based diagnosis is testing. Testing can be characterized as a "black box" experiment. Each black box has an associated set of input and output terminals. The correct functioning of the black box must be determined by applying stimuli to the input terminals and observing responses, which are called *terminal characteristics*, on the output terminals. The terminal characteristics may be electrical (such as a straight-line relationship between voltage and current for a resistor), combinational (such as an AND gate), sequential (such as a counter), or even complex systems (such as a microprocessor on a chip). As the functions of the component become more complex, the testing problem becomes critical, for there is less direct control and less direct observability of internal behavior. Manipulation of external inputs must establish a certain condition in a component deep in the recesses of the black box, and the outputs of that component must be propagated to the output terminals. With increasing system complexity, not only are there more components, but each component is also harder to test.

Testing covers multiple activities, not just maintenance, during the stages in the life of a digital system (see Table 1–2, p. 6). During the first stage, *specification and design*, the faults of most concern are logic errors in the algorithms. During the *prototype development* stage, any number of failures are possible, including logical design errors, wiring mistakes, incorrect timing—all of which can lead to different functional behavior. Failed components can also cause altered functional behavior. The former, designated as a *logical fault*, can be significantly more difficult to test than the latter, termed a *structural fault*. With logical faults, the proper algorithm must ultimately be distinguished from any arbitrary algorithm. Here testing involves many similarities to proving programs correct; however, given a correct design, there are many fewer faulty behaviors caused by a malfunction. The component interconnections limit the number of realizable fault behaviors. In prototype development, the final

conceivably contain a record of every operation performed by the system. In practice, event logs contain only a subset of system event records, although they almost always include all detected errors; hence, the common misnomer, *error log*. Examples of normal system events are network and bus traffic loads, process completions or aborts, and devices going on and off line. Examples of abnormal events are errors originating in such devices as central processors, disk drives, controllers, buses, memories, and other subsystems.

errors in the design and proposed implementation are sought by testing. Physical connectivity may cause timing errors and coupling between multiple signal lines. Subjecting a small number of systems to design maturity testing (described in Chapter 1) establishes baseline failure manifestations and MTTF.

During the *manufacturing* and *installation* stages of a system, the main goal is acceptance testing. Here, problems of design have been resolved, and testing focuses on the mass-produced black boxes. The faults are primarily structural, but there may be any number of them resulting from the assembly process. When a system malfunctions during the *operational* stage, maintenance testing is used to isolate and repair faults. This form of testing is perhaps the easiest form of testing, since at this stage there are few structural faults. Frequently, maintenance tests are run during system idle time to detect failures and increase confidence in the correct functioning of the system. As mentioned in Chapter 1, there is a significant trend toward remote diagnosis, either to pinpoint failures before dispatching field service personnel or to issue instructions for customer repair.

At any of the stages of system life, testing can occur at each level in the physical hierarchy defined in Chapter 1. It is extremely important to understand at what level and stage a testing technique is aimed. Thus, Figure 4–1 classifies types of testing by hierarchical level and temporal stage. Note that the figure has been simplified by combining some of the levels and stages given in Chapter 1, where system-level testing at all of the stages was briefly discussed. The following sections discuss testing techniques in more detail according to the three stages given in Figure 4–1.

Design Stage

During this stage, the first priority is to produce a correct design, which is usually accomplished by testing to exercise or validate the design. During the initial phase, goals are set for product reliability. These goals are derived either from prior experience with similar products or from market trends. As the first prototypes are completed, a test is set up to determine whether the design has the potential of reaching the

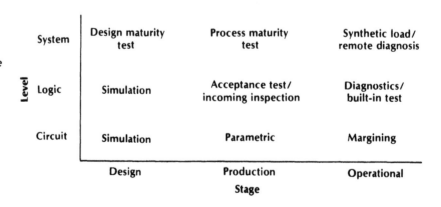

FIGURE 4–1

Testing as a function of system level and life cycle stage

Level	Design	Production	Operational
System	Design maturity test	Process maturity test	Synthetic load/ remote diagnosis
Logic	Simulation	Acceptance test/ incoming inspection	Diagnostics/ built-in test
Circuit	Simulation	Parametric	Margining

Stage

specification goals. As pointed out in Chapter 1, a design maturity test (DMT), sometimes called a reliability qualification test (RQT), estimates the mean time to failure (MTTF) for a new product before it is committed to volume manufacture. During the DMT, repetitive and systematic problems are isolated and corrected. The DMT is applied to a set of sample devices for a period of time (typically 10 to 50 units for one to six months) simulating actual field operation. The number of units and the test time are a function of the goal MTTF and the number of failures observed. After the fundamental causes of failure are found and corrective action is taken, the test procedure is continued until the estimated MTTF of the test sample meets the specifications with a certain statistical confidence.

Design Validation. Exercising software to locate design errors or "bugs" has its origins mingled with the origins of programming [ACM, 1976]. These techniques not only apply to software but also to hardware during the requirement and design stages. Techniques such as bench checking, peer review, and design walk-throughs were discussed as software fault avoidance techniques.

Testing techniques can be grouped into functional (black box) and structural (white box) approaches. In functional testing, the system is treated as a black box, with no knowledge of the internal structure available. One approach in black-box testing revolves around boundary value analysis. The observation has been made that regions in which systems change sign from positive to negative or reach their minimum or maximum values are those where programmers are likely to make mistakes. Design-based functional testing approaches use the design hierarchy both to provide partitioning for testing and to suggest input combinations. Cause-effect graphing generates test cases from high-level specifications. For example, if 8 bits are used to formulate the input stimuli, there are 256 "types" of input whose responses can be collected into effect classes. Thus, a decision table can be formulated that relates the input "types" to the output "effect classes."

Structural testing, on the other hand, utilizes information about the internal organization not only to simplify test set generation but also to remove from consideration behavior that cannot be generated as a permutation of the existing structure. The structure is used to create the effectiveness of test data. The general term *test coverage* is used as a figure of merit. Coverage can be based upon the percentage of the structure that is exercised. Several attributes of the structure can be used to calculate the coverage. Branches, paths, and decision-to-decision paths can all be used as a basis for measuring coverage.

Coverage can be dynamically determined by seeding the code with counters that are incremented each time they are passed. After execution of the test, counters that contain zero indicate branches and/or a path that were not exercised. Coverage can also be based upon complexity of the software structure and is measured by either graph complexity or software science [Halstead, 1979].

The effectiveness of the testing process can be estimated by injecting errors [Acree et al., 1982; Acree, 1980; Adrion, Branstad, and Cheriavsky, 1982; Budd et al., 1980]. Error seeding is the process of inserting faults (errors) into the software during debugging. When the acceptable percentage of the seeded errors is found, the debugging effort ceases. It is assumed that the unseeded errors (programmers' errors) are found at the same rate as the seeded errors, and thus error seeding provides a measure of the number of unfound errors. Mutation analysis is used as a measure of test program coverage. Faults (mutations), which are a slight perturbation of a program statement (such as changing a plus sign to a minus sign), are inserted one at a time into lines of code. Test sets are run to determine if the mutation is detected, thus gaining a measure of the test effectiveness.

Alternatively, the program can be analyzed statically without the application of test inputs. For example, flow analysis identifies undefined variables that are potential sources of design errors. Symbolic execution generates equations at various points of the program that can be used as verification conditions for formal proofs. However, symbolic execution grows exponentially in complexity if there are loops in the code.

Lower Confidence Level Test. The lower confidence level test ensures that when an accepted decision is made, the mean time to failure is at least the specified value within the lower confidence level certainty. The typical lower confidence level is 90 percent. The test does not say that 90 percent of the systems will have a mean time to failure greater than the specified mean time to failure. Rather it expresses a probability that the actual system mean time to failure is at least the specified value.

The lower confidence level MTTF is given by

$$\theta_L = \frac{2T}{\chi^2_{2r,\alpha}} \tag{1}$$

where T is the total number of hours of operation for all units and χ is the chi-squared value with $2r$ degrees of freedom at the α level of confidence. The number of observed failures is $r - 1$.

Example. The following data depicts a system whose specified mean time to failure is one year (8760 hours):

Total Test Hours	Total Failures	MTTF Estimate	90 Percent LCL
8,760	1	8,760	2,252
17,520	2	8,760	3,306
26,280	3	8,760	3,922
35,040	4	8,760	4,380

The estimated MTTF is the total number of hours divided by the total number of failures. Even though the system has an MTTF of one year, our confidence in that value grows slowly from only one quarter of that value for one year of testing to only half of that value after four unit-years of testing.

Alternatively, we can solve Eq. 1 for the total number of hours required to pass the test as a function of the number of failures. The following data illustrates the large number of unit test time required to pass the 90% lower confidence level test:

Number of Failures	Total Test Time to Accept in Multiples of Specified MTTF	Number of Failures	Total Test Time to Accept in Multiples of Specified MTTF
0	2.3	6	10.55
1	3.89	7	11.75
2	5.3	8	13
3	6.7	9	14.2
4	8	10	15.4
5	9.25		

For example, if there are no observed failures, we require 2.3 times the specific mean time to failure of system hours to be 90 percent confident that the actual system MTTF is better than the specified value. Figure 4–2 depicts the slow asymptotic growth of the 90 percent lower confidence level to the actual specified mean time to failure by normalizing and extending the values in the total test hours given in the table above. This slow asymptotic growth implies either a long test period or a large number of units under test to accumulate the required unit test hours. Since this time is unacceptably long, other tests were developed to prove product MTTF.

Sequential Probability Ratio Test. Rather than pick a specific target mean time to failure, the amount of test time can be shortened by specifying a range for the mean time to failure. The sequential probability ratio test (SPRT) has been developed and used in procuring military systems. The SPRT defines a number of parameters [Mil Handbook 781]:

• Upper bound on MTTF; θ_0, which is the value above which the manufacturer believes is the useful life of the product.

FIGURE 4–2

The asymptotic approach of the 90 percent LCL to the actual MTTF

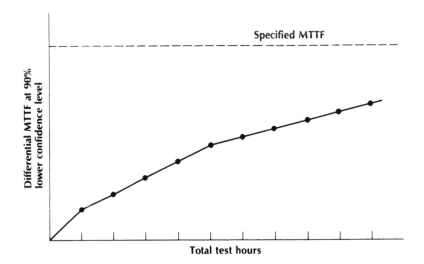

- Minimal acceptable MTTF, θ_1, which is the value below which the product will be noncompetitive in the marketplace.
- Producers' risk, α, which is the probability that a product with a true MTTF = θ_0, will be rejected.
- Consumers' risk, β, which is the probability that a product with a true MTTF = θ_1, will be accepted.

A ratio of θ_0 and θ_1 between 1.5 and 3—termed the *discrimination ratio, d*—is typically used. Consumers' and producers' risk are commonly taken to be 20 percent.

The concept of sequential tests is derived from the expected number of failures in an observation period T. For electronic equipment with a constant failure rate hazard function that follows the Poisson distribution the probability of K failures in time $[0,t]$ is given by

$$P(K) = (\lambda t)^K \frac{e^{-\lambda t}}{K!} \tag{2}$$

In order to conform to the notation in Mil Handbook 781, we will replace k by r and λ by $1/\theta$ where λ is failure rate and $1/\theta$ is the mean time to failure. These substitutions yield

$$P(r) = \left(\frac{t}{\theta}\right)^r \frac{e^{-t/\theta}}{r!} \tag{3}$$

This equation predicts the number of failures expected to be observed in time t. By substituting θ_0 for a lower bound and θ_1 for a lower bound we can form the ratio

$$P_{\text{ratio}} = \frac{P_1(r)}{P_2(r)} = \left(\frac{\theta_0}{\theta_1}\right)^r e^{-(1/\theta_1 - 1/\theta_0)t} \tag{4}$$

This ratio is constantly evaluated throughout the test. If the ratio is larger than a specified constant A, the test is stopped and the hypothesis rejected. On the other hand, if the ratio becomes less than B, the test is terminated with an accept decision. In between, results are inconclusive and the testing needs to be continued. In equation form, the test criteria become

$$B < P_{\text{ratio}} < A \tag{5}$$

$$\text{where } A = \frac{(1 - \beta)(d + 1)}{2\alpha d} \tag{6}$$

$$B = \frac{\beta}{1 - \alpha}$$

The extra factor of $(d + 1)/(2d)$ in the term A is a correction factor arising from the fact that the test is truncated. By taking natural logarithms and solving for r we can get the a linear relationship in time.

Figure 4–3 is a standard test plan for a discrimination ratio of 2 (i.e., θ_0/θ_1 is equal

FIGURE 4–3

The sequential test plan for α = β = 20 percent and discrimination ratio d = 2.0 [From Mil Handbook 781]

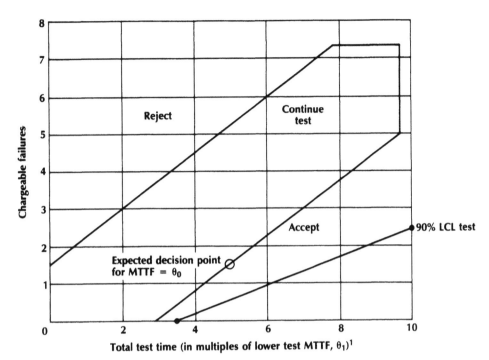

Chargeable failures	Standardized Termination time, t^2	
	Reject at $t_R \leq$	Accept at $t_A \geq$
0	N/A	2.80
1	N/A	4.18
2	.70	5.58
3	2.08	6.96
4	3.46	8.34
5	4.86	9.74
6	6.24	9.74
7	7.62	9.74
8	9.74	N/A

Accept-reject criteria

[1]Total test time is the summation of operating time of all units included in test sample.
[2]To determine the actual termination time, multiply the standardized termination time (t) by the lower test MTTF (θ_1).

FIGURE 4–4

The sequential test plan for $\alpha = \beta = 30$ percent and discrimination ratio $d = 2.0$

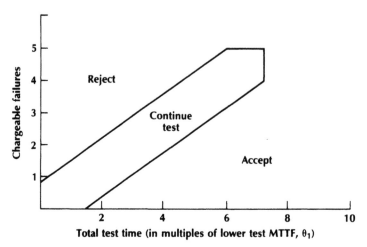

to 2) and 20 percent risk factor. The test time is given in multiples of the lower mean time to failure, θ_1. The table gives the expected times for making accept or reject decisions as a function of the number of observed failures. By way of comparison, the 90 percent lower confidence level test is indicated on the same graph, and it depicts much longer times to make a decision. As the risk values get larger, the region of ambiguity (continue testing) grows smaller, as depicted in Figure 4–4.

The continue testing region is defined by two straight lines as given in Eq. 7:

$$a + bt < \text{continue testing} < c + bt \tag{7}$$

where the intercepts a, c and the slope b are given by Eq. 8.

$$a = \frac{\ln B}{\ln(\theta_0/\theta_1)} \qquad c = \frac{\ln A}{\ln(\theta_0/\theta_1)} \qquad b = \frac{1/\theta_1 - 1/\theta_0}{\ln(\theta_0/\theta_1)} \tag{8}$$

Figure 4–5a expresses the probability of acceptance by the test if the true MTTF is as specified. Thus, we see that if the true MTTF is the lower bound, its probability of acceptance is only 0.2, whereas if the true MTTF is the upper bound, there is a probability of 0.8 of accepting—in other words, consumers' and producers' risks. Figure 4–5b is the expected test time as a function of MTTF. Therefore, if the true MTTF is the upper bound θ_0, we can expect a test time of 2.4 θ_0 as the expected decision point. This point was plotted on Figure 4–3.

The mathematical development of these curves can be found in Mil Handbook 781. The test is truncated when there are r failures such that r is the smallest integer that satisfies Eq. 9:

$$\frac{\chi^2_{2r,(1-\alpha)}}{\chi^2_{2r,\beta}} \geq \frac{\theta_1}{\theta_2} \tag{9}$$

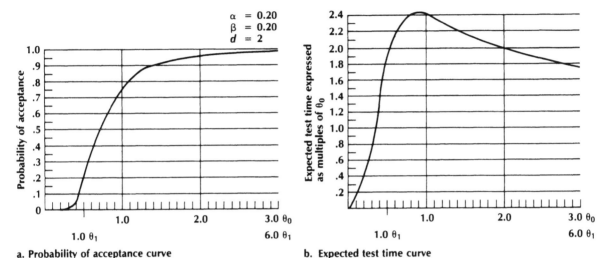

FIGURE 4-5 *True MTTF expressed as multiples of θ_0, θ_1 [From Mil Handbook 781]*

This value is r_0. The maximum test time (T_0) is given by Eq. 10:

$$T_0 = \frac{\theta_0 \chi^2_{2r_0,(1-\alpha)}}{2} \tag{10}$$

Weibull Sequential Test. The previous two types of tests are used when the failure rate is constant with time (an exponential distribution). When reliability growth is occurring, the failure rate is not constant, so those test methods are conservative. J. T. Duane [1964] was one of the first to model reliability growth processes in the development cycle. The model provides a deterministic approach to reliability growth such that the MTTF versus operating hours falls along a straight line when plotted on log-log paper.

The Duane model is essentially the Weibull distribution when the failure rate is decreasing with time during the infant mortality period. (See Holcomb and North [1985].) When the failure rate or hazard rate (instantaneous failure rate) is plotted versus time, it becomes a straight line on log-log graph paper. When the hazard rate is decreasing, the slope of the line is negative and the Weibull shape parameter is less than one. From Chapter 2,

$$\text{Hazard rate} = z(t) = \alpha\lambda(\lambda t)^{\alpha-1} \tag{11}$$

The concept of the Weibull sequential test is similar to the SPRT except the hazard rate does not have to be constant. The equations are similar, but the continue test region is defined by two curved lines, not by straight lines. The equations for these lines are

$$\text{Accept number of failures} = -\frac{(K4 - K3)Nt^{1-A} - \ln[1-(\alpha/\beta)]}{\ln(K3/K4)} \tag{12}$$

$$\text{Accept number of failures} = -\frac{(K4 - K3)Nt^{1-A} - \ln[\alpha/(1-\beta)]}{\ln(K3/K4)} \tag{13}$$

where $K3 = \dfrac{t_0^A}{\theta_0(1 - A)}$

$K4 = \dfrac{t_0^A}{\theta_1(1 - A)}$

A = Growth rate
N = Sample size
t_0 = Time at which the MTTF is tested

Rearranging Eqs. 12 and 13 and using the definitions in Eq. 8 yields

$$\text{Accept number of failures} = a + b\frac{t_0^A}{1-A}Nt^{1-A} \tag{14}$$

$$\text{Reject number of failures} = c + b\frac{t_0^A}{1-A}Nt^{1-A} \tag{15}$$

Figure 4–6 compares a sequential probability ratio test with

$\theta_0 = 40{,}000$ hours $\theta_1 = 20{,}000$ hours $\alpha = \beta = 20\%$

to the Weibull sequential test with

$A = 0.7$ $N = 100$ $t_0 = 1000$

Note that the SPRT requires fewer failures to reach an accept or reject decision.

STRIFE Test. Of particular interest is the final system test. Examination of repair histories has shown that failures can be grouped into three main categories: random component

FIGURE 4–6
Comparison of sequential tests, assuming a constant failure rate (SPRT) and a decreasing failure rate (Weibull) [Courtesy of Digital Equipment Corporation]

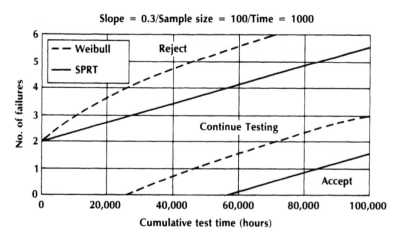

failures, production-related failures, and design-related failures. Random component failure represents the ultimate attainable MTTF. This is the number that Mil Handbook 217 attempts to predict. Failures caused by production and design add to this basic failure rate and prevent the product from realizing its full potential. Manufacturers typically use burn-in tests on 100 percent of the production units to weed out production errors related to minor variations in workmanship and process fluctuations. Burn-in may also discover residual design errors.

Burn-in tests are usually applied for short periods of time under normal system stresses (e.g., the designed voltage, clock, etc.). STRIFE testing (from stress and life) was derived to detect difficult-to-find design errors. STRIFE tests are conducted on a number (10 or more) of engineering or production prototypes during the development process. External stresses (thermal, electrical, and mechanical) are applied that slightly exceed those experienced by the product under normal conditions. The stress reveals areas of weakness and the observed failures are analyzed and corrected to decrease their probability of recurrence [Punches, 1986; Institute of Environmental Sciences, 1981].

> *Example.* Figure 4–7 depicts the results of a survey of 33 Hewlett Packard products for which failure histories had been established. The products are divided into four groups—one that had received minimal (no burn-in or STRIFE) testing, depicted by line 1; products that had received STRIFE tests but no burn-in (line 2); products that had received burn-in but no STRIFE tests (line 3); and products that had received both STRIFE and burn-in tests (line 4). Burn-in alone was shown to improve product reliability by 30 to 60 percent.
>
> STRIFE testing alone improved reliability by 30 to 50 percent. In both groups (and in the control group), the failure curve leveled off at the 24- to 30-month point, and, in all cases, some production-related errors were found and fixed by natural attrition (e.g., problems detected and reported in warranty and subsequently corrected). Products that were burned-in and STRIFE tested were the most reliable, and the failure curve for these products leveled off at the 6- to 12-month point [Punches,* 1986].

Production Stage

As pointed out in Chapter 1, defects should be located and eliminated at the earliest possible stage of production; the cost of a defect increases by a factor of 10 with each inspection stage that fails to identify it [Hotchkiss, 1979; Craig, 1980].

Parametric Testing. At the circuit level, incoming inspection may vary from simple electrical parametric and functional tests to stress tests that force infant mortalities. Stress testing can include vibration, over-voltage, burn-in, and thermal shock (see

---

* Punches is a pseudonym, and the author has not been identified to allow independent confirmation of the published data appearing in Figure 4–7.

FIGURE 4-7

A comparison of failure rates of minimally tested products, STRIFE tested products, burn-in tested products, and products that have been burn-in and STRIFE tested [From Punches, 1986; reprinted by permission of Hewlett Packard]

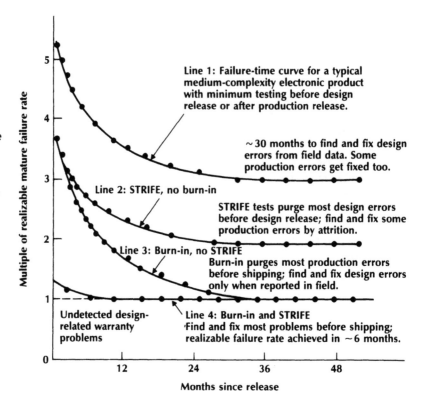

Line 1: Failure-time curve for a typical medium-complexity electronic product with minimum testing before design release or after production release.

~ 30 months to find and fix design errors from field data. Some production errors get fixed too.

Line 2: STRIFE, no burn-in

STRIFE tests purge most design errors before design release; find and fix some production errors by attrition.

Line 3: Burn-in, no STRIFE

Burn-in purges most production errors before shipping; find and fix design errors only when reported in field.

Undetected design-related warranty problems

Line 4: Burn-in and STRIFE
Find and fix most problems before shipping; realizable failure rate achieved in ~ 6 months.

(y-axis) Multiple of realizable mature failure rate

(x-axis) Months since release

Chapter 2). The more extensive the testing, the more costly the incoming inspection. For mass-produced, low-cost systems, incoming inspection is often less than 100 percent because only randomly selected lots are tested.

Some typical parametric tests used to determine whether components meet vendors' electrical specifications are as follows:

Typical MOS Parametric Tests

Gate-oxide breakdown voltage
Drain-to-substrate breakdown voltage
Drain-to-source punchthrough voltage
Gate-to-source threshold voltage
Drain current at 0 gate voltage
Drain current at specified operating voltage
Gate-to-source leakage current
Drain-to-substrate leakage current
Transconductance at specified operating voltage
Drain-source resistance

Figure 4–8 illustrates a computer-driven test system for driving and measuring electrical parameters [Howard and Nahourai, 1978]. A relay matrix is used to configure the sources and measuring instruments to the pin configuration of the unit under test. Parametric testing is most often done by the IC manufacturer or by a system house when it initially qualifies an IC vendor's process.

Acceptance Testing. The largest body of theory has been developed for logic-level acceptance testing. Usually single structural stuck-at-logical-0/1 faults are assumed. A means must be provided for generating stimulus and checking responses in the unit under test (UUT). Table 4–1 categorizes the varied approaches to testing. In general, any stimulus generation approach could be used with any response checking approach; however, certain stimulus/response approach pairs have been more widely adopted than others.

The stimulus/response can be generated off-chip or on-chip. If they are off-chip, they may be dynamically generated or precomputed and stored. Table 4–1 provides the framework for discussing the various testing approaches developed.

The simplest form of response checking is to compare the outputs of the UUT with those of a known good component (exclusive-OR testing). The input stimuli could be generated by incrementing a counter to produce all possible combinations (exhaustive testing). Exhaustive testing is practical for only the smallest circuits. Williams and Parker [1979] give an example of an exhaustive test of an LSI circuit with n inputs and m latches, which requires a minimum of 2^{n+m} tests. For $n = 25$ and $m = 50$ there are $2^{75} = 3.8 \times 10^{22}$ patterns. At 1 microsecond per pattern, the test would require over a billion years.

FIGURE 4–8
Block diagram of an automated parametric test system [Adapted from Howard and Nahourai, 1978]

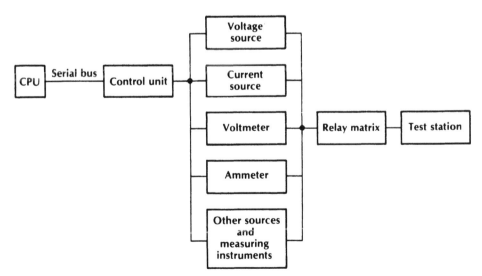

TABLE 4–1
Approaches to stimulus generation and response checking

Stimulus Generation	Response Checking
Exhaustive	Exclusive OR
Random	Stored
	Compact testing: transition counting and signature analysis
Stored	
Simulation: deductive, parallel, and concurrent	Predicted response
	Fault dictionary
Algorithmically generated	
Algebraic: Boolean difference	
Path sensitization: *D*-algorithm	
On-chip	On-chip

Alternatively, the stimuli could be generated randomly (probabilistic testing). In probabilistic testing, a predetermined number of inputs are generated and properties of the output are observed. The output properties are then compared with stored characteristics of the good circuit. This response checking is termed *compact testing* because responses are not stored or checked in detail; only summary statistics are checked. Summary statistics include counting the number of 1's produced and/or the number of transitions. If the count exceeds a predetermined threshold, the component is declared functional. The number, which is arrived at statistically, is chosen to yield a specific confidence level [Williams and Parker, 1979].

A variation of compact testing is *signature analysis* [Nadig, 1977]. In signature analysis, a set of known inputs is dynamically applied to the UUT. The outputs are either displayed for visual comparison with a known good pattern or sensed by computer for comparison with a stored pattern. If the patterns produced by the most likely failures are stored, signature analysis can also be used for fault diagnosis. Often output patterns are summarized by feeding the sequence of outputs into feedback shift registers (FSR), such as those used in the generation and checking of serial codes (see Chapter 3). The FSR output is a function of all the response bits, no matter how long the test sequence may be. Although it is theoretically appealing, in practice compact testing usually provides low fault coverage. In any event, the fault coverage is extremely hard to estimate. Consequently, effort has focused on the systematic generation of input stimuli.

Systematic test-set generation starts with a list of all faults of concern. The fault set usually consists of all single stuck-at-logical-0/1 faults. A test for each fault is generated in turn. Once a fault list and a set of tests have been generated, it is possible to select a minimal set of tests to detect all faults or to determine which fault is present [Kautz, 1968].

Tests can be generated by simulation, algebraic methods, and path sensitization. In *simulation*, faults are inserted into the simulation of the circuit. Both the faulty and the good circuits are simulated until their outputs differ [Seshu and Freeman, 1962]. This is primarily a trial-and-error approach. Faulty behavior may be deduced from a logic simulator by comparing the simulated output of each component with the faulted output. Alternatively, the nonfaulty and several faulty circuits could be simulated and compared in parallel. In concurrent simulation, circuit components are copied and simulated every time the faulty output differs from the good circuit [Grason and Nagle, 1980].

For each test, the predicted output is stored for use in response checking. If the responses of faulty and good circuits are tabulated into a fault dictionary, field service personnel can use the dictionary to diagnose to the field replaceable unit. Chang, Smith, and Walford [1974] describe the LAMP system used to create fault dictionaries for the computers used in the Bell System.

An alternative to simulation is algorithmic generation of the stimulus. One *algorithmic approach* is based upon an algebra of differences. Sellers, Hsiao, and Bearnson [1968a] and Susskind [1972] describe an algebraic approach called the *Boolean difference*. Figure 4–9 illustrates a circuit and a minimal test set for all single stuck-at faults. Each line has a separate identification number and can be stuck-at either logical 0 or 1. The abstract model makes no assumption about electrical connectivity; thus, a stuck-at fault on line 5 does not imply anything about line 3. In practice, certain faults, such as an open metalization, will comply with this abstraction while others, such as a short-to-ground, may cause several lines to be in error.

A test for a fault is one in which the faulty circuit's output differs from that of the good circuit. Consider line 5 stuck-at-1 in Figure 4–9. The first test, 100, should produce an output of 0. With line 5 stuck-at-1, the output is 1. Hence, 100 is a test for line 5 stuck-at-1 (as well as for other faults).

The Boolean difference for a line, i, is defined as the exclusive-OR of the function with line i taking on the values of both 1 and 0:

$$\frac{dF}{dx_i} \triangleq F(x_1, x_2, \ldots, x_{i-1}, 1, x_{i+1}, \ldots, x_n) \oplus F(x_1, x_2, \ldots, x_{i-1}, 0, x_{i+1}, \ldots, x_n)$$

The Boolean difference generates all tests such that a change in the value of x_i results in a change in the value of F. For the example in Figure 4–9,

$$\frac{dF}{dx_5} = (x_1 x_4 + x_6 x_7) \oplus x_6 x_7$$

FIGURE 4–9
A circuit for test generation

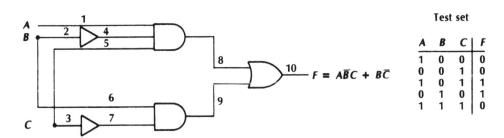

Setting $dF/dx_5 = 1$ yields all the tests for line 5:

$$1 = (x_1x_4 + x_6x_7) \oplus x_6x_7 = (\bar{x}_1 + \bar{x}_4)(\bar{x}_6 + \bar{x}_7)x_6x_7 + (x_1x_4 + x_6x_7)(\bar{x}_6 + \bar{x}_7) = x_1x_4\bar{x}_6 + x_1x_4\bar{x}_7$$

For $x_1x_4\bar{x}_6 = 110$, $F = x_5$, and for $x_1x_4\bar{x}_7 = 110$, $F = x_5$. The corresponding input tests are

$ABC = 100$ for x_5 stuck-at-1

$ABC = 101$ for x_5 stuck-at-0

Path sensitization techniques are essentially an intelligent form of simulation. In path sensitization, all components along a path from the fault to an output are placed in a state such that the output changes value only as a function of the value of the faulty component. To complete the test, the conditions to sensitize the path are driven back, by means of consistency checks, to corresponding conditions on the network inputs. In all these methods, once a test has been generated, a post process determines which other faults in the fault list have also been detected and then it eliminates them from the list. In Figure 4–9, in order to propagate x_5 to the output, lines 1 and 4 have to be 1 and line 9 has to be 0. Driving these values back toward the circuit inputs implies that $A = 1$, $B = 0$.

The path sensitization approach has been formalized in the *D*-algorithm [Roth, 1966; Roth, Bouricius, and Schneider, 1967]. A symbol, *D*, is defined to be equal to 1 in the good circuit and to be equal to 0 in a bad circuit ($\bar{D}$ is 0 in the good circuit and 1 in a bad circuit). Each elementary gate has its function redefined in terms of the symbol *D*, as shown in Table 4–2. First, *D* is placed on the line for which a test is to be generated, and then it is propagated to circuit outputs one step at a time. An implication step sets values on other circuit lines required to realize the state specified by the propagation step. The propagation/implication cycle is repeated until either *D* or $\bar{D}$ is propagated to the circuit outputs. If at least one test exists, the *D*-algorithm is guaranteed to find it.

Starting with $\bar{D}$ on line 5 (line 5 stuck-at-1) of Figure 4–9, the three propagation steps from line 5 to line 8 to line 10 could be tabulated as shown in Figure 4–10. The *D* is propagated through each elementary gate in turn without regard to the state of other gates. The implication steps assign values to other circuit lines. For example, in order for line 8 to take a value $\bar{D}$, lines 1 and 4 must be 1. The fact that line 4 is 1 implies that line 2 is 0. Contradictions (such as a line taking on both a 0 and a 1 value) signal the nonexistence of a test.

In any algorithmic test-generation technique, once a test for a fault has been found, the list of faults the test has detected is compared with the original fault list. Tested faults are thus removed and the fault list is shortened. Significant work has been done to reduce the length of the original fault list by grouping faults into equivalence classes (that is, members of the class are indistinguishable) [McCluskey and Clegg, 1971].

Example. Figure 4–11 shows the relationships among six faults for a two-input AND gate and their respective test sets. The test set for lines 1, 2, and 3 stuck-at-0 is

TABLE 4–2
The D-algorithm definition of elementary gate functions in terms of the symbol D

AND			Inverter		OR		
Input 1	Input 2	Output	Input	Output	Input 1	Input 2	Output
1	1	1	1	0	1	1	1
1	0	0	0	1	1	0	1
0	1	0	D	$\bar{D}$	0	1	1
0	0	0	$\bar{D}$	D	0	0	0
1	D	D			1	D	1
D	1	D			D	1	1
1	$\bar{D}$	$\bar{D}$			1	$\bar{D}$	1
$\bar{D}$	1	$\bar{D}$			$\bar{D}$	1	1
0	D	0			0	D	D
D	0	0			D	0	D
0	$\bar{D}$	0			0	$\bar{D}$	$\bar{D}$
$\bar{D}$	0	0			$\bar{D}$	0	$\bar{D}$
D	D	D			D	D	D
$\bar{D}$	$\bar{D}$	$\bar{D}$			$\bar{D}$	$\bar{D}$	$\bar{D}$
$\bar{D}$	D	0			$\bar{D}$	D	1
D	$\bar{D}$	0			D	$\bar{D}$	1

Source: Data from Roth, 1966; and Roth, Bouricius, and Schneider, 1967, © 1967 IEEE.

the same. Hence, these are equivalent faults and it is sufficient to generate a test for only one of them. Another relationship between faults is that of dominance. Because the test set for line 3 stuck-at-1 includes the tests for lines 1 and 2 stuck-at-1, line 3 stuck-at-1 dominates those two faults. The dominating fault is automatically tested for if all the dominated faults are tested. Thus, instead of six faults on the original fault list for this two-input AND gate, only three are required: line 3 s-a-0, line 1 s-a-1, and line 2 s-a-1. In general, for elementary gates of N inputs, only $N + 1$ faults need to be on the original fault list instead of the $2(N + 1)$ single faults, provided the single-fault assumption is being used.

FIGURE 4–10
The D-algorithm applied to line 5 stuck-at-1 in Figure 4–9

Step	1	2	3	4	5	6	7	8	9	10
Initial test on Line 5	x	x	x	x	$\bar{D}$	x	x	x	x	x
Implication on other gate inputs	x	x	$\bar{D}$	x	$\bar{D}$	x	x	x	x	x
Propagate to Line 8	x	x	$\bar{D}$	x	$\bar{D}$	x	x	$\bar{D}$	x	x
Implication on other gate inputs	1	0	$\bar{D}$	1	$\bar{D}$	x	x	$\bar{D}$	x	x
Propagate to Line 10	1	0	$\bar{D}$	1	$\bar{D}$	x	x	$\bar{D}$	x	$\bar{D}$
Implication on other gate inputs	1	0	$\bar{D}$	1	$\bar{D}$	0	0	$\bar{D}$	0	$\bar{D}$

A	B	C	F
1	0	$\bar{D}$	$\bar{D}$

b. Test

a. Forward propagation and implication

I. THE THEORY OF RELIABLE SYSTEM DESIGN

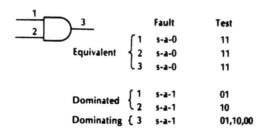

FIGURE 4–11
Equivalence and dominance relations among faults

	Fault	Test
Equivalent		
1 s-a-0		11
2 s-a-0		11
3 s-a-0		11
Dominated		
1 s-a-1		01
2 s-a-1		10
Dominating 3 s-a-1		01,10,00

The reduction of fault lists for multiple faults has also been addressed [Bossen and Hong, 1971]. Circuits exist, however, for which a test set for all single structural faults will not detect certain multiple faults. Fault models other than s-a-0, s-a-1 have also been used. The bridging fault, frequently caused by a solder bridge, is a common fault type in digital system fabrication [Mei, 1974]. Special fault models developed for memories look for sensitivity to multiple-bit patterns. Some of these tests and their complexity as a function of the number of bits are as follows:

Test	Complexity
Checkerboard pattern of 1's and 0's	N
Walking pattern	$N^{3/2}$
Galloping 1's and 0's (dynamic test)	N^2
Ping pong	N^2

Test-set generation algorithms based on gate level and the stuck-at fault model are not applicable to VLSI complexity. Williams and Parker [1979] have observed that the computer run time to perform test generation and fault simulation is related to the number of logic gates by a cubic law: $T = kn^3$. Hence, there have been efforts to test systems at higher levels of functionality [Breuer and Friedman, 1980; Thatte and Abraham, 1978]. The purpose of functional testing is to validate the correct functional operation of a digital system with respect to its functional specification. Ideally, the tests developed are based solely on the specification and are capable of validating any implementation that is alleged to perform the specified function. Functional testing not only reduces test-generation complexity, but also, being free of implementation details, allows one test set to serve for implementations produced by multiple vendors. Indeed, manufacturers of LSI chips will not release the implementation details of their chips lest they be copied. Thus, the user of LSI chips who by necessity deals with multiple sources has no recourse but functional testing. Research in functional testing has focused on microprocessors.

Robach and Saucier [1980] proposed a testing method based on a data transfer description of each instruction executed by the microprocessor. Each instruction of a microprocessor is represented by an abstract execution graph (AEG). Memory elements (could be a memory location or a general purpose register) and data manipulation functions are represented as nodes in the AEG.

Terminal nodes for an AEG include the source nodes and sink nodes corresponding to the instruction's data read and write sets. In general, information supplied by source nodes flows through the data manipulation nodes into sink nodes.

The AEG of an instruction is verified for the presence of three types of errors:

1. Any source node in an AEG may be improperly selected.
2. Any sink node in an AEG may be improperly selected.
3. The selection of functional nodes of the AEG is faulty.

The generality of this method comes from the detailed data flow information in the AEGs. It includes faults that cover register selection and faulty data manipulation. However, faults that will change the AEG structure are not included. The quality of tests generated from an AEG is difficult to determine because of the fact that there is no explicit functional level fault model.

Thatte and Abraham [1980] proposed a method to test microprocessors that makes use of a register transfer level (RTL) description. This method was enhanced by Brahme and Abraham [1984]. In this approach, a microprocessor is represented as a directed graph where the nodes represent the microprocessor's register (e.g., general purpose registers, processor status register). A directed arc between nodes indicates the flow of data between the corresponding registers. Arcs are labeled indicating the instruction that causes the transfer to occur. Two special nodes, *in* and *out*, represent the microprocessor's controllable and observable data points respectively. Each register is labeled according to its distance from the out node.

The faults represented in this approach included changes in the following:

Register decoding function
Data transfer function
Data manipulation function
Instruction decoding function
Instruction sequencing function

The approach could be applied to a wide range of microprocessors.

The test generator developed by Lai [1981] and Lai and Siewiorek [1983] represents a more general approach to functional level testing. The method utilizes a system representation, called state transformation graph (STG), that includes a detailed representation of the control flow within the digital system. The result is a test generation system that is not only applicable to microprocessors but also to other general digital systems. Data tokens in the STG are used to represent control flow. The STG also uses low-level primitive test sets that can be precomputed and that take into consideration the actual circuit implementation.

Fault modeling with the system is done at two levels. The first level addresses faults within node and path primitives. Each node or path within the STG may exhibit functional level faults. Test requirements for coverage of these faults within the nodes or paths are accomplished through the use of a database with a complete test set for each primitive. The second level fault model is at the graph level, and it gives the number of nodes and paths that can be faulty at any time. In Lai [1981], it is assumed that only one node or path is faulty at any one time.

The literature abounds with surveys on test-set generation: Breuer and Friedman [1976], Chang, Manning, and Metze [1970], Friedman and Menon [1971], Hennie [1968], and Bennetts and Lewin [1971] are examples. More recent research has focused on generating tests and checking responses directly on the semiconductor chip, so that chips could test themselves without reliance on external support. Such self-testing chips could alleviate both production and operational testing. One approach [Bozorgui-Nesbat and McCluskey, 1980] partitions the logic into small groups for exhaustive testing. A counter on the group inputs generates all possible input combinations. An FSR on the group outputs is compared with a hard-wired constant to provide the matching function.

System-Level Testing. The evaluation of a fault-tolerant system includes both functional and reliability measures. Functional measures are relatively straightforward, but analyses of reliability require measures of such quantities as component reliability, fault coverage, error-detection coverage, and other difficult-to-measure factors. These unique measures typically require special methods, such as fault insertion [Carter, 1986; NASA, 1979a, 1979b; SAE, 1986], to estimate their value.

Fault insertion has been studied extensively for a number of objectives, as indicated in Table 4–3. In the studies summarized in the table as well as others, the two most common means of fault insertion have been simulation of the hardware and physical fault insertion. Fault simulation has occurred at all the levels discussed in Chapter 1 [Bryant, 1984; McGough, Swern, and Bavuso, 1983; Northcutt, 1980; Silberman and Spillinger, 1986]. Physical fault insertion has been used to determine fault coverage of test programs [Avizienis and Rennels, 1972], fault latency [Finelli, 1987; Shin and Lee, 1986], and fault detection efficiency [Crouzet and Decouty, 1982; Lala, 1983; Schuette et al., 1986]. Table 4–4 presents a matrix of advantages and disadvantages of four fault insertion methods:

1. Software simulation, which involves fault insertion by code modifications or special functions of the simulation engine.
2. Hardware emulation, which uses hardware representative of the system under test, such as an engineering prototype, as a basis for study.
3. Fault emulation, which attempts to initiate fault behavior through software control of the hardware or special capabilities built into the hardware.
4. Physical fault insertion, which involves the inducement of faults through special hardware built for the actual system under test.

Physical fault insertion has been used extensively in system validation, with the typical means of fault insertion being pin-level stuck-ats and inverted faults [Avizienis and Rennels, 1972; Crouzet and Decouty, 1982; Decouty, Michel, and Wagner, 1980; Lala, 1983; Schuette et al., 1986; Shin and Lee, 1986; Stiffler and Van Doren, 1979]. With an SSI/MSI realization of a system, pin-level stuck-ats closely represent failures that have been observed to occur in such devices, but with LSI and VLSI realizations, failures may be remote from the input/output pins. At these higher levels of integration, fault insertion seldom claims to accurately portray physical faults, but the hope is that they provide a first approximation to the metrics under study. Palumbo and Finelli

TABLE 4–3 *Fault insertion studies*

Objective/Study	Target	Method/Level	Goal
Test coverage evaluation			
Kurlak and Chobot, 1981	GE MCP-701 CPU	Physical faults with FMEA analysis	Evaluation of watchdog timer
Generation of fault dictionaries			
Goetz, 1972	ESS Microstore	Simulation/gate level	Detection and coverage measure
Error propagation and latency			
Courtois, 1979	MC 6800	Simulation/op-code (RT) level	Detection time
Finelli, 1987	FTMP Engineering Model	Permanent physical/gate level	Fault recovery distributions
McGough, Swern, and Bavuso, 1981	Bendix Simplex BDX-930	Simulation/gate and pin level	Coverage measurement
Error-detection schemes			
Crouzet and Decouty, 1982; Decouty, Michel, and Wagner, 1980	GORDINI: Fault Tolerant micro	Physical/pin (gate and RT) level	Tool and methodology development
Schuette et al., 1985	MC 68000	Transient, physical/bus (RT) level	Evaluation of error-detection techniques
System evaluation			
Avizienis and Rennels, 1972	JPL–Star breadboard	Permanent and transient physical/pin (gate) level	Estimate of detection, recovery parameters, coverage
Czeck, Segall, and Siewiorek, 1987	FTMP Engineering Model	Fault emulation/RT level	Methodology study
Lala, 1983	FTMP Engineering Model	Physical/pin (gate) level	System and coverage evaluation
Yang et al., 1985	iAPX 432	Fault emulation/memory words (RT)	Coverage of TMR

Source: Czeck, 1991.

[1987] hypothesized that pin-level stuck-at faults produce error behavior similar to that caused by internal devices. Initial empirical results are conclusive; the hypothesis holds well for 85 percent of the data, but other data call for rejection.

Although actual faults may be remote from the pin boundaries, promising results have been reported with pin fault insertion of LSI and VLSI devices, and other abstract fault insertion methods. Schuette et al., [1986] inserted transient faults on the data, address, and control lines of an MC68000 bus, representing faults within the data and control sections of the processor. With this fault insertion ability, two error-detection schemes were evaluated. Yang et al. [1985] inserted faults into an iAPX 432 to evaluate software-implemented TMR; the faults were generated by altering bits in the program or data areas in memory using the debugger. Czeck, Segall, and Siewiorek [1987] inserted faults in an FTMP triad by causing one processor to execute special code,

TABLE 4–4 *Fault insertion methods*

	Method			
	Software Simulation	Hardware Emulation (Breadboard)	Fault Emulation	Physical Fault Insertion
Advantages	Access to system at any level of detail; fault types and control are unlimited.	Representative hardware with favorable access and monitoring	True hardware and software in use	True hardware and software in use
Disadvantages	Simulation time explosion; lack of tools limit ability.	Implementation and other parameters will change with deployed system.	Fault types are limited.	VLSI limits access and monitoring points; task is difficult.

Source: Czeck, 1991.

thus triggering the error-detection mechanisms. This method was able to duplicate some hardware fault insertion results presented by Lala and Smith [1983] and Lala [1983]. However, even with these results, McGough and Swern [1981, 1983] and McGough, Swern, and Bravuso [1983] illustrated a distinct gap between gate-level and component-level fault types, as discussed in Chapter 2.

Fault insertion has been used in areas other than hardware test generation and verification. Within the Sperry Univac 1100/60 [Boone, Liebergot, and Sedmak, 1980], fault insertion capabilities are built into the system to verify the functionality of the fault detection, isolation, and recovery mechanisms. Fault insertion is activated during system idle time and can insert faults in the processor, memory, and I/O unit. These fault insertion capabilities are under operating system control and require no external hardware.

Design for Testability. It has long been recognized that it is easier to derive test sets for some circuits than for others. Attempting to define easy-to-test properties has led to a new discipline called *design for testability*. Table 4–5 lists four stages of testability design. Each stage has an increasing effect upon the original design until ultimately a totally new design is created. Bennetts and Scott [1976] and Grason and Nagle [1980] discuss in detail techniques for each of these stages. Only a cursory review will be provided here.

The first stage in testability design is to develop test sets for an existing design. The faults assumed are usually of the single stuck-at structural variety. The Boolean difference and *D*-algorithm are among the approaches used for combinational circuits. Sequential circuits are more difficult to test because of feedback. Approaches for combinational circuits have been extended to sequential circuits by replicating logic and treating the sequential circuit as a cascade of combinational circuits.

TABLE 4–5
*Stages in design
for testability*

Stage	Combinational	Sequential
Test set for unmodified circuit	Structural faults	Extension of combinational approaches for structural faults
		Functional faults
Minimum modification to existing circuit	Add a small number of test points	Add synchronizing sequence
		Add distinguishing sequence
		Break selected feedback
Extensive modification to existing circuit	Improve controllability	Make combinational LSSD
	Improve observability	
New design	Reed-Muller expansion	Fail-safe design
	Totally self-checking circuits	

Example. Figure 4–12a depicts a typical sequential circuit. In Figure 4–12b the combinational logic has been replicated three times, representing three transitions in the state of the original circuit. The inputs in Figure 4–12b actually correspond to a sequence of three inputs to the original sequential circuit. Note that a single fault in the original circuit (such as a stuck-at-1 on a next-state line) would correspond to a multiple fault (a stuck-at-1 on all three copies of the next-state line) in the expanded circuit. Furthermore, there is no guarantee that the combinational logic test generation algorithms can find a test in three state transitions. The whole process may have to be repeated for multiple-state transitions until a test, if any, can be found. The increased number of faults to be considered and the additional complexity of the replicated logic make sequential circuit testing much more complicated than combinational circuit testing.

Another approach to sequential testing is based on a fault model that is different from the structural model. The sequential circuit is represented as a functional state table, regardless of its implementation. Faults are simply changes in the next state or the output for an entry in the state table. Single structural faults may exist that are not representable by a single functional fault, and vice versa. The testing approach is to derive a sequence that ensures that each state and each transition between states exist. By assuming that faults cannot introduce new states, a test sequence (on the order of N^3 symbols, where N is the number of states) is generated such that no sequential machine of fewer states could respond correctly [Hennie, 1964].

The second stage in testability adds a small amount of logic to the existing circuit. For combinational logic, this usually takes the form of insertion of a test point or control point. Test points are added at critical positions (such as flip-flop outputs,

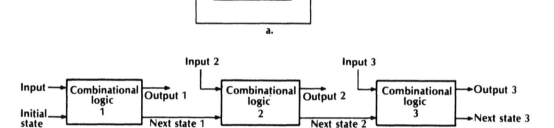

FIGURE 4–12 *A sequential circuit replicated three times as a combinational circuit*

sources of large fan-out, buses, and deeply buried components) to increase observability. Control points (such as flip-flop inputs, large fan-in points, buses, and deeply buried information paths) are added to increase control. For sequential circuits, extra pins or logic may be added to produce synchronizing (set circuit to a known state) or distinguishing sequences. In addition, feedback lines may be broken by the insertion of independently controlled blocking gates.

The third stage starts with the original circuit, but adds extensive modifications; any amount is possible, but 5 to 20 percent is typical. If sufficient logic is added, only three tests would be required for combinational logic circuits [Bennetts and Scott, 1976]. Often, however, it is not possible to make the extensive modifications, and a more practical approach is required. Grason and Nagle [1980] have summarized the types of added logic that can assist testing of printed circuit boards:

- Test points: edge connectors, dual in-line package (DIP) sockets, terminal posts, tristate drivers, IC clips
- Pull-up resistors
- Pin amplification: input demultiplexers, output multiplexers, parity trees
- Blocking gates
- Control and observation switching
- Disconnection structures: edge connectors, DIP sockets, tristate drivers, blocking gates
- Test-state register
- Power-up reset
- Scan-in/scan-out shift registers

Test points can utilize pins at the edge of boards, sockets accessible to plug-in of automatic test equipment, internal posts accessible by clips, tristate drivers to break or connect a line, and signal clips placed over an integrated circuit. Pull-up resistors can be used to isolate power supplies, providing constant logical values that allow the line to be forced to the opposite logical value.

A major problem is to provide enough pins for observing or controlling the circuit. A small number of output pins can be driven by a multiplexer so that a large number of internal points can be sequentially observed. Likewise, a demultiplexer on a set of inputs can be used to drive a large set of controllability points. Parity trees can be used to summarize the state of a large number of points (like the on-board data reduction used in signature analysis). Blocking gates can be used to break feedback in sequential circuits or to partition a combinational circuit. Lines that are difficult to control or observe can be multiplexed with an easily controlled/observed line. In test mode, the easily controlled/observed line is tied directly to the difficult line.

Often circuits are easier to test if they are partitioned into smaller circuits. Techniques similar to test-point addition can be used to partition (disconnect) the circuit. Circuit test-mode control information (such as the control of blocking gates, tristate drivers, and multiplexers) may be more extensive than the number of test points that can be added. Test-mode information is relatively static and can often be derived from an on-board test-state register. Finally, a power-up signal can often be used to set a predetermined state into the sequential logic.

As mentioned before, many sequential testing strategies are based upon transforming the sequential circuit into a combinational circuit. One such technique uses scan-in/scan-out shift registers and is termed level sensitive scan design (LSSD) by IBM. Figure 4–13 illustrates the use of LSSD in the IBM 4341 [Frechette and Tanner, 1979]. Every latch is replaced by a latch pair. During normal operation the second latch is invisible. During test mode, the latch pairs are tied together into a shift register controlled by a separate clock (in this case provided by a support processor). The latch pairs partition the logic into sections composed only of combinational logic. In test-mode operation the test mode is set, test input data are shifted in, the normal mode is set, one system clock pulse is applied, the test mode is set again, and the result of the test is shifted out for analysis. LSSD makes the system state almost completely observable and controllable. Test-set generation is the same as for combinational logic, for which there already exist many practical results. Few extra pins are required and IBM reports the extra logic cost to be somewhere between 5 and 20 percent of the total cost. A major disadvantage is that stimulus application and response checking is slow. A variation of LSSD is the Visibility Bus, which provides observability only in the VAX-11/780 and VAX-11/750 (see Chapter 7).

A summary of suggestions given by Grason and Nagle [1980] on where to add hardware follows.

1. Make sequential circuit components such as counters, shift registers, and control flip-flops initializable. Some ways of providing initializability are to wire control signals or testpoints to component clear or preset inputs, or to provide direct-load capabilities. Do not tie both the set and preset inputs of flip-flops to a common permanent logic signal.

2. Make counter chains controllable and observable in a reasonably short test sequence. For example, break long counter chains during test mode by inserting testpoints in the carry-propagate/count-control lines. This is especially important in

FIGURE 4–13

An example of LSSD [Adapted from Frechette and Tanner, 1979]

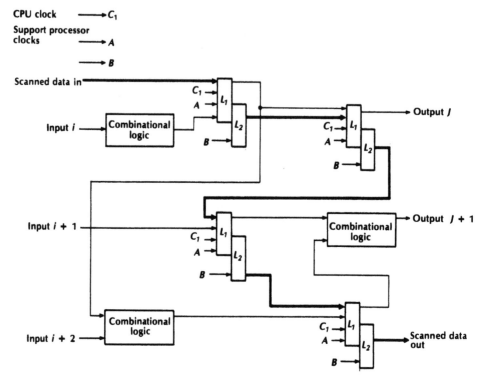

the case of clock countdown circuits that are used to provide control inputs for the rest of the circuit. In the latter case it may even be wise to provide testpoints to bypass the counters entirely during portions of the test.

3. On-board clock oscillators should be made disconnectable during test mode. This can be done by disconnecting their output with a testpoint or by socketing them for removal during test mode.

4. If one-shots are used, control and observe their outputs with testpoints.

5. Try to break global feedback loops during test mode. Blocking gates can be used for this, rather than more costly testpoints.

6. Use added hardware to partition the circuit into functionally independent subcircuits for testing. This is especially important for separating digital and analog subcircuits. One method is to place testpoints between subcircuits.

7. Break reconvergent fan-out paths when they interfere with testability.

8. Place testpoints at locations of high fan-out or high fan-in.

9. Route logic drives of lamps and displays to testpoints so that the tester can check for correct operation. Make keyboard and switch outputs accessible to the test machine by breaking with testpoints.

10. In circuits containing microprocessors and other LSI devices, use testpoints to enhance controllability and observability of address buses and data buses, important control signals such as the reset and hold inputs to the microprocessor, and bus tristate control. In particular, the address and data terminals of RAMs and ROMs should be easily accessible.

The following is a summary of design guidelines for testability from Grason and Nagle [1980] that do not require added hardware:

1. Avoid the use of asynchronous sequential circuits. Edge-triggered D-type flip-flops are preferable to other types of flip-flops. These are synchronous, and behave merely as clocked data delays during testing.
2. Avoid one-shots when possible.
3. Avoid unnecessary wired-OR or wired-AND connections. When these must be used, try to employ gates from the same IC package to enhance fault locations.
4. Use elements in the same IC package when designing a series of inverters.
5. Try to assign gates in a feedback loop to the same IC package.

The final stage in design for testability is to develop new designs with unique properties. These designs should have a small test-set size that is easy to generate. Bennetts and Scott [1976] describe the Reed-Muller expansion for realizing combinational circuits. This test-set size and contents are derived by inspection.

Some of the techniques described in Chapter 3 can be used for on-line testing. In particular, Carter, Wadia, and Jessep [1972] introduce an algebra for totally self-checking circuits and an algorithm for producing them from the regular Boolean description. The physical realization of these circuits is usually twice as complex as nonself-checking circuits (roughly comparable to dual-rail logic or duplication). However, there are important classes of these checkers that are only about as complex as the nonredundant Boolean realization. Anderson and Metze [1973] explore such a class of check circuits for data encoded in m-of-n codes (see Chapter 3).

For sequential machines, it is possible to encode states in such a way that the machine does not make a mistake. There are two general approaches. The first constructs the sequential machine such that any error drives the machine into an error state from which it cannot escape. Thus, the machine remains in essentially a do-nothing state and no further outputs are issued. The second approach is the so-called fail-safe [Tohma, Ohyama, and Sake, 1971] sequential machine. One of the two possible outputs is designated as fail-safe, and the occurrence of that output is used in such a way that no damage is done if that output is wrong. The other output value can always be assumed correct, even in the presence of a fault. Consider the example of a traffic light, mentioned in Chapter 3 in the section on fail-safe logic design. Whenever green appears, it is correct, even if there are internal failures. When red appears, it is either correct or the result of an internal failure.

Several theoretical models have been developed for the application of tests to isolate a faulty subsystem. The goal of these models is to isolate the faulty component as quickly as possible [Brule, Johnson, and Kletsky, 1960; Chang, 1965, 1968]. If subsystems are given the capability of diagnosing each other, then it becomes possible to construct a system that could diagnose (and perhaps reconfigure) itself automatically; however, the application of test sets requires the setting of inputs and the observation of outputs. In systems with parallel data paths, the "hooks" necessary to set and observe results are many bits wide and costly to implement; the number of these hooks should be kept to a minimum.

Preparata, Metze, and Chien [1967] treat the case of subsystem interconnection for diagnosis when each subsystem is completely capable of testing another subsystem. Kime [1970], combining the work of Kautz [1968] and Preparata, Metze, and Chien, extends the possible outcomes of a test (passed, failed) to include the incomplete test—a test whose output is indeterminate under the influence of a fault (that is, it is unknown whether the test will pass or fail when the fault is present). This corresponds to a don't-know condition. Procedures for determining the diagnostic resolution (i.e., the smallest unique unit in which the test isolates a fault) of a set of tests are then developed. Subsequent work by Kime and others treats the cases in which subsystems are not identical.

Field Operation Stage

The final phase of system life is in the field. Field service must respond to both real and customer-perceived failures. Because of the complex nature of systems, it is not unusual for the false-alarm rate to be two to four times higher than the actual fault rate. Therefore, one goal of design for maintainability is to decrease the rate of false alarms.

Another problem is illustrated by the typical time to repair (TTR) distribution in Figure 4–14. It is common for 5 percent of calls to consume 35 percent of the time spent in repair. This time to repair "tail" is very costly. Hard failures are easy to diagnose and repair; more subtle errors are often caused by interactions between systems components and are also a function of system load. Diagnostics are unable to reproduce the events leading up to the error.

When the time to repair a system has gone beyond a threshold (typically, four hours), a second person, usually a more experienced troubleshooter, can be dispatched to assist in the repair process. Subsequently, a third and even a fourth person might be dispatched in an attempt to limit customer downtime. A more realistic view of the cost of repair is the number of labor hours involved in repair; for example, two people for one hour yields two labor hours. Figure 4–15 depicts a typical labor hours to repair (LH) distribution corresponding to the TTR distribution in Figure 4–14. The tail on the LH caused by problem systems is even more pronounced than the TTR tail. Hence, the second goal of design for maintainability is to decrease the tails on the TTR (affecting customer downtime) and LH (affecting cost of maintenance) distributions.

The maintenance philosophy is a function of the total set of design decisions, including design choices for fault tolerance and design for testability. The great variety

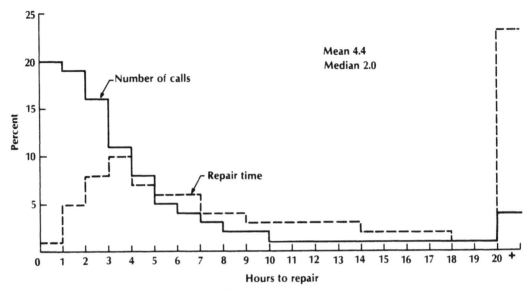

FIGURE 4–14 *Time to repair distribution*

of possible combinations of design choices makes it very difficult to provide a comprehensive set of guidelines for design for maintainability. The following incomplete, unordered list of suggestions may be used to stimulate the generation of ideas.

• Once a suspect subsystem has been identified (through error-detection logic, periodic diagnostics, error reports, and the like), the first consideration is to determine whether a fault is actually present. Verification should start with the smallest set of logic that can perform useful functions. In a processor, the minimum functionality might be execution of move constant, compare, and branch instructions. Functions are verified incrementally.

• Each subsystem should be testable as a stand-alone environment. For example, communications devices should have a test mode that wraps the sending port around to a receiving port. The sending and receiving logic can be tested without the aid of other subsystems.

• Because of the availability of low-cost LSI technology, most subsystems have at least one microprocessor. The addition of a microprocessor simplifies the design of self-tests for the subsystem. These tests should include the microprocessor (check-summing its memory) as well as error-detection/reporting circuitry that is normally not exercised.

• The next suggestion is to provide information that will eliminate lengthy repairs by increasing observability and controllability of internal signals (as with the LSSD and visibility bus discussed under design for testability).

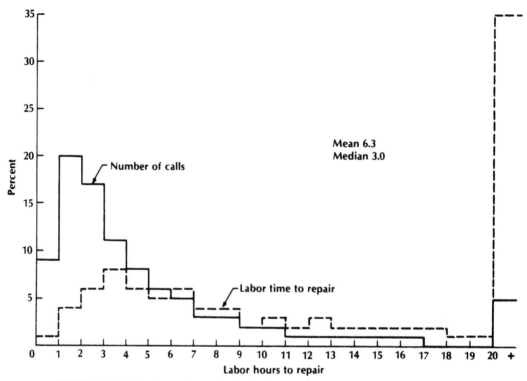

FIGURE 4–15 *Labor hours to repair distribution*

• Another suggestion for gaining information is to provide error logging and reporting. Often a diagnostic program cannot recreate an error event because it does not stress the system in the same way that the operational program does. Indeed, often the operational program is the best diagnostic. Error logging captures information about the state of the system at the time of the error, thus providing clues to the source of the error. Error logging makes it possible to perform automatic trend analysis. A program can periodically scan the error log, looking for patterns (such as multiple-read retries to one head of a disk). Trend analysis can be used in all systems, whether they contain little or extensive error-detection logic.

• A suggestion aimed at the repair process involves minimizing or eliminating use of external test equipment. Such test equipment is difficult to transport, time-consuming to hook up and may perturb the system to the point of masking the fault. Even options such as a diagnostics control store should be avoided, because its installation changes the system configuration (perhaps even necessitating removal of a board to make room).

• A very important suggestion related to maintenance is the selection of an FRU. Typically, FRUs are printed circuit boards or LSI chips. The physical layout of the system should provide for easy access and replacement of the FRUs. If the maintenance strategy calls for verification with the cabinet open or the FRU on an extender board, the subsystem should operate correctly under these conditions (power should still be applied and timing margins should still be met). If on-line repair is mandated, care should be taken to minimize human error, such as the switching off of the wrong power supply. Telettra builds telephone switching equipment that supports on-line repair [Morganti, 1978]. The power pins on each card are slightly longer than the signal pins. Furthermore, there is enough mechanical resistance in card insertion to allow enough time for capacitors to charge up and electrical equilibrium to be reached prior to logic-signal contact with the rest of the system. On removal, the logic signals are disconnected prior to power disruption. The cards are keyed to prevent incorrect orientation or insertion into the incorrect slot; thus, there are never any ill-formed logic signals in the system caused by the insertion/removal of a card. In addition, the processor is logically notified when a card is not present.

• The repair strategy should be one of replacement rather than swapping. In replacement the faulty FRU is uniquely identified. FRU swapping, sometimes called the "shotgun" approach, removes and substitutes several components at a time. Mostly on the basis of guesswork, components are substituted, sometimes en masse, until the system again functions properly. Swapping increases TTR/LH averages and spare-inventory costs. More spare FRUs are required because all removed FRUs are suspect. The workload on repair facilities is also increased. The swapping strategy was popular in the early days of computing, but it is no longer economically justifiable with today's more complex systems.

• The final suggestion is to provide a support processor to serve as a hub for maintenance activities. When provided with remote access, the support processor can help eliminate tails on the TTR and LH distributions and also decrease both. Given an average transit time of one hour from a field service office to a customer site and a TTR of two hours, an average field service engineer can make two repairs a day. Even if the TTR were halved there would still be only two repairs per day because of the constraint of an eight-hour work day. Thus, savings can be realized by reducing transit time and eliminating false alarms through the use of remote diagnosis (RD).

For an example of the final suggestion, consider a VAX system with an RD option, as described in Chapter 1. When a customer perceives a failure, the data disk is dismounted, a diagnostic disk is mounted, the RD option is switched to remote, and the customer telephones the diagnostic center, which dials up the target VAX. The RD option gives the engineer visibility to the implementation registers, microsequencer, back-plane bus, and other internal components. The engineer can then run and interpret diagnostics as if on-site. The RD option greatly reduces false alarms. The experience of the RD center personnel tends to insure that the field engineer is dispatched with the appropriate repair kit and expertise. Multiple trips for additional spare parts or additional expertise are greatly reduced. The RD center can also run extensive diagnostics under control of an RD computer when the customer is not using the computer. For remote diagnosis to be most effective, the system should be designed with RD in mind.

The IBM 4341 also uses a support processor to perform on-line analysis of errors [Frechette and Tanner, 1979]. The maintenance and support processor logs environmental factors such as power-line transients, electrostatic discharge, and internal machine temperatures. The 4341 processor is implemented using the level sensitive scan design (LSSD) technique. There are approximately 5,000 latch pairs in the CPU, 300 of which are used solely to aid fault diagnosis. In the diagnostic mode, the data latch is transferred to the scan latch, capturing the state of the machine for the support processor. The latch pairs are linked together to form shift registers called *scan rings*. The support processor subsequently can serially shift out the scan latch data. Thus, when the checking circuitry detects an error dynamically (such as with parity or duplication), the state of the machine is captured. There is no need to recreate the failure. When error notification occurs, the support processor reads the scan latches, determines the error type, attempts recovery via retry for transient errors, records failure information in an error log on a diskette, and, in the case of hard faults, invokes error-log analysis microcode, whose 17,000 bytes analyze the error logs to identify the faulty FRU. Chapter 7 describes the support processor used in IBM 3090 systems.

SYMPTOM-BASED DIAGNOSIS

Analysis of system error files indicates that many permanent hardware failures are preceded by a period of instability. Frequently, the period of instability can be detected by observing trends. If a characteristic symptom can be identified in the trend data, the diagnostic time and hence the period of instability can be reduced. This approach is often called *trend analysis* or *symptom-based diagnosis*.

Methods of Analysis

One trend analysis method employs a data grouping or clustering technique called tupling [Tsao and Siewiorek, 1983]. *Tuples* are clusters, or groups, of event-log entries exhibiting temporal or spatial patterns of features. The approach to the data clustering technique called *tuple extraction*, or *tupling*, is based on the observation that because computers have mechanisms for both hardware and software detection of faults, single error events can propagate through a system, causing multiple entries in the event log. Tuple extraction clusters these entries into tuples, collections of machine events whose logical grouping is based primarily on their proximity in time and in hardware space. A tuple may contain from one to several hundred event-log entries.

Tupling Example. The validity of tuple clustering algorithms was studied via sensitivity analysis using 330 machine-days of event-log data collected from three different DEC

TOPS-20 computing systems with 58,305 event-log entries. Tuples were formulated off-line. Two procedures were used to determine whether the current event-log entry belonged to the tuple that was currently being formed or was the start of a new tuple. The first procedure coalesced the current entry with the existing tuple if it occurred within 2.8 minutes of the previous entry. The second procedure allowed coalescing of entries within 22.5 minutes of the previous entry if certain conditions about lack of physical device location and error-entry-type were met. The times were chosen in view of the fact that a single fault can trigger several related log entries. These log entries, depending on the level of hardware or software that generates them, can be dispersed in time from a few seconds to several hours or days. The intent of the temporal clustering is to group all the events associated with a single fault or a set of related faults, and to exclude unrelated events.

The sensitivity study showed that the first clustering procedure was used over 95 percent of the time in deciding whether or not an event-log entry belonged in a tuple. The results of the study indicated that although the contribution of the second clustering procedure is small, it should remain an integral part of the clustering algorithm.

Formation into tuples reduces the number of logical entities in an event log by approximately a factor of 20 (e.g., from 58,305 entries into 3,060 single entries and the remaining 55,245 entries grouped in 2,452 tuples). The median entry count for the multiple entry tuples is three, and the spanning time for the medium tuple is on the order of three minutes. Five categories of tuple types were identified: normal operational status reports; normal device errors (e.g., soft disk errors) that are usually self-recoverable; recoverable system crashes; known hard failure symptoms; and finally, the totally unexpected, or tuples of such rarity that their symptoms were known to only a few engineers.

In order to further reduce the volume of log information and to demonstrate the validity of the "hierarchy of significance" of data in a tuple, matching algorithms were used to determine the uniqueness of a tuple. Five different matching algorithms, which used various amounts of information from the tuple attribute hierarchy, were examined. The first algorithm, which matched on error-entry-type and bug-halt-name, as well as on certain error register bits, was the most exacting and most rigorous matching algorithm. The least rigorous algorithm matched only on error-entry-type and bug-halt-name, while excluding multiple occurrences of the same error-entry-type and ignoring the arrival order of entry types.

A few tuple types accounted for a large number of tuples encountered. Depending on the matching algorithms used, the number of unique tuples varied from 41 percent down to 6 percent, on average a further decrease in information complexity of a factor of 10. The 2,452 tuples in the preceding example were categorized into 255 different tuple types. Four tuple types accounted for 65.2 percent of the tuple occurrences. In most cases, 75 percent of the unique tuple types appeared at least once in the first 15 percent of the observation period. Once normal system behavior is characterized by tuple types, this information can be expunged from the event log, leaving only abnormal symptoms. Thus, instead of 200 event-log entries per day to analyze, there may be only one or two. Furthermore, symptoms of disk failure were seen in the event logs up to two weeks prior to catastrophic failure.

The concept of observing system trends for failure prediction was investigated by Nassar [1985]. A methodology that involves three types of analysis was outlined. In the first analysis, an average error distribution for each error type was calculated. This was used as an indication of whether or not a trend was associated with an error type. In the second analysis, error distributions for all error types were obtained for intervals between crashes. Both average and individual error distributions between crashes demonstrated increasing error generation rates prior to the crash. A failure prediction algorithm based on the detection of large error clusters—that is, a threshold number of errors—was proposed. The algorithm may be used to give a last moment warning so emergency procedures can be initiated to minimize any potential damage resulting from the failure. The third analysis examines the failure/CPU utilization relationship as suggested by previous work. It was shown that there is a break point above which the system devotes most of its time to scheduling and memory allocation. The I/O and paging rates abruptly increase, which in turn strongly increases the probability of device failures and system crashes. Preliminary results using an average of 113 errors for each prediction over six months of data were analyzed showing a 60 percent chance of success. Although this method has been neither thoroughly tested nor implemented, at least the results clearly indicate that failure prediction based on an increase in error rate, a threshold error number, a CPU utilization threshold, or a combination of these factors may be feasible.

A probabilistic model has been developed to characterize the relationship among errors recorded in a system error log [Iyer, 1986]. The model was used to automatically detect symptoms of frequently occurring persistent errors in two large Control Data Cyber systems. It was shown that 85 percent of the identified error symptoms, each utilizing a total of 36 errors,* corresponded to permanent system faults. Several steps are involved in constructing the model. First, error records that report the same conditions (i.e., same type of error and same machine state) are grouped to form a cluster. Error clusters occurring within a small time interval are gathered to form error groups. Error groups occurring within 24 hours and having at least two error records in common are called *events*. Second, probability measures are used to validate and quantify the strength of relationships among errors, error clusters, error groups, and events, where joint and individual probabilities based on the frequency of occurrences (according to past data) are calculated. If the joint probability is larger than the product of all the individual probabilities, errors are likely to be related, therefore appearing together. Records that are common to most of the groups in an event are identified as the symptom of an event, permitting automatic identification of the cause of a persistent fault.

---

* In many systems errors will be reported by multiple error checkers. Tuples automatically cluster multiple error reports into a single event corresponding to the original error.

The following table summarizes some of the studies on trend analysis [Lin, 1988]:

Reference	Approach	Average Number of Events	Percentage of Success
Iyer, 1986	Joint probability	36	85%
Nassar, 1985	Thresholds on error numbers and CPU utilization	113	60%
Weibull	Statistical Weibull fit	25	—
Lin, 1988	Dispersion frame technique	5	88%

This table, which includes (Weibull distribution) and the dispersion frame technique (described next), lists the approach, the average number of events required to identify a trend, and the percentage of success in applying the approaches. Although the data sets adopted from individual sources are different, the table nevertheless shows that the DFT uses the least number of data points, given that similar instrumentation techniques are used. Moreover, the small set of rules (i.e., five rules) derived from the error log successfully predicts almost 90 percent of the hard failures with sufficient prior information.

DFT Example. A distributed on-line monitoring and predictive diagnostic system has been developed for the campus-wide Andrew file system at Carnegie Mellon University. The file server hardware is composed of a SUN 2/170 (or SUN 3/280) workstation with Motorola 68010 (or 68020) microprocessor, a Xylogics 450 disk controller, and Fujitsu Eagle disk drives each accommodating up to 800 megabytes. Each file server has at most two disk controllers and each controller supports up to two disk drives. According to published statistics, the mean time between failures (MTBF) of the disk drive is 20,000 hours, and the mean time to repair (MTTR) is 30 minutes. Therefore, when the file system is run at full capacity, with 52 disk drives spreading over 13 file servers, one could expect a hard disk failure in the file system every 400 hours.

Sources of information for data analysis include the automatic error log, collected by the on-line predictive diagnostic system, and an operator's log. Data collected from February 1986, the first date of file server operation, until January 1988 was used for studying the characteristics of various faults. The increasing number of file servers placed in service over the twenty-two-month period resulted in a total of 20 machine-years of data. It was shown that the typical error log contained events that were caused by a mixture of transient and intermittent faults. The operator's log contained permanent failure information, as well as repair actions attempted to remedy the problem.

Chapter 2 demonstrated that the failure distribution of transient faults can be characterized by the Weibull function with a decreasing error rate, and that the failure distribution of intermittent faults is typified by an increasing error rate. Moreover, 25 errors are typically required to give an accurate estimate of the Weibull parameters satisfying the chi-square goodness-of-fit test requirements. Users will not tolerate such a large number of errors, and subsequent system crashes, prior to an attempted repair. Hence, the dispersion frame technique (DFT) was developed. The DFT is based upon the observation that electromechanical and electronic devices experience an increasing error rate prior to catastrophic failure. The technique determines the relationship between error occurrences by examining their closeness in time and space, and it utilizes dispersion frames (DF) and error dispersion indices (EDI). A dispersion frame is the interarrival time between successive error events of the *same* error type. The error dispersion index is defined as the number of error occurrences in a DF irrespective of error type. A highly related group of errors exhibits a high EDI.

Based on successive applications of space and time partitioning to the event log, the DFT first extracts events pertinent to each device, and then groups events according to time. The heuristics are activated when a dispersion frame between 150 and 200 hours is encountered. This threshold is also observed as the mean interarrival times between errors depicted in the data [Lin, 1988], where the smallest mean is 154 hours. Thus, the threshold was chosen to be one week's time—that is, 168 hours—to avoid potential cyclic patterns caused by daily dependencies on workload. The DFT is illustrated in Figure 4–16 and can be described as follows:

1. For each device, a time line of the five most recent error occurrences for that device is drawn. The DFT is activated when a frame size less than 168 hours is encountered. Figure 4–16 shows the error events *i-4*, *i-3*, *i-2*, *i-1*, and *i*.
2. Centered around each error occurrence on the time line are the dispersion frames of previous interarrival times. Frame (*i-3*) is the interarrival time between event *i-4* and *i-3*, and frame (*i-2*) is the interarrival time between event *i-3* and *i-2*. Frame (*i-3*) is centered around error event *i-3*, *i-2*, and frame (*i-2*) is centered around error *i-2*, *i-1*, etc.
3. The number of errors in each frame is measured and designated as the error dispersion index. Figure 4–16 shows that the error dispersion index is 3 for frame (*i-3*), and 2 for frame (*i-2*).
4. A pending-failure warning is issued under the following conditions:
   a. *3,3 rule*: when two consecutive indices from the same frame exhibit an error dispersion index of at least 3—such as frame (*i-3*) in Figure 4–16

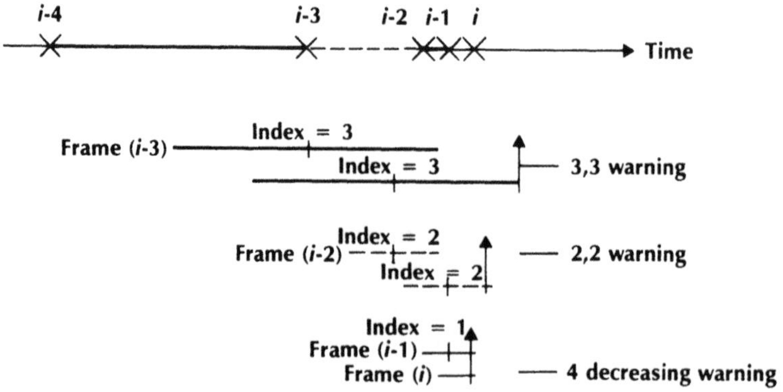

FIGURE 4–16
Dispersion frame technique [From Lin, 1988]

    b. *2,2 rule*: when two consecutive indices from two successive frames exhibit an error dispersion index of at least 2—such as frames (*i*-3) and (*i*-2)

    c. *4 decreasing rule*: when there are four monotonically decreasing frames and at least one frame is half the size of its previous frame—such as frame (*i*-3); frame (*i*-2), which is less than half of frame (*i*-3); frame (*i*-1); and frame (*i*)

    d. *2-in-1 rule*: when a dispersion frame is less than one hour

    e. *4-in-1 rule*: when four error events occur within a 24-hour frame.

5. Several iterations among steps 2, 3, and 4 are usually performed before a warning can be issued.

Although three of the preceding conditions, termed the *DFT rules*, are triggered in the preceding example, in practice, interarrival times between errors are not uniformly decreasing. These five rules were extracted from the intersection of the conditions of the intermittent errors leading to each of the 29 permanent failures in the file system. Moreover, they were designed to identify local error patterns that can be shown mathematically to cover a range of values for the α parameter of the Weibull distribution. The range of α associated with each rule is derived in the following paragraphs. To illustrate, consider five errors with interarrival times represented by the following frames: $2w$ = frame (*i*-3), x = frame (*i*-2), y = frame (*i*-1), z = frame (*i*). Further, assume $2w$ is 40 units.

• *3,3 Rule*: The 3,3 rule sets up the following relationships between the frames. The combinatorial equations to be solved are $w > x + y$ and $w > y + z$. Possible values for $2w$, x, y, and z are depicted by the family of DF curves in Figure 4–17a in which the envelope of the graph is denoted by squares. The envelope for the error rate covers a range from increasing to decreasing, resulting in an α value that can be locally less than, equal to, or greater than one. This sequence of DFs of error events is termed a *band* and covers a wide range of α values.

• *2,2 Rule*: The relationships between the frames yield the following combinatorial equations: $w > x$, $w > y$, $x > 2y$, $x > 2z$, $x + y > w$, and $y + z > x/2$. Possible values of $2w$, x, y, and z are depicted in Figure 4–17b, showing a mixture of increasing and

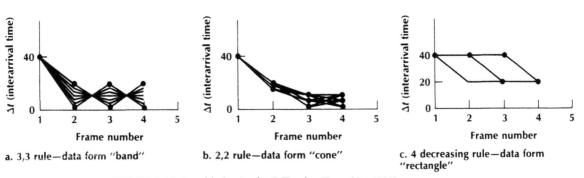

a. 3,3 rule—data form "band"   b. 2,2 rule—data form "cone"   c. 4 decreasing rule—data form "rectangle"

FIGURE 4–17 *Local behavior for DFT rules [From Lin, 1988]*

constant error rates. This range of DFs of error events is termed a *cone* shape with α values greater than or equal to one.

• *4 Decreasing Rule*: The relationships for 4 decreasing rule are $2w > x > y > z$. Also, at least one frame is half the size of its previous frame. Figure 4–17c depicts a *rectangular* envelope representing the worst case values. The range of DFs covers α values strictly greater than one.

• *2-in-1 and 4-in-1 Rules*: For completeness, the 2-in-an-hour rule is termed a *dimple*, and has the shape of a sharp transition in the slope of the DFs. The 4-in-a-day rule is termed a *valley*, and is in the form of a sharp slope followed by a relatively flat portion.

A total of 28 rules were fired during the 22-month period of data analysis: 7 from the 3,3 rule, 3 from the 2,2 rule, 4 from the 4 decreasing rule, 5 from the 4-in-a-day rule, and 9 from the 2-in-an-hour rule. Table 4–6 shows the frequency with which each of the rules fired during the fault prediction analysis for each device. Two numbers are listed under each rule: the number of total firings and the number of times that particular rule was first to detect the trend. Although the 4-in-1 rule (four events in one day) did not succeed in issuing the first warning, it nevertheless was activated five times prior to repairs. Since each rule was fired more than once and for more than one device, some degree of confidence is generated in the generality and robustness of the individual rules. Furthermore, no single rule is adequate to identify all the trends. However it is speculated that only a small rule set will be required.

Table 4–6 also lists the number of total repairs, the number of events with prior error log information (i.e., five or more events), the number of successful predictions, and false alarms for each device. Two conclusions can be drawn. First, the DFT can be used to distinguish intermittent from transient errors for both electromechanical and electronic devices. Second, the interarrival pattern captured through DFT exhibits the same characteristics used by the traditional statistical analysis for fault prediction. The high success prediction rate of 88 percent using a small set of rules and a maximum number of five events among the events with recorded information shows that the DFT is very effective when coupled with good system instrumentation. Failures were predicted an average of 160 hours prior to repair activity.

Impact of Symptom-Based Diagnosis

During the second half of the decade of the 1970s, Digital Equipment Corporation started a shift from specification-based diagnosis, in which the field service engineer would execute diagnostic programs in an attempt to recreate the failure, to symptom-based diagnosis, in which error data is analyzed to capture information about the failure. The latter approach, termed symptom-directed diagnosis (SDD), is based upon techniques similar to those outlined in the previous section and is embodied in programs such as SPEAR (systems package for error analysis and reporting) [SPEAR, 1986] and VAXsim-PLUS. These programs analyze error log data using heuristically established rules to locate the failing FRU. Figure 4–18a depicts the distribution of on-

TABLE 4–6 *Rule firing and effectiveness of DFT in fault prediction study*

Device	Frequency of DFT Rules Fired										Effectiveness of DFT			
	3,3		2,2		4 Decreasing		4-in-a-Day		2-in-an-Hour		Total Repairs	With Prior Information	Prediction Succeeded	False Alarms
	Total	First	Total	First	Total	First	Total	First	Total	First				
Disk	3	2	1	1	2	2	3	0	7	2	7	5	5	2
Mem	1	1	1	1	1	1	1	0	1	1	7	4	4	2
CPU	1	1	1	1	0	0	0	0	0	0	7	3	3	0
Disk controller	2	2	0	0	1	1	1	0	1	0	8	5	3	1

Source: Lin, 1988.

site time spent by a field engineer when specification-based diagnosis was prevalent. The vast majority of the time was spent executing diagnostic programs and observing the system to identify the problem, whereas only 10 percent of the time was spent making the physical repair, and a further 15 percent of the time was devoted to validating that the repair activity fixed the original problem. SDD, in conjunction with the DEC Remote Diagnostic Center, analyzes the system prior to dispatching a field service engineer; this results in a two-thirds decrease in on-site time, as depicted in Figure 4–18b. SDD is not only a powerful technique for reducing repair time but also it quickly identifies problems, thereby decreasing the number of system crashes and increasing system availability.

FIGURE 4–18
Comparison of on-site repair time distributions (excluding travel time) for the "failure recreate" or specification-based approach to field service and the "failure capture" or symptom-based approach [Courtesy of Digital Equipment Corporation]

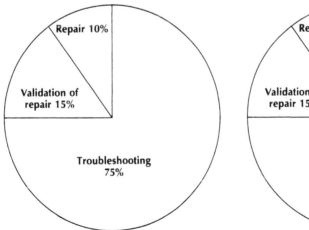
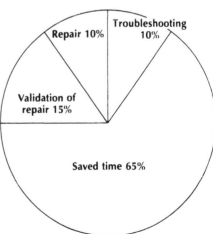

SUMMARY

This chapter focused on maintainability in general and testing in particular. The physical hierarchy of abstract levels and the temporal stages in a system's life, both introduced in Chapter 1, were used to organize the discussion. Specification-based diagnosis, frequently referred to as testing, is primarily focused at the lower levels of abstraction (through the logic level) and the earlier stages in the development of a system (through installation). While specification-based diagnosis is frequently applied at the system level and during operational life, the large variation in system configurations and operational environments diminishes the effectiveness of this approach.

Symptom-based diagnosis is rapidly becoming the preferred approach for system-level diagnosis during operational life. Based upon the observation that systems typically exhibit a period of potentially increasing unreliability prior to catastrophic failure, trends can often be identified and used to isolate the faulty field replaceable unit. If the system has been designed to tolerate these intermittent faults, the user will perceive no system outages during diagnosis. Trend analysis develops a model of normal system behavior and watches for a shift that signifies the onset of abnormal behavior. Since normal system workloads tend to stress systems differently than specification-based diagnostics, these workloads will uncover problems that are not stimulated by test programs. Trend analysis can also adaptively learn the changing normal usage pattern of individual systems.

REFERENCES

ACM, 1976; Acree, 1980; Acree et al., 1982; Adrion, Branstad, and Cheriavsky, 1982; Anderson and Metze, 1973; Avizienis and Rennels, 1972; Bennetts and Lewin, 1971; Bennetts and Scott, 1976; Boone, Liebergot, and Sedmak, 1980; Bossen and Hong, 1971; Bozorgui-Nesbat and McCluskey, 1980; Brahme and Abraham, 1984; Breuer and Friedman, 1976, 1980; Brule, Johnson, and Kletsky, 1960; Bryant, 1984; Budd et al., 1980; Carter, 1986; Carter, Wadia, and Jessep, 1972; Chang, 1965, 1968; Chang, Manning, and Metze, 1970; Chang, Smith, and Walford, 1974; Chin and Lee, 1986; Courtois, 1979; Craig, 1980; Crouzet and Decouty, 1982; Czeck, 1991; Czeck, Segall, and Siewiorek, 1987; Decouty, Michel, and Wagner, 1980; Duane, 1964; Finelli, 1987; Frechette and Tanner, 1979; Friedman and Menon, 1971.

Goetz, 1972; Grason and Nagle, 1980; Halstead, 1979; Hennie, 1964, 1968; Hokomb and North, 1985; Hotchkiss, 1979; Howard and Nahourai, 1978; Institute of Environmental Sciences, 1981; Iyer, 1986; Kautz, 1968; Kime, 1970; Kurlak and Chobot, 1981; Lai, 1981; Lai and Siewiorek, 1983; Lala, 1983; Lala and Smith, 1983; Lesser and Shedletshy, 1980; Lin, 1988; Maxion and Siewiorek, 1985; McCluskey and Clegg, 1971; McGough and Swern, 1981, 1983; McGough, Swern, and Bavuso, 1981; Mei, 1974; Mil Handbook 781; Morganti, 1978.

Nadig, 1977; NASA, 1979a, 1979b; Nassar, 1985; Northcutt, 1980; Palumbo and Finelli, 1987; Preparata, Metze, and Chien, 1967; Punches, 1986; Robach and Saucier, 1980; Roth, 1966; Roth, Bouricius, and Scheider, 1967; SAE, 1986; Schmid et al., 1983; Schuette et al., 1986; Sellers, Hsiao, and Bearnson, 1968a; Seshu and Freeman, 1962; Shin and Lee, 1986; Silberman and Spillinger, 1976; SPEAR, 1986; Stiffler and Van Doren, 1979; Susskind, 1972; Thatte and Abraham, 1978, 1980; Tohma, Ohyama, and Sake, 1971; Tsao, 1983; Tsao and Siewiorek, 1983; Williams and Parker, 1979; Yang et al., 1985.

PROBLEMS

1. Draw an SPRT graph for $\alpha = \beta = 0.1$ and a discrimination ratio of 2. Compare this graph with the others given in the text and comment upon the amount of testing time required as a function of the risk factors.

2. Two SPRT plans have been suggested:

   Plan A: $\alpha = \beta = 0.3$. Discrimination ratio = 2.
   Plan B: $\alpha = \beta = 1.0$. Discrimination ratio = 3.

   Comment upon the amount of testing time expected for Plan A and Plan B. Which plan would you prefer if you were the manufacturer? Which would you prefer if you were the consumer?

3. Use the following parameters:

   $\alpha = 0.10 \quad \beta = 0.10 \quad \theta_1 = 100$ hours $\quad \theta_0 = 200$ hours

   Calculate the discrimination ratio, accept-reject criteria, truncation points, and the slope and ordinate intercepts of the test plan curves. Plot the test plan.

4. Assume incoming components have a defective rate of 0.01.
   a. Without incoming screening, what is the probability that a 500-chip system will be defective after assembly?
   b. What fraction of the defective components would have to be removed by incoming screening if the probability that the 500-chip system will not be defective is 0.8?
   c. If the cost of screening incoming chips is one-tenth the cost of locating a defective chip in the assembled system, at what defect rate (assuming screening is 100 percent effective) is incoming screening more cost effective than no screening?

5. Use the Boolean difference to find all the tests in the circuit in Figure P4–1 for the following:

   Line 2 stuck-at-0
   Line 6 stuck-at-0

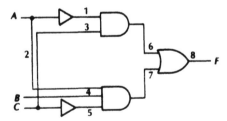

FIGURE P4–1

6. For the circuit in Figure P4–1, use the D-algorithm to find a test for the following:

   A stuck-at-1
   Line 7 stuck-at-1

   What other faults do these tests also detect?

7. Find a minimal test set for the circuit in Figure P4–1. (Hint: This is a minimal cover problem; see Kautz [1968] for further information if required.)

8. Create the Reed-Muller implementation for the circuit in Figure P4–1.

9. Create a controllable version of the circuit in Figure P4–1, and list the five required tests (including control points).

10. For the circuit pictured in Figure P4–2, generate a test for the following:

Line 8 stuck-at-0
Line 1 stuck-at-0

Explain your approach in each case.

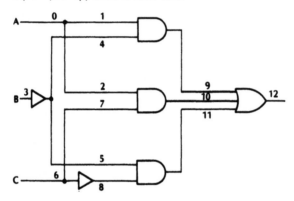

FIGURE P4–2

5 EVALUATION CRITERIA

Stephen McConnel and Daniel P. Siewiorek

INTRODUCTION   A method of evaluation is required in order to compare the redundancy techniques presented in Chapter 3 and make subsequent design trade-offs. Evaluation criteria are often loosely referred to as *reliability*. Reliability, however, can mean many things, and thus a difficulty arises in the measurement and interpretation of reliability. To people in business, a computer is reliable when paychecks are printed on time and contain no errors. To scientists, a computer is reliable if it has enough computing power available to process experimental numerical data. Space scientists consider a spacecraft's on-board computer reliable when the mission (perhaps years in length) is successfully completed. Finally, airline personnel and others consider an on-board control computer reliable if it makes no decisions with fatal consequences. The major difference among these users is the application-dependent interpretation of what a reliable system does. The great variety of applications has engendered a large number of reliability measures, both quantitative and qualitative. Often, several measures are required to describe a system adequately.

This chapter introduces criteria for evaluating system reliability and availability. The chapter also develops modeling techniques that can be used to obtain reasonable predictions for the criteria. Figure 5–1 presents a taxonomy of these modeling techniques. The reliability branch utilizes different modeling techniques depending on the operating assumptions, such as failure to exhaustion and failure with repair. *Failure to exhaustion* is used for unattended operation where repair is not possible—the system fails when all redundancy has been consumed. *Failure with repair,* on the other hand, is based on two separate but concurrent processes: the failure process and the repair process. Failure to exhaustion can be modeled by the combinatorial techniques shown in the reliability branch of Figure 5–1. The availability branch uses a variety of models for systems with repair. As shown in the figure, various Markov models can be used to evaluate both reliability and availability criteria.

A number of issues related to the use of modeling techniques are raised in this chapter, and various software programs that have been written to assist in reliability evaluation are reviewed. The final section of the chapter considers several applications of the modeling techniques: nonredundant components, redundancy-enhanced chip yield, system performance/reliability trade-offs, and system design.

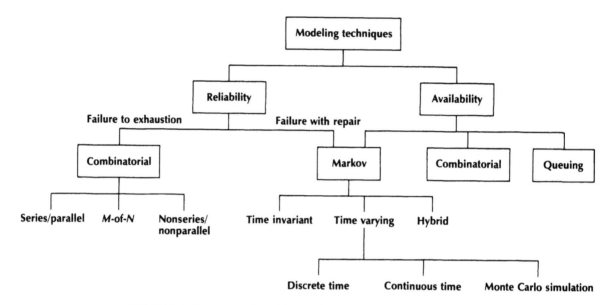

FIGURE 5–1 *Taxonomy of modeling techniques*

SURVEY OF EVALUATION CRITERIA: HARDWARE

Evaluation criteria for system hardware reliability can be classified according to two basic techniques, deterministic and probabilistic modeling, as shown in Table 5–1. Four levels of modeling are customarily used.

The highest level of modeling is the *system level,* in which the entire system is considered as a black box. After statistics are gathered about events such as failures of a certain kind, a model can be suggested to fit the data as closely as possible. Modeling at this level requires an enormous amount of data.

At the next level, the *module level,* the system is subdivided into several modules that have mutually independent failures. The system model is obtained by a composite of the models for the modules. Modeling is most often performed at the module level. Redundant systems are then modeled in terms of their nonredundant subsystems.

The next lowest level is the *gate level.* It is seldom necessary to model a system below the gate level. However, if the redundancy is introduced at a lower level, the *component level* of modeling is required, where components are such items as transistors, diodes, and resistors. The failure rate and reliability functions of individual components were discussed in Chapter 2.

Of the two modeling techniques listed in Table 5–1, the simplest is the *deterministic model.* In this model, the minimum number of component failures that can be tolerated without system failure is taken as the figure of merit for the system. Deterministic modeling can result in wasted resources and unbalanced system design because highly reliable components must be replicated as many times as the low-reli-

TABLE 5–1
Evaluation criteria for system reliability

Model	Criteria
Deterministic	Survive at least k component failures
Probabilistic	*Functions*
	Hazard (failure rate) function, $z(t)$
	Reliability, $R(t)$
	Mission time, $MT(r)$
	Repair rate, μ
	Availability, $A(t)$
Probabilistic	*Single parameters*
	Mean time to failure (MTTF)
	Mean time to repair (MTTR)
	Mean time between failures (MTBF)
	Coverage
Probabilistic	*Comparative measures*
	Reliability difference $\quad R_2(t) - R_1(t)$
	Reliability gain $\quad R_2(t)/R_1(t)$
	Mission time improvement $\quad MT_2(r)/MT_1(r)$
	Reliability improvement index $\quad \log R_{old}/\log R_{new}$

ability components. The only common use of the deterministic model in practice is to specify that no *single* component failure should cause the system to fail.

Probabilistic modeling, based on relative component failure and repair rates, is most frequently used to evaluate hardware reliability. Probabilistic modeling is the primary method of evaluating system reliability/availability. The probabilistic evaluation criteria listed in Table 5–1 are discussed in the following subsections.

Probabilistic Model Functions

Hazard Function. The hazard function refers to the time-dependent failure rate of hardware components (see the bathtub curve in Figure 1–4, which depicts the failure rate as a function of time). Denoted as $z(t)$, the hazard function is sometimes called the hazard rate or the force of mortality and is usually measured in failures per million hours.

For a known distribution, the hazard function is mathematically defined by

$$z(t) \triangleq \frac{pdf}{1 - CDF}$$

For electronic components on the normal-life portion of the bathtub curve, the failure rate is assumed to be constant. Thus, the exponential hazard function is applicable:

$$z(t) = \lambda$$

For the periods of infant mortality and component wearout, the Weibull hazard function* is often used:

$$z(t) = \alpha\lambda(\lambda t)^{\alpha-1}$$

The Weibull shape parameter α and the scale parameter λ, which are used in both hazard functions, are constants specific to a particular component.

For the nonredundant constant-failure-rate model, the system hazard function is the sum of the component failure rates, as discussed in Chapter 2. For the combination of Weibull processes and for redundant systems with either model, the relationship is much more complex. The hazard function is easy to measure in ascertaining the operational reliability of physical systems because it can be calculated from a histogram of times between failures.

In keeping with the probabilistic nature of the concepts of failue rate and hazard function, the failure of electronic components is assumed to follow a general Poisson distribution:

- The probability of one failure during an interval Δt is approximately $z(t)\Delta t$.
- The probability of two or more failures during an interval Δt is negligible.
- Failures are independent.

Defining $m(t) = \int_0^t z(x)\,dx$, Ross [1972] has shown that the probability of k failures in time $[0,t]$ is given by

$$\frac{e^{-m(t)}[m(t)]^k}{k!}$$

The expected value (or mean) of the number of failures in time $[0,t]$ is

$$E[k] = \sum_{k=0}^{\infty} k\,\frac{e^{-m(t)}[m(t)]^k}{k!} = m(t)$$

The variance is

$$\text{Var}[k] = E[k^2] - (E[k])^2 = m(t) = E[k]$$

For a constant failure rate λ, $m(t) = \lambda t$. Thus,

$$P\{k \text{ failures in time } [0,t]\} = \frac{e^{-\lambda t}(\lambda t)^k}{k!}$$

$$E[k] = \text{var}[k] = \lambda t$$

For the Weibull hazard function $z(t) = \alpha\lambda(\lambda t)^{\alpha-1}$, $m(t) = (\lambda t)^{\alpha}$. Therefore,

$$P\{k \text{ failures in time } [0,t]\} = \frac{e^{-(\lambda t)^{\alpha}}(\lambda t)^{k\alpha}}{k!}$$

$$E[k] = \text{var}[k] = (\lambda t)^{\alpha}$$

---

* As noted in Chapter 2, the exponential function is equivalent to the Weibull function with α equal to one.

Reliability Function. The reliability function of a system, denoted $R(t)$, is defined as the probability that the system will perform satisfactorily from time zero to time t, given that operation commences successfully at time zero. It is a monotonically decreasing function whose initial value is one. The reliability function can be used to derive many of the other reliability measures detailed here.

Given the general Poisson distribution developed previously, the reliability function for a single component becomes

$$R(t) \triangleq P\{0 \text{ failures in time } [0,t]\} = e^{-m(t)}$$

For a constant failure rate, substitute λt for $m(t)$. Then,

$$R(t) = e^{-\lambda t}$$

If a system does not contain any redundancy—that is, if every component must function properly for the system to work—and if component failures are statistically independent, then the system reliability is the product of the component reliabilities and is thus also exponential. Furthermore, the failure rate of the system is the sum of the failure rates of the individual components. Therefore,

$$R_{sys}(t) = \prod_{i=1}^{n} R_i(t) = \prod_{i=1}^{n} \exp(-\lambda_i t) = \exp\left(-\left(\sum_{i=1}^{n} \lambda_i\right)t\right)$$

where there are n components.

For the Weibull hazard function, substitute $(\lambda t)^{\alpha}$ for $m(t)$

$$R(t) = \exp(-(\lambda)t)^{\alpha}$$

The Weibull model is more flexible but less tractable than the exponential when large groups of components are involved. The reliability function for a group of components is

$$R_{sys}(t) = \exp\left(-\left[\sum_{i=1}^{n} (\lambda_i t)^{\alpha_i}\right]\right)$$

The sum must be performed for each new value of t, resulting in lengthy calculations. It is also difficult, if not impossible, to integrate analytically, which affects the other reliability measures discussed here.

For the general hazard function, recall that $m(t) = \int_0^t z(x)\, dx$. Thus,

$$R(t) = \exp\left(-\int_0^t z(x)\, dx\right)$$

$$R_{sys}(t) = \exp\left(-\left[\sum_{i=1}^{n} \left(\int_0^t z_i(x)\, dx\right)\right]\right)$$

As noted earlier, the Weibull function is more accurate than the exponential function for components subject to wear and aging (increasing failure rates) or for those that improve with time, as the weaker members of the population are culled out (decreasing failure rates). When extremely accurate reliability predictions are needed, sample components are tested to find the underlying distribution (Weibull or otherwise) and the value of pertinent parameters. This testing is necessary because different kinds of components experience different distributions, as do similar components from different manufacturing lots or manufacturers.

Mission Time Function. The mission time function, $MT(r)$, gives the time at which system reliability falls below the level r. The mission time function is particularly well suited for applications with a minimum lifetime requirement either due to impossible or prohibitively expensive repair or due to fixed intervals between maintenance. Such applications include spacecraft computers, undersea cable repeaters, and commercial airliner avionics systems, all of which have stringent reliability requirements.

The relationship between $R(t)$ and $MT(r)$ is given by

$$R[MT(r)] = r$$

$$MT[R(t)] = t$$

For a constant failure rate $[z(t) = \lambda]$, the component mission time function is easily shown to be

$$MT(r) = \frac{-\ln r}{\lambda}$$

A nonredundant system with n components therefore has

$$MT(r) = \frac{-\ln r}{\sum\limits_{i=1}^{n} \lambda_i}$$

For a more complex hazard function or for a redundant system, the mission time function is much more difficult to compute.

Repair Rate Function. The repair rate function should be taken into consideration in accurate models of system reliability. Repair activity, however, is not as easily modeled analytically as failure mechanisms. Many factors affect the rate at which repair occurs, including human ability, travel time, diagnostic capabilities, and parts availability. Despite the lack of strong theoretical backing, probabilistic models usually assume a repair rate analogous to the failure rate discussed already. For the purposes of this text, the repair rate function is treated similarly to the hazard (failure rate) function and is generally denoted $z_r(t)$. The form and parameter values of this function can be measured for existing systems or estimated from experience with comparable situations.

For a Weibull repair rate function, μ is used for the scale parameter ($= \lambda$ in the failure rate function) and β is used for the shape parameter ($= \alpha$ in the failure rate function). The solution of a reliability model with both failure and repair rates requires the use of Markov models, which are discussed later in this chapter. These models usually assume that repair of a failed system restores it such that the failure rate of the repaired system is the same as if no failure had occurred. In the case of the exponential model (constant hazard rate) process, this is completely true. The assumption is less valid for the Weibull process, but is usually made in order to provide analytic solutions.

Availability Function. For systems that can be repaired, the availability function defines the probability that the system is operational at any given time. Expressed symbolically as $A(t)$, availability differs from reliability $R(t)$ in that any number of system failures can have occurred prior to that time. As a result, the availability function has a nonzero constant (steady-state) term. For a constant failure rate λ and a constant repair rate μ, the steady-state availability can be expressed as

$$A_{ss} = \frac{\mu}{\lambda + \mu}$$

The exact form of the availability function requires the solution of the appropriate Markov model, which will be derived later in the chapter.

Probabilistic Single-Parameter Models

Reliability and availability equations, even for simple systems with repair, are often too complex to comprehend except (perhaps) in graphic form. Therefore, single-parameter metrics have been proposed to summarize these continuous-time equations.

Mean Time to Failure. Measuring the mean time to failure (MTTF) for components was discussed in Chapter 2. For components, the MTTF of a system is the expected time of the first system failure in a population of identical systems, given successful startup at time zero. It assumes a new (perfect) system at time zero. For the reliability functions used here, the MTTF is defined as

$$MTTF = \int_0^\infty R(t) \, dt$$

Reliability functions of complex redundant systems require numeric integration techniques, as do the Weibull reliability functions because of their nonintegrability. However, the MTTF is still relatively easy to determine by means of numerical integration of the reliability function on a computer. Although the MTTF, in theory, applies only to a large population of systems, it is also useful as a measure for a given design (population of one).

For an example of MTTF calculation, consider a nonredundant system with n components, each with individual constant failure rate λ_i:

$$MTTF = \int_0^\infty R(t) \, dt = \int_0^\infty \exp\left(-\left(\sum_{i=1}^n \lambda_i\right)t\right) dt$$

Hence,

$$MTTF = \frac{1}{\sum_{i=1}^n \lambda_i}$$

This direct relationship between the MTTF and the system failure rate is one reason the constant-failure-rate assumption is often made even when supporting data are scanty.

Mean Time to Repair. The mean time to repair (MTTR) is often used to measure the repairability of a system. It is the expected time for repair of a failed system or subsystem. The MTTR is related to the repair rate discussed previously much as MTTF is related to the failure rate. As with the repair rate, MTTR is not easily modeled analytically, and it must usually be measured or estimated.

As indicated for exponential distributions, MTTF = $1/\lambda$ and MTTR = $1/\mu$. The steady-state availability, A_{ss}, defined earlier, can be rewritten in terms of these parameters:

$$A_{ss} = \frac{MTTF}{MTTR + MTTF}$$

Mean Time Between Failures. The term mean time between failures (MTBF) is often mistakenly used in place of mean time to failure (MTTF). The MTBF is the mean time between failures in a system with repair, and it is thus derived from a combination of repair and failure processes. The easiest approximation for MTBF is

MTBF = MTTF + MTTR

This expression should be exact for nonredundant systems, but it can only be approximate for redundant systems because the interplay of multiple failures usually causes the repair rate to change.

Coverage. Coverage is a concept serving diverse purposes, with two major meanings: quantitative and qualitative. The quantitative meaning is used most often in reliability modeling of redundant systems. In its quantitative sense, coverage is the probability that the system successfully recovers from a specific type of failure. Quite often, coverage is the probability that a particular class of fault is successfully detected before a complete system corruption occurs. Other typical uses include the probability of successful takeover by backup systems and the noncorruption of checkpoint (restart) variables.

The qualitative meaning of coverage specifies the types of errors against which a particular redundancy scheme guards. For example, the coverage of Hamming single-error-correcting/double-error-detecting code is correction for all single-bit errors in a code word and detection of all double-bit errors and some multiple-bit errors. Jack et al. [1975] develop this measure of coverage for a variety of both error-detection and error-correction techniques.

Probabilistic Comparative Measures

A major use of the evaluation criteria discussed so far is to compare different systems or different models of the same system. Such comparisons generally involve arithmetic differences of the measures or ratios between the measures. The four common comparative measures shown in Table 5–1 are

Reliability difference: $R_{new}(t) - R_{old}(t)$
Reliability gain: $R_{new}(t)/R_{old}(t)$
Mission time improvement: $MT_{new}(r)/MT_{old}(r)$, where MT is the time the system is above the reliability, r
Reliability improvement index: $\log R_{old}/\log R_{new}$

The use of these and similar measures is illustrated later in the Motorola 6809 design example in the final section of this chapter.

SURVEY OF EVALUATION CRITERIA: SOFTWARE

Software reliability assessment is part of the more general area of software quality assessment [Mohanly, 1973]. Effective mechanisms for measuring software quality are required because of the high cost of software development and maintenance. Estimates indicate that over 90 percent of the total computing dollars spent annually are for software. The development of techniques for measuring software reliability has been motivated mainly by project managers, who need not only ways of estimating the manpower required to develop a software system with a given level of performance but also techniques to determine when this level of performance has been reached. Most software reliability models presented to date are still far from satisfying these two needs in a general context.

Most models assume that the software failure rate will be proportional to the number of bugs or design errors present in the system, and they do not take into account that different kinds of errors may contribute differently to the total failure rate. Eliminating one significant design error may double the mean time to failure, whereas eliminating ten minor implementation errors (bugs) may have no noticeable effect.

Even assuming that the failure rate is proportional to the number of bugs and design errors in the system, no model considers the fact that the failure rate will then be related to the workload of the system. For example, doubling the workload without changing the distribution of input data to the system may double the failure rate.

Software reliability models can be roughly grouped in four categories: time domain, data domain, axiomatic, and other models.

Time Domain Models

Models formulated in the time domain attempt to relate software reliability (characterized, for instance, by an MTTF figure under typical workload conditions) to the number of bugs present in the software at a given time during its development. Typical of this approach are the models presented in Shooman [1973], Musa [1975], and Jelinsky and Moranda [1973]. Removal of implementation errors should increase MTTF, and correlation of bug-removal history with the time evolution of the MTTF value may allow the prediction of when a given MTTF value will be reached. The main disadvantages of time domain models are that bug correction can generate more bugs, and that software unreliability can be caused not only by implementation errors but also by design (specification) errors, characterization, and simulation during testing of typical workload.

The Shooman model [Shooman, 1973] attempts to estimate the software reliability—that is, the probability that no software failure will occur during an operation time interval [0,t]—from an estimate of the number of errors per machine-language instruction present in a software system after T months of debugging. The model assumes that at system integration there are E_i errors present in the system and that the system is operated continuously by an exerciser that emulates its real use. The hazard function after T months of debugging is assumed to be proportional to the remaining errors in the system. The reliability of the software system is then assumed to be

$$R(t) = e^{-CE(r,T)}$$

where $E(r,T)$ is the remaining number of errors in the system after T months of debugging, and C is a proportionality constant. The model provides equations for estimating C and $E(r,T)$ from the results of the exerciser and the number of errors corrected.

The Jelinsky–Moranda model [Jelinsky and Moranda, 1973] is a special case of the Shooman model. The additional assumption is made that each error discovered is immediately removed, decreasing the remaining number of errors by one. Assuming that the amount of debugging time between error occurrences has an exponential distribution, the density function of the time of discovery of the ith error, measured from the time of discovery of the $i - 1$th error, is

$$p(t_i) = \lambda(i) \exp(-\lambda(i)t_i)$$

where $\lambda(i) = f(N - i + 1)$ and N is the number of errors originally present. The model gives the maximum likelihood estimates for N and f.

An extension of the Jelinsky–Moranda model has been given by Wolverton and Schick [1974]. It assumes that the error rate is proportional not only to the number of errors but also to the time spent in debugging, so that the chance of discovery increases as time goes on. Another extension is given in Thayer, Lipow, and Nelson [1978], in which more than one error can be detected in a time interval, with no correction being made after the end of this interval. The new maximum likelihood estimators of N and f are also given.

All the models presented so far attempt to predict the reliability of a software system after a period of testing and debugging. In a good example of an application of this type of model, Miyamoto [1975] describes the development of an on-line realtime system for which a requirement is that the mean time between software errors (MTBSE) has to be longer than 30 days. The system will operate on a day-to-day basis, 13 hours a day. (It will be loaded every morning and reset every evening.) The requirement is formulated such that the value of the reliability function, $R(t)$, for $t = 13$ hours has to be greater than $e^{-[13/\text{MTBSE}]} = 0.9672$.

Miyamoto also gives the variations in time of the MTBSE as a function of the debugging time. The MTBSE remained at a very low value for most of the debugging period, jumping to an acceptable level only at the end. The correlation coefficient between the remaining number of errors in the program and the failure rate was 0.77, but the scatter plot shown is disappointing and suggests that the correlation coefficient between the failure rate and any other system variable could have given the same value. In the same paper, Miyamoto describes in detail how the system was tested.

Most of the models mentioned thus far take into account the fact that in the process of fixing a bug, new errors may be introduced in the system. The final number given is usually the mean time between software errors, but only Miyamoto points out that this number is valid only for a specific set of workload conditions.

Other models used to study the improvement in reliability of a software item during its development phase exist, such as Littlewood [1975], where the execution of a program is simulated with continuous-time Markov switching among smaller programs. This model also demonstrates that under certain conditions in the software system structure, the failure process will be asymptotically Poisson. Another Markov model is given in Trivedi and Shooman [1975], where the most probable number of errors that will have been corrected at any time t is based on preliminary modeling of the error occurrence and repair rates. The model also provides predictions of the availability and reliability of the system at time t. Schneidewind [1975] describes a model that assumes that the failure process is described by a nonhomogeneous Poisson process. The rate of error detection in a time interval is assumed to be proportional to the number of errors present during that interval. This leads to a Poisson distribution with a decreasing hazard rate.

Design diversity has been proposed as a means of tolerating design errors (see Chapter 3). A common assumption in software reliability models is that design errors are independent. However, data from design diversity experiments [Finelli, 1988; Knight and Leveson, 1986; Schnell and Leveson, 1988; see also Chapter 2] indicate correlations between design errors due to ambiguities in the specification and common misinterpretations of the specifications. Eckhardt and Lee [1985, 1988] provide a model for design diversity that also takes into account common mode errors.

Data Domain Models

Another approach to software reliability modeling is the data domain technique. The first model of this kind is described in Nelson [1973]. In principle, if sets of all input data values upon which a computer program can operate are identified, an estimate of the reliability of the program can be obtained by running the program for a subset of input data values. A more detailed description of data domain techniques is given in Thayer, Lipow, and Nelson [1978]. In Schick and Wolverton [1978], the time domain and data domain models are compared. However, different applications tend to use different subsets of all possible input data values, yielding different reliability values for the same software system. This fact is formally taken into account in Cheung [1980], where software reliability is estimated from a Markov model whose transition probabilities depend on a user profile. Techniques for evaluating the transition probabilities for a given profile are given in Cheung and Ramamoorthy [1975].

In the Nelson model [1973], a computer program is defined as a computable function, F, defined on the set $e = \{E_i, i = 1, \ldots, N\}$. E includes all possible combinations of input data values, with each E_i being a sample of data values needed to make a run of the program. Execution of a program produces, for a given value of E_i, the function value $F(E_i)$.

In the presence of bugs or design errors, a program actually implements F'. Let E_e be the set of input data values such that $F'(E_e)$ produces an execution failure (execution terminates prematurely, fails to terminate, or the results produced are not acceptable). If N_e is the number of E_i in E_e, then

$$p = \frac{N_e}{N}$$

is the probability that a run of the program will result in an execution failure. Nelson defines the reliability, R, as the probability of no failures, or

$$R = 1 - p = 1 - \frac{N_e}{N}$$

This model takes into account that the inputs to a program are not selected from E with a priori probability, but rather according to some operational requirement. This requirement may be characterized by a probability distribution $\{P_i: i = 1, \ldots, N\}$, P_i being the probability that the selected input is E_i. If we define the auxiliary variables Y_i to have the value zero if a run with E_i is successful and to have the value one otherwise, we have

$$p = \sum_{i=1}^{N} P_i Y_i$$

where P is again the probability that a run of the program will result in an execution failure. A mathematical definition of the reliability of a computer program is given as the probability of no execution failures after n runs:

$$R(n) = R^n = (1 - p)^n$$

The model elaborates on how to choose input data values at random from E according to the distribution P_i to obtain an unbiased estimator of $R(n)$. In addition, if the execution time for each E_i is also known, the reliability function can be expressed in terms of the more conventional probability of no failure in a time interval, $[0,t]$.

Chapter 6 in Thayer, Lipow, and Nelson [1978] extends the previous models to take into account how the testing input data sets should be partitioned. Also discussed are the uncertainty in predicting reliability values, the effect of software error removal, and the effect of program structure.

Axiomatic Models

Models in which software reliability (and software quality in general) is postulated to obey certain universal laws are known as axiomatic models [Ferdinand, 1974; Fitzsimmons and Love, 1978]. Although such models have generated great interest, their general validity has never been proven, and at most, they only give an estimate for the number of bugs present in a program.

The best-known axiomatic model is the so-called "Software Science"* developed by Halstead [Fitzsimmons and Love, 1978]. Halstead used an approach very similar to that of thermodynamics to provide quantitative measures of program level, language level, algorithm purity, program clarity, effect of modularization, programming effort, and programming time. In particular, the estimated number of bugs in a program is given by the expression

$$B = K\left(\frac{V}{EO}\right)$$

where K is a proportionality constant, V is the volume of the implementation of an algorithm, and EO is the mean number of mental discriminations between errors made by the programmer. V is given by

$$V = N \log_2 (n)$$

where N is the program length and n the size of the vocabulary defined by the language used. More specifically,

$$N = N1 + N2$$

$$n = n1 + n2$$

where $n1$ = number of distinct operators appearing in a program

$n2$ = number of distinct operands appearing in a program

$N1$ = total number of occurrences of the operators in a program

$N2$ = total number of occurrences of the operands in a program

EO has been empirically estimated to have a value around 3000

Although unconventional, the measures proposed by "Software Science" are easy to compute, and in any case, it is an alternative for estimating the number of bugs in a software system. The following table shows the correlation coefficients between the real and predicted numbers of bugs found in a software project for several experiments according to Software Science theory:

Reference	Correlation Coefficient Between Predicted and Real Numbers of Bugs	
Funami and Halstead, 1975	0.98, 0.83, and 0.92	
Cornell and Halstead, 1976	0.99	
Fitzsimmons and Love, 1978	System A	0.81
	System B	0.75
	System C	0.75
	Total	0.76

* Many publications have either supported or contradicted the results proposed by "Software Science," including a special issue of the *IEEE Transactions on Software Engineering* [Halstead, 1979].

There are significant correlations with error occurrences in the programs, although the data reported by Fitzsimmons and Love (obtained from three General Electric software development projects totaling 166,280 statements) show weaker correlation than the original values reported by Halstead.

Other Models

The model presented in Costes, Landrault, and Laprie [1978] is based on the fact that for well-debugged programs the occurrence of a software error results from conditions on both the input's set of data and the logical paths encountered. These events, then, can be considered random and independent of the past behavior of the system, that is, with constant failure rate. Also, because of their rarity, design errors or bugs may have the same effect as transient hardware faults.

The model is built on the following assumptions:

1. The system initially possesses N design errors or bugs that can be totally corrected by N interventions of the maintenance team.
2. The software failure rate is constant for a given number of design errors present in the system.
3. The system starts and continues operation until a fault is detected, then passes to a repair state: If the fault is caused by a hardware transient, the system is put into operation again after a period of time for which the probability density function is assumed to be known; if the fault is due to a software failure, maintenance takes place, during which the error may be removed, more errors may be introduced, or no modifications may be made to the software.

The model computes the availability of the system as a function of time by use of a semi-Markovian theory. That is, the system will make state transitions according to the transition probabilities matrix, and the time spent in each state is a random variable whose probability density function (PDF) either is assumed to be known or is measurable.

The main result presented in Costes, Landrault, and Laprie [1978] is how the availability of the system tends toward the asymptotic availability (availability of the system when all the design errors have been removed) as the design errors are being removed under some restrictive conditions. The minimum availability is shown to depend only on the software failure rate at system integration, and not on the order of occurrence of the different types of errors. The presence of different types of design errors only extends the time necessary to approach the asymptotic availability. The mathematics involved for the model are complex, requiring numerical computation of inverse Laplace transforms for the transition probabilities matrix, and it is not clear that the parameters needed to simulate a real system accurately can be easily measured from a real system.

Finally, there have been some attempts to model fault-tolerant software through module duplication [Hecht, 1976] and warnings about how not to measure software reliability [Littlewood, 1979]. None of the models characterize system behavior accurately enough to give the user a figure of guaranteed level of performance under general workload conditions. They estimate the number of bugs present in a program, but do not provide any accurate method to characterize and measure operational system unreliability due to software. There is a large gulf between the variables that can be easily measured in a running system and the number of bugs in its software. Instead, a cost-effective analysis should allow precise evaluation of software unreliability from variables easily measurable in an operational system, without knowledge of the details of how the software has been written.

RELIABILITY MODELING TECHNIQUES: COMBINATORIAL MODELS

Combinatorial modeling is a failure-to-exhaustion approach, in which the system is divided into nonoverlapping modules. Each module is assigned either a probability of working, P_i, or a probability as a function of time, $R_i(t)$. The goal is to derive the probability, P_{sys}, or function, $R_{sys}(t)$, of correct system operation. The following assumptions are made:

1. Module failures are independent.
2. Once a module has failed, it is assumed always to yield incorrect results.
3. The system is considered failed if it does not satisfy the minimal set of functioning modules.
4. Once the system enters a failed state, subsequent failures cannot return the system to a functional state.

This last property, called *coherency*, is mathematically defined by Esary and Proschan [1962] in terms of a structure function $\phi(x)$. x is a vector composed of elements x_1, x_2, . . . , x_n, where each x_i is one if module i is functional, and zero if module i is failed. A coherent system satisfies the following properties:

$\varphi(1, 1, . . . , 1) = 1$, when all modules function, the system must function

$\varphi(0, 0, . . . , 0) = 0$, when all modules fail, the system fails

$\varphi(x) \geq \varphi(y)$, whenever $x_i \geq y_i \forall_i$, $i = 1, 2, . . . , n$

Failure-to-exhaustion models typically enumerate all the states of the system (where a state is a pattern of failed and working modules) that meet or exceed the requirements of the minimal module set. Combinatorial counting techniques are used to simplify this enumeration. The following three subsections treat commonly used combinatorial modeling techniques for series/parallel systems, M-of-N systems, and complex systems.

Series/Parallel Models

Most frequently, reliability evaluation involves a series or parallel combination of independent systems. Figure 5–2a illustrates a serial string of modules, all of which must operate for the system to function correctly. The modules could be resistors,

FIGURE 5–2
n module
connections

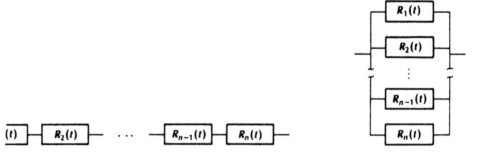

a. Series connection   b. Parallel connection

fuel valves, computers, or any other components. If $R_i(t)$ is the reliability of module i and if the modules are assumed independent, then the overall system reliability is

$$R_{series}(t) = \prod_{i=1}^{n} R_i(t) \tag{1}$$

Hence, the failure probability, denoted by Q, of a series system can be written as

$$Q_{series}(t) = 1 - R_{series}(t) = 1 - \prod_{i=1}^{n} R_i(t) = 1 - \prod_{i=1}^{n} [1 - Q_i(t)] \tag{2}$$

The parallel configuration in Figure 5–2b fails only if all the systems fail. The probability of failure is

$$Q_{parallel}(t) = \prod_{i=1}^{n} Q_i(t) \tag{3}$$

The system reliability is

$$R_{parallel}(t) = 1 - Q_{parallel}(t) = 1 - \prod_{i=1}^{n} Q_i(t) = 1 - \prod_{i=1}^{n} [1 - R_i(t)] \tag{4}$$

Note the duality between R, Q; between Eqs. 1 and 3; and between Eqs. 2 and 4. For some systems it may be easier to work with failure probability than with reliability. Eqs. 1 through 4 can be applied recursively to complex series/parallel configurations to arrive at an overall reliability function.

Figure 5–3 depicts two different interconnections of four components. These configurations have been used in aerospace systems for providing redundant trans-mission paths between terminals t_1 and t_2 where each working path has to contain at least one good component. The modules may be resistors, diodes (such as the com-ponent quadding used in the Orbital Astronomical Observatory), or valves controlling fuel flow to a rocket motor. The configuration in Figure 5–3a tolerates more patterns of shorted components (such as shorted resistors and diodes or stuck-at-open fuel valves) than does the configuration in Figure 5–3b.

FIGURE 5–3
Two forms of series/parallel interconnection

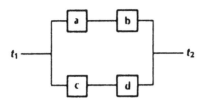

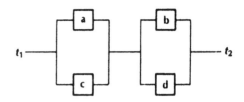

Shorts tolerated: a, b, c, d, ac, ad, bc, bd

Opens tolerated: a, b, c, d, ab, cd

a. Designed to tolerate short failures

Shorts tolerated: a, b, c, d, ac, bd

Opens tolerated: a, b, c, d, ab, ad, bc, cd

b. Designed to tolerate open failures

Both configurations tolerate all single shorts and double shorts (ac, bd). Configuration a also tolerates double shorts (ad, bc). In a dual manner, configuration b tolerates more patterns of open components (such as open resistors and diodes or stuck-at-closed fuel valves). In particular, configuration b tolerates the double-open failures of (ad, bc) for which configuration a fails. Now consider the case where blocks (a, c) are processors and (b, d) are memories. For the system to operate, at least one processor-memory pair is required. Configuration a represents a computer with a standby spare. Figure 5–4a illustrates the application of the series reliability equation.

Now, applying the parallel reliability equation

$$R_{short}(t) = 1 - (1 - R_aR_b)(1 - R_cR_d) \qquad (5)$$

Note that the R_i's may be either a single value such as a probability of success, or a function of time. In this text, the function notation $R_i(t)$ is reserved for special cases. R_i may be interpreted as either a single numbered probability or a function. Applying the parallel reliability equation to configuration b (Figure 5–4b) results in

$$R_{open} = [1 - (1 - R_a)(1 - R_c)][1 - (1 - R_b)(1 - R_d)]$$

Letting $R_a \ldots R_d = R_m$ yields

$$R_{short} = 2R_m^2 - R_m^4 \qquad (6)$$

and

$$R_{open} = 4R_m^2 - 4R_m^3 + R_m^4$$

FIGURE 5–4
Applying the series/parallel formulas to Figure 5–3

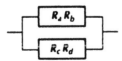

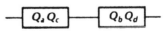

a. Series interconnection model for Figure 5-3a

b. Parallel interconnection model for Figure 5-3b

By mathematical manipulation of Eq. 6, it can be shown that

$$R_{open} > R_{short}$$

for all $t > 0$.

Now consider the case of n modules in parallel, only one of which is required to function. The other $n - 1$ modules represent spares. The spares can be operating in parallel or, as is more often the case, standing by to replace the operating module when it fails. The form of Eq. 3 suggests that as n grows large, $Q_{parallel}$ becomes close to perfection. For example, for $R_{parallel}$ to be within ϵ of 1.0, choose n such that

$$n = \frac{\ln \epsilon}{\ln Q} \tag{7}$$

for $\epsilon = 10^{-6}$ and $Q_m = 0.1$, $n = 6$.

Eqs. 3 and 4, however, assume that the detection of the failed operating module and the switchover of a standby spare occur flawlessly. This assumption is not valid in complex systems, in which even failure detection is far from perfect (a typical diagnostic program, for example, may detect only 80 to 90 percent of possible faults). As a result, the concept of coverage [Wyle and Burnett, 1967; Bouricius, Carter, and Schneider, 1969a, 1969b] has been introduced. In this context, coverage is defined as the conditional probability that a system recovers, given there has been a failure. What constitutes proper recovery is a strong function of the intended application. It may mean merely establishing a workable hardware system configuration (such as telephone switching processors) or it may demand that no data be lost or corrupted (such as in transaction processing computers, used in banks).

Let coverage be denoted by c. Then, for a system with two modules,

$$R_{sys} = R_1 + cR_2(1 - R_1) \tag{8}$$

The first term is the probability that the first module survives. The second term is the probability that the first module fails, with the second still functioning, and a successful switchover was accomplished. Note that if $c = 1$ and $R_1 = R_2 = R_m$, $R_{sys} = 2R_m - R_m^2 = 1 - (1 - R_m)^2$. If the modules are identical, then Eq. 8 can be generalized to

$$R_{sys} = R_m \sum_{i=0}^{n-1} c^i(1 - R_m)^i \tag{9}$$

This geometric progression can be evaluated by noting, for $0 < x < 1$, that

$$\sum_{i=0}^{n} x^i = \frac{1 - x^{n+1}}{1 - x}$$

Hence,

$$R_{sys} = R_m \left(\frac{1 - c^n(1 - R_m)^n}{1 - c(1 - R_m)} \right) = R_m \left(\frac{1 - c^n Q_m^n}{1 - cQ_m} \right)$$

For R_{sys} to be within ϵ of 1.0, choose n such that

$$n = \frac{\ln\left[1 - \dfrac{(1 - \epsilon)(1 - cQ_m)}{R_m}\right]}{\ln(cQ_m)} \tag{10}$$

Returning to the example where $R_{sys} = 1 - \epsilon$ for $\epsilon = 10^{-6}$, $R_m = 0.9$, and $c = 1.0$, it was shown that $n = 6$ was sufficient. Now assume a nonperfect, but still high, coverage of $c = 0.99$. Even for $n = \infty$, R_{sys} from Eq. 9 is only 0.99889. For a more conservative coverage of $c = 0.9$, the maximum value for R_{sys} with $n = \infty$ is 0.989.

Table 5–2 lists the values of system reliability expressed by Eq. 9 as a function of module reliability (R_m), coverage (c), and number of modules (n). Two things should be noted from this table. First, as in all redundancy techniques, the initial application of redundancy produces a major decrease in system unreliability. Factors of 10 or more are not uncommon. In a comparison of R_m with R_{sys} for $n = 2$, the ratios of unreliability vary from a high of 9.09 to a low of 1.67. However, once n is increased to 4, the great majority of the system reliability improvement has been realized. Second, the single most important parameter is coverage. For high values of coverage (such as 0.99) and a moderate number of modules (say, four to six), system reliability is almost indepen-dent of module reliability over a wide range. Although coverage is a mathematically concise concept, it is often impossible to measure (or indeed even estimate) in practice because so many factors influence the final value of c.

The MTTF of a standby sparing system can be derived by integrating Eq. 9:

$$\text{MTTF }(n \text{ modules}) = \int_0^\infty R_m \sum_{i=0}^{n-1} c^i(1 - R_m)^i dt$$

which can be rewritten for exponential reliability as

$$\text{MTTF }(n \text{ modules}) = \text{MTTF }(n - 1 \text{ modules}) + \int_0^\infty R_m c^{n-1}(1 - R_m)^{n-1} dt$$

$$= \text{MTTF }(n - 1 \text{ modules}) + \int_0^\infty e^{-\lambda t} c^{n-1}(1 - e^{-\lambda t})^{n-1} dt \tag{11}$$

$$= \text{MTTF }(n - 1 \text{ modules}) + \frac{c^{n-1}}{n\lambda} = \frac{1}{\lambda c}\sum_{i=1}^{n}\frac{c^i}{i}$$

The nth spare's contribution to MTTF is c^{n-1}/n times that of a single module. If c is not very close to 1.0, the added spare's contribution to MTTF is negligible.

The impact of improving coverage can also be demonstrated using mission time improvement. Setting Eq. 4, with t replaced by It, equal to Eq. 9, yields

$$1 - Q_m(It)^n = R_m(t)\left(\frac{1 - c^nQ_m(t)^n}{1 - cQ_m(t)}\right)$$

Solving for I gives

$$I = \frac{1}{\lambda t}\ln\left\{1 - \left[1 - R_m(t)\left(\frac{1 - c^nQ_m(t)^n}{1 - cQ_m(t)}\right)\right]\right\} \tag{12}$$

TABLE 5–2 *Standby system reliability for various values of module reliability, coverage, and number of spares*

		Coverage								
		0.99			0.9			0.8		
R_m	n	2	4	∞	2	4	∞	2	4	∞
0.9		0.9891	0.9988	0.9989	0.9810	0.9889	0.9890	0.9720	0.9782	0.9783
0.8		0.9584	0.9960	0.9975	0.9440	0.9746	0.9756	0.9280	0.9518	0.9524
0.7		0.9079	0.9880	0.9957	0.8890	0.9538	0.9589	0.8680	0.9180	0.9211
0.6		0.8376	0.9689	0.9934	0.8160	0.9218	0.9375	0.7920	0.8731	0.8824
0.5		0.7475	0.9307	0.9901	0.7250	0.8718	0.9091	0.7000	0.8120	0.8333

Figure 5–5 shows the tabulations and plot for the value of $R_m(t) = 0.9$ in Eq. 12. Both illustrate the high sensitivity to the coverage parameter c.

A more general reliability model of a system with standby sparing has been described by Bouricius [Bouricius et al., 1971]:

$$R(t;s,c,q,\lambda,\mu) = R[t;(s-1),c,q,\lambda,\mu] + \int_0^t \frac{\partial\{-R[u;(s-1),1,q,\lambda,\mu]\}}{\partial u}$$

$$\times (c^s e^{-\mu u} e^{-q\lambda(t-u)} du)$$

where q = the number of on-line modules required
s = the initial number of spare modules
$(q + s)$ = the total number of modules in the system
c = the probability of successful replacement by a spare (coverage)
λ = failure rate of an on-line module
μ = failure rate of a standby module*

This model does not explicitly include the reliability of the switch, detection elements, and control circuitry (SDC unit). If any failure in the SDC unit is assumed to cause a system failure, the reliability of the system is

$$R_{SDC}(t) \cdot R(t;s,c,q,\lambda,\mu)$$

Where compensating failures can occur, the coverage factor, c, is sometimes modified to include the effect of some or all failures in the SDC unit. The increased ease of modeling, however, is gained at the cost of decreased accuracy.

M-of-N Models

M-of-N systems are a generalization of the parallel model. However, instead of requiring only one of the N modules for the system to function, M modules are required.

---

* Spare modules that are unpowered (cold spares) may have a lower failure rate than on-line modules or powered-up spare modules (hot spares).

FIGURE 5–5
Potential mission time improvement with coverage increase from C to 1.0

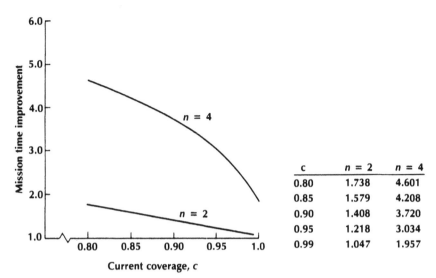

c	n = 2	n = 4
0.80	1.738	4.601
0.85	1.579	4.208
0.90	1.408	3.720
0.95	1.218	3.034
0.99	1.047	1.957

Consider triple modular redundancy (TMR), in which two of three must function in order for the system to function. Thus, for module reliability, R_m,

$$R_{TMR} = R_m^3 + \binom{3}{2} R_m^2(1 - R_m) \tag{13}$$

Eq. 13 enumerates all the working states. The R_m^3 term represents the state in which all three models function. The $\binom{3}{2}R_m^2(1 - R_m)$ term represents the three states in which one module is failed and two are functional. Because the modules are assumed to be identical, all three states need not be enumerated. Any combination of two of the three modules is enumerated by the 3-take-2 combinatorial coefficient, denoted by $\binom{3}{2}$ where

$$\binom{N}{M} = \frac{N!}{(N - M)!M!}$$

The M-of-N model can be generalized as follows: If there are N identical modules with the reliability of each module R_m (R_m may be a single number, such as a probability of success, or may be a function of time), and if a task requires k modules, the system can tolerate up to $N - k$ failures, and the reliability of such a system is

$$R = \sum_{i=0}^{N-k} \binom{N}{i} R_m^{N-i}(1 - R_m)^i$$

Nonseries/Nonparallel Models

Sometimes a "success" diagram is used to describe the operational modes of a system. Figure 5–6a depicts a success diagram that is not directly reducible by application of

FIGURE 5–6
Diagrams for non-series/nonparallel connections

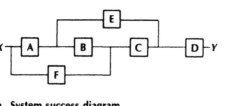

a. System success diagram

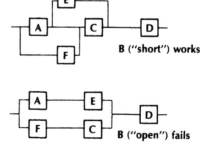

b. Reduced model with B replaced

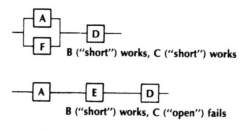

c. Further reduction with B and C replaced

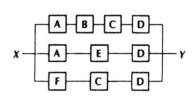

d. Reliability block diagram (RBD) of part a

the series/parallel formulas. Each path from terminal *x* to terminal *y* represents a configuration that leaves the system successfully operational. The exact reliability can be derived by expanding around a single module

$$R_{sys} = R_m \cdot P(\text{system works}|m \text{ works}) + (1 - R_m) \times P(\text{system works}|m \text{ fails}) \quad (14)$$

where the notation $P(s|m)$ denotes the conditional probability "*s* given *m* has occurred."

If module B is selected for expansion, Eq. 14 yields the two reduced diagrams in Figure 5–6b. In one, module B is replaced by a "short" (module B works); in the other, module B is replaced by an "open" (module B is failed and not available). Using the series/parallel reductions on the case where B is failed yields

$$R_{sys} = R_B \cdot P(\text{system works}|B \text{ works})$$
$$+ (1 - R_B) \{R_D[1 - (1 - R_A R_E)(1 - R_F R_C)]\} \quad (15)$$

The case for module B working has to be further reduced. Expanding around module C yields

$$P(\text{system works}|B \text{ works}) = R_C\{R_D[1 - (1 - R_A)(1 - R_F)]\} + (1 - R_C)(R_A R_D R_E)$$

Thus,

$$R_{sys} = R_B[R_C R_D(R_A + R_F - R_A R_F) + (1 - R_C)R_A R_D R_E]$$
$$+ (1 - R_B)[R_D(R_A R_E + R_F R_C - R_A R_C R_E R_F)]$$

Letting $R_A \ldots R_F = R_m$ yields

$$R_{sys} = R_m^6 - 3R_m^5 + R_m^4 + 2R_m^3$$

If the success diagram becomes too complex to evaluate exactly, upper- and lower-limit approximations on R_{sys} can be used. An upper bound on system reliability is [Esary and Proschan, 1962]:

$$R_{sys} \leq 1 - \Pi(1 - R_{\text{path } i}) \tag{16}$$

where $R_{\text{path } i}$ is the serial reliability of path i. Eq. 16 calculates the system reliability as if all paths were in parallel. Placing the paths in parallel yields a reliability block diagram (RBD). Figure 5–6d shows the RBD for the success diagram of Figure 5–6a. Eq. 16 is an upper bound because the paths are not independent. That is, the failure of a single module affects more than one path. Eq. 16 is a close approximation when $R_{\text{path } i}$ is small. Hence,

$$R_{sys} \leq 1 - (1 - R_A R_B R_C R_D)(1 - R_A R_E R_D)(1 - R_F R_C R_D)$$

Letting $R_A \ldots R_F = R_m$,

$$R_{sys} \leq 2R_m^3 + R_m^4 - R_m^6 - 2R_m^7 + R_m^{10} \tag{17}$$

The RBD method can be altered to yield an exact result.

Because the paths are not independent, perform the multiplication in Eq. 16 by replacing R_m^i with R_m. That is, an individual module can only have its reliability raised to the first power:

$$R_{sys} = R_A R_B R_C R_D + R_A R_E R_D - R_A R_B R_C R_D R_E$$
$$+ R_C R_D R_F - R_A R_C R_D R_E R_F - R_A R_B R_C R_D R_F + R_A R_B R_C R_D R_E R_F$$

Letting $R_A \ldots R_F = R_m$,

$$R_{sys} = R_m^6 - 3R_m^5 + R_m^4 + 2R_m^3$$

which is the same result obtained from Eq. 15. Setting all R_i's to R_m has to occur after the multiplication; otherwise, individual R_i's would be raised to higher than the first power and the result would be a lower bound. For obtaining exact reliability, the RBD approach is more suitable to noncomputerized calculations, because simplifying assumptions (such as $R_i = R_m$ for all i) can be made before algebraic expansion.

Esary and Proschan [1962] also define a lower bound in terms of the minimal cut sets of the system. Given that a minimal cut set is a list of components such that removal of any component from the list (by changing the component from operational to failed) will cause the system to change from operational to failed, a lower bound is given by

$$R_{sys} \geq \Pi(1 - Q_{cut\ i}) \tag{18}$$

where $Q_{cut\ i}$ is the probability that the minimal cut i does not occur. The minimal cut sets for Figure 5–6a are D, AC, AF, CE, and BEF. Assuming all modules are identical,

$$R_{sys} \geq R(1 - (1 - R)^2)^3(1 - (1 - R)^3)$$

and

$$R_{sys} \geq 24R^5 - 60R^6 + 62R^7 - 33R^8 + 9R^9 - R^{10}$$

EXAMPLES OF COMBINATORIAL MODELING

In this section, we use the M-of-N combinatorial model to illustrate several pitfalls commonly encountered during modeling, including incorrect conclusions drawn from single-parameter summaries and the effect of extra logic (voters) on redundant system reliability, more detailed modeling, and more accurate modeling.

Pitfalls with Using a Single Model

To compare different redundant systems, it is often desirable to summarize their models by a single parameter. The reliability may be an arbitrarily complex function of time, and the selection of the wrong summary parameter could lead to incorrect conclusions. Consider, for example, TMR and MTTF. For the nonredundant system,

$$R_{simplex} = e^{-\lambda t}$$

$$MTTF_{simplex} = \frac{1}{\lambda}$$

For TMR with an exponential reliability function,

$$R_{TMR} = (e^{-\lambda t})^3 + \binom{3}{1}(e^{-\lambda t})^2(1 - e^{-\lambda t}) = 3e^{-2\lambda t} - 2e^{-3\lambda t}$$

$$MTTF_{TMR} = \frac{3}{2\lambda} - \frac{2}{3\lambda} = \frac{5}{6\lambda} < \frac{1}{\lambda} = MTTF_{simplex}$$

Thus, by the MTTF summary, TMR is worse than a simplex system.

Figure 5–7 plots the reliability functions for a simplex computer and a redundant computer (TMR processor and Hamming coded memory). Even though there is more area under the nonredundant curve (e.g., MTTF), the redundant system maintains a higher reliability for the first 6000 hours of system life. Hence, functions such as mission time improvement have been utilized to compare redundant systems in subregions of their operational life. The redundant computer in Figure 5–7 operates at or above a probability of success of 0.8, 66 percent longer than the simplex computer. The S-shaped curve is typical of redundant systems; usually there is a well-defined "knee." Above the knee, the redundant system has spare components that tolerate failures

FIGURE 5–7
Relation of reliability function, mission time, and mission reliability

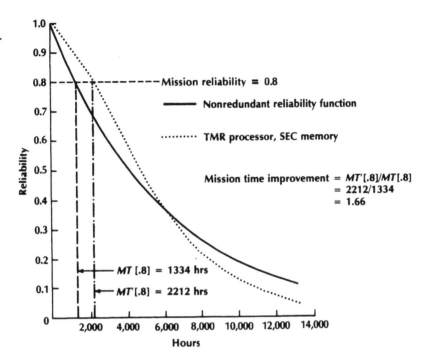

and keep the probability of system success high. Once the system has exhausted its redundancy, however, there is merely more hardware to fail (voters, switches, and other elements that support the redundancy) than in the nonredundant system. Thus, there is a sharper decrease in the redundant system's reliability function.

When modeling redundant systems with repair, single parameters such as MTTF may again be appropriate since the repair process replenishes the redundancy. There is no exhaustion phenomenon. This topic is discussed later in the chapter.

Effect of Extra Logic in Redundant Systems*

In adding redundancy to a system, care must be taken that the extra logic to control the redundancy does not actually decrease the overall system reliability. Ingle and Siewiorek [1976] model various switches proposed for hybrid redundancy and show that the switch is a significant factor in determining the overall system reliability. A hybrid redundancy scheme with a TMR core may have a maximum attainable reliability for only one or two spares. Adding spares complicates the switch enough to cause the system reliability actually to decrease. There are conditions under which the switch becomes so complex that simple TMR would yield a better solution.

Consider the hybrid redundancy with a TMR voter described in Chapter 3. If only

---

* This section is based on Ingle and Siewiorek [1976].

one of the three TMR core modules (those currently being voted on) is assumed to fail at a time, the system fails only if all the modules fail or if all but one module fails. The reliability of the hybrid system with a TMR core and $n - 3$ spares is

$$R_{\text{hybrid}} = R_v \cdot R_{sw}[1 - nR_m(1 - R_m)^{n-1} - (1 - R_m)^n]$$

where R_t and R_{sw} are the voter and switch reliabilities, respectively. Subtracting the system reliability for n modules from that for $n + 1$ modules gives

$$R_{sw}[1 - (n + 1) \cdot R_m(1 - R_m)^n - (1 - R_m)^{n+1}]$$
$$- R_{sw} \cdot [1 - nR_m(1 - R_m)^{n-1} - (1 - R_m)^n] = R_{sw} \cdot nR_m^2(1 - R_m)^{n-1}$$

This expression is positive for any $0 < R_m < 1$ and $n \geq 1$. Therefore, under the assumption that R_{sw} is independent of n, adding modules increases the system reliability.

The switch typically becomes more complex as more modules are added, although the dependence of the switch complexity on n will be a function of the particular design. A reasonable assumption, however, is that switch complexity grows nearly

FIGURE 5–8
R_{sys} as a function of n and module reliability R for hybrid redundancy, α = 0.1 [From Ingle and Siewiorek, 1976; © 1976 IEEE]

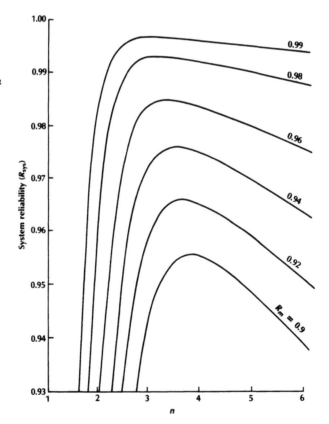

linearly with n; that is, the addition of each module to the system increases switch complexity by a constant amount [Siewiorek and McCluskey, 1973a]. Consequently, as a more realistic assumption, we will consider the R_{sw} to be p^n, where p is the reliability of the switch component that must be added when a module is added. Further, let $p = R_m^\alpha$, where α is used to relate the relative complexities of the incremental switch component to the basic module. Hence, the system reliability is

$$R_{hybrid} = R_m^{n\alpha}[1 - nR_m(1 - R_m)^{n-1} - (1 - R_m)^n]$$

Figure 5–8 shows the variation of R_{hybrid} as a function of n, R_m (basic module reliability), and α. All curves exhibit a definite maximum. The optimum value, n_{max}, of the number of modules for maximum R_{sys} is higher for lower R_m or lower α. Differentiating R_{hybrid} with respect to n and equating the resultant expression to zero yields

$$\alpha \ln R_m = Q_m^{n-1}[R_m + (\alpha \ln R_m + \ln Q_m)(nR_m + Q_m)]$$

where $Q_m = 1 - R_m$.

This equation may be numerically solved for n_{max}. Values of n_{max} for hybrid redundancy are plotted in Figure 5–9, which shows that n_{max} is about 4 to 6 for most practical cases. Thus, only one to three spares should be used. In Figure 5–9, n_{max} exceeds 6 only for $\alpha \leq 10^{-3}$. Given that α is the complexity of the switch component compared with that of the module, more than three modules need be used only when the module is more than 1000 times as complex as the switch. For the iterative cell switch component that consists of 22 equivalent gates [Siewiorek and McCluskey, 1973b], the module will contain about 22,000 gates. A central processor of a computer has this complexity.

FIGURE 5–9

n_{max} as a function of α for hybrid redundancy [From Ingle and Siewiorek, 1976; © 1976 IEEE]

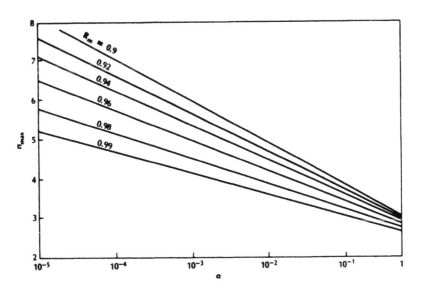

FIGURE 5–10
*R_{sys} for various
schemes as a func-
tion of m (for R_m
= 0.9, α = 0.1)
[From Ingle and
Siewiorek, 1976;
© 1976 IEEE]*

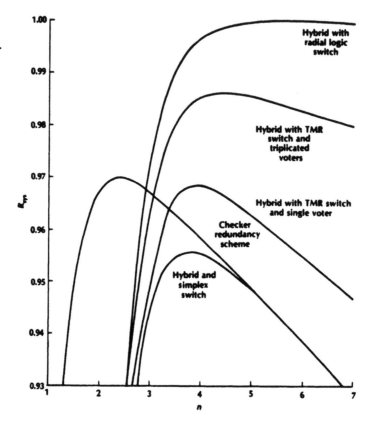

Figures 5–10 and 5–11 illustrate similar trends for variations of the hybrid scheme:

Hybrid redundancy
Checker redundancy scheme [Ramamoorthy and Han, 1973]
TMR switch with single voter
TMR switch with triplicate voter
Switch with Hamming coded states [Ogus, 1973]
Switch implemented with radial logic [Klaschka, 1969]

A switch with Hamming coded states does not appear on Figure 5–10 because its maximum reliability (at m = 3 for R = 0.9) is only 0.75.

Effect of More Detailed Modeling*

Eq. 13 is the classical model for TMR. The effect of nonperfect voters can readily be incorporated into Eq. 13 if voters are assigned to module inputs [von Neumann, 1956; Brown, Tierney, and Wasserman, 1961; Teoste, 1962]. Because each voter drives exactly

---

* This section is based on Siewiorek [1975].

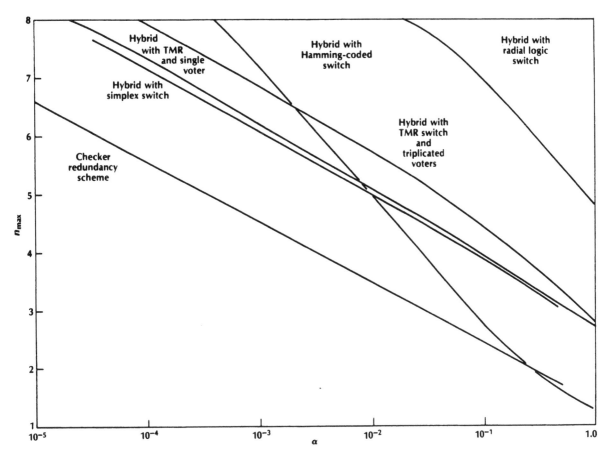

FIGURE 5–11 n_{max} *for various schemes as a function of* α *(for $R_m = 0.9$, $\alpha = 1.0$) [From Ingle and Siewiorek, 1976; © 1976 IEEE]*

one module input, a voter failure has the same effect as a module failure. If R_v is the voter reliability, then the effective module reliability (for a two input module) in Eq. 13 becomes $R_v^2 R_m$. The classical model can be rewritten as

$$R_{TMR} = R_v^6 R_m^3 + 3R_v^4 R_m^2(1 - R_v^2 R_m) \tag{19}$$

Eq. 19 is still pessimistic, for there are many cases in which a majority of the modules may have failed and yet the system would not be failed. For example, consider two failed modules for the system shown in Figure 5–12. Assuming that module 1 has a permanent logical one on its output and module 3 has a permanent logical zero output, the network will still realize its designed function. Such multiple module failures that do not lead to system failures are called *compensating module failures*.

Taking into account these double, and even triple, module failure cases can often

FIGURE 5–12
*Classical triple
modular redun-
dancy [From Sie-
wiorek, 1975;
© 1975 IEEE]*

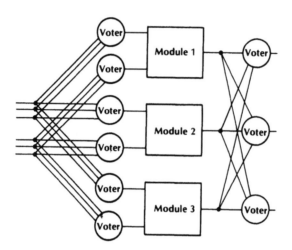

lead to a substantially higher predicted reliability than the classical reliability model. With a better reliability model, some systems may be found to be overdesigned for their specific mission because an inadequate reliability model was used.

Siewiorek [1975] developed a model based on stuck-at interconnection failures. For TMR, the model takes the form

$$R_{TMR} = R_m^3 + 3R_m^2(1 - R_m) + R_m f_2 + f_3$$

where f_2 and f_3 are complex expressions for double and triple module failures.

An exact model is based on the concept of functionally equivalent faults [Mc-Cluskey and Clegg, 1971; Schertz and Metze, 1972]. A less complex and less accurate alternative is based on fault dominance [Mei, 1970]. Table 5–3 summarizes the results. The fault-equivalence model increases the predicted mission time by at least 40 percent over the classical model for even simple systems. The fault-dominance model shows up to a 75 percent improvement for slightly more complex networks.

Effect of More Accurate Modeling*

Figure 5–12 shows TMR in its simplest configuration, with triplicated modules followed by triplicated voters. Systems whose nonredundant form may be represented by a serial cascade of modules are referred to as *serial TMR*.

Reliability modeling becomes more complex when fan-in and fan-out are considered and when not all module inputs are driven by voters. Several investigators have addressed the problem of modeling the reliability of TMR and multiple-line systems. There have been two basic approaches. The first approach is to approximate the system by a serial TMR system, modeling the system as a cascade of single-input single-output

* This section is adapted from Abraham and Siewiorek [1974].

TABLE 5-3
Mission time improvement of the fault-equivalence reliability model and fault-dominance reliability model over the classical reliability model for various modules

Module Type	R_m					
	0.75	0.8	0.85	0.9	0.95	0.99
Single-NAND gate						
Equivalence model	1.476	1.477	1.481	1.484	1.491	1.496
Dominance model	1.358	1.382	1.405	1.439	1.472	1.491
Two NAND gates						
Equivalence model	1.494	1.497	1.510	1.515	1.526	1.539
Dominance model	1.355	1.384	1.414	1.452	1.492	1.531
Four-Level Full						
Binary Tree						
Dominance model	1.405	1.451	1.505	1.575	1.663	1.766
Multiple-fault model	1.300	1.318	1.389	1.361	1.386	1.408
Dominance plus multiple	1.442	1.485	1.535	1.598	1.692	1.771
Exclusive-OR						
Dominance model	1.196	1.207	1.214	1.232	1.246	1.259
Priority Encoder						
Dominance model	1.228	1.244	1.263	1.283	1.304	1.324

Source: From Siewiorek, 1975; © 1975 IEEE.

modules, adding extra voters if required [Brown, Tierney, and Wasserman, 1961; Teoste, 1962; Rhodes, 1964; Longden, Page, and Scantlebury, 1966; Lyons and Vanderkulk, 1962; Gurzi, 1965]. A variation of this first approach [Rubin, 1967] models systems as serial cells and inserts fictitious module trios where required to make all the cells serial cells; then it alters the standard serial voter-module reliability formula to approximate the effect of these added fictitious modules.

The second basic approach is to develop a bound on the system reliability by treating TMR as a coherent system. (The concept of coherent systems defined previously was introduced by Esary and Proschan [1962].) One property of coherent systems is that, having once failed, the system or component cannot work properly again. A *system cut* is defined as a set of components whose failure causes system failure. A *minimal cut* is a cut from which no members can be deleted without the set losing the property of being a system cut. The value obtained by taking the product, over all minimal cuts, of the probability that the cut does not occur is a lower bound on coherent system reliability.

Jensen [1964] uses matrix manipulation to establish the minimal cuts of a system. However, if there are n modules in the nonredundant system, Jensen's method in the worst case requires on the order of n^3 operations and on the order of n^2 storage locations just to set up the matrices for determining the minimal cuts.

Another approach is to use an algorithm that divides the system into independent cells; that is, any nonfatal pattern of failures in a cell that leaves a cell operational does not interact with a nonfatal pattern of failures in another cell to cause system failures. The system reliability is then the product of the reliability of the independent cells. Figure 5–13 illustrates the partitioning of a complex system into cells (voters are represented by circles and modules by squares). Voter 1 has to be in the same cell as voter 2. If the indicated voters were in different cells, voters 1 and 2 would be nonfatal cell failures, but the system would fail because modules 3 and 4 receive potentially faulty inputs. The cell reliability is calculated by

$$R_{cell} = \sum_{i=0}^{N_v} \sum_{j=0}^{N_m} F(i,j) R_v^{3N_v - i}(1 - R_v)^i R_m^{3N_m - j}(1 - R_m)^j$$

Here, N_v and N_m are the number of voters and modules, respectively, in the cell; $F(i, j)$ is a complicated function of the cell structure; and

$$R_{sys} = \prod_{i=1}^{k} R_{cell_i}$$

The algorithm in Abraham and Siewiorek [1974] calculates the exact classical reliability of TMR networks (that is, the reliability of a coherent system as defined in Esary and Proschan [1962]). The results of this algorithm can be compared with the previously defined approaches: serial cell and minimal cut set.

Consider a 16-register multiplexed data bus system in which the contents of a data register can be supplied to any one of 16 general-purpose registers. Figure 5–14 shows a TMR configuration of the data register to register transfer along one path.

In the serial reliability model, the reliability of a serial cell is given by Eq. 13. For nonperfect voters, Eq. 13 becomes

$$R_{cell} = 3(R_m R_v)^2 - 2(R_m R_v)^3 \tag{20}$$

where R_v is the voter reliability.

Figure 5–14 is more complicated than a cascade of serial cells. One approach to

FIGURE 5–13
Partitioning a TMR system network into cells [From Abraham and Siewiorek, 1974; © 1974 IEEE]

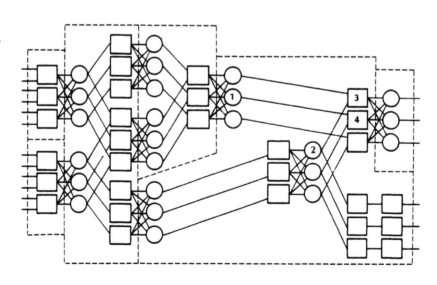

FIGURE 5–14
*The TMR configu-
ration for one bit
of the data register
to register fan-out
block, with only
one path shown
[From Abraham
and Siewiorek,
1974; © 1974 IEEE]*

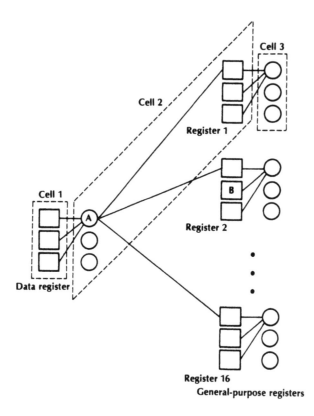

General-purpose registers

include fan-in/fan-out in the serial cell reliability model is to assign the voters to the modules they drive [Roth et al., 1967], because a voter failure affects only the module it drives. Cell 2 of Figure 5–14 shows one way to assign voters to the driven modules.

Now the serial cell reliability model for the network of Figure 5–14 can be developed. The reliability of a module "end cell" such as cell 1 can be derived from Eq. 20 by letting $R_v = 1$. Similarly, setting $R_m = 1$ in Eq. 20 yields the reliability of voter end cells such as cell 3. Next, assume $R_m = R_v$. This simplification is not crucial, and similar results are obtainable when R_v and R_m retain their separate identities. The end cell reliability is thus $3R_m^2 - 2R_m^3$. The serial cell reliability model for the system of Figure 5–14 would consist of 17 end cells (16 voters and 1 module), and 16 serial cells like cell 2, each of which share the one-voter trio. The system reliability is thus modeled by

$$R_{\text{serial}} = (3R_m^2 - 2R_m^3)^{17} (3R_m^4 - 2R_m^6)^{16} \tag{21}$$

For the case of fan-in there are still 17 end cells (16 modules and 1 voter). The fan-in portion would consist of 16 overlapping serial cells. Thus, Eq. 21 represents the serial cell model for both fan-in and fan-out.

For the minimal cut set reliability model, the lower bound on system reliability is given by Esary and Proschan [1962]:

$$R_{sys} \geq \prod_{\forall i \in I} (1 - Q_{cut\ i})$$

such that i is a minimal cut where $Q_{cut\ i}$ is the probability that the minimal cut does not occur; that is, all the components composing the minimal cut do not fail. Consider Figure 5–14. A minimal cut is a set of modules whose failure causes the system to fail. All minimal cuts consist of either two voters ($Q_{cut} = Q_v^2$), two modules ($Q_{cut} = Q_m^2$), or one voter and one module ($Q_{cut} = Q_v Q_m$). Note that $Q_v = 1 - R_v$ and $Q_m = 1 - R_m$.

There are three ways in which two modules can fail in the module end cell and 16×3 ways in which two voters can cause system failure in the voter end cells. In the fan-out portion, there are three double-voter failures, 3×16 double-module failures, and $3 \times 2 \times 16$ single-voter and single-module failures (such as voter A and module B) whose failure would cause system failure. Hence, the minimal cut reliability model for fan-out is

$$R_{mcs} = (1 - Q_v^2)^{51}(1 - Q_m^2)^{51}(1 - Q_v Q_m)^{96} = [1 - (1 - R_m)^2]^{198} \tag{22}$$

Now consider the case of fan-in. There are 16×3 ways in which two modules can cause system failure in the 16 module end cells and three ways for two voters in the voter end cell. In the fan-in portion, there are three double-module failures, $3 \times 16 \times 2$ single-voter and single-module failures, 3×16 double-voter failures in the same voter trio, and $3 \times 2 \times \sum_{i=1}^{15} i$ or 720 ways in which two-voter failures from different

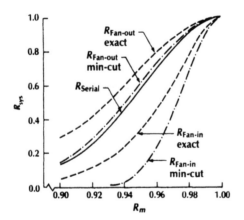

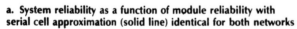

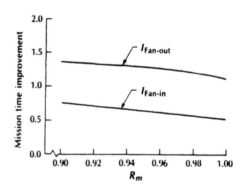

a. System reliability as a function of module reliability with serial cell approximation (solid line) identical for both networks

b. Mission time improvement over serial cell approach with exact reliability model

FIGURE 5–15 *Reliability models for the 1:16 fan-out network of Figure 5–14 and a 16:1 fan-in network [From Abraham and Siewiorek, 1974; © 1974 IEEE]*

voter trios can interact to cause system failure. Thus, the minimal cut reliability model for fan-in is

$$R_{mcs} = (1 - Q_v^2)^{771}(1 - Q_m^2)^{51}(1 - Q_vQ_m)^{96} = [1 - (1 - R_m)^2]^{918} \qquad (23)$$

The system reliability for the three approaches for the system in Figure 5–14 is plotted as a function of module reliability in Figure 5–15a.

Now consider a case of 16:1 fan-in, such as an arithmetic and logic unit (ALU) multiplexer that takes data from one of 16 registers as an input to an ALU. The three models for this fan-in network are also depicted in Figure 5–15a. The minimal cut lower bound is a rather poor predictor of system reliability, whereas the serial cell approach predicts the same system reliability for both fan-in and fan-out systems.

Figure 5–15b shows a plot of mission time improvement when I is the ratio of the exact model to the serial cell model. It can be seen that a mission time improvement of 50 percent for the 1:16 fan-out system can be obtained with the more accurate reliability model. If the serial cell model is used, the resultant system is overdesigned by 50 percent, for it could meet its mission time specification with less reliable components. In the case of 16:1 fan-in, the system has only 50 percent of designed mission time.

RELIABILITY AND AVAILABILITY MODELING TECHNIQUES: MARKOV MODELS

A powerful tool for modeling systems composed of several processes (such as a failure process and a repair process) is the Markov model. As Figure 5–1 indicates, Markov models are a basic tool for both reliability and availability modeling. This section introduces the underlying mathematics. It will be shown how minor variations to the Markov model can change an availability model into a reliability model or model different repair strategies such as single or multiple field service engineers.

The two central concepts of this model are state and state transition. The *state* of a system represents all that must be known to describe the system at any instant. For reliability models, each state represents a distinct combination of working and failed modules. If each module is in one of two conditions—working or failed—then the complete model for a system of n modules has 2^n states. As time passes, the system goes from state to state as modules fail and are repaired. These changes of state are called *state transitions*. Discrete-time models require all state transitions to occur at fixed intervals, and they assign probabilities to each possible transition. Continuous-time models allow state transitions to occur at varying, random intervals, with transition rates assigned to possible transitions. For reliability models, the transition rates are the module hazard functions and repair-rate functions, possibly modified by coverage factors.

Time-Invariant Markov Models

The basic assumption underlying Markov models is that the probability of a given state transition depends only on the current state. For continuous-time Markov processes, the length of time already spent in a state does not influence either the probability distribution of the next state or the probability distribution of remaining time in the same state before the next transition. These very strong assumptions imply that the waiting time spent in any one state is geometrically distributed in the discrete-time case, or exponentially distributed in the continuous-time case [Howard, 1971]. Thus, the Markov model naturally fits with the standard assumption that failure rates are constant, leading to exponentially distributed interarrival times of failures and Poisson arrivals of failures.

Figure 5–16a is a graphic representation of the two-state discrete-time Markov model. The labeled nodes correspond to the states of the modeled system, and the directed arcs represent the possible state transitions. The information conveyed by the model graph is often summarized in a square matrix P, whose elements P_{ij} are the probabilities of a transition from state i to state j. The probabilistic nature of the matrix requires that each row of the matrix must sum to one, and that all elements of the matrix must be nonnegative. The transition probability matrix for the model of Figure 5–16a is

$$
\begin{array}{cc}
\text{Current} & \text{New} \\
\text{State} & \text{State}
\end{array}
$$

$$
\begin{array}{cc}
 & 0 \quad\quad 1
\end{array}
$$

$$
\begin{array}{c}
0 \\
1
\end{array}
\begin{bmatrix}
1 - q_e & q_e \\
q_r & 1 - q_r
\end{bmatrix} = P
$$

The discrete-time model is solved by a set of linear equations based on the transition probability matrix. In vector notation, these equations are defined as

$$\overline{P}(k + 1) = \overline{P}(k)P$$

In more explicit form, the equations for the model of Figure 5–16a are

$$[p_0(k + 1), p_1(k + 1)] = [p_0(k), p_1(k)] \begin{bmatrix} 1 - q_e & q_e \\ q_r & 1 - q_r \end{bmatrix}$$

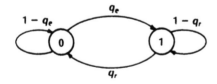

0, 1—States
q_e, q_r — State transition probabilities

a. Two-state discrete-time Markov model

$\lambda\Delta t$, $\mu\Delta t$—State transition probabilities
λ, μ—State transition rates

b. Two-state differential Markov model

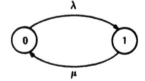

λ—Failure rate
μ—Repair rate

c. Two-state continuous-time Markov model

FIGURE 5–16 *Markov models*

Multiplying into separate equations yields

$$p_0(k + 1) = (1 - q_e)p_0(k) + q_r p_1(k)$$

$$p_1(k + 1) = q_e p_0(k) + (1 - q_r)p_1(k)$$

The n-step transition probability matrix that contains the probabilities of transitions from one state to another in exactly n transition intervals is given by P^n. In general, to find the probability distribution of a transition from one state to another in no more than k steps, $f_{ij}(k)$, state j can be made a "trapping" state, with p_{jj} set equal to one, and the analysis is straightforward.

The continuous-time Markov model can be derived from the discrete-time model by taking the limit as the time-step interval approaches zero. Consider a single system with constant failure rate Λ that can be repaired with constant repair rate μ. Let $p_0(t)$ and $p_1(t)$ be the probabilities of being in the nonfailed state and the repair state, respectively. The transactions between states can be represented as in Figure 5–16b. From the figure we can write the following transition matrix:

$$P = \begin{bmatrix} 1 - \lambda\Delta t & \lambda\Delta t \\ \mu\Delta t & 1 - \mu\Delta t \end{bmatrix}$$

The probability of being in state 0 or 1 at time $t + \Delta t$ can be formulated by multiplying the probability at time t by the transition matrix

$$[p_0(t + \Delta t), p_1(t + \Delta t)] = [p_0(t), p_1(t)] \begin{bmatrix} 1 - \lambda\Delta t & \lambda\Delta t \\ \mu\Delta t & 1 - \mu\Delta t \end{bmatrix}$$

Performing the indicated multiplication yields a system of equations

$$p_0(t + \Delta t) = (1 - \lambda\Delta t)p_0(t) + \mu\Delta t p_1(t)$$

$$p_1(t + \Delta t) = \lambda\Delta t p_0(t) + (1 - \mu\Delta t)p_1(t)$$

Rearranging and dividing by Δt produces

$$\frac{p_0(t + \Delta t) - p_0(t)}{\Delta t} = -\lambda p_0(t) + \mu p_1(t)$$

$$\frac{p_1(t + \Delta t) - p_1(t)}{\Delta t} = \lambda p_0(t) - \mu p_1(t)$$

Taking the limit as Δt approaches zero generates a set of simultaneous differential equations (the Chapman–Kolmogorov equations):

$$\frac{dp_0(t)}{dt} = \dot{p}_0(t) = -\lambda p_0(t) + \mu p_1(t)$$

$$\frac{dp_1(t)}{dt} = \dot{p}_1(t) = \lambda p_0(t) - \mu p_1(t)$$

(24)

In matrix form,

$$[\dot{p}_0(t), \dot{p}_1(t)] = [p_0(t), p_1(t)] \begin{bmatrix} -\lambda & \lambda \\ \mu & -\mu \end{bmatrix}$$

or

$$\vec{\dot{P}}(t) = \vec{P}(t) \times T \tag{25}$$

The set of equations (continuous-time Chapman–Kolmogorov equations) can be written by inspection of a transition diagram without self-loops or Δt's. Consider Figure 5–16c. The change in state 0 is minus the flow out of state 0 times the probability of being in state 0 at time t plus the flow into state 0 from state 1 times the probability of being in state 1. The equation for the change in state 1 is derived in a similar manner.

The set of equations in 24 can be solved by use of the LaPlace transform of a time domain function, given by

$$L\{f(t)\} = f^x(s) = \int_0^\infty f(t)e^{-st}dt$$

The LaPlace transform reduces ordinary, constant-coefficient linear differential equations to algebraic equations in s. The algebraic equations are solved and transformed back into the time domain.

Taking the LaPlace transform of Eq. 24 using Table 5–4 gives

$$sp_0^x(s) - p_0(0) = -\lambda p_0^x(s) + \mu p_1^x(s)$$
$$sp_1^x(s) - p_1(0) = \lambda p_0^x(s) - \mu p_1^x(s) \tag{26}$$

where $p_0(0)$ is the value of $p_0(t)$ at $t = 0$. The algebraic equations in Eq. 26 can be solved by any linear equation-solving technique such as Kramer's rule or Gaussian elimination. Using matrix algebra, Eq. 26 can be written as

$$[p_0(0), p_1(0)] = [p_0^x(s), p_1^x(s)] \begin{bmatrix} s + \lambda & -\lambda \\ -\mu & s + \mu \end{bmatrix}$$

or

$$\vec{P}(0) = \vec{P}^x(s)[sI - T] = \vec{P}^x(s)A$$

where I is the identity matrix and T is the differential matrix derived earlier. Thus,

$$\vec{P}^x(s) = \vec{P}(0)[sI - T]^{-1} = \vec{P}(0)A^{-1}$$

To derive A^{-1} from A, recall that element a_{ij}' of A^{-1} can be calculated as

$$a_{ij}' = \frac{\text{cofactor}_{ji}(A)}{\det A}$$

Here, cofactor$_{ji}$ (A) is defined as cofactor$_{ji}(A) \triangleq (-1)^{i+j} \times$ determinant of matrix formed by removing row j and column i from A; det A is the determinant of A.

TABLE 5–4
Common LaPlace transforms

f(t)	f*(s)	f(t)	f*(s)
1. k	$\dfrac{k}{s}$	6. $f(t) + g(t)$	$f^*(s) + g^*(s)$
		7. $\dot{f}(t)$	$sf^*(s) - f(0)$
2. $\delta(t)$ [unit impulse]	1	8. $tf(t)$	$-\dot{f}^*(s)$
3. e^{-at}	$\dfrac{1}{s+a}$	9. $\int_0^t f(\tau)d\tau$	$(1/s)f^*(s)$
4. $\dfrac{t^{n-1}}{(n-1)!}e^{-at}$	$\dfrac{1}{(s+a)^n}$	10. $\dfrac{1}{t}f(t)$	$\int_s^\infty f(\sigma)d\sigma$
5. $kf(t)$	$kf^*(s)$	11. e^{At}, A = matrix	$[sI + A]^{-1}$

Note: $f(0)$ denotes the value of $f(t)$ at time $t = 0$.

For our example,

$$A = \begin{bmatrix} s + \lambda & -\lambda \\ -\mu & s + \mu \end{bmatrix}$$

$$\det A = s^2 + \lambda s + \mu s$$

$$A^{-1} = \frac{\begin{bmatrix} s + \mu & \lambda \\ \mu & s + \lambda \end{bmatrix}}{s^2 + \lambda s + \mu s}$$

Assuming that the system starts out in the operational state, then $P(0) = [1,0]$. So,

$$\overline{P}^*(s) = [1,0]\begin{bmatrix} \dfrac{s + \mu}{s^2 + \lambda s + \mu s} & \dfrac{\lambda}{s^2 + \lambda s + \mu s} \\ \dfrac{\mu}{s^2 + \lambda s + \mu s} & \dfrac{s + \lambda}{s^2 + \lambda s + \mu s} \end{bmatrix}$$

or

$$p_0^*(s) = \frac{s + \mu}{s^2 + \lambda s + \mu s}$$

$$p_1^*(s) = \frac{\lambda}{s^2 + \lambda s + \mu s}$$

The general form of the transforms calculated by this stage in the solution process is that of a rational fraction in s, which is a ratio of two polynomials in s:

$$f^*(s) = \frac{N(s)}{D(s)}$$

The inverse transform of a rational fraction is obtained by the following process.

1. If the degree of the numerator is greater than or equal to the degree of the denominator, divide the denominator into the numerator until the degree of the remainder is one less than that of the denominator. The result is

$$f^x(s) = N_q(s) + \frac{N_r(s)}{D(s)}$$

The inverse transform of $N_q(s)$ can be found by using relationships 2 and 7 from Table 5–4 and adding to the remaining solution because of relationship 6. (For our example, this step is unnecessary, as is usually the case. Even when required, the degree of $N_q(s)$ is almost never higher than one or two.)

2. The roots of the denominator polynomial $D(s)$ must be found. In general, the roots may be either real or complex, and there may be multiple occurrences of distinct roots. For our example, we shall assume that all roots are real and distinct. This is usually the case, and other cases can be found using similar techniques. If $D(s)$ is a second-degree polynomial, the two roots can be found by direct use of the quadratic formula. Otherwise, the roots can be extracted using such techniques as Horner's method or Lin's method.

3. After finding the roots $-a_1, -a_2, \ldots, -a_r$ of $D(s)$, the rational fraction $N_r(s)/D(s)$ must be expanded into

$$\frac{N_r(s)}{D(s)} = \frac{N_r(s)}{(s + a_1)(s + a_2) \cdots (s + a_r)} = \frac{k_1}{s + a_1} + \frac{k_2}{s + a_2} + \cdots + \frac{k_r}{s + a_r}$$

where r is the degree of $D(s)$ and k_i is a constant associated with the ith root. This expansion is called the partial fraction expansion of the rational fraction. The easiest way to find each constant k_i is to cancel the $(s + a_i)$ factor in $D(s)$ and evaluate the modified fraction for $s = -a_i$:

$$k_i = \frac{N_r(-a_i)}{(a_1 - a_i)(a_2 - a_i) \cdots (a_{i-1} - a_i)(a_{i+1} - a_i) \cdots (a_r - a_i)}$$

After obtaining the partial fraction expansion, the inverse transform is found by applying relationships 3 through 6 from Table 5–4.

Returning to our example, after following the preceding steps, we find the partial fraction expansions of the transforms:

$$p_0^x(s) = \frac{\dfrac{\mu}{\lambda + \mu}}{s} + \frac{\dfrac{\lambda}{\lambda + \mu}}{s + \lambda + \mu}$$

$$p_1^x(s) = \frac{\dfrac{\lambda}{\lambda + \mu}}{s} - \frac{\dfrac{\lambda}{\lambda + \mu}}{s + \lambda + \mu}$$

Taking the inverse transforms gives

$$p_0(t) = \frac{\mu}{\lambda + \mu} + \frac{\lambda}{\lambda + \mu} e^{-(\lambda + \mu)t}$$

(27)

$$p_1(t) = \frac{\lambda}{\lambda + \mu} - \frac{\lambda}{\lambda + \mu} e^{-(\lambda + \mu)t}$$

where $p_0(t)$ is the time-dependent probability that the system is in the operational state, defined earlier as the availability function $A(t)$. The availability consists of a steady-state term and an exponentially decaying transient term. As noted earlier, for a non-redundant system with failure rate λ and repair rate μ, the steady-state availability is $\mu/(\lambda + \mu)$. Figure 5–17 plots $A(t)$ for an MTTF of 1000 hours ($\lambda = 0.001$) and an MTTR of 10 hours ($\mu = 0.1$). The steady-state value is reached in a very short time.

If only the steady-state solution is sought, the required computation is substantially less than that for the time-dependent solution. The differential equations in Eq. 24 are changed to algebraic equations by replacing $\dot{p}_0(t)$ and $\dot{p}_1(t)$ by zero, $p_0(t)$ by p_0, and $p_1(t)$ by p_1. That is, there is no rate of change in steady state, and the state probabilities

FIGURE 5–17
Availability as a function of time

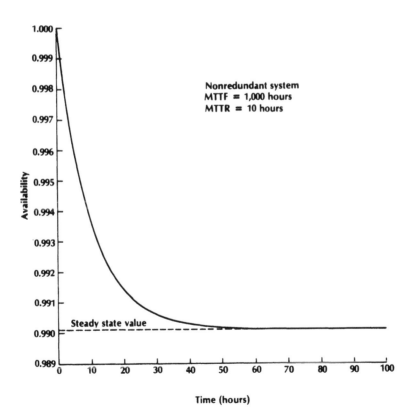

have reached their equilibrium values. Thus, p_0 is the steady-state probability of proper system operation, if a solution exists. Applying these changes to Eq. 24 yields

$$0 = -\lambda p_0 + \mu p_1$$

$$0 = \lambda p_0 - \mu p_1$$

or

$$p_1 = \frac{\lambda}{\mu} p_0 \tag{28}$$

The condition that $p_0 + p_1 = 1$ is required to solve Eq. 28. Thus,

$$p_0 + \frac{\lambda}{\mu} p_0 = 1$$

or

$$p_0 = \frac{1}{1 + \dfrac{\lambda}{\mu}} = \frac{\mu}{\lambda + \mu}$$

which is the result obtained earlier.

The reliability function can also be represented as a Markov model by making the system-failed state a trapping state; that is, once the failed state is entered, the probability of exiting is zero. Figure 5–18 depicts the transition probabilities for the single-system model. The differential equations become

$$\dot{p}_0(t) = -\lambda p_0(t)$$
$$\dot{p}_1(t) = \lambda p_0(t) \tag{29}$$

The T matrix can be written by inspection:

$$T = \begin{bmatrix} -\lambda & \lambda \\ 0 & 0 \end{bmatrix}$$

$$\bar{P}(0) = \bar{P}^x(s)[sI - T] = \bar{P}^x(s) \times A$$

$$\bar{P}(0) = \bar{P}^x(s) \begin{bmatrix} s + \lambda & -\lambda \\ 0 & s \end{bmatrix}$$

$$\bar{P}^x(s) = \bar{P}(0)A^{-1}$$

Letting $\bar{P}(0) = [1,0]$ yields

$$\bar{P}^x(s) = [1,0] \frac{\begin{bmatrix} s & \lambda \\ 0 & s + \lambda \end{bmatrix}}{s^2 + \lambda s}$$

$$p_0^x(s) = \frac{s}{s^2 + \lambda s}$$

FIGURE 5–18
*Markov model for
single system with-
out repair*

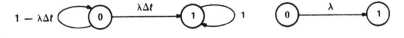

a. Discrete-time (differential) model   b. Continuous-time model

$$p_1^x(s) = \frac{\lambda}{s^2 + \lambda s}$$

Simplifying and performing partial fraction expansion yields

$$p_0^x(s) = \frac{1}{s + \lambda}$$

$$p_1^x(s) = \frac{1}{s} - \frac{1}{s + \lambda}$$

Taking the inverse transform gives the final solutions:

$$p_0(t) = e^{-\lambda t}$$

$$p_1(t) = 1 - e^{-\lambda t} \tag{30}$$

Eq. 30 could also have been derived from the properties of the exponential distribution and the fact that $p_0 + p_1 = 1$. In addition, Eq. 30 is simply Eq. 27 with μ set equal to zero (an infinite repair rate). The steady-state solution to Eq. 29 yields

$$p_0 = 0$$

$$p_1 = 1 - p_0 = 1$$

Now consider a dual-processor system with repair. Figure 5–19a gives the Markov model. There are four states, corresponding to both functioning, one functioning and one not, and both failed. Two field service engineers and perfect coverage are assumed. If the processors and field service engineers are identical, the model can be collapsed as in Figure 5–19b. In general, if there are n components in a system that may be either functional or failed, the Markov model will have 2^n states and a system of 2^n equations to solve. Computational complexity can be reduced by using symmetry to coalesce states. Furthermore, solutions may be limited to finding only the probability of occupying one state of interest (the all-failed state) instead of the probabilities of all states.

To solve the model in Figure 5–19c, which assumes a single field service engineer (and perfect coverage), by inspection,

$$T = \begin{bmatrix} -2\lambda & 2\lambda & 0 \\ \mu & -\lambda - \mu & \lambda \\ 0 & \mu & -\mu \end{bmatrix}$$

FIGURE 5–19
Markov models for dual system with repair

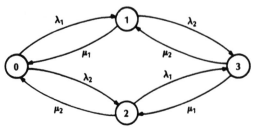
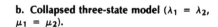
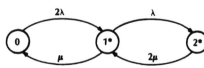

a. **Full four-state model**

b. **Collapsed three-state model** ($\lambda_1 = \lambda_2$, $\mu_1 = \mu_2$).

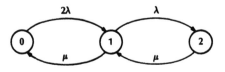
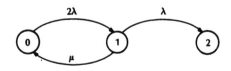

c. **Single repairman model**

d. **Reliability model**

Therefore,

$$A = \begin{bmatrix} s + 2\lambda & -2\lambda & 0 \\ -\mu & s + \lambda + \mu & -\lambda \\ 0 & -\mu & s + \mu \end{bmatrix}$$

The solution requires finding the inverse of this matrix, which also requires finding the determinant:

$$\det A = s^3 + (3\lambda + 2\mu)s^2 + (2\lambda^2 + 2\lambda\mu + \mu)s$$

$$A^{-1} = \frac{\begin{bmatrix} \det\begin{bmatrix} s+\lambda+\mu & -\lambda \\ -\mu & s+\mu \end{bmatrix} & -\det\begin{bmatrix} -2\lambda & 0 \\ -\mu & s+\mu \end{bmatrix} & \det\begin{bmatrix} -2\lambda & 0 \\ s+\lambda+\mu & -\lambda \end{bmatrix} \\ -\det\begin{bmatrix} -\mu & -\lambda \\ 0 & s+\mu \end{bmatrix} & \det\begin{bmatrix} s+2\lambda & 0 \\ 0 & s+\mu \end{bmatrix} & -\det\begin{bmatrix} s+2\lambda & 0 \\ -\mu & -\lambda \end{bmatrix} \\ \det\begin{bmatrix} -\mu & s+\lambda+\mu \\ 0 & -\mu \end{bmatrix} & -\det\begin{bmatrix} s+2\lambda & -2\lambda \\ 0 & -\mu \end{bmatrix} & \det\begin{bmatrix} s+2\lambda & -2\lambda \\ -\mu & s+\lambda+\mu \end{bmatrix} \end{bmatrix}}{\det A}$$

$$A^{-1} = \frac{\begin{bmatrix} s^2 + (\lambda + 2\mu)s + \mu^2 & 2\lambda s + 2\lambda\mu & 2\lambda^2 \\ \mu s + \mu^2 & s^2 + (2\lambda + \mu)s + 2\lambda\mu & \lambda s + 2\lambda^2 \\ \mu^2 & \mu s + 2\lambda\mu & s^2 + (3\lambda + \mu)s + 2\lambda^2 \end{bmatrix}}{s^3 + (3\lambda + 2\mu)s^2 + (2\lambda^2 + 2\lambda\mu + \mu)s}$$

If we assume that $P(0) = [1,0,0]$, then

$$p_2^x(s) = \frac{2\lambda^2}{s^3 + (3\lambda + 2\mu)s^2 + (2\lambda^2 + 2\lambda\mu + \mu^2)s} \tag{31}$$

(If the initial state is known with certainty, and only one state probability is of interest, then only one element of A^{-1} needs to be calculated, a potentially large savings in effort.) $p_2(t)$ is the probability of the system's being in the failed state at time t. The availability function $A(t)$ is therefore equal to $1 - p_2(t)$. Alternatively, $A(t)$ could be calculated by solving for $p_0(t) + p_1(t)$, which increases the amount of computation required.

Since the degree of the numerator (0) is obviously less than the degree of the denominator (3), the next step in the solution is to find the roots of the denominator. Since one root is zero, using the quadratic formula gives

$$-a_1 = 0$$

$$-a_2 = -\frac{1}{2}(3\lambda + 2\mu) - \frac{1}{2}\sqrt{\lambda^2 + 4\lambda\mu}$$

$$-a_3 = -\frac{1}{2}(3\lambda + 2\mu) + \frac{1}{2}\sqrt{\lambda^2 + 4\lambda\mu}$$

Next, finding the partial fraction expansion yields

$$p_2^x(s) = \frac{k_1}{s} + \frac{k_2}{s + a_2} + \frac{k_3}{s + a_3}$$

where $k_1 = \dfrac{2\lambda^2}{a_2 a_3} = \dfrac{2\lambda^2}{2\lambda^2 + 2\lambda\mu + \mu^2}$

$$k_2 = \frac{2\lambda^2}{-a_2(a_3 - a_2)} = \frac{4\lambda^2}{\lambda^2 + 4\lambda\mu + (3\lambda + 2\mu)\sqrt{\lambda^2 + 4\lambda\mu}}$$

$$k_3 = \frac{2\lambda^2}{-a_3(a_2 - a_3)} = \frac{4\lambda^2}{\lambda^2 + 4\lambda\mu - (3\lambda + 2\mu)\sqrt{\lambda^2 + 4\lambda\mu}}$$

Taking the inverse transform gives

$$p_2(t) = k_1 + k_2 e^{-a_2 t} + k_3 e^{-a_3 t}$$

As noted earlier, $A(t) = 1 - p_2(t)$. Therefore,

$$A(t) = 1 - k_1 - k_2 e^{-a_2 t} - k_3 e^{-a_3 t}$$

$$A(t) = \frac{2\lambda\mu + \mu^2}{2\lambda^2 + 2\lambda\mu + \mu^2} - \frac{4\lambda^2 \exp\left(-(1/2)[(3\lambda + 2\mu) + \sqrt{\lambda^2 + 4\lambda\mu}]t\right)}{\lambda^2 + 4\lambda\mu + (3\lambda + 2\mu)\sqrt{\lambda^2 + 4\lambda\mu}}$$

$$- \frac{4\lambda^2 \exp\left(-(1/2)[(3\lambda + 2\mu) - \sqrt{\lambda^2 + 4\lambda\mu}]t\right)}{\lambda^2 + 4\lambda\mu - (3\lambda + 2\mu)\sqrt{\lambda^2 + 4\lambda\mu}}$$

The steady-state availability is

$$A_{ss} = 1 - k_1 = \frac{2\lambda\mu + \mu^2}{2\lambda^2 + 2\lambda\mu + \mu^2} \tag{32}$$

As discussed earlier, the steady-state availability alone can be found more easily by substituting zero for $\dot{\vec{P}}(t)$ and $\vec{P}$ for $\vec{P}(t)$ in Eq. 25.

The availability model in Figure 5–19c can be transformed into a reliability model by making state 2 a trapping state (see Figure 5–19d). Then the solution proceeds as follows:

$$T = \begin{bmatrix} -2\lambda & 2\lambda & 0 \\ \mu & -\lambda - \mu & \lambda \\ 0 & 0 & 0 \end{bmatrix}$$

$$A = \begin{bmatrix} s + 2\lambda & -2\lambda & 0 \\ -\mu & s + \lambda + \mu & -\lambda \\ 0 & 0 & s \end{bmatrix}$$

$$\vec{P}^x(s) = \vec{P}(0) \times A^{-1}$$

For $\vec{P}(0) = [1,0,0]$, we need to calculate only a'_{13} in order to find $R(t) = 1 - p_2(t)$:

$$p_2^x(s) = a'_{13} = \frac{\text{cofactor}_{31}(A)}{\det A}$$

$$p_2^x(s) = \frac{\det \begin{bmatrix} -2\lambda & 0 \\ s + \lambda + \mu & -\lambda \end{bmatrix}}{(s + 2\lambda)(s + \lambda + \mu)s - 2\lambda\mu s}$$

$$p_2^x(s) = \frac{2\lambda^2}{s^3 + (3\lambda + \mu)s^2 + 2\lambda^2 s}$$

$$p_2^x(s) = \frac{2\lambda^2}{s(s + a_2)(s + a_3)} \qquad (a_1 = 0, \text{ by inspection})$$

where the roots are

$$-a_2 = -\frac{1}{2}(3\lambda + \mu) + \frac{1}{2}\sqrt{\lambda^2 + 6\lambda\mu + \mu^2}$$

$$-a_3 = -\frac{1}{2}(3\lambda + \mu) - \frac{1}{2}\sqrt{\lambda^2 + 6\lambda\mu + \mu^2}$$

Expanding the partial fractions yields

$$p_2^x = \frac{k_1}{s} + \frac{k_2}{s + a_2} + \frac{k_3}{s + a_3}$$

where $k_1 = \dfrac{2\lambda^2}{a_2 a_3} = 1$

$$k_2 = \frac{2\lambda^2}{-a_2(a_3 - a_2)} = \frac{4\lambda^2}{\lambda^2 + 6\lambda\mu + \mu^2 - (3\lambda + \mu)\sqrt{\lambda^2 + 6\lambda\mu + \mu^2}}$$

$$k_3 = \frac{2\lambda^2}{-a_3(a_2 - a_3)} = \frac{4\lambda^2}{\lambda^2 + 6\lambda\mu + \mu^2 + (3\lambda + \mu)\sqrt{\lambda^2 + 6\lambda\mu + \mu^2}}$$

the desired reliability function is

$$R(t) = 1 - p_2(t)$$

Therefore, taking the inverse of the LaPlace transform gives

$$R(t) = -k_2 e^{-a_2 t} - k_3 e^{-a_3 t}$$

$$R(t) = \frac{4\lambda^2 \exp\left(-(1/2)(3\lambda + \mu - \sqrt{\lambda^2 + 6\lambda\mu + \mu^2})t\right)}{(3\lambda + \mu)\sqrt{\lambda^2 + 6\lambda\mu + \mu^2} - \lambda^2 - 6\lambda\mu - \mu^2}$$

$$- \frac{4\lambda^2 \exp\left(-(1/2)(3\lambda + \mu + \sqrt{\lambda^2 + 6\lambda\mu + \mu^2})t\right)}{(3\lambda + \mu)\sqrt{\lambda^2 + 6\lambda\mu + \mu^2} + \lambda^2 + 6\lambda\mu + \mu^2}$$

In review, continuous-time Markov models are solved using the Chapman–Kolmogorov differential equations

$$\vec{P}(t) = \vec{P}(t)T$$

where $\vec{P}(t)$ = vector of state probability functions

$$\vec{P}(t) = \frac{d\,\vec{P}(t)}{dt}$$

T = differential state-transition rate matrix

The elements of T are easily derived from the graph of the Markov model. For $i \neq j$, t_{ij} is the state-transition rate (possibly zero) from state i to state j. Each diagonal element t_{ii} is minus the sum of all transition rates leaving state i. Thus, the rows of T all add up to zero, making it a differential matrix.

Using LaPlace transforms, the differential equations are changed into algebraic equations:

$$\vec{P}^x(s) = \vec{P}(0)A^{-1}$$

$$A = [sI - T]$$

After solving the set of linear algebraic equations, the final solutions are obtained by applying the inverse LaPlace transform.

Symbolic Solutions to Time-Invariant Markov Models. Another way of computing the steady-state solutions of Markov models is to consider the average transition times from each state to every other state and the average transition time from state i to state j as X_{ij}. These steady-state transition times can then be used to compute the steady-state probabilities p_i. The probability p_i will be the ratio of the average before a transition out of that state and the time between visits of that state. If we define the sum of the λ_{ij} leaving state i as Λ_i, then

$$p_i = \frac{1}{\Lambda_i X_{ii}}$$

The Λ_i can easily be computed from the transition rate matrix. The average transition times X_{ij} can be computed by adding the average time until a transition out of state i (Λ_i) and the sum of the transition times from the states adjacent to i to state j (X_{kj}) weighted by the probabilities of making the transition from i to k:

$$X_{ij} = \frac{1}{\Lambda_i} + \sum_{k=0,k\neq j}^{n} \frac{\lambda_{ij}}{\Lambda_i} X_{kj}$$

For an n state model, this produces a total of n^2 equations and n^2 unknowns. If Gaussian elimination is used to solve the model we find that the order of complexity is $O(n^6)$. Notice though that equations degrade into n independent sets of n equations in n unknowns, one for each value of j. This reduces the order of complexity to $O(n^4)$. Typically we do not need all of the X_{ii}, and need only solve for one or two states.

Average transition times X_{ij} can also be used to estimate the MTTF of a system. If i is the initial state and j is the failed state (assuming all the failed states have been collapsed to a single state), then the X_{ij} will be the MTTF for that system.

When doing analysis by hand, there are several short cuts that can be made to reduce the number of equations to be solved. For example, consider the Markov model in Figure 5–20a. This model represents a uniprocessor system with failure prediction. State 0 represents the OK state, 1 represents a state where a failure has

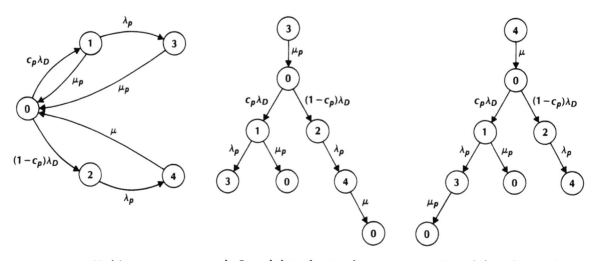

a. Model   b. Expanded tree for state three   c. Expanded tree for state four

FIGURE 5–20 *Markov availability model for uniprocessor system [From Hansen, 1988]*

been predicted, 2 represents a state where a failure is about to occur but has not been detected, and states 3 and 4 are the failed states for predicted and unpredicted failures. We would like to solve for the availability, by finding $p_0 + p_1 + p_2$. The easiest way to do this is to solve for $p_3 + p_4$ and subtract from one.

We can solve for p_3 by expanding the model into a tree with node 3 as the root as shown in Figure 5–20b. The tree is formed by tracing all of the arcs in the model and stopping when a node is repeated. We then write an equation for the root node and each internal node that is repeated as a leaf node. To get p_3, we first need to compute X_{33}. The result will be the average time before leaving this node, $1/\mu_p$, plus the average time to go from node 0 to node 3 (X_{03}). All of the terms comprising a time have the same common divisor (the Λ for that node), so we can write the equation as 1, plus the transition times from each of the child nodes to the destination node, with each weighted by the transition rate for that arc. Thus, the equation for node 3 is

$$X_{33} = \frac{1 + \mu_p X_{03}}{\mu_p}$$

The internal node 0 is repeated as a leaf node, so we must write an equation for it as well (notice that the simplification $\lambda_D = c_p \lambda_D + (1 - c_p)\lambda_D$ has been made):

$$X_{03} = \frac{1 + c_p \lambda_D \dfrac{1 + \mu_p X_{03}}{\lambda_p + \mu_p} + (1 - c_p)\lambda_D \left(\dfrac{1}{\lambda_p} + \dfrac{1}{\mu} + X_{03}\right)}{\lambda_D}$$

If we then solve these two simultaneous equations, we find

$$X_{33} = \frac{1}{\mu_p} + \frac{\dfrac{1}{\lambda_D} + (1 - c_p)\left(\dfrac{1}{\lambda_p} + \dfrac{1}{\mu}\right) + c_p\left(\dfrac{1}{\mu_p + \lambda_p}\right)}{c_p \lambda_p / (\mu_p + \lambda_p)}$$

Thus, the steady-state probability of being in state 3 is

$$p_3 = \frac{1/\mu_p}{X_{33}} = \frac{c_p \lambda_p}{\lambda_p c_p + \mu_p(\mu_p + \lambda_p).\left[\dfrac{1}{\lambda_D} + (1 - c_p)\left(\dfrac{1}{\lambda_p} + \dfrac{1}{\mu}\right) + c_p\left(\dfrac{1}{\mu_p + \lambda_p}\right)\right]}$$

We can do a similar analysis for state 4 using the tree in Figure 5–20c. The state 4 equations are

$$X_{44} = \frac{1 + \mu X_{04}}{\mu}$$

$$X_{04} = \frac{1 + c_p \lambda_D \left[\dfrac{1}{\lambda_p + \mu_p} + \dfrac{\mu_p}{\lambda_p + \mu_p} X_{04} + \dfrac{\lambda_p}{\lambda_p + \mu_p}\left(\dfrac{1}{\mu_p} + X_{04}\right)\right] + (1 - c_p)\lambda_D \dfrac{1}{\lambda_p}}{\lambda_D}$$

The final solution is

$$p_4 = \frac{1/\mu}{X_{44}} = \frac{1 - c_p}{(1 - c_p)\left(1 + \dfrac{\mu}{\lambda_p}\right) + \dfrac{\mu}{\lambda_D} + c_p \dfrac{\mu}{\mu_p}}$$

Combining the results, we get the availability

$$1 - \frac{c_p \lambda_p}{\lambda_p c_p + \mu_p(\mu_p + \lambda_p)\left[\frac{1}{\lambda_D} + (1 - c_p)\left(\frac{1}{\lambda_p} + \frac{1}{\mu}\right) + c_p\left(\frac{1}{\mu_p + \lambda_p}\right)\right]}$$

$$- \frac{1 - c_p}{(1 - c_p)\left(1 + \frac{\mu}{\lambda_p}\right) + \frac{\mu}{\lambda_D} + c_p\frac{\mu}{\mu_p}}$$

Time-Varying Markov Models

A useful generalization of the Markov process for reliability modeling is to allow state-transition probabilities to change over time. This causes difficulties in analysis, since it generally makes the use of transform analysis impossible. Nevertheless, if failure rates (or repair rates) are functions of time, the techniques discussed in this section can be used.

Discrete-Time Equations. These equations define $q_{ij}(m,n)$ as the probability that the system is in state j at time n given that it was in state i at time m ($m \leq n$). For consistency, $Q(m,m) = I$. With this notation, in matrix form the Chapman–Kolmogorov equation is

$$Q(m,n) = Q(m,k)Q(k,n) \qquad m \leq k \leq n$$

Letting $k = n - 1$,

$$Q(m,n) = Q(m,n - 1)Q(n - 1,n)$$

Defining $P(n) = Q(n,n + 1)$,

$$Q(m,n) = Q(m,n - 1)P(n - 1) \tag{33}$$

This equation can be expanded recursively

$$Q(m,n) = Q(m,n - 2)P(n - 2)P(n - 1)$$

$$Q(m,n) = Q(m,n - 3)P(n - 3)P(n - 2)P(n - 1)$$

yielding the final solution

$$Q(m,n) = \prod_{i=m}^{n-1} P(i) \tag{34}$$

For $m = 0$ and all $P(i) = P$, this becomes P^n, as given earlier.

Continuous-Time Equations. These equations define the difference operator as

$$\Delta_n f(n) = f(n + 1) - f(n)$$

Then,

$$\Delta_n Q(m,n - 1) = Q(m,n) - Q(m,n - 1)$$

From Eq. 33,

$$\Delta_n Q(m,n - 1) = Q(m,n - 1)P(n - 1) - Q(m,n - 1) \qquad (35)$$

$$\Delta_n Q(m,n - 1) = Q(m,n - 1)[P(n - 1) - I]$$

Defining the differential matrix gives

$$T(n) = P(n) - I$$

Eq. 35 is rewritten as

$$\Delta_n Q(m,n - 1) = Q(m,n - 1)T(n - 1) \qquad (36)$$

Eq. 36 is the difference-equation form of the Chapman–Kolmogorov equation for discrete-time Markov processes. The continuous-time Chapman–Kolmogorov equations are directly derived from this equation. Defining $Q(\tau,t)$ as the continuous-time interval transition probability matrix analogous to the discrete-time interval multi-step translation probability matrix $Q(m,n)$ defined earlier, the matrix form of the Chapman–Kolmogorov equation is

$$Q(\tau,t) = Q(\tau,\rho)Q(\rho,t)$$

In differential equation form, this becomes

$$\dot{Q}(\tau,t) = Q(\tau,t)T(t) \qquad (37)$$

Eq. 37 is a more general form of Eq. 25. If $\tau = 0$, Eq. 25 is obtained by summing:

$$p_j(t) = \sum_{i=1}^{N} q_{ij}(0,t)p_i(0)$$

The solution to Eq. 36 comes from basic differential equation theory

$$Q(\tau,t) = \exp \left(\int_{\tau}^{t} T(\rho)d\rho \right) \qquad (38)$$

Obtaining explicit solutions from this may be quite difficult. If $\tau = 0$ and $T(t) = T$ for all values of t, Eq. 38 becomes

$$Q(t) = e^{Tt}$$

which is a reformulation of the solution using LaPlace transforms that was discussed in the section on time-invariant Markov models.

Numerical integration techniques are used to solve Eq. 38 because of its complexity [Stiffler, Bryant, and Guccione, 1979]. An alternative method is to approximate the continuous-time process with discrete-time equivalents. Because numerical integration involves some degree of approximation anyway, this is frequently a good choice. The major difficulty is that many transition rates that are effectively zero in the continuous-time differential transition rate matrix assume small but nonzero probabilities in the discrete-time transition probability matrix. Consider the model of Figure 5–19c. A discrete-time approximation has to consider the probability of two failures during the same interval. This cross-coupled transition probability can be ignored for continuous-time models because of the infinitesimal time-steps involved.

For converting from continuous-time hazard functions (failure and repair rate functions) to discrete-time hazard functions, a discrete-time probability distribution must be found that corresponds to the continuous-time distribution defined by that hazard function. The corresponding parameters can then be calculated for the desired time-step Δt. For the Weibull distribution function mentioned earlier,

$$pdf = f(t) = \alpha\lambda(\lambda t)^{\alpha-1} \exp\left(-(\lambda t)^{\alpha}\right)$$

Recall that a corresponding discrete Weibull function exists (see Chapter 2):

$$pmf = f(k) = q^{k^{\alpha}} - q^{(k+1)^{\alpha}}$$

Given that $f(k)$ is defined as the probability of an event (failure) occurring between time Δt and time $(k + 1)\Delta t$ for some chosen interval size Δt, this probability mass function can be expressed as

$$f(k) = P[\text{no event by } k\Delta t] - P[\text{no event by } (k + 1)\Delta t]$$

$$f(k) = R(k) - R(k + 1)$$

where $R(k)$ is the reliability function. Substituting the continuous-time equivalents yields

$$f(k) = R(k\Delta t) - R[(k + 1)\Delta t]$$

$$f(k) = \exp\left(-(\lambda k\Delta t)^{\alpha}\right) - \exp\left(-[\lambda(k + 1)\Delta t]^{\alpha}\right)$$

Rearranging terms gives

$$f(k) = [\exp\left(-(\lambda\Delta t)^{\alpha}\right)]k^{k^{\alpha}} - [\exp\left(-\lambda\Delta t\right)]^{(k+1)^{\alpha}}$$

which makes it obvious that

$$q = \exp\left(-(\lambda\Delta t)^{\alpha}\right)$$

and that α does not change between the continuous-time distribution and the discrete-time equivalent. The transition probabilities are now given by

$$z(n) = 1 - q^{(n+1)^{\alpha}} - n^{\alpha}$$

Consider the reliability model of Figure 5–21a, which is the same as that shown in Figure 5–19d except that the failure and repair rates have been replaced by Weibull hazard functions. In the equivalent discrete-time model displayed in Figure 5–21b, the complexity of terms is greater, particularly due to the joint probabilities of state transitions.

After deriving the transition probability matrix function $P(n)$ from the model graph the final solution can be derived from Eq. 34. Figure 5–22 plots the solution of Eq. 34

a. Continuous-time model

b. Discrete-time model

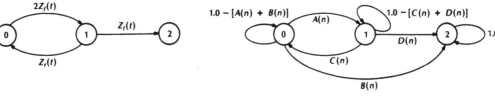

$$Z_f(t) = \alpha\lambda(\lambda)^{\alpha-1}$$
$$Z_r(t) = \beta\mu(\mu)^{\beta-1}$$

$$A(n) = 2Z_f(n)[1 - Z_f(n)] \quad D(n) = Z_f(n)[1 - Z_r(n)]$$
$$B(n) = [Z_f(n)]^2 \quad Z_f(n) = 1 - q_f^{(n+1)^\alpha - n^\alpha}; \ q_f = e^{-(\lambda\Delta t)^\alpha}$$
$$C(n) = [1 - Z_f(n)]Z_r(n) \quad Z_r(n) = 1 - q_r^{(n+1)^\beta - n^\beta}; \ q_r = e^{-(\mu\Delta t)^\beta}$$

FIGURE 5–21 *Dual system with a single field service engineer: time-varying transition rates*

for representative values of α with $\beta = 1$. For purposes of comparison, failure processes of equal means are used throughout. The values of λ are changed along with the values of α to maintain a constant value for the mean of each process. The reliability curves plotted in Figure 5–22 are based on a module MTTF of 100 time-steps and a module MTTR of 10 time-steps. The following table lists discrete Weibull parameter values:

α	q_f	β	q
0.6	0.922319	1.0	0.90
0.8	0.972515	1.0	0.90
1.0	0.990000	1.0	0.90
1.2	0.996285	1.0	0.90
2.0	0.999921	1.0	0.90

The differences in reliability caused by changing the value of α_f (and adjusting other parameters to maintain a constant module MTTF) are highlighted in Figure 5–23, which plots the reliability difference using $\alpha_f = 1.0$ as the baseline system. Two features are generally discernible from these curves. First, for values of α_f less than one, the system reliability is less than that for α_f equal to one for some period. This is followed by a much longer period during which the reliability of systems with α_f less than one is greater than the reliability of systems with α_f equal to one. (Similar but opposite effects are evident for systems with α_f greater than one.) The second feature is that as α_f gets farther from 1.0, the magnitude of deviation in the curves becomes larger. Significant deviations in reliability occur even for relatively small deviations in α_f.

These examples of Markov analysis have been given to illustrate the analysis procedure. The interested reader is referred to more comprehensive analysis such as Howard [1971] and Shooman [1968, 1991] for additional solution techniques and examples.

Monte Carlo Simulation. The techniques considered so far are insufficient to obtain results for even quite minor changes in the modeling assumptions. In the issue of failure process renewal, for example, it seems obvious that a repaired module should

FIGURE 5–22
Reliability of dual-redundant systems

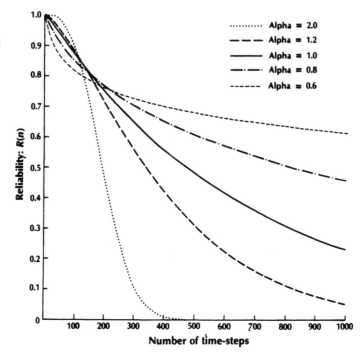

FIGURE 5–23
Reliability differences between exponential and Weibull for a dual-redundant system

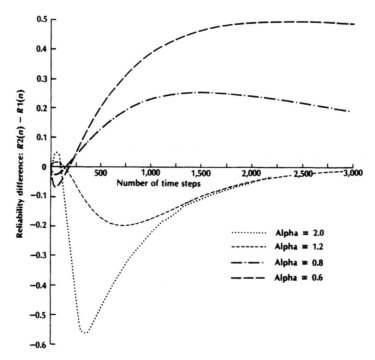

be "as good as new," but that is *not* the assumption behind the model of Figure 5–21. In that model, the failure processes $z_A(t)$ (or $z_A(n)$) are not reset to time $t = 0$ ($n = 0$) when a module is repaired. This fact can make a dramatic difference in the failure rates. In the Weibull hazard function, for α less than one, the failure rate asymptotically approaches zero; for α greater than one, it grows without limit. Thus, the failure rate immediately following a repair can vary tremendously under the two modeling assumptions (of course, for constant failure rates there is no difference in effect between the two assumptions). Consider the discrete Weibull hazard function:

$$z(n) = 1 - q^{(n+1)^\alpha - n^\alpha}$$

If this failure process is reset (renewed) whenever a repair occurs, then the conditional hazard function of the process given the renewal time N_r is

$$z(n) = 1 - q^{(n-N_R+1)^\alpha - (n-N_R)^\alpha}$$

In general, the hazard function of the failure process with renewal is given by

$$z(n) = 1 - \sum_{k=0}^{n} (q^{(n-k+1)^\alpha - (n-k)^\alpha}) P\{N_R = k|n\}$$

The second factor in the summation is the conditional probability that the renewal time has any particular value given the current time. Calculation of this value depends on the entire past history of the system, which makes it intractable to compute in practice. Therefore, a new technique to attack the problem of reliability modeling is needed.

A standard method of studying the reliability of systems that are too complex to model analytically is to simulate their performance and examine the results [Almassy, 1979; Yakowitz, 1977]. The basis of such "Monte Carlo" simulation schemes is a pseudo-random number generator that produces a sequence of numbers between 0 and 1. This sequence approximately follows the uniform distribution. For good results, simulations should be run on two or more independent pseudo-random number generators, and the generators used should be thoroughly tested [Knuth, vol. 2, 1969].

Figure 5–24 shows the reliability model of a dual-redundant system. Because of the need to distinguish between failures and repairs of the individual modules, a full four-state model is necessary. Otherwise, this model is the same system as Figures 5–19d and 5–21b. From the model graph, the transition probability matrix function $P(n; N_A, N_B, M_A, M_B)$ is defined. Each simulation run follows the following algorithm.

1. Establish global initialization:

   $i = $ current state $= 0$

   $N_A = N_B = M_A = M_B = $ renewal times $= 0$

   $n = $ current time $= -1$

2. Set loop variables:

   $n = n + 1$

   $j = $ next state $= -1$

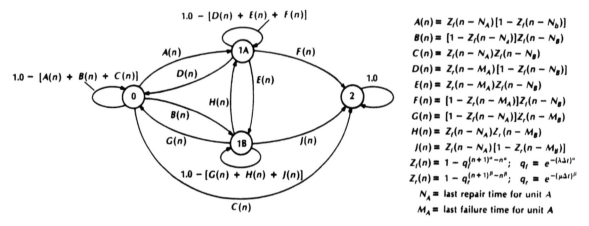

FIGURE 5–24 *Model of dual system with failure and repair process renewals*

x = cumulative probability = 0

R = next pseudo-random number in sequence

3. Test for next state:

(a) $j = j + 1$

(b) $x = x + p_{ij}(n; N_A, N_B, M_A, M_B)$

(c) If $R > x$, then go to (a)

4. Find next state:

If $i \neq j$, then set one of $\{N_A, N_B, M_A, M_B\}$ to $n + 1$

$i = j$

If $i \neq$ a trapping (failed) state, then go to step 2

5. Output the value of n for this simulation run.

For each value of α used in the preceding example of time-varying Markov processes (0.6, 0.8, 1.0, 1.2, 2.0), 3000 simulations were performed, using three pseudo-random number generators for 1000 simulations apiece. Figure 5–25 plots the empirical reliability curves for a dual-redundant system with independent failure and repair process renewals, using the same parameter values (q_f, α, q_r, β) as for Figure 5–22; only the modeling assumption concerning process renewals was changed. Figure 5–26 plots the corresponding reliability difference curves. The reliabilities of systems with α_f not equal to one diverge quite sharply under the two different modeling assumptions. The general shapes of the curves remain much the same, but the magnitude of the deviation is much smaller in the second time period (underestimation for α_f less than one and overestimation for α_f greater than one) for the systems with error-process renewals (although comparable in the earlier time frame). Also, the crossover points are significantly delayed for the systems with error-process renewals, compared to the systems without renewals.

FIGURE 5–25
Simulated reliability of dual system

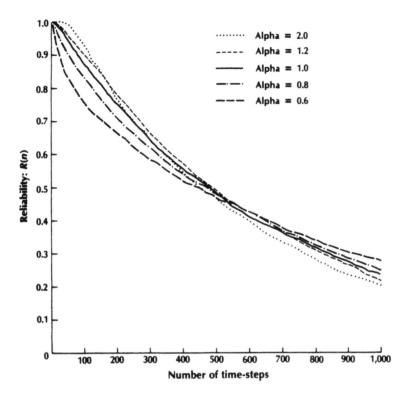

If the exponential (constant error rate) assumption is used for reliability modeling, significant deviations between predicted and experimental reliability will occur whenever the data indicate that failures follow a nonconstant error rate. The extent of deviation from exponential model results depends both on the explicit form of the failure rate (hazard) function and on whether the failure process is renewed whenever a repair occurs.

Hybrid Models Using Measured Statistics

The measures traditionally used to compare systems do not take into account the performance of the system whose reliability is being measured. Table 5–5 lists the results obtained from nine different experiments whose specific goal was to gain experience on systems reliability. Data for the first system [Yourdon, 1972] are from a summary of failure statistics on a Burroughs 5500 over a 15-month period starting in April 1969. Limited information is available about the cause of each failure. One category, for example, includes system failures resulting from unexpected I/O interrupts. These failures were recorded whenever the software responded to an interrupt signifying that some I/O action had taken place but discovered that it had no record of having initiated such action. Thus, there was an indication of some form of hardware

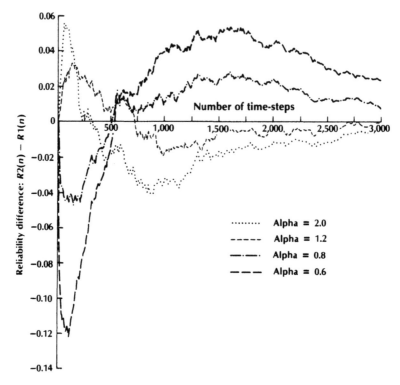

or software error, but the particular cause for the failure (hardware or software) remained unknown.

The data for the second system, reported in Lynch, Wagner, and Schwartz [1975], are from the first 13 months of operation of a system called Chi/OS developed by the Chi Corporation for the Univac 1108 between 1970 and 1973. There is no explanation of how such an accurate distinction between hardware and software failures was obtained.

Reynolds and Kinsbergen [1975] reported data obtained over three years from a dual IBM 370/165 installed at Hughes Aircraft Company to handle a mixed batch and time-sharing load.

The fourth system is at the Stanford Linear Accelerator Center (SLAC), where the main workload is processed as a multistream background batch. The system consists of a foreground host (IBM 370/168) and two background batch servers (IBM 370/168 and IBM 360/91) and is designed to be highly available and reconfigurable.

The CMU-10A is an ECL PDP-10 used in the Computer Science Department at Carnegie-Mellon University. The data for the CRAY-1 were reported in Keller [1976]; those for the three generic UNIVAC systems were reported in Siewiorek and Rennels [1980]. The data on the SUN-2 workstation and the Tandem systems is derived from Chapter 2.

Table 5–5 gives, when available, a mean time to restart (MTTS) value in hours (that is, the mean time to system failure); a mean number of instructions to restart (MNIR), which is an estimate of the mean number of instructions executed from system start up until system failure; and the percentages of system failures caused by hardware faults, software faults, and faults whose cause could not be resolved. The information about execution rates needed to compute the MNIR value was obtained from Phister [1979]. Note that the MNIR has increased over time, exhibiting a growth of about four orders of magnitude from 1975 to 1985.

Obviously, the numbers in Table 5–5 do not convey much information. A MTTS figure alone does not reveal the impact of unreliability on system use. Compare, for example, the CRAY-1 [Russel, 1978] with the CMUA [Bell et al., 1978]. Although the CRAY-1 crashes twice as often as the CMUA, it can operate continuously at rates above 138 million instructions per second (MIPS), whereas the CMUA operates at 1.2 MIPS. Hence, the CMUA executes $\approx 10^{10}$ instructions between crashes, whereas the CRAY-1 executes $\approx 10^{12}$ instructions between crashes. Inconsistencies like these suggest that reliability modeling and measuring should be closely related with the characterization of the performance of the system under study.

Integrated performance-reliability models appear in the literature. In Meyer, Furchtgot, and Wu [1979], a performance measure called *performability* gives the probability that a system performs at different levels of "accomplishment." Gay and Ketelsen [1979] model systems with Markov processes to estimate the probability of their being in one of several capacity states. This approach is similar to the one previously taken in Beaudry [1978], who introduced the concept of "computation reliability" as a measure that takes into account the computation capacity of a system in each possible operational state. Finally, Chou and Abraham [1980] provide a performance availability model for gracefully degrading systems with critically shared resources.

TABLE 5–5
Reliability experience of several commercial systems

System	MTTS (hours)	MNIR	Percent Hardware Faults	Percent Software Faults	Percent Unknown
B 5500	14.7	2.6×10^{10}	39.3%	8.1%	52.6%
Chi/05 (Univac 1108)	17	6.7×10^{10}	45	55	—
Dual 370/165	8.86	2.8×10^{11}	65	32	3
SLAC	20.2	2.3×10^{11}	73.3	21.6	5.1
CMU-10A	10	4.3×10^{10}	—	—	—
CRAY-1	4	1.9×10^{12}	—	—	—
UNIVAC (large)	—	—	51	42	7
UNIVAC (medium)	—	—	57	41	2
UNIVAC (small)	—	—	88	9	3
SUN-2	650	2.3×10^{12}	—	—	—
Tandem	35,000	2.5×10^{14}	19	43	—

Source: Modified from Castillo, 1980.

Reliability as a Function of System Workload. Consider now Figure 5–27, which shows the expected elapsed time required to execute a program for a time-sharing system at three different times of day. The curves were obtained as follows. From April 3 to July 2, 1979, a CPU bound program (basically a loop that computes several fast Fourier transforms with no I/O involved and small memory requirements) was executed three times daily. The program required 10 seconds of run-time (T min = 10 sec), and the actual elapsed time for each execution was recorded in the histogram of T use at each of these three times of day.

The mean time to system crash was measured for the same period. This value of mean time to crash was substituted as $1/\lambda$ in the model given in Castillo and Siewiorek [1980]. The $1/\lambda$ value was measured at noon (mean time to crash $1/\lambda$ = 9.6 hours), 4:00 p.m. ($1/\lambda$ = 11 hours), and 4:00 a.m. ($1/\lambda$ = 33 hours). A down-time value of 5 minutes was assumed in all cases. These three values of the mean time to fatal failure were

FIGURE 5–27
Expected elapsed time versus the minimum time required to execute a program [From Castillo and Siewiorek, 1980; © 1980 IEEE]

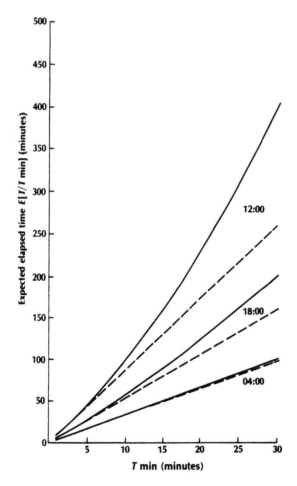

computed by assigning 2-hour time slots around each of the three times of day and counting the number of system restarts in each of the slots during the same three months for which the histograms of T use were computed.

Figure 5–27 plots the value of the expected elapsed time required to execute a program at these three times of day for different values of the minimum CPU time required to execute the program (T min). The expected elapsed time includes the effect of workload and unreliability, for it takes into account the time wasted by a system restart due to software or hardware transient errors.

For each curve, the dashed straight line represents the values of the expected elapsed time due only to workload (the expected elapsed time in the absence of errors), and the solid line represents the total expected elapsed time. The figure shows that at 12:00 noon the contribution due to restarts for a program requiring 30 minutes of CPU time amounts to over 40 percent of the total elapsed time. The curves have been obtained assuming that the time to system crash can be characterized with an exponentially distributed random variable with constant λ. But for the same curves, different values of λ are used at different times of day. This suggests that in models for time-sharing systems the failure rate is a periodic function of time.

Modeling Reliability and Workload. A workload-dependent model presented in Butner and Iyer [1980] assumes a linear dependency between failure rate and workload. The workload is characterized by a periodic function of time. The PDF becomes an exponential "modulated" by a periodic function.

$$P_p(t < \tau) = 1 - e^{-K_p \tau} e^{-F_p U_p(\tau)}$$

where F_p = load-induced failure rate
    $U_p(\tau)$ = instantaneous load value

This model, referred to as the *periodic model,* assumes a periodic utilization function $u(t) = m(t)$. It further assumes that the instantaneous value of the system failure rate is a linear function of this utilization function. That is,

$$\lambda_p(t) = s_p m(t) + c_p$$

Castillo [1980] shows that under this assumption the PDF of the time to system crash is given by

$$P(t < \tau) = 1 - e^{-(s_p m + c_p)\tau} e^{\ln \phi(\tau)}$$

where $\phi(\tau)$ is a periodic function of time.

A closer study of the utilization functions of critical resources in time-sharing systems reveals, however, that it is an oversimplification to assume that they can be approximated by a purely periodic function. Figure 5–28 shows the sampled values of the fraction of time spent executing the operating system for five consecutive weekdays in a time-sharing computing system. There are reasons to assume that the instantaneous value of the system-failure rate should follow the variations of the fraction of time in the operating system.

FIGURE 5–28
Fraction of time in the operating system during five consecutive week- days

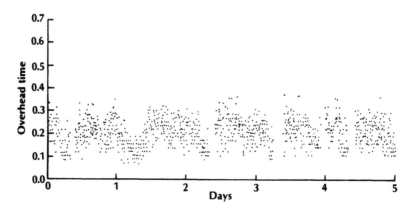

First, assume a constant-failure rate for the primary memory of a digital computing system operating in a stable environment under time-sharing policy. That the transient failure rate in a memory is constant is a reasonable assumption. There is also justification for thinking that certain complex devices may follow an exponential failure law [Barlow and Proschan, 1965, pp. 18–22]. Because the physical characteristics of the memory ICs do not change with time (at least during the effective life cycle of modern digital computing systems), the origin of these transients must lie in external sources, such as radiation, the presence of noise (possibly impulsive) in the power supply, or in the limitations of the manufacturing process.

In fact, Geilhufe [1979] has reported that MOS memory devices exhibit nonrecurring bit failures caused by α-particles emitted from small amounts of radioactive elements present in IC packaging material. The failure rate for this kind of failure is, of course, constant. Now assume that a transient memory failure has higher probability of leading to a system crash when the central processor is executing the operating system than when it is executing in user mode. A memory failure when the CPU is executing in user mode may affect a user process but will not crash the system.

The *system* failure rate due to transient memory failures will then depend on the ratio of the number of memory references while in the operating system to the total number of memory references per unit time. Because it is well known that operating system overhead increases with workload, the previous ratio will also be a nondecreasing function of the system workload, increasing in turn the observed system failure rate. The result is that the observed system failure rate due to transient memory failures should be equal to the sum of a component following the operating system overhead variations in time (or, indirectly, workload variations in time) plus a constant, workload-independent component. (Even if the system is idle, there may still be memory errors that corrupt, for example, the clock interrupt subroutine.)

Even if a computing system is not always equally sensitive to the presence of hardware errors, there are still arguments to support the idea that the apparent system-failure rate should depend on the workload. In practice, in most computing systems a component failure will be noticed only if the component is used. A time-sharing system with no load that spends most of its time in a wait state and only a fraction of the time executing the clock interrupt routine may sustain several failures and still not report any errors if the minimal hardware configuration required to execute these basic functions is not affected. The idea here is not that failures will be caused by increased utilization (although in some cases this situation is certainly possible), but that they will be detected by an increase in system utilization. This effect has also been referred to as *error latency* [Shedletsky and McCluskey, 1973].

Analogous arguments lead to the expectation that the rate of system failures caused by software unreliability will depend on how much the software is used. System software failures result from either of two conditions: The (static) input data to a program module present some peculiarities that the program is not able to handle, or the software is not capable of handling some time-dependent (dynamic) sequence in the input data stream. In a time-sharing system, the only software capable of provoking a system failure is the operating system. This software executes in a privileged processor state, and a software error that corrupts some critical information in the operating system data structures may lead to a system crash. However, because nobody knows a priori what these errors are, it is less likely that the system finds one of these combinations in its input stream under low load than in a high load situation (that is, small amounts of input data to process per unit time probably exercises software that has been more thoroughly debugged). Again, the observed system-failure rate has to depend on the system load. Furthermore, upon correct system operation, a user program is prevented from accessing any resource for which it has not been given explicit permission by the operating system. Consequently, it is not necessary to consider the effects of user programs.

Assuming that the failure rate is workload-related, and given the workload measured in Figure 5–28, a utilization function of the following form is thus appropriate for modeling a time-sharing system:

$$u(t) = m(t) + z(t)$$

where $m(t)$ = periodic function of time
$z(t)$ = zero-mean stationary Gaussian process

Castillo [1980] shows that, under the assumption that

$$\lambda_i(t) = s_i[m(t) + z(t)] + c_i$$

the following expression is obtained for the PDF of the time to system failure:

$$P(t < \tau) = 1 - \exp\left(-(\lambda_c + \sigma_{c1} + \sigma_{c2})\tau - \left(\frac{\sigma_{c1}}{\beta_1}\right)\right.$$
$$\left.(1 - e^{-\beta_1\tau}) - \left(\frac{\sigma_{c2}}{\beta_2}\right)(1 - e^{-\beta_2\tau}) + \ln \phi(\tau)\right)$$

where $\phi(\tau)$ is a periodic function of time depending only on $m(t)$, and the additional assumption is that the autocorrelation function of $z(t)$ is of the form

$$R_{zz}(t) = \alpha_1 e^{-\beta_1 t} + \alpha_2 e^{-\beta_2 t}$$

This model is termed *cyclostationary* because it is obtained from a cyclostationary utilization function (that is, the utilization function $u(t)$ is a stochastic process with periodic mean and autocorrelation functions).

Table 5–6 summarizes the reliability functions and hazard functions of the two preceding models (periodic and cyclostationary), along with the exponential and Weibull distributions. The fifth distribution in Table 5–6 is a simplified version of the distribution obtained with the cyclostationary model, considering only one exponential in the hazard function and neglecting the periodic component $\phi(\tau)$. This last distribution is particularly important because it has a known LaPlace transform that makes it suitable for Markov modeling (neither the Weibull distribution nor the distributions obtained from the periodic and cyclostationary models have known LaPlace transforms). Castillo [1980] has shown that both the cyclostationary and simplified cyclostationary models have substantially better statistical fits to measured data than the exponential, Weibull, and periodic models.

EXAMPLES OF MARKOV MODELING

This section applies Markov modeling techniques and assumptions to a common structure, a simple triple modular redundant system. In TMR, correct operation continues as long as two of the three modules are working properly. A second module failure causes the system to fail.

TABLE 5–6 *Reliability and hazard function of five failure models*

Model	Reliability Function	Hazard Function
Exponential	$R_e(\tau) = e^{-\lambda_e \tau}$	$h_e(\tau) = \lambda_e$
Weibull	$R_w(\tau) = \exp\left(-(\lambda_w \tau)^{\alpha_w}\right)$	$h_w(\tau) = \dfrac{\alpha_w \lambda_w}{(\lambda_w t)^{1-\alpha_w}}$
Periodic	$R_p(\tau) = \exp\left(-\lambda_p \tau e^{-f_p u(\tau)}\right)$	$h_p(\tau) = \left[\lambda_p + F_p \dfrac{\partial u(\tau)}{\partial \tau t}\right]$
Cyclostationary	$R_c(\tau) = e^x$ where $x = \left[-(\lambda_c + \sigma_{c1} + \sigma_{c2})\tau - \dfrac{\sigma_{c1}}{\beta_1}(1 - e^{-\beta_1 \tau})\right.$ $\left. - \dfrac{\sigma_{c2}}{\beta_2}(1 - e^{-\beta_2 \tau}) + \ln \phi(t)\right]$	$h_c(\tau) = \lambda_c - \sigma_{c1}(1 - e^{-\beta_1 \tau}) - \sigma_{c2}(1 - e^{-\beta_2 \tau}) + \dfrac{1}{\phi(t)}\dfrac{\partial \phi(t)}{\partial t}$
Simplified Cyclostationary	$R_m(\tau) = \exp\left(-(\alpha_m - \gamma_m)\tau - (\gamma_m/\beta_m)[1 - e^{-\beta_m \tau}]\right)$	$h_m(\tau) = \alpha_m - \gamma_m[1 - e^{-\beta_m \tau}]$

Source: From Castillo, 1980.

Time-Invariant or Constant Failure Rates

A repair strategy of calling in a field service engineer whenever a module fails produces a Markov model like that shown in Figure 5–29a. By inspection, the differential transition rate matrix is

$$T = \begin{bmatrix} -3\lambda & 3\lambda & 0 \\ \mu & -2\lambda - \mu & 2\lambda \\ 0 & 0 & 0 \end{bmatrix}$$

where λ = module failure rate
μ = repair rate

From this, the LaPlace transform $p_2(s)$ is calculated (assuming that $\overline{P}(0) = [1,0,0]$):

$$p_2(s) = \frac{6\lambda^2}{s[s + (1/2)(5\lambda + \mu - \sqrt{\lambda^2 + 10\lambda\mu + \mu^2})][s + (1/2)(5\lambda + \mu + \sqrt{\lambda^2 + 10\lambda\mu + \mu^2})]}$$

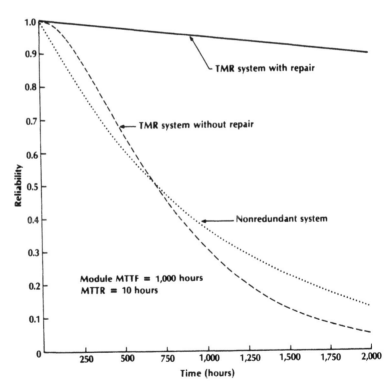

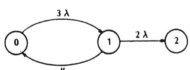

a. Markov model   b. Comparison with nonredundant system

FIGURE 5–29 *TMR system reliability*

Expanding the partial fractions, taking the inverse of the LaPlace transform, and subtracting from one produces the reliability function:

$$R(t) = \frac{5\lambda + \mu + \sqrt{\lambda^2 + 10\lambda\mu + \mu^2}}{2\sqrt{\lambda^2 + 10\lambda\mu + \mu^2}} \exp\left(-(1/2)(5\lambda + \mu - \sqrt{\lambda^2 + 10\lambda\mu + \mu^2})t\right)$$

$$- \frac{5\lambda + \mu - \sqrt{\lambda^2 + 10\lambda\mu + \mu^2}}{2\sqrt{\lambda^2 + 10\lambda\mu + \mu^2}} \exp\left(-(1/2)(5\lambda + \mu + \sqrt{\lambda^2 + 10\lambda\mu + \mu^2})t\right)$$

Integrating this function to find the MTTF produces

$$\text{MTTF} = \frac{5\lambda + \mu + \sqrt{\lambda^2 + 10\lambda\mu + \mu^2}}{(5\lambda + \mu)\sqrt{\lambda^2 + 10\lambda\mu + \mu^2} - \lambda^2 - 10\lambda\mu - \mu^2}$$

$$- \frac{5\lambda + \mu - \sqrt{\lambda^2 + 10\lambda\mu + \mu^2}}{(5\lambda + \mu)\sqrt{\lambda^2 + 10\lambda\mu + \mu^2} + \lambda^2 + 10\lambda\mu + \mu^2}$$

Adding together and simplifying gives

$$\text{MTTF} = \frac{5\lambda + \mu}{6\lambda^2}$$

Rearranging this expression yields

$$\text{MTTF} = \frac{5}{6\lambda} + \frac{\mu}{6\lambda^2}$$

Thus, the MTTF of a TMR system with repair is equal to the MTTF of a TMR system without repair *plus* an additional term due to the repair activity.

Consider the effect of redundancy and repair on the reliability of a module with a failure rate of one per 1000 hours ($\lambda = 0.001$) and a repair rate of one per 10 hours ($\mu - 0.1$). Figure 5–29b plots the reliability curves of a nonredundant system, a TMR system without repair, and a TMR system with repair for these parameter values. The MTTF calculations show the following results:

$$\text{Nonredundant MTTF} = \frac{1}{\lambda} = 1000 \text{ hours}$$

$$\text{TMR without repair MTTF} = \frac{5}{6\lambda} = 833 \text{ hours}$$

$$\text{TMR with repair MTTF} = \frac{5}{6\lambda} + \frac{\mu}{6\lambda^2} = 17,5000 \text{ hours}$$

Thus, while redundancy alone reduces the MTTF by about 17 percent, the strategy of on-line repair allows the system MTTF to increase by a factor of 17. This strongly suggests that redundant systems should be designed to allow on-line repair whenever possible.

Time-Varying Failure Rates

If the failure and repair processes vary with time according to the Weibull distribution, a model such as that shown in Figure 5–30 applies. Solving this model for the same parameter values as used earlier in the dual-redundant system model (on page 323), that is, a module MTTF of 100 time-steps and an MTTR of 10 time-steps, generates the family of reliability curves shown in Figure 5–31. Figure 5–32 plots the difference between the reliability of systems with α not equal to one and systems with α equal to one (constant failure rates). It is evident that the patterns in these plots are the same as those that appeared in the dual-redundant system reliability plots in Figures 5–22 and 5–23.

Another comparative measure mentioned previously in this chapter is mission time improvement. Instead of comparing the system reliabilities at fixed intervals, mission time improvement compares the amount of time different systems require to fall to fixed levels of reliability. The calculations are performed by taking the ratio between the mission time of the system under study and the mission time of some baseline system. For our purposes, the baseline system is the nonredundant system with the same parameters as the TMR system under consideration. This is the usual way of using mission time improvement to evaluate different redundant system designs.

The following table lists the mission time improvement factors at several reliability levels:

	Reliability			
α	0.90	0.80	0.70	0.60
0.6	4.50	2.88	3.13	3.62
0.8	3.33	3.14	3.12	3.23
1.0	3.30	2.82	2.74	2.70
1.2	2.93	2.55	2.34	2.27
2.0	1.97	1.73	1.61	1.53

Two patterns are broadly discernible. First, an increasing value for α results in a

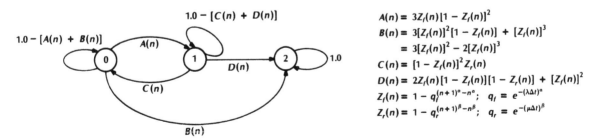

$$A(n) = 3Z_f(n)[1 - Z_f(n)]^2$$
$$B(n) = 3[Z_f(n)]^2[1 - Z_f(n)] + [Z_f(n)]^3$$
$$= 3[Z_f(n)]^2 - 2[Z_f(n)]^3$$
$$C(n) = [1 - Z_r(n)]^2 Z_r(n)$$
$$D(n) = 2Z_r(n)[1 - Z_r(n)][1 - Z_f(n)] + [Z_f(n)]^2$$
$$Z_f(n) = 1 - q_f^{(n+1)^\alpha - n^\alpha}; \quad q_f = e^{-(\lambda \Delta t)^\alpha}$$
$$Z_r(n) = 1 - q_r^{(n+1)^\beta - n^\beta}; \quad q_r = e^{-(\mu \Delta t)^\beta}$$

FIGURE 5–30 *TMR model with time-varying failure and repair rates*

FIGURE 5–31
*Reliabilities of
TMR system with
Weibull failure
processes*

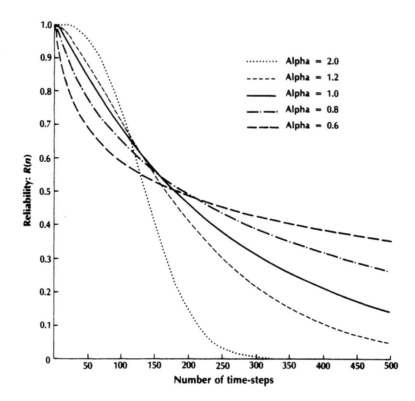

FIGURE 5–31
Reliabilities of TMR system with Weibull failure processes

decreasing value of the mission time improvement. Second, while the mission time improvement values decrease monotonically for α greater than or equal to one, they hit a minimum point and start increasing again for the values of α less than one.

Failure Process Renewals: Monte Carlo Simulation

If the individual failure processes are renewed (reset to time zero) whenever a corresponding repair occurs, then a simulation model like the one developed earlier for a dual-redundant system is needed. Figure 5–33 shows the model for the simple TMR system under discussion. The simulation process is similar to that discussed for the previous model with 1000 runs from each of three pseudo-random number generators for five different values of α. A rough check on the validity of the simulation results is provided by comparing the mission times for several levels of reliability of the analytic solution and the simulation solution for α equal to one. The values should be in close agreement, because the constant failure rate (exponential) process is memoryless, as the following comparison table confirms:

FIGURE 5–32
Reliability differ-
ences for TMR
system

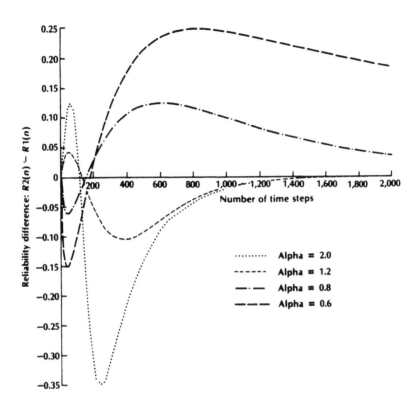

	Mission Time	
Reliability	Analytic Solution	Monte Carlo Solution
0.99	7	7
0.90	34	34
0.80	63	63
0.70	97	94
0.60	136	130
0.50	182	179
0.40	238	234
0.30	310	304
0.20	412	412
0.10	587	581

Figure 5–34 shows the empirical reliability curves for the simulated systems; Figure 5–35 plots the empirical reliability difference curves. The same patterns are evident in these plots as in the earlier dual-redundant system and TMR system reliability and reliability difference plots. The degree of convergence for system reliabilities under the assumption of failure process renewals is even greater for the TMR systems than for the dual-redundant systems.

FIGURE 5–33
TMR model with failure process renewals

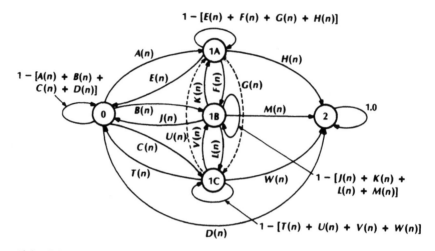

$$A(n) = Z_f(n - N_A)[1 - Z_f(n - N_B)][1 - Z_f(n - N_C)]$$
$$B(n) = [1 - Z_f(n - N_A)]Z_f(n - N_B)[1 - Z_f(n - N_C)]$$
$$C(n) = [1 - Z_f(n - N_A)][1 - Z_f(n - N_B)]Z_f(n - N_C)$$
$$D(n) = Z_f(n - N_A)Z_f(n - N_B)[1 - Z_f(n - N_C)]$$
$$\quad + Z_f(n - N_A)[1 - Z_f(n - N_B)]Z_f(n - N_C) + \cdots$$

$$E(n) = \cdots$$
$$Z_f(n) = q_f^{(n+1)^\alpha - n^\alpha}; \quad q_f = e^{-(\lambda \Delta t)^\alpha}$$
$$Z_r(n) = q_r^{(n+1)^\beta - n^\beta}; \quad q_r = e^{-(\mu \Delta t)^\beta}$$

$N_A =$ Time of last transition from state 1A to state 0

FIGURE 5–34
Reliabilities of simulated TMR system

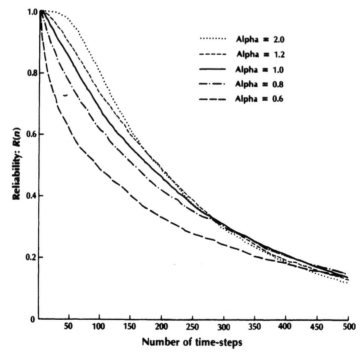

FIGURE 5–35
Reliability differences for simulated TMR system

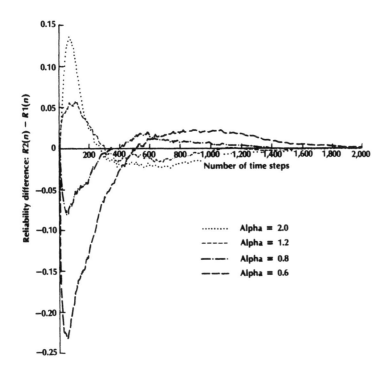

Although Figures 5–23 and 5–26 (the reliability difference plots for the dual-redundant system) show a superficially different pattern from those for the TMR system (Figures 5–32 and 5–35), the changes from the analytical time-varying Markov model to the Monte Carlo simulation models are actually quite similar. In both cases, the magnitudes of deviation for the initial period of overestimation for α less than one (underestimation for α greater than one) increase slightly with the assumption of error-process renewals. After the initial period of error, the magnitudes after the crossover points are much smaller. These crossover points are also delayed for the models assuming error-process renewals, in contrast with the simpler models.

The following mission time improvement factors for TMR systems with failure process renewals are calculated in the same way as those in the previous section:

	Reliability			
α	0.90	0.80	0.70	0.60
0.6	6.00	2.80	2.33	2.52
0.8	3.60	3.33	3.18	3.11
1.0	3.30	2.81	2.66	2.48
1.2	2.81	2.63	2.49	2.53
2.0	2.00	1.87	1.82	1.88

The first trend noted previously, that an increasing value of α results in a decreasing value for the mission time improvement, is not so evident. The second trend is almost reversed: for α greater than one, the mission time improvement hits a minimum point and starts increasing again, whereas for α less than one, the decline in mission time improvement values is almost monotonic.

The deviation of the mission time improvement for $\alpha = 0.8$ compared with $\alpha = 1.0$ is of interest because some data collected on transient errors have yielded experimental values in that range (see Chapter 2 and McConnel, Siewiorek, and Tsao [1979]). The TMR model without failure-process renewal shows a ratio increasing from just over 1.0 to almost 1.4. With failure-process renewals, there is no steady increase in the ratio. The ratio between the mission time improvement for $\alpha = 0.8$ to that for $\alpha = 1.0$ ranges from between 1.1 and 1.2 for the TMR model with failure-process renewals. If the calculations had been made assuming α equal to one in the baseline system, the deviations shown by these ratios would be even greater.

These examples show that even in models of simple structures, serious differences exist between exponential models and models based on Weibull processes with non-constant hazard functions.

AVAILABILITY MODELING TECHNIQUES

In general, modeling the availability of systems with repair requires the use of Markov models. If certain restrictions are made, however, special techniques can be used that are easier to apply. This section presents two such methods. The first permits calculation of the system availability function $A_{sys}(t)$, given the module availability functions $A_i(t)$ for any arbitrary structure, provided that the module availabilities are independent. The second uses queuing theory to obtain the steady-state availability for a structure composed of identical modules with constant failure rates. Both of these restricted models (as well as the general Markov model) assume that redundant structures are designed for on-line repair.

Combinatorial Models

The reliability function $R(t)$ and the availability function $A(t)$ are both probability functions, although they have different asymptotic behavior. Because they are both probabilities, the combinatorial modeling techniques developed earlier in this chapter for system reliability calculations apply equally well to calculating system availability if three basic assumptions are met:

1. The system design is coherent—that a module failure never causes the system to have increased availability.
2. Individual modules are always in one of two states—working or failed.
3. Individual module availabilities must be statistically independent.

For the last condition to hold, there is only one allowable repair strategy: One repairman is called for each failed module, and repair proceeds on failed modules while the remainder of the system continues to function (on-line repair). This also dictates the size of the subdivision into modules that are used in the model. Separate repairmen may be a reasonable assumption for minicomputer-sized modules, but probably not for individual memory or I/O cards, and certainly not for individual memory or logic chips.

To illustrate the application of combinatorial modeling to system availability, consider the Markov model of Figure 5–36. The differential transition rate matrix defined by this model graph is

$$T = \begin{bmatrix} -3\lambda & 3\lambda & 0 & 0 \\ \mu & -2\lambda - \mu & 2\lambda & 0 \\ 0 & 2\mu & -2\mu - \lambda & \lambda \\ 0 & 0 & 3\mu & -3\mu \end{bmatrix}$$

Solving this for an initial state vector of $\vec{P}(0) = [1,0,0,0]$, using the Markov model solution techniques developed earlier, produces the following state probability functions:

$$p_0(t) = \frac{\mu^3 + 3\lambda\mu^2 e^{-(\lambda+\mu)t} + 3\lambda^2\mu e^{-2(\lambda+\mu)t} + \lambda^3 e^{-3(\lambda+\mu)t}}{(\lambda + \mu)^3}$$

$$p_1(t) = \frac{3\lambda\mu^2 + 3\lambda\mu(2\lambda - \mu)e^{-(\lambda+\mu)t} + 3\lambda^2(\lambda - 2\mu)e^{-2(\lambda+\mu)t} - 3\lambda^3 e^{-3(\lambda+\mu)t}}{(\lambda + \mu)^3}$$

$$p_2(t) = \frac{3\lambda^2\mu + 3\lambda^2(\lambda - 2\mu)e^{-(\lambda+\mu)t} - 3\lambda^2(2\lambda - \mu)e^{-2(\lambda+\mu)t} + 3\lambda^3 e^{-3(\lambda+\mu)t}}{(\lambda + \mu)^3}$$

$$p_3(t) = \frac{\lambda^3 - 3\lambda^3 e^{-(\lambda+\mu)t} + 3\lambda^3 e^{-2(\lambda+\mu)t} - \lambda^3 e^{-3(\lambda+\mu)t}}{(\lambda + \mu)^3}$$

The Markov model can be interpreted in any of three ways. First, it may represent a system that requires all three modules in order to work properly. For this case, the availability function is

$$A(t) = p_0(t)$$

The alternative way to derive this function (derived earlier in Eq. 27 as the solution for the two-state Markov model with initial state vector $\vec{P}(0) = [1,0]$) is to consider the system as a series connection of three independent identical modules, each with availability:

$$A_m(t) = \frac{\mu}{\lambda + \mu} + \frac{\lambda}{\lambda + \mu}e^{-(\lambda+\mu)t}$$

FIGURE 5–36
Markov model of system with three modules

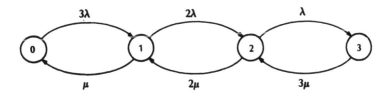

The equation for series connection of the availability block diagram produces

$$A_{sys}(t) = \prod_{i=1}^{3} A_i(t) = [A_m(t)]^3$$

$$= \left(\frac{\mu + \lambda e^{-(\lambda+\mu)t}}{\lambda + \mu}\right)^3$$

$$= \frac{\mu^3 + 3\lambda\mu^2 e^{-(\lambda+\mu)t} + 3\lambda^2\mu e^{-2(\lambda+\mu)t} + \lambda^3 e^{-3(\lambda+\mu)t}}{(\lambda + \mu)^3}$$

which is the same result as obtained by solving the Markov model.

The second interpretation of the Markov model is that it represents a simple TMR system such as the one modeled for reliability earlier (see Figure 5–29a). For the two-of-three model, the availability defined by the Markov model solution is

$$A(t) = p_0(t) + p_1(t)$$

The combinatorial solution proceeds as follows:

$$A_{sys}(t) = \sum_{i=0}^{1} \binom{3}{i} [A_m(t)]^{3-i}[1 - A_m(t)]^i$$

$$= \binom{3}{0} [A_m(t)]^3 + \binom{3}{1}[A_m(t)]^2[1 - A_m(t)]$$

$$= 3[A_m(t)]^2 - 2[A_m(t)]^3$$

$$= \frac{3(\mu + \lambda e^{-(\lambda+\mu)t})^2}{(\lambda + \mu)^2} - \frac{2(\mu + \lambda e^{-(\lambda+\mu)t})^3}{(\lambda + \mu)^3}$$

$$= \frac{3(\lambda + \mu)(\mu + \lambda e^{-(\lambda+\mu)t})^2 - 2(\mu + \lambda e^{-(\lambda+\mu)t})^3}{(\lambda + \mu)^3}$$

$$= \frac{\mu^3 + 3\lambda\mu^2 + 6\lambda^2\mu e^{-(\lambda+\mu)t} + 3\lambda^2(\lambda - \mu)e^{-2(\lambda+\mu)t} - 2\lambda^3 e^{-3(\lambda+\mu)t}}{(\lambda + \mu)^3}$$

Careful examination shows that this combinatorial solution for $A_{sys}(t)$ is indeed equal to that derived from the Markov model.

The remaining system modeled by Figure 5–36 is a module with two spares, which is otherwise expressed as a parallel structure in the availability block diagram. The availability function derived from the Markov model is

$$A(t) = p_0(t) + p_1(t) + p_2(t) = 1 - p_3(t)$$

The solution as a parallel system with three modules is as follows:

$$A_{sys}(t) = 1 - \prod_{i=1}^{3} [1 - A_i(t)] = 1 - [1 - A_m(t)]^3 = 1 - \left(\frac{\lambda}{\lambda + \mu} - \frac{\lambda}{\lambda + \mu} e^{-(\lambda+\mu)t}\right)^3$$

$$= 1 - \frac{\lambda^3 - 3\lambda^3 e^{-(\lambda+\mu)t} + 3\lambda^3 e^{-2(\lambda+\mu)t} - \lambda^3 e^{-3(\lambda+\mu)t}}{(\lambda + \mu)^3}$$

Again, the results obtained from the combinatorial and Markov model solutions match.

The combinatorial *M-of-N* formula assumes that all modules have identical availability. This is *not* necessary for the series/parallel approach. Also, the methods discussed obviously apply equally to calculating steady-state availability, which is the next topic of discussion.

Queuing Models

Several of the Markov models in Figure 5–37 have already been discussed in this chapter. All are members of an important class of Markov process models known as *birth-and-death processes*. The defining characteristics of birth-and-death processes are

1. State transitions occur only between "adjacent" states; that is, for state N (not an end state), transitions occur only to state $N - 1$ or $N + 1$.
2. Both "birth" transitions (N to $N + 1$) and "death" transitions (N to $N - 1$) follow a Poisson process.
3. The probability of both a "birth" and a "death" occurring simultaneously is negligible.

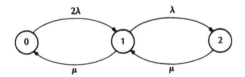

a. Two modules, one repairperson

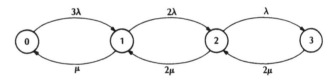

d. Three modules, two repairpersons

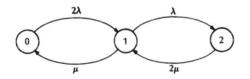

b. Two modules, two repairpersons

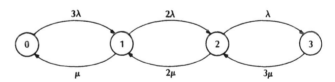

e. Three modules, three repairpersons

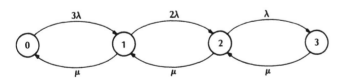

c. Three modules, one repairperson

FIGURE 5–37 *Markov models for two and three module systems for different numbers of field service engineers*

Figure 5–38a shows the general infinite birth-and-death process, and Figure 5–38b the general finite birth-and-death process.

A very fruitful application of birth-and-death processes has been the study of waiting-line behavior, or queuing theory. Queues, or waiting lines, are common in daily life: the checkout line at the grocery store, the line of customers waiting to be seated at a restaurant, the innumerable lines of students at college registration. The queue involved here consists of a finite population of modules that fail randomly while entering a waiting line to be repaired by a finite (possibly smaller) number of repair personnel. This queuing model is known as the machine-repair, multiple-repair per-sonnel model and is named the M/M/c/K/K Queuing System. This cryptic nomenclature is decoded as follows:

1. The first letter describes the interarrival time distribution for failures ("birth"). The "M" (which stands for Markov, or the memoryless property of the exponential distribution) means that failures follow an exponential distribution.
2. The second letter gives the distribution for service (repair) time, again exponential for this model.
3. The third term is the maximum number of repair personnel.
4. The fourth term is the maximum number of failed modules that can be serviced, either immediately or after waiting for the next available repair person.
5. The last term (which is always equal to the fourth term in this model) is the population size, that is, the total number of modules in the system.

Figure 5–39 shows the general form of the Markov model that fits the M/M/c/K/K queuing system. All modules are assumed to have the same (constant) failure rate λ, and all repair personnel work at the same (constant) rate μ.

For the model shown in Figure 5–39, the limiting (steady-state) state probabilities p_n are defined by the following recurrence equation:

$$p_n = \left(\frac{\lambda_n}{\mu_n}\right) p_{n-1} \qquad n = 1, 2, 3, \ldots, K \tag{39}$$

FIGURE 5–38
Birth-and-death process Markov models

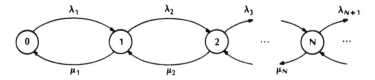

a. Infinite population model

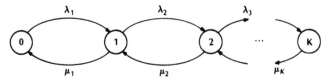

b. Finite population model

with

$$p_0 = 1 - \sum_{n=1}^{K} p_n$$

The specific adaptation of Eq. 39 to the M/M/c/K/K queue of Figure 5–39 is

$$p_n = \left(\frac{K - n + 1}{n}\right)\left(\frac{\lambda}{\mu}\right) p_{n-1} \qquad n = 1, 2, 3, \ldots, c$$

$$p_n = \left(\frac{K - n + 1}{c}\right)\left(\frac{\lambda}{\mu}\right) p_{n-1} \qquad n = c + 1, \ldots, K$$

(40)

Solving these in terms of p_0 yields

$$p_n = \binom{K}{n}\left(\frac{\lambda}{\mu}\right)^n p_0 \qquad n = 1, 2, \ldots, c$$

$$p_n = \frac{n!}{c! c^{n-c}} \binom{K}{n}\left(\frac{\lambda}{\mu}\right)^n p_0 \qquad n = c + 1, \ldots, K$$

(41)

and

$$p_0 = 1 - \left[\sum_{n=1}^{c} \binom{K}{n}\left(\frac{\lambda}{\mu}\right)^n p_0 + \sum_{n=c+1}^{K} \frac{n!}{c! c^{n-c}} \binom{K}{n}\left(\frac{\lambda}{\mu}\right)^n p_0\right]$$

(42)

$$p_0 = \frac{1}{\displaystyle\sum_{n=0}^{c} \binom{K}{n}\left(\frac{\lambda}{\mu}\right)^n + \sum_{n=c+1}^{K} \frac{n!}{c! c^{n-c}} \binom{K}{n}\left(\frac{\lambda}{\mu}\right)^n}$$

The limiting state probabilities p_n ($n = 0, 1, \ldots, K$) are used to calculate the steady-state availability A_{sys}. For an M-of-N system structure, the equation for A_{sys} is

$$A_{sys} = \sum_{n=0}^{N-M} p_n = 1 - \sum_{n=N-M+1}^{N} p_n$$

(43)

The first model of Figure 5–37 (two modules, one repair person) was solved in the section on time-invariant Markov models. Applying Eq. 42 to this M/M/1/2/2 queue gives

$$p_0 = \frac{1}{1 + \binom{2}{1}\left(\frac{\lambda}{\mu}\right) + \frac{2!}{1!}\binom{2}{2}\left(\frac{\lambda}{\mu}\right)^2} = \frac{\mu^2}{\mu^2 + 2\lambda\mu + 2\lambda^2}$$

FIGURE 5–39
*Model for
M/M/c/K/K queuing
system*

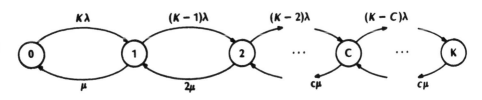

Using Eq. 40 yields

$$p_1 = 2\left(\frac{\lambda}{\mu}\right)p_0 = \frac{2\lambda\mu}{\mu^2 + 2\lambda\mu + 2\lambda^2}$$

$$p_2 = \left(\frac{\lambda}{\mu}\right)p_1 = \frac{2\lambda^2}{\mu^2 + 2\lambda\mu + 2\lambda^2}$$

If Figure 5–37 represents a dual-redundant system, then

$$A_{sys} = p_0 + p_1$$

$$A_{sys} = \frac{\mu^2 + 2\lambda\mu}{\mu^2 + 2\lambda\mu + 2\lambda^2}$$

which is the result obtained in the section on time-invariant Markov models, Eq. 32.

If the repair strategy is changed to call a second repair person when a second module fails, the model of Figure 5–37b results, a M/M/2/2/2 queue. For this model,

$$p_0 = \frac{1}{1 + \binom{2}{1}\left(\frac{\lambda}{\mu}\right) + \binom{2}{2}\left(\frac{\lambda}{\mu}\right)^2} = \frac{\mu^2}{\mu^2 + 2\lambda\mu + \lambda^2}$$

$$p_1 = 2\left(\frac{\lambda}{\mu}\right)p_0 = \frac{2\lambda\mu}{\mu^2 + 2\lambda\mu + \lambda^2}$$

$$p_2 = \frac{1}{2}\left(\frac{\lambda}{\mu}\right)p_1 = \frac{\lambda^2}{\mu^2 + 2\lambda\mu + \lambda^2}$$

The system availability for a dual-redundant structure now becomes

$$A_{sys} = \frac{\mu^2 + 2\lambda\mu}{\mu^2 + 2\lambda\mu + \lambda^2}$$

This new availability is greater than that of the previous model because of the smaller λ^2 term in the denominator; that is, access to more repair persons improves the availability.

Figure 5–37d shows an example of an M/M/2/3/3 queue where the number of repair persons is greater than one but less than the number of modules.

$$p_0 = \frac{1}{1 + \binom{3}{1}\left(\frac{\lambda}{\mu}\right) + \binom{3}{2}\left(\frac{\lambda}{\mu}\right)^2 + \frac{3!}{2!2}\binom{3}{3}\left(\frac{\lambda}{\mu}\right)^3} = \frac{\mu^3}{\mu^3 + 3\lambda\mu^2 + 3\lambda^2\mu + 1.5\,\lambda^3}$$

$$p_1 = 3\left(\frac{\lambda}{\mu}\right)p_0 = \frac{3\lambda\mu^2}{\mu^3 + 3\lambda\mu^2 + 3\lambda^2\mu + 1.5\lambda^3}$$

$$p_2 = \left(\frac{\lambda}{\mu}\right)p_1 = \frac{3\lambda^2\mu}{\mu^3 + 3\lambda\mu^2 + 3\lambda^2\mu + 1.5\lambda^3}$$

$$p_3 = \frac{1}{2}\left(\frac{\lambda}{\mu}\right)p_2 = \frac{1.5\,\lambda^3}{\mu^3 + 3\lambda\mu^2 + 3\lambda^2\mu + 1.5\lambda^3}$$

Using this to model a system with two spares (one-of-three), the steady-state system availability is

$$A_{sys} = p_0 + p_1 + p_2$$

$$A_{sys} = \frac{\mu^3 + 3\lambda\mu^2 + 3\lambda^2\mu}{\mu^3 + 3\lambda\mu^2 + 3\lambda^2\mu + 1.5\,\lambda^3}$$

Considering the system modeled by Figure 5–37e to be a TMR structure, the resulting steady-state availability should be the same as the constant terms in the example solved using combinatorial techniques. For the M/M/3/3/3 queue,

$$p_0 = \frac{1}{1 + \binom{3}{1}\left(\frac{\lambda}{\mu}\right) + \binom{3}{2}\left(\frac{\lambda}{\mu}\right)^2 + \binom{3}{3}\left(\frac{\lambda}{\mu}\right)^3} = \frac{\mu^3}{\mu^3 + 3\lambda\mu^2 + 3\lambda^2\mu + \lambda^3}$$

$$p_1 = 3\left(\frac{\lambda}{\mu}\right) p_0 = \frac{3\lambda\mu^2}{\mu^3 + 3\lambda\mu^2 + 3\lambda^2\mu + \lambda^3}$$

$$p_2 = \left(\frac{\lambda}{\mu}\right) p_1 = \frac{3\lambda^2\mu}{\mu^3 + 3\lambda\mu^2 + 3\lambda^2\mu + \lambda^3}$$

$$p_3 = \frac{1}{3}\left(\frac{\lambda}{\mu}\right) p_2 = \frac{\lambda^3}{\mu^3 + 3\lambda\mu^2 + 3\lambda^2\mu + \lambda^3}$$

$$A_{sys} = p_0 + p_1 = \frac{\mu^3 + 3\lambda\mu^2}{\mu^3 + 3\lambda\mu^2 + 3\lambda^2\mu + \lambda^3} = \frac{\mu^3 + 3\lambda\mu^2}{(\mu + \lambda)^3}$$

This result is indeed the constant term from the solution derived earlier.

SOFTWARE ASSISTANCE FOR MODELING TECHNIQUES

As reliability and availability modeling techniques gained wider acceptance, software packages were developed to simplify the analysis of complex systems. These packages support the two major modeling techniques: combinatorial and Markov. Since the underlying mathematics is the same, these packages can be used for both reliability and availability modeling with a suitable change in assumptions.

Software for Combinatorial Models

Existing algorithms and programs for calculating combinatorial models may be roughly cast into one of two classes based on the form of the input data and type of problem being considered. The first class of algorithms and programs accepts the graph of the physical (or logical) interconnections of system components and calculates fairly simple probabilistic measures for the system. Typically, the system is a computer communication network, and the vertices of the interconnection graph denote the computers while the arcs denote the communication links. Either arcs or vertices or both are assumed to fail stochastically. Usually all failing elements are considered homogeneous, with identical probabilities of failure.

Two common probabilistic measures computed for such a system are

The probability that some specific pair of vertices will have at least one communication path between them at all times

The probability that the operative arcs always contain a spanning of the network

Frank and Frisch [1970] and Wilkov [1972] present good tutorial papers on the subject. These types of network reliability calculation problems have been shown to be NP-hard in the case of general networks [Rosenthal, 1977; Ball, 1980].

The second class of algorithms and programs accepts as input some intermediate representation that encodes the behavior of the system under consideration. This representation, from which the system reliability or availability is computed, is expected to be derived by human computation from the system interconnection structure and functionality requirements before being input to the program. Reliability graphs and fault trees are the most commonly used intermediate representations. The system interconnection graph may or may not be isomorphic to the derived intermediate representation. Fault trees are used as aids in failure modes effects and criticality analysis (FMECA). Reliability graphs are more often used to compute numerical values of reliability (also termed *network reliability analysis* in the literature).

Shooman [1970] shows that these two intermediate representations are equivalent. The kinds of problems addressed here are far more general than the simple networks of the first class. Generalization is made possible by the fact that reliability graphs and fault trees are hand-derived from a knowledge of the system. Lapp and Powers [1977] describe work toward automating synthesis of fault trees for chemical engineering systems. The literature on the analysis of reliability graphs and, in particular, fault trees, is vast; the references here serve as a bare introduction [Misra, 1970; Gandhi, Knove, and Henley, 1972; Satyanarayana and Prabhaker, 1978; Aggarwal and Rai, 1978; Bennetts, 1975].

CARE II. CARE II (Computer-Aided Reliability Estimation II), developed at the Raytheon Company under contract to NASA [Raytheon, 1974, 1976], implements a very general combinatorial model for systems consisting of one or more subsystems or stages. Each stage contains a number of identical modules configured as a set of active devices with spares. CARE II handles hard and transient faults, reconfiguration with degraded performance, and coverage. Two operating modes are allowed for each stage: fully operational and degraded but partially operational. The coverage model depends on three conditional probabilities:

1. D is the probability that a fault is detected, given that one occurs.
2. I is the probability that a fault is correctly isolated, given that it is detected.
3. R is the probability that the system recovers from a fault, given that it was properly isolated and that sufficient spares still exist.

The inputs to CARE II are the reliability parameters for the modules within each stage and a description of the coverage detection/isolation/recovery mechanisms. The output includes coverage specification and contributions, system reliability and unreliability (both tables and plots), MTTF, mission time, and several other measures. CARE II is a very versatile program, limited largely by its combinatorial approach, which precludes repair.

ADVISER. Work by Kini [1981] advanced the state of the art with respect to computation of computer system reliability or availability at the processor-memory-switch (PMS) [Bell and Newell, 1971] level of design. Kini and Siewiorek [1982] describe a program named ADVISER (ADVanced Interactive Symbolic Evaluator of Reliability), which computes the symbolic system reliability expression given

> The interconnection graph (PMS diagram) of the system
> The reliability or availability of each *class* of identical system components
> A simple statement of system functionality requirements

The program assumes that the arbitrary system PMS diagram is represented as a nondirected graph whose vertices are labeled with the corresponding system component names. However, the organization of the program does not preclude a directed graph model. Component behavior is lumped into the vertices, which are subject to stochastic failures, whereas the edges of the graph are perfect and represent only the topology of the interconnection. Hence, the failure of a component implies the removal from the graph of the corresponding vertex and all arcs incident on it. Components are assumed to be binary-state entities. The communication axiom, fundamental to the calculation paradigm of ADVISER, states roughly that functioning components belonging to the component classes distinguished by the statement of functionality requirements must at all times be able to communicate in order for the system to be functional. Only hard-failure reliability is computed, and the effects of coverage are not modeled.

An example illustrates the operation of ADVISER. Figure 5–40 shows a simple dual-processor system with a duplicated fast interprocessor bus that also allows access to shared dual-ported memories. Each processor also has its own I/O bus with a disk and local memory. The Boolean requirements expression in the figure distinguishes four of the component classes (processor, local memory, disk, and shared memory) and states that *at least* one component from each of the four classes must be functioning at all times if the system is to be functional. A requirements expression may also contain a disjunction, such as 1 of P and 1 of MD and (1 of MS or 1 of ML). During the course of the computation, ADVISER takes into account all component classes not mentioned in the requirements expression, whose members must be functional in the various system success states.

ADVISER begins its analysis by detecting symmetries in the interconnection graph. Two subgraphs will be symmetric if they are isomorphic, and corresponding vertices of the subgraphs represent components drawn from the same class of identical system components. Any symmetries found will enable the calculations for one member of a group of symmetric subgraphs to be used as templates for the results concerning the other members of the group. The graph is then segmented into subgraphs for which special calculation techniques are known. When these known subgraphs are removed

FIGURE 5–40
Sample PMS diagram and requirements expression input to ADVISER

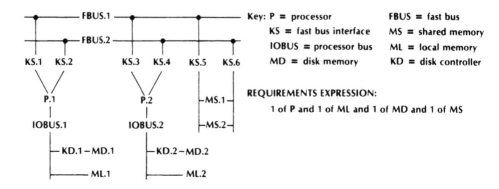

Key: P = processor   FBUS = fast bus
KS = fast bus interface   MS = shared memory
IOBUS = processor bus   ML = local memory
MD = disk memory   KD = disk controller

REQUIREMENTS EXPRESSION:
1 of P and 1 of ML and 1 of MD and 1 of MS

from the original interconnection graph, the remaining vertices and edges form a subgraph, called the *kernel,* for which special techniques are not known, and which is therefore treated with simple pathfinding algorithms to compute reliability or availability.

In our example, the atomic requirement, 1 of ML, can be satisfied by the functioning either of ML.1 in one subgraph or of ML.2 in the other, but no components of class ML are available in the kernel. In the case that ML.1 is functioning, then, to be useful, it must be available to the rest of the system in the other segments. This implies that IOBUS.1 and P.1 must be functional. The symbolic probability expression for this is $R_{P.1}R_{IPBUS.1}R_{ML.1}$. The probability expression in the case of ML.2 functioning in the other (symmetric) subgraph is identical in form. Each satisfaction of an atomic requirement produces such a symbolic probability expression. The atomic requirements—1 of P, 1 of ML, and 1 of MD—are each satisfied by two of the three segments of the graph. The atomic requirement, 1 of MS, is satisfied only by the kernel. Thus, there is a total of eight cases in which the system is functional.

ADVISER contains algorithms that accept symbolic probabilities of events, such as are generated for the preceding cases, and produces other symbolic probabilities for the conjunction or disjunction of those events. By using these algorithms, it is possible to assemble the probabilities of the analyzed functional cases to obtain the reliability of the system. The symbolic probabilities and the eventual symbolic system-reliability function are maintained in sum-of-products canonical form within ADVISER.

The output of ADVISER consists of the text of a FORTRAN function that computes the symbolic reliability function assembled by the program. Figure 5–41 shows the FORTRAN output from ADVISER for the PMS of Figure 5–40. The block of comments preceding the function definition of RSYS (the name is user-assignable) is simply a reproduction of the salient input data for the problem. The type definitions identify the classes of identical components in the PMS structure and give the parameters for the reliability of a representative member of each class. Components may be described as having exponential, Weibull, constant, and external reliability functions. In the last case, ADVISER inserts a user-supplied function that computes the component reliability. Failure rates (or the scale parameter, in the Weibull case) are under the LAMBDA column and are in units of per-million-hours. The numbers in this example were arbitrarily chosen.

The definition of the function itself initializes variables to the value of component class probabilities at the time, which is given as the function parameter. Some expressions are computed and assigned to temporary variables. These expressions represent the templates for the various symbolic probabilities derived for symmetric subgraphs of the interconnection graph. Finally, the expression that gives the system reliability is computed and the resultant floating-point number is returned as the value of the function. Continuation lines are preceded by a dollar-sign in column six, and the variable MODREL is especially useful when printing of the reliability function requires more continuation lines than are allowed by the FORTRAN compiler. As evident from Figure 5–41, combinatorial equations quickly explode in complexity, thus necessitating software assisted computation. ADVISER can also calculate availability if the component function describes the component's availability.

Software for Markov Models

As with combinatorial modeling, programs have been written using Markov modeling to assist in evaluating general classes of system structures. Six of these programs deserve special mention. A more comprehensive survey of modeling software can be found in Johnson and Malek [1989].

ARIES. ARIES (Automated Reliability Interactive Estimation System), developed at UCLA by Ng and Avizienis [1980], implements a general time-invariant Markov model for systems similar to those covered by CARE II. The structures handled consist of a series of one or more independent subsystems or stages, each containing a number of identical modules that either are active or serve as spares. Systems can be reconfigured by adding, deleting, or replacing stages, or by modifying the values of some parameters. The inputs to ARIES include the following:

The initial numbers of active and spare modules
The number of repair facilities for each stage
The failure rates for active and spare modules and the repair rates for the repair facilities
The coverage factors for recovery from failed spares
The number and sequence for allowed degradations and the coverage factors for degraded configurations

The program outputs several measures, including MTTF, mission time, and reliability plots or tables. ARIES is very general in the type of redundant structures it can model, and is limited primarily by the assumption of distinct eigenvalues for the Markov differential transition matrix.

CARE III. CARE III (Computer-Aided Reliability Estimation III), developed at Raytheon [Stiffler, Bryant, and Guccione, 1979], implements a time-varying Markov model for

FIGURE 5–41

*FORTRAN output
from ADVISER*

```
C-------------------------------------------------------------------------
C ** FORTRAN Module for Reliability Function evaluation
C **       produced by ADVISER on Sunday, 18 Jan 81 at 17:32:37 for [4,1367]
C-------------------------------------------------------------------------
C ** Task Title: EXPMS.PMS -- An example PMS to demonstrate ADVISER.
C
C ** Requirements on the Structure were:
C
C      (1-OF-P AND 1-OF-ML AND 1-OF-MS AND 1-OF-MD)
C
C ** Component-Type definitions for this task:
C
C    INDEX  TYPENAME    PRINTNAME    REL.FN.    PARAMS
C    -----  --------    ---------    -------    ------
C      0    FASTBUS     FBUS         Expon.     Lambda= .00010000
C      1    K.FBUS      KS           Expon.     Lambda=6.00000000
C      2    M.SHARED    MS           Expon.     Lambda=10.00000000
C      3    M.LOCAL     ML           Expon.     Lambda=10.00000000
C      4    CPU         P            Weibull    Lambda=8.00000000
C                                               Alpha= .95000001
C      5    IOBUS       IOBUS        Expon.     Lambda= .00010000
C      6    DISK        MD           Expon.     Lambda=10.00000000
C      7    K.DISK      KD           Expon.     Lambda=6.00000000
C
C ** PMS Structure Definitions for this task:
C
C    INDEX  NAME       TYPE         NNEIG      NEIGHBORS
C    -----  ----       ----         -----      ---------
C      0    FBUS.1     FASTBUS        3        (KS.1, KS.3, KS.5)
C      1    FBUS.2     FASTBUS        3        (KS.2, KS.4, KS.6)
C      2    KS.1       K.FBUS         2        (FBUS.1, P.1)
C      3    KS.2       K.FBUS         2        (FBUS.2, P.1)
C      4    KS.3       K.FBUS         2        (FBUS.1, P.2)
C      5    KS.4       K.FBUS         2        (FBUS.2, P.2)
C      6    KS.5       K.FBUS         3        (FBUS.1, MS.1, MS.2)
C      7    KS.6       K.FBUS         3        (FBUS.2, MS.1, MS.2)
C      8    P.1        CPU            3        (KS.1, KS.2, IOBUS.1)
C      9    P.2        CPU            3        (KS.3, KS.4, IOBUS.2)
C     10    IOBUS.1    IOBUS          3        (P.1, KD.1, ML.1)
C     11    IOBUS.2    IOBUS          3        (P.2, KD.2, ML.2)
C     12    ML.1       M.LOCAL        1        (IOBUS.1)
C     13    ML.2       M.LOCAL        1        (IOBUS.2)
C     14    KD.1       K.DISK         2        (MD.1, IOBUS.1)
C     15    KD.2       K.DISK         2        (MD.2, IOBUS.2)
C     16    MD.1       DISK           1        (KD.1)
C     17    MD.2       DISK           1        (KD.2)
C     18    MS.1       M.SHARED       2        (KS.5, KS.6)
C     19    MS.2       M.SHARED       2        (KS.5, KS.6)
C
C-------------------------------------------------------------------------
C
C *** Begin Reliability Function evaluation code;
      REAL FUNCTION RSYS (T);
      IMPLICIT REAL (A-Z)

      WEIBUL(LAMBDA,ALPHA,TIME)=EXP(-(LAMBDA*1E-6*TIME)**ALPHA)

      FBUS = EXP(-0.000100 * 1E-6 * T)
      KS = EXP(-6.000000 * 1E-6 * T)
      MS = EXP(-10.000000 * 1E-6 * T)
      ML = EXP(-10.000000 * 1E-6 * T)
      P = WEIBUL( 8.000000 , 0.950000 , T )
      IOBUS = EXP(-0.000100 * 1E-6 * T)
      MD = EXP(-10.000000 * 1E-6 * T)
      KD = EXP(-6.000000 * 1E-6 * T)
```

FIGURE 5–41
(continued)

```
C ** End of expressions for calculating individual reliabilities;
    XXX0 = ML * P * IOBUS
    XXX2 = P * IOBUS * MD * KD
    XXX4 = ML * P * IOBUS * MD * KD
C ** End of template evaluating expressions;

    MODREL = 0

    MODREL = 8.0 * FBUS * KS**2 * MS * XXX4  +  8.0 * FBUS * KS**3
$ * MS * XXX0 * XXX2  -  4.0 * FBUS * KS**2 * MS**2 * XXX4  -
$8.0 * FBUS * KS**3 * MS * XXX0 * XXX4  -  8.0 * FBUS * KS**3 *
$MS * XXX4 * XXX2  +  4.0 * FBUS * KS**3 * MS * XXX4**2  -  4.0
$ * FBUS * KS**3 * MS**2 * XXX0 * XXX2  +  4.0 * FBUS * KS**3 *
$MS**2 * XXX0 * XXX4 + 4.0 * FBUS * KS**3 * MS**2 * XXX4 * XXX2
$  -  2.0 * FBUS * KS**3 * MS**2 * XXX4**2  -  4.0 * FBUS**2 *
$KS**4 * MS * XXX4  -  4.0 * FBUS**2 * KS**4 * MS * XXX4**2  +
$2.0 * FBUS**2 * KS**4 * MS**2 * XXX4  -  4.0 * FBUS**2 * KS**6
$ * MS * XXX0 * XXX2  +  2.0 * FBUS**2 * KS**4 * MS**2 * XXX4**2
$  +  8.0 * FBUS**2 * KS**5 * MS * XXX4**2  +  4.0 * FBUS**2 *
$KS**6 * MS * XXX0 * XXX4  +  4.0 * FBUS**2 * KS**6 * MS * XXX4
$ * XXX2  -  6.0 * FBUS**2 * KS**6 * MS * XXX4**2  +  2.0 * FBUS
$**2 * KS**6 * MS**2 * XXX0 * XXX2  -  2.0 * FBUS**2 * KS**6 *
$MS**2 * XXX0 * XXX4  -  2.0 * FBUS**2 * KS**6 * MS**2 * XXX4 *
$XXX2  +  3.0 * FBUS**2 * KS**6 * MS**2 * XXX4**2  -  4.0 * FBUS
$**2 * KS**5 * MS**2 * XXX4**2
C **  End of System Reliability computation;


    RSYS = MODREL
    RETURN
    END
```

ultrareliable redundant systems. The system structures handled by CARE III are like those handled by CARE II and ARIES. Two new assumptions are made; one is more restrictive than ARIES, and one is more general. The first assumption is that the user is interested only in extremely reliable (system failure rates less than 10^{-10} per hour) systems with short mission times (no longer than 10 hours) and no repair during missions. Typical target systems are flight-critical avionics computers for future aircraft. The second, more general assumption is that failures follow a Weibull distribution. CARE III handles not only hard failures but also intermittent and transient faults. It also implements an extensive coverage model based on that of CARE II. The inputs to CARE III include the module-failure parameters (both α and λ for the Weibull function) for each stage and the coverage parameters. The output includes both tables and plots of the system reliability and unreliability. The generality of CARE III is limited by the assumption of both extremely high mission reliability and no repair during a mission.

SAVE. SAVE (System AVailability Estimator), developed by IBM [Goyal et al., 1986], uses analytical and simulation techniques to solve time-invariant Markov models for systems with and without repair. Steady-state availability is given in analytical form derived from solving the set of simultaneous linear equations derived from the Markov model. Sparse matrix techniques are used to solve Markov models containing tens of thousands of states. The Markov model can also be solved using Monte Carlo simulation. The user specifies failure and repair rates, the Markov chain (described in numerical or symbolic format), and the system operational states using assertions, reliability block diagrams, or fault trees. SAVE is limited to constant failure and repair rates and systems exhibiting only permanent failures.

HARP. HARP (Hybrid Automated Reliability Predictor) was developed concurrently with SAVE with Trivedi serving as a bridge between the projects [Geist and Trivedi, 1983]. It uses analytical and simulation techniques to model repairable and nonrepairable systems subject to permanent and transient faults. The fault/error handling model can be expressed as a CARE III, ARIES, or an extended stochastic petri net, among others. The fault occurrence and repair model is a Markov model with exponential, Weibull, or general distributions for transition rates [Bavuso et al., 1987].

SHARPE. SHARPE employs analytical techniques to solve systems with and without repair [Sahner and Trivedi, 1987]. SHARPE utilizes a hierarchical model to reduce the state space explosion, and it provides reliability and availability in symbolic form. It can solve series-parallel reliability block diagrams, fault trees, cyclic and acyclic Markov chains, and acyclic semi-Markov chains. Solutions for models at one level can be used as inputs to a higher level. Models are of the form of a polynomial and the variable t where each term in the polynomial is multiplied by e^{xt}.

SURE. SURE (Semi-Markov Unreliability Range Evaluator), a reliability model generator that generates the reliability model from a functional and structural description, has been developed [McCann and Palumbo, 1988; Butler, 1986; Butler and White, 1988]. It produces upper and lower bounds on the probability of entering a trapping state in a semi-Markov model as a function of the means and variances of the transitions. The bounds are generated in algebraic form. SURE assumes that permanent failures are modeled by a slowly varying exponential transition, while recovery processes are modeled by fast general transitions.

APPLICATIONS OF MODELING TECHNIQUES TO SYSTEMS DESIGNS

The previous portions of this chapter have provided a taxonomy of modeling techniques. The purpose of this section is to illustrate how these techniques can be used to evaluate design trade-offs through the use of four examples.

The first example is the use of error-correcting codes to enhance the reliability of memory. The example demonstrates how the initial application of a redundancy technique produces the largest improvement in reliability. However, the application of redundancy to one portion of the system may significantly change the distribution of unreliability. In particular, the memory example demonstrates how a portion of the system that formerly had only a small contribution to unreliability may become the dominant contributor.

While redundancy techniques were originally conceived for improving reliability during operational life, they have also been employed to tolerate defects during the manufacturing stage. The second example illustrates how spare redundancy can be used to tolerate defects in semiconductor chip manufacturing. The example demonstrates how the same combinatorial modeling techniques used to model memories during the operational stage can be used to model random logic chips during the manufacturing stage.

With attention focused on enhancing reliability, it is easy to lose sight of the impact that redundancy techniques and failures have on system performance. The third example models the performance of a redundant memory system when failures are present. The twin goals of reliability and performance are central to contemporary systems design.

The fourth example presents a methodology of iteratively improving a system design until the reliability goals are met. A single-board computer and a workstation illustrate how the techniques presented in Chapter 3 can be combined. These examples also demonstrate how reliability modeling techniques can be utilized to evaluate a complex system.

The examples illustrate a methodology for modeling a complex system. First the failure modes and their probabilities have to be identified. The failure modes could be from any source including operational life failures and manufacturing defects. The most likely failure modes are modeled with respect to their impact on the redundancy technique. Finally, the model is used to systematically explore the design trade-off space defined by the model and expected parameter values.

Redundancy to Enhance Memory Reliability*

Current digital systems design is dominated by use of memory chips in the form of main memories, register files, caches, and microstores. Thus, improvement in memory reliability will greatly affect overall system reliability.

The first step in reliability design is to decide what failure modes will be tolerated. Determination of the relative frequency of failure modes is best made from analyzing field failure data. However, field failure data may take years to collect, and its applicability to the current design situation may be questionable. Nevertheless, the failure mode data provides guidance. Usually two reliability models are derived: one for the expected failure modes and a second for the worst case failure modes. A brief survey of memory chip failure modes will illustrate how field data can be used to select the appropriate level of modeling.

Memory-Chip Failure Modes. There are few data on semiconductor memory-chip failure modes during operating life. Most semiconductor manufacturers are more interested in the physical failure mechanisms than in the functional characteristics of a failure. What data are available come mostly from screening, burn-in, and, to a lesser extent, high-temperature accelerated-life tests [Texas Instruments, n.d.; Pascoe, 1975; Rickers, 1975–76; Gear, 1976]. Not surprisingly, the data show that memory-chip failure modes are dependent on technology, process, and device design and thus may vary widely. Failure mode distributions also change with time for a given device as the fabrication

---

* This section is adapted from Elkind and Siewiorek [1978]. Also available in Elkind and Siewiorek [1980].

process matures.* Nevertheless, there is good evidence that the whole-chip failure mode (complete inability to store and/or retrieve data) is not the dominant failure mode for most chips. Rather, single-bit, row, and column failure modes seem to be the effect of the majority of chip failures. This fact motivates the formulation of the following error-correcting-code (ECC) memory models.

Error-Correcting Memory Model Parameters. The models presented in this section cover any single-error correction scheme for any size memory and are developed in such a way that the reliability of all the control, correction, and interface circuitry for the memory system is included, thus modeling the reliability of the entire memory system. A formula is derived that can be used to calculate the reliability function, mean time to failure (MTTF), and the hazard function efficiently under any of the various failure mode assumptions. A modification of the model allows inclusion of the effect of failures already present.

Three of the models in this section are for error-correcting-code (ECC) memory reliability, based on a different assumption of dominant memory-chip failure mode. Two of the models provide upper (assuming all failures are single bit) and lower bounds (assuming all failures are whole chip) for the reliability of an ECC memory. The fourth, presented for comparison, is a model for the nonredundant memory. All the models assume that component failures in the memory-support circuitry cannot be survived. Many current commercial memory designs prove the validity of this assumption. Two error-correcting schemes, Hamming codes and block codes, illustrate how a general model can be applied to different error correcting codes. The memory reliability model differentiates between two types of memory words. The first, called a *logical word*, is the word that the system using the memory requires. The second, called a *physical word*, is made up of one or more logical words in addition to whatever coding bits are required.

For Hamming codes a k-bit word has c coding bits (which may or may not include the extra bit for double-error detection) added to it. The total number of bits is $n = (k + c)$. Several logical words may be combined into a larger physical word for error encoding, thus decreasing the number of coding bits in the memory. If j logical words occupy a physical word that includes e coding bits, the physical word size becomes $n = (kj + e)$, and the number of physical words in an x-logical word memory is $w = (x/j)$.

Block codes are widely used for sequential-access memory systems, but have seen little or no use in other types of memories. In this scheme, each word has a parity bit appended (horizontal parity bit) and j words of k bits are grouped to form a block. Each block has an extra word associated with it, each of whose $(k + 1)$ bits is the parity bit for the appropriate bit slice of the block (vertical parity bits). The total number of bits in the physical word is $n = (k + 1) \times (j + 1)$, and for an x-logical word memory

---

* The Texas Instruments data indicate that 92 percent of the failures observed were single-bit failures. This proportion has since declined as a result of process improvements; however, the dominant portion of all failures for these chips is still due to partial-array failures.

there are $w = (x/j)$ physical words. In the case of a single error, a horizontal parity error is found and the vertical word reconstructed. The intersection of the horizontal parity error and vertical parity error pinpoint the bit to be corrected. This method also detects double errors not in the same logical word.

Both the Hamming-coded and block-coded memories contain n-bit physical words and w physical words in the memory. The only difference between these two or any other SEC schemes as far as the model is concerned is that n and w vary. In each case, the memory can tolerate no more than one failure in the n bits of a given word in a w-word memory. This common property is the one upon which the following development is based.

Error-Correcting Memory Model: Single-Bit Failure. The single-bit failure mode (SBFM) model assumes that single-memory bit-cell failures dominate and thus provides an upper bound on system reliability by assuming that individual bit failures are independent. In this case, up to one failure per word, or w total failures, can be tolerated. Since single-bit failures are assumed to be independent events, with each cell following the exponential failure law with failure rate λ_b and reliability function R_b. Each n-bit word can tolerate the failure of a single bit. Thus, the reliability R_g of a given word is

$$R_g(t) = R_b^n + n(1 - R_b)R_b^{(n-1)}$$

For a w memory, the array reliability is

$$R_{asb}(t) = [nR_b^{(n-1)} - (n - 1)R_b^n]^w$$

Fault-free operation of the memory requires that the selection, control, and decoding circuitry be functioning correctly. It is assumed that these also follow exponential failure processes, with total failure rate λ_s. The reliability of the complete memory is then expressed as

$$R_{msb}(t) = e^{-\lambda_s t}[ne^{-(n-1)\lambda_b t} - (n - 1)e^{-n\lambda_b t}]^w$$

The mean time to failure of the memory is

$$\text{MTTF}_{sb} = \int_0^\infty e^{-\lambda_s t}[ne^{-(n-1)\lambda_b t} - (n - 1)e^{-n\lambda_b t}]^w \, dt$$

The integral is evaluated as

$$\text{MTTF}_{sb} = \int_0^\infty e^{-\lambda_s t}e^{-\lambda_b(n-1)w}[n - (n - 1)e^{-\lambda_b t}]^w \, dt$$

Next, the substitutions are

$$x = e^{-\lambda_b t} \qquad dx = -\lambda_b e^{-\lambda_b t}dt \qquad x|_{t \to \infty} = 0 \qquad x|_{t=0} = 1$$

To further simplify the integral, let

$$m = (n - 1)w + \frac{\lambda_s}{\lambda_b} - 1$$

and

$$v = -(n - 1)$$

The integral becomes

$$\text{MTTF}_{sb} = -\frac{1}{\lambda_b} \int_1^0 x^m (n + vx)^w \, dx$$

which has the recursive solution

$$\text{MTTF}_{sb} = -\frac{1}{\lambda_b} \left\{ \frac{x^{(m+1)}(n + vx)^w}{m + w + 1} + \frac{nw}{m + w + 1} \int x^m (n + vx)^{(w-1)} dx \right\} \Big|_1^0$$

After one more recursion, the equation becomes

$$\text{MTTF}_{sb} = -\frac{1}{\lambda_b} \left\{ \frac{x^{(m+1)}(n + vx)^w}{m + w + 1} \right.$$

$$\left. + \frac{nw}{m + w + 1} \left[\frac{x^{(m+1)}(n + vx)^{(w-1)}}{m + w} + \frac{n(w - 1)}{m + w} \int x^m (n + vx)^{(w-2)} dx \right] \right\} \Big|_1^0$$

More simplifications are now possible:

$$f_i = (m + w + 1) - i = wn + \frac{\lambda_s}{\lambda_b} - i$$

$$g_i = w - i + 1,$$

$$y = n + vx$$

With some rearranging, the MTTF$_{sb}$ equation reduces to

$$\text{MTTF}_{sb} = -\frac{1}{\lambda_b} \left\{ \frac{x^{(m+1)}y^{g_1}}{f_0} + \frac{ng_1}{f_0} \left[\frac{x^{(m+1)}y^{g_2}}{f_1} + \frac{ng_2}{f_1} \int x^m y^{g_3} dx \right] \right\} \Big|_1^0$$

The final term in the recursion is

$$ng_w \int x^m y^{g_{(w+1)}} dx = \frac{ng_w x^{(m+1)}}{f_w}$$

Thus, $x^{(m+1)}$ can be factored out, giving

$$\text{MTTF}_{sb} = \frac{x^{(m+1)}}{\lambda_b f_0} \left\{ y^{g_1} + \frac{ng_1}{f_1} \left[y^{g_2} + \frac{ng_2}{f_2} \left(\dots \frac{ng_w}{f_w} \dots \right) \right] \right\} \Big|_1^0$$

When $x = 0$, $x^{(m+1)} = 0$, and when $x = 1$, $x^{(m+1)} = 1$ and $y^{g_i} = [n - (n - 1)]^{g_i} = 1$, thus yielding

$$\text{MTTF}_{sb} = \frac{1}{\lambda_b f_0} \left\{ 1 + \frac{ng_1}{f_1} \left[1 + \frac{ng_2}{f_2} \left(\dots \frac{ng_w}{f_w} \dots \right) \right] \right\}$$

A final reorganization yields an iterative formula:

$$\text{MTTF}_{sb} = \frac{1}{\lambda_b} \left(\frac{1}{f_0} + \frac{ng_1}{f_0 f_1} + \cdots + \frac{n^w g_1 \cdots g_w}{f_0 f_1 \cdots f_w} \right) \tag{44}$$

This form of solution is preferred because of its easy and direct iterative implementation on a computer or calculator. Usually, only the first few terms need to be computed, for the value of successive terms quickly drops to zero and the number of terms is bounded by w.

The MTTF of the memory array alone is obtained by setting $\lambda_s/\lambda_b = 0$. Eq. 44 offers a quicker means of calculating ECC memory MTTF than either the earlier methods of numerical integration or Monte Carlo simulation. Eq. 44 also lends itself well to exploring reliability properties of ECC memories. This topic is discussed later.

It is important to note that in solving the integral, m is assumed to be an integer, which in turn constrains λ_s/λ_b to also be an integer. In almost all cases this constraint is not a problem, because normally $\lambda_s \gg \lambda_b$.

The hazard function $z(t)$ expresses the instantaneous failure rate of a population. At a given time it measures the ratio of the instantaneous rate of change in reliability to the current reliability. A constant hazard function implies that the percentage change in reliability is constant through time. The corresponding reliability function is exponential. An increasing hazard function implies that the percentage change in reliability grows larger with time, and can be thought of as accelerating (rather than just increasing) unreliability. An increasing hazard function is inherent in redundant systems. Intuitively, as a redundant system approaches the limit of its tolerance to failures, it becomes more unreliable than it was when new. The hazard function for the SBFM model can be shown to be

$$z_{sb}(t) = \lambda_s + \lambda_b wn(n-1) \frac{1 - e^{-\lambda_b t}}{n - (n-1)e^{-\lambda_b t}}$$

Error-Correcting Memory Model: Whole-Chip Failure. This model assumes that the dominant failure mode is complete functional failure of memory chips. It provides a lower bound on system reliability, since bit failures are not assumed to be independent but to occur d at a time, where d is the number of bits on a chip. Only w/d total failures* of this type can be tolerated. The whole-chip failure mode (WCFM) and row- (or column-) failure mode (RFM) models have the same form as the SBFM model. If the whole-chip failure mode is dominant, the design must apportion no more than one bit per chip per physical word. A similar restriction applies in the case of a dominant-row (or column) failure mode. The models here assume these restrictions.

In the WCFM model, the parameter h replaces the parameter w of the SBFM model. For a w-word memory of n-bit physical words implemented with d-bit chips, $h = w/d$. In effect, the memory is organized into rows of n chips each, every row containing d words; h is then the number of such rows. λ_c, the memory-chip failure

---

* Assuming a $d \times 1$-bit memory chip, one bit per physical word per chip.

rate, takes the place of λ_b, the bit-failure rate. These substitutions apply in the reliability, MTTF, and hazard formulas.

The RFM model also derives from the SBFM model. For a w-word memory of n-bit physical words implemented with d-bit memory chips having q bits per row (column), w of the SBFM model is replaced by $p = (wg)/d$, which is the number of one-word-wide sets of rows (columns) in the memory architecture. λ_b is replaced by λ_r, the row (column) failure rate.

Error-Correcting Memory Model: Failures Present. A variation of the preceding MTTF formula should be useful in maintenance planning. Assume that β failures are present at time zero. These failures are of the type assumed to be dominant; that is, single-bit, whole-chip, or row (column). The expression for the MTTF of an SBFM model is

$$\text{MTTF}_{sb \cdot \beta} = \frac{1}{\lambda_b}\left(\frac{1}{f_0} + \frac{ng_1}{f_0 f_1} + \cdots + \frac{n^\alpha g_1 \cdots g_\alpha}{f_0 \cdots f_\alpha}\right)$$

where $f_i = nw - \beta + (\lambda_s/\lambda_b) - i$
$\quad g_i = w - \beta - i + 1$
$\quad \alpha = w - \beta$

The forms for the WCFM and RFM models follow using the previously defined substitutions.

Nonredundant Memory Model. The model for nonredundant memory (NR) is based on the assumptions that components have exponential failure processes and that any component failure results in complete memory failure. The support and storage array circuitry have failure rates λ_{enr} and λ_a, respectively. The reliability of the entire memory is then expressed by

$$R_{mnr} = e^{-(\lambda_{enr} + \lambda_a)t}$$

The MTTF of the memory is

$$\text{MTTF}_{nr} = \frac{1}{\lambda_{enr} + \lambda_a}$$

The nonredundant memory has the constant hazard function:

$$z_{nr}(t) = \lambda_{enr} + \lambda_a$$

Example: ECC Memory Reliability Exploration via the Models. The single-bit failure mode, whole-chip failure mode, and nonredundant memory models will be compared for Hamming and block coding SEC schemes. The comparison measures are the MTTF, the hazard function $z(t)$, and the reliability function $R(t)$. When specific values for memory-chip reliability are used, they are based on the failure rates for 4096-bit chips found in the following table:

Chip λ_c	Bit λ_b
0.005	0.0000122
0.2	0.0000488
0.5	0.000122
3.0	0.000732
5.0	0.00122

Source: From Elkind and Siewiorek, 1980; © 1980 IEEE.

These ranges cover observed failure rates for state-of-the-art chips.

The reliabilities of control circuitry for error-correcting and nonredundant memories are derived from the models depicted in Figures 5–42 and 5–43, assuming the use of standard SSI/MSI logic. These memories are assumed to be "bare-bones" memories of relatively simple design. Assume a nonredundant k-bit per word memory of w words. Hamming single-error-correcting capabilities are added to it as shown in Figure 5–42 by increasing the array size to include the coding bits. Extra control and data manipulation facilities (MUXes, parity trees, XORs, and registers) are added to perform error correction and detection, as well as error coding when writing into the memory. When j logical words are combined into a larger physical word to limit the increase in array size, extra logic in the form of wider data paths, more complex coding/decoding circuitry, and a final one-of-j switch is needed.

In the block-coded memory shown in Figure 5–43 the control circuitry is more complex than for the Hamming code. The total support circuitry required is less, however, because the coding/decoding logic for block codes is less complex than for a Hamming code. For example, only one parity tree is needed in the block-coded memory, whereas the Hamming-coded memory needs several. The block code also requires fewer redundant bits than the Hamming code. The block-code decoder works

FIGURE 5–42
Hamming-coded memory model [From Elkind and Siewiorek, 1980; © 1980 IEEE]

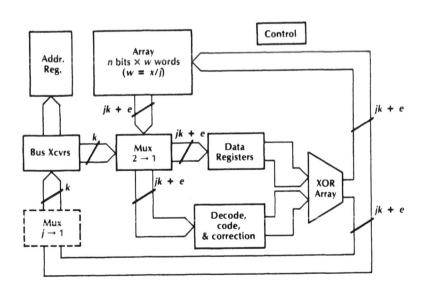

FIGURE 5–43
*Block-coded RAM
model [From El-
kind and Siewio-
rek, 1980; © 1980
IEEE]*

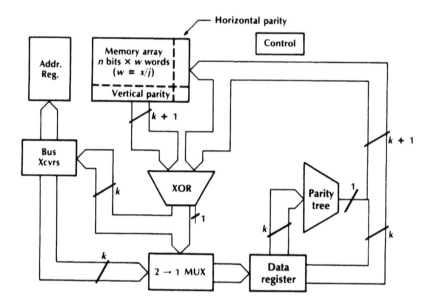

in the following manner. When a word is read and XORed with zeros being fed into the other leg of the XOR array (zero is the XOR identity operator), the parity tree calculates the parity. If there is an error, the vertical parity for the block is calculated by successively XORing words from the memory block with what is already in the register. The results of the new vertical parity point to the bit in error.

If more than one horizontal or vertical parity bit in the block indicates an error, a multiple-bit failure has occurred and the error is unrecoverable. In the case of a write, the horizontal parity is calculated and the vertical parity is updated simply by XORing the new and old data words with the old vertical parity word. Because writes to memory occur only 10 to 30 percent of the time, degradation due to vertical parity update is small. However, the block code is particularly effective for read-only memory because the extra complication on writes is not necessary. The vertical parity word could be stored in a separate memory array, thus allowing the update of the vertical parity word to proceed in parallel with the data write.

Block coding of small memories presents some problems because of the relatively large physical word size and the small number of physical words in the memory. Tolerance of whole-chip failure modes requires an allocation of no more than one bit per block per chip. When whole-chip failure modes are dominant, block codes are efficient only for large memories. For a small memory, the number of memory chips is fixed by the number of bits in a block. A large number of chips with relatively few bits on each must be used. The same disadvantage applies less stringently for row/column failure modes. For single-bit failure modes there is no such problem.

The comparisons that follow use support reliabilities calculated from these model memory designs of Figures 5–42 and 5–43. The comparisons will be made in terms of MTTF and the hazard functions.

Hamming Code MTTF. In comparisons of the SBFM and WCFM models, a normalized MTTF is used in order to avoid dependence on specific reliabilities of the current or any other technology. The normalized measure is obtained by multiplying the MTTF formulas by λ_b. When this is done the MTTF becomes a function of the ratio λ_s/λ_b instead of being a function of λ_s and λ_b. MTTF$_{wc.norm}$ is still dependent on the number of bits per chip.

It is possible to normalize the nonredundant memory MTTF in the same way, assuming that the ratio $r = \lambda_{enr}/\lambda_s$ is known. The normalized MTTF for the nonredundant memory becomes

$$\text{MTTF}_{nr.norm} = \frac{1}{r(\lambda_s/\lambda_n) + wn}$$

Figure 5–44 shows the normalized MTTF curves plotted against the ratio λ_s/λ_b. These curves are for 16-bit logical word memories of 16K and 64K words in the SBFM and WCFM (assuming 4096 bits per chip) ECC models and the nonredundant memory model. The figure illustrates a factor of 20 to 30 superiority in MTTF predicted for the SBFM over the WCFM model for small values of λ_s/λ_b, with the size memories modeled. As λ_s/λ_b increases, the ECC memory MTTF becomes essentially that of the support circuitry (which would plot as a line with unity negative slope). Thus, the limiting factor on the memory reliability is the support-circuitry reliability.

The plot in Figure 5–44 also shows that the ratio λ_s/λ_b at which the array reliability can be ignored in computing MTTF is lower for the SBFM than for the WCFM model. This difference becomes greater for larger chip size. For λ_s in the range from 1 to 100

FIGURE 5–44
Comparison of MTTF [From Elkind and Siewiorek, 1980; © 1980 IEEE]

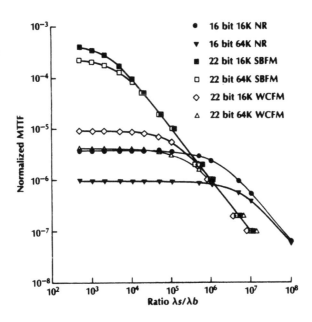

failures per million hours this corresponds to a λ_s/λ_b of 10^4 to 10^6 for the λ_b values given earlier. This is well into the range where the SBFM assumption shows that the memory reliability can be modeled as simply as that of the support circuitry, and just at or below that range for the WCFM assumption. To interpret Figure 5–44 in terms of a specific memory-chip technology, divide the vertical scale by λ_b.

The normalized MTTF for the nonredundant memory (assuming $r = \lambda_{enr}/\lambda_s = 0.1$) shows the same behavior as the ECC memories: the MTTF is limited by the support circuitry MTTF, although at a higher value of λ_s/λ_b. It also illustrates the fact that by the time

$$\frac{\lambda_s}{\lambda_b} \geq \frac{wk}{1 - r}$$

the nonredundant memory becomes more reliable than ECC memory, and that for large λ_s/λ_b, its MTTF is greater by the factor $1/r$. Thus, the formulas and derived curves such as Figure 5–44 can be used to select the appropriate memory organization as a function of λ_s/λ_b and the failure mode assumptions.

Hamming Code Hazard Function. Based on the calculated support failure rates, the hazard functions for 32-bit logical word memories of 16K and 64K words were calculated for the SBFM and WCFM models and the nonredundant memory model. Figure 5–45a plots the results. The assumed bit failure rate is $\lambda_b = 0.000122$ failures per million hours.

For the SBFM model, the hazard is nearly constant for the 80 years shown, and the two different-size memories exhibit an almost total hazard function dominance by the support circuitry's constant hazard function $z(t) = \lambda_s$. The WCFM model exhibits very different behavior for this ratio of λ_s/λ_b. For both sizes of memory the hazard functions increase throughout the 80 years, with a rapid rise in the first 10 to 20 years as the memory array hazard function grows and eventually dwarfs the contribution of the support circuitry's constant hazard function. At the end of 15 to 25 years, the WCFM models have larger hazards than do the models for the nonredundant memories of the same (logical) size. The nonredundant memories exhibit constant hazard functions dominated by the greater constant hazard of the memory array alone ($\lambda_a \gg \lambda_{enr}$).

Figure 5–45b demonstrates the effect of varying λ_b while holding λ_s constant (i.e., more reliable memory for the same support technology, thus increasing λ_s/λ_b). The memory modeled is a 16-bit logical-word memory of 32K words. For larger λ_b the memory array hazard function becomes more important and the SBFM model begins to exhibit the same qualities as the WCFM model in Figure 5–45. Below some λ_b the nonredundant memory model has a consistently lower hazard function. Its hazard function never gets as large as the Hamming code hazard function.

Block Code Hazard Function. A block-coded memory of 64K logical words, with 16 words per block, was compared against a Hamming SEC-coded memory of the same (logical) size, but having one logical word per physical word [Elkind and Siewiorek,

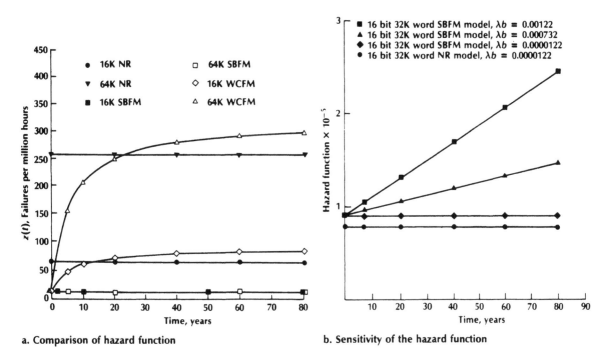

a. Comparison of hazard function

b. Sensitivity of the hazard function

FIGURE 5–45 *Plots of hazard functions [From Elkind and Siewiorek, 1980; © 1980 IEEE]*

1980]. The SBFM model was used for both memories. The Hamming-coded memory had a hazard function that was approximately constant at 9 failures per million hours over 80 years. The block-coded memory, on the other hand, had a hazard function that increased from 4.5 to 7.5 failures per million hours over 80 years. The block code's greater departure from a constant hazard function was due to its larger, and hence less reliable, code word size. This was more than compensated for by the less complicated support circuitry; over the entire period modeled, the block code memory hazard function remained lower than the Hamming code hazard function. Thus, the block-code memory design is more reliable, and requires fewer memory chips than the Hamming-code memory design.

ECC Redundancy on Memory: Summary. The way in which memory chips fail affects the reliability of single-error-correcting memories. It also dictates the choice of models for memory system reliability. When the dominant failure mode, chip failure rate, and control failure rate are known, the preceding models can be used in making trade-off analyses in memory system design.

ECC memories are not inherently more reliable than nonredundant memories. With very reliable memory chips, the limiting factor is the reliability of the support circuitry. When using standard SSI/MSI logic, Hamming code support circuitry has a failure rate several times that of the support circuitry for an equivalent nonredundant memory. Using more reliable LSI logic for ECC support would greatly improve the total ECC memory reliability.

Block-coded memories have several desirable properties. When SSI/MSI support circuitry is used, they can be more reliable than Hamming code memories. The memory redundancy required is less than that for Hamming codes. Even though large Hamming words (many logical words per physical word) could be used, the decoding/encoding for such large code sizes would be complex and slow. The block code, however, does have disadvantages that limit applicability. Writing into a block-coded RAM takes longer (although Hamming codes with multiple words per physical word have a similar problem). This would be offset somewhat if serial direct memory access (DMA) devices are used. The stored data are already encoded, for DMA devices usually perform block transfers; thus, reading from tape or disk would have no degradation. Block-code error correction also takes longer, but the resultant degradation is negligible. Another limitation is that some double errors (those in the same logical word) cannot be detected. Finally, although some chip (or row/column) failure modes are to be tolerated, the block coding scheme is board-space efficient only for large memories. Even with these limitations, the block code is still suitable for many RAM and ROM applications.

Redundancy to Enhance Chip Yield

This section uses combinatorial modeling techniques to evaluate duplication as a means of yield improvement. As pointed out in Chapter 2, semiconductor technology continues to produce increased densities and chip sizes. As chip size increases and defect density remains constant, however, the chip yield diminishes. Redundancy on the chip has been suggested as an effective means to increase yield [Tammaru and Angell, 1967]. Indeed, several semiconductor manufacturers already provide spare bits and control electronics on memory parts [Posa, 1980]. The redundancy is configured after wafer probe, but before final assembly. Polysilicon fuses or a second layer of metallization provide the means for handwiring the configuration. The redundancy may vary from as little as 1 percent to over 25 percent. The redundancy requires additional chip area, raising the question of how much improvement of chip yield redundancy will actually provide.

Chip-Manufacturing Defect Modes. In the absence of redundancy, one or more defects in a chip cause it to be discarded. There are three basic types of defects [Murphy, 1964]:

1. *Area defects*, which are caused by such faults as diffusion or masking errors, surface layer inversion, and general contamination, and which affect whole slices or areas larger than the chip size
2. *Line defects*, which are caused by scratches during the handling of a chip
3. *Spot defects*, which are highly localized, and which are caused by imperfections during the diffusion or masking process

The last category is the most common and is the predominant cause for discarding the chip.

Manufacturing-Yield Parameters and Nonredundant Model. In several attempts to predict chip yield, the assumptions for defect density range from a simple Poisson distribution to a compound (or mixed) Poisson distribution [Murphy, 1964; Stapper, 1973; Warner, 1974; Gupta, Porter, and Lathrop, 1974]. Using the simple Poisson distribution to illustrate the usefulness of redundancy on a chip, let D be the defect density measured in number of spot defects per unit area. Assuming that the defect centers obey the Poisson probability distribution and are independent, then, if the effective circuit area is A, the probability that the device is good is

$$p = e^{-DA}$$

The defect density D itself is not constant. Let $f(D)$ be the normalized distribution function of D. Then the overall yield, Y, is

$$Y = \int_0^\infty e^{-DA} f(D) \, dD \tag{45}$$

On the basis of experiences in the field, Murphy [1964] has claimed that the distribution function, $f(D)$, may be assumed to be the bell-shaped curve shown in Figure 5–46. The curve can be further approximated by a δ-function, or a triangular function. For our purposes, the bell-shaped curve is approximated by

$$f(D) = \frac{D}{D_0^2} \quad \text{for } 0 \leqslant D \leqslant D_0$$

$$\tag{46}$$

$$f(D) = \frac{2D_0 - D}{D_0^2} \quad \text{for } D_0 \leqslant D \leqslant 2D_0$$

Evaluating the integral in Eq. 45, using $f(D)$ from Eq. 46, produces

FIGURE 5–46
Normalized distri-
bution function of
chips in defect
densities

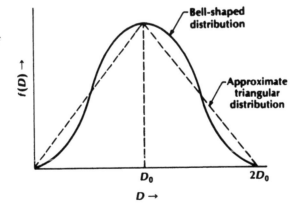

$$y = \frac{1 - e^{-D_0 A}}{D_0 A} \qquad (47)$$

Figure 5–47 shows the yield as a function of $D_0 A$.

Manufacturing Yield Model for Duplication. Now consider replication as a means of improving yield. A circuit is logically divided into n sections of identical complexity, as shown in Figure 5–48. Each section is then duplicated, and simple switching circuitry is added to each pair of sections to allow selection of a good section after testing for spot defects. Assuming that the area required for a circuit is directly proportional to its complexity, let the complexity of the logic added to each section be α times the complexity of the section. The parameter α includes the additional circuitry required to control the functions of the chip (such as a shift register to control which duplicate sections are being used). The probability that there is at least one good section to use is

$$e^{-D\alpha A/n}(2e^{-DA/n} - e^{-2DA/n})$$

Because there are n such sections, the probability that the chip is good is

$$p = e^{-D\alpha A}(2e^{-DA/n} - e^{-2DA/n})^n \qquad (48)$$

Again, using the expression for yield,

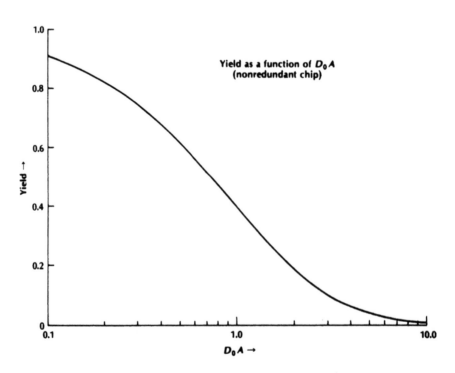

FIGURE 5–47
Yield as a function of $D_0 A$ (nonredundant chip)

Yield as a function of $D_0 A$
(nonredundant chip)

Yield →

$D_0 A$ →

FIGURE 5–48
Proposed redundancy to enhance yield

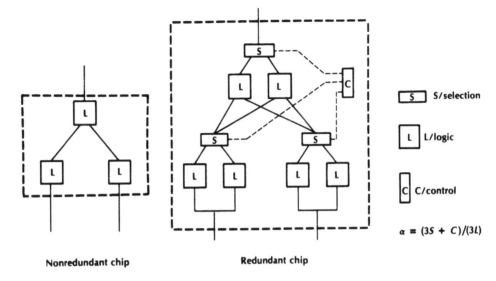

Nonredundant chip   Redundant chip

S   S/selection

L   L/logic

C   C/control

$\alpha = (3S + C)/(3L)$

$$Y_r = \int p f(D) dD$$

we can determine Y_r, the yield of a chip with redundancy.

The integration of terms in Eq. 48 presents difficulties. The solution is obtained by first expanding the bracketed terms using the binomial theorem. The expression can then be integrated with comparative ease:

$$Y_r = \sum_{i=0}^{n} \binom{n}{i} 2^{n-i}(-1)^i \left(\frac{1 - e^{D_0 b}}{D_0 b}\right)^2 \tag{49}$$

where $b = A\left(1 + \alpha + \frac{1}{n}\right)$

Example: Duplication and Chip-Yield Exploration via the Models. The expression for Y_r remains very complex. It is best evaluated numerically, and then compared with Y. Figure 5–49 shows the yield of a redundant chip as a function of $D_0 A$ for $n = 2$. The yield of a nonredundant chip with the same $D_0 A$ is also depicted with the curves for $\alpha = 1.0$, $\alpha = 0.5$, $\alpha = 0.1$, and $\alpha = 0$. As expected, the Y_r for the worst case of $\alpha = 1.0$ (the selection and switch circuitry comparable to the original circuits) is less than that of the nonredundant chip. Significant increases in Y_r are observed as α reduces to 0.5, and further to 0.1. Any further gains, however, are marginal, for there is only a slight increase in Y_r as α is allowed to approach zero. For a typical LSI microprocessor circuit (0.2 in. × 0.2 in.) with mean defect density D_0 about 6.4 defects per sq. cm. [Muehldorf, 1975], the yield of a nonredundant chip as predicted by Eq. 47 is 24 percent. With duplication after dividing the circuit into two sections ($n = 2$) and with $\alpha = 0.1$,

FIGURE 5–49

Yield Y_r as a func-
tion of $D_0A(n = 2)$

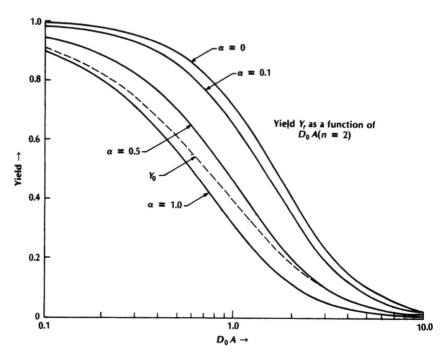

Yield Y_r as a function of $D_0 A(n = 2)$

the yield will increase to 42 percent, a factor of 1.75 increase in yield for a small increase in complexity.

In Figure 5–50 Y is plotted allowing n to vary with $\alpha = 0.5$. Again, the yield of the nonredundant chip is also depicted for comparison. Although the yield increases with n, the maximum increase is at low values of n (two and four), with larger numbers of divisions providing diminishing returns. This fact is also obvious in Figure 5–51, where Y_r is depicted as a function of n for $D_0A = 1.5$. Once again, for $\alpha = 1.0$ the yield is less than that of a nonredundant chip.

Alternatively, redundancy can be used to enhance logic complexity while maintaining a given level of yield (the production point established for maximizing return). The preceding equations can be used to estimate the degree to which logic complexity can be increased while maintaining a constant yield.

If there are N possibles on a wafer, for the nonredundant case the number of good possibles is

$$NY_0 \tag{50}$$

where Y_0 is nonredundant yield. For the redundant case there are $NY_r/[2(1 + \epsilon) + \alpha]$ possibles, where ϵ represents an increase in logic complexity over the nonredundant circuit and Y_r is the redundant yield.

FIGURE 5–50
Yield Y_r as a function of $D_0 A(\alpha = 0.5)$

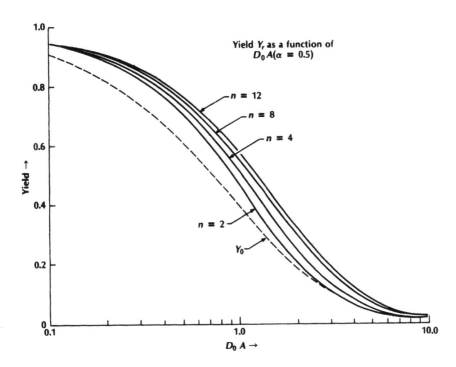

Yield Y_r as a function of $D_0 A(\alpha = 0.5)$

$n = 12$

$n = 8$

$n = 4$

$n = 2$

Y_0

Yield →

$D_0 A$ →

FIGURE 5–51
Yield Y_r as a function of $n(D_0 A = 1.5)$

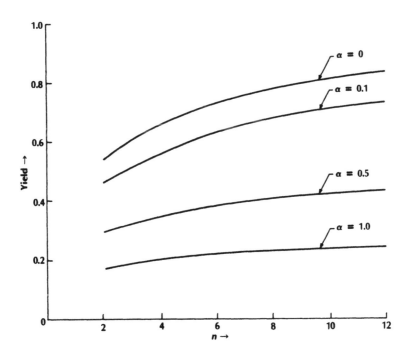

$\alpha = 0$

$\alpha = 0.1$

$\alpha = 0.5$

$\alpha = 1.0$

Yield →

$n →$

If the redundant and nonredundant number of possibles are equated, we have

$$Y_0 = \frac{Y_r}{2 + \alpha + 2\epsilon} \tag{51}$$

where Y_r is a function of ϵ.

The second column of Table 5–7 lists the value of D_0A beyond which redundancy is better than nonredundancy as a function of the number of sections, n. For larger values of D_0A, redundancy yields more possibles. When there are only two sections ($n = 2$), the nonredundant design always yields a larger number of possibles. For $n = 3$, $D_0A = 1.78$ for break-even, while D_0A is as small as 1.1 for $n = 8$. In order to see what the maximum potential gain is through the use of redundancy, D_0A was allowed to become arbitrarily large. The third column of Table 5–7 lists the limiting value of $Y_r/Y_0(2 + \alpha)$ for $\alpha = 0.1$. For $n = 8$ the number of possibles increases by almost a factor of 2.2.

Converting the increased number of possibles from redundancy to increase the nonredundant circuit size yields solutions to Eq. 51. The fourth column of Table 5–7 lists the limiting value of ϵ for arbitrarily large D_0A, and the fifth column lists the relative size (nonredundant = 1) of the resultant redundant chip. The table shows that a potential increase of 114 percent in the nonredundant circuit complexity can be achieved through use of redundancy and a chip 4.49 times larger than the nonredundant circuit without sacrificing the number of possibles from a wafer. This, however, is a maximum potential, and the number of possibles (yield) at that point might be unacceptably low. If D_0A were 2.4, for example, the yield would be 0.143 for the nonredundant circuit. For a redundant circuit with the same yield and $n = 3$, the number of extra possibles would be only 0.04 instead of the limiting value of 0.17.

Other redundancy schemes to enhance yield can be evaluated using the combinatorial techniques presented in the sections on series/parallel systems, M-of-N systems, and reduction of nonseries/nonparallel cases.

Modeling the Performance Impact of Redundancy and Failures

This section illustrates how combinatorial modeling techniques can be used to predict the performance of systems which include redundancy. Adding redundancy to a system often affects performance. A triplication-with-voting scheme such as C.vmp (see Chapter 10), for example, incurs the gating delay of the voter. Such gate delays are easy to measure and model. Main-memory cycle time degradation, due to the addition of error-checking logic, is easy to calculate. The system degradation is usually small because the processor-memory bandwidth is normally not fully utilized. Parallel operations and relative frequency of use, however, generally make performance degradation modeling more difficult.

Another difficulty is determining the effect on performance when there are (covered) failures present in a functioning redundant system. In some cases (as in backup systems) there is no additional degradation beyond the time required for system reconfiguration. In others, performance becomes degraded, such as when extra time

TABLE 5–7 *Use of redundancy to increase nonredundant circuit complexity, holding number of possibles per wafer constant*

Number of Sections in Chip, n	Value of D_0A (number of defects) Beyond Which Complete Duplication Yields More Possibles	Limiting Value (as D_0A approaches infinity) of Relative Number of Possibles Complete Duplication	Limiting Value of Original Circuit Complexity Increase (ϵ) for which Compete Duplication Yields Same Number of Possibles Wafer	Chip Size of Resultant Redundant Chip Relative to Nonredundant Chip
2	None	0.94	—	—
3	1.78	1.17	0.86	3.90
4	1.40	1.40	0.91	4.01
6	1.20	1.80	1.14	4.49
8	1.10	2.18	1.01	4.22

is required for correction, or fewer resources are left to accomplish tasks. The impact of single-error correcting codes for main memory or microstore on system reliability was discussed earlier. The effect such ECC memories have on system performance serves as an example of performance-degradation modeling. Chapter 10 provides additional examples.

Model of Main-Memory Performance with Redundancy. Because most error checking can be carried out in parallel with the use of data, there is usually no performance change in an error-free state. This is the case if no irreversible actions (such as an overwriting of information needed to restart the current operation) occur before the error checking has been completed, and if the hardware has stall/restart capabilities. Most processor/main memory systems and vertically coded microemulators belong in this class. Most register-transfer level results are not latched until the end of a microcycle, leaving enough time for error checking in most designs. On the other hand, a horizontally microcoded machine with a short microcycle and a very large word width would not allow retry, because the propagation time through the several XOR levels required for ECC checking would be greater than the microcycle time. This should not be the case very often, however. This section focuses on the effect of recoverable memory errors on system performance.

Model of Main-Memory Performance in the Presence of Errors. Assume that the access frequency is not uniform throughout the memory, so that some memory segments, such as those containing parts of the operating system kernel, are more likely to be accessed than others. Suppose that each location i has access probability P_i, and that there are n errors in a w word memory. The expected memory access time can be expressed as a function of the cycle time c and the cycle time degradation caused by an error, ϵc:

$$\sum_{i=1}^{w} P_i \left(1 - \frac{n}{w}\right) c + \sum_{i=1}^{w} P_i \left(\frac{n}{w}\right)(c + \epsilon c) = c \left(1 + \frac{n\epsilon}{w}\right) \tag{52}$$

since $\Sigma P_i = 1$. Thus, the expected degradation of the memory access time is $n\epsilon/w$.

Figure 5–52 illustrates the effects of errors on memory access time for several values of n and w. Two types of ECC memory are represented: a Hamming code memory with an ϵ of one (one full extra memory cycle to correct an error) and a block-coded memory with an ϵ of 64 (reading all words in the block to determine the vertical parity). The performance degradation is negligible (less than 1 percent) for the Hamming code, whereas the degradation becomes significant for the block code only when n becomes large.

FIGURE 5–52

Memory access degradation [From Elkind and Siewiorek, 1980; © 1980 IEEE]

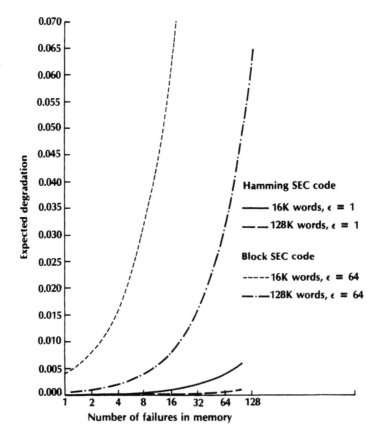

TABLE 5–8
Timing data and resulting degradation for PDP-11 computer systems

| System | Time (in microseconds) | | System Degradation | |
	Memory Access	Average Instruction Execution	D_s (% of D_m)	D_s for $m = 4$, $\epsilon = 64$, $w = 16K$
LSI-11	0.400	5.883	14.7%	0.0023
PDP-11/40	0.600	4.096	31.6	0.0049
PDP-11/34	0.940	3.129	64.9	0.0101

Source: Elkind and Siewiorek, 1980; © 1980 IEEE.

Example: Main-Memory Performance Degradation. The degradation of system performance depends on how often the memory is accessed. A system with a low memory bandwidth utilization will exhibit less degradation than one whose bandwidth is almost saturated. Table 5–8 compares the degradation in three different PDP-11 systems. The data in the first two columns, drawn from Snow and Siewiorek [1978], are the result of dynamic measurements of PDP-11 programs. Another result from the same source is that an average of 2.16 memory references occur for each instruction. If T_m is the memory access time, T_I the average instruction execution time, and D_m the expected memory access time degradation, the expected system degradation D_s is

$$D_s = \frac{D_m T_m (2.16)}{T_I} \tag{53}$$

Based on this formula, the third column of Table 5–8 lists the proportion of memory degradation that comes through as system degradation. The system performance degradation is less than the memory performance degradation in all cases. For the LSI-11 and the PDP-11/10, a large memory degradation must occur before its effects are noticeable. The system degradation effects are more noticeable on the PDP-11/34, which comes close to saturating the processor-memory bandwidth. Therefore, even though the memory performance degradation is more serious for block codes than for Hamming codes, as shown in Figure 5–52, overall system performance is comparable over wide ranges of failure situations. Using Eqs. 52 and 53, the data in the last column of Table 5–8 were calculated assuming four failures in a 16K word block-code memory with 64 word blocks. The degradation is negligible (1 percent) even in the PDP-11/34.

Model of Microstore Performance in the Presence of Errors. Microstore reliability is becoming more important as the use of microcoded system design increases. The growing size of microstores being used and the subsequent effect on system reliability make error-coding techniques more attractive. Unlike main memory, in which degraded segments can be left unallocated, degraded sections of microcode are permanently allocated and will continue to affect system performance until repaired.

The following table [Elkind and Siewiorek, 1980] summarizes the characteristics of a microcoded machine.

Microstore Model: Allocation and Access Frequency

Purpose	Size	P (access)	No. of Occurrences in Microstore
Fetch	F	1	1
Interrupt service	S	1	1
Addressing mode	A_j	P_j	a
Instruction	I_k	P_k	i

$$\text{Total memory } w = F + S + \sum_{j=1}^{a} A_j + \sum_{k=1}^{i} I_k$$

It is assumed that all F (fetch) and S (interrupt) service microwords are executed during each macrocycle. The expected macrocycle time M_0 with no errors present can be shown to be

$$E[M_0] = (F + S + \overline{A} + \overline{I})m$$

where m is the microcycle time, $\overline{A}$ is the average number of microwords needed to access the operands, and $\overline{I}$ is the average number of microwords to execute the instruction.

Formulating the performance degradation model entails two additional assumptions: first, the probability distribution of errors is uniform over all memory words; second, an error code with one logical word per physical word is being used. If the number of microcycles needed to correct a word with an error is ϵ and there are n errors in the memory, the expected macrocycle time is

$$E[M_n] = E[M_0] \left(1 + \frac{n\epsilon}{w}\right) \tag{54}$$

The derivation is similar to that of Eq. 52. Thus, the expected performance degradation is $n\epsilon/w$, as with main memory. This result has been shown to hold for block codes also.

Example: Microstore Performance Degradation. Consider three computers with microstores of 256, 1,024, and 4,096 words, with $\epsilon = 1$ (Hamming code) and $\epsilon = 16$ (block code, 16 words per block), and with three failures. The expected degradation can be calculated as in Elkind and Siewiorek [1978]. Degradation is negligible for the Hamming code (1.7 percent for $w = 256$; 0.3 percent for $w = 1,024$; and 0.1 percent for $w = 4,096$). In the block-code design, degradation is negligible when the block size is small in relation to the memory size (1.2 percent for $w = 4,096$). In the other cases it is more noticeable (4.7 percent for $w = 1,024$, and 18.8 percent for $w = 256$).

Given a microcoded machine like the one characterized in the previous tabulation, the probability distribution of the performance degradation with n errors present can be computed. Figure 5–53 shows this distribution for two slightly different machines, as well as a listing of their characteristics. Addressing mode and instruction frequencies

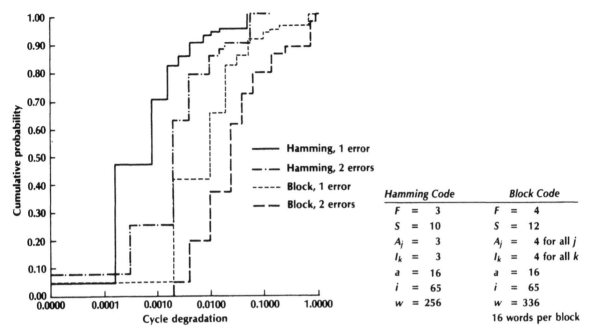

FIGURE 5–53 *SEC microstore distribution of degradation [From Elkind and Siewiorek, 1980; © 1980 IEEE]*

were drawn from a study of PDP-11 program traces [Snow and Siewiorek, 1978]. The microstore is divided into sections for *F*, *S*, and each of the addressing modes and instructions. A vector, $\bar{f}$ represents a given error pattern, with an element for each of the microstore divisions. The expected degradation was calculated for each $\bar{f}$ possible in Elkind and Siewiorek [1978, 1980].

For the Hamming coded machine, the probability of negligible (less than 1 percent) degradation is 93 percent. The probability that the degradation is less than the expected degradation (0.0039) from Figure 5–53 is 86 percent. The probability of noticeable degradation (more than 5 percent), is only 5 percent, whereas severe degradation does not occur.

A second curve in Figure 5–53 details the probability distribution for the machine when two errors are present. Although there is a possibility of severe degradation (more than 10 percent), the probability is small (0.24 percent) while there is an 86 percent probability that the degradation will be less than 1 percent. The other two curves in Figure 5–53 are for the block-coded microstore. Its performance degradation is more severe than that of the Hamming coded microstore. With one error present, the probability of severe degradation (more than 10 percent) is about 8 percent, whereas the probability of negligible degradation (1 percent or less) is only 65 percent. When two errors are present, the chance of a severe performance loss is 17 percent, and that of a benign failure drops to 40 percent.

Performance of Redundant Memory: Summary. When data are used in parallel with error checking, error-correcting-code memories can have performances similar to nonredundant memories if no failures are present. In the majority of cases, error-correcting-code memories experience negligible performance degradation in the presence of failures. The preceding results can be used to predict such degradation. These results, coupled with the failure-present MTTF predictor developed earlier in the section on the effect of nonredundant components, should be useful in planning memory system maintenance.

The Use of Modeling in Systems Design

So far we have used a variety of techniques to model isolated redundancy techniques or individual subsystems such as memory. In the design of a system, a variety of models must be used. This section illustrates how the failure rate models in Chapter 2 can be combined with the combinatorial models of this chapter to evaluate various combinations of reliability techniques from Chapter 3 to design a single board computer and a workstation. A design space is generated and evaluated for both computers.

An incremental improvement method is often used to design a cost-effective system. This technique gives rise to the two related problems of choosing which part of the system design to improve and deciding how best to improve that section in accord with the design goals. The MIL-HDBK-217 parts-count model provides one way to pinpoint hard-failure problem areas in a nonredundant system. The least reliable module (or functional area) will necessarily have the largest module failure rate.

The most effective target for improvement is not always the one with the highest failure rate, however. Control logic, for example, is exceedingly difficult to add redundancy to without complete redesign. The techniques that work for random logic, such as quadded logic [Tryon, 1962] and triplication with voting (TMR), unfortunately involve massive amounts of redundancy. Quadded logic uses four times the normal number of gates; TMR requires three times that number. TMR also requires a majority voter on each of the output lines, which is a significant disadvantage if there are a large number of output lines. Thus, regularity of structure is an important factor in the choice of fault-tolerance techniques.

The failure-rate-analysis method becomes at least partially invalid with redundancy, because the reliability function is no longer a simple exponential. Approximations are feasible in practice. Often, the redundant portion of a system can be assumed to be perfect with respect to other portions of the system.

Design Example: A Motorola 6809 Single Board Computer. This example illustrates a possible iterative improvement method utilizing a Motorola 6809 processor-based single-board computer and only two redundancy techniques. Chapter 7 will illustrate the type of analysis that can be performed during the design of a system, specifically the VAX-11/750.

The evaluation criteria for the example are cost and mission time for 0.95 reliability (MT[0.95]). Manufacturing cost, in terms of chip count, is the easiest property to model. In the early design stage it is usually taken to be just the materials cost of a design. Quite often the design is optimized for minimal materials cost alone, although other costs can also be used. Total manufacturing cost or user purchase price is important. Repair, spare parts, and operating costs can also be significant. Attempts to predict these and other costs over the lifetime of a system, or life-cycle cost (LCC) models, usually predict present value, total, or annual costs of combinations of purchase, financing, repair, inflation, and all other possible costs and factors. The number of different models is staggering (IEEE [1977] provides some examples). No single LCC model applies to all problems and viewpoints. Chapter 6 discusses economic criteria in more detail. Chip count will be used as the cost function in this example.

The 6809, an 8-bit microprocessor, provides the computation element for this simple single board computer design. This design exercise will employ a simple algorithm for making design changes. The two techniques in the algorithm's catalog are single-error-correcting/double-error-detecting (SEC/DED) codes and triple modular redundancy (TMR) with voting, the two most commonly used fault-tolerance techniques. The site chosen for applying a redundancy technique is the module with the lowest effect mean time to failure (MTTF), determined by the Lambda program (discussed in Chapter 2). The site choice can be done in a recursive fashion, using the subarea having the lowest MTTF within the area having the lowest MTTF, and so on, until a suitable site is found for applying one of the techniques. Finally, if the mission time shows a decline from the previous step, the algorithm requires the designer to return to the previous step and try again. This algorithm uses only mission time and MTTF as evaluations; it ignores other factors such as cost and performance.

Figure 5–54 shows the single board computer (SBC) discussed here. It consists of a 6809 processor, an external bus interface, input/output (I/O) devices, and a memory consisting of a 64K bit PROM and three 16K RAM chips.

Initial Improvement: Adding SEC/DED Encoding to the Memory. Evaluating the initial design is the first step in reliability enhancement. This is accomplished by preparing the parts list for the SBC, categorized by function, then running the list through Lambda. Table 5–9 shows the results. The system has an MTTF of 47,109 hours and an

FIGURE 5–54
Simple Motorola 6809 single board computer design

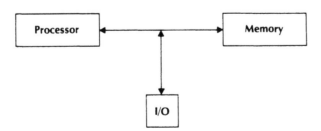

TABLE 5–9
Results of Lambda
MTTF analysis of
basic Motorola
6809 single-board
computer

(Quantity)/Module	MTTF for Single Module	Mission Reliability	Mission Time
(1) SINGLE.BOARD	4.711E+04	0.9999	5
(1) PROCESSOR	7.868E+05	0.999	49
(1) MICRO.PROC	9.527E+05	0.995	239
(1) PROC.SUPP	4.518E+06	0.99	474
(1) IO.INTERFACE	4.653E+05	0.98	952
(1) IO.SUPPORT	1.949E+06	0.95	2417
(1) MC.CHIPS	6.112E+05	0.9	4966
(1) BUS.INTERFACE	1.880E+06	0.8	10510
(1) MEMORY	5.789E+04	0.7	16800
(1) MEM.SUPPORT	5.231E+05		
(1) PROM.SUPPORT	3.174E+06		
(1) RAM__ROM.CHIPS	6.645E+04		

MTTF: 47109.2 hrs.
Mean Time to Part Failure: 47102.9 hrs.
Est. number parts: 73.8   Est. number pins: 714

$MT[0.95]$ of 2417 hours. The MTTF of the MEMORY module is an order of magnitude lower than any other module in the system, making it the most logical place for initial improvement. The strategy chosen is to use a Hamming SEC/DED code for the memory words. Each 8-bit memory word is encoded into a 13-bit code word. The extra circuitry (control, encoding/decoding, and so forth) is designed assuming a 13-bit Hamming encoding/decoding LSI chip will be used. In addition to the encoding/decoding chip, two data buffers are required to provide for communication between the memory and the rest of the system. The resulting design is checked by Lambda. Table 5–10 shows the resultant MTTF of 137,832 hours, and $MT[0.95]$ is now 7080 hours, a 193 percent increase over the original, nonredundant system.

The original (nonredundant) design used 74 ICs; the 13-bit ECC memory version uses 81. The difference results from the extra support circuitry and the memory chips for the redundant code bits. The result is a total increase in cost of around 9 percent.

The code word size can be increased (and extra memory bits for coding decreased) by combining two 8-bit memory words into a 21-bit SEC/DED code word. This represents a savings of 1 memory chip over the 13-bit ECC version. However, the control and coding/decoding functions become more complex. The net cost savings over the 13-bit code memory are nil. There is no change in the system mission time, and the MTTF actually decreases by 35 hours. The memory cycle time on reads increased over the 13-bit code because there are more levels in the decoding trees. On writes, the 21-bit word must first be read, decoded, and then reencoded and rewritten with the new word replacing half the code word; this process takes almost twice as long as a nonredundant memory. Thus, the 13-bit SEC/DED code is the best improvement to make for the size of memory involved.

Triplication of the IO.INTERFACE. The Lambda output from the previous step (see Table 5–10) shows that the IO.INTERFACE has the shortest MTTF, excluding the MEMORY, which has already been augmented by redundancy. Because the I/O device outputs are limited in number and easily identifiable (they connect to the system data bus), the next attempt at improvement is to triplicate these devices and vote on their data bus outputs. Triplication requires eight voters, one per bidirectional data line. To force synchronization of all three copies of the devices, synchronizing voters [McConnel and Siewiorek, 1981] will be employed on the data bus. Figure 5–55 is a block diagram of the resulting modified system. Table 5–11 shows the Lambda evaluation results. The mission time, *MT*[0.95], declined by 2 percent to 6914 hours. Thus, by the rules of the algorithm, a return to the previous design is required.

Triplication of the PROCESSOR. Turning again to Table 5–10, note that although the processor module exhibits a higher MTTF than the IO.INTERFACE, it also consists of fewer devices. The device failure rate of the single processor chip, while lower than

TABLE 5–10
Results of Lambda MTTF analysis of Motorola 6809 SBC with SEC memory

(Quantity)/Module		MTTF for Single Module	Mission Reliability	Mission Time
(1) SINGLE.BOARD	R	1.378E+05	0.9999	20
(1) PROCESSOR		7.868E+05	0.999	147
(1) MICRO.PROC		9.527E+05	0.995	703
(1) PROC.SUPP		4.518E+06	0.99	1387
(1) IO.INTERFACE		4.653E+05	0.98	2793
(1) IO.SUPPORT		1.949E+06	0.95	7080
(1) MC.CHIPS		6.112E+05	0.9	14530
(1) BUS.INTERFACE		1.880E+06	0.8	30780
(1) MEMORY	R	3.022E+05	0.7	49190
(1) MEM.SUPPORT		5.231E+05		
(1) ECC.PROM	R	1.384E+08		
(1) ECC__TPB	RF	1.384E+08		
(2) ROM.CTRL		6.349E+06		
(1) RAM__ROM.ECC	R	7.077E+05		
(1) ECC__RAM.MEM	RF	8.882E+06		
(6) RAM.CHIP		4.207E+05		
(1) ECC__ROM.MEM	RF	8.005E+06		
(2) ROM__MEM.CHIP		1.263E+05		
(1) ECC.SUPPORT		7.215E+05		

Flags after module name:
R = module has redundant submodules
RF = module is defined by REL.FN

MTTF: 137832.6 hrs.
Mean Time to Part Failure: 26548.6 hrs.
Est. number parts: 80.8   Est. number pins: 910

FIGURE 5–55
Motorola 6809 SBC
with SEC memory
and triplicated I/O

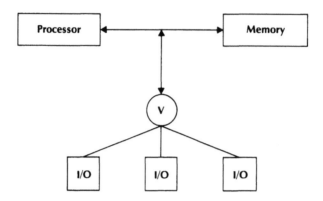

the failure rate of the combined I/O devices, is larger than the failure rate of any single I/O device. Triplication with voting is again attempted, this time for the processor. Simple voters are used for each data and address line on the processor.

Table 5–12 shows the results of the Lambda evaluation. Although the MTTF for the system declined by nearly 5 percent, the *MT*[0.95] is now 7246 hours, a 5 percent increase. According to the algorithm, this is a successful step in the design improvement. Looking again at Table 5–11, no other areas for improvement can be found, since the only module that has yet to be modified is the BUS.INTERFACE, which possesses an MTTF that is an order of magnitude larger than any other module, even in its original configuration.

Analyses of the Example. This treatment of the 6809 processor-based SBC follows only one of the possible routes through the design space. Figure 5–56 shows other routes, for which each of the design points was evaluated. In the following discussion, each point is specified by the combination of the path and step indices from the figure. For example, the SBC with ECC memory and TMR processor added is denoted by B2. The SBC with a TMR I/O is denoted by the index C1.

Figure 5–57a graphs the *MT*[0.95] versus the number of ICs in the design for each design configuration shown in Figure 5–56. Path B portrays the path of the simple algorithm through the design space. The sole aim of the algorithm is mission time improvement. The net improvement in the example was 200 percent, of which 193 percent occurred in the first step, adding the SEC memory. Thus, the algorithm attained the mission time improvement goal.

The effect of the choice of design goal is graphically illustrated by Figure 5–57b, which shows a design space for this example with the MTTF as the chosen design goal to be improved. The decision to triplicate the processor actually reduces the MTTF of the system, and would be rejected if MTTF were to be improved. Thus, while design B2 has the highest *MT*[0.95] in the design space, design B1 would be preferred if MTTF is the desired design goal.

TABLE 5–11
Results of Lambda
MTTF analysis of
Motorola 6809 SBC
with SEC memory
and triplicated I/O

(Quantity)/Module		MTTF for Single Module	Mission Reliability	Mission Time
(1) SINGLE.BOARD	R	1.310E+05	0.9999	20
(1) PROCESSOR		7.868E+05	0.999	137
(1) MICRO.PROC		9.527E+05	0.995	684
(1) PROC.SUPP		4.518E+06	0.99	1367
(1) IO.INTERFACE	R	3.621E+05	0.98	2734
(1) IO.SUPPORT		1.949E+06	0.95	6914
(1) TMR.MC.CHIPS	R	4.344E+05	0.9	14180
(1) TMR.6821	RF	2.433E+06	0.8	29960
(3) PIA		2.919E+06	0.7	47780
(1) TMR.6840	RF	2.424E+06		
(3) PTM		2.909E+06		
(1) TMR.6850	RF	2.744E+06		
(3) ACIA		3.293E+06		
(1) TMR.DECODE		5.544E+05		
(1) BUS.INTERFACE		1.880E+06		
(1) MEMORY	R	3.022E+05		
(1) MEM.SUPPORT		5.231E+05		
(1) ECC.PROM	R	1.384E+08		
(1) ECC__TPB	RF	1.384E+08		
(2) ROM.CTRL		6.349E+06		
(1) RAM__ROM.ECC	R	7.077E+05		
(1) ECC__RAM.MEM	RF	8.882E+06		
(6) RAM.CHIP		4.207E+05		
(1) ECC__ROM.MEM	RF	8.005E+06		
(2) ROM__MEM.CHIP		1.263E+05		
(1) ECC.SUPPORT		7.215E+05		

Flags after module name:
    R = module has redundant submodules
    RF = module is defined by REL.FN

MTTF: 131001.3 hrs.
Mean Time to Part Failure: 24507.0 hrs.
Est. number parts: 138.9   Est. number pins: 1788

The path followed by the simple algorithm is not necessarily optimal, although it appears to be in this instance. The order in which techniques are applied strongly affects the final design that is chosen. For example, reconsider Figure 5–57a in which the goal was *MT*[0.95]. Had design C1 or A1 instead of B1 been implemented as the first application of fault tolerance, the final design would have been B3, representing ECC on the memory and triplication of both the processor and I/O devices. The relative success of design B2 as compared to B3 would never have been detected in these instances.

TABLE 5-12
Results of Lambda MTTF analysis of Motorola 6809 SBC with SEC memory and triplicated processor

(Quantity)/Module		MTTF for Single Module	Mission Reliability	Mission Time
(1) SINGLE.BOARD	R	1.314E+05	0.9999	20
(1) PROCESSOR	R	4.694E+05	0.999	147
(1)TMR.PROC	R	5.136E+05	0.995	723
(1) TRIPLE.MP	RF	7.939E+05	0.99	1426
(3) U.PROC		9.527E+05	0.98	2861
(1) TMR.DECODER		1.155E+06	0.95	7246
(1) PROC.SUPP		4.518E+06	0.9	14810
(1) IO.INTERFACE		4.653E+05	0.8	31150
(1) IO.SUPPORT		1.949E+06	0.7	49410
(1) MC.CHIPS		6.112E+05		
(1) BUS.INTERFACE		1.880E+06		
(1) MEMORY	R	3.022E+05		
(1) MEM.SUPPORT		5.231E+05		
(1) ECC.PROM	R	1.384E+08		
(1) ECC__TPB	RF	1.384E+08		
(2) ROM.CTRL		6.349E+06		
(1) RAM__ROM.ECC	R	7.077E+05		
(1) ECC__RAM.MEM	RF	8.882E+06		
(6) RAM.CHIP		4.207E+05		
(1) ECC__ROM.MEM	RF	8.005E+06		
(2) ROM__MEM.CHIP		1.263E+05		
(1) ECC.SUPPORT		7.215E+05		

Flags after module name:
R = module has redundant submodules
RF = module is defined by REL.FN

MTTF: 131447.7 hrs.
Mean Time to Part Failure: 24611.0 hrs.
Est. number parts: 108.8   Est. number pins: 1354

Design Example: SUN-2/50 Workstation. The simple algorithm was similarly applied to the SUN-2/50 workstation (the design used as the basis for the fault intolerance design examples in Chapter 3). As in the preceding SBC example, SEC/DED and TMR were the two techniques employed for fault tolerance. In this exercise, *MT*[0.95] was again chosen as the goal to be improved by the algorithm. Thus, any design modification that increased system *MT*[0.95] was accepted. As before, at each step the module with the lowest relative MTTF was chosen as the area for improvement.

Figure 5-58 shows the design space of possible *MT*[0.95] improvements for the SUN-2/50 workstation. Figure 5-59 graphs the *MT*[0.95] and MTTF versus the number of ICs in the design for each design alternative in Figure 5-58. Error-correcting codes are relied upon for the majority of MTTF improvements because the workstation design

FIGURE 5–56
*Design space for
the fault-tolerant
Motorola 6809 SBC*

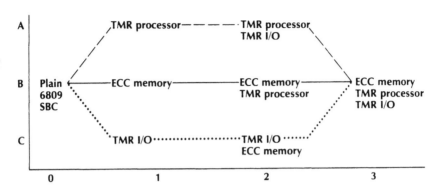

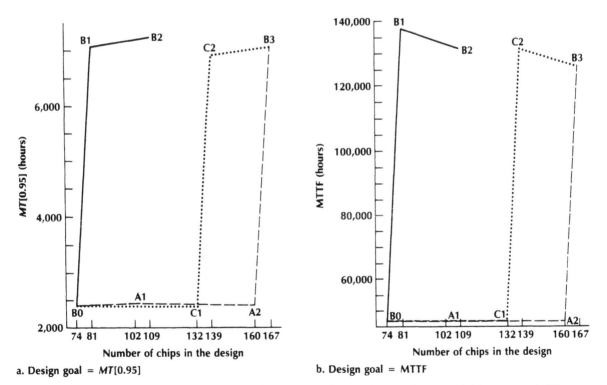

a. Design goal = $MT[0.95]$ b. Design goal = MTTF

FIGURE 5–57 *Design space for the Motorola 6809 SBC as a function of chip count and different
evaluation functions: MT and MTTF*

FIGURE 5–58
Design space for the fault-tolerant SUN-2/50 workstation

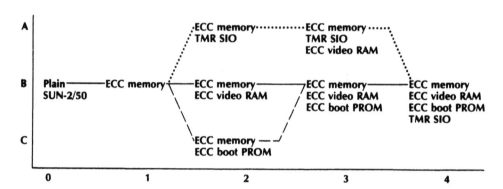

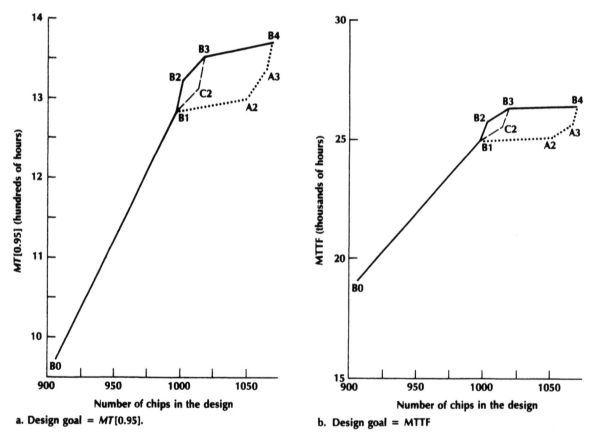

FIGURE 5–59 *Design space for the SUN-2/50 workstation as a function of chip count and different evaluation functions: MT and MTTF*

is very memory-intense. Regardless of the path chosen by the algorithm or the goal specified by the user, the final design chosen is B4, which represents ECC on the memory, boot PROM, and video RAM and triplication of the SIO.

One can, however, evaluate the relative efficiency of the path that is chosen. The goal of the simple algorithm is to maximize the $MT[0.95]$ of the system. It is desirable for each step in the process to result in the maximum relative improvement in $MT[0.95]$ possible. However, it is necessary to evaluate the performance of the algorithm not only in relation to mission time improvement but also relative to the cost incurred by the added redundancy. One possible measure is

$$I_n = \frac{MT[0.95]_n - MT[0.95]_{n-1}}{c_n - c_{n-1}}$$

$MT[0.95]_n$ is the mission time of the design resulting from the nth successful step, and c_n is the cost of the design (in this example, the number of ICs). The graph of Figure 5–60 shows the performance of the evaluation of this example, where the simple algorithm followed path B in Figure 5–58. The plot is monotonic decreasing, which

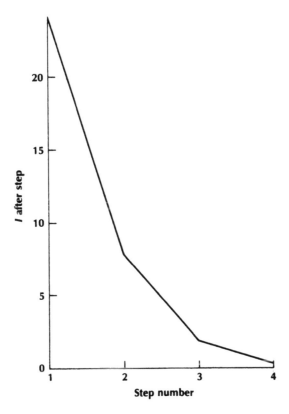

FIGURE 5–60
Performance of the simple algorithm for design improvement with MT [0.95] as goal

indicates that each step is the most cost effective of those performed. In this sense, then, the algorithm performs well.

Figure 5–61a shows the graph of I_n for each of the three paths shown in Figure 5–59a. Note that two of the paths are not monotonically decreasing, indicating that the ordering of the applications of redundancy did not result in the maximum increase in reliability per step. Figure 5–61b shows the graph of I_n for each of the three paths shown in Figure 5–59b (which graphed MTTF versus IC count). Notice that none of the paths are monotonically decreasing, indicating that a different ordering of redundancy applications should be used if increased MTTF is the goal.

For both of the examples in this chapter, the exploration of the design space minimized the number of design trade-offs (such as redundancy techniques) in order to illustrate the methodology. Inclusion of additional redundancy or fault-intolerant techniques (such as changing environmental, temperature, and quality factors as in Chapter 3) would yield a much richer design space. The practicing engineer must consider all these alternatives.

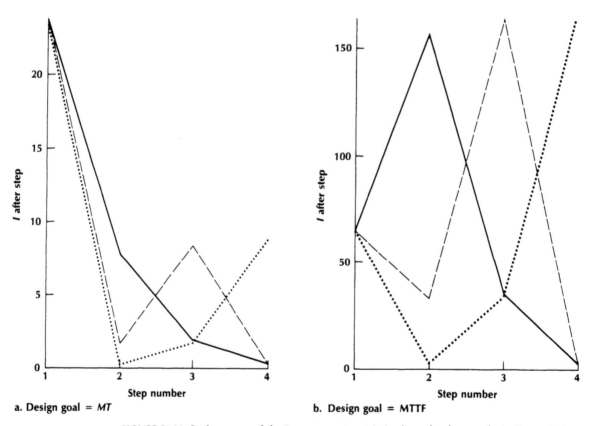

a. Design goal = MT

b. Design goal = MTTF

FIGURE 5–61 *Performance of the improvement metric I_n along the three paths in Figure 5–58*

SUMMARY

This chapter introduced a number of evaluation criteria for reliable computing structures. The modeling examples in this chapter provided several lessons about the use of redundancy to enhance reliability:

- Frequently, multiple evaluation criteria are required for adequate comparison of alternative designs. The most frequently used criterion—MTTF—is particularly poor for evaluating massively redundant systems. The reliability curve for a redundant system exhibits a sharp knee when all the fault tolerance has been exhausted. The redundant system is much more likely to fail, because there are more components than in a nonredundant system, and the next component failure causes a system failure.
- The first application of redundancy to a system produces the largest absolute increase in reliability. The point of diminishing returns is usually reached by redundancy factors of five or less.
- Care must be taken to model the entire system. The addition of extra logic to manage redundancy may actually result in a less reliable system than the nonredundant one.
- Often, apparent system reliability will improve as a result of using more detailed models. Although modeling effort increases rapidly with the level of detail, more effort in modeling can produce a less overdesigned, more cost-effective system.
- Values for mathematically concise parameters (such as coverage) are often difficult or impossible to predict. Indeed, the gross parameters may oversimplify the situation. An engineering "guesstimate," coupled with a sensitivity analysis (varying the parameter over a best case/worst case range to determine effects on the model) can isolate parameters that need further refinement.
- Fault-intolerant techniques should not be neglected. Extra care in component specification and screening may cost less than many forms of redundancy.
- Above all, a balanced approach is required. All portions of a system should be considered, not simply the CPU or memory. Furthermore, a mixture of fault-tolerant techniques usually produces a more effective design than application of one technique throughout the system. Each technique should be applied to the portion of the system that best matches its properties (such as codes to portions of systems that deal in vectors of data—memory, registers, bus, data paths).
- System comparison techniques are stressed rather than absolute numbers because the reliability function of a module frequently is not known at system design time.

REFERENCES

Abraham and Siewiorek, 1974; Aggarwal and Rai, 1978; Almassy, 1979; Ball, 1980; Barlow and Proschan, 1965; Bavuso, 1984; Bavuso et al., 1987; Beaudry, 1978; Bell and Newell, 1971; Bell et al., 1978; Bennetts, 1975; Bouricius, Carter, and Schneider, 1969a, 1969b; Bouricius et al., 1971; Brown, Tierney, and Wasserman, 1961; Butler, 1986; Butler and White, 1988; Butner and Iyer, 1980.

Castillo, 1980; Castillo and Siewiorek, 1980; Cheung, 1980; Cheung and Ramamoorthy, 1975; Chou and Abraham, 1980; Cornell and Halstead, 1976; Costes et al., 1981; Costes, Landrault, and Laprie, 1978.

DEC, 1971, 1972; Eckhardt and Lee, 1985, 1988; Elkind, 1980a, 1980b; Elkind and Siewiorek, 1978, 1980; Esary and Proschan, 1962; Ferdinand, 1974; Finelli, 1988; Fitzsimmons and Love, 1978; Frank and Frisch, 1970; Funami and Halstead, 1975.

Gandhi, Knove, and Henley, 1972; Gay and Ketelsen, 1979; Gear, 1976; Geilhufe, 1979; Geist and Trivedi, 1983; Goyal et al., 1986; Gupta, Porter, and Lathrop, 1974; Gurzi, 1965; Halstead, 1979; Hecht, 1976; Horowitz, 1975; Howard, 1971.

IEEE, 1977; Ingle and Siewiorek, 1976; Jack et al., 1975; Jelinsky and Moranda, 1973; Jensen, 1964; Johnson and Malek, 1989; Keller, 1976; Kini, 1981; Kini and Siewiorek, 1982; Klaschka, 1969; Knight and Leveson, 1986; Knuth, 1969.

Lapp and Powers, 1977; Levine and Meyers, 1976; Littlewood, 1975, 1979; Longden, Page, and Scantlebury, 1966; Lynch, Wagner, and Schwartz, 1975; Lyons and Vanderkulk, 1962; McCann and Palumbo, 1988; McCluskey and Clegg, 1971; McConnel and Siewiorek, 1981; McConnel, Siewiorek, and Tsao, 1979; Mei, 1970; Meyer, Furchtgot, and Wu, 1979; Misra, 1970; Miyamoto, 1975; Mohanly, 1973; Muehldorf, 1975; Murphy, 1964; Musa, 1975.

Nelson, 1973; Ng and Avizienis, 1980; Ogus, 1973; Pascoe, 1975; Peterson and Weldon, 1972; Phister, 1979; Posa, 1980; Ramamoorthy and Han, 1973; Raytheon, 1974, 1976; Reynolds and Kinsbergen, 1975; Rhodes, 1964; Rickers, 1975–76; Rosenthal, 1977; Ross, 1972; Roth et al., 1967; Rubin, 1967; Russel, 1978.

Sahner and Trivedi, 1987; Sanders and Meyer, 1986; Satyanarayana and Prabhakar, 1978; Schertz and Metze, 1972; Schick and Wolverton, 1978; Schneidewind, 1975; Schnell and Leveson, 1988; Shedletsky and McCluskey, 1973; Shooman, 1968, 1970, 1973, 1991; Siewiorek, 1975; Siewiorek and McCluskey, 1973a, 1973b; Siewiorek and Rennels, 1980; Snow and Siewiorek, 1978; Stapper, 1973; Stiffler, Bryant, and Guccione, 1979.

Tammaru and Angell, 1967; Teoste, 1962; Texas Instruments, n.d.; Thayer, Lipow, and Nelson, 1978; Trivedi and Shooman, 1975; Tryon, 1962; Tsao, 1982; von Neumann, 1956; Wang and Lovelace, 1977; Warner, 1974; Wilkov, 1972; Wolverton and Shick, 1974; Wyle and Burnett, 1967; Yakowitz, 1977; Yourdon, 1972.

PROBLEMS

1. Assume that the failures of three computers A, B, and C, are independent, exponential distributed random variables with failure rates $\lambda_A = 1/800$, $\lambda_B = 1/1,300$, and $\lambda_C = 1/1,300$ failures per hour respectively.
   a. What is the probability that at least one system fails in a four-week period?
   b. What is the probability that all three systems fail in a four-week period?
2. Calculate the reliability of the structure in Figure P5–1 between points A and B. Assume all modules have a reliability of R.

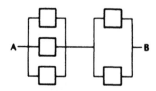

FIGURE P5–1

3. Consider the system success diagram in Figure P5–2.

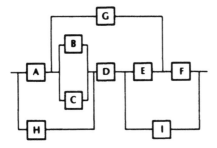

FIGURE P5–2

a. List all possible working paths in the form of a reliability block diagram.
b. Derive the upper bound for system reliability given by

$$R_{sys} \leq 1 - \prod_{i=1}^{j} (1 - R_{path\ i})$$

c. Derive the lower bound for system reliability from the minimal cut set:

$$R_{sys} \geq \prod_{i=1}^{k} (1 - Q_{cut\ i})$$

d. Derive the exact reliability formula.
e. Simplify the preceding results if all modules exhibit the same reliability R.

4. Assume that the probabilities f_0 (probability of a relay or MOS transistor failure in open position) and f_s (probability of a failure in short position) and that the system can tolerate a short between points A and B (that is, a short failure is acceptable but an open failure is not). Choose one of the following to describe the reliability of the structure in Figure P5–3.

FIGURE P5–3

a. $1 - f_0$ b. $(1 - f_0)^2$ c. $1 - 2f_0$ d. $1 - f_0^2$

5. With f_0 and f_s as in Problem 4, assume that a short between A and B may be tolerated. Choose one of the following to describe the reliability of the structure in Figure P5–4.

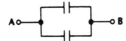

FIGURE P5–4

a. $1 - f_0$ b. $(1 - f_0)^2$ c. $1 - 2f_0$ d. $1 - f_0^2$

6. Given that $f_0 = f_s$, assume that a short between A and B is tolerated and that Y is known to have failed already. Choose one of the following to describe the reliability of the structure in Figure P5–5.

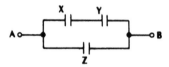

FIGURE P5–5

a. $1 - (f_0/2)$ b. $1 - [(f_0 + f_s)/2]$ c. $0.5(2 - f_0)(1 - f_0)$ d. $0.5(1 - f_0)^2$
e. $1 - 0.5 f_0 - 0.5 f_0^2$

7. The connection between points A and B is to be controlled. The circuit in Figure P5–6 is used instead of a single relay or MOS transistor in order to achieve highly reliable control. The probability of failing in an open position is f_0, and the probability of a failure in a short position is f_s. Assume that statistically, the reliabilities of the relay/transistors are mutually independent. What is the reliability of this network? Find the conditions under which this network is more reliable than a single relay/transistor between A and B.

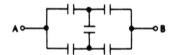

FIGURE P5–6

8. If the reliability of a module is R_m and if a perfect arbiter chooses between the outputs of a pair of identical independent modules, which of the following describes the reliability of a system?
a. R_m^2 b. $R_m^2 + 0.5 R_m$ c. $R_m^2 + 0.5 R_m(1 - R_m)$ d. R_m

9. The reliability of a nonredundant system ranges between 0.2 and 1; that is, below 0.2 the system is considered failed. To achieve unconditional improvements in reliability through triple modular redundancy, the system is divided into m modules of identical reliability. If voters are perfect, which of the following is the minimum value of m?
a. 2   b. 3   c. 4   d. 5

10. With an imperfect voter, the maximum system reliability in a TMR scheme with triplicated voters resulted from dividing the system into eight modules before triplication. If the mean time to failure for the original system was 800 hours, which of the following represents the MTTF for a voter?
a. 100 hours   b. 800 hours   c. 3200 hours   d. 6400 hours

11. Assume a perfect voter and a perfect switch in a TMR scheme with two spares. What is the reliability of the TMR scheme at the time when the reliability of a single module is 0.5?
a. 0.5   b. 0.1875   c. 0.8125   d. 1.0

12. Assume a perfect switch and an imperfect voter in a TMR scheme with S spares. Which of the following will show a maximum reliability at the time when module reliability is 0.7?
a. $S = 1$ b. $S = 2$ c. $S = 3$ d. $S = 4$

13. The inputs of a two input AND gate may be stuck-at-0 or stuck-at-1 with probabilities f_0 and f_s, respectively. If $f_s = 0$ and if the inputs are totally random, which of the following represents the reliability of the output?

   a. $1 - f_0$ b. $(1 - f_0)^2$ c. $1 - 0.5f_0 + 0.25f_0^2$ d. $1 - 1.5f_0 + 0.75f_0^2$

14. With f_0 and f_s as defined in Problem 13 and with $f_0 \neq 0$, what is the reliability of the output of an AND gate (with $f_s \neq 0$)?

   a. $1 - f_s$ b. $(1 - f_s)^2$ c. $1 - 0.5f_s + 0.25f_s^2$ d. $1 - 1.5f_s + 0.75f_s^2$

15. If the failures in a system are known to alternate (that is, a stuck-at-0 failure is followed by a stuck-at-1 failure, and so on), how many failures can a 7MR scheme tolerate?

   a. 3 failures   b. 4 failures   c. 5 failures   d. 6 failures

16. A variation of a hybrid redundancy scheme associates a spare with a specific module; that is, a spare, S_i, can replace only the module M_i and no other. For a TMR system with three such spares, which of the following represents the difference between the reliabilities of the variant system and of the hybrid system (with reliability of a module $= R_m$, $Q_m = 1 - R_m$)?

   a. 0   b. 1   c. $3R_m^3 Q_m^3 + 3R_m^4 Q_m^2$ d. $3R_m^2 Q_m^4$ e. $6R_m^3 Q_m^3 + 12R_m^2 Q_m^4$

17. The following reliability model has been proposed for the system in Figure P5–7:

$$R_{sys} = R_v(3R_p^2 - 2R_p^3)(3R_m^2 - 2R_m^3)$$

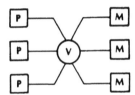

FIGURE P5–7

where R_v, R_p, and R_m are the voter, processor, and memory reliability, respectively. Several factors are ignored in this model. Ignoring each factor makes the model either pessimistic or optimistic. List at least four of these factors and explain their effect on the model.

18. Consider a TMRed register file composed of eight 16-bit words in Figure P5–8.

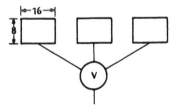

FIGURE P5–8

   a. Assuming only single-bit failures, write the system reliability function, R_{TMR}, in terms of the bit reliability, R_b, and the voter reliability, R_v.

   b. Now assume that the register file is protected by a 21-bit (16 data bits and 5 check bits) single-error-correcting Hamming code as shown in Figure P5–9. Write the system reliability function R_{SEC}, in terms of the bit reliability, R_b, and the encoder/decoder reliability, R_e.

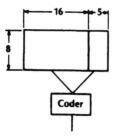

FIGURE P5-9

c. Assume $R_v = R_e = 1$. Pick a value of R_b for which $R_{TMR} > R_{SEC}$. Also pick a value of R_b for which $R_{SEC} > R_{TMR}$. Which scheme, TMR or SEC, would you recommend using and why? [Hint: The functions are well behaved and intersect only at one value of R_b.]

19. a. Derive the expression given in this chapter for the reliability of a hybrid redundant system with a TMR core.
    b. Generalize this expression to hybrid redundancy with an NMR core.
    c. What is the effect of including coverage? Consider two cases: TMR with one spare and TMR with $m - 3$ spares.

20. a. As an alternative to the conventional hybrid system with a TMR core and a single spare, the organization in Figure P5-10 is proposed. In this scheme the spare, a, can replace only module 1 and no other. If the voter and the switching circuits are perfect, show that the reliability of the system is

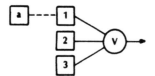

FIGURE P5-10

$$R_m^4 + 4R_m^3 (1 - R_m) + 3R_m^2 (1 - R_m)^2$$

where R_m is the reliability of a module. [Hint: With the three original modules denoted by numbers 1, 2, 3 and the spare by a, a failure tree showing all permutations for the preceding system is shown in Figure P5-11.]

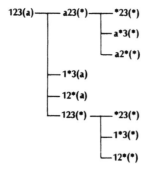

FIGURE P5-11

b. Using the tree approach (or otherwise), what is the reliability of the system in Figure P5–12? (This is an alternative to a hybrid scheme with a TMR core and two spares. The spares are once again dedicated, spare *a* to module 1 and spare *b* to module 2.)

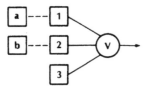

FIGURE P5–12

21. If we denote the expression in Problem 20 by R_d [that is, $R_d = R_m^4 + 4R_m^3(1 - R_m) + 3R_m^2(1 - R_m)^2$] and the reliability of the switching circuits by R_{swd}, then we may model the system reliability as

$$R_{sysd} = R_{swd} \cdot R_d$$

We may also model the reliability of a hybrid scheme with one spare, R_{hyb}, as a product of the switch reliability, R_{swh}, and the probability of having two or more good modules in the core of the system. Assume that all modules are identical and that the reliability is R_m ($= e^{-\lambda t}$). The ratio of the circuit complexity of the switch in the hybrid scheme to the complexity of a single module is denoted by α. Assuming that failure rates are directly dependent on the complexity, we may write $R_{swh} = R_m^\alpha$. Realizing that the switching circuits in a dedicated spare system need to attain only half the number of states required by switching circuits in a hybrid system with a single spare, we estimate the complexity ratio to be half also; that is, $R_{swd} = R_{swh}^{0.5}$. For $\alpha = 0.1$, plot the mission time improvement of R_{hyb} over R_{sysd} as a function of R_m. [Use $R_{swd}(R_m)$ as R_{sysmin}, the minimum required system reliability that defines the mission time.] For the plots, use logarithmic scale for R_m if you prefer. From the plot, determine the range of R_m during which R_{hyb} is better than R_{sysd}. Repeat for $\alpha = 0.01$. (Note: $\alpha = 0.01$ implies that the basic modules are 100 times as complex as the switch in the hybrid system. If the switch had 10 gates, the module would have 1,000 gates. Compared with the LSI-11, how big is the module?)

22. Consider two redundant systems based on voting in Figure P5–13. System a does bus-level voting on every P-M transfer. System b is a multiprocessor that votes after each subtask by mutual communications over interfaces T. Develop a reliability model for each system. State your assumptions. Which system is better? [Hint: This problem is purposely left open-ended. At the highest level of modeling the systems appear identical. Drive the modeling to a low enough level to illustrate the differences in the systems.]

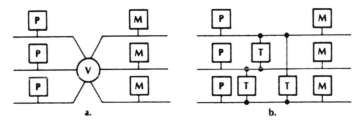

FIGURE P5–13

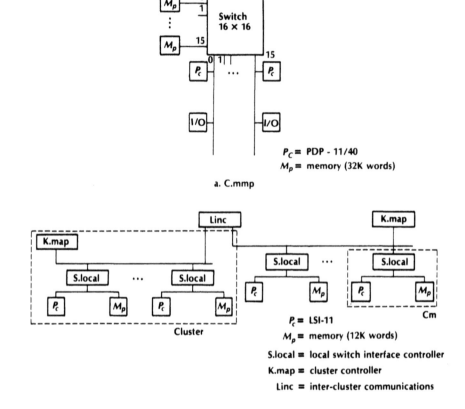

a. C.mmp

b. Computer module system (Cm*) with two clusters.

FIGURE P5–14

23. Figures (a) and (b) in Figure P5–14 depict two computer structures, C.mmp and Cm*. Besides being multiprocessor systems, the two structures may also be viewed as fault-tolerant structures with redundant processing power. Consider the 16-processor, 16-memory C.mmp and a two-cluster, 8-processor-per-cluster Cm* organization. For a task that requires at least four processors and at least 48K words of memory, compare the reliabilities of C.mmp and Cm* using various modeling techniques. Assume that the recovery processes are imperfect and the probability of recovery given a failure is a function of the size of the system. Suggest a model for the probability of recovery. A parts-count model of the components of the two systems yields the failure rates shown in Table P5–1. Make reasonable assumptions where necessary, such as assuming that the failure rate of K.map includes that of the inter-Cm bus. [Note: Although a single-memory port of 64K words of C.mmp seems sufficient for the task, a single-port with multiple processors is a highly unbalanced system and not only slows down the system but also is extremely susceptible to transient failures. Therefore, assume that at least as many memory ports as the number of processors are required for reliable operation of C.mmp.]

TABLE P5–1

Component	Failure Rate (failure per 10^6 hrs.)	Component	Failure Rate (failure per 10^6 hrs.)
C.mmp		CM*	
PDP-11/40	56.9	LSI-11 processor	29.9
Processor associated circuitry		Memory (12K words; semiconductor)	69.4
(RELOC box, processor interface)	20.3	K.map	131.0
Memory box (32K words)	159.6	Linc	34.8
Memory associated circuitry/port	9.8	S.local	24.0
(Priority decode, etc.)			
Switch	507.6		

24. Consider a dual-redundant system that normally operates with both units running. Error detection is achieved by comparing the outputs of the two units. If either unit fails, the probability that the failure is isolated correctly so that the remaining unit (and system) continues to run properly is c (coverage = c). The system can therefore fail in two ways: both units fail (exhaustion of spares) or one unit fails in a bad way (coverage failure). Assume that each unit exhibits failure rate λ and repair rate μ. [Note: Whenever a coverage failure occurs, both units are considered to have failed, and repair—with rate μ—starts on each. The first one to be repaired brings the system as a whole back up, while repair continues on the other.)
    a. Draw the complete four-state transition diagram for the system and give the corresponding T matrix.
    b. Reduce the transition diagram to three states and give the corresponding T matrix.
    c. Derive the steady-state availability for the three-state model.
25. Consider the dual-redundant system discussed in this chapter. Assume now that when both systems have failed, two field service engineers are called in, one for each system. Furthermore, assume that the dual system is configured as a main unit with a backup. Whenever the main unit fails, there is only the probability c (coverage = c) that the backup comes on-line successfully to keep the system going. Whenever the backup fails, the system will continue to operate if the main unit is working, or will fail if the main unit has already failed without yet being repaired. Both the main unit and the backup unit exhibit failure rate λ and repair rate μ. [Note: Whenever the main unit fails and the backup does not come on-line due to a coverage failure, both units are considered to have failed, and repair—with rate μ—starts on both. The first one to be repaired brings the system as a whole back up, while repair continues on the other.]
    a. Draw the complete four-state transition diagram.
    b. Draw the three-state transition diagram obtained by merging the states with a single failed unit.
    c. Derive the availability function $A(t)$ for the three-state model.
    d. Derive the reliability function $R(t)$, first drawing the modified three-state transition diagram.

26. Tandem Computers, Inc., introduced a multiple computer system in 1975 for critical appli-cations, characterized by a high cost for loss of computer power. A prime example is electronic funds transfer where interest is charged by the hour and one company estimated a $300,000 revenue loss per hour of computer down time. The structure of a dual processor Tandem Non-Stop system is shown in Figure P5–15. The computers communicate via the intercomputer dynabus. The system is considered failed only if both computers are down at the same time (assume the Dynabus never fails).

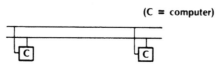

(C = computer)

FIGURE P5–15

   a. Assume that the failure rate is exponential with $\lambda = 1/1000$ failures per hour. Also assume that computer repair is exponential, with μ repairs per hour. Develop the Markov model for the system with λ, μ as parameters. What is the probability that the system is failed for $\mu = 1/48$? Draw a graph of probability of failure versus μ.
   b. What is the expected time to failure for the system?
27. Reformulate the analysis in the redundancy to enhance chip yield section for a RAM chip employing the redundancy technique of your choice.
28. Consider the system success diagram in Figure P5–16.

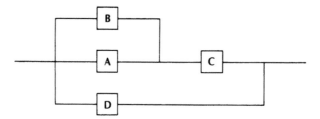

FIGURE P5–16

   a. Derive the exact reliability formula in terms of A, B, C, D.
   b. Simplify the formula assuming $A = B = C = D = R$.
   c. Check your answer by calculating the reliability formula by an alternative method.
29. Derive an equation for the mission time—that is, $MT(r)$—for the Weibull function.
30. Consider a system with n modules that tolerates two failures.
   a. Write and simplify the reliability equation for this system.
   b. Assuming module reliability is exponentially distributed with failure rate λ, calculate and simplify the MTTF for this system.
31. The design goal is an SEC memory for a 16-bit minicomputer with memory mapping. The memory is to be a 128M-word memory, built with 1M-bit MOS RAMs. Assume that the ambient temperature is 30°C, components are of quality class C, the environment is ground fixed, and single-bit failures are the dominant mode of memory-chip failures.
   a. To save on memory chips, a 39-bit SEC/DED Hamming code is to be used (its parity-check matrix is given in Figure P5–17). Design the correction/detection/encoding tree, holding register, correction circuit, and other data path elements shown in the block diagram in

Figure 5–42. Use 7400 series TTL and do not bother with pin numbers (this is a rough design). Assume control circuitry of 10 SSI chips ($\approx$ 8 gates per chip) and 5 MSI chips ($\approx$ 15 gates each). Evaluate this design using the MIL-217 model and techniques discussed in this chapter.

FIGURE P5–17

b. Design a block-coded memory with a better MTTF. Assess the difference in cost in number of chips (if any). Assume 10 MSI and 15 SSI chips for auxiliary circuitry, and design the data-path elements shown in the block-code memory diagram in Figure 5–43. Justify your choice of block size.

c. Discuss the relative performance (not reliability) of the two designs, both with and without errors present. Can the vertical parity words be kept in a separate memory so that they can be accessed in parallel with the data on writes? How does this affect the performance? Discuss the conditions under which you would choose each design.

32. Redesign the error-checking code memory of Problem 31 to allow it to switch in two spare-bit planes. Evaluate the effect on the memory system cost, performance, and reliability.

6 FINANCIAL CONSIDERATIONS

This chapter discusses several fundamental financial considerations in the development, acquisition, and operation of a computer system, and it explains why knowledge of these costs is important to the designer of a computer system or component. These financial considerations can also guide the owner or operator of a computer system in assessing the effects of a system's reliability and maintainability on the cost of ownership.

Several fundamental terms and concepts will be defined and used as parameters in mathematical models. Of primary interest are discounted cash-flow cost of ownership models, maintenance cost models, maintainability feature-decision analysis techniques, and life-cycle cost models.

FUNDAMENTAL CONCEPTS

Maintenance Costs

Maintenance cost is the cost associated with keeping a computer system functioning according to operational specifications. This very complex topic should not be trivialized by the designer; maintenance cost constitutes a significant proportion of the cost of owning a computer, and it is under at least the indirect control of the designer.

Installed Base. From the point of view of the maintenance provider, an important factor in the calculation of maintenance cost is the *installed base*. This is the number of systems (as a function of time) that the manufacturer is required to service. Some customers may elect self-maintenance or third-party service (by someone other than the manufacturer); these systems are not included in the installed base. (The fact that some customers may have fixed-price contracts and that others pay for each service call is potentially significant in terms of field service revenue, but has no real importance to the designer.) The installed base can be estimated from three basic parameters: the shipment rate, contract penetration rate, and contract renewal rate.

- *Shipment rate* is the number of units sold, shipped, and installed in the field, as a function of time. Typically, the value of the frequency distribution is low at the beginning and end of product life and very high in the middle.
- *Contract penetration rate* is the percentage of customers who elect to have the manufacturer service their system; it does not include those who either self-maintain or go to a third party. This discussion makes no distinction between per-call (parts and labor) and fixed-price contract customers. Contract penetration is

normally quite high for medium- to large-scale systems, ranging from 85 to 95 percent.

• *Contract renewal rate*, the last important parameter in determining installed base, takes into account the fact that not all customers renew their commitment to service from the manufacturer.

Example. Table 6–1 is an example of an installed base calculation with an assumed three-year shipment rate (in quarters), a 75 percent contract penetration rate, and a 90 percent renewal rate. Seventy-five percent of the customers receiving systems take out a contract. Thus, 45 of the 60 systems shipped in the first quarter become part of the installed base, 150 of the 200 shipped in the second quarter, and so on. The last column shows the accumulation of these contracts in the installed base.

By the fifth quarter, 90 percent of the 45 contracts coming up for renewal are actually renewed, resulting in the attrition of approximately five contracts. The last column in the fifth quarter shows the addition of 1,050 contracts (from new shipments) to the installed base, minus the attrition of five.

In the ninth quarter, the attrition is 10 percent of the fifth quarter's new contracts (105), plus 10 percent of the 40 remaining contracts opened in the first quarter. Figure 6–1 restates Table 6–1 graphically.

Sources of Maintenance Costs

Labor Expense. Labor represents the largest expenditure in computer servicing. Even the most efficient field service organizations have an average round-trip travel time to and from the customer's site (that is, totally unproductive time) on the order of 1.5 hours. At $100 or more per hour, fully burdened, a service call costs the service provider $150 before any work is performed. Labor expense depends on mean time between

TABLE 6–1
Example of installed base calculation

Quarter	Shipments	New Contracts	First Year Attrition	Second Year Attrition	Total Contracts
1	60	45			45
2	200	150			195
3	1000	750			945
4	1400	1050			1995
5	1400	1050	5		3040
6	1400	1050	15		4075
7	1400	1050	75		5050
8	1200	900	105		5845
9	600	450	105	4	6186
10	300	225	105	14	6292
11	0	0	105	68	6119
12	0	0	90	95	5934

FIGURE 6–1

Example of in-stalled base curve

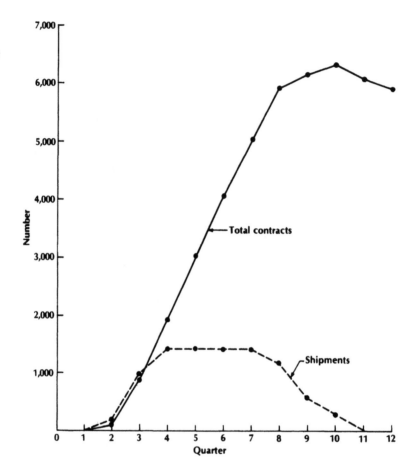

failures, mean time to repair, preventive maintenance (PM) interval, mean time to preventive maintenance, travel times, average labor cost, and support ratio (a measurement of the amount of assistance needed on a particular service call). The following formula is a rough estimate of the annual labor expense involved in servicing a computer system:

$$ALE = (CPH)(8760)\left(\frac{MTTR + TTR}{MTBF} + \frac{MTPM + TTPM}{MTBF}\right)$$

where ALE = annual labor expense
      CPH = cost per hour for labor
      8760 = number of hours in a year
      MTTR = mean time to repair.
      TTR = travel time for a repair call
      MTBF = mean time between failures

MTPM = mean time to perform preventive maintenance
TTPM = travel time for a preventive maintenance call
MTBP = mean time between preventive maintenance

Assume that the labor cost per hour is $100, the MTTR is 2.5 hours, and the MTPM is 4.5 hours. Further assume a travel time of 1.5 hours for a repair and 0.5 hour for a PM (it is usually assumed that because several simultaneous PMs can be scheduled in advance, the cost of travel time can be apportioned among several devices). For an MTBF of 4000 hours and an MTBP of 5000 hours, the annual labor expense is

$$\text{ALE} = (100)(8760)\left(\frac{2.5 + 1.5}{4000} + \frac{4.5 + .5}{5000}\right) = (100)(8760)(.001 + .001) = \$1752$$

Material Expense. The next largest expense for computer servicing is for materials, particularly the cost of the field replaceable unit (FRU). The choice between a logical and physical partitioning of the system is crucial for a system designer, for it directly affects both the maintainability and cost of ownership of the system. The cost impact can be estimated from the cost and reliability of each FRU as follows:

Total Cost = $\sum[(\text{FRU cost})_i(\text{FRU failure rate})_i]$

This formula, however, estimates only the cost of replacing failed hardware. For the service provider, there are also other costs:

- *Inventory costs* are the costs associated with keeping a supply of spare parts; they consist of all the costs of maintaining a supply depot, including order processing costs and the fully burdened cost per square foot of the building.
- *Level of service costs* are an important consideration in determining inventory costs; that is, level of service is the conditional probability that a part is in stock, given a failure of that part. If the MTBP of each part and its field population are known, a relatively straightforward statistical calculation can determine how many parts of each type to have in stock to attain a given level of service.

Other Expenses. Two additional expenses have a bearing on the cost of maintaining a computer system:

- Training costs include service personnel who must be trained. Whether the owner self-maintains the system or purchases field service externally, this cost is ultimately borne by the system owner. Because training and course development can be a significant expense, it is important to design a system that minimizes the amount of special training necessary.
- *Depreciation of capital equipment* can be significant. If special test equipment is required to service the computer system, the cost of that equipment must be taken into account by both the system purchaser and the designer. For example, such equipment is frequently written off during a period of five years, using the double-declining balance method.

   The double-declining method expenses the cost of the equipment at a rate double that of a linear method, but it applies this rate to the remaining balance instead of to the original amount. Thus, a straight-line depreciation over five years would be 20 percent per year. A double-declining balance would write off 40 percent in the first year, 40 percent of the remainder (40 percent of 60 percent, or 24 percent) the next year, and 40 percent of the remainder (40 percent of 36 percent, or 14.4 percent) the third year. Because this series is infinite, it is customary to divide the remainder evenly between the last two years; thus, 10.8 percent of the original cost is written off in each of the last two years.

Cost of Customer Ownership

Cost of ownership is the true total cost of owning a computer system, not just the acquisition cost. It includes a multitude of factors, such as purchase cost, maintenance cost, and costs of downtime, site preparation, storage media and supplies, power, environmental conditioning, and operating personnel. Maintenance cost alone can easily equal the purchase price after just five years of operations.

The other costs of operation can render the purchase cost relatively insignificant. Consider especially the cost of downtime. Presumably, all computer systems are purchased in order to increase productivity and efficiency. If a computer system is properly utilized (consistently loaded at or near full capacity), an interruption in service will inevitably lead to a loss of money or time, which normally equates to loss of revenue.

It is difficult to present a generalized model of the cost of downtime because it varies greatly with the application. In some systems it is negligible; in others, it far outweighs any other financial considerations. Finally, in some applications its value cannot be computed because the survival of priceless things (such as human life) depends upon the computer's continuous operation. The following are examples of systems in which the cost of downtime is high:

- *On-Line Billing System:* In an on-line billing system used, say, by a telephone company for recording charges on long distance calls, the lost revenue when the system is down is practically unrecoverable, and typically substantial. In this case, a "lost-revenue-per-hour" figure should be arrived at by the system's financial analysts and factored into the cost of ownership.
- *Airline Reservation System:* It is more difficult to establish a quantitative measure of lost bookings due to this system's failure, but it can obviously be significant.
- *Electronic Funds Transfer:* When money is being transmitted electronically, there is a great danger that system failure (including loss of data integrity) can lead to large losses.
- *Life-Support Systems:* In systems such as those for monitoring hospital intensive care patients, system failure at an inopportune time can lead to loss of life. With the increasing use of computers in medical care and biomedical engineering, the incidence of loss of life due to computer failures is bound to increase. The cost is, of course, impossible to assess. Systems that deal with transportation (such as flight control systems) and building management (such as fire alarm and containment systems) also belong in this category.

• *National Defense Systems:* Computers now form the backbone of the defense of entire countries. In one incident, a minicomputer failure resulted in an indication that a Russian missile attack on the United States was taking place. The system was designed to fail "safely"—that is, to indicate an attack when it failed—with the premise being that an indication of attack when none is occurring is better than no indication of attack when one is occurring. Fortunately, the system required adequate cross-checks before counteroffensive measures could be taken, and the failure was discovered before any potentially devastating actions occurred.

Net Present Value. A simplified economic model of the cost of computer ownership assumes an initial cash purchase, followed by periodic maintenance payments. It is possible to compute the true cost of ownership as the present value of these outlays. Present value is a financial concept that takes the time value of money into account; that is, if you receive $10 today and put it into a savings account for a year at a 10 percent effective annual interest rate, in a year you will have $11. Conversely, if you are promised $11 one year from today, its present value is only $10.

The rate used to calculate present value is known as the discount rate. Assuming a discount rate of 10 percent, the present value of a dollar received or expended one year from now is

$$\frac{1}{(1 + 0.10)}$$

The present value of a dollar received or expended two years from now has a present-value factor of

$$\frac{1}{(1 + 0.10)^2}$$

and so on.

Net Present Value Example: Assume an initial cost of $1 million, an annual maintenance cost of $100,000, an income tax rate of 34 percent, a write-off over five years using the double-declining balance method, and a discount rate of 10 percent. The following table gives the cost of ownership (in thousands of dollars):

(1)	(2)	(3)	(4)	(5)	(6)	(7)
					Present-	
	Maintenance			After-Tax	Value	Discounted
Year	Cost	Depreciation	Net	Cash Flow	Factor	Cash Flow
1	100	400	−300	−198	0.909	−93
2	100	240	−140	−92	0.826	−40
3	100	144	−44	−29	0.751	−11
4	100	108	−8	−5	0.683	−2
5	100	108	−8	−5	0.621	−2
						Total −148

The amount in column 3 is the depreciation on the capital outlay according to the double-declining balance method. Column 4 is the difference between columns 2 and 3, or the net expense. Column 5 shows the after-tax cash flow (the expenses are deductible from the company's income tax). Column 6 shows the present-value factors. Column 7 is the product of columns 5 and 6. After subtracting the sum of column 7 from the initial outlay of $1 million, the cost of ownership is $852,000.

Alternatives to Net Present Value. There are several alternatives to assessing cost of ownership by the net present value method. The first is the *payback method*, which assumes no time value of money and thus simply adds (or subtracts) the yearly net values to the initial investment. The payback period is then defined as the time at which the cumulative cash flows reach zero.

A better alternative is *internal rate of return* (IRR). To determine the internal rate of return, the discount value is assumed to be unknown, and an iterative procedure is performed to discover the discount rate at which the net-present value equals zero. The company establishes a minimum IRR, and if the IRR is greater than this minimum, it is a desirable investment.

COST MODELS

Field Service Overview

In many computer companies, *field service* (hardware and software) is a business unit with independent responsibility for profit and loss. The expense the company incurs when repairing equipment under warranty accumulates in the field service department. Because each company's financial structure varies, it is impossible to generalize about the field service business units, but it is important to realize that field service revenues can be a significant proportion of corporate revenues, in some cases approaching 30 percent. For a large end-user minicomputer company or mainframe manufacturer, field service personnel typically account for 20 to 30 percent of the total personnel.

Field service is a labor intensive business, and travel time is also a very significant part of the expense. The cost of field service is determined primarily by product traits (reliability, diagnosability, and the like). The business can be further characterized by a potentially lengthy and strong commitment to the customer. There are inherent risks in charging fixed contract prices: loss of profits if the price is set too low, and loss of business to third-party maintenance organizations if the price is too high.

There is also a growing set of legal considerations about which to worry. What if a client company loses substantial revenue because of the failure of a computer? What if property damage results from a computer malfunction? What if personal injury occurs as the result of an unsafe design? In one case, a small data processing company was located near a fire station. Electromagnetic emissions from some of the computer equipment were interfering with the fire department's radio communications. The problem was remedied before any damage was done, but the consequences of a computer's interfering with the reporting of a major fire could have been critical. The number of individual litigations, class action suits, and government regulations is likely to increase as computers and the consequences of their malfunctions proliferate.

Maintenance Cost Models

Maintenance cost models estimate the variable costs associated with servicing a particular system or part of a system. A variable cost is one that varies in direct proportion to the number of service calls received, as distinct from a fixed cost, which is incurred independently of the number of calls received. Typically, a variable cost is the cost of a particular replacement part for a broken computer system. An example of a fixed cost is the cost of a piece of test equipment which is required whether or not anything ever actually breaks.

Typical parameters in a maintenance cost model are

Mean time between failures

Mean time to repair

Travel time associated with the service call, perhaps computed at some average rate

Material consumed, such as replacement parts and lubricants

Preventive maintenance performed, either on a regular basis or in conjunction with a repair action

Cost of labor

The results of such a calculation would provide a rough estimate of the cost per unit time of maintaining a system or part of a system. This type of model ignores fixed (front-end) costs and can be expected to estimate only variable costs.

Maintenance Cost Model Example: A comprehensive model that includes these fixed costs, as well as items such as salvage value, has been developed by Xerox and is reported in Pierce [1977]. Alternative designs can easily be analyzed, as the histograms in Figure 6–2 demonstrate. This case involved comparison of three alternative packaging schemes. The overall life costs were shown to be less for one large, relatively expensive board than for a system partitioned into smaller boards; the smaller boards had decreased reliability resulting from the increase in number of connectors.

Sensitivity analyses evaluate the effect of various parameters on profitability. Figure 6–3 shows an example.

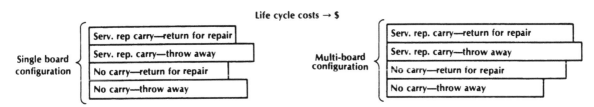

FIGURE 6–2 *Life-cycle costs of alternative configurations*

FIGURE 6–3
Profit sensitivities

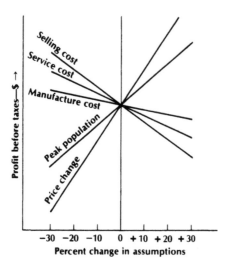

Other trade-off studies performed with this model sought answers to the following questions:

- Should the diagnostic hardware for the system be included as part of the system hardware or carried by the field engineer?
- Should a unit replaced in the field be repaired and recirculated or discarded?
- Should a given availability goal for a subassembly be achieved by improving its reliability or its maintainability?
- At what level (region, district, branch, or individual person) should a spare part be stocked?

Table 6–2 lists the input and output data for the model by Pierce [1977].

Maintenance Cost Model with Risks. Risk factors could be added to the preceding model, in the form of probability distributions expected for each of the parameters. Adding risk factors would take into account the fundamentally random nature of failures. The model parameters could be established to give minimum cost (with appropriate confidence levels), average cost, and so on.

The outputs would be a probability distribution of the expected maintenance costs instead of a point estimate. This type of model facilitates a simple sensitivity analysis, answering such questions as the following:

- What happens to the cost of maintenance if the MTBF is 10 percent higher than the estimate?
- What happens to the cost of maintenance if the MTTR is decreased by 15 minutes?

Maintainability Feature Analysis: The Feature Failure-Mode Matrix. A feature failure-mode matrix is a technique to evaluate a series of maintainability features for their effect on

TABLE 6–2
Input and output parameters for a maintenance cost model

Primary Data Inputs	Primary Data Outputs
Part data	1. Increase in number of service personnel by year
1. Unit cost	2. Number of spares replaced per year
2. Repair cost	3. Average cost of a spare item
3. Repair transportation cost	4. Mean corrective maintenance time
4. Power-on hours	5. Number of spares returned from the field per year
5. Repair turnaround time	6. Number of additional spares needed per year
6. Repair attrition	7. Number of spares shipped to the field per year
7. Part population	8. Number of nonrepairable parts
8. Erroneous replacements	9. Number of parts in field inventory
9. Replacement rates (MTBF)	10. Number of parts returned from the repair facility
10. Reliability growth	11. Initial cost of parts per year
11. On-site time to repair	12. Initial parts depreciation/tax recovery per year
12. Salvage value	13. Cost of replaced spare parts per year
Business economic factors	14. Tax recovery from replaced parts per year
1. Life-cycle period	15. Cost of service labor per year
2. Corporation-selected depreciation	16. Shipping cost of failed parts per year
3. Corporate tax rate	17. Cost of vendor repair of failed parts per year
4. Service personnel labor rate	18. Shipping cost of spares per year
5. Part cost improvement	19. Salvage value of nonrepair parts
6. Machine placements	
7. Machine workload per service personnel	
Program option controls	
1. Detailed or summarized output	
2. Supplemental quarterly output	
3. Unit cost vs. reliability indifference routine	
4. Part repair or discard evaluation	
5. Service rep carry part or no-carry evaluation	
6. Computations without present value, depreciation, and tax influences	

Source: Pierce, 1977.

the cost of maintaining a given system or device. For example, for a hypothetical digital tape unit, engineering can generate a list of potential maintainability features such as data path loop-around, error simulation, internal parity, speed check, skew check, and power check. Field service can provide a list of failure modes (projected from experience with previous similar designs) such as permanent/intermittent data path errors, faulty controller, faulty error logic, faulty head preamplifier, faulty servos, and faulty power supply. These features and modes are then put in matrix form, as shown in Table 6–3.

At each intersection of a feature and a failure mode in the matrix is an estimate of the time that would be saved when repairing this failure, were the feature present. In the last column is the estimated percent of failures resulting from each of the

TABLE 6–3 *A feature failure-mode matrix*

Failure Mode	Feature							% of System Failures
	Data Path Loop-Around	Error Simulation	Internal Parity	Speed Check	Skew Check	Power Check	Reel LEDs	
Permanent Data Path	74	24	74					11
Intermittent Data Path			168					2
Controller								6
Error Logic	24	54	24					6
Head Preamp	84		84					10
Servos				390	210		66	25
Power Supply						90		5
Minutes Saved	18	6	21	97.5	52.5	4.5	16.5	

defined failure modes. In the last row, a projection of the total time saved by each maintainability feature is obtained by taking the column weighted averages.

The decision about whether to include a particular feature in the final design would proceed as follows: From an estimate of the base parameters of the design (MTBF, MTTR, MTPM), calculate the projected decrease in MTTR due to the feature. Using an appropriate cost model with sales projections, calculate the present value of incorporating this feature. Compare this result with the cost of including this feature in the design, including development cost and the cost of the hardware for all the units to be shipped, expressed in present value. Incorporate the feature if the difference between the life-cycle cost savings and the feature's cost is positive.

Life-Cycle Cost (LCC) Models

Life-cycle cost models take into account the total product business profile: the cost of purchase of the computer system, maintenance, supplies, environmental controls, power, and so on. Every expense associated with owning a computer is considered. Such a model enables an organization to evaluate design alternatives with regard to effects on life-cycle cost and to make a choice that minimizes that cost. Figure 6–4 shows how revenues and expenses (the difference of which is defined as income) might vary over time. Engineering expenses dominate the first years, and manufacturing and service expenses begin to take over as sales revenues increase. Even after manufacturing has ceased, service expenses and revenues continue for a long time, with (it is hoped) a net positive income.

Typical inputs to an LCC model might be

Shipment forecasts over the planned life of the product
Contract penetration (the percentage of customers electing to purchase service contracts) and renewal (percentage renewing each year) rates
List price of the system
Warranty period

FIGURE 6–4

Cost and income distribution over the life of a system

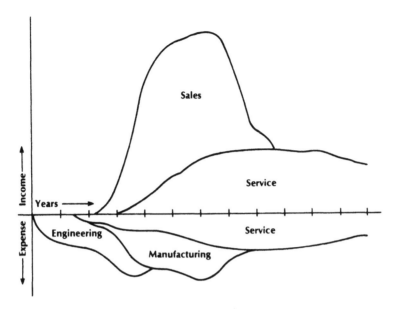

Spares requirements (number of spare parts kits required per system, cost per kit)

Installation expenses (labor and material expense per installation), expenses incurred due to DOA (dead-on-arrival) parts, and other installation difficulties

MTTR, varying over time as experience with repairing the system increases

Labor costs per corrective and preventive maintenance action

MTBF, several values for a sensitivity analysis

Travel time

An estimate of average material cost per failure

Training costs

Capital equipment costs

Spare parts inventory carrying expense

The result of such an analysis would be a tabulation of maintenance cost as a function of MTBF (or other independent variables), profit and loss information, and warranty expense estimates, all with discounted cash flows.

Life-Cycle Cost Model Example: Table 6–4 lists the five-year expense forecasts for manufacturing costs of a hypothetical piece of equipment under a base case (6 months MTBF) and two alternatives (8.5 and 10 months MTBF). The basic assumption is that increased reliability requires a higher manufacturing cost and results in a higher field MTBF and lower field MTTR. This example assumes that the system manufacturing cost was $11,000 in the base case, $300 more for the first alternative, and $800 more for the second alternative.

Table 6–4 also lists the service costs for the base case and the two alternatives over the five-year planned shipments of the product. There is a decrease in service

TABLE 6–4 *Cost forecasts as a function of time with different MTBFs (base: 6 months, alternative 1: 8.5 months, alternative 2: 10 months)*

Quarter	Shipments	Manufacturing Costs			Service Costs		
		Base ($K)	Alt. 1 ($K)	Alt. 2 ($K)	Base ($K)	Alt. 1 ($K)	Alt. 2 ($K)
0	—	—	—	—	17	17	17
1	1	11	11.3	11.8	425	425	425
2	4	44	45.2	47.2	196	177	170
3	73	803	824.9	861.4	554	493	462
4	354	3,894	4,000.2	4,177.2	847	757	709
5	612	6,732	6,915.6	7,221.6	909	818	773
6	820	9,020	9,266.0	9,676.0	1,179	1,045	992
7	990	10,890	11,187.0	11,682.0	1,243	1,075	1,007
8	1,000	11,000	11,300.0	11,800.0	1,576	1,309	1,239
9	1,000	11,000	11,300.0	11,800.0	1,777	1,481	1,361
10	1,000	11,000	11,300.0	11,800.0	1,852	1,527	1,401
11	1,000	11,000	11,300.0	11,800.0	2,042	1,673	1,521
12	1,000	11,000	11,300.0	11,800.0	2,194	1,776	1,609
13	1,000	11,000	11,300.0	11,800.0	2,336	1,876	1,693
14	1,000	11,000	11,300.0	11,800.0	2,484	1,981	1,782
15	1,000	11,000	11,300.0	11,800.0	2,626	2,081	1,866
16	1,000	11,000	11,300.0	11,800.0	2,609	2,044	1,831
17	650	7,150	7,345.0	7,670.0	2,448	1,866	1,651
18	447	4,917	5,051.1	5,274.6	2,345	1,767	1,542
19	320	3,520	3,616.0	3,776.0	2,265	1,677	1,464
20	229	2,519	2,587.7	2,702.2	2,224	1,633	1,419

costs due to increased MTBFs and an associated increase in manufacturing costs. From a life-cycle cost point of view, which alternative is preferable?

Table 6–5 lists the discounted expenses (manufacturing' and service') over the shipment life of the product. At the bottom of the primed columns is the discounted present value of service and manufacturing costs and their total for the base case and two alternatives:

- The total discounted present value for the base case (6 months MTBF and $11,000 manufacturing cost) is $109,277,600.
- The total discounted present value for Alternative 1 (8.5 months MTBF and $11,300 manufacturing cost) is $108,152,300.
- The total discounted present value for Alternative 2 (10 months MTBF and $11,800 manufacturing cost) is $110,849,300.

This analysis shows that Alternative 1 has the best financial profile, because it has the lowest total life-cycle cost, and Alternative 2 has the lowest service cost (about 2 percent less than Alternative 1). Is it worth the investment?

TABLE 6–5 *Discounted cost forecasts*

Quarter	Base System Manufac-turing ($K)	Base System Manufac-turing' ($K)	Base System Service ($K)	Base System Service' ($K)	Alternative 1 (42% Improvement in MBTF) Manufac-turing ($K)	Alternative 1 Manufac-turing' ($K)	Alternative 1 Service ($K)	Alternative 1 Service' ($K)	Alternative 2 (67% Improvement in MTBF) Manufac-turing ($K)	Alternative 2 Manufac-turing' ($K)	Alternative 2 Service ($K)	Alternative 2 Service' ($K)
0			17	17.0			17	17.0			17	17.0
1	11	10.5	425	406.1	11.3	10.8	425	406.1	11.8	11.3	425	406.1
2	44	40.2	196	178.9	45.2	41.3	177	161.6	47.2	43.1	170	155.2
3	803	700.4	554	483.2	824.9	719.5	493	430.0	861.4	751.4	462	403.0
4	3,894	3,245.4	847	705.9	4,000.2	3,333.9	757	630.9	4,177.2	3,481.5	709	590.9
5	6,732	5,360.9	909	723.9	6,915.6	5,507.1	818	651.4	7,221.6	5,750.8	773	615.6
6	9,020	6,863.1	1,179	897.1	9,266.0	7,050.3	1,045	795.1	9,676.0	7,362.3	992	754.8
7	10,890	7,917.0	1,243	903.7	11,187.0	8,133.0	1,075	781.5	11,682.0	8,492.8	1,007	732.1
8	11,000	7,640.9	1,576	1,094.7	11,300.0	7,849.3	1,309	909.3	11,800.0	8,196.6	1,239	860.6
9	11,000	7,300.7	1,777	1,179.4	11,300.0	7,499.8	1,481	982.9	11,800.0	7,831.7	1,361	903.3
10	11,000	6,975.7	1,852	1,174.4	11,300.0	7,165.9	1,527	968.3	11,800.0	7,483.0	1,401	888.4
11	11,000	6,665.1	2,042	1,237.3	11,300.0	6,846.8	1,673	1,013.7	11,800.0	7,149.8	1,521	921.6
12	11,000	6,368.3	2,194	1,270.2	11,300.0	6,542.0	1,776	1,028.2	11,800.0	6,831.5	1,609	931.5
13	11,000	6,084.8	2,336	1,292.2	11,300.0	6,250.7	1,876	1,037.7	11,800.0	6,527.3	1,693	936.5
14	11,000	5,813.8	2,484	1,312.9	11,300.0	5,972.4	1,981	1,047.0	11,800.0	6,236.7	1,782	941.8
15	11,000	5,555.0	2,626	1,326.1	11,300.0	5,706.5	2,081	1,050.9	11,800.0	5,958.9	1,866	942.3
16	11,000	5,307.6	2,609	1,258.9	11,300.0	5,452.4	2,044	986.3	11,800.0	5,693.6	1,831	883.5
17	7,150	3,296.4	2,448	1,128.6	7,345.0	3,386.3	1,866	860.3	7,670.0	3,536.1	1,651	761.2
18	4,917	2,165.9	2,345	1,033.0	5,051.1	2,225.0	1,767	775.7	5,274.6	2,323.5	1,542	679.3
19	3,520	1,481.5	2,265	953.3	3,616.0	1,521.9	1,677	705.8	3,776.0	1,589.3	1,464	616.2
20	2,519	1,013.0	2,224	894.4	2,587.7	1,040.6	1,633	656.7	2,702.2	1,086.7	1,419	570.6
Present values		89,806.4		19,471.2		92,255.7		15,896.6		96,337.8		14,511.5
	Total present value = $109,277.6				Total present value = $108,152.3				Total present value = $110,849.3			

LCC Model with Generalized Data Elements. Common LCC models require detailed and precise analysis of the system's characteristics and its operating environment. It is a difficult task to compare alternative designs, for much information must be collected and entered in the model for each alternative. Eames and Spann [1977] have developed a method that uses cursory system descriptions to produce timely and comprehensive LCC data to support design decisions.

• **Implied Characteristics:** The system is first classified according to the following implied characteristics.

> *Reliability*, developed from a parts stress analysis, from past engineering data and estimates, or from a parts-count reliability prediction model
> *Maintainability*, determined from maintainability scores described in MIL-HDBK-472, Procedure III

Availability, pertaining to a nonredundant functional entity and related to its reliability and maintainability by

$$A_e = \frac{MTTF}{(MTTF + MTTR)}$$

The system availability can then be estimated by taking the product of the availabilities of each functional entity, A_e, provided that system operation is dependent upon concurrent and continuous functioning of each entity and that the functional entities are independent in terms of failures and repairs.

• **Cost Categories:** The reliability, maintainability, and availability data are then incorporated in an LCC model that includes the following cost categories:

Investment costs, which include acquisition, development, initial installation, as well as initial and replaceable spares

Operating and support costs, which include organizational level maintenance, intermediate and depot level maintenance, inventory management, support equipment, personnel training, management and technical data, and new facilities

Table 6–6 lists a description of the variables used and the resulting equations, with suggested typical values for the constants.

Cost of Downtime Model. Often an organization has to decide whether new equipment is justified. One approach is to calculate the downtime over the life of the system for several configurations. The difference in LCC and downtime represents the cost of avoiding downtime by using each configuration.

A method for computing the cost of downtime is to determine the optimum nonredundant system and divide the total LCC by the number of hours in the system design life. The optimum nonredundant system is defined as a system with no redundancy, but with maintainability and fault-intolerant features optimized for minimum life-cycle cost. Eames and Spann [1977] cite an example of a system whose design life is 10 years, with a total LCC of $10 million. If the system is being used 24 hours a day, the user of the system is paying

$$\frac{\$10M}{87,600} = \frac{\$114.16}{hour}$$

for the use of the system. Therefore, it must be worth at least this amount to keep the system running.

Cost of Downtime Example*: Consider a large computer-aided instruction (CAI) system, consisting of keyboards, video terminals, tape units, line printers, software, and various controllers and display generation equipment. Each of these system com-

---

* This example is adapted from Eames and Spann [1977].

ponents is first assigned to one of two categories: electromechanical and large electronic assemblies, and printed circuit boards and small electronic assemblies. LCC analyses are performed with the parameters described in Table 6–6. The system is first considered in its optimum nonredundant form; Table 6–7 shows the results for three different part quality grades.

Next, the effects of various kinds and degrees of redundancy are considered. Table 6–8 compares the results for commercial grade components. Column A restates the results of the optimum nonredundant analysis. Column B shows three variations

TABLE 6–6 *A simple life-cycle cost model and its parameters*

Variables	Value	Constants	Value
NUM: Number of equipment items	Input	FIXILQ: Fraction of failures repaired at intermediate level (IL) branch office by quantity	0.20
PRICE: Initial price	Input		
TFAIL: Failure rate for total quantity of equipment item (I), F/MHR	Input	FIXDLQ: Fraction of failures repaired at depot level (DL) by quantity	0.20, 0.50
QUANT: Total quantity of equipment item (I)	Input	AILRS: Average IL repair material cost percent of PRICE	0.05
HOURS: Total life cycle operating hours per equipment item	Input	AILRT: Average IL repair time, mh	5.0
LABOR: Average labor rate $/MH	50.00	ADLRS: Average DL repair material cost percent of PRICE	0.10
RPPTIP: Ratio of system purchase price to sum of PRICE(I)	0.40	ADLRT: Average DL repair time, mh	5.0
DEVELS: Cost of development	Input	AOLRT: Average organizational level (OL) factory repair time, mh	5.0
INSTAS: Cost of initial installation material and equipment, $	Input	AOLRTS: Average OL repair material cost percent of PRICE	0.20
MTTF: Mean Time To Failure for the whole system	Input	TRIP: Cost to make service trip	100
TQUANT: Total quantity of systems to be made to amortize development costs	Input		

Equations

Acquisition = (RPPTIP)Σ[PRICE (I) × QUANT (I)]

Development = DEVELS/TQUANT

Initial installation = INSTAS

Initial and replaceable spares =
(0.05 + HOURS × 6.0E-6) × Acquisition

Organizational level maintenance =
int (HOURS/MTTF) × {Σ[TFAIL(I) × MTTF × 1.0E-6 ×
(1.0 − FIXDLQ − FIXILQ) × X(I)] + TRIP}

  Where X(I) = AOLRTS × PRICE (I) + AOLRT ×
LABOR

Intermediate and depot level maintenance =
int (HOURS/MTTF) (Σ{TFAIL(I) × MTTF × 1.0E-6 ×
[FIXILQ × V(I) + FIXDLQ × W(I)]} + TRIP)

  Where V(I) = AILRS × PRICE(I) + AILRT × LABOR

  and W(I) = ADLRS × PRICE(I) + ADLRT × LABOR

Inventory management = 4.0 × (Initial Installation)

Support equipment = 0

Personnel training = 0

Management and technical data = 0

New facilities = 0

Source: This model is a modified version of one proposed in Eames and Spann, 1977.

TABLE 6-7
Example of effects of component quality levels on LCC

Parts Quality Grade:	Commercial	MIL-Spec	Hi-Rel
Total FRUs:	1,600	1,600	1,600
Availability:	0.979624	0.993635	0.997444
Mean Uptime:	24 Hrs.	78 Hrs.	195 Hrs.
Acquisition	$2,560,000	$2,900,244	$ 4,400,516
Development	207,999	207,999	207,999
Initial installation	84,979	84,979	84,979
Initial and replacement spares	2,880,000	3,262,804	4,950,596
Organization level maintenance	125,974	122,017	120,968
Intermediate and depot level maintenance	430,346	147,256	84,849
Inventory management	309,287	309,287	309,287
Support equipment	185,000	185,000	185,000
Personnel training	0	0	0
Management and technical data	200,804	196,638	195,530
New facilities	0	0	0
Life-cycle cost	$6,984,389	$7,416,224	$10,539,720
Cost to avoid downtime		$360/hr.	$11,484/hr.

Source: Eames and Spann, 1977; © 1977 IEEE.

TABLE 6-8 *Example of effects on LCC of reliability improvement via redundancy*

Configuration:	A. Optimum Simplex Analysis — Series	B. 9-out-of-10 Redundancy 11% Redundancy	63% Redundancy	100% Redundancy
Total FRUs:	1600	1617	1706	1777
Availability:	0.979624	0.981619	0.991583	0.999540
Mean uptime:	24 Hrs.	24 Hrs.	58 Hrs.	1.085 Hrs.
Acquisition	$2,560,000	$2,588,423	$2,730,836	$2,844,423
Development	207,099	216,412	225,545	235,674
Initial installation	84,979	85,086	85,619	86,046
Initial and replacement spares	2,880,000	2,908,423	3,050,636	3,164,423
Organization level maintenance	125,974	127,374	134,372	139,970
Intermediate and depot level maintenance	430,346	435,125	459,034	478,163
Inventory management	309,287	309,287	309,287	309,287
Support equipment	185,000	185,000	185,000	185,000
Personnel training	0	0	0	0
Management and technical data	200,804	202,291	209,710	215,649
New facilities	0	0	0	0
Life-cycle cost	$6,984,389	$7,057,421	$7,389,939	$7,658,635
Cost to avoid downtime		$392/hr.		

Source: Eames and Spann, 1977; © 1977 IEEE.

of a 9-out-of-10 redundancy scheme: 11 percent of the system with 9-out-of-10 redundancy, the rest simplex; 63 percent with 9-out-of-10 redundancy, the rest simplex; and 100 percent with 9-out-of-10 redundancy. Columns C and D show similar analyses with 4-out-of-5 and 1-out-of-2 redundancies in various portions of the system.

The ratio of LCC change to the change in system downtime yields the value of avoiding downtime for each of these approaches. Figure 6–5 shows these values graphically.

SUMMARY

It is for a financial reason of one sort of another that any fault-tolerant system is designed and built. Calculating the costs and/or benefits of a given high reliability, maintainability, or availability design is a complex task. This chapter has explained important financial concepts related to the purchase, operation, and servicing of a computer system. Also explained were several mathematical techniques, including discounted cash-flow cost-of-ownership calculations, maintenance cost and life-cycle cost models, and a method to assess the cost effectiveness of maintainability features.

This chapter should give the design engineer an adequate understanding of the principles necessary for a rudimentary analysis of the financial considerations for a given system. More sophisticated problems can be handled by financial analysts and management scientists.

REFERENCES

Eames and Spann [1977]; Pierce [1977].

C. 4-out-of-5 Redundancy			D. 1-out-of-2 Redundancy		
12% Redundancy	65% Redundancy	100% Redundancy	18% Redundancy	75% Redundancy	100% Redundancy
1640	1839	2000	1760	2560	3200
0.981619	0.991562	0.999484	0.981616	0.991453	0.999186
26 Hrs.	58 Hrs.	967 Hrs.	26 Hrs.	58 Hrs.	613 Hrs.
$2,624,000	$2,943,906	$3,199,903	$2,816,000	$ 4,095,896	$ 5,119,392
216,527	226,437	237,812	217,151	231,049	249,533
85,219	86,419	87,379	85,939	90,739	94,579
2,944,000	3,263,906	3,519,903	3,136,000	4,415,898	5,439,892
129,122	144,869	157,466	138,571	201,557	251,946
441,110	494,905	537,931	473,384	688,559	860,683
309,287	309,287	309,287	309,287	309,287	309,287
185,000	185,000	185,000	185,000	185,000	185,000
0	0	0	0	0	0
204,143	220,845	234,209	214,167	280,971	334,412
0	0	0	0	0	0
$7,138,408	$7,875,624	$8,468,890	$7,575,499	$10,498,950	$12,845,220
	$865/hr.			$3,468/hr.	

FIGURE 6–5
Cost to reduce downtime [From Eames and Spann, 1977; © 1977 IEEE]

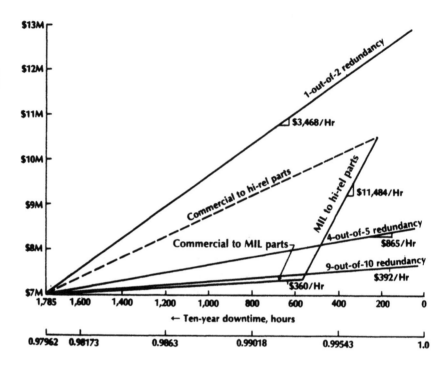

PROBLEMS

1. Suppose that you are issuing maintenance contracts on a new system with the following shipment schedule:

Quarter	Shipments
1	50
2	250
3	1250
4	4000
5	5000
6	5000
7	5000
8	2000
9	1000
10	500
11	0
12	0

If the contract penetration rate is 50 percent and the annual contract renewal rate is 75 percent, calculate the resulting number of contracts in each quarter.

2. What is the cost of owning a system purchased for $500,000, with an annual cost of maintenance of $40,000? Assume a discount rate of 10 percent and a tax rate of 35 percent, with the system depreciated over five years, using the double-declining balance method.

3. Consider the feature failure-mode matrix (Table 6–3). Suppose that the development costs associated with each feature are as follows:

Data Path Loop-Around	$1000
Error Simulation	$8500
Internal Parity	$1500
Speed Check	$2000
Skew Check	$5000
Power Check	$7400
Reel LEDs	$9000

Assume that the MTBF of the device remains at a constant 5,000 hours, and that a minute of repair time saved is worth $5. Ignoring the time value of money, which features should be incorporated into the device if you are going to ship a total of 100 units? 1000 units? 10,000 units? Assume the manufacturing cost per unit is $1000 and the system lifetime is five years.

II THE PRACTICE OF RELIABLE SYSTEM DESIGN

Part I presented the techniques used in fault-tolerant computer design. Part II illustrates how various system designers have combined these techniques into successful fault-tolerant architecture. Each chapter is devoted to a significant application of fault-tolerant computers and provides background information describing attributes of the application area as well as typical operational configurations and procedures. The heart of each chapter is a series of case studies on actual fault-tolerant systems written by experts in the design of each system. Most of the case studies were explicitly written for this book. The authors illustrate how the form of their systems was derived from the initial system goals as well as from characteristics of the intended application.

The ultimate use of the system affects not only the design philosophy but also the trade-offs between design alternatives. The cost of fault tolerance must be weighted against the cost of error. Error costs include the cost of downtime as well as the cost of incorrect computation. Some attributes of system usage that directly affect design philosophy include: Is the system to be highly reliable or highly available? Do all outputs have to be correct, or only data committed to long-term storage? How familiar must the user be with the architecture and software redundancy? Is the system dedicated so that attributes of the application can be used to simplify fault-tolerant techniques? Is the system constrained to use existing components? Even if the design is new, what is the cost and/or performance penalty to the user who does not require fault tolerance? Is the design stand-alone or are there other processors that can be called upon to assist in times of failure?

Rather than enumerate a long list of design goals addressed by an architecture, it is more insightful to group fault-tolerant architectures by their intended applications. Architectures designed for the same application area not only have similar design goals but also have similar features designed to respond to these goals. Despite these similarities, the detailed designs can differ significantly. Part II presents case studies for architectures organized into four application areas: general-purpose computing, high availability, long life, and critical computations. We feel this organizational feature of Part II will provide more insight for readers as they compare and contrast systems with similar design goals.

GENERAL-PURPOSE COMPUTING

General-purpose computing is the most familiar application to the computer user. Programs from a wide variety of disciplines—ranging from engineering analysis to business and from computational science to databases—can simultaneously co-exist in a general-purpose computer. Since no single computational model exists and the interactions between applications are unknown, attributes of the applications cannot be used to detect or recover from errors. Thus, general-purpose computers represent both the biggest challenge and the largest opportunity because of their pervasive use throughout business and science. General-purpose computers define the minimum that can be expected from a fault-tolerant computer. Their users are more forgiving of failure. Occasional errors that disrupt processing for several seconds are tolerable as long as automatic restart follows.

Chapter 7 provides case studies of high-end general-purpose computers designed by the two largest computer companies. The first two generations of Digital Equipment Corporation's VAX family are summarized so that the reader can gain an appreciation for the time rate of change of fault-tolerant features employed in mid-range and high-end computer systems. International Business Machine's 3090 mainframes form the other major case study. The case studies emphasize design trade-offs (VAX), hardware manufacturing (3090), operating system software (3090), diagnosis (VAX), maintenance (VAX), and repair. These activities are common to all computer systems regardless of their degree of fault tolerance. Features built into commercial systems represent the minimal attributes to which all fault-tolerant systems should aspire.

HIGH-AVAILABILITY SYSTEMS

High-availability systems share resources when the occasional loss of a single user is acceptable but a system-wide outage or common database destruction is unacceptable. Not only must the source of errors be rapidly detected but also corrective action must be swiftly implemented to minimize downtime. Indeed, downtime required to install new software releases is often unacceptable, thus necessitating a well-conceived approach to incrementally updating running software.

Chapter 8 compares and contrasts the evolution of three high-availability computer families that employ multiple copies of processors, memory, and input/output to detect and/or tolerate errors. The AT&T Switching Systems pioneered duplication and matching techniques in the domain of real-time switching of telephone calls. A model of the process for establishing and maintaining a telephone call provides the basis for several application-specific fault-tolerant techniques that could be used to detect and recover from errors. The other two case studies—the Tandem family and the Stratus family—focus on the transaction processing computational model that has been successfully applied to such diverse applications as electronic funds transfer, inventory management, and airline reservation systems. The similarities in end-user applications provide a unique opportunity to compare and contrast a software-intensive approach (Tandem) to a hardware-intensive solution (Stratus).

LONG-LIFE SYSTEMS

There are many mobile systems (such as airplane, ship, and mass transit systems) that depart from a central facility for a period of time and return. Stocking spares and maintenance expertise are most cost-effective if maintenance can be postponed until the mobile unit returns to the central facility. Since on-site repair may be difficult, the use of redundancy is more cost-effective than unscheduled maintenance. For some systems like spacecraft, maintenance could be postponed for the entire system life.

Chapter 9 focuses on long-life unmanned spacecraft systems which cannot be manually maintained over the operating life—frequently five or more years. Often, as in spacecraft monitoring of planets, the peak computational requirement comes at the end of system life. These systems are highly redundant and are equipped with enough spares to survive the mission with the required computational power. Error detection, diagnosis, and reconfiguration may be performed automatically (on the spacecraft) or remotely (from ground stations). While a substantial period of downtime might occur, serious operational mistakes or exhaustion of resources cannot be tolerated and must be removed through careful design. The Galileo spacecraft, which will orbit Jupiter and inject a probe into Jupiter's atmosphere, exemplifies the design of long-life redundant systems.

CRITICAL COMPUTATIONS

The most stringent requirement for fault tolerance is in real-time control systems in which faulty computations can jeopardize human life or have high economic impact. Not only must computations be correct but also recovery time from faults must be minimized. Specially designed hardware and software operate with concurrent error detection so that incorrect data never leave the faulty module.

Chapter 10 illustrates critical computations in two diverse domains. SIFT (Software-Implemented Fault Tolerance) is an avionic computer designed to control dynamically unstable aircraft. The design goal is a failure probability of less than 10^{-9} for a ten-hour mission. C.vmp is a real-time computer designed for process control. Triplication of off-the-shelf components combined with a specially designed voter yields a system with a measured mean time to crash six times longer than a nonredundant system constructed from the same components.

In conclusion, we feel these four categories cover the spectrum of contemporary applications for fault-tolerant computing systems. These categories have been refined into more numerous subcategories in the literature, and in the future, we can expect the introduction of new categories as computing systems are applied to even more innovative applications.

7 GENERAL-PURPOSE COMPUTING

INTRODUCTION   We have all had some interaction with general-purpose computing such as direct access to a mainframe timesharing system, workstation, or personal computer. General-purpose computing indirectly touches our everyday lives in many ways, ranging from the preparation of our utility bills to the use of cash registers at our favorite restaurants. Thus, the concept of general-purpose computing needs no introduction. However, people may not realize the degree that fault tolerance is used in these systems.

While occasional errors that disrupt processing for several seconds are tolerable as long as automatic recovery follows, the frequency of severe outages such as system crashes must be reduced. In addition, user programs are becoming more sophisticated and require more instructions to be executed to complete a task. Table 7–1 depicts the two attributes of most interest to users: mean time to crash (MTTC) and mean number of instructions executed (MNIE) between crashes. Both numbers have been steadily increasing. Note that the MNIE between crashes must increase at a faster rate than the MNIE per user task in order for useful work to be done. One way to increase MNIE is through the use of fault tolerance. Table 7–1 illustrates that a substantial gap exists between the capabilities of a general-purpose computer and a high-availability system such as Tandem. Nevertheless, improvements continue to be made in general-purpose computing as illustrated by the 26 percent per year compounded improvement in mean time to hard failures per MIPS (million instructions per second) per year for IBM mainframes (Figure 1–7).

Since general-purpose computers must execute a wide range of applications, one cannot depend upon particular attributes of the application (such as transactions processing) to improve fault tolerance. Thus, the redundancy techniques employed in general-purpose computers can be utilized in any fault-tolerant machine. Therefore, general-purpose computing is an appropriate place to start our in-depth case studies of fault-tolerant computers. In this introduction, we first consider a generic general-purpose computer and briefly look at two leading vendors of general-purpose computers—DEC and IBM—in preparation for the case studies that follow.

GENERIC COMPUTER   From its inception, the computer has been divided into three main sections: processor, main memory, and input/output. Most contemporary computers have augmented this structure by adding a fast memory (called a *cache*) between the processor and main memory. Since each section has unique attributes, they typically employ slightly different fault-tolerant strategies. Error-detection mechanisms in a typical system include the following:

TABLE 7–1
*Number of
instructions
executed between
system crashes for
several systems*

System	Mean Time To Crash MTTC (hours)	Mean Number Instructions Executed MNIE ($\times 10^{10}$)
B5500 [Yourdon, 1972]	15	3
PDP-10 [Castillo, 1980]	10	4
Chi/05 (Univac 1108) [Lynch, Wagner, and Schwartz, 1975]	17	7
Dual 370/165 [Reynolds and Kinsberger, 1975]	9	28
SLAC	20	23
CRAY-1 [Keller, 1976]	4	190
Sun II [Lin, 1988]	1000	720
Tandem [Grey, 1987]	16,000	5760

- *Memory*: Double-error-detecting code on memory data and parity on address and control information
- *Cache*: Parity on data, address, and control information
- *Input/Output*: Parity on data and control
- *Processor*: Parity on data paths, parity on control store, and duplication and comparison of control logic.

As can be seen, the dominant error-detection mechanisms are parity on multibit logic and duplication of random logic. Based on the assumption that most errors are transient, recovery consists primarily of retry by the error-detection mechanisms:

- *Memory*: Single error-correction code on data and retry on address or control information parity error
- *Cache*: Retry on address or control information parity error and disable portions of cache on data parity errors
- *Input/Output*: Retry on data or control parity errors
- *Processor*: Retry on control store parity error, invert sense of control store, and macroinstruction retry

Instead of attempting a number of retries immediately after an error is detected, systems typically pause so that the source of a transient error (such as power supply instability) can die out. The pause usually ranges from 5 milliseconds to 5 seconds. The pause value can be set to cope with site-dependent conditions. Hard failures are typically tolerated in main memory through ECC; in the cache, through performance degradation; and in the control store, by inverting the bits in the microinstruction, if required for a bit to match a stuck-at value.

With the advent of low-cost microprocessors, it became cost-effective to concentrate in a console processor the functionality traditionally provided by front console switches and maintenance panels. Once the basic functionality was provided for system control, expansion to include functionality for reliability followed naturally. A console processor typically consists of a 50K to 100K-instructions-per-second processor, a small amount of novolatile ROM (such as 4K words), RAM (up to 256K words), secondary storage (floppy disk), remote access port, and interfaces to buses and control signals internal to the CPU. Some of the functionality associated with console processors [Kunshier and Mueller, 1980] includes:

- System console
- System boot
- System quick tests of boot path
- Error logger
- Diagnostic tool: microdiagnostics, scan/set/compare internal state, fault injection, and remote diagnosis
- Error recovery: writable control store reload, transplant state to another processor, and reconfiguration

The maintenance strategy for general-purpose computers has evolved over time as more error-detection and -correction techniques have been added. Table 7–2, for example, sketches the evolution of IBM's maintenance strategy. Techniques are listed

TABLE 7–2
Evolution of IBM maintenance strategy

Machine	Era	Techniques
650	Late 1950s	6 internal checkers; stand-alone diagnostics on punched cards; light and switch panels
1401	Early 1960s	20 internal checkers; stand-alone diagnostics; light and switch panels
S/360-50	Mid-1960s	75 internal checkers; OLTEP (on-line test executive program); microdiagnostics; log fault data to main memory; EREP (error recording and edit program) for outputting logged data; maintenance panel
370/168 Mod 3	Early 1970s	Error-detection circuits; OLTEP; microdiagnostics for fault isolation; service processor, including trace unit (to trace up to 199 fixed and 8 movable logic points over 32 machine cycles for intermittent or environmental faults)
303X	Mid-1970s	Error-detection circuits; OLTS (on-line functional tests); console and processor microdiagnostics; EREP; scope loops; support processor, including trace and remote (telephone) access to log data and trace information
4341	Late 1970s	Error-detection circuits; 25,000 shadow latches; support processor (error logging and environmental monitoring)
3090	Mid-1980s	Error-detection circuits; error-correction circuits; recovery techniques; console and processor microdiagnostics; processor controller (duplicated for availability); fault isolation circuits; fault threshold and isolation analysis; autocall and remote access to service information and remote service console; EREP; on-line tests; reconfiguration capability; internal machine environment monitoring

for a representative machine from each major era. These techniques can be loosely grouped in three major categories: internal hardware error-detection circuits, diagnostics (including software and microcode), and display (such as lights, error logs, and tracing). The IBM strategy has evolved from "failure re-creation" to "failure capture," to "failure recovery." Prior to the S/370, IBM field service engineers attempted to re-create the failure by running diagnostics, sometimes in conjunction with varying voltage and clock frequency, until the failure reoccurred. The system was placed in a tight programmed loop to produce a continuous failure condition for analysis. In failure capture, hardware circuits detect errors, and information about the current status of the machine state is logged for subsequent analysis. In failure recovery, the information captured by the detection circuits is utilized by recovery techniques, in hardware, microcode, and software, to allow the application or job to complete. The information is also logged at a remote support facility to assist engineering design activity.

DEC

The DEC family of VAX computers is the subject of the first case study in this chapter. A generic VAX implementation is composed of a processor connected to memory and I/O devices by a backplane bus. Bus adapters convert I/O bus protocols to the backplane bus protocol. A set of internal system registers is associated with each subunit (cache, memory, translation buffer, backplane, etc.). Most subunits are associated with up to four types of registers: configuration/control, status, data, and diagnostic/maintenance. The *configuration/control register* contains information on the state of the element (checking enabled, reporting enabled, and so forth). The *status register* contains flags summarizing the state of the element, including error reports. *Data registers* capture relevant information about the system state when an error is detected (for example, the address used on cache look-up when a cache parity error is detected). Finally, the *diagnostic/maintenance register* contains control and status information generated by the error-detection and -correction logic.

The console subsystem of a VAX provides control (halt, restart, initialize, etc.) over the processor as well as access to internal system registers. It has a mass storage device containing the main system bootstrap code and some diagnostics. The console subsystem also has access to the visibility bus, which makes several hundred internal logic signal values visible to the microdiagnostics.

The main memory in VAX systems is protected by error-correcting code (ECC). An optional backup battery preserves the contents of memory over short-term power failures.

VAX systems also have a port for remote diagnosis, an integral part of the VAX maintenance philosophy. A typical VAX maintenance scenario is as follows. Disk-resident user mode diagnostics periodically execute under the VMS operating system. The goal of user mode diagnostics is to exercise and detect functional errors in memory, bus adapters, device controllers, and disk drives. Errors reported by user-mode diagnostics or hardware check circuits prompt a customer call to Digital's Remote Diagnostic Center (RDC). The customer replaces the removable disk media with diagnostic and scratch disks, turns a key on the front of the console to REMOTE, and calls the RDC (unauthorized access is not possible). The RDC engineer calls the customer's processor, logs on to the system, and begins to execute a script of diagnostics. Micro- and macrodiagnostics can be loaded from the diagnostic disk and executed. The error log can be examined, memory locations deposited or examined, and so on. If the diagnostic disk is not operable, the diagnostics can be loaded from the console subsystem mass storage device or downline-loaded over the phone. The RDC attempts to isolate the failure to a subsystem. If the processor is faulty, the diagnostics on the console subsystem mass storage device are executed to verify the processor status.

The RDC notifies the local field service office of the failing subsystem. Upon arrival at the customer's site, a field service engineer replaces the faulty board and reverifies the system. If the failing subsystem is the processor, microdiagnostics are loaded into the writable control store.

Remote diagnosis has at least three major advantages: (1) faster mean time to repair, especially when the problem is trivial and can be resolved over the remote link; (2) faster resolution of difficult problems, because the person at the RDC is an expert in VAX system fault determination; and (3) greater certainty that the field service engineer is sent to the site with the correct part in hand.

The DEC VAX architecture defines several Reliability, Availability, and Maintainability Program (RAMP) features that must appear in every member of the VAX computer family. Other RAMP features are implementation-specific. The case study first introduces the architecturally defined features. Next implementation-specific RAMP features for the first (VAX-11/780 and VAX-11/750) and second (VAX 8600 and VAX 8700) generation VAXes are compared and contrasted. The impact of differing design philosophies is also explored.

A significant amount of detail is given for the VAX family for two reasons. The first reason is that it is the first case study, and thus it provides background for the other case studies. Any of the techniques and procedures employed in the VAX can be utilized in any computing system. The second reason is that the implementations employ the two major approaches to fault management: fault intolerance (VAX-11/750 and VAX 8700) and fault tolerance (VAX-11/780 and VAX 8600). Thus, not only can the two approaches be contrasted but also their evolution between two generations can be observed.

IBM

The IBM case study describes in detail the reliability, availability, and serviceability (RAS) features of the IBM 308X and 3090 processor complexes. Part I of the case study, by Siewiorek, focuses on hardware, while Part II, by C.T. Connolly, describes software recovery mechanisms. The goal of both hardware and software is high availability with minimized impact of failures. Four stages of corrective action are identified, each with successively larger impact on users: transparent recovery, one user affected, multiple users affected, and down. The recovery structure of successively higher severity stages is common in systems with high-availability goals or in real-time data processing environments in which temporary loss of data is tolerable. The current IBM strategy of first-failure data capture is evident in the design of both hardware and software. The IBM 3090 series includes the following features:

- *Reliability*: Low intrinsic failure-rate technology; extensive component burn-in during manufacture; dual processor controller that incorporates switchover; dual 3370 direct-access storage units that support switchover; multiple consoles for monitoring processor activity and for backup; LSI packaging that vastly reduces number of circuit connections; internal machine power and temperature monitoring; chip sparing in memory to replace defective chips automatically
- *Availability*: Two or four central processors; automatic error detection and correction in central and expanded storage, including single-bit error correction and double-bit error detection in central storage, as well as double-bit error correction and triple-bit error detection in expanded storage; storage deallocation in 4 kB increments under system program control; ability to vary channels off-line in one-channel increments; instruction retry; channel command retry; error-detection and fault-isolation circuits that provide improved recovery and serviceability; multipath I/O controllers and units
- *Data integrity*: Key controlled storage protection (store and fetch); critical address storage protection; storage error checking and correction; processor cache error handling; parity and other internal error checking; segment protection (S/370 mode); page protection (S/370 mode); clear reset of registers and main storage; automatic remote support authorization; block multiplexer channel command retry; extensive I/O recovery by hardware and control programs
- *Serviceability*: Automatic fault isolation (analysis routines) concurrent with operation; automatic remote support capability (auto call to IBM if authorized by customer); automatic customer engineer and parts dispatching; trace facilities; error logout recording; microcode update distribution via remote support facilities; remote service console capability; automatic validation tests after repair; customer problem analysis facilities

The listed hardware error-detection, error-correction, and monitoring circuits are used in the following maintenance scenario. The processor controller analyzes the error-detection data and develops a field replaceable unit (FRU) call or a maintenance action plan. Automatically, at the customer's option, the processor controller establishes a data link for service. A field service engineer receives the FRU information and goes to the site with the appropriate part or parts needed to effect the repair. For additional information, the customer engineer can communicate via data link with a central data base (called RETAIN) for the latest service tips. A field technical support center specialist can use the data link to monitor remotely and/or control diagnostics on the IBM 3090.

THE DEC CASE

RAMP in the VAX Family

DANIEL P. SIEWIOREK

At the time of the inception of the VAX architecture, concerns for reliability, availability, and serviceability were gaining momentum. This case study focuses on DEC's RAMP (Reliability, Availability, and Maintainability Program) features in four different implementations of the VAX architecture. Briefly summarized in Table 7–3, these implementations are treated chronologically, by date of introduction, rather than by model number.*

The case study is divided into four sections. The first section deals with RAMP features at the VAX architectural level; that is, the level at which the attributes of the system are visible to the programmer. The next two sections describe implementations in two different generations: the first generation, composed of the VAX-11/780 and VAX-11/750, and the second generation, composed of the VAX 8600 and VAX 8700. Design, which is evolutionary in each VAX implementation, is built upon previous experiences. Thus, each generation has an archetypical implementation that not only capitalizes on experience, but also allows sharing of peripheral devices.

The discussion of the individual implementations includes the design philosophy and a brief summary of the RAMP features. The design philosophy subsections focus on the major new contribution of each implementation:

- VAX-11/780: Permanent failure detection, diagnosis, and reporting
- VAX-11/750: Reliability modeling to guide the design process
- VAX 8600: Intermittent/transient fault detection and correction via retry to increase mean time to crash
- VAX 8700: Design integrity through simplification

As each contribution proved successful in practice, it was used in subsequent VAX implementations. However, to simplify the discussion in this case study, each contribution is only described in detail in the first implementation that made extensive use of it.

The final section in this case study summarizes the RAMP features in each generation by means of a comparison table.

THE VAX ARCHITECTURE

Compatibility between members of a computer family is essential. The need for compatibility at the architectural level is the most pronounced, but there are also substantial benefits from similarities between implementations. Similarities can reduce costs of training, documentation, and repair.

The VAX architecture defines both error-detection mechanisms, which generate either exceptions or interrupts, and registers that capture error-related information. These architectural features, coupled with a maintenance architecture based on remote diagnosis, allow VAX implementations to share a common approach to repair as outlined in the following subsections.

---

* Historically, the various implementations of the VAX architecture have been assigned designations relative to their performance.

TABLE 7–3 *Comparison of VAX-11/750, 11/780, 8600, and 8700 implementations*

Component	VAX-11/750 (1980)	VAX-11/780 (1978)	VAX 8600 (1985)	VAX 8700 (1987)
Processor				
Relative performance	0.6	1.0	4.0	6.0
Relative cost	0.4	1.0	3.1	3.8
Control store				
Word length	78 bits, 2 parity	96 bits, 3 parity	86 bits, 2 parity	140 bits, 3 parity
Number of words	6K ROM, 1K RAM	4K ROM, 1K RAM	8K RAM	16K RAM
Microcycle time	320 nsec	100 nsec	80 nsec	42 nsec
Data path width	32 bits	32 bits	32 bits	32 bits
Instruction lookahead buffer	8 bytes	8 bytes	8 bytes	16 bytes
Cache				
Size and organization	4 kB, direct-mapped	8 kB, 2-way set associative	16 kB, 2-way set associative	65 kB, direct-mapped
Cycle time	320 nsec	290 nsec	80 nsec write back	45 nsec write through
Effective main memory cycle time	400 nsec/32 bits	1800 nsec/64 bits	384 nsec/128 bits	270–540 nsec/ 128 bits
Address translation buffer				
Size (number of entries)	512	128	512	1024
Main memory				
Physical address bits	24	29	29	29
Physical size (words)	2 MB in 256-kB increments	8 MB in 256-kB increments	260 MB	128 MB in 16-MB increments
Battery backup option	10 min for 2 MB	10 min for 4 MB	10 min	10 min
Cycle time				
Read	800 nsec/32 bits	800 nsec/64 bits	500 nsec more than cache	495–1260 nsec/ 256 bits
Write	640 nsec/32 bits	800 nsec/64 bits	—	270–540 nsec/ 128 bits
ECC	7-bit ECC/32-bit word	8-bit ECC/64-bit word	7-bit ECC (over data and address)/32-bit word	7-bit ECC/32-bit word
I/O				
Max. system I/O rate	5 MB/sec	13.3 MB/sec with 2 memory controllers	26.6 MB/sec	30 MB/sec
I/O bus	Unibus	Unibus	SBI	BI
Number	1	Up to 4	Up to 2	Up to 4
Weight	400 lbs	1100 lbs	—	1700 lbs
Max. AC power consumption	1700 W	6225 W	7000 W	6500 W

Exceptions and Interrupts

The VAX architecture defines two ways to invoke execution of software outside the explicit flow of control. The first, resulting from internal events (usually related to the current instruction under execution), is called an *exception*. The second, resulting from external events, is called an *interrupt*. The VAX architecture specifies three types of exceptions: aborts, faults, and traps.

1. *Aborts* are the most severe form of exception. When an instruction is aborted, the machine registers and memory may be left in an indeterminate state. Because system state is destroyed, the instruction cannot be correctly restarted, completed, simulated, or undone.

2. *Faults* leave the machine registers and memory in a consistent state. Once the fault is eliminated, the instruction may be restarted and the correct results obtained. Faults restore only enough state to allow restarting. The state of the process may not be the same as before the fault occurred.

3. A *trap* occurs at the end of the instruction that generated the exception. The machine registers and memory are consistent and the address of the next instruction to execute is stored on the machine stack. The process can be restarted with the same state as before the trap occurred.

Several arithmetic exceptions are architecturally defined. These exceptions deal primarily with overflow/underflow and illegal operations:

Arithmetic Exceptions

Exception	Type	Exception	Type
Integer overflow	Trap	Decimal overflow	Trap
Integer divide by zero	Trap	Subscript range	Trap
Floating overflow	Trap	Floating overflow	Fault
Floating/decimal divide by zero	Trap	Floating divide by zero	Fault
Floating underflow	Trap	Floating underflow	Fault

The floating point faults differ from the traps in that the faults do not affect the destination operand.

Table 7–4 lists the VAX architecturally defined exceptions. Each exception represents a unique memory location where an address is stored. The address points to the start of a software routine unique to the corresponding exception. Exceptions may store information about their type on the system stack to help guide the software in restarting the system. Some exceptions are triggered by consistency checks and detect primarily software errors. Other exceptions are detected by hardware and represent hardware or environmentally induced errors. The next few paragraphs provide more details for the entries in Table 7–4.

The machine check is the most damaging exception. It is triggered when internal CPU error-checking circuitry detects an exceptional condition. The processor may be restartable if the exception is related to redundant logic whose sole purpose is to improve machine performance (such as instruction cache or instruction look-ahead buffer).

The VAX has four defined modes of access: kernel, executive, supervisor, and user. These modes are used to grant or deny privileges, such as access to portions of memory or execution of specific instructions. The VAX architecture also defines an extensive virtual-to-physical address translation. Associated with each memory page is a protection code. The system mode and address

Name	Type	Parameters
Machine check	Abort/trap	Length parameter and error-specific data are pushed onto the stack, if possible.
Kernel stack not valid	Abort	No parameters
Access control violation	Fault	Virtual address causing the fault is pushed onto the kernel stack.
Translation not valid	Fault	Virtual address causing the fault is pushed onto the kernel stack.
Reserved or privileged instruction	Fault	No parameters
Customer reserved instruction	Fault	No parameters
Reserved operand	Fault/abort	No parameters
Reserved addressing mode	Fault	No parameters
Power fail	Interrupt	No parameters
Trace pending	Fault	No parameters
Breakpoint instruction	Fault	No parameters
Corrected memory read data	Interrupt	No parameters
Memory write timeout	Interrupt	No parameters
Arithmetic	Trap/fault	Type code is pushed onto stack.
Interval timer	Interrupt	No parameters
Console terminal receive	Interrupt	No parameters

request must match the code, or a translation-not-valid fault results. Table 7–5 lists the various allowable system modes and access rights.

An exception occurs if an access to the kernel, or most privileged stack, encounters a memory-access violation (such as no access or attempted write to a read-only page) or if the translation from virtual address to physical address is not valid.

Execution of reserved or privileged instructions (such as improper system state) triggers faults. Faults may be caused by attempted use of a reserved operand format or reserved addressing mode; that is, an ill-formed instruction and addressing mode.

Power failure causes an interrupt so that machine state can be saved for a clean power-up sequence.

When the Trace bit is enabled, the system faults after every instruction execution. Tracing is used for performance evaluation or debugging.

The breakpoint fault is also associated with debugging. The breakpoint instruction can be placed anywhere in the software flow and is designed to restore control to the user for examining the state of the program.

Two interrupts report memory-related problems: an error on read-from-memory is corrected by an error-correcting code, and no memory responded to a write request (such as nonexisting memory).

Error Reporting and Control Registers

In addition to exceptions, the architecture also defines several processor registers. Of the architecturally defined registers, the ten registers detailed in Table 7–6 are related to RAMP functionality. The numbers in angle brackets indicate the number of bits in each field. The interval counter has a one-microsecond resolution and can be used by diagnostics for timing critical functions.

TABLE 7–5
VAX architectural access rights

Protection Code	System Mode			
	Kernel	Executive	Supervisor	User
0000	No	No	No	No
0001		Unpredictable		
0010	R/W	No	No	No
0011	RO	No	No	No
0100	R/W	R/W	R/W	R/W
0101	R/W	R/W	No	No
0110	R/W	RO	No	No
0111	RO	RO	No	No
1000	R/W	R/W	R/W	No
1001	R/W	R/W	RO	No
1010	R/W	RO	RO	No
1011	RO	RO	RO	No
1100	R/W	R/W	R/W	RO
1101	R/W	R/W	RO	RO
1110	R/W	RO	RO	RO
1111	RO	RO	RO	RO

Key: No—No access   R/W—Read/write access   RO—Read only access

The time-of-year clock is used to put a time stamp on software objects, such as entries of Error information into a file (error log), for post-error analysis.

A console terminal is defined via data and control/status register pairs for the transmit/receive functions. A system ID register provides information that can be used to isolate failures to the manufacturing process. Finally, the processor status word contains control for enabling tracing and various arithmetic exceptions.

Remote Diagnosis

Remote diagnosis is an integral part of the VAX maintenance philosophy. In a typical VAX maintenance scenario, disk-resident user-mode diagnostics periodically execute under the VMS operating system to exercise and detect functional errors in memory, Massbus adapters, Unibus adapters, device controllers, and device drives. Errors reported by user-mode diagnostics or hardware check circuits prompt a customer call to DEC's Remote Diagnostic Center (RDC). The customer replaces the removable disk media with a diagnostic and scratch disk, turns a key on the front console to "remote," and calls the RDC; unauthorized access is not possible. The RDC engineer calls the customer's processor, logs onto the system, and begins to execute a script of diagnostics. Micro- and macrodiagnostics can be loaded from the diagnostic disk and executed, the error log can be examined, memory locations deposited or examined, and so on. If the diagnostic disk is not operable, the diagnostics can be loaded from the console subsystem mass storage device or down-line loaded over a telephone line. The RDC will attempt to isolate the failure to a subsystem. If the CPU is faulty, the diagnostic on the console subsystem mass storage device is executed to verify the CPU status.

The RDC advises the local field service office of the failing subsystem. At the customer's site, field service replaces the faulty board and reverifies the system. If the failing subsystem is the CPU, microdiagnostics are loaded into the writable control store.

TABLE 7-6 *Details of RAMP-related VAX architecturally defined processor registers*

Register	Subfields	Comments
Interval counter <31:0>		1 μsec resolution
Next interval counter <31:0>		Loaded into interval counter when counter overflows
Interval clock control and status	Error	Second overflow occurs before first serviced
	Interrupt request	Set on counter overflow
	Interrupt enable single clock	Advances counter one step
	Transfer	Loads counter from next interval counter
	Run	Increments counter
Time of year <31:0>		
Console subsystem receiver control and status	Ready, interrupt enable	
Console receiver data buffer	Data <31:0>	
Console subsystem transmit control and status	Done, interrupt enable	
Console subsystem transmit data buffer	Data <31:0>	
System ID	System type <7:0>	
	ECO level <7:0>	
	Manufacturing plant <3:0>	
	System serial number <11:0>	
Processor status word	Trace pending	Initiates trace trap at end of current instruction
	First part done	Set by microcode on certain instructions to indicate instruction may be restarted from that point if instruction is interrupted
	Current mode <1:0>	User, supervisor, executive, kernel
	Previous mode <1:0>	
	Interrupt priority level of CPU <4:0>	
	Enable decimal overflow exceptions	
	Enable floating underflow exceptions	
	Enable integer overflow exceptions	
	T	Trace
	N	Negative condition code
	Z	Zero condition code
	V	Overflow condition code
	C	Carry condition code

Remote diagnosis has at least three major advantages:

- Faster MTTR, especially when the problem is of a trivial nature and can be resolved over the remote diagnostic link
- Faster resolution of difficult problems, because the person at the RDC is an expert in VAX system fault determination
- Much greater certainty that the field service engineer arrives with the correct part

All diagnostics can be run either at the site or remotely. In a building-block approach, the console subsystem first verifies its own operation; then the system hard core (CPU, backplane interconnect, and memory controller) is checked by loading microdiagnostics into the writable control store. Macro-level tests on the I/O bus adapters and peripheral controllers are run next, followed by the peripheral device diagnostics.

Functional level tests—that is, isolation to the failing major unit—can generally be performed on-line with the operating system. Faulty field-replaceable units can then be identified by stand-alone fault-isolation diagnostics.

Automatic on-line error logging is an integral part of every VAX system. A snapshot of the system is taken upon occurrence of a CPU, memory, I/O, or software error, with two exceptions. First, if a long time has elapsed with no errors, only the time of day is logged. Second, if the number of errors from the ECC memory exceeds a certain threshold (due to a permanent correctable failure in a frequently accessed location), no more entries are made for a period of time. The operating system has a special utility routine that converts the log into a readily analyzed form.

FIRST-GENERATION VAX IMPLEMENTATIONS

Archetypical Implementation

Figure 7–1 illustrates an archetypical implementation of a first–generation VAX. The CPU is interconnected to memory and I/O devices by a backplane bus. I/O devices reside on either the Unibus or Massbus. The latter is a high-speed block-transfer bus used primarily for block-oriented mass storage devices such as disks and tapes. Bus adapters convert Unibus or Massbus protocols to the backpanel bus protocol.

The backpanel bus is optimized for bandwidth rather than for minimum response time. Thus, the various ports to the backplane (Unibus, Massbus, CPU, and memory) are provided with

FIGURE 7–1
Archetypical first–generation VAX implementation

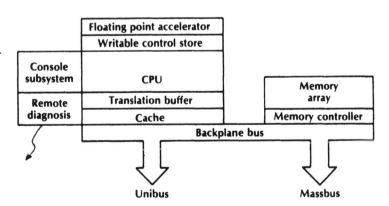

buffers. The buffers can support one of two purposes: They can smooth data flow between buses or devices with different data rates, or they can reduce bus accesses by holding frequently used data items.

Two standard options are the floating point accelerator (FPA) and the writable control store (WCS). Although the CPU microcode implements the full floating-point instruction set, the FPA provides data paths specifically tailored to executing floating-point operations. The FPA is logically invisible to software and affects only the instruction execution rate. The WCS supports microcode changes and additions. The WCS can also be used for microdiagnostics.

The console subsystem serves as a system console. The system console terminal provides control (halt, restart, initialize, and so on) over the CPU, as well as access to internal system registers. The console subsystem also has a mass storage device containing the main system bootstrap code and some diagnostics. Finally, a port is provided for remote diagnosis (RD). The RD port provides all the functionality of the console subsystem to a remote site.

The control store of each CPU has associated parity bits. Each CPU has three buffers: instruction lookahead, cache, and address translation. The instruction buffer serves two purposes. First, it decomposes the highly variable instruction format into its basic components; second, it constantly fetches ahead of CPU execution to reduce delays in obtaining the instruction components. The cache stores away frequently used data so that subsequent accesses to a datum do not incur the memory-fetch delay. The virtual-to-physical address translation specified in the VAX architecture requires several table lookups and memory fetches. The address translation buffer is a cache of recent virtual-to-physical address translations.

The main memory is protected by error-correcting code and has a battery backup option that preserves the contents of memory over short-term power failures.

I/O consists of Unibus and Massbus adapters. The adapters contain buffers that smooth data flow between the slower data rate Unibus/Massbus and the higher data rate backplane interconnect and also serve as assembly/disassembly stations for differences in data path widths; for example, the Unibus and Massbus deal in 16-bit words while the main memory has either 32-bit words for the VAX-11/750 or 64-bit words for the VAX-11/780. The adapters also contain tables for mapping Unibus/Massbus physical addresses into backplane interconnect physical addresses.

VAX-11/780 Implementation

Design Philosophy. At the time of its inception, the VAX instruction set was at least an order of magnitude more complex than anything previously implemented by DEC.* Thus, a major concern was the detection and identification of permanently failed components. A committee was formed to establish RAMP goals, with members representing diagnostic engineering, documentation, field service, hardware development, manufacturing, marketing, software development, software support, and software quality management.

The committee developed a maintenance philosophy that centers on the console subsystem. The VAX-11/780 introduced two important RAMP-related buses, the ID (internal data) bus and V-bus (visibility bus), which are tied into the console subsystem. The console subsystem is composed of an LSI-11 microcomputer with 16 kB of RAM and 8 kB of ROM, a hard copy terminal, a floppy disk, and a remote diagnostic port. The LSI-11 performs a self-test on power-up. The LSI-11 can examine and deposit values in internal processor registers via the ID bus. Registers

---

* For example, a typical PDP-11 (the immediate forerunner of the VAX) required less than 15K bits of microcode to implement. The VAX-11/780 required 468K bits of microcode.

accessible to the ID include configuration control, error summary, error data, and maintenance registers. The V-bus makes almost 600 internal logic signal values visible to the microdiagnostics.

The VAX-11/780 maintenance philosophy can be understood by examining the registers associated with each hardware error-detection or -correction element. In general, each element can be associated with the four types of registers: configuration/control, status, data, and diagnostic/maintenance.

Registers for processor elements reside either internally to the processor or on the ID bus. Registers for other ports on the SBI (such as memory, Unibus adapters, Massbus adapters) reside in the main memory address space. The functionality provided by these registers solves two maintenance problems: providing a means by which to test the error-detection/correction circuitry and alerting the system when a second error occurs before a first error has been properly handled.

RAMP Features: Error Detection/Correction. Figure 7–2 shows the major functional blocks in the VAX-11/780 implementation. Random logic is implemented in standard, low-power Schottky SSI/MSI; memory consists of standard MOS LSI memory chips. The main memory array is protected by ECC. The data cache, translation buffer, control store, and WCS memory arrays are protected by multiple parity bits for error detection. Several special-purpose buses interconnect the various functional blocks.

The synchronous backplane interconnect (SBI) joins the CPU, memory, and I/O subsystems. As its name implies, the SBI is a synchronous bus with a minor cycle time of 200 nanoseconds. The data path is 32 bits wide. During each 200-nanosecond minor cycle, either 32 bits of data or 30 bits of physical address can be transferred. Because read or write operations require the transmission of both address and data, two SBI minor cycles are required to complete the transaction. The SBI protocol also provides for 64-bit operations in three minor cycles, one address and two data. The CPU and I/O devices use the 64-bit mode whenever possible.

Each minor cycle is checked by two parity bits. One covers the 32 address/data lines; the other covers 12 control information lines. During each minor cycle the receiver checks and confirms parity. Each SBI interface checks bus arbitration and SBI protocol. Any irregularities are reported to the CPU. The CPU also maintains a history of the last 16 SBI cycles. Any SBI error condition preserves the history for diagnostic purposes.

RAMP Features: Controllability/Observability. The RAMP features are controlled by writing (setting) bits in control registers associated with each error detector/corrector. Information about an error is observed by reading status registers.

Cache. The Cache Parity Error Register contains the parity-bit values of the cache data and tag fields. Another bit assists recovery software by indicating whether the CPU or instruction buffer caused the cache parity error.

Translation Buffer. Three registers are associated with control, status, and data of the translation buffer (TB). TB Register 0 can disable TB halves; that is, Force Replace. The Force Miss and TB Hit fields (in the TB Data Register) can be used by diagnostics to check TB functionality; the Force TB Parity Error (in the TB Data Register) coupled with the TB Parity Error Status bits (in TB Register 1) can be used to test the TB parity checkers. Finally, the TB Data Register captures relevant information about a virtual address that caused a protection violation.

Writable Control Store. The WCS includes address/control and data registers. When the Data Register $\langle 31:0 \rangle$ is written, the contents are loaded into the control store word designated by the Address $\langle 12:0 \rangle$, and the word location is pointed to by Counter $\langle 1:0 \rangle$ in the WCS Address/Control

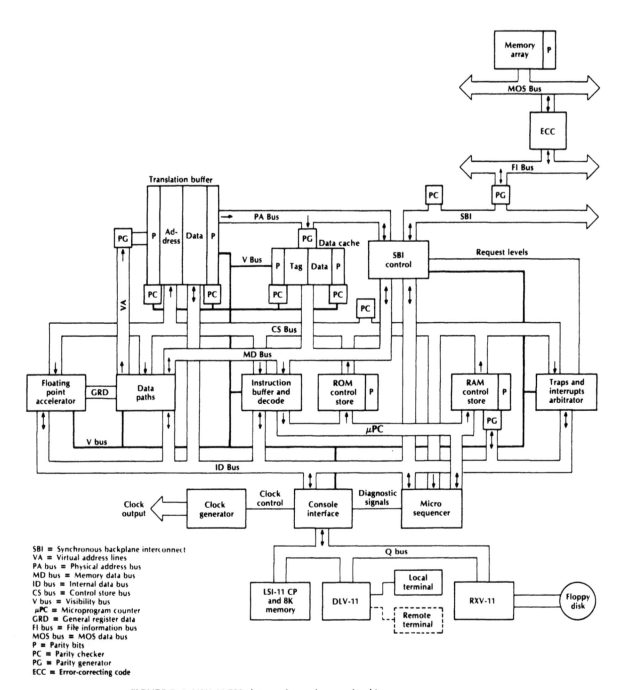

SBI = Synchronous backplane interconnect
VA = Virtual address lines
PA bus = Physical address bus
MD bus = Memory data bus
ID bus = Internal data bus
CS bus = Control store bus
V bus = Visibility bus
μPC = Microprogram counter
GRD = General register data
FI bus = File information bus
MOS bus = MOS data bus
P = Parity bits
PC = Parity checker
PG = Parity generator
ECC = Error-correcting code

FIGURE 7–2 *VAX-11/780 data paths and error checking*

Register. The Invert Parity bit causes the parity generated by the Data $\langle 31{:}0 \rangle$ word to be placed in the WCS in a complemented form. Thus, the control store bus (parity checker and CPU Error Status Register) can be tested by use of this bit. The WCS can be loaded with microdiagnostics to assist in fault isolation.

Control Store. The CPU Error Status Register holds the control store parity error summary; that is, which third of the control store caused a parity error. In conjunction with the microbreak register, the CPU Error Status Register can be used to identify the faulty control store chip. The value of internal condition codes is made available to facilitate checking of condition code operations. Finally, the arithmetic trap code is captured to aid software recovery from arithmetic errors.

SBI. Every port on the SBI has a register that summarizes errors detected on the SBI. The SBI Fault Status Register records these errors as seen by the processor in 7 bits. One bit records parity errors. Two bits record SBI protocol errors: The Unexpected Read Response bit is set if data are placed on the bus in response to a read command not seen by the CPU; the Multiple Transmitter bit is set if more than one transmitter was seen. The SBI Fault bit is set if the CPU sees a fault signal asserted by an SBI port; that is, if the SBI port detected an SBI parity error. Setting the Interrupt Enable bit allows an SBI fault to interrupt the CPU. The Transmitter During Fault bit is set if the CPU was transmitting when an error was detected. This bit allows the software to isolate the error. The Error First Pass bit is used to detect the occurrence of a second SBI fault prior to complete handling of the first fault.

The silo is a history of selected 32 bits from each of the last 16 SBI cycles. The silo is frozen (locked) whenever a fault is signalled on the SBI confirmation lines or when a condition defined by the Silo Comparator Register has been met. The silo can be used in postfault analysis of subtle problems such as intermittents.

The Silo Comparator Register allows the definition of predetermined conditions to trigger loading of the SBI silo. The silo can be loaded unconditionally or upon matches in SBI subfields: port ID, ID and Tag, ID and Tag and Mask. When the silo is full, it is frozen (locked), a bit is set, and an interrupt is generated if the Interrupt Enable bit is set.

The SBI Error Register contains further SBI status information. Bits indicate whether the memory corrected a single-bit error (Corrected Read Data bit, CRD) or detected a double error (Read Data Substitute bit, RDS). RDS errors can cause an interrupt to the processor. Also recorded are SBI timeouts and parity errors detected on cycles requested by the CPU (SBI error confirmation). The SBI Error Register distinguishes whether the SBI error was triggered by a regular CPU request or an instruction prefetch request made by the instruction buffer (IB). The IB requests are for performance reasons only, and errors can be tolerated by simply flushing the IB. Errors associated with other performance-related buffers such as the TB and cache are easily tolerated because they cause no change in system state; that is, they are logically transparent to the system.

The SBI Maintenance Register contains bits for forcing error conditions in various CPU subsystems. The various error-detection circuits can be tested by these forced-error conditions. SBI errors are simulated by forcing Write Sequence, Unexpected Read Data, and Timeouts. Cache operation can be checked by observing the Cache Match field while invalidating cache entries and forcing cache misses. Permanent failures in the cache can be configured out by disabling cache halves or disabling the cache altogether. Cache disabling is achieved by specifying where new entries are to be placed upon a cache miss.

Finally, the microbreak register can be used to stop the microsequencer in specific regions of microcode.

Main Memory. There are three main memory registers. Register A contains the memory port's fault status of the SBI. This field is identical to the corresponding fields in the CPU SBI Fault Status Register. Similar fields reside in the Unibus adapter and Massbus adapter registers. The remaining Register A fields deal with memory configuration and power status.

Register B contains additional memory configuration (such as Memory Starting Address), status (such as ascertaining whether battery backup allowed the memory to ride through a power loss), and maintenance fields. The memory controller is buffered and can have up to four reads and four writes in progress. The File Pointer fields can be used to check the functionality of these buffers. ECC check logic can be tested by forcing the ECC bits to be replaced by the contents of the Substitute ECC Bits ⟨7:0⟩ field.

Register C has two fields that capture the address and syndrome of the memory word in error. Both fields are locked until the error is serviced. The Error Log Request bit identifies the memory controller in error for the error-handling subroutine. A set High Error Rate bit indicates that a second error occurred before the first was serviced. Finally, error correction on reads can be disabled by the Inhibit CRD bit.

Unibus. Six registers are associated with the Unibus adapter (UBA). The Configuration Register records the standard SBI fault status. The Control Register contains interrupt enable bits for reporting Unibus errors to the CPU.

The Unibus Status Register records several situations. The Read Data and Command Transmit timeouts are checks on the Unibus timeout circuitry. The bits are set if the SBI has not responded within 100 microseconds and the Unibus timeout of 10 microseconds has failed to cancel the request. The Read Data Substitute bit is set if a Unibus request ends in an uncorrectable error: No data are transmitted to the Unibus, the Unibus times out, and a Unibus nonexisting-memory error is recorded. The Command Transmit Error bit is set when the SBI cycle causes an error on the confirmation lines. Finally, parity errors on the internal UBA data paths or in the address translation memory are recorded. Data associated with errors are captured in the Failed Map Entry and Failed Unibus Address Registers. Subsequent errors do not overwrite the Failed Map Entry Register until the first error has been cleared.

The Diagnostic Control Register has bits to inhibit parity on the data and map registers. If data with an even number of ones are used, the odd-parity checking circuitry is tested. The Microsequencer OK bit is used to detect when the microsequencer is caught in a loop.

Massbus. The Massbus adapter (MBA) contains four registers. The Configuration/Status Register records the standard SBI fault status. The Control Register has a Maintenance Mode bit that allows for testing the Massbus without any devices attached. An Interrupt Enable bit allows reporting of Massbus errors to the CPU. The Status Register records SBI, device, and Massbus parity errors. The Diagnostic Register allows exercising of MBA parity-check circuits and testing of the Massbus by reading and writing of selected Massbus fields.

RAMP Features: Console Subsystem. Several RAMP-related console commands are available to probe and test the CPU. The examine/deposit command allows reading and setting of most of the CPU registers. In addition to the ID bus error registers, almost 600 internal logic signals are observable over the V-bus.

The V-bus is composed of 7 channels. Table 7–7 lists the logic associated with each channel. Figure 7–3 depicts the operation of a V-bus channel. When requested, the internal logic signals are entered in a shift register, which is emptied into a register for examination and display.

Other console commands enable execution of micro- and macrodiagnostics: single-stepping a state, a bus cycle, or an instruction at a time; setting microbreaks; and CPU clock margining.

TABLE 7–7
V-bus channels and associated logic

Channel	Logic	Signals
0	Microsequencer	101
1	Data paths, arithmetic section	60
2	Data paths, data and exponent section	92
3	Instruction decode, instruction buffer, translation buffer data matrix	85
4	Cache and translation buffer address matrix, cache data matrix	103
5	SBI control	93
6	Floating point accelerator: control, exponent processor, and fraction adder	43

RAMP Features: Micro- and Macrodiagnostics. The microdiagnostics are stored on floppy disks accessible to the LSI-11 console processor, which can load them into the WCS. The field service engineer gives the console a TEST command. The first portion of the microdiagnostics sizes the system and prints out system configuration information. Upon completion, it prompts the engineer to load a new floppy disk. Table 7–8 lists a sample of the commands available to the engineer. The microdiagnostics consist of a series of "go-chains." Detection of a disagreement initiates a fault tree analysis, which uses the V-bus to isolate the failure. The V-bus is read only (thus requiring the machine to be in a known state before applying the next test) and is normally used only by the microdiagnostics.

The Diagnostic Supervisor allows the engineer to control and run macrodiagnostic programs through a command line interpreter in either stand-alone or user (on-line) mode. At the beginning of each diagnostic program, the Diagnostic Supervisor requests information from the engineer, such as the unit to be tested For example, a User Environment Test Package (UETP) can be employed for on-line diagnostics. A scratch tape or disk is mounted on the peripheral device to be tested. The UETP simulates a user load on the selected device. The number of simulated users is a function of the peripheral device type and the amount of memory in the system.

The error log is another tool available to the engineer. Information about exceptions is automatically captured by the hardware and entered into a disk file. The engineer can select printouts of the error log by device and error class. Error classes include hardware (such as machine checks, corrected read data, read data substitute, SBI alerts, and SBI faults), configuration

FIGURE 7–3
V-bus block diagram

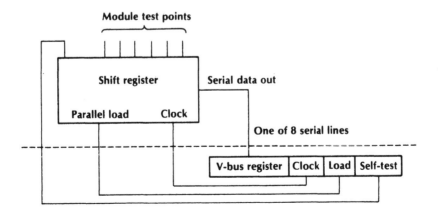

TABLE 7–8
Sample of microdiagnostic monitor commands

Command	Action
HALT	Halts CPU
INIT	Initializes
UNJAM	Clears SBI
LOAD <CODE>	Loads a macrodiagnostic
RUN <CODE>	Executes a macrodiagnostic
Diagnose/Test : 2F/PASS : 2	Executes microdiagnostic test 2F twice in succession
SET/CLEAR SCMM : <ADDRESS>	Sets/clears micromatch; loads address into micromatch register
SET STEP STATE/BUS/INSTRUCTION	Enables single-stepping
SET CLOCK FAST/SLOW/NORMAL/ EXTERNAL	Selects CPU clock speed and source
EXAMINE	
ID : <ADDRESS>	Registers on ID bus
V-bus : <CHANNEL>	Displays contents of specified V-bus channel
RA/RC	Scratch-pad registers
LA/LC	Latches
DR/QR/SC/FE/VA	Registers
PC	Program counter
DEPOSIT	Exists for all except the V-bus and PC. (There is a deposit for the physical address register.)

changes (such as mount and dismount of peripherals), and system information (such as system startup time, crashes, software bug checks). The engineer can select one of five report formats:

- *Rollup,* a summary of the number of errors by each device
- *Brief,* a brief description of each error entry, including device, type of error, and time
- *Cryptic,* the contents of associated registers for hardware and device errors
- *Standard,* the complete information on each error
- *Unknown,* the full information on unknown, invalid, and undefined errors

Because the ID bus is not accessible to the VAX-11/780 instruction set, an error log format has been defined that places several key registers on the kernel stack when an error occurs. ID bus registers include the CPU Error Status, D Register, and TB Error Registers 0 and 1. SBI-related processor registers include SBI Error, SBI Timeout Address, and Cache Parity Registers. The virtual address, program counter, and microprogram counters are also stored. Finally, an error summary indicates the type of error that caused the machine check:

CP/IB read timeout or error confirmation
CP/IB TB parity error
CP/IB read data substitute fault
CP/IB cache parity error
Control store parity error abort
Microcode "not supposed to get here" abort

Machine checks force the microsequencer to trap. The error-handling microcode first copies the registers to be logged into temporary registers accessible on the ID bus. Subsequently, the registers are logged onto the machine stack. If the error-handling microcode finds the Error First

Pass bit set in the SBI Fault Status Register, the CPU is halted. Data related to the first error are found in the ID temporary registers; those related to the second error are found in the corresponding error/status registers. Both sets of data are readable by the console subsystem.

VAX-11/750 Implementation

The VAX-11/750 is the second implementation of the VAX architecture. Although the VAX-11/780 implementation influenced the design team, the VAX-11/750 differs from its predecessor in several major respects.

Design Philosophy. Several global design goals were set even before the design team was established. These global design goals placed constraints on implementation and RAMP design trade-offs.

The targeted market determined the cost and performance goals: one-third to one-half the cost and 60–70 percent of the native mode performance of the VAX-11/780. The 11/750 needed at least 50 percent of the 11/780 performance to achieve a performance/cost ratio improvement so that three years' difference in technology would be aggressively utilized.

The improved performance/cost ratio dictated the use of dense circuitry to decrease signal delays and decrease area, which is directly related to cost. The design specified the extended hex board (12″ × 15″) used on the VAX-11/780. To achieve a density increase over the 11/780, a new random logic technology was selected. Custom-designed 48-pin gate arrays (400 bipolar gates plus 44 transceivers per chip) were to be used. (See Figure 7–4.) Each hex board could hold up to 50 gate array chips. Table 7–9 lists the characteristics and utilization of the gate array chips.

To take advantage of mass production and standardization, several 11/780 features were adopted, including use of the same operating system, functional diagnostics, Unibus/Massbus I/O, and—as nearly as possible—the same maintenance/repair procedure.

Also, to reduce cost, the 11/750 was specified as a bounded system with limited expansion capacity. In contrast with the 11/780, which can be configured with multipled cabinets, the 11/750 CPU/Memory/IO adapters were to be contained in a single cabinet. Figure 7–5 shows a system diagram. The synchronous backplane bus was dubbed CMI (Comet Memory Interconnect). Primarily for performance reasons, the CMI was limited to eight ports and a length of six inches. The CPU, memory controller, one Unibus adapter, WCS, and the Remote Diagnostic Module (RDM) were dedicated ports. The other three ports could be allocated to Massbus and/or Unibus adapters, multiport memory, or directly interfaced DMA (direct memory access) devices. The

FIGURE 7–4
VAX-11/750 gate array technology [Courtesy of Digital Equipment Corporation]

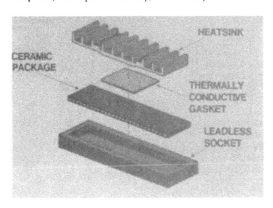

a. Exploded view of gate array assembly

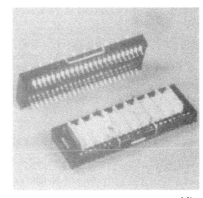

b. Two complete gate array assemblies

TABLE 7–9
VAX-11/750 gate array technology

Characteristic	Utilization	Total Used	Unique Types
Technology: Low-power bipolar Schottky	CPU, memory controller	55	27
Die size: 0.215″ × 0.244″	Floating point accelerator	28	7
Package: 48 pins	Massbus adapter	12	5
Circuitry: 400 identical 4-input NAND gates 44 I/O transceiver gates			
Speed per gate: 5 to 10 nsec			

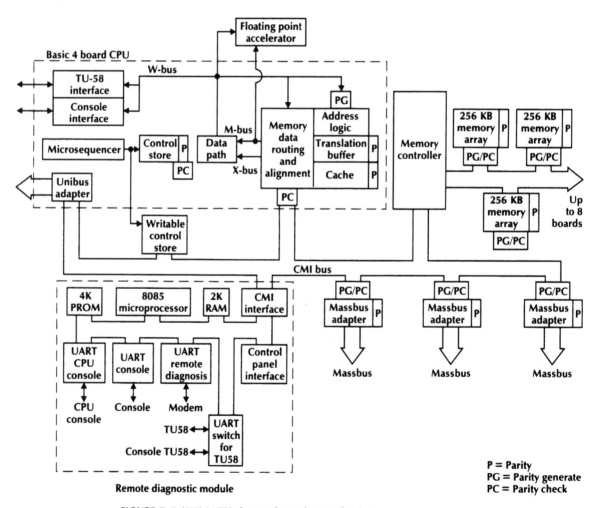

FIGURE 7–5 *VAX-11/750 data paths and error checking*

memory controller could handle up to eight memory array cards of 128 kB or 256 kB each for a maximum system memory of 2 MB.

Custom gate array, RAM, and ROM chips were used extensively to keep board densities high. To minimize the number of custom gate array designs, a bit-sliced approach was adopted. Depending on logic complexity, each gate array handled 4, 8, or 16 bits of data.

Thus, the design is dominated by LSI, RAM, and ROM chips. Almost 95 percent of the chips were of LSI complexity, and over 45 percent represented a new technology: the gate arrays.

Chip-level repair is a key design philosophy. A board-swap repair strategy usually ties up as many boards in field service repair kits and in transit to/from repair depots as there are in functioning CPUs. Because of the high cost of large, LSI-intense boards, a board-swap strategy would have required too large an investment in inventory. Given that the gate array chips represented a complexity comparable to that of an early 1970s SSI printed circuit board and that those earlier diagnostics were targeted at a board-level resolution (that is, the FRU was a board), chip-level repair was deemed practical. Even if only 20 percent of failures were repaired by chip replacement in the field, the reduced inventory costs for boards would offset the chip socket cost. To facilitate field repair, a special leadless chip socket was used. Because sockets potentially increase costs and also increase CPU failure rate, the question of socket failure rate had to be adequately resolved with the socket vendor to insure that more problems were not introduced than were solved. A special V-bus (like that in the 11/780) chains together the outputs of the gate array chips. The goal is resolution to a path containing three to five gate arrays and other MSI chips in 98 percent of the cases. When chip replacement fails, the board will be swapped.

The VAX-11/750 was the first DEC designed processor which used failure rate prediction and reliability modeling from the beginning of the design process. Procedures developed during the VAX-11/750 design were refined and applied to subsequent VAX implementations.

The MIL-HDBK-217B reliability model was not accurate in predicting failure rates for the LSI components. The first RAMP-related problem was to devise better estimates of component failure rates. Better estimates were essential because of the effect of MTTF predictions on maintenance and repair strategies.

The failure rate of RAM chips could be estimated from the failure rates observed by memory engineering during the high-temperature, accelerated-life testing of memory chips from potential vendors. Although accelerated-life testing has shortcomings (see Chapter 2), it provided the most up-to-date data available.

The gate array failure rate was more difficult to estimate. There was no similar technology inside Digital Equipment Corporation. Even data on random logic LSI were difficult to acquire. The major random logic LSI chip used by DEC at that time was the LSI-11 NMOS chip set. One potential source of information was DEC's Field Service Labor Activity Reporting System (LARS). Each field service call is recorded according to system identity, time to repair, type of call (such as installation, preventive maintenance, repair), and module failure action (such as adjust, repair, replace, trouble-shoot). The total number of DEC systems reported in LARS is not known. A second system, Regional Customer Obligation File (RCOF), is composed of systems under contract whose configurations were known. With LARS and RCOF, MTTR and mean time between calls (MTBC) can be estimated. Because the system duty cycle was not known, MTTF calculations were "guesstimates" at best. Furthermore, because of the small size of systems employing them, LSI-11s rarely appeared in RCOF or even LARS. One solution was to obtain data from a controlled environment. Carnegie-Mellon University and DEC entered into cooperative research in multiprocessors based on LSI-11s. The LSI-11 data presented in Chapter 2 were collected and compared for consistency with data on RAM chip MTTFs culled from several sources. Complexity derating for LSI was developed and applied to the preliminary design.

Table 7–10 lists estimates for the chip and board failure rates. Even though the design evolved, the relative failure rates did not change significantly. In fact, during design maturity testing the basic CPU was tested to 90 percent of its initially predicted failure rate at a 90 percent confidence level.

One of the first RAMP design studies was the sensitivity of system failure rate to the junction temperature of the gate array transistors. Whereas the gate arrays were designed for up to two watts of power dissipation, the actual transistor junction temperature was unknown. Indeed, no gate array chip had been fabricated at that time, and the semiconductor process was just being defined. The results of the temperature-sensitivity study are as follows:

Sensitivity of CPU Failure Rate to Gate Array Junction Temperature

Gate Array Junction Temperature	Relative Failure Rate of CPU
50° C	1.00
60° C	1.05
70° C	1.15
80° C	1.30

The sensitivity to high junction temperatures reinforced and economically justified the addition of heat sinks for the gate array chips.

The following conclusions were drawn from the initial reliability study:

1. For a 2-MB system, main memory chips would account for 71 percent of the system failure rate. The application of Hamming code (which to a first-order approximation removes the memory chips as a source of error; see Chapter 5) improved CPU/memory MTTF (under a failure-to-exhaustion model) by a factor of almost 3.5.
2. The control store board represented 57 percent of the CPU failure rate. Of that total, 82 percent was microstore; thus, a total of 47 percent of the CPU failure rate was attributable to the microstore. Fifty-six percent of the CPU failure rate and 51 percent of the CPU/memory control failure rate consisted of RAM and ROM failures.

A series of fault-tolerant techniques was proposed for the RAMs/ROMs in the CPU. Figure 7–6 shows a Lambda analysis of the standard VAX-11/750 processor. The control store accounts for 55 percent of the RAM/ROM failure rate and 30 percent of the total failure rate. Table 7–11 lists the improvements predicted for application of a series of ECCs to the RAM/ROM arrays in the CPU plus memory controller. With these modifications, a factor of two improvements in

TABLE 7–10

Reliability analysis of preliminary VAX-11/750 design

Chip Type	Number	Failure Rate (%)	Board	Failure Rate (%)
Gate array	97	41	Data path	10.4
4K ROMs	16	9	Control store	43.6
8K ROMs	56	47	Memory interface	29.0
64-bit RAMs	32	2	Floating point accelerator	16.9
512-bit ROM	1	0		99.9
SSI/MSI	12	1		
	214	100		

FIGURE 7–6

Lambda analysis of failure rates in VAX 11/750 three-board CPU and memory controller

```
            LSI=   16.000   ROM=   16.000   RAM=   16.000
E =   1.000   Q =   16.000   L =    1.000   T =   40.000

MODULE                                               PERCENTAGE
COMET.CPU.PLUS.MEMORY.CONTROL                           100.000
        Data.Path.Module                                16.187
            Misc                                 42.643
            ROM.AND.RAM                          27.007
            GATE.ARRAY                           30.271
        Memory.Interface.Cache                          25.038
            Misc                                 30.003
            ROM.AND.RAM                          48.648
            GATE.ARRAY                           21.349
        Unibus.Interface                                14.158
            Misc                                 58.633
            ROM.AND.RAM                          20.905
            GATE.ARRAY                           20.462
        Control.Store                                   29.908
            Misc                                  5.657
            ROM.AND.RAM                          94.343
        Memory.Controller                               14.717
            Misc                                 64.169
            ROM.AND.RAM                          25.237
            GATE.ARRAY                           10.594

# of chips =   662.000   # of gates =   33361.000   # of bits =   732416.000
```

- -

SUMMARY ROLLUP BY COMPONENT TYPE

TYPE	# of CHIPS	PERCENTAGE
SSI	180.000	10.824
MSI	142.000	22.809
LSI	67.000	14.914
ROM	150.000	35.179
RAM	123.000	16.274
MOS	.000	.000
BIP	662.000	100.000

MTTF was predicted for a cost of 11 gate array chips.* A point of diminishing returns was reached after applications of ECC to the control store, TB, and data cache.

Full Hamming coding was too expensive in terms of board area for the control store. Block-code correctors are susceptible to multiple-bit failures. Because the control store was to be implemented by four-bit-wide chips, the relative failure rate of multiple bits was an additional unknown in establishing the effectiveness of a block-code corrector. It was therefore decided to disperse the resource commitment to RAMP throughout the CPU.

RAMP Features: Error Detection/Correction. Parity was provided on the cache and each half of the TB. Upon error detection, the appropriate TB half could be disabled, thus providing a form of fault tolerance in exchange for performance degradation.

In the control store, two parity bits are used to improve the diagnostic resolution of the chip in error. Field service would have at most 10 suspect ROM chips instead of 20 (hardware captures the microaddress that triggered the parity error as well as to which half of the control store the error occurred in). Main memory is protected by ECC.

* A gate-level design for a block-code corrector chip (see Chapter 3) was the basis for this chip estimate. No performance degradation was anticipated in the case of no failures. The overall parity detection was fast enough to freeze the processor and perform microinstruction retry after correction.

TABLE 7-11
Projected improvements in applying ECC to the RAM/ROM arrays in the three-board 11/750 CPU and memory controller

Configuration	Change in Failure Rate (%)	Relative Failure Rate	Extra Chips Required
Stock 11/750	—	1.00	—
ECC control store	28	0.72	4
ECC memory interface/cache	12	0.58	4
ECC data path	4		
ECC Unibus	3		
Interface	3	0.49	3
ECC memory controller	3		

The extensive use of gate arrays, the decreased visibility of logic signals because of LSI gate densities, and the higher board costs result in a repair strategy based on microdiagnostics, a V-bus, sockets for the gate array chips, and chip-level repair. The bounded, single-cabinet environment results in reduced complexity and the use of fault intolerant techniques. To reduce complexity, the same microsequencer that implements the VAX architecture also services the console subsystem.

RAMP Features: Controllability/Observability. Because there is no separate console processor in the VAX-11/750, there is no equivalent to the ID bus. All registers are located in either the processor (accessible by the special Move-To/From-Processor Register instructions) or the main memory address space.

Cache. Because the cache is direct-mapped, the Cache Disable Register only controls turning the cache on or off. The Cache Error Register records whether the tag or data recorded the parity error. The Lost Error bit indicates that a second cache error occurred before the first one was serviced. The Cache Hit/Miss bit indicates the status of the last reference.

Translation Buffer. The TB Disable Register controls the replacement strategy on a TB miss. Replacement can be random or forced to one half of the TB. The latter case can be used to disable half of the TB and allows reconfiguration around a permanent failure. The Force Miss bits, coupled with the TB Hit/Miss bit (in the Machine Check Status Register) can be used by diagnostics to check the TB's functionality. Finally, the TB Register records the address that caused the last protection violation. This data can be used by system software to repair or isolate software errors.

CMI. As mentioned, no parity or error checking was deemed necessary on the CMI due to its sheltered environment and implementation similarity to other data paths in the CPU. Hence, there are no registers to control or report CMI errors in the CPU or, for that matter, any CMI port.

Main Memory. Three registers are associated with the ECC main memory. Control/Status Register 0 (CSR 0) contains the address and syndrome of the last detected error. Two bits record whether an error was correctable or uncorrectable. The address and syndrome of an uncorrectable error overwrites the address and syndrome of a correctable error. The Uncorrectable Error/Information Lost bit records the occurrence of a second uncorrectable error before the first was serviced. The address and syndrome of this second error will not overwrite the address and syndrome of the first error.

CSR 1 contains control and maintenance bits. Single correctable errors can be ignored by setting the Inhibit Reporting Correctable Errors bit. The Page Mode Address bits specify the memory page affected by the other maintenance-mode bits. The Page Mode bit controls whether the whole memory is involved or just the specified page. Check bits are used to replace or make accessible the ECC bits associated with a word in main memory. The Diagnostic Check Mode allows for substitution on a memory read of the Check Bits field for the ECC bits stored in memory, providing a means of testing the ECC check logic. During writes, the newly generated ECC bits are stored in both memory and Check Bits (6:0). The Diagnostic Check Mode bit can operate only on a single page whose address is specified by the Page Address field. While in Diagnostic Check Mode, read errors in other memory pages will not be logged into CSR 0. The Error Disable Mode turns off error detection, correction, and logging. ECC can be disabled for the entire memory of a single page, depending on the value of the Page Mode bit.

CSR 2 contains memory configuration information such as the starting address of memory, the validity of memory contents after a power failure, and the presence of memory array boards.

Unibus. The Unibus adapter has only one RAMP related-register: the Buffered Data Path Control and Status Register. Only nonexisting memory and uncorrectable ECC errors are recorded.

Massbus. The Massbus adapter has three RAMP-related registers. The Control Register has a Maintenance Mode bit that allows exercising the Massbus without requiring an attached peripheral. When the bit is set, all Massbus devices detach from the bus. The Interrupt Enable bit allows reporting of Massbus-related errors to the CPU.

The MBA Status Register has three groups of signals. The first group records errors associated with the CMI portion of the access: corrected ECC, no response, and error. The second group deals with Massbus-related errors: control bus hung, nonexistent drive, data late, miss transfer, Massbus parity, and programming. A programming error is logged if a second MBA operation is attempted before completion of the first. The third group logs errors associated with logic in the MBA: page map and data path parity errors.

The MBA Diagnostic Register allows setting of incorrect parity on the Massbus, page map, or MBA data path, and reading or writing of selected Massbus fields.

Processor. The Machine Check Error Summary Register records the region of the machine where the error was reported; that is, the CMI, TB, or Unibus. It also records whether the error occurred on a CPU fetch or an IB prefetch. Transient errors associated with the IB prefetch can be recovered from by simply flushing the IB.

The Machine Check Status Register gives detailed information about bus and TB errors. The CMI can be disabled. Memory errors that are logged include nonresponding memory, ECC corrected read data, and uncorrectable ECC errors. A Lost Error bit is set if a second error occurs before the first error is serviced. TB errors include the parity bit in error as well as the status (hit or miss) of the last translation.

When an internal error is detected, status information is automatically placed on the machine stack for software analysis and error logging:

Byte Count (length of information on stack)
Error Summary code
Virtual Address Register (operand address)
Program Counter
Memory Data Register
Saved Mode Register (CPU mode during fault)
Read Lock Timeout Register

TB Group Parity (subfield of Machine Check Status Register)
Cache Error Register
Bus Error Register (subfield of Machine Check Status Register)
Machine Check Error Summary Register
Backup Program Counter (address of instruction)
Program Status Word

The error summary code pinpoints the region of the system where the error occurred:

Control Store Parity Error
Cache Parity Error
Memory Error
Corrected Memory Data
Write Bus Error
Bad Instruction Register Decode

RAMP Features: Micro- and Macrodiagnostics. The following levels of diagnostic actions are employed in the VAX-11/750:

- Level 1: User-mode macrodiagnostics run under the VMS (virtual memory system) operating system, such as line printer, card reader, terminal, tape, disk, instruction set
- Level 2: Macrodiagnostics executed under Diagnostic Supervisor while VMS is still operational; used in acceptance tests
- Level 3: Macrodiagnostics executed under the Diagnostic Supervisor with the CPU operating in a stand-alone mode; used in Unibus diagnostics
- Level 4: Macrodiagnostics executing stand-alone without the Diagnostic Supervisor; used in instruction set diagnostics
- Level 5: Microdiagnostics executing in a stand-alone mode
- Micro-verify: PROM resident microdiagnostics executed upon system initialization (a sanity check of the data path and memory interconnect modules)

The Remote Diagnostics Module plays a critical role in the 11/750 RAMP philosophy. Because the 11/750 console interface is provided by microcode executed in the main microsequencer, a CPU failure would bring the system completely down. A large percentage of the CPU hardware has to be functioning correctly in order to respond to console commands such as examine registers, deposit values, and single step. The RDM uses a separate microprocessor that can read the W-bus (for access to the CPU registers) and single-step (either single clock or single instruction) the CPU. It can also write via DMA over the CMI. The RDM contains a small 64-word WCS for executing microdiagnostics stored on a TU-58 cassette. It can also force arbitrary microaddresses, thus using the CPU control store to provide more microdiagnostics. A typical scenario would be to set up the CPU registers by DMA write into memory, execute some CPU microcode through forced microaddresses and clock control, set up a microtest via the forced microaddress and clock control, and observe results via the W-bus.

In a typical maintenance scenario on the VAX-11/750, disk-resident, user-mode diagnostics periodically execute under the virtual memory system to exercise and detect functional errors in memory, MBA, UBA, device controllers, and device drives. Errors reported by User Mode diagnostics or hardware check circuits prompt a customer call to the Remote Diagnostic Center (RDC). The customer replaces the removable disk media with a diagnostic and scratch disk. The RDC engineer calls the customer's processor and loads macrodiagnostics from the diagnostic disk. If the disk is not operable, the diagnostics can be loaded from the TU-58 or down-line loaded over the telephone. The RDC attempts to isolate the failure to a subsystem. If the CPU is faulty, the diagnostic on the TU-58 is executed to verify the CPU status.

The RDC advises the local field service office of the failing subsystem. At the customer's site, field service performs a board-swap and reverifies the system. If the failing subsystem is the CPU, microdiagnostics are loaded into the 64-word WCS on board the RDM. Multiple TU-58 cassettes are used to accommodate the extended length of the microdiagnostics (the VAX-11/780 microdiagnostics occupy five floppy disks). Length is also the reason that microdiagnostics are not down-line loaded from the RDC to attempt CPU failure isolation at the board or chip level. The 64-word WCS is loaded to set up data paths, registers, and the like, then overlaid with a series of tests. Each test exercises a single gate-array function. Results of tests are observed on the W-bus or V-bus. The RDM also monitors output of the control store. In the case of control store failure, parity pinpoints the failure to 10 chips. A microstore image stored on the TU-58 is used for comparison when the RDM accesses the faulty microstore word.

The microdiagnostics isolate the failure to between three and five gate array chips. If the malfunction persists after chip replacement, the board is swapped. The board is also swapped if one of the nonsocketed SSI/MSI chips fails.

SECOND-GENERATION VAX IMPLEMENTATIONS

Archetypical Implementation

The second-generation VAXs represented an evolutionary growth by enhancing the features found in the first-generation implementations. Features such as the following were retained:

- High performance backplane bus
- Block-oriented I/O buses attached to the backplane bus via buffered bus adapters
- Writable control store for flexibility and effective field modifications
- Separate console subsystem with visibility buses
- Remote diagnosis
- Instruction prefetch buffer, address translation buffer, and cache to boost performance
- ECC on main memory
- Logging of hardware and software detected errors

In order to meet the goal of providing substantially more performance than the previous generation, a high-speed logic technology and a highly concurrent implementation architecture were developed.

While the first generation relied upon bipolar TTL, the second generation introduced the higher speed emitter-coupled logic (ECL) technology to the VAX family. The characteristics of the basic building blocks for the VAX 8600 and VAX 8700 are as follows:

ECL Building Blocks: Motorola Macro Cell Array Characteristics

Technology: Emitter-coupled logic
Package: 68 pins
Circuitry: 106 cells from a library of macros (up to 1192 equivalent gates)
Speed per gate: 1.2–1.8 nsec
Power dissipation: 5 W

These characteristics of the Motorola macro cell array (MCA) should be contrasted to the TTL gate array technology used in the VAX-750 (Table 7.9). The enhanced gate speed directly translated to a factor of 4 to 8 in decreased cycle time. The macro cell is an extension of the gate array concept. Each cell contains a number of unconnected transistors and resistors that can be interconnected to form "macros." The macro cell library is composed of standard logic elements such as dual D-type flip-flops, dual full adders, quad latches, input and output cells, and so on. If full adders and latches are used in each cell, a single MCA may contain 1192 equivalent gates. Typical power dissipation is 4.4 milliwatts per equivalent gate.

Figure 7–7 depicts the archetypical implementation of a second–generation VAX. The CPU has been divided into three autonomous units: I-box, E-box, and M-box. The I-box prefetches instructions and operands and decodes them for later execution by the E-box. The M-box interfaces the memory and I/O to the I- and E-boxes. The M-box also contains the translation buffer and cache. A number of buses interconnect the various boxes so that they may all work concurrently. All data movement between the processor and the memory array and I/O subsystem occurs through the memory data bus connecting the M-box with the I-box. The I-box receives the instruction and operand stream over the memory data bus. The operands are then passed to the E-box over the instruction/operand bus. The E-box supplies the address and data resulting from the instruction execution to the M-box over the virtual address and write data buses, respectively. The M-box holds the results in cache or writes them to the memory array if appropriate.

The VAX-11/780 prefetches instructions whenever a cache cycle is available. Thus, the next opcode is ready for decoding as soon as the results from the previous instruction are stored. One possible scenario is depicted in Figure 7–8a. The second generation implementations extended this simple pipelining to the entire instruction. The M-, I-, and E-boxes, along with the buses, form a deeper pipeline wherein several instructions are in different stages of execution at the same time. Figure 7–8b depicts the execution of a sequence of instructions in this pipeline.

FIGURE 7–7

Archetypical second-generation VAX implementation [Courtesy of Digital Equipment Corporation]

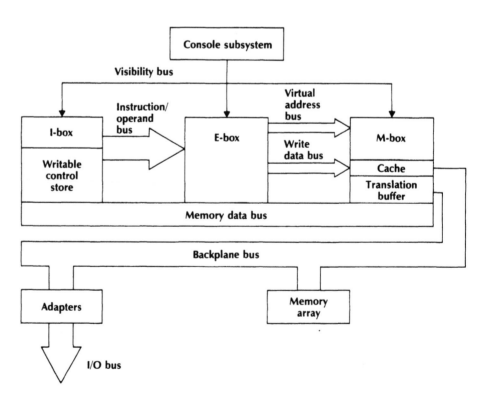

FIGURE 7–8
*Example instruc-
tion pipelines
[Courtesy of Digi-
tal Equipment Cor-
poration]*

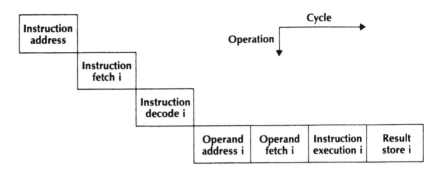

a. VAX 11/7/80

Unit							
Instruction address	Instruction address						
Instruction fetch		Instruction fetch i					
Instruction decode			Instruction decode i				
Operand address				Operand address i			
Operand fetch					Operand fetch i		
Instruction execution						Instruction execution i	
Result store							Result store i

b. VAX 8600

As an example, consider the ADDL2 (R0), R1 instruction execution in the VAX 8600 [Fossom, McElry, and English, 1985]:

1. *Instruction Address*: The PC sends out the address for instruction i, ADDL2.
2. *Instruction Fetch*: The I-box fetches the ADDL2 from the instruction stream in memory.
3. *Instruction Decode*: The I-box uses the opcode from ADDL2 to address the decode RAM.
4. *Operand Address*: The I-box gets the virtual address of the first operand from register R0 and sends it to the M-box.
5. *Operand Fetch*: The M-box translates the virtual address into a physical address, retrieves the data from the cache, and sends it to the I-box. (If the cache does not have the data, the procedure must wait at this stage for the M-box to get the data from storage.)

6. *Instruction Execution*: The E-box receives operands from the cache and R1 and adds them.
7. *Result Store*: The E-box stores the result in R1. (If the result were to be stored in memory, the I-box would supply the address.)

Even though this instruction takes seven cycles to execute, a sequence of instructions can store a result in a register every cycle.

Due to the increased complexity of the second generation over the first generation, RAMP became an even more pronounced design consideration. The second generation has two to three times the gate count of the first generation. Efforts were mounted to minimize errors throughout the life cycle of the implementation. The various types of errors and the techniques used are as follows:

Type of Error	Error Handling Technique
Design errors	Timing verification tools, signal integrity
Manufacturing errors	Burn-in parts, electrostatic discharge control
Field failures	Airflow analysis, failure-rate prediction, environmental monitoring, remote diagnosis, visibility bus, ECC memory, error-detecting/correcting circuits

Verification of the design prior to construction helped to minimize design errors. Due to the high switching speeds of ECL gates that can cause even small pieces of etch to become transmission lines, a detailed timing analysis was required to insure sufficient timing margins. A custom timing analysis program was thus employed by the VAX 8600 and the VAX 8700 teams. The circuit density also aggravated noise and crosstalk problems, so special care was taken to protect the logic through careful shielding and grounding.

Failures due to manufacturing errors were decreased through incoming screening and burn-in of parts. Since ECL circuits are easily damaged by electrostatic discharge, handling procedures were established to reduce this damage. Throughout the entire design process, careful attention was devoted to thermal profiles. Physical placement coupled with airflow analysis established the case-ambient temperature for each chip. The Lambda program (see Chapter 2) was then used to predict the failure rate of individual components. The results of the Lambda analysis were used to reposition high failure rate components and/or justify heat sinking of the components. A sophisticated Environmental Monitoring Module was designed to shut down the system in an orderly way, if it sensed overvoltage, overcurrent, or overtemperature conditions. The EMM was also designed to shut down the system if a loss of air flow is detected and to help isolate intermittent faults by margining voltage and timing. Finally, an array of error-detection and -correction techniques, coupled with a visibility bus and remote diagnosis, were developed to assist in quick, accurate diagnosis of failed components.

Implementation of VAX 8600

Design Philosophy. The designers of the VAX 8600 were not only concerned about detecting/diagnosing permanent faults, but also with increasing the mean time to crash. In order to improve MTTC, the number of error detectors was increased to include extension to portions of the machine uncovered in the first generation implementations. Designers carefully analyzed the boundaries between error detectors to provide overlap; that is, the check performed by one error detector, such as parity, only occurs after the information is protected by the second error detector, such as duplication. Due to the dominance of transient and intermittant faults, retry was selected as the primary error-correction technique since it was considered to be the most economical approach to increasing MTTC.

Another design principle is that incorrect information is only considered an error if an attempt is made to use or store the data. For example, if corrupted data is detected during a write-back to the memory from the cache, a fault will not be logged. The software will experience a fault if it attempts to consume the corrupted data or to store it on disk. Thus, data is stored with a corrupted data tag, which marks it for later detection.

Since the VAX 8600 is heavily pipelined, unique opportunities and challenges have resulted. For example, four copies of the general-purpose registers were provided for performance reasons. Thus, if one general register set detected a parity error, it can easily be "corrected" by updating from one of the other register sets. On the other hand, since several instructions can be partially executed in the pipeline at any given time, a detected error must be mapped to the appropriate instruction and that instruction backed up and retried without disturbing the other partial results. There are many design decisions that have been uniformly applied across the boxes. An overview of the common features used in the various boxes is given next.

- Substantial attention was placed on signal integrity and thermal profiles. A careful budget was drawn up for noise margin with an allocation for each identified contributor to noise including: load reflections, crosstalk, interconnect mismatch impedance, simultaneous switching of outputs, power supply noise on signal line, signal and power-resistive voltage drops, gate feedthrough, and output voltage variations due to thermal differences. Since the signal input and output levels shift with changes in temperature, constraining the noise contribution due to temperature gradients required limiting the air temperature difference between any two devices connected together to 10° C. Design rules were established for the maximum power dissipation for any three-inch high column of chips on a board. Thermal profiles were extensively analyzed with special MCA parts having a diode serve as an internal thermometer. Plastic pseudo boards are installed in all unused slots to prevent the cooling air from taking the path of least resistance through the gaps.

- All memories and buses are checked by parity. Furthermore, parity continuity is carried through all the major data paths. Parity is kept not only for data, but also for physical addresses and microcode. Bad data in a writable memory, such as control store or table look-up constants, are corrected by the console processor from the files it uses during machine initialization.

- Address parity and a bad data flag are "folded" into the error-correcting code for the main memory and the cache. Thus, not only are incorrectly accessed words (that is, address parity mismatched) but also data that was stored corrupted (that is, a data path's parity error is detected prior to storing in memory) can be identified.

- Instruction retry is used to recover from transient and intermittent errors.

- Errors are dynamically logged and analyzed by the Standard Package for Error Analysis and Reporting (SPEAR). By analyzing trends, failures can be more accurately isolated to field replaceable units.

- Memory, under software control, is dynamically reconfigured to exclude bad pages.

- The F-box continually tests itself when not in use. If an error is detected, the floating point unit can be configured out and its functionality replaced by E-box microcode.

- A diagnostic bus provides the console with access to hundreds of internal logic signals.

• The EMM determines that all modules are in the proper place through electronic keying. It also detects the ambient temperature of the incoming air and the temperature gradient across the card cage. An overheated regulator, a failed blower, inadequate air flow, inadequate output voltage, or dangerously high temperature gradients will cause the EMM to shut the system down. Instead of monitoring the power cord, the EMM monitors the internal 300-volt DC level. This internal voltage is an indirect measure of the energy stored by capacitors in the system. When the voltage reaches a level at which there is just enough energy remaining to perform a power fail sequence, an AC power failure is signaled.

• Diagnostics isolate failures to a board with a high probability with subsequent depot levels servicing isolating to within 10 chips on average.

Since most VAX instructions store results only upon completion, errors in most cases cause only intermediate results to be lost. There are five program counters in the system:

1. Instruction prefetcher address stream pointer
2. Program counter, which points to the current byte being processed in the instruction stream
3. Current program counter, which points to the instruction currently being decoded
4. I-box starting address, which points to instruction-fetching operands
5. E-box starting address, which points to the instruction being executed

For most instructions, the program state must be restored to what it was prior to the execution of the instruction if the instruction is to be successfully retried. The program state consists of those general-purpose registers that have been modified and the instruction starting address. The general-purpose register modifications are kept in the RLOG. The RLOG has enough entries to allow register restoration for multiple instructions. The program counter for the instruction in question is restored from either the current program counter, the I-box starting address, or the E-box starting address. The effected general-purpose registers are restored from the RLOG. If the instruction cannot be retried, the software process containing it must be retried, or in the worst case, the system would need rebooting.

Each of the boxes has its own microstore and microsequencer. Much of the error reporting and recovery is implemented in microcode. If an error related to the currently executing instruction occurs, the microcode is trapped. It then collects the error information, fixes the error condition, backs up the affected instruction for later restart, and enters the machine check software.

The sequence of events triggered by the detection of a hardware error includes:

• Hardware logic detects the error and latches it in an internal hardware status register.
• An error signal is sent to the E-box to invoke a microtrap to start the error-handling microcode (EHM).
• The EHM retrieves the state of all the error and status registers and builds an error stack frame in the E-box scratch pad.
• The EHM passes the stack frame to the operating system to initiate recovery, if possible.
• The operating system formats the stack frame into an error record, which is written out to the disk on the system event file. The failing operation is restarted if possible.
• The service engineer executes SPEAR to determine error trends and schedule the required maintenance to correct the source of intermittent problems before they become solid. The periodic analysis of the system event file can be performed remotely from the RDC.

In the case of fatal errors that cause a system crash, the console processor retrieves the state of the CPU at the time of the crash. When the system is restarted, the operating system writes the snapshot into the system event file for subsequent analysis by SPEAR. If the system is unable to restart, a second snapshot is taken by the console software and made available to the service engineer to perform a manual crash analysis.

Two types of error events have been identified: synchronous and asynchronous. Synchronous errors have a direct relationship to the current value of the program counter. For example, consider a TB miss on a prefetch of an instruction. If a branch instruction occurs in the instruction buffer ahead of the translation buffer miss and the branch is taken, the translation buffer miss will not be a problem and should not be reported. Thus, a delay must be introduced prior to sending the translation buffer miss signal to the E-box, which performs memory management operations. Only when the instruction that caused the prefetch translation buffer miss is to be executed should the fault be reported. Synchronous faults are reported via E-box microtraps.

Asynchronous errors, on the other hand, are ones for which the value of the program counter has no definite relationship. These are usually reported through interrupts. An example is a parity error on a cache write-back operation. When an error is detected, it may not be known whether it should be reported synchronously or asynchronously. In this case, both a microtrap and an interrupt error-logging mechanism is initiated. For example, in the case of a parity error on an instruction prefetch, if the E-box executed the branch prior to using the bad data, the synchronization error will never be reached and the fault will be logged through an interrupt. Thus, the microtrap condition will be cleared by the execution of the branch. If, however, the E-box attempts to execute the prefetch instruction with the parity error, an E-box microtrap will occur, and the trap routine will clear the interrupt.

Figure 7–9 provides an overview of the VAX 8600 implementation architecture. There are four boxes—I (instruction), F (floating point), E (execution), and M (memory)—and eight buses: I-box virtual address, E-box virtual address, operand, write, memory data, adapter, array, and SBI. A brief description of each box follows [VAX 8600/8650, 1986]:

- *I-Box*: The I-box prefetches instructions to load an 8-byte IB; prefetches operands required by the E-box and F-box; decodes instructions and provides fork addresses to the E-box's microsequencer; maintains program counter registers for instruction restart, instruction stream fetches, and operand fetches; calculates operand addresses; executes branch instructions to modify program control; stores E-box and F-box results in memory via the memory data bus; and maintains the RLOG and scoreboard to unwind the general-purpose registers prior to instruction retry. The I-box is controlled by a microsequencer whose microcode resides in a 50-bit-wide, 256-word-deep WCS. The I-box is implemented on three boards.
- *E-Box*: The E-box executes the VAX's instruction set, handles exceptions and interrupts, and handles memory management functions to refill the translation buffer when the M-box detects a translation buffer miss or an access violation. The E-box is controlled by a microsequencer whose microcode resides in a 92-bit-wide, 8K-word-deep WCS. An integral part of the microcode is an error handling microroutine that is invoked to handle all errors detected within the CPU. The E-box is implemented on six boards.
- *F-Box*: The F-box is a hardware option to speed up the execution of floating point instructions. It is controlled by two microsequencers one of which has a 48-bit-wide, 512-word-deep WCS, and the second has a 40-bit-wide, 512-word-deep WCS. The F-box is implemented on two boards.
- *M-Box*: The M-box provides the entry and exit point for all data to and from the CPU. Data can come from the internal memory array via the array bus or from the I/O subsystem via the adapter bus. It contains the translation buffer and the cache. It services requests from the I-box or E-box to fetch instructions, fetch operands, and write results. It also provides the

FIGURE 7–9

*VAX 8600 data
paths and error
checking*

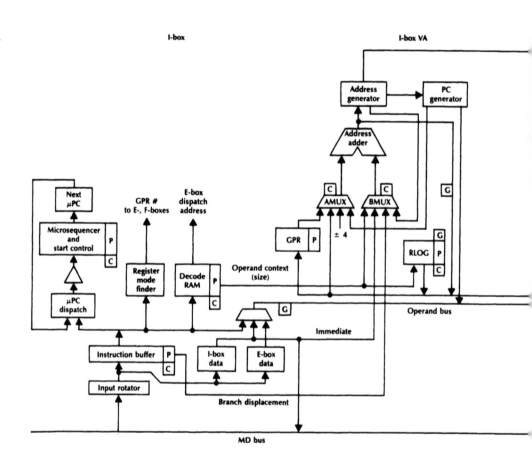

C bus – console bus
MD bus – Memory Data bus
VA bus – Virtual Address
MPS – Modular Power Supply
EMM – Environmental Monitor Module
TB – Translation Buffer
GPR – General Purpose Registers
μPC – Microprogram Counter
P – Parity bits
PC – Parity Checker
PG – Parity Generator
ECC – Error-correcting Code

facilities for direct memory access transfers to/from the I/O subsystem. It is controlled by a microsequencer whose WCS is composed of 80-bit-wide, 256-word-deep entries. The M-box is implemented on three boards.

• The VAX 8600 is composed of four boxes: the I-box for instruction fetch and decoding, the E- and F-boxes for instruction execution, and the M-box, which serves as an interface to the system memory.

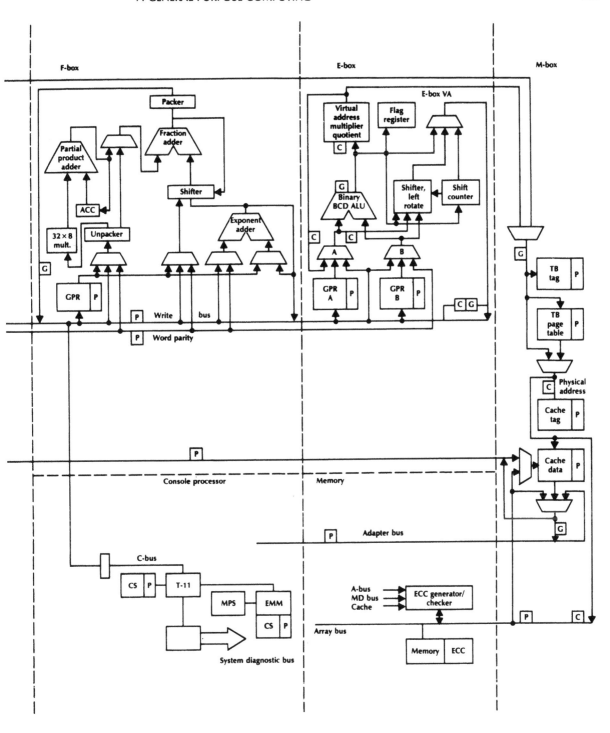

As in the VAX implementations described earlier in this case study, the VAX 8600 is also a memory-intensive design. In addition to data storage such as caches, translation buffers, registers, and instruction decoding memories, the vast majority of the control logic resides in the micro-sequencers provided by each box. Microcode integrity and sequencing are amenable to inexpensive parity error checking. In addition, the parity is continued from the data storage elements through the data paths and checked prior to consumption by the appropriate box.

Since so much of the machine is "soft" and contained in writable memories, the system console plays a vital role in initialization and error handling. The console subsystem is composed of a T-11 (PDP-11) CPU with 256 kB of program memory protected by byte parity and 8 kB of read-only memory for system cold start. It contains three UARTs to interface to the local console, the remote diagnostic center, and the EMM. A check-summed C-bus provides the interface between the console subsystem and E-box. A system diagnostic bus (SDB) provides the console with observability/controllability access to over 2000 internal signals. The SDB provides the equivalent functionality to the V-bus in the VAX-11/780. The following steps must be taken upon system initialization:

1. The Intel 8085 microprocessor in the EMM checks the state of the module-keying circuits to determine whether they are all inserted correctly. If there are no errors, the power supply is turned on to provide DC power to the console module.
2. The console subsystem executes code from its read-only memory to perform hard core checks on the console processor, console processor memory, and load path to the console processor floppy disk.
3. The console processor loads its software from the floppy disk and continues the power-on sequence in coordination with the EMM microprocessor.
4. The console processor loads the various writable control stores in the central processor boxes. The console also sizes the internal memory subsystem and loads a mapping memory in the M-box to allow memory and I/O subsystem access.
5. The command file is read from the console floppy disk, which loads the operating system boot-loader program.
6. The operating system boot program loads a secondary boot program in the system disk, which, in turn, loads and starts the operating system kernel.

There are eight main buses in the system:

1. Array bus, which interfaces the memory array cards to the M-box
2. SBI bus (synchronous backplane interconnect used in the VAX-11/780), to which prior generation I/O peripherals are attached via adapters
3. I-box virtual address bus, which carries virtual addresses from the I-box to the M-box during instruction fetch, operands fetch, and I-box write operation
4. E-box virtual address bus, which carries virtual addresses from the E-box to the M-box during E-box operand references and certain memory management routines
5. Memory data bus, which carries data from both reads and writes to the M-box
6. Operand bus, which carries operands from the I-box to the E-box and F-box
7. Write bus, which carries results from the execution units to memory (via the I-box) or to the general-purpose registers
8. Adapter bus, which interfaces the CPU to the I/O subsystem

RAMP Features: Error Detection/Correction. The VAX 8600 utilizes many fault-tolerant techniques [Bruckert and Josephson, 1985]. These techniques are summarized for each of the boxes in Table 7–12.

TABLE 7-12 *VAX 8600 error-detection/correction features*

I-Box	E-Box	F-Box	M-Box
Parity	Parity	Parity	Parity
Microstore	Microstore	Microstore	Microstore
General-purpose	Microstack	General-purpose	Microstack
registers	General-purpose registers	registers	Microaddress
Instruction buffer	Memory control function	Decode memory	Cache (tag, data, written bits)
Decode memory	memory	Other	Translation buffer (tag, data,
RLOG	Buses parity checked	Self-tests during	valid bits)
Data path	Operand bus	idle	Cycle condition code
Buses parity checked	Write bus	Correction	Buses parity checked
Operand bus	Console bus	Microstore	Array bus
Write bus	Correction		Adapter bus
Correction	Microstore		Other error detection
Microstore	General-purpose register		Microstack overflow/underflow
	copy		Force bad parity
	Instruction retry		Enable/disable error-detection
	Data path parity checked		and reporting mechanisms
	Output parity of multiple		Multiple error while servicing
	ALUs		first error
	Shifter		Correction
	AMUX, active source		ECC on main memory, cache
	recorded		over data, address parity,
	BMUX, active source		and bad data bit
	recorded		Write back corrected data on an
	Other		error
	CPU keep-alive signal		
	Error insertion: static and		
	dynamic		

I-Box. The WCS is 51 bits wide and protected by a parity bit. Data from the write bus is parity checked on the output of the AMUX prior to consumption by the address adder. Data from the address adder to be placed upon the write bus has its parity generated. Similarly, data placed on the operand bus has parity generated. If the data is being passed through from the memory data bus (byte parity), the four parity bits are collapsed into a single parity bit for the word parity on the operand bus. The I-box's copy of the general-purpose registers, the IB, and the decode memory, which provides the starting address for the microsequence corresponding to macroinstructions, are all protected by parity, which is checked upon usage for the various memories.

Parity on data is carried through the registers and data path and checked just prior to consumption by the address adder. Since all sources to the address adder do not provide parity, a separate control signal indicates when parity is valid to prevent spurious signals. (This form of partial checking is defined in Chapter 3.)

The RLOG is a special-purpose 11-bit-wide, 16-entry-deep memory that records which general-purpose registers have been modified (and by how much) by self-modifying addressing modes (e.g., auto increment and auto decrement) of the macroinstructions currently in the pipeline. An entry mark is entered into the RLOG at the beginning of each macroinstruction. During the instruction execution, an entry is made for each operand specifier that modifies a general-purpose register. These entries record the general-purpose register number, the amount of modification, and a valid bit that indicates that the modification has taken place. When the pipeline has to be restarted due to an error condition detected by a partially executed instruction, the RLOG is used to regenerate the state of the pipeline prior to the error detection. Consider the case where the M-box has detected an error. The M-box causes the E-box to microtrap. Part of the error-handling microcode in the E-box issues a stop command to the I-box so that no further updating of the program counter registers and no further memory requests (i.e., preventing further memory errors) are made. The E-box reads and saves all of the M-box error registers and attempts to correct the source of the error. The E-box decides how many instructions should be restarted and what the restart address should be. The I-box uses the RLOG to restore the pipeline state to what it was just prior to encountering the error. The latest RLOG entry is read out, and if the valid bit is set, the general-purpose register specified in the entry is modified according to the context; that is, the size is added to or subtracted from the indicated register. Unwinding continues until the I-box sees a first bit set. The E-box then restarts the I-box by issuing a command to flush the prefetch buffers and another command to restart instruction fetching.

E-Box. The main microstore for the system resides in the E-box. Both microinstructions and the microstack are checked by parity. When a microstore parity error is detected, a signal is sent to the console processor. The console software stops the CPU clocks and retrieves the address of the microinstruction in error from a microprogram counter save register accessible via the visibility channel. Next the console processor retrieves all 92 bits of the microinstruction in error via the system diagnostic bus. Using ECC tables stored in memory, the console software corrects the bad microinstruction and shifts the corrected results back to the control store. The console then initiates a read of the same microinstruction location to verify that the parity error has been corrected and restarts the system clocks.

All buses interfaced to the E-box (operand bus, write bus, and C-bus), as well as both copies of the general-purpose registers and the memory containing the definition of memory control functions, are checked by parity. When the E-box is writing to the M-box, it generates the parity for the data on the write bus and sends it directly to the M-box. The write bus data is routed through the I-box and sent to the M-box via the memory data bus.

Data paths have a number of parity checks to determine errors on operands presented to the data operators as well as the results from the data operators. The ALU is replicated three times. One copy feeds the virtual address multiplier quotient (VAMQ) unit, one copy feeds the shifter, and one copy is used to generate the condition codes. The VAMQ and the condition code ALU generate parity on their results for comparison to detect ALU errors. The parity from the shifter is generated over the results of the shift operation and exclusive-ORed with those inputs to the shifter that were not used in the operation. The shifter result parity is compared to the shifter ALU parity to detect errors in the shift operation. The inputs to the shifter are parity checked at the AMUX and BMUX. The active source to the multiplexers at the time of parity errors is also captured to help isolate the cause of the error.

VAX macroinstructions can be retried as described in the section on the I-box. When a parity error is detected in one copy of the general register set, it can be corrected by selecting and using the data in the other register set. A CPU keep-alive signal is asserted by the E-box every time its microcode starts the execution of a new macroinstruction. If the E-box fails to set the flag before a software timer (approximately 300 milliseconds) expires in the console, the console intervenes by stopping the CPU clocks. A keep-alive failure sequence is initiated to crash the system, collect error information from all units in the CPU, log the error information, and reboot the CPU.

The data from all these errors is collected into a scratch-pad register for examination by the error-handling microcode. The pattern of parity errors and active sources at the time of error detection creates a signature that can be used to help isolate the origin of the error. For example, assume that the following bits were set: in the E-box Data Parity Status Register (EDPSR), the general-purpose register copy B parity error, the operand bus parity error, and the E-box control store (EBCS) and the EDP parity error indicating that the ALU was input to the VAMQ when the parity error occurred. The fault most likely lies in the general-purpose register B RAMs, the B input side of the ALU, or the parity error-detection logic itself.

There is also special logic in the E-box to test the error-detection logic. Error insertion (EIS) registers are used to enable specific error conditions in the Diagnostic Fault Insertion Register, which can be used to dynamically insert the error while the system is running. EIS registers can be used by the console processor over the system diagnostic bus to statically set and test the various error checkers. EIS registers can be set up over the SD bus by the console for triggering insertion of the error at some later time. An 11-bit binary upcounter is used to specify when the error should be inserted. A 5-bit Control Register specifies which events should increment the counter; for example, increment every master clock period or increment on various stall or delay events in the CPU pipeline.

There are times when the error-detection and -reporting mechanisms should be disabled. For example, consider a single-bit permanent failure in memory. A single memory page, such as in low memory where interrupt vectors are stored, may not be eligible for mapping out. The single-bit failure is correctable, but to prevent a known problem from filling up the system error log, the operating system may choose to inhibit reporting of correctable errors.

F-Box. The F-box is a hardware option for speeding up the execution of floating point arithmetic instructions and some instructions involving integer multiplication. If enabled, this option overrides the E-box floating point microcode and uses dedicated hardware. The operation of the F-box is transparent to system-level software. Two microsequencers control the floating point data paths, and their control stores are checked by parity. The F-box copies of the general-purpose registers, as well as the decoder RAM providing the microroutine starting address for the floating point macroinstructions, are also protected by parity. Parity generation is provided by the fraction adder. When the E-box or I-box updates the F-box copy of the general-purpose registers, the byte parity provided by the write bus is stored with the data. If the F-box writes the general-purpose registers, the data has to be routed through the fraction adder so that the parity may be calculated.

When the F-box is idle it executes a self-test. The type of test is dependent upon the length of time the current instruction in the E-box will take to execute. The data for the tests consists of constants from the F-box scratch-pad registers or the current data on the operand bus. The self-test compares the results to the expected value and sets an error flag if there is a difference. The exponent logic is not subject to the self-test. Self-tests include the following:

- *Data Path Tests.* Data from the operand bus is added to zero, then subtracted from itself.
- *Branch Test.* Using constants from the scratch-pad registers, an exponent difference of three is set up to test the branch for exponent differences less than 32.
- Scratch-Pad Data Path Test. A constant from the scratch-pad registers is added to zero and subtracted from itself.
- Add Self-Test with Operand A Greater than Operand B. Two constants from the scratch pad

are added, the result normalized and rounded, and then compared to the expected result stored in the scratch pad by subtraction.

- Add Self-Test with Operand A Less than Operand B. (The test is the same as in the previous item.)
- Subtract Self-Test. Two constants from the scratch-pad registers are subtracted. The result has more than seven leading zeros and must be normalized and rounded.
- Double-Precision Add Self-Test. Two double-precision constants with unlike signs are added.
- Multiplier Data Path Test. A constant from the scratch-pad is multiplied by one and normalized. The normalized result is subtracted from the original constant.

M-Box. All read/write memories in the M-box are protected by parity. Parity is generated when the memory is threatened and is checked when the memory is read. Errors in microsequencer operations are detected by parity on microaddresses, microinstructions, and the microaddress stack. Furthermore, attempts to push onto a full microstack or pop from an empty microstack are also detected. Transactions across the array bus and adapter bus are protected by parity. In the case of the adapter bus, there is separate parity over the address, data, and control. Furthermore, errors during access of input/output registers are separately identified. The TB has parity over Data, Tag, and Valid Bit fields. There are times when state must be remembered across a sequence of microinstructions. For example, the memory access rights of the current translated page address must be checked on every fetch from memory. This "residual" information is available from the cycle condition code memory. This writable memory is composed of 18 bits of data and 2 parity bits.

The two-way set associative cache is composed of 1000 entries each of 16 bytes. The cache data is protected by byte parity and there are parity bits over the tag and written bit. Both the TB and cache normally contain redundant copies of information. In the case of a TB, a parity error could be considered the same as a TB miss, thus evoking the virtual-to-physical address translation microcode to recalculate the final physical address. The recomputed translation is loaded into the TB, thus correcting nonpermanent errors. In most systems, the cache is merely a copy of data in the main memory. Thus, a parity error in the cache could be treated as a miss and the backup copy of the data retrieved from main memory.

However, in the VAX 8600 a "write-back" replacement policy is used to minimize the amount of traffic between the processor and the memory. In a write-back, cache data that has been modified in the cache is only written back to memory when the cache location is to be replaced. Thus, there are times when the data in the cache is the only valid copy in the system. When byte parity detects an error on cache data, a single-bit error-correction/double-bit error-detection code is utilized to restore the data. The byte parity is used for high-speed error detection; the ECC is only utilized when an error is present. The cache and main memory utilize the same ECC. The ECC is formulated over 32 bits of data, the address parity bit, and a bad data bit. Neither the address parity bit nor the bad data bit is stored in the memory: They are only used in generation and checking operations. Five of the ECC check bits use even parity and the other two use odd parity.

The alternating parity between the check bits detects the case of all zero or all one errors that might be generated by "floating" signal lines due to a timing or selection error. When a word is fetched, check bits are formulated from the data retrieved, the parity of the address presented to the memory, and a zero representing the phantom bad data bit. If the check bits indicate a Bad Address bit, it is assumed that for some reason the wrong word was fetched from memory; that is, the word that was actually addressed was not selected. Indication that the bad data bit is in error implies that a known bad data element was stored and becomes visible to the application program. If this location had been overwritten prior to use, the original creation of the bad data would have been logged but there would have been no stoppage of user-level programs since no one had tried to consume the bad data.

Most ECC memories will correct data on a read, but for performance reasons, will not write back the corrected results to memory. The VAX 8600 not only corrects data, but writes it back so that there is a low probability that errors will saturate the ECC. The M-box also keeps track of whether a second error has occurred before the E-box has finished servicing the first. The condition of high-arrival rate of errors is considered fatal.

RAMP Features: Micro- and Macrodiagnostics. There are four levels of diagnostics in the VAX 8600. The Microhardcore is a test program based in the console microprocessor, which is initially executed to test all the key data and control facilities necessary to successfully load and run microdiagnostics. The microdiagnostic programs permit isolation of faults to an FRU. The micro-diagnostics are executed on the boxes in the following order: E-box, M-box, I-box, and F-box. Finally, the memory array diagnostics and the I/O diagnostics are executed. They verify the operation of all the control stores in the CPU along with the basic tests of the E-box, F-box, I-box, and M-box microsequencers. Composed of 98 tests, they are organized into eight groups that provide isolation to the box and module for failure in the hardcore logic. The microdiagnostics are loaded into the E-box control store and, once started, communicate the results to the console processor and display them for interpretation by the service engineer. The VAX macrodiagnostics functionally test the CPU and I/O subsystems. Most of the I/O subsystem macrodiagnostics are available in both stand-alone and on-line test programs.

Perhaps the best diagnostic is the VMS operation system itself. VMS logs error entries in the system event file for on-line analysis. These errors can trigger on-line macrodiagnostic programs for functional testing of the hardware without taking down the operating system.

VAX 8700 Implementation

Design Philosophy. The VAX 8700 has a close cultural heritage with the VAX-11/750. Performance is achieved through a faster cycle time and decreasing the number of cycles per instruction execution. Reliability results from design simplicity and fault avoidance techniques.

Design integrity flows from a chief architect through a structured, top-down design methodology. Detailed specifications are written for the entire system before any logic is designed. The entire system is thoroughly simulated prior to generating any hardware. Simulation shifted the majority of debugging to the design phase. Plots of cumulative bugs detected are used to demonstrate the stability of the design.

The diagnostics are debugged on the simulator prior to availability of the hardware. Thus, the diagnostics are available for hardware design verification as well as providing test vectors for manufacturing checkout. Not only is the cost of a prototype saved but also development time is decreased. As a result, the design required fewer engineering change orders.

The VAX 8700 designers projected the system-level reliability requirements backwards to identify the reliability requirements for individual components. Once component-level goals were identified, steps were taken to improve factors affecting component reliability through design and component level specification. Careful attention was paid to component selection and specification, with emphasis on removal of early life failures. A sequential burn-in process was specified and made part of vendor agreements. This process included accelerated burn-in at elevated temperature followed by testing with additional burn-in for failing lots. Only after component reliability was demonstrated were the burn-in requirements reduced to decrease component costs. It was found that most lots have no failures in contrast with the few maverick lots exhibiting a large number of failures. A sequential burn-in was effective in eliminating these maverick lots.

Thermal analysis was performed to insure that no component exceeded the defined junction temperature. Thermal characteristics were the major factor in the selection of ceramic packaging for the macro cell arrays (MCAs). A simple, effective, and inexpensive heat sink was devised for the larger power-dissipating components. A thermal conductive epoxy was developed to attach a four-finned, circular heat sink tower that could be placed in the airflow path in any orientation. Heat sinks for components other than MCAs were determined not to be cost effective. The VAX 8700 program benefited from extensive thermal studies and thermal analysis CAD tools developed by the VAX 8600 project. The VAX 8700 logic modules were placed in wind tunnels that simulated cabinet airflow, and an infra-red scan of the modules was used to identify hot spots and verify that no components exceeded their thermal design parameters.

Prototype modules were built to verify the technology, determine the ability of vendors to supply the technology, and validate the CAD tools and design rules. Finished printed circuit board modules and backplanes were built, extensively exercised, and the results fed back to the design process. The backplane and board technology test cases proved to be valuable in influencing the final design. Early test cases showed that the FR4 board material was inappropriate for backplanes since the solder reflow process used to attach module connectors caused excessive Z-axis expansion, damaging the backplanes beyond repair. The final backplane design utilized polyimid, which was less susceptible to Z-axis expansion. Subtle Z-axis expansion problems can result in difficult-to-diagnose intermittent backplane connections. No problems were discovered with the nine-layer printed circuit board test case, indicating that the less-expensive FR4 material was appropriate for printed circuit boards. MCA test cases were used to validate the design rules used in the CAD process. Masks were built from test cases and sent to the actual release and manufacturing processes.

The VAX 8700 project introduced a program of 100 percent high-potential testing. This high-voltage stress test was effective in identifying void defects in the resin of the printed circuit board module. Elimination of boards with resin voids was necessary to reduce the possibility that a stressed-printed circuit board would slowly smolder and burn. This problem had been previously seen on a small number of systems.

Manufacturing personnel were integrated with the design effort from the beginning. Rather than following the tradition of engineering's assembling the first hardware model, manufacturing generated all copies of the VAX 8700, thus accelerating the learning curve for manufacturing. One problem discovered during this process was that the zero insertion force connectors for the logic modules lacked the "wiping" action of friction-type connectors. Thus, strict cleaning techniques were developed to avoid contamination and module reseating problems.

Studies of previous systems found a considerable number of failures that were attributable to electrostatic discharge (ESD). The ESD protection program that was developed included the following:

- Modules assembled in designated ESD protection areas with conductive flooring and clothing
- ESD ground "swipes" provided on logic card cages to dissipate electrostatic charge from modules prior to insertion into the backplane and to protect logic modules already seated in the backplane
- Shipping containers designed to reduce ESD damage in handling
- Wrist straps provided in the CPU cabinet, allowing the field service engineer and the module container to be grounded during service activities
- Modules electrically keyed to prevent improper insertion

Field service personnel had long recognized that many installation problems result from the subtleties of grounding when cabling together CPUs, mass storage devices, and peripherals. Particularly difficult problems occur when equipment comes from different vendors. There are three types of ground interconnection topologies: single-point (star), multi-point (ground plane), and hybrid (mixture of the two). Single-point and multi-point are difficult to use in large systems, hence the hybrid is the topology of choice.

First, the sources of ground-conducted noise must be identified and reduced. Second, the various ground networks must be designed and provision made for interconnection [Kement and Brand, 1987]. There are four sources of noise:

• Switching Power Regulators. Operating at 50 kHz, these regulators produce current spikes (di/dt) up to 1000 amperes per microsecond and voltage slews (dv/dt) up to 2000 volts per microsecond. Noise currents from the high voltage slew rates are generated across the parasitic capacitance of the foil safety shield between windings of the power transformer. The leakage inductance associated with the primary transformer windings coupled with this capacitance to form a series-resonant circuit. Currents of 2 amperes are observed. Noise is reduced by adding dampening resistance, which reduces the Q of the resonant circuit. International safety regulations strictly limit the amount of the fault-current in this impedance path. A ferrite bead is inserted on the shield of the ground lead. The bead does not block the fault currents from a short circuit but reduces the noise current.

• Power Line Filter. Leakage inductance from the choke in the filter combines with capacitors to create a resonant circuit energized by current pulses from the switching power converters. The Q is reduced by adding a ferrite bead resistor or separating logic returns and chassis grounds as far as possible.

• Power Converter. Parasitic inductance causes a noise voltage due to the changing current which rings at 10–30 MHz. A ferrite bead is placed on the switching diodes to dampen the oscillations.

• Radiated Magnetic Flux. Dying currents produce a collapsing magnetic field, which induces voltage in other conductors. A noise measured in volts can be induced across as little as two inches of circuit board etch. A modular power supply converter reduces noise by making the high-current loop area as small as possible, thus minimizing radiated magnetic flux. Copper Faraday shields and ground plane circuit boards are also used.

The timing (±5%) and voltage margining provided by the Environmental Monitor Module are very effective in isolating marginal RAM chips. The EMM also allows troubleshooting of power and environmental problems via remote diagnosis.

The revision level of each module is readable. An automatic verification of module revision incompatibilities insures that only compatible modules can be assembled into the same backplane. This provision also enables the remote diagnostic center to dispatch the field service engineer with the proper module level revision to facilitate repairs.

Figure 7–10 depicts the data paths in the VAX 8700. The system is composed of 186 MCAs of 28 unique types. The general-purpose registers are implemented in a special four-value logic, 1800-gate equivalent chip that is 50 percent faster than an MCA. RAM uses 10–15-nanosecond ECL. The loop formed from the register file to the ALU back to the register file determines the CPU cycle time. Traditional CPUs cascade multiple function units, such as an ALU and a shifter, adding to the delay through this loop. The VAX 8700 arranges the functional units in parallel resulting in two advantages. First, any given operation only traverses one functional unit yielding a short clock cycle of 45 nanoseconds. Second, multiple function units can be loaded with the

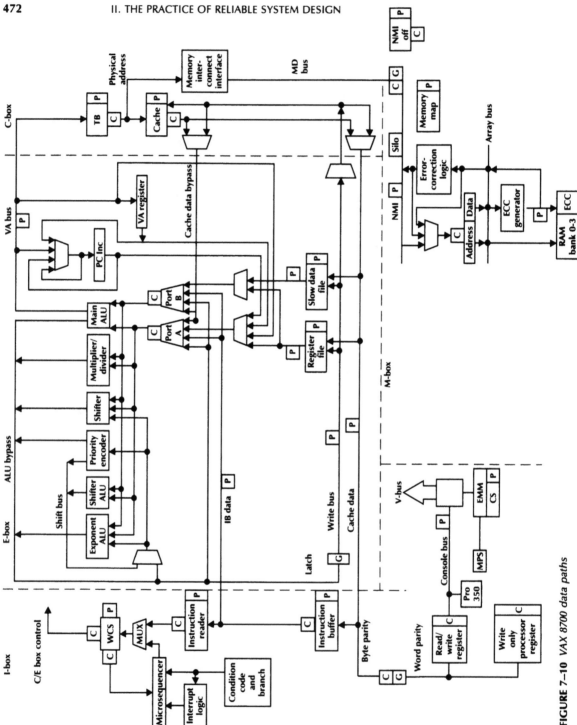

FIGURE 7–10 *VAX 8700 data paths*

same data allowing parallel operation (for example, the parallel manipulation of the exponent and martissa of a floating point number).

There are four boxes—I (instruction), E (execution), C (cache), and M (memory)—and seven buses: cache data, write data, instruction buffer data, virtual address, ALU bypass, cache bypass, and memory data. The bypass buses supply data directly to the ALU instead of waiting for it to be retrieved from a register file or cache.

A brief description of each box follows [Burley, 1987]:

• *I-Box*: The I-box buffers prefetched VAX instruction in the IB and receives data from the cache. It performs instruction decoding by table look-up in RAM and supplies the E-box with instruction stream-embedded data via the IB data bus. Decoding and control of the microinstructions is performed in a five-stage microinstruction pipeline (produce microinstruction address; look-up control store 0; broadcasting control store 1 and 2 look-up and register read; ALU function; register write and cache operation). It monitors and services microtraps, interrupts, and exceptions. A silo in the microsequencer keeps the address of the microinstructions in the pipeline, so they can be re-executed upon completion of microtraps. Microtraps can be caused by parity errors in the control store, virtual address, translation buffer tag, and buses. The microcode resides in a 143-bit-wide, 16K-word-deep WCS loaded from the console subsystem. The I-box is implemented on three boards.

• *E-Box*: The E-box handles all arithmetic, logical, and bit-shift operations. The program counter, general registers, and processor registers reside in the E-box. It controls data transfers between the C-box, I-box, and clock-module registers. It also provides the condition code information to the I-box microsequencer. The E-box is implemented on three boards.

• *C-Box*: The C-box is the processor's interface to the Nautilus Memory Interconnect (NMI) and contains the Cache and TB. The C-box is implemented on two boards.

• *M-Box*: The M-box contains the memory protected by a SEC/DED code. The memory array bus can supply over 50 mBytes/second.

Also, two CPUs can be combined in a dual processor configuration. One processor is logically designated the primary. Since hardware is symmetric, a fail over to the other CPU provides added availability in a dual processor configuration.

RAMP Feature: Error Detection/Correction. As in the VAX-11/750, the VAX 8700 is a memory-intensive design. Memory is used for the WCS, caches, TB, registers, and instruction decoding. The control store parity is over both address and data so that address decoder failure can be detected. Over half of the CPU predicted failure is in memory chips. Thus, parity is provided on all memory chips and data paths yielding error detection for the majority of the CPU logic.

I-Box, E-Box, C-Box. Table 7–13 summarizes the dynamic error checkers implemented in the VAX 8700. The error checkers are organized by the functional partitions in the processor design. Typically, with each functional partition there is an associated error register where the error conditions are recorded. The second column in Table 7–13 briefly summarizes the detected errors. The third column depicts where the errors are reported. An R indicates that the error is reported in the processor register (usually the error register associated with that functional partition), which is accessible to the VAX macroinstructions if the VAX microsequencer is functional. A V indicates that the error report can be found on a V-bus, which is accessible by the console processor. The fourth column of the table illustrates how the error is reported to the central processor. Errors can be reported via a microtrap or a branch to a special microaddress, either of which could occur internally to a VAX macroinstruction. Note that some errors are reported

TABLE 7–13 *Error checkers on the VAX 8700*

Portion of Machine	Errors Detected	Where Reported	How Reported	Effect
I-Box	Decoder RAM output parity	R/V	Microtrap	Abort
	CS0, 1, 2, parity	R/V	Microtrap	Abort
	Console processor received data parity	R	Microtrap	Abort
	Console processor transmit data parity	R	Microtrap	Abort
	Processor register parity (register file)	R	Microtrap	Abort
	IB parity	R	Special Address	Abort
	Memory broken	—	Special Address	Fault
	Prefetch broken	R	Special Address	Fault
	"Mustn't Be" microaddress	R	Microbranch	Abort
E-Box	A/B side byte parity, plus indication of source	R/V	Microtrap	Fault if source or cache; abort otherwise
C-Box	TB tag parity	R	Microtrap/interrupt	Fault
	Cache tag parity	R	Microtrap/interrupt	Fault
	NMI sequencer parity	R/V	Microtrap/interrupt	Abort
	PA (TB data) parity	R	Microtrap/interrupt	Fault
	Memory data parity	R	Microtrap/interrupt	Fault
	VA parity	R/V	Microtrap/interrupt	Fault
	Bad read data	R	Microtrap/interrupt	Fault
	Bad PIBA data	R	Microtrap/interrupt	Fault
	NMI data parity	R	Microtrap/interrupt	Fault
NMI	CPU read timeout	R	Microtrap	Fault
	Write timeout	R	Interrupt	Fault
	Parity on address/data/command	R/V	Interrupt	Fault
	No response	R	Interrupt	
	Timeouts (interlock, busy, no return read data, no access to bus)	R	Interrupt	
	Return data w/o read		Interrupt	Fault
	Incomplete R/W data	R	Microtrap	
Memory	ECC	R	Interrupt	
	Internal error	R	Interrupt	
	Higher error rate	R	Interrupt	
	Interlock timeout	R	Interrupt	
	Memory map parity	—	—	

by more than one mechanism. The final column of Table 7–13 lists the impact of the associated error on execution of software processes. A fault is potentially recoverable without disturbance to the executing process. An abort cannot be recovered from and will result in the termination of the process or even the operating system. Figure 7–10 summarizes the error checkers in the VAX 8700. A P on a bus or memory array indicates that the structure has associated parity. C indicates where parity bits are checked, while G indicates sites of parity bit generation. Parity generators are normally located at regions of code conversion. For example, the arithmetic and logic units are not checked by parity, and hence, the outputs are not protected by a code. Prior to writing on the W-bus, parity is generated. As another example, the VAX 8700 central data paths are protected by byte parity. The NMI employs word-wide parity, thus necessitating a generator from the byte-wide parity code to the word-wide parity code. Note that the VAX 8700 employs a detect-error-on-use strategy so that bad data would never be used in a calculation.

NMI. The NMI backplane bus shares a strong cultural heritage with the VAX-11/780 synchronous backplane interconnect. The NMI has parity bit on the 32 address/data lines and a parity bit over the function and ID fields. Other errors detected by the NMI ports include write and read sequence errors. A write sequence error is generated when a responder does not receive enough write data. That is, there are not enough write data cycles to complete the specified transaction. A read sequence error is a requester that does not receive enough read data (too few read data cycles) to complete the transaction. When a CPU or I/O adapter detects one of these errors, it asserts a fault detected line on the bus. Fault prevents further loading of the NMI transaction silo. This silo, containing 256 locations, holds a history file of the last 256 bus cycles including the faulting cycle. The states of the arbitration, function, ID mask, confirmation, and address/data bits are stored for each cycle in the silo. Various timeout errors are reported by interrupts. Timeouts include no return data on the read, no access to the bus, and continuous assertion of busy/no response/interlocked. In addition, the NMI sequencers microcode is protected by a parity bit.

VAXBI. The VAX 8700 took advantage of a new bus to provide reliable interconnection to I/O, the VAXBI. The predecessor to the VAXBI was the VAX Unibus. Introduced with the PDP-11 in 1970, the Unibus was enhanced many times over its lifetime—but a formal specification was not available until 1986. Thus, numerous compatibility and configuration problems arose. A complete specification of the VAXBI was made prior to any hardware design. Specification, especially electrical, had to be independent of any physical configuration. A bus is implemented as a group of transmission lines that are perturbed by the loading of connectors for modules and by the modules themselves. Particular attention was paid to physical layout to control capacitance, the clock, which is provided by a custom designed ECL differential receiver, and to grounding the chip and board for noise immunity. The VAXBI interface chip includes self-test functions and performs bus error detection and handling. Each chip monitors to bus protocol and reports any abnormal bus cycles to assist in diagnosis.

The VAXBI is also culturally compatible with the NMI and VAX-11/780 SBI. It is a synchronous bus with a 32-bit address/data path protected by parity. Parity is also checked on the node ID on arbitration cycles and during idle bus cycles. Each master is required to compare transmitted data with data received at its node during cycles when it is the only source of data on the bus. The transaction is aborted if the transmitted data does not match the received data. This comparison detects any driver failures as well as the event that a transient caused two masters to take the bus. Illegal confirmation codes, which are asserted in response to a bus transaction, have encodings that are apart by Hamming distance 2. Thus, single errors on the confirmation lines are detected. BI ports are constantly checked for proper protocol sequencing. BI transactions that have produced errors can be retried. On initialization, each BI port executes a self-test. The results of these self-tests are reported on a bus error line. During the normal self-test, the port must respond within ten seconds or be considered broken. A fast self-test with a 250-millisecond limit is also defined for time-critical real time applications.

For all error-detection mechanisms, there must be a way to induce an error in a controlled manner so that the proper functioning of the error detection mechanism itself could be determined. Furthermore, data captured in hardware registers from an error is frozen until software can access the information. Thus, if a second error occurs before the first can be processed, the data from the first error is still maintained and the data from the second error is lost. Frequently, the occurrence of a second or subsequent errors prior to the system's ability to process the first error is indicated in a separate errors-occurring-too-fast flag.

Console Subsystem. As in first generation VAXes, the console subsystem is a vital link in initialization and fault diagnosis. The console is used for booting, depositing/examining, enabling/disabling, initialization, loading, probing (for example, examining the V-bus), setting, displaying, microstepping, and testing the central processor complex.

The console subsystem communicates with the central processor over the cache data bus. Additional state is available to the console subsystem through the V-bus. The V-bus is a slow-speed bus consisting of 16 data lines and 2 control lines that allow the console processor to read selected logic levels in the CPU modules. It is used mainly during the execution of microdiagnostics and during system initialization. Normally, the V-bus is used when the system clocks are stopped. The console processor controls and reads the V-bus by means of two registers: the V-bus Control Register and the V-bus Access Register. The 16 data lines allow 16 separate visibility channels to be read by the console, and 8 V-bus channels can be read by the console at a time. Each channel goes to one of the 8 CPU boards. The console reads V-bus data from a module by first shifting an address onto the V-bus address line one bit at a time. The address is held in the module in a shift register and is used to select the single V-bus data bit that is transmitted on the module's V-bus data line. Thus, each CPU module must have a shift register to capture the V-bus data address supplied by the console.

There must also be one or more data multiplexers that selects the V-bus data bit specified by the address. A tail bit is provided in the serial address stream, which is readable by the console. When testing the V-bus channel, the console shifts both a one and a zero tail bit through the shift register and reads each back to verify that the V-bus channel is operating correctly. A successful test also verifies that a module is installed in the slot. Furthermore, because the tail bit address is different for each module, the test verifies that the correct module is installed in the slot. In addition to internal logic values, the module's revision number is also accessible over the V-bus channel. The number of V-bus address bits for each module varies from three to ten.

Also accessible to the console subsystem is the Environmental Monitoring Module. The EMM is a microprocessor-based unit that monitors the power and environmental conditions within the VAX 8700 system. The EMM responds to console processor commands during power-up and power-down sequencing, initialization, and battery backup operations. The EMM is controlled by an Intel 8085A 8-bit microprocessor with its own ROM and RAM. The RAM provides the working storage area and contains the software registers addressable by the console processor. The RAM is protected by parity, and when an error is detected, the 8085 program counter is reset to zero and a self-test, similar to that performed at power-up, is executed. The EMM monitors voltage, ground currents, cabinet temperature, battery status, and air flow. It can margin the voltage on individual DC regulators. The EMM performs a power shutdown when the environmental parameters are not within allowable specifications established by the console subsystem.

The EMM also ensures that CPU logic modules are only plugged into appropriate backplane slots. The module placement verification is a two-step process. The first step uses a module key test to ensure that there are no modules inserted in a slot that cause damage to the module and power supply. The modules within a group have similar power requirements and cannot be damaged provided the module is installed in the correct grouping. A key sense signal is a single wire looped from the EMM to the computer backplane and back. The EMM compares the key sense input with an internal reference voltage and asserts a signal that holds the EMM in a reset state if an error is detected. Holding the EMM in a reset state keeps the EMM from receiving power-on commands from the console. The EMM checks to see if the module power pins match the backplane power pins. Failure of the module key test illuminates the Key Fault LED on the front of the EMM. When the key test verifies that the modules are installed in the correct grouping

FIGURE 7–11
Bottom-up testing [Courtesy of Digital Equipment Corporation]

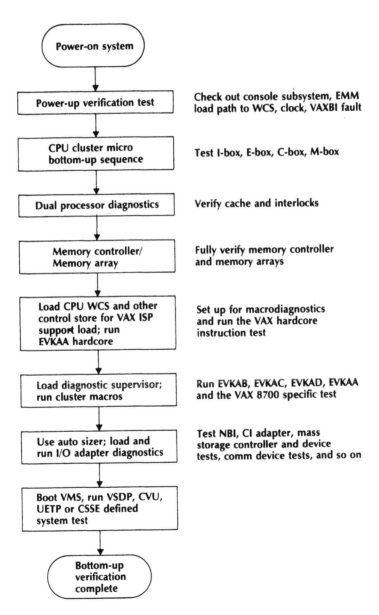

Power-on system

Power-up verification test — Check out console subsystem, EMM load path to WCS, clock, VAXBI fault

CPU cluster micro bottom-up sequence — Test I-box, E-box, C-box, M-box

Dual processor diagnostics — Verify cache and interlocks

Memory controller/ Memory array — Fully verify memory controller and memory arrays

Load CPU WCS and other control store for VAX ISP support load; run EVKAA hardcore — Set up for macrodiagnostics and run the VAX hardcore instruction test

Load diagnostic supervisor; run cluster macros — Run EVKAB, EVKAC, EVKAD, EVKAA and the VAX 8700 specific test

Use auto sizer; load and run I/O adapter diagnostics — Test NBI, CI adapter, mass storage controller and device tests, comm device tests, and so on

Boot VMS, run VSDP, CVU, UETP or CSSE defined system test

Bottom-up verification complete

and power supply, the visibility bus is used to determine that the correct module is inserted into the clock and CPU slots. The V-bus test that is used to determine the correct module placement within the CPU group will not work if the clock module is not installed in the correct slot. Thus, the console subsystem can report a variety of information on the CPU status, including clock on/off, clock period, power on/off, power margins, running/halted, remote port enabled/disabled, battery back-up present, module keying okay/wrong, auto-start enabled/disabled, auto power on, and auto boot.

RAMP Features: Micro- and Macrodiagnostics. The console subsystem is central to the VAX 8700 diagnostic function. The console system periodically exchanges "I'm alive" messages with the CPU. If the CPU halts, the console system can initiate a diagnosis of the CPU through the V-bus. It can reload the WCS. The loading of the control store is protected by a check sum.

Figure 7–11 depicts the steps in a complete bottom-up test sequence. A console subsystem self-test determines whether the Pro-380 (a PDP-11–based computer system) is capable of executing the console software. The power supply, clocks, and load paths to the WCS are also exercised. The micromonitor is a program that is part of the console software. It is used to load, control, and monitor both console-based and WCS-based microdiagnostics. Separate microdiagnostics are run for the I-box, E-box, C-box, and M-box. Next, logic specific to the dual processor configuration is exercised followed by the memory controller and memory arrays. Subsequently, the macrodiagnostics are loaded. Macrodiagnostics are used to test and isolate problems in the CPU kernel, I/O subsystem, I/O adaptors, and I/O devices. EVKAA functionally verifies a kernel of the VAX instruction set. EVKAB is a basic instruction exerciser for integer arithmetic, variable

TABLE 7–14 *Common VAX RAMP features*

Feature/Example	Benefit	Aids MTTF	Aids MTTR
Processor consistency checking Arithmetic traps, memory-address protection, limit checking, reserved opcodes	Limits damage due to hardware or software errors	Yes	Yes
Interval timer 1 μsec resolution	Used by diagnostics to test time-dependent functions	No	Yes
Disk error correcting codes (RP05, RP06, and RK06) Detection of all errors up to 11 bits; correction of single burst up to 11 bits	Tolerates transient and media related faults	Yes	Yes
Peripheral write-verify checking hardware Read after write, followed by comparison	Detects error	No	Yes
Track offset retry hardware Upon error, retry of read (If retry fails, disk head is offset for retry.)		Yes	Yes
Bad block handling Removal of bad disk blocks from use by VMS operating system		Yes	Yes
On-line error logging Records exceptional conditions in an error log, including time and system state	Aids permanent and intermittent fault isolation	No	Yes

length bit fields, control instructions, queue instructions, character strings, and decimal strings. EVKAC exercises the floating point unit. The VAX 8700 system-specific cluster exercisor tests internal processor register access, processor power failure, processor halts, user WCS, machine checks, and dual processor communication. The testing process concludes by exercising the I/O adaptors and I/O peripherals. It is also possible to remotely access the console subsystem for the purpose of running diagnostics.

Summary of Two Generations of VAX Implementations

Table 7–14 lists the RAMP features common to all VAX implementations. In addition to describing the benefit of each feature, the table indicates whether the feature improves MTTF and/or MTTR.

Table 7–15 lists the RAMP-related features that vary in the VAX-11/750 and VAX-11/780 implementations. Table 7–16 provides a similar comparison between the VAX 8600 and VAX 8700.

TABLE 7–15 *Comparison of VAX-11/750 and VAX-11/780 features*

Feature	VAX-11/750	VAX-11/780	Benefit	Aid MTTF	Aid MTTR
Fault intolerance					
Air flow	Blowers	Blowers	Lowers chip junction temperature	Yes	No
LSI	Memory chips, 90% of CPU logic functions implemented as custom gate array	Memory Chips	Fewer boards, more reliability per function over SSI/MSI; lower power consumption—hence, cooler junction temperatures	Yes	Yes
Cabling	Card cage fixed mounted and not on slides; no internal cables; connections through backplane; no cables to cards.		Fewer pluggable connectors to fail	Yes	Yes
Physically bounded system	Yes	No	Limited number of system configurations (CPU and memory in one cabinet results in greater control of environmental factors such as temperature and electromagnetic interference.)	Yes	Yes
Sensors and indicators	Power loss, temperature, air flow	Power loss	Protects system from damage resulting from emergency conditions	Yes	Yes
Modular power supply	Yes	Yes	Easy replacement	No	Yes

(continues)

TABLE 7–15 (continued)

Feature	VAX-11/750	VAX-11/780	Benefit	Aid MTTF	Aid MTTR
Fault tolerance					
Main memory	7-bit ECC per 32-bit word	8-bit ECC per 64-bit word	Tolerates transient and permanent failures (Logging of error information allows quick fault isolation.)	Yes	Yes
Control store	2 parity bits: 1 even parity, 1 odd parity, over disjoint subfields of the 78-bit-wide control store	3 parity bits; 1 per 32 bits of control store	Provides tolerance of transient errors as well as partial isolation to the failing chip	No	Yes
	Microverify		Control store resident check of data paths, registers, and other portions of the system boot path; ensures proper boot of system if passed.	No	Yes
Translation buffer	2-way set-associative; 4 parity bits for each set: 1 over 15-bit tag and valid bit; 3 over disjoint subfields of 15-bit page frame number, 4-bit protection, and modify bit	2-way set-associative; 6 parity bits for each set: 3 over 16-bit tag, valid, modify, and 4-bit protection: 3 over 21 bits of page-frame number	Provides faulty chip isolation; tolerates transients by recalculating TB contents; tolerates permanent failures by disabling one set	Yes	Yes
Cache	Direct-mapped cache: 5 parity bits, 1 over 12-bit tag and valid bit: 4 over 32 data bits (byte parity)	2-way set-associative; 7 parity bits per set: 3 over 12-bit tag and valid bit: 4 over 32 data bits (byte parity)	Provides faulty chip isolation; tolerates transients by refetching cache contents; tolerates permanent failures by disabling cache (11/750) or one set (11/780).	Yes	Yes
Synchronous backplane interconnect	None	2 parity bits: 1 over 32-bit data/address field, 1 over 12 bits of control information	Detects errors and isolates to faulty bus port; transients tolerated by bus level retry	No	Yes
		Silo captures last 16 bus cycles	Isolates faulty chips	No	Yes
Unibus adapter	None	Parity on data paths and Unibus map	Provides faulty chip isolation; transients tolerated by retry	No	Yes

TABLE 7–15 *(continued)*

Feature	VAX-11/750	VAX-11/780	Benefit	Aid MTTF	Aid MTTR
Massbus	Data and control bus lines parity; data buffer parity	Data and control bus lines parity	Provides faulty chip isolation; transients tolerated by retry	No	Yes
Watchdog timer	None	In LSI-11 console processor	Detects hung machine and allows automatic restart	No	No
Clock margining	None	Change clock speed	Aids isolation of timing problems	No	Yes
Maintenance registers	Machine check error summary Cache error Machine check status	SBI fault status SBI silo comparator SBI error, SBI timeout address, SBI maintenance buffer, translation parity	Aids fault isolation	No	Yes
Visibility bus	Internal signals made available to microdiagnostics	Internal signals made available to the console or microdiagnostics	Aids fault isolation	No	Yes
Chip sockets	Gate array	None	Allows replacement of individual gate array chips	No	Yes
Remote Diagnostic Module	Load/examine critical machine registers	Load/examine critical machine registers; single-step sequencer	Provides remote, expert troubleshooting	No	Yes
	Monitors control store output for control store verification	Clock margining			
	Error status registers readable over W-bus	Error status registers readable over ID bus			
	Monitor Memory Data Register to verify memory-CPU transfers and opcode undergoing execution	Access to V-bus			
	Visibility of cache and translation buffer contents to insure correct functionality	Microdiagnostics loadable into WCS			
	Access to V-bus; on-board 64-word writable control store for microdiagnostics				

TABLE 7-16 *Comparison of VAX 8600 and VAX 8700 features*

Feature	VAX 8600	VAX 8700	Benefit	Aid MTTF	Aid MTTC	Aid MTTR
Fault intolerance						
Air flow	Blowers	Blowers	Lowers chip junction temperature	Yes	No	No
VLSI	Motorola cell arrays, memory chips	Motorola cell arrays, memory chips	Fewer boards; more reliability per function; lower power consumption—hence, cooler junction temperatures	Yes	No	Yes
Heat sinks	Yes	Yes	Conducts heat away from chips resulting in cooler junction temperatures	Yes	No	No
CPU complexity	12 boards, 126 MCAs	8 boards, 186 MCAs	Lower overall failure rate; isolation to field replaceable unit	Yes	No	Yes
Sensors and indicators	MM to observe power loss, temperature, air flow	MM to observe voltage, temperature, air flow	Protects system from damage resulting from emergency conditions	Yes	No	Yes
Modular power supply	Yes	Yes	Easy replacement	No	No	Yes
Fault tolerance						
Main memory	7-bit ECC over 32-bit data word, address parity, bad data bit	7-bit ECC per 32-bit word	Tolerates transient and permanent failures (Logging of error information allows quick fault isolation.)	Yes	Yes	Yes
	5 bits even parity; 2 bits odd parity		Detects all zero, all one errors due to timing or selection error	No	No	Yes
Control stores	Parity on control store in each of E-, M-, I-, F-boxes (E-, M-boxes also check microaddress and microstack parity.)	3 parity bits over 140-bit control store	Provides detection of transient errors as well as partial isolation of failing chip	No	No	Yes
	Corrects errors detected in E-box microstore; retry on I-, F-boxes.		Provides tolerance of transient errors	No	Yes	Yes

TABLE 7–16 *(continued)*

Feature	VAX 8600	VAX 8700	Benefit	Aid MTTF	Aid MTTC	Aid MTTR
Translation buffer	Direct mapped; parity on Tag, Data, and Valid Bit fields	Parity over tag, physical address	Provides faulty chip isolation; tolerates transients by recalculating TB contents; tolerates permanent failures by disabling portion of TB	Yes	Yes	Yes
Cache	2 way set associative: parity over tag and written bit; byte parity on datam for error detection, ECC for error correction	Direct mapped code; parity over tag and 32 data bits (byte parity)	Provides faulty chip isolation; tolerates transients by refetching cache contents (8700) or error correction code (8600)	Yes	Yes	Yes
	ECC bits a mixture of even/odd parity		Detection of all zero, all one errors due to timing or selection error			
Backplane bus	Parity on address, data; timeout	Word parity on NMI address/data; parity on 5-bit command field; timeout on read/write, interlock, busy	Detects errors and isolates to faulty bus port; transients tolerated by retry	No	Yes	Yes
		Last 256 bus cycles captured by silo	Isolates faulty chips	No	No	Yes
I/O bus	Parity on address, data, and control	Parity on BI address/data, node ID; proper protocol sequencing check	Provides faulty chip isolation; transients tolerated by retry	No	Yes	Yes
Data paths	Parity on decode RAM, general register sets, instruction buffer, ALU input with source indicated, CCC, RLOG, ALU, shifter	Parity on decode RAM, general register file, instruction buffer, ALU input with source indicated	Provides faulty chip isolation	No	No	Yes
	Redundant copies of general-purpose registers		Restores contents of one register set from a redundant copy without loss of user data	No	Yes	No

(continues)

TABLE 7–16 (continued)

Feature	VAX 8600	VAX 8700	Benefit	Aid MTTF	Aid MTTC	Aid MTTR
Internal buses	Byte parity on write, memory data, operand, adapter buses; check sum on console bus	Byte parity on write, cache data, MD, IB data, VA, console buses	Provides faulty chip isolation	No	No	Yes
Instruction retry	RLOG of register modifications restored prior to retry		Tolerates transients errors without loss of user data	No	Yes	No
Watchdog timer	In LSI-11 console processor	In PC-350 console processor	Detects hung machine and allows automatic restart	No	No	No
Clock and voltage margining	In Environmental Monitoring Module	In Environmental Monitoring Module	Aids isolation of marginal chips	No	No	Yes
Error logging	Error-handling microcode	Error-handling microcode	Preserves state of error and status registers at time of error into an error stack frame to assist in diagnosis	No	No	Yes
Visibility/ diagnostic bus	Over 2000 internal signals available to console processor	8 channels of internal signals available to console processor	Aids fault isolation	No	No	Yes
Error insertion	Static and dynamic error insertion	Static write-wrong parity	Ensures correct operation of error-detection circuits	No	No	Yes
Remote diagnostics	Yes	Yes	Provides remote, expert troubleshooting	No	No	Yes

REFERENCES   Bell and Strecker, 1976; Bell et al., 1970; Bruckert and Josephson, 1985; Burley, 1987; Castillo, 1980; Fossom, McElry, and English, 1985; Grey, 1987; Keller, 1976; Kement and Brand, 1987; Kunshier and Mueller, 1980.

Lin, 1988; Lynch, Wagner, and Schwartz, 1975; Reynolds and Kinsberger, 1975; Strecker, 1978; *VAX 8600/8650*, 1986; Yourdon, 1972.

THE IBM CASE

Part I: Reliability, Availability, and Serviceability in IBM 308X and IBM 3090 Processor Complexes

DANIEL P. SIEWIOREK*

In 1982 IBM introduced the 308X line of high-performance processors that refined the standard for uniprocessor reliability. Employing a high-density packaging technology called *thermal conduction module* (TCM), coupled with advanced fault detection/tolerant techniques, field operational MTTF has been measured, by an independent publisher of computer reliability statistics, in excess of 70,000[†] hours. As measured by the same independent publisher, the higher performance IBM 3090 series MTTF averages above 40,000 hours.

This level of quality requires improved technology, more attention to detail, and a commitment permeating the entire design, manufacturing, and field operation cycle. Both major approaches to improving reliability, availability, and serviceability (RAS)—fault avoidance and fault tolerance—are used. Over 25% of the IBM 3090 circuits are for RAS.

Fault avoidance is fundamentally incorporated through the design and manufacturing of the physical components. Part I of this case study introduces the TCM technology, describes the manufacturing process, and discusses the fault tolerant aspects of the IBM 3090 implementation architecture. Part II of the IBM case study, by C. T. Connelly, covers software recovery management.

TECHNOLOGY

The TCM technology has its roots in the solid logic technology (SLT) of the mid 1960s. Discrete devices are bonded to a ceramic substrate. Each SLT unit corresponds roughly to a logic element (e.g., gates, flip-flops, and so on). The key attributes of TCM technology used in the IBM 3090E series of the late 1980s are summarized as follows:

- *Chip*: 180 solder pads, 612 ECL circuits per chip
- *Substrate*: Ceramic material, 1800 I/O pins, 18,000 chip pads, 36 or 38 layers, 470,000 vias for layer to layer connections, 130 m of wire
- *Thermal conduction module*: 15 × 15 × 6 cm, 525 W maximum, 30,000 circuits on a logic-predominant TCM, 32 kB on array-predominant TCM, up to 132 chips per TCM
- *Board*: 60 × 70 cm, 600-A capacity, 20 or 22 layers, 9 TCMs, 1.5 km of wiring

The basic chip employs bipolar ECL logic (the IBM 308X series employs transistor-transistor logic (TTL) while the IBM 3090 series utilizes emitter-coupled logic (ECL)) in master slice arrays of up to 612 circuits each. One hundred of the circuits can be used to drive signals off the chip. The 612 circuits in the master-slice chip are customized into a unique logic chip by the final layer of metalization. A logic circuit is roughly equivalent to one and one-half or two gates.

In addition to the 612 circuit master-slice chips, custom-designed array chips are used to implement the general registers, local working registers, buffer storage, and control storage. For some array chips, extra circuit areas may be provided to enhance yield. In those cases, address

* *Acknowledgments*: The author acknowledges Louise Nielsen, whose dynamic management style provided access to the required information; Doug Bossen, Kate Connolly, Bob Meeker, Dick Merral, Larry Miller, Les Parker, Frank Sera, and Nandakumar Tendolkar, all of whom took time to provide a "crash" course on the IBM 3090; and Stan Dickstein, who critiqued the many drafts of this portion of the IBM case study for accuracy. The MTTF field measurements were provided by Larry J. Martin of Reliability Research, Inc.
† Field measurement courtesy of Larry Martin, Reliability Research, Inc.

circuits off the chip are used to direct data to good circuit areas on the chip. Each logic chip and array chip has a unique part number. The chips are mounted upside down onto a ceramic substrate. The bonding is performed by reflowing solder balls attached to the 96 signal and 84 power chip-pads that match a corresponding pattern on the ceramic substrate.

The ceramic substrate is a 36- or 38-layer chip carrier with room for up to 132 chips. The mixture of chips between logic and array determine the number of chips that can be mounted upon a substrate. For example, a substrate might contain 90 chips, divided between 53 logic sites and 37 array sites. The average ceramic substrate in the IBM 3090 has 60% of the sites occupied by logic and 40% occupied by array chips. The average substrate contains approximately 470,000 vias for interlayer connections and 130 meters of wiring. Array chip sites are wired to select the good areas of bits. If an array chip has to be replaced, the solder is reflowed, the faulty chip is removed, and another chip with the same pattern of good areas soldered in. Of the 1800 input/output pins emerging from the bottom of the ceramic substrate, 1200 are used for signals and 600 for power.

A cross-section of the TCM is shown in Figure 7–12. The TCM has a helium-filled module cap that provides a thermal conduction path from the back of each chip, via one contacting piston per chip, to the cap. The cap is in contact with the water-cooled cold plate (water jacket), which is removable for module service without disconnecting the supply of circulating water. A separate coolant distribution unit is used to pump water (at approximately 24° C) through the cold plate. The TCM maintains a circuit junction temperature in the range of 40° C to 85° C. The maximum thermal load is 6.3 W per chip and a maximum total of 525 W per TCM.

The TCM represents the minimal field replaceable unit. An IBM 3090 central processing unit is composed of 9 TCMs mounted on a large 60 × 70 centimeter board. The 9-module board for the 3090 is depicted in Figure 7–13. TCMs are interconnected by up to 1500 m of wiring through 20 or 22 layers of the board. In the 22-layer board, 8 are for signals, 12 are for power, one is for engineering changes, and one is for actual module connection.

MANUFACTURING   Figure 7–14 depicts the manufacturing flow for TCMs. During the design process, level-sensitive scan design (LSSD) latches are used to test the logic. After design validation (which includes design rule and testability checks), the general test development system generates test vectors automatically for stuck-at logic faults. The automatically generated tests typically achieve greater

FIGURE 7–12
Thermal conduc-
tion module with
water-cooled
cold plate
[© International
Business Machines
Corporation; re-
printed with per-
mission]

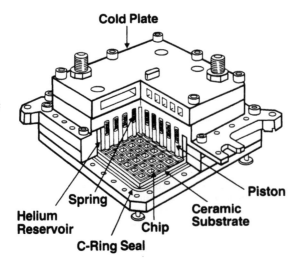

FIGURE 7–13
*Central processor
TCM board
[© International
Business Machines
Corporation; re-
printed with per-
mission]*

FIGURE 7–14
TCM manufactur-
ing flow
[© International
Business Machines
Corporation; re-
printed with per-
mission]

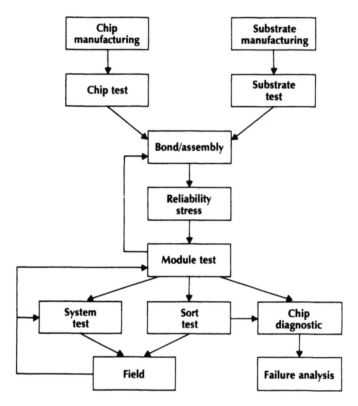

than 99% coverage of the stuck-at faults. Tests for array chips are generated by hand, through the cooperative effort of the design engineer and the test engineer. The test is written in a high-level language for compilation into the test machine language. Since each processor design only requires two to three different types of array chips, the hand generation of test patterns does not require extensive labor.

The wafer test is under computer control. There are typically five to ten different part numbers per wafer. Functional and parametric tests are applied to each chip on the wafer and the results of the test are examined by an AI (artificial intelligence) system to determine if further tests are required. The AI system captures experience from engineers at analyzing the outcome of tests. If no retesting is required, the host computer generates a map of good chips for subsequent dicing and packaging. The remainder of the wafer (now called a carcass) is stored for several months in case a downstream problem occurs with the chips that might require investigation of the original wafer. The manufacturing date, known as the "vintage," becomes a portion of the chip's history in case future diagnosis indicates a weakness in the processing of a batch of wafers. Every chip in every TCM in every board has a corresponding history file to assist in future diagnosis of process-related weaknesses. The die defect levels for field failures are so low that each failure needs to be thoroughly examined to pinpoint its cause. The rationale for this extensive attention to detail is to make future chips more reliable.

The following categories of logic tests for logic and array chips are used:

Logic Chip	Array Chip
DC stuck patterns	AC pattern sensitivity
Power supply margining	Power supply margining
Parametric testing of input/output pads	Parametric testing of input/output pads
Single- or multiple-test temperature test	Multiple temperature
AC assurance	Mean performancing monitoring

The logic chips are tested for stuck-at faults using the LSSD logic. Tests are also performed at different power supply voltages and at different temperature levels. There are parametric tests for the electrical characteristics of the input/output paths. Since each die represents only a small portion of the processors functionally, it is difficult to define an AC functional test for each logic chip. Thus AC assurance tests are performed on a wafer basis by examining special test structures such as transistors and inverter loops. The measured values of the parameters of these devices and the frequency achieved by the inverter loop determine whether the wafer is accepted or rejected. The long-term strategy includes AC functional tests for each individual die.

The memory chips have a more limited class of functions and are fully tested for AC pattern sensitivity. Tests are also conducted under variation of power supply and temperatures. Electrical parameters of the input/output paths are also determined. The mean performance of the memory cells on the array chips are also monitored and recorded.

Another expert system employs knowledge from diverse sources (for example, electrical test data, visual inspection data, test pattern failure, and so on) to diagnose minor and major problems in the manufacturing line. In addition, this expert system picks the best candidates among the failed chips for detailed historical analysis. The system uses frames to capture the gross signature of the problem. Frames are matched to identify whether the problem has occurred before or is unique.

Once the chips and substrates have been tested, they are assembled into a TCM as is depicted in the center of Figure 7–14. The heart of the bond/assembly/test is the reliability stress performed by a custom-made accelerated module run-in system that performs power on cycling and temperature stress of the TCMs. The run-in process brings out infant mortalities due to latent chips/process manufacturing defects, such as interlevel shorts, opens/shorts/bridges in metalization, open collector contacts, and open vias. The substrate is mounted into a base plate over which is placed a helium-filled hat containing pistons that contact the chips. A heater applies thermal stress to the hat, under control of a temperature sensor built into the TCM substrate. Nominal power voltages are applied to the chips, along with random signal inputs to simulate normal operation. Substrates go through several thermal cycles which include a period of time to ramp up to temperature, a dwell time at temperature, and a ramp down interval similar to ramp up. The maximum chip temperature is limited by the physical properties of the chip and is under control of a closed loop system. An acceleration factor, which is custom calculated for each TCM, is used to convert test hours to the equivalent power-on hours using the Arrhenius equation. Thus, all chips on the TCM are burned in for a period equivalent to at least 1400 normal operating hours for the predominant failure mechanism.

After the reliability stress operation the substrate is tested. (Periodically a small sample of substrates are tested prior to reliability stress and tested a second time after application of stress to determine what failures may have been injected by the stress process.) The substrates are immersed in a liquid fluorocarbon coolant to remove the heat dissipated by the chips. Each of the chips is tested sequentially using the LSSD logic. Tests of a complete substrate and its chips take approximately ten minutes. The test takes three forms: (1) check of termination, opens, and shorts (power off); (2) check of the analog parameters (power on); and (3) application of the LSSD test patterns for determining the presence of stuck-at faults (power on).

Next, the substrates are assembled into TCMs and placed into a system, and for the first time the logic chips undergo AC functional testing. The system tests include the following:

- Visual inspection and continuity checks
- DC verification tests, including set-up, execution, and checking of results for stuck-at fault test using LSSD
- Dynamic microcode tests of arrays and functional elements
- Architectural program tests, using randomly generated interleaved instruction streams
- Stress tests, including plus-and-minus variations of the three voltage supplies (eight possible combinations), increases/reductions in system clock cycle, and electrostatic discharge for grounding and noise-immunity tests

If a TCM is suspected of a difficult to diagnose problem, it is placed into a machine where all other TCMs are known to be good. Defect isolation tests, the same as the system level tests performed on new modules, are made on the difficult TCMs. These tests attempt to replicate the failure by dynamically cycling the system to the point where the failure is first observed. Data is collected on the conditions causing the failure (instructions and operands), and the system state is recorded at each cycle. The LSSD latches are scanned out, and the data is compared to a scan-out of a working part. Thus, the failing logic blocks are isolated, and the failing component is sent to physical analysis.

Sophisticated equipment is used for failure analysis including gas chromatographs and infrared spectrophotometers that can separate and identify organic molecules; an atomic absorption spectrometer that can detect presence of metals in solutions in concentrates of a few parts per million; and scanning electron microscopes that can magnify images up to 200,000 times. As an example, an electrical short in a TCM board was tracked to a hole in a glass fiber used to make the glass epoxy boards. Each glass epoxy board has millions of glass fibers—each smaller in diameter than the human hair—totaling 16,000 kilometers in length.

For each generation of a product or manufacturing line, samples are taken of failing devices that are first detected at the system level. Simple sampling for detailed analysis at an early phase of the program included the following: 300–400 chip samples from system detected failures during initial manufacturing; 150–200 system-detected chip failures from preannounce and early field operational systems; and 25–75 manufactured and field operational TCM boards.

The extensive testing and analysis that takes place prior to general availability of the IBM processors leads to dramatic improvement in product quality. Figure 7–15 illustrates observations at a particular point in the integration of components into the system during preproduction manufacturing. Here the defect rate found under dynamic testing of circuit chips is shown over several months. The observations start when the quantity of test machines is sufficient for statistical significance. As shown in the figure, during the initial testing, an increase in failure rate was observed in interval 8. A process change was found to have had the negative effect on quality. The test and analysis process permitted early removal of the cause of reduced quality, as illustrated in the return to the trend by interval 10. Thereafter, the initial improvement trend continues.

Failure analysis information obtained during design tests is used to inform chip manufacturing process changes. Relative decreases in the defective rate is due to the manufacturing learning curve. Similar learning occurs for boards and systems. Tracking of quality is employed at each

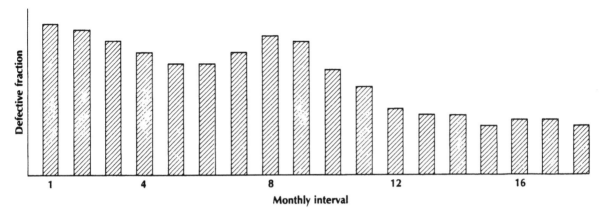

FIGURE 7–15 *Monthly chip defect rates observed during active system test [© International Business Machines Corporation; reprinted with permission]*

level of manufacturing and product integration and on processor complexes in the field after general availability.

Figure 7–16 depicts the cumulative hazard function, as a function of power-on hours, for one type of fault found on chips. The various curves represent the relative changes in cumulative hazard as process changes are made. Each curve traces the experience with chips made by a particular version of the general process. The initial increase in the cumulative hazard function is due to infant mortalities. Figure 7–17 depicts the fit of a Weibull function to the infant mortality portion of a cumulative hazard function.

A prime IBM objective is to achieve in each successive processor better quality (MTBF) when measured against a comparable predecessor machine. This objective is pursued even if the successor provides a large increase in function. After the new model becomes available to customers, the observation of quality continues, using data derived from field maintenance activity. Major field replaceable units (FRUs) removed during repairs are returned to the plant of origin for detailed analysis to establish the cause of failure. Results of these investigations are fed back into the manufacturing and design process to assure maintenance of quality over the life of the product.

Many stages in the manufacturing process are automated. Figure 7–18 depicts the car-on-track conveyor network used in manufacturing IBM 3090s. As each board enters the manufacturing building, wheel assemblies are mounted so it can be moved easily from the conveyor cars to the stations. A bar code label is affixed to each board to enable a computer to track the boards through the manufacturing system. The conveyor system is built on a spine concept, where a main transfer track runs 70% of the length of the building. Spurs branch off the spine at each of nine sectors. The sectors consist of more than 90 manual or robotic assembly, test, and inspection stations. Ten IBM Series/1 computers select the next operation for each board. They also track each serialized board through the sectors, issue commands to modular process controllers (MPCs) and receive tracking confirmations from bar code readers on each spur.

In all, 53 MPCs receive commands from the IBM Series/1 computers and send signals to the track and special devices. They also inform the IBM Series/1 computers of completions. A main track car delivers the boards to the sectors on a priority set by the computers. Then the spur cars move the boards to test and repair stations within each sector. The boards are rotated or flipped

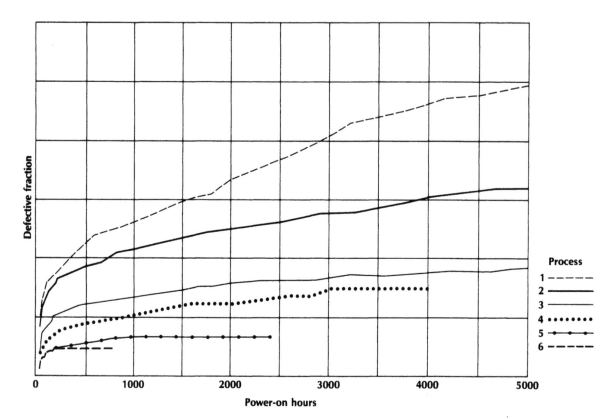

FIGURE 7–16 *Cumulative hazard function for stuck faults, showing improvement in chip failure rates with process changes [© International Business Machines Corporation; reprinted with permission]*

to the proper orientation for each job. At most, workers have to push or pull the boards off the conveyor cars to the workstation. Once the operator enters the board in the computer system, the system tracks the board's movement through the sectors. At each spur or equipment stop, the bar code label is read to the computer, and the sector operators know the location of the boards.

After manufacture, replacement boards and TCMs are packaged in specialized containers. The boards are placed in oversized "suitcases" riding on heavy duty wheels. The TCMs are attached by insulating screws to an insulating handle which forms the back of TCM carrier. The carriers are placed in foam-packed shipping containers. TCM containers simplify field replacement. After the faulty TCM is removed, the new TCM is removed from its container with the field engineer only touching the insulating handle. Once the TCM is in place, it is properly grounded and protected from damage due to static electricity discharges. Power and cooling are provided to the new TCM and the replacement is completed.

FIGURE 7–17
Infant mortality modeled by a Weibull function [© International Business Machines Corporation; reprinted with permission]

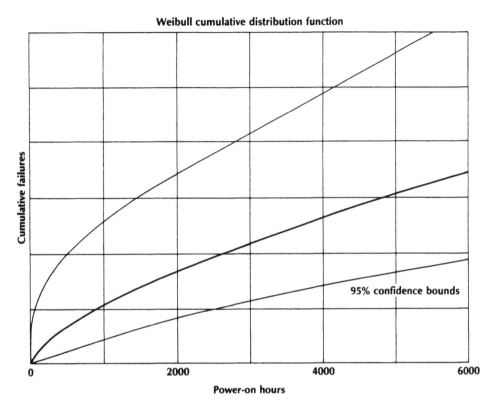

Weibull cumulative distribution function

95% confidence bounds

Power-on hours

OVERVIEW OF THE 3090 PROCESSOR COMPLEX

The IBM 3090 series of processors utilizes TCM technology to construct uni, dual, quad, and hex processor configurations. Table 7–17 summarizes the characteristics of the seven models in the IBM 3090 enhanced family. Figure 7–19 depicts an overview of a dual processor IBM 3090 system. Each processor occupies a single board holding nine TCMs. Two boards may be mounted on a frame. A switch or "system controller" serves to connect the processors, memory, and input/ output. The system controller occupies its own board composed of six TCMs. All system input and output travels through the channel subsystem, which is implemented partly in TCMs and partly in card-on-board technology. Operating under the IBM System/370 extended architecture, there may be up to four logical paths to an I/O device. Any free path can be used to access a device. All I/O channels are accessible to the central processors in a complex. Therefore, should a central processor fail, there is no loss of paths to I/O devices. The power and coolant distribution unit (PCDU) distributes 400 hertz power and cooling water to the IBM 3090 processor complex. The IBM 3092 processor controller acts as a console processor for initializing the system as well as error recording and recovery.

Heat is removed from the IBM 3090 processor complex via the IBM 3097 PCDU. The PCDU circulates distilled water throughout the TCMs. The distilled water is returned to the PCDU for cooling in a heat exchanger, which is connected to an external chilled water supply. Segregation of the distilled water loop ensures that contaminants from the external chilled water supply cannot enter or clog the TCM cold plate. Coolant is circulated by a pump. Any pump malfunction

FIGURE 7–18
*IBM's 3090 mechanized conveyor network
[© International Business Machines Corporation; reprinted with permission]*

TABLE 7–17
Family of IBM 3090 enhanced processors

Model	Number of Processors	Maximum Central Storage (Mbytes)	Maximum Extended Storage (Mbytes)	Number of I/O Channels	Performance (MIPS)[1]
120E	1	32	128	24	7.5
150E	1	64	128	24	10.1
180E	1	64	256	32	15.6
200E	2	128	1024	64	31.2
300E	3	128	1024	64	46.0
400E	4 (MP)	256	2048	128	61.5
600E	6 (MP)	256	2048	128	79

[1]Data from *Computer World* "Hardware Roundup."

FIGURE 7–19
Overview of IBM 3090 processor complex [© International Business Machines Corporation; reprinted with permission]

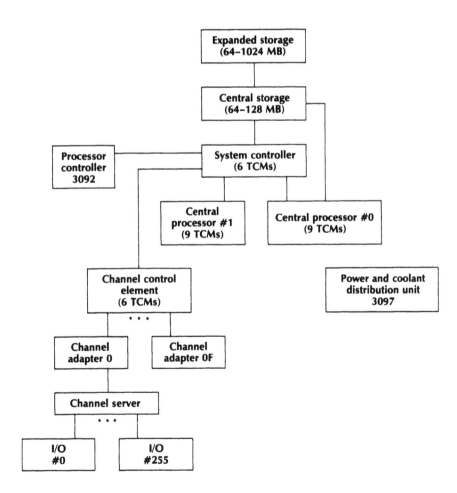

is detected and an alternate pump is automatically switched into the coolant circuit for continued operation.

Overview of the IBM 3090 Error Recovery

This description of error recovery principles is based on information published about the IBM 308X series of processors. The IBM 3090 series employs the same principles although details may differ. Errors in an IBM 3090 are first detected by built-in hardware error checkers, then system software, and occasionally by humans. It is estimated that the IBM 3081 processor unit has the ability to instantaneously detect 90% of hardware failures [Tendolkar and Swann, 1982]. For the TCM technology, it was estimated that intermittents were three times more likely than permanent failures [Tendolkar and Swann, 1982].

Figure 7–20 provides an overview of the steps to recover from a hardware failure. If an error is detected by hardware, information about the event is logged, prior state is restored, and a retry attempted. A fundamental principle of error recovery is to capture as much data about the error event as possible and to analyze that data rather than try to recreate the error during the service action. Since intermittent and transient faults occur much more frequently than permanent failures, it is highly likely that the hardware retry will be successful. If a retry is unsuccessful, first the system software and then, if necessary, the operator attempt to recover. The recovery mode is dependent on the severity of the error. In all cases, the recovery attempts are logged for subsequent analysis. For a discussion of software-directed recovery (the middle column in Figure 7–20) see Part II of this case study.

The placement of error checkers determines the probability of not only detecting and isolating a fault to a single FRU, but also whether the error is caught before memory elements are written with bad data, thus precluding a simple retry of the operation. In order to detect errors prior to writing of corrupt information to registers, a large number of domains is required. The 3081 processor unit has over 1000 domains.

Determining the placement of error checkers and their use in diagnosis is based upon the concept of error detection/fault isolation and direct-isolation domains (DIDs) [Bossen and Hsiao, 1982; Tendolkar and Swann, 1982]. Figure 7–21 depicts two memory arrays, several registers, and a decoder protected by three checkers. The checkers define the boundaries of fault confinement regions as depicted in the figure. If the checkers catch all faults in the areas they protect, then fault isolation merely requires stopping the machine upon the first error detection and identifying the checker and, hence, the domain in which the error occurred.

It is very difficult to make the DID boundaries coincide with physical boundaries. For example, the logic in Figure 7–21 might be physically partitioned into FRUs, as shown in Figure 7–22. The effectiveness of the error checkers is determined by the error-detection (ED) percentage and their fault-isolation (FI) coverage. The goal for the ED/FI methodology is to detect the maximum number of errors and isolate their occurrence to the minimum number of FRUs.

Consider the correspondence between the DIDs and the FRUs as depicted in Table 7–18. If checker 1 in DID1 detected an error, the syndrome would be C1, and FRU1 would be the most likely candidate for replacement. Now consider an error detected by checker 2. FRUs 1, 2, 3, and 4 are implicated by syndrome C2. Since the goal for the IBM 3081 processor unit was an average of 1.2 TCM replacement per failure [Tendolkar and Swann, 1982], DIDs themselves were insufficient for the fault-isolation goals. The checker information was augmented by active source identification (ASID) information. In many cases, the combination of ASID information and the checker syndromes is sufficient to uniquely identify the FRU. For example, if checker 2 in Figure 7–22 is triggered and if register 3 supplies the input to register 2, the implicated set would be

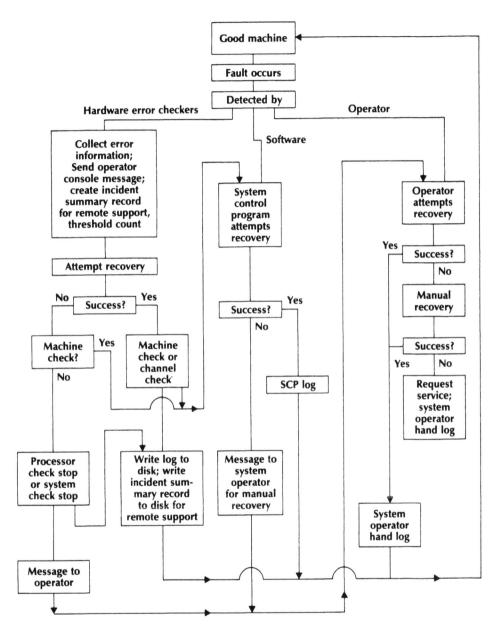

FIGURE 7–20
*IBM 3090 hardware error recovery steps
[© International Business Machines Corporation; reprinted with permission]*

reduced from FRUs 1, 2, 3, and 4 to FRUs 3 and 4. If further isolation is required and if the fault is intermittent and retry is successful, the information from multiple errors can be used to attempt further diagnostic resolution. Consider a second error in the above example, which triggers checker 2, but now the ASID indicates memory array 2. FRUs 1, 2, 3 from the second error would isolate the failure to FRU 3.

FIGURE 7–21
Logic partitioned by direct-isolation domains [© International Business Machines Corporation; reprinted with permission]

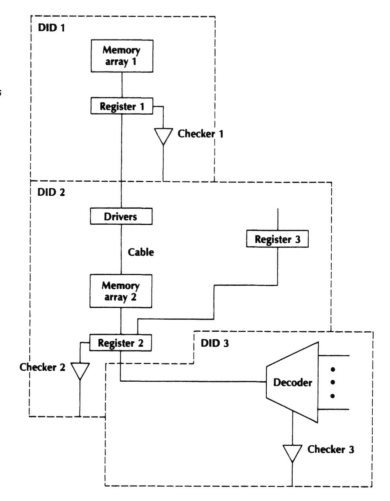

The concept of DIDs and error-detection coverage of checkers was used to mathematically model the ED/FI approach [Bossen and Hsiao, 1982]. The relative failure probability of the various logic elements composing the DID were calculated, as well as the probability the checker would detect a failure, to yield an estimate for the probability of error detection and the weighted average of the number of implicated FRUs. The checker design and placement was iterated, and in the case of the IBM 3081, the system error-detection coverage increased from 60% in early design stages to greater than 90% in the final design [Bossen and Hsiao, 1982].

Processor

Figure 7–23 gives an overview of the data path RAS features in the IBM 3090 processor complex. The central processor is composed of an instruction/data cache, an instruction prefetch and decoding unit, an instruction execution unit, and a control store composed of 8K words of 144

FIGURE 7–22
Logic partitioned by field replace-able unit
[© International Business Machines Corporation; re-printed with per-mission]

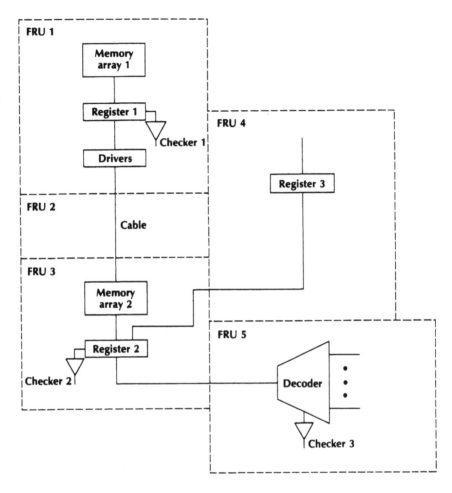

bits of read only memory and 1K words of 146 bits read/write memory. The cache is four-way set associative, with 128 bytes per line. A separate translation look-aside buffer contains 256 translated addresses to speed virtual address translation. An optional vector facility allows the central processor to handle up to 32 element vectors.

The goal of RAS in the central processor is to detect errors, log information for subsequent analysis, and retry the operation. Figure 7–24 summarizes the retry process. Successful retry requires the logic support station (LSS) and the processor controller, as depicted in Figure 7–25. The LSS has access to all of the LSSD scan rings on the processor board. When an error checker is triggered, the LSS stops the processor clocks, the LSS interrupts the processor controller, the processor controller error handler and recovery microcode access the appropriate scan ring and retry back-up buffers, and the processor controller microcode analyzes the information. If retry is permitted, the appropriate back-up values are loaded into the registers via the scan logic, and the processor clocks are reenabled.

TABLE 7–18

Mapping of direct-isolation domains to field replaceable units

Function	DID	FRU	Syndrome	Function	DID	FRU	Syndrome
Memory array 1	1	1	C1	Memory array 2	2	3	C2
Register 1	1	1	C1	Register 2	2	3	C2
Checker 1	1	1	C1	Checker 2	2	3	C2
Drivers	2	1	C2	Register 3	2	4	C2
Cable	2	2	C2	Decoder	3	5	C3
				Checker 3	3	5	C3

The following checkers are utilized in the central processor:

• Byte parity on data path registers
• Parity checks on input/output of adders
• Eight parity bits on 146 bit-wide microstore
• Parity on microstore addresses
• Encoder/decoder checks
• Illegal pattern checks
• Single-bit error detector in cache for data received from memory

Memory

The system control element is a crossbar switch that allows the various system components to intercommunicate. The central storage is composed of 64-bit data words protected by single error-correcting and double error-detecting code. Blocks of memory can be reallocated on 4K boundaries further prolonging the useful life of the memory array. The memory array has 450 latches interconnected into a scan ring to assist hard fault diagnosis. Due to the large size of central storage, the hardware-assisted memory tester (HAMT) is built in. The HAMT validates memory upon power-up.

The HAMT can also be directed to store-fetch-compare data from deallocated pages in memory in order to collect evidence on hard or intermittent failures. When the HAMT completes this operation, it interrupts the processor controller. The processor controller issues commands to the HAMT over a serial scan bus. Central storage errors are also corrected by a double-complement algorithm in the storage controller.

A double-complement algorithm extends the error-correction capability of an error-correction code. For example, consider the traditional single error-correcting/double error-detecting, odd-weight-column code. If the redundancy in the code is used totally for error detection, up to three errors can be detected. If the location of the errors is known, the extra information can be used to transform a random error process into an "erasure channel" and the code can then detect and correct t errors. See Chapter 3.

The following example of the double-complement algorithm shows an 8-bit word:

Original word	1 1 0 0 1 1 0 0	
Hard and soft faults	0 S	
Read R	0 1 0 0 1 1 1 0	Double error
Write R̄	1 . 0 1 1 0 0 0 1	
Read W	0 0 1 1 0 0 0 1	
Form W̄	1 1 0 0 1 1 1 0	Single error
Hard erasure: R ⊕ W̄	1 0 0 0 0 0 0 0	
Soft error	0 0 0 0 0 0 1 0	

FIGURE 7–23
Overview of data path RAS features in the IBM 3090 processor complex [© International Business Machines Corporation; reprinted with permission]

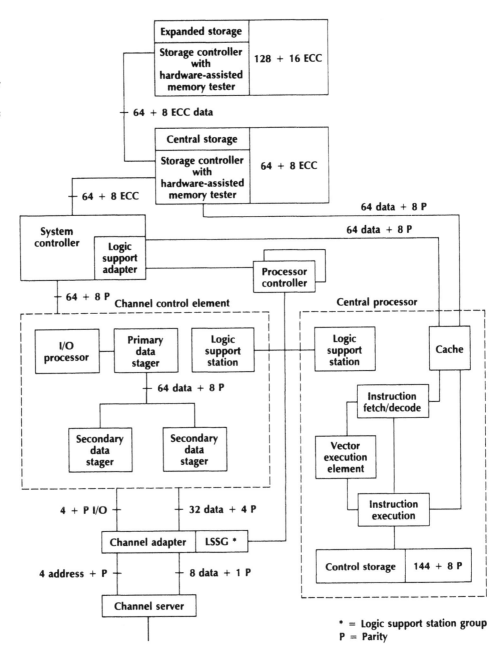

FIGURE 7–24
*Flowchart of retry-
on-error process
[© International
Business Machines
Corporation; re-
printed with per-
mission]*

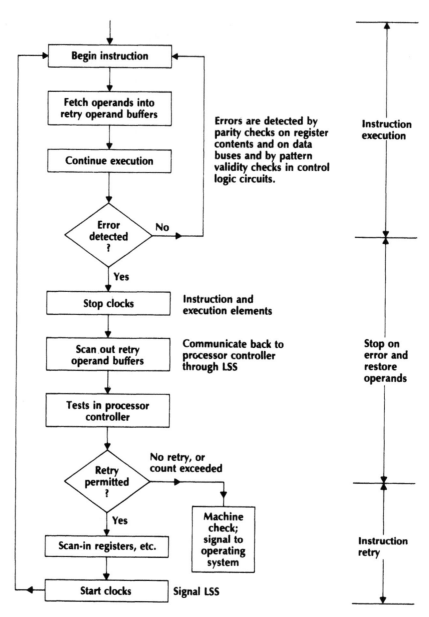

Errors are detected by
parity checks on register
contents and on data
buses and by pattern
validity checks in control
logic circuits.

Instruction and
execution elements

Communicate back to
processor controller
through LSS

Instruction
execution

Stop on
error and
restore
operands

Instruction
retry

The most significant bit has a hard failure of zero, and the next to last least significant bit has a soft error. The word that is read would have two bits flipped, and the triple error-detecting code would detect that there was a multiple error present. In order to determine if any of the errors are permanent, the data word is complemented, written back, reread, complemented, and exclusive-ORed with the originally read data. The only bits that would not have changed through this whole operation would be permanently stuck-at bits. The exclusive-OR operation would

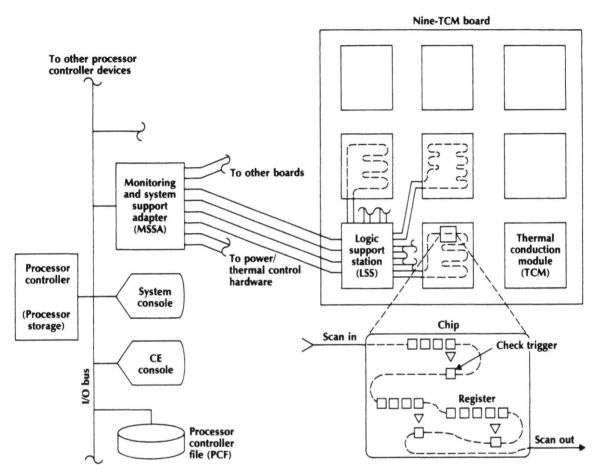

FIGURE 7–25 *Relationship of processor controller and logic support system [© International Business Machines Corporation; reprinted with permission]*

identify the permanently failed bit. The complemented word read back would now indicate a single error due to the original soft failure, which would be correctable by regular Hamming code techniques. The code can also detect all four bit errors that occur on a single memory card.

The expanded storage is also composed of 128-bit data words protected by a triple-bit error-detection and two-bit error-correction code. The expanded storage operates as a fast paging device by buffering disk pages that cannot currently fit into central storage. The expanded storage controller performs error detection and error correction activities.

Input/Output

The channel control element is composed of an input/output processor and primary and secondary data stagers for multiplexing and demultiplexing data to the system controller. The channel subsystem logs error information as well as microcode-recorded traces. The traces record the recent history at key hardware signal levels. Each TCM in the channel control element has a trace array controlled by the logic support station. Each array has 64 entries. The trace arrays are refreshed with new data on each cycle, freezing only on detected errors or deliberate intervention. The channel subsystem concurrently exercises single channels or simulates high I/O activity. If a problem is suspected on a single channel, diagnostic tests can be run on that channel by means of concurrent single channel service. All other channels are available for normal operation. I/O simulation allows the testing of all channel server circuitry through the use of wrap-around cables.

The microcode for the I/O processor is loaded from the system area in central storage. The system area is initialized upon machine startup. Thus any logical errors in the I/O processor code are easily handled through normal microcode distribution medium.

Upon error detection, the channel subsystem logs the information. The channel subsystem makes no attempt to retry the I/O operation in progress when the error occurred. Soft errors can normally be logged and ignored. Hard errors must be analyzed, because the reporting element cannot recover without assistance. Whereas soft errors do not stop the clocks to capture trace data, hard errors do cause trace data to be collected. Hard errors are not reported as machine check errors unless the error is not recoverable or the error threshold has been exceeded. When the I/O processor detects a hard error, it stops the I/O clocks and informs the processor controller by means of a hard interrupt. Using the same procedure defined in Figure 7–24 for the central processor, the processor controller examines the error and retry latches; if retry is possible, the processor controller uses the input/output processor's retry buffers to restore the channel control element to the state prior to the failing instruction. If the retry is successful, the input/output processor informs the processor controller by means of a soft interrupt.

The channel server is composed of an arithmetic logic unit, 8 kilobytes of data memory, a writable control store of 16 kilobytes, and an interface card. The byte multiplexer channels have 4 kilobytes of data memory while the block multiplexer channels have 8 kilobytes. There is odd parity on the channel server microword. A channel server can handle up to 256 individual devices. A maintenance register accessible to the processor controller allows for enabling/disabling of I/O trace. The I/O trace includes the I/O data and tag busses. In general, the channel subsystem is protected from end to end via data path parity, parity on address and control information fields, and positive acknowledgment of single-line control requests. Illegal and incomplete protocol sequences are also detected as soft errors.

Soft errors are usually detected by microcode. Hard errors detected by a channel server cause the channel server to enter an error hard-stop state. When a LSS detects a channel server in an error hard-stop state, it sends a hard interrupt to the processor controller. The I/O processor retry microcode attempts to preserve data integrity, prevent hung and missing interruptions, recover the channel subsystem, and report errors for analysis. Errors detected by the channel control element do not stop the channel, but eventually cause one or more channel servers to enter an error hard-stop state.

Processor Controller

An IBM 3092 processor controller is responsible for initialization and control of the IBM 3090 processor complex. The IBM 3092 initializes the other system components including sequencing power, validating error-free operation of memory, recording failing memory locations, and establishing the hardware system area (HSA), which includes a copy of the processor microcode, I/O device configuration, message buffers, tables, directories, and trace information. During normal operation, the IBM 3092 monitors voltage levels, coolant temperatures, and water flow. The IBM 3090 can switch in the alternative water pump if the coolant flow is reduced. It can also shut down the processor complex due to high temperature readings. The IBM 3092 logs error symptoms, correlates multiple symptoms, and analyzes errors to isolate the failing FRU. When automatic error recovery fails or the error count exceeds the allowable thresholds, failure information is displayed on the system console.

The IBM 3092 is a dual processor that can either control two processor complex sides in "partitioned" mode or act as an active and standby pair in "single-image" mode. In the latter mode, the standby processor monitors the active processor and automatically takes over upon failure.

Service Aids

The IBM 3090 processor complex has a comprehensive set of microcode for manipulating error information (logging, display, and analysis), exercising, and verifying the results of repair activity. The IBM 3090 processor complex maintenance microcode is summarized as follows:

- Error Logging and Analysis Routines: Management, fault isolation, and FRU replacement
- Diagnostic Tests and Exercises: Memory array, channel, cache, processor complex, and online test stand-alone executive program (OLTSEP)
- Verification: Array, service board, scan ring, and repair validation

Error Logging and Analysis Routines. An overview of the fault-isolation process is shown in Figure 7–26. When an error is detected, it is reported to the processor controller via an interruption. Depending on the circumstances, the error data is reported via data in certain registers, and the system continues to run. In many instances, the failing element (central processor, storage controller, channels, and so forth) stops and error-related information is scanned out, the processor controller microcode then analyzes the information, retry data is scanned in, and the operation is retried. In rare instances, the system stops for scan-out and analysis of the error-related information prior to operation retrial.

In every instance, error data is captured and analyzed, and the affected FRU or units are identified. The processor controller microcode analyzes the error-related system state data recorded by the error handler as well as the contents of certain registers, status information, and so on. An 8-byte reference code results from this analysis. The code is used to identify the unique area of hardware that contains the failing logic. The code is also used to distinguish between unique/identical error occurrences. Sometimes, as in the case of power/thermal events, the reference code is used as a pointer to procedures that narrow down the FRU identification. A table entry is created and includes the reference code, along with the locations and part numbers of the FRUs believed to be the likely causes of the event. Intersection analysis is used to compare the FRUs called out by the current table entry with the FRUs called out by related, previous entries. If an overlap is found, the count of occurrences in the previously generated table entry is updated on the assumption that the original error has recurred. If no intersection is found, the new table entry is retained for the error. Management microcode allows service personnel to manipulate the table entries by requesting those associated with a particular fault or FRU or time period.

If the failing operation cannot be successfully re-executed or if the frequency of an error exceeds some limit that varies with component category, an automatic call is made to a central service facility (RETAIN), subject to approval by customer operations staff. The message transmitted gives all necessary FRU information to the local service representative who is dispatched to service the machine. Note that due to the effectiveness of retry, the customer may not have

FIGURE 7–26
*Fault-isolation
process
[© International
Business Machines
Corporation; re-
printed with per-
mission]*

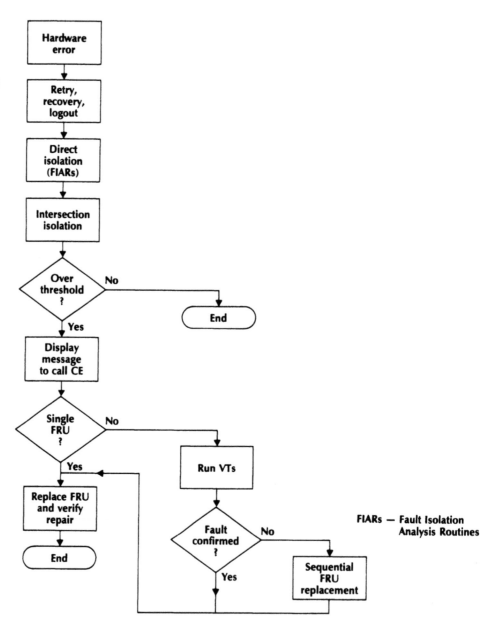

perceived a problem prior to notification of the service representative; such calls can be deferred at the convenience of the customer.

If the error threshold is exceeded and the failing FRU has not been isolated, fault isolation microcode automatically selects and invokes validation tests (VTs) based on the FRUs called out in the table entries built during error analysis.

If a single FRU is still not identified, the sequential FRU replacement (SFR) policy is applied. The SFR specifies which FRUs to replace during the first call. If the same error occurs within two weeks, the remaining FRUs are replaced. If the error occurs in more than two weeks, it is considered to be due to a new fault, since the probability of a second failure is now greater than missing the FRU on the first call.

Diagnostic Tests and Exercises. Diagnostic tests and exercisers exist for the main components of the IBM 3090 processor complex. Diagnostic and validation tests run hardware elements and themselves establish the source of any errors that occur. Exercisers run the system and employ the error log-out analysis described above to establish the source of errors. The memory array test identifies defective memory cards and maps single-bit errors (in the case of main storage) for each memory array card. The test consists of a combination of microcode and special test hardware located in the storage controller. The channel diagnostic tests utilize the microprocessor built into each channel server. The microprocessor is tested for proper functionality first. A subset of channel microdiagnostic tests can be run concurrently on a single channel server that is in single-channel-service mode while the user has access to the remainder of the system. A full set of microdiagnostic tests requires the user to relinquish the channel subsystem. The exerciser programs check out functionality while running the system at speed. Finally, the On-Line Test Stand-Alone Executive Program (OLTSEP) is used to run on-line tests for I/O device interfaces.

Verification. Validation tests are single-cycle tests that check combinational logic paths between source and sink LSSD scan register latches. Verification tests attempt to recreate the hardware error or verify that the replaced FRU is operating correctly. Tests include the functional logic in the TCM, intra-TCM connections, and special logic, such as memory arrays, caches, and clocks. A scan ring diagnostic test also verifies that there are no breaks in the scan ring, the scan ring is of appropriate length, and that the scan ring is independent of all other scan rings in the TCM.

Processor Controller and Power/Thermal Subsystems. A set of maintenance facilities similar to that for the 3090 processor complex exists for the 3092 processor controller. These include analysis routines, functional exercisers (for memory, channel, and I/O adaptors) and verification tests (for processor, channel, storage, I/O adaptors, and power control hardware). The standby processor is continuously exercised using functional tests for the processor, memory array, channel, and I/O adaptor. In-line tests exist for the communication adaptor and the disk.

The power/thermal control tests are run during the power-on cycle. These tests can also be run under user control to verify that the power/thermal control and monitoring hardware are working.

Other Facilities. There are other facilities which enhance the maintainability of the IBM 3090 processor complex. A patch facility provides the capability to install, test, and remove microcode patches for any part of the 3090 processor complex. Trace hardware captures the state of key hardware signals for each cycle for at least the last 64 cycles. The trace function can be set to start and stop on several different conditions to determine the status of the system before an error occurs. The monitor mode allows a remote support facility to monitor the on-site service and system consoles. History files are kept for all repair and validation activities.

REFERENCES   Bossen and Hsiao, 1982; Tendolkar and Swann, 1982.

THE IBM CASE

Part II: Recovery Through Programming: MVS Recovery Management

C.T. CONNOLLY*

INTRODUCTION

Since the days of System/360, numerous changes have affected the nature and scope of operating system recovery. The acronym RAS (reliability, availability, and serviceability) came into widespread acceptance at IBM as the replacement for the subset notion of recovery management. The change in scope can be attributed to both technological advances and the natural extension to requirements as viewed by the user of the system. This case study describes the reliability, availability, and serviceability philosophy for IBM's large systems as well as indicates the direction of future enhancements to today's systems. Specific emphasis will be placed on the key RAS functions of the Multiple Virtual Storage/Extended Architecture (MVS/XA) system. All concepts presented in this chapter are relevant to the MVS/ESA architecture.[†]

The demand for continually available systems spurred the advances in the RAS of IBM's large systems. Numerous availability and serviceability enhancements have been incorporated into each release of MVS/XA, adding to those already provided by its predecessor, MVS/370. The effort to provide higher system availability is demonstrated by the fact that an estimated 30% of MVS/XA code is dedicated to providing system recovery and recovery services for applications use.

The trend of the past twenty years indicates that both hardware and software have become increasingly more reliable. The processors and operating systems have improved dramatically. New functions contribute to improved system RAS because each new hardware and software feature must conform to specific RAS design criteria. Even though the software and hardware have become more efficient and reliable, the dependency on their reliability and availability has continued to increase by an even greater degree.

Today's architecture is capable of communicating significant hardware malfunctions to the operating system. Once this information is presented, the operating system will attempt to recover the hardware element with the least impact to the system or work it is performing. Some of these recovery processes are, in fact, transparent to the users of the system. For example, the 3090 processor supports a function known as frame deallocation. When a double bit storage error is detected by the hardware, the MVS/XA operating system's storage manager proceeds to copy the data from the affected frame to another frame, marking the frame with the error as unusable. This process is totally transparent to the users of the system.

The fact that today's system recovery is more robust than that of the System/360 era will be taken for granted with the introduction of more clever means to achieve fault tolerance. In addition, once an error is encountered, it is of utmost importance to provide sufficient data to

* Acknowledgments: The author acknowledges the assistance of Barbara A. Marshall and Robert R. Rogers, who critiqued this portion of the case study and provided valuable technical insights. The diagram depicting first-failure data capture was drafted by Lisa M. Bidstrup and Michael J. Keyes.

† Due to space limitations, it is possible only to identify the main features of the key components that implement the MVS/XA RAS strategy. It is also necessary that the reader have some prior familiarity with 370-XA processors and MVS/XA. Also, since each release of MVS/XA contributes further enhancements to RAS, it is worth noting that at the time of writing, MVS SP 2.2.0 is the current release and that it supports IBM 438X, 308X, and 3090 processors.

diagnose the problem without recreating the scenario to gather more documentation. For example, messages must be indicative of the problem and the need for a system dump should be limited to the most serious of error conditions.

Staffing is admittedly the largest portion of any data processing budget. Consequently, the amount of time spent deciphering messages, reading dumps, and recreating problems must be drastically reduced over the next few years. More trivial tasks will be automated. The automation of operations and problem diagnosis are key to a continually available system.

RAS OBJECTIVES

IBM's MVS/XA adheres to specific development processes, whereby the RAS function is an integral part of the design and development of a new and significantly changed function (i.e., where more than a third of an existing function is changed).

The specific connotation of RAS as viewed from the MVS/XA perspective includes, but is not limited to, the following:

- *Reliability = High Initial Quality*: Errors should be prevented through "doing it right the first time." The development process incorporates a quality plan that stipulates the explicit actions that will be taken to ensure a high-quality product. Software engineering techniques, extensive reviews, and testing are used to ensure initial quality.
- *Availability = Toleration of Errors*: Higher availability is provided by minimizing the impact of an unscheduled system interruption with minimal or no disruption to the rest of the system. Error isolation is accomplished by incorporating the RAS design attributes as noted later in the section on MVS/XA software error recovery.
- *Serviceability = Allowance for Timely Fixes*: The users of large systems should not have to spend an inordinate amount of time debugging vendor problems. Towards this end, the system must generate a precise error description that enables the user to perform problem determination rapidly. This concept, known at IBM as first-failure data capture (FFDC), is essential to the serviceability of any hardware or software product. In addition to providing sufficient error data at the first instance of the failure, it should be relatively easy to identify duplicate problems and to diagnose unique ones. Simplification of error diagnosis is accomplished via the numerous service aids and diagnostic tools provided in MVS/XA.

The following sections describe recovery management in general and then elaborate on specific recovery mechanisms used by the hardware and software. For completeness, a discussion of MVS serviceability facilities and availability topics are included.

OVERVIEW OF RECOVERY MANAGEMENT

The objective of recovery management* is to enhance system availability in the event of an unscheduled system interruption that could have the consequence of disrupting users of the system. The initial priority is to reduce the number of unscheduled system interruptions resulting from either machine malfunctions or programming errors. The second priority is to isolate and minimize the impact of such interruptions when they do occur. If recovery is not possible to accomplish, then it is necessary to preserve information related to the error for subsequent diagnosis. Recording, either through error records or system dumps, is an essential aspect of recovery management.

---

* This section was inspired by the paper "Recovery Through Programming System/360 and System/370" written by Donald L. Droulette [Droulette, 1971].

Sources of Errors

Errors can be introduced into the system from a variety of sources. The primary origins of an error are as follows: processor, channels, I/O devices, software, and operations personnel. For the sake of brevity, environmental errors will not be discussed here.

General Recovery Techniques

System recovery procedures can be programmed to take advantage of functions which allow the error to be circumvented or minimized. Some of these functions are:

- *Instruction Retry*: Many malfunctions are intermittent in nature and, therefore, the probability is high that a retry of the instruction will result in successful execution and recovery. This technique is applicable to I/O, CPU, and main storage errors.
- *Refreshing Main Storage*: If an instruction retry is not possible, then the error recovery routine could refresh main storage. The recovery routine achieves this by loading a new copy of the affected module into main storage.
- *Selective Termination*: The recovery termination manager is capable of detecting which problem program was executing and encountering an error. It can terminate that program while allowing others to continue. This function results in the loss of a particular job; however, the system remains available for the remaining jobs executing.
- *I/O Recovery*: Error recovery procedures are created for the different I/O devices. When an I/O error occurs, the related error recovery procedure will attempt I/O retry. If the retry to a specific device is not possible, then another channel path or control unit will be selected. If the I/O device medium encountered the malfunction, then data sets may be switched, if possible.
- *Operator Errors*: Some system outages can be traced to procedural and/or operator errors. It is IBM's direction to minimize these errors by automating more of the trivial tasks done by the operator and by supplying tools for installations use in order to achieve this goal. (Refer to the bibliography for additional details on automated operations.)

These techniques are just a few of the mechanisms by which continuous system operation can be achieved. The following sections describe additional hardware and software recovery mechanisms in greater detail.

Levels of Recovery

To handle the severity of an error appropriately, a hierarchy of recovery management exists. The four levels of recovery are

1. Functional recovery: Retry the interrupted operation.
2. System recovery: Terminate the affected task.
3. System-supported restart: Prepare for re-IPL (initial program load).
4. System repair: Require stop for repair.

Figure 7–27 illustrates this hierarchy. The outcome of recovery procedures I, II, or III determines the level at which recovery will be accomplished.

Using a machine check interrupt as an example, the first level of recovery is functional recovery. At this level, the interrupted operation is retried. If successful, then the incident would be transparent to the user. The second level, system recovery, involves termination of the affected task as well as repair or clean-up of the environment (i.e., selective termination). The next level,

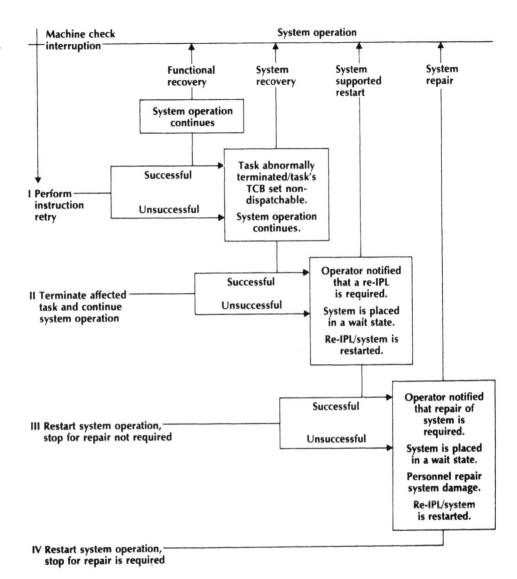

FIGURE 7–27
Levels of error recovery [From Droulette, 1971]

system-supported restart, requires an IPL, which involves the use of system restart facilities. Both the system job and data queues are preserved by the system restart facilities. In the most critical case, the system is halted for repair. For difficult problems, serviceability data provided in the form of dumps, error records, and console logs are essential for rapid error diagnosis.

MVS/XA HARDWARE ERROR RECOVERY

MVS/XA facilities are presented data about hardware failures and allow recovery of operations that fail due to processor, I/O device or channel errors. While processing of software errors is done entirely by the Recovery/Termination Manager (RTM) of MVS/XA, hardware failures are handled by several facilities. The following are some of the most significant hardware recovery mechanisms:

- Processor: Machine Check Handler and Alternate CPU Recovery
- I/O device: Missing Interrupt Handler, Dynamic Device Reconfiguration, and Hot I/O Recovery
- Channel subsystem: Alternate Path Recovery and Subchannel Logout Handler

Each of these mechanisms is discussed in the following subsections. Additionally, mention will be made of the recovery scenario facility, which is a new hardware feature available on the 3090 processors.

Processor Hardware Error Recovery

Machine Check Handler (MCH). Figure 7–28 depicts the flow of recovery processing for hardware malfunctions handled by the operating system. There are three sources of machine checks: (1) processor, (2) I/O subsystem, and (3) storage. As illustrated in the figure, the MCH will pass control to the RTM, the I/O Supervisor (IOS) or the Real Storage Manager (RSM) depending on the source of the machine check and the severity of the problem. There are three classes of machine checks:

1. Soft (least severe type): Typically, a report of an error from which the hardware has already recovered is generated. In general, the operation of the current task is not impacted. Soft errors can be repressed if desired.
2. Hard: The current instruction and/or contents of hardware data areas (for example, registers) are invalidated.
3. Terminating: A malfunction has occurred that impacts the operation of a processor.

All soft errors are correctable by the hardware but their occurrence can degrade performance. Therefore, a threshold of soft errors is monitored. Each event is written to the system error-recording data set, SYS1.LOGREC. When the threshold is reached, the processor is disabled for that class of machine checks until the next IPL. There are two types of soft errors: Either the hardware detects the problem and the system can recover (system recovery, SR), or a continuous degradation in system performance is determined (degradation, DG).

In the case of a hard error (for example, the current instruction could not complete), control is passed from the MCH to the RTM. The RTM invokes the associated recovery routines and either enables retry or terminates the unit of work. In either case, a record of the event is passed to the error-recording data set, SYS1.LOGREC. The RSM handles any storage-related machine checks, while the IOS manages problems in the I/O subsystem. There are multiple types of hard machine checks:

- System damage (SD): A malfunction has caused the processor to lose control over the operation to the extent that the cause of error cannot be determined.
- Instruction processing damage (PD): A malfunction has occurred in the processing of an instruction.
- Invalid PSW or registers (IV): The hardware was unable to store the PSW or registers at the time of error. Any error (even a soft machine check) is treated as a hard machine check because the operating system does not have a valid address to use and resume operation.
- Timing facility damage: TOD clock (TC), Processor timer (PT), and Clock comparator (CC).

FIGURE 7–28
MVS/XA handling
of machine checks

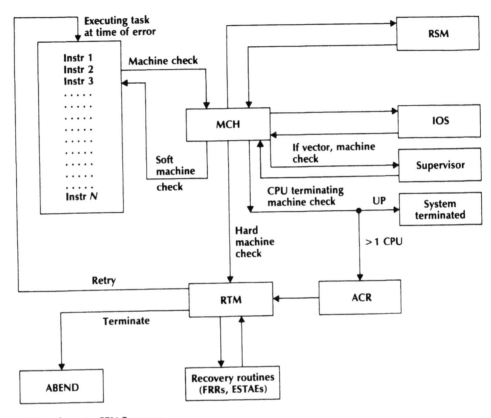

ACR – Alternate CPU Recovery
UP – Uniprocessor
MCH – Machine Check Handler
MP – Multiprocessor
RTM – Recovery/Termination Manager
RSM – Real Storage Manager
IOS – I/O Supervisor

If the threshold for hard machine checks is exceeded, processor operation cannot continue. On a multiprocessor system, the processor will be configured offline via alternate CPU recovery. Another processor will attempt to continue the unit of work that was executing at the time of failure. Typically, HMCs will result in a task being terminated, and the processor will continue to operate.

   In the case of a terminating machine check, which is an unrecoverable failure of the processor (or the channel subsystem on a dyadic machine), two scenarios are possible. On a uniprocessor, a terminating machine check will place the system into a disabled wait state, requiring a re-IPL in order to proceed. In a multiprocessor environment, if the hardware detects the terminating machine check, the processor is placed in a check stop state and a malfunction alert to an operative processor is generated. If the operating system determines that a processor has encountered a terminating error, it will signal the other processors via a SIGP (signal processor) emergency signal. Regardless of the source of the alert signal, the recovery action is the invocation of the alternate CPU recovery function of MVS/XA on a multiprocessor.

Alternate CPU Recovery (ACR). Due to the predominance of multiprocessors in today's large systems environment, an elaboration on the ACR facility of MVS/XA seems appropriate. ACR is invoked to recover from errors requiring a processor to be removed from a multiprocessing configuration. It is initiated in three separate ways:

1. The hardware will issue a malfunction alert from a failing processor when that processor experiences a terminating machine check.
2. The operating system will issue an emergency signal from the MCH of a processor experiencing channel subsystem damage.
3. The operator can initiate the ACR in response to the excessive spin loop timeout message.

Once invoked, the ACR removes the failing processor by marking its related control areas in the operating system as inactive. The ACR then initiates the release of resources held on the failing processor via a call to the RTM and subsequent execution of recovery routines for the task that was executing on the failing processor. It is possible that the task may fully recover despite the hardware error experienced. The ACR then communicates to the service processor to physically remove the processor from the hardware configuration. Finally, the ACR records the incident in SYS1.LOGREC and issues a message to the operator. Figure 7–29 illustrates the flow of control through the MCH and ACR for recovery induced by the operating system.

Recovery of a Vector Facility (VF). The VF, which adds an additional set of instructions to MVS/XA, is a feature exclusive to the 3090 processor. This facility dynamically associates a compute-intensive instruction with a vector processor. Although the VF is a new hardware feature, it fits into the existing recovery design for hardware errors. In the event that a VF encounters an error, the operating system will be presented with a machine check interrupt. Through the recovery processing of the system, the unit of work will be recovered, if possible, for subsequent processing on another VF in the configuration. If the VF cannot be recovered or the threshold for VF errors has been reached, then the operating system will remove the VF from the configuration. In the event that the system has no VF online, then any jobs requiring a VF are swapped out until a facility is available again.

I/O Device Hardware Error Recovery

Missing Interrupt Handler (MIH). The IOS of MVS/XA is interrupt driven. If it expects to receive an interrupt from a specific device but doesn't within a specified time interval, a missing interrupt condition occurs. The MIH attempts to determine the cause and correct the situation so that system performance is not impacted. Typically, missing interrupts are caused by temporary errors somewhere along the I/O path. Usually, clearing and restarting the I/O operation is all that is required to resume normal operation.

The time intervals are device dependent. Although IBM supplies defaults in SYS1.PARMLIB, the user can optionally customize that information for an installation. The MIH does not initiate recovery until two intervals have passed.

Dynamic Device Reconfiguration (DDR). The DDR provides the system and user the capability to circumvent an I/O failure by attempting to (1) move a demountable volume (tape or direct-access storage device, DASD) from one device to another or (2) substitute one unit record device (reader, punch, or printer) for another. DDR is invoked by the IOS after the device-dependent error

FIGURE 7–29
System-induced re-
covery

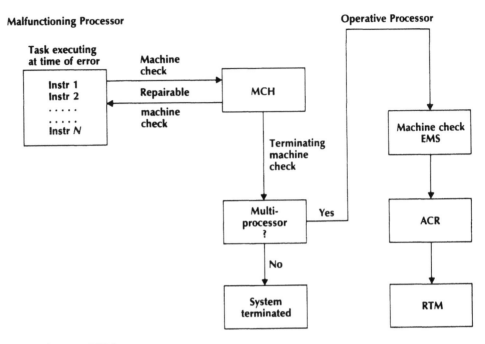

ACR – Alternate CPU Recovery
EMS – Emergency Signal
MCH – Machine Check Handler
RTM – Recovery/Termination Manager

recovery procedures post a permanent error on tape or removable DASD, where the probable cause is not damaged media. DDR requests are processed without shutting down the system and may eliminate the need to terminate a job.

The system or operator can initiate a DDR swap. When a permanent I/O error occurs, DDR initiates a swap along with a proposed alternate device to take over the processing of the device on which the error occurred. The operator has the option to accept the swap and proposed device, accept the swap but select another device, or refuse the swap. The operator may wish to initiate a swap via the SWAP command in the following circumstances: (1) The device cannot be made ready; (2) there is a need to substitute one unit record device for another; or (3) a device needs to be taken off-line for some reason. Regardless of the source of the swap, retry is initiated.

Hot I/O Recovery. A "hot" I/O situation is defined as repeated, unsolicited interrupts from the same I/O device with the same status information without any intervening successful I/O operation. The phenomenon appears as a system loop with the potential of exhausting system storage because the system is unable to process the interrupts as fast as they occur. To prevent the potential outage, an unsolicited interrupt threshold is monitored. Once exceeded, the IOS first tries recovery at the device level by issuing the clear subchannel instruction. If that does clear the "hot" I/O condition, then the system initiates full recovery based on the information prescribed by the installation in SYS1.PARMLIB or provided by the operator response to appropriate hot I/O messages (for example, invoke error recovery procedures for channel path recovery). Finally, a series of additional recovery actions may be taken as specified in the SYS1.PARMLIB (for example, logically remove the device from the configuration). As a consequence the IOS discontinues I/O activity to the offending device.

Channel Subsystem Hardware Error Recovery

Alternate Path Recovery (APR). In an MVS/XA system, it is possible to connect DASDs to the system through multiple channel paths and control units. This is done for performance and availability. In the event that a control unit or channel path failure prohibits a DASD from being accessed by the system, APR attempts to rectify the situation. The APR encompasses the detection, analysis, and recovery from the error. First, the IOS ensures the ownership of the device to a specific system. This is done because DASDs can be shared among multiple MVS/XA systems. The APR then attempts to recover the I/O operation over an alternate path, if one exists. If no alternate paths are available, the I/O request is terminated in error, and no subsequent requests to the device are allowed. Typically, permanent errors are recorded to SYS1.LOGREC so that service can be applied if needed. Without the APR, many of these situations could cause a multisystem failure due to shared DASDs.

Subchannel Logout Handler (SLH). The SLH also contributes to recovery management in MVS/XA. Formerly known as the channel check handler (in MVS/370), the SLH reduces the impact of subchannel malfunctions on systems running MVS/XA. It is an integral part of the IOS that aids in recovering from subchannel errors and informs the operator or system maintenance personnel when errors occur.

The SLH receives control after a channel malfunction is detected. It analyzes the type and extent of the error using information stored by the channel. When an error condition occurs, the SLH allows the device-dependent error recovery procedures to retry the failing I/O, forcing the retry on an alternate subchannel (if one is available). Records describing the error are written to the SYS1.LOGREC data set. The SLH performs no error recovery itself; it does not retry any operation or make any changes to the system. Recovery from the subchannel errors is performed only by the device-dependent routines.

MVS/XA Software Error Recovery

RAS Design Attributes. MVS/XA and subsystems running on MVS/XA must protect themselves from abnormal conditions, both from failures within themselves and errors propagated to them for handling. The MVS/XA software recovery mechanisms enable the systems and subsystems to provide the level of protection desired due to the support available for a myriad of recovery scenarios. By adhering to the RAS design guidelines, MVS/XA and its subsystems can achieve an intrinsically reliable system. Some of the key RAS design guidelines are as follows:

• *Isolation/Protection*: The general techniques for isolation/protection include the physical and logical separation of code, control blocks, buffers, etc., between software components.

• *Error Detection*: The propagation of errors and the resulting unpredictable later failures can be prevented by verifying critical input data, monitoring for potential problems, and by performing extensive damage assessment upon actual detection of an error.

• *Recovery*: Functional recovery is the cornerstone of MVS/XA software error recovery philosophy as well as the objective of continuous operations. Whenever an error is encountered, the operating system provides the capability for any program to recover itself and to isolate the error to the offending unit of work. Ideally, damage should be minimized to the interactive user or job subtask involved. As part of the component's recovery process, cleanup of critical resources is required so that subsequent requests can be handled successfully.

• *Repair/Refresh of Key System Data Areas*: Data structures managed by the component are repaired and refreshed during recovery from abnormal terminations of the task and/or address space as well as during restart situations (recovery from wait states or loops). "Refresh" refers to the concept of creating a new copy of either a module or control block by acquiring main storage and loading in another copy of the module or control block.

• *Termination/Restart*: If adequate cleanup can be performed, then components can be restarted after a catastrophic error with minimal impact on the users and system. The system dump facility is an example of a function which has been specifically designed to be restartable.

• *Serviceability*: Components ensure their serviceability by providing sufficient data at the first occurrence of an error whenever possible. The notion of first-failure data capture is discussed further in the section on MVS/XA serviceability.

• *Quality*: High availability is directly related to the quality exercised during the development process and testing of each new function.

• *Dynamic Update/Migration*: Dependencies on an IPL or restart to synchronize changes should be avoided whenever possible. In addition, data structures should be designed to allow independent integration of new product releases.

Recovery/Termination Management (RTM). MVS/XA facilitates both software error recovery as well as recovery for errors propagated to it from the hardware. The primary mechanism for both types of recovery is the RTM function of MVS/XA as illustrated in Figure 7–30. The RTM allows MVS/XA to deal with the damage caused by the failure without having detailed knowledge of the source of the error.

FIGURE 7–30
Recovery process-ing overview

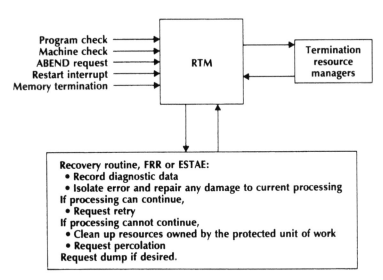

FRR – Functional Recovery Routine
ESTAE – Extended Specify Task Abnormal Exit

Some software errors are detected by the hardware and passed to MVS/XA in the form of program checks. Some program checks (e.g., page faults) are normal operation. Others are intended for serviceability and monitoring (e.g., program event recording or monitor calls). Program checks that indicate error conditions are converted to ABENDs (abnormal terminations) and further processed by the RTM. The RTM controls the processing of errors through its communication with recovery routines, resource managers, and the restart function.

Other software errors are detected by the programs themselves, such as invalid input. These errors are processed by the RTM via the ABEND process.

Recovery Routines. Recovery routines, which are capable of intercepting the error, should isolate the error, provide serviceability data, diagnose the cause of the error and repair damage if possible. There are two primary types of recovery routines: functional recovery routines and task recovery routines, known in MVS/XA as ESTAEs (Extended Specify Task Abnormal End). Further details on recovery routines are provided below.

Resource Managers. Resource managers are specifically invoked to perform repair and cleanup after a recovery routine has executed due to an error. Resource managers are called by the RTM for both normal and abnormal terminations of tasks and address spaces.* The resource managers are provided by each component or subsystem that manages a critical system resource. Names of resource manager routines are kept in a list and called by the RTM when a task is being terminated. Additional installation supplied resource managers can be added.

Restart Function (RF). The RF is an operator-initiated recovery, typically used to break out of a loop or restartable wait state. Some analysis is performed by the RF prior to invoking the RTM to attempt software recovery.

RTM Processing. The MVS/XA operating system and its subsystems must protect themselves from ABENDs. Due to the pervasiveness of recovery protection throughout the system, multiple levels of nested recovery routines are allowed. Typically a recovery routine has two options: (1) Retry at the next sequential instruction (or special code written to handle the error), or (2) pass control (i.e., "percolate" the error) to the next level of recovery.

For example, an accounting program may have a recovery routine protecting it. If it analyzes the error and cannot assure a successful retry, it may percolate the error to the accounting subsystem recovery routine. The RTM utilizes the following hierarchical structure to invoke recovery routines: *functional recovery routines*, intended for use by any authorized programs such as the operating system and key subsystems, and *task recovery routines* (ESTAEs), which can be established by any program, regardless of authorization.

Figure 7–30 illustrates the operation and function of the RTM. Some functions performed by the RTM are as follows

- Monitors the flow of software recovery processing
- Passes control to associated recovery routines, both functional and task recovery routines
- Provides dumping services and recording to SYS1.LOGREC, the system error record data set
- Enables user programs to establish their own recovery

---

* The range of virtual addresses that the operating system assigns to a program (or user) is called an address space. A normal address space termination signifies that the program completed successfully or the user has successfully logged off the system. In the event of an abnormal termination, the RTM receives control for appropriate recovery processing (i.e., route control to related recovery routines, etc.). The terms "address space termination" and "memory termination" are synonymous.

- Works in conjunction with the MCH for hardware failure recovery
- Provides recursion protection (including recovery for recovery routines) during error handling

Some of the conditions under which the RTM is invoked are:

- Hardware-detected errors: machine checks and program checks
- Software-detected errors: abnormal task terminations and abnormal memory terminations
- Operator-detected errors: restart interrupt

The RTM is a highly complex component of the operating system and can be conceptually subdivided into two primary subcomponents, RTM1 and RTM2. RTM1 interfaces with the MCH on software recovery for hardware failures, routes control to functional recovery routines, and invokes RTM2 for ABENDs, if recovery has been unsuccessful. RTM2 passes control to task-level recovery routines and routes control to resource managers, if terminating a task.

Checkpoint/Restart. Long-running jobs, such as accounting and scientific programs, can be extremely expensive to rerun from the beginning in the event of an error. These programs can be restarted at an earlier point in the program execution, at a programmer-provided checkpoint, where the program should be correct. MVS provides this checkpoint/restart facility via the JCL (Job Control Language) and an interface for routines to request checkpoints from application programs. Checkpoint/Restart limits the impact of any kind of error which results in an abnormal termination of a program. Large data base applications typically provide internal checkpointing.

Hardware Facilities for Software Errors. MVS/XA exploits specific features of the hardware 370-XA architecture to further enhance recovery from software errors. Examples of hardware facilities which extend software recovery are as follows.

- *Prefix Save Area (PSA) Protect*: The PSA protect contains critical information about the MVS/XA operating system and the processor. The PSA occupies the first 4 kilobytes of virtual and real storage. It includes fixed storage locations for such things as the contents of the new program status words (PSWs), register save areas for system routines, and pointers to important control blocks. It is always fixed in real storage and never paged out. The PSA Protect hardware facility ensures that no program can store into the critical portion of the PSA used for hardware/software communications.

- *Page Protect*: Similar protection is provided for critical system code by this hardware facility, which allows any virtual page to be designated as read-only.

- *Storage Keys*: Under MVS/XA, the information in real storage is protected from unauthorized use by means of multiple storage protect keys. A control field in storage called a key is associated with each 4K frame of real storage. The protect key controls which programs can modify the frame. When a request is made to change the contents of a real storage location, the key associated with the location is compared to the storage protect key "owned" by the program, which appears in the current PSW. If the keys match or the PSW key is 0 (the master key), then the request is allowed. Otherwise, the system rejects the request and presents a program check interrupt.

- *Program Event Recording (PER)*: The PER facility demonstrates the ability of the processor and operating system to take immediate action for a specific event that is potentially linked to a difficult-to-diagnose error condition. Hardware notifies the operating system of specific events that the operating system would like to intercept. Specifically, the PSW, which controls the processor's execution of instructions, contains a PER indicator. When the PER indicator is on, the processor may inform the operating system that one of the following conditions has occurred: (1) The instruction executed was fetched from a storage location that falls within a specific range of addresses; (2) the instruction executed is a successful branch instruction; or (3) the altered storage location falls within a specific range of addresses. The PER indicator is supplemented by information contained in control registers, which reflect the type(s) of events to monitor as well as the address range of interest. After the processor recognizes the PER event, control is given to the Serviceability Level Indication Processing (SLIP) facility of MVS/XA. The SLIP mechanism, mentioned in the next section, exploits the PER facility in its trapping of events for error diagnosis.

Excessive Spin Loop Detection. First, a definition of "excessive spin" is required. It is common for system code to briefly enter a tight loop in order to synchronize with events happening on another processor in a multiprocessor system. Since spin durations are expected to be brief, excessive spin is a potential error indicator. Possible indications of an excessive spin vary depending on the perspective of the processor. The detecting, or "spinning," processor waiting on the failing processor may have attempted a SIGP (signal processor), whereby the operating system on one processor attempts to communicate with the other processor to either obtain a resource or complete a function. The failing processor may be experiencing a disabled loop, disabled wait state, stopped state, or undetermined state. Once the system detects an excessive spin loop situation, it is reported to the operator via the Disable Console Communication (DCC) facility. The operator has the option of allowing the system to resume normal processing by waiting an additional period of time or by invoking Alternate CPU Recovery.

Excessive spin loop detection is a system recovery mechanism that handles both hardware and software induced errors, although software errors are more likely to be the cause.

MVS/XA SERVICEABILITY FACILITIES

This section describes some of the diagnostic facilities available with MVS/XA for problem determination and resolution.

- **Error Recording:** A key aspect of providing serviceability data is the sufficiency and repeatability of the data. Figure 7–31 illustrates MVS/XA's First-Failure Data Capture facilities. The recording of error information to SYS1.LOGREC for post processing by the Environmental Record Editing and Printing Program (EREP) serves multiple purposes. Reports can be generated to analyze a specific incident or to observe trends, such as temporary errors from DASD. In either case, the repeatability of the data is essential to screen duplicates from first-time occurrences, thereby saving system programmer resources. Repeatable data is provided in the form of symptom strings within the error record. Users can abstract the symptom strings to do duplicate problem searches on IBM's problem management data base. If the error is a known problem, then the fix is identified to the user for application. With MVS/XA SP 2.2.0, a new service, SYMREC, became available. SYMREC, an acronym derived from symptom record service, allows authorized programs to record a symptom record from their mainline to SYS1.LOGREC. The symptom record is an architected record that consequently provides cross-system consistency for programs that run in different operating systems environments. A symptom record from the mainline program is preferable to recording symptom strings from recovery routines when an error is encountered that does not warrant the overhead of ABEND processing. In either case, a symptom needs to reflect the error information at the first occasion of the failure.
- **Dumping Services:** There are two primary types of dumps: system and user dumps. A recovery routine may request a dump to ensure that sufficient documentation is provided to analyze an error situation. To avoid redundant analysis of system dumps, MVS/XA has a duplicate dump suppression facility known as dump analysis and elimination (DAE).

FIGURE 7–31
First-Failure Data
Capture facilities

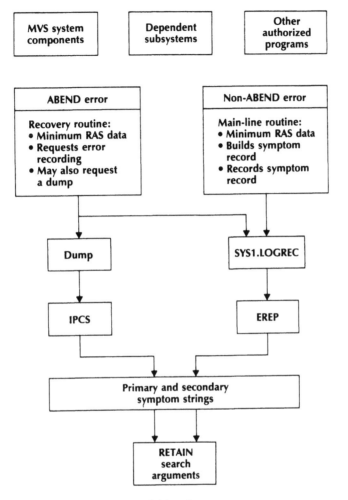

SYS1.LOGREC – Error record data set
IPCS – Interactive Problem Control System (on-line dump viewing)
RETAIN – IBM's problem tracking data base

- **Traces:** System and component traces enable the programmer to analyze the sequence of events that may have culminated in an error. Users can also perform their own customized tracing of the system and its components via the GTF (generalized trace facility). Traces are typically captured within a dump to supplement the documentation of an error. They can also be invoked by the operator as a stand-alone function.
- **SLIP (Serviceability Level Indication Processing):** SLIP is a mechanism that aids in problem diagnosis by allowing programmers to trap an error condition and to take immediate action, such as a dump or trace, when the error occurs. SLIP traps can intercept two classes of system events: (1) PER (program events recording) events and (2) error events. PER events have been described in the section on hardware facilities for software errors. Examples of error events are program checks, machine checks, abnormal address space terminations

(MVS/XA components request that the RTM terminate an address space and clean up its resources), ABENDS, and restart interruptions (the operator presses the restart key on the console). When SLIP processing completes, either the interrupted program regains control or it is abnormally terminated.

- **IPCS (Interactive Problem Control System):** System programmers can increase their productivity in analyzing dumps via the IPCS, which permits on-line dump viewing. One of the features of IPCS is the invocation of specific post dump analysis routines which could be further enhanced in the future to limit the need for human analysis of dumps.

AVAILABILITY

Above and beyond the provision of more reliable hardware and software, specific facilities have evolved to focus on the issue of system availability. The facilities mentioned here are not the only means of addressing availability. They imply a continued direction in IBM's large systems in the realm of availability.

- **Extended Recovery Facility (XRF):** The large systems environment is evolving towards continuous system operations. MVS/XA offers the XRF enhancement, which is based on the redundancy concept, for use by the Information Management System and the Customer Information Control System. In the event of either a scheduled or unscheduled outage, the XRF triggers a takeover of the production system by an alternate system. The objective is to maintain the production workload, regardless of system disruptions. Prior to a takeover the alternate system allocates a portion of its resources to checkpointing and monitoring the production system. The remaining portion of the alternate system is meanwhile doing productive work. Typically, the alternate system is dedicated to less critical work should it be required to take over from a production system.
- **System Availability Manager (SAM):** The SAM provides a monitoring and reporting mechanism for key production applications. It measures the availability of the production application in terms of ABENDs, re-IPLs, and system stalls. If used correctly, the user can identify actions needed to tune or adjust its production environment.
- **MVS Alternate Console Support:** Adherence to suggested configuration guidelines can help to increase system availability. For example, the MVS/XA master console and its alternate should be attached sharing the least number of common hardware elements (e.g., separate control units and channel paths). In an MVS/XA environment, the system automatically switches to the alternate console if the master console encounters a hardware problem. The impact of this recovery is the avoidance of a re-IPL and operator intervention. If the master console and alternate are not configured on separate hardware, then the ability of the operator to communicate with the operating system in certain recovery situations is affected. In the instance of hot I/O or a spin loop, the Disabled Console Communication Facility (DCCF) attempts to alert the operator. If the DCCF is unable to issue messages to the master console (or alternate), the entire system or one CPU, depending on the problem, is placed in a restartable wait state. To recover from the wait state, the operator must invoke recovery procedures that may require manual intervention. By configuring the master and alternate consoles as recommended, the potential for encountering this recovery scenario for the restartable wait state is reduced.
- **IOGEN Restructure:** MVS/XA has introduced an initial step towards dynamic systems management with the SP 2.2.0 release. This release contains a restructure of the IOGEN process. Previously, an IOGEN was part of the SYSGEN process. Today, however, a systems programmer can reconfigure the system whenever convenient. The new configuration is effective at

the next IPL. The direction is to eliminate the need for the IPL and to facilitate such dynamic change management so that planned outages will no longer be required to install maintenance and new function.

- **Reduced Role of the Operator:** Unattended operations is a relatively recent objective in the large systems environment. An aspect of automated operations is the handling of messages requiring operator response. More actions will be taken under program control, limiting the operator involvement to the exceptional cases.

   In MVS/XA, the Message Processing Facility (MPF) serves as a message suppression/automation tool. In addition to automating existing functions normally done by an operator or systems programmer, the design of new functions is challenged to address minimal interfaces. Samples and examples are provided for the user of MP to select for a specific installation. To supplement the function of MP and to extend the user's capability to automate remote operations, IBM has created the NetView product. Additional information on NetView and automated operations can be obtained from the bibliography.

SUMMARY

The future of the large systems environment is contingent upon the reliability, availability, and serviceability features of its hardware and software. This case study provided an overview of what is currently available in the MVS/XA–3090 processor arena. MVS/XA provides total system recovery by the functional recovery built into the hardware and software and the sophisticated communication between the hardware and software components. A wide range of errors are recoverable that were not previously possible in the days of OS/360, nor MVS/370.

BIBLIOGRAPHY

IBM Reference Library: *MVS/XA Recovery & Reconfiguration Guide* (GC28-1160); *MVS/XA SPL: System Macros & Facilities* (GC28-1150); *MVS/XA DPL: Supervisor Services & Macros* (GC28-1150); *3090 Processor Complex: Hardware Recovery Guide* (SC38-0051); *Automated Operations Using Standard S/NM Products* (GG24-3083); *Automated Operations Implementation Guide* (GG24-3111); *MPF/NetView Migration and Automation* (GG24-3113); *Automated System Operations for MVS/XA Systems* (GG24-3142); *Automated System Operations for High Availability: Concepts & Examples* (GG66-0260); *NetView R2 General Information and Planning* (GC30-3463).

REFERENCE

Droulette, 1971.

8 HIGH-AVAILABILITY SYSTEMS

INTRODUCTION Dynamic redundancy is the basic approach used in high-availability systems. These systems are typically composed of multiple processors with extensive error-detection mechanisms. When an error is detected, the computation is resumed on another processor. The evolution of high-availability systems is traced through the family history of three commercial vendors: AT&T, Tandem, and Stratus.

AT&T SWITCHING SYSTEMS AT&T pioneered fault-tolerant computing in the telephone switching application. The two AT&T case studies given in this chapter trace the variations of duplication and matching devised for the switching systems to detect failures and to automatically resume computations. The primary form of detection is hardware lock-step duplication and comparison that requires about 2.5 times the hardware cost of a nonredundant system. Thousands of switching systems have been installed and they are currently commercially available in the form of the 3B20 processor. Table 8–1 summarizes the evolution of the AT&T switching systems. It includes system characteristics such as the number of telephone lines accommodated as well as the processor model used to control the switching gear.

Telephone switching systems utilize natural redundancy in the network and its operation to meet an aggressive availability goal of 2 hours downtime in 40 years (3 minutes per year). Telephone users will redial if they get a wrong number or are disconnected. However, there is a user aggravation level that must be avoided: users will redial as long as errors do not happen too frequently. User aggravation thresholds are different for failure to establish a call (moderately high) and disconnection of an established call (very low). Thus, a telephone switching system follows a staged failure recovery process, as shown in Table 8–2.

Figure 8–1 illustrates that the telephone switching application requires quite a different organization than that of a general-purpose computer. In particular, a substantial portion of the telephone switching system complexity is in the peripheral hardware. As depicted in Figure 8–1, the telephone switching system is composed of four major components: the transmission interface, the network, signal processors, and the central controller. Telephone lines carrying analog signals attach to the voice band interface frame (VIF), which samples and digitally encodes the analog signals. The output is pulse code modulated (PCM). The echo suppressor terminal (EST) removes echos that may have been introduced on long distance trunk lines. The PCM

TABLE 8–1
Summary of installed AT&T telephone switching systems

System	Number of Lines	Year Introduced	Number Installed	Processor	Comments
1 ESS	5,000–65,000	1965	1,000	No. 1	First processor with separate control and data memories
2 ESS	1,000–10,000	1969	500	No. 2	
1A ESS	100,000	1976	2,000	No. 1A	Four to eight times faster than No. 1
2B ESS	1,000–20,000	1975	>500	No. 3A	Combined control and data store; microcoded; emulates No. 2
3 ESS	500–5,000	1976	>500	No. 3A	
5 ESS	1,000–85,000	1982	>1,000	No. 3B	Multipurpose processor

TABLE 8–2
Levels of recovery in a telephone switching system

Phase	Recovery Action	Effect
1	Initialize specific transient memory.	Temporary storage affected; no calls lost
2	Reconfigure peripheral hardware. Initialize all transient memory.	Lose calls being established; calls in progress not lost
3	Verify memory operation, establish a workable processor configuration, verify program, configure peripheral hardware, initialize all transient memory.	Lose calls being established; calls in progress not affected
4	Establish a workable processor configuration, configure peripheral hardware, initialize all memory.	All calls lost

signals are multiplexed onto a time-slotted digital bus. The digital bus enters a time-space-time network. The time slot interchange (TSI) switches PCM signals to different time slots on the bus. The output of the TSI goes to the time multiplexed switch (TMS), which switches the PCM signals in a particular time slot from any bus to any other bus. The output of the TMS returns to the TSI, where the PCM signals may be interchanged to another time slot. Signals intended for analog lines are converted from PCM to analog signals in the VIF. A network clock coordinates the timing for all of the switching functions.

The signal processors provide scanning and signal distribution functions, thus relieving the central processor of these activities. The common channel interface signaling (CCIS) provides an independent data link between telephone switching systems. The CCIS terminal is used to send supervisory switching information for the

FIGURE 8–1

Diagram of a typical telephone switching system

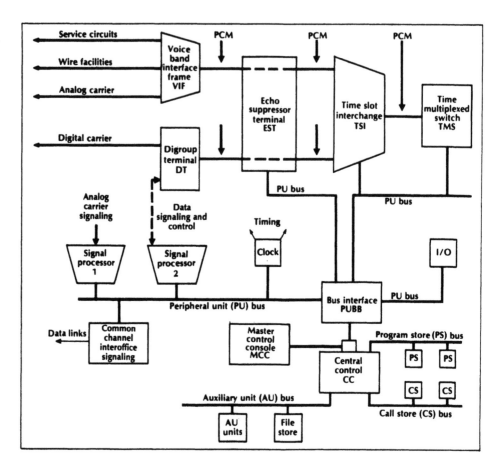

various trunk lines coming into the office. The entire peripheral hardware is interfaced to the central control (CC) over AC-coupled buses. A telephone switching processor is composed of the central control, which manipulates data associated with call processing, administrative tasks, and recovery; program store; call store for storing transient information related to the processing of telephone calls; file store disk system used to store backup program copies; auxiliary units magnetic tapes storage containing basic restart programs and new software releases; input/output (I/O) interfaces to terminal devices; and master control console used as the control and display console for the system. In general, a telephone switching processor could be used to control more than one type of telephone switching system.

The history of AT&T processors is summarized in Table 8–3. Even though all the processors are based upon full duplication, it is interesting to observe the evolution from the tightly lock-stepped matching of every machine cycle in the early processors to a higher dependence on self-checking and matching only on writes to memory. Furthermore, as the processors evolved from dedicated, real-time controllers to mul-

TABLE 8–3 *Summary of AT&T Telephone Switching Processors*

Processor/ Year Introduced	Complexity (Gates)	Unit of Switching	Matching	Other Error Detection/Correction
No. 1, 1965	12,000	PS, CS, CC, buses	Six internal nodes, 24 bits per node; one node matched each machine cycle; node selected to be matched dependent on instruction being executed	Hamming code on PS; parity on CS; automatic retry on CS, PS; watch-dog timer; sanity program to determine if reorganization led to a valid configuration
No. 2, 1969	5,000	Entire computer	Single match point on call store input	Diagnostic programs; parity on PS; detection of multiword accesses in CS; watch-dog timer
No. 1A, 1976	50,000	PS, CS, CC, buses	16 internal nodes, 24 bits per node; two nodes matched each machine cycle	Two-parity bits on PS; roving spares (i.e., contents of PS not completely duplicated, can be loaded from disk upon error detection); two-parity bits on CS; roving spares sufficient for complete duplication of transient data; processor configuration circuit to search automatically for a valid configuration
No. 3A, 1975	16,500	Entire computer	None	On-line processor writes into both stores; m-of-$2m$ code on micro-store plus parity; self-checking decoders; two-parity bits on registers; duplication of ALU; watch-dog timer; maintenance channel for observability and controllability of the other processor; 25% of logic devoted to self-checking logic and 14% to maintenance access
3B20D, 1981	75,000	Entire computer	None	On-line processor write into both stores; byte parity on data paths; parity checking where parity preserved, duplication otherwise; modified Hamming code on main memory; maintenance channel for observability and controllability of the other processor; 30% of control logic devoted to self-checking; error-correction codes on disks; software audits, sanity timer, integrity monitor

tiple-purpose processors, the operating system and software not only became more sophisticated but also became a dominant portion of the system design and maintenance effort.

The part I of the AT&T case study in this chapter, by Wing Toy, sketches the evolution of the telephone switching system processors and focuses on the latest member of the family, the 3B20D. Part II of the case study, by Liane C. Toy, outlines the procedure used in the 5ESS for updating hardware and/or software without incurring any downtime.

TANDEM COMPUTERS, INC.

Over a decade after the first AT&T computer-controlled switching system was installed, Tandem designed a high-availability system targeted for the on-line transaction processing (OLTP) market. Replication of processors, memories, and disks was used not only to tolerate failures, but also to provide modular expansion of computing resources. Tandem was concerned about the propagation of errors, and thus developed a loosely coupled multiple computer architecture. While one computer acts as primary, the backup computer is active only to receive periodic checkpoint information. Hence, 1.3 physical computers are required to behave as one logical fault-tolerant computer. Disks, of course, have to be fully replicated to provide a complete backup copy of the database. This approach places a heavy burden upon the system and user software developers to guarantee correct operation no matter when or where a failure occurs. In particular, the primary memory state of a computation may not be available due to the failure of the processors. Some feel, however, that the multiple computer structure is superior to a lock-step duplication approach in tolerating design errors.

The architecture discussed in the Tandem case study, by Bartlett, Bartlett, Garcia, Gray, Horst, Jardine, Jewett, Lenoski, and McGuire, is the first commercially available, modularly expandable system designed specifically for high availability. Design objectives for the system include the following:

- "Nonstop" operation wherein failures are detected, components are reconfigured out of service, and repaired components are configured back into the system without stopping the other system components
- Fail-fast logic whereby no single hardware failure can compromise the data integrity of the system
- Modular system expansion through adding more processing power, memory, and peripherals without impacting applications software

As in the AT&T switching systems, the Tandem architecture is designed to take advantage of the OLTP application to simplify error detection and recovery. The Tandem architecture is composed of up to 16 computers interconnected by two message-oriented Dynabuses. The hardware and software modules are designed to be fast-fail; that is, to rapidly detect errors and subsequent terminate processing. Software modules employ consistency checks and defensive programming techniques. Techniques employed in hardware modules include the following:

Checksums on Dynabus messages
Parity on data paths
Error-correcting code memory
Watch-dog timers

All I/O device controllers are dual ported for access by an alternate path in case of processor or I/O failure. The software builds a process-oriented system with all communications handled as messages on this hardware structure. This abstraction allows the blurring of the physical boundaries between processors and peripherals. Any I/O device or resource in the system can be accessed by a process, regardless of where the resource and process reside.

Retry is extensively used to access an I/O device. Initially, hardware/firmware retries the access assuming a temporary fault. Next, software retries, followed by alternative path retry and finally alternative device retry.

A network systems management program provides a set of operators that helps reduce the number of administrative errors typically encountered in complex systems. The Tandem Maintenance and Diagnostic System analyzes event logs to successfully call out failed field-replaceable units 90 percent of the time. Networking software exists that allows interconnection of up to 255 geographically dispersed Tandem systems. Tandem applications include order entry, hospital records, bank transactions, and library transactions.

Data integrity is maintained through the mechanisms of I/O "process pairs"; one I/O process is designated as primary and the other is designated as backup. All file modification messages are delivered to the primary I/O process. The primary sends a message with checkpoint information to the backup so that it can take over if the primary's processor or access path to the I/O device fails. Files can also be duplicated on physically distinct devices controlled by an I/O process pair on physically distinct processors. All file modification messages are delivered to both I/O processes. Thus, in the event of physical failure or isolation of the primary, the backup file is up-to-date and available.

User applications can also utilize the process-pair mechanism. As an example of how process pairs work, consider the nonstop application, program A, shown in Figure 8–2. Program A starts a backup process, A1, in another processor. There are also duplicate file images, one designated primary and the other backup. Program A periodically (at user-specified points) sends checkpoint information to A1. A1 is the same program as A, but knows that it is a backup program. A1 reads checkpoint messages to update its data area, file status, and program counter.

The checkpoint information is inserted in the corresponding memory locations of the backup process, as opposed to the more usual approach of updating a disk file. This approach permits the backup process to take over immediately in the event of failure without having to perform the usual recovery journaling and disk accesses before processing resumes.

Program A1 loads and executes if the system reports that A's processor is down (error messages sent from A's operating system image or A's processor fails to respond

FIGURE 8–2
Shadow processor in Tandem

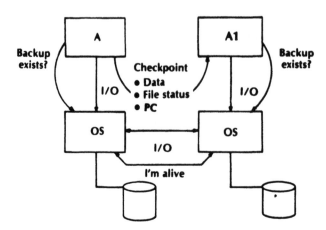

to a periodic "I'm alive" message). All file activity by A is performed on both the primary and backup file copies. When A1 starts to execute from the last checkpoints, it may attempt to repeat I/O operations successfully completed by A. The system file handler will recognize this and send A1 a successfully completed I/O message. Program A periodically asks the operating system if a backup process exists. Since one no longer does, it can request the creation and initialization of a copy of both the process and file structure.

A major issue in the design of loosely coupled duplicated systems is how both copies can be kept identical in the face of errors. As an example of how consistency is maintained, consider the interaction of an I/O processor pair as depicted in Table 8–4. Initially, all sequence numbers (SeqNo) are set to zero. The requester sends a request to the server. If the sequence number is less than the server's local copy, a failure has occurred and the status of the completed operation is returned. Note that the requested operation is done only once. Next, the operation is performed and a checkpoint of the request is sent to the server backup. The disk is written, the sequence number incremented to one, and the results checkpointed to the server backup, which also increments its sequence number. The results are returned from the server to the requestor. Finally the results are checkpointed to the requester backup, which also increments its sequence number.

Now consider failures. If either backup fails, the operation completes successfully. If the requester fails after the request has been made, the server will complete the operation but be unable to return the result. When the requester backup becomes active, it will repeat the request. Since its sequence number is zero, the server test at step 2 will return the result without performing the operation again. Finally, if the server fails, the server backup either does nothing or completes the operation using checkpointed information. When the requester resends the request, the new server (that is, the old server backup) either performs the operation or returns the saved results. More information on the operating system and the programming of nonstop applications can be found in Bartlett [1978].

TABLE 8–4
Sample process-pair transactions

Step	Requester SeqNo = 0	Requester Backup SeqNo = 0	Server SeqNo = 0	Server Backup SeqNo = 0
1	Issue request to write record ───►		
2			If SeqNo < MySeqNo, then return saved status	
3			Otherwise, read disk, perform operation, ──────► Saves request checkpoint request	
4			Write to disk SeqNo = 1 ──────────────► Saves result checkpoint result	SeqNo = 1
5	◄────────────────────────────────────── Return results		
6	Checkpoint ──────► SeqNo = 1 results		

Source: Bartlett, 1981; © 1981 ACM.

STRATUS COMPUTERS, INC.

Whereas the Tandem architecture was based upon minicomputer technology, Stratus entered the OLTP market five years after Tandem by harnessing microprocessors. By 1980, the performance of microprocessor chips was beginning to rival that of minicomputers. Because of the smaller form factor of microprocessor chips, it was possible to place two microprocessors on a single board and to compare their output pins on every clock cycle. Thus, the Stratus system appears to users as a conventional system that does not require special software for error detection and recovery. The case study by Steven Webber describes the Stratus approach in detail.

The design goal for Stratus systems is continuous processing, which is defined as uninterrupted operation without loss of data, performance degradation, or special programming. The Stratus self-checking, duplicate-and-match architecture is shown in Figure 8–3. A module (or computer) is composed of replicated power and backplane buses (StrataBus) into which a variety of boards can be inserted. Boards are logically divided into halves that drive outputs to and receive inputs from both buses. The bus drivers/receivers are duplicated and controlled independently. The logical halves are driven in lock-step by the same clock. A comparitor is used to detect any disagreements between the two halves of the board. Multiple failures that affect the two independent halves of a board could cause the module to hang as it alternated between buses seeking a fault-free path. Up to 32 modules can be interconnected into a system via a message-passing Stratus intermodule bus (SIB). Access to the SIB is by dual 14 megabyte-per-second links. Systems, in return, are tied together by an X.25 packet-switched network.

FIGURE 8–3

The Stratus pair-and-spare architecture

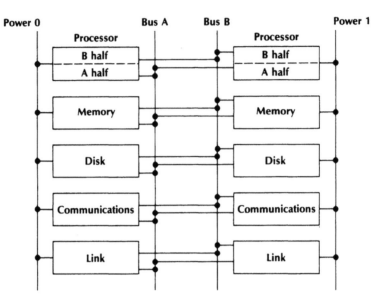

Now consider how the system in Figure 8–3 tolerates failure. The two processor boards (each containing a pair of microprocessors), each self-checking modules, are used in a pair-and-spare configuration. Each board operates independently. Each half of each board (for example, side A) received inputs from a different bus (for example, bus A) and drives a different bus (for example, bus A). Each bus is the wired-OR of one-half of each board (for example, bus A is the wired-OR of all A board halves). The boards constantly compare their two halves, and upon disagreement, the board removes itself from service, a maintenance interrupt is generated, and a red light is illuminated. The spare pair on the other processor board continues processing and is now the sole driver of both buses. The operating system executes a diagnostic on the failed board to determine whether the error was caused by a transient or permanent fault. In the case of a transient, the board is returned to service. Permanent faults are reported by phone to the Stratus Customer Assistance Center (CAC). The CAC reconfirms the problem, selects a replacement board of the same revision, prints installation instructions, and ships the board by overnight courier. The first time the user realizes there is a problem is when the board is delivered. The user removes the old board and inserts the new board without disrupting the system (that is, makes a "hot" swap). The new board interrupts the system, and the processor that has been running brings the replacement into full synchronization, at which point the full configuration is available again. Detection and recovery are transparent to the application software.

The detection and recovery procedures for other system components are similar, although the full implementation of pair-and-spare is restricted to only the processor and memory. The disk controllers contain duplicate read/write circuitry. Communications controllers are also self-checking. In addition, the memory controllers monitor the bus for parity errors. The controllers can declare a bus broken and instruct all boards to stop using that bus. Other boards monitor the bus for data directed to them. If the board detects an inconsistency but the memory controllers have not declared the bus broken, the board assumes that its bus receivers have failed and declares itself failed.

The Stratus hardware approach is attractive in that it does not require on-line recovery from faults. The spare component continues processing until its fault counterpart can be replaced. No data errors are injected into the system; hence, no software recovery mechanisms are required for the pair-and-spare components. Complexities caused by checkpointing/restart programming and other software fault-tolerant considerations are eliminated. In addition to ease in programming, the Stratus approach to maintenance reduces the yearly service cost to 6 percent of life-cycle cost, as compared to an industrial average of 9 percent.

REFERENCES   Bartlett, 1978, 1981.

THE AT&T CASE

Part I: Fault-Tolerant Design of AT&T Telephone Switching System Processors

W.N. TOY

INTRODUCTION   Except for computer systems used in space-borne vehicles and U.S. defense installations, no other application has a higher availability requirement than a stored-program–controlled (SPC) telecommunications switching system. SPC systems have been designed to be out of service no more than a few minutes per year. Furthermore, design objectives permit no more than 0.01 percent of the telephone calls to be processed incorrectly [Downing, Nowak, and Tuomenoksa, 1964]. For example, when a fault occurs in a system, few calls in progress may be handled incorrectly during the recovery process.

At the core of every system is a single high-speed central processor [Harr, Taylor, and Ulrich, 1969; Browne et al., 1969; Staehler, 1977]. To establish an ultrareliable switching environment, redundancy of system components, including duplication of the processor itself, is the approach taken to compensate for potential machine faults. Without this redundancy, a single component failure in the processor might cause a complete failure of the entire system. With duplication, a standby processor takes over control and provides continuous telephone service.

When the system fails, the fault must be quickly detected and isolated. Meanwhile, a rapid recovery of the call processing functions (by the redundant component(s) and/or processor) is necessary to maintain the system's high availability. Next, the fault must be diagnosed and the defective unit repaired or replaced. The failure rate and repair time must be such that the probability is very small for a failure to occur in the duplicate unit before the first unit is repaired.

ALLOCATION AND CAUSES OF SYSTEM DOWNTIME

The outage of a telephone (switching) office can be caused by facilities other than the processor. While a hardware fault in one of the peripheral units generally results in only a partial loss of service, it is possible for a fault in this area to bring the entire system down. By design, the processor has been allocated two-thirds of the system downtime. The other one-third is allocated to the remaining equipment in the system.

Field experience indicates that system outages due to the processor may be assigned to one of four categories, as shown in Figure 8–4 [Staehler and Watters, 1976]. The percentages in this figure represent the fraction of total downtime attributable to each cause. The four categories are as follows.

• *Hardware Reliability*: Before the accumulation of large amounts of field data, total system downtime was usually assigned to hardware. We now know that the situation is more complex. Processor hardware actually accounts for only 20 percent of the downtime. With growing use of stored program control, it has become increasingly important to make such systems more reliable. Redundancy is designed into all subsystems so that the system can go down *only* when a hardware failure occurs simultaneously in a unit and its duplicate. However, the data now show that good diagnostic and trouble location programs are also very critical parts of the total system reliability performance.

• *Software Deficiencies*: Software deficiencies include all software errors that cause memory mutilation and program loops that can only be cleared by major reinitialization. Software faults are the result of improper translation or implementation of the original algorithm. In some cases, the original algorithm may have been incorrectly specified. Program changes and feature additions are continuously incorporated into working offices. Software accounts for 15 percent of the downtime.

• *Recovery Deficiencies*: Recovery is the system's most complex and difficult function. Deficiencies may include the shortcomings of either hardware or software design to detect faults when they occur. When the faults go undetected, the system remains extensively impaired until the trouble is recognized. A recovery problem can also occur if the system is unable to properly isolate a faulty subsystem and configure a working system around it.

The many possible system states that may arise under trouble conditions make recovery a complicated process. Besides those problems already mentioned, unforeseen difficulties may be

FIGURE 8–4
System outage allocation

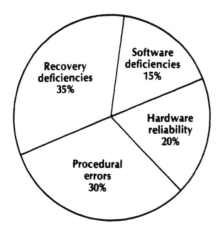

encountered in the field and lead to inadequate recovery. Because of the large number of variables involved and because the recovery function is so strongly related to all other components of maintenance, recovery deficiencies account for 35 percent of the downtime.

• *Procedural Errors*: Human error on the part of maintenance personnel or office administrators can also cause the system to go down. For example, someone in maintenance may mistakenly pull a circuit pack from the on-line processor while repairing a defective standby processor. Inadequate and incorrect documentation (for example, user's manuals) may also be classified as human error. Obviously, the number of manual operations must be reduced if procedural errors are to be minimized. Procedural errors account for 30 percent of the downtime.

The shortcomings and deficiencies of current systems are being continually corrected to improve system reliability.

DUPLEX ARCHITECTURE

When a fault occurs in a nonredundant single processor, the system will remain down until the processor is repaired. In order to meet reliability requirements, *redundancy* is included in the system design, and continuous, correct operation is maintained by duplicating all functional units within the processor. If one of the units fails, the duplicated unit is switched in, maintaining continuous operation. Meanwhile, the defective unit is repaired. Should a fault occur in the duplicated unit during the repair interval, the system will, of course, go down. If the repair interval is relatively short, the probability of simultaneous faults occurring in two identical units is quite small. This technique of redundancy has been used throughout each AT&T switching system.

The first-generation electronic switching system (ESS) processor structure consists of two store communities: program store and call store. The program store is a read-only memory, containing the call processing, maintenance, and administration programs; it also contains long-term translation and system parameters. The call store contains the transient data related to telephone calls in progress. The memory is electrically alterable to allow its data to be changed frequently. In one particular arrangement, shown in Figure 8–5b, the complete processor is treated as a single functional block and is duplicated. This type of single-unit duplex system has two possible configurations: Either processor 0 or processor 1 can be assigned as the on-line working system, while the other unit serves as a standby backup. The mean time to failure (MTTF), a measure of reliability, is given by the following expression [Smith, 1972]:

$$MTTF = \frac{\mu}{2\lambda^2}$$

where μ = repair rate (reciprocal of the repair time)
λ = failure rate

The failure rate (λ) of one unit is the sum of the failure rates of all components within the unit. For medium and small ESS processors, Figure 8–5a shows a system structure containing several functional units that are treated as a single entity, with λ still sufficiently small to meet the reliability requirement. The single-unit duplex configuration has the advantage of being very simple in terms of the number of switching blocks in the system. This configuration simplifies not only the recovery program but also the hardware interconnection by eliminating the additional access required to make each duplicated block capable of switching independently into the on-line system configuration.

In the large 1ES switching system, which contains many components, the MTTF becomes

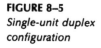

FIGURE 8–5
Single-unit duplex configuration

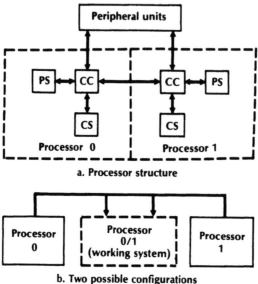

a. Processor structure

b. Two possible configurations

too low to meet the reliability requirement. In order to increase the MTTF, either the number of components (failure rate) or the repair time must be reduced. Alternatively, the single-unit duplex configuration can be partitioned into a multi-unit duplex configuration, as shown in Figure 8–6. In this arrangement, each subunit contains a small number of components and can be switched into a working system. The system will fail only if a fault occurs in the redundant subunit while the original is being repaired. Since each subunit contains fewer components, the probability of two simultaneous faults occurring in a duplicated pair of subunits is reduced. The MTTF of the multi-unit duplex configuration can be computed by considering the conditional probability of the failure of a duplicate subunit during the repair time of the original subunit.

An example of a multi-unit duplex configuration is shown in Figure 8–6. A working system is configured with a fault-free CCx-CSx-CSBx-PSx-PSBx-PUBx arrangement, where x is either subunit 0 or subunit 1. This arrangement means there are 2^6, or 64, possible combinations of system configurations. The MTTF is given by the following expression:

$$MTTF = \frac{r\mu}{2\lambda^2} \tag{1}$$

and

$$r = \frac{1}{(\lambda_{CC}/\lambda)^2 + (\lambda_{CS}/\lambda)^2 + (\lambda_{CSB}/\lambda)^2 + (\lambda_{PS}/\lambda)^2 + (\lambda_{PSB}/\lambda)^2 + (\lambda_{PUB}/\lambda)^2} \tag{2}$$

The factor r is at a maximum when the failure rate (λ_i) for each subunit is the same. In this case,

$$\lambda_{CC} = \lambda_{CS} = \lambda_{CSB} = \lambda_{PS} = \lambda_{PSB} = \lambda_{PUB} = \lambda_i \tag{3}$$

or

$$\lambda_i = \frac{\lambda}{s} \qquad\qquad\qquad (4)$$

where s = number of subunits in Eq. (2)

$s = 6$

$r = s$

At best, the MTTF is improved by a factor corresponding to the number of partitioned subunits. This improvement is not fully realized, since equipment must be added to provide additional access and to select subunits. Partitioning the subsystem into subunits, as shown in Figure 8–6, results in subunits of different sizes. Again, the failure rate for each individual subunit will not be the same; hence, the r-factor will be smaller than 6. Because of the relatively large number of components used in implementing the 1ESS switch processor, the system is arranged in the multi-unit duplex configuration in order to meet the reliability requirement.

Reliability calculation is a process of predicting, from available failure rate data, the achievable reliability of a system and the probability of meeting the reliability objectives for telephone switching applications. These calculations are most useful and beneficial during the early stages of design in order to assess various types of redundancy and to determine the system's organi-

FIGURE 8–6
Multi-unit duplex configuration

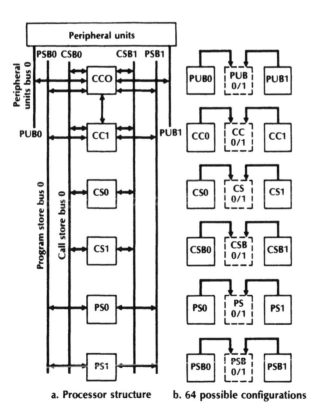

a. Processor structure   b. 64 possible configurations

zation. In the small and medium switches, the calculations support the use of single-unit duplex structures. For large systems, it is necessary to partition the system into a multi-unit duplex configuration.

FAULT SIMULATION TECHNIQUES

One of the more difficult tasks of maintenance design is fault diagnosis. The maintenance design's effectiveness in diagnostic resolution can be determined by simulation of the system's behavior in the presence of a specific fault. By means of simulation, design deficiencies can be identified and corrected prior to any system's deployment in the field. It is necessary to evaluate the system's ability to detect faults, to recover automatically back into a working system, and to provide diagnostics information when the fault is within a few replaceable circuit packs. Fault simulation, therefore, is an important aspect of maintenance design.

There are essentially two techniques used for simulating faults of digital systems: physical simulation and digital simulation. Physical simulation is a process of inserting faults into a physical working model. This method produces more realistic behavior under fault conditions than digital simulation does. A wider class of faults can be applied to the system, such as a blown fuse or shorted backplane interconnection. However, fault simulation cannot begin until the design has been completed and the equipment is fully operational. Also, it is not possible to insert faults that are internal to an integrated circuit.

Digital fault simulation is a means of predicting the behavior under failure of a processor modeled in a computer program. The computer used to execute the program (the host) is generally different from the processor that is being simulated (the object). Digital fault simulation gives a high degree of automation and excellent access to interior points of logic to monitor the signal flow. It allows diagnostic test development and evaluation to proceed well in advance of unit fabrication. The cost of computer simulation can be quite high for a large, complex system.

The physical fault simulation method was first employed to generate diagnostic data for the Morris Electronic Switching System [Tsiang and Ulrich, 1962]. Over 50,000 known faults were purposely introduced into the central control to be diagnosed by its diagnostic program. Test results associated with each fault were recorded. They were then sorted and printed in dictionary format to formulate a trouble-locating manual. Under trouble conditions, by consulting the manual, it was possible to determine a set of several suspected circuit packs that might contain the defective component. Use of the dictionary technique at the Morris system kept the average repair time low and made maintenance much easier.

The experience gained in the physical fault simulation was applied and extended in the 1ESS switch development [Downing, Nowak, and Tuomenoksa, 1964]. Each plug-in circuit pack was replaced by a fault simulator that introduced every possible type of single fault on the replaced package one at a time and then recorded the system reaction on magnetic tape. This procedure was followed for all circuit packs in the system. In addition to diagnostic data for dictionaries, additional data were collected to determine the adequacy of hardware and software in fault detection and system recovery. Deficiencies were corrected to improve the overall maintenance of the system.

A digital logic simulator, called LAMP [Chang, Smith, and Walford, 1974], was developed for the 1A system, and it played an important role in the hardware and diagnostics development of the 1A Processor. LAMP is capable of simulating a subsystem with as many as 65,000 logic gates. All classical faults for standard logic gates are simulatable with logic nodes stuck-at-0 or stuck-at-1. Before physical units are available, digital simulators can be very effective in verifying the design, evaluating diagnostic access, and developing tests. Physical fault simulation has been demonstrated in the System 1 processor to give a very realistic behavior under fault conditions. The integration of both techniques was employed in the development of the 1A processor to take advantage of both processes. The use of complementary simulation allows faults to be simulated physically (in the system laboratory) and logically (on a computer). Most of the deficiencies of one simulation process are compensated for by the other. The complementary method provides both a convenient method for validating the results and more extensive fault simulation data than is possible if either process is used individually. Figure 8–7 shows the complementary process of fault simulation used in the 1A Processor development [Bowman et al., 1977; Goetz, 1974]. Maximum diagnostic performance was achieved from an integrated use of both simulation methods.

FIGURE 8–7
Complementary fault simulation system

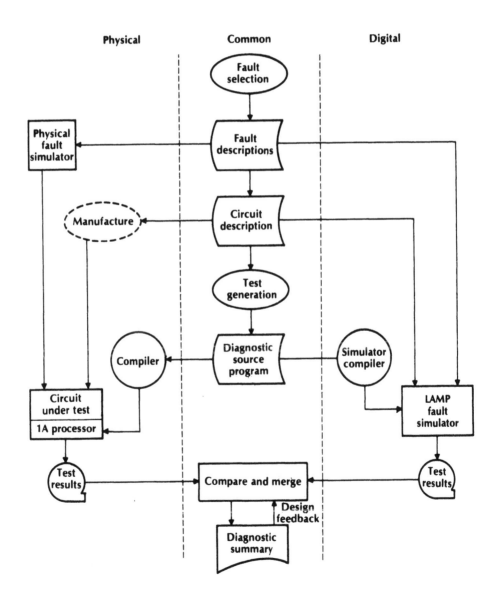

**FIRST-
GENERATION ESS
PROCESSORS**

The world's first stored-program–controlled switching system provided commercial telephone service at Morris, Illinois, in 1959 for about a year on a field-trial basis [Keister, Ketchledge, and Lovell, 1960]. The system demonstrated the use of stored program control and the basic maintenance philosophy of providing continuous and reliable telephone service. The trial established valuable guides for designing a successor, the 1ESS switch.

1ESS Switch Processor (No. 1 Processor)

The 1ESS switching system was designed to serve large metropolitan telephone offices, ranging from several thousand to 65,000 lines [Keister, Ketchledge, and Vaughan, 1964]. As in most large switching systems, the processor represents only a small percentage of the total system cost. Therefore, performance and reliability were of primary importance in the design of the No. 1 processor; cost was secondary. In order to meet the reliability standards established by electro-mechanical systems, all units essential to proper operation of the office are duplicated (see Figure 8–6). The multi-unit duplex configuration was necessary to increase the MTTF of the processor because of the large number of components in each of the functional blocks.

Even with duplication, troubles must be found and corrected quickly to minimize exposure to system failure due to multiple troubles. All units are monitored continually so that troubles in the standby units are found just as quickly as those in the on-line units. Monitoring is accomplished by running the on-line and standby units in synchronous and match mode of operation [Downing, Nowak, and Tuomenoksa, 1964]. Synchronization requires that clock timing signals be in close tolerance so that every operation in both halves is performed in step, and key outputs are compared for error detection. The synchronization of duplicated units is accomplished by having the on-line oscillator output drive both clock circuits. There are two match circuits in each central control (CC). Each matcher compares 24 bits within one machine cycle of 5.5 microseconds. Figure 8–8 shows that each matcher has access to six sets of internal nodes (24 bits per node). In the routine match mode, the points matched in each cycle are dependent upon the instruction that is being executed. The selected match points are those most pertinent to the data processing steps that occur during a given machine cycle. The two matchers in each CC compare the same sets of selected test points. If a mismatch occurs, an interrupt is generated, causing the fault-recognition program to run. The basic function of this program is to determine which half of the system is faulty. The suspected unit is removed from service, and the appropriate diagnostic program is run to pinpoint the defective circuit pack. The capability of each CC to compare a number of internal nodes provides a highly effective means of detecting hardware errors.

The No. 1 Processor was designed during the discrete component era (early 1960s), using individual components to implement logic gates [Cagle et al., 1964]. The CC contains approximately 12,000 logic gates. Although this number appears small when compared to large-scale integration (LSI) technology, the No. 1 Processor was a physically large machine for its time. The match circuits capable of comparing internal nodes are the primary tools incorporated into the CC for diagnosing as well as detecting troubles. Specified information can be sampled by the matchers and retained in the match registers for examination. This mode of operation obtains critical data during the execution of diagnostic programs.

The early program store used permanent magnet twister (PMT) modules as basic storage elements [Ault et al., 1964]. PMTs are a form of ROM in which system failures cannot alter the information content. Experience gained from the Morris field test system, which used the less reliable flying spot store, indicated that Hamming correction code was highly effective in providing continuous operation. At the time of development, it was felt that PMT modules might not be

FIGURE 8–8

*No. 1 Processor's
CC match access*

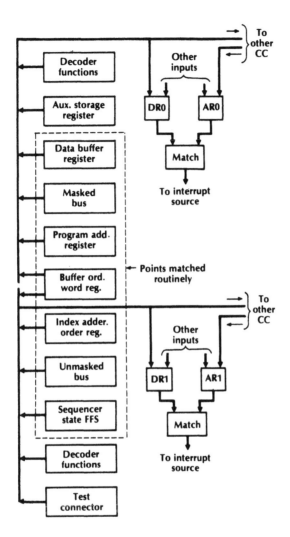

reliable enough. Consequently, the program store word included additional check bits for single-bit error correction (Hamming code). In addition, an overall parity check bit that covers both the data and their addresses is included in the word. The word size consists of 37 bits of information and seven check bits. When an error is corrected during normal operation, it is logged in an error counter. Also, detection of a single error in the address or a double error in the word will cause an automatic retry.

The call store is the temporary read and write memory for storing transient data associated with call processing. Ferrite sheet memory modules are the basic storage elements used in implementing the call store in the 1ESS switch [Genke, Harding, and Staehler, 1964]. The call store used in most No. 1 offices is smaller than the program store. (At the time of design, the cost per bit of call store was considerably higher than that of program store.) Also, ferrite sheet memory modules were considered to be very reliable devices. Consequently, single-bit error detection rather than Hamming correction code was provided in the call store.

There are two parity check bits: one over both the address and the data, and the other over the address only. Again, as in the program store, automatic retry is performed whenever an error is detected, and the event is logged in an error counter for diagnostic use.

Troubles are normally detected by fault-detection circuits, and error-free system operation is recovered by fault recognition programs [Downing, Nowak, and Tuomenoksa, 1964]. This requires the on-line processor to be capable of making a proper decision. If this is not possible, an emergency action timer will time out and activate special circuits to establish various combinations of subsystems into a system configuration. A special program that is used to determine whether or not the assembled processor is sane takes the processor through a series of tests arranged in a maze. Only one correct path through the maze exists. If the processor passes through successfully, the timer will be reset, and recovery is successful. If recovery is unsuccessful, the timer will time out again, and the rearrangement of subsystems will be tried one at a time (for example, combination of CC, program store, and program store bus systems). For each selected combination, the special sanity program is started and the sanity timer is activated. This procedure is repeated until a working configuration is found. The sanity program and sanity timer determine if the on-line CC is functioning properly. The active CC includes the program store and the program store bus.

2ESS Switch Processor (No. 2 Processor)

The No. 2 Processor was developed during the mid-1960s [Spencer and Vigilante, 1969]. The 2ESS switch was designed for medium-sized offices ranging from 1,000 to 10,000 lines. The processor's design was derived from experience with the common stored program of a private branch exchange (PBX), the No. 101 [Seley and Vigilante, 1964]. Since the capacity requirement of the 2ESS switch was to be less than that of the 1ESS switch, cost became one of the more important design considerations. (Reliability is equally important in all systems.) The 2ESS switch contains much less hardware than the 1ESS switch. Understandably, its component failure rate is also substantially lower. Its CC contains approximately 5000 gates (discrete components). To reduce cost and increase reliability, resistor-transistor logic (RTL) gates were chosen for the 2ESS processor, since resistors are less expensive and more reliable than diodes [the No. 1 Processor used diode-transistor logic (DTL)].

Because the No. 2 Processor's CC, program store, and call store are smaller, they are grouped together as a single switchable block in the single-unit duplex configuration shown in Figure 8–5. Calculations indicate that its MTTF is approximately the same as the No. 1 multi-unit duplex structure, with each of the functional blocks and associated store buses grouped together as a switchable block. The use of only two subsystem configurations considerably reduces the amount of hardware needed to provide gating paths and control for each functional unit. Moreover, the recovery program is simplified, and the reliability of the system is improved.

The No. 2 Processor runs in the synchronous and match mode of operation [Beuscher et al., 1969]. The on-line oscillator output drives both clock circuits in order to keep the timing synchronized. The match operation is not as extensive as it is in the No. 1 Processor. For simplicity, there is only one matcher in the No. 2 Processor; it is located in the nonduplicated maintenance center (see Figure 8–9). The matcher always compares the call store input register in the two CCs when call store operations are performed synchronously. A fault in almost any part of either CC quickly results in a call store input register mismatch. This mismatch occurs because almost all data manipulation performed in both the program control and the input-output control involves

FIGURE 8–9

*No. 2 Processor's
CC match access*

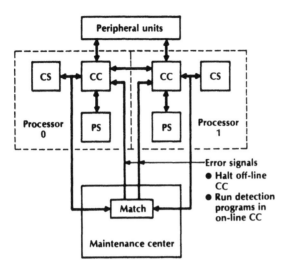

processed data returning to the call store. The call store input is the central point by which data eventually funnel through to the call store. By matching the call store inputs, an effective check of the system equipment is provided. Compared to the more complex matching of the No. 1 Processor, error detection in the No. 2 Processor may not be as instantaneous, since only one crucial node in the processor is matched. Certain faults in the No. 2 Processor will go undetected until the errors propagate into the call store. This interval is probably no more than tens or hundreds of microseconds. During such a short interval, the fault would affect only a single call.

The No. 2 Processor matcher is not used as a diagnostic tool as is the matcher in the No. 1 Processor. Therefore, additional detection hardware is designed into the No. 2 Processor to help diagnose as well as detect faults. When a mismatch occurs, the detection program is run in the on-line CC to determine if it contains the fault. This is done while the standby processor is disabled. If a solid fault in the on-line processor is detected by the mismatch detection program, the control is automatically passed to the standby processor, causing it to become the on-line processor. The faulty processor is disabled and diagnostic tests are called in to pinpoint the defective circuit pack.

The program store also uses PMT modules as basic storage elements, with a word size of 22 bits, half the width of the No. 1 Processor's word size. Experience gained in the design and operation of the No. 101 PBX showed that PMT stores are very reliable. The additional protection provided in the No. 1 Processor against memory faults by error correction was not considered to be as important in the No. 2 Processor. Thus, the need to keep the cost down led to the choice of error detection *only*, instead of the more sophisticated Hamming correction code.

Error detection works as follows: One of the 22 bits in a word is allocated as a parity check bit. The program store contains both program and translation data. Additional protection is provided by using odd parity for program words and even parity for translation data. This parity scheme detects the possibility of accessing the translation data area of memory as instruction words. For example, a software error may cause the program to branch into the data section of the memory and execute the data words as instruction words. The parity check would detect this problem immediately. The program store includes checking circuits to detect multiple-word access. Under program control, the sense amplifier threshold voltage can be varied in two discrete amounts from its nominal value to obtain a measure of the operating margin. The use of parity check was the proper choice for the No. 2 Processor in view of the high reliability of these memory devices.

The No. 2 Processor call store uses the same ferrite sheet memory modules as the No. 1 Processor. However, the No. 2 Processor's data word is 16 bits wide instead of 24. Fault detection depends heavily upon the matching of the call store inputs when the duplex processors run in the synchronous mode. Within the call store circuit, the access circuitry is checked to see that access currents flow in the right direction at the correct time and that only two access switches are selected in any store operation, ensuring that only one word is accessed in the memory operation. Similarly, threshold voltages of the sense amplifiers may be varied under program control to evaluate the operating margins of the store. No parity check bit is provided in the call store.

Each processor contains a program timer that is designed to back up other detection methods. Normally, the on-line processor clears the timer in both processors at prescribed intervals if the basic call processing program cycles correctly. If, however, a hardware or software trouble condition exists (for example, a program may go astray or a longer program loop may prevent the timer from being cleared), the timer will time out and automatically produce a switch. The new on-line processor is automatically forced to run an initialization restart program that attempts to establish a working system. System recovery is simplified by using two possible system configurations rather than the multi-unit duplex system.

SECOND-GENERATION PROCESSORS

The advent of silicon integrated circuits (ICs) in the mid-1960s provided the technological climate for dramatic miniaturization, improved performance, and cost-reduced hardware. The term *1A technology* refers to the standard set of IC devices, apparatus, and design tools that were used to design the No. 1A Processor and the No. 3A Processor [Becker et al., 1977]. The choice of technology and the scale of integration level were dictated by the technological advances made between 1968 and 1970. Small-scale integration (SSI), made possible by bipolar technology, was capable of high yield production. Because of the processor cycle time, high-speed logic gates with propagation delays from 5–10 nanoseconds were designed and developed concurrent with the No. 1A Processor.

No. 1A Processor

The No. 1A Processor, successor to the No. 1 Processor, was designed primarily for the control of large local and toll switches with high processing capabilities (the 1A ESS and 4ESS switches, respectively) [Budlong et al., 1977]. An important objective in developing the 1A ESS switch was to maintain commonality with the 1ESS switch. High capacity was achieved by implementing the new 1A integrated technology and a newly designed system structure. These changes made possible an instruction execution rate that is four to eight times faster than the No. 1 Processor. Compatibility with the 1ESS system also allows the No. 1A Processor to be retrofitted into an in-service 1ESS, replacing the No. 1 Processor when additional capacity is needed. The first 1A Processor was put into service in January, 1976, as control for a 4ESS toll switch in Chicago. Less than one year later, the first 1A ESS system was put into commercial operation. By 1988, about 2000 systems were in service.

The No. 1A Processor architecture is similar to its predecessor in that all of its subsystems have redundant units and are connected to the basic CC via redundant bus systems [Bowman et al., 1977]. One of the No. 1A Processor's major architectural differences is its program store

[Ault et al., 1977]. It has a writable RAM instead of PMT ROM. By combining disk memory and RAM, the system has the same amount of memory as a system with PMT, but at a lower cost. Backup copy of program and translation data is kept on disk. Other programs (e.g., diagnostics) are brought to RAM as needed; the same RAM spare is shared among different programs. More important is the system's ability to change the content of the store quickly and automatically. This ability considerably simplifies the administration and updating of program and translation information in working offices.

The additional disk (file store) subsystem adds flexibility to the No. 1A Processor [Ault et al., 1977], but it also increases the complexity of system recovery. Figure 8–10 shows the multi-unit duplex No. 1A Processor. This configuration is similar to the No. 1 Processor arrangement (see Figure 8–6) with a duplicated file store included. The file store communicates with the program store or call store via the CC and the auxiliary unit bus. This communication allows direct memory access between the file store and the program store or the call store. The disk file and the auxiliary unit bus are grouped together as a switchable entity.

Error detection is achieved by the duplicated and matched synchronous mode of operation, as in the No. 1 Processor. Both CCs operate in step and perform identical operations. The

FIGURE 8–10
*No. 1A Processor
configuration*

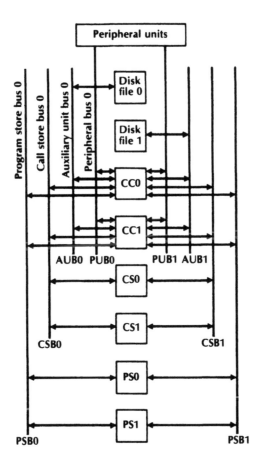

matching is done more extensively in the 1A to obtain as complete a check as possible. There are two match circuits in each processor. Each matcher has the ability to compare 24 internal bits to 24 bits in its mate once every machine cycle. (A machine cycle is 700 nanoseconds.) Any one of 16 different 24-bit internal nodes can be selected for comparison. The choice is determined by the type of instruction that is being executed. Rather than compare the same nodes in both CCs, the on-line and the standby CCs are arranged to match different sets of data. Four distinct internal groups are matched in the same machine cycle to ensure the correct execution of any instruction.

The No. 1A Processor design is an improvement of the No. 1 Processor design. The No. 1A Processor incorporates much more checking hardware throughout various functional units, in addition to matching hardware. Checking hardware speeds up fault detection and also aids the fault recovery process by providing indications that help isolate the faulty unit. The matching is used in various modes for maintenance purposes. This capability provides powerful diagnostic tools in isolating faults.

The program store and call store use the same hardware technology as in the No. 1 Processor. The CC contains approximately 50,000 logic gates. While the initial design of the stores called for core memories, they have been replaced with semiconductor dynamic MOS memories. The word size is 26 bits (24 data bits and 2 parity check bits). In the No. 1 Processor, the program store and the call store are fully duplicated. Because of their size, duplication requires a considerable amount of hardware, resulting in higher cost and increased component failures. To reduce the amount of hardware in the No. 1A Processor's store community, the memory is partitioned into blocks of 64K words, as shown in Figure 8–11. Two additional store blocks are provided as roving spares. If one of the program stores fails, a roving program store spare is substituted, and a copy of the program in the file store is transferred to the program store replacement. This type of redundancy has been made possible by the ability to regenerate data stored in a failing unit. Since a program store can be reloaded from the file store in less than a second, a roving spare redundancy plan is sufficient to meet the reliability requirement. As a result, Hamming correction code was not adopted in the No. 1A program store. However, it is essential that an error be detected quickly. Two parity check bits are generated over a partially overlapped, interleaved set of data bits and address. This overlapping is arranged to cope with particular memory circuit failures that may affect more than one bit of a word.

The 1A call stores contain both translation data backed up on the file stores and call-related transient data that are difficult to regenerate. The roving spare concept is expanded for the call stores to include sufficient spares to provide full duplication of transient data. If a fault occurs in a store that contains translation data, one of the duplicated stores containing transient call data is preempted and loaded with the necessary translation data from the duplicate in the file store. A parity check is done in the same manner as in the program store, using two check bits.

FIGURE 8–11
No. 1A Processor's program store structure

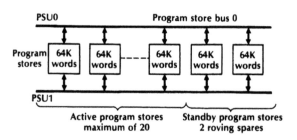

The combination of writable program store and file store provides a very effective and flexible system architecture for administrating and implementing a wide variety of features that are difficult to obtain in the 1ESS system. However, this architecture also complicates the process of fault recognition and recovery. Reconfiguration into a working system under trouble conditions is an extensive task, depending on the severity of the fault. (For example, it is possible for the processor to lose its sanity or ability to make proper decisions.) An autonomous hardware processor configuration (PC) circuit is provided in each CC to assist in assembling a working system. The PC circuit consists of various timers that ensure that the operational, fault recovery, and configuration programs are successfully executed. If these programs *are not* executed, the PC circuit controls the CC-to-program memory configuration, reloading program memory from file store when required, and isolating various subsystems from the CC until a working system is obtained.

No. 3A Processor

The No. 3A Processor was designed to control the small 3ESS switch [Irland and Stagg, 1974], which can handle from 500 to 5,000 lines. One of the major concerns in the design of this ESS was the cost of its processor. The low cost and high speed of integrated logic circuitry made it possible to design a cost-effective processor that performed better than its discrete component predecessor, the No. 2 Processor. The No. 3A project was started in early 1971. The first system cut into commercial service in late 1975.

Because the number of components in the No. 3A Processor is considerably fewer than in the No. 1A Processor, all subsystems are fully duplicated, including the main store. The CC, the store bus, and the store are treated as a single switchable entity, rather than individual switchable units as in the No. 1A Processor. The system structure is similar to the 2ESS switch. Experience gained in the design and operation of the No. 2 provided valuable input for the No. 3 Processor design.

The 3A design makes one major departure from previous processor designs: It operates in the nonmatched mode of duplex operation. The primary purpose of matching is to detect errors. A mismatch, however, does not indicate *where* (in which one of the processors) the fault has occurred. A diagnostic fault-location program must be run to localize the trouble so that the defective unit can be taken off line. For this reason, the No. 3A Processor was designed to be self-checking, with detection circuitry incorporated as an integral part of the processor. Faults occurring during normal operation are discovered quickly by detecting hardware. Detection circuitry eliminates the need to run the standby system in the synchronous and match mode of operation or the need to run the fault recognition program to identify the defective unit when a mismatch occurs.

The synchronous and match mode arrangement of the No. 1 Processor and the No. 2 Processor provides excellent detection and coverage of faults. However, there are many instances (for example, periodic diagnostics, administration changes, recent change updates, and so on) when the system is not run in the normal match mode. Consequently, during these periods, the system is vulnerable to faults that may go undetected. The rapid advances in integrated circuit technology make possible the implementation of self-checking circuits in a cost-effective manner. Self-checking circuits eliminate the need for the synchronous and match mode of operation.

Another new feature in switching system processor design is the application of the micro-program technique in the No. 3A [Storey, 1976]. This technique provides a regular procedure of implementing the control logic. Standard error detection is made part of the hardware to achieve a high degree of checkability. Sequential logic, which is difficult to check, is easily implemented as a sequence of microprogram steps. Microprogramming offers many attractive features: It is simple, flexible, easy to maintain, and easy to expand.

The No. 3A Processor paralleled the design of the No. 1A Processor in its use of an electrically alterable (writable) memory. However, great strides in semiconductor memory technology after the No. 1A became operational permitted the use of semiconductor memory, rather than the core memory, in the 3A.

The 3A's call store and program store are consolidated into a single store system. This consolidation reduces cost by eliminating buses, drivers, registers, and controls. A single store system no longer allows concurrent access of call store and program store. However, this disadvantage is more than compensated for by the much faster semiconductor memory. Its access time is 1 microsecond (the earlier PMT stores had an access time of 6 microseconds).

Normal operation requires the on-line processor to run and process calls while the standby processor is in the halt state, with its memory updated for each write operation. For the read operation, only the on-line memory is read, *except* when a parity error occurs during a memory read. A parity error results in a microprogram interrupt, which reads the word from the standby store in an attempt to bypass the error.

As discussed previously, the No. 2 Processor (first generation) is used in the 2ESS switch for medium-sized offices. It covers approximately 4,000 to 12,000 lines with a call handling capability of 19,000 busy-hour calls. (The number of calls is related to the calling rate of lines during the busy hour.) The microprogram technique used in the No. 3A Processor design allows the No. 2 Processor's instruction set to be emulated. This emulation enables programs written in the No. 2 assembly language to be directly portable to the No. 3A Processor. The ability to preserve the call processing programs permits the 2ESS system to be updated with the No. 3A Processor without having to undergo a complete new program development.

The combination of the No. 3A Processor and the peripheral equipment of the 2ESS system is designated as the 2B ESS switch. It is capable of handling 38,000 busy-hour calls, twice the capability of the 2ESS switch [Mandigo, 1976], and can be expanded to cover about 20,000 lines. Furthermore, when an existing 2ESS system in the field exceeds its real-time capacity, the No. 2 Processor can be taken out and replaced with the No. 3A Processor. The retrofit operation has been carried out successfully in working offices without disturbing telephone service.

Self-checking hardware has been integrated into the design to detect faults during normal system operation. This simplified fault recognition technique is required to identify a subsystem unit when it becomes defective. Reconfiguration into a working system is immediate, without extensive diagnostic programs to determine which subsystem unit contains the fault. The problem of synchronization, in a much shorter machine cycle (150 nanoseconds), is eliminated by not having to run both processors in step. The No. 3A Processor uses low-cost ICs to realize its highly reliable and flexible design.

General Systems Description. The general system block diagram of the No. 3A Processor is shown in Figure 8–12. The CC, the main store, and the cartridge tape unit are duplicated for reliability. These units are grouped as a single switchable entity rather than individual switchable units. The quantity of equipment within the switchable block is small enough to meet the reliability requirements; therefore, the expense and complexity of providing communication paths and control for switchable units within the system are avoided. Each functional unit was designed to be as autonomous as possible, with a minimum number of output signal leads. Such autonomy provides the flexibility necessary to expand the system and make changes easily.

As shown in Figure 8–12, the standard program store and call store are combined as a single storage unit to reduce cost. Although the processors are not run in the synchronous and match

FIGURE 8–12

No. 3A Processor organization

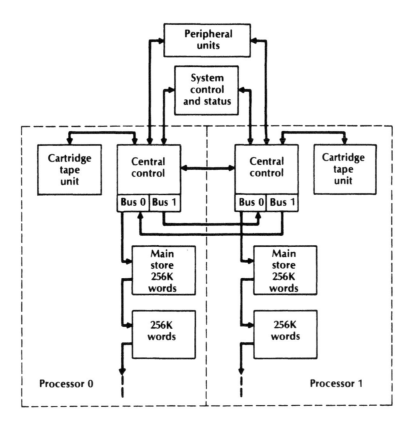

mode of operation, both stores (on-line and standby) are kept up to date by having the on-line processor write into both stores simultaneously when call store data are written or changed. Because of the volatile nature of a writable memory, low-cost bulk storage backup (cartridge tape) is required to reload the program and translation data when the data are lost due to a store failure. The pump-up mechanism, or store loader, uses the microprogram control in conjunction with an I/O serial channel to transfer data between the cartridge tape unit and the main store. Other deferrable, infrequently used programs (that is, diagnostics or growth programs) are stored on tape and paged in as needed.

The system control and status panel, a nonduplicated block, provides a common point for the display of overall system status and alarms. Included in this unit is the emergency action circuitry that allows the maintenance personnel to initialize the system or force and lock the system into a fixed configuration. Communication with the processor takes place via the I/O serial channel.

General Processor Description. Figure 8–13 shows a detailed block diagram of the CC. It is organized to process input data and handle call processing functions efficiently. The processor's design is based on the register type of architecture. Fast-access storage in the form of flip-flop registers provides short-term storage for information that is being used in current data processing operations. Sixteen general-purpose registers are provided as integral parts of the structure.

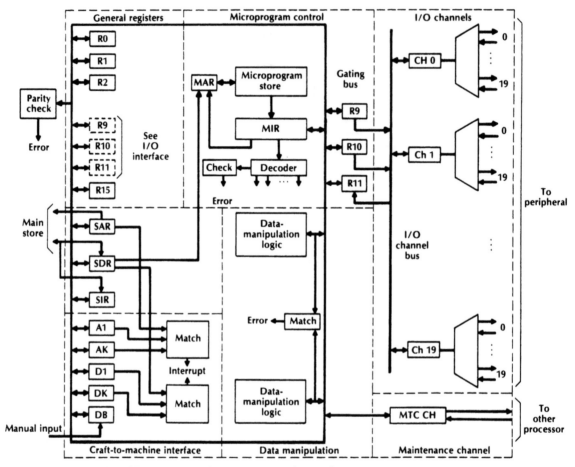

FIGURE 8–13 *No. 3A Processor's central control*

Microprogram control is the heart of the No. 3A Processor. It provides nearly all of the complex control and sequencing operations required for implementing the instruction set. Other complicated sequencing functions are also stored in the microprogram memory; for example, the bootstrap operation of reloading the program from the backup tape unit, the initializing sequence to restart the system under trouble conditions, the interrupt priority control and saving of essential registers, the emergency action timer and processor switching operation, and the craft-to-machine functions. The regular structure of the microprogram memory makes error detection easier. The microprogram method of implementation also offers flexibility in changing control functions.

The data manipulation instructions are designed specifically for implementing the call processing programs. These instructions are concerned with logical and bit manipulation rather than with arithmetical operations. However, a binary ADD is included in the instruction repertoire for adding two binary numbers and for indexing. This instruction allows other arithmetical operations to be implemented conveniently by the software combinations of addition and logical operations, or by a microprogram sequence if higher speed is essential. The data manipulation logic contains rotation, Boolean function of two variables, first zero detection, and fast binary ADD.

The remaining function blocks in Figure 8–13 deal with external interfaces. The 20 main I/O channels, each with 20 subchannels, allow the processor to control and access up to 400 peripheral units by means of 21-bit (16 data, 2 parity, and 3 start code bits) serial 6.67-MHz messages. The system is expandable in modules of one main channel (20 subchannels). The I/O structure allows up to 20 subchannels (one from each main channel) to be active simultaneously. In addition, the craft-to-machine interface, with displays and manual inputs, is integrated into the processor. This interface contains many of the manual functions that will assist in hardware and software debugging. The control logic associated with this part of the processor is incorporated as part of the microprogram control. Lastly, the maintenance channel enables the online processor to control and diagnose the standby processor. The use of a serial channel reduces the number of leads interconnecting the two processors and causes them to be loosely coupled. This loose coupling facilitates the split mode or stand-alone configuration for factory test or system test.

Hardware Implementation. Maintenance has been made an integral part of the 3A CC design. It uses the standard 1A ESS logic family with its associated packaging technology [Becker et al., 1977]. Up to 52 silicon integrated circuit chips (SICs), each containing from 4 to 10 logic gates, can be packed on a 3.25" × 4.00" 1A ceramic substrate. The substrate is mounted on a 3.67" × 7" circuit board with an 82-pin connector for backplane interconnections. In the 3A CC, the 53 1A logic circuit packs average about 44 SICs, resulting in an average of 308 gates per circuit pack, or a total of 16,482 gates. Figure 8–14 shows a detailed functional diagram of the 3A CC and the percentage of logic gates used in each function unit.

Another insight into how the gates are used in the 3A is shown in Figure 8–15. The figure shows the relationship between working gates, maintenance access gates, and self-checking logic. The working gates are the portion that contributes to the data processing functions, while the maintenance access gates provide the necessary access to make the CC maintainable (that is, maintenance channel and control panel). The self-checking gates are required to implement the parity bits, the check circuits, and the duplicate circuits that make the CC self-checking. As indicated, about 30 percent of the logic is used for checking. The design covers a high degree of component failures. It is estimated that about 90–95 percent of the faults would be detected by hardware error detection logic. Certain portions of the checkers, timers, and interrupt logic are not checked. These circuits are periodically exercised under program control to ensure that they are fault-free.

THIRD-GENERATION 3B20D PROCESSOR

The 3B20D Processor is the first designed for a broad range of AT&T applications. Its development is a natural outgrowth of the continuing need for high availability, real-time control of electronic switching systems for the telecommunications industry. The 3B20D architecture takes advantage of the increased efficiency and storage capabilities of the latest integrated-circuit technology to significantly reduce its maintenance and software development costs.

Figure 8–16 shows the trend of processors for AT&T switching systems for the past three decades. The first-generation processors, the No. 1 and the No. 2, were designed specifically for controlling large (several thousand to 65,000 lines) and medium (1,000–10,000 lines) telephone offices. The predominant cost of these systems, as in most early systems, was the cost of the hardware. The advent of silicon integrated circuits in the mid-1960s was the technological advance needed for dramatic performance improvements and cost reductions in hardware. Integrated circuits led to the development of the second generation of processors (the No. 1A and the No.

FIGURE 8–14
No. 3A Processor's CC gate count

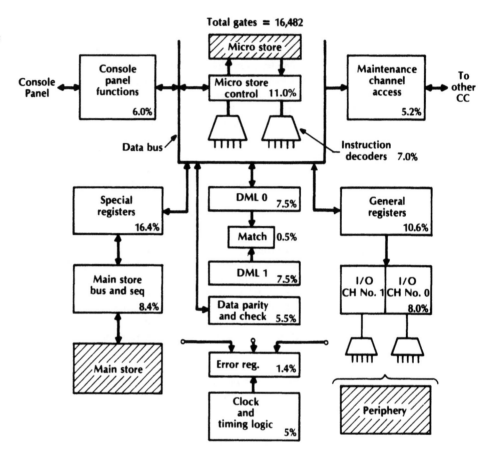

FIGURE 8–15
Logic gates in No. 3A Processor's CC (total gates = 16,482)

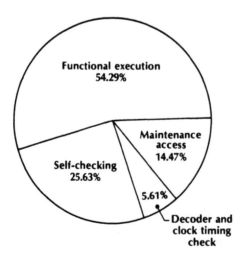

FIGURE 8–16
Processor trends for AT&T switching systems

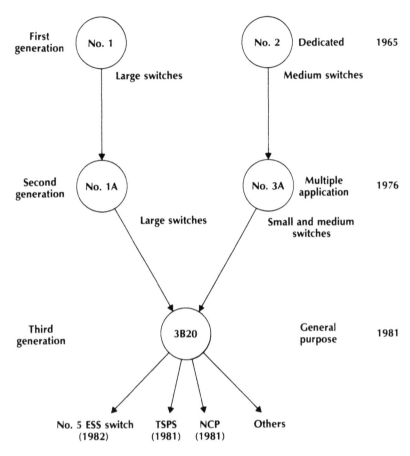

3A). These processors, unlike the first-generation machines, were designed for multiple applications; the third-generation machines have even greater capabilities.

The 3B20D Processor, the first member of the third generation, is a general-purpose system. Its versatile processing base fulfills the varied needs of telecommunications systems. Several thousand 3B20D sites are currently providing real-time data base processing for enhanced 800 service, network control point systems, high-capacity processors for the traffic service position system, the central processor in the administration module for the 5ESS systems, and support processors for the 1A ESS and 4ESS systems.

Overview of 3B20D Processor Architecture

The successful deployment and field operation of many electronic switching systems and processors (notably the No. 3A) have contributed to the design of the 3B20D. Previous systems have demonstrated the simplicity and robustness of duplex configurations in meeting stringent reliability requirements [Toy, 1978; Storey, 1976]. Hence, a duplex configuration forms the basic structure for both the hardware and software architecture for the 3B20D. The 3B20D processor also has a concurrent, self-checking design [Toy and Gallaher, 1983]. Extensive checking hardware is an integral part of the processor. Faults that occur during normal operation are quickly discovered by detection hardware. Self-checking eliminates the need for fault-recognition programs to identify the defective unit when a mismatch occurs; therefore, the standby processor is not required to run synchronously. System maintenance is simplified because reconfiguration into a working system is immediate. Another advantage of the self-checking design is that it permits more straightforward expansion from simplex to duplex or to multiple processor arrangements.

As opposed to the hardware-dominated costs of the first- and second-generation processors, the costs of the 3B20D, as is typical of current systems, are dominated by software design, updating, and maintenance expenditures. To reduce these costs as much as possible, the 3B20D supports a high-level language, a customized operating system, and software test facilities. By combining the software and hardware development efforts, an integrated and cost-effective system has evolved.

Figure 8–17 shows the general block diagram of the 3B20D Processor. The CC, the memory, and the I/O disk system are duplicated and grouped as a switchable entity, although each CC may access each disk system. The quantity of equipment within the switchable block is small enough to meet stringent reliability requirements, thus avoiding the need for complex recovery programs. Each CC has direct access to both disk systems; however, this capability mainly provides a valid data source for memory reloading under trouble conditions. The processors are not run in the synchronous and match mode of operations as is done in early systems. However, both stores (on-line and standby) are kept current by memory update hardware that acts concurrently

FIGURE 8–17
3B20D Processor general block diagram

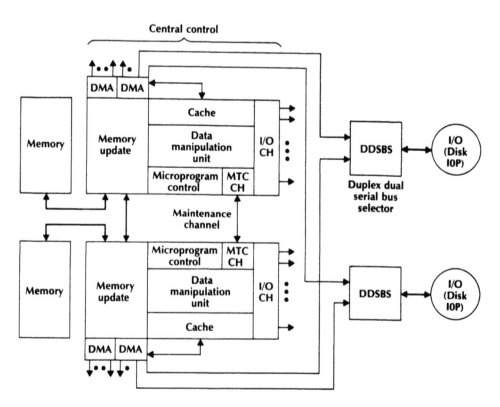

with instruction execution. When memory data is written by the CC, the on-line memory update circuit writes into both memories simultaneously. Under trouble conditions, the memory of the standby processor contains up-to-date information; complete transfer of memory from one processor to another is not necessary.

The direct memory access (DMA) circuits interface directly with the memory update circuit to have access to both memories. A DMA write also updates the standby memory. Communication between the DMA and the peripheral devices is accomplished by using a high-speed dual serial channel. The duplex dual serial bus selector allows both of the processors to access a single I/O device. For maintenance purposes, the duplex 3B20D CCs are interconnected by the maintenance channel. This high-speed serial path provides diagnostic access at the microcode level. It transmits streams of microinstructions from the on-line processor to exercise the standby processor. Other microinstructions from an external unit help diagnose problems.

The 3B20D Processor

The 3B20D Processor performs all the functions normally associated with a CPU and other functions, including duplex operation, efficient emulation of other machines, and communication with a flexible and intelligent periphery [Rolund, Beckett, and Harms, 1983]. The microprograms in the processor minimize the amount of hardware decoding and simplify the control structure. There is substantial flexibility in the choice of instruction formats that may be interpreted.

The CPU is a 32-bit machine with a 24-bit address scheme. Most of the data paths in the CC are 32 bits wide and have an additional 4 parity check bits. The CC architecture is based on registers; multiple buses allow concurrent data transfers. Separate I/O and store buses allow concurrent memory access and I/O operations. A block diagram of the central control is shown in Figure 8–18. These functions and subsystems control the CC and all interactions with it.

The microprogram control subsystem provides nearly all the complex control and sequencing operations required for implementing the instruction set. The microcode supports up to three different emulations in addition to its native instruction set. Other complicated sequencing functions are stored in the microinstruction store, or microstore. The microcontrol unit sequences the microstore and interprets each of its words to generate the control signals specified by the microinstruction. Execution time depends on the complexity of the microinstruction. Each microinstruction is allocated execution times of 150, 200, 250, and 300 nanoseconds. The wide 64-bit word allows a sufficient number of independent fields within the microinstruction to perform a number of simultaneous operations. Some frequently used instructions are implemented with a single microinstruction.

The data manipulation unit (DMU) contains the rotate mask unit (RMU) and the arithmetic logic unit (ALU), as shown in Figure 8–19. These units perform the arithmetic and logic operations of the system. The RMU rotates or shifts any number of bits from positions 0 through 31 through a two-stage, barrel-shift network. In addition, the RMU performs AND or OR operations on bits, nibbles, bytes, half words, full words, and miscellaneous predefined patterns. The RMU outputs go directly into the ALU. The ability of the RMU to manipulate and process any bit fields within a word greatly enhances the power of the microcode.

The other component of the DMU is the ALU, which is implemented using AMD Company's 2901 ALU slices. The 2901s are bipolar 4-bit ALUs (see Figure 8–20) [AMD, 1979]. Eight 2901 chips provide two key elements: the 2-port, 16-word RAM and the high-speed ALU. Data in any of the 16 words addressed by the 4-bit A-address input can be used as an operand to the ALU. Similarly, data in any of the 16 words defined by the 4-bit B-address input can be simultaneously read and used as a second operand to the ALU. Because the internal 16-word RAM is dedicated as general

FIGURE 8–18
3B20D Processor's central control

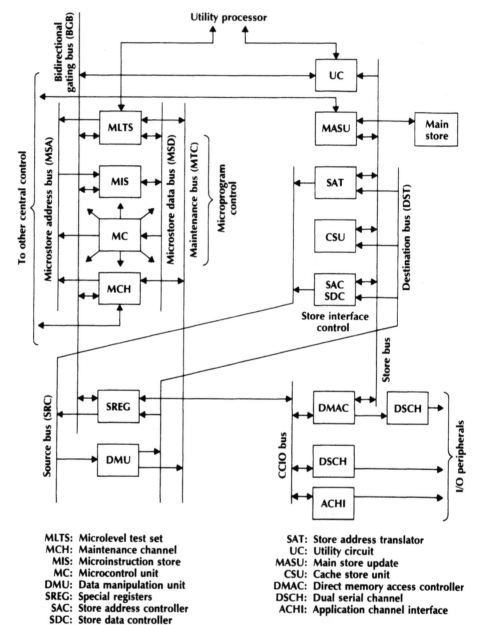

MLTS: Microlevel test set
MCH: Maintenance channel
MIS: Microinstruction store
MC: Microcontrol unit
DMU: Data manipulation unit
SREG: Special registers
SAC: Store address controller
SDC: Store data controller

SAT: Store address translator
UC: Utility circuit
MASU: Main store update
CSU: Cache store unit
DMAC: Direct memory access controller
DSCH: Dual serial channel
ACHI: Application channel interface

FIGURE 8–19

3B20D Processor's data manipulation unit

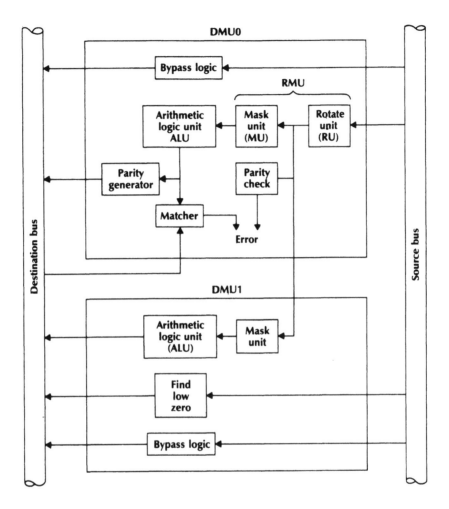

FIGURE 8–19

3B20D Processor's data manipulation unit

registers, the result can be directed to the RAM word specified by the B-address, thus optimizing the performance speed of the arithmetic and logical operations involving general registers and the output of the RMU.

The logic blocks of Figure 8–19 depict the self-checking capability of the RMU and ALU. The first-stage byte rotate unit of the RMU is checked for byte parity, which it preserves; the mask unit, including the second-stage bit rotate, is checked by duplication. The ALU is also checked by duplication. The data is taken from one ALU, and parity is generated from the other. The data from one ALU is also matched with that from the duplicate. The underlying self-checking strategy, illustrated here and used throughout the CPU, is to use parity checking where parity is preserved and duplication of logic where parity is not preserved.

The special registers (SREG) associated with the operation of the CC are external to the DMU, unlike the 16 general registers inside the DMU that are available to the programmer. Most of the special registers are not explicitly specified by the 3B20D instruction set. They are characterized by their special dedicated functions and receive their inputs from sources other than

FIGURE 8–20
AMD's 2901 internal architecture

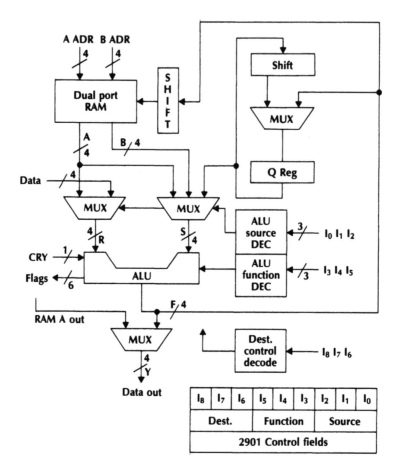

the internal data bus. They control and direct the operation of the processor. Some of the special registers are (1) error register, (2) program status word, (3) hardware status register, (4) system status register, (5) interrupt register, and (6) timers. In addition to these registers, a 32-word RAM that is available only at the microcode level is provided within the SREG block. It is used for scratch-pad space, and it is preassigned registers, such as those that support memory management, to facilitate and enhance the power of microprogram sequences.

The *store interface circuit* controls the transfer of data and instructions from system memory to the CC. Two controls, the store address control and the store data control, handle memory addressing, update the program counter, and fetch instructions. Associated with the SAC are the program address, the store address register, and the store control register. Associated with the store data control are the store data register, the store instruction register, and the instruction buffer. These circuits ensure a continuous flow of instructions to the microcontrol unit.

Memory mapping is required in the implementation of a virtual address multiprogramming system. The store address translation (SAT) facility is the mechanism that provides memory mapping between a program-specific virtual address and its corresponding physical address.

Address translation hardware is included in the SAT by the address translation buffer to facilitate memory management [Hetherington and Kusulas, 1983].

The cache store unit is an optional circuit that improves overall system performance by reducing the effective memory access time. The cache is a four-way, set-associated memory containing 8K bytes.

The main store update unit provides a multiport interface to the memories as both DMA and CC circuit attempt to use the memory. The update circuit arbitrates asynchronous requests from the on-line CC and the on-line DMA. The cross-coupling between the memory update units permits the on-line CPU to access either memory, or both memories, for concurrent write operations.

The main store uses dynamic memory devices and high-speed, TTL-compatible, gate-array integrated circuits. It consists of a single circuit board main store controller and up to 16 mega-bytes may be equipped within the central control frame. Throughout the central control, byte parity is maintained over each byte of the data word. By adding four error-correction code bits in a modified form of Hamming code (in addition to the byte parity bits), the main store performs single-bit error correction and double-bit error detection.

Input/output interfacing is done in several ways in the CC. The communication path between the CC and the I/O channels is through the central control input/output (CCIO) bus, which is a local, high-speed, direct-coupled, parallel bus. Direct memory access between the main store and peripheral units is provided by a direct memory access controller (DMAC) that communicates with intelligent peripheral units via dual serial channels (DSCHs). I/O channels, including user-specific interfaces, can be connected directly to the CC by means of the CCIO bus. Two standard interfaces are the DSCH, a high-speed, multiport serial interface, and the application channel interface (ACHI). The ACHI is a high-throughput, parallel bus, peripheral communication path.

The maintenance channel circuit provides diagnostic access to the CC at the microinstruction level. It also controls basic fault recovery and system sanity functions in the off-line processor.

Craft Interface

The maintenance interface is commonly referred to as the craft interface [Barton and Schmitt, 1983] in the telecommunications industry. The craft interface of the 3B20D is markedly different from previous systems developed at Bell Laboratories because it relies almost exclusively on video displays and keyboard controls. The earlier systems have key-lamp panels and teletypewriters in their master control centers.

The craft interface includes hardware, firmware, and software that enable maintenance personnel to obtain the status of, and exert control over, the system. Status information is presented visually as graphical displays and text messages on various terminals and printers; audible alarm circuits can also be connected to the 3B20D. System control is exerted primarily through a keyboard attached to the video display terminal. System control is also possible from remote locations, called switching control centers. The data links to the remote sites use the international standard message protocol (X.25) because of its low vulnerability to noise and other data communication failures. The adoption of the X.25 message protocol standardizes remote access to the 3B20D processor for packet switching networks.

Figure 8–21 is a functional block diagram of the craft interface. Each of the duplex processors is connected to both input/output processors (IOPs), which, as mentioned previously, support up to 16 peripheral controllers. The IOP software driver contains handlers that deal with the specialized functions of the peripheral controllers. Maintenance personnel use the read-only

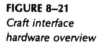

FIGURE 8–21
*Craft interface
hardware overview*

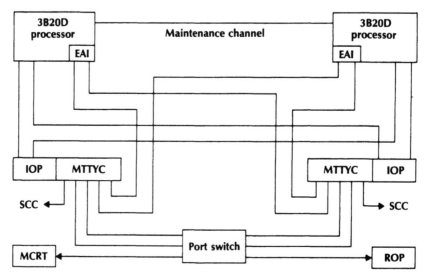

printer (ROP) and the maintenance CRT (MCRT). The ROP logs all important status messages. The MCRT is a keyboard display terminal. The system contains only one ROP and one MCRT because the port switch keeps the ROP and the MCRT connected to the active on-line processor.

All capabilities of the craft interface are accessible from a remote switching control center by means of a dedicated data link. The data link is duplicated; it includes a primary link and a backup link. Both links use the CCITT X.25 communication protocol. The MCRT, ROP, and X.25 links are attached to a peripheral controller known as the maintenance teletype controller (MTTYC). The craft interface handler controls the transfer of data to and from the peripheral devices associated with the MTTYC. The MTTYC is connected directly to the emergency action interface (EAI) in the central processor. The EAI menu on the MCRT gives basic status information and manual control of the processor regardless of DMERT (operating system, see the following section) software sanity; this access is controlled totally by the firmware in the MTTYC. This reliable, high-capacity data link for remote maintenance makes the 3B20D well suited for unattended operation.

DMERT: The UNIX RTR Operating System

The operating system used in the 3B20D is the duplex multi-environment real-time (DMERT) operating system, which is now called the UNIX RTR operating system [Kane, Anderson, and McCabe, 1983; Grzelakowski, Campbell, and Dubman, 1983]. It has a process-oriented structure that emphasizes high data availability. It is designed for both real-time and time-shared operations. The basic architecture of the DMERT operating system is based on an earlier system named MERT [Lycklama and Bayer, 1978] and the UNIX operating system [Ritchie and Thompson, 1978]. Both the UNIX and the MERT operating systems were developed to execute on commercial equipment. Currently, the UNIX operating system is widely used, and the MERT operating system has been replaced by its duplex successor, the DMERT operating system. Experience gained from the operating system of the earlier No. 3A Processor, a real-time monitor known as the extended operating system (EOS) [Elmendorf, 1980], also benefited the designers of the DMERT system.

The DMERT operating system has a sophisticated architecture that draws on the proven design concepts of the EOS, MERT, and UNIX operating systems (see Figure 8–22).

Application programmers may add code at the kernel process, supervisor process, and user levels. The multilevel structure makes the DMERT operating system flexible and efficient in its use of real time. The structure of the virtual machines permits the management of both real-time applications and time-shared background tasks. For example, Figure 8–23 shows how telephone switching software is allocated to the different levels. The operating system maintains a process hierarchy based on 16 execution levels. Time-critical functions such as the I/O drivers, fault recovery, and call processing are implemented at the kernel process level. A kernel process may belong to levels 3 through 15 (levels 0 through 2 are reserved for the time-sharing environment). By means of this hierarchical execution-level structure, applications are able to customize their control and distribution of real time.

The portion of real time that is not used by the kernel or kernel processes is time shared among supervisor and user processes. Deferrable jobs such as traffic reports, recent changes, and diagnostics are implemented at the highest user level. Processes supporting the time-sharing environment are run at execution level 2. These processes are run just beneath the real-time hierarchy; they gain control of the processor only after all the real-time work is completed. By supporting both real-time and time-sharing environments, the DMERT operating system makes efficient use of its physical resources.

Fault Recovery

When any of the unique fault detection circuits detects an error condition, an error interrupt (or error report in the case of certain peripherals) is registered in the processor. The most severe error interrupts result in automatic hardware sequences that switch the processing activity between the processors (hard switch). Less severe errors result in micro-interrupts that activate the microcode and software to recover the system. This layered approach that constitutes the recovery

FIGURE 8–22
Bases of DMERT architecture

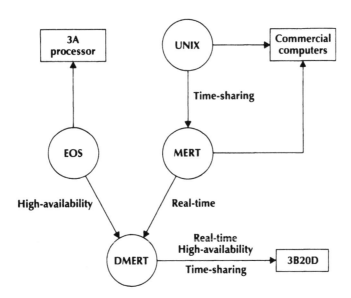

FIGURE 8–23
Example of DMERT multi-environment structure

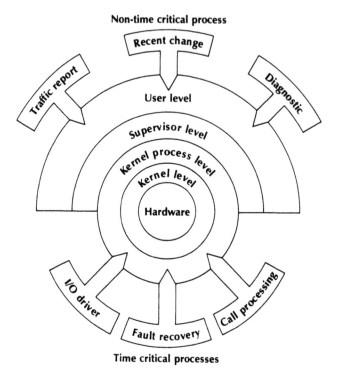

architecture is depicted in Figure 8–24 [Hansen, Peterson, and Whittington, 1983]. Microcode provides low-level access to the hardware, and the recovery software provides the high-level control mechanisms and decision making.

Figure 8–25 illustrates the principal architecture and features of the recovery software. The bootstrap and initialization routines contain a fundamental set of microcode and software algorithms that control initializations and recoveries. These actions are stimulated by a maintenance restart function (MRF), which represents the highest-priority microinterrupt in the system. An MRF sequence may be stimulated from either hardware or software recovery sources.

The fault recovery and system integrity packages control fault detection and recovery for hardware and software, respectively. The error interrupt handler is the principal hardware fault recovery controller. It receives all hardware interrupts and controls the recovery sequences that follow. The configuration management program (CONFIG) determines whether an error is exceeding the predetermined frequency thresholds. If a threshold is exceeded, CONFIG requests a change in the configuration of the processor to a healthy state. Thus, CONFIG serves as an error-rate analysis package for both hardware and software errors.

Hardware Fault Recovery. The 3B20D Processor has built in self-checking circuitry that detects hardware faults as soon as they occur. This circuitry simplifies recovery, since early detection limits the damage done by the fault. Faults in this category indicate that the processor is no longer capable of proper operation and result in an immediate termination of the currently running processor and a switch to the standby processor. Since the standby processor does not

FIGURE 8–24
Recovery software structure

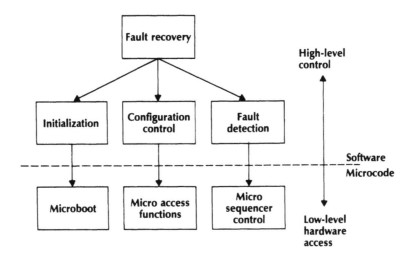

FIGURE 8–25
Fault recovery architecture

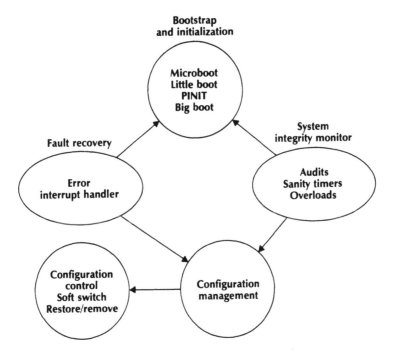

match the active processor instruction by instruction, an initialization sequence is required to start execution properly.

Some types of faults and errors are not severe enough to justify an immediate termination and switch of the processors. Examples of errors of this kind are hardware faults detected in the standby processor memory and software errors such as write-protection violations. Other errors in this category are the hardware faults that are handled by the self-correcting circuitry. Although most units have self-checking circuits, some units (such as main memories) have fault rates that justify the addition of self-correcting capabilities. Disks also are self-correcting through the use of cyclic redundancy codes. All errors in this class are reported to the recovery system as error interrupts.

All error interrupts are reported to CONFIG. Errors are logged against the failing unit, and error rates are compared to allowed error thresholds. If the affected threshold is exceeded, further action is required based on several factors, including the importance of the faulty unit and whether a mate exists for it. If the faulty unit is essential to the system and a mate unit is available, the faulty unit is removed from service and scheduled for diagnostic testing. If there is no available mate unit, the faulty unit is initialized and returned to service until the mate is restored. When the mate is restored, it is switched on line and the faulty unit is scheduled for diagnostic testing. In the case of essential units, it is better to have a faulty unit than no unit. Unessential units are removed from service and scheduled for diagnostic testing whenever their error thresholds are exceeded.

Each processor has a sanity timer that causes an initialization if it expires. The active processor maintains both its own timer and the timer of the standby unit. If the active processor cannot recover from a fault, the sanity timer triggers the initialization of the standby processor.

Special Microcode for Recovery. A large fraction of the microcode in the central control handles system recoveries. Most of this recovery microcode is in ROM because most of the recovery functions are required, regardless of the past history of the CC or its boot devices. Functions that are required even if the CC is not ready to execute its instruction set include microinterrupt processing, maintenance channel assists, and microcode to initialize hardware systems.

Microinterrupt processing handles errors in the address translation buffer to micro-instruction store sequence. Maintenance channel assists allow one processor to access the other processor. Microcode initializes the hardware systems; additional recovery microcode that resides in writable microstore (WMS) extends the processor's instruction set to provide convenient diagnostic and recovery software access instructions. When diagnostic performance requirements do not justify a special instruction, a microstore scratch area is made available. Arbitrary microsequences loaded into the scratch area are then executed as special tests or functions. Before the software can run, however, the WMS must be loaded from disk. The WMS is loaded as part of the processing of the MRF microinterrupt.

Software Fault Recovery. Software fault recovery is architecturally similar to hardware fault recovery. Each major unit of software has associated with it error detection mechanisms (defensive checks and audits), error thresholds, and error recovery mechanisms (failure returns, audits, and data correction and initialization techniques). Both the system integrity monitor (SIM) and the error interrupt handler (EIH) oversee the proper execution of the process. An error threshold in SIM ensures that a process does not put itself into an infinite execution loop or excessively consume a system resource (for example, message buffers). The EIH, through the use of hardware and microcode detectors, ensures that processes do not try to access memory outside defined limits or execute restricted instructions. Each process has initialization and recovery controls (analogous to hardware) to effect recoveries. Figure 8–26 illustrates this software recovery architecture.

If recovery actions result in the removal of hardware units, diagnostics are dispatched automatically to analyze the specific problem. Audits are the software counterparts for hardware diagnostics; the major difference is that routine audits run more frequently than diagnostics, and they correct certain errors.

Software Audits. The DMERT audit package verifies the validity of critical data structures. Most audits exist throughout the system within the processes that control the data to be audited. In some cases, several audits are invoked consecutively to form a sequenced mode audit. Most requests for running audits come from an audit control structure, the audit manager.

Audits in the DMERT operating system verify data, not functions. The basic types of auditable data are system resources and stable data. Though most of the auditable data in the operating system reside in the kernel, additional data reside in critical processes such as the file manager and device drivers. Smaller amounts of auditable data reside in supervisor processes, such as the UNIX operating system and the process manager.

Some audits, scheduled on a regular basis, are known as routine audits; others, scheduled on request, are known as demand audits. Audits within the DMERT operating system include the following:

• The *message buffers audit* finds and frees lost message buffers; that is, messages that have been on the queue of a process for extended periods of time.

FIGURE 8–26
Software fault re-
covery architecture

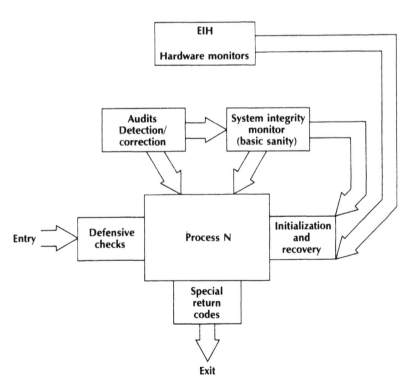

- The *scheduler audit* checks for linkage errors in the ready and not-ready lists of the scheduler.
- The *memory manager audit* recovers lost swap space and corrects any overlap of swap space.
- The *file manager audit* checks all internal file manager structures, including task blocks, buffers, and the mount table. It corrects the information and can back out aborted tasks to free their resources.
- The *file system audit* is demanded by the file manager whenever a file system is mounted in the read/write mode. It checks and corrects the file system's super block, free list and its free-block bit map. The audit verifies the integrity of the mounted file systems concurrent with their use.

System Initialization. When a maintenance restart interrupt occurs, a long sequence of microsteps begins to establish system sanity. Both processors may be in their maintenance restart function (MRF) sequence at the same time, and each may try to become the active processor. The MRF code decides which processor should become active and whether to do an off-line initialization or an on-line initialization. If a processor determines that it has just powered up, it clears main store and does an off-line initialization unless it is forced on line by an operator command.

A number of tests are made on data in the operating status register to select one of four possible actions: (1) processor initialization, (2) stop and switch, (3) microboot, or (4) tapeboot. The simplest actions are initializing a processor and stopping and switching to the other processor. Switching to another processor is accomplished by sending a switch command over the maintenance channel to the other processor. If an initialization does not recover the system to an operational state, another and more severe initialization is triggered automatically. The initialization interval determines whether escalating is necessary. Any initialization that occurs within the initialization interval (that is, within a specified time interval after an initialization) escalates to the next higher level. The length of the initialization interval is a system generation parameter that is established by the application.

The *microboot program* uses information on the DMERT disk to initialize the writable microstore and read in the first software boot program, called "little boot." To do this, it must first select the disk drive to use as the boot device. If the craft interface has forced either the primary or the secondary boot device active, it uses that device. Otherwise, the microboot program selects a disk drive based on the state of the initialization status control bits in the system status register. Alternate boots use alternate devices. Microcode is read from the disk and then copied to the writable microstore. Finally, the little boot program is read from the boot partition and given control.

The *tapeboot program* is a complex sequence of microcode that is used only when requested manually from the craft interface. Its function is to create a new system disk from tape. Tapeboot initializes the tape device and disk drive selected by the craft interface and initializes the writable microstore from tape. The load disk tape program is read from tape into main store; memory management tables are created to allow it to run the hardware complex without the operating system present. The load disk tape program then reads the tape to make a DMERT disk image.

Emergency Mode. The emergency mode on the 3B20D refers to the facilities and procedures that prevent the system from experiencing a total outage. For example, emergency facilities are applied when the system is unable to recover automatically. The most frequent emergencies encountered include duplex failures of the control unit, duplex failures of the system disks, duplex failures of the essential I/O devices, and failures of fault recovery to find a working configuration of the hardware. Other problems that require the emergency mode include software faults that do not allow the system to operate properly, errors that destroy the integrity of the disks, and software overwrites that introduce catastrophic errors into the software.

Emergency mode capabilities are built into the system to address problems that may cause the failure of the 3B20D as a system. The emergency action interface (EAI) on the 3B20D provides manual initialization capabilities that can recover the system from several of the conditions mentioned above. The EAI allows the maintenance personnel to demand a specific processor and disk configuration if a certain configuration is causing problems. The EAI also allows the craft to reconfigure the system to handle maintenance hardware failures. For example, the craft may inhibit error sources and sanity timers through EAI commands, thus allowing recovery from certain maintenance failures even though both processors are affected. The EAI also provides capabilities for craft initializations to deal with the loss of subsystem capabilities.

The 3B20D provides other emergency mode capabilities through the port switch select, the disk power inverter select, and the unit power switches. These devices are used by maintenance personnel to reconfigure the system manually to handle certain problems. Under unstable boot-strap conditions, the 3B20D outputs diagnostics information called *processor recovery messages*. These messages provide a general set of diagnostics in the event of a complete system outage.

The final backup repair procedure consists of the dead start diagnostics. Primarily used as installation tools, the dead start diagnostics allow a nonworking processor to be repaired from a remote host processor.

Fault Diagnostics

As with earlier processor designs, 3B20D processor diagnostics detect faults efficiently and effectively, provide consistent test results, protect the contents of memory, do not interfere with normal system operation, allow automatic trouble location, and are easy to maintain and update. To meet these design objectives, the diagnostic control structure is an integral part of the DMERT operating system and supports the evolutionary stages of development [Quinn and Goetz, 1983].

Diagnostic Environments. As shown in Figure 8–27, the 3B20D Processor may be diagnosed from several execution environments. During the early phase of its development, a local host computer was used to support hardware, software, and diagnostic design. This arrangement continues to be used in factory testing. Later in the development phase, more efficient use was made of the host computer by providing access to a remote 3B20D Processor over a dial-up telephone line. In the final development stage (the standard duplex system configuration), the active control unit was capable of diagnosing its own peripheral controllers and the standby control unit. Each of these access arrangements is discussed below.

Figure 8–27a shows three local host access arrangements. In the first arrangement, diagnostic programs executing in a host computer send test inputs and receive test results through a standard communication port to a microlevel test set (MLTS). The MLTS connects directly to the 3B20D control unit backplane and provides complete access to and control of the processor's microprogram control circuitry. The second access arrangement uses a circuit designed to simulate the central control input/output (CCIO) internal bus. The CCIO bus simulator (BS) is accessible using a standard communication input port. A dual serial channel (DSCH) connected to the CCIO/BS can then communicate directly with a maintenance channel (MCH), the circuit designed for control unit access. Like the MLTS, the MCH can access the central control at a low level. Only the MCH, however, is used in the duplex configuration; it communicates with either another MCH or a DSCH. As shown, the CCIO/BS-DSCH access path is also used to diagnose the IOP and the disk file controller (DFC). The third access arrangement is used when the local host is a 3B20D processor. The path in this case is from the DSCH of the host processor to the MCH, IOP, or DFC of the target machine.

The DSCH communicates over distances of approximately 100 feet. Remote host (Figure

FIGURE 8–27
3B20D Processor's diagnostic environments

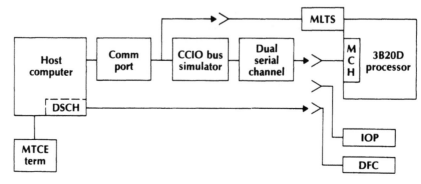

a. Local host

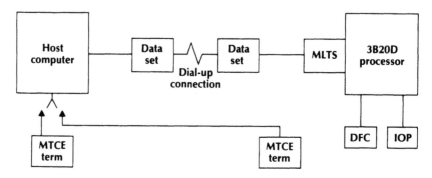

b. Remote host

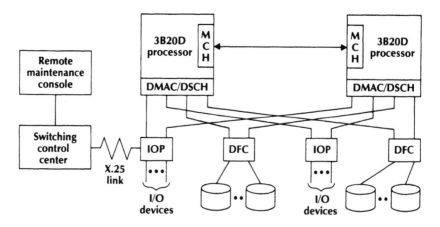

c. Duplex mode

8–27b) access arrangements are used for diagnosing over longer distances. Using data sets and a telephone line, tests stored and executed on a remote computer are applied through the MLTS to the control unit. Peripheral controllers (IOP and DFC) may also be diagnosed by downloading tests into the control unit and executing them. Although remote host diagnostics are useful when a local host is unavailable, execution performance is limited by the transmission facilities used.

The primary diagnostic execution environment is the duplex mode of the 3B20D (Figure 8–27c). The active (on-line) processor acts as a local host for diagnosing the standby (off-line) processor. A link between maintenance channels provides the access path for testing the control unit. In the duplex mode, the DFC and IOPC are diagnosed from the on-line control unit using the operational interface path, which is a DSCH attached to the direct memory access controller. Tests of the links from the off-line processor to the peripherals may also be run under the control of the active processor. As shown in Figure 8–27c, the duplex system configuration also supports remote monitoring and control of diagnostics over a dedicated link to a switching control center.

Diagnostic Control Structure. The diagnostic control structure is depicted in Figure 8–28. The modules that provide access to the equipment configuration data base (ECD) are at the kernel

FIGURE 8–28
Diagnostic control structure

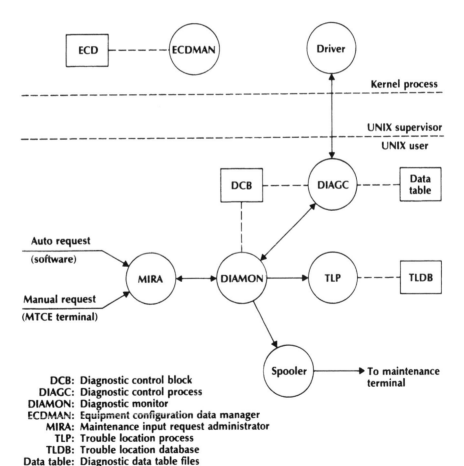

DCB: Diagnostic control block
DIAGC: Diagnostic control process
DIAMON: Diagnostic monitor
ECDMAN: Equipment configuration data manager
MIRA: Maintenance input request administrator
TLP: Trouble location process
TLDB: Trouble location database
Data table: Diagnostic data table files

process level. All the information relevant to the diagnostic tests that should be applied to each hardware unit is contained in the ECD. This information includes the name of each hardware unit; its subsystem, subunits, and their logical interconnections; equipage options; and auxiliary information such as channel address and baud rate. Whenever a circuit design is originated or updated, diagnostic tests are designed and appropriate ECD changes are made.

The UNIX operating system supervisor resides at the supervisor level and provides a protected environment and operating system service for the higher-level processes. The modules operating under the UNIX operating system that pertain exclusively to diagnostics are the maintenance input request administrator (MIRA), the diagnostic monitor (DIAMON), the diagnostic control process (DIAGC), and the trouble-locating process (TLP). Output messages from the diagnostic structure are sent to the system spooler for printing.

The MIRA schedules and dispatches all the maintenance requests. MIRA has two queues, a waiting queue and an active queue, to administer maintenance requests. Requests are serviced according to their priorities and the availability of resources. Manual requests have higher priorities than requests initiated automatically. For each service request, MIRA creates a DIAMON process and sends it a message. When the request is completed, DIAMON sends a message back to MIRA. Interfaces are provided in MIRA to administer routine exercise requests and inputs from the error interrupt handler (EIH). Execution of each diagnostic is directed from start to finish by DIAMON.

DIAGC is a generic name that refers to a class of diagnostic control processes. The DIAGC is a unit or application-dependent module that controls the execution of tests. DIAGC contains all the application-dependent task routines, translates the interpretive diagnostics, and provides the interface with DIAMON. A unit's diagnostic phase table (DPT) contains the name of a particular DIAGC process to be used in the diagnosis. DIAMON imposes no limit on the number of processes that may interface with it.

If the diagnostic request specifies the TLP option, the trouble-locating process is invoked after the diagnostic testing is completed. The TLP compares characteristics of the failures found by the diagnostics with a resident data base of fault signatures. In each data table, the tests are partitioned into groups. A test failure in a group sets a flag bit, called a key, which is permanently assigned to the group. The TLP searches the results of the diagnostics and, based on the phase and key information, creates an ordered list of the closest signatures and, ultimately, of the suspected faulty equipment. This approach makes the data base and sorting processes less sensitive than earlier methods of testing changes to circuits and marginal failures. During the development of the 3B20D, the trouble-locating data base (TLDB) was generated by physically inserting faults into units in a test laboratory. The TLDB of operational systems can be modified directly by inserting information into the test data table.

Diagnostic Features. The combination of hardware access circuits and modular control programs just discussed provides the 3B20D Processor with considerable maintenance flexibility. Tests are selected according to the type of circuit under diagnosis. Requests may diagnose an entire unit, a particular subunit, or all the subunits in a specified community. Individual test phases or ranges of phases may be executed and the results printed with optional amounts of detail. Some diagnostic test phases, because of their long execution time requirements or their dependence on the availability of other system hardware resources, are restricted to manual initializations. Interactive features, such as stepping, pausing, and looping, facilitate difficult repairs. Units are restored to service automatically if they pass all tests. Several host computer versions of the software are supported, along with application-dependent interfaces.

Diagnostics are initiated manually or automatically. Manual requests may be entered from a local maintenance terminal or through a work station at a switching control center that is connected to the processor with a synchronous data link. Automatic requests originate from other software modules, including the error interrupt handler, the routine exercise scheduler, and the application software modules.

Evaluation. The stringent availability requirements of AT&T applications using the 3B20D Processors have a significant effect on all the aspects of the system design. The diagnostic and maintenance designers were actively involved in meeting these requirements from the initial architectural planning and requirements generation. Many hardware features monitor system integrity, detect errors, reconfigure the system, and facilitate repairs. Although some of the features isolate faults during pack repairs, most are used at the system level to effect repairs through circuit pack replacement. Diagnostics, the primary repair capability for the system, makes extensive use of these hardware features for control and observation of the circuitry.

During the development of the processor, diagnostic tests were generated manually and with the aid of hardware logic simulators. To ensure that the diagnostics met the objective of detecting 90 percent of the simulated faults, an extensive evaluation process was carried out. Thousands of faults were inserted at the dual-in-line (DIP) package terminals (pins). These faults provided timely and effective feedback on the design of the diagnostic tests and the development of the trouble-locating data base.

Operational Results of 3B20D Processor

The 3B20D Processors have been in commercial operation since September, 1981. The performance of the 3B20D improved tremendously during the first two years of operation. Figure 8–29 shows the results of field data accumulated over many machine operating hours during early

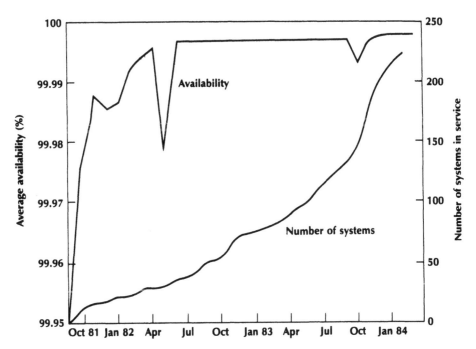

FIGURE 8–29
Observed availability and number in service of 3B20D Processors

years of operations [Wallace and Barnes, 1983]. When the first system began commercial service, outages occurred because of software and hardware faults that could only be corrected with field experience. The availability factor improved as the processor design matured and the operating personnel gained experience.

Figure 8–30 shows downtime data for three AT&T processors, including the 3B20D. The experience gained in the design and field operation of earlier electronic switching systems (notably the No. 1A and the No. 3A Processors) has contributed to the design of the 3B20D. The reliability (downtime) curves show that each processor approached its downtime objective more quickly than its predecessor [Wallace and Barnes, 1983]. The data has been smoothed and fit to an exponential decay function for the comparison.

SUMMARY

In order to achieve the reliability requirements, all AT&T switch subsystem units are duplicated. When a hardware failure occurs in any of the subunits, the processor is reconfigured into a working system around the defective unit. The partitioning of subsystem units into switching blocks varies with the size of the processor. For the medium- or small-sized processors, such as the No. 2 or the No. 3, the central control, the main memory, the bulk memory, and the store bus are grouped as a single switchable entity. A failure in one of the subunits is considered a failure in the switchable block. Since the number of components within a switchable block is sufficiently small, this type of single-unit duplex configuration meets the reliability requirement. For larger processors, such as the No. 1 or the No. 1A, the central control, the program store, the call store, the store buses, and the bulk file store are treated individually as switchable blocks.

FIGURE 8–30
Downtime versus time since introduction for three high-availability processors

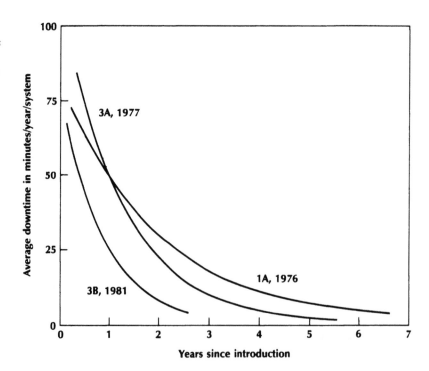

This multi-unit duplex configuration allows a considerable number of combinations in which a working system can be assembled. The system is down only when two simultaneous failures occur, one in the subunit and the other in the duplicate subunit. A greater fault tolerance is possible with this configuration. This type of configuration is necessary for the large processor because each subunit contains a larger number of components.

The first generation of processors, which includes the No. 1 and the No. 2, have provided commercial service since 1965 and 1969, respectively. The No. 1 Processor serves large telephone offices (metropolitan); the No. 2 Processor is used in medium-sized offices (suburban). Their reliability requirements are the same. Both processors depend on integrated maintenance software, with hardware that must (1) quickly detect a system failure condition, (2) isolate and configure a working system around the faulty subunit, (3) diagnose the faulty unit, and (4) assist the maintenance personnel in repairing the unit. The primary detection technique is the synchronous and match mode of operation of both central controls. Matching is done more extensively in the No. 1 than in the No. 2, since cost is one of major considerations in the design of the No. 2 Processor. In addition to matching, coding techniques, diagnostic access, and other check logic have been incorporated into the basic design of these processors to realize the reliability objectives.

The widespread acceptance of the 1ESS and 2ESS switching systems has created the need for a second generation of processors: the No. 1A and the No. 3A. They offer greater capability and are also more cost effective. Both processors use the same integrated circuit technology. The 1A Processor extends its performance range by a factor of 4 to 8 times over the No. 1 Processor by using faster logic and faster memory. The 1A design takes advantage of the experience gained in the design and operation of the No. 1 Processor. The No. 1A Processor provides considerably more hardware for error detection and more extensive matching of a large number of internal nodes within the central control. The design of the No. 3A Processor has benefited by the experience gained from the No. 2 Processor. A major departure in the design of the 3A Processor from the design of earlier processors is the nonsynchronous and the nonmatch mode of operation. The No. 3A Processor uses self-checking as the primary means of error detection. Another departure is in the design of the No. 3A Processor's control section: It is microprogrammed. The No. 3A Processor's flexibility permits emulation of the No. 2 Processor quite easily.

The third-generation systems are dominated by software design, updating, and maintenance expenditures. The 3B20D Processor is a general-purpose, high-availability machine that supports many types of applications. A comprehensive set of software tools and facilities improves programming productivity and reduces the cost of software development and maintenance. The hardware architecture efficiently supports high-level languages, particularly the C language. The UNIX RTR operating system was designed concurrently with the hardware to meet the needs of switching and telecommunication systems. Its architecture permits time-critical, real-time code to coexist with time-shared background tasks. An important provision in the 3B20D Processor is a complete set of maintenance facilities, from error detection through fault recovery and diagnostics. Approximately 30 percent of the internal control logic is devoted to self-checking. Self-checking allows concurrent error detection and immediate recovery. In March, 1988, over 1000 5ESS systems and more than 20 million telephone lines were in commercial use, serving the smallest remote switching module of hundreds of lines to the largest office of 85,000 lines with high-quality services.

REFERENCES AMD, 1979; Ault et al., 1964, 1977; Barton and Schmitt, 1983; Becker et al., 1977; Beuscher et al., 1969; Bowman et al., 1977; Browne et al., 1969; Budlong et al., 1977; Cagle et al., 1964; Chang, Smith, and Walford, 1974.

Downing, Nowak and Tuomenoksa, 1964; Elmendorf, 1980; Genke, Harding, and Staehler, 1964; Goetz, 1974; Grzelakowski, Campbell, and Dubman, 1983; Hansen, Peterson, and Whittington, 1983; Harr, Taylor, and Ulrich, 1969; Hetherington and Kusulas, 1983.

Irland and Stagg, 1974; Kane, Anderson, and McCabe, 1983; Keister, Ketchledge, and Lovell, 1960; Keister, Ketchledge, and Vaughan, 1964; Lycklama and Bayer, 1978; Mandigo, 1976; Quinn and Goetz, 1983; Ritchie and Thompson, 1978; Rolund, Beckett, and Harms, 1983.

Seley and Vigilante, 1964; Smith, 1972; Spencer and Vigilante, 1969; Staehler, 1977; Staehler and Watters, 1976; Storey, 1976; Toy, 1978; Toy and Gallaher, 1983; Tsiang and Ulrich, 1962; Wallace and Barnes, 1983.

THE AT&T CASE

Part II: Large-Scale Real-Time Program Retrofit Methodology in AT&T 5ESS® Switch

L.C. TOY*

Modern telephone systems are continuously undergoing changes to take advantage of rapid advances in hardware technology. In addition, new features are continuously being developed and incorporated as integral parts of the system. The additions and changes must be implemented in real time without disrupting the customer's telephone service. The procedures and methodology utilize the distributed and redundant architecture of the 5ESS Switching System to update and/or grow the system, while at the same time providing continuous service.

In this case study, the architecture of the 5ESS electronic switching system is described briefly, and then considerations for replacement of the resident software in the 5ESS system and how the process is implemented are discussed. The focus is on major software replacement.

5ESS SWITCH ARCHITECTURE OVERVIEW

The 5ESS switch is a fully digital switching system with a distributed processing and switching architecture [5ESS, 1986; Smith and Andrews, 1981; Davis et al., 1981]. It is comprised of an administrative module, a communications module, and one or more switching modules and/or remote switching modules (Figure 8–31). These three basic elements can be configured to cover the complete range of applications, from remote switching modules to large-capacity telephone exchanges [Byrne and O'Reilly, 1985]. The system is highly reliable: Because of the fault-tolerant architecture, the administrative module and switching modules experience only a few minutes of downtime per year [Allers et al., 1983].

• **Switching Module (SM):** Over 95 percent of call processing is handled by the switching module, which is the basic growth unit of the system. In addition to providing circuit and packet switching functions, the switching module connects all external lines, trunks, and special services circuits. Remote switching modules can be located at a considerable distance from the main body of the switch and can be used singly or grouped in clusters to serve groups of up to 10,000 subscribers. Time-division switching is performed in the time slot interchange unit, while most of the call processing is done in the switching module processor unit. Each switching module

* The author acknowledges M.A. Gauldin and F.B. Strebendt, for their assistance and encouragement, and E.E. Haselrick and M.G. D'Souza, for providing reference materials. Development of the retrofit capability resulted from the contributions of many people within AT&T Bell Laboratories and AT&T Technologies.

FIGURE 8–31
5ESS remote switching module capabilities

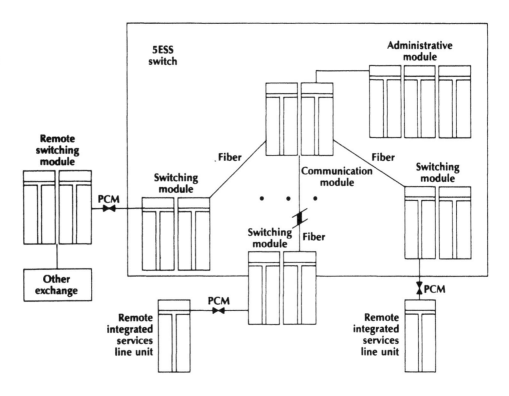

has a time slot interchange unit and a switching module processor unit but may differ from other switching modules in the types and quantities of peripheral equipment (line unit, trunk unit, digital carrier line unit, and digital line trunk unit). All common equipment in the switching module is duplicated for reliability purposes. Optical fiber network, control, and timing links connect the switching modules to the communications module.

• **Communications Module (CM):** The control-message communication facilities between the switching modules and the administrative module and between any two switching modules are provided by the communication module. The communications module contains a time-multiplexed switch and a message switch. Digital paths for switched connections between the switching modules are provided by the time-multiplexed switch. The message switch passes control messages between any two switching modules and between the switching modules and the administrative module. For reliability, both the time-multiplexed switch and the message switch are duplicated. The initial design of the communications module supported one switching module. A new communications module that supported 30 switching modules was then followed by a communications module with the capacity of 48 switching modules [Anderson et al., 1987]. A large communications module that supports 192 switching modules is now available. Call routing functions now exist in the communications module.

• **Administrative Module (AM):** The administrative module collects traffic and billing data. Many functions not related to call processing, such as fault detection, diagnostics, and fault recovery, are performed by the administrative module, which uses a 3B20D computer [Toy and Gallaher, 1983]. The administrative module consists of a duplicated administrative processor, an input/output processor to interface with terminals, printers, data links and tape units, and a duplicated disk file controller to which the disks are connected. Disk interfaces are SCSI (small computer system interface) standard.The duplicated administrative processors in the administrative module work in active/standby configuration so that if a fault occurs in the active unit, the standby unit can be switched into service. The disk memory provides mass storage for programs and data [Haglund and Peterson, 1983]. The input/output processor allows technicians to interface with the system via video display units and a master control center.

SOFTWARE
REPLACEMENT

With the 5ESS switch, replacement of the resident software and/or hardware is done in real time to minimize the impact on customer service and call processing. A conversion process occurs when one generation of the switch's features is upgraded to accept new hardware or software. The generation change marks a change in the *generic*. The conversion process is referred to as a *generic retrofit* [Bauer, Croxall, and Davis, 1985]. The generic retrofit capability in the 5ESS switch provides the method and support software for replacing the resident software, the associated databases, and the read-only memory firmware for the switching modules, while maintaining adequate service and reliability.

Several factors must be taken into consideration before a 5ESS switch is retrofitted. First, to minimize impact on customers, retrofitting of software and most hardware occurs at separate times in the 5ESS switch. Consequently, either the old hardware must be compatible with the new software or the new hardware must be compatible with the old software.

Second, due to the distributed processor architecture of the 5ESS system, there are periods of time when the software release in the administrative module is different from that in one or more switching modules. The messages that pass between processors fall into three categories: (1) messages that must pass through regardless of software release, (2) messages that involve the switching module read-only memory software, and (3) all other messages. Messages in the first category establish the links between the administrative module and switching modules and are needed so that other messages can be exchanged. The second category consists of those messages related to initializing the switching modules with data.

A third consideration is evolution of the two databases that exist in the 5ESS switch. The Office Dependent Data contains such information as routing information and subscriber information. The Equipment Configuration Data contains information about the 3B20D hardware and peripheral equipment, such as the video display units and disk drives. Each exchange customizes these two databases to fit the particular configuration. Due to structural changes that are needed to support new features, the databases must be evolved from a format compatible with the old software release to one compatible with the new software release. The 5ESS system's generic retrofit capability supports the evolution of these customized databases.

Software Replacement Processes

The 3B20D/UNIX* RTR system provides system update facilities to support the introduction of new versions of UNIX RTR and application software [Wallace and Barnes, 1984]. The system update software provides a flexible mechanism that can be used by a variety of applications, including the 5ESS switch and allows the inclusion of application-dependent processing. The system update software places all new generic data into the system and makes final preparations prior to initializing the system from the new generic. After initialization, complete propagation of the new generic into the system occurs.

During each step of the update process, the system update software provides an opportunity

---

* UNIX is a registered trademark of UNIX System Laboratories, Inc.

for application-dependent processing by transferring control to an application process. To regain control, the system update process monitors the application-dependent process. Each time the application-dependent process is invoked, the system update process waits a specified time for its completion. The application process sends an acknowledgment message to the system update process that indicates the amount of time it requires for processing. If the application-dependent process does not finish within the allocated time, the system update process sends a software termination signal to the application process, informs the office technicians of any error, and stops the stage.

A separate process exists for each step of the update procedure. Communication between the system update processes is accomplished through use of a binary log file. The first entry in the log file specifies the number of entries in the file. Each system update process will write beginning, ending, and application-dependent entries in the log file. Information contained in the beginning and ending entries for each process includes the date and time of the entry, the process identification, and the type of update process that is making the entry. In addition, the ending entry contains the completion code of the stage, which indicates success or failure, and error codes that provide more specific information about what errors occurred.

The application-dependent process maintains an ASCII log file. An entry for each stage of the retrofit exists in the application-dependent process's log file. Each entry specifies the stage of the retrofit, the starting and ending times of the stage, and the completion code that indicates the type of error, if any, that occurred. The log file also contains information about processing specific to each stage.

Stages in 5ESS Switch Software Replacement

Replacement of software in the 5ESS switch consists of four major stages: advance preparation, preparation, initialization, and evaluation (Figure 8–32). The advance preparation stage occurs

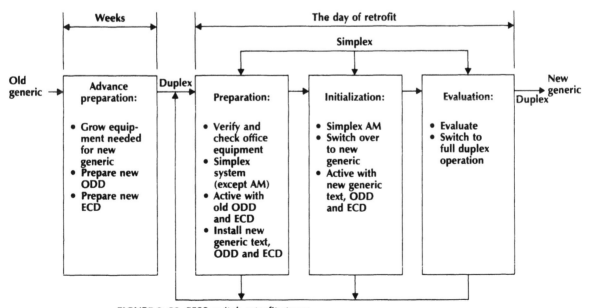

FIGURE 8–32 *5ESS switch retrofit stages*

weeks prior to the actual day of retrofit and consists of growing in equipment needed for the new generic and preparing the new databases. The system remains in duplex operation during this time. The preparation, initialization, and evaluation stages occur on the day of retrofit. The system is simplexed during the preparation stage and is duplexed after evaluation of the new generic. After verifying and checking the office equipment for reliability, the new generic text and databases are installed. The system is then initialized and evaluated. During these stages of software replacement, the exchange is able to back out any changes made and revert to the old software if the need should arise. The UNIX RTR system update and 5ESS switch application-dependent software are utilized during the preparation, initialization, and evaluation stages.

Advance Preparation Stage. During the advance preparation stage, the exchange is evaluated to verify that it is properly equipped to perform a retrofit. At this time, any hardware that is required for the new generic to be operational is grown into the system. Additional memory for the administrative module and switching modules is also grown if needed. Also during this stage, a series of tests designed to diagnose and verify the operation of devices and equipment used to read in and store the new generic, equipment units essential to the retrofit, and hardware and software units needed to recover the system from an outage are executed. This testing ensures that there is a low probability of trouble attributable to existing system faults in subsequent stages of the retrofit.

Evolution of the office-dependent data (ODD) [Barclay, Dossey, and Nolan, 1986] and Equipment Configuration Data (ECD) databases takes place during this time interval. Database evolution is the process of converting a database used by one generic to a format required by a different generic. The ODD stores most of the 5ESS switch office data and contains information on subscriber lines, trunks, routing, and features. Information about the 3B20D hardware and 5ESS switch terminal configurations is stored in the ECD. While the ECD resides strictly in the administrative module, the ODD is distributed among the administrative module and switching modules. Evolution is required when structural changes occur in the databases (for example, when relations or attributes are added in the new database). Both the ODD and ECD databases are evolved off site.

Two dumps, the preliminary and final, are taken of the ODD and ECD. The preliminary dump is used to identify major inconsistencies in the databases. Fixes from the preliminary dump are then applied to the databases, and a final dump is taken and used to create the new generic's databases.

Office Dependent Data Evolution. The first step in ODD evolution is to back up the database to ensure that the disk copy is identical to the copy in main memory. Backups of the ODD for evolution cause changes made to the database to be logged so that they can be later evolved and applied to the new ODD. The ODD for the administrative module and all switching modules are copied to tape and shipped to a center responsible for evolving the databases. At the center, the ODD is decompiled from binary form to the original ASCII input. The ASCII input is then evolved to the new generic format and compiled into binary. The evolved ODD is then shipped back to the exchange.

The new generic database is created from a *snapshot* of the ODD. While the old generic database is being evolved to the new generic format, changes are continuously being made to the database in the exchange. Changes to the ODD are made by the exchange (recent changes, RCs) [Fuhrer, Shen, and Yates, 1986] or originated by the customer (customer originated recent changes, CORCs). An example of a CORC is when someone forwards his or her incoming calls to a different number.

At the same time that an RC or CORC is being applied to the database, it is doubly logged for recovery reasons [Locher, Pfau, and Tietz, 1986] and for retrofit purposes. The retrofit log file is in binary format and contains the database relation name and the updated tuple data. Each time the ODD is backed up on disk, the CORCs are automatically flushed from the administrative module and switching modules and are appended to the retrofit log files. Each time a relation gets inserted, updated, or deleted, the relation is logged in the switching module's memory buffers. The CORCs are sorted by timestamp; only the most recent transaction of a particular CORC is retained. The buffers are then shipped to the administrative module and will be written to disk the next time a database backup occurs. At the time of retrofit, these logged changes are evolved to a format compatible with the structure of the new generic's database. These evolved changes are then applied to the new database once the system is initialized on the new generic. Both the old and new generic databases are synchronized (Figure 8–33).

Equipment Configuration Data Evolution. A copy of the exchange's ECD is made to tape and is sent to an off-site processing center for evolution (Figure 8–34). Off-line tools are provided to extract certain exchange options from the ECD automatically. These options are applied to a *base* ECD that contains data items common to all 5ESS systems with the same generic to obtain a customized database. A process in the administrative module dumps the ECD, converts it to ASCII format, and loads it onto tape. A process on an off-site processor extracts the options from the tape and applies them to new base ECD via customization scripts. Since some options may not be customized in the new database, an audit report is sent, along with the new database, to the exchange. The audit report tells which fields have not been customized and allows the technicians to customize the fields after initialization on the new generic.

FIGURE 8–33
Customer-originated recent changes and recent changes reapplications

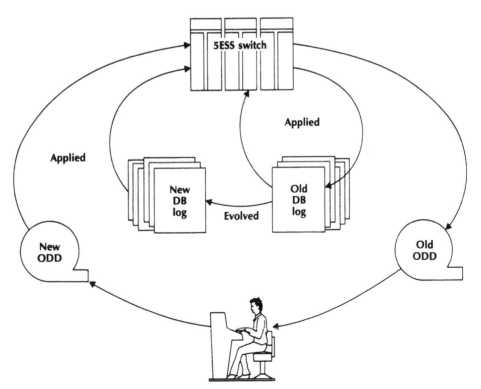

FIGURE 8–34
*Equipment config-
uration data evolu-
tion*

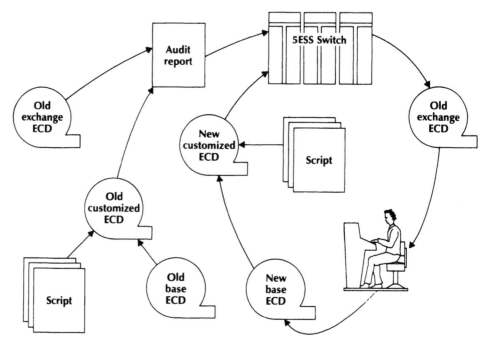

Preparation. This stage prepares the exchange for the actual retrofit and begins during the morning of the planned cutover to the new generic. The exchange verifies that it has installed the latest software and hardware updates and that all temporary overwrites to main memory are installed permanently or removed. The system is then backed up and it is verified that the exchange is running in duplex configuration (Figure 8–35). Diagnostics on equipment that is critical for retrofit are executed during this stage. At this time, billing data are collected and transmitted to a central location over a data link or are dumped to tape.

After the technician enters the command to start the retrofit, the application process sets the generic retrofit indicator on the maintenance control center and creates its log file. During this stage, the new generic and associated databases are read in from tape onto the secondary set of disks (Figure 8–36). The system update process determines the disks for which a set of tapes is targeted. It then removes the disks from service and marks the system off line in the ECD. This prevents restoral of the disks and will protect the new generic data from being overwritten. The remaining active disks continue to serve the live office; changes made to the active disks are not made to the off-line disks. The disks will remain simplex until the system is committed to the new generic.

A special device file provides mapping and allows the system update process to access the off-line disks. Each sequence of tapes contains a volume table of contents that defines which partitions the remaining data belong in. The offset of the data within the disk partition is determined from the physical disk address contained in the tape header and the starting address of the partition obtained from the volume table of contents.

During this stage, the system update process writes several types of log file entries. The beginning entry also includes the path name of the input device, the path name of the destination

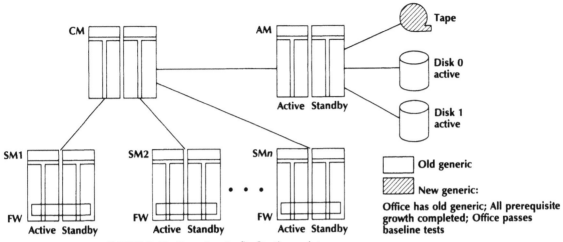

FIGURE 8–35 Generic retrofit: Starting point

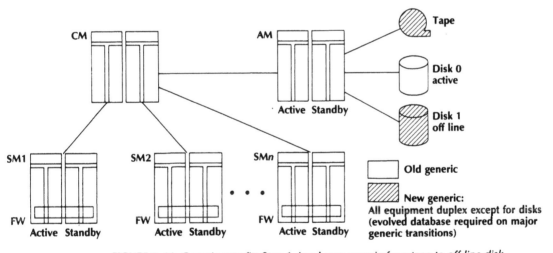

FIGURE 8–36 Generic retrofit: Step 1, Load new generic from tape to off-line disk

volume table of contents, and information that will be used to access the new generic's ECD and the old and new generic's system update log files. Log file entries are also made that indicate the disks that are being updated, the partitions on disk that are being updated, and information related to the tapes that are being read. Before the ending entry for this stage is written, an application-dependent process entry with the process identification number is written.

Files used by the old generic and needed by the new generic are copied from the active disk to the off-line disk by the application process. The destination off-line partition is mounted, and then the files are copied over. The application process writes an entry in its log file specifying the names of the files it tried to copy and whether it was successful in doing so. Once the new generic text and database tapes have been read, the duplicated module processors in each switching module are simplexed so that the generic dependent firmware may be replaced (Figure 8–37). One side of the switching module is forced active and continues processing calls. The other side of the switching module is unavailable and is pumped with the new generic, which is stored on the off-line disks (Figure 8–38).

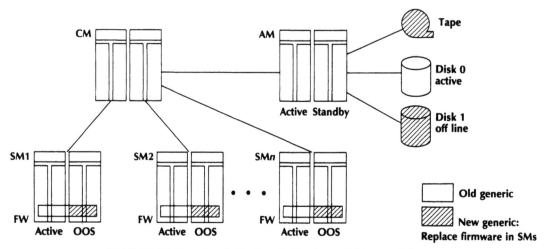

FIGURE 8–37 *Generic retrofit: Step 2, Simplex switching modules*

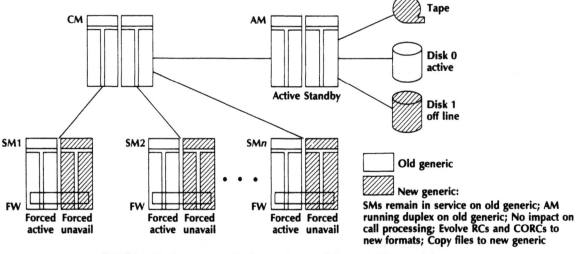

FIGURE 8–38 *Generic retrofit: Step 3, Pump off-line switching modules*

A process in the administrative module coordinates all requests to perform switching module pumps. It queues and prioritizes pump requests and invokes a special process to mount the off-line partitions to make the new generic software accessible for pumping. This special process uses the mknod and mount system calls to create special device files and mount point directories on the active disks. The partitions on the off-line disk are then mounted on the mount point directories. After the off-line partitions have been mounted, a third process in the administrative module controls the transfer of the data from disk to the switching modules via the 3B memory. A process in each switching module sets up and releases the data path for pumping. The process then performs hashsum checks of the memory on the unavailable side. Throughout this stage, the active processor of each switching module is still in service on the old generic, the administrative module is running duplex on the old generic, and there has been no impact on call processing.

At this point in time, the new generic's ODD is out of date with the ODD for the old generic. Changes that have been made to the ODD by the technician or the customer are logged and are evolved to a format compatible with the new generic database. The evolved RCs and CORCs are then copied by the application process from the active disk to the off-line disk.

Initialization Stage. During this stage, the switching modules are switched over from the old generic side to the new generic side and are initialized. The application process is responsible for changing the switching modules from the old generic side to the new one. The application log file entry for this stage contains information about whether the switch was successful for each switching module.

Messages other than ones used to establish the links between the administrative module and the switching modules are throttled in the communication module. The administrative module is the last processor to be initialized, since it needs to retain control over switching the switching modules to the new generic and to monitor their progress. Limited verification of the new ODD is done prior to initializing the switching modules on the new generic.

To protect the disks containing the old generic, the system update process accesses the new ECD on the off-line disks and marks the active disks off line. After the system is initialized, the disks containing the new generic will be active and the disks containing the old generic will be off line (Figure 8–39). The application and system update processes copy over their log files at this time. The system update process then requests the technician to initialize the system using the new generic disks. At any point in the retrofit, the exchange personnel can decide to return to the old generic and databases. The old software is available until the last stage in retrofit; thus, it is a very short process to abort the retrofit.

Evaluation Stage. Operation on the new generic is verified during this stage. Prior to duplexing the disks and switching modules, the technicians want to ensure that the new system is operational. The administrative module is restored to duplex operation. The new ODD is brought up to date with the old database by applying the evolved changes. The length of this stage, during which call processing is unaffected, is determined by local practice (Figure 8–40).

When the technicians are satisfied with the stability of the new system, the exchange is committed to full duplex operation. The new firmware is loaded in the side of the switching modules containing the old firmware, and both the switching modules and disks are restored to duplex operation (Figure 8–41). The system update process marks the off-line disks out of service in the ECD so that UNIX RTR facilities can be used to restore the disks.

The application process is responsible for checking that the switching modules are duplexed and for clearing the generic retrofit indicator on the maintenance control center. It prints out and then destroys its log file. At the completion of this stage, the system update process removes

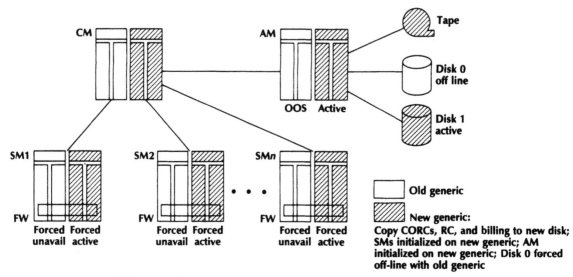

FIGURE 8–39 *Generic retrofit: Step 4, Initialization*

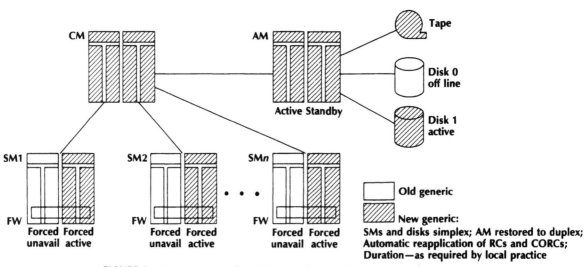

FIGURE 8–40 *Generic retrofit: Step 5, Verify operation on new generic*

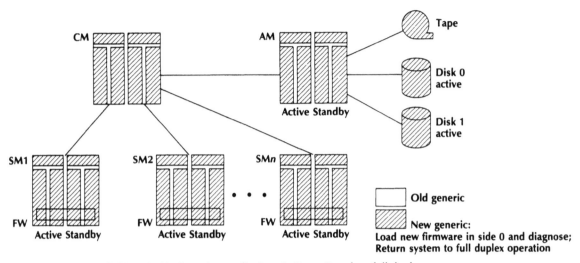

FIGURE 8–41 *Generic retrofit: Step 6, Commit and go full duplex*

its log file, since the update is finished and the system update processes no longer need to communicate.

In rare instances, the exchange personnel will decide to return to the old generic. This is simple to do prior to duplexing the disks, and a backout procedure is provided if necessary. The retrofit process is reversed and the disks that contain the old generic are re-initialized. The disks that contain the new generic are marked inaccessible and are then overwritten with the old generic.

SUMMARY

A much less desirable alternative to the generic retrofit process is to bring the system to a stop, load in new tapes, and then undergo a full initialization of the system. Long system downtimes would result from using this method, and there would be no mechanism for evolving the databases or recent changes. In addition, system integrity would not be guaranteed.

Generic retrofit takes advantage of the duplicated nature of the 5ESS switch in order to minimize impact on call processing and system reliability. It provides a way to read in the new software and databases while the switch is still running on the old generic. Call processing is uninterrupted during most of the initialization of the switching modules with the new generic.

All hardware growth and software changes occur at separate times. Hardware that is essential for the new generic to be operational is grown prior to retrofit and must be compatible with the new generic.

Because structural changes may occur in the databases, they are evolved from their old generic format to one that is compatible with the new generic. Changes made to the ODD are logged and automatically applied to the new generic database. The retrofit process provides databases compatible with the new generic that contain basically the same information as the old.

The architecture of the 5ESS system enables a smooth transition to a new generic that contains new features and hardware without a noticeable service interruption to subscribers. The process has been well tested and has been very successful. As of August, 1987, there were 137 exchanges retrofitted from the 5E1 to the 5E2(1) generic, 215 exchanges retrofitted from the 5E2(1) to the 5E2(2) generic, and 70 exchanges retrofitted from the 5E2(2) to the 5E3(1) generic.

REFERENCES   Allers et al., 1983; Anderson et al., 1987; Barclay, Dossey, and Nolan, 1986; Bauer, Croxall, and Davis, 1985; Byrne and O'Reilly, 1985; Davis et al., 1981; 5ESS, 1986; Fuhrer, Shen, and Yates, 1986; Haglund and Peterson, 1983; Locher, Pfau, and Tietz, 1986; Smith and Andrews, 1981; Toy and Gallaher, 1983; Wallace and Barnes, 1984.

THE TANDEM CASE

Fault Tolerance in Tandem Computer Systems

JOEL BARTLETT, WENDY BARTLETT, RICHARD CARR, DAVE GARCIA, JIM GRAY, ROBERT HORST, ROBERT JARDINE, DOUG JEWETT, DAN LENOSKI, AND DIX McGUIRE

The increasing trend for businesses to go on line stimulated a need for cost-effective computer systems with continuous availability [Katzman, 1977]. The strongest demand for general-purpose, fault-tolerant computing was in on-line database transaction and terminal-oriented applications. In the early 1970s, vendors and customers demanding continuous availability configured multiprocessor systems as hot standbys (see Figure 8–42). This configuration preserved previous development effort and compatibility by introducing devices, such as I/O channel switches and interprocessor communications adapters, to retrofit existing hardware. These architectures, however, still contained many single points of failure. For example, a power supply failure in the I/O bus switch, or an integrated circuit failure in any I/O controller on the I/O bus switch channel, would cause the entire system to fail. Other architectures used a common memory for interprocessor communications, creating another single point of failure. Typically, these architectures did not even approach the problems of on-line maintenance, redundant cooling, or a power distribution system that tolerates brownout conditions. Furthermore, these systems lacked thorough data integrity features, leading to problems in fault containment and possible database corruption.

As late as 1985, conventional, well-managed, transaction-processing systems failed about once every two weeks for about an hour [Mourad and Andrews, 1985; Burman, 1985]. This failure rate translates to 99.6 percent availability, a level that reflects a considerable effort over many years to improve system availability. When the sources of faults were examined in detail, a surprising picture emerged: Faults come from hardware, software, operations, maintenance, and the environment in about equal measure. Hardware could operate for two months without generating problems; software was equally reliable. The result was a one-month mean time between failures (MTBF). But if operator errors, errors during maintenance, and power failures were included, the MTBF fell below two weeks.

In contrast, the goal of Tandem is to build systems with a MTBF measured in years*—more than two orders of magnitude better than conventional designs. The key design principles of the system were, and still are, the following:

- *Modularity*: Both hardware and software are based on modules of fine granularity that are units of service, failure, diagnosis, repair, and growth.

---

* The original goal was to build a system with 100-year MTBF.

FIGURE 8–42
*An example of
early fault-tolerant
architectures*

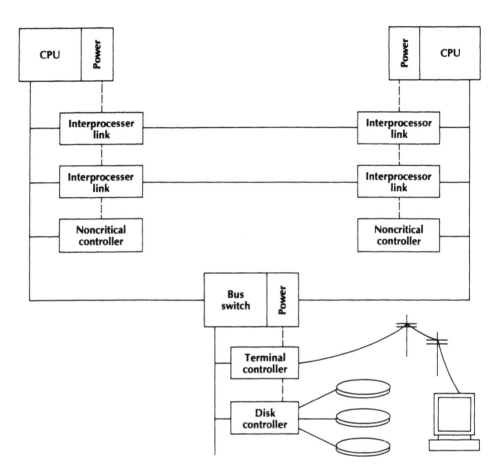

- *Fail-Fast Operation*: Each module is self-checking; when it detects a fault, the module stops.
- *Single Fault Tolerance*: When a hardware or software module fails, another module immediately takes over the failed module's function, giving a mean time to repair measured in milliseconds. For processors or processes, this takeover means that a second processor or process must exist. For storage modules, it means that the modules and the paths to them are duplexed.
- *On-line Maintenance*: Hardware and software can be diagnosed and repaired while the rest of the system continues to deliver service. When the hardware, programs or data are repaired, they are reintegrated without interrupting service.
- *Simplified User Interfaces*: Complex programming and operations interfaces can be a major source of system failures. Every attempt has been made to simplify or automate interfaces to the system.

This case study presents Tandem NonStop and Integrity systems, viewed from the perspective of these key design features.

HARDWARE Multiple hardware modules and multiple interconnections among those modules provide a basis for fault-tolerant operation. Two modules of a certain type are generally sufficient for hardware fault tolerance because the probability of a second independent failure during the repair interval of the first is extremely low. For instance, if a processor has an MTBF of 10,000 hours (about a year) and a repair time of 4 hours, the MTBF of a dual-path system increases to about 10 million hours (about 1000 years). If more than two processors were added, the further gains in reliability would be obscured by system failures related to software or system operations.

• *Modularity*: Modularity is important to fault-tolerant systems because individual modules must be replaceable on line. Keeping modules independent also makes it less likely that a failure of one module will affect the operation of another module. Increasing performance by adding modules allows customers to expand the capacity of critical systems without requiring major outages to upgrade equipment.

• *Fail-Fast Logic*: Fail-fast logic is defined as logic that either works properly or stops. Fail-fast logic is required to prevent corruption of data in the event of a failure. Hardware checks (including parity, coding, and self-checking), as well as firmware and software consistency checks, provide fail-fast operation.

• *Serviceability*: As mentioned before, maintenance is a source of outages. Ideally, the hardware should have no maintenance. When maintenance is required, it should require no special skills or tools.

• *Price and Price/Performance*: Commercial pressures do not permit customers to pay a high premium for fault tolerance; if necessary, they will use ad-hoc methods for coping with unreliable, but cost-effective, computers. Vendors of fault-tolerant systems have no special exemption from the requirement to use state-of-the-art components and architectures, frequently compounding the complexity already required by fault tolerance.

Hardware Architecture

The Tandem NonStop computer system was introduced in 1976 as the first commercial fault-tolerant computer system. Its basic architecture is shown in Figure 8–43. The system includes from 2 to 16 processors, connected by dual buses collectively known as the Dynabus interprocessor bus. Each processor has its own memory, containing its own copy of the operating system. The processors communicate with one another through messages passed through the Dynabus mechanism. The system can continue operation despite the loss of any single component. Each processor has its own input/output bus. Dual-ported controllers connect to I/O buses from two different processors. An ownership bit in each controller selects which of its ports is currently the primary path. When a processor or I/O bus failure occurs, all controllers that are designated as primary on that I/O bus switch to their backup paths. The controller configuration can be arranged so that in a multiprocessor system, the failure of a processor causes that processor's I/O workload to be spread out over the remaining processors. All subsequent systems have been upward-compatible with this basic design.

Processor Modules

The primary components of a system are its processor modules, each of which includes an instruction processing unit (IPU), memory, I/O channel, and Dynabus interprocessor bus interface. The design of the system's processor module is not much different from that of any traditional processor, with the addition of extensive error checking to provide fail-fast operation.

FIGURE 8–43
*Original Tandem
system architec-
ture, 1976*

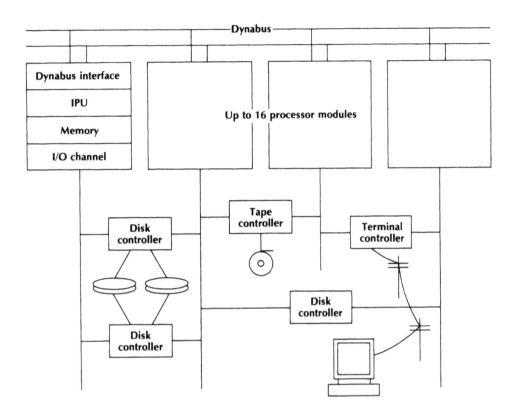

Each processor operates independently and asynchronously from the rest of the processors. Another novel engineering requirement is that the Dynabus interfaces must prevent a single-processor failure from disabling both buses. This requirement focuses on the proper selection of a single component type: the buffer that drives the bus. This buffer must be well behaved when power is removed from the processor module to prevent errors from being induced on both buses.

The power, packaging, and cabling must also be carefully considered. Parts of the system are redundantly powered through diode ORing of two different power supplies. In this way, I/O controllers and Dynabus controllers tolerate a power supply failure. To allow on-line maintenance and modular growth, all boards are designed for *hot insertion;* that is, they can be inserted while the slot is powered. Battery backup power is standard in all systems. It preserves the system state for several hours in case of power failure.

The evolution of these processors is summarized in Table 8–5. Features common to all processors are described in the following sections. More details about the individual processors appear later in this case. Each processor provides a basic set of instructions that includes operations on bits, integers, decimal numbers, floating-point numbers, and character strings; procedure calls and exits; I/O operations; and interprocessor SENDS to streamline the performance of the message-based operating system. All instructions are 16 bits long. The Tandem NonStop I was designed as a stack-oriented, 16-bit processor with virtual memory. This instruction set has evolved to an upward-compatible, 32-bit addressing machine. Program binaries from the

TABLE 8–5 Summary of Tandem NonStop processor evolution

Processor Feature	NonStop I (1976)	NonStop II (1981)	TXP (1983)	VLX (1986)	CLX 600 (1987)	CLX 700 (1989)	Cyclone (1989)	CLX 800 (1991)
Processor								
MIPS/IPU	0.7	0.8	2.0	3.0	1.0	1.5	10.0	2.2
Instructions	173	285	285	285	306	306	306	306
Technology	MSI	MSI STTL	MSI, Fast PAL	ECL, Gate array	Custom 2µ CMOS	Custom 1.5µ CMOS	ECL, Gate array	Custom 1µ CMOS
Cycle time	100 ns	100 ns	83 ns	83 ns	133 ns	91 ns	45 ns	61 ns
Microstore	—	8K × 32b	Two level: 8K × 40b, 4K × 84b	10K × 120b, dual	14K × 56b	14K × 56b	8K × 160b std, 8K × 160b pairs	14K × 56b
Cache (data and instructions)	—	—	64 KB, direct map	64 KB, direct map	64 KB, direct map	128 KB, direct map	2 × 64 KB, direct map	192 KB, direct map
Gates (approx)	20K	30K	58K	86K	81K	81K	275K	81K
Processor boards	2	3	4	2	1	1	3	1
Processors/system	2–16	2–16	2–16	2–16	1–6	2–8	2–16	2–16
Memory								
Virtual	512 KB	1 GB	1 GB	1 GB	1 GB	1 GB	2 GB	1 GB
Physical	2 MB	16 MB	16 MB	256 MB	32 MB	32 MB	2 GB	32 MB
Per board	64 KB 384 KB	512 KB 2 MB 4 MB	2 MB 8 MB	8 MB 16 MB 48 MB	4 MB (on processor board) 8 MB	8 MB (on processor board) 8 MB	32 MB 64 MB	32 MB (on processor board)
Max. boards	2	2	4	2	1	1	2	0
Cycle time	500 nsec/2 B	400 nsec/2 B	666 nsec/8 B	416 nsec/8 B	933 nsec/8 B	637 nsec/8 B	495 nsec/16 B	414 nsec/8 B
Input Output								
Interprocessor bus speed	2 × 13 MB/sec	2 × 13 MB/sec	2 × 13 MB/sec	2 × 20 MB/sec	2 × 20 MB/sec	2 × 20 MB/sec	2 × 20 MB/sec	2 × 20 MB/sec
Channel speed	4 MB/sec	5 MB/sec	5 MB/sec	5 MB/sec	3 MB/sec	4.4 MB/sec	2 × 5 MB/sec	4.4 MB/sec

† Additional 225 nsec if CAM miss.

NonStop I will run on a Cyclone. The processor implementations have been fairly conventional, using a mix of special-purpose hardware for basic arithmetic and I/O operations, along with microcode to implement higher-level functions. Two novel features are the special hardware and microinstructions to accelerate the sending and receipt of messages on the Dynabus. The performance of these instructions has been a key component of the success of the message-based operating system.

Memory, as originally implemented, was designed to support a 16-bit minicomputer. In 1981, designers added a 32-bit addressing scheme to provide access to 4-MB code space (for users), multiple 127.5-MB data spaces (for users), 4-MB code space (for the operating system), and 1-GB (2 GB for Cyclone) of virtual data space (for the operating system). The code and data spaces in both the user and the system areas are logically separate from one another.

In order to make processors fail-fast, extensive error checking is incorporated in the design. Error detection in data paths typically is done by parity checking and parity prediction, while checking of control paths is done with parity, illegal state detection, and self-checking. Loosely coupling the processors relaxes the constraints on the error-detection latency. A processor is required to stop itself only in time to avoid sending incorrect data over the I/O bus or Dynabus. In some cases, to avoid lengthening the processor cycle time, error detection is pipelined and does not stop the processor until several clocks after the error occurs. Several clocks of error-detection latency are permitted in the architecture, but cannot be tolerated in systems in which several processors share a common memory. In addition, the true fail-fast character of all processors eliminates the need for instruction retry in the event of errors.

Dynabus Interprocessor Bus

The Dynabus interprocessor bus is a set of two independent interprocessor buses. All components that attach to either of the buses are kept physically distinct so that no single component failure can contaminate both buses simultaneously. Bus access is determined by two independent interprocessor bus controllers. Each of these controllers is dual-powered in the same manner as an I/O controller. The Dynabus controllers are not associated with, nor physically part of, any processor. Each bus has a two-byte data path and several control lines associated with it. No failed processor can independently dominate bus utilization upon failure because, to electrically transmit onto the bus, the bus controller must agree that a given processor has the right to transmit.

The original Dynabus, connecting from 2 to 16 processors, was designed with excess capacity to allow for future improvements in processor performance without redesign of the bus. The same bus is used on the NonStop II, introduced in 1980, and the NonStop TXP, introduced in 1983. The NonStop II and NonStop TXP processors can even plug into the same backplane to operate in a single system with mixed processors. A full 16-processor TXP system does not drive the bus near saturation. A new Dynabus was introduced with the VLX system. It provides peak throughput of 40 megabytes per second, relaxes the length constraints of the bus, and has a reduced manufacturing cost due to improvements in its clock distribution. It was, again, overdesigned to accommodate the higher processing rates predicted for future processors. The CLX and Cyclone systems also use this bus.

For any given interprocessor data transfer, one processor is the sender and the other is the receiver. To transfer data over the Dynabus interprocessor bus, the sending processor executes a send instruction. This instruction specifies the bus to be used, the intended receiver, and the number of bytes to be sent. Up to 64 kilobytes can be sent in a single send instruction. The sending processor continues to execute the send instruction until the data transfer is completed, during which time the Dynabus interface control logic in the receiving processor is storing the data in memory. In the receiving processor, this activity occurs concurrently with program execution. Error recovery action is taken in case the transfer is not completed within a specified timeout interval. In the Dynabus design, the more esoteric decisions are left to the software (for example, alternate path routing and error recovery procedures): Hardware, then, implements fault detection and reporting [Bartlett, 1978].

Fiber-Optic Extension Links

In 1983, a fiber-optic bus extension (FOX) was introduced to link systems together in a high-speed local network. FOX allows up to 14 systems of up to 16 processors each to be linked in a ring structure, for a total of 224 processors. The maximum distance between adjacent nodes is 1 kilometer on the original FOX and 4 kilometers with FOX II, which was introduced on the VLX processor. A single FOX ring can mix NonStop II, TXP, VLX, and Cyclone processors. The interconnection of systems by FOX links is illustrated in Figure 8–44. Each node in the group can accept or send data at rates of up to 4 MB/sec.

The FOX connection is based on a store-and-forward ring structure. Four fibers are connected between a system and each of its two neighbors. Each interprocessor bus is extended by a pair of fibers, allowing messages to be sent in either direction around the ring. The four paths provided between any pair of systems ensure that communication is not lost if a system is disabled (perhaps because of a power failure) or if an entire four-fiber bundle is severed.

The ring topology also has advantages over a star configuration because a ring has no central switch that could constitute a single point of failure and because cable routing is easier with a ring than with a star. In a ring structure, bandwidth increases as additional nodes are added. The total bandwidth available in a FOX network depends on the amount of pass-through traffic. In a 14-node FOX ring, if each node sends to other nodes with equal probability, the network has a usable bandwidth of 10 MB/sec. When there is no pass-through traffic, the bandwidth increases to 24 MB/sec. Theoretically, an application generating 3 kB of traffic per transaction, at 1000 transactions per second, would require a FOX ring bandwidth of only 3 MB/sec. In this situation, the FOX network would use less than 30 percent of the total available bandwidth. Transaction processing benchmarks have shown that the bandwidth of FOX is sufficient to allow linear performance growth in large multinode systems [Horst and Chou, 1985; Englert, 1989].

Fiber-optic links were chosen to solve both technical and practical problems in configuring large clusters. Fiber optics are not susceptible to electromagnetic interference, so they provide a reliable connection even in noisy environments. They also provide high-bandwidth communication over fairly large distances (4 km/hop). This capability lessens the congestion in the computer room and allows many computers in the same or nearby buildings to be linked. FOX links allow computer sites to physically isolate nodes by housing them in different buildings, thereby providing a degree of fault isolation and protection against disaster. For example, a fire in the computer room in one building would not affect nodes in other buildings.

Dynabus+ Fiber-Optic Dynabus Extension

With the introduction of the Cyclone system in 1989, Tandem made two additional uses of fiber-optic links. Their use between peripheral controllers and I/O devices is described later in this case. Their use as an interprocessor link within a system (as compared with FOX, which is an intersystem link) is described here.

FIGURE 8–44
*Tandem system ar-
chitecture, 1990*

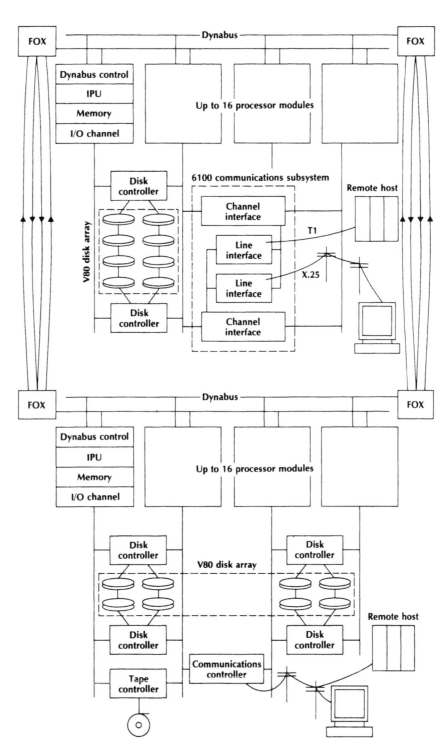

Cyclone processors are grouped into sections, each containing up to four processor modules. The sections may be geographically distributed up to 50 meters. Within a section, the normal (backplane) Dynabus interface is used. Sections within a system are connected in a ring arrangement, similar to the FOX arrangement.

Individual Dynabus+ fiber-optic links are capable of 12.5-MB/sec bandwidth, a good match for the 20-MB/sec bandwidth of the Dynabus. While increasing performance was not the major design goal of Dynabus+, the design has resulted in additional aggregate interprocessor bus bandwidth, up to 160 MB/sec in a system. Each section contains its own Dynabus controllers, so message traffic local to the section can proceed concurrently with local traffic in other sections. In addition, intersection traffic can proceed concurrently on the multiple fiber-optic links.

The Dynabus+ system is transparent to all levels of software except the maintenance subsystem (described later in this case). The system is self-configuring when power is first applied: Maintenance processors within each cabinet determine the configuration and routing rules. In the event of a failure of any of the fiber-optic links or interface logic boards, the system reconfigures itself, establishes new routing paths, and notifies the maintenance subsystem. In addition, a VLX interface to Dynabus+ allows intermixing VLX and Cyclone processor modules within a system. This feature allows an existing VLX customer to add Cyclone processors to a system, providing a smooth upgrade path.

Evolutionary Changes

Processor architecture has evolved to keep pace with technology. These improvements include (1) expansion of virtual memory to 1 GB (NonStop II system) and to 2 GB (Cyclone system), (2) incorporation of cache memory (TXP system), (3) expansion of physical memory addressability to 256 MB (VLX system) and to 2 GB (Cyclone system), (4) incorporation of separate instruction and data caches (Cyclone system), (5) incorporation of superscalar architecture (Cyclone system) [Horst, Harris, and Jardine, 1990], and (6) incorporation of an independent instruction fetch unit with dynamic branch prediction (Cyclone system).

Technological improvements include evolution from core memory to 1-Mb dynamic RAM and evolution from Schottky TTL (NonStop I and II systems) to programmable array logic (TXP system) [Horst and Metz, 1984] to bipolar gate arrays (VLX and Cyclone system) to silicon-compiled custom CMOS (CLX system) [Lenoski, 1988].

The Tandem multiprocessor architecture allows a single processor design to cover a wide range of processing power. Having processors of varying power adds another dimension to this flexibility. For instance, for approximately the same processing power, a customer can choose a two-processor VLX system, a three-processor TXP system, or a four-processor CLX-700 system. Having a range of processors extends the range of applications from those sensitive to low-entry price to those with extremely high-volume processing needs. In a different performance range, the customer may choose a four-processor Cyclone system or a 16-processor VLX system.

Peripherals

In building a fault-tolerant system, the entire system, not just the processor, must have the basic fault-tolerant properties of dual paths, modularity, and fail-fast design, as well as good price/performance. Many improvements in all of these areas have been made in peripherals and in the maintenance subsystem. The basic architecture provides the ability to configure the I/O system to allow multiple paths to each I/O device. With dual-ported controllers and dual-ported peripherals, there are actually four paths to each device. When disks are mirrored, there are eight paths that can be used to read or write data.

In the configurations illustrated in Figure 8–44, there are many paths to any given disk. Typically, two controllers access each disk, and each controller is attached to two processor channels. Software is used to mirror disks; that is, data is stored on two disks so that if one fails, the data is still available on the other disk. Consequently, the data can be retrieved regardless of any single failure of a disk drive, disk controller, power supply, processor, or I/O channel.

The original architecture did not provide as rich an interconnection scheme for communications and terminals. The first asynchronous terminal controller was dual-ported and connected to 32 terminals. The terminals themselves were not dual-ported, so it was not possible to configure the system so that it would withstand a terminal controller failure without losing a large number of terminals. The solution for critical applications was to have two terminals nearby that were connected to different terminal controllers.

The 6100 Communications Subsystem. The 6100 communications subsystem, introduced in 1983, helped reduce the impact of a failure in the communications system. The 6100 consists of two dual-ported communications interface units (CIUs) that communicate with I/O buses from two different processors (see Figure 8–44). Individual line interface units (LIUs) connect to both CIUs and to the communications line or terminal line. With this arrangement, CIU failures are completely transparent, and LIU failures result in the loss of only the attached line or lines. An added advantage is that each LIU can be downloaded with a different protocol in order to support different communications environments and to offload protocol interpretation from the main processors.

The 6100 communications subsystem is configured to have up to 45 LIUs. Each LIU can support up to 19.2 Kb/sec of asynchronous communication or 64 Kb/sec of synchronous communication. Redundant power supplies and cooling fans provide an extra margin of fault tolerance and permit on-line replacement of components.

Disk Subsystem. Modularity is standard in peripherals. It is common to mix different types of peripherals to match the intended application. In on-line transaction processing (OLTP), it is desirable to select increments of disk capacity and of disk performance independently. OLTP applications often require more disk arms per megabyte than are provided by traditional large (14″) disks. This requirement may result in customers' buying more megabytes of disk than they need in order to avoid queuing at the disk arm.

In 1984, Tandem departed from traditional disk architecture by introducing the V8 disk drive. The V8 was a single cabinet that contained up to eight 168-MB, 8″ Winchester disk drives in six square feet of floor space. Using multiple 8″ drives instead of a single 14″ drive provided more access paths and less wasted capacity. The modular design was more serviceable because individual drives could be removed and replaced on line. In a mirrored configuration, system software automatically brought the replaced disk up to date while new transactions were underway.

Once a system can tolerate single faults, the second-order effects begin to become important in system failure rates. One category of compound faults is the combination of a hardware failure and a human error during the subsequent human activity of diagnosis and repair. The V8 reduced the likelihood of such compound hardware-human failures by simplifying servicing and eliminating preventative maintenance.

In fault-tolerant systems design, keeping down the price of peripherals is even more important than in traditional systems. Some parts of the peripheral subsystem must be duplicated, yet they provide little or no added performance. For disk mirroring, two disk arms give better read performance than two single disks because the seeks are shorter and because the read work is spread evenly over the two servers [Bitton and Gray, 1988; Bitton, 1989]. Write operations, on the other hand, do demand twice as much channel and controller time. Also, mirroring does double the cost per megabyte stored. To reduce the price per megabyte of storage, the XL8 disk drive was introduced in 1986. The XL8 had eight 9″ Winchester disks in a single cabinet and had a total capacity of 4.2 GB. As in the V8 drive, disks within the same cabinet could be mirrored, saving the costs of added cabinetry and floor space. Also, like the V8, the reliable sealed media and modular replacement kept maintenance costs low.

The V80 disk storage facility replaced the V8 in 1988. Each of the V80's eight 8″ disk drives has a formatted capacity of 265 MB. Thus, each cabinet can hold 2.7 GB of unformatted storage, or 2.1 GB of formatted storage. Externally, the V80 resembles the V8, housed in a single cabinet that occupies six square feet of floor space. The internal design of the V80, however, extends the capacity and reliability of the V8 with a fully checked interface to the drives. Furthermore, the design reduces by a factor of five the number of external cables and connectors between the storage facility and the control unit.

The disk drive interface is based on the emerging industry-standard IPI-2 interface design, which has parity checking on data and addressing to ensure the integrity of data and commands. (The previous SMD-based design provided only data parity.) IPI's parallel and batched data and command interface between the disks and their controller allow higher data transfer rates (2.4 MB/sec) and reduced interrupts. A radial connection between the controller and the drives eliminates possible drive interaction that could occur with conventional bus structures. The fivefold reduction in the number of external cables and connections is achieved by placing the control logic in the disk cabinet. Within the cabinet, a new interconnect design has reduced by a factor of five the number of internal cables and connections.

In 1989, the XL80 replaced the XL8 in similar fashion, doubling the storage capacity per drive and also moving to an IPI-2 storage interface. In addition, the XL80 cabinet contains sensors for inlet air temperature, power supply and board voltages, and fan operation; this information is polled periodically by the cabinet's maintenance subsystem and reported to the peripheral controller when an exception condition exists. A fully configured XL80 disk subsystem, including storage modules, power supplies, and cooling fans, appears in Figure 8–45.

Peripheral Controllers. Peripheral controllers have fail-fast requirements similar to processors. They must not corrupt data on either of their I/O buses when they fail. If possible, they must return error information to the processor when they fail. In terms of peripheral fail-fast design, the Tandem contribution has been to put added emphasis on error detection within the peripheral controllers. An example is a VLSI tape controller that uses dual, lock-stepped Motorola 68000 processors with compare circuits to detect errors. It also contains totally self-checked logic and self-checking checkers to detect errors in the ad-hoc logic portion of the controller. Beyond this contribution, the system software uses end-to-end checksums generated by the high-level software. These checksums are stored with the data and are recomputed and rechecked when the data is reread.

The single-board controller supporting the V80 and the XL80 disks uses CMOS VLSI technology. The controller is managed by dual, lockstepped Motorola 68010 microprocessors that provide sophisticated error-reporting and fault-isolation tools. The controller is contained on a single board. Thus, it requires only half the I/O slots of previous controllers.

Other efforts to reduce peripheral prices include the use of VLSI gate arrays in controllers to reduce part counts and improve reliability and the use of VLSI to integrate the stand-alone 6100 communications subsystems into a series of single-board controllers. The Tandem evolution of fault tolerance in peripherals is summarized in Table 8–6.

FIGURE 8–45
XL80 disk subsystem (front view)

PROCESSOR MODULE IMPLEMENTATION DETAILS

The following sections outline the implementation details of each of the Tandem processors summarized in Table 8–5.

NonStop I

The NonStop I processor module, introduced in 1976, included a 16-bit IPU, main memory, Dynabus interface, and an I/O channel. Physically, the IPU, I/O channel, and Dynabus control consisted of two PC boards that measured 16″ × 18″, each containing approximately 300 integrated circuit packages. These boards employed Schottky TTL circuitry. The processor module was

TABLE 8–6
Tandem evolution of peripheral fault tolerance

Year	Product	Contribution
1976	NonStop I system	Dual-ported controllers, single-fault tolerant I/O system
1977	NonStop I system	Mirrored and dual-ported disks
1982	INFOSAT	Fault-tolerant satellite communications
1983	6100 communications subsystem	Fault-tolerant communications subsystem
1983	FOX	Fault-tolerant, high-speed, fiber-optic LAN
1984	V8 disk drive	Eight-drive, fault-tolerant disk array
1985	3207 tape controller	Totally self-checked VLSI tape controller
1985	XL8 disk drive	Eight-drive, high-capacity/low-cost, fault-tolerant disk array
1986	TMDS	Fault-tolerant maintenance system
1987	CLX	Fault-tolerant system that is 98 percent user-serviceable
1988	V80 storage facility	Reduced disk cabling and fully-checked disk interfaces
1988	3120 disk controller	Totally self-checked VLSI disk controller
1989	XL80 storage facility	Reduced disk cabling, fully-checked disk interfaces, environmental monitoring within disk cabinet
1989	Fiber-optic interconnect for V80 and XL80	Reduced cabling to a minimum, reduced transmission errors

viewed by the user as a stack-oriented, 16-bit processor, with a demand paging, virtual memory system capable of supporting multiprogramming.

The IPU was a microprogrammed processor consisting of (1) an execution unit with ALU, shifter, register stack, and program counter, (2) a microprogram sequencer with 1024 32-bit words stored in ROM, (3) address translation maps supporting system code and data, and current user code and data segments, (4) main memory of up to 512 KB, (5) 96 KB memory boards with single-error correction and double-error detection, and (6) battery backup for short-term main memory ride-through of power outages of up to 4 hours.

The heart of the I/O system is the I/O channel. In the NonStop I, all I/O was done on a direct memory access basis. The channel was a microprogrammed, block-multiplexed channel; individual controllers determine the block size. The channel did not execute channel programs, as on many systems, but did transfer data in parallel with program execution. The memory system priority always permitted I/O accesses to be handled before IPU or Dynabus accesses. The maximum I/O transfer was 4 KB.

Dual-Port Controllers. The dual-ported I/O device controllers provided the interface between the NonStop I I/O channel and a variety of peripheral devices using distinct interfaces. While these I/O controllers were vastly different, depending on the devices to which they interfaced, there was a commonality among them that fitted them into the NonStop I architecture. Each controller contained two independent I/O channel ports implemented by IC packages that were physically separate from each other so that no interface chip could simultaneously cause failure of both ports. Logically, only one of the two ports was active. The other port was utilized only in the event of a path failure to the primary port. An ownership bit, as illustrated in Figure 8–46, indicated to each port if it was the primary port or the alternate.

Ownership changed only when the operating system issued a Take-Ownership I/O command. Executing this special command caused the I/O controller to swap its primary and alternate port designation and to do a controller reset. Any attempt to use a controller that was not owned by a given processor resulted in an ownership violation. If a processor determined that a given controller was malfunctioning on its I/O channel, it could issue a Disable-Port command that logically disconnected the port from that I/O controller. This disconnection did not affect the ownership status. Thus, if the problem was within the port, the alternate path could be used, but if the problem was in the common portion of the controller, ownership was not forced on the other processor.

Fault-Tolerant I/O Considerations. The I/O channel interface consisted of a 2-byte data bus and control signals. All data transferred over the bus was parity checked in both directions, and errors were reported through the interrupt system. A watch-dog timer in the I/O channel detected if a nonexistent I/O controller was addressed or if a controller stopped responding during an I/O sequence. The data transfer byte count word in the channel command entry contained four status bits, including a protect bit. When this bit was set on, only output transfers were permitted to this device.

Because I/O controllers were connected between two independent I/O channels, it was very important that word count, buffer address, and direction of transfer be controlled by the processor instead of within the controller. If that information were kept in the controller, a single failure could fail both processors attached to it. Consider what would happen if a byte count register were located in the controller and the count did not decrement on an input transfer. It

FIGURE 8–46
Ownership circuitry and logic

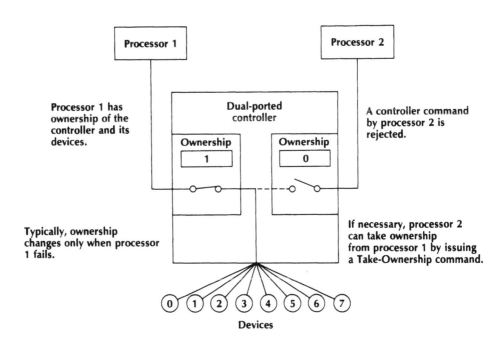

would be possible to overwrite the buffer and render system tables meaningless. The error would propagate to the other processor upon discovery that the first processor was no longer operating.

Other error conditions that the channel checked for were violations of I/O protocol, attempts to transfer to absent pages (it is the operating system's responsibility to lock down the virtual pages used for I/O buffering), uncorrectable memory errors, and map parity errors.

NonStop II

The NonStop II was a compatible extension of the NonStop I. The major changes from the NonStop I processor module were the introduction of a 32-bit addressing scheme and a diagnostic data transceiver processor. The software for the NonStop II system was upward-compatible with the NonStop I system. Thus, application programs written for the NonStop I system could be run on the NonStop II system.

The IPU was implemented using Schottky TTL logic using a microinstruction cycle time of 100 nsec. Instructions were added to support 32-bit extended addressing. An optional floating point instruction set was also added for high-speed scientific calculations; eventually, these instructions became a standard part of the instruction set. The instruction sets were implemented on microcode in a high-speed control store, which had 8K 32-bit words of loadable storage and 1K words of read-only storage. The loadable part of the control store was initialized when the operating system was loaded. Before loading the control store, the system performed a set of diagnostic routines to verify that the processor was operating correctly. The processor's internal data paths and registers were parity-checked to ensure data integrity. The IPU featured a two-stage pipeline that allowed it to fetch the next instruction while executing the current instruction.

Memory boards for the NonStop II system contained 512 KB, 2 MB, or 4 MB of storage. Up to four of these boards, in any combination, could reside in one processor for a maximum of 16 MB. A fully configured 16-processor system allowed up to 64 boards with a total of 256 MB of memory. The memory access time was 400 nsec. Each memory word was 22 bits long. Six bits of the word provided an error-correction code that enabled the system to correct any single-bit error and detect any double-bit error. The error-correction code also checked the address sent from the IPU to ensure that the memory access was valid.

I/O Channel. Each processor module contained a separate processor dedicated to I/O operations. Because the I/O processor operated independently from the IPU, I/O transfers were extremely efficient and required only a minimum of IPU intervention. The channel was a burst multiplexor. Every I/O device controller was buffered, allowing data transfers between main memory and the controller buffer to occur at full memory speed. I/O transfers had a maximum length of 64 KB. The high-speed I/O channels used burst-multiplexed direct memory access to provide transfer rates of up to 5 MB/sec. Thus, the aggregate burst I/O rate of a fully configured 16-processor system was 80 MB/sec.

The I/O processor supported up to 32 device controllers. Depending on the type, device controllers could support up to eight peripheral units. Therefore, as many as 256 devices could be connected to a single processor. Multipoint communication lines were treated as a single device, so each processor could support very large terminal configurations. I/O device controllers were intelligent devices. This intelligence allowed them to relieve the central processing unit of many routine functions such as polling synchronous terminals, checking for data transmission errors, and so forth.

Diagnostic Data Transceiver. The diagnostic data transceiver (DDT) was a separate microprocessor included as part of each processor module. The DDT provided two distinct functions:

1. The DDT allowed communication between a processor module and the operations and service processor (OSP), which supports both operational and maintenance functions, such as running diagnostics. (More about the OSP appears in the section on maintenance facilities and practices later in this case.)
2. The DDT monitored the status of the central processing unit, Dynabus interface, memory, and the I/O processor, and reported any errors to the OSP.

Virtual Memory. The virtual memory addressing scheme, introduced by the NonStop II processor, is used by all subsequent processors. It converted the system from 16-bit addressing to 32-bit addressing. This addressing is supported by the instruction set and is based on segments that contain from 1 to 64 pages each. A page contains 2048 bytes. Each processor can address up to 8192 segments, providing a billion bytes (1 GB) of virtual memory address space (later extended to 2 GB on the Cyclone processor, introduced in 1989).

The instruction set supports standard and extended addressing modes. The standard 16-bit addressing mode provides high-speed access within the environment of an executing program. The extended 32-bit addressing mode allows access to the entire virtual memory space by privileged processes. Programs written in Pascal, C, COBOL85, and the Transaction Application Language (TAL) can use extended addressing for access to large data structures.

The instruction set supports two types of extended addressing: absolute and relocatable. Absolute extended addressing is available only to privileged users such as the operating system itself. Absolute addresses can address any byte within the virtual memory. Relocatable extended addresses are available to all users. This form of addressing can reference any byte of the current process's data space, as well as one or more private relocatable extended data segments. Each extended data segment can contain up to 127.5 MB.

To provide efficient virtual-to-physical address translations, each NonStop II processor included 1024 high-speed map registers. The memory maps contained absent, dirty, and referenced bits to help the software manage virtual memory.

Maintenance. A major feature of the NonStop II system was the OSP located in a console supplied with the system. In addition to serving as an operations interface for communication with the system, the OSP was a powerful diagnostic and maintenance tool. The OSP is described later in this section.

NonStop TXP Processor

While the NonStop II system extended the instruction set of the NonStop I system to handle 32-bit addressing, it did not efficiently support that addressing mode. The existing 5 MB/s I/O channel and 26 MB/s Dynabus interprocessor bus offered more than enough bandwidth to handle a processor with two to three times the performance. The existing packaging had an extra processor card slot for future enhancements, and the existing power supplies could be reconfigured to handle a higher powered processor. The NonStop TXP processor module, introduced in 1983, was designed in this environment.

The main problems concerned designing a new micro-architecture that would efficiently support the 32-bit instructions at much higher speeds, with only 33 percent more printed circuit board area and the existing backplane. This design involved eliminating some features that were not critical to performance and finding creative ways to save area on the PC board, including strategic uses of programmable array logic and an unusual multilevel control-store scheme.

The performance improvements in the NonStop TXP system were attained through a combination of advances in architecture and technology. The NonStop TXP architecture used dual

16-bit data paths, three levels of macro-instruction pipelining, 64-bit parallel access from memory, and a large cache (64 KB/processor). Additional performance gains were obtained by increasing the hardware support for 32-bit memory addressing. The machine's technology includes 25-nsec programmable array logic, 45-nsec 16K static RAM chips, and Fairchild Advanced Schottky Technology (FAST) logic. With these high-speed components and a reduction in the number of logic levels in each path, a 12-MHz (83.3 nsec per microinstruction) clock rate could be used.

The TXP's dual data-path arrangement increased performance through added parallelism, as shown in Figure 8–47. A main ALU operation could be performed in parallel with another operation done by one of several special modules. Among these modules were a second ALU to perform both multiplications and divisions, a barrel shifter, an array of 4096 scratch-pad registers, an interval timer, and an interrupt controller. Other modules provided interfaces among the IPU and the interprocessor bus system, I/O channel, main memory, and a diagnostic processor.

The selection of operands for the main ALU and the special modules was done in two stages. In the first stage, data was accessed from the dual-ported register file or external registers and placed into two of the six registers. During the same cycle, the other four pipeline registers were loaded with cache data, a literal constant, the result of the previous ALU operation, and the result of the previous special-module operation. In the second stage, one of the six pipeline registers was selected for each of the main ALU inputs, and another one of these registers was selected for each special-module operand. Executing the register selection in two stages, so that the register file could be two-ported rather than four-ported, greatly reduced the cost of multiplexers and control storage; the flexibility in choosing the required operands was unimpeded.

The dual 16-bit data paths tended to require fewer cycles than a single 32-bit path when manipulating byte and 16-bit quantities. However, the paths did require slightly more cycles when manipulating 32-bit quantities. A 32-bit add took two cycles rather than one, but the other data

FIGURE 8–47
Parallel data paths of the TXP processor [Horst and Metz; © 1984 by McGraw-Hill]

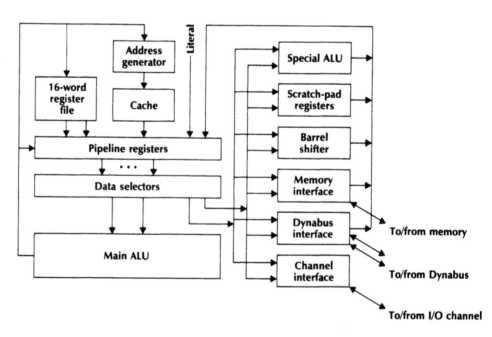

path was free to use the two cycles to perform either another 32-bit operation or two 16-bit operations. Measurements of transaction-processing applications showed that the frequencies of 32-bit arithmetic were insignificant relative to data-movement and byte-manipulation instructions, which were handled more efficiently by the dual data paths than by a single 32-bit data path. Most instructions include enough parallelism to let the microcode make effective use of both data paths.

To control the large amount of parallelism in the NonStop TXP processor, a wide control-store word was required. The effective width of the control store was over 100 bits. To reduce the number of RAMs required, the control store was divided between a vertical control store of 8K 40-bit words and a horizontal control store of 4K 84-bit words. The vertical control store controlled the first stage of the microinstruction pipeline and included a field that addressed the horizontal control store, whose fields controlled the pipeline's second stage. Lines of microcode that required the same or similar horizontal controls could share horizontal control-store entries.

Unlike microprocessor-based systems that have microcode fixed in read-only memory, the NonStop TXP system microcode was implemented in RAM so that it could be changed along with normal software updates and so that new performance-enhancing instructions could be added. Because instructions were pipelined, the TXP processor could execute its fastest instructions in just two clock cycles (167 nsec). The processor could also execute frequently used load and branch instructions in only three clock cycles (250 nsec).

Each NonStop TXP processor had a 64-KB cache holding both data and code. A 16-processor NonStop TXP system had a full megabyte of cache memory. To determine the organization of the cache, a number of measurements were performed on a NonStop II system using a specially designed hardware monitor. The measurements showed that higher cache hit ratios resulted with a large, simple cache (directly mapped) than with a smaller, more complex cache (organized as two-way or four-way associative). Typical hit ratios for transaction processing on the NonStop TXP system fell in the range of 96 percent to 99 percent. Cache misses were handled in a firmware subroutine, rather than by the usual method of adding a special state machine and dedicated data paths for handling a miss. Because of the large savings in the cache hardware, the cache could reside on the same board as the primary data paths. Keeping these functions proximal reduced wiring delays, contributing to the fast 83.3-nsec cycle time.

The cache was addressed by the 32-bit virtual address rather than by the physical address, thus eliminating the extra virtual-to-physical translation step that would otherwise be required for every memory reference. The virtual-to-physical translation, needed to refill the cache on misses and to store through to memory, was handled by a separate page table cache that held mapping information for as many as 2048 pages of 2 KB each (see Figure 8–48).

Manufacturing and Testing. The NonStop TXP processor was implemented on four large PC boards using high-speed FAST logic, PALs, and high-speed static RAMs. Each processor module had from one to four memory boards. Each memory board contained up to 8 MB of error-correcting memory. A 16-processor NonStop TXP system could therefore contain up to 256 MB of physical memory.

The NonStop TXP system was designed to be easy to manufacture and efficient to test. Data and control registers were implemented with shift registers configured into several serial-scan strings. The scan strings were valuable in isolating failures in field-replaceable units. This serial access to registers also made board testing much faster and more efficient because the tester could directly observe and control many control points. A single custom tester was designed for all four IPU boards and for the memory-array board.

FIGURE 8–48

TXP memory access

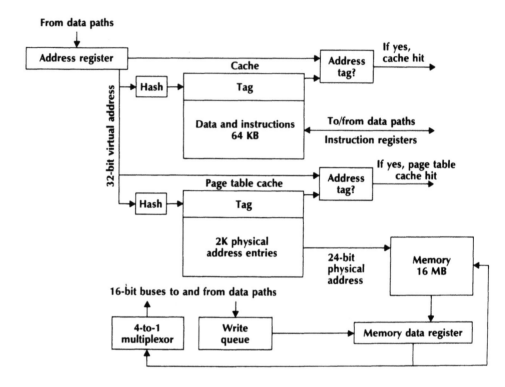

VLX Processor Module

The VLX processor module combines advanced VLSI technology with the fault-tolerant features of its predecessors. This processor module uses emitter-coupled logic (ECL) gate array technology to implement its dual path structure and other extensions to the TXP system. These features include dual interleaved control store; 83.3-nsec cycle time; 64-KB direct-mapped, store-through cache with 16-byte block size; hardware cache fill; 256-MB physical memory addressing; up to 96 MB of physical memory with 48-MB memory boards; on-line power and temperature monitoring; four-stage instruction pipeline, supporting single clock instruction execution; and dual 20-MB/sec Dynabus interprocessor bus.

One of the VLX processor module's printed circuit boards appears in Figure 8–49. The VLX IPU uses 32-bit native addressing and 64-bit main memory transfers to improve upon the transaction throughput of its predecessors, move large amounts of data, and lower the cost per transaction. Failed component sparing in cache memory allows a single malfunctioning component to be replaced by means of a logical switch to a spare; thus, a single point of failure does not require a service call.

Chips in the VLX processors contain up to 20,000 circuits, producing modules with over three times the density of the TXP processor. This increased density adds functions that enhance error checking and fault correction, as well as performance. By making it possible to reduce the number of components and interconnections, the increased density improves both performance and reliability. VLX processor gate arrays use ECL for enhanced internal performance and TTL for

FIGURE 8–49 *Printed circuit board from VLX processor module*

input/output functions. Each VLX processor includes 31 ECL/TTL gate arrays spread over only two modules.

Maintenance. A major goal of the VLX processor was to reduce the cost of servicing the system. This goal was accomplished in several ways.

Traditional mainframe computers have error-detection hardware as well as hardware that allows instructions to be retried after a failure. This hardware is used both to improve availability and to reduce service costs. The Tandem architecture does not require instruction retry for availability; processors can be fail-fast. The VLX processor is the first Tandem processor to incorporate a kind of retry hardware, primarily to reduce service costs.

In the VLX processor, most of the data-path and control circuitry is in high-density gate arrays, which are extremely reliable. This design leaves the high-speed static RAMs in the cache and the control store as the major contributors to processor unreliability. Both the cache and the control store are designed to retry intermittent errors, and both have spare RAMs that can be switched in to continue operating despite a hard RAM failure [Horst, 1989].

The cache provides store-through operation, so there is always a valid copy of cache data in main memory. A cache parity error just forces a cache miss, and the correct data is refetched from memory. The microcode keeps track of the parity error rate; when this rate exceeds a threshold, the microcode switches in the spare RAM. The VLX control store has two identical copies to allow a two-cycle access of each control store starting on alternate cycles. The second copy of control store is also used to retry an access in case of an intermittent failure in the first copy. Again, the microcode switches a spare RAM on line once the error threshold is reached. Traditional instruction retry was not included due to its high cost and complexity relative to the small improvement in system MTBF it would yield.

There is also parity checking on all data paths, single-bit error correction and double-bit error detection on data in memory, as well as single-bit error detection on addresses. Bus control lines are checked for line errors, and hardware consistency checks are used throughout the system.

Each processor contains a microprocessor-based diagnostic interface, which ensures that the processor is functioning properly before the operating system receives control. Pseudo-random scan diagnosis is conducted to provide a high level of coverage and a short execution time. Correct operation of the processor is verified before processing begins.

The VLX system cabinet, shown in Figure 8–50, is divided into four sections: the upper card cage, the lower card cage, the cooling section, and the power supply section. The upper card cage contains up to four processors, each with its own I/O channel and private memory. The lower card cage contains up to 24 I/O controller printed circuit (PC) cards, where each controller consists of one to three PC cards. The cooling section consists of four fans and a plenum chamber

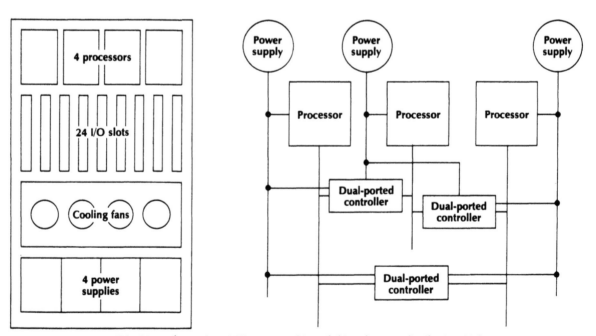

FIGURE 8–50 *NonStop VLX system cabinet (left) and power distribution (right)*

that forces laminar air flow through the card cages. The power supply section contains up to four power supply modules. Multiple cabinets can be bolted together.

For the VLX system, the Tandem Maintenance and Diagnostic System (TMDS) replaced the operations and service processor used on the NonStop II and TXP processors. Information about TMDS appears later in this case, in the section on maintenance facilities and practices.

CLX Processor Module

The CLX system was designed to fill the need for a low-cost distributed system. The design goal was to provide user serviceability, modular design, and fault tolerance with lower service and maintenance costs. The CLX is based on a custom CMOS chip set developed using silicon compilation techniques [Lenoski, 1988]. The original CLX-600 processor was introduced in 1987 and is based on 2.0-μ CMOS. The silicon compiler allowed the processor chip to be retargeted into 1.5-μ CMOS for the CLX-700 and into 1.0-μ CMOS for the CLX-800. The CLX-700, introduced less than 18 months after the 600, raised performance by 50 percent, and the CLX-800 raised performance again by nearly 50 percent. The description in this section is based on the latest CLX-800.

All CLX processors have a similar micro-architecture that integrates the features of both traditional board-level minicomputers and high-performance VLSI microprocessors. This hybrid design incorporates several novel structures, including a single static RAM array that serves three functions: writable control store, data cache, and page table cache. The processor also features intensive fault checking to promote data integrity and fault-tolerant operation.

A fully-equipped, single-cabinet CLX system contains two processor boards with optional expansion memory, six I/O controllers, five 145-MB to 1-GB disk drives, and one cartridge tape drive. Dual power supplies and cooling fans are also included in the cabinet. The entire system operates within the power, noise, and size requirements of a typical office environment. To expand the system, the customer simply adds more I/O or processor cabinets to the basic configuration. The CLX system architecture appears in Figure 8–51. A view of the actual cabinet appears in Figure 8–52.

As with the other Tandem processors, each CLX processor communicates with other processors over two interprocessor buses (IPBs). Each bus operates synchronously on 16-bit wide data, and each provides a peak bandwidth of 20 MB/sec. The two buses transfer data independently of one another, providing a total bandwidth of 40 MB/sec for a maximum of eight processors. Processors communicate with I/O devices either through a local I/O bus or through the interprocessor bus (IPB) to another processor and its I/O bus. Each processor contains a single asynchronous, burst-multiplexed I/O bus that transfers data at a maximum rate of 4.4 MB/sec to a maximum of 16 controllers. As with the other processors, these controllers are dual-ported and can be driven by either of the processors to which they are attached.

The CLX uses a multifunction controller (MFC) based on a Motorola 68010 microprocessor to control dual small computer system interfaces (SCSI) that support up to five disk drives and one tape drive. The MFC runs its own real-time operating system kernel that coordinates independent disk control, tape control, synchronous and asynchronous communication, and remote maintenance tasks. The CLX processor module's printed circuit board appears in Figure 8–53. Through the maintenance buses, maintenance and diagnostic information can flow among the system control panel, processors, multifunction controllers, and environmental monitors. Enhanced diagnostic software and careful design of all replaceable units allows customers to service 98 percent of all component failures.

FIGURE 8–51
*CLX system
architecture*

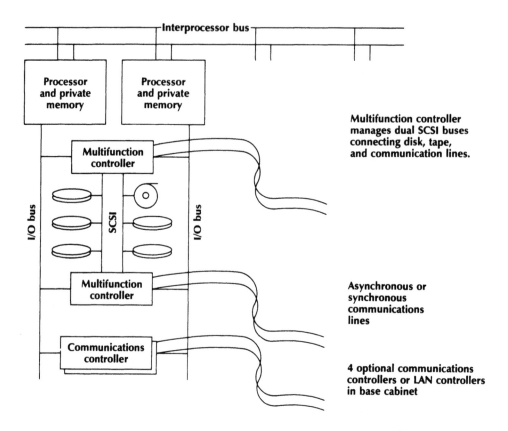

Multifunction controller
manages dual SCSI buses
connecting disk, tape,
and communication lines.

Asynchronous or
synchronous
communications
lines

4 optional communications
controllers or LAN controllers
in base cabinet

The processor logic resides within six custom CMOS chips, allowing the processor and main memory to be implemented in a single board. A block diagram of the processor appears in Figure 8–54. The chip set was designed using a silicon compiler supplied by Silicon Compiler Systems Corporation. The two IPU chips are identical, running in lock-step to form a fully self-checking module. These chips provide the complete IPU function. They work together with a single bank of static RAM that serves as the microcode control store, page table cache, and data/instruction cache. The RAM provides for 14K × 7B of microcode and scratch pad memory, 4K entries of page table cache, and 192 KB of instruction/data cache.

The MC chip includes the control and ECC logic (SEC/DED) to interface with the up to 32 MB of on-board dynamic memory. This chip contains FIFO buffers to hold data in transit to and from the main-memory dynamic RAMs, using nibble mode access. The chip also features a wraparound mode to support high-speed memory-to-memory block transfers.

Each processor has one IPB chip per interprocessor bus. Each chip contains a 16-word in-queue and a 16-word out-queue. These queues work with on-chip state machines for sending and receiving interprocessor message packets asynchronous to processor execution.

The IOC chip contains the data latches and logic to control a burst-multiplexed, asynchronous I/O bus. The I/O bus is primarily controlled by the IPU, but it can also handle DMA transfer polling and selection without microcode intervention. The bus also includes priority-encoding logic to support the fair servicing of I/O interrupts.

FIGURE 8–52
*CLX system cabi-
net (front view
showing from top
to bottom: car-
tridge tape drive
and SCSI disk
drives, two proces-
sor modules with
memory and I/O
boards, dual fans,
power supplies,
and batteries for
memory power)*

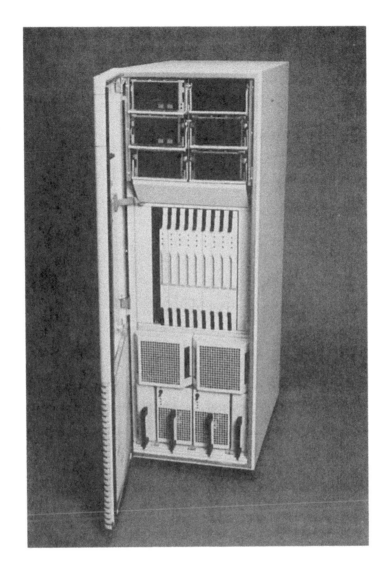

FIGURE 8–52
*CLX system cabi-
net (front view
showing from top
to bottom: car-
tridge tape drive
and SCSI disk
drives, two proces-
sor modules with
memory and I/O
boards, dual fans,
power supplies,
and batteries for
memory power)*

The final component of the processor is a Motorola 6803-based maintenance and diagnostic processor. This processor furnishes overall control of the main processor, as well as a diagnostic and error-reporting path for the main processor through the maintenance buses.

The IPU architecture for the CLX, as mentioned earlier, is a blend of features found in both minicomputer and microcomputer architectures. The IPU chip's external interface is similar to that of a VLSI microprocessor. For example, the interface features one address bus, one data bus, and one status bus, along with miscellaneous signals, such as an interrupt request, memory wait

FIGURE 8–53 *Printed circuit board for CLX-600 processor module, showing dual, lock-stepped IPU chips (bottom center)*

controls, and three-state bus controls. Minicomputer features, however, appear in the size of the address bus, which is 18 bits wide, and the data bus, which is 60 bits wide.

The IPU chip interface merges many buses that would normally be separate in a minicomputer architecture. In particular, a bus cycle on the CLX can execute any of the following functions: microcode control store access, instruction or data cache access, page table cache access, main memory access, microcode scratchpad memory access, and special module (IPB, IOC, MDP) access. Merging these buses reduced the cost of the processor by decreasing the number of static RAM parts and their associated support logic and by reducing the number of pins needed on the IPU chips. If this merging were not implemented carefully, however, performance would have degraded significantly. To reduce the bandwidth required on the buses and to minimize the impact on performance, the designers employed a variety of techniques, including the use of a small on-chip microcode ROM, a virtually-addressed cache, nibble-mode DRAM with block operations to the main memory controller, and high-level control operations for special modules.

The on-chip micro-ROM is most important in reducing the impact from the merged bus structure. The micro-ROM contains 160 words of microcode, with an identical format to the off-chip microcode. This ROM is addressed either by the microcode PC or through an explicit index

FIGURE 8–54
*CLX processor
block diagram*

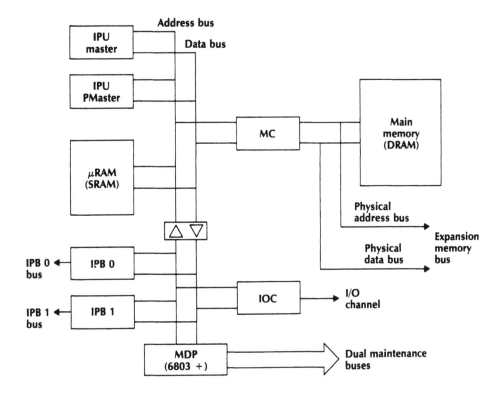

specified in the previous line of microcode. The microcode PC addressing is used to implement the inner loops of IPB and IOC transfers, cache filling routines, and block memory moves. The explicit index is used for short sequences of common microcode. These lines overlay otherwise sequential lines of external microcode. Use of these ROM lines does not conflict with other micro-operations.

The virtually-addressed cache reduces the number of page-table accesses; thus, it decreases the required bandwidth to the shared micro-RAM. Likewise, the use of block-mode commands to the memory controller reduces the number of memory commands needed during cache filling and block moves. Finally, the use of higher-level commands to the IPB and IOC reduces the control transfers needed to receive and transmit data to these devices. The on-chip micro-ROM, together with these other features, reduces the penalty of using a single bus approach from over 50 percent to less than 12 percent.

The main alternative to the micro-ROM used on the CLX would be an emulation scheme in which a subset of instructions is implemented entirely by internal ROM, and the remaining instructions are emulated by a sequence of the simpler instructions. The micro-ROM scheme has two chief benefits when compared with emulation techniques. First, it provides much higher performance when the amount of ROM space is limited relative to the number of instructions that must be implemented. Second, the dispatch of each instruction is to external writable control store, enabling any ROM microcode errors to be corrected externally (although with some performance penalty).

Data Integrity Through Fail-Fast Operation. In a NonStop system, fail-fast hardware operation is essential to providing fault tolerance at the system level. Fail-fast operation requires that faults do not escape detection and that the processor is halted before a fault is propagated. The CLX's processor module uses a variety of error-checking strategies to provide extensive fault coverage.

The IPU chip itself is covered by a duplicate-and-compare scheme. This scheme minimizes the amount of internal logic required for a high degree of coverage, and it maximizes the utilization of existing library elements in the silicon compiler CAD system. The implementation of the IPU's duplicate-and-compare logic appears in Figure 8–55. The CLX's scheme improves the fault coverage of other duplicate-and-compare schemes by providing for a cross-coupling of data and parity outputs. One chip, designated the data master, drives all data outputs, while the other chip, designated the parity master, drives all parity outputs. This action ensures that both chips' outputs and checking logic are active and that latent errors in the checking logic cannot lead to an undetected double failure. The parity outputs of the IPU also cover the address and data lines connecting the IPU to other parts of the processor and the micro-RAM.

Within the memory system, ECC with encoded address parity provides checking of all memory system data paths. In addition, redundant state machines are contained in the MC chip

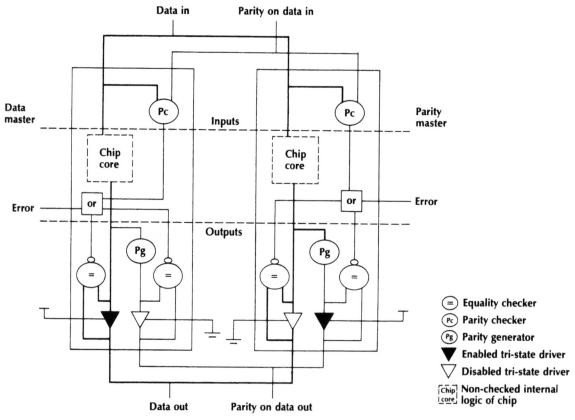

FIGURE 8–55 *CLX processor's cross-coupled checking*

and in the external RAS/CAS generation logic. The state transitions of these machines are encoded into CRC registers whose outputs are compared. The resulting structure produces a high fault coverage for both the data and control sections of main memory.

The IOC and IPB provide for parity protection of the data and control lines to which they are interfaced. In addition, they are protected by end-to-end checksums supported in software; these checksums guarantee the integrity of their respective buses.

Cyclone Processor Module

The design goals of the Cyclone system were to significantly increase performance, while providing improvements in serviceability, manufacturability, installability, and overall cost of ownership. The Cyclone processor, introduced in 1989 [Horst, Harris, and Jardine, 1990], provides more than three times the performance of the VLX, yet it retains full object-code compatibility. About half of the performance improvement is due to higher clock rates, and the other half is due to the new micro-architecture. Much of the architectural improvement is due to the ability to execute up to two instructions per clock cycle, a technique that has been called *superscalar* [Jouppi and Wall, 1989]. Other improvements are due to parallel data paths and new designs for the caches and main memory.

Cyclone Technology. The technology for Cyclone is a combination of ECL for speed, CMOS for high density, and TTL for standard interfaces and buses. The ECL gate arrays, jointly developed by Tandem and Advanced Micro Devices, contain approximately 5000 gate equivalents. These gate arrays are implemented in 155-pin, grid-array packages. The pins can be individually programmed for TTL or ECL interfaces.

The processor is implemented on three 18″ × 18″ circuit boards, with a fourth board holding either 32 MB or 64 MB of main memory. A second, optional, memory board allows expansion up to a total of 128 MB of main memory per processor (with 1 Mb DRAMs). The circuit boards have eight signal layers, four of which have controlled impedance for routing ECL signals.

Like the VLX, Cyclone uses an interleaved control store, allowing two clock cycles for access. The control store is implemented in 16K × 4 CMOS SRAMs, surface-mounted on a double-sided ceramic substrate, which is then vertically mounted on the main boards.

Cyclone Processor Architecture. The superscalar design of the Cyclone processor was necessitated by the fact that the VLX processor executes many frequent instructions in a single clock cycle, and the goal of three times VLX performance could not realistically be achieved based on cycle time only. Such a fast cycle time would involve higher risk, lower reliability, and higher product cost. Thus, Cyclone needed to break the one-cycle-per-instruction barrier. At peak rates, the Cyclone processor executes two instructions per clock cycle. To do this, it incorporates an independent, asynchronous instruction fetch unit (IFU), separate large caches for instructions and data, a deep pipeline, and a dynamic branch prediction mechanism. A block diagram of the Cyclone processor is shown in Figure 8–56.

The IFU operates independently of the rest of the processor. It fetches up to two instructions per clock cycle from the instruction cache, decodes the instructions to determine whether they are candidates for paired execution, and presents a microcode entry address for either a single instruction or a pair of instructions to the control unit and data unit for execution. It also assists in the execution of branching instructions and of exception handling. Up to 16 different instructions can be in some stage of execution at any point in time. The IFU is shown in more detail in Figure 8–57.

The Cyclone processor uses a dynamic branch prediction mechanism for conditional

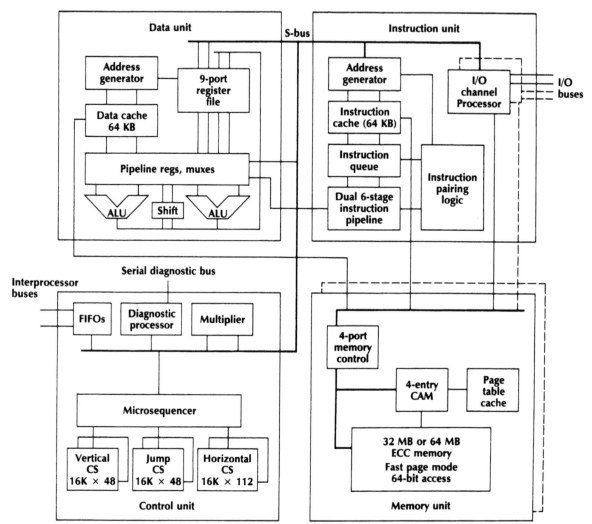

FIGURE 8–56 *Cyclone processor block diagram [Chan and Horst, 1989; reprinted by permission from CMP Publications]*

branches. This mechanism relies on the premise that when a particular branch instruction is repeatedly encountered, it will tend to be taken (condition met) or not taken (condition not met) the same direction each time. An extra bit for each instruction is included in the instruction cache. This bit records the branch direction actually taken by the last execution of each branch instruction in the cache. When a branch is fetched from the instruction cache, the IFU predicts that the branch will choose the same path as the previous time, so it continues prefetching along the predicted path. When the branch instruction later enters the execution pipeline, the microcode determines whether the prediction was correct. If so, it does nothing. If not, the microcode directs the IFU to back up and resume instruction fetching along the other path. Modeling has

FIGURE 8–57
Cyclone instruction fetch unit

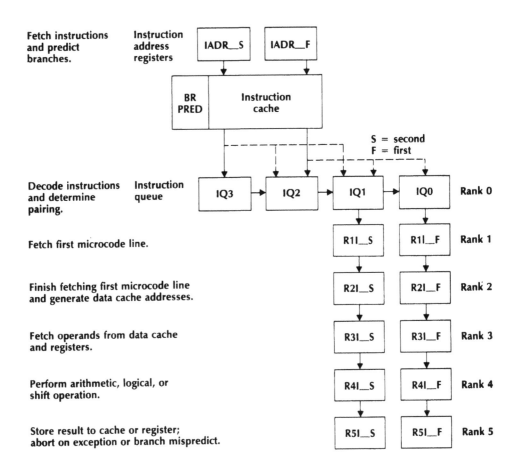

shown that this mechanism would be correct between 85 percent and 95 percent of the time. The result is an average cost of 1.3 to 1.9 cycles per branch instruction. In addition, because the branch prediction occurs early in the prefetch queue, branches may be executed in a pair with the previous instruction, the sequentially following instruction, or the target instruction.

The Cyclone data path uses two 16-bit ALUs, similar to the TXP and VLX, but with two major differences. First, the two ALUs are connected with the register file in a very general way. This interconnection is necessary for the execution of many of the instruction pairs, but it is also quite useful in improving the performance of many complex, multicycle instructions as well. In addition, the two ALUs can be linked together so that 32-bit arithmetic can be accomplished in a single clock cycle.

Both the instruction cache and the data cache are capable of fetching two adjacent 16-bit words in a single cycle, regardless of alignment. This feature, along with the instruction pairing, the nine-port register file, the 32-bit ALU capability, and the deep pipeline, allows the execution of a double (32-bit) load instruction and a 32-bit arithmetic instruction, as a pair, in a single clock cycle.

The Cyclone sequencer is similar to the VLX sequencer in that two copies of the control store are used to allow two-cycle access time. In addition to allowing the use of slower, denser CMOS RAM parts, the two copies provide backup for each other. In the event of an error in fetching a word from control store, the alternate bank is automatically accessed. If the error is a soft error, one of the banks can be refreshed from the other bank. In the event of a hard failure, a spare RAM can be switched in. Part of the control store is duplicated yet again (four total copies). This duplication allows both potential paths of a microcode branch to be fetched simultaneously, thus minimizing the penalty for microcode choices.

In the Cyclone processor, virtual addresses are sent directly to the main memory. A four-entry, content-addressable memory (CAM) compares each access to the row address that previously addressed a bank of DRAM. When the addresses match, the DRAM column address is generated by a few bits from the CAM plus the address offset. Translation from virtual to physical address is performed only on a CAM miss. Since the translation is performed infrequently, it was possible to implement the page table cache (translation look-aside buffer) in relatively slow, but dense, CMOS static RAMS.

For both increased bandwidth and increased connectivity, Cyclone allows the connection of up to four I/O channels per processor, whereas previous Tandem processors allowed only one channel. Two channels are supplied on the instruction unit board, while an additional two channels are available on an optional board. The maximum Cyclone processor thus contains six boards (three processor, two memory, one optional I/O).

Cyclone Fault Tolerance, Data Integrity, and Reliability Features. Parity checking is used extensively to detect single-bit errors. Parity is propagated through devices that do not alter data, such as memories, control signals, buses, and registers. Parity prediction is used on devices that alter data, such as arithmetic units and counters. Predicted parity is based strictly on a device's data and parity inputs; it does not rely on the device's outputs, which may be faulty. Thus, an adder might generate an erroneous sum, but the parity that accompanies the sum will correspond to the correct result. Parity checkers downstream will then detect the error. Invalid-state checking or duplication-and-comparison are used in sequential state machines.

The hardware multiplier is protected by a novel technique similar to recomputation with shifted operands (RESO) [Sohi, Franklin, and Saluja, 1989]. After each multiplication, a second multiplication is initiated with the operands exchanged and one operand shifted. Microcode compares the two results whenever the multiplier is needed again or before any data leaves the processor. Unlike other implementations of RESO, these checking cycles incur almost no performance penalty because they occur concurrently with unrelated execution steps.

If the processor hardware detects a fault from which it cannot recover, it shuts itself down within two clock cycles, before it can transmit any corrupt data along the interprocessor bus or I/O channel. The error is flagged in one or more of the approximately 300 error-identification registers, allowing quick fault isolation to any of the 500 hardware error detectors in each processor. Like the VLX, Cyclone processors include spare RAM devices in all of the large RAM arrays, such as caches and control stores. These devices are automatically switched in to replace hard-failed RAMs.

Cyclone systems make extensive use of fiber-optic interconnections, which, among other advantages, increase reliability. The Dynabus+ fiber links between sections were described earlier in this case. In addition, Cyclone systems use fiber optic links between the disk controllers and the disk units themselves and between the communications controllers and outboard communications concentrators.

The Cyclone approach to diagnostics is similar to the approach taken on VLX, but it goes beyond in many respects. Test coverage of microprogrammed diagnostic routines has been dramatically increased, and more support has been added for pseudo-random scan test. Together, these changes improve the ability to automatically diagnose faults on line and quickly pinpoint the field-replaceable unit responsible for the fault. In addition, a guided-probe facility, which leads factory personnel through the diagnostic process, enhances the product's manufacturability.

Like the VLX processor, the Cyclone processor is implemented primarily in ECL gate arrays, although Cyclone's arrays are considerably more dense. Because of this added density and the increased clock speed, Cyclone's gate arrays dissipate up to 11 watts. In order to cool these devices without resorting to liquid cooling, Cyclone uses an *impingement* air-cooling technique. Instead of blowing chilled air across the circuit board, Cyclone's boards include an orifice plate, which serves to focus the incoming air onto the hottest components. This design is shown in Figure 8–58. The result is that Cyclone's devices, in spite of dissipating much more power, operate at a junction temperature 10°C cooler than those in the VLX, significantly increasing reliability.

FIGURE 8–58
Cyclone printed circuit board showing impingement cooling

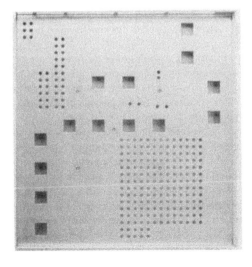

INTEGRITY S2   While Tandem's traditional NonStop architecture provides efficient fault tolerance through its fail-fast hardware and proprietary Guardian operating system, some computing environments require an open standards-based operating system and fault tolerance based strictly in hardware (e.g., the telecom industry). Tandem's Integrity S2 was designed to meet the needs of these markets.

The primary design objective for Integrity S2 was to provide a fault-tolerant on-line user-serviceable UNIX-based system [Jewett, 1991]. Application portability at the source level was a requirement as well as support for an industry standard peripheral bus. Furthermore, no single hardware failure should corrupt the data stored or manipulated by the system. Last, but certainly not least, among the major design objectives was the recognition that the operating system would represent a single point of failure.

System Architecture

A depiction of the machine architecture is provided in Figure 8–59. The system is divided into a number of customer-replaceable units (CRUs). Every CRU in the system is designed to be hot-pluggable. This permits on-line removal of fault CRUs and on-line insertion of replacement CRUs.

The system consists of a triplicated processor-local memory system contained on three central processor CRUs (CPCs). Duplexed triple modular redundant controllers (TMRCs) provide a large secondary main memory (global memory) and serve as the nexus for the I/O operations of the machine. The CPCs connect to the TMRCs over the reliable system bus (RSB). Duplexed input/output packetizers (IOPs) provide the interface for a superset of an industry standard I/O bus (VME) on one side and an interface to the TMRC on the other. The interconnection between the IOPs and the TMRCs is called the reliable I/O bus (RIOB). The IOPs are the conduit through which all I/O in the machine flows. Each IOP produces a bus that is called the NonStop-V+, which is a high data integrity variant of the popular VME bus. Ordinary VME controllers are connected to the system via a bus interface module (BIM). The BIM provides a dual-ported path from a peripheral controller to each IOP.

Each CPC consists of a 33.33-MHz oscillator driving an R2000 processor, R2010 floating point coprocessor, 128 KB of split instruction and data caches, local memory and RSB interface. In addition, the CPC contains a DMA machine used to transfer blocks of data between local memory and the secondary memory store, a minimum of 8 MB of on-board DRAM, augmented with hardware write-protection logic and an RSB interface. The DMA engine transfers packets of memory between local and global memory and accumulates a checksum of the data during the transfer. Upper layers of the system software use this checksum to provide end-to-end checking for disk transfers.

The clocks of the three processing modules have no fixed-phase relationship that is maintained by the system. The processors operate independently, but are kept in logical phase via proprietary synchronization logic. Two different time domains are relevant to synchronization: virtual and physical. Virtual time is measured by the passage of instructions on a given CPC. The independent processing modules are designed to execute the same instruction stream in virtual time. These instruction streams proceed until such time as the processing complex needs to access a resource beyond the CPC boundary. All such non-CPC resource requests generate RSB transactions that are voted at the TMRC. Voted read operations inherently bring the processors into closer alignment in physical time because there is a single logical copy of the data.

Since the machine can operate within the bounds of the cache and local memory subsystem for long periods of time, another synchronization mechanism is required. The progress of the processors is monitored on each CPC by a set of counters which are incremented as the machine

FIGURE 8–59
Integrity S2 archi-tecture

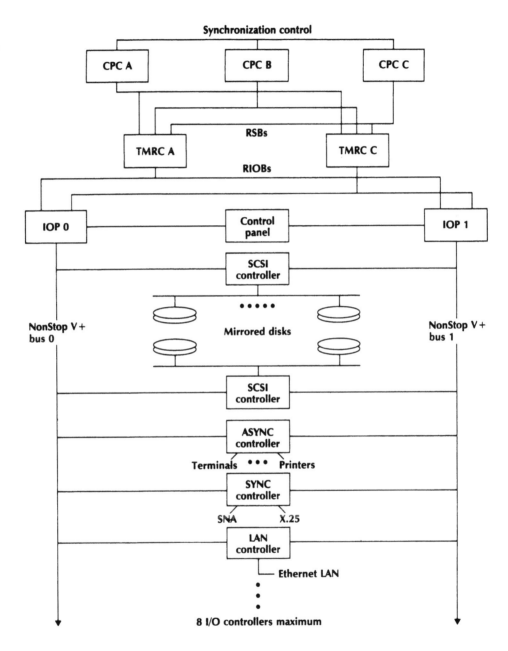

pipeline advances. Periodically (every 2047 instructions), each of the processors is stalled until all of the processors arrive at the synchronization point or a timeout expires. In addition, the arbiter for the local bus on the CPC ensures that all machines execute reads and writes in the same temporal order.

The technique devised to provide precise presentation of exceptions to each of the processors involves instruction counting. As the pipeline of the processor advances, a number of counters are incremented. In the current system, interrupts can be presented every 64 instructions. The process of collecting, distributing, voting and presenting exceptions on specific modulos of an instruction counter guarantees that all processors will field the exception at the same virtual time.

The TMRC contains up to 128 MB of global memory and interfaces to the CPC via the RSB and to the IOPs via the RIOB. The TMRC also contains the cause, mask, and clear registers for the interrupt mechanism. Having the TMRC serve as the repository for causes of exceptions presents a uniform view of interrupts to the processors.

A central role that the TMRC has in system operations is voting the RSB transactions. All processor transactions that are external to the CPC are voted on a bit-by-bit basis and the vertical OR of these results implicate the errant CPU module. The voting circuit is duplicated and compared and any self-check error halts the board. During system operation one of the TMRCs is designated as primary and the other as backup. The primary TMRC provides the data in the case of a read operation and both TMRCs perform all write operations. All TMRC registers and static RAMs are protected by even byte parity. The memory is word organized, and the even parity of the word address of the datum is hashed into every byte of data parity in order to detect addressing failures in the memory controller.

The nonvolatile memory (EPROM) on the TMRC is not parity protected, but is checksummed by the software. All of the data paths on each TMRC are protected by even parity hashed among the four data bytes. State machines are protected using either parity or duplication. Scrubbers, implemented in the operating system, are used to detect, and correct if possible, latent errors in both local and global memory.

Like the TMRC, the IOP is designed to be a self-checking fail-fast CRU. The system has two IOPs, each of which can support the full complement of peripheral controllers. If an IOP fails, software arranges for the peripheral controllers to become bound to the other IOP and system operation continues. The data path on the IOP is checked using techniques analogous to those described for the TMRC.

All peripheral controller-initiated bus transactions result in NonStop-V+ transactions that are translated into RIOB bus transactions by the IOP. In order to prevent errant peripheral controllers from writing or reading inappropriate global memory cells, the IOP contains an access and validation RAM (AVRAM). This AVRAM is a direct-mapped cache that translates virtual VME addresses into physical RIOB addresses. During the translation process, the IOP checks the permission bits in the AVRAM entry to see if the specific peripheral controller is permitted to read or write the appropriate physical RIOB address.

The power subsystem was also designed to be fault-tolerant. Batteries are provided to support continued system operation during power failures. Redundant bulk supplies drive independent 36 V_{DC} rails to protect against bulk failures. Redundant batteries drive dual 24 V_{DC} rails to protect against battery failures. The DC-DC converters use these four independent DC rails to produce the requisite DC voltage required by a specific CRU.

Software Architecture

Since one of the basic design goals of the system was to use an existing UNIX kernel as the basis for the operating system, the system software architecture was based on an industry standard implementation of UNIX. A major addition that was made in the kernel was a two-tiered memory management system to support the local/global bifurcation of the main memory system. This virtual memory system treats local memory as the main memory pool with global memory serving as a backing paging pool. Finally, pages in global will be swapped to disk if global memory is in short supply. The text, most of the data and per process stacks for the kernel reside in local memory. User processes text, data and stacks may also reside in local memory.

I/O operations are launched on behalf of user processes by the operating system. The operating system arranges for the data to be moved to the appropriate destination for the user process. If the source of the data for a write operation is in local memory then a buffer is allocated in global memory and the data is moved from local to global by the special purpose DMA hardware implemented on the CPC and TMRC. Similarly, if the destination of a read operation is in local memory, the data transfer performed by the operating system uses this DMA engine after the data is placed in global memory by the peripheral controller. The collection of services that assist in providing the illusion of fault-free operation to the system is called subscription based services. An entity in the operating system that required notification of an event calls a function to subscribe to the occurrence of that event. If the event occurs, a function specified by the caller is invoked with parameters that depend on the particular event type.

Faults that occur within the processor memory complex (CPC and TMRC) are known as core faults. The hardware guarantees that the operating system can continue to execute instructions to effect repair of the system, but the operating system must identify the faulting component and take the appropriate recovery action.

A core fault is indicated to the processors via a high priority interrupt. The processors then use the private-write mechanism to distribute a global view of the faulting condition. The private-write mechanism allows the processors to store private, possibly asymmetric, non-voted data in the global memory without causing the voting mechanism to register a fault.

Once a common view of the cause is obtained by each of the three processors, low-level exception processing code follows a deterministic parsing mechanism of the hardware status. This parse results in an implication of the offending CRU, which precipitates an action based on the type and severity of fault and the current configuration graph of the system. Typical actions are, in order of likelihood, incrementing a threshold counter, logging an event to the event reporting mechanism, or finally removing a CPC or TMRC.

Faults beyond the core, namely in the IOP or peripheral controllers, are handled by the I/O fault handling layer. IOP failures are typically recoverable. At any given moment a collection of controllers is bound to either IOP via the BIM, and the system can still access the controller via the alternate path.

A key to high availability in replicated systems is the ability to repair the system on-line. The operating system support for such repair activity is called reintegration. Consider CPC integration. A newly inserted CPC runs a power-on self-test (POST) from its local EPROM to verity the health of the board. The remaining processors agree to reintegrate and copy a small amount of local state to global memory. The processors then issue a soft reset (an operation supported by the RSB and TMRC, and hence voted) that results in all three CPCs entering reset. The CPCs notice that this is a soft reset operation and, after initializing some local state, find the communication block deposited by the operating system in global memory and load the program counter and stack pointer. The operating system now has control again and it proceeds to move a copy routine into each processor's local memory. Then, the processors use the local-global DMA engine to move pages from local to global and back, using the voting mechanism to bring the contents of all three local memory arrays into agreement. After this copying process is completed, normal execution resumes. Note that processing is suspended during the copy period of CPC reintegration. This is slightly more than one second on an 8-MB local memory system.

Unlike the processor, TMRC reintegration takes place during normal machine operation and only borrows cycles from the machine in small chunks that are controlled by the system administrator. The first phase of TMRC reintegration just copies global memory to a global memory buffer and back to global memory using the local-global DMA engine. During this phase, the IOPs believe that the replacement TMRC is off-line. The replacement TMRC returns "good" status for all RSB TMRC reads and writes.

In the second phase, the replacement TMRC remains a write-only memory. The processors lock the RIOB, copy a packet from global to local and back to global using the DMA engine. The RIOB is unlocked, and the process is repeated until the entire memory array has been restored. During the entire IOP revive process, both TMRCs accept writes from the CPCs and IOPs. This guarantees that the memories are consistent after the copying process is complete.

The standard UNIX operating system assumes perfect hardware and software. A failure in either the hardware or the kernel will result in an unconditional loss of all services (a "panic"). Given this collection of self-imposed constraints, a fault recovery model based on forward recovery was adopted. The kernel uses consistency checks as a fault-detection mechanism through approximately 1000 ASSERTs. An ASSERT is simply a macro that ensures that an expression is true. In the standard UNIX kernel, the failure of an ASSERT results in a system panic. Recovery from an assertion failure is provided using an assertion-specific forward recovery routine. These recovery routines are guided by data structure audit routines. Data structure audit routines determine the validity and consistency of various data structures.

A provably correct implementation of any version of UNIX has yet to be produced. A reliable "panic" mechanism was implemented to greatly increase the probability that various disk resident data structures are consistent upon reboot from an unrecoverable operating system fault. To accomplish this, the hardware write-protection feature is used to lock a number of critical kernel data structures during the panic procedure. Then, a number of kernel data structure consistency checks are performed and only those data structures that pass the various validity checks are subsequently utilized. The dirty blocks in the buffer pool are written to disk using a polled version of the disk driver. This ensures that a minimal amount of the system structure is used to accomplish the write operation. Finally, an image of the kernel is written to the disk using the PROMs. Experience shows that this procedure greatly increases the probability of the file systems being in a consistent state upon reboot.

In sum, the Integrity S2 incorporates numerous hardware and software techniques appropriate to a commercial, standards-dominated marketplace which demands fault tolerance. Fault tolerance has been accomplished without compromising the programmatic interface, operating system or system performance.

MAINTENANCE FACILITIES AND PRACTICES

Tandem's tools, facilities, and practices for hardware maintenance have evolved considerably in the last ten years. Over time, the trend has been increasingly to share maintenance responsibility with its customers, making it easier for customers to resolve hardware problems quickly on their own.

Early Methods

Early maintenance systems were based mainly on the use of on-line diagnostic tests to isolate the causes of readily apparent failures. Subsequent systems, however, moved toward the ability to detect failures automatically, analyze them, report upon them, and track their repair.

The first diagnostic and maintenance tools were very primitive. For example, to support the NonStop I systems, only a set of lights and switches was available on each processor for communicating error information and for resetting and loading the processor. In 1979, the Diaglink diagnostic interface was introduced to permit access to the system from remote maintenance sites. Diaglink featured an asynchronous modem. With Diaglink, customer engineers could remotely examine customers' systems, obtain system status by running operating system utilities, and execute diagnostics with customer assistance for remote, low-level debugging.

Operations and Service Processor (OSP)

The NonStop II system replaced Diaglink with an operations and service processor (OSP). The OSP was a microcomputer system that communicated with all processors and a maintenance console. The OSP offered all of the capabilities of Diaglink, as well as additional features to diagnose failures and to operate a system remotely. The OSP enabled operations and support personnel to obtain an internal view of the status of each processor.

The OSP communicates with the diagnostic data transceiver (DDT) included as a part of each processor module in the system. This communication allows the operator to diagnose software and hardware problems through the operator's console. The DDT monitors the status of the Dynabus interface, I/O channel processor, memory, and IPU, including the internal data paths. For example, the DDT enables the operator to put the processor in single-step mode and monitor the contents of its registers before and after execution of a specific instruction.

The OSP includes a built-in modem that can connect it to a remote terminal or to another OSP. This connection allows an operator or customer engineer to diagnose and possibly even correct problems from the remote site. A remote customer engineer can, for example, run microdiagnostics residing on a local OSP. Alternatively, the customer engineer can download diagnostics from the remote OSP to the local OSP, remotely reset and load processors, and display error information. For the TXP system, the OSP was enhanced to include an asynchronous modem, improved microdiagnostics, more remote operations capability, and additional remote support capabilities.

Tandem Maintenance and Diagnostic System. For the VLX system, the Tandem Maintenance and Diagnostic System (TMDS) replaced the OSP. TMDS provides a framework for problem detection with the VLX system, which was intended to reduce the cost of ownership in various ways [White, 1987]. A major aspect of this attack on costs was improved diagnostic and maintenance facilities. TMDS permitted the elimination of front panel lights and switches from the system design, dramatically streamlining maintenance activities. Unlike its predecessors, TMDS operated on line without requiring significant system resources. It provided a uniform interface to many diagnostic subsystems [Troisi, 1985].

By the time of the VLX system, the maintenance strategy had evolved beyond real-time monitoring of system components to include automatic on-line fault analysis and automatic dial-out for on-line support by remote service centers [Eddy, 1987]. TMDS was based on that strategy. Today, although it is known primarily for its use on the VLX, CLX, and Cyclone systems, TMDS is compatible with all NonStop systems. It runs under the Guardian operating system and is distributed automatically to all customers.

Through pervasive instrumentation, an internal fault-tolerant maintenance and diagnostic subsystem continuously monitors the system's processors, power supplies, and cabinet environments. When the Guardian operating system or an I/O process detects a change of state or an irregular event, it writes an event signature to an event log on disk. Then, TMDS examines each event signature. If further study seems advisable, TMDS starts a module known as an automatic fault analyzer. Thus, TMDS supports both active testing of components and symptom-based fault analysis.

TMDS fault analyzers relieve the customer of the need for an intimate knowledge of hardware, status codes, or specific error values. TMDS uses if-then-rule–based algorithms to evaluate events against a knowledge base, automating many of the detection, interpretation, and reporting tasks previously required of a console operator. The knowledge base contains a range of acceptable component states and environmental factors. If the fault analyzer finds that an event falls within the acceptable range, TMDS saves the fault analysis in a local log (a catalog of system events and patterns that can aid future troubleshooting).

However, if a fault analyzer detects an event that suggests an active or potential problem, TMDS transmits a signal to a fault-tolerant service processor called the remote maintenance interface (RMI). The RMI consists of dual Motorola 68000–based processors that communicate with each other and with other subsystems over dual bit-serial maintenance buses. The processors, FOX controllers, and power supply monitors all connect to the maintenance buses. The RMI supports all the functions of the old OSP, but does so as a much more compact unit—two circuit boards residing in one of the cabinets (VLX and Cyclone) or a part of the MFC (CLX). Through a synchronous protocol, a special communication process, and a password requirement, the RMI also greatly reduces the risk of unauthorized users gaining access to the system through the diagnostic facility.

When it receives a problem signal, the RMI alerts the on-site operator and, on the CLX, VLX, or Cyclone system, optionally dials out to a Tandem National Support Center (TNSC). Tandem staffs two such centers: one to service sites in North America and one for sites in Europe. Other TNSCs are planned as business needs for them develop.

Through the RMI, either the on-site operator or the remote analysts and engineers at the TNSC can review the event log, run diagnostics, test components, and isolate and diagnose the problem. On newer equipment, these actions include detecting out-of-spec intake and exhaust cabinet temperatures, malfunctioning disks or tape controllers, and faulty fans. TMDS also uses processor diagnostics to test power supplies, clocks, and batteries. If necessary, the TNSC can dispatch a field service engineer for on-site troubleshooting or part replacement. The TNSC staff has identified and diagnosed the problem, so the service engineer is very likely to arrive with the correct replacement part in hand.

TMDS also allows analysts and engineers to run on-line diagnostics to identify problems that fault analyzers don't cover. In fact, many diagnostics can be run while the device that is being studied is on line. In the worst cases, only the problem device needs to be shut down; under previous diagnostic systems, both the device and its controlling processor needed to be shut down. In any case, testing with TMDS only minimally affects the system's performance. Processing continues unhindered by the diagnostic tests, unless a processor itself is being evaluated.

The following steps illustrate how TMDS operates if a tape I/O process detects an error event involving a tape unit:

1. The tape I/O process immediately creates an error event and sends it to the TMDS event log.
2. TMDS signals the fault analyzer.
3. The fault analyzer localizes the error to a particular controller board.
4. The fault analyzer writes additional error information to the event log, specifying the probable FRU, the controller address, and the terminal error code. All of these actions take place within seconds.
5. After completing the analysis, TMDS dials out to the TNSC.
6. The TNSC dials back in to verify the analysis.

7. The TNSC dispatches a customer engineer to replace the controller board.

8. TMDS records the replacement in the event log.

TMDS event logs and the reports generated by the remote intervention are archived in a centralized support database. This database contains a history of service requests, diagnoses, and support actions for hardware and software. Experts periodically scrutinize the database, seeking out diagnostic patterns and irregularities that they can use to improve system maintenance.

TMDS continues to evolve, incorporating many new features. One of these features is a built-in self-test (BIST) method that uses pseudo-random test vectors and scan-path design [Garcia, 1988]. On the CLX, the pseudo-random test covers several custom ICs, commercial MSI logic, a static RAM array, and their interconnects. The BIST also does a functional test of the dynamic RAM main memory and its control logic. The test is controlled by maintenance processor software, simplifying the processor board hardware dedicated to the BIST. With the BIST, hardware problems on the CLX processor can be detected and reported to TMDS without requiring downloaded, handwritten diagnostics.

In the Cyclone system, the power and environmental monitoring facilities have been significantly enhanced. In addition to sensing more components (voltages both on the circuit boards and at the power supply outputs, intake and outlet air temperatures, battery condition, and fan rotation), sensors are polled much more frequently, and most sensors are replicated to allow differentiation between a failing component and a failing sensor. In addition, Cyclone's maintenance subsystem can detect the physical presence or absence of many components, such as cables, power supplies, fans, and bus terminators. Both the logical address and physical location (which cabinet and which slot within the cabinet) are automatically available to the maintenance subsystem so that failed components can be easily identified and reliably replaced.

SOFTWARE

Overview

In the preceding discussion of the evolution of the Tandem system, the careful reader will find no mention of fault-tolerant hardware modules. In fact, one of the primary design criteria for Tandem hardware is to make it *fault intolerant*. Any incorrectly functioning hardware module should detect the problem and, as quickly as possible, shut itself down. There are a few exceptions to this rule, such as error-correcting main memory, but the fundamental design of the Tandem system is to connect *fail-fast* hardware with fault-tolerant software.

Fault tolerance normally implies hardware redundancy. While this is true for a Tandem system, the net additional cost to the customer has been kept surprisingly low due to the many innovative features of the Tandem system. In most cases, the redundant modules each perform useful work in their own right and, except when they have failed, contribute to the capacity of the system. Failing modules can be replaced while the system is running. The net effect of a hardware failure is, at worst, a short period of slightly degraded performance. A system with a normal amount of excess capacity will survive a failure without any noticeable effect.

The key to fault tolerance without wasted redundancy is the Guardian operating system. The following sections describe the many components of Guardian, from the kernel (process and memory management and message system) to the transaction manager, networking support, and NonStop Structured Query Language (SQL). Each makes an important contribution, not only to the functionality of the Tandem system, but also to the support of fault tolerance.

Fault tolerance would be of little value without data integrity; business demands accurate record keeping, and an inconsistent database is often worse than no database at all. Furthermore, a business that depends on its computer system must be able to grow that system at least as fast as the business. The following sections also describe how the system has been engineered to prevent data corruption and to provide expandability.

Guardian: An Integrated OLTP Operating System

A basic difference between Guardian and other systems is the very high level of software integration. Although there is the usual layering of software function, these layers are relatively closely tied together and interdependent. This approach has its costs, but the resulting efficiency, coupled with a high level of functionality, is unique in the computer industry. There are many software components that contribute to the fault tolerance, data integrity, expandability, and basic functionality of the Tandem system. In this section, we will give a general overview of the Guardian elements that differentiate Tandem from other systems.

• The *kernel* includes the usual support for the management of processes, memory, interprocess communication, names, time, peripheral I/O, process synchronization, and debugging. In addition, the kernel detects failures of any processor, interprocessor bus, or I/O channel and performs recovery. Several innovative techniques are used to synchronize the independent processors and to provide a consistent view of time and system state, despite failures and communication delays. Finally, the kernel supports the management of process pairs, which are the keystone of both hardware and software fault tolerance.

• The *file system* hides the distributed nature of the system from application processes and presents a conventional view of peripheral I/O devices. Communication with I/O devices and other processes is accomplished without regard to the location of the resource, be it in the same processor, another processor in the same system, or a processor in a remote system. The file system also provides checkpoint and retry mechanisms for hiding the effects of hardware and software failures from the application process.

• *I/O processes* manage peripheral devices and react to component failures by routing access over working paths and devices and then notifying operators and customer engineers about the need to repair or replace the failing component. I/O processes receive messages from application processes (via the file system) and perform the requested operations on physical devices. In the view of the application programmer, the I/O process and the device it manages are indistinguishable. There are dozens of different I/O processes, each designed to manage a particular class of device.

• The *disk process* is probably the single most important component of the system. It provides data integrity and reliable access to data despite processor, channel, controller, or media failure. It supports mirrored disks efficiently, making good use of the dual access paths to data. It supports four types of file structures, as well as SQL tables; it supports file partitioning, alternate indices, data security, and main memory cacheing for both reading and writing of data. It supports full transaction management, including two-phase locking and two-phase commit protocols. Last, but far from least, it can execute those parts of SQL queries that require data local to one disk, greatly reducing message traffic for many applications.

• The *transaction management facility* (TMF) coordinates the processing of disk accesses and updates, ensuring the requirements for atomicity, consistency, isolation, and durability. An application can, in a very simple manner, request multiple database updates in many physical locations, possibly thousands of miles apart, and be assured that either all or none of them will be performed; during the transaction, other applications will always have a consistent view of the database, never being able to see only some of the updates and not others. TMF protects the database from total media failure (including the loss of a mirrored disk pair) through the technique of on-line dumping and roll-forward of the transaction log. TMF also supports the remote duplicate database facility, which can quickly recover from the loss of an entire computing facility.

• The *transaction processing monitor* (Pathway) provides a flexible method for managing customer applications in a distributed system. Pathway automatically distributes application processes (called servers) to the available processors and, in the event of a processor failure, redistributes the applications to the remaining processors. Any work that was lost or compromised by the failure is automatically restarted after being rolled back to its initial state. Customer programming is straightforward and is not required to perform any special operations to achieve full fault tolerance.

• The *network control process and line handler processes* (Expand) manage communications between a system and a network of other Tandem systems. To a user on one node of a network, the rest of the network appears as a seamless extension of the local system. The requirement for local autonomy may impose access barriers, and communication delays may impose performance penalties; otherwise, it is as easy to manage distributed applications and databases as it is to manage local ones.

Fundamental System Structure

A Tandem system is composed of from 2 to 16 independent processors connected by a dual, high-speed interprocessor bus (IPB). Guardian, Tandem's proprietary operating system, has two primary responsibilities: (1) to maintain a consistent view of the system while allowing each processor to exercise independent autonomy, and (2) to provide general services for its clients and the processes and particularly to provide an efficient and reliable means of communication between them.

The first responsibility of the operating system requires that each processor establish and maintain communication with the other processors of the system. Continuous availability of the IPB is a fundamental assumption, since the processors must coordinate many operations and notify each other of changes in system state. If any two processors are not able to communicate with each other for any period, it is likely that they will have inconsistent views of the system state; one or the other must be restarted. Thus, a dual (fault-tolerant) IPB is an important requirement.

Except for the lowest-level functions of process dispatching, message transmission, and interrupt processing, all work in the system is managed by one or more processes. System processes manage process creation and termination, virtual memory, security, performance measurement, event management, diagnostics, and debugging. I/O processes manage access to peripheral devices and are responsible for dealing with failing components. Application and utility processes direct the operation of the system towards some useful purpose.

Messages are the primary method for process-to-process interaction, eliminating the need for applications to deal with the multiple-computer organization of the system. To applications, the system has the appearance of a conventional uniprocessor programmed in conventional programming languages such as COBOL85, Pascal, C, and FORTRAN. Processes interact with one another using a client-server protocol typical of the remote procedure call protocols that are common in workstation-server LANS today. This client-server design is well accepted today, but fifteen years ago it was considered novel.

Fault tolerance is provided by duplication of components in both the hardware and the software. Access to I/O devices is provided by process pairs consisting of a primary process and a backup process. The primary process must checkpoint state information to the backup process so that the backup can take over if a failure occurs. Requests to these devices are routed using the logical process name so that the request is always routed to the current primary process. The result is a set of primitives and protocols that allow recovery and continued processing in spite of bus, processor, I/O controller, or I/O device failures. Furthermore, these primitives provide access to all system resources from every process in the system.

Initialization and Processor Loading. System initialization starts with one processor being *cold loaded* from a disk attached to that processor; any processor can be used for this operation, as long as it is connected to a disk with a copy of the operating system image file. The image file contains the code of the kernel and the system processes that are automatically started when each processor is loaded. Once any processor is loaded, it is then used to load the other processors via the IPB. All processors other than the first can be loaded in parallel. Should a processor fail or be removed for maintenance, it can be reloaded by any other processor. There is no essential difference between an initial load of a processor and a later reload of a processor after it has been repaired. A processor reload operation does not interfere with the operation of application processes.

Each processor receives an identical copy of the kernel and other system-level software, but a different processor configuration, depending upon the peripheral devices attached to the processor. Each processor will start the appropriate I/O processes to manage the attached devices. Once a processor's software and configuration is loaded, it passes through a phase in which it is synchronized with the other processors. Basically, this synchronization involves transmitting a consistent copy of the system state to the processor. Once this is accomplished, the processor becomes a fully independent entity. There is no master processor.

Processor Synchronization. Although Tandem computer systems are designed to tolerate any single fault, either hardware or software, multiple failures do sometimes occur, either through multiple hardware errors (unlikely), software errors (likely), operation errors (more likely), or during maintenance periods. Even when multiple faults occur, only a portion of the system (some disk volumes and/or processors) becomes unusable until it can be repaired and reintegrated into the system.

Two different mechanisms are provided for dealing with multiple faults: processor synchronization and transactions. The following sections describe the issues of processor synchronization. In addition to a simple algorithm to detect processor failure, Guardian also has three more complex algorithms to ensure that all processors of a system have closely agreeing views of processor configuration, replicated data, and time. Each of these algorithms requires a minimum of communication and is sufficiently robust without resorting to the cost and complexity of solving the Byzantine Generals problem.

I'm-Alive Protocol. Once two or more processors are loaded, they must continually check on each other's health. Because the processors are designed to be fail-fast, they respond to any internal error by shutting down completely and refusing to communicate with the outside world until receiving an explicit signal that they are ready to be reloaded. Thus, it is up to the remaining processors to detect a failure through the absence of any response from the failed processor.

Using the I'm-Alive protocol, each processor transmits a short message to each processor, including itself, at least once every second, over each of the two IPBs (the message to itself verifies that the sending and receiving bus circuitry is functioning). Every two seconds, each processor checks to see that it has received at least one message from each processor in the interval. Any missing messages imply that a processor is not healthy and has probably failed. Normally, any processor would immediately declare such a processor down and proceed to cancel all outstanding communication with that processor.

Regroup Protocol. Experience showed, however, that there are rare instances in which one processor might merely be a little late in sending out its I'm-Alive messages. This situation usually occurs when recovery from power failure or other high-priority error recovery momentarily usurped a processor. Because the I'm-Alive intervals are not synchronized between processors, a late I'm-Alive might result in a processor's being declared down by some processors and not by others. Such a case, termed a *split-brain* situation, could lead to a lack of database integrity. Thus, a Regroup algorithm was implemented to handle these cases with as little disruption as possible. In essence, the slow processor is given a second chance. Whenever any processor detects a missing I'm-alive message, all processors (including the suspect processor, if able) exchange messages to decide which processors are healthy. After two broadcast rounds, the decision is made and all processors act on it.

Global Update Protocol. Certain information, notably the destination control table (described later), is replicated in each processor and must be identical in each processor. Updates to replicated information, however, originate in multiple processes and multiple processors. Consistency of an update depends upon *atomicity* [Gray, 1979], which demands that (1) any update is completed within a maximum time, (2) either all replicated copies are updated or no copy is updated, and (3) all updates occur serially.

In Tandem systems, atomic update is guaranteed by the Global Update protocol [Carr, 1985]. All such updates are performed by the Guardian kernel so that high-priority processes cannot delay the completion of an update within a maximum time. All updates must first be sent to a locker processor, which ensures that updates occur serially and also ensures that an update is propagated to all processors even if the originating processor fails, including simultaneous failure of the updating and locker processors.

Time Synchronization. An OLTP system is designed to record and control real-world events at the time they actually occur. An important part of the information processed is the current time. Furthermore, it is important that the sequence in which events occur can be reconstructed from timestamps associated with each event.

Although it is clearly difficult to have coordinated clocks in a widely distributed system, initial attempts to synchronize time on a local Tandem system showed that this is not a simple problem either. Although it is no great problem to keep clocks within seconds of each other, synchronization of a multiprocessor system requires that no message that can be sent from processor A, with A's clock time T, should arrive at processor B before B's clock time has reached T. Otherwise, time would appear to move backwards.

A novel algorithm [Nellen, 1985, 1986] passes time-adjustment packets from processor to processor; each processor not only adjusts its own clock to the average time of all processors, but it also calculates its clock error relative to the average and makes adjustments on a continual basis. This algorithm ensures that the average time does not fluctuate wildly when a processor fails and is replaced by a processor with a different speed clock.

The provision for an external clock can extend the local synchronization algorithm to geographically distributed Tandem systems. Electronic clocks that monitor a broadcast time standard can keep Tandem systems synchronized to less than the time it takes them to communicate with each other.

Guardian Kernel Services

Now that the basic problem of maintaining consistency between the distributed processors has been addressed, we can turn to the performance of useful work. As in all modern systems, Guardian supports the concurrent execution of multiple independent processes. What distinguishes Guardian is its heavy dependence on messages to coordinate the operations of processes. Messages are essential for the operation of both system-level software and customer applications.

The design of the system was strongly influenced by Dijkstra's "THE" system [Dijkstra, 1968] and Brinch Hansen's implementation of a message-based operating system nucleus [Brinch Hansen, 1970]. Both hardware and software have been optimized to facilitate the sending of messages between processors and between processes. The heavy dependence upon messages, in preference to other communication and synchronization mechanisms, has been very important in the design of a system that is both distributed and smoothly expandable. Customer applications can be easily grown by simply adding more processors, disks, and other peripherals, without changing software or even reloading the system.

Because of the message-based structure, the applications are unaware of the physical configuration of the system. An application accesses a directly connected peripheral and a remotely connected peripheral in exactly the same way: Messages are exchanged with the peripheral's manager (an I/O process); the I/O process is also unaware if the requestor is in the same or a different processor.

Efficient messages have also been a key element in implementing fault tolerance. System-level software uses messages to *checkpoint* information critical to data integrity and continued operation in the event of a failure. Applications are generally unaware that a failure has occurred because messages can be automatically rerouted from a failing component to a functioning one.

Processes

A process is an independently executable entity that consists primarily of shareable program code, private memory, and the process state vector. The process state vector includes the program counter, registers, privileges, priority, and a microsecond timer that is incremented only when the process is executing.

Once a process begins execution in some processor, it remains in that processor until it is terminated. Each process in the system has a unique identifier or name by which other processes may communicate with it on a network-wide basis. Messages to a process are addressed to its identifier, and so the identifier provides a network-wide and fault-tolerant method for process addressing.

Guardian maintains a destination control table that is identical in all processors of a system. This table relates the name of a process with its location (that is, its processor and process number) so that messages to a process can be routed in an efficient manner.

Processes scheduling uses a pure priority mechanism with preemption. Scheduling is round robin within a priority class. Considerable care is taken to avoid the priority inversion problem in which a low-priority client makes a request of a high-priority server, thereby promoting its work to high priority. This problem is unique to message-based systems and must be solved in order to provide a global priority scheduling mechanism.

Memory Management

Each process has a virtual address space containing its program and a process data stack. A program consists of *user code* and an optional *user library*. The user library is an object code file that can be shared by processes that execute different user code program files. All processes within a processor executing the same program share memory for object code. The process data stack is private to the process and cannot be shared.

Processes may allocate additional *extended memory segments*, which have a maximum size of 127.5 MB each. A process may access its data stack and one extended segment concurrently. If multiple extended segments are allocated, the process must explicitly request that a particular segment be placed in use when it is required.

Data in extended segments may be shared with other processes in two different ways:

1. A read-only segment is a method of accessing the contents of a file as if it were main memory, using virtual memory to load the information on demand. Such segments can be shared among all processes in all processors, although multiple copies of the data may exist in different processors.

2. A read-write segment can be shared only by processes in a single processor, since it would be impractical to update multiple copies in different processors.

The sharing of read-write data among customer application processes is discouraged so that fault containment is maintained and so that the system load can be distributed by the placing processes in idle processors. Guardian does not provide interprocess concurrency control (other than via messages) necessary for coordination of updates to shared memory.

The Guardian memory manager supports virtual memory using demand paging and a clock replacement strategy [Carr, 1982]. It intentionally does not support load (thrashing) control, as the performance requirements of on-line transaction processing do not permit the paging or swapping of processes commonly found in interactive time-sharing systems.

Interprocess Messages

The basic message system protocol follows the requestor-server model. One process sends a message with a request to another process and waits for a response. The second process services the request and replies with a result as depicted in Figure 8–60. This is considered to be a single message and can also be viewed as a remote procedure call. Naturally, this basic mechanism also suffices for simple datagrams or for transferring bulk data (up to 60 KB per message) in either direction.

Multi-threaded requestor processes may have many messages outstanding to collections of server processes. Multi-threaded server processes may accept multiple requests and reply to each in any desired order. Any process may operate concurrently both as a client and as a server. For application processes, access to the message system is through the file system, which provides some protection from abuse of privileged mechanisms and simplifies the interface for sending messages. System processes, on the other hand, generally use the message-system primitives directly, as these provide better performance.

The simplest use of messages is for application processes to access peripheral devices; the programmer is generally unaware that messages are involved, as the program makes a simple read or write of data on a file. If, for example, the file is a disk file, then the read/write request will send a message to the manager of the disk, known as the *disk process*.

It is simple for a process to masquerade as a device manager. An example of this is the printing spooler process: Applications send print output messages to a spooler (which pretends to be a physical printer process) and stores them for printing later; the spooler then sends the output, again via messages, to a true physical printer process. The application programmer need not be concerned with whether the message system routes the messages to the spooler process

FIGURE 8–60

*Process concepts
in the Guardian
operating system*

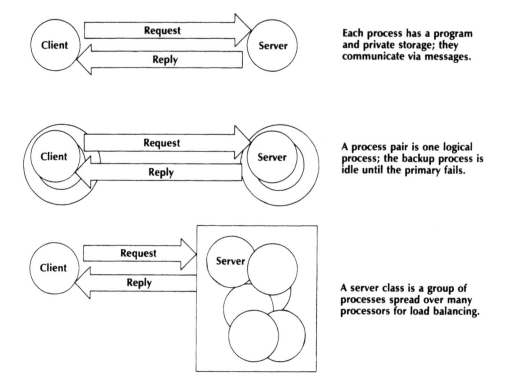

Each process has a program
and private storage; they
communicate via messages.

A process pair is one logical
process; the backup process is
idle until the primary fails.

A server class is a group of
processes spread over many
processors for load balancing.

or directly to an I/O process controlling a physical printer; only the process name must be changed to choose the destination process. A more interesting use of messages is in the structuring of applications as a network of communicating processes, which is described in the section on Pathway.

In the Tandem system, messages are a fundamental mechanism for providing fault tolerance:

• The *communication protocol* for the interprocessor buses tolerates any single bus error during the execution of any message-system primitive. A communication failure will occur only if the sender or receiver processes or either of their processors fails. Any bus errors that occur during a message-system operation are automatically corrected without involving the communicating processes.

• The *process-pair mechanism*, as described in the next section, provides fault-tolerant access to peripheral devices despite processor, channel, or even most software failures. A request message that is being processed by the failing component is automatically resent to the backup component; the application is not even aware that this has happened and need not make any provision for it.

Memory moves rather than the interprocessor buses are used for communication between processes in the same processor, but there is no apparent difference to the communicating processes. In addition to messages between processes, Guardian also implements simpler *control* messages, which are for communication between processor kernels. Control messages are used as a basis of the full message-system protocol, as well as an inexpensive mechanism to maintain synchronization between processors.

Guardian and the IPB are highly optimized for the processing of interprocess messages, especially for short messages of 2 KB or less. A message between processes in different processors is only marginally more expensive than an intraprocessor message. In fact, an interprocessor message usually has a shorter *elapsed* time than an intraprocessor message, since both sender and receiver processes can execute in parallel.

A final advantage of the message system is its transparent support of both short- and long-haul networks. Except for the inevitable communication delays, the client and server can detect no apparent difference between accessing a local disk file (or process or printer) and a remote one [Uren, 1986]. The message-system and file-system protocols are precisely the same in both the local and remote cases.

Tolerating Software Faults

Systems whose fault tolerance is based solely on hardware mechanisms can be designed to provide high reliability and to continue to function in the presence of hardware component failures. Unfortunately, a high percentage of computer system failures are due to software.

Unlike the situation with hardware components, it is possible to develop perfect, defect-free, failure-proof software. It is only a matter of cost to the manufacturer and inconvenience to the customer, who must wait much longer for some needed software to be delivered. In the commercial world, customers demand a continuous flow of new software and improvements to old software. They demand that this be done quickly (more quickly than the competition) and at a reasonable price. New software systems are inevitably more functional and more complex than the systems they replace.

The use of structured programming and higher-level languages has not eliminated software errors because they have enabled the building of larger and more complicated programs. Methods to improve software quality, such as code inspections and structured testing techniques, are effective, but they only reduce the number of errors; they do not eliminate them. Therefore, in practice, even with significant care taken in software development processes, software faults are inevitable. In fact, as previously stated, software failures are typically more common than hardware failures.

Software fault tolerance leads, indirectly, to better software quality and data integrity. At Tandem, system programmers are encouraged to make numerous consistency checks and, if a problem is detected, to *halt* the processor. (Tandem's system software probably has one of the highest densities of processor-halt instructions in the industry.) The system programmer knows that, for almost all consistency problems, the backup processes (described in the next section) will continue to provide service to the customer. This consistency checking has two direct effects:

1. When contamination of system data structures is detected, the processor is immediately shut down, reducing the chance that the database can become contaminated.
2. All significant errors in system software become very visible, and since the entire processor state is frozen and dumped when an error is detected, it is easier to uncover the cause of the error. Thus, errors that affect system stability and data integrity are found and corrected in a very timely manner. The result is higher-quality software and fewer failures that need to be tolerated.

Process pairs provide fault-tolerant execution of programs. They tolerate any single hardware fault and most transient software faults. (Transient software faults are those caused by some untimely combination of events, such as a resource shortage that occurs at the same time that an I/O error must be handled.) Most faults in production software are transient [Gray, 1985], since the simpler programming errors are weeded out during testing. Process pairs allow fail-fast programs to continue execution in the backup process when the software bug is transient.

Process Pairs

The key to both hardware and software fault tolerance is the *process pair* [Bartlett, 1981]. A process pair consists of a *primary* process, which does all the work, and a *backup* process, which is passive but is prepared to take over when the primary process fails. (See Figure 8–61.) This arrangement is analogous to having a standby processor or computer system, except that, if properly arranged, the cost of the backup process is far less than the cost of the primary process. Generally, the memory requirements and processor time consumption is a small fraction (usually about 10 percent) of the primary process.

A typical process pair is started in the same way as an ordinary process: as a single process executing in a single processor. The process then notifies the operating system that it would like to create a clone of itself, using the same program file, in another processor. The second process is also started in a very ordinary fashion, but with two small differences:

1. The second process receives an initial message that informs it that it is a backup process; the process then goes into a passive mode, accepting messages only from the primary or from Guardian (to notify the backup that either the primary process or its processor has failed).
2. Both the primary and backup process share a single name, and for each name, the destination control table registers both the primary and backup processes; all communication to the process pair is routed to the primary process.

While the primary process executes, the backup is largely passive. At critical points, the primary process sends *checkpoint* messages to the backup.

Checkpoint messages have two different forms; a process pair will normally use either one or the other, but not both. For application software, a simple form of checkpointing is provided. Checkpoints copy the selected process state, at carefully chosen takeover points, from the pri-

FIGURE 8–61
Diagram of system structure

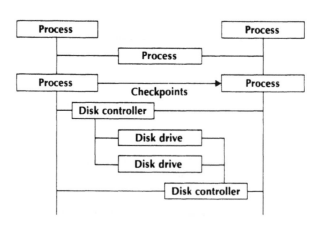

These processes represent application programs that are communicating with one another and with device servers.

These two processes are a pair controlling a mirrored disk.

mary to the backup. Updating the process state of the backup is performed solely by the system software at the command of the primary process; the backup process is completely passive.

At a checkpoint, usually immediately before or after some important I/O operation, the primary and backup are functionally identical. If the primary fails, the backup begins executing at the point at which the last checkpoint occurred. For most system software, such as I/O processes, checkpoint messages contain functional updates to the process state. The backup processor must interpret these messages and apply appropriate updates to its own local data structures; this is sometimes referred to as an *active* backup. Although the program code is identical, the contents of memory can be entirely different. A typical checkpoint would indicate that a file has been opened or closed, but, in the case of the disk process, most updates to important files also will involve a checkpoint.

The active backup approach is more complicated, but it has several advantages. Less data is transmitted on each checkpoint, and information that the backup can obtain from other sources (such as a disk file) need not be checkpointed. For software fault tolerance, the active backup is better because the backup must manage its own state, and errors in the primary process are less likely to contaminate the backup [Borr, 1984].

Since the process pair shares a single name, it appears to all other processes as a single process. When a message is sent to it, the message system automatically consults the destination control table to determine which process is primary and routes the message to that location. When the primary process fails for some reason, the backup becomes the primary, the destination control table is changed, and all messages are directed to the new primary process. The new primary has already received checkpoints that describe the current openers of the process, so those openers need do nothing to re-establish communication.

There are potential race conditions in which a server process pair has performed some request and has not replied to the client when a failure occurs. When the outstanding request is resent to the new primary process, it might perform the same operation a second time, possibly causing an inconsistency. This problem is eliminated by associating sequence numbers with each request and having the new primary simply make duplicate responses to already-processed requests.

Similar problems could occur if a client process pair performs a checkpoint and then makes requests to a server. If a failure occurs, the backup client takes over and makes duplicate requests to the server. These requests are handled using the same sequence numbering scheme. During normal operation, the sequence numbers are used for duplicate elimination and detection of lost messages in case of transmission error [Bartlett, 1978].

I/O Processes

Most processes can execute on any processor. The exceptions are I/O processes because they manage devices, and each device is connected to two processors via dual-ported device controllers. When a device is configured, an I/O process pair is automatically defined for the device; one member of the pair resides in each processor connected to the device. The configuration parameters may state which processor is the normal primary access path to the device, but this choice can be altered by the operator for testing and performance tuning. In the case of a processor, channel, or controller port failure, the process that still has access to the device will take over control, and all application requests will be routed to it.

When a request for an operation such as a file open or close occurs, the primary process sends this information to the backup process through the message system. These checkpoints ensure that the backup process has all information needed to take over control of the device. Process pairs provide a uniform way to access I/O devices and all other system-wide resources. This access is independent of the functions performed within the processes, their locations, or their implementations. Within the process pair, the message system is used to checkpoint state changes so that the backup process can take over in the event of a failure. A process pair for a mirrored disk volume appears in Figure 8–61.

Disk Process

Although the overall design of an OLTP application may be very complex, it is essentially composed of many simple servers that require a minor amount of computation and perform a large number of database accesses and updates. To achieve high performance in this environment requires a great deal of sophistication in the design of the database management software. In this section, we are able to give only a broad outline of the myriad responsibilities and functions of the disk process, but it clearly has the most demanding task of any component of the system.

Each disk process pair must manage a pair of mirrored disks, each connected to two controllers, which are in turn connected to two processor channels. Thus, there are eight possible paths to the data, any component of which may fail; even in the rare case of a multiple failure, the disk process must attempt to use all available resources to provide continuous access to the data.

Mirrored Disks. Mirrored disks are, as the name implies, identical images of one another. It would appear that this is a situation in which fault tolerance requires a redundant (and expensive) resource that contributes nothing to system capacity. (The value of data integrity in most cases, however, justifies the expense of the redundant disks.) Fortunately, however, even though the redundant disk does not contribute to storage capacity, it usually contributes significantly to processing capacity. When data must be read from disk, the disk process can use either of the two disks, usually the disk that offers the shorter seek time. Multiple read requests can be processed concurrently, and, if one disk is busy, then the other disk can be used. Because duplexed disks offer shorter seeks, they support higher read rates than two ordinary disks [Bitton, 1989].

Any write operation must be made to each of the mirrored disks and requires that both disks seek to the same cylinder (thereby reducing the chance of having a short seek on the next read). Consequently, disk writes are considerably more expensive than reads, but, when performed in parallel, they are not much slower than a write to a single disk. The proper use of disk cache, particularly when protected by transaction management, can eliminate a large majority of disk writes without sacrificing data integrity.

Customers who consider all or part of their database to be a noncritical resource may have unmirrored disks on a disk-by-disk basis. Modern disks are very reliable, and, even when drives fail, it is exceedingly rare that the data are lost. Many activities, such as software development, would not be seriously impacted by the rare unavailability of a disk.

Disk Cache. Each disk process can be allotted many megabytes of main memory for disk cache. In 1990, the upper limit was 56 MB per disk volume, but this will steadily increase, along with the size of main memory. The disk process uses the cache to hold recently accessed disk pages and, under normal circumstances, can satisfy most read requests without performing any physical I/O operation. The disk process can service many requests concurrently, so it is not unusual for it to satisfy a half-dozen requests from cache while it is performing a single real disk I/O.

The worst case for cache management is an application that performs random accesses to a very large database. The probability that it re-uses a recently accessed page in cache is quite low. Experience, however, shows that the typical application usually has, at most, one such file in addition to numerous smaller files that are also accessed in each transaction; thus, the ratio of cache-hits to physical I/Os remains quite good. Even in the case of the large file, traversing the B-tree index structure to find a data record might normally require three physical I/Os that can be saved by cacheing the index blocks.

Although cache has an obvious benefit in reducing read I/O operations, the situation is not so clear with write operations. There are many situations in which disk file updates are made to blocks that were recently updated; if only part of a block is being updated, this clearly saves a read to get the unchanged parts of the block. More significantly, if updated blocks could be kept in main memory and written to disk only when convenient, many disk writes could be eliminated. On a conventional system, we couldn't do this because a processor failure would lose a large number of disk updates and corrupt the entire database.

In Tandem systems, we might consider checkpointing disk updates to the backup disk process, which is much cheaper than performing an actual I/O. If a processor failed, the backup could make sure that the updates were written to disk. This approach, however, would not be safe enough, since it is possible for a long power failure, or simple bad luck, to cause a multiple failure and loss of an unacceptable number of database updates. Luckily, there is a solution to this problem, but we must postpone its discussion until we have covered the basics of transactions.

Partitioning. If an OLTP application has a high transaction rate and each transaction accesses a particular file, the load on the disk process, even with perfect cacheing, may be too large to sustain on a single processor. As with the application, it is necessary to be able to distribute the database access load across the processors easily. (In general, dynamic load redistribution has not proved necessary, but it must be easy to redistribute in a static manner.)

The concept of file partitioning is not new, but the disk process and file system cooperate to provide a simple and flexible solution. Any file can be simply partitioned by issuing a few commands specifying the key ranges of each partition. To the applications, the partitioned file appears as a single file, and the file system redirects any read or write request to the proper partition, depending on the key of the record. If a partition becomes too full, or too busy, it can be split by subdividing its key range and moving the appropriate records to the new partitions.

The partitions of a file can be distributed throughout a network, and, thus, a distributed database can be created and maintained in a manner that is completely invisible to the applications, while maintaining excellent performance when accessing local data. For example, one could easily construct a 50-partition file, one for each of the United States, and physically locate each partition on a separate Tandem system in each state. On each system, local state data could be processed very efficiently, but every application process could have access to the full database as if it were a single file, subject only to the inevitable communication delays.

Locking and Transaction Protection. An OLTP application may have hundreds of independent servers performing concurrent accesses to the same set of files; the disk process must support file and record locks, for both shared and exclusive access. Locks can be obtained through explicit application request or through the operation of transaction management, which automatically provides atomicity and isolation of all database accesses in a transaction. More about transactions appears later.

File System. The file system is a set of system routines that execute in the application process and manage communication with I/O processes and other application processes. For access to I/O devices, the file system hides the process-and-message structure, and the application program appears to be issuing direct requests to a local I/O supervisor. That is, the file system provides a procedure call interface to the remote I/O processes, masking the fact that they are remote procedure calls. The application is unaware of the distributed nature of the system. In order to implement partitioned files, the file system automatically manages requests. It implements buffering so that many sequential operations can be satisfied with one request to the I/O process.

The file system implements the first level of system security, as it does not allow an application to send a message to an I/O (or application) process unless the application has first identified itself with an Open message that contains an authenticated user name. If the server process denies access to the object, the file system will not permit further messages (except for Open messages) to be sent.

The file system manages timeout and retransmission of requests; it sends the message to the backup server process if the primary fails. In addition, if the client is a process pair, the file system manages checkpointing of the process state to the backup process.

NonStop SQL

The file system and the disk server cooperate to process Structured Query Language (SQL) database operations in an integrated and efficient manner [Tandem Data Base Group, 1988]. The file system manages the SQL processing in the client and performs all the high-level operations such as sort, join, and aggregation. The disk process understands simple constructs, such as table, field, and expression, and will do low-level SQL operations on the data. Thus, operations can be performed at whatever level promotes the best efficiency. For example, the SQL statement

    UPDATE ACCOUNT SET BALANCE = BALANCE + :DEPOSIT-AMOUNT
        WHERE ACCOUNT_NUMBER = :ACCOUNT-ID;

can be processed with a single message to the disk process. There is no need for the application to fetch the information, update it, and send it back to the disk process. In another example, the statement

    SELECT FIELDA, FIELDE FROM TABLEX WHERE FIELDA + FIELDB > FIELDC;

allows filtering to be performed at the disk process, minimizing the transfer of data to the application.

NonStop SQL is designed specifically to handle OLTP applications while achieving good performance. Because it is integrated with other system software, it can be used for OLTP applications in a geographically distributed network of systems. SQL tables can be partitioned across systems in a network. Also, applications can run at one network node while accessing and updating data at another node. Furthermore, the applications themselves can be distributed. With NonStop SQL, fault tolerance derives from the basic mechanisms of process pairs, mirrored disk, and geographically distributed systems, along with node autonomy and transaction support. All transactions, local and network, are protected for consistency and error recovery.

From a fault-tolerance perspective there are two novel things about NonStop SQL. First is the design goal of node autonomy. The system is designed so that if the client and server can communicate, then the client can access the data. This simple requirement implies that all the metadata describing the file must be replicated with the file. If the file is partitioned among many nodes of the network, the catalog information describing the file must be replicated at all those nodes.

The second requirement is that no administrative operations on the data are allowed to take the database off line. For example, taking an archive dump of the database must be done while the data are being accessed, reorganizing the data must be done on line, and so on. Many administrative tasks are not yet on line, but a major focus of current efforts is to make all administrative operations completely on line.

SQL allows data administrators to attach integrity constraints to data; these may take the form of *entity constraints* that limit the values a record may have or *referential integrity constraints* that constrain the relationships among records in different tables. Placing the constraints on the data is more reliable than depending on the application program to make such checks. Updates to the data that would violate these entity constraints are rejected.

Transactions

The work involved in a computation can be packaged as an atomic unit by using the transaction monitoring facility (TMF) (Figures 8–62, 8–63). This facility allows an application to issue a Begin-Transaction request, make numerous database accesses and updates in multiple files, on multiple disks, and on multiple network nodes, and then issue an End-Transaction request [Borr, 1981]. The system guarantees that the work of the transaction will be ACID, defined as follows [Haerder and Reuter, 1983].

- *Atomic*: Either all of the database updates will be performed, or none of them will be; for example, if a transaction moves money from one bank account balance to another, the end result will never be more or less money on the books.
- *Consistent*: Each successful transaction preserves the consistency of the database.
- *Isolated*: Events within a transaction must be hidden from other transactions running concurrently; otherwise, a failing transaction could not be reset to its beginning.
- *Durable*: Once committed, the results of the transaction must survive any failure.

Should the application or Guardian (that is, the disk process or TMF) detect a problem that compromises the transaction, either one may issue Abort-Transaction, which will cause any

FIGURE 8–62
Structure of the transaction monitoring facility

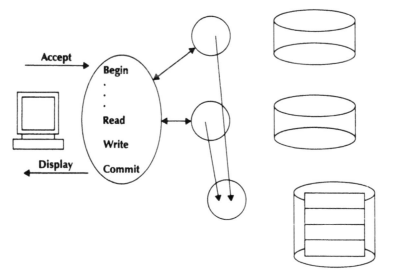

Accept

Begin
.
.
.
Read
Write
Display Commit

Undo-redo log of
old value and
new value
of each updated
record

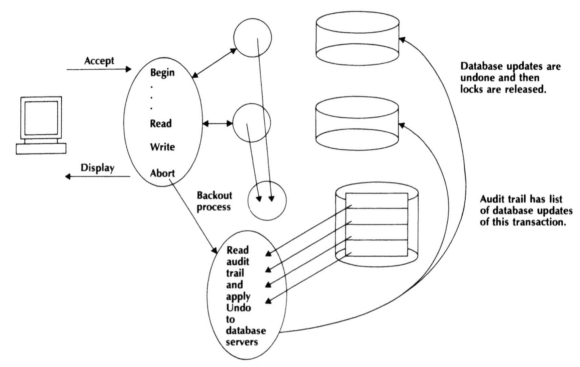

Accept

Begin
.
.
.
Read

Write

Display

Abort

Backout
process

Read
audit
trail
and
apply
Undo
to
database
servers

Database updates are
undone and then
locks are released.

Audit trail has list
of database updates
of this transaction.

FIGURE 8–63 *TMF transaction backout structure*

database updates to be undone. The system can manage thousands of concurrent transactions, keeping them all isolated from one another. The application program need not concern itself with the locking protocol, as the required locking operations are well defined and performed automatically.

The work of a transaction can be distributed to multiple processes. As we shall see, it is normal to structure an application as client processes directing numerous server processes, each designed to perform some simple part of the transaction. Once the client has issued Begin-Transaction, all requests to servers are marked as belonging to the transaction; all database updates by the servers become part of the single transaction until the client issues the End-Transaction or Abort-Transaction request.

When a client issues Begin-Transaction, the system creates a unique *transaction identifier* and uses it to tag all messages and all database requests. If a tagged message is accepted by a server, all of its messages and database requests receive the same tag. Database locks acquired by the client or its servers are also tagged by the transaction identifier.

During a transaction, disk processes hold the updates in their caches. If there is insufficient cache, the disk process may update the database before the transaction completes, but first it must generate *undo* and *redo* records that allow the transaction to be either undone in case it aborts or redone in case it commits and a later failure occurs. When the client issues End-Transaction, each disk process with updates for the transaction must generate undo and redo log records before it updates the disk.

The undo and redo records are written to specially designated transaction log files called the *audit trail*. Normally, these files are on disks that are separate from the database, and the undo and redo records must be written to the audit trail disk before the main database is updated. Thus, even a total system failure will not lose transactions that are committed or allow the database to become inconsistent. Even if a mirrored disk pair is destroyed, the database and all transactions can be recovered from an archival copy of the disk and the transaction log. Any process participating in the transaction can unilaterally abort it. The system implements two-phase locking and uses a nonblocking, grouped, presumed-abort, two-phase commit protocol.

It might appear that support of transactions adds considerable overhead to the basic operations of accessing and updating the database. Surprisingly, TMF *improves performance*, while enhancing fault tolerance and data integrity. As described previously, updates to a database should be written to disk immediately in order to prevent their loss in case of a failure. This increases disk traffic and lengthens transaction response time.

When database operations are protected by TMF, a description of all updates is written to the audit trail; it becomes unnecessary for the disk process to write the updates to the database, except when it is convenient to do so. As soon as the audit trail records are reliably stored on disks, the application can be notified that the updates have been permanently recorded and will survive any failure. Writing the updates to the audit trail is considerably more efficient than writing the updates to the database because many updates from a single transaction (and, in a busy system, from multiple concurrent transactions) are blocked together and written in a single I/O operation. Further, the audit trail is written sequentially and writing is performed with a minimum of seeks, while database updates are random-access and imply numerous seeks. Finally, the disk process performs less checkpointing to its backup because uncommitted updates do not need to be protected against processor failures.

The result of these effects is that the logging and recovery of TMF is a net savings over the less functional store-thru-disk cache. TMF converts random main memory database access to sequential accesses, dramatically reducing the density of I/O transfers. Benchmarks have demonstrated that I/O density can be reduced by a factor of two or three when TMF is used [Enright, 1985].

While the Tandem system provides high availability through single-fault tolerance, TMF provides multiple-fault tolerance for the critical element of transaction processing systems: the database. Although multiple faults are exceedingly rare, the consequent cost of database loss is very high.

Before the introduction of TMF, application programmers relied on process pairs and forward error recovery to provide fault tolerance. Whenever an error was detected, the backup process resumed the computation from the last checkpoint. Process pairs were difficult to design and implement and reduced the productivity of application programmers. Applications implemented with TMF are much simpler to program and achieve the equivalent level of fault tolerance. Because transactions imply an automatic locking protocol, it is much easier to maintain a consistent database.

Process pairs are still an important concept and are used for system and I/O processes, as well as for specialized utility processes such as the print spooler. They are the fundamental basis on which TMF and other system software are built so that the customer can write fault-tolerant applications without regard for fault tolerance.

Transaction Processing Monitor

Applications are structured as client (requestor) and server processes. The clients are responsible for presentation services and for managing the user interface. Such user interfaces range from a forms-oriented interface to an electronic mail or home banking system, to real-time interfaces where the user is an automated warehouse, gas pump, or telephone switch. The servers are programmed to perform specific functions, usually a set of related database accesses and updates. In the electronic mail example, one server looks up names while another is responsible for routing messages to other network nodes and to gateways. In the gas pump example, one server does user authentication while another does billing. Typically, applications are structured as hundreds of services. Breaking an application into requestors and servers promotes software modularity, allows on-line change and growth of applications, and exploits the multicomputer architecture. With the advent of intelligent terminals (workstations, automated teller machines, and other computers acting as clients and servers), the client is migrating to the workstation, and the client-server architecture is becoming the standard structure for all transaction processing applications.

The application designer specifies the programs and parameters for each client and server. The servers can be programmed in any language, but the clients have traditionally been programmed in a COBOL dialect called Screen COBOL. This interpretive language automatically manages transactions and process pairs. In case the client process fails for any reason, the backup process takes over, reprocesses the input message if necessary, and redelivers the output message. This gives exactly-once semantics to transaction processing. Screen COBOL relieves the application programmer from needing to understand how to write process pairs. It is the most common way that customers get message integrity.

The transaction processing monitor, Pathway (Figure 8–64), is responsible for managing the application's requestors and servers. It creates requestors and servers at system startup, maintains a configuration database that can be altered on line by operator commands, and load balances the system by creating and deleting server instances as the load changes and as processors come and go from the system.

Process Server Classes

To obtain software modularity, computations are broken into several processes. For example, a transaction arriving from a terminal passes through a line-handler process (for instance, X.25), a protocol (for example, SNA), a presentation services process to do screen handling, an application process that has the database logic, and several disk processes that manage disks, disk buffer pools, locks, and transaction audit trails. This method breaks the application into many small modules, which serve as units of service and of failure. If one unit fails, its computation switches to its backup process.

If a process performs a particular service (for example, acting as a name server or managing a particular database), then traffic against this server is likely to grow as the system grows. Gradually, the load on such a process will increase until it becomes a bottleneck. Such bottlenecks can be an impediment to linear growth in performance as processors are added. The concept of process *server class* is introduced to circumvent this bottleneck problem.

A server class is a collection of processes that all perform the same function, typically spread over several processors. Such a collection can be managed by Pathway. Requests are sent to the class rather than to individual members of the class. As the load increases, members are added to the class. If a member fails or if one of the processors fails, the server class migrates into the remaining processors. As the load decreases, the server class shrinks. Hence, process server classes are a mechanism for fault tolerance and for load balancing in a distributed system [Tandem, 1985]. The application designer specifies the program, parameters, minimum size, maximum size, and distribution of the server class. Pathway reads this configuration database at

FIGURE 8–64

*The structure of
the Pathway trans-
action processing
monitor*

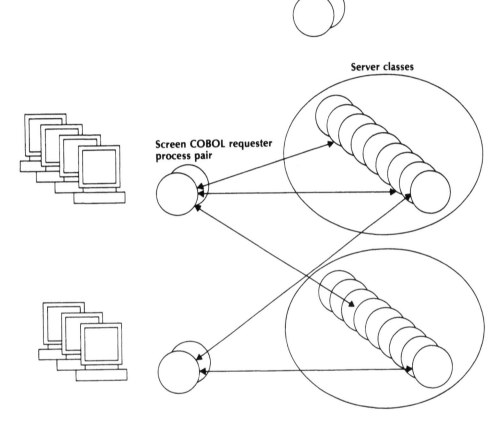

system startup and manages the server class, growing it as the load increases and shrinking it as the load decreases.

Networking

The process- and message-based structure of Guardian naturally generalizes to a network operating system. A proprietary network, called Expand [Tandem, 1987], enlarges the original 16-processor design to a 4080-processor (255-node) network. Expand uses a packet-switched, hop-by-hop routing scheme to move messages among nodes; in essence, it connects all of the IPBs of remote systems. Expand is now widely used as a backbone for corporate networks or as an intelligent network, acting as a gateway among other networks. The fault tolerance and modularity of the architecture make it a natural choice for these applications. Increasingly, the system software supports standards such as SNA, OSI, MAP, SWIFT, TCP/IP, Named Pipes, and so forth. These protocols run on top of the message system and appear to extend it.

The fault tolerance provided by the system extends to the network. Networking software allows a session to continue even if a communication link breaks. For example, SNAX, Tandem's implementation of IBM's System Network Architecture, provides continuous operation by transparently checkpointing at key points the internal information needed to sustain operation. This enables SNAX to maintain all active sessions in the event that a single processor or line fails. Similar provisions exist in the open system interconnection software.

Fault tolerance also underlies the distributed systems management products for globally managing NonStop systems and Expand networks. For example, with the event management subsystem, an event recorder process executing as a NonStop process pair provides for graceful recovery from single-process failures. That is, if the primary event recorder process fails or is stopped, the backup process continues recording in the appropriate event logs.

Disaster Protection

In conventional disaster recovery operations, when a disaster happens, people at a standby site retrieve the database tapes from archival storage, transfer them to the standby site, establish a compatible operating system environment, restore the data from tape to disk, switch communication lines to the backup site, and restart application programs. This is a complex, labor-intensive, and error-prone process that commonly takes from 12 to 48 hours. The issues surrounding disaster recovery change dramatically when one moves from a traditional batch environment to the world of on-line transaction processing. OLTP customers require recovery within a matter of seconds or minutes with little or no lost transactions or data. Symmetric network and application designs based on the remote duplicate database facility (RDF) software give this kind of disaster protection.

Operations personnel can use RDF to get applications back on line within five minutes after a disaster. RDF stores the database at two systems, typically at two distinct geographic sites. For each data item there is a primary copy and a backup copy of record. All updates are made to the primary copy, and the TMF log records for the primary are sent to the site that holds the backup copy of the record, where they are applied to the backup copy of the data. The customer can select one of three options for the sending of these log records:

• **2-Safe:** No lost transactions at takeover. In this case, the transaction is recorded at both sites prior to committing the transaction to the client. It implies slightly longer response times because of the added network delay.

• **1-Safe:** The last few transactions may be lost at takeover because they were not recorded at the backup site. 1-safe has better response time and may be appropriate if each transaction is of little value or is easily reconstructed at a later time.

• **Electronic Vaulting:** The log of the system is simply transmitted to a remote site and stored there. It is not applied to the remote database until there is an actual disaster. This is similar to the standby site scheme, but avoids the movement of data to the standby site when the disaster happens.

RDF makes it possible to maintain a current, on-line copy of the database at a secondary node, as illustrated in Figure 8–65. The secondary database can be located nearby or across the nation. The use of RDF is completely transparent to the application programmer. Any TMF application can be converted to an RDF application without change. Only the database configuration and operations procedures change [Lyon, 1990].

To support its backup capabilities, RDF monitors and extracts information from TMF audit files and sends this information over the Expand network to a corresponding RDF process on the

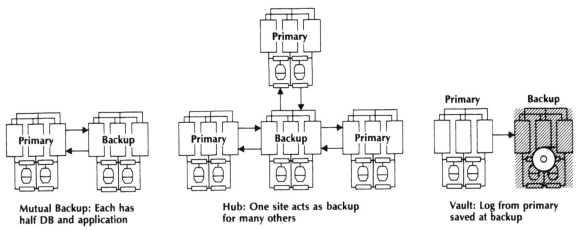

Mutual Backup: Each has
half DB and application

Hub: One site acts as backup
for many others

Vault: Log from primary
saved at backup

FIGURE 8–65 *Remote duplicate database facility*

second node. This extraction usually takes place within seconds of the audit's being created by TMF. The RDF process on the second node receives the audit transactions and stores them in disk buffers. Another RDF process on the second node then applies these transactions to the database, thus maintaining the duplicate database. The second copy of the database is usually current within seconds of the primary database. Updating activities on the second database can be temporarily suspended without compromising the integrity of the on-line backup process. The audit transactions accumulate in disk buffers at the secondary site until updating is resumed. Then all accumulated updates are automatically applied in the correct sequence.

RDF has some additional fault-tolerance benefits. If one of the sites needs to be taken off line for a software upgrade, hardware upgrade, facilities move, or just a fire drill to test the disaster recovery facility, the load can be switched to the other node without interrupting service.

Operating System Summary

The innovative aspects of the Guardian operating system do not entail new concepts; instead, they are a synthesis and integration of preexisting ideas. Of particular importance are the low-level abstractions: processes and messages. These abstractions allow all processor boundaries to be hidden from both application programs and most system software. These initial abstractions are the key to the system's ability to tolerate failure. They also provide the configuration independence that is necessary in order for system and application software to run on systems of many sizes. Process pairs are a natural extension of the process concept to fault-tolerant execution. Transactions have been integrated with the operating system and appear as a natural part of the execution environment. Spooling the transaction log to a remote site is the basis of the disaster recovery facility. Extending the message-based system to a long-haul network makes it geographically distributed.

The operating system provides the application programmer with general approaches to process structuring, interprocess communication, and failure tolerance. Much has been documented about structuring programs by using multiple communicating processes, but few operating systems support such structures.

Finally, the design goals of the system have been demonstrated in practice. Systems with from 2 to 200 processors have been installed and are running on-line applications. Many of these systems are members of multinode networks. They are recovering from failures and failures are being repaired on line, with little or no impact on the system users.

Application Software

Application software provides a high-level interface for developing on-line transaction processing applications to run on the low-level process-message-network system described in the preceding sections. The basic principle is that the simpler the system, the less likely the user is to make mistakes [Gray and Anderson, 1985]. For data communications, high-level interfaces are provided to paint screens for presentation services. Furthermore, a high-level interface is provided to SNA to simplify the applications programming task. For database management, the relational data model is adopted, and the NonStop SQL software provides a variety of easily implemented functions. A relational query language integrated with a report writer allows quick development of ad hoc reports.

System programs are written in the transaction application language (TAL), which is a high-level, block-structured language similar to ALGOL or Pascal; TAL provides access to machine instructions where necessary. Most commercial applications are written in COBOL85 or developed through application generators. In addition, the system supports FORTRAN, Pascal, C, BASIC, MUMPS, and other specialized languages. A binder allows programmers to combine modules from different languages into a single application, and a symbolic debugger allows them to debug in the source programming language. The goal, however, is to reduce such low-level programming by moving to application-specific, fourth-generation languages.

A menu-oriented application generation system, Pathmaker, guides developers through the process of developing and maintaining applications. Whenever possible, it generates the application code for clients and servers based on the contents of an integrated system dictionary. The application generator builds most clients from the menu-oriented interface, although the user can tailor the client by adding COBOL statements. The template for the servers is also automatically generated, but customers must add the semantics of the application, generally using COBOL. Servers access the relational database either through COBOL record-at-a-time verbs or through set-oriented relational operators. Using automatically generated clients and the transaction mechanism, customers can build fault-tolerant distributed applications with no special programming required. Pathmaker provides maximum protection against failures through its reliance on TMF.

Ongoing investigations support the hypothesis that, as programmers migrate from language to language, human error rates remain nearly constant. That is, a programmer will produce about the same number of errors for every 1000 lines of code, regardless of the language being used. Thus, the higher the level of language a programmer uses, the smaller the number of errors in the object code. On this basis, Tandem urges its customers to use high-level tools like the Pathmaker application generator and other products that incorporate fourth-generation language concepts for OLTP program development. These tools include SQL Forms from Oracle, Applications By Forms from Ingres, and Focus from Information Builders. These tools greatly simplify the programmer's work.

New application software is under development that takes advantage of the growing number of personal computers and other workstations in the business world. This influx of desktop computers has dramatically influenced the way that business people do their computing. As these machines become faster and provide more memory and disk storage, businesses are expected to want system software for them that parallels software running on mainframes and minicomputers. This software, in turn, will generate a growing number of applications.

As stressed earlier in this section, customers demand good price/performance from fault-tolerant systems. Each Cyclone processor can process about 25 standard transactions per second. Benchmarks have demonstrated that 32 processors have 32 times the transaction throughput of one processor; that is, throughput grows linearly with the number of processors, and the price per transaction declines slightly [Tandem Performance Group, 1988]. Tandem believes a 50-processor Cyclone system is capable of 1000 transactions per second. The price per transaction for a small system compares favorably with other full-function systems. This price per transaction demonstrates that single-fault tolerance need not be an expensive proposition.

OPERATIONS

Errors that originate with computer operators are a major source of faults. Operators are often asked to make difficult decisions based on insufficient data or training. The system attempts to minimize operator actions and, where required, directs the operator to perform tasks and then checks the operator's actions for correctness [Gray, 1990]. Nevertheless, the operator is in charge and dictates what orders the computer must follow. This relationship poses a dilemma to the system designer: how to limit the actions of the operator. First, all routine operations are handled by the system. For example, the system automatically reconfigures itself in the case of a single fault. The operator is left with only exceptional situations. Single-fault tolerance reduces the urgency of dealing with failures of single components. The operator can be more leisurely in dealing with most single failures.

Increasingly, operators are given a simple and uniform high-level model of the system's behavior that reflects physical real-world entities, such as disks, tapes, lines, terminals, applications, and so on, rather than control blocks and other abstractions. The interface is organized in terms of actions and exception reports. The operator is prompted through diagnostic steps to localize and repair a failed component.

Maintenance problems, discussed earlier in this chapter, are very similar to operations. Ideally, there would be no maintenance. Single-fault tolerance allows hardware repair to be done on a scheduled basis rather than as soon as possible, since the system continues to operate even if a module fails. This approach reduces the cost and stress of conventional maintenance. The areas of single-fault-tolerant operations and single-fault-tolerant maintenance are major topics of research at Tandem.

SUMMARY AND CONCLUSIONS

Single-fault tolerance is a good engineering tradeoff for commercial systems [Horst and Gray, 1989]. For example, single disks are rated at an MTBF of five years. Duplexed disks, which record data on two mirrored disks connected through dual controllers to dual processors, raise the MTBF to 5000 years (theoretical) and 1500 years (measured). Triplexed disks would have a theoretical MTBF of over one million years, but because operator and software errors dominate, the measured MTBF would probably be similar to that of duplexed disks.

Single-fault tolerance through the use of fail-fast modules and reconfiguration must be applied to both software and hardware. Processes and messages are the key to structuring software into modules with good fault isolation. A side benefit of this design is that it can utilize multiple processors and lends itself to a distributed system design. Modular growth of software and hardware is a side effect of fault tolerance. If the system can tolerate repair and reintegration of modules, then it can tolerate the addition of brand new modules. In addition, systems must tolerate operations and environmental faults.

Fault tolerance can also be applied to open standard-based systems. These systems provide the benefit of application transparent fault tolerance at the cost of additional hardware resources and a decreased resilience to software faults.

REFERENCES   Bartlett, 1978, 1981; Bitton, 1989; Bitton and Gray, 1988; Borr, 1981, 1984; Brinch Hansen, 1970; Burman, 1985; Carr, 1981, 1985; Chan and Horst, 1989; Dijkstra, 1968; Eddy, 1987; Englert, 1989; Enright, 1985; Garcia, 1988; Gray, 1979, 1985, 1990; Gray and Anderson, 1985; Haerder and Reuter, 1983; Homan, Malizia, and Reismer, 1988; Horst, 1989; Horst and Chou, 1985; Horst and Gray, 1989; Horst, Harris, and Jardine, 1990; Horst and Metz, 1984; Jewett, 1991; Jouppi and Wall, 1989.

Katzman, 1977; Lenoski, 1988; Lyon, 1990; Mourad and Andrews, 1985; Nellen, 1985, 1986; Sohi, Franklin, and Saluja, 1989; Tandem, 1985, 1987; Tandem Database Group, 1988; Tandem Performance Group, 1988; Tom, 1988; Troisi, 1985; Uren, 1986; White, 1987.

THE STRATUS CASE

The Stratus Architecture

STEVEN WEBBER*

The fault-tolerant computer industry uses many terms that have different meanings for different people. The following definitions are of particular importance in this report on Stratus architecture.

• *Hardware fault tolerance* is the technique of applying hardware alone to effect fault-tolerance. Commercially available hardware fault-tolerant solutions include voting systems and systems such as those developed by Stratus that utilize two levels of duplexing—one for checking and one for fault-tolerance. Successful hardware fault-tolerant solutions require no effort on the part of application programmers to effect fault-tolerance. Hardware fault-tolerant computers are programmed as if they were simple, nonfault-tolerant computers.

• *Software fault tolerance* is the technique of applying software programs to effect fault-tolerance. These techniques typically include checkpointing information between different computers within a computer network so that some other back-up computer can take over when the primary computer fails. The majority of commercially available fault-tolerant products rely on software fault tolerance.

• *Software fault recovery*, or the ability of a system to recover from software faults, refers to the techniques brought into play when a software failure is recognized. These techniques preserve the integrity of the execution environment. They are independent of hardware fault tolerance, providing an additional level of protection for a different class of failures.

• *Critical on-line computing* refers to systems that run a company's most important business operations and manage the delivery of their most important products and services to customers. The system directly contributes to a business's profitability, revenue growth, or competitive advantage; it is the direct interface between a business and its customers; it provides constantly changing data relied upon for decisions in real time by many users; it is responsible for individual transactions of enormous financial value or business importance.

* The author acknowledges Kippi Fagerlund, who edited the draft manuscript, and also Marc Sill and Greg Baryza, who provided some of the artwork. The evolution of Stratus products is the result of the efforts of many people, including Bob Reid, Ken Wolff, Kurt Baty, Ron Dynneson, Joe Samson, Gardner Hendrie, Mike Grady, Larry Johnson, Jerry Stern, Janice Lacy, Bob Freiburghouse, Richard Barnes, Paul Green, Otto Newman, Herb Robinson, Neil Swinton, Doug Steinfeld, Jim Murry, Jim Bush, John Bongiovanni, and Jim Filreis.

• *Data integrity* refers to the consistency of multiple database records and files. Data integrity is usually a concern only after a system interruption. Fault tolerance does not guarantee data integrity. Data integrity is typically achieved through transaction protection.

• *Data corruption* is the contamination or alteration of data without any indication that the data is no longer correct. The kind of fault tolerance provided by Stratus systems protects against data corruption in nearly all cases. Most other systems, even fault-tolerant ones, provide minimal means of protection against or detection of corrupted data, and often the data is irrevocably corrupted before the detection hardware can stop it.

• *Transaction protection (TP)* is the ability to perform a sequence of database and communications operations in an *atomic* way such that if any changes are made to a database or sequence of databases, all associated changes that are part of the transaction are instituted. TP is independent of fault tolerance. A complete TP system must include its own recovery capabilities so that the integrity of the database after a system failure is guaranteed. Some TP systems do not provide fault-tolerant features. When hardware failures occur, such systems go down, but when service is restored, the database is made consistent such that each transaction prior to the failure is applied or lost. Even hardware fault-tolerant TP systems must provide mechanisms in addition to the normal system fault tolerance to guarantee database integrity against nonhardware-related system crashes.

• *On-line transaction processing (OLTP)* refers to a TP system's performing sequences of transactions in real time as on-line users, machinery, or other computers wait. Typical OLTP applications include 24-hour banking networks, airline reservation systems, manufacturing support programs, and point-of-sale terminal networks.

System downtime is typically broken up into the following categories.

• *Hardware failures*—failures of hardware that cause the system to stop running: As a result, the application (solution for which the computer was purchased) is not available. Usually, hardware failures lead to some degree of system degradation or failure. The degradation often manifests itself as poorer performance (response time and/or throughput) and occasionally results in the unavailability of selected data. The degradation may also result in the inaccessibility of selected devices.

• *Operating system software crashes*—failure of the software resulting in a system crash: After a failure of this type, the system must somehow reinitialize all or part of itself. Often, the failure is data-dependent and will crash multiple systems or continue to crash a system until some manual corrective action is taken. In other cases, the failure is unreproducible and is brought out only by the juxtaposition of relatively rare events (often related to I/O or communications error situations that are difficult to test). If the failure is unreproducible, retrying or restarting the system usually works, although there may be no insight as to why the system crashed.

• *Operational downtime*—SYSGEN, missing or improper operator intervention: Operators usually have high-level privileges (access or permission not granted to most users) and can inadvertently cause considerable damage.

• *Application software problems*—failure of the application software leading to the inability of the end-users to do their work: The operating system may remain operational, but the application must reinitialize itself or be reinitialized by explicit operator intervention. The fact that the system remains up is of little consequence to the end-users.

• *Database maintenance and backup*—the maintenance and support of database systems often results in periods of time when the database is not available for normal use: Registering new users, adding new structures, and backing up a database often requires that the database be made unavailable. As with application system software problems, the availability of the system without the database is of limited value.

   • *Environmental problems*—problems with electrical power, air conditioning, earthquakes, floods or other storms, smoke, contaminants, or sabotage.

   • *Communications failures*—failure of communications lines used to interconnect systems.

   • *Field service*—removal of parts of the system or the disabling of the entire system for such activities as repairing failed components, running preventive maintenance, and running diagnostics.

   • *Software installation*—the unavailability of part of the system or an entire system while new software is installed: Software installations fall into two main groups, installation of basic operating system software (which usually requires a reboot) and installation of application software (which rarely requires a reboot but usually requires the application to be quiesced or stopped).

   • *Hardware installation*—the installation of new hardware to expand or upgrade a configuration.

The design of a modern computer system must minimize or eliminate downtime in all of these areas.

   The statistical breakdown of the occurrence of downtime as a result of the various factors listed previously is different in nearly all published reports. Two trends are clearly important, however. First, hardware (including that of nonfault-tolerant systems) is becoming more reliable, resulting in less downtime. Second, operational downtime (including operator errors and system downtime for performing such activities as installing new hardware or software and running preventive maintenance on some component of the system) seems to be on the increase.

   Another important trend is that software tends to become more stable and reliable the longer it is in the field without significant functional improvement. Software stability is one of the most important factors leading to software reliability. Modern software practices (structured design techniques such as design reviews, documentation, and code; use of modern development tools; object oriented programming; more extensive testing) have led to software products that are initially significantly more reliable, but the highest levels of reliability of most software are achieved only after fixing problems as they are encountered.

   Another important issue relating to the availability of systems is environmental quality. For example, it is becoming increasingly difficult to get high-quality, continuous electrical power. Today's computer systems must not only be more forgiving of power fluctuations but must also be able to survive (ride through) brief power outages.

STRATUS SOLUTIONS TO DOWNTIME

Stratus has addressed potential downtime problem areas as follows.

   • **Hardware Failures:** The Stratus hardware fault-tolerant architecture isolates users from almost all hardware failures.

   • **Operating System Software Crashes:** System crashes are minimized (but not completely eliminated) with the use of software fault recovery procedures.

   • **Operational Downtime:** Operational downtime is almost completely eliminated due to the lack of need for a SYSGEN; that is, hardware and software configuration occurs automatically. An operator needs to do little to run the system.

TABLE 8–7
Introduction of major Stratus hardware products

Year	Product	Significant New Features
1981	FT200	2-CPU 68000-based (2 logical CPUs/board); up to 16 MB of memory; user and executive CPUs (not symmetric); 20-slot main chassis; powerfail recovery
1984	XA400	4-CPU 68010–based (4 logical CPUs/board); symmetric multiprocessing
1984	XA600	6-CPU 68010–based (6 logical CPUs/3 boards); symmetric multiprocessing; 8-KB cache/CPU; floating point assist in hardware; 40-slot main chassis
1987	XA2000 110-160	1- to 6-CPU 68020–based (1 logical CPU/board); up to 96 MB of memory; 64-KB cache/CPU; floating point coprocessor; dynamic processor upgrades; enhanced powerfail ride-through
1988	XA2000 50–70	4-CPU 68020–based (4 logical CPUs/board); generalized I/O controller; 10-slot chassis; fault-tolerant I/O communications bus
1989	XA2000 30	Single-CPU 68030–based (1 logical CPU/board) "midplane" eliminates need for many cables and simplifies service; 6-slot chassis; integrated peripheral package; increased customer serviceability
1990	XA2000 210-260	1- to 6-CPU 68030–based (1 logical CPU/board); up to 256 MB of memory; 128-KB intelligent cache/CPU; bus-watching for cache consistency

• **Application System Software Problems:** Stratus provides highly structured, powerful interfaces for transaction processing and forms management. These interfaces can simplify application development and lower the risk of the application's introducing errors.

• **Environmental Problems:** Using sophisticated powerfail recovery procedures, powerfail ride-through, and battery backup, Stratus systems avoid or minimize most power-related environmental problems. Stratus systems usually require no special air conditioning.

• **Field Service:** Nearly all Stratus hardware can be replaced while the system is fully operational, minimizing the impact of field service on system availability. Boards, disks, fans, power supplies, and line adapters (interfaces to peripherals of all types) can be replaced on line while the system is running. Most replacements can be installed by customers, although some assemblies require trained field service personnel. Self-diagnosing boards clearly indicate broken parts. Specific failures are reported automatically to the Stratus Customer Assistance Center (CAC) through the remote service network (RSN) (using autodialing modems). Field service is simple and reliable.

• **Software Installation:** Installing basic operating system software (excluding device drivers) requires a system reboot. Most other software (including most device drivers) can be installed while the system is fully operational. To install new application software, however, it is often necessary for the application itself to quiesce or reach a clean point.

• **Hardware Installation:** Table 8–7 lists the major hardware products Stratus has introduced since 1981. Most Stratus hardware can be replaced on line while the system runs at full capacity. Further, any configuration expansions (including adding disks, memory boards, communications lines, and additional processors anywhere within a Stratus computer network) can be performed while the system is fully operational. The ability to dynamically expand or change the hardware configuration of a system is becoming increasingly important due to the need for frequent changes in many critical on-line systems.

ISSUES OF FAULT TOLERANCE

A fault-tolerant system must be designed to withstand failures of all types. This means that the architecture and design of system software must be fault resilient and that every hardware component of the system must be, in some way, redundant.

Software Issues

Stratus has taken several approaches to solving the problem of system software reliability. First, from the beginning the Stratus architecture has included a mechanism that gives the system software designers powerful analysis tools and capabilities. The Stratus system automatically records information about every system crash and forwards this information or makes it available to the CAC or operations system personnel through the RSN. Stratus learns of every customer system crash automatically, and therefore has more knowledge of software problems than other companies. The system continuously logs system and error activity. These logs are valuable for analyzing many system outages.

Second, Stratus uses software fault recovery techniques to enable the operating system to recover from software bugs within the system. These techniques are described in detail later.

Finally, Stratus has used modern software development techniques, including use of high-level languages, extensive design and code reviews, testing for both quality and performance, and significant customer involvement in new hardware and software products. The use of tools and compilers avoids many classical errors (for example, forgetting to recompile all programs when an include file changes or forgetting to initialize a variable).

Hardware Issues

Most fault-tolerant systems provide some method of recovery from the failure of a major hardware component, but basic components are often overlooked. Specific critical components include power, buses (often printed circuits), disks, printed circuit boards, and the clock.

Table 8–8 describes the redundancy techniques of Stratus system components. The following paragraphs describe how Stratus has addressed failures of these components.

Power. Power failures occur within the computer itself as well as outside of it. Uninterrupted power sources solve only the external problem. The failure of a power supply or the cables or buses that distribute the power to the active components will crash most systems. A complete solution requires that power from separate sources be fed through different power supplies to separate logic boards over different buses.

Techniques that use special chips to provide duplicate, self-checking circuitry do not satisfactorily address the problem of power failures. Such chips use a single power source. This solution to protect against internal chip logic errors is becoming less practical as a means for achieving fault tolerance as computer chips become more reliable. Most failures today occur above the chip level. Similarly, triply redundant voting systems do not solve the power problem unless each voting circuit and logic unit derives power from a separate source.

Buses. Architectures that use a bus must have a duplicate bus to protect against failure. A bus can fail because of a mechanical problem, such as a short in the bus interface logic. Systems that use some form of local area network must have duplicate media and interfacing logic. Furthermore, local area network systems must provide software to automatically manage failures in the

TABLE 8–8
Stratus system components

Component	Type/Width	Bandwidth/Speed	Redundancy Technique
Processor	68000	8 MHz	Self-checking; lockstep pairs
	68010	8 MHz	
	68020	16 MHz	
	68030	24 MHz	
Memory	8 MB	—	Self-checking logic for
	16 MB	—	control; ECC for data;
	32 MB	—	lockstep pairs
StrataBus	32 bits data	64 MB/sec	Duplicated; parity on groups of signals
StrataLink	—	1.4/2.8 MB/sec	Self-checking; duplicated
I/O controllers	Communications	600 Kb/sec	Self-checking; lockstep pairs
	IOP	4 MB/sec	Self-checking; lockstep pairs or duplicated
	Disk	1.2 MB/sec	Self-checking; duplicated
	Tape	600 KB/sec	Self-checking
Devices	Disks	—	Duplicated
	Terminals	—	None
	Tapes	—	—

media. Without such software, application programmers must take on what should be a system function.

Disks. All fault-tolerant computers provide some form of disk redundancy. Some systems provide the option of mirroring entire volumes; others allow mirroring of partial volumes. Since disks are far less volatile than main memory, many applications and users rightfully feel secure only after their data is safely stored on one or more disks.

Boards. Failure of a single component on a computer board usually has one of two effects: the entire board breaks in some way recognizable by the rest of the system, or worse yet, the error goes unnoticed. In most systems, either situation eventually leads to a crash of the module containing the board. A truly fault-tolerant computer must protect against **any** error of this type.

Clocks. Although very reliable, clock circuits which generate and distribute clocking signals to the various components of the system must be considered when designing a fault-tolerant system.

SYSTEM ARCHITECTURE OVERVIEW

A Stratus computer *system* consists of up to 32 *modules* connected through a Stratus intermodule bus (*StrataLink*). The StrataLink, a redundant, coaxial, proprietary interconnect mechanism, is used for system expansion. Using StrataLink, the Stratus operating system provides a global system view for all devices in the system. It also provides "message passing" between cooperating processes. The StrataLink restricts modules to a geographic proximity of a few miles, but typically the modules are linked into a system in a single building or a few adjacent buildings. The StrataLink consists of two independent coaxial "links." Each link runs at 1.4 megabytes per second, providing an intermodule throughput capability of 2.8 megabytes per second. The system software continuously uses both links, thereby recognizing immediately if one of the links fails. If a link does fail, the throughput drops to 1.4 megabytes per second.

A Stratus *network* consists of several systems connected using an X.25 packet switched network or the StrataLink hardware. Figure 8–66 illustrates an X.25 packet switched network of four systems (4 groups of 14 modules total connected with StrataLinks).

Each module within a system is a complete computer; Figure 8–67 illustrates a typical Stratus module. Each module is bus-oriented, containing a Stratus backplane or midplane that implements a proprietary fault-tolerant module bus called a *StrataBus*. A module also contains one or more processor board pairs, one or more memory board pairs, and pairs of I/O controllers connected to various peripheral devices, including disks, tapes, and communications interfaces. A module contains its own redundant power supplies, battery backup subsystem, and various card cages for I/O line adapters and I/O controlling logic.

The Basic Module Bus

The major boards of a Stratus module interface with the StrataBus. The StrataBus has 32 logical slots and is implemented in various Stratus modules with 6, 10, 20, or 40 physical slots. (The 40-slot chassis supports logical board stacks that contain multiple physical boards.) The StrataBus uses an arbitration scheme that, in its simplest form, provides bus priority as a function of bus slot number. Even-numbered slots within the bus derive power from a subsystem that is totally independent of the power subsystem used by the odd-numbered slots of the bus. This partitioning of slots into disjoint, isolated sets enables a module to survive the complete failure of either of its power subsystems.

The power for the boards derived from these power supplies consists of unregulated 24 V_{DC}. Each board regulates this power to the necessary levels. By placing the power regulation function on each board, it is possible to remove and insert boards from the StrataBus while the

FIGURE 8–66
A typical network

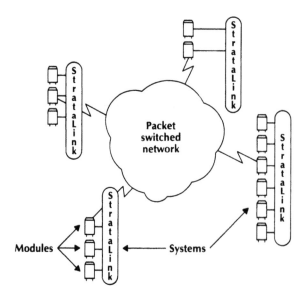

FIGURE 8–67
A Stratus 40-slot module

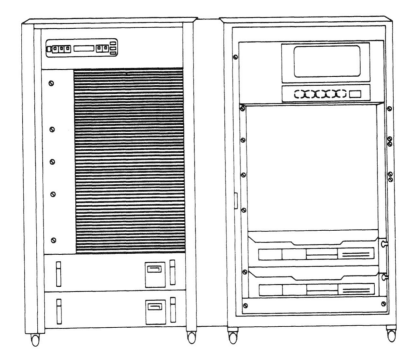

bus is fully powered. No components of the system need to be disabled to remove or insert a board.

The StrataBus is a synchronous bus. The system clocking function drives all circuitry in the system and is distributed using a single bus signal. This clock signal generates a standard bus tick of 125 nanoseconds (8 MHz). The bus protocol provides for extensive overlapping/pipelining, allowing a new bus request of up to 64 bits of data on every 125-nanosecond tick. This yields a maximum bus bandwidth of 64 megabytes per second. (The system clocking function generates higher frequencies for boards running at rates faster than 8 MHz.)

Nearly every signal on the bus is duplicated. The bus is actually viewed as two independent buses, bus A and bus B, each with its own power, ground, data, address, and control lines. Parity protects the lines of each bus.

Each major system board simultaneously interfaces with both buses. A board drives the same data on both buses and reads data from both buses if they are both enabled. (The hardware automatically instructs all boards to ignore a suspect bus.)

A power supply for each bus powers pullup resistors to effect an *open collector* technology. Unless driven to a 1 state by at least one board, each bus signal represents a logical 0.

Bus Monitoring by Memory Boards. The various parity signals on the StrataBus detect bus failures or bus-related failures of boards that interface with the bus. Controller logic performs the detection within the memory boards. If multiple pairs of memory boards exist within a module, all such boards monitor the bus for problems. If a memory board detects a problem on either bus, it declares that bus broken and instructs all boards to stop using the bus (by asserting signals on bus lines). This bus monitoring detects such failures as an open bus line, a shorted bus line, or the failure of a bus driver on one of the boards plugged into the bus. Such bus driver failures cannot be detected by the on-board checking logic, as the drivers are enabled and disabled by the comparator logic and are thus logically beyond it (see Figure 8–69). The bus drivers are the only logic on a major board not covered by the self-checking logic of the board.

If the memory subsystem detects a subsequent failure of the single working bus, that bus is declared broken and the originally broken bus is declared good. The buses alternate in this manner until system software tests the buses and places them both back in service. Alternating between failing buses provides a simple recovery strategy for transient bus errors. If the original failed bus has a hard failure, implying that both buses have simultaneously failed, the module is inoperable.

Power Subsystem

Each power supply has an associated battery backup system. The battery system works in two modes: It either powers all boards within the module, or it powers only the memory boards. The power supplies monitor the AC power and interrupt the system when they detect a power failure. The system software reacts to a power failure indication by saving in main memory all information needed by boards in the system. In 90–95 percent of all power failures, power returns within a few seconds. If the AC power-sensing hardware detects a failure of this type, the system simply continues with what it was doing before the power failure was first detected.

The battery systems have enough capacity to power the entire module (excluding disk and tape drives) for up to six seconds during a power outage. After six seconds, if the AC power has not returned, the system quiesces all boards and instructs the hardware to supply power only to the memory boards. In this extended battery backup mode, the system is not operational, but its complete state is preserved. If power is restored within an hour or two, depending on the amount of memory that must be backed up by battery, the system software restores the system to its state at the time of the power interruption. All I/O that did not complete is restarted.

During the first few seconds of a power outage (while the system is still operating), the disks are not powered and begin to cycle down. This typically leads to normal, recoverable disk errors that are retried when the power is fully restored. No data can be damaged.

With the large memory sizes supported by Stratus modules, there is not enough time to save all of memory to disk before it becomes necessary to switch to the low power usage mode, which supports only memory. The battery system has insufficient power to support all disks in an operational state. Additional batteries can be configured to provide recovery from arbitrarily long power outages.

System Boards

The boards that interface to the StrataBus have several common features. First, they all operate synchronously at a simple multiple of the common system frequency. First-generation boards run at 8 MHz, but newer boards operate at up to 24 MHz.

Second, all boards are self-checking and auto-isolating. The boards check themselves for component errors on every clock tick and will not place data on the bus if a board finds itself to be in error. This self-checking is typically performed by duplicating the logic on the board and running both sets of logic independently but synchronously. The outputs of these independent logic networks then run through onboard comparator circuits that enable the bus drivers. The self-checking logic automatically causes a board to break. A failed board is said to be *broken* or *red-lighted.* (When a board breaks, a red LED on the front of the board lights to identify it.) A broken board never drives data onto the buses.

Third, each board must provide its own power regulation to convert the unregulated 24 V$_{DC}$ available from the bus to usable TTL levels.

Fourth, each board is self-identifying, providing system software with coded information describing the board's type, the revision level of the board, the revision level of the PROM software on the board (if any), and a limited amount of board repair history. This information is critical to the software that puts reinserted boards on line. If the boards are incompatible, the system does not accept the new board.

Fifth, all boards that interface to the StrataBus must obey a set of common interface conventions used by the Stratus maintenance and diagnostic software for testing, initializing, and enabling boards in the system. The common interface allows the operating system software to monitor and diagnose boards plugged into the bus through a common mapped I/O space—a special range of virtual memory addresses—which is interpreted similarly for all boards. (Each slot within the backplane has a set of addresses associated with it that control the board in that slot. These addresses are referenced to enable, disable, test, remove, and restore the board.)

One specific requirement of this self-checking feature is that both halves of a board must behave totally deterministically. Any logic must progress from state to state with each clock tick totally deterministically. In particular, *don't care states* (bits that can apparently harmlessly assume either a 0 or a 1) are not allowed, since they may yield conflicting values in the comparator logic on the boards.

Figure 8–68 depicts the general layout of a Stratus self-checking board. The A connector connects to bus A, the B connector connects to bus B, and the C connector connects to external

FIGURE 8–68
A self-checking board

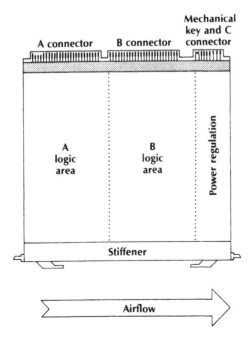

logic, such as an I/O bus, the maintenance panel (in the case of CPU boards), or to other boards of the same type (as is the case for memory boards).

Figure 8–69 is a block diagram of the typical checking logic for a self-checking board. The comparator logic (represented by the question mark in Figure 8–69) enables and disables the bus drivers. If a compare mismatch occurs, the bus drivers are immediately disabled, and no data is allowed out on the buses.

Boards within a Stratus system nearly always occur in pairs. Such boards are referred to as *partners*. Major boards operate in two ways: either in synchronous lockstep with a partner board or only logically paired with a partner board. When operating in synchronous lockstep, proprietary Stratus hardware and software synchronize both self-checking boards of the pair; thus, both boards (including a total of four sets of logic) do exactly the same thing on any bus cycle. This requires that the boards behave completely deterministically with respect to any conditions that can arise. In essence, the same requirements that apply to self-checking boards (mainly total determinism of the logic) apply to boards in synchronous lockstep.

Two boards running in synchronous lockstep read the same values from the StrataBus simultaneously. Output signals are logically ORed on the StrataBus. For example, two client partner boards ask for a bus cycle (arbitration for the bus) at exactly the same time (on the same cycle) by asserting their intention to use the bus. If the arbitration network grants the bus to the pair of boards, they both place the address for a read or write on the bus at the next clock tick. Two ticks later, the client boards or the responding boards (usually memory controllers) place the data on the bus. The data is taken off the bus one tick later.

Boards that interface with such devices as disks, tapes, and the StrataLink operate in a logically paired state. Such boards are not synchronized in lockstep with their partners; rather, they rely on operating system software for an equivalent function. (The two halves of the board must be synchronized.) Disk mirroring with dedicated disk controllers uses this method. Software ensures that mirrored disks contain duplicate, consistent copies of data. This software is com-

FIGURE 8–69

The logic of a self-checking board

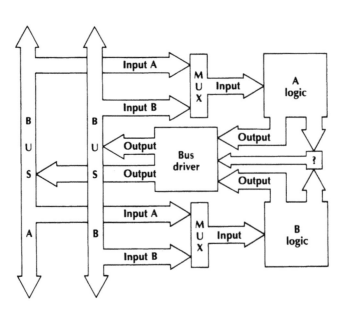

pletely invisible and inaccessible to application code (and most operating system code) and therefore need not concern application and operating system developers. The placement of partner boards in even-odd slots of the StrataBus chassis is not required by the architecture, but it is required to protect against power supply failures.

Off-Board I/O Interface Buses

The I/O controller boards usually connect to some form of I/O bus. The type of bus is a function of the type of controller. The dedicated disk controllers have several interface options such as Stratus proprietary and SMD. The tape and StrataLink controllers each interface to a single device and do not have an associated bus. The programmable StrataBus interface (PSI) controller has a Stratus proprietary bus. The communications controllers interface to Stratus proprietary buses, some of which are fault tolerant. The I/O processor (IOP) boards interface to a Stratus proprietary fault-tolerant bus.

Any controllers that run in lockstep with a partner and interface to nonfault-tolerant buses must have special logic to interface to the bus. This guarantees that all four sets of logic (two sets on each board of the partnered pair) see the same data. This scheme is typically implemented using (1) latches on the logic interfacing to the bus, (2) conservative timing assumptions so that clocking signals from the bus lead to all four sets of logic seeing the same data, and more recently, (3) reflexive checking logic on the controller boards. The reflexive checking logic trades special signals between the partnered boards at each clock tick to make sure that the boards are still synchronized. The signals traded are basic board cycle signals, the earliest indicators that the boards are out of synchronization. If the boards do go out, the hardware stops one of the boards automatically. This reflexive checking guards against failing devices connected to one of the nonfault-tolerant buses.

Line adapters, or I/O adapters (IOAs), plug into the various I/O buses and interface with devices or communications lines. These come in many types: full modem asynchronous, null modem asynchronous, synchronous, or high-speed synchronous. The IOAs usually contain microprocessors and significant amounts of memory for loading protocol-specific code to drive that particular device or communications line.

The IOP utilizes a sophisticated, self-checking, duplexed I/O bus, called the *P/Q bus*, to interface to the IOAs. This is a duplicated address/data multiplexed bus. The same bus signals are used for both address and data, and there are two separate sets of signals. The bus is limited to 20 feet in length and supports 4 megabytes per second transfer speeds. Both the P and the Q buses use parity for checking. Each bus has four function code lines, again protected by parity. The bus design is expandable to 8 megabytes per second.

The P/Q bus protects against any single-bit asynchronous glitch and any multibit failure on a single bus. The bus uses loop-back checking to ensure that a bus has what was placed on it, bus-to-bus comparison (P versus Q) to see if both buses have the same data, and continual checking for errors by every board on the bus. Each IOA has a pair of custom gate arrays to implement the special bus protocols and checking logic. The P/Q bus can accept white noise on any data line and continue to run. Figure 8–70 illustrates the logical configuration of I/O.

Major Board Types

Stratus supports three major board types: processors, memory boards, and I/O controllers. The processor and memory boards run in lockstep. Some I/O controllers run in lockstep, and some run logically paired.

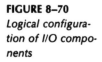

FIGURE 8–70
Logical configuration of I/O components

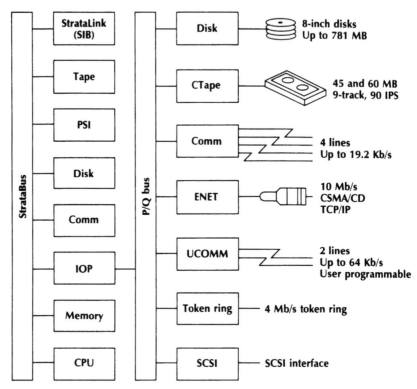

Processors. Stratus has several processor board products, all based on the same principles. The operating system software supports multiple processors executing out of a common shared memory system (often referred to as *symmetric multiprocessing*). This provides significant performance improvements over single-CPU configurations. For applications that require more CPUs than the maximum supported by a single module, Stratus resorts to the same architecture other computers use for expansion: loosely-coupled configurations linked together over some high-speed interconnect, using a combination of message passing and remote procedure calls.

Memories. Stratus system memory is contained on memory packages of one-, two-, or three-board stacks. Such stacks are called a board since they behave as a single unit and use one logical slot in the StrataBus chassis. A memory board contains controller logic that interfaces to the StrataBus and drives the memory chips. Memory currently comes in 4-, 8-, 16-, and 32-megabyte packages. All memory is protected by single-bit error-correcting, double-bit error-detecting (ECC) logic.

    Memory can be configured in one of two ways: *simplexed* or *duplexed*. When configured in a simplexed manner, the memory is not fault tolerant, although it can survive single-bit errors. When configured in a duplexed manner, the memory is fault tolerant. The simplexed configuration is provided for customers who want to configure more memory at certain times while knowingly sacrificing fault tolerance. Memory can be switched between fully duplexed and simplexed and back to fully duplexed again while the system operates. Figure 8–71 illustrates various configu-

FIGURE 8–71
Methods of du-plexing and sim-plexing memory

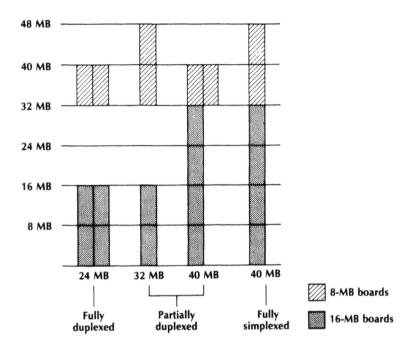

The ECC logic on the memory boards behaves differently, depending on whether or not the memory is duplexed. If the memory is duplexed, a board detecting an ECC error immediately declares itself temporarily broken, allowing the remaining partner board to continue operating. Operating system software tests the broken board, and if the error appears to be transient, the board is reduplexed with its partner. If the memory board is running simplexed when the ECC error occurs, the error is corrected, and the client board receives the correct data two cycles later. The board is not reported as broken in this case.

When a memory board is reduplexed with its partner, the additional memory controller is placed into a listening state; it does not drive data onto the bus. This state allows a special bus cycle to read from the good memory and immediately write back to both memory boards. A background system process sweeps through all memory using this cycle, allowing normal operations to continue while a memory board is added to the system. More recently manufactured memory boards can perform this update operation automatically (after diagnostic system software instructs them to do so).

I/O Controllers. As previously mentioned, I/O controller boards operate in one of two ways. Synchronously lockstepped boards include the various models of communications controllers,

rations of the same set of four memory boards, two of which are 16 megabytes and two of which are 8 megabytes.

the IOP, and the PSI. If one of the boards of such a pair fails or is removed from the system physically, the other board continues to process what the two boards were doing in parallel.

Logically paired I/O controller boards perform different physical tasks simultaneously for peripherals such as disk and tape. The operating system software ensures that applications are presented with a fault-tolerant base on which to work. The most interesting board type handled in this way is the *disk controller*. (Stratus supports disks with the IOP, as well as with dedicated disk controllers. The basic algorithms that follow apply to either.)

Disks. Disks are grouped into logical volumes of up to 10 pairs of disks. The disks in a logical volume need not all be of the same type. Each disk in the logical volume is usually, but not necessarily, duplexed or mirrored with another disk. A disk and its corresponding partner disk are called a *duplexed pair*. Duplexed pairs must be of the same disk type.

Standard configurations assign the two disks of a duplexed pair to different disk controller boards. This configuration provides two completely independent hardware paths for accessing the two copies of data. The controlling logic, electrical power to drive the logic, bus interfaces, and cabling system are also duplicated. The operating system software uses several techniques to ensure that both disks of a duplexed pair contain exactly the same data and that if one disk fails, its replacement is brought up to date automatically.

CRC Checks for Disk Blocks. Each block of data written to disk is checksummed, and the checksum is written to the disk with the data. This allows the hardware to detect problems related to cables and connectors and failures that were not detected by the disk hardware. The checksums are examined by logic in the disk controller, which is itself self-checking, providing an additional guarantee of data integrity.

Bad Block Remapping. Stratus software keeps a list of blocks that are unusable—either because the manufacturer declared them unusable or because Stratus diagnostic software determined they were unusable during the manufacturing process or normal operation. In either case, the operating system allocates another block on the disk from a pool (on each disk) reserved for this purpose and uses this alternate block whenever references are made to the failed block. The software uses the alternate disk block address for all accesses to the disk. The remapping is done whenever a read or write fails and retries are unsuccessful. The knowledge of this remapping is isolated to limited software in the disk system.

When a write failure occurs, the data is simply kept in memory and written to the newly allocated block. When a read fails, the data is read from the other disk and then written back to an alternate block on the disk that had the read failure.

SCSI disk manufacturers now build this type of facility (or a variant of it) into the drives that Stratus purchases and incorporates into its systems.

Reads from a Duplexed Pair. The operating system can read from either of two disks containing the same data. Depending on load, activity, and reference patterns, appropriate disk selection algorithms can lead to an effective disk performance improvement. One algorithm that Stratus uses is simple: If both disks are idle (no real or queued activity to the disk), the operating system selects the disk positioned closest to the cylinder on which the data resides. If one disk is busy, the operating system selects the other disk. If both disks are busy, a disk is selected at random and the operating system uses a finer-grained disk sorting algorithm.

Fast and Normal Disk Recovery. Stratus hardware and software can diagnose a particular failure when it occurs. Two cases are significant: a controller (which can be controlling several disk drives) fails, or a single drive fails.

In the case of a controller failure, the system continues to operate by reading from and writing to the disks connected to the controller partner that is interfacing with the mirrored disks. When the failed controller is replaced (on line, while the system is fully operational), the operating system automatically brings the disks connected to that controller in synchronization with the disks that were in use while the controller was out of service. Stratus calls this updating operation *disk recovery*. The operating system performs it automatically upon recognition of the replacement controller in the module. Basically, disk recovery consists of copying data from the good (consistent, complete) disk to the bad (inconsistent, incomplete) disk.

Stratus provides two forms of disk recovery. The first, *fast disk recovery*, is used when a controller, rather than a drive, fails. In this case, most of the data that exist on the drives connected to that controller are valid. As soon as the controller fails, the operating system software begins tracking all writes to the disks connected to that controller. When the controller is later replaced, the system need only update the blocks that were modified while the controller was missing or broken. Any data that may have been modified while the controller was broken are copied from the good disk, thereby guaranteeing consistency of data on both disks.

The second form of disk recovery, *normal disk recovery*, is used when the entire disk must be updated from its partner. Normal disk recovery is necessary, for example, if the drive itself must be replaced. The system software copies all used blocks from the valid disk to the new disk while the system operates. During the recovery period, the software forces writes to both disks (while reading only from the good disk), guaranteeing that, when the recovery pass is complete, the disks are synchronized.

Disk Writes. Most operating system developers do not worry about failure scenarios to the degree that developers of fault-tolerant systems must. Two issues are of particular interest because they demonstrate Stratus's concern for guaranteeing data integrity.

The first relates to serial writes; the second relates to verified writes. The Stratus disk software must, as noted, manage the writing of each data block to two separate disks. Writing could be done in parallel (overlapping the I/O), since totally separate I/O paths are available.`Instead, the operating system does not usually begin the second write of the two until it knows that the first write has completed without error. This strategy protects against an extended power failure while a parallel write is done to both disks. Such a power failure, in rare cases, could lead to blocks being written incorrectly as the write logic within the disk drives loses power. Incorrectly written blocks, in turn, could lead to the destruction of both copies of a piece of data.

Writes are also verified to guarantee that the data is reliably on disk. The second check, referred to as *disk verify*, is provided on most vendors' disk hardware.

Stratus provides the option of allowing selected disks to run without verifying writes. A parallel write option will be available in the future.

Synchronizing Boards

When a Stratus module is initialized, all boards that are running in lockstep must be synchronized. The concept is fairly simple: get the four sets of logic to do exactly the same thing. The actual implementation is a bit tricky. The system starts up with all intelligence isolated to one of the main CPUs of the system. Tie-breaking hardware effectively runs exactly one CPU at first. All other boards initialize themselves but remain off line. The running CPU surveys the hardware in the system, using the mapped I/O space that is part of the common interface to each board that interfaces with the StrataBus. The CPU brings the other boards within the system on line one by one.

Before a CPU can run, it must synchronize its two halves: All registers, caches, memory cells, and microprocessors must be provided with the same data. The CPU initializes these items before enabling the comparator logic that would otherwise force the board off-line as broken. Memories must be brought on line by the initializing CPU before any I/O (other than primitive character I/O to a terminal) can be accomplished.

Reflexive Checking

The term *reflexive checking* describes the interboard communication performed by certain pairs of boards to guarantee they are synchronized. If the boards get out of synchronization, one of them is forced off line automatically by the hardware so that the boards' signals, which are ORed on the bus, do not confuse other boards in the system. This logic typically exchanges selected control state indicators that change frequently (at least every tick) during operation of the boards.

Periodic Tests

The comparator logic on self-checking boards can fail. Such a failure has two manifestations: either a false failure can be reported, or a true failure can be missed. A false failure indication is harmless to the system, but even so, it is immediately detected and indicated—the board goes broken. Failure to diagnose a real problem is also harmless as long as the partner board is working. If a single failure occurs, one of the buses is receiving the correct data from both boards. The failing board can fail in one of two ways. First, it can place a 0 on the bus when it should place a 1, in which case the partner board overrides it by placing the correct data on the bus with an OR signal. Second, it can place a 1 on the bus when it should (and its partner does) place a 0 on the bus. In this case, the memory controllers detect the problem using the parity-checking logic and declare that bus broken.

   The board can also be broken in such a way that no data at all are being placed on the bus; for example, the on-board power system could be broken. If this is the case, the bus monitoring software run by the maintenance process detects the problem. The board does not appear to be on line. Note that the state of the bus logic is such that a 0 is assumed if nothing is driving the bus (as would be the case if the board had no power).

RECOVERY SCENARIOS

With this background, it is easy to understand how Stratus achieves its fault tolerance while meeting so many of its corporate product goals. Once an entire system is initialized and all duplexed components are synchronized with their partners, the following failures are insignificant both to system availability and capacity.

   • **Board Failure:** When a component or materials failure associated with a board occurs, the failing board automatically drops out while its partner continues to run. The partner does not take over, as would be the case with a backup component; instead, it continues the actions it was performing synchronously with its partner. One board, rather than two, is ORing signals to the bus and responding to other bus requests. The operating system software hides the unavailability of the failed board for boards not running in lockstep. After the failed board takes itself off line, the system increments a fault count associated with the board and recalculates the board's mean time between failures (MTBF) based on any earlier failures. If the MTBF is less than an administratively set value, the board is marked for replacement, and the RSN is invoked to report the board as a failed component. If the calculated MTBF is still greater than acceptable parameters, the board performs a series of self-tests. If it fails these tests, the failure is not transient, and the replacement process is initiated. If the board passes these self-tests, it is either reduplexed with its partner board (for synchronously lockstepped boards) or logically brought back into service (for logically paired boards).

• **Power Supply Failure:** If one of the two Stratus power supplies within a module fails, all of the boards driven by that power supply drop out while their partner boards continue to run at full capacity. If either power supply is operational, no battery backup hardware is needed.

• **Operational Downtime:** Operational downtime because of improper action as a result of a hardware failure is almost unheard of. The board that failed is self-identifying, so it is unlikely that the wrong board will be removed for repair. Further, all board replacements are performed while the system is fully operational. It typically requires no more than a few seconds to integrate the replacement board into the module. No time is lost waiting for someone to notice that the system has failed in some way. When a failure does occur, it results in no downtime, and notification (including the CAC, usually responsible for initiating the correct repair action) is automatic.

• **Field Service:** The classical outages due to field service (shotgunning by trying to guess what might be wrong and restarting the system to see if the guess was correct) do not exist with Stratus systems. The self-diagnosing and self-identifying nature of the boards makes this approach obsolete. No preventive maintenance is required for the central system components and therefore no downtime results. As mentioned previously, repair of the system by replacing boards does not affect system operation.

• **Hardware Installation:** Installing new hardware to expand or upgrade a module or system does not require any downtime. In fact, when new hardware is dynamically added, the system automatically makes such hardware available to already running applications. For example, additional processor boards can be added to a system, and the software can immediately benefit from the increase in processing power (due to the symmetric multiprocessing architecture of the operating system). Similarly, memory boards and disks can be dynamically added to a live configuration and are then immediately available for application use (without rebooting the system).

ARCHITECTURE TRADEOFFS

The entire Stratus architecture reflects tradeoffs between simplicity, ease of maintenance, lifetime system costs, logistics concerns, and technology trends on one hand and slight increases in product cost on the other hand. The resulting products clearly justify such tradeoffs.

First, the Stratus solution requires more hardware. Any truly fault-tolerant system requires more hardware than a conventional system, but a Stratus system needs, in some cases, four times the amount of hardware. However, the cost of hardware (primarily logic chips) that Stratus must quadruplicate is low and is decreasing, becoming a less significant part of the total cost of a computer system, particularly when measured over the lifetime of the system. The components with the most significant hardware costs (mainly on-line memory and peripherals) need only be duplicated (or, in the case of disks, redundant in some way), and any truly fault-tolerant computer has these same requirements.

Second, to design circuits that use Stratus concepts, logic chips must be totally deterministic. This has been problematic in the past, but it is becoming less so, as chip manufacturers become more aware of the needs of architectures built on Stratus concepts. Stratus has received commitments from several chip manufacturers for the future production of chips with totally deterministic behavior.

Third, since the logic circuits depend on total synchronization, anything that detracts from this synchronization can be a potential problem. The primary sources of difficulty in this area are new revisions of chips (new masks, usually to fix bugs). Chips that behave slightly differently from earlier revisions are harmless to all other architectures, but to the Stratus architecture, they can be devastating. (If the differing chips are on the same board, the board automatically diagnoses the difference and stops itself. If the differing chips are on separate boards, the boards cannot be synchronized or stay synchronized.) Therefore, Stratus must be sensitive to the revision level of the chips that are placed on boards. Extensive onboard self-identification hardware allows the operating system software to reject boards that do not meet synchronization requirements.

STRATUS SOFTWARE

The Stratus approach to fault tolerance does not depend on a particular operating system; however, software must be capable of managing disk mirroring, redundant intermodule connections, and the diagnostics and maintenance functions necessary to test, remove, and install replacement or expansion hardware. Further, as noted earlier, extensive work is needed to improve the quality and fault tolerance of system software. This work includes a well-structured development process, of course, but Stratus has been able to transcend normal quality levels with its extensive knowledge of system failure scenarios (through the RSN) and with the use of software fault-recovery techniques described later.

Stratus chose to develop its own proprietary operating system, the Virtual Operating System (VOS). When VOS was developed, no other commercially available operating system provided the necessary features. These features include support for the following: multiple processors running in a tightly coupled, shared main memory configuration; disk mirroring; a file system that supports all high-level features of COBOL, as well as transaction-protected files; worldwide networking, providing a single system view of thousands of modules; and the previously mentioned features needed for fault tolerance.

Stratus has since decided to support the UNIX operating system, as well as VOS. The following discussion refers specifically to VOS, but all of the concepts leading to high-quality software are also used in the Stratus UNIX offering, FTX.

Processes

VOS is a process-oriented operating system based on a procedure-call model. It differs from other general-purpose operating systems in its support for multiple processors, emphasis on the client/server model, ability to provide transaction-protected distributed databases, management of fault-tolerant issues such as disk mirroring, and its relative newness.

Programs run within processes that call upon the operating system to complete tasks. A typical call to the operating system does not switch processes (as would be the case with a message-based operating system); rather, it verifies that the arguments to the operating system entry are valid and optionally switches the process to a higher level of privilege. For intermodule or intersystem calls, call arguments are placed in a message that is sent to the appropriate server module. Message-passing primitives are also provided for interprocess communication, particularly for applications that may grow to require multiple modules. These message-passing primitives are vital to the recommended method of developing applications: a client/server process organization.

Processes play a key role in application development but also are a means of implementing some of the basic concepts of Stratus fault tolerance. System processes are created, usually at module initialization time, to manage the diagnostics and maintenance of the hardware. Similarly, system processes are created to interface to the remote service network (RSN).

System processes also implement VOS networking. Server processes perform remote file operations for the benefit of client processes. This client/server relationship is similar to the client/server relationship recommended for applications. Any process, however, can be a client process merely by requesting some remote operation that must be processed by a server on some other module. The difference between VOS message passing and pure message passing in other operating systems is that local requests do not require the client/server process switch and other overhead. VOS becomes a message-passing (distributed) operating system only for off-module requests. Finally, an important use of processes is to implement the distributed transaction management required by any transaction processing system.

Access Control

VOS provides extensive access control facilities to protect data and access to modules and systems in general. Access control lists, passwords, data encryption, and privilege levels protect data.

Distributed Transaction Protection

An important attribute that contributes to the success of VOS in the OLTP marketplace is its ability to support the concept of a *distributed transaction*. A distributed transaction requires interaction between client processes that typically start and commit transactions, server processes acting on behalf of the client processes, and transaction processing (TP) overseer processes that manage transaction processing, including the TP log files and TP recovery after a module interruption.

The TP overseer processes on each module communicate using message passing and remote procedure calls to effect a *two-phase commit protocol*. This protocol guarantees that the distributed databases involved in a transaction are kept consistent, even when some modules involved in the transaction may be unavailable for extended periods of time.

The methods used by Stratus involve TP log files that contain afterimages of the database, flushed to disk at commit time. These log files are applied to the real database files as time permits. VOS also provides the ability to back up transaction-protected files during operation and to perform database roll-forward after a system interruption.

Software Fault Recovery

Since software problems are a primary cause of unavailable applications, Stratus has devised methods of software fault recovery that make its operating system more resilient than most other systems. The extensive data structure locking needed to implement full support for multiple tightly-coupled CPUs is the basis for the operating system strategy. Since every shared data structure within the operating system must be protected from simultaneous updates by multiple CPUs, an extensive locking protocol is necessary. If a data structure is not locked, it is in a consistent state. If a data structure is write locked (where a distinction exists between read locks and write locks), it is potentially inconsistent.

If a fault occurs within a process that is executing within the kernel, or if the process detects a problem through the use of its own checking software, fault recovery procedures that check which data structures might be inconsistent are automatically invoked. The check simply sees which data structures are write locked by the faulting process. Each lock has an associated procedure to call in case the fault recovery software detects the lock set at recovery time.

By establishing recovery procedures for each locked data structure and by defining the data structures so that the called recovery procedures can determine how to make the data structure consistent, many operating system software bugs can be rendered harmless. Many key software packages within the operating system have been designed to operate using this software fault recovery strategy.

Diagnostic Software

Several processes are created to manage the diagnostics, reporting, and maintenance of the hardware. The key processes are the maintenance process and the diagnostic process. The maintenance process determines if a significant event (such as a board failure or the removal or insertion of a board) has occurred. When the maintenance process detects a significant event, the diagnostic process is notified and directed to test the hardware involved.

The maintenance process uses two distinct techniques to determine when events of interest occur. The first technique uses a hardware interrupt signal generated by a board when it breaks. This interrupt is referred to as a *red-light interrupt*. Since a board could break in such a way that it might not be able to set this interrupt, the maintenance process also uses another technique. This second technique polls all boards plugged into the StrataBus to determine if any boards have been inserted, removed, or broken. The typical polling interval is 10 seconds.

When the maintenance process notices a change, it places a request in the diagnostic queue serviced by the diagnostic process. The queue entries typically request the diagnostic process to test a piece of hardware. However, software must occasionally be downloaded into a line adapter before it can be fully tested. The diagnostic process also performs this action. If a piece of hardware is diagnosed as broken, the hardware is left off line and the RSN notifies the Stratus Customer Assistance Center (CAC). If the board error appears to be transient, it is placed back on line and synchronized with its partner if necessary. If too many transient errors are encountered in a specified period of time, the board is declared broken, and the software initiates the process of calling for a replacement board.

System Log Files

One last system process that plays a role in the overall diagnostic management of a module is the overseer process. Among other things, it maintains various log files that record events of interest to system operation. The log files of primary interest are the *system error log* and the *hardware log*. These files are written to by the system at appropriate times by buffering messages in operating system space. The overseer process then copies the messages into actual files. The hardware log file consists of hundreds of message types, all adhering to a standard, formatted structure. All log messages are time stamped. Application software can be notified whenever a message is placed in these files and can therefore reflect these messages to a terminal or some other file. When the RSN packages a message to send to the CAC about a failed piece of hardware, the log files are scanned, and any entries within the file related to the failed hardware are copied into the package sent to the CAC.

As noted earlier, the RSN plays an important role in improving the reliability of Stratus software by notifying the Stratus CAC whenever a system interruption occurs. This gives Stratus engineering personnel extensive insights into the types of problems that occur in the field. Whenever a module is booted, it sends a message to the CAC over the RSN indicating why the reboot occurred. If the reboot was triggered by a software crash, the reason for the crash is available through the remote dump analysis software available through the RSN. In general, the reboot messages provide a complete and accurate tracking of the availability of Stratus systems. This information is used to continuously improve upon the target of continuous availability.

**SERVICE
STRATEGIES**

One of the important design issues for VOS and for Stratus hardware was the strategy for servicing the computers. The following paragraphs compare the Stratus approach to the then current approaches of other computer companies. (Since the introduction of Stratus systems, some of the techniques described have been adopted by other companies.)

The Classical Repair Approach

A classical approach to computer repair follows a scenario such as the following:

1. Someone notices that something is wrong. Either the computer does not seem to be giving the right answers, or it seems to have crashed.
2. Someone, usually a vendor field engineer, tries to determine what might be broken. The problem may be hardware- or software-related.
3. If hardware is suspected, a shotgun approach is often used, whereby boards are replaced singly or in groups in an effort to determine where the problem lies. To aid in determining which boards may be problematic, diagnostic programs are often run, usually requiring a dedicated machine.
4. An attempt is made to check whether or not the fix has been effective. Often, this amounts to little more than seeing if the system seems to work. Such a method is rarely exhaustive, scientific, or conclusive.
5. If the problem still exists or recurs within a few days or weeks, the process loops back to step 2 again.

The disadvantages with this scheme are obvious. The process is expensive, time-consuming, error-prone, unconvincing, and usually makes the system unavailable for extended periods of time.

The Stratus Service Approach

The Stratus approach contrasts with the classical approach in many ways. Hardware errors and software errors may be distinguished with complete confidence. If there is no red light on any board, the problem is a software problem. If there is a red light on a board, that board is broken. If the board failed because of a transient error, the system has already tried to reinstate it into the system several times before giving up and leaving the red light on. (There is no need to diagnose what is wrong with the board; it will not be repaired until it is brought back to the Stratus manufacturing facility.)

The RSN (Remote Service Network) plays a key role in Stratus maintenance. The RSN software provides a means for computers at Stratus customer sites to inform the Stratus CAC of broken or failing hardware automatically. It also provides a communications path for such activities as remote maintenance by CAC personnel, exchange of files, on-line updates, and bug fixes.

The CAC periodically uses the RSN to poll sites; to gather configuration information, error statistics, and system release information; and to check on the consistency of software versions. Customer sites use the RSN to ask both technical and nontechnical questions of CAC personnel. The RSN also informs Stratus publications personnel about problems with or suggestions for manuals.

Many customers are concerned about the implicit access to their files that the RSN might provide to CAC personnel. Extensive protection is built into the RSN software facility, and most customers are completely satisfied with the level of protection provided.

When a hardware error does occur, the RSN immediately informs the Stratus CAC. Appropriate local operations personnel can arrange for immediate notification on their terminals as well.

The advantages to the Stratus approach are clear. First, errors do not result in emergency situations; the system continues to run at full capacity. Second, since the repair can usually be made by onsite, untrained staff personnel, there is a considerable customer savings. The parts necessary for the repair are typically sent to the site automatically from the Stratus manufacturing facility using overnight courier. After repair, these parts undergo a complete testing cycle as rigorous as the initial manufacturing of the parts.

SUMMARY

The introduction of computer systems based on the Stratus architecture provides businesses of all types with new levels of system availability and serviceability. The architecture has proven portable to new I/O systems and faster chip technologies. It provides a platform on which software not cognizant of issues of fault tolerance can provide continuously available solutions. Finally, it provides relief to the ever-increasing threats of rising service costs and quality degradation. Stratus systems and their customers enjoy the highest satisfaction for service and quality.

9   LONG-LIFE SYSTEMS

Spacecraft are the primary example of systems requiring long periods of unattended operation. Unlike most other applications, spacecraft must control their environment (such as electrical power, temperature, and stability) directly. Thus, one must treat all aspects of a spacecraft (for example, structural, propulsion, power, analog, and digital) when designing for reliability.

Spacecraft missions range from simple (such as weather satellites in low earth orbit) to sophisticated (such as deep-space planetary probes through uncharted environments). Within this range are low earth-orbit sensing, low earth-orbit communication or navigation, low earth-orbit scientific, synchronous orbit communication, and deep-space scientific satellites.

Each spacecraft is unique and specifically designed for its mission. Frequently, only one or two copies of the spacecraft are built. As an aid to understanding the specialized approaches to using fault tolerance in spacecraft, a generic spacecraft will be described, followed by a detailed case study of two generations of deep-space planetary probes.

GENERIC SPACECRAFT

A typical spacecraft can be divided into the following five subsystems.

• **Propulsion:** The propulsion system controls the stability and orientation of the spacecraft. Multiple, often redundant, chemical or pressurized-gas thrusters are most frequently used. Occasionally, spacecraft employ a spin for stability instead of the active control provided by thrusters.

• **Power:** The generation and storage of electrical energy must be closely monitored and controlled because all other spacecraft systems operate on electricity. Most often, spacecraft electrical systems consist of solar cells and battery storage. The batteries carry the system through loss of sun or loss of orientation periods. Control of solar cell orientation, battery charging, power transients, and temperature is the most time-consuming task for the spacecraft computers.

• **Data Communications:** Data communications are divided into three, often physically distinct, channels. The first is commands from the ground to the spacecraft via the uplink. It is even possible to reprogram a spacecraft computer by means of the uplink. The other two channels are from the spacecraft to the ground (downlinks). One downlink carries data from the satellite payload; the second carries telemetry data about the spacecraft subsystems (temperature, power supply state, and thruster events).

• **Attitude Control:** A dedicated computer is often used to sense and control the orientation and stability of the spacecraft.

• **Command/Control/Payload:** All aspects of spacecraft control are usually centered in a single command/control computer. This computer is also the focus for recovery from error events. Recovery may be automatic or controlled from the ground via uplink commands.

Typically, each subsystem is composed of a string of stages. As an example, Table 9–1 lists seven stages in a representative power subsystem. Solar panels are physically oriented by tracking motors. Power is delivered to the spacecraft via slip rings. A charge controller automatically keeps the batteries at full potential; a power regulator smooths out voltage fluctuations; and a power distributor controls the load connected to the power subsystems. At each stage, redundancy is used to tolerate anticipated fault modes. To reduce complexity, usually only the output of a string is reported via telemetry.

Table 9–2 lists the attributes of the five generic spacecraft subsystems for three representative spacecraft: RCA's Defense Meteorological Satellite Program (DMSP), JPL's (Jet Propulsion Laboratory) *Voyager,* and JPL's *Galileo.* DMSP relays weather photographs from a polar orbit. *Voyager* is a deep-space probe used in the Jupiter and Saturn planetary fly-bys [Jones, 1979]. *Galileo* is a Jupiter orbiter and probe mission. (See the case study that follows.)

We will use DMSP, a simple spacecraft, as a running example to illustrate the discussion of generic spacecraft architectures, redundancy techniques, and error-management procedures. Each spacecraft has a unique architecture for interconnecting the generic subsystems as well as interfacing the subsystems to the payload designed to carry out the mission of the spacecraft. Figure 9–1 depicts the interconnection of the generic subsystems in DMSP with the telemetry and meteorology sensor subsystems. (The propulsion subsystem has not been shown in order to simplify the example.)

A standard set of redundancy techniques, each tailored to a generic subsystem, has evolved through several generations of spacecraft. A representative set of techniques for each generic subsystem includes the following.

TABLE 9–1 *Typical power subsystem*

Stage	Redundancy	Stage	Redundancy
Tracking solar array	Extra capacity; series/parallel connections of individual solar cells allowing for graceful degradation	Batteries	Series/parallel connections; diode protection
		Power regulation	Redundant spares
		Power distribution	Automatic load shedding
Solar array drive	Redundant drive elements and motors		
Slip-ring assembly	Parallel rings for power transfer		
Charge controller	Automatic monitoring and control of battery charge state		

TABLE 9-2 *Attributes of DMSP, Voyager, and Galileo spacecraft*

Spacecraft	System Characteristics	Propulsion	Power	Data Communications	Attitude Control	Command and Payload
Defense Meteorological Satellite Program (DMSP)	Meteorological 3-axis stabilized sun-synchronous, polar orbit; Mission life: 2 years	Pressurized N$_2$ and hydrazine thrusters	Sun-tracking solar array; Cd battery 300 W minimum average power	Telemetry downlink: 2 or 10 Kbps; Payload data downlink: 3 links at 1–2.7 Mbps; Uplink: 1 Kbps command or 100 Kbps; 6 antennae (1 per link)	Star, earth, and sun sensors; Four reaction wheels; magnetic torque ring coils; Redundant processors	Command rate: 1 Kbps; Redundant, ground programmable computers, 16K 16-bit words each; Downlink data encrypted
Voyager	Planetary probe 3-axis stabilized; Mission life: 7 years	Hydrazine thrusters	3 radioactive thermal generators; 430 W at Jupiter	2 downlinks; 1 uplink; 2 antennae (high gain and low gain)	Redundant sun sensors and Canopus trackers	Command rate: 16 bps; Redundant computers, 4K words each; Data storage on board
Galileo	Planetary orbiter, spun and despun sections; Mission life: 4 years	Bi-propellant thrusters and engine	Two radioisotope thermoelectric generators; 972 W at mission end	2 downlinks: 40 Kbps and up to 134 Kbps; 1 uplink: 32 bps; 2 antennae (high gain and low gain)	Redundant sun sensors and star scanner	Command rate: 32 bps; 19 microprocessors with total of 360 KB of memory; 9 scientific instruments controlled by microprocessors

FIGURE 9–1

Interconnection of major subsystems in RCA's Defense Meteorological Satellite Program (DMSP) block 5D-1 spacecraft

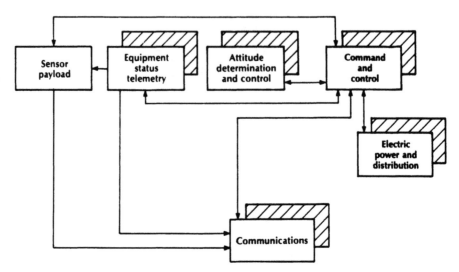

- *Propulsion:* Redundant thrusters, including multiple valves for propellant flow control, automatic switchover based on excessive attitude change rates, multiple commands required to initiate any firing sequence
- *Power:* Redundant solar cell strings, batteries, power buses; automatic load shedding
- *Data Communications:* Redundant transponders; digital error-detection and -correction techniques, switch from directional to omni antennae for backup
- *Attitude Control:* Redundant sensors, gyros, and momentum wheels; automatic star reacquisition modes
- *Command/Control:* Hardware testing of parity, illegal instructions, memory addresses; sanity checks; memory checksums; task completion timed; watch-dog timers; memory write protection; reassemble and reload memory to map around the memory failures

Table 9–3 lists typical redundancy in spacecraft subsystems as a function of mission. For nondemanding missions, reduced complexity of design is a way of meeting system reliability goals.

Returning to our specific example of DMSP (Figure 9–1), we see that standby redundancy is used in all but the sensor payload. The standby spares are cross-strapped so that either unit can be switched in to communicate with other units. This form of standby redundancy is called *block redundancy* because redundancy is provided at the subsystem level rather than internally to each subsystem.

When an error is detected, spacecraft systems enter a unique error management procedure. When an error has been detected in a generic spacecraft, it automatically enters a "safe" or "hold" mode. All nonessential loads on the power subsystems are shed. Normal mission sequencing and solar array tracking are stopped. The spacecraft

TABLE 9–3 *Typical redundancy in spacecraft subsystems as a function of mission*

Mission Subsystem	Low Earth Orbit Sensing	Low Earth Orbit Navigation or Communication	Low Earth Orbit Scientific	Synchronous Orbit Communications	Deep Space Scientific
Propulsion	⟵	{ Station keeping maneuvers via ground commands } { Redundant thrusters and leak detection } ⟶			Backup system Leak detection and automatic switching
Power	⟵	{ Redundant batteries { Low-voltage detection and load shedding } ⟶		Overload protection Low-voltage dropout	Overload protection
Data communication	⟵	{ Redundant links } ⟶		Low-rate telemetry and commands	Redundant data and command channels Omni antennae for backup
Attitude control Command and payload	⟵	{ Safe hold and ground fix } ⟶ Multiple repeaters	Fault-tolerant on-board data processing	Automatic Multiple repeaters and graceful degradation	Automatic High reliability design

is oriented to obtain maximum solar power. Meanwhile, ground personnel must infer which failures could cause the output behavior of each of the strings. A possible failure scenario is selected as most likely, and a reconfiguration (termed a "work-around") of the spacecraft subsystems is devised. A command sequence implementing the work-around is sent to the satellite. Depending on the severity of the failure, this procedure may take days, or even weeks, to complete.

Responses to faults in generic spacecraft vary from automatic in hardware for critical faults (such as power, clocks, and computer), to on-board software for serious faults (such as attitude and command subsystems), to ground intervention for non-critical faults. Faults can be detected by one of several means:

- *Self-Tests:* Subsystems perform self-tests, such as checksums on computer memories.
- *Cross-Checking Between Units:* Either physical or functional redundancy may be used. When a unit is physically duplicated, one is designated as on-line and the other as monitor. The monitor checks all outputs of the on-line unit. Alternatively, there may be disjoint units capable of performing the same function. For example, there is usually a set of sensors and actuators for precision attitude control. Attitude may also be less precisely sensed by instruments with other primary functions. The less precise calculation can be used as a sanity check on the more precise units.

• *Ground-Initiated Special Tests:* These tests are used to diagnose and isolate failures.
• *Ground Trend Analysis:* Routine processing and analysis of telemetry detect long-term trends in units that degrade or wear out.

DMSP uses block redundancy, cross-checking on attitude control, routine self-testing, automatic load shedding upon undervoltage detection, and block switching under ground control. Internally detected error conditions include memory parity, memory address, arithmetic overflow, and illegal transfer.

With this background we can examine the evolution of two generations of planetary probes to Jupiter.

DEEP-SPACE PLANETARY PROBES

The two *Voyager* spacecraft missions launched in 1977 were designed to investigate four of the five outer planets of the solar system. Typically, the planetary encounter phase of each mission lasted 100 days, and was composed of a 30-day "observatory" phase (regular periodic observations of the planetary system), a 30-day "far-encounter" phase (observation of the planet's satellites and spacecraft reorientation in order to calibrate various field and particle sensing instruments), a 10-day "near-encounter" phase (high-resolution observations, intense data gathering, and Sun/Earth occultations), and a 30-day "post-encounter" phase similar to the initial "far-encounter" phase. Between encounters, the spacecraft calibrated instruments, gathered interplanetary "cruise science" data, such as field and particle information, and prepared for the next encounter.

The *Voyager* spacecraft primarily used block redundancy for fault tolerance, as is depicted in Figure 9–2. The attitude control subsystem (ACS) is composed of redundant computers: one is an unpowered standby spare. The command and control subsystem (CCS) is also a redundant computer, but the standby is powered and monitors the on-line unit. Cross-strapping and switching allow reconfiguration around failed components. The CCS executes self-testing routines prior to issuing commands to other subsystems. Memory is only 4K words; the tape recorders are used for storage of scientific data only; and new programs for memory must be loaded from the ground.

Error detection in the *Voyager* ACS is composed of the following:

• Failure of CCS to receive "I'm-Healthy" report every 2 seconds
• Loss of celestial (Sun and Canopus) reference
• Failure of power supply
• Failure to rewrite memory every 10 hours
• Thruster failure (spacecraft takes longer to turn than expected)
• Gyro failure
• Parity error on commands from CCS
• Incorrect command sequence
• Failure to respond to command from CCS

FIGURE 9–2

Voyager *system block diagram*

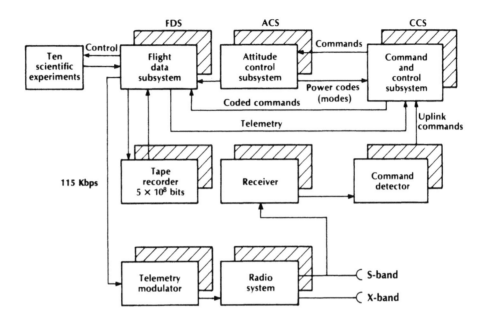

Error detection in the CCS includes the following hardware and software tests.

- Hardware: Low voltage; primary command received before previous one processed; attempt to write into protected memory without override; processor sequencer reached an illegal state
- Software: Primary output unit unavailable for more than 14 seconds; self-test routine not successfully completed; output buffer overflow

A follow-on to the *Voyager* Jupiter fly-by mission is the *Galileo* Jupiter orbiting and probe insertion mission. Figure 9–3 depicts a block diagram of the major subsystems in the *Galileo* orbiter. As can be seen, the *Galileo* architecture borrows heavily from the experiences gained with the *Voyager* system. Block redundancy is used throughout the ten subsystems comprising the orbiter. All but the command and data subsystem (CDS) operate as an active/standby pair. The CDS operates as active redundancy, wherein each block can issue independent commands or the blocks can operate in parallel on the same critical activity. The major departure from the *Voyager* architecture is the extensive use of microprocessors in the *Galileo* orbiter. A total of 19 microprocessors with 320 KB of random access memory and 41 KB of read only memory form a distributed system communicating over an 806 kHz data bus. Nine scientific instruments add eight further microprocessors to the total system. The bus is used to pass network-like messages between sources and destinations. Due to the volatile nature of the RAM, a further requirement for the *Galileo* orbiter has memory Keep-Alive inverters to maintain power to the CDS and to the attitude and articulation control subsystem

FIGURE 9–3
*Galileo orbiter
block diagram*

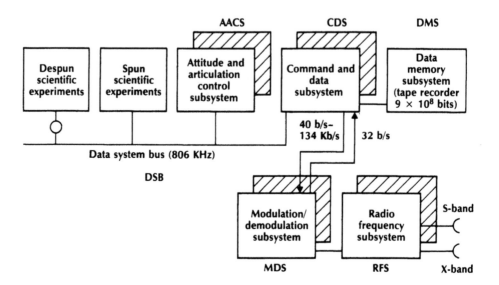

memories in case of power faults. The orbiter accommodates a total of nine scientific instruments (five fields and particles and four remote sensing science). Due to the nature of the phenomena to be measured, field and particle instruments demand a spinning platform to make total spherical observations, while the remote science instruments require very accurate and very stable pointing. These requirements produced a dual-spin structure in which a portion of the spacecraft is spun at three to ten revolutions per minute, while the other portion is held in a stable fixed configuration.

Power is transmitted across the spun/despun interface via slip rings, while rotary transformers are used for data signals. The downlink data rates vary as a function of the experiment. Nonimaging science experiments require a high-quality bit-error rate (less than five times 10^{-5}) and are encoded in a Golay (24, 12) error-correcting code. Imaging experiments can use a lower quality bit-error rate (less than five times 10^{-3}). The orbiter has been designed to operate reliably and autonomously in the harsh Jovian radiation and electrostatic discharge environments during the critical phase of relaying probe data and orbit insertion.

The *Galileo* spacecraft has few hardware error-detection mechanisms. Faults are detected by monitoring the performance of various spacecraft subsystems. The following is a partial list of error-detection mechanisms [Keksz, 1984]:

- Test of event durations including transfers between subsystems and transition between all spin and spun/despun modes
- Parity or checksum errors on messages
- Unexpected command codes
- Loss of "Heartbeat" between the AACS and the CDS
- Spin rates above or below set values

- Loss of sun or star identification detected by no valid pulse from acquisition sensor for a given period of time
- Too great an error between control variable setting and measured response

The on-board fault-protection software is designed to alleviate the effects and symptoms of faults rather than to pinpoint the exact faults themselves. Fault identification and isolation is performed by ground intervention.

The *Galileo* mission was scheduled to fly from the space shuttle in May of 1986. However, the *Challenger* explosion postponed the launch until 1990. The case study, by Kocsis, explores the architecture developed for the *Galileo* orbiter.

OTHER NOTEWORTHY SPACECRAFT DESIGNS

Several prototype spacecraft computers have been designed and/or constructed to explore the frontiers of fault-tolerant techniques. Noteworthy among this group are STAR, FTSC, and FTBBC. A single mission to make a grand tour of the outer solar system by taking advantage of a rare alignment of the five outer planets was designed during the late 1960s. In support of the grand tour mission, the Jet Propulsion Laboratory designed and breadboarded the STAR (Self-Test And Repair) computer [Avizienis et al., 1971]. STAR primarily used hardware subsystem fault-tolerant techniques, such as functional unit redundancy, voting, power-spare switching, coding, and self-checks. Task-level rollback was also incorporated in the design, which represented the most advanced fault-tolerant techniques in the 1960s.

Another fault-tolerant uniprocessor designed as a satellite computer is the FTSC (Fault Tolerant Spaceborne Computer) [FTSC, 1976]. FTSC is a 32-bit, general-purpose computer with a 60K memory and 5-microsecond average instruction execution time. Error-detection/correction codes and bit-sliced sparing are extensively used to tolerate failures.

With the advent of microprocessors, emphasis has shifted to multiple-computer spacecraft. The FTBBC (Fault-Tolerant Building-Block Computer) is an experimental set of VLSI chips that allow construction of reliable multiprocessors with standard microprocessor and memory LSI chips. The new chips provide ECC circuitry for memory and duplication/comparison for processors [Rennels, 1980].

REFERENCES

Avizienis et al., 1971; FTSC, 1976; Jones, 1979; Keksz, 1984; Rennels, 1980.

THE *GALILEO* CASE

Galileo Orbiter Fault Protection System

ROBERT W. KOCSIS*

The *Galileo* spacecraft, originally intended to be launched by the Shuttle Transportation System in 1986, was delayed until 1990. In 1992, when the spacecraft is approximately 150 days out from

* *Acknowledgment*: The research described in this case study was carried out by the Jet Propulsion Laboratory, California Institute of Technology, under contract with the National Aeronautics and Space Administration.

Jupiter, the probe will be separated from the orbiter and enter Jupiter's atmosphere. The orbiter will acquire data from the probe for real-time transmissions back to Earth and recording on an orbiter tape recorder. Following acquisition of the probe data, the orbiter will perform a maneuver such that it will go into orbit about Jupiter. For the following 20 months, the orbiter will explore Jupiter, its moons, and the surrounding space environment, using a complement of fields and particles and imaging instruments. The mission will be executed with a single spacecraft (no backup), and its success is predicated on the probe relay and Jupiter orbit insertion events that must occur even in the presence of faults.

This case study focuses on the orbiter system and does not discuss the probe. It presents the orbiter system fault-protection design with emphasis on the fault-protection associated with the attitude and articulation control subsystem and the command and data subsystem, as well as the orbiter sequences. Problems in the fault-protection design, as uncovered by analyses and testing on the spacecraft, are discussed, together with some example problems and their resolution.

THE *GALILEO* SPACECRAFT

The *Galileo* spacecraft, shown in Figure 9–4, consists of an orbiter vehicle and a probe vehicle. The orbiter is dual-spun and consequently divided into two major sections: the spun and despun sections. The spun section is dominated by a 4.8-meter high-gain antenna used for transmitting data and receiving signals at S- and X-band frequencies. A low-gain antenna, with a broad beam width, is located on the axis of the high-gain antenna for use during near-Earth operations and as a backup for cases where the spacecraft may not be pointed directly at Earth. Electrical power, on the order of 600 watts, is derived from two general-purpose heat-source radioisotope thermoelectric generators mounted on separate 5-meter booms. Fields and particles instruments are mounted on a boom at points 3 meters and 11 meters from the orbiter's centerline. The majority of the orbiter's electronics is located in structural compartments behind the high-gain antenna. The retro propulsion module, used for all attitude control and propulsive maneuvers, is an integral part of the spun section; it consists of propellant and pressurant tanks, together with necessary valves and regulators, a 400-newton rocket engine, and 10-newton thrusters mounted in groups of six on two 2-meter booms.

The despun section consists of the probe vehicle, a relay antenna for receiving data from the probe, selected electronics, and a scan platform with imaging instruments. The scan platform has two degrees of freedom: one from motion of the stator about the spin axis of the orbiter; the other about an orthogonal axis integral with the platform. The spun and despun sections are joined via a spin bearing assembly that contains bearings for mechanical interfacing and slip rings and rotary transformers for electrical interfacing. A more detailed description of the orbiter system is given in Jones and Landano [1983] and Landano and Easter [1984].

ATTITUDE AND ARTICULATION CONTROL SUBSYSTEM

The attitude and articulation control subsystem (AACS) is responsible for maintaining the spin rate of the spun section, pointing the spin vector, despinning the stator as required, pointing the scan platform, controlling the propulsion isolation valves and heaters, and firing the 10-N thrusters and 400-N engine.

A functional block diagram of the AACS is shown in Figure 9–5. Most of the AACS elements are standby block redundant. Central to the AACS are the attitude control electronics (ACEs), which are block redundant and consist of memory (both are powered at the same time), processor, and I/O. The ACE controls the AACS configuration; monitors its health; performs processing, telemetry, and command functions; and provides AACS fault protection. The heart of each ACE is a high-speed 2500 ATAC-16 processor and memory containing 32K 16-bit words of RAM and 1K words of ROM. The elements of the AACS on the spun side (rotor) in addition to the ACE include

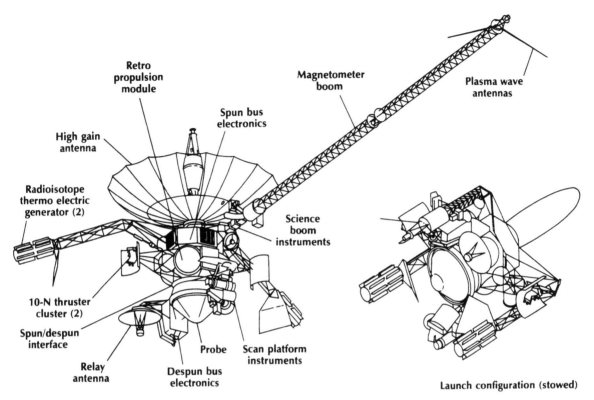

Retro
propulsion
module

Magnetometer
boom

Plasma wave
antennas

Spun bus
electronics

High gain
antenna

Radioisotope
thermo electric
generator (2)

Science
boom
instruments

10-N thruster
cluster (2)

Spun/despun
interface

Relay
antenna

Probe

Despun bus
electronics

Scan platform
instruments

Launch configuration (stowed)

FIGURE 9–4 Galileo *spacecraft configuration*

the acquisition sun sensors (AS), which enable AACS to point the spin vector toward the sun and provide off-sun spin rate estimates; the star scanner (SS), which provides celestial references for determining the attitude of the spacecraft; the propulsion drive electronics (PDE), which contain the switching logic for controlling valves and engines within the propulsion module; and the linear boom actuators (LBA), which control the position of the RTG booms for adjusting the inertial properties of the spacecraft.

On the despun (stator) side is the DEUCE (despun control electronics), which provides communication between the actuators and sensors on the stator and the ACEs on the rotor via rotary transformers on the spin bearing assembly (SBA). Gyros (GSS) are located on the scan platform for accurate pointing control and execution of turns; the pointing of the scan platform is controlled by the scan actuator subassembly (SAS). The accelerometer transducer subassemblies (ATS) are used to determine changes in velocity for axial ΔV maneuvers. The gyro and accelerometer electronics (GE and AE, respectively) are also located on the stator.

The AACS has internal fault protection that can be enabled or disabled by command. Most of this internal fault protection consists of reasonableness checks, such as rates too high or too low or time too long to achieve desired state, position errors. This strategy is implemented through the use of threshold monitors. Fault protection, which requires system-level action (more than one subsystem involved), is effected through alert codes to the command and data subsystem

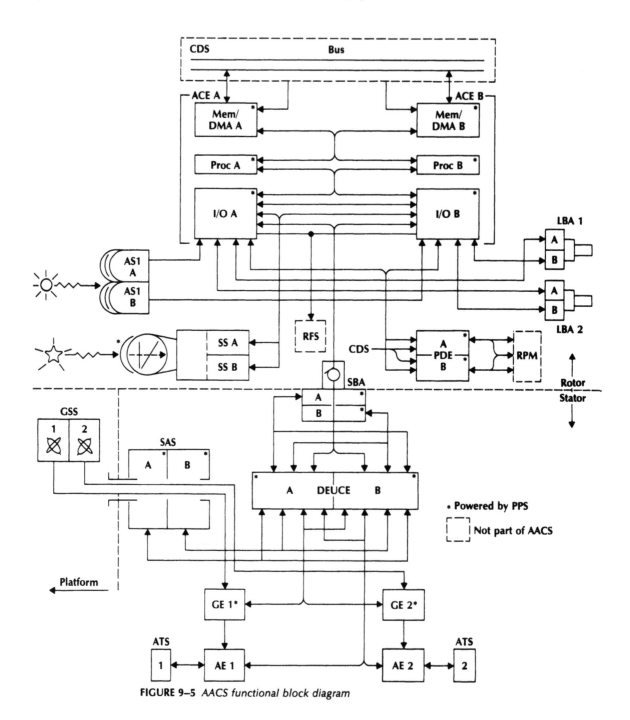

FIGURE 9–5 *AACS functional block diagram*

(CDS), as discussed later in the section on AACS/CDS interactions. There are two exceptions, however, where AACS takes unilateral system-level action in response to detected faults. In the event that AACS does not receive any time messages or commands from CDS for a specified time period, AACS assumes that CDS is "lost" and informs CDS of the detected fault. Barring any response from CDS, AACS will safe the scan platform behind a sun shade to protect the imaging instruments, select the low-gain antenna, and point the spin vector toward the sun, placing the spacecraft in a commandable and reasonably safe state. The other instance of AACS system-level fault-protection action involves the scan platform and the associated science imaging instruments. If the scan platform is commanded so that the boresight of the instruments passes within 30° of the sun, AACS will abort the pointing and safe the scan platform behind the sunshade in order to protect the instruments from possible sun damage.

COMMAND AND DATA SUBSYSTEM

The CDS is the center of activity on board the orbiter. The CDS is actively redundant, with two parallel strings running at all times, and has responsibility for the following functions: (1) decoding of uplink commands; (2) execution of commands and sequences; (3) execution of system-level fault-protection responses; (4) collection, processing, and formatting of telemetry data for downlink transmission; and (5) movement of data between subsystems via a data bus. The primary hardware elements of CDS are shown in Figure 9–6. The CDS employs six 1802 microprocessors and has 176K 8-bit words of RAM. There are four microprocessors and 144K of RAM on the spun side and two microprocessors and 32K of RAM on the despun side.

As shown in Figure 9–6, each CDS string is composed of the same functional elements. The hardware command decoders (HCDs) receive command data from the active command detector unit of the modulation/demodulation, subsystem, decode these data, and transfer the decoded data to the high-level modules (HLMs) and the critical controllers (CRCs). Each HLM contains an 1802 microprocessor and a 32K RAM and is responsible for the following functions: (1) uplink command processing; (2) maintenance of the spacecraft clock; (3) movement of data over the data system bus; (4) execution of stored sequences (time-event tables); (5) telemetry control; and (6) error recovery including system fault-protection monitoring and response. Each of the four low-level modules (LLMs) contains an 1802 microprocessor and a 16K RAM; two LLMs are on the spun side, two on the despun side. The LLMs collect and format engineering data from the subsystems and transfer them to the bulk memories (BUMs) for output over the downlink, provide the capability to issue coded and discrete commands to spacecraft users, recognize out-of-tolerance conditions on status inputs, and perform some system fault-protection functions. The BUMs and data management subsystem bulk memories (DBUMs) contain 16K and 8K RAMs, respectively. The BUMs and DBUMs provide storage for sequences and contain various buffers for telemetry data and interbus communication. The CRCs provide the mechanism for controlling the configuration of CDS elements and subsystem users to the two data system buses, supplying enable signals to certain critical events (for example, probe separation), and controlling CDS write protects. The Golay coders (GCs) provide Golay encoding of data via hardware, while the timing chains (TCs) and phase lock loops (PLLs) establish timing within the CDS.

Fault protection within CDS falls into two categories: internal or subsystem level and system level. CDS internal fault protection includes data parity checks, periodic self-tests and block redundancy of hardware elements. CDS has a variety of hardware and software error indicators from which it can determine the severity of the fault and the appropriate response or action to take. Faults from a CDS perspective can be divided into three categories: (1) Faults impairing the fundamental operation of the CDS as it relates to telemetry and command processing and fault-protection response capability, which are classified as *privileged errors*, such as power outage; (2) faults affecting activities essentially external to CDS fundamental operation but may impact

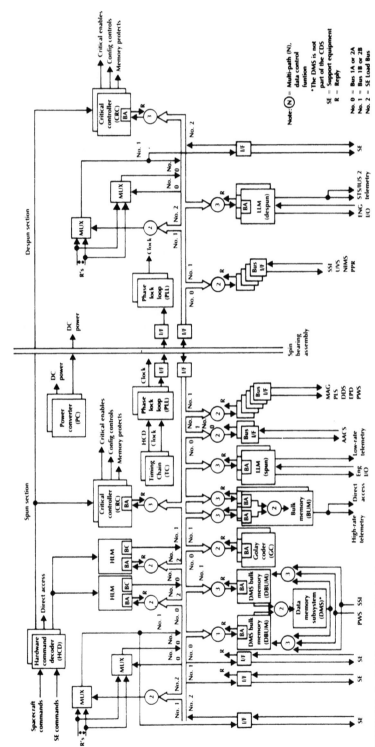

FIGURE 9-6 CDS hardware block diagram

spacecraft-level activities are classified as *nonprivileged errors*, such as error in a science sequence load; and (3) faults not interfering with CDS operation, which are classified as *message-only errors*. The CDS response to these errors involves system considerations and is presented in summary form in Table 9–4.

Basically, for critical operation, at least one CDS string must continue executing the critical sequence regardless of fault conditions. For noncritical operations, it is appropriate to stop sequencing and safe the spacecraft. In order to actualize this philosophy, some form of communication between redundant CDS strings is required. This communication is accomplished by having a status flag in each HLM that can be interrogated by the other HLM. The flag will indicate if a CDS string is down and has therefore stopped processing. There is also interstring communication with regard to a CDS string requesting safing of the spacecraft (S/C); that is, a string requesting S/C-safing will notify the other string to request S/C-safing also so that the two strings are coordinated.

Since the CDS is the center of all command, telemetry, and sequencing activity, it followed that system fault-protection responses should be resident in CDS and under CDS control. The system fault protection resident in CDS consists of monitors that look for fault indications and responses that are time-ordered sequences of commands designed to isolate and correct a fault condition. The monitors and responses can be separately enabled and disabled by ground command to provide for an adaptable system fault-protection response. The monitors also include persistence checks—that is, a fault condition must last for a specified time before a response is requested—so that the fault responses will be not triggered by spurious, transient indications.

The system fault-protection responses that are specifically related to AACS are discussed under AACS/CDS interactions (alert code responses and heartbeat loss). The remaining responses are as follows:

• *S/C-safing* terminates all sequencing, turns off power loads to take S/C to a minimum power state, stops propulsive maneuvers, establishes a low-power downlink, turns on heaters to place spacecraft subsystems (primarily science instruments) in a thermally safe state, and commands S/C to a commandable configuration if required. It calls RPM thermal safing, which is described later. S/C-safing is a service routine; that is, it is called by other fault-protection

TABLE 9–4
CDS HLM generalized fault response matrix

	Privileged Error		Nonprivileged Error	
	Critical OP Mode and Marked Sequence	Standard OP Mode or No Marked Sequence	Critical OP Mode and Marked Sequence	Standard OP Mode or No Marked Sequence
Other String Up	Down	Down	Effectual down	Safe
Other String Down	Rollback	Safe	Rollback	Safe
	Message-Only Error			
	Enqueue a message for downlink			

Key: Down—inhibit string processing except for ADMIN and CAP VMs; Rollback—restart the critical sequence; Safe—request system fault protection to Safe and request other string to Safe; Effectual down—inhibit nonprivileged functions and set "down" indicator

responses and, as such, does not have a monitor. Furthermore, this response is designed to place the spacecraft in a safe, commandable state from any noncritical initial state. S/C-safing is disabled during critical sequences, since critical activity must by definition continue.

• *Undervoltage recovery* monitors whether the CDS has experienced a power-on-reset (POR) and/or whether the power subsystem has indicated an undervoltage on the primary power bus. The basic response is to terminate sequencing and turn off power loads in an effort to remove a possible fault and to provide power margin to blow fuses. If the operational mode is noncritical, the response uses a portion of the S/C-safing response to safe the spacecraft and requests RPM thermal safing. If the operational mode is critical (see discussion under Sequences and Fault Protection for critical and noncritical operation), the call to S/C-safing and RPM thermal safing is not made, and the response conditions the spacecraft to a state consistent with the ongoing critical activity (downlink configuration established, science instruments initialized, subsystems in a thermally safe state). A special version of undervoltage recovery is used during the critical launch sequence to perform the same basic functions.

• *Data management subsystem (DMS) recovery* is a service routine, called by undervoltage recovery, which places the DMS, a tape recorder, in a commandable, safe state in the event of a CDS POR. For critical operations, the DMS is placed in the appropriate mode (record or rewind) consistent with the ongoing critical sequence.

• *Launch monitor* handles coded messages sent to CDS by the Centaur injection vehicle. The coded message is validated and, if correct, the appropriate segment of the launch sequence is initiated.

• *Retro propulsion module (RPM) thermal safing* is a service routine called by those fault-protection algorithms that reduce net spacecraft power consumption. Excess power is diverted into heaters near the RPM propellant tanks. This response regulates the amount of power into the RPM by turning selected power loads on or off to prevent a thermally induced over-pressurization of the RPM tanks. The action taken by this response is commandable from the ground to match varying power states.

• *RPM over pressure (O/P)* monitors the temperatures and pressures of the RPM propellant tanks. In the event a regulator fails so that the tanks become over-pressurized, the response will isolate the pressurant from the propellant tanks by actuating a pyrotechnic valve and requesting S/C-safing. If the tanks become overheated, which could lead to a thermally induced over-pressurization, the response will call S/C safing, which in turn calls RPM thermal safing to safe the spacecraft and thermally safe the RPM.

• *Radio frequency loss (RF Loss)* monitors the status of the downlink elements in the radio frequency subsystem (RFS). In the event of a fault, the response takes progressive measures to clear the fault until ultimately selecting the associated redundant units (exciters and transmitters) and thereby restoring the downlink. If a possible power change (e.g., high power to low power) is made, a call to S/C-safing and therefore to RPM thermal safing is made.

• *Command loss (CMD Loss)* monitors the receipt of valid ground commands. If a valid command is not received by a predetermined time (selectable from the ground), it is assumed that there has been a failure in the uplink so that the spacecraft cannot be commanded. The response switches to the low-gain antenna, waits three hours, commands the spacecraft to point to the sun (in order to achieve a commandable attitude), and on three-hour centers requests S/C-safing and switches redundant elements of the RFS critical to the receipt of commands (for example, command detector units and receivers). The three-hour waits between reconfigurations provide time for the ground to attempt to command the spacecraft in each new configuration.

The response continues to execute over and over again until terminated by the receipt of a valid command.

• *Temperature control monitor* checks the temperatures of selected elements that are determined to have particularly critical temperature requirements. The basic response is to turn associated heaters on or off if the monitored temperatures are too low or too high.

• *Science alarm monitors*—one for the energetic particle detector (EPD) and one for the plasma subsystem (PLS)—check the status words from the instruments. If a fault is detected in the PLS, the response is to turn the instrument off. For the EPD, the response is to turn the instrument off and turn bias power and a replacement heater on. These responses place the instruments in a benign, safe state.

Supporting descriptions of system fault protection responses can be found in Larman [1983].

AACS/CDS INTERACTIONS

In addition to the nominal command and telemetry interfaces between AACS and CDS, AACS sends special coded messages to CDS for processing and subsequent action. Some of these messages from AACS are used directly for fault-protection responses resident in CDS. These AACS messages fall into three categories: power codes, alert codes, and heartbeat.

Power codes from AACS to CDS are messages that AACS requires the switching of power (on/off) to an element or elements within its subsystem. Particular examples are the turning on/off of heaters on the thrusters or the powering of the propulsion drive electronics, which is required for the execution of maneuvers. Although not directly related to fault-protection responses, power codes will be sent from AACS to CDS as part of reconfiguration responses following a fault. In response to these power codes, CDS issues the appropriate command to the power subsystem.

Alert codes are coded messages sent by AACS to CDS to indicate a change in state or the detection of a fault condition within AACS. There are 17 defined alert codes. Some of these alert codes, such as Earth Acquired/Not Acquired and Inertial Reference Loss, do not result in direct fault protection responses by CDS, but are used to determine if a particular response is appropriate. In the case of the Inertial Reference Loss alert code, for instance, a word in CDS memory is changed to reflect a "lost" condition and is checked by other fault-protection responses to ensure that AACS is not commanded to the inertial mode under this circumstance. Other alert codes, such as Thruster Firing Imminent or Maneuver Complete, indicate the occurrence or onset of normal activity. However, the majority of alert codes are sent as the result of faults detected within AACS that may require a system-level fault-protection response by CDS. Of particular note is the AACS POR alert code, which results in one of the most complex and interactive responses executed by CDS. This alert code is sent by AACS after the occurrence of a power outage so that AACS comes up in a power-on-reset state (POR) and requires commands in order to be reconfigured to an operational state. The basic approach is to configure AACS via CDS command to a safe, operational state consistent with the mode AACS was in at the time of the fault. In the case of critical mode operation, the AACS state will vary with time and the CDS response will depend on the time in the critical sequence at which the fault occurred. The method of implementing this time-dependent response is discussed in the section on sequences and fault protection. A complete list of alert codes, together with the basic responses, is given in Table 9–5.

Finally, AACS sends a "heartbeat" to CDS to indicate that the attitude control electronics (ACE) is functioning. Under normal operation, this heartbeat is sent to CDS every 666 milliseconds. There are defined valid heartbeat patterns for AACS operating in RAM or ROM. If a valid heartbeat is not received for a specified period of time (on the order of 5 seconds, which serves as a

TABLE 9–5 *AACS alert codes*

Alert Code	Alert Code Description	Basic CDS Response
0	NO-OP (No Alert)	None
1	Commanded Maneuver Complete	Record status; test as required for appropriate fault protection response
2	Maneuver Abort	Safe the spacecraft*
3	AACS POR	Noncritical: Initialize AACS; safe the spacecraft
		Critical: Initialize AACS as required by sequence
4	Command Error	Safe the spacecraft*
5	CDS Loss	Reconfigure AACS electronics via heartbeat loss response
6	Thruster Firing Imminent	Safe selected science instruments to protect from contamination
7	Thruster Firing All Clear	Prepare selected science instruments to resume data gathering
8	ROM Entry	Safe the spacecraft*
9	Inertial Reference Loss	Record status; test as required for appropriate fault protection response
10	Celestial Reference Loss	Safe the spacecraft*
11	Celestial Reference Reacquire	Record status
12	Earth Acquired	Record status
13	Earth Not Acquired	Record status; if not Earth acquired, command sun point and select low-gain antenna as part of S/C-Safing response
14	Bit FLIP POR	See AACS POR
15	Command Constraint Violation	Safe the spacecraft*
16	Sun Constraint Violation	Record status
17	Thruster Swap	Record status (available for check by sequence)

*The Spacecraft is safed by executing the S/C-safing response.

persistence check to obviate responses to spurious conditions), CDS will execute the Heartbeat Loss algorithm, which switches ACE I/Os, processors, and memories until a valid heartbeat is restored. This fault protection response uses redundant elements within AACS to restore a failed ACE.

SEQUENCES AND FAULT PROTECTION

As used on the *Galileo* orbiter, sequences are time-ordered lists of commands loaded into the on-board CDS memory and executed by CDS in order to perform specific spacecraft activities. These sequences can be science-gathering sequences, propulsive maneuver sequences, calibration sequences, probe checkout and release sequences, or the mission-critical launch and relay/JOI (Jupiter Orbit Insertion) sequences. From a fault-protection design perspective, the sequences are divided into two categories: critical and noncritical.

Noncritical sequences are not time critical and can therefore be aborted and executed at a later time without failing to achieve the primary mission objectives of returning probe data and getting into an orbit about Jupiter. Consequently, the fault-protection design for noncritical sequences is to terminate sequencing in the event of a fault and place the spacecraft in a minimum power, thermally safe, commandable state. The CDS resident S/C-safing algorithm achieves this desired safe state in all cases. There is some logic built into some noncritical sequences to check certain status bits in CDS memory that can indicate the occurrence of a fault; if a fault is detected in this manner by the sequence, an error message is sent to CDS, resulting in termination of the sequence and safing of the spacecraft.

Critical sequences must be executed correctly within the specified time period in order to achieve primary mission objectives; they cannot be aborted and executed at a later time. As such, there are two critical sequences: launch and relay/JOI. The launch sequence takes the spacecraft through the STS launch, the Centaur injection, separation from Centaur, the deployment of the spacecraft elements, and the attainment of a safe, stable attitude. The relay-JOI sequence ensures acquisition of probe data and the insertion of the orbiter into orbit about Jupiter. The fault-protection design for both of these critical sequences is basically the same. The sequence is run in parallel on both CDS strings with CDS in the critical mode. If one CDS string should fail, the remaining string is capable of successfully completing the sequence. Furthermore, if one CDS string goes down, the remaining string will do all it can to continue the sequence even if it encounters errors; it will not go down. There is within CDS a *rollback* feature for critical sequences so that if a significant error or CDS POR occurs, the CDS will go back to a special mark in the sequence and reissue the commands from that mark; in this way, it is ensured that nothing in the sequence is missed even if the CDS was momentarily down.

The system fault-protection interaction with the critical sequences is quite complex. Only that system fault protection that is absolutely required is enabled; in particular, S/C-safing is disabled. Undervoltage recovery and AACS POR responses are the most complex and required the incorporation of a special design feature: *flags*. The power state of the spacecraft and the state of AACS vary with time as the critical sequence progresses. In the event of a fault, which could occur at any time, the spacecraft must be restored to a state compatible with what existed at the time of the fault so that the sequence can continue in a normal sense. Consequently, there are instructions in the sequence that set parameters (flags) within CDS to specific values, depending on the state of the spacecraft at that time. These flag-setting instructions are usually at the beginning of significant transitions. If a fault occurs, and undervoltage recovery or AACS POR is entered, CDS will check the flag and issue the appropriate response from a list of possible responses. The end result is an integrated system fault-protection design that draws on the fault-protection features of the subsystems and the sequences.

FAULT-PROTECTION DESIGN PROBLEMS AND THEIR RESOLUTION

Two methods were employed to test and verify the system fault-protection design. The first method was started in October 1984 and involved sitting down with AACS and CDS software and hardware designers, sequence designers, and system fault-protection engineers to walk through the software code for postulated fault scenarios and verify that the responses and states achieved were proper and correct. The process was very tedious and time-consuming and lasted some seven months. The findings made the effort worthwhile: Several problems were uncovered, primarily involving timing of responses between AACS and CDS. Changes to the software were implemented based on these findings. One case in point involved a fault scenario wherein AC power to CDS was interrupted, causing a POR in CDS. When both the hardware and software responses and associated delays were laid out for both CDS and AACS, it was determined that CDS could be down long enough to miss power codes and alert codes that were being sent by AACS. Consequently, CDS could miss mission-critical signals from AACS and therefore not initiate the proper fault response. This timing problem led to a redesign of the AACS to CDS interface for alert codes and power codes. In particular, alert codes are now held by AACS for CDS to read for 8 seconds (as opposed to 3 seconds) to give CDS adequate time to recover. A handshake was instituted for the power code interface between AACS and CDS, whereby AACS sends a power code to CDS and must receive an echo of that power code from CDS or repeat the process three times before proceeding to the next power code.

Rigorous testing of the system fault-protection design was conducted on the integrated spacecraft beginning in 1985. Although the testing was difficult, it provided an ideal opportunity to verify the system fault-protection design with actual hardware and software responses. The first step was to test individual fault-protection algorithms by injecting appropriate faults without sequences running. The next step was to introduce faults while the sequences were active. Much was learned and many problems and unexpected responses were encountered. Most of the problems involved race conditions wherein fault-protection responses were either too late or too early relative to subsystem or sequence events to achieve the desired state. To cite an example, a test of the relay/JOI sequence on the spacecraft in September 1985 involved the introduction of an AACS POR just prior to the critical orbit insertion rocket engine firing. The CDS responded properly to the AACS POR fault; however, AACS's internal processing of one of the fault-protection commands had a time delay (instituted to accommodate another requirement) that resulted in terminating the engine burn after the sequence had started the burn. Consequently, the engine burned for only 40 seconds instead of the required 40 minutes. If this had happened in flight, the orbiter would *not* have gone into orbit around Jupiter. The problem was resolved by moving the time of the engine burn in the sequence by 2 minutes to ensure that there was adequate time for the fault protection response to complete in the worst case.

SUMMARY

The *Galileo* orbiter system fault-protection design integrates system fault protection with the fault protection designed into the AACS, CDS, and mission sequences. The system fault protection has been analyzed and tested on the spacecraft. Several redesign efforts and retests were instituted. The critical launch sequence and several noncritical sequences have successfully passed fault-protection testing. The critical relay/JOI sequence still has fault protection-related problems that will require analyses and testing on a special test bed composed of AACS, CDS, and power subsystems. This test bed is required since the spacecraft will not be available for further testing.

The AACS/CDS fault-protection code walkthroughs, although tedious and time-consuming, proved to be of great value. The process is necessary, and there are plans currently being pursued to develop computerized tools to aid in the analysis of fault-protection responses and their interaction with ongoing sequences.

REFERENCES

Jones and Landano, 1983; Landano and Easter, 1984; Larman, 1983.

10 CRITICAL COMPUTATIONS

Real-time control represents the most challenging application for fault-tolerant computer designers since faulty computations can cause the loss of human life or expensive equipment. Fault-tolerant computers have been designed for several real-time applications:

- Flight control of commercial airlines, military fighters, and space shuttles.
- Safety monitors in nuclear power plants, high-speed trains, and hospitals.
- Continuous process control in chemical plants, oil well drilling/pumping, and metal forming.

Since real-time controllers are often embedded into these larger systems, the fault-tolerant computers most often go unnoticed.

Not only must real-time controllers not make computation errors, they must also produce results on strict deadlines. These deadlines are frequently only milliseconds apart. Thus, error detection and recovery time must be minimized. Specially designed hardware operates with concurrent error detection so that incorrect data never leaves a faulty module.

Historically, the only fault-tolerant technique that could rapidly recover from any form of error has been massive replication and voting. The replication can be in either hardware or software. Hardware replication and voting can be applied at any level in the digital hierarchy, although it has most often been used at the processor level. Software approaches use replication in time or space. Repeated execution (time redundancy) is usually impractical in situations with strict deadlines. Hence, software is typically replicated on different computers, with software voting on messages carrying the computed results between processors.

A key issue in replicated systems is synchronization, regardless of whether voting is conducted in hardware or software. The various copies must be kept in lock-step, and the voting must be performed in a timely manner. If the copies become inconsistent, substantial effort may be required to return them to identical behavior. This chapter contains two case studies: one based on hardware voting, and the other based on software voting.

C.vmp   C.vmp (Computer, voted multiprocessor) is a triplicated microprocessor system designed for real-time control environments. The design goals for the system included the ability to tolerate permanent and transient faults; fault survival that should be transparent to user software; no lost time due to recovery from faults; the use of off-the-shelf components; and the dynamic trading of performance for reliability.

To be consistent with the design goals of modularity and software transparency, bus-level voting was selected as the major fault-tolerance mechanism. There are three processor-memory pairs, and each pair is connected via a bus. The voter cuts all three buses between the processors and the memories. Voting occurs every time the processors access the bus to either send or retrieve information. C.vmp is thus a multi-processor system capable of fault-tolerant operation. In independent mode, C.vmp executes three separate programs. C.vmp can synchronize its redundant hardware and start executing a critical section of code as a single processor system either under the control of an external event or under the control of one of the processors. With the voter active, the three buses are voted on and the result of the vote is sent out. Any disagreements among the processors will thus not propagate to the memories, and vice versa. Since voting is a simple act of comparison, the voter is memoryless. Disagreements are caught and corrected before they have a chance to propagate.

Bus-level voting only works if information passes through the voter. One issue is whether the processor registers will circulate through the voter. Traces of program behavior indicate that on average a register is loaded or stored to memory approximately every 20 instructions and subroutines are called approximately every 40 instructions (thereby saving the program counter on the stack in memory). The only register that normally is not saved or written into is the stack pointer. To maintain fault tolerance, the system must periodically save and reload the stack pointer. Thus, normal program behavior can keep the registers circulating through the voter.

There are two levels of synchronization used in C.vmp to keep the three processors in step: bus signal synchronization and processor clock synchronization. The voter uses the bus reply signal to synchronize the three buses, as it is asserted by an external device (memory and I/O devices) once every bus cycle. Thus, processors can stay in step if they receive bus reply concurrently. The four-phase processor clocks are synchronized on every phase zero.

An important parameter in the design of fault-tolerant computers is the amount of performance degradation suffered to obtain greater reliability. In a triplicated architecture such as C.vmp, the obvious loss of two-thirds of the available computing power is unavoidable. This was the reason C.vmp was made flexible enough to switch between voting (fault-tolerant) mode and independent (high-performance) mode. However, this fundamental loss because of triplication is not the only loss; the voter cutting and buffering all the bus lines introduces delays of 80 to 140 nanoseconds in the signals between the processors and the memories.

Since the bus is not utilized 100 percent of the time, the average slow-down viewed by a program can be substantially less. A set of test programs with representative mixes of instructions and addressing modes run on C.vmp resulted in performance degradation of about 16 to 19 percent when compared to the standard processor from which it is constructed. In exchange, C.vmp exhibited a mean time to crash that is five to six times greater than the nonredundant processor measured in the same environment. C.vmp executes an unmodified version of the DEC RT-11 operating system. Although composed of almost 150 SSI chips in a wire-wrap version, the voter has been reimplemented in a custom LSI chip with four bus lines per 48-pin package, thus decreasing voter complexity to approximately 10 custom LSI chips plus 20 SSI chips.

There are two major reasons for studying C.vmp. First, it illustrates the process by which a simple technique (triplication) is translated into a working system. Numerous problems, including synchronization, require solution before even simple techniques are reduced to practice. Auxiliary functions, such as error status information, enabling/disabling of the redundancy, and initialization, must support the technique. From the detailed C.vmp implementation, the reader may be able to extrapolate the higher level descriptions of more complex systems into plausible implementations. The second reason for considering C.vmp is to explore the consequences of redundancy on system performance. Several methods of predicting and measuring performance are provided.

SIFT

SIFT (Software-Implemented Fault Tolerance), designed by SRI International, was intended for real-time control of aircraft. Due to concerns over fuel efficiency and performance, the aircraft of the future will be dynamically unstable. The loss of computer control for even a few milliseconds could lead to disaster. Thus, these experimental systems are designed for a failure probability of 10^{-9} during a 10-hour mission. An interesting problem arises from this reliability goal: How does one verify that a system meets its design specifications? 10^{-10} failures per hour translates into 1.14 million operating years before failure. The approach taken in SIFT is to mathematically prove the correctness of the system software.

As the name implies, software-implemented fault tolerance relies primarily on software mechanisms to achieve reliability. The hardware consists of independent computers communicating with other computers over unidirectional serial links. Thus, for N computers, there are $N(N-1)$ links. The SIFT software is divided into a set of tasks. The input to a task is produced by the output of a collection of tasks. Reliability is achieved by having tasks done independently by a number of computers. Typically, the correct output is chosen by a majority vote. If all copies of the output are not identical, an error has been detected. Such errors are recorded for use by the executive for determining faulty units and system reconfiguration. Voting is performed only on the input data to tasks rather than on every partial result. Thus, the tasks need to be only loosely synchronized (for example, to within 50 microseconds).

Consider two application tasks, with task A receiving its inputs from task B. Task A receives the majority voted input from three copies of task B provided by the executive. When task A finishes, it places its output into a buffer so that the executive can provide the majority voted data as input to the next task. The number of processors executing a task can vary with the task and even with the execution instance of the task.

The SIFT project has to solve a number of challenging problems, including distributed clock synchronization, reaching consensus on system health in the presence of faults, and the mathematical proof of software correctness. Several significant theoretical issues, such as the Byzantine General's Problem, were identified and formalized during the SIFT project. It is significant to note that these theoretical issues have been observed in real fault-tolerant systems.

THE C.vmp CASE

A Voted Multiprocessor

DANIEL P. SIEWIOREK, VITTAL KINI, HENRY MASHBURN, STEPHEN McCONNEL, AND MICHAEL TSAO

A design study was initiated in the summer of 1975 to examine fault-tolerant architectures in industrial environments. Major attributes of this environment were electromagnetic noise, less knowledgeable users, and nonstop operation. From these attributes the following design goals were established.

• *Permanent and Transient Fault Survival:* The system should have the capability to continue correct operation in the presence of a permanent hardware failure (a component or subsystem failure) and in the presence of transient errors (a component or subsystem that is lost for a period of time due to the superposition of noise on the correct signal).

• *Software Transparency to the User:* The user should not know that he or she is programming a fault-tolerant computer, with all fault tolerance being achieved in the hardware. This would allow the user to rely on established software libraries, increasing the reliability of the software itself.

• *Capable of Real-Time Operation:* A fault should be detected and corrected within a short period from the time the fault actually occurs.

• *Modular Design to Reduce Downtime:* The hardware should be able to operate without certain sections activated. Hence, maintenance could be performed without having to halt the machine. Modularity includes the design of separate power distribution networks to be able to deactivate selected sections of the machine. The use of modules in the design also has the virtue of allowing the user to upgrade, in steps, from a nonredundant to a fully fault-tolerant computer.

• *Off-the-Shelf Components:* To decrease the amount of custom-designed hardware, to be able to rely on an established software library, and to allow systematic upgrading to a fault-tolerant system, the computer should primarily employ off-the-shelf components. Further, as illustrated in Siewiorek et al. [1978b], advantage can be taken of the greater reliability of high production volume components.

• *Dynamic Performance/Reliability Tradeoffs:* The fault-tolerant computer should have the capability, under operator or program control, to dynamically trade performance for reliability.

SYSTEM ARCHITECTURE

Actual System Configuration

To be consistent with the design goals of modularity and software transparency, bus level voting was selected as the major fault-tolerance mechanism. (See Siewiorek, Canepa, and Clark [1976] for a more detailed discussion leading up to the selection of voting.) That is, voting occurs every time the processors access the bus to either send or retrieve information. There are three processor-memory pairs, each pair connected via a bus, as depicted in Figure 10–1. A more precise definition of C.vmp would therefore be a multiprocessor system capable of fault-tolerant operation. C.vmp is in fact composed of three separate machines, capable of operating in independent mode, executing three separate programs. Under the control of an external event or under the control of one of the processors, C.vmp can synchronize its redundant hardware, and start executing the critical section of code.

With the voter active, the three buses are voted upon and the result of the vote is sent out. Any disagreements among the processors will, therefore, not propagate to the memories and vice versa. Since voting is a simple act of comparison, the voter is memoryless. Disagreements are caught and corrected before they have a chance to propagate. The nonredundant portion of the voter does not represent a system reliability bottleneck, as will be shown later. However, the voter may be totally triplicated if desired. With voter triplication even the voter can have either a transient or a hard failure and the computer will remain operational. In addition, provided that the processor is the only device capable of becoming bus master,* only one bidirectional voter is needed, regardless of how much memory or how many I/O modules are on the bus. Voting is done in parallel on a bit-by-bit basis. A computer can have a failure on a certain bit in one bus, and, provided that the other two buses have the correct information for that bit, operation will continue. There are cases, therefore, where failures in all three buses can occur simultaneously and the computer would still be functioning correctly.

FIGURE 10–1

C.vmp configuration and connection to Carnegie-Melon University facilities

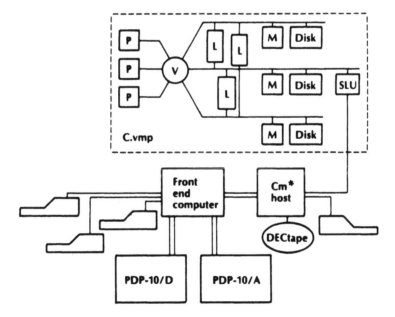

* Note that this restriction prohibits the use of direct memory access devices. If such devices were allowed to communicate only with the processors and the memory (not other I/O devices), a second voter between the memory and the I/O devices on the bus would be sufficient to retain fault tolerance.

Bus level voting* works only if information passes through the voter. Usually the processor registers reside on the processor board and are not voted upon. The PDP-11, for example, has six general-purpose registers, one stack pointer, and one program counter. However, after tracing over 5.3 million instructions over 41 programs written by five different programmers and using five different compilers, the following average program behavior was discovered [Lunde, 1977]:

1. On the average, a register is loaded or stored to memory every 24 instructions.
2. A subroutine call is executed, on the average, every 40 instructions, thus saving the program counter on the stack.
3. The only register that normally is not saved or written into is the stack pointer. To maintain fault tolerance, the system must periodically save and reload the pointer.

Thus normal program behavior can be counted on to keep the registers circulating through the voter.

To present a detailed description of the voter, a brief digression to explain the DEC LSI-11 Q-bus is necessary [DEC, 1975b]. The 36-signal bus uses a hybrid of synchronous and asynchronous protocols. Every bus cycle begins synchronously with the processors placing an address on the time multiplexed data/address lines (DAL):

1. SYNC goes high and all the devices on the bus latch the address from the DAL lines. The address is then removed by the processor, terminating the synchronous position of the bus cycle.
2. In the event of an input cycle (DATI shown in Figure 10–2), the processor activates DIN on the bus.
3. The addressed slave responds by placing a data word on the DAL lines and asserting RPLY.
4. The processor latches the data word and terminates DIN and SYNC.
5. In the event of an output cycle (DATO), after removing the address, the processor places a data word on the bus and activates DOUT.
6. When the slave device has read the word, it activates RPLY.
7. The processor responds by terminating DOUT and SYNC.

Voter Modes of Operation

The multiplexed paths through the voter are shown in Figure 10–3. Figure 10–3a shows the case for the (unidirectional) control lines. Signals generated by the processor are routed from bus

---

* This bus-level voting scheme can be contrasted with the Draper Laboratory Symmetric Fault-Tolerant Multiprocessor [Hopkins and Smith, 1975; see also Hopkins, Smith, and Lala, 1978]. In SFTMP, memory and processor triads are interconnected by a triplicated serial bus. Program tasks are read from a memory triad into local memory in a processor triad where execution takes place. After execution the results are transferred back to memory triads. The major architectural differences from C.vmp are as follows: serial bus rather than parallel bus, thus degrading performance; voting only takes place on transfers from and to memory triads; errors in the processors may accumulate to the point that their results are not comparable; programmer has to partition problems into tasks and provide for transfer to processor triads. SFTMP has up to 14 processors that can be dynamically assigned to four triads (two are spares). When a processor fails, it can be replaced in its triad by another processor. However, processors cannot operate independently of triads to improve throughput. Another voting design is described by Wakerly [1976]. The described system is based on an Intel 8080 microprocessor and has an output address and data bus and an input (from memory to processor) data bus. The major difference from C.vmp is that only a unidirectional voter is employed, on the input data bus. Thus, only information flow from memory to processor is voted upon. There is no consideration of I/O, apart from an assertion that each I/O device on the bus requires a separate voter.

FIGURE 10–2

DATI cycle for LSI-11 computer

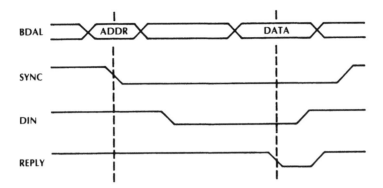

receivers to multiplexers, which allow either signals from all three buses or signals from only bus A to pass to the voting circuit. The output of the voting circuit always feeds a bus driver on external bus A but is multiplexed with the initially received signals on buses B and C. This arrangement allows all three processor signals to be voted on and sent to all three external buses; the signal from only processor A to be "broadcast" to all three external buses; and the independent processor signals to be sent to the separate external buses, albeit with extra delay on bus A.

• *Voting Mode:* The transmitting portion of each of the three buses is routed into the voter, and the result of the vote is then routed out to the receiving portion of all three buses. In addition to the voting elements, the voter has a set of disagreement detectors. These detectors, one for each bus, activate whenever that bus has lost a vote. By monitoring these disagreement detectors, one can learn about the kinds of failures the machine is having.

• *Broadcast Mode:* Only the transmitting portion of bus A is sampled, and its contents are broadcast to the receiving portions of all three buses. This mode of operation allows selective triplication and nontriplication of I/O devices, depending on the particular requirements of the user. The voter has no idea which devices are triplicated and which are not. The only requirement is that all nontriplicated devices be placed on bus A. To handle nontriplicated devices, two extra lines are added to bus A. One is a special copy of RPLY for use by nontriplicated devices instead of the standard bus A RPLY, and the other is a special copy of the interrupt request line (IRQ).

• *Independent Mode:* Buses B and C are routed around the voting hardware. Bus A is routed to feed its signals to all three inputs of the voting elements. In this mode C.vmp is a loosely coupled multiprocessor. Switching between independent and voting modes allows the user to perform a performance/reliability tradeoff. The unidirectional control signals generated by devices on the external buses are handled the same way as processor signals, except that the direction (external-processor) has been changed.

Figure 10–3b shows the more complex case of the bidirectional data/address lines. Two sets of bus transceivers replace the sets of receivers and transmitters used before, and another level of multiplexing has been added. The received signals from both sets of transceivers are fed into a set of multiplexers that choose which direction the signals are flowing. After passing through the set of multiplexers and the voter circuit, the voted signal goes through a latch that ensures that bus timing specifications are met. From there the signals pass onto the opposite bus from

FIGURE 10–3

C.vmp voter multi-plexing

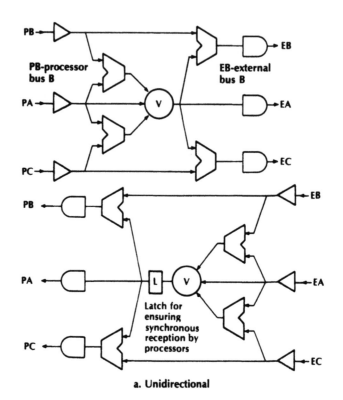

a. Unidirectional

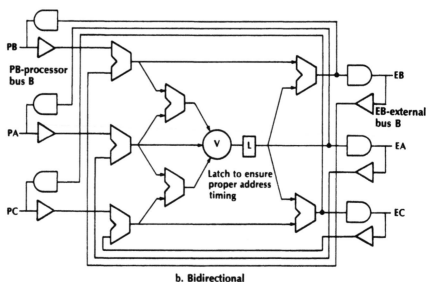

b. Bidirectional

which they were initially received. (Note that the drivers on the receiving bus are disabled to avoid both sinking and sourcing the same signal.)

Peripheral Devices

In most cases, triplicating a device simply means plugging standard boards into the backplane, as is the case with memory. In some cases, however, the solution is not quite so simple. An example of a device that has to be somewhat modified is the RX01 floppy disk drive. The three floppies run asynchronously. Therefore, there can be as much as a 360° phase difference in the diskettes. Since the information does not arrive under the read heads of the three floppies simultaneously, the obvious solution to this problem is to construct a buffer whose size is large enough to accommodate the size of the sectors that are being transferred. A disk read operation would then occur as follows [DEC, 1975c].

1. The track and sector number to be read are loaded into the three interfaces, and the read command is issued.
2. The three floppies load their respective buffers asynchronously.
3. The processors wait until the three buffers are loaded and then synchronously empty the buffers into memory. A write operation would be executed in a similar fashion.

The main synchronization problem is to find out when all three floppies have completed their tasks or when one of the floppies is so out of specification that it can be considered failed. Once this is determined the done signals are transmitted to the three buses simultaneously.

When in independent mode, the three processors must be able to communicate to each other. For this reason there are three full-duplex, single-word transfer, fully interlocked parallel interfaces in the system (labeled L in Figure 10–1). These interfaces provide data transfer between the separate processors (in independent mode) at rates up to 180 KB/sec [DEC, 1975b]. They are used for software synchronization of the processors prior to reestablishment of voting mode, in addition to straight data transfers.

ISSUES OF PROCESSOR SYNCHRONIZATION

Dynamic Voting Control

A major goal in the design of C.vmp was to allow dynamic tradeoff between reliability and performance. Ideally, when reliability is of less importance, the machine should be able to split into a loosely coupled multiprocessor capable of much greater performance. Conversely, when reliability becomes crucial, the three processors ought to be able to resynchronize themselves and resume voting. Consideration of dynamic voting-mode control led to the following features:

- In transiting from voting to independent mode, a simple change in the multiplexing control signals causes the next instruction to be fetched and executed independently by the three processors.
- In order to insure proper synchronization of all processors in transiting from independent to voting mode, a delayed transition forces an interrupt, presumably after each processor has had ample time to execute a wait instruction. (Wait halts the processor until an interrupt occurs.)

Two bits are provided in the voter-control register for voter-mode control. The first, a read-only bit, monitors the state, returning 0 if voting and 1 if not. The other, a read/write bit, chooses the desired mode. Each processor has a copy of the voter-control register, and a vote is taken on the mode-control bit. This control register is accessed, like any I/O device register, as a specific memory location (in this case, 167770).

Dynamic voting-mode control has been demonstrated by a test program. When in voting mode, setting the appropriate bit in the control register causes the three processors to split apart and begin executing separately. To resynchronize the processors, a simple handshaking protocol is used, in which each processor waits for both of the others to signal permission before clearing the control bit. (A more sophisticated protocol would provide for a timeout if one of the processors has failed, with efforts to recover from such a situation.) After clearing its copy of the control bit, each processor releases control of its bus and ceases execution via a wait instruction. The ensuing interrupt generated by the voter then serves to resynchronize the three processors, and the first instruction of the interrupt-service routine is the first instruction executed in voting (fault-tolerant) mode.

Bus Control Signal Synchronization

There are two levels of synchronization used in C.vmp to keep the three processors in step: bus signal synchronization and processor clock synchronization. The first type of synchronization deals with the bus control signals. The voter uses RPLY to synchronize the three buses, since it is asserted by an external device (memory and I/O devices) once every bus cycle. Thus processors can stay in step if they receive RPLY concurrently. A set of possible voting circuits is shown in Figure 10–4. (The boxes labeled V are voters, and the boxes labeled T are delays.) The first voter is the one used for the data/address lines. The other voters attempt to maintain synchronization of five critical control lines (SYNC, DIN, DOUT, IAK, and RPLY)* by waiting an appropriate period of time for a lagging control signal. (The delay is selected not only long enough that a lagging device is far enough out of specification to be suspect but also short enough not to degrade performance severely. For maintaining processor synchronization, a value for *T* of at least one microcycle (400 nsec) is desirable since processors are most likely to slip just one microcycle in the five to ten microcycles between bus cycles, rather than to become several microcycles out of synchronization.)

FIGURE 10–4
*Synchronizing
voter circuits*

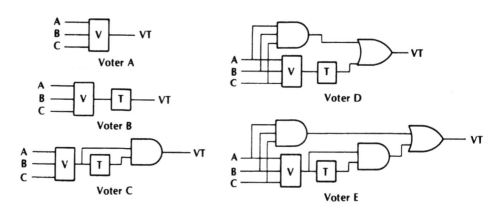

* SYNC is used to clock the address lines and is left asserted for the remainder of the bus cycle; DIN indicates a read cycle; DOUT indicates a write cycle; IAK is used to acknowledge receipt of an interrupt request; and RPLY is asserted to indicate that the device has responded to the request indicated by the previous four signals.

The first circuit considered for synchronizing the five control lines was voter A in Figure 10–4. This circuit was rejected because it provides no synchronization at all: If a signal fails high, the voter passes the first of the other two to be asserted without regard to the second. Thus, if the two remaining processors get at all out of step, the voting process fails.

The second circuit, voter B in Figure 10–4, provides a measure of synchronization by waiting a time T for the third signal after two have been asserted. However, performance is degraded because this delay occurs even when all three processors are working and synchronized. Also, control signals will continue to be asserted after they should be in relation to the data on the bus, thus failing to meet bus specifications. (RPLY is asserted after DATA is invalid; see Figure 10–5.)

The third circuit, voter C in Figure 10–4, fixes the problem of meeting bus specifications by having a slow-rising, fast-falling delay after the voter. However, performance is still degraded by the presence of the delay even when all is well.

The fourth circuit, voter D in Figure 10–4, addressed the performance problem by providing a second path through the voter for when all three processors are working. However, the delay used after the voter to provide synchronization still causes the signal to fail bus specifications and also causes some amount of unavoidable performance degradation. (RPLY is asserted after DATA is invalid; see Figure 10–5.)

The last circuit, and the one used (voter E in Figure 10–4), combines the features of the previous two. Thus, a slow-rising, fast-falling delay is used in order to meet bus specifications, and a second path through the voter is provided for optimal performance when all is well. Note that the fast-falling feature of the delay not only allows bus specifications to be met but also removes any performance degradation caused by the voting process when all three signals are in step. This circuit was used for SYNC, DIN, DOUT, IAK, and RPLY in C.vmp. The value for T is about 400—500 nsec for SYNC, DIN, DOUT, and IAK, and about 75–100 nsec for RPLY. This method allows the three processors to receive RPLY within 5 nsec of each other and thus to stay synchronized.

System Clock

Perhaps the most critical timing problems encountered in the design of C.vmp were the synchronization of the four-phase processor clocks and of the memory refresh* timing oscillators. This part of the design was left untriplicated in C.vmp because of its very small size, hence high reliability, relative to the rest of the machine. The original design, shown in Figure 10–6a, used the oscillators on processor A to drive the clock circuits on all three processors, and the decoded clock signals of processor A to feed the voter and to synchronize the phases of the other two processors by forcing phase one when processor A was in phase one. This original design worked fairly well, as processors B and C were closely synchronized, but the extra loading placed on the clocks of processor A caused them to lag several nanoseconds behind, a significant figure for pulses of duration less than 100 nsec. This lag resulted in sufficient unreliability that the mean time between crashes in voting mode was never more than five minutes. Therefore, a new clock circuit, shown in Figure 10–6b, was installed in the voter to drive and synchronize the processor clocks. All three processors were wired exactly the same way, needing only three wires to be changed on each board. Since this change was made, the mean time between software discernible disagreement has been over 250 h, with one run of more than 900 h before crashing.

---

* Note that the LSI-11 uses dynamic MOS RAM memory, which requires continual refreshing. This is normally done by processor microcode at regular intervals of about 1.67 msec.

FIGURE 10–5
DATI bus cycle with desynchro- nized processors

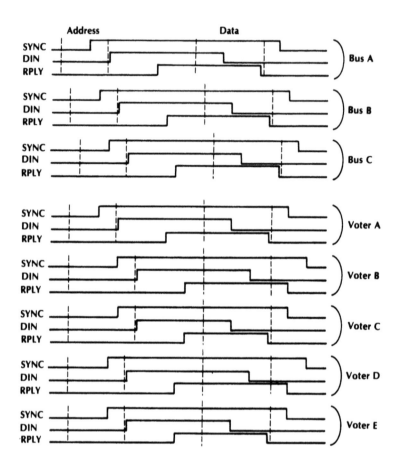

Initial measurements using the disagreement detection circuit attached to all the bus control lines showed no errors on any of the three buses over periods ranging from 8 h to 40 h. (Note that data/address lines were not included.) This indicates that the processors are well synchronized by the current design.

PERFORMANCE MEASUREMENTS

Processor Execution/Memory Fetch Time

An important parameter in the design of fault-tolerant computers is the amount of performance degradation suffered to obtain greater reliability. In a triplicated architecture such as C.vmp, the obvious loss of two-thirds of the available computing power is unavoidable. This loss was the reason why C.vmp was made flexible enough to switch between voting (fault-tolerant) mode and independent (high-performance) mode. However, this fundamental loss due to triplication is not the only loss: The voter cutting and buffering all the bus lines introduces delays of 80–140 nsec in the signals between the processors and the memories.

Because the LSI-11 is a clocked machine, these delays are not too significant in and of themselves. However, the latching of RPLY from slave devices on the external buses in order to

FIGURE 10–6
Processor clock synchronization

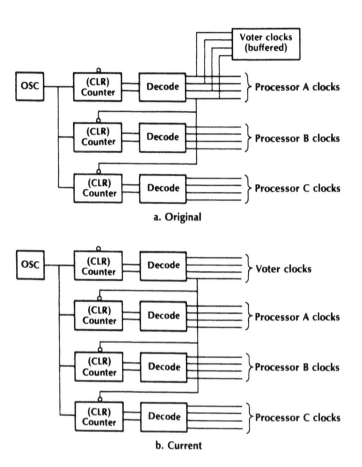

a. Original

b. Current

preserve processor synchronization turns out to be the more dominant degradation factor. The voter latches RPLY one clock phase (100 nsec) before the processors to allow sufficient latch settling time for minimizing the probability of a runt pulse [Chaney, Ornstein, and Littlefield, 1972]. The delays in the control lines due to the voter cause the external RPLY to return during the phase on which the processors sample RPLY but *after* the voted RPLY has already been latched. Thus, the voted processors must wait one more clock cycle (four phases/400 nsec) to receive their RPLY after asserting SYNC than would a nonredundant LSI-11. The same sort of delay happens on the falling edge of RPLY, causing up to two clock cycles to be lost in one complete bus cycle. These losses could likely be prevented by more careful selection of timing components within the voter and, more important, by choosing different timing on the memory boards.

Measurements were taken on the various bus cycles to learn what amount of degradation actually was occurring. These measurements, and all others presented later, were taken on the voted processor (C.vmp) and on either processor B (PBB) or C (PCC) in independent mode. (Note that in independent mode, bus A passes through the entire voter via the broadcast multiplexing, while both buses B and C pass through only a bus receiver/driver pair. Comparison tests with other LSI-11s showed that processors B and C operated fully as fast in independent mode as a

TABLE 10–1
Normalized instruction phases

Phase	C.vmp	PCC	C.vmp/PCC
Fetch	7.00	6.00	1.167
Source	2.69	2.09	1.287
Destination	3.68	3.22	1.143
Execution	3.53	3.53	1.000
Total	16.90	14.84	1.139
Time (μsec)	6.760	5.936	

standard LSI-11.) The degradation within bus cycles introduced by the voter ranges from 27 percent to 67 percent, with 40 percent degradation for the most common (read) cycles.

As the LSI-11 does not saturate its bus, the above figures are worse than the overall processor degradation. A second step in measuring degradation was to check the different phases of instruction execution. Tests were made using the MOV, TST, and BR instructions* as typical double operand, single operand, and zero operand instructions. From this data, a prediction can be made of performance degradation by using instruction frequency data provided by Snow and Siewiorek [1978]. Table 10–1 summarizes the calculations, showing that the voting process should degrade instruction execution performance by roughly 14 percent.

The third stage for measuring performance was to run a set of test programs with representative mixes of instructions and addressing modes to test the validity of the above model. Table 10–2 compares the triplicated processor with a single LSI-11, both without faults and with certain induced faults. These faults were in the two most critical bus control signals, SYNC and RPLY, and represented worst-case failures. Each signal was forced to be either always asserted (hi) or never asserted (lo) on one of the three buses.

As illustrated by Table 10–2, a degradation in performance of about 16–19 percent can be expected, as compared to a standard LSI-11. This figure is somewhat larger than predicted by the above model, which can be attributed to the greater degree of degradation in such functions as memory refresh, which is done by the processor microcode (18.5 percent) and also to normal deviations of programs from the standard instruction mix.

The measurements involving the four failure modes show that only certain failures will cause further degradation: those that cause the processor's synchronizing signals (for example, SYNC, DIN, and DOUT) never to be asserted. Even in these extreme cases, only another 12–14 percent slowdown is experienced. Most faults, however, would not degrade the speed at all but just the future reliability. For instance, the loss of power to a bus would force all signals to ground, which is the active assertion level (hi) on the LSI-11 bus. Only lo failures in the five bus control signals that require synchronization will cause any degradation. (Recall that there are a total of 36 bus lines.)

Disk Access Time

The last performance measurements involved the floppy disks used for mass storage on C.vmp. Access time to a particular position on a rotating memory is assumed to be directly proportional

* MOV loads the destination from the source, TST examines the destination for various conditions, and BR causes an unconditional transfer of control.

TABLE 10–2

*Sample program execution times**

Unit	DVKAA (msec)	DZKMA (min)	QSORT (sec)
LSI-11	18.51	7:03	11.9
C.vmp (normal)	21.4	8:23	14.0
C.vmp (RPLY hi)	21.4	8:23	14.0
C.vmp (RPLY lo)	21.4	8:23	14.0
C.vmp (SYNC hi)	21.4	8:23	14.1
C.vmp (SYNC lo)	23.6	9:20	15.6
C.vmp/LSI-11	1.157	1.189	1.176
C.vmp/LSI-11	1.324	1.276	1.311 (SYNC lo)

*DVKAA is the basic instruction diagnostic, testing all instructions and addressing modes. DZKMA is the memory diagnostic, and would tend to make more memory references than average. QSORT is an example of compiler-produced code, being an integer sorting program coded in BLISS-11.

to the initial position of the disk. Since the hardware makes no attempt to synchronize disk rotation, access to the triplicated disks will take the maximum of the three times. In general, for *n* disks, the access time is given by

$$T_n = MAX(t_1, t_2, \ldots, t_n)$$

Assuming that each access time *t* is uniformly distributed over the normalized range [0, 1], the expected value for access time is

$$T_n = \frac{n}{n + 1}$$

So for a single disk ($n = 1$), we can expect to wait 0.5 rotation and for the triplicated disk ($n = 3$), 0.75 rotation, giving a 50 percent degradation in access time for the triplicated disks over the nontriplicated disk for random accesses. This figure was verified to an extent by experimental data. In reading 50 sectors in a random pattern from the same physical track, the triplicated machine experienced about 51 percent degradation, a very close confirmation. However, if the track was also chosen at random for each of the 50 sectors, the triplicated machine was only 18 percent slower than the single-disk system. The model failed to consider that, although sector access time is affected by the diskettes' being out of phase, track access time is the same, regardless of triplication.

Another shortcoming of the disk performance model based only on consideration of the diskettes' being out of phase with each other is the impact of the resulting slowdown on nonrandom disk access patterns. The impact of this can be much more severe (or much less severe) than predicted, depending on the pattern of nonrandom disk accesses. For instance, the RT-11 floppy disk software uses a 2:1 interleaving of sectors in order to minimize access time for sequential file storage.* The extra delay due to voting causes this interleaving to be insufficient

* 2:1 interleaving means that only every other sector on a track is read when reading sectors sequentially. As some amount of time is necessary to read the data into memory after it has been fetched from the diskette, this allows all 26 sectors of a track to be read in just two revolutions rather than in 26 revolutions.

for achieving much speedup in accesses, as illustrated by Figure 10–7. Waiting for all three drives to read a sector can cause the first two drives to overrun the next sector in sequence before the third drive has read the initial sector. Thus, part of an additional revolution is required on the next sector read. For the example shown, a nontriplicated disk drive requires only 0.375 revolution to read sectors 1 and 3, while the triplicated drive needs 1.75 revolutions. The specific values depend on the number of sectors per revolution, the access pattern (and interleaving scheme), and the degree to which the three disks of the triplicated drive are out of phase.

Table 10–3 summarizes timing data collected by a program that was written to test different interleaving schemes. A number of consecutive logical sectors were read, which mapped into the same number of physical sectors in the pattern dictated by the desired interleaving. In addition, a test program was assembled under RT-11, using its 2:1 interleaving, to examine the impact of increased disk latency on typical operations. Figure 10–8 plots access time versus interleaving factor for reading 1000 sectors sequentially. The data indicate that perhaps the best sequential file access could be achieved for triplicated disks using 8:1 interleaving. The point to be made about replicated disk access time is that it is very pattern sensitive: Very little degradation due to replication occurs in sequential accesses without interleaving, but great degradation is seen when interleaving is used. Instead of the factor of 10 speedup available with 2:1 interleaving on a single disk, only a factor of roughly 1.5 is possible (using 8:1 interleaving) on a triplicated disk.

FIGURE 10–7
Effects of disk tri-plication on sequential access (2:1 interleaving)

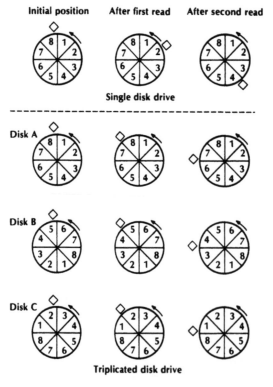

TABLE 10–3
Disk timing tests (in seconds)

Sectors	Interleave	C.vmp	PBB	C.vmp/PBB
10	1:1	1.69	1.66	1.021
10	2:1	1.55	0.17	9.218
50	1:1	8.51	8.06	1.055
50	2:1	7.66	0.81	9.403
1,000	1:1	171.2	159.9	1.071
1,000	2:1	153.9	14.6	10.540
Assembly	2:1	109.6	15.8	6.937

FIGURE 10–8
Disk access time versus interleaving factor

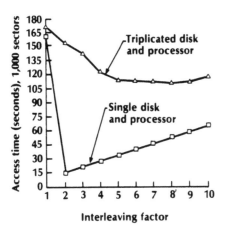

OPERATIONAL EXPERIENCES

Operating History

Implementation of C.vmp has been completed and stable performance achieved. The software is a standard, unmodified, single-user, diskette-based, real-time operating system (RT-11). The system has been utilized under actual load conditions with students doing projects in an introductory real-time programming course. The students were supplied with an RT-11 software manual and a short paper on C.vmp specific data (i.e., location of the power switches, reminder to load three diskettes, etc.). To these users, C.vmp successfully appeared as a standard LSI-11 uniprocessor running standard software.

C.vmp System Reliability

C.vmp has repeatedly demonstrated hard-failure survival by bus power switching and board removal (see comments later about on-line maintenance). Another aspect of fault tolerance is transient-fault survival. The only transients that should cause C.vmp to crash are those that occur simultaneously in more than one module. According to the data from Cm* presented in Siewiorek et al. [1978a], such transients make up 17 percent of the total, occurring roughly every 1,000 h. The mean time to crash should equal or exceed this figure. Indeed, as the hardware situation

TABLE 10–4 *C.vmp crash data (in hours)*

Month	Worst Case					Best Case				
	Mean	Std. Dev.	Median	Number	Uptime	Mean	Std. Dev.	Median	Number	Uptime
August	64.8	91.9	28.0	5	323.8	81.0	96.1	34.6	4	323.8
September	108.7	139.6	35.6	4	434.9	217.4	132.4	217.4	2	434.9
October	35.5	51.1	19.8	16	568.3	142.1	44.5	125.7	4	568.3
November	49.3	33.0	52.0	10	492.9	246.5	167.3	246.5	2	492.9
December	204.8	191.6	113.1	3	614.5	614.5	0.0	614.5	1	614.5
January	95.4	104.3	70.5	7	667.7	—	—	—	0	667.7
February	258.8	78.6	258.8	2	517.6	517.6	0.0	517.6	1	517.6
March	298.3	276.4	298.3	2	596.7	—	—	—	0	596.7
April	352.4	114.2	352.4	2	704.7	704.7	0.0	704.7	1	704.7
Total	96.5	167.8	30.6	51	4921.1	328.1	470.8	114.3	15	4921.1

has been stabilizing, C.vmp's reliability has been increasing toward this order of magnitude. Table 10–4 summarizes C.vmp crash data for the nine-month period from August 1, 1977, to April 30, 1978. Note that software- or user-caused crashes have not been included in the data. Also, repeated crashes (ones due to the same cause) have been removed. Due to uncertainty as to the exact causes of many crashes, dual tables have been constructed, giving the best-case and worst-case figures. Crashes that may have been software- or user-caused are included in the worst-case but not in the best-case data. The voter-induced transient failures are due mainly to construction. The wire-wrap boards used in the voter are prone to socket failures. These sockets are being systematically replaced, with a consequent improvement in mean time to crash (MTTC). With permanent construction techniques (for example, printed circuit boards), the voter should be removed as a source of system crashes.

One measure of transient fault survival lies in the severity of the methods necessary for recovery. Five levels of recovery exist:

1. Continue execution at the same location without any change to processor registers or memory.
2. Restart the program in memory, which will also reset the I/O devices and processor registers.
3. Reload the program into memory, also resetting the I/O devices and processor registers.
4. Reset the processors and reload the program.
5. Debug the hardware to whatever extent is required to restore stable operation.

Table 10–5 summarizes this data in correspondence to the entries of Table 10–4.

It is interesting to note that the majority of crashes required relatively little effort to recover from. Only a few required the processor to be actually reset, and several required only the resident monitor to be restarted. All the cases of debugging involved socket failures in the voter boards and seem to be getting less frequent.

On-Line Maintenance

The success of the voting mechanism has been established by experiments with powering down buses and removing components, while still having the system as a whole continue operating.

TABLE 10–5 *C.vmp crash recovery data*

Month	Worst Case					Best Case				
	Continue	Restart	Reload	Reset	Debug	Continue	Restart	Reload	Reset	Debug
August	0	1	3	0	1	0	0	3	0	1
September	0	0	2	0	2	0	0	0	0	2
October	0	5	7	1	3	0	0	1	0	3
November	0	1	7	1	1	0	0	0	1	1
December	0	0	2	0	1	0	0	0	0	1
January	0	7	0	0	0	0	0	0	0	0
February	0	1	0	0	1	0	0	0	0	1
March	0	2	0	0	0	0	0	0	0	0
April	0	2	0	0	0	0	1	0	0	0
Total	0	19	21	2	9	0	1	4	1	9

With a bus powered down, the associated processor and memory are, of course, lost, but the system keeps working. Defective components (if they exist) can be replaced and the bus powered back up. Contents of the newly restored memory can be brought into agreement with the other copies by providing a read/write memory background job. Normal operation suffices to resynchronize the processor, since it starts executing code randomly until it gets in execution phase with the other two processors.

Actual experiments have included removing memory boards from one, two, or even all three buses (different 4K banks of memory from different buses). Also, a processor was removed, and the machine kept running. Even with one of the processors missing and a different 4K bank of memory removed from each bus, the machine continued in operation.

The only problem encountered with these experiments was that restoring power to a bus sometimes caused a crash. All three buses, and even the voter itself, draw power from the same +5-V supply. The transients on the power lines associated with turning on an LSI-11 processor, 12K of memory, and assorted I/O interfaces are the cause of the crashes. (These transients arise from the sudden demand for 7–10 A current for the various components on each bus.) Independent power supplies, as would be desirable in any case for a fault-tolerant computer, are necessary to correct this problem.

The ability described above to power down selective sections of C.vmp in order to remove or replace defective modules is certainly a strength of the system in terms of high availability.

REFERENCES

Chaney, Ornstein, and Littlefield, 1972; DEC, 1975b, 1975c; Hopkins and Smith, 1975; Hopkins, Smith, and Lala, 1978; Lunde, 1977; Siewiorek, Canepa, and Clark, 1976; Siewiorek et al., 1978a, 1978b; Snow and Siewiorek, 1978; Wakerly, 1976.

THE SIFT CASE

Design and Analysis of a Fault-Tolerant Computer for Aircraft Control

JOHN H. WENSLEY, LESLIE LAMPORT, JACK GOLDBERG, MILTON W. GREEN, KARL N. LEVITT, P.M. MELLIAR-SMITH, ROBERT E. SHOSTAK, AND CHARLES B. WEINSTOCK*

This case study describes ongoing research whose goal is to build an ultra-reliable fault-tolerant computer system named SIFT (Software-Implemented Fault Tolerance). In the first section, we describe the motivation for SIFT and provide some background for our work. The remainder of the case describes the actual design of the SIFT system.

MOTIVATION AND BACKGROUND

Modern commercial jet transports use computers to carry out many functions, such as navigation, stability augmentation, flight control, and system monitoring. Although these computers provide great benefits in the operation of the aircraft, they are not critical. If a computer fails, it is always possible for the air crew to assume its function or for the function to be abandoned. In other cases, the safety of the flight depends upon active controls derived from computer outputs. Computers for this application must have a reliability that is comparable with other parts of the aircraft. The frequently quoted reliability requirement is that the probability of failure should be less than 10^{-9} per hour in a flight of ten hours' duration. This reliability requirement is similar to that demanded for manned space-flight systems.

A highly reliable computer system can have applications in other areas as well. In the past, control systems in critical industrial applications have not relied solely on computers, but have used a combination of human and computer control. With the need for faster control loops and with the increased complexity of modern industrial processes, computer reliability has become extremely important. A highly reliable computer system developed for aircraft control can be used in such applications as well. Our objective in designing SIFT was to achieve the reliability required by these applications in an economical manner. Moreover, we wanted the resulting system to be as flexible as possible. (See Murray, Hopkins, and Wensley [1977] for a review of reliability requirements associated with flight control computers.)

When failure rates are extremely small, it is impossible to determine their values by testing. Therefore, testing could not be used to demonstrate that SIFT meets its reliability requirements. It was necessary to *prove* the reliability of SIFT by mathematical methods. The need for such a proof of reliability was a major influence on the design of SIFT.

Background

Our work on SIFT began with a study of the requirements for computing in an advanced commercial transport aircraft [Ratner et al., 1973; Wensley et al., 1973]. We identified the computational and memory requirements for such an application and the reliability required for the safety of the aircraft. The basic concept of the SIFT system emerged from a study of computer architectures for meeting these requirements.

The second phase in the development of the SIFT system was the complete design of the hardware and software systems [Wensley, 1972; Wensley et al., 1976]. This design was expressed formally by rigorous specifications that describe the functional intent of each part of the system.

* *Acknowledgments:* The authors wish to acknowledge the following people: William H. Kautz, Marshall Pease, Lawrence Robinson (all of the Computer Science Laboratory), Nicholas D. Murray, Billy Dove, Earl Migneault, Sal Bavuso, Brian Lupton, and Larry Spencer (all of NASA-Langley Research Center).

A major influence during this phase was the hierarchical design methodology developed at SRI [Robinson et al., 1976]. A further influence was the need to use formal program proving techniques to ensure the correctness of the software design.

The next phase of the development called for the building of an engineering model and the carrying out of tests to demonstrate its fault-tolerant behavior. The engineering model was intended to be capable of carrying out the calculations required for the control of an advanced commercial transport aircraft. SRI was responsible for the overall design, the software, and the testing, while the detailed design and construction of the hardware was done by Bendix Corporation.

The study of fault-tolerant computing has in the past concentrated on failure modes of components, most of which are no longer relevant. The prior work on permanent stuck-at-1 or stuck-at-0 faults on single lines is not appropriate for considering the possible failure modes of modern LSI circuit components, which can be very complex and affect the performance of units in very subtle ways. The SIFT design approach makes no assumptions about the failure modes, distinguishing only between failed and nonfailed units. Since the primary method of detecting errors is the corruption of data, the particular manner in which the data are corrupted is of no importance. This has important consequences for failure-modes-and-effects analysis (FMEA), which is only required at the interface between units. The rigorous, formal specification of interfaces enables us to deduce the effects on one unit of improper signals from a faulty unit.

Early work on fault-tolerant computer systems used fault detection and reconfiguration at the level of simple devices, such as flip-flops and adders. Later work considered units such as registers or blocks of memory. With today's LSI units, it is no longer appropriate to be concerned with such small subunits. The unit of fault detection and of reconfiguration in SIFT is a processor/memory module or a bus.

Several low-level techniques for fault tolerance, such as error-detection and -correction codes in memory, are not included in the design of SIFT. Such techniques could be incorporated in SIFT but would provide only a slight improvement in reliability.

SIFT CONCEPT OF FAULT TOLERANCE

System Overview

As the name Software-Implemented Fault Tolerance implies, the central concept of SIFT is that fault tolerance is accomplished as much as possible by programs rather than by hardware. Fault tolerance includes error detection and correction, diagnosis, reconfiguration, and the prevention of a faulty unit from having an adverse effect on the system as a whole.

The structure of SIFT hardware is shown in Figure 10–9. Computing is carried out by the main processors. Each processor's results are stored in a main memory that is uniquely associated with the processor. A processor and its memory are connected by a conventional high bandwidth connection. The I/O processors and memories are structurally similar to the main processors and memories but are of much smaller computational and memory capacity. They connect to the input and output units of the system which, for this application, are the sensors and actuators of the aircraft.

Each processor and its associated memory form a *processing module*, and each of the modules is connected to a multiple bus system. A faulty module or bus is prevented from causing faulty behavior in a nonfaulty module by the fault isolation methods described in the next section.

The SIFT system executes a set of *tasks*, each of which consists of a sequence of *iterations*. The input data to each iteration of a task are the output data produced by the previous iteration of some collection of tasks (which may include the task itself). The input and output of the entire

FIGURE 10–9

*Structure of the
SIFT system*

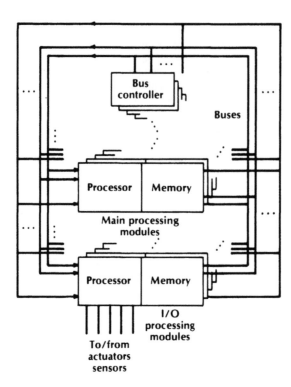

system is accomplished by tasks executed in the I/O processors. Reliability is achieved by having each iteration of a task independently executed by a number of modules. After executing the iteration, a processor places the iteration's output in the memory associated with the processor. A processor that uses the output of this iteration determines its value by examining the output generated by each processor that executed the iteration. Typically, the value is chosen by a two-out-of-three vote. If all copies of the output are not identical, then an error has occurred. Such errors are recorded in the processor's memory, and these records are used by the executive system to determine which units are faulty.

SIFT uses the iterative nature of the tasks to economize on the amount of voting by voting on the state data of the aircraft (or the computer system) only at the beginning of each iteration. This produces less data flow along the buses than with schemes that vote on the results of all calculations performed by the program. It also has important implications for the problem of synchronizing the different processors. We must ensure only that the different processors allocated to a task are executing the same iteration. This means that the processors need be only loosely synchronized (for example, to within 50 μsec), so we do not need tight synchronization to the instruction or clock interval.

An important benefit of this loose synchronization is that an iteration of a task can be scheduled for execution at slightly different times by different processors. Simultaneous transient failures of several processors will, therefore, be less likely to produce correlated failures in the replicated versions of a task.

The number of processors executing a task can vary with the task and can be different for the same task at different times—for example, if a task that is not critical at one time becomes critical at another time. The allocation of tasks to modules is, in general, different for each module. It is determined dynamically by a task called the global executive, which diagnoses errors to determine which modules and buses are faulty. When the global executive decides that a module has become faulty, it reconfigures the system by appropriately changing the allocation of tasks to modules. The global executive and its interaction with the individual processors is described later under The Software System.

Fault Isolation

An important property required in all fault-tolerant computers is that of fault isolation: preventing a faulty unit from causing incorrect behavior in a nonfaulty unit. Fault isolation is a more general concept than damage isolation. Damage isolation means preventing physical damage from spreading beyond carefully prescribed boundaries. Techniques for damage isolation include physical barriers to prevent propagation of mechanical and thermal effects and electrical barriers (for example, high-impedance electrical connections and optical couplers). In SIFT, such damage isolation is provided at the boundaries between processing modules and buses.

Fault isolation in SIFT requires not only isolating damage, but also preventing a faulty unit from causing incorrect behavior either by corrupting the data of the nonfaulty unit or by providing invalid control signals. The control signals include those that request service, grant service, effect timing synchronization between units, etc.

Protection against the corruption of data is provided by the way in which units can communicate. A processing module can read data from any processing module's memory, but it can write only into its own memory. Thus a faulty processor can corrupt the data only in its own memory and not in that of any other processing modules. All faults within a module are treated as if they have the same effect: namely, that they produce bad data in that module's memory. The system does not attempt to distinguish the nature of a module fault. In particular, it does not distinguish between a faulty memory and a processor that puts bad data into an otherwise nonfaulty memory.

Note that a faulty processor can obtain bad data if those data are read from a faulty processing module or over a faulty bus. Preventing these bad data from causing the generation of incorrect results is discussed in the section on fault masking.

Fault isolation also requires that invalid control signals not produce incorrect behavior in a nonfaulty unit. In general, a faulty set of control signals can cause two types of faulty behavior in another unit: (1) The unit carries out the wrong action (possibly by doing nothing), and (2) the unit does not provide service to other units.

In SIFT these two types of fault propagation are prevented by making each unit autonomous, with its own control. Improper control signals are ignored, and time-outs are used to prevent the unit from hanging up, waiting for a signal that never arrives. The details of how this is done are discussed under The SIFT Hardware.

Fault Masking

Although a faulty unit cannot cause a nonfaulty processor to behave incorrectly, it can provide the processor with bad data. In order to completely mask the effects of the faulty unit, we must ensure that these bad data do not cause the processor to generate incorrect results. As we indicated, this is accomplished by having the processor receive multiple copies of the data. Each copy is obtained from a different memory, over a different bus, and the processor uses majority voting to obtain a correct version of the data. The most common case is the one in which a processor obtains three copies of the data, providing protection from a single faulty unit.

After identifying the faulty unit, the system is reconfigured to prevent that unit from having any further effect. If the faulty unit is a processing module, then the tasks that were assigned to it are reassigned to other modules. If it is a bus, then processors request their data over other buses. After reconfiguration, the system is able to withstand a new failure, assuming that there are enough nonfaulty units remaining.

Because the number of processors executing a task can vary with the task and can be changed dynamically, SIFT has a flexibility not present in most fault-tolerant systems. The particular application field, aircraft control, is one in which different computations are critical to different degrees, and the design takes advantage of this.

Scheduling

The aircraft control function places two types of timing requirements on the SIFT system:

- Output to the actuators must be generated with specified frequency.
- Transport delay (the delay between the reading of sensors and the generation of output to the actuators based upon those readings) must be kept below specified limits.

To fulfill these requirements, an iteration rate is specified for each task. The scheduling strategy must guarantee that the processing of each iteration of the task will be completed within the time frame of that iteration. It does not matter when the processing is performed, provided that it is completed by the end of the frame. Moreover, the time needed to execute an iteration of a task is highly predictable. The iteration rates required by different tasks differ, but they can be adjusted somewhat to simplify the scheduling.

Four scheduling strategies were considered for SIFT: (1) Fixed preplanned (nonpreemptive) scheduling, (2) priority scheduling, (3) deadline scheduling, and (4) simply periodic scheduling. Of these, fixed preplanned scheduling, in which each iteration is run to completion (traditional in-flight control applications), was rejected because it does not allow sufficient flexibility.

The priority-scheduling strategy, commonly used in general-purpose systems, can meet the real-time requirements if the tasks with the fastest iteration rates are given the highest priorities. Under this condition, it is shown in Melliar-Smith [1977] that all tasks will be processed within their frames, for any pattern of iteration rates and processing times, provided the processing load does not exceed ln(2) of the capacity of the processor (up to about 70 percent loading is always safe).

The deadline-scheduling strategy always runs the task whose deadline is closest. It is shown in Melliar-Smith [1977] that all the tasks will be processed within their time frames provided the workload does not exceed the capacity of the processor (100 percent loading is permissible). Unfortunately, for the brief tasks characteristic of flight-control applications, the scheduling overhead eliminates the advantages of this strategy.

The simply periodic strategy is similar to the priority strategy, but the iteration rates of the tasks are constrained so that each iteration rate is an integral multiple of the next smaller rate (and thus of all smaller rates). To comply with this requirement, it may be necessary to run some tasks more frequently than their optimum rate, but this is permissible in a flight control system. It is shown in Melliar-Smith [1977] that if the workload does not exceed the capacity of the processor (100 percent loading is possible), then simply periodic scheduling guarantees that all tasks will complete within their time frames.

The scheduling strategy chosen for the SIFT system is a slight variant of the simply periodic method, illustrated by Figure 10–10. Each task is assigned to one of several priority levels. Each priority level corresponds to an iteration rate, and each iteration rate is an integral multiple of the next lower one. In order to provide very small transport delays for certain functions and to allow rapid detection of any fault that causes a task not to terminate, the scheme illustrated in Figure 10–10 is modified as follows. The time frame corresponding to highest priority level (typically 20 msec) is divided into a number of subframes (typically 2 msec). The highest-priority tasks are run in specific subframes so that their results can be available to other tasks run in the next subframe, and they are required to complete within one subframe.

Processor Synchronization

The SIFT intertask and interprocessor communication mechanism allows a degree of asynchronism between processors and avoids the lockstep traditional in ultrareliable systems. Up to 50 μs of skew between processors can readily be accommodated, but even this margin cannot be assured over a 10-hour period with free-running clocks unless unreasonable requirements are imposed on the clocks. Thus, the processors must periodically resynchronize their clocks to ensure that no clock drifts too far from any other.

For reliability, the resynchronization procedure must be immune to the failure of any one clock or processor and to a succession of failures over a period of time. In order to guarantee the high reliability required of SIFT, we cannot allow a system failure to be caused by any condition whose probability cannot be quantified, regardless of how implausible that condition may seem. This means that our synchronization procedure must be reliable in the face of the worst possible behavior of the failing component, even though that behavior may seem unrealistically malicious. We can only exclude behavior that we can *prove* to be sufficiently improbable.

FIGURE 10–10
A typical schedule

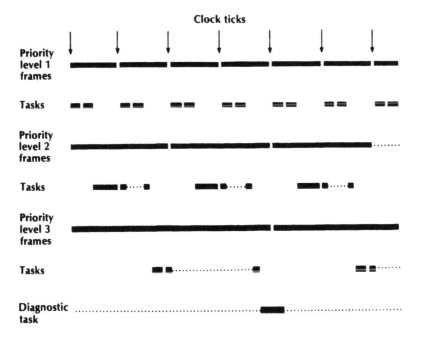

The traditional clock resynchronization algorithm for reliable systems is the median clock algorithm, requiring at least three clocks. In this algorithm, each clock observes every other clock and sets itself to the median of the values that it sees. The justification for this algorithm is that, in the presence of only a single fault, either the median value must be the value of one of the valid clocks or else it must lie between a pair of valid clock values. In either case, the median is an acceptable value for resynchronization. The weakness of this argument is that the worst possible failure modes of the clock may cause other clocks to observe different values for the failing clock. Even if the clock is read by sensing the time of a pulse waveform, the effects of a highly degraded output pulse and the inevitable slight differences between detectors can result in detection of the pulse at different times.

In the presence of a fault that results in other clocks seeing different values for the failing clock, the median resynchronization algorithm can lead to a system failure. Consider a system of three clocks A, B, and C, of which C is faulty. Clock A runs slightly faster than clock B. The failure mode of clock C is such that clock A sees a value for clock C that is slightly earlier than its own value, while clock B sees a value for clock C that is slightly later than its own value. Clocks A and B both correctly observe that the value of clock A is earlier than the value of clock B. In this situation, clocks A and B will both see their own value as the median value, and therefore not change it. Both the good clocks A and B are therefore resynchronizing onto themselves, and they will slowly drift apart until the system fails.

It might be hoped that some relatively minor modification to the median algorithm could eliminate the possibility of such system-failure modes. However, such hope is groundless. The type of behavior exhibited by clock C above will doom to failure any attempt to devise a reliable clock resynchronization algorithm for only three clocks. It can be proved that, if the failure-mode behavior is permitted to be arbitrary, then there cannot exist any reliable clock resynchronization algorithm for three clocks. The impossibility of obtaining exact sychronization with three clocks is proved in Pease, Shostak, and Lamport [1980]. The impossibility of obtaining even the approximate synchronization needed by SIFT has also been proved, but the proof is too complex to present here. The result is quite general and applies not only to clocks but to any type of integrator that is subject to minor perturbations as, for example, inertial navigation systems.

Although no algorithm exists for three clocks, we have devised an algorithm for four or more clocks that makes the system immune to the failure of a single clock. The algorithm has been generalized to allow the simultaneous failure of M out of N clocks when $N > 3M$. Here, we only describe the single-failure algorithm, without proving it correct. (Algorithms of this type often contain very subtle errors, and extremely rigorous proofs are needed to ensure their correctness.) The general algorithm, and the proof of its correctness, can be found in Pease, Shostak, and Lamport [1980].

The algorithm is carried out in two parts. In the first part, each clock* computes a vector of clock values, called the *interactive consistency vector*, having an entry for every clock. In the second part, each clock uses the interactive consistency vector to compute its new value.

A clock p computes its interactive consistency vector as follows. The entry of the vector corresponding to p itself is set equal to p's own clock value. The value for the entry corresponding to another processor q is obtained by p as follows:

1. Read q's value from q.
2. Obtain from each other clock r the value of q that r read from q.

---

* In the following discussion, a clock is assumed to be capable of logical operations. In SIFT, such a clock is actually a processor and its internal clock.

3. If a majority of these values agree, then the majority value is used. Otherwise, the default value NIL (indicating that q is faulty) is used.

One can show that if at most one of the clocks is faulty, then (1) each nonfaulty clock computes exactly the same interactive consistency vector, and (2) the component of this vector corresponding to any nonfaulty clock q is q's actual value.

Having computed the interactive consistency vector, each clock computes its new value as follows. Let δ be the maximum amount by which the values of nonfaulty processors may disagree. (The value of δ is known in advance and depends upon the synchronization interval and the rate of clock drift.) Any component that is not within δ of at least two other components is ignored, and any NIL component is ignored. The clock then takes the median value of the remaining components as its new value. Since each nonfaulty clock computes exactly the same interactive consistency vector, each will compute exactly the same median value. Moreover, this value must be within δ of the original value of each nonfaulty clock.

This is the basic algorithm that the SIFT processors use to synchronize their clocks. Each SIFT processor reads the value of its own clock directly and reads the value of another processor's clock over a bus. It obtains the value that processor r read for processor q's clock by reading from processor r's memory over a bus.

Reliability Prediction

A sufficiently catastrophic sequence of component failures will cause any system to fail. The SIFT system is designed to be immune to certain likely sequences of failures. To guarantee that SIFT meets its reliability goals, we must show that the probability of a more catastrophic sequence of failures is sufficiently small.

The reliability goal of the SIFT system is to achieve a high probability of survival for a short period of time (for example, a 10-hour flight) rather than a large mean time before failure (MTBF). For a flight of duration T, survival will occur unless certain combinations of failure events occur within the interval T or have already occurred prior to the interval T and were undetected by the initial checkout of the system. Operationally, failures of the latter type are indistinguishable from faults that occur during the interval T.

To estimate the probability of system failure, we use a finite-state, Markov-like *reliability model* in which the state transitions are caused by the events of fault occurrence, fault detection, and fault handling. The combined probability of all event sequences that lead to a failed state is the system failure probability. A design goal for SIFT is to achieve a failure rate of 10^{-9} per hour for a 10-hour period.

For the reliability model, we assume that hardware-fault events and electrical transient-fault events are uncorrelated and exponentially distributed in time (constant failure rates). These assumptions are believed to be accurate for hardware faults because the physical design of the system prevents fault propagation between functional units (processors and buses) and because a multiple fault within one functional unit is no more serious than a single fault. The model assumes that all failures are permanent (for the duration of the flight), so it does not consider transient errors. The effects of uncorrelated transient errors are masked by the executive system, which requires a unit to make multiple errors before it considers the unit to be faulty. It is believed that careful electrical design can prevent correlation of transient errors between functional units. The execution of critical tasks in loose synchronism also helps protect against correlation of fast transient errors. Failure rates for hardware have been estimated on the basis of active component counts, using typical reliability figures for similar hardware. For the main processors, we obtain the rate 10^{-4} per hour; for I/O processors and buses, we obtain 10^{-5} per hour.

For a SIFT system with about the same number of main processing modules, I/O processing modules, and buses, it can be shown that the large difference in failure rates between a main processing module and an I/O processing module or bus implies that we need only consider main processing module failures in our calculations. We can therefore let the state of the system be represented in the reliability model as a triple of integers (h, d, f) with $h \leqslant d \leqslant f$, where such a state represents a situation in which f failures of individual processors have occurred, d of those failures have been detected, and h of these detected failures have been handled by reconfiguration. As illustrated in Figure 10–11, there are three types of possible state transition:

- $(h, d, f) \rightarrow (h, d, f + 1)$, representing the failure of a processor
- $(h, d, f) \rightarrow (h, d + 1, f)$, $d < f$, representing the detection of a failure
- $(h, d, f) \rightarrow (h + 1, d, f)$, $h < d$, representing the handling of a detected failure

The first two types of transition (processor failure and failure detection, represented in Figure 10–11 by straight arrows) are assumed to have constant probabilities per unit time. However, the third type of transition (failure handling, represented in Figure 10–11 by wavy arrows) represents the completion of a reallocation procedure. We assume that this transition must occur within some fixed length of time τ.

A state (h, d, f) with $h < d$ represents a situation in which the system is reconfiguring. To make the system immune to an additional failure while in this state is a difficult problem, since it means that the procedure to reconfigure around a failure must work despite an additional, undetected failure. Rather than assuming that this problem could be solved, we took the approach of trying to insure that the time τ that the system remains in such a state is small enough to make it highly unlikely for an additional failure to occur before reconfiguration is completed. We therefore made the pessimistic assumption that a processor failure that occurs while the system is reconfiguring will cause a system failure. Such failures are represented by the double-fault transitions indicated by asterisks in Figure 10–11. In our calculations, we assume that each of these transitions results in a system failure.

We have calculated the probability of system failure through a double-fault transition and also through reaching a state with fewer than two nonfaulty processors, for which we say that

FIGURE 10–11
The reliability model

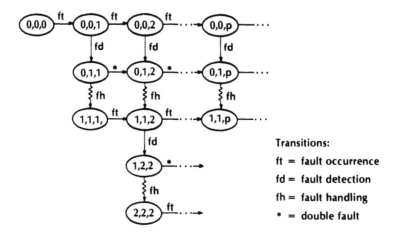

Transitions:

ft = fault occurrence
fd = fault detection
fh = fault handling
* = double fault

the system has failed because it has run out of spares.† A brief summary of these failure probabilities for a five-processor system is shown in Table 10–6.

THE SIFT HARDWARE

The SIFT system attempts to use standard units whenever possible. Special design is needed only in the bus system and in the interfaces between the buses and the processing modules.

The major parameters of the SIFT system are shown in Table 10–7. The Engineering Model column indicates the system intended for initial construction, integration, and testing. The "Maximum" column indicates the limits to which the engineering model can be expanded with only the procurement of additional equipment.

As described previously, the fault-tolerant properties of SIFT are based on the interconnection system between units and on the software system. The particular design of the processors

† The probability of system failure because of multiple *undetected* faults has not been computed precisely, but is expected to be comparable to the double fault values.

TABLE 10–6
Failure probabilities for a five-processor system (T = 10 hours)

Failure Cause	Failure Probability
Exhaustion of spares	5×10^{-12}
Double fault (τ = 100 msec)	7×10^{-11}
Double fault (τ = 1 sec)	7×10^{-10}

TABLE 10–7 *Major parameters of the SIFT system, engineering model*

System Parameters	Engineering Model	Maximum	System Parameters	Engineering Model	Maximum
Main processors	5*	8	Main Memories		
Main memories	5	8	Word length	16 bits	Same
I/O processors	5	8	Capacity	32K words	64K
I/O memories	5	8	Type	Semiconductor	Same
Buses	5	8		RAM**	
External interfaces	5	8	I/O Processors		
Main processors			Word length	8 bits	Same
Word length	16 bits	Same	Type	Intel 8080	Same
Addressing capability	32K words	64K	I/O Memories		
			Word length	8 bits	Same
Speed	500K IPS	Same	Capacity	4K bytes	Same
Arithmetic modes	Fixed point	Same	Buses		
	Double length		Speed	< 10 msec per word	Same
	Floating point			Bit serial	
Type	Bendix BDμ	Same	I/O Interfaces		
			Type	1553A MIL-STD	Same

*In addition, a spare unit of each type is to be built.
**Program memory would be ROM for actual flight use.

and memories is irrelevant to our discussion of fault tolerance. We merely mention that the main processors and memories are based on the BD*microX* computer, an LSI-based, 16-bit computer designed and manufactured by Bendix Corporation specifically for avionics or similar applications. The I/O processors are based on the well-known 8080 microprocessor architecture.

To help the reader understand the operation of the units and their interaction with one another, we describe the operation of the interconnection system in abstract terms. Figure 10–12 shows the connections among processors, buses, and memories. The varying replications of these connections are shown for each type of unit. Within each unit are shown a number of abstract registers that contain data or control information. Arrows that terminate at a register indicate the flow of data to the register. Arrows that terminate at the boundary of a unit indicate control signals for that unit.

We explain the operation of the interconnection system by describing how a processor *p* reads a word of data from location *w* of memory *m* via bus *b*. We assume normal operation, in which no errors or time-outs occur. Processor *p* initiates the Read operation by putting *m* and *w*

FIGURE 10–12
An abstract view of data transfers

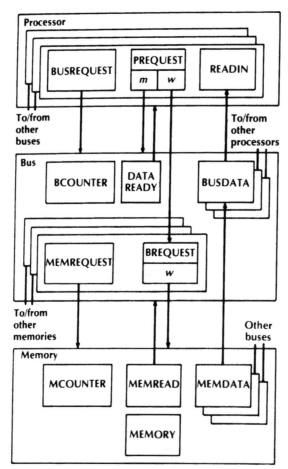

into the register Prequest (p, b). Note that every processor has a separate Prequest register for each bus to which it is connected. When this register is loaded, a Busrequest line is set to request attention from the appropriate bus. The processor must now wait until the requested bus and memory units have completed their part of the operation.

Each bus unit contains a counter-driven scanner that continuously scans the Prequest and Busrequest lines from processors. When the scanner finds a processor that requires its attention (Busrequest high), it stops, and the bus is said to have been *seized* by that processor. The bus's counter then contains the identifying number of the processor that has seized it. When seized, the bus transfers the value w from the processor to a register connected to memory m. When this transfer has been completed, the Memrequest line is raised, calling for attention from the memory. The bus then waits for the memory to complete its actions.

Memory units contain counter-driven scanners that operate in the same manner as those in the bus units, that is, they continuously scan all buses to determine which of them (if any) is requesting service. When a request is detected, the memory is said to be seized, and it reads the value w from the bus. The memory then reads the contents of its location w into Memdata register and raises the Memread line to inform the bus that the data are available. The memory leaves the state of Memdata and Memread unchanged until it detects that the Memrequest line from the bus has dropped, indicating that the bus has received the data from the Memdata register. The memory then drops the Memread line and resumes scanning the buses for further requests.

When the bus detects that the Memread line from the memory is up, it transfers the data in the Memdata register to the Busdata register, drops the Memrequest line, and raises the Dataready line, indicating to the processor that the data are available. The bus leaves the state of the Busdata and Dataready lines unchanged until it detects that the Busrequest line from the processor has dropped, indicating that the processor has received the data word. The bus then drops the Dataready line and resumes scanning the processors for further requests.

Meanwhile, the processor that made the original request has been waiting for the Dataready line to be raised by the bus, at which time it reads the data from the Busdata register. After completing this read, it drops the Busrequest line and continues with other operations. These actions have left the units in their original states. They are therefore ready to take part in other data transfer operations.

The precise behavior of the units can be described by abstract programs. Table 10–8 is an abstract program for the processor-to-bus interface unit.* It shows the unit's autonomous control and the manner in which the unit requests service. Note how time-outs are used to prevent any kind of bus or memory failure from hanging up the unit. Abstract programs for the other units are similar.

The interconnection system units designed especially for the SIFT system are (1) the processor-to-bus interfaces, (2) the buses, and (3) the bus-to-memory interfaces. These units all operate autonomously and contain their own control, which is implemented as a simple microprogrammed controller. For example, the bus control scanner that detects the processors' requests for service is controlled by a microprogram in a programmable read-only memory (PROM). The contents of this PROM are used for two purposes: first, part of the data is fed back to the PROM's address register to determine which word of the PROM is to be read next; second, part of the data is used as logic signals that control the operation of the unit in which the PROM resides.

---

* This program is only meant to illustrate the unit's main features; it does not accurately describe the true behavior of the unit.

TABLE 10–8

Abstract program for processor-to-bus interface unit

Data:
  READIN(p,b)
  A set of registers, one for each bus b, that receive data read from another processor.

  PREQUEST(p,b)
  A set of registers, one for each bus b, that hold the parameters of a request to read one word from another module's memory over that bus.

  BUSREQUEST(p,b)
  A set of booleans that indicate a request from bus b.

  ― ― ―

  A constant that is the maximum time a processor will wait for a bus action.

  BUS FAIL(p,b)
  A boolean indicating that processor p timed-out before receiving data from bus b.

External Data (generated by other units):
  DATAREADY, BUSDATA from BUS module

Abstract Program:
  REQUEST(p,b) := m,w
  D := REALTIME
  WAIT ON (DATAREADY (b) OR REALTIME > (D + - - -))
  IF DATA READY (b)
    THEN BEGIN READIN(p,b) := BUSDATA(b)
                BUSREQUEST(p,b) := FALSE
                WAIT ON ((DATA READY = FALSE)
                          OR (REALTIME > (D + - - -))
    END
  ELSE BEGIN BUS REQUEST := FALSE
              BUSFAIL(p,b) := TRUE
    END

For example, this second part could contain data to open gates to allow the flow of information from one unit to another. Input signals to the controller are applied to some of the bits of the PROM's address register, thereby affecting which PROM words are read.

The interface units consist mainly of a few registers, the controller, and the gates necessary to effect the data flow. The bus with its controller contains a larger set of such gates, since each bus can allow data flow from every memory to every processor. We estimate that the complexity of a bus unit, consisting of a bus together with all its interfaces, is about 10 percent of that of a main processing module. The logical structure is such that an LSI version of an entire bus unit will be practical for future versions of SIFT. However, the engineering model is a mixture of LSI and MSI (medium-scale integration) technology.

The design of the interfaces permits simultaneous operation of all units. For example, a processor can simultaneously read data from its memory and from another memory, while at the same time another processor is reading from the first processor's memory. Such simultaneous operation is limited only by contention at a memory unit. This contention is handled by conventional cycle-stealing techniques and causes little delay, since the memory cycle time is small (250 nsec) compared to the time needed to transfer a full word through the bus (10 μsec).

Since several processors may attempt to seize the same bus, or several buses may attempt to seize the same memory, a processor may have to wait for the completion of one or more other operations before receiving service. Such waiting should be insignificant because of the small amount of data that is transmitted over the buses.

THE SOFTWARE SYSTEM

The software of SIFT consists of the application software and the executive software. The application software performs the actual flight-control computations. The executive software is responsible for the reliable execution of the application tasks and implements the error-detection and reconfiguration mechanisms discussed in the section on SIFT concept of fault tolerance. Additional support software to be run on a large support computer is also provided.

From the point of view of the software, a processing module, with its processor, memory, and associated registers, is a single logical unit. We will therefore simply use the term "processor" to refer to a processing module for the rest of the case study.

The Application Software

The application software is structured as a set of iterative tasks. As described in the subsection Scheduling, each task is run with a fixed iteration rate that depends on its priority. The iteration rate of a higher-priority task is an integral multiple of the iteration rate of any lower-priority task. Every task's iteration rate is a simple fraction of the main clock frequency.

The fact that a task is executed by several processors is invisible to the application software. In each iteration, an application task obtains its inputs by executing calls to the executive software. After computing its outputs, it makes them available as inputs to the next iteration of tasks by executing calls to the executive software. The input and output of a task iteration will consist of at most a few words of data.

The SIFT Executive Software

Formal specifications of the executive software have been written in a rigorous form using the SPECIAL language [Robinson and Roubine, 1977] developed at SRI. These formal specifications are needed for the proof of the correctness of the system discussed in the next section. Moreover, they are also intended to force the designer to produce a well-structured system. Good structuring is essential to the success of SIFT. A sample of these SPECIAL specifications is given in the Appendix to this case. The complete formal specification is omitted here. Instead, we informally describe the important aspects of the design.

The SIFT executive software performs the following functions:

1. Run each task at the required iteration rate.
2. Provide correct input values for each iteration of a critical task (masking any errors).
3. Detect errors and diagnose their cause.
4. Reconfigure the system to avoid the use of failed components.

To perform the last three functions, the executive software implements the previously described techniques of redundant execution and majority voting described in the section on the SIFT, concept of fault tolerance. The executive software is structured into three parts: the global executive task, the local executive, and the local-global communicating tasks.

One global executive task is provided for the whole system. It is run just like a highly critical application task, being executed by several processors and using majority voting to obtain the output of each iteration. It diagnoses errors to decide which units have failed and determines the appropriate allocation of tasks to processors.

Each processing module has its own local executive and local-global communicating tasks. The local-global communicating tasks are the error-reporting task and the local reconfiguration task. Each of these tasks is regarded as a separate task executed on a single processor rather than as a replication of some more global task, so there are as many separate error-reporting tasks and local reconfiguration tasks as there are processors.

Figure 10–13 shows the logical structure of the SIFT software system. The replication of tasks and their allocation to processors is not visible. Tasks communicate with one another through buffers maintained by the local executives. Note that the single global executive task is aware of (and communicates with) each of the local executives but that the local executives communicate only with the single (replicated) global executive task and not with each other. In this logical picture, application tasks communicate with each other and with the global executive but not with the local executives.

Figures 10–14 and 10–15 show where the logical components of Figure 10–13 actually reside within SIFT. Note how critical tasks are replicated on several processors. For the sake of clarity, many of the paths by which tasks read buffers have been eliminated from Figures 10–14 and 10–15.

The Local-Global Communicating Tasks. Each processor runs its local reconfiguration task and error-reporting task at a specified frequency, just like any other task. These two tasks communicate with the global executive via buffers.

The local executive detects an error when it obtains different output values for the same task iteration from different processors.* It reports all such errors to the error-reporting task. The error-reporting task performs a preliminary analysis of these errors and communicates its results to the global executive task. These results are also used by the local executive to detect possibly faulty units before the global executive has diagnosed the errors. For example, after several error reports involving a particular bus, the local executive will attempt to use other buses in preference to that one until the global executive has diagnosed the cause of the errors.

The local reconfiguration task maintains the tables used by the local executive to schedule

---

* It can also detect that a time-out occurred while reading from the memory of another processing module.

FIGURE 10–13

Logical structure of the SIFT software system

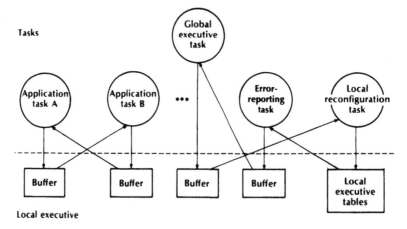

FIGURE 10–14
Arrangement of application tasks within SIFT configuration

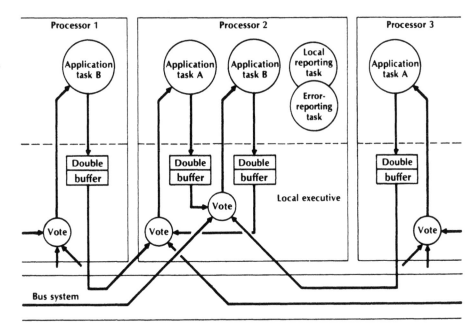

FIGURE 10–15
Arrangement of executive tasks within SIFT configuration

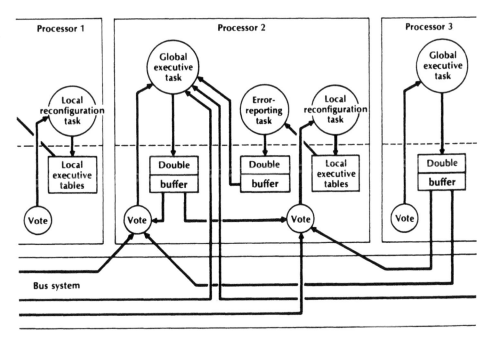

the execution of tasks. It does this using information provided to it by the global executive. The interaction of the global executive and the local-global communicating tasks is as follows:

1. Error handler in each processor puts reports in error table.
2. Error reporter task in each processor reads error table and decides what conditions to report to the global executive. This report is put in a buffer.
3. Global executive (triplicated) reads each processor's buffer over three buses (to guard against bus errors) and votes for a plurality.
4. Global executive, using the diagnosis provided by the error reporter, determines what reconfiguration, if any, is necessary. If a reconfiguration is necessary, a report is put in a buffer.
5. Local reconfiguration task in each processor reads report from each of the global executive buffers and votes to determine plurality.
6. Local reconfiguration task changes the scheduling table to reflect the global executive's wishes.

The Global Executive Task. The global executive task uses the results of every processor's error task to determine which processing modules and buses are faulty. The problem of determining which units are faulty is discussed in the subsection on fault detection. When the global executive decides that a component has failed, it initiates a reconfiguration by sending the appropriate information to the local reconfiguration task of each processor. The global executive may also reconfigure the system as a result of directives from the application tasks. For example, an application task may report a change of flight phase that changes the criticality of various tasks.

To permit rapid reconfiguration, we require that the program for executing a task must reside in a processor's memory before the task can be allocated to that processor. In the initial version of SIFT, there is a static assignment of programs to memories. The program for a critical task usually resides in all main processor memories, so the task can be executed by any main processor.

The Local Executive. The local executive is a collection of routines to perform the following functions: (1) run each task allocated to it at the task's specified iteration rate; (2) provide input values to and receive output values from each task iteration; and (3) report errors to the local executive task. A processor's local executive routine can be invoked from within that processor by a call from a running task, by a clock interrupt, or by a call from another local executive routine. There are four types of routines.

1. The *error-handler routine* is invoked by the voter when an error condition is detected. It records the error condition in a *processor/bus error table,* which is used by the error-reporting task described above.

2. The *scheduler routine* is responsible for scheduling the execution of tasks. Every task is run at a prespecified iteration rate that defines a sequence of time frames within which the task must be run. (For simplicity, we ignore the scheduling of the highest-priority tasks in subframes that was mentioned under Scheduling.) A single iteration of the task is executed within each of its frames, but it may be executed at any time during that frame. The scheduler is invoked by a clock interrupt or by the completion of a task. It always runs the highest-priority task allocated to the processor that has not yet finished executing the iteration for its current time frame. Execution of a task may be interrupted by the clock, in which case its state is preserved until execution is resumed, possibly after the execution of a higher-priority task. A task that has completed its current iteration is not executed again until after the start of its next time frame.

3. The *buffer-interface routines* are invoked by a task when it generates output for an

iteration. These routines put the output into a buffer reserved for that task. These output values are used by the voter routines to obtain input for the tasks. Because a task may be run at any time during its time frame, the double-buffering scheme shown in Figure 10–16 is used. Each buffer consists of a double buffer. In any one time frame, one of the buffers is available for new data that is being generated by the task, while the other contains the data generated last time frame. It is the latter values that are used to provide input to other tasks (and possibly to the same task). At the start of the next time frame, the buffers are switched around. Provision is also made for communication between processors operating at different frequencies.

4. The *voter routine* is invoked by a task to obtain the inputs for its current iteration. The task requests a particular output from the previous iteration of second task, which may be the same task. The voter uses tables provided by the local reconfiguration task to determine what processors contain copies of that output and in which of their buffers. It reads the data from each of these buffers and performs a majority vote to obtain a single value. If all the values do not agree, then an error has occurred, and the error reporter is called.

Fault Detection

Fault detection is the analysis of errors to determine which components are faulty. In SIFT, fault detection is based on the processor/bus error table, an m by n matrix, where m is the number of processors and n the number of buses in the system. Each processor has its own processor/bus error table that is maintained by its local executive's error handler. An entry $Xp[i,j]$ in processor p's table represents the number of errors detected by processor p's local executive that involve processor i and bus j. Suppose that processor p is reading from processor q using bus r. There are five distinct kinds of errors that cause a matrix value to change:

1. The connection from bus r to processor q is faulty.
2. The connection from processor p to bus r is faulty.
3. Bus r is faulty.
4. Processor q is faulty.
5. Processor p is faulty.

FIGURE 10–16
The double-buffering mechanism

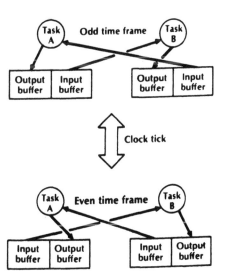

Processor p's error-reporting task analyzes the processor/bus error table as follows to determine if any of these cases hold. Let $e > 0$ be a threshold of errors that will be tolerated for any processor/bus combination. It can deduce that case 1 holds if the following conditions all hold: (1) $Xp[q,r] > e$; (2) there exists a bus j such that $Xp[q,j] \leq e$; and (3) there exists a processor i such that $Xp[i,r] \leq e$. Either case 2 or 3 may hold if $Xp[i,r] > e$ for all active processors i. These two cases can only be distinguished by the global executive task, which has access to information from all the processors. (Case 3 holds if all active processors report bus r faulty; otherwise case 2 holds.) The error handler can deduce that case 4 holds if $Xp[q,j] > e$ for all active buses j. The error handler cannot be depended upon to diagnose case 5, since the failure of the processor executing it could cause the error handler to decide that any (or none) of the other four cases hold.

Once the error handler has performed this analysis, the appropriate action must be taken. In case 1, processor p will stop using bus r to talk to processor q. In cases 2 and 3, processor p will stop using bus r, and will report to the global executive that bus r is faulty. In case 4, processor p will report to the global executive that processor q is faulty.

The global executive task makes the final decision about which unit is faulty. To do this, it reads the faulty processor reports provided by the error-reporting task. If two or more processors report that another processor is faulty, then the global executive decides that this other processor has indeed failed. If two or more processors report that a bus is faulty, then the global executive decides that the bus has failed.

The global executive may know that some unit produced errors but be unable to determine which is the faulty unit. In that case, it must await further information. It can obtain such information by allocating the appropriate diagnostic tasks. If there is a faulty unit (and the error reports were not due to transient faults), then it should obtain the necessary information in a short time.

It can be shown that in the presence of a single fault, the above procedure cannot cause the global executive to declare a nonfaulty unit to be faulty. With the appropriately malicious behavior, a faulty unit may generate error reports without giving the global executive enough information to determine that it is faulty. For example, if processor p fails in such a way that it gives incorrect results only to processor q, then the global executive cannot decide whether it is p or q that is faulty. However, the majority-voting technique will mask these errors and prevent a system failure.

The Simulator

To facilitate debugging of the executive, a simulator was constructed. The simulator uses five asynchronous processes, each running a SIFT executive and a toy set of application tasks. The controlling process simulates the actions of the SIFT bus system and facilitates interprocess communications. Faults are injected, either at the processor or the bus levels, and a visual display of the system's behavior is provided. This gives us a means of testing software in the absence of the actual SIFT hardware.

THE PROOF OF CORRECTNESS

Concepts

Estimates of the reliability of SIFT are based on the assumption that the software operates correctly. Since we know of no satisfactory way to estimate the probability that a piece of software is incorrect, we are forced to try to guarantee that the software is indeed correct. For an asynchronous multiprocess system such as SIFT, the only way to do this is to give a rigorous mathematical proof of its correctness.

A rigorous proof of correctness for a system requires a precise statement of what it means for the system to be correct. The correctness of SIFT must be expressed as a precise mathematical statement about its behavior. Since the SIFT system is composed of several processors and memories, such a statement must describe the behavior of many thousands of bits of information. We are thus faced with the problem that the statement of what it means for the SIFT software to be correct is too complicated to be humanly comprehensible.

The solution to this problem is to construct a higher-level view of the SIFT system that is simpler than the actual system. Such a view is called a *model*. When stated in terms of the simple model, the requisite system properties can be made comprehensible. The proof of correctness is then performed in two steps: (1) We first prove that the model possesses the necessary correctness properties, and (2) we then prove that the model accurately describes the SIFT system [Shostak et al., 1977].

Actually, different aspects of correctness are best expressed in terms of different models. We use a hierarchy of models. The system itself may be viewed as the lowest-level model. In order to prove that the models accurately describe the SIFT system, we prove that each model accurately describes the next lower-level one.

Models

We now make the concept of a model more precise. We define a model to consist of a set S of possible states, a subset S_0 of S consisting of the set of possible initial states, and a *transition relation* $\to$ on S. The relation $s \to s'$ means that a transition is possible from state s to state s'. It is possible for the relations $s \to s'$ and $s \to s''$ both to hold for two different states s' and s'', so we allow nondeterministic behavior. A *possible behavior* of the system consists of a sequence of states $s_0, s_1, \ldots$ such that s_0 is in S_0 and $s_i \to s_{i+1}$ for each i. Correctness properties are mathematical statements about the possible behaviors of the system.

Note that the behavior of a model consists of a linear sequence of transitions, even though concurrent operations occur in the SIFT system. Concurrent activity can be represented by the transitions that change disjoint components of the state so that the order in which they occur is irrelevant.

Each state of the model represents a collection of states in the real system. For example, in the reliability model discussed in the subsection on reliability prediction, the state is a triple of integers (h,d,f) that contains only the information that f processors have failed, d of those failures have been detected, and h of the detected failures have been handled. A single-model state corresponds to all possible states the system could reach through any combination of f failures, d failure detections, and h reconfigurations.

We now consider what it means for one model to accurately describe a lower-level one. Let S, S_0, and $\to$ be the set of states, set of initial states, and transition relation for the higher-level model, and let S', S_0', and $\to'$ be the corresponding quantities for the lower level model. Each state of the lower-level model must represent some state of the higher-level one, but different lower-level states can represent the same higher-level one. Thus there must be a mapping REP: $S' \to S$, where REP (s') denotes the higher-level state represented by s'.

Having defined a correspondence between the states of the two models, we can require that the two models exhibit corresponding behavior. Since the lower-level model represents a more detailed description of the system, it may contain more transitions than the higher-level one. Each transition in the lower-level model should either correspond to a transition in the higher-level one or describe a change in the system that is invisible in the higher-level model. This requirement is embodied in the following two conditions.

1. REP (S_0') is a subset of S_0.
2. For all s', t' in S', if $s' \rightarrow t'$, then either (a) REP (s') = REP (t') or (b) REP (s') $\rightarrow$ REP (t').

If these conditions are satisfied, then we say that REP defines the lower-level model to be a *refinement* of the higher-level one.

If a model is a refinement of a higher-level one, then any theorem about the possible behaviors of the higher-level model yields a corresponding theorem about the possible behaviors of the lower-level one. This is used to infer correctness of the lower-level model (and ultimately, of the system itself) from the correctness of the higher-level one.

A transition in the higher-level model may represent a system action that is represented by a sequence of transitions in the lower-level one. For example, the action of detecting a failure may be represented by a single transition in the higher-level model. However, in a lower-level model (such as the system itself), detecting a failure may involve a complex sequence of transitions. The second requirement means that in order to define REP, we must define some arbitrary point at which the lower-level model is considered to have detected the failure. This problem of defining exactly when the higher-level transition takes place in the lower-level model is the major difficulty in constructing the mapping REP.

The Reliability Model

In the reliability model, the state consists of a triple (h,d,f) of integers with $h \leq d \leq f \leq p$, where p is the number of processors. The transition relation $\rightarrow$ is described in the subsection on reliability prediction, as is the meaning of the quantities h, d, and f.

Associated with each value of h is an integer $sf(h)$, called its *safety factor*, which has the following interpretation. If the system has reached a configuration in which h failures have been handled, then it can successfully cope with up to $sf(h)$ additional (unhandled) failures. That is, the system should function correctly so long as $f - h$, the number of unhandled failures, is less than or equal to $sf(h)$. The state (h,d,f) is called *safe* if $f - h \leq sf(h)$.

To demonstrate that SIFT meets its reliability requirements, we must show two properties:

1. If the system remains in a safe state (one represented by a safe state in the reliability model), then it will behave correctly.
2. The probability of the system's reaching an unsafe state is sufficiently small.

Property 2 is discussed in the subsection on reliability prediction. The remainder of this section describes our approach to proving property 1.

The reliability model is introduced specifically to allow us to discuss property 2. The model does not reflect the fact that SIFT is performing any computations, so it cannot be used to state any correctness properties of the system. For that a lower-level model is needed.

The Allocation Model

An Overview. SIFT performs a number of iterative tasks. In the *allocation model*, a single transition represents the execution of one complete iteration of all the tasks. As described in the subsection on scheduling, most tasks are not actually executed every iteration cycle. For the allocation model, an unexecuted task is considered to perform a null calculation, producing the same result it produced during the previous iteration.

The input used by a task in its tth iteration is the output of the $(t - 1)$ iteration of some (possibly empty) set of tasks. Input to SIFT is modeled by a task executed on an I/O processor that produces output without requiring input from other tasks. The output that an I/O processor produces is simply the output of some task that it executes.

In the allocation model, we make no distinction between main processors and I/O processors. Bus errors are not represented in the model. SIFT's handling of them is invisible in the allocation model and can be represented by a lower-level model.

The fundamental correctness property of SIFT (property 1) is stated in terms of the allocation model as follows: If the system remains in a safe state, then each nonfaulty processor produces correct output for every critical task it executes. This implies the correctness of any critical output of SIFT generated by a nonfaulty I/O processor. (The possibility of faulty I/O processors must be handled by redundancy in the external environment.)

The allocation of processors to tasks is effected by the interaction of the global executive task, the local-global communicating tasks, and local executives, as described in the previous section. The output of the tth iteration of a local-global communicating task uses as input the output of the $(t - 1)$ iteration of the global executive. During the tth iteration cycle, the local executive determines what the processor should be doing during the $(t + 1)$ cycle; that is, what tasks it should execute and what processor memories contain the input values for each of these tasks. The processor executes a task by fetching each input from several processor memories, using a majority vote to determine the correct value and then computing the task's output.* We assume that a nonfaulty processor will compute the correct output value for a task if majority voting obtains the correct value for each of the task's inputs.

The only part of the executive software that is explicitly represented in the allocation are the local-global communicating tasks. Although each processor's local-global communicating task is treated in SIFT as a separate task, it is more convenient to represent it in the allocation model as the execution on that processor of a single replicated task whose output determines the complete allocation of tasks to processors.

The States of the Allocation Model. We now describe the set of states of the allocation model. They are defined in terms of the primitive quantities listed below, which are themselves undefined. (To show that a lower-level model is a refinement of the allocation model, we must define these primitive quantities in terms of the primitive quantities of that lower-level model.) The descriptions of these quantities are given to help the reader understand the model; they have no formal significance.

- P, a set of processors, represents the set of all processors in the system.
- K, a set of tasks, represents the set of all (critical) tasks in the system.
- LE, an element of K, is the single task that represents all the local-global communicating tasks, as described above.
- e, a mapping from the cross-product of K and the set of nonnegative integers into some unspecified set of values, describes what the SIFT tasks should compute. The value of $e(k,t)$ represents the correct output of the tth iteration cycle of task k. It is a primitive (undefined) quantity in the allocation model because we are not specifying the actual values the tasks

---

* The fault diagnosis performed by the global executive is not represented in the allocation model.

should produce. (These values will, of course, depend upon the particular application tasks SIFT executes and the inputs from the external environment.)
  • sf, the safety factor function introduced in the reliability model, remains a primitive quantity in the allocation model. It can be thought of as a goal the system is trying to achieve.

We define the allocation model state to consist of the following components.* (Again, the descriptions are to assist the reader and are irrelevant to the proof.)

  • t, a nonnegative integer, represents the number of iteration cycles that have been executed.
  • F, a subset of P, represents the set of all failed processors.
  • D, a subset of F, represents the set of all failed processors whose failure has been detected.
  • c, a mapping from $P \times K$ into some unspecified set of values, denotes the output of task k as computed by processor p. The value $c(p,k)$ is presumably meaningless if p did not execute the tth iteration of task k.

The Axioms of the Model. We do not completely describe the set of initial states S_0 and the transition relation $\rightarrow$ for the allocation model. Instead, we give the following list of axioms about S_0 and $\rightarrow$. Rather than give their formal statement, we simply give here an informal description of the axioms. (Uninteresting axioms dealing with such matters as initialization are omitted.)

  1. The value of $c(p,LE)$ during iteration cycle t, which represents the output of the tth iteration of processor p's local-global communicating task, specifies the tasks that p should execute during cycle $t + 1$ and the processors whose memories contain input values for each such task.
  2. If a nonfaulty processor p executes a task k during iteration cycle t, and a majority of the copies of each input value to k received by p are correct, then the value $c(p,k)$ it computes will equal the correct value $e(k,t)$.
  3. Certain natural assumptions are made about the allocation of tasks to processors specified by $e(LE,t)$. In particular, we assume that (a) no critical tasks are assigned to a processor in D (the set of processors known to be faulty), and (b) when reconfiguring, the reallocation of tasks to processors is done in such a way that the global executive never knowingly makes the system less tolerant of failure than it currently is.

To prove that a lower-level model is a refinement of the allocation model, it will suffice to verify that these axioms are satisfied.

The Correspondence with the Reliability Model. In order to show that the allocation model is a refinement of the reliability model, we must define the quantities h, d, and f of the reliability model in terms of the state components of the allocation model—thereby defining the function REP. The definitions of d and f are obvious; they are just the number of elements in the sets D and F, respectively. To define h, we must specify the precise point during the execution of the allocation model at which a detected failure is considered to be handled. Basically, the value of h is increased to $h + 1$ when the reconfiguration has progressed to the point where it can handle $sf(h + 1)$ *additional* errors. (The function sf appears in the definition.) We omit the details.

The Correctness Proof. Within the allocation model, we can define a predicate $CF(t)$ that expresses the condition that the system functions correctly during the tth iteration cycle. Intuitively, it is the statement that every nonfaulty processor produces the correct output for every task it executes. The predicate $CF(t)$ can be stated more precisely: If $e(LE,t - 1)$ indicates that p should

---

* To simplify the discussion, one component of our actual model has been omitted.

execute a task k in K during the tth iteration cycle, and p is in $P - F$, then the value of $c(p,k)$ after the tth iteration equals $e(k,t)$. (A precise statement of how $e(LE, t - 1)$ indicates that p should execute task k requires some additional notation, and is omitted.)

We can define the predicate SAFE(t) to mean that the system is in a safe state at time t. More precisely, SAFE(t) means that after the tth iteration cycle, $sf(h) \geq f - h$, where f and h are defined above as functions of the allocation model state. The basic correctness condition for SIFT can be stated as: If SAFE(t') is true for all t' with $0 \leq t' \leq t$, then $CF(t)$ is true.

A rigorous proof of this theorem has been developed, based upon the axioms for the allocation model. The proof is too long and detailed to include here.

SUMMARY

The SIFT computer development is an attempt to use modern methods of computer design and verification to achieve fault-tolerant behavior for real-time, critical control systems. We believe that the use of standard, mass-produced components helps to attain high reliability. Our basic approach, therefore, involves the replication of standard components, relying upon the software to detect and analyze errors and to dyamically reconfigure the system to bypass faulty units. Special hardware is needed only to isolate the units from one another, so a faulty unit does not cause the failure of a nonfaulty one.

We have chosen processor/memory modules and bus modules as the basic units of fault detection and reconfiguration. These units are at a high enough level to make system reconfiguration easy and are small and inexpensive enough to allow sufficient replication to achieve the desired reliability.

By using software to achieve fault tolerance, SIFT allows considerable flexibility in the choice of error handling policies and mechanisms. For example, algorithms for fault masking and reconfiguration can be easily modified on the basis of operational experience. Novel approaches to the tolerance of programming errors, such as redundant programming and recovery blocks [Randell, 1975], can be incorporated. Moreover, it is fairly easy to enhance the performance of the system by adding more hardware.

While designing SIFT, we have been concerned with proving that it meets its stringent reliability requirements. We have constructed formal models with which to analyze the probability of system failure, and we intend to prove that these models accurately describe the behavior of the SIFT system. Our effort has included the use of formal specifications for functional modules.

Although the design described in this case has been oriented toward the needs of commercial air transports, the basic architectural approach has a wide applicability to critical real-time systems. Future work may extend this approach to the design of fault-tolerant software and more general fault-tolerant control systems.

APPENDIX: SAMPLE SPECIAL SPECIFICATION

This appendix contains an example of a formal specification extracted from the specifications of the SIFT executive software. The specification is written in a language called SPECIAL, a formally defined specification language. SPECIAL has been designed explicitly to permit the description of the results required from a computer program without constraining the programmer's decisions as to how to write the most efficient program.

The function that is specified here is the local executive's voter routine, described informally in the section on the software system. This function is called to obtain a value from one of the buffers used to communicate between tasks. The value required is requested over the bus system from every replication of this buffer, and a consensus value that masks any errors is formed and returned to the calling program. Errors are reported, and provision is made for buses that do not obtain a value (due to a nonresponding bus or memory) and for the possibility that there is no consensus.

```
OVFUN read_buffer (buffer_name i;address k;value safe)
                  [processor a;task t]
                  -> result r;                                    [1]

EXCEPTIONS                                                        [2]
       CARDINALITY(activated_buffers(a,i))=0;
       0>k OR k>=buffer_size(i);

EFFECTS
   EXISTS SET_OF response                                        [3]
          w=responses(a, activated_buffers(a,i),k):
     EXISTS SET_OF response
          z={response b|b INSET w AND b.flag} :

       IF(EXISTS value v;                                        [4]
             SET_OF response x|
             x ={response c|c INSET (w DIFF z)
                        AND c.val = v}:

         FORALL value u:                                         [5]
             SET_OF response y|
             y={response d|d INSET (w DIFF x DIFF z)
                        AND d.val=u}:
         CARDINALITY (x) > CARDINALITY (y))

       THEN(EXISTS value v;                                      [6]
              SET_OF response x|
              x={response c|c INSET (w DIFF z)
                         AND c.val=v}:

         FORALL value u;                                         [6]
             SET_OF response y|
             y={response d|d INSET (w DIFF x DIFF z)
                        AND d.val=u}:
         CARDINALITY(x) > CARDINALITY(y);

         EFFECTS_OF errors(a, w DIFF x);                         [7]
         r=v)

       ELSE(EFFECTS_OF errors(a,w);                              [8]
            r=safe);
```

Specification Notes

The following notes are keyed to statements in the specification.

[1] The function 'read_buffer' takes three arguments and returns a result. The buffer_name 'i' is the name of a logical buffer that may be replicated in several processors, while the address 'k' is the offset of the required word in the buffer and 'safe' is the value to be returned if no consensus can be obtained. The parameters 'a' and 't' need not be explicitly cited by the caller of this function but are deduced from the context.

[2] Exception returns will be made if there are no active instances of the named buffer or if the offset is not within the buffer.

[3] A response is obtained by interrogating a buffer in another processor. Each response is a record (also known as a "structure") containing a value field ("val") and flag field ("flag"), the latter set if no response was obtained from the bus or store. The set 'w' of responses is the set obtained from all of the activated buffers known to processor 'a.' The set 'z' is the subset of no-response responses.

[4] First we must check that a plurality opinion exists. This section hypothesizes that there exists a consensus value 'v' together with the subset of responses 'x' that returned that value.

[5] Here we consider all other values and establish for each of them that fewer responses contained this other value than contained the proposed consensus value.

[6] Having established that a consensus value exists, we may now validly construct it, repeating the criteria of stages 4 and 5. It is important to note that these are not programs but logical criteria. The actual implementations would not repeat the program.

[7] This section requires that any responses not in the set 'x' (the set 'x' is the set reporting the consensus value) should be reported as errors, and the result is the consensus value 'v.' The expression

EFFECTS_ OF errors(a, w DIFF X)

indicates a state change in the module that contains the 0-function "errors." The specification indicates that an error report is loaded into a table associated with processor "a."

[8] If there is no consensus value, as determined by stages 4 and 5, then all the responses must be reported as errors, and the safe value returned as the result.

REFERENCES   Floyd, 1967; Melliar-Smith, 1977; Murray, Hopkins, and Wensley, 1977; Pease, Shostak, and Lamport, 1980; Randell, 1975; Ratner et al., 1973; Robinson and Roubine, 1977; Robinson et al., 1976; Shostak et al., 1977; Wensley, 1972; Wensley et al., 1973, 1976.

III A DESIGN METHODOLOGY AND EXAMPLE OF DEPENDABLE SYSTEM DESIGN

Part I provided the underlying theory for reliable systems design. Part II described in detail the design of eight dependable systems. By studying both the evolutionary changes within a product family and the differences in competitive product families we can gain some insight into how dependable systems are designed.

Consider the example of an art student. The student can study the basic techniques of colors, textures, application of materials, perspective, and direction of light sources. The student can also study completed works of art for composition, contrast, and mood. However, mastery of basic techniques and art appreciation does not transform a student into an artist. The situation is the same for a would-be designer of dependable systems. Knowledge of both the basic techniques and previous designs does not guarantee that a designer can produce a quality design. What is missing is a methodology for mixing, combining, and contrasting the large number of techniques into a coherent design. Design is a dynamic process with alternatives constantly being weighted and traded off against each other. The artifact represents the final state of that design process. The reasons for the final form are usually not documented by the designer and hence are not available to fill out the student's education.

The purpose of Part III is to introduce some of that dynamic experience called design. The first essay by Siewiorek and Johnson provides an eight-step methodology for the systematic design of dependable systems. This design strategy provides a top-down methodology for combining the numerous techniques described in earlier chapters into a balanced and unified system design. The book culminates with the case study, by Bruckert and Bissett, that describes the design process that produced Digital Equipment Corporation's VAXft 310 high-availability computer system.

11 A DESIGN METHODOLOGY

Daniel P. Siewiorek and David Johnson

INTRODUCTION

After the presentation of numerous techniques and evaluation criteria, the question remains, how can these techniques be applied to produce a coherent, balanced system design? This chapter attempts to answer that question by proposing a top-down design methodology and illustrating its application in a detailed example, the VAXft 310.

A DESIGN METHODOLOGY FOR DEPENDABLE SYSTEM DESIGN

The methodology consists of eight steps:

1. Define system objectives.
2. Limit the scope.
3. Define the layers of fault handling.
4. Define reconfiguration and repair boundaries.
5. Design the fault-handling mechanisms.
6. Identify the hardcore.
7. Evaluate the design against the objectives.
8. Return to Step 3 and iterate the design if necessary.

Each of the first six steps is discussed in detail in the following subsections.

Define System Objectives

As illustrated in Chapter 5, there are multiple objectives in the design of computing systems: Cost, performance, and reliability. The first decision in the design of a new system is where in the cost/performance/reliability space the system is to be positioned. There are three generic system types in the evaluation space. The first is the traditional point product, which evaluates to a single cost/performance/reliability number. The second is a family of products that requires more resources (hence, cost) to deliver more performance. Examples include a computer family such as the IBM 3090 or the DEC VAX. It is nearly impossible to modify cost and performance without altering reliability. Generally, higher performance systems have lower reliability because of the extra components. The third approach is to add resources in a modular fashion. In the Tandem and Stratus systems of Chapter 8, for example, processors, memory, and I/O can be replicated to enhance performance. These resources can also be utilized to enhance reliability (shadow computers in the case of Tandem and spare processor/memory components in the case of Stratus). Thus, there is a trend toward products that occupy a volume in the evaluation space to which resources can be added to enhance performance or reliability or both.

Although the cost/performance design space is relatively well understood, the reliability dimension is not. However, it is possible to evaluate system reliability and fault-tolerant capabilities by using such key measures as system availability, fault coverage (completeness of fault detection), granularity of fault isolation, probability of system survival for a given period, extent of graceful degradation of service, range of applications covered by the design, and division of fault-tolerant responsibilities among hardware, system software, and application programs.

The definition of system objectives imposes the needs of the selected set of applications onto the key fault-tolerant metrics. It is extremely important to establish the system objectives as early as possible. These objectives help to limit the overwhelming number of design alternatives by restricting the design space, and by providing the criteria for making design decisions. Without a well-defined set of objectives, the design process will fail to focus, and inconsistent design decisions may be made.

Limit the Scope

In order to make intelligent design tradeoffs, the scope of the system objectives must be limited. Numerous environmental factors must be selected to refine the system objectives defined earlier. These environmental assumptions will intensify the focus of the design and limit the system development effort. Environmental factors include the following issues:

- What is the maintenance strategy? Is field repair possible? Is on-line repair required? What is acceptable as a field replaceable unit (component, module, subsystem)? What is the response time of the field service people?
- What parts of the system will the fault-tolerant design encompass (central system, I/O devices, power)?
- What are the relative failure rates for various parts of the system?
- What are the dominant failure modes in the system?
- What types of failures will be considered? Single or multiple concurrent faults? What is the ratio of transient to permanent faults? What error sources are considered (external environment, hardware, software, operator)?

Define the Layers of Fault Handling

Systems are composed of a hierarchy of levels. Faults and errors may be generated at any of the levels in the hierarchy. Indeed, mechanisms for each of the ten stages in handling a fault (confinement, detection, masking, retry, diagnosis, reconfiguration, recovery, restart, repair, and reintegration) can be proposed at each level. Figure 11-1 is an incomplete example of a hypothetical system composed of five hierarchical levels. Typical errors, typical techniques for the detection and recovery stages of fault handling, and typical error response times are also given. If an error is not detected

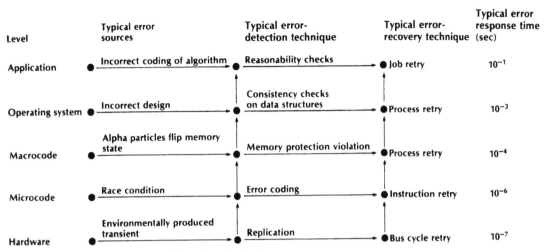

Level	Typical error sources	Typical error-detection technique	Typical error-recovery technique	Typical error response time (sec)
Application	Incorrect coding of algorithm	Reasonability checks	Job retry	10^{-1}
Operating system	Incorrect design	Consistency checks on data structures	Process retry	10^{-3}
Macrocode	Alpha particles flip memory state	Memory protection violation	Process retry	10^{-4}
Microcode	Race condition	Error coding	Instruction retry	10^{-6}
Hardware	Environmentally produced transient	Replication	Bus cycle retry	10^{-7}

FIGURE 11–1 Levels in a hypothetical system

at the level in which it originated, the detection of the error is left to higher levels. Similarly, if the current level lacks the capacity to recover from a particular detected error, appropriate information about the detected error must be passed onto a higher level.

As an undetected error propagates up the levels in the hierarchy, it affects an increasing amount of system state and data structures. Longer response times to an error mean that the error manifestations have become more diverse. The error recovery becomes more complex. If left totally to software, error recovery routines may easily become more complex than the application software.

Error-detection techniques should be established at the various boundaries to ensure that the coverage holes from one level to the next do not align. Figure 11–2 graphically depicts several levels in a system, each with "holes" in its coverage. The existence of holes represents trade-offs between fault-tolerant design goals such as speed of recovery and granularity of fault isolation, and system constraints such as cost and available technology. However, awareness of the system's hierarchical structure allows the design to handle all faults, some immediately and others after reflection to higher levels of the system.

When error correction is performed at the lower levels, a straightforward combinational recovery can be attempted. For example, the state affected by the current level can be double buffered, so that the prior state is released only upon successful completion of the operation at this level. If an error is detected, the buffered prior state can be used to retry. The higher this solution is applied in the system hierarchy, the more state that has to be buffered and the longer the time between checking for errors and the greater the opportunity for the error to interact with healthy activities, causing incorrect decisions. The longer an error, and hence a physical fault, goes undetected, the more data structures in the system may be polluted.

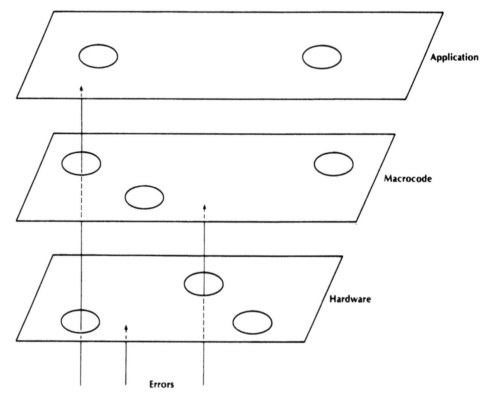

The situation is even more critical in a multiprocessor, where memory and data structures are shared by several concurrently executing processes. Errors can be multiplied by nonfailed components that make incorrect decisions or initiate incorrect operations based on the erroneous information.

Define Reconfiguration and Repair Boundaries

Next, conceptual and physical boundaries for error confinement and isolation must be specified. In order to produce a coherent design strategy, these boundaries must reflect the previously defined system objectives, such as modularity and maintenance/repair strategies. Ideally, boundaries drawn for each level in the hierarchy define nonoverlapping regions.

The percentage of faults detected is the single most important factor in successful recovery. An undetected error usually results in incorrect information's crossing system boundaries and ultimately to a system failure.

Once the confinement boundaries have been established, the repair and reconfiguration boundaries can be drawn. The repair and reconfiguration regions are placed to maximize the effectiveness of the recovery procedures. Before establishing the repair and reconfiguration regions it is important to review the general procedure for recovery.

The purpose of reconfiguration/recovery is to return the system to an operational state. This new operational state should have as many of the original hardware resources available as possible, and the transition to this new state should have minimal impact on normal system operation. Figure 11–3 depicts the generalized reconfiguration/recovery procedure employed at each level in the system hierarchy. After an error has been detected, the faulted operation is frozen (halted). This guarantees that corrupted information cannot leave the faulty reconfiguration/repair region. Next an attempt is made to reestablish the correct operation of the hardware. If the fault is transient, correct operation can resume after the transient interference has subsided. If the fault is permanent, it may be possible to resume operation by reconfiguring around the faulty reconfiguration/repair region. Next the faulted operation is rolled back and the operation retried. The correction phase of recovery ends when either the operation has been successfully retried or there are no more alternatives for correcting the situation. If the faulted operation cannot be completed, any shared resources damaged or left in an inconsistent state are locked. Next the error is reported by signaling the next higher level in the hierarchy. The final step is restart. If recovery was successful, control moves to the next operation. Otherwise control passes up to the next higher level in the recovery hierarchy.

Typically, recovery takes one of two forms: retry (good for transient error correction and permanent failure detection) and standby-sparing/graceful degradation. In the

FIGURE 11–3
Generalized recovery procedure

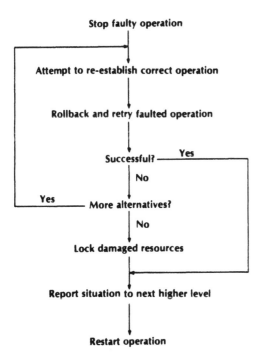

latter case, the computation is moved to another part of the system and restarted. Enough information must be retained so that the restart can be executed cleanly without interference from the side effects of the partially completed first instantiation.

Design the Fault-Handling Mechanisms

Now mechanisms can be designed for each of the ten fault-handling stages at each of the system levels. The previous steps in the design methodology resulted in the definition of regions for fault isolation and subsequent recovery. The partitioning establishes the ideal recovery, reconfiguration, and repair regions in the system. It also describes the extent and the completeness of detection and recovery mechanisms at each level in the system. Hence, system partitioning will provide the higher-level guidelines during the design of the detection and recovery mechanisms, ensuring that the fault-handling mechanisms are applied in a unified manner in support of the system objectives.

The mechanisms are aimed at containing errors at the defined conceptual boundaries. Generally, smaller boundaries are more costly in terms of hardware or time but allow for more complete recovery. At the hardware levels the goal is to effect recovery without software intervention. At the software levels the goal is to prevent incorrect data from passing across boundaries.

Location and isolation of a failure can be achieved by analyzing the state of the system when the error was detected. The activity of the error-associated components should be stopped and their intermediate state frozen. A mechanism should be provided to notify some other components in the system of the stoppage. Some nonaffected intelligence can examine the state information, exercise the components, and initiate a recovery. Thus, at each conceptual boundary the object should be controllable and observable. If the fault cannot be resolved by the existing state, a diagnostic sequence can be initiated.

Identify the Hardcore

At this point in the design process it is very important to evaluate the effectiveness of the fault-tolerant mechanisms. This evaluation is based on three checkpoints:

- Are all the fault-handling mechanisms in the system exercised as part of normal operation?
- Do the detection mechanisms provide the desired level of fault coverage?
- Are there any common-mode failures (single-point dependencies) that undermine the detection and recovery mechanisms?

Failures are detected only when an erroneous piece of information is processed. If any portion of the system is not exercised as a part of normal operation, then latent faults may accumulate. The presence of these latent faults may violate the environmental assumptions (such as no concurrent multiple failures) made earlier in the design process. Two areas of a system where latent faults could occur are the detection and recovery mechanisms, and memory locations that are used only during software recovery. An evaluation of the system fault coverage is important because the detection and recovery circuits that were just added to the design may not be fault tolerant. Indeed, they may not be covered by the fault-detection mechanisms or they may have introduced common-mode failures. These circuits may need to be self-checking or covered by periodic testing.

The VAXft 310 case study, which follows, illustrates the design methodology outlined here.

THE VAXft 310 CASE

A Fault-Tolerant System by Digital Equipment Corporation

WILLIAM BRUCKERT AND THOMAS BISSETT*

The market's perception of the requirements for a fault-tolerant computer system is becoming more demanding. The older generation of fault-tolerant computers had single points of hardware failure, required extensive application programming, and imposed high cost penalties. The newer generation of fault-tolerant computers has no single points of hardware failure, operates transparently to an application, and has lower cost penalties. Today, fault tolerance need not be a type of system, but rather an attribute of a computer. Consequently, the user can purchase the system that provides the desired level of fault tolerance.

A fault-tolerant computer system is measured in terms of the degree to which the attributes of data integrity, computational integrity, availability, and recovery time are realized. Table 11–1 represents the attributes of fault tolerance and describes how they are realized in a conventional and a fault-tolerant computer system. The relative importance of each of these attributes depends

TABLE 11–1 Comparison of conventional and fault-tolerant systems

Attributes of Fault Tolerance	Conventional System	Fault-Tolerant System
Data integrity	Data protection usually limited to memory and buses; parity on buses, checking codes, message protocols	No corruption caused by a single point of failure; duplication, parity on buses, checking codes, message protocols
Computational integrity	Limited checking of logical and arithmetic functions; parity on microcode, parity on data paths	No corruption caused by a single point of failure; replicated computations
Availability	95.0% to 98%	99.999$^+$%
Recovery time	Seconds to minutes	Less than 1 second

* The authors wish to thank the many members of the VAXft 310 program for their willingness to review this material. A special thanks goes to Ted Flessa who assisted in the writing of this chapter and provided much guidance in the art of technical writing.

on the requirements of an application. The effects of recovery time, data integrity, and computational integrity vary from application to application. Different solutions provide different mixtures of these attributes. For some applications, recovery times on the order of 5–10 seconds are perfectly acceptable. In other cases, rapid recovery (on the order of milliseconds) is required.

Given the need for an application-independent, fault-tolerant platform, a basic design tenet was to implement a hardware-intensive, rather than a software-intensive, fault-tolerant system. The primary reasons for this decision were the following:

- Software fault tolerance is difficult to achieve without some significant constraints (such as requiring software to be written as an on-line transaction processing (OLTP) application).
- Hardware fault tolerance provides the fastest recovery time.
- Hardware fault tolerance provides the greatest degree of transparency to the application.
- An OLTP environment should be in addition to hardware fault tolerance rather than the basic means to accomplish it.
- A hardware-based, fault-tolerant implementation allows the features of software fault tolerance to be layered on top of the hardware, producing a highly protected environment.

When designing a fault-tolerant system, it is often difficult to insure that the recovery procedure is correct. Obviously, any error in the fault recovery procedures can compromise the fault tolerance of a system. When recovery is performed at a low level, it is inherently less complex and has fewer interactions. At the hardware level, error recovery can be as simple as a bus cycle retry. However, when an error propagates from the hardware through the microcode, to the macrocode, and into the operating system, the error manifestations become more diverse, and the error recovery becomes more complex.

DEFINING DESIGN GOALS AND REQUIREMENTS FOR THE VAXft 310

The VAXft 310 is a fault-tolerant computer system that supports up to nine transactions per second. This system uses unique and conventional fault-tolerant techniques, such as trace memory for error analysis and hardware redundancy, to provide a continuously operating computer environment.

By designing the hardware architecture with redundant modules and error-checking mechanisms, the system insures that a high degree of fault tolerance is met by providing the following three functions:

- Error capture—the detection and reporting of an error
- Error recovery—removing the effects of an error
- Faulted device restoration—returning the system to full redundancy

Error capture is achieved by fault detection and fault confinement. *Error recovery* is achieved by bus retry or fault isolation and fault reconfiguration. *Faulted device restoration* is achieved by fault repair and reintegration.

Top-level goals provided the parameters against which all ensuing design decisions were made. The three top goals were (1) to provide a fault-tolerant system based on the VAX architecture, (2) to provide a fault-tolerant system that is transparent to the application, and (3) to provide a fault-tolerant system that complements existing VAX product offerings.

Thus, to a user, the system must be a VAX that transparently provides the attributes of fault tolerance. The computer was required to provide a level of availability and fault tolerance distinctly greater than existing DEC systems. Existing products already provide a range of capability from conventional to highly available; the VAXft 310 would augment DEC's range of capability to include hardware fault tolerance.

Before beginning the detailed design, many key characteristics of a fault-tolerant system were identified as essential to meet customer needs:

• *No single point of failure:* No single failure in any piece of hardware can bring down the system. (This requirement includes AC line cords, circuit breakers, and oscillators.)

• *No single point of repair:* Although modules and power supplies fail the most frequently, all components of a computer system can fail (for example, the input circuit breaker). When the system is running and there is no single point of failure, it is essential to avoid the problem of having to bring down the system to effect repairs.

• *Quick mean time to repair:* After the failure of a module, the system is vulnerable to a second failure until the first module has been repaired. The implementation of a low mean time to repair (MTTR) requires the system to detect a fault, isolate it to a specific field-replaceable unit (FRU), and inform the service facility so that a replacement can be made.

• *Protection against accidental errors:* The system should be designed to protect itself from the effects of service and operator errors. However, not all circumstances can be foreseen; therefore, it is important to provide operators with the means to override these protections. At the same time, the system must not be made so easy to override that it does not provide a fair measure of protection. It is important that all repair actions should place the system in as little jeopardy as possible. By configuring the system as two separate cabinets, repair actions on one cabinet are physically isolated from the hardware in the other cabinet that is still executing the operating system.

• *Self-checking checkers:* The first fault in the system could be in the checking mechanism. When this occurs, the machine will no longer be able to detect an error, a fault will go unnoticed, and the application will fail. If a checker can fail in an undetected fashion, there must be some other means of testing the functionality of a checker. The solution is on-line testing of a checker. Self-checking checkers remove the risk of a checker failing, without adding the complexity of on-line hardware testing, while insuring system integrity.

• *Single-Ethernet capability* (with a fault-tolerant connection to a single Ethernet cable): This capability is needed to provide continuous service to devices on the Ethernet that have only a single connection.

• *Multiple-Ethernet capability* (with a fault-tolerant connection to each Ethernet cable): The transmission of messages across multiple Ethernets under DECnet would be load balanced, and if one of the Ethernets fails, the system would failover to another Ethernet. The failover should be automatic, rapid, and transparent to the application.

• *Fault-tolerant synchronous communications control:* There must be the ability to provide the option for DDCMP, SDLC/HDLC, X.25 and other protocols such that, if a single controller fails, the system will failover to another controller.

• *AC power input tolerance:* Since AC input power failures are the most common reason for system downtime, the system must be able to tolerate brownouts, sequences of brief power outages, and longer-term power outages of up to 15 minutes. This protection was to extend beyond memory alone, to include the ability to run disk storage peripherals.

VAXft 310 OVERVIEW

The VAXft 310 is a hardware-intensive implementation of a fault-tolerant architecture. The system is comprised of two duplicate systems, called *zones*. Each zone is a fully functional computer with enough elements to run an operating system. (Depending upon the configuration, the mass storage devices either are part of a zone or are an additional set of resources.) The two zones, referred to as zone A and zone B, are shown in Figure 11–4, which illustrates the duplication of the system components. Each zone contains several modules interconnected by a backplane. The two independent zones are connected by duplicated crosslink cables. The cabinet of each zone also includes a battery, a power regulator, cooling fans, and an AC power input. Each zone's hardware has sufficient error checking to detect all single faults within that zone.

The system components are duplicated in two dimensions: intrazone duplication for checking purposes and interzone duplication providing redundancy. In *intrazone duplication,* the CPUs and other elements are duplicated for checking purposes, but operate as a single logical element. Duplicated elements within a zone never operate independently of one another. *Interzone duplication* is done for redundancy purposes rather than for checking. For example, the failure of a single CPU in zone A will result in both CPUs in zone A being removed from service. The pair of CPUs in zone B will continue system operation.

In the normal mode of fault-tolerant operation, both zones execute the same instruction at the same time (lock-step operation). The two zones are kept in lock-step synchronization by treating each zone's CPU as a deterministic machine. Two deterministic machines, starting from the same state and receiving the same input, will produce the same results. Any divergence from this lock-step operation is a key mechanism for determining that a fault has occurred. The two zones operate in lock-step except (1) when initially booting the system and (2) when a zone's CPU module or a complete zone is disabled.

When the two zones are operating in lock-step, they comprise a single fault-tolerant system running a single copy of the operating system. If a zone is removed from operation, the remaining zone executes the system software. The removal and reintegration of a zone is managed by the

FIGURE 11–4
Dual-zone VAXft 310

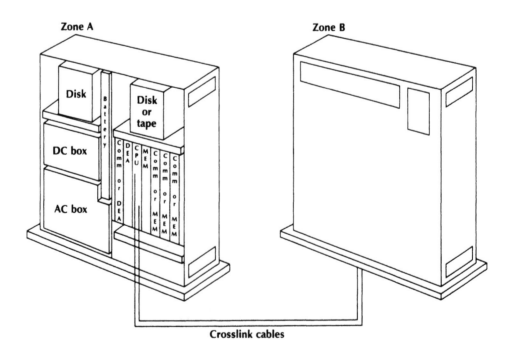

system software and is totally transparent to application software. From the application's per-spective, this system appears as one CPU with two I/O buses. Each I/O bus has a set of controllers that has a redundant counterpart on the other I/O bus. The system software handles all of the duplication of system components so that multiple sets of I/O devices are not visible to the application.

The Zones

The dual-zone system uses various methods to check for correct operation. Checking always involves some form of redundancy. When there is 100 percent redundancy, the method of checking is by direct comparison. That is, if the two results are equal then the answer is correct, and if the two answers are unequal, then the answer is incorrect.

In each zone, the portion of the system using duplication has similar elements connected together, side by side, and is referred to as the dual-rail portion of the system. (See Figure 11–5 for a representation of the system's dual-rail architecture.) However, at times the redundancy is only partial and the checking method is an error-detection code. When changing from one form

FIGURE 11–5
VAXft 310 dual-rail architecture

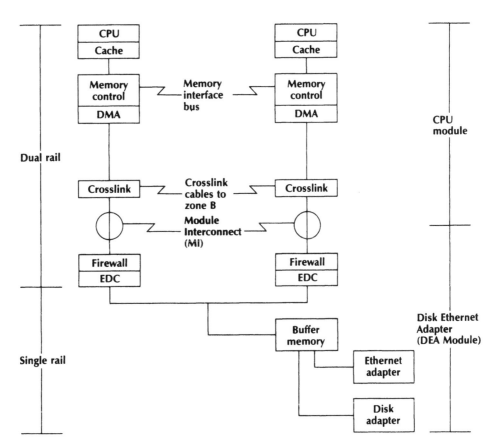

of checking to another, the checkers are located so that one form of checking can be applied before the previous form of checking is removed.

Within each zone, there are seven module slots for four types of modules: CPU, memory, Disk and Ethernet Adapter (DEA), and communications. In each zone, a backplane interconnects the modules. In normal configurations, the two zones contain identical modules.

Each zone communicates with the other zone through a crosslink cable. The crosslink has two communication ports, the parallel and serial crosslinks. The serial crosslink is used when the two zones are not in lock-step, the parallel crosslink when both zones are in lock-step.

CPU Module. The CPU module contains the CPU, floating point unit, memory controller, and crosslink. As shown in Figure 11–5, the dual-rail architecture runs from the processor chips down into the I/O modules. In each zone, the dual-rail has connections to the following system components: crosslink cables between zones, the backplane (module interconnect–MI) running between the CPU and I/O module, and portions of the memory interface bus to main memory. The dual rails in each zone connect: One CPU, one memory controller, one crosslink, one module interconnect, and one Firewall. During proper operation, the data on both rails is the same, operating at a peak bandwidth of 33 MB/sec.

Memory Module. The memory module connects to the CPU module by a memory interface bus and supports the full VAX physical address space. There is support for up to four memory arrays (32 MB to 128 MB), with each memory array containing 32 MB of error correction code (ECC) memory. Duplicate address and control lines from the CPU module are checked during read/ write. Also, the data's ECC is checked on the memory array during reads and writes.

DEA Module. The DEA module contains the following components: Ethernet controller, Digital Storage Systems Interconnect (DSSI) bus, system console terminal, and remote terminal interfaces. Each DEA module is connected to the CPU module in its zone by the dual-rail module interconnect (MI). A Firewall chip supports a single MI interface. Two Firewalls are used on each I/O module, one for each rail of the MI. The Firewalls prevent errors in the single-rail portion of the DEA module from propagating into the dual-rail machine and those in the dual-rail machine from propagating into the single-rail portion.

Ethernet Controller. The Ethernet controller is part of the DEA module; connection to a single Ethernet cable requires two Ethernet controllers, one in each zone. Redundant Ethernet connections (dual) are also supported, allowing fault-tolerant networks to be configured. If a failure occurs on one Ethernet cable, the system will transparently failover to the other Ethernet cable. Redundant Ethernet connections require a second pair of controllers.

DSSI Bus. The DSSI bus supports connections to host adapters (an adapter that issues requests), disk drives, and tape drives. The DSSI bus supports up to eight connections. For systems with smaller disk capacity requirements, a single host adapter is used with either two servers (disk or tape) in the CPU cabinet. For larger disk requirements an expander cabinet is used. In the expanded system configuration, the DSSI bus is connected between the two zones, providing dual paths (two hosts) to every drive. The operating system is cognizant of both paths. If one path fails, the operating system uses the alternate path. The operating system occasionally attempts to use the faulted path to see if it has started working.

The advantage of the two-host configuration is that any single point of failure cannot disable both hosts. Thus, only failures of the disk expander cabinet and the bus can result in the loss of a string of devices. This two-host configuration prevents the loss of volume shadowing operations for most failures and ensuing repair operations.

The disk drives perform optimization, error recovery, and bad block replacement. Each drive holds 381 MB of data. The maximum number of devices that can be configured is eleven, giving a total of 1.9 GB of shadowed (2 copies of all data) storage with the RF31, or 4.1 GB unshadowed. The disk drives are available in fixed-mount and routinely removable shock-mounted canisters. The storage expansion cabinet supports up to five fixed-mount, 5¼", full-height storage devices and one routinely removable storage device. The basic system supports two routinely removable storage devices.

System Console. The system console is a combination of hardware and software that provides the following functions:

- Provides input to the operating system as a common user terminal
- Enables the user to issue console commands
- Boots the system either automatically or interactively
- Installs the VMS operating system
- Examines the control and status registers and runs diagnostic tests
- Enables the user to view messages from the console program, diagnostics, and VMS
- Provides remote dial-in or dial-out capability

The console is configured redundantly, with one connection in each zone of the system. During normal operations only one terminal is required. However, during repair of a system, two terminals are needed. One is used to manage the system, while the other is used to manage the zone under repair. Each zone can support one local and one remote console, for a total of four possible console terminals. Terminals can be hardcopy, or video with or without a printer. The remote terminal allows dial-in communications from DEC's Remote Diagnostic Center (RDC).

Communications Module. Up to four synchronous communications controllers may be installed in a zone. Each controller supports two lines. These lines can be interconnected between controllers in separate zones, providing complete redundancy to the line.

Synchronous lines can be connected to the system in one of three ways.

- A single line can be brought into the system and connected to a single controller. However, if a fault occurs in the zone to which the line is attached, access to that line is lost.

- Using two synchronous communication controller boards, a single line can be connected to both controllers using a Y-connector (see Figure 11–6). A Y-connected line maintains service through all system failures, including failures of line drivers and receivers. In this mode of operation, the fault recovery is transparent to the application code.

- Two independent lines, without replicated controllers, can be connected from one system to another. A failure detected in one line can be bypassed by using the other line.

Each synchronous controller is downline loadable and supports two lines at up to 64 KB with full modem control. Protocols supported include HDLC (X.25), DDCMP (DECnet), SDLC (SNA/IBM), and BISYNC. Also, synchronous communications can be supported through Ethernet-based microservers and gateways. Asynchronous communications are supported on the Ethernet through terminal servers.

Configuring the Modules

With seven module slots for each zone, up to 14 logic modules can be configured in each system. Each zone must contain a CPU module, an identical amount of memory, and at least one DEA

FIGURE 11–6
Y-connector for communications module

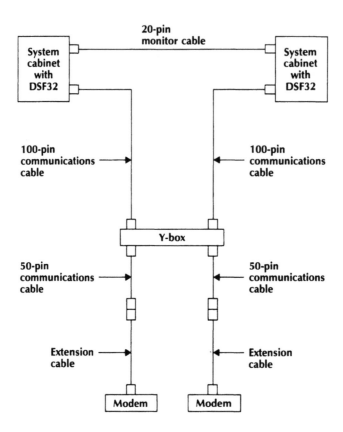

module. I/O adapters and disks need not be configured redundantly (one per zone). Each zone can include one CPU module, one to four memory array modules (32 MB each), one to two DEA modules, and zero to four synchronous communication controllers.

Power Supply

Each zone and each expansion cabinet contains its own battery backup (an internal UPS). Since all system elements have battery backups, the system has the ability to tolerate any AC power disturbances up to full outages of fifteen minutes' duration. If full power returns within fifteen minutes the system continues to operate. The system uses AC input as its primary power source. The battery will be recharged or trickle charged whenever AC power is present. The system can withstand multiple power-on/off cycles until the battery is drained. Also, the system notifies the console in the event of any power fluctuation and has the ability to send an autonotification message to the user upon transfer to internal battery power. This message allows the system manager or operator to take the appropriate action (such as switching to an external generator to power the system).

Operating System and Other Software

The VAXft 310 is a VAX system and, as such, supports, without change, all layered and application software that runs on VAX-supported operating systems. The operating systems and application software simply run on a fault-tolerant platform, taking advantage of all the hardware-intensive, fault-tolerant capabilities provided by the VAXft 310. The system boots on the standard VMS kernel used by all VAX processors and requires the VAXft System Services, a layered product, to provide completely fault-tolerant functionality.

Booting

The system can be configured to boot automatically or manually. The automatic reboot has safeguards to insure that only one copy of the operating system is running, even if the two zones cannot communicate. Many factors are considered to make sure that two zones do not boot at the same time. These considerations include the following:

- Are the zones connected?
- Is the other zone powered off?
- Has the other CPU previously failed?
- Is the other zone being repaired?

Before the start of the boot process, the two zones are independent computers cabled together but logically disconnected. The system logically looks like Figure 11–7. If both zones are available, the clocks in both zones are brought into synchronization. The nonbooting zone releases its I/O devices to the booting zone, thus causing the CPU/memory pair for the nonbooting zone to be disconnected from the I/O structure of the machine. Consequently, the booting zone is in control of all I/O. The system is booted on one CPU, and the other zone's CPU and memory

FIGURE 11–7
System before boot, with no logical connection between zones

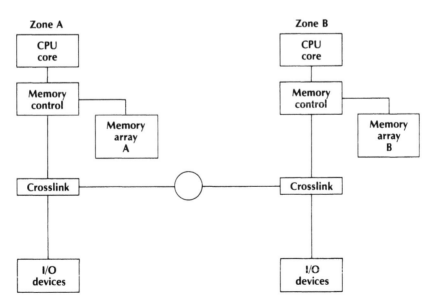

modules are left out of the booting process. During the boot process, the system configuration logically looks like Figure 11–8. Up to this point in the boot process, the only communication possible between the CPUs in the different zones has been through the serial crosslink. The serial crosslink is a replicated, full-duplex, asynchronous serial link between the CPUs.

Resynchronization

Memory synchronization is a system process that makes the memory contents in both zones equal. The memory in the zone where the operating system is running can be designated memory A. The memory in the zone where the operating system is not running can be designated memory B. During the resynchronization process the system configuration logically looks like Figure 11–9.

While the operating system is running, the contents of memory A must be transferred into memory B. This copy operation starts at the bottom of memory A and continues until the top of memory A is reached. However, the copy operation alone does not achieve memory equality. While the copy is being performed, the operating system is still running; therefore, memory write operations are occurring. These writes can be to locations in memory A that were previously copied to memory B; thus, memory B no longer has an up-to-date copy of those pieces of data. The hardware solves this problem by sending any write performed by memory A across to memory B by way of the parallel crosslink.

Once the memory has been copied, the operating system moves all its state information into main memory. (Note that these values are also being sent to memory B as described above.) Once the state information is in main memory, the two CPUs simultaneously perform a hardware reset. The CPUs in both zones then restore the system context from main memory. The system continues operation with both zones in lock-step, as shown in Figure 11–10.

FIGURE 11–8
System during boot, with zone B having no connection to I/O devices

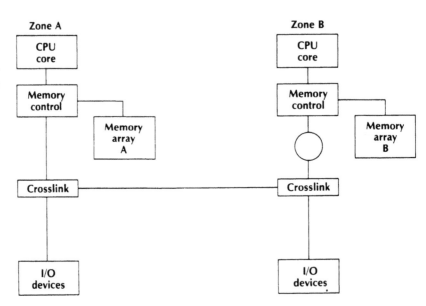

FIGURE 11–9
System during re-synchronization, with zone B having no connection to memory

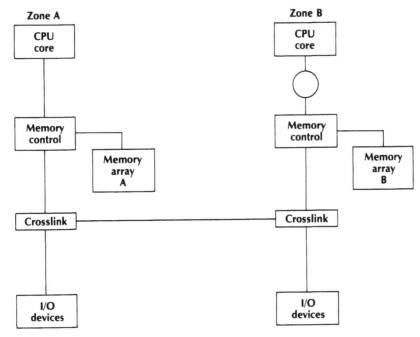

FIGURE 11–10
Operation of two-zone system, with both CPU modules acting as one logical CPU

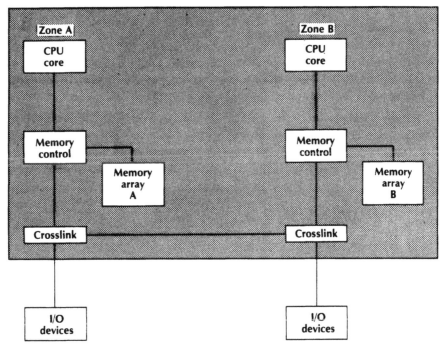

Fault Management

Fault management consists of error detection, recovery, and faulted device restoration. The hardware provides the error detection and error confinement. If a fault is transient, the system notes that an error occurred, and continues. If after a retry the fault is still present, the fault is declared solid and the offending hardware is no longer utilized by the system. The system utilizes trace memory to determine the faulty hardware. The trace memory system is described in detail in the next section. Even if all hardware retries are successful, a device is removed from service by the operating system if retries are too frequent. In the case of a recovery from either a transient or a hard fault, the operating system insures data integrity before passing data to an application.

Service

Fault-tolerant systems support mission-critical applications in which the cost of downtime is extremely high. System failures occur when one element fails, and prior to the repair of that element, the redundant element also fails. The time from when an element fails until it is repaired has a very significant impact on the predicted MTBF of the system.

The system has been designed for ease of repair while minimizing risks associated with service mistakes. It has been designed so that repairs can be made to one zone while the other zone continues normal system operation. The following features facilitate early detection for system faults and ensure quick repair:

- Autonotification, whereby the system dials out and reports failures to Digital Field Service, or to the user organization's service capability, or to both
- Isolation and reporting of faults down to the single FRU
- Thresholding, whereby the system can manage intermittent hardware faults by logging the errors and continuing in operation with full redundancy
- Repair of the system without interruption of the running application
- Ease of maintenance, with all subsystems being front-accessible for ease of access and repair and with modules having fault indicators on board for easy identification of the failing FRU.
- Swapping of DSSI disks and tapes without special tools or shutting down a zone of the system

DETAILS OF VAXft 310 OPERATION

Error Handling

The two basic tasks that error recovery mechanisms perform are recovery of the faulted operation and identification of the repair action to be taken. Recovery from an error requires knowing what operation faulted. Repair of a system requires knowing which FRU failed.

The design of error recovery mechanisms must take into account the profile of the faults. Current data indicate that transient faults occur more frequently than solid faults. Since transient faults, by definition, are not repeatable, only the information collected at the time of a fault is available for fault isolation. If sufficient information for isolation is collected for transient faults, it is also sufficient for solid faults. Therefore, error isolation was designed for transient faults.

Recovery from transient faults does not require the removal of the element that faulted. When recovering from a transient fault, a retry will be successful. However, the recovery from solid faults cannot be a simple retry; rather, an alternate element must be used to replace the failed one. If transient faults occur too frequently, a transient fault is reclassified as a solid fault.

Trace Memory System. In many cases, knowing which error occurred also identifies the failing FRU. When this is not sufficient, additional data is available from trace memories. The trace memories are bus monitors that capture bus activities. When a fault is detected, the trace memories cease capturing bus activity, so the trace memories hold a snapshot of the bus activity just prior to and after the fault. The trace memories are located in the dual-rail portion of the system and, thus, occur in pairs. If the trace data from a pair of memories is equal, a fault did not pass through that point. If the trace data is not equal, a fault passed through that point of the machine. The fault can be isolated by noting the transition from equal to unequal. If there is no transition from equal to unequal, the fault entered the system prior to the location of the first trace memory.

Error Recovery Mechanisms. In this system, there are three types of error recovery mechanisms.

• *Standard adapter error handling* is used with the single rail portion of I/O devices. The adapter software handles adapter errors that are detected by the interface chips. Typical types of adapter errors are EDC errors on incoming data, a timeout on an operation, and so on. Recovery from an adapter error involves retrying operations and, if a retry is not successful, failing over to an alternate unit.

• *Automatic hardware retries* are performed when a fault is detected during an I/O read or I/O write operation. A reset is performed to clear out any latent effects of the fault, and then the operation is retried. If the fault was transient, the retry will succeed. For occasional transient faults, retries are sufficient to keep the machine running with no loss of redundancy. If operation failed because one CPU pair was in error, the faulted CPU/memory pair is removed from the system configuration by the hardware. Removal occurs prior to the retry, and the retry will therefore be successful. The other zone's CPU is notified of the fault by activating the software error handler. Note that a CPU/memory pair will be removed from the system even if the fault on the CPU/memory pair is transient. The CPU and memory context cannot be guaranteed after such a fault. The CPU/memory pair is therefore removed from the system. It can be brought back in by running the resynchronization process.

• *The software error handler* activates any time an error is detected. For transient faults, the software handler keeps a threshold count and logs the event. If the fault is solid or the transient fault activity exceeds a given threshold, the software error handler will remove the failing element from the system configuration.

Fault Detection Mechanisms. The system contains both dual-rail and single-rail structures. The rail structure of a zone is shown in Figure 11–11. For the dual-rail areas of the system, hardware cross-checking is used to detect faults. Fault detection on single-rail logic is done with error-detection codes (EDC). The main memory fault detection mechanism is hardware based and described in further detail in the section on the memory controller.

The fault detection mechanism for the single-rail I/O modules is a combination of hardware and communication protocols. The system performs I/O operations by sending and receiving message packets. The packets are exchanged between the CPU and various servers that include disks, Ethernet, and synchronous lines. These message packets are formed and interpreted in a fault-tolerant environment (that is, the duplicated self-checked processors). After a packet is formed, it is transmitted through an I/O subsystem to the packet's final destination. The final destination can be an Ethernet, a disk drive on the DSSI bus, or a synchronous line.

The packets of data are transferred from the CPU module to the I/O module by a direct memory access (DMA) engine. When a packet is transferred, an appropriate EDC is calculated

FIGURE 11–11
*Rail architecture of
the VAXft 310*

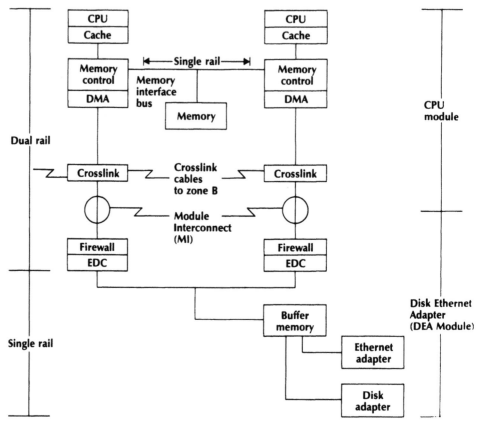

on the packet. Once the packet is placed on the I/O module, the CPU directs the I/O module to deliver the packet to its final destination. Reads and writes to an I/O register are used to control this routing of packets. When the CPU module converses with the I/O registers, a failure of either a read or writer operation cannot compromise packet integrity. A faulty I/O register read or write operation can result in one of the following: no error, a corrupted packet, or a lost packet.

For example, a packet of information destined for the Ethernet is initially formed inside the main memory, and then it is moved with the DMA operation into I/O buffer memory. Note that there is a duplication of the data path from the memory controller to the I/O Firewall chip (see Figure 11–11). The I/O buffer memory is not duplicated; therefore an EDC is appended to maintain checking. On transmitted packets, this EDC is generated in the firewalls and is appended to the packet. The packet is then transmitted by the adapter. The receiving adapter is responsible for checking the validity of the packet's EDC.

Incoming packets are placed into the I/O buffer memory with the EDC still appended. When the data is transferred by the DMA engine to main memory, the EDC is checked by the firewalls. Thus, the EDC is retained on incoming packets until duplicate data streams are available for checking. The packet that is placed into main memory has the same degree of data integrity as it had coming into the system.

The details of recovering from faults, once detected, are different for each of the I/O module's adapters. However, all of the adapters must (1) use an alternate path or device if a solid fault is detected and (2) recover from duplicate or missing packets.

CPU Module and Memory Module Details

The CPU module is part of the system's dual-rail architecture. In each zone, the CPU module has identical CVAX CPUs, memory controllers, and crosslink interfaces that are interconnected by independent, identical, internal buses.

The CPU and memory are treated as a single functional unit. There is no provision for a CPU in one zone to operate the memory in the other zone; to do so would impose a significant performance impact. The systems must be configured with equal amounts of memory in both zones. The CPU/memory pair is composed of the CPU core, the memory controller, the main memory, and the crosslink. The CPU, memory controller, and crosslink are full, dual-rail implementations that are replicated for self-checking. However, the main memory is far too expensive and bulky to replicate on a rail-by-rail basis. Thus, for main memory, robust error checking and correction, rather than duplication, are used to achieve the required fault tolerance.

CPU Core. In each zone, the CPU core exists on each of the zone's two rails. It consists of the following elements: CVAX processor chip, floating point processor, 32 KB cache, 160 KB code ROM, 32 KB EEPROM, and 8 KB local scratch-pad memory.

The CVAX chip set is a CMOS implementation of the VAX architecture (CVAX). A floating point accelerator is part of the chip set. The CVAX has a 1 KB internal cache memory, which is supplemented by an external 32 KB cache.

Each rail of the CPU module contains the ROM code necessary to run the system console, diagnostics, and the bootstrap loader. This code can be modified or enhanced through a code patch space provided by a 32 KB EEPROM. This EEPROM also contains system parameters, such as serial numbers, network IDs, and boot parameters. Each rail also has a local scratch-pad memory for use for console, diagnostics, boot, and error processing.

Neither the memories, buses, nor processors require special checking codes because their outputs are replicated on the dual-rail CPU module. An error in any of the cache memories results in the two rails of the CPU module not producing the same outputs; this will be caught by the checking logic in the memory controllers.

Memory Controller. The memory controller is responsible for handling the interface between the processor, the memory arrays, and the crosslink. Both the processor and the crosslink are dual-rail structures, while the memory arrays are a single-rail structure. The memory controller provides the following capabilities:

- Interface of the processor to main memory
- Interface of the processor to I/O structure
- Arbitration of DMA transfers for main memory
- DMA transfer to I/O adapters
- Main memory checking
- Lock-step detection of errors between the dual-rail processors
- Hardware error recovery

The conventional interface functions listed here are not discussed in any further detail because they have no real impact on the fault tolerance of the system. However, the details for the following capabilities of memory control are presented: DMA transfers, main memory checks, lock-step detection, and hardware error recovery.

DMA Transfers. The DMA engine is a conventional design that includes a source and destination address, as well as a transfer length. DMA transfers occur between two main memories and an I/O buffer memory. Thus, there are three memories involved in a normal DMA operation: the main memory of zone A, the main memory of zone B, and the I/O buffer memory. These memories are shown in Figure 11–12. The DMA engine is implemented so that a failure in any one of these three pieces will result in the corruption of only one zone's memory or an unsuccessful transfer.

In this system, the DMA activity is restricted to a single I/O module at a time. The DMA engines in both zones' memory controllers are given a queue describing the DMA functions that are to be performed. The DMA engine extracts a request from this queue and completes it before

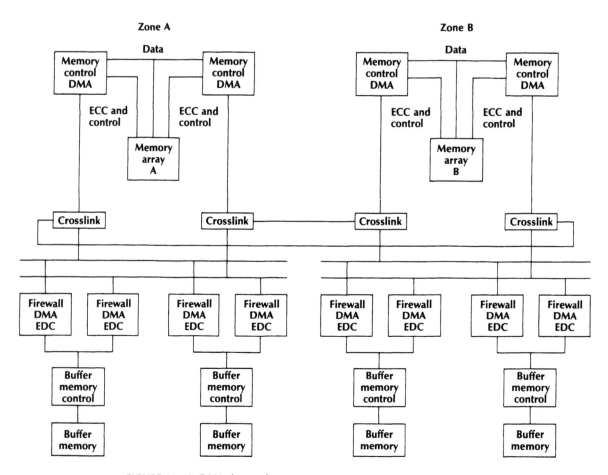

FIGURE 11–12 *DMA data paths*

going back to the queue for another request. A DMA operation involves a DMA setup followed by a number of data subtransfers. Setup defines the standard DMA parameters such as address and transfer length. Setup also selects the I/O module and defines the DMA data path through the crosslinks. When the DMA data subtransfers are started, no routing information is passed along with the data, since the setup already selected the correct data path. Subtransfers are bursts of data occurring at main memory bandwidth.

Each DMA request involves both zones' main memories and a single I/O module. All subsequent DMA subtransfers will be with the selected I/O module until the DMA engine does the setup for the next request. The structure of the DMA engine in the main memory controller and the I/O buffer memory includes a main memory address counter/pointer or an I/O buffer memory address counter/pointer (either source or destination depending upon data direction), as well as a transfer byte counter.

The following four examples illustrate the value of using this structure for the DMA engine.

1. During a DMA write of main memory, a fault in one zone's main memory-addressing logic will result in writing the wrong location in that particular main memory. Neither I/O buffer memory nor the other zone's main memory are destroyed. Therefore, the recovery procedure is to remove the corrupted CPU/memory pair from the system configuration.

2. During a DMA read of main memory, a fault in a zone's main memory-addressing logic results in the I/O buffer memory containing a corrupted packet. The zone's main memory that experienced the addressing error will be removed from the system, and the packet will be recopied to the I/O buffer memory using only the other zone's main memory.

3. During a DMA write of main memory, a fault in an I/O buffer memory results in both main memories having a corrupted data packet detected with EDC. Recovery is accomplished by re-accessing the data. The original data is still available in either the I/O buffer memory or on the device being assessed (that is, the disk).

4. During a DMA read of main memory, a fault in the I/O buffer memory-addressing logic results in corrupting the I/O buffer memory. The recovery for this is to either recopy the data, or failout the I/O adapter with the corrupted buffer memory and use the alternate I/O adapter to re-issue the DMA read of main memory data.

Main Memory Checks. There are a variety of checking schemes used in the memory controller and in main memory. The schemes were chosen based on the type of coverage that is needed. For DRAM cells, single-bit errors are expected due to alpha particle collisions. Therefore single-bit errors need to be corrected as well as detected. This requires some form of error-correcting code. Addressing errors can affect the integrity of a single DRAM chip all the way up to the entire memory subsystem. Replication of the addressing logic provides a simple and consistent means of covering addressing across all levels. The connections between the memory controllers and the memory module are shown in Figure 11–13.

Three different checks are done at the memory interface: ECC detection and correction, data comparison, and address and control comparison. The data in main memory is protected by an ECC code. This code is capable of detecting any double-bit error and correcting any single-bit error. When data is read from main memory, the memory array checks the correctness of the ECC on data that is retrieved from the DRAMs. The memory controllers also check the ECC code received from the memory array. If the memory controllers and the memory array do not all agree that the last read was either good or in error, then a CPU/MEMORY fault has occurred for that CPU/memory pair. This is done to protect from failures that the ECC code is not capable of detecting. For example, if a memory data bus driver fails, multiple bits could be in error, but the

FIGURE 11–13
Memory interface

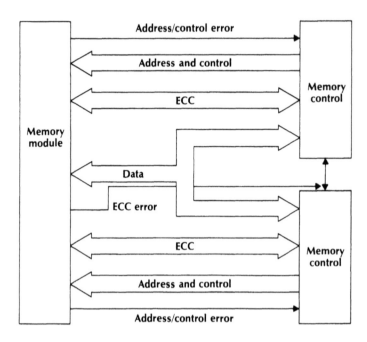

memory control chips could both indicate a correctable single-bit error. This is because the memory array is looking at the data before the drivers; thus, the memory array will not see the errors introduced by the drivers. A single-bit error will be corrected by the memory controllers. This correction occurs without affecting access time and, consequently, it does not affect lock-step operation. Single-bit error correction only insures that the system uses correct data; it does not correct the main memory location.

A single-bit error experienced on one zone's memory does not occur on the other zone's memory because the system is using two totally separate main memory arrays. After a single-bit error has been corrected, the rewrite of the faulted memory location must be done to prevent the single-bit error from becoming a double-bit error. (A double-bit error will also cause a CPU/MEMORY fault for a CPU/memory pair.) This rewrite must be performed without causing the system to lose lock-step operation. The rewrite operation is handled as a background task of the system. Each memory array maintains the address of the memory location read with an error. Thus, when the rewrite is performed, there can be up to eight memory locations flagged as needing correction (up to four modules in each of two zones). A special set of communication registers is built into the system to let each zone share the unique data it possesses (in this case, the memory addresses) without losing instruction lock-step. Basically, both zones write to a register in their own zones with the zone-unique data. Then, both zones read zone A's register and both zones read zone B's register. Both zones then know the complete list of all memory locations that need to be updated. When processing updates to the memory locations, both zones must rewrite every location on the list; rewriting corrects the memory location of the zone that has the error, but it is harmless to the other zone's memory.

During a write, the ECC code is generated in each memory controller and passed in duplicate to the memory arrays. The ECC received from both memory controllers must match. An ECC is also produced by the memory array using the received data. The ECC that is generated must match the pair of ECC codes received from the memory controllers. the memory array does not perform any comparison of the data from the memory controllers. Rather, one memory controller drives the data onto the memory bus, and both memory controllers read and check the data.

The memory array receives redundant address and control signals from the memory controllers. The address and control signals are checked for all memory operations. Any errors produce a CPU/MEMORY fault and remove the failing CPU/memory pair from the system configuration. The memory array uses a number of schemes internally to prevent latent faults from causing undetectable errors. The control engine in the memory array is replicated and checked against itself. Additionally, the control lines to the DRAM chips are laid out in a serial path in the printed circuit etch. The control lines are driven by one of the control engines. Both control engines check the control lines to insure that the end of the path received the same signals as the beginning. Any failures in the control engines will cause a CPU/MEMORY fault.

Lock-Step Detection. The memory data bus is connected between the CPU cores and is used as a comparison point for detecting lock-step failure within a zone. This connection can easily be seen in Figure 11–11. If the operation is destined for main memory, then the lock-step detection is done by the main memory checking that has been previously described. For I/O operations, the address and data are placed in successive cycles on the memory bus for checking by the memory controllers. Thus, in combination with main memory checking, complete coverage (at the point where data first leaves the CPU core) is provided for detecting the failure of lock-step operation for a CPU/memory pair.

Hardware Error Recovery. The same checking hardware that provides lock-step detection also insures that data sourced by the I/O adapters will not be rail unique (each rail having unique data) at the time of entry into the CPU core. Any time rail-unique data is read by the CPU core, the hardware automatically substitutes zeroes for data, insuring that the processors will not take different execution paths due to erroneous data. The adapter error-handling software can deal with incorrect data read from the I/O adapters, as long as the incorrect data is consistent and the I/O adapter notifies the adapter software.

Any error that indicates a difference between two core CPUs on a module is nonrecoverable. Any error that can corrupt the contents of main memory or allow corrupted data to reach the CPU core is nonrecoverable. In the case of a nonrecoverable error, the CPU/memory pair is automatically taken off line by the hardware. The contents of main memory or any CPU registers cannot be guaranteed after a nonrecoverable fault. Therefore, a complete restoration of the memory and CPU state must be performed. Before this can happen, the fault's profile must be determined as either a transient or a solid fault. The restoration of the CPU/memory pair is performed by the resynchronization process.

The effects of a failed I/O operation are confined. After an error is detected, either by the I/O module or the memory checks previously described, the operation can be retried by the hardware. On a retry, a special reset is issued to initialize the logic connecting the memory controller to the I/O module. This reset is important because it removes any latent effects of the fault. The operation is then re-issued. If the error does not reoccur, the fault is declared transient and the system continues operating. However, if the error occurs again, the fault is declared as solid, and a system routine is activated to analyze the error data and remove the failing module from service.

Crosslink. The crosslink provides the communications path between the CPU/memory pairs and the I/O subsystem. The crosslinks are also responsible for the interconnections between the two zones. The crosslink causes data moving to or from the I/O subsystem to experience exactly the same propagation delay (regardless of the source or destination zone). The crosslink on each rail of the CPU module is connected to the memory controller, the crosslink cable, and a zone's module interconnect (MI) bus. The MI bus supports up to five I/O modules.

The crosslink provides two different data paths between the zones: serial and parallel. The serial path is used to communicate between the two zones when the zones are not operating in lock-step. (This usually occurs prior to zone synchronization.) The parallel path provides the interconnect between zones when the zones are operating in lock-step.

The basic function of the crosslink is twofold: It can cause the I/O adapters of both zones to communicate with only one zone's CPU module, and it can cause the CPU modules to synchronously read and write to all I/O adapters. The crosslink functions are clock synchronization between zones, system initialization support, error reporting between zones, and interrupt coordination between zones.

Clock Synchronization. The system has two oscillators, one in each zone. Before the two zones can be operated as a single system, the clocks must be brought into synchronization. Clock reference signals from the other zone are available in each zone. One zone is selected as the clock master and the other as the clock slave. The clock in the master zone runs at a fixed frequency. The clock in the slave zone phase locks its oscillator to the master's oscillator. Each zone monitors a phase detector to verify phase lock. If a phase error is detected, the operating system remains running in one zone and the other zone is shut down. System software is then activated to reconfigure the I/O adapters.

System Initialization. The crosslinks are responsible for sequencing the resets that are required for powerup, error recovery, resynchronization, and disabling modules. There are three types of resets in the machine: soft, hard, and clock. A soft reset clears the paths between the CPU/memory pairs and the I/O subsystem prior to a retry of a failed bus operation. A hard reset sets all the hardware back to a known state, such as a power-up initialization. A clock reset is used to align the internal clock generators in various chips.

The resets are not tied between zones because this would result in a single point of failure for the system. The resets for a zone are controlled by that zone's CPU module so that the correct behavior for independent, lock-step operation is achieved. When both zones are running in lock-step, both zones are executing the same sequences and recovering from the errors. Whether requested by hardware or software, both zones will issue the reset request at the same time. When the operating system is running totally within a single zone, there is no need to coordinate resets between zones. When the system is operating with one CPU/memory pair and both I/O zones, the resets to I/O must be propagated between zones. (The nonoperational CPU can reset only itself and not the I/O in its zone.)

There is only one case where the CPU in one zone has reset authority over the CPU in the other zone. After the memories have been copied during the resynchronization process, the master CPU initiates a reset sequence that simultaneously puts both CPU modules through a hard reset. At the completion of the reset, the designation between master CPU and slave CPU is removed; then, each CPU module manages all resets for its zone.

Error Reporting Between Zones. The crosslink provides an exchange of the current error status between zones. This exchange allows both zones to activate error recovery procedures in lock-step. A priority scheme is used to encode the errors so that each zone sees the most important error it experienced, as well as the most important error the other zone experienced. The errors reported between zones are the following.

• A *clock phase error,* as previously explained, is when the oscillators between zones lose phase lock. This loss results in an automatic termination of the parallel crosslink data path. System software sets the oscillator in each zone as a clock master to prevent the faulted oscillator from affecting the accuracy of the system clocks. The zone with the faulted oscillator will enter console mode and wait for a repair action. The nonfaulted zone will continue running the operating system and all applications. The system configures out the I/O adapters that physically reside in the no longer accessible zone and uses the alternate adapters to access devices.

• A *CPU/MEMORY fault* is the error reported when the memory controllers determine that the CPU/memory pair is no longer a valid computing device. When this error is encountered, the zone with the fault automatically becomes the slave and the nonreporting zone becomes the master, and the hardware automatically performs the reconfiguration of the I/O bus paths at the crosslink. Any bus operation in progress at the time of the error will be retried. The hardware reconfiguration of the system is completed prior to the retry, so the retry operation will complete successfully.

• An *I/O miscompare* is the error reported when a fault is detected during a CPU core access of I/O. I/O miscompares are caused by faults in the path between CPUs and I/O adapters. When this error is detected, the buses are reset and the operation is retried. The system is then notified of the success or failure of this retry. If the retry was unsuccessful, software error handling is invoked to switch to an alternate adapter.

• A *DMA error* is reported when a fault is detected during a DMA operation. The DMA operation is terminated and error-handling software is activated to process the error information. The error-handling software will either retry the DMA operation or reconfigure the system.

In addition to reporting errors between zones, the crosslink is also responsible for coordinating the freezing and unfreezing of the trace memory system. When a zone reports an error to a crosslink, the trace data collection is stopped throughout that zone. If the two zones are running in lock-step, the trace memories in both zones are stopped at the same time. When the error-handling software has finished with the trace memory data, the capture process is unfrozen in both zones.

Interrupt Coordination Between Zones. The two CPU/memory pairs receive the same interrupt at the same time in order to maintain lock-step operation. The crosslinks scan for the highest-priority interrupt in their own zone. The crosslinks also exchange interrupt levels between zones and provide both CPU/memory pairs with the highest interrupt level of the two zones. The interrupt logic is set up so that if there is a failure in some part of its circuitry, the crosslink can declare an improper interrupt sequence. Error-handling software is used to threshold I/O adapters and the CPU/memory pairs on improper interrupt sequences; when the threshold is exceeded, the offender is removed from the system configuration.

I/O Modules

All I/O modules use the same interface chip (Firewall) to attach to the MI bus. The Firewall provides a fault-tolerant interface between the synchronous MI bus and the asynchronous microprocessor bus on the I/O module. The Firewall is so named because it prevents errors occurring in the I/O modules from corrupting data in the CPU/memory pairs. The Firewall provides a number of features, including EDC generation/checking hardware, dual bus error checking, and trace reader.

As explained in the subsection on DMA transfers, EDC codes play an important role in providing data integrity for I/O data packets. The EDC generator/checkers reside in the Firewall chip. For each different supported EDC, two versions of the generator/checker are provided. One version of the EDC generator/checker supports parallel calculation, and the other supports serial calculation. Parallel calculation is required to keep up with the DMA transfer throughput of the system, and serial calculation is necessary to finish the EDC calculation when the parallel width is not a multiple of the packet size. For example, calculating a cyclic redundancy check over 49 bytes is handled by doing a parallel calculation over 48 bytes, followed by a serial calculation using the last byte.

Dual MI buses connect to an I/O module, one MI bus to each Firewall chip. A single microprocessor bus provides an interface between the adapters on the I/O module to both Firewalls. One Firewall controls the microprocessor bus based on commands received from its MI bus. The other Firewall monitors the microprocessor bus to verify proper operation of that bus. Any errors detected on the microprocessor bus are reported to the memory controller.

Each rail of a zone is connected to a different trace bus. Each trace memory has its own trace address on the zone's serial trace bus. The trace reader in the Firewall provides access to the trace memories for that rail. The microprocessor on a zone's DEA module accesses the trace memory, using the Firewalls of that module to read both rails. As the data is read, the microprocessor performs the comparison between the rails and produces a comparison signature for that zone. The error-handling software running in the CPU modules reads the trace signature from the DEA module in each zone and analyzes the results.

Notice that there is no restriction on the microprocessor using rail-unique data, because the microprocessor is single rail and is not in lock-step with any other microprocessor in the system. The rail-unique data is moved into the single-rail I/O module through a bus structure that is totally separate from the MI bus. Once the data has been moved to a single-rail environment, the CPU module can safely access the data.

SUMMARY

The goal for the VAXft 310 was to provide a hardware-intensive, fault-tolerant VAX system to satisfy the demands of the fault-tolerant marketplace. The VAXft 310 supplies transparent application fault tolerance with no single point of hardware failure. This concept was also extended to include no single point of repair. Thus, any part of the system can be replaced without terminating the operating system.

The major architectural cornerstones that are present in the VAXft 310 hardware design are physically separate zones, dual-rail checking, ECC/EDC checking, support systems (environmental monitoring and battery backup), hardware redundancy, fault-isolation hardware, and fault-tolerant system services.

The design relies heavily upon detection and recovery mechanisms already present in VAX systems, such as the disks and Ethernet. In some areas, such as memory, conventional error detection was augmented with additional checking to overcome shortcomings of these mechanisms. Finally, entirely new checking and recovery mechanisms were added when conventional checking and recovery techniques were neither sufficient nor extensible; for example, the duplication of the CPU chips for checking and the duplication of the CPU modules for redundancy. Table 11–2 represents examples of implementation techniques that DEC used to satisfy the design goals.

TABLE 11–2 *Techniques used to meet the VAXft 310 design goals*

Digital Implementation	Design Goal Satisfied	Reason
Battery backup	High system MTBF	Most common cause of conventional system outages
Two cabinets	No single point of repair	All components replaceable without outage; minimizes service errors
Two cabinets	High system MTBF	Reduces servicing risks
CVAX chip set	VAX architecture	Supports VMS and over 6400 applications
Dual CPUs	Compute integrity	Duplication for checking
Two CPU modules	High system MTBF	Duplication for redundancy
Lock-step CPU operation	High system MTBF	Rapid failover
I/O CRC protection	Data integrity	Allows protection of data while still using standard interface components

APPENDIXES

APPENDIX A

Error-Correcting Codes for Semiconductor Memory Applications:
A State-of-the-Art Review

C. L. Chen and M. Y. Hsiao*

This appendix presents a state-of-the-art review of error-correcting codes for computer semiconductor memory applications. The construction of four classes of error-correcting codes appropriate for semiconductor memory designs is described, and for each class of codes the number of check bits required for commonly used data lengths is provided. The implementation aspects of error correction and error detection are also discussed, and certain algorithms useful in extending the error-correcting capability for the correction of soft errors such as α-particle-induced errors are examined in some detail.

INTRODUCTION

In recent years *error-correcting codes* (ECCs) have been used increasingly to enhance the system reliability and the data integrity of computer semiconductor memory subsystems. As the trend in semiconductor memory design continues toward higher chip density and larger storage capacity, ECCs are becoming a more cost-effective means of maintaining a high level of system reliability [Levine and Myers, 1976; Richard, 1976; Lala, 1979; Ferris-Prabhu, 1979].

A memory system can be made fault tolerant with the application of an error-correcting code; i.e., the mean time between "failures" of a properly designed memory system can be significantly increased with ECC. In this context, a system "fails" only when the errors exceed the error-correcting capability of the code. Also, in order to optimize data integrity, the ECC should have the capability of detecting the most likely of the errors that are uncorrectable.

Error-correcting codes used in early computer memory systems were of the class of *single-error-correcting* and *double-error-detecting* (SEC-DED) codes invented by R. W. Hamming [Hamming, 1950]. An SEC-DED code is capable of correcting one error and detecting two errors in a codeword. The double-error-detecting capability serves to guard against data loss. In 1970, a new class of SEC-DED codes called *odd-weight-column* codes was published by Hsiao [Hsiao, 1970]. With the same coding efficiency, the odd-weight-column codes provide improvements over the Hamming codes in speed, cost, and reliability of the decoding logic. As a result, odd-weight-column codes have been widely implemented by IBM and the computer industry worldwide [Hsiao et al., 1981; Lin and Costello, 1983; Basham, 1976; Morris, 1980]. Examples of systems which incorporate these codes are the IBM 158, 168, 303X, 308X, and 4300 series, Cray I, Tandem, etc. There are also various standard part numbers of these codes offered by many semiconductor manufacturers [Siewiorek and Swarz, 1982] (for example, the AM2960 and AMZ8160 of Advanced Micro Devices, the MC68540 of Motorola, the MB1412A of Fujitsu, and the SN54/74 LS630, LS631 of Texas Instruments).

The number of errors generated in the failure of a memory chip is largely dependent on the chip failure type. For example, a cell failure may cause one error, while a line failure or a total

* Acknowledgment: The authors gratefully acknowledge the contributions made by D. C. Bowen.

chip failure in general causes more than one error. For ECC applications, the memory array chips are usually organized so that the errors generated in a chip failure can be corrected by the ECC. In the case of SEC-DED codes, the one-bit-per-chip organization is the most effective design. In this organization, each bit of codeword is stored in a different chip; thus, any type of failure in a chip can corrupt, at most, one bit of the codeword. As long as the errors do not line up in the same codeword, multiple errors in the memory are correctable.

Memory array modules are generally packaged on printed-circuit cards with current semi-conductor memory technology, and usually a group of bits from the same card form a portion of an ECC codeword, as illustrated in Figure A–1. With this multiple-bit-per-card type of organization, a failure at the card-support-circuit level would result in a byte error, where the size of the byte is the number of bits feeding from the card to a codeword. In this type of configuration, it is important for data integrity that the ECC be able to detect byte errors [Bossen, Chang, and Chen, 1978]. A SEC-DED code is in general not capable of detecting all single-byte errors. However, a class of SEC-DED codes capable of detecting all single-byte errors can be constructed [Reddy, 1978; Chen, 1983a]. These are called *single-error-correcting double-error-detecting single-byte-error-detecting* (SEC-DED-SBD) codes.

There are certain design applications where the memory array cannot be organized in one-bit-per-chip fashion because of cost or other reasons such as system granularity or power restrictions. As chip density increases, it becomes more difficult to design a one-bit-per-chip memory system. For a multiple-bit-per-chip type of memory organization, a *single-byte-error-correcting double-byte-error-detecting* (SBC-DBD) code [Berlekamp, 1968; Peterson and Weldon, 1972; Reed and Solomon, 1960; Kasami, Lin, and Peterson 1967; Wolf, 1969; Bossen, 1970] would be more effective in error correction and error detection.

System reliability generally tends to decrease as the capacity of a memory system increases. To maintain the same high level of reliability, a *double-error-correcting triple-error-detecting* (DEC-TED) code may be used. However, this type of code requires a larger number of check bits than an SEC-DED code and more complex hardware to implement the functions of error correction and error detection [Lin and Costello, 1983; Berlekamp, 1968; Peterson and Weldon, 1972].

An error-correcting code can be used to correct "soft" errors as well as hard errors. Soft errors are temporary errors such as α-particle-induced errors that disappear during the next memory write operation. With a maintenance strategy that allows the accumulation of hard errors, a high soft error rate would cause a high *uncorrectable error* (UE) rate. To reduce the UE rate that involves soft errors, an SEC-DED code can be modified to correct two hard errors or a combination

FIGURE A–1
A 4-bit-per-card memory array

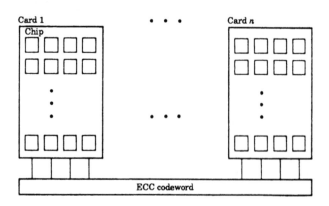

of one hard and one soft error [Carter and McCarthy, 1976; Sundberg, 1978; Lala, 1978; Nelson, 1982; Bossen and Hsiao, 1980].

In this appendix we review the current status of error-correcting codes for semiconductor memory applications and present the state of the art by describing the construction of four classes of error-correcting codes suitable for this type of design application. These four classes are SEC-DED codes, SEC-DED-SBD codes, SBC-DBD codes, and DEC-TED codes. For each class of code we provide the number of check bits required for commonly used data lengths, information that is particularly useful to designers for system planning. We also discuss the implementation aspects of error correction and error detection for these classes of error control codes. In addition, we describe a number of algorithms useful in extending the error-correcting capability of codes for the correction of soft errors such as α-particle-induced errors and other temporary errors.

BINARY LINEAR BLOCK CODES

A binary (n,k) linear block code is a k-dimensional subspace of a binary n-dimensional vector space [Lin and Costello, 1983; Berlekamp, 1968; Peterson and Weldon, 1972]. An n-bit codeword of the code contains k data bits and $r = n - k$ check bits. An $r \times n$ *parity check matrix* **H** is used to describe the code. Let $\mathbf{V} = (v_1, v_2, \ldots, v_n)$ be an n-bit vector. Then **V** is a codeword if and only if

$$\mathbf{H} \cdot \mathbf{V}' = 0 \tag{1}$$

where V' denotes the transpose of **V**, and all additions are performed modulo 2.

The *encoding* process of a code consists of generating r check bits for a set of k data bits. To facilitate encoding, the **H** matrix is expressed as

$$\mathbf{H} = [\mathbf{P}, \mathbf{I}_r] \tag{2}$$

where **P** is an $r \times k$ binary matrix and $\mathbf{I}_r$ is the $r \times r$ identity matrix. Then the first k bits of a codeword can be designated as the data bits, and the last r bits can be designated as the check bits. Furthermore, the ith check bit can be explicitly calculated from the ith equation of the set of r equations in (1). A code specified by an **H** matrix of (2) is called a *systematic code*.

Any binary $r \times n$ matrix **H** of rank r can always be transformed into the systematic form of (2). Since the rank of **H** is r, there exists a set of r linearly independent columns. The columns of the matrix can be reordered so that the rightmost r columns are linearly independent. Applying elementary row operations [Peterson and Weldon, 1972] on the resultant matrix, a matrix of (2) is obtained. The systematic code obtained is equivalent to the code defined by the original **H** matrix. Figure A–2(a) is an example of the parity check matrix of a (26,20) code in a nonsystematic form. Note that the last six columns of the matrix are linearly independent. The submatrix of the

FIGURE A–2
(26,20) code: (a) nonsystematic form; (b) system-atic form

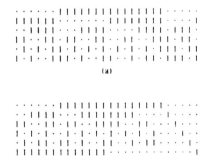

six columns can be inverted. The multiplication of the inverse of the submatrix and the transpose of the parity check matrix results in a matrix of systematic form shown in Figure A–2(b).

A word read from the memory may not be the same as the original codeword written in the same location. Let $U = (u_1, u_2, \ldots, u_n)$ be the word read from the memory. The difference between U and the original codeword V is defined as the *error vector* $E = (e_1, e_2 \ldots, e_n)$; i.e., $U = V + E$. The *i*th position of U is in error if and only if e_i is nonzero.

The *decoding process* consists of determining whether U contains errors and determining the error vector. To determine whether U is in error, an *r*-bit *syndrome* S is calculated as follows:

$$S = H \cdot U' = H \cdot (V' + E') = H \cdot E' \qquad (3)$$

If S is an all-zeros vector, the word U is assumed to be error-free. If S is a nonzero vector, it is used to determine the error vector.

The error-correcting capability of a code is closely related to the *minimum distance* of the code. The *weight* of a codeword is the number of nonzero components in the codeword. The *distance* between two codewords is the number of components in which the two codewords differ. The minimum distance *d* of the code is the minimum of the distances of all pairs of codewords. For a linear code, the minimum distance of the code is equal to the minimum of the weights of all nonzero codewords [Lin and Costello, 1983; Berlekamp, 1968; Peterson and Weldon, 1972]. A code is capable of correcting *t* errors and detecting *t* + 1 errors if and only if $d > 2t + 1$.

In semiconductor memory applications, the encoding and the decoding of a code are implemented in a parallel manner. In encoding, the check bits are generated simultaneously by processing the data bits in parallel. In decoding, the syndrome is generated using the same hardware for the generation of the check bits. The error vector is then generated by decoding the syndrome bits in parallel. Finally, the errors are corrected by subtracting the error vector from the fetched word. The subtraction is accomplished by the bit-by-bit exclusive-or (XOR) of the components of the two vectors.

The reliability function of a memory system that employs an error-correcting code can be handled either analytically or through Monte Carlo methods [Levine and Meyers, 1976; Richard, 1976; Lala, 1979; Ferris-Prabhu, 1979; Mikhail, Bartoldus, and Rutledge, 1982; Chen and Rutledge, 1984; Libson and Harvey, 1984]. For a system with a simple architecture, an analytical approach may be possible. However, for a memory system consisting of hierarchical arrays, the memory reliability function is too intractable to handle analytically. Monte Carlo methods are considered a general approach to study the effectiveness of error-correcting codes and other fault-tolerant schemes [Chen and Rutledge, 1984; Libson and Harvey, 1984].

To demonstrate the reliability improvement obtainable with ECC, we consider three memory systems of four megabytes. The first system consists of eight memory cards and is designed with a parity check on each set of eight data bits. The second system consists of 18 memory cards and is designed with a (72,64) SEC-DED code. The last system consists of 20 memory cards and is designed with an (80,64) DEC-TED code. The memory chips for the systems are 16K-bit chips with 128 bit lines and 128 word lines in each chip. Each memory card contains an array of 32 × 9 chips for the first system, and an array of 32 × 4 chips for the other two systems. The failure rates of the chips and the card-support circuits are assumed to be the same as those described in Chen and Rutledge [1984]. When a UE occurs, the strategy is to replace the card that contains the UE and that has the largest number of defective cells.

The modeling tool of Chen and Rutledge [1984] is used to simulate the reliability of the three memory systems. The results of the simulation are shown in Table A–1. The improvement factor of ECC over the parity check scheme on the number of UEs is over 15 for SEC-DED code and over 84 for DEC-TED code.

TABLE A–1

Average number of uncorrectable errors (UEs) with three memory systems employing different error control schemes: parity check, SEC-DED code, and DEC-TED code

Time (× 10^3 hrs.)	Parity Check	SEC-DED	DEC-TED
0–10	49	3.2	0.56
0–20	81	5.2	0.96
0–30	111	6.9	1.3
0–50	168	9.3	2.0
0–80	253	13	2.9

Parity check: (9,8) code.   SEC-DED: (72,64) code.   DEC-TED: (80,64) code.

SEC-DED CODES

The minimum distance of a single-error-correcting and double-error-detecting (SEC-DED) code is greater than or equal to four. Since an *n*-tuple of weight three or less is not a codeword, from Eq. (1) the sum of a set of three or fewer columns of the **H** matrix must be nonzero. In other words, any set of three columns of the **H** matrix are linearly independent. Thus, the **H** matrix of a SEC-DED code must satisfy the following conditions:

A1. The column vectors of the **H** matrix are nonzero and are distinct.

A2. The sum of two columns of the **H** matrix is nonzero and is not equal to a third column of the **H** matrix.

Note that the sum of two odd-weight *r*-tuples is an even-weight *r*-tuple. A SEC-DED code with *r* check bits can be constructed with its **H** matrix consisting of distinct nonzero *r*-tuples of odd weights. This is an odd-weight-column code of Hsiao [1970].

The maximum code length of an odd-weight-column code with *r* check bits is 2^{r-1}, for there are 2^{r-1} possible distinct odd-weight *r*-tuples. This maximum code length is the same as that of a SEC-DED Hamming code. The maximum number of data bits *k* of a SEC-DED code must satisfy $k \leq 2^{r-1} - r$. The following table lists the number of check bits required for a set of data bits:

Data Bits	Check Bits
8	5
16	6
32	7
64	8
128	9
256	10

Figure A–3 shows examples of SEC-DED codes used in some IBM systems.

Most of the SEC-DED codes for semiconductor memory applications are *shortened codes* in that the code length is less than the maximum for a given number of check bits. There are various ways of shortening a maximum-length SEC-DED code. Usually a code designer constructs a shortened code to meet certain objectives for a particular application. These objectives may include the minimization of the number of circuits, the amount of logic delay, the number of part numbers, or the probability of miscorrecting triple errors [Hsiao, 1970].

In a write operation, check bits are generated simultaneously by processing the data bits in a parallel manner according to Eqs. (1) and (2). In a read operation, syndrome bits are generated

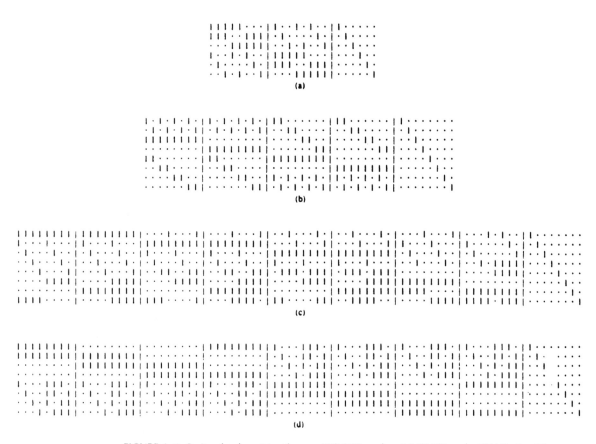

FIGURE A–3 *Parity check matrix of some SEC-DED codes: (a) (22,16) code (IBM System/3); (b) (40,32) code (IBM 8130); (c) (72,64) code (IBM 3033); (d) (72,64) code (IBM 3081)*

simultaneously from the word read according to Eq. (3). Typically the same XOR tree is used to generate both the check bits and the syndrome bits (see Figure A–4).

An algorithm for correcting single errors and detecting multiple errors is described as follows:

1. Test whether S is **0**. If S is **0**, the word is assumed to be error-free.
2. If S ≠ **0**, try to find a perfect match between S and a column of the H matrix. The match can be implemented in n r-way AND gates.
3. If S is the same as the ith column of **H**, then the ith bit of the word is in error.
4. If S is not equal to any column of **H**, the errors are detected as uncorrectable (UE).

This algorithm applied to a SEC-DED code corrects all single errors and detects all double errors. Multiple-bit errors may be detected or falsely corrected. The extent of multiple errors detected depends on the structure of the code.

As shown in Figure A–5, hardware implementation of the error correction and detection

FIGURE A–4
Generation of check bits and syndrome bits

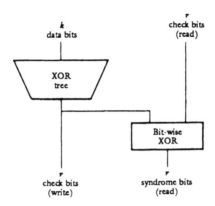

FIGURE A–5
Error detection and correction block diagram

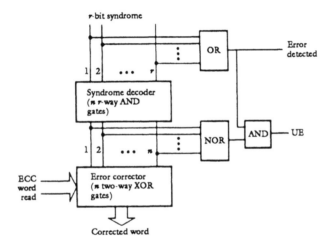

mainly consists of an *r*-way OR gate for testing nonzero syndrome, *n r*-way AND gates for decoding syndromes, an *n*-way NOR gate for generating UE signal, and *n* two-way XOR gates for inverting the code bit in error. Additionally, an *n*-bit data register and control logic for timing are required.

A UE signal can also be generated based on the logical OR of the minterms of all UE syndromes. A subset of all UE syndromes is the set of even-weight syndromes caused by even numbers of errors. This subset of syndromes can be recognized by an *r*-way XOR gate.

The failure of a common logic support in the memory may result in an all-ones or an all-zeros pattern in a codeword. In this case, the error vector in general contains a multiple number of errors that are not detectable by an SEC-DED code. To prevent this kind of data loss, the code can be constructed or modified so that an all-ones or an all-zeros *n*-tuple is not a codeword. For example, if the check bits are inverted before the codeword is written into the memory, then all the codewords stored in the memory are nonzero. In general, the detection of all-ones and all-zeros errors can be achieved by inverting a subset of the check bits [Basham, 1976].

SEC-DED-SBD CODES

In some applications it is required that the memory array chips be packaged in a *b*-bits-per-chip organization. A chip failure or a word-line failure in this case would result in a byte-oriented error that contains from 1 to *b* erroneous bits. Byte errors can also be caused by the failures of the supporting modules at the memory card level. The class of SEC-DED codes that are capable of detecting all single-byte errors (SEC-DED-SBD codes) may be used to maintain data integrity in these applications.

The **H** matrix of an SEC-DED-SBD code can be divided into N blocks of $r \times b$ submatrices, $\mathbf{B_1}, \mathbf{B_2}, \ldots, \mathbf{B_n}$, where $\mathbf{B_i}$ represents the parity checks for byte position i. From (3), the syndrome of a byte error at position i is a sum of the columns of $\mathbf{B_i}$ that correspond to the bit error positions within the byte. The syndromes of all possible byte errors at position i are the sum of all possible combinations of the columns of $\mathbf{B_i}$. Let $\langle \mathbf{B_i} \rangle$ denote the sums of all possible nonzero linear combinations of the columns of $\mathbf{B_i}$. Each member of $\langle \mathbf{B_i} \rangle$ should be nonzero and should not be equal to a column of $\mathbf{B_j}$, for $j \neq i$. Otherwise, the byte error at position i will be mistaken as no error or as a correctable single error at position j. Thus, the **H** matrix of an SEC-DED-SBD code must satisfy the conditions A1 and A2 given previously, as well as the following condition:

A3. Each vector of $\langle \mathbf{B_i} \rangle$ is nonzero and is not equal to a column vector of $\mathbf{B_j}$, for $j \neq i$.

For $b \leq 4$, most of the SEC-DED codes for practical applications can be *reconfigured* to detect single-byte errors. The reconfiguration involves the regrouping or rewiring of the bit positions of the original code. Since the same encoding and decoding hardware can be used, no additional hardware is required if an SEC-DED code can be reconfigured for single-byte error detection. Figure A–6 illustrates some examples of SEC-DED-SBD codes. The codes in Figures

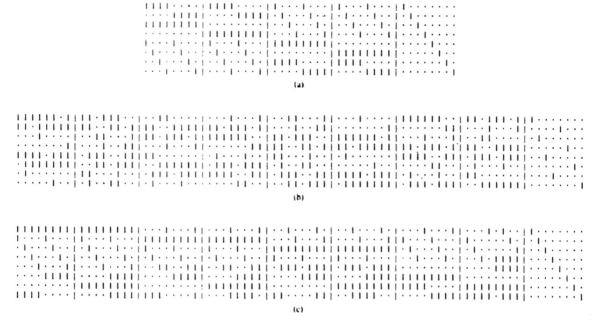

FIGURE A–6 *Examples of SEC-DED-SBD codes: (a) (40,32) code, b = 4; (b) (72,64) code, b = 4; (c) (72,64) code, b = 3 and b = 4*

A–6(a) and (b) are obtained from those in Figures A–3(b) and (d) by reconfiguration, and the code in Figure A–6(c) is the same as that in Figure A–3(c). The (72,64) codes of Figure A–6 are those used in IBM systems 3081 and 3033.

Techniques for the construction of SEC-DED-SBD codes have been presented in Reddy [1978] and Chen [1983a]. Let $N(r,b)$ be the code length in b-bit bytes. For $b = 3$, it is shown in Chen [1983a] that optimal codes with $N(r,3) = \lfloor 2^{r-1}/3 \rfloor$, where $\lfloor x \rfloor$ denotes the integer part of x, can be constructed. For other values of b, the construction of the longest code for a given r is an open question. A list of the code lengths of some known SEC-DED-SBD codes is given in Table A–2.

SBC-DBD CODES For a memory system packaged in a b-bits-per-chip organization, the reliability provided by a SEC-DED code may not be acceptable. To increase the reliability, a byte-oriented error-correcting code may be used [Berlekamp, 1968; Peterson and Weldon, 1972; Reed and Solomon, 1960; Kasami, Lin, and Peterson, 1967; Wolf, 1969; Bossen, 1970]. In this section, we discuss the construction and implementation of single-byte-error-correcting and double-byte-error-detecting (SBC-DBD) codes.

A codeword of an SBC-DBD code consists of N b-bit bytes. A binary b-tuple is considered an element of the finite field $GF(2^b)$ of 2^b elements [Lin and Costello, 1983; Berlekamp, 1968; Peterson and Weldon, 1972]. For example, all binary 3-tuples can be assigned as the elements of $GF(8)$:

$$0 = 0\ 0\ 0$$
$$x^0 = 1\ 0\ 0$$
$$x^1 = 0\ 1\ 0$$
$$x^2 = 0\ 0\ 1$$
$$x^3 = 1\ 1\ 0$$
$$x^4 = 0\ 1\ 1$$
$$x^5 = 1\ 1\ 1$$
$$x^6 = 1\ 0\ 1$$

In the finite-field representation of b-tuples, the sum of two elements is the bit-by-bit XOR of the two associated b-tuples. The product of two elements X^i and X^j is X^k with $k = i + j \bmod (2^b)$ $- 1$. For example, $X^3 + X^6 = (1\ 1\ 0) + (1\ 0\ 1) = (0\ 1\ 1) = X^4$, and $X^3 \cdot X^6 = X^2$ from the above list of elements of $GF(8)$.

With the finite-field representation, an SBC-DBD code is a linear code over $GF(2^b)$ with a minimum distance $d \geq 4$. The code can also be defined by the parity check matrix **H** of Eqs. (1) and (2), with the components of the matrices and vectors considered elements of $GF(2^b)$.

TABLE A–2
Code length in bytes for some SEC-DED-SBD codes

r	\multicolumn{7}{c}{b}
	3	4	5	6	7	8	9
$b + 1$	2	2	3	3	3	3	3
$b + 2$	5	6	7	8	9	10	11
$b + 3$	10	12	15	16	18	20	22
$b + 4$	21	26	31	36	41	46	51
$b + 5$	42	52	63	72	82	92	102
$b + 6$	85	106	127	148	169	190	211

Let h_i, $1 \le i \le N$, be the column vectors of the **H** matrix. The SBC-DBD code must satisfy the following conditions:

B1. $h_i \ne X \cdot h_j$ for $i \ne j$, $X \in GF(2^b)$.
B2. $h_i + X_1 \cdot h_j \ne X_2 \cdot h_f$, for distinct i, j, f, and $X_1, X_2 \in GF(2^b)$.

Let r be the number of check bytes of an SBC-DBD code over $GF(2^b)$. For $r = 3$, a code of length $N = 2 + 2^b$ bytes can be constructed by extending a Reed-Solomon code of length $(2^b) - 1$ [Berlekamp, 1968; Peterson and Weldon, 1972; Reed and Solomon, 1960; Kasami, Lin, and Peterson, 1967; Wolf, 1969]. The parity check matrix of the code can be expressed as

$$\mathbf{H} = \begin{bmatrix} \mathbf{I} & \mathbf{I} & \mathbf{I} & \cdots & \mathbf{I} & \mathbf{I} & \mathbf{O} & \mathbf{O} \\ \mathbf{I} & \mathbf{T} & \mathbf{T}^2 & \cdots & \mathbf{T}^{2^b-2} & \mathbf{O} & \mathbf{I} & \mathbf{O} \\ \mathbf{I} & \mathbf{T}^2 & \mathbf{T}^4 & \cdots & \mathbf{T}^{2(2^b-2)} & \mathbf{O} & \mathbf{O} & \mathbf{I} \end{bmatrix} \tag{4}$$

where **I** is the $b \times b$ identity matrix, **O** is a $b \times b$ all-zero matrix, **T** is the $b \times b$ companion matrix of X, and X is a *primitive element* of $GF(2^b)$ [Berlekamp, 1968; Peterson and Weldon, 1972]. If X is a root of the *primitive polynomial* $P(X) = a_0 + a_1X + a_2X^2 + \cdots + a_{b-1}X^{b-1}$, the companion matrix of X is

$$\mathbf{T} = \begin{bmatrix} 0 & 0 & \cdots & 0 & a_0 \\ 1 & 0 & \cdots & 0 & a_1 \\ 0 & 1 & \cdots & 0 & a_2 \\ \cdot & \cdot & \cdots & \cdot & \cdot \\ \cdot & \cdot & \cdots & \cdot & \cdot \\ 0 & 0 & \cdots & 1 & a_{b-1} \end{bmatrix}$$

For example, the companion matrix of X in the GF(8) listing on p. 779 is

$$\mathbf{T} = \begin{bmatrix} 0 & 0 & 1 \\ 1 & 0 & 1 \\ 0 & 1 & 0 \end{bmatrix}$$

and the **H** matrix for a (10,7) SBC-DBD code with $b = 3$ is shown in Figure A-7.

Using the **H** matrix of Eq. (4), the last three column positions of **H** can be designated as the positions of check bytes and the other column positions of **H** can be designated as data byte positions. The check bytes can be generated with an XOR tree just as in the case of SEC-DED codes. The syndrome can also be generated with the same XOR tree. For decoding, the syndrome **S** is divided into three parts, S_1, S_2, S_3. Each S_i consists of b bits and represents the parity check equations for the ith row of Eq. (4). From Eq. (3), if **E** is a single-byte error pattern at data byte position i, then **E** is a unique solution to the following three equations:

$$S_1 = E'$$

$$S_2 = T^i \cdot E'$$

$$S_3 = T^{2i} \cdot E'$$

On the other hand, if **E** is a byte error pattern at check byte position i, where $i = 1$, 2, or 3, then $E = S_i'$ and the other two subsyndromes are zeros. The following steps can be taken to find the correctable single-byte error patterns and to detect multiple uncorrectable byte errors.

FIGURE A–7
*(10,7) SBC-DBD
code with b = 3*

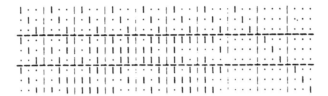

1. If **S** is a zero vector, assume that there is no error. If **S** is nonzero, go to step 2.
2. If one of the subsyndromes $S_i \neq \mathbf{0}$, and the other two subsyndromes are zero, $i = 1, 2, 3$, the check byte position i with error pattern S is assumed. Otherwise, go to step 3.
3. Assume that $\mathbf{E} = S_i'$. Find i that satisfies $0 \leq i < N - 4$, $\mathbf{T}^i \cdot \mathbf{E}' = \mathbf{S}_2$ and $\mathbf{T}^{2i} \cdot \mathbf{E}' = \mathbf{S}_3$. If i has a solution, the byte error with pattern **E** at data byte position i is assumed. If i has no solution, then an uncorrectable error is detected.

A block diagram for the generation of the error pointers for the code of Figure A–7 is shown in Figure A–8.

The extended Reed-Solomon codes defined in Eq. (4) are optimal in that no other SBC-DBD codes with three check bytes contain more data bytes. However, there exists only one code for a given byte size b. When b is small, the code may be too short for memory applications. For example, the code for $b = 2$ can only accommodate six data bits. This code certainly is not practical for most applications. In order to increase the code length for a given b, additional check bits are required.

Techniques for the construction of SBC-DBD codes for $r > 3$ can be found in [Berlekamp, 1968; Peterson and Weldon, 1972; Dao, 1973; Keneda and Fujiwara, 1982]. Table A–3 lists the minimum number of check bits required for some known SBC-DBD codes.

DEC-TED CODES

A memory system with a large capacity or with high chip failure rates may use a double-error-correcting and triple-error-detecting (DEC-TED) code to meet its reliability requirements. A DEC-TED code is also attractive for a memory with a high soft error rate. Although there are schemes [Carter and McCarthy, 1976; Sundberg, 1978; Lala, 1978; Nelson, 1982; Bossen and Hsiao, 1980], to be discussed in a subsequent section, for an SEC-DED code to correct hard-hard and hard-

FIGURE A–8
*Generation of error
vectors for a (10,7)
SBC-DBD code
with b = 3*

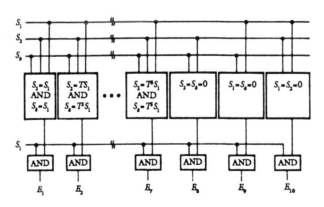

Bits per Byte	Data Bits per ECC Word			
	16	32	64	128
2	8	10	10	12
3	9	12	12	12
4	12	12	14	16
$b > 5$	$3b$	$3b$	$3b$	$3b$

soft types of double errors, these schemes cannot correct double soft errors and they require the interruption of a normal memory read operation. With a DEC-TED code, any combination of hard and soft double errors, including double soft errors, can be corrected automatically without system interruption.

A minimum distance of a DEC-TED code is at least equal to six. The parity check matrix **H** of a DEC-TED code must have the property that any linear combination of five or fewer columns of **H** is not an all-zeros vector.

A class of DEC-TED binary linear block codes can be constructed according to the theory of BCH codes [Lin and Costello, 1983; Berlekamp, 1968; Peterson and Weldon, 1972; Bose and Ray-Chaudhuri, 1960; Hocquenghem, 1959]. Let X be a root of a primitive binary polynomial $P(X)$ of degree m. The powers of X can be considered elements of $GF(N)$, $N = 2^m$, and can be expressed as binary m-tuples. A binary code defined by Eq. (1) with the following parity check matrix is a DEC-TED code:

$$\mathbf{H} = \begin{bmatrix} 1 & 1 & 1 & \cdots & 1 \\ 1 & X & X^2 & \cdots & X^{N-2} \\ 1 & X^3 & X^6 & \cdots & X^{3(N-2)} \end{bmatrix} \tag{5}$$

The powers of X in **H** are expressed in m-tuples. Since there are $2m + 1$ linearly independent row vectors in **H**, the number of check bits of the code is $2m + 1$. The code length is equal to $N - 1$. The code can be extended to length N by adding a column of 1 followed by $2m$ zeros. Figure A–9(a) shows the parity check matrix of a (31,20) code constructed from Eq. (5).

A full-length BCH code can be shortened by deleting a number of columns from its **H** matrix. The shortened code has a minimum distance at least as large as the original code. The number of check bits of the shortened code may be less than the original code when proper bit positions are deleted [Goethals, 1971; Chen, 1972]. In particular, let **Y** be a row vector in the space generated by the row vectors of **H**. Deleting the column positions of **H** where the corresponding positions of **Y** are ones, then the shortened **H** matrix has one fewer linearly independent row vector and the shortened code has one fewer check bit than the original code. The following table lists the number of check bits required for some DEC-TED BCH codes:

Data Bits	Check Bits
8	9
16	11
32	13
64	15
2^m	$2m + 3$

FIGURE A–9
Parity check matrix of a (31,20) code: (a) nonsystematic form H; (b) systematic form H1

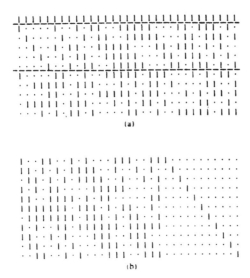

(a)

(b)

The **H** matrix defined by Eq. (5) can be transformed into the systematic form of Eq. (2) for the generation of check bits (see Figure A–9 for an example). Let **H1** be the parity check matrix in systematic form, and **T** be an $r \times r$ transformation matrix that satisfies

$$H = T \cdot H1 \tag{6}$$

The generation of check bits from matrix **H1** can be implemented with an XOR tree. For decoding, it is convenient to define the syndrome **S** from (3) with the **H** matrix instead of the **H1** matrix. The syndrome can be generated using an XOR tree associated with the **H** matrix. Thus, two separate XOR trees are used to generate check bits and syndrome bits. The syndrome can also be generated by first generating **S1** from Eq. (3) with the **H1** matrix, then multiplying matrix **T** by **S1**. Using this approach, the same XOR tree can be used to generate check bits and **S1**. The validity of this procedure follows directly from Eq. (6).

The syndrome **S** can be divided into three parts, S_0, S_1, and S_2, where S_0 consists of one bit, and S_1 and S_2 consist of m bits. Let the bit positions of the code be assigned as the powers of X. Assume that E_1 and E_2 are the positions of two erroneous bits. Then $S_0 = 0$ and $S_1 = E_1 + E_2$, $S_2 = E_1^3 + E_2^3$. Since $S_1^3 + S_2 = E_1^2 E_2 + E_1 E_2^2 = E_2 E_2 S_1$, the error positions E_1 and E_2 are roots of the quadratic equation

$$S_1 y^2 + S_1^2 y + (S_1^3 + S_2) = 0 \tag{7}$$

On the other hand, if there is only one error, then $S_0 = 1$ and the error position is the root of the linear equation $y + S_1 = 0$.

The major part of the error correction is to find the error positions from the syndrome. Once the error positions are known, the errors are corrected by inverting the data bits at the error positions. The error positions are determined by solving Eq. (7). If $S_0 = 0$, and Eq. (7) has two solutions, then the solutions are the positions of two errors. If $S_0 = 1$, and Eq. (7) degenerates to a linear equation, then the solution is the position of a single error. Uncorrectable errors are detected if Eq. (7) has no solution when $S_0 = 0$, or Eq. (7) does not degenerate into a linear equation when $S_0 = 1$.

There are various schemes for solving Eq. (7) [Howell, Gregg, and Rabins, 1977; Yamato and Tana, 1978; Golan and Hlavicka, 1983]. The equation can be solved algebraically using hardware that implements finite-field operations as in Howell, Gregg, and Rabins [1977]. It can also be solved by substituting all possible solutions into the equation, as in Golan and Hlavicka [1983]. Another approach is to store the error positions of correctable errors in a table. The syndrome is used as the address to the table of error positions [Yamato and Tana, 1978].

EXTENDED ERROR CORRECTION

Errors in semiconductor memory can be broadly divided into hard errors and soft errors [Nelson, 1982; Bossen and Hsiao, 1980]. Hard errors are caused by stuck faults or by permanent physical damage to the memory devices. Soft errors are temporary errors or α-particle-induced errors that will be erased during the next data storage operation. For this discussion, the errors that will stay in their locations during the next few write cycles are considered hard errors.

Error-correcting codes can be used to correct hard as well as soft errors. However, the maintenance strategy for a system may allow the hard errors to accumulate. The presence of errors in the memory increases the probability of uncorrectable errors (UE) due to the lineup of multiple errors in a codeword. The UE rate can be reduced by periodically scheduled repair service. It can also be reduced by extending the conventional error correction to some of the otherwise uncorrectable errors. The latter approach is especially attractive when the soft error rates are high, because it does not require the replacement of memory components. The extended error-correction schemes are discussed in this section.

The errors for which locations but not values are known are called *erasures* [Berlekamp, 1968; Peterson and Weldon, 1972]. Erasures are easier to correct than random errors. Let t and e be the number of random errors and erasures, respectively, that a code is capable of correcting; then the minimum distance d of the code must satisfy [Berlekamp, 1968; Peterson and Weldon, 1972]

$$2t + e < d \qquad (8)$$

For example, an SEC-DED code is capable of correcting one random error and one erasure.

In memory applications, the hard errors can be considered erasures if their locations can be identified. To locate the erasures of a particular word in the memory, we may apply some test patterns to the memory. Assume that any binary pattern can be written into the memory. An example is shown in Table A–4 for finding the locations of erasures with two test patterns, T_1 and T_2, of length 8, where T_2 is the complement of T_1. Before the test patterns are written into and read out of the memory, the word originally stored in the memory is read out and stored in a temporary storage. The erasure vector is obtained by the complement of T_1(READ) + T_2(READ).

TABLE A–4
Example of locating erasures

Direction of Stuck Faults	1 0 – – – – – 1
T_1 (WRITE)	1 1 0 0 1 1 0 0
T_1 (READ)	1 0 0 0 1 1 0 1
T_2 (WRITE)	0 0 1 1 0 0 1 1
T_2 (READ)	1 0 1 1 0 0 1 1
T_1 (READ) + T_2 (READ)	0 0 1 1 1 1 1 0
ERASURE ERROR	1 1 0 0 0 0 0 1

The locations of the erasures are indicated by the ones in the erasure vector. Since T_1 can be arbitrarily chosen, we may also use the word that originally stored in the memory as T_1. This approach for locating the erasures, known as the *double complement algorithm*, saves one write and one read operation. An example of the algorithm is shown in Table A–5.

Some system designs permit only the codewords to be written into the memory [Carter and McCarthy, 1976; Sundberg, 1978; Bossen and Hsiao 1980]. If the complement of a codeword is not a codeword, then the approaches just described for the identification of erasures are not applicable. In this case, one solution is to design codes with some special properties [Carter and McCarthy, 1976; Sundberg, 1978]. Another solution is to employ three test patterns in locating the erasures [Bossen and Hsiao, 1980]. The test patterns are chosen in such a way that they contain at least one 1 and one 0 in every bit position. It can be shown that three test patterns are sufficient to satisfy this condition for any linear code.

Once the locations of the erasures are identified, algorithms can be designed to correct the hard and soft errors, provided that the number of errors satisfies Eq. (8). Assume that the double complement algorithm is applicable for locating the erasures. The following procedure can be used to correct up to two hard errors or a combination of one hard and one soft error for a SEC-DED code:

1. Read word T_1 from a memory location.
2. If a single error in T_1 is detected by the ECC logic, the error in the word is corrected, and the corrected codeword is sent out to its destination.
3. If uncorrectable errors in T_1 are detected by the ECC logic, the complement of T_1 is written into the same memory location. Then the word from the same memory location is read and complemented. Let the resultant word be T_3 (see Table A–5).
4. If a single error in T_3 is detected by the ECC logic, the error is corrected. The corrected word is sent out to its destination and is also written into the same memory location.
5. If no error is detected by the ECC logic, T_3 is assumed error free. T_3 is sent out to its destination and is also written into the same memory location.
6. If uncorrectable errors are detected by the ECC logic, the original word is declared uncorrectable.

Note that double soft errors are not correctable by this procedure. All single errors are corrected at the normal speed. The correction of hard-hard and hard-soft types of double errors takes more time because additional write and read operations are involved. The procedure can be modified or refined to correct additional multiple hard errors [Carter and McCarthy, 1976; Nelson, 1982]

TABLE A–5
Example of double complement algorithm

Original word = T_1 (WRITE)	1 1 0 0 1 1 0 0
Hard and soft errors	H – – – – – S –
T_1 (READ)	0 1 0 0 1 1 1 0
T_2 (WRITE) = $\overline{T_1 \text{ (READ)}}$	1 0 1 1 0 0 0 1
T_2 (READ)	0 0 1 1 0 0 0 1
T_1 (READ) + T_2 (READ)	0 1 1 1 1 1 1 1
Erasure error	1 0 0 0 0 0 0 0
$T_3 = \overline{T_2 \text{ (READ)}}$	1 1 0 0 1 1 1 0
Soft error = $T_3 + T_1$ (WRITE)	0 0 0 0 0 0 1 0

at the expense of speed and cost. The procedure can also be extended to correct multiple errors beyond the random error-correcting capability of SBC-DBD codes and DEC-TED codes.

The procedure just described derives the information on erasures at the time when the double error occurs. A different method is to store the information on the erasure errors in a table [Sundberg, 1978]. This approach increases the speed of correcting double errors. However, the table has to be constantly updated to reflect the true status of the erasures in the memory.

There are other schemes for the correction of multiple erasures [Tsybakov, 1975; Kuznetsov, Kasami, and Yamamura, 1978; Chen, 1983b]. These schemes involve the design of codes with additional check bits, which are used to mask the erasures in decoding. For example, a (76,64) code can be designed to correct double erasures and single random errors, and to detect double random errors [Kuznetsov, Kasami, and Yamamura, 1978].

CONCLUSIONS

Advances in semiconductor technology have brought about very high levels of integration, especially in the memory area where circuit densities are up to 256K bits per chip. In VLSI memory, higher density usually means a reduced signal-to-noise margin. It also increases the likelihood of soft errors due to radiation and other sources. Error-correcting codes have provided a very effective solution to these problems. They have become an essential part of modern memory design. In the future, the ECC could even be an integral part of the memory chips that manufacturers would offer.

In this appendix, we have described the essentials of the principal error-correcting codes used in semiconductor memory design applications. The class of SEC-DED codes is currently most widely used throughout the industry. However, more powerful codes such as SBC-DBD and DEC-TED codes are quite likely to be used in future commercial systems.

REFERENCES

Basham, 1976; Berlekamp, 1968; Bose and Ray-Chaudhuri, 1960; Bossen, 1970; Bossen, Chang, and Chen, 1978; Bossen and Hsiao, 1980; Carter and McCarthy, 1976; Chen, 1972, 1983a, 1983b; Chen and Rutledge, 1984; Dao, 1973; Ferris-Prabhu, 1979; Goethals, 1971; Golan and Hlavicka, 1983; Hamming, 1950; Hocquenghem, 1959; Hong and Patel, 1972; Howell, Gregg, and Rabins, 1977; Hsiao, 1970; Hsiao et al., 1981; Kasami, Lin, and Peterson, 1967; Keneda and Fujiwara, 1982; Kuznetsov, Kasami, and Yamamura, 1978; Lala, 1978, 1979; Levine and Myers, 1976; Libson and Harvey, 1984; Lin and Costello, 1983; Mikhail, Bartoldus, and Rutledge, 1982; Morris, 1980; Nelson, 1982; Peterson and Weldon, 1972; Reddy, 1978; Reed and Solomon, 1960; Richard, 1976; Siewiorek and Swarz, 1982; Sundberg, 1978; Tsybakov, 1975; Wolf, 1969; Yamato and Tana, 1978.

APPENDIX B

Arithmetic Error Codes: Cost and Effectiveness Studies for Application in Digital System Design

Algirdas Avizienis*

The application of error-detecting or error-correcting codes in digital computer design requires studies of cost and effectiveness tradeoffs to supplement the knowledge of their theoretical properties. General criteria for cost and effectiveness studies of error codes are developed, and results are presented for arithmetic error codes with the low-cost check modulus $2^n - 1$. Both separate (residue) and nonseparate (AN) codes are considered in this appendix. The class of multiple arithmetic error codes is developed as an extension of low-cost single codes.

METHODOLOGY OF CODE EVALUATION

Scope of the Problem

In this paper the name *arithmetic error codes* identifies the class of error-detecting and error-correcting codes which are preserved during arithmetic operations. Given the digital number representations, x, y, an arithmetic operation $*$, and an encoding $f: x \rightarrow x'$, we say that f is an arithmetic-error code with respect to $*$ if and only if there exists an algorithm $A*$ for coded operands to implement the operation $*$ such that

$$A * (x', y') \equiv (x * y)'$$

The definition applies to single-operand operations and multioperand operations as well, i.e.,

$$A * (x') \equiv (* x)'$$

and

$$A * (x'_1, x'_2, \ldots, x'_n) \equiv (x_1 * x_2 * \cdots * x_n)'$$

must be satisfied in those cases.

Arithmetic error codes are of special interest in the design of fault-tolerant computer systems, since they serve to detect (or correct) errors in the results produced by arithmetic processors as well as the errors which have been caused by faulty transmission or storage. The same encoding is applicable throughout the entire computing system to provide *concurrent diagnosis*, i.e., error detection which occurs concurrently with the operation of the computer. Real-time detection of transient and permanent faults is obtained without a duplication of arithmetic processors.

The economic feasibility of arithmetic error codes in a computer system depends on their cost and effectiveness with respect to the set of arithmetic algorithms and their speed requirements. The choice of a specific code from the available alternatives further depends on their relative cost and effectiveness values. This paper presents the results of an investigation of the

* Acknowledgments: The author wishes to acknowledge stimulating discussions with D. A. Rennels, D. K. Rubin, J. J. Wedel, and A. D. Weeks of the Jet Propulsion Laboratory, Pasadena, California.

cost and effectiveness of arithmetic error codes in digital system design. Other new results include several classes of multiple arithmetic error codes. The investigation was stimulated by the need for low-cost real-time fault detection in the fault-tolerant STAR computer [Avižienis, 1968; Avižienis et al., 1971]. Favorable results led to the choice of arithmetic encoding of both data words and instruction addresses in this machine. Preliminary reports on parts of the results have been made on several occasions previously [Avižienis, 1964, 1965, 1966a, 1966b, 1967a, 1967b, 1969].

The Criteria of Cost

For the purposes of this paper a "perfect" computer is a reference computer in which logic faults do not occur. The specified set of arithmetic algorithms is carried out with prescribed speed and without errors. For a given algorithm, word length, and number representation system of the perfect computer the introduction of any error code will result in changes that represent the *cost* of the code. The components of the cost are discussed below in general terms applicable to all arithmetic error codes.

Word Length. The encoding introduces redundant bits in the number representation. A proportional hardware increase takes place in storage arrays, data paths, and processor units. The increase is expressed as a percentage of the perfect design. "Complete duplication" (100 percent increase) is the encoding which serves as the limiting case.

The Checking Algorithm. This tests the code validity of every incoming operand and every result of an instruction. A correcting operation follows when an error-correcting code is used. The cost of the checking algorithm has two interrelated components: the hardware complexity and the time required by checking. The complete duplication case requires only bit-by-bit comparison: other codes require more hardware and time. Provisions for fault detection in the checking hardware itself are needed and add to the cost.

The Arithmetic Algorithms. An encoding usually requires a more complex algorithm for the same arithmetic operation than the perfect computer. This cost is expressed by the incremental time and hardware required by the new algorithm. The reference case of complete duplication does not add any cost of this type (the algorithms are not changed, but they are performed in two separate processors). The set of arithmetic algorithms which is usually provided in a general-purpose processor is discussed in the section on Fault Effects in Binary Arithmetic Processors.

The Criteria of Effectiveness

An *arithmetic error* occurs when a logic fault causes the change of one or more digits in the result of an algorithm. A *logic fault* is defined to be the deviation of one or more logic variables from the values specified in the perfect design. Logic faults differ in their duration, extent, and nature of the deviation from perfect values. The effectiveness of an arithmetic error code in a computer may be expressed in two forms: as a direct *value effectiveness*, and as a design-dependent *fault effectiveness*.

Value Effectiveness. The most direct measure of effectiveness is the listing of the error values that will be detected or corrected when the code is used. These values are determined by the properties of the code and are independent of the logic structure of the computer in which the code will be used. Value effectiveness for 100 percent detection (or correction) of some class of error values has been the main measure of arithmetic codes. For example, *single*-error detection (or correction) is said to occur when *all* (100 percent) errors of value

$$\pm cr^i \quad 0 < c < r \quad 0 < i < n - 1$$

are detected (or corrected) in an n-digit, radix-r number [Brown, 1960; Peterson, 1961, pp. 236–244]. There is no direct reference for algorithms or their implementation. The present study considers value effectiveness with less than 100 percent detection. Such codes may be useful when their cost is low and when other means of fault tolerance supplement the codes in a computer.

Fault Effectiveness. The purpose of arithmetic error codes in digital systems is to detect the occurrence of logic faults. The detection enables the system to initiate corrective action (error correction, diagnosis, program restart, etc.). In order to assess the effectiveness of fault detection, the value effectiveness of a code must be translated into a measure of *fault effectiveness* for one or more specified types of logic faults. The translation is performed separately for every algorithm and requires an *error table* for every type of fault. The error table is generated from the description of the logic implementation of the algorithm α. The specified fault ϕ is applied to every logic circuit which is used by the algorithm. Every application yields an *error value* E (or a *set* of error values $\{E\}$) by which the fault will change the perfect value S of the result to the actual (incorrect) value $S* = S + E$. The error table $T(\alpha, \phi)$ lists all error values together with their relative frequencies of occurrence during the compilation of $T(\alpha, \phi)$. A comparison of $T(\alpha, \phi)$ with the detectable error values of the given code f shows which entries of the error table are not detectable. The fault effectiveness of f with respect to (α, ϕ) is the *percentage* of all occurrences of ϕ which will be detected (or corrected) when f is employed. Less than 100 percent fault-effective codes are of interest when their cost is low, because other methods of fault tolerance (especially program restarts) can be used to reinforce the codes [Avižienis, 1968; Avižienis et al., 1971]. If the fault effectiveness for (α, ϕ) is not sufficient, it may be improved by redesigning the implementation of α to eliminate some or all of the undetectable entries of $T(\alpha, \phi)$.

During the compilation of the error table $T(\alpha, \phi)$ an application of the fault ϕ to a logic circuit changes the radix-r, n-digit perfect result $s \equiv (s_{n-1}, \ldots, s_1, s_0)$ to an "actual" (incorrect) result $s*$ which differs from the s in at least one digit. The digit changes which have taken place are described by the error number $e \equiv (e_{n-1}, \ldots, e_1, e_0)$ defined digitwise as

$$e_i = s*_i - s_i \quad \text{for } 0 \leq i \leq n - 1$$

The digits of e are in the range $-r + 1 \leq e_1 \leq r - 1$, and e itself represents the error value E in the range

$$-(r^n - 1) \leq E \leq r^n - 1$$

When e is recorded to have the minimum number of nonzero digits, this minimum number is defined to be the *arithmetic distance* between s and $s*$, as well as the *arithmetic weight* of e [Peterson, 1961, pp. 236–244]. The weight of an error value has been employed to indicate its relative probability (single, double, etc.). The results of the following sections show that the weight of an error number is data dependent in some algorithms and therefore not suitable as a general criterion of fault effectiveness.

Classes of Logic Faults

Single Faults. A single logic fault is the deviation of one logic variable from the design value. During an interval of time ΔT_i (to be called a *use*) it has two possible forms: a) the logic variable is "stuck-on-zero" (abbreviated S0) when it assumes the actual value 0 instead of the design value 1; and b) the logic variable is "stuck-on-1" (abbreviated S1) when it assumes the actual value 1 instead of the design value 0.

The circuits that are used to store, transmit, or generate digit values during an algorithm will be called *digit circuits*. A single fault is said to be *local* if its immediate effect changes the value of only one digit, i.e., the local fault in position $i(0 \leq i \leq n - 1)$ of a radix-r operand adds the value

$$cr^i \qquad -r + 1 \leq c \leq r - 1$$

to the affected number. The value of the error number is either cr^i, or an arithmetic function of cr^i, determined by the location of the fault and the microprogram of the algorithm. A single fault which immediately affects more than one digit is *distributed*. Its effect is expressed as the cumulative effect of two or more local faults.

One-Use and Repeated-Use Faults. With respect to the microprogram of the algorithm, there are one-use and repeated-use faults. The fault is a *one-use* fault when the faulty digit circuit is used only once before the checking algorithm is performed. Iterative algorithms (multiplication, division, byte-serial addition, etc.) employ the same digit circuits repeatedly in order to generate the result; if one of these circuits is faulty, a *repeated-use* fault results. Repeated-use faults differ according to their one-use effectiveness, duration, and determinancy. The fault is ineffective during the use ΔT_i if the fault-induced value is identical to the design value. The fault is *transient* if it does not exist during one or more of the uses; otherwise it is *permanent*. A transient fault is equivalent to a permanent fault that is ineffective during some uses; consequently, transient faults are a subset of permanent faults. Some types of failures cause the logic value at a point to become uncertain, and it is interpreted randomly as either one or zero during the repeated uses of the faulty circuit. In these cases neither a constant S0 nor a constant S1 fault exists for all uses; the fault is *indeterminate* and is called "stuck-on-X," abbreviated SX. An indeterminate fault has the combined effect of two transient faults (one S0, the other S1) affecting the same variable.

Cumulative Fault Effects. A multiple (double, triple, etc.) fault occurs when two or more faulty logic variables exist during the same algorithm. Its effect is expressed as the cumulative effect of two or more single faults. A review of the fault model shows that the effect of any fault is equivalent to the cumulative effect of a set of local one-use faults. The *basic fault* is defined to be a local one-use fault (either S0 or S1 at ΔT_i). In the study of fault effectiveness, the effect of a basic fault is determined for every digit circuit and every algorithm of a processor or storage array. The effect of any other fault is then determined in two steps: *a*) identify the set of basic faults which corresponds to the given fault; and *b*) determine the effect (error value, or set of possible error values) of the given fault by applying sequentially the basic faults identified in step *a*.

The classification of faults is summarized in Figure B–1.

FAULT EFFECTS IN BINARY ARITHMETIC PROCESSORS

Basic Faults in Parallel Arithmetic

The set of arithmetic algorithms which is provided in a general-purpose processor includes at least the eight algorithms listed in Table B–1 either separately or as parts of composite algorithms, multiplication, and division. In this section we determine the error magnitudes due to the existence of a basic (local, one-use) fault in a digit circuit of a radix-2 processor. A parallel design is assumed, in which the algorithms of Table B–1 use the digit circuits of the processor only once, and the faults are single-use faults. The error magnitudes $|E|$ which can be generated by a basic fault and their arithmetic weights are presented in Table B–1. The radix-2 operands are n binary digits long $(0 \leq i \leq n - 1)$. Two systems for the representation of negative numbers are consid-

FIGURE B–1
Classification of logic faults

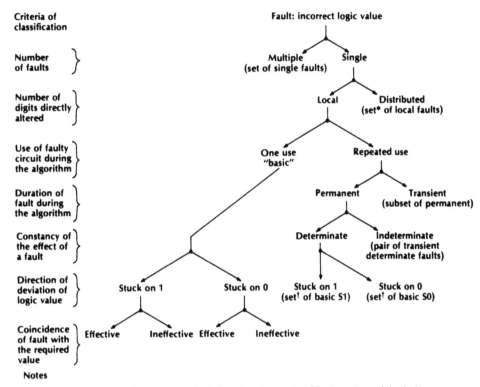

Criteria of classification

Number of faults }

Number of digits directly altered }

Use of faulty circuit during the algorithm }

Duration of fault during the algorithm }

Constancy of the effect of a fault }

Direction of deviation of logic value }

Coincidence of fault with the required value }

Fault: incorrect logic value

Multiple (set of single faults) — Single

Local — Distributed (set* of local faults)

One use "basic" — Repeated use

Permanent — Transient (subset of permanent)

Determinate — Indeterminate (pair of transient determinate faults)

Stuck on 1 — Stuck on 0 — Stuck on 1 (set[†] of basic S1) — Stuck on 0 (set[†] of basic S0)

Effective — Ineffective — Effective — Ineffective

Notes
* Membership of set determined by logical design of the net and by the nature of the fault
[†] Membership of set determined by algorithm being implemented

ered: complements with respect to $N_1 = 2^n - 1$ (one's complements), and complements with respect to $N_2 = 2^n$ (two's complements). All operands and results are treated as unsigned integer values for checking purposes. The transfer (A1) is included in every other algorithm; thus the $|E| = 2^i$ of a transfer may occur in every case. If the same register is used to hold an operand and the result, a repeated-use fault may result.

Table B–1 shows that error magnitudes of weights greater than one occur for a single basic fault. In (A2)–(A5) they assume the form $c2^i$, with $1 \le c \le 2^{k+1} - 1$; that is, the nonzero digits in the error number are contained in at most $k + 1$ adjacent positions. In modulo N addition and subtraction, every $|E| = 2^i$ with weight 1 has an associated $|E| = N - 2^i$, usually with weights 2 or 3. The origins of error values with weights greater than 1 are discussed next.

Arithmetic Shifts (A2, A3). These are subject to basic faults that affect the values of the end digits. In the k-digit right shift (A3) for both complement systems, the left-end digit x_{n-1} is replicated k times. A fault in x_{n-1} or the setting circuit affects $k + 1$ left-end digits of the results, giving

$$|E| = \sum_{n-1-k}^{n-1} 2^i$$

TABLE B–1 *Magnitudes due to a basic fault in a parallel binary processor*

	Number System			
	$N_1 = 2^n - 1$ (one's complement)		$N_2 = 2^n$ (two's complement)	
Algorithm	Error Magnitude $|E|$	Weight W	Error Magnitude $|E|$	Weight W
A1 Transfer (applies also to A2–A7 below)	2^i	1	2^i	'1
A2 Left shift, k digits	$2^k - 1$	2	$2^k - 1$	2
A3 Right shift, k digits	$2^{n-1-k}(2^{k+1} - 1)$	2	$2^{n-1-k}(2^{k+1} - 1)$	2
A4 Range extension, k digits	$2^{n-1}(2^{k+1} - 1)$ $2^n(2^k - 1)$	2 2	$2^{n-1}(2^{k+1} - 1)$ $2^n(2^k - 1)$	2 2
A5 Range contraction, k digits ($1 \le c \le 2k - 1$)	$c2^{n-k}$ $2^{n-1-k}(2^{k+1} - 1)$	$1 \le w \le \lfloor k/2 + 1 \rfloor$ 2	$c2^{n-k}$ $2^{n-1-k}(2^{k+1} - 1)$	$1 \le w/2 \le \lfloor k/2 + 1 \rfloor$ 2
A6 Modulo N addition or modulo N subtraction	$2^n - 1 - 2^i$	2, ($i = 0, n - 1$) 3, ($1 \le i \le n - 2$)	$2^n - 2^i$	1, ($i = n - 1$) 2, ($0 \le i \le n - 2$)
A7 Additive inverse (complementation)	2^i	1	2^i Also see (A6)	1
A8 Roundoff, k digits Also see (A6) for case (a)	2^k	1	2^k	1

In the k-digit left shift (A2), k new digits are filled in at the right end. They are equal to x_{n-1} for $N_1 = 2^n - 1$, and they are zero for $N_2 = 2^n$. In both cases, a fault will generate

$$|E| = \sum_0^{k-1} 2^i$$

Range Extension and Contraction. In the k-digit range extension (A4), k identical digits equal to x_{n-1} are attached at the left end. An incorrect value of x_{n-1} will give

$$|E| = \sum_{n-1}^{n-1+k} 2^i$$

A fault in the sensing circuit will give

$$|E| = \sum_{n}^{n-1+k} 2^i$$

The value $|E| = 2^i(n \le i \le n + k - 1)$ occurs when one of the new digits is altered by a fault. The k-digit range contraction (A5) is the inverse operation, in which k identical digits ($x_{n-1}, \ldots, x_{n-k}$) are removed at the left end when they are equal to the leftmost remaining digit x_{n-k-1}. An incorrect removal gives $|E| = c2^{n-k}$, with $1 \le c \le 2^k - 1$. An incorrect value of x_{n-k-1} (e.g., 1 instead of 0) causes the removal of k identical digits (e.g., all 1s), giving

$$|E| = \sum_{n-k-1}^{n-1} 2^i$$

Modulo N Addition or Subtraction (A6). This requires the "casting out" of N or of $-N$ from the sum or difference, respectively. A basic fault which locally generates $|E| = 2^i$ may cause an error in the "casting out," either by causing it unnecessarily, or by inhibiting it when it should take place. In both cases $|E| = N - 2^i$ occurs; its weight is 1, 2, or 3, depending on N and i.

The Additive Inverse (A7). This is the fixed subtraction $N - X$, called "complementation." For $N_1 = 2^n - 1$ it is the digitwise negation of x. For $N_2 = 2^n$, the negation of x is followed by the addition of 1 to the least significant digit, and the addition errors of (A6) may also occur.

Roundoff (A8). The roundoff of k digits ($i = 0, \ldots, k - 1$) is implemented by one of three methods: a) range test of $x_{k-1}, \ldots, x_0$ followed by the addition of 0 or 1 to x_k; b) always setting x_k to 1; and c) truncation (without arithmetic). Cases a and b both may have $|E| = 2^k$; case a is also subject to the addition error of (A6).

Repeated-Use Faults in Binary Processors

Two classes of algorithms are subject to repeated-use faults: algorithms (A1)–(A8) of Table B–1 in a byte-serial arithmetic processor, and multiplication and division in a parallel processor.

In a byte-serial processor, the kb digits' long operands enter the processor in a sequence of k bytes, and the digit circuits are used k times. The length of each byte is $b > 1$ digit. The value of k is variable in some processors. A permanent local fault will affect the same relative position $h(0 \le h \le b - 1)$ within each byte. The fault may be ineffective during some of the k uses.

Of the algorithms in Table B–1, byte-serial processing directly affects (A1)–(A3), (A6), and (A7). The error magnitudes 2^i and $N - 2^i$ are replaced by the sets of possible error magnitudes $\{|E_c|\}$ and $\{N - |E_c|\}$, with

$$E_c = \sum_{j=0}^{k-1} d_j 2^{bj+h}$$

where $d_j = 0$ if the fault is ineffective for the jth byte, $d_j = 1$ for an effective S1, and $d_j = -1$ for an effective S0. There are $2^k - 1$ nonzero magnitudes $|E_c|$ for a determinate (S0 or S1) local fault, and $(3^k - 1)/2$ nonzero magnitudes $|E_c|$ for an indeterminate (SX) local fault. Which one of the $2^k - 1$ or $3^k - 1$ nonzero sets of the coefficients d_j occurs is determined by the digit values of the operand or operands. An equal frequency of occurrence is assumed here. The arithmetic weights W are in the following ranges: 1) for $|E_c|$: $1 \le W \le k$; 2) for $2^n - |E_c|$: $2 \le W \le k + 1$; and 3) for $(2^n - 1) - |E_c|$: $2 \le W \le k + 2$. The end-condition errors of the shifts (A2) and (A3), the range algorithms (A4) and (A5), and the roundoff (A8) do not differ from the parallel case ($k = 1$, $b = n - 1$) and the results of Table B–1 apply.

Parallel multiplication and division may be intolerably slowed down by the checking of individual additions and shifts; therefore, the repeated-use error magnitudes are of interest. It is assumed that the partial products or partial remainders are not checked, but returned to the accumulator as operands for the next step. The effect of a local fault in the digit circuits is cumulative, and different positions of the results are affected by successive steps because of the shifting. The set of expected error magnitudes is determined by the details of the algorithm.

Most readily susceptible to analysis are algorithms that employ fixed shifts of b bits. In this case the error numbers caused by a local fault in the digit circuits are the same as those developed during an addition or shift in a byte-serial processor with byte length b. End-condition setting in shifts, multiplier digit recoding, and quotient digit selection may contribute additional error values. More error values are also contributed by the multiple-forming circuits which shift the multiplicand (or divisor) left to obtain the multiples 2, 4, 8, etc. For example, a fault in the multiplicand register with provisions to add $c_j = 0, \pm 1, \pm 2$ times the operand to the partial product during the jth step affects one of two adjacent positions $(i, i + 1)$ of the sum. The sets of possible error magnitudes are $\{|E|\}$ and $\{N - |E|\}$, with

$$E = \sum_{j=0}^{k-1} c_j d_j 2^{bj}$$

where b is the length of one right shift. The set of error magnitudes for any given variation of an algorithm and logic structure of the processor is obtained as the cumulative effect (sum) of appropriately shifted contributions of the error magnitudes in Table B–1.

LOW-COST RADIX-2 ARITHMETIC CODES

Implementation of Arithmetic Error Codes

Arithmetic error codes are classified into separate and nonseparate codes [Garner, 1966]. Both classes possess many common properties, but differ significantly in their implementation. The nonseparate code considered is the AN code [Brown, 1960; Peterson, 1961], which is formed when an uncoded operand x is multiplied by the *check modulus* A to give the coded operand Ax. The separate codes are the *residue code* [Peterson, 1958], and the *inverse residue code* [Avižienis, 1967a, 1969], which is a previously unexplored variant of the residue code. The inverse residue code has significant advantages in fault detection of repeated-use faults. The modulo A inverse residue encoding for a number x attaches a check symbol x'' to form the pair (x, x''). The value of x'' is X'':

$$X'' = A - (A|X) = A - X'$$

where $A|X$ designates the modulo A residue of X. $A|X$ is the value X' of the check symbol x' employed in modulo A residue encoding (x, x'). The inverse residue code is a separate code, since it has no arithmetic interaction between x and x'' [Garner, 1966], and should not be confused with the nonseparate systematic subcodes of AN codes [Henderson, 1961; Garner, 1966].

The set of undetectable error magnitudes $|E_m|$ (called *misses* in the subsequent discussion) for both AN and residue codes consists of all multiples of the check modulus A:

$$|E_m| = KA \qquad K = 1, 2, \ldots, \lfloor (r^n - 1)/A \rfloor$$

for n-digit radix-r operands. The effectiveness and the cost of arithmetic checking depends very strongly on the choice of the check modulus A. The *checking algorithm* which establishes whether a detectable (or correctable) error exists in the result z for both classes of codes computes the modulo A residue $A|Z$, where Z is the unsigned integer value of z. The increase in word length is the same for both classes of codes. For radix-2 it is $\lceil \log_2 A \rceil$ bits.

The most significant differences of implementation are caused by the property of separateness. For residue codes, the operands x, y and their check symbols x', y' enter separate (*main* and *check*) processors which produce the main result z (value Z) and the check result z' (value Z'). The checking algorithm computes $A|Z$ and compares it to Z'. If the values are equal, either the correct result has been obtained, or a miss has occurred. Disagreement indicates a fault in either the main or the check processor; the uncertainty precludes fault location and error correction without supplementary procedures. An exception in the check procedure occurs for division $X \div Y$ which produces the quotient Q and the remainder P. The checking algorithm computes both $A|Q$ and $A|P$. The check processor computes the value $(A|Q) \cdot Y' + (A|P)$ which is compared to X' for equality [Garner, 1958]. The *inverse residue code* differs from the residue code in only one respect: the check result has the value $Z'' = A - (A|Z)$ when an error has not occurred. The checking algorithm computes $A|Z$ and forms the check sum $F = A|[(A|Z) + Z'']$, where $F = 0$ indicates that either the result is correct, or a miss has occurred.

For the nonseparate AN code the checking algorithm computes $A|Z$, where Z is the value of a result. $A|Z = 0$ indicates either a correct result or a miss. A nonzero $A|Z$ indicates a fault: for certain choices of A the value of $A|Z$ indicates the error value E for error correction [Brown, 1960; Peterson, 1961; Garner, 1966]. The algorithms of the processor are designed to compute with product-coded numbers [Avižienis, 1966b]. All intermediate steps of the algorithms must preserve product coding in order to retain the error-checking properties in the result. The hardware cost of AN codes is in the greater complexity of the main processor, while for residue codes it is in the separate check processor.

The Low-Cost Checking Algorithm

A practical checking method must satisfy both cost and effectiveness constraints. For radix-2 numbers, every odd integer $A > 1$ will detect weight 1 error magnitudes. The search for values of A which have a low-cost checking algorithm identified the class of *low-cost* arithmetic codes [Avižienis, 1964] which employ check moduli of the form

$$A = 2^a - 1 \quad \text{with integer } a > 1$$

The parameter a is called the *group length* of the code. Since division is a complex algorithm, the checking algorithms for most odd $A > 1$ are relatively costly and slow. The check modulus $2^a - 1$ is an exception because the congruence

$$K_i r^i \equiv K_i \text{ modulo } (r - 1), \quad r = 2^a$$

allows the use of modulo $2^a - 1$ summation of the k groups (a-bit segments of value K_i, with $0 \le K_i \le 2^a - 1$) that compose the ka-bit number Z to compute the *check sum* $(2^a - 1)|Z$. Division by A is replaced by an "end-around carry" addition algorithm, which "casts out $2^a - 1$'s" in a byte-serial or parallel implementation.

It is also important to note that the low-cost check moduli $2^a - 1$ are exceptionally compatible with binary arithmetic. A complete set of algorithms has been devised for AN-coded operands [Avižienis, 1964, 1967a], and an experimental byte-serial processor with four-bit bytes, $ka = 32$, $a = 4$, and $A = 15$ has been constructed for the STAR computer [Avižienis, 1966b, 1968]. While AN codes are limited to one's complement ($N = 2^n - 1$) algorithms, the two's complement ($N = 2^n$) algorithms can be carried out as well with the separate residue and inverse residue codes, which also display implementation advantages for multiple-precision algorithms. A set of algorithms for a two's complement inverse residue code processor (including multiple precision) has been developed to replace the AN code processor of the STAR computer [Avižienis et al., 1971].

Fault Effectiveness: One-Use Faults

It was already noted that the check moduli $2^a - 1$, with $a > 1$, will detect all weight 1 error magnitudes 2^j with $0 \le j \le ka - 1$. Furthermore, all error values which can be confined within $a - 1$ adjacent bits of the error number (bursts of length $a - 1$ or less) will be detected, since their error magnitudes are $g2^j$, with g in the range $1 \le g \le 2^{a-1} - 1$. Only one error magnitude (out of $2^a - 1$ possibilities) confined within a adjacent bits is undetectable (that described by a adjacent 1's). This is important with respect to algorithms (A1)–(A5) of Table B–1, which contains error magnitudes of the forms $(2^k - 1)2^j$ and $(2^{k+1} - 1)2^j$. The choice of $a \ge k + 2$ will guarantee complete fault detection for these algorithms.

For operands of length $n = ka$ bits, the check modulus $2^a - 1$ will detect the one's complements $(2^{ka} - 1) - |E|$ of all detectable error magnitudes $|E|$. Some weight 2 error magnitudes will not be detected: the undetectable error numbers are caused by one S1 and one S0 basic fault with a certain separation. The fraction f_2 of undetected weight 2 error magnitudes for $a > 2$ is

$$f_2 = (k - 1)a/[2a(ka - 3) + 6/k]$$

For $a > 2$, $f_2 < 1/2a$ holds [Avižienis, 1964]. For example, given $ka = 24$, $a = 3$ yields $f_2 = 0.166$, $a = 4$ yields $f_2 = 0.118$, and $a = 6$ yields $f_2 = 0.071$. The case of $a = 2$ is an unfavorable exception, yielding $f_2 \cong 0.5$ for any value of k. The analysis may be continued for higher weights, due to several independent basic faults; however, errors due to repeated use of a single faulty circuit are of more immediate interest.

Fault Effectiveness: Determinate Repeated-Use Faults

For the case of a determinate local repeated-use fault discussed earlier in the section on Repeated-Use Faults in Binary Processes above, which considers kb bits long operands processed in k bytes of b bits each, an analytic solution indicates very effective fault detection for the choice $b = a$ [Avižienis, 1965]. All possible $2^k - 1$ error magnitudes (and their one's complements) are detected by the check modulus $2^a - 1$ for $k < 2^a - 1$. Only one miss (undetectable error) occurs when $k = 2^a - 1$; the count of misses ϵ for $k \geq 2^a - 1$ is given by the expression

$$\epsilon = \sum_{j=1}^{\lceil k/(2a-1) \rceil} k!/[j(2^a - 1)]![k - j(2^a - 1)]!$$

For example, the check modulus $\alpha = 15$ with byte length $b = 4$ allows no misses for words up to $n = 56$ bits, and $\alpha = 31$ with $b = 5$ up to $n = 150$ bits. The expressions for the miss count ϵ are derived by considering all possible ways in which result value $2^a - 1$ consisting of all ones can be generated by modulo $2^a - 1$ summation of k contributions of either 0 or 2^h, with $0 \leq h \leq a - 1$.

For any choice of the pair (a, b) and the word length $n = kb = ca$, it has been shown that the first miss occurs when the word length reaches the value

$$n' = c'a(2^{a;k'} - 1)$$

where $c'a = k'b$ is the least common multiple of a and b [Avižienis, 1965]. Consequently, the maximum value of n' results when $k' = 1$, giving $b = c'a$, and

$$n'_{max} = c'a(2^a - 1) = b(2^a - 1)$$

The choice of $b = 2a$ will double the "safe length"; for example, $\alpha = 15$ and $b = 8$ allows no misses for words up to 112 bits, and $\alpha = 7$ and $b = 6$ up to 36 bits. The minimum value of n' is obtained when a and b are relatively prime: in this case we have $n'_{min} = ab$.

The effectiveness of any choice of the pair (a, b) can be expressed in terms of the percentage of misses along all possible $2^k - 1$ error magnitudes which can be caused by a local determinate fault. Given a miss count ϵ, the *miss percentage* is obtained as $100\epsilon/(2^k - 1)$, where $n = kb$ is the word length of the operands. The miss percentages for various word lengths are obtained using a computer program which tabulated all misses for word lengths up to $k = 18$ bytes, check lengths $2 \leq a \leq 12$, and byte lengths $2 \leq b \leq 10$ and $b = 12$ [Avižienis, 1965]. The maximum word length of 18 bytes results in a total of $2^{18} - 1 = 262{,}143$ possible nonzero error magnitudes. In selected cases the maximum word length was extended to 20 bytes, i.e., $2^{20} - 1 = 1{,}048{,}575$ possible nonzero error magnitudes. The miss percentages (for the same values of b) were also tabulated for 11 moduli A which detect all weight 2 and 5 check moduli which detect all weight 2 and 3 error magnitudes [Peterson, 1961, pp. 236–44]. The word lengths used were n, with the requirement that $2^n - 1$ should be divisible by A.

The results of the tabulation (available in Avižienis [1965]) show that for a and b relatively prime, the percentage of misses rapidly becomes $100/(2^a - 1)$ after the first miss which occurs at word length $n' = ab$ (the minimal case). For other pairs (a, b), the miss percentages beyond the word length n' tend to overshoot $100/(2^a - 1)$ and then go below $100/(2^a - 1)$ with increasing word length. The weight 2 and weight 2, 3 detecting check moduli A display miss percentages which are comparable to those of relatively prime (a, b).

Fault Effectiveness: Indeterminate Repeated-Use Faults

A local indeterminate fault (used m times) will contribute to the error magnitude in one of 3^m possible ways. During each use the contribution will be 0, 2^i, or -2^i with various values of i. For the same repeated-use model as used in the preceding section, the choice $b = a$, and the word length ka, the number of misses ϵ' due to the indeterminate fault (excluding the determinate subset) is given by the expression

$$\epsilon' = \sum_{j=1}^{\lfloor k/2 \rfloor} k!/2[(k - 2j)!](j!)^2$$

The total count of possible nonzero error magnitudes is $(3^k - 1)/2$. The miss percentage $100\epsilon'/2(3^k - 1)$ is highest for $k = 2$ and gradually decreases with increasing k. For values $k \geq 2^a - 1$ the determinate subset contributes the miss count ϵ, and the total number of misses is $\epsilon + \epsilon'$. We also note that the value of ϵ' is independent of a. Table B–2 lists the miss percentages (excluding the determinate subset) for the byte counts $2 \leq k \leq 12$.

Given any pair (a, b), the first miss due to an indeterminate fault (excluding the determinate subset) occurs when the word length exceeds the least common multiple of a and b; that is, the first miss occurs for the word length n'', where

$$n'' > c'a$$

where $c'a = k'b$ is the least common multiple. Consequently, the maximum safe length n is attained for a and b relatively prime, with $n''_{max} > ab$. In this case the first miss is due to the determinate subset and occurs for $n'' = ab$. For other choices of the pair (a, b) we observe

$$n''_{max} < n'_{max}$$

TABLE B–2
Miss percentages for byte counts 2 ≤ k ≤ 12

k	$(3^k - 1)/2$	ϵ'	Miss %
2	4	1	25.00
3	13	3	23.08
4	40	9	22.50
5	121	25	20.66
6	364	70	19.23
7	1093	196	17.93
8	3280	553	16.86
9	9841	1569	15.94
10	29524	4476	15.16
11	88573	12826	14.48
12	265720	36894	13.88

The total miss percentages $100(\epsilon' + \epsilon)/2(3^k - 1)$ are of interest in the cases $b \neq a$ as well. An exhaustive tabulation by means of a computer program was performed for word lengths up to $k = 12$ bytes; that is, $(3^{12} - 1)/2 = 265{,}720$ nonzero error magnitudes were considered. The check lengths were again $2 \leq a \leq 12$, and the byte lengths were $2 \leq b \leq 10$ and $b = 12$. It was observed that for relatively prime pairs (a, b) the miss percentages were close to $100/(2^a - 1)$, becoming greater for pairs with common divisors, and reaching the maximal values of Table B–2 for $b = a$ and $b = c'a$. Complete results of the tabulation are presented in Avižienis [1965].

It is noted that the most favorable choices of pairs (a, b) in the determinate faults are the least desirable choices for indeterminate faults, and vice versa. The choice of the most suitable values therefore depends on the relative frequencies of these two types of faults.

Repeated-Use Faults in Residue Codes

The results of the preceding sections on repeated-use faults apply directly to the fault effectiveness of the low-cost AN codes $(2^a - 1)X$. The low-cost residue codes in the byte-serial processor suffer a serious disadvantage because of a new variety of an undetectable repeated-use determinate fault. The miss occurs when the check symbol x' of value $(2^a - 1)|X$ uses the same digit circuits as the operand x. In this case, the fault affects the relative position $h(0 \leq h \leq b - 1)$ in x', as well as in every byte of x, and a compensating error may occur. In the preferred choice $b = a$, the miss will occur whenever the position h in x' and *exactly one* position in x are altered by an S0 or S1 fault. For example, consider the modulo 15 residue encoding

$x = 0010, 0011, 0101 \qquad x' = 1010$

An S1 fault sets the rightmost $(h = 0)$ bit to 1 in every byte of x and in x' (boldface indicates changed bits) to give $x*$, $x'*$:

$x* = 0011, 0011, 0101 \qquad x'* = 1011$

The checking algorithm yields $15|X* = 1011$ which is equal to $X'*$, and a "compensating miss" occurs which is independent of the length of x as long as only one byte in x is affected.

The compensating miss is eliminated by the use of the *inverse* residue code in which $X'' = (2^a - 1) - X'$ is substituted for X'. Consider the preceding example with the inverse residue $X'' = 1111 - 1010 = 0101$ replacing X'. The same S1 fault causes

$x* = 0011, 0011, 0101 \qquad x''* = 0101$

The check yields $15|X* = 1011$: adding $X''*$ modulo 15 gives the result 0001 which indicates an error, since it is not equal to 1111.

The fault remains detectable even when one change each occurs in x and x'. Consider the previous example with a new operand y and its inverse residue y'':

$y = 1000, 1101, 0101 \qquad y'' = 0100$

The check gives $15|Y = 1011$, and $15|Y + Y'' = 1111$, i.e., no error. The previous S1 fault causes

$y* = 1001, 1101, 0101 \qquad y''* = 0101$

The check gives $15|Y* = 1100$ and $15|Y* + Y''* = 0010$, indicating an error.

The compensating miss does not occur because the change $0 \to 1$ in y' corresponds to the change $1 \to 0$ in y'. The first miss will occur when $y*$ consists of 14 bytes, each containing a zero in the rightmost position $n = 0$, and y' also has a zero in $h = 0$. All results of the determinate fault effectiveness study are directly applicable to the low-cost inverse residue codes. This result led to the choice of modulo 15 inverse residue codes for both data words and address parts of instructions in the fault-tolerant STAR computer [Avižienis et al., 1971].

MULTIPLE ARITHMETIC ERROR CODES

Multiple Low-Cost Codes

The preceding section treated *single* codes which use only one check modulus. A study of fault-locating properties of the low-cost codes led to the observation that the use of *multiple* codes with two or more check moduli could provide complete fault location, corresponding to error correction [Avižienis, 1965, 1967a]. Continued study of multiple encodings has led to the development of several new varieties of arithmetic error codes, first discussed in Avižienis [1969].*

First it is shown that a single low-cost check modulus $2^a - 1$ has partial error-location properties in both AN and residues codes. Consider the error value pairs ($0 \leq i \leq ka - 1$):

$$\{2^i; \ -(2^{ka} - 1) + 2^i\} \qquad \{-2^i; \ (2^{ka} - 1) - 2^i\}$$

that may be caused by a basic fault during a transfer or one's complement additive inverse, shift, or addition (the operand is ka bits long). Writing the value of 2^i as a radix-2^a number, we have

$$2^i = 2^h 2^{ja}, \qquad h = i - ja.$$

The index $h = i - ja$ is called the *intra-group index* and j is called the *group index*. Their ranges are

$$0 \leq h \leq a - 1 \qquad 0 \leq j \leq k - 1$$

It is evident that

$$2^a | 2^h 2^{ja} = 2^a | [-(2^{ka} - 1) + 2^h 2^{ja}] = 2^h$$

$$2^a | (-2^h 2^{ja}) = 2^a | [(2^{ka} - 1) - 2^h 2^{ja}] = (2^a - 1) - 2^h$$

The sign and the intra-group index h are uniquely identified for the error values $\pm 2^i$, even if the value of the end-around carry is incorrect due to the addition of $\pm 2^i$. The a-bit residue 2^h has a single 1 digit, and $(2^a - 1) - 2^h$ has a single 0 digit. For example, (with $h = 3$, $a = 4$) the residue is 1000 for the error 2^{3+4j}, and 0111 for -2^{3+4j}.

In the case of AN low-cost codes, the modulo $2^a - 1$ checking algorithm directly yields the check sum residues described above. In the case of residue low-cost codes, the main result X and the check result X' are computed. The checking algorithm must compute the a-bit check sum F:

$$F = (2^a - 1) | [(2^a - 1) | X + (2^a - 1) - X']$$

A correct result (X, X') will yield the all ones form of $F = 0$. It is readily shown that an erroneous main result $X \pm 2^i$ yields $F = (2^a - 1) | (\pm 2^h)$, identical to the check sums of the AN code. An erroneous check result $(2^a - 1) | (X' \pm 2^h)$ yields $F = (2^a - 1) | (\mp 2^h)$, and the sign information becomes ambiguous: 1000 indicates the error $+2^{3+4j}$ in the main result, or the error -2^3 in the

---

* Multiple arithmetic encodings have been recently described in Rao [1970] and Rao and Garcia [1971]. It must be noted that the use of multiple check moduli for single-error correction was first described in Avižienis [1965, pp. 12–13] and [1967a, pp. 36–37], and details were presented in Avižienis [1969], considerably prior to Rao [1970] and Rao and Garcia [1971]. Papers by Avižienis [1965, 1967a] and additional communication on the topic were supplied to Garcia at a UCLA short course in April 1968.

check result. The ambiguity is eliminated by the inverse residue codes which use $X'' = (2^a - 1) - X'$ as the check result. The check sum for the inverse residue code is

$$G = (2^a - 1)|[(2^a - 1)|X + X'']$$

When X'' is correct, $G = 0$ is represented by the all ones form. An error in the main result X gives the same check sum as for the residue code. An erroneous check result has the value $(2^a - 1)|(X'' \pm 2^h)$, which replaces X'' and yields the check sum $G = (2^a - 1)|(\pm 2^h)$. Both the sign and the intra-group index h are known. The group index j remains unknown; it is also not known whether the check result or the main result is in error.

The preceding result has two applications. First, it has been used to derive the miss percentage equations for repeated-use faults in the section above on Low-Cost Radix-2 Arithmetic Codes. Second, it has led to the observation that the use of more than one low-cost check modulus will permit the unique identification of the bit index i of the error values $\pm 2^i$, and subsequent error correction, while using only the low-cost check moduli $2^{a_1} - 1$, $2^{a_2} - 1$, etc. [Avižienis, 1965, 1967a].

The check modulus $A^i = 2^{a_i} - 1$ has the group length of a_i bits. Given the pair (a_1, a_2) with GCD $(a_1, a_2) = 1$, there will be $a_1 a_2$ distinct pairs of intra-group indices

$$\{h_1, h_2\}, \quad 0 \le h_1 \le a_1 - 1$$
$$0 \le h_2 \le a_2 - 1$$

For example, $a_1 = 3$ and $a_2 = 4$ yield twelve pairs of indices:

$$h_1 = |2, 1, 0|2, 1, 0|2, 1, 0|2, 1, 0|$$

$$h_2 = |3, 2, 1, 0|3, 2, 1, 0|3, 2, 1, 0|$$

The same observation applies to sets of three or more group lengths $\{a_1, a_2, \ldots, a_m\}$ which are pairwise prime. The length of the binary number for which distinct sets of intra-group indices $\{h_1, h_2, \ldots, h_m\}$ exist is p bits, while the encoding requires s bits, with

$$p = \prod_{i=1}^{m} a_i \text{ and } s = \prod_{i=1}^{m} a_i$$

For example, the choice of $a_1 = 3$, $a_2 = 4$, $a_3 = 5$ will give $p = 3 \cdot 4 \cdot 5 = 60$ distinct sets of three intra-group indices with $s = 3 + 4 + 5 = 12$ bits used for encoding [Avižienis, 1965, 1967a].

The effect of the m-tuple low-cost code with m pairwise prime group lengths $\{a_1, a_2, \ldots, a_m\}$ is the same as the effect of a code with a single check modulus $2^p - 1$ with respect to single-error correction and double-error detection for error values $\pm 2^i$ and $\mp(2^p - 1 - 2^i)$ over $0 \le i \le p - 1$. Burst-error detection is 100 percent effective for all bursts up to and including $s - 1$ adjacent positions. Most important, the m separate low-cost checking algorithms are retained by an m-tuple low-cost code. One low-cost check is sufficient to detect the error values for which correction is possible; the other checks need to be performed only when an error is indicated and may share the same hardware.

Both AN and residue codes are suitable for multiple low-cost encoding. In the case of ordinary and inverse residue codes, the use of more than one check modulus resolves whether the error is in the main or in the check result: if only one check result indicates an error, it is incorrect; if all check results indicate an error, then it is traced to the bit i in the main result by the set of intra-group indices. The sign ambiguity of single residue codes is eliminated, and correction takes place either in the main result, or in the incorrect residue. An important difference between multiple low-cost residue and AN codes is the length of the uncoded information word. The nonseparate AN codes allow $p - s$ information bits, while the separate residue codes allow p information bits, with the s check bits added on as separate check symbols. Residue codes with the same number of check bits provide the same performance for a longer information word. The separateness of residue codes leads to a simpler design of the main processor which deals with uncoded operands, rather than with multiples of the check moduli which are used in the AN code processor.

The use of two or more low-cost check moduli permits multiple "mixed" low-cost encodings. A *mixed low-cost code* is a single or multiple low-cost AN code (p bits long) with a low-cost residue encoding (single or multiple) of the AN-coded words. Given the moduli $\{A_1, \ldots, A_m\}$, the mixed codes possess the same error-location properties as the corresponding *uniform* (AN or residue) multiple codes. For an example, consider the moduli $\{7, 15, 31\}$, with $a_1 = 3$, $a_2 = 4$, $a_3 = 5$. The uniform residue code has $p = 3 \cdot 4 \cdot 5 = 60$ information bits and $s = 3 + 4 + 5 = 12$ check bits. The uniform AN code has $p - s = 48$ information bits encoded with $A = 7 \cdot 15 \cdot 31 = 3255$; however, the checking algorithms remain separate modulo 7, 15, 31 low-cost checks. Six versions of the mixed code are available: three with double-residue encoding: (7, 15), (7, 31), (15, 31); and three with single-residue encoding: (7), (15), (31). In all six cases the AN-coded word must remain $p = 60$ bits long; e.g., the AN code with $A_3 = 31$ has 55 information bits and 5 check bits, plus the 7 check bits of the double residue code with $A_1 = 7$, $A_2 = 15$. The error location algorithm uses the intra-group indices as in the uniform codes; an error in the main result is identified by the AN code check.

"Hybrid-Cost" Forms of Multiple Codes

In this section it is shown that the partial error-location property of the low-cost codes provides a low-cost extension of the range of other (non-low-cost) error-correcting codes. *Hybrid-cost* arithmetic error codes are multiple codes with a set of moduli $\{A_1, A_2, \ldots, A_m\}$ which includes one or more low-cost check moduli A_i, as well as one or more non-low-cost check moduli A_j' with the properties of error correction [Brown, 1960; Peterson, 1961, pp. 236–44; Henderson, 1961; Garner, 1966].

A hybrid-cost code (for example, the double code with moduli A, A') offers two advantages over one error-correcting check modulus A'. First, the low-cost code (modulo $2^a - 1$) checking algorithm alone is sufficient to detect errors which are corrected by A'. Second, suitable choices of the pairs (A, A') permit the use of the intra-group index h of the low-cost code ($h = 0, 1, \ldots,$ $a - 1$) to extend the range covered by A'. Given a single-error-correcting check modulus A' with the period of g bits, and the low-cost check modulus $A = 2^a - 1$ such that GCD $(g, a) = 1$, it is evident that the intra-group index h extends the range of the hybrid-cost code to $p' = g \cdot a$ bits. For example, $A' = 23$ gives distinct values of the residue $23|(\pm 2^i)$ for $0 \le i \le 10$, $11 < i < 21$, etc., identifying uniquely the index i and the sign of $\pm 2^i$ for an 11-bit operand [Brown, 1960]. Together with $A = 2^a - 1$, the length for unique identification of the index and sign is $11a$ bits as long as GCD $(11, a) = 1$ [Avižienis, 1969]. The use of $f \le 2$ low-cost check moduli $(A_1, \ldots, A_f)$ with some A' will give the combined effect of the f-tuple low-cost code with the error-correcting properties of A', as long as the check moduli have pairwise GCD $= 1$.

Three distinct classes of f-tuple hybrid-cost codes (with $f \ge 2$) can be identified: 1) uniform AN codes; 2) uniform residue codes; and 3) mixed (AN + residue) codes. The codes are similar to low-cost multiple codes described previously with the exception that one or more check moduli A_j' are non-low-cost. Differences between the three classes of codes appear in their implementation. The hybrid-cost AN codes $AA'X$ have the disadvantage of a costlier and slower implementation of arithmetic algorithms, since A' is not a low-cost check modulus. The hybrid-cost residue codes avoid these difficulties because they are separate. The use of more than one check modulus resolves the question whether the error is in the main or in the check result. In a double hybrid-cost residue code with the check moduli (A,A') the low-cost modulo A check is carried out each time for error detection. An error indication initiates the modulo A' check. If the latter does not indicate an error, then the modulo A check result is incorrect, and correction of the check result follows. If the modulo A' check result also indicates an error, then the main result is corrected, using both check results.

The mixed hybrid-cost codes have two major variants: 1) low-cost AN code with modulo A' residue encoding; 2) error-correcting $A'X$ code with modulo-A low-cost residue encoding. The first variant gives simple algorithms in the main processor, but must resolve the problem (existing also for hybrid-cost residue codes) of checking the error-correcting modulo A' residue if the modulo A' check is used only after detection using low-cost A. The second variant (preferably with inverse residue code) gives simple residue checking for error detection, but requires complex algorithms in the main processor which operates on multiples of the non-low-cost check modulus A'. Other minor variants of mixed hybrid-cost codes are created when two or more check moduli are used for the AN part and/or the residue part. Each part, in turn, can be low cost or hybrid cost.

In conclusion it is noted that the use of multiple low-cost and hybrid-cost arithmetic encodings offers a variety of implementations. Fault location and error correction by means of multiple encodings employs the low-cost codes alone as well as to extend the range covered by error-correcting codes. It is also important to observe that multiple encodings permit the use of residue codes for error correction, since they distinguish whether the error is in the main result or in one of the check results. This information is not available with one residue and the generally less convenient nonseparate AN codes have to be used in single encodings. Detailed consideration of multiple encodings is presented in Avižienis [1969]. Finally, it should be noted that the concepts of multiple encoding (AN, residue, and mixed) are applicable to multiple non-low-cost check moduli as well.

REFERENCES

Avižienis, 1964, 1965, 1966a, 1966b, 1967a, 1967b, 1968, 1969; Avižienis et al., 1971; Brown, 1960; Garner, 1958, 1966; Henderson, 1961; Peterson, 1958, 1961; Rao, 1970; Rao and Garcia, 1971.

APPENDIX C

Design for Testability—A Survey

Thomas W. Williams and Kenneth P. Parker*

This appendix discusses the basics of design for testability. A short review of testing is given along with some reasons why one should test. The different techniques of design for testability are discussed in detail. These include techniques that can be applied to today's technologies and techniques that have been recently introduced and will soon appear in new designs.

INTRODUCTION

Integrated Circuit Technology is now moving from Large-Scale Integration (LSI) to Very-Large-Scale Integration (VLSI). This increase in gate count, which now can be as much as factors of three to five times, has also brought a decrease in gate costs, along with improvements in performance. All these attributes of VLSI are welcomed by the industry. However, a problem never adequately solved by LSI is still with us and is getting much worse: the problem of determining, in a cost-effective way, whether a component, module, or board has been manufactured correctly [Breuer, 1976; Chang, Manning, and Metze, 1970; Friedman and Menon, 1971;

The testing problem has two major facets:

Test generation [Test Generation]
Test verification [Simulation]

Test generation is the process of enumerating stimuli for a circuit which will demonstrate its correct operation. Test verification is the process of proving that a set of tests are effective towards this end. To date, formal proof has been impossible in practice. Fault simulation has been our best alternative, yielding a quantitative measure of test effectiveness. With the vast increase in circuit density, the ability to generate test patterns automatically and conduct fault simulation with these patterns has drastically waned. As a result, some manufacturers are foregoing these more rigorous approaches and are accepting the risks of shipping a defective product. One general approach to addressing this problem is embodied in a collection of techniques known as "Design for Testability" [Designing for Testability].

Design for Testability initially attracted interest in connection with LSI designs. Today, in the context of VLSI, the phrase is gaining even more currency. The collection of techniques that comprise Design for Testability are, in some cases, general guidelines; in other cases, they are hard and fast design rules. Together, they can be regarded essentially as a menu of techniques, each with its associated cost of implementation and return on investment. The purpose of this paper is to present the basic concepts in testing, beginning with the fault models and carrying through to the different techniques associated with Design for Testability which are known today in the public sector. The design for testability techniques are divided into two categories [Williams and Parker, 1979]. The first category is that of the ad hoc technique for solving the testing problem.

* Acknowledgments: The authors wish to thank D. J. Brown for his helpful comments and suggestions. The assistance of Ms. B. Fletcher, Ms. C. Mendoza, Ms. L. Clark, Ms. J. Allen, and J. Smith in preparing this manuscript for publication was invaluable.

803

These techniques solve a problem for a given design and are not generally applicable to all designs. This is contrasted with the second category of structured approaches. These techniques are generally applicable and usually involve a set of design rules by which designs are implemented. The objective of a structured approach is to reduce the sequential complexity of a network to aid test generation and test verification.

The first ad hoc approach is partitioning [Akers, 1977; HP-b; Hayes, 1974; Lippman and Donn, 1979]. Partitioning is the ability to disconnect one portion of a network from another portion of a network in order to make testing easier. The next approach which is used at the board level is that of adding extra test points [Hayes, 1974; Hayes and Friedman, 1973]. The third ad hoc approach is that of Bus Architecture Systems [HP-a; Nadig, 1979]. This is similar to the partitioning approach and allows one to divide and conquer—that is, to be able to reduce the network to smaller subnetworks which are much more manageable. These subnetworks are not necessarily designed with any design for testability in mind. The fourth technique which bridges both the structured approach and the ad hoc approach is that of Signature Analysis [HP-a; Nadig, 1979; White, 1978; Frohwerk, 1977]. Signature Analysis requires some design rules at the board level, but is not directed at the same objective as the structure approaches are—that is, the ability to observe and control the state variables of a sequential machine.

For structured approaches, there are essentially four categories which will be discussed—the first of which is a multiplexer technique [Ando, 1980; Funatsu, Wakatsuki, and Arima, 1975], Random Access Scan, which has been recently published and has been used, to some extent, by others before. The next techniques are those of the Level-Sensitive Scan Design (LSSD) [DasGupta, Eichelberger, and Williams, 1978; Eichelberger and Williams, 1978, 1977; Eichelberger et al. 1978; Williams and Angell, 1973; Williams, 1978] approach and the Scan Path approach which will be discussed in detail. These techniques allow the test generation problem to be completely reduced to one of generating tests for combinational logic. Another approach which will be discussed is that of the Scan/Set Logic [Stewart, 1977]. This is similar to the LSSD approach and the Scan Path approach since shift registers are used to load and unload data. However, these shift registers are not part of the system data path and all system latches are not necessarily controllable and observable via the shift register. The fourth approach which will be discussed is that of Built-In Logic Block Observation (BILBO) [Koenemann, Mucha, and Zwiehoff, 1979] which has just recently been proposed. This technique has the attributes of both the LSSD network and Scan Path network, the ability to separate the network into combinational and sequential parts, and has the attribute of Signature Analysis—that is, employing linear feedback shift registers.

For each of the techniques described under the structured approach, the constraints, as well as various ways in which they can be exploited in design, manufacturing, testing, and field servicing will be described. The basic storage devices and the general logic structure resulting from the design constraints will be described in detail. The important question of how much it costs in logic gates and operating speed will be discussed qualitatively. All the structured approaches essentially allow the controllability and observability of the state variables in the sequential machine. In essence, then, test generation and fault simulation can be directed more at a combinatorial network, rather than at a sequential network.

Definitions and Assumptions

A model of faults which is used throughout the industry that does not take into account all possible defects, but is a more global type of model, is the Stuck-At model. The Stuck-At model [Breuer, 1976; Chang, Manning, and Metze, 1970; Friedman and Menon, 1971] assumes that a logic gate input or output is fixed to either a logic 0 or a logic 1. Figure C–1(a) shows an AND gate which is fault-free. Figure C–1(b) shows an AND gate with input "A," Stuck-At-1 (S-A-1).

The faulty AND gate perceives the "A" input as 1, irrespective of the logic value placed on the input. The pattern applied to the fault-free AND gates in Figure C–1 has an output value of 0 since the input is 0 on the "A" input and 1 on the "B" input, and the AND'ing of those two leads to a 0 on the output. The pattern in Figure C–1(b) shows an output of 1, since the "A" input is perceived as a 1 even though a 0 is applied to that input. The 1 on the "B" input is perceived as a 1, and the results are AND'ed together to give a 1 output. Therefore, the pattern shown in Figures C–1(a) and (b) is a test for the "A" input, S-A-1, since there is a difference between the faulty gate (faulty machine) and the good gate (good machine). This pattern 01 on the "A" and "B" inputs, respectively, is considered a test because the good machine responds differently from the faulty machine. If they had the same response, then that pattern would not have constituted a test for that fault.

If a network contained N nets, any net may be good, Stuck-At-1 or Stuck-At-0; thus all possible network state combinations would be 3^N. A network with 100 nets, then, would contain 5×10^{47} different combinations of faults. This would be far too many faults to assume. The run time of any program trying to generate tests or fault simulate tests for this kind of design would be impractical.

Therefore, the industry, for many years, has clung to the single Stuck-At fault assumption. That is, a good machine will have no faults. The faulty machines that are assumed will have one, and only one, of the stuck faults. In other words, all faults taken two at a time are not assumed, nor are all faults taken three at a time, etc. History has proven that the single Stuck-At fault assumption, in prior technologies, has been adequate. However, there could be some problems in LSI—particularly with CMOS using the single Stuck-At fault assumption.

The problem with CMOS is that there are a number of faults which could change a combinational network into a sequential network. Therefore, the combinational patterns are no longer effective in testing the network in all cases. It still remains to be seen whether, in fact, the single Stuck-At fault assumption will survive the CMOS problems.

Also, the single Stuck-At fault assumption does not, in general, cover the bridging faults [Mei, 1974] that may occur. Historically again, bridging faults have been detected by having a high level—that is, in the high 90 percent—single Stuck-At fault coverage, where the single Stuck-At fault coverage is defined to be the number of faults that are tested divided by the number of faults that are assumed.

FIGURE C–1
Test for input stuck-at fault: (a) fault-free AND gate (good machine); (b) faulty AND gate (faulty machine)

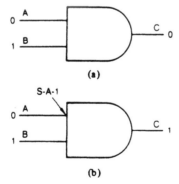

The VLSI Testing Problem

The VLSI testing problem is the sum of a number of problems. All the problems, in the final analysis, relate to the cost of doing business (dealt with in the following section). There are two basic problem areas:

Test generation
Test verification via fault simulation

With respect to test generation, the problem is that as logic networks get larger, the ability to generate tests automatically is becoming more and more difficult.

The second facet of the VLSI testing problem is the difficulty in fault simulating the test patterns. Fault simulation is that process by which the fault coverage is determined for a specific set of input test patterns. In particular, at the conclusion of the fault simulation, every fault that is detected by the given pattern set is listed. For a given logic network with 1000 two-input logic gates, the maximum number of single Stuck-At faults which can be assumed is 6000. Some reduction in the number of single Stuck-At faults can be achieved by fault equivalencing [Boote and McCluskey, 1971; Boote, 1972; McCluskey and Clegg, 1971; Mei, 1970; Schertz and Metze, 1972]. However, the number of single Stuck-At faults needed to be assumed is about 3000. Fault simulation, then, is the process of applying every given test pattern to a fault-free machine and to each of the 3000 copies of the good machine containing one, and only one, of the single Stuck-At faults. Thus fault simulation, with respect to run time, is similar to doing 3001 good machine simulations.

Techniques are available to reduce the complexity of fault simulation; however, it still is a very time-consuming, and hence, expensive task [Sellers, Hsiao, and Bearnson, 1968; Manning and Chang, 1968; Parker, 1979; Seshu and Freeman, 1962; Szygenda, 1972; Ulrich and Baker, 1974; Ulrich, Baker, and Williams, 1972].

It has been observed that the computer run time to do test [Goel, 1980] generation and fault simulation is approximately proportional to the number of logic gates to the power of 3;[*] hence, small increases in gate count will yield quickly increasing run times. Equation (1)

$$T = KN^3 \tag{1}$$

shows this relationship, where T is computer run time, N is the number of gates, and K is the proportionality constant. The relationship does not take into account the falloff in automatic test generation capability due to sequential complexity of the network. It has been observed that computer run time just for fault simulation is proportional to N^2 without even considering the test generation phase.

When one talks about testing, the topic of functional testing always comes up as a feasible way to test a network. Theoretically, to do a complete functional test ("exhaustive" testing) seems to imply that all entries in a Karnaugh map (or excitation table) must be tested for a 1 or a 0. This

---

[*] The value of the exponent given here (3) is perhaps pessimistic in some cases. Other analyses have used the value 2 instead. A quick rationale goes as follows: with a linear increase k in circuit size comes an attendant linear increase in the number of failure mechanisms (now yielding k squared increase in work). Also, as circuits become larger, they tend to become more strongly connected such that a given block is affected by more blocks and even itself. This causes more work to be done in a range we feel to be k cubed. This fairly nebulous concept of connectivity seems to be the cause for debate on whether the exponent should be 3 or some other value.

means that if a network has N inputs and is purely combinational, then 2^N patterns are required to do a complete functional test. Furthermore, if a network has N inputs with M latches, at a minimum it takes 2^{N+M} patterns to do a complete functional test. Rarely is that minimum ever obtainable; and in fact, the number of tests required to do a complete functional test is very much higher than that. With LSI, this may be a network with $N = 25$ and $M = 50$, or 2^{75} patterns, which is approximately 3.8×10^{22}. Assuming one had the patterns and applied them at an application rate of 1 μs per pattern, the test time would be over a billion years (10^9).

Cost of Testing

One might ask why so much attention is now being given to the level of testability at chip and board levels. The bottom line is the cost of doing business. A standard among people familiar with the testing process is: If it costs $0.30 to detect a fault at the chip level, then it would cost $3 to detect that same fault when it was embedded at the board level; $30 when it is embedded at the system level; and $300 when it is embedded at the system level but has to be found in the field. Thus if a fault can be detected at a chip or board level, then significantly larger costs per fault can be avoided at subsequent levels of packaging.

With VLSI and the inadequacy of automatic test generation and fault simulation, there is considerable difficulty in obtaining a level of testability required to achieve acceptable defect levels. If the defect level of boards is too high, the cost of field repairs is also too high. These costs, and in some cases, the inability to obtain a sufficient test, have led to the need to have "Design for Testability."

DESIGN FOR TESTABILITY

There are two key concepts in Design for Testability: controllability and observability. Control and observation of a network are central to implementing its test procedure. For example, consider the case of the simple AND block in Figure C–1. In order to be able to test the "A" input Stuck-At 1, it was necessary to control the "A" input to 0 and the "B" input to 1 and be able to observe the "C" output to determine whether a 0 was observed or a 1 was observed. The 0 is the result of the good machine, and the 1 would be the result if you had a faulty machine. If this AND block is embedded into a much larger sequential network, the requirement of being able to control the "A" and "B" inputs to 0 and 1, respectively, and being able to observe the output "C," be it through some other logic blocks, still remains. Therein lies part of the problem of being able to generate tests for a network.

Because of the need to determine if a network has the attributes of controllability and observability that are desired, a number of programs have been written which essentially give analytic measures of controllability and observability for different nets in a given sequential network [Dejka, 1977; Goldstein, 1979; Keiner and West, 1977; Kovijanic, 1979; Stephenson and Grason, 1976].

After observing the results of one of these programs in a given network, the logic designer can then determine whether some of the techniques, which will be described later, can be applied to this network to ease the testing problem. For example, test points may be added at critical points which are not observable or which are not controllable, or some of the techniques of Scan Path or LSSD can be used to initialize certain latches in the machines to avoid the difficulties of controllability associated with sequential machines. The popularity of such tools is continuing to grow, and a number of companies are now embarking upon their own controllability/observability measures.

AD HOC DESIGN FOR TESTABILITY*

Testing has moved from the afterthought position that it used to occupy to part of the design environment in LSI and VLSI. When testing was part of the afterthought, it was a very expensive process. Products were discarded because there was no adequate way to test them in production quantities.

There are two basic approaches which are prevalent today in the industry to help solve the testing problem. The first approach categorized here is Ad Hoc, and the second approach is categorized as a Structured Approach. The Ad Hoc techniques are those techniques which can be applied to a given product, but are not directed at solving the general sequential problem. They usually do offer relief, and their cost is probably lower than the cost of the Structured Approaches. The Structured Approaches, on the other hand, are trying to solve the general problem with a design methodology, such that when the designer has completed his design from one of these particular approaches, the results will be test generation and fault simulation at acceptable costs. Structured Approaches lend themselves more easily to design automation. Again, the main difference between the two approaches is probably the cost of implementation and hence, the return on investment for this extra cost. In the Ad Hoc approaches, the jobs of doing test generation and fault simulation are usually not as simple or as straightforward as they would be with the Structured Approaches, as we shall see shortly.

A number of techniques have evolved from MSI to LSI and now into VLSI that fall under the category of the ad hoc approaches of "Design for Testability." These techniques are usually solved at the board level and do not necessarily require changes in the logic design in order to accomplish them.

Partitioning

Because the task of test pattern generation and fault simulation is proportional to the number of logic gates to the third power, a significant amount of effort has been directed at approaches called "Divide and Conquer."

There are a number of ways in which the partitioning approach to Design for Testability can be implemented. The first is to mechanical partition by dividing a network in half. In essence, this would reduce the test generation and fault simulation tasks by 8 for two boards. Unfortunately, having two boards rather than one board can be a significant cost disadvantage and defeats the purpose of integration.

Another approach that helps the partitioning problem, as well as helping one to "Divide and Conquer" is to use jumper wires. These wires would go off the board and then back on the board, so that the tester and the test generator can control and observe these nets directly. However, this could mean a significant number of I/O contacts at the board level which could also get very costly.

Degating is another technique for separating modules on a board. For example, in Figure C–2, a degating line goes to two AND blocks that are driven from Module 1. The results of those two AND blocks go to two independent OR blocks—one controlled by Control Line 1, the other with Control Line 2. The output of the OR block from Control Line 1 goes into Module 2, and the output of Control Line 2 goes into Module 3. When the degate line is at the 0 value, the two Control Lines, 1 and 2, can be used to drive directly into Modules 2 and 3. Therefore, complete controllability of the inputs to Modules 2 and 3 can be obtained by using these control lines. If those two nets happen to be very difficult nets to control, as pointed out, say, by a testability

---

* Williams and Parker, 1979.

FIGURE C–2
Use of degating logic for logical partioning

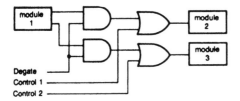

measure program, then this would be a very cost-effective way of controlling those two nets and hence, being able to derive the tests at a very reasonable cost.

A classical example of degating logic is that associated with an oscillator, as shown in Figure C–3. In general, if an oscillator is free-running on a board, driving logic, it is very difficult, and sometimes impossible, to synchronize the tester with the activity of the logic board. As a result, degating logic can be used here to block the oscillator and have a pseudo-clock line which can be controlled by the tester, so that the dc testing of all the logic on that board can be synchronized. All of these techniques require a number of extra primary inputs and primary outputs and possibly extra modules to perform the degating.

Test Points

Another approach to help the controllability and observability of a sequential network is to use test points [Hayes, 1974; Hayes and Friedman, 1973]. If a test point is used as a primary input to the network, then that can function to enhance controllability. If a test point is used as a primary output, then that is used to enhance the observability of a network. In some cases, a single pin can be used as both an input and an output.

For example, in Figure C–4, Module 1 has a degate function, so that the output of those two pins on the module could go to noncontrolling values. Thus the external pins which are dotted into those nets could control those nets and drive Module 2. On the other hand, if the degate function is at the opposite value, then the output of Module 1 can be observed on these external pins. Thus the enhancement of controllability and observability can be accommodated by adding pins which can act as both inputs and outputs under certain degating conditions.

FIGURE C–3
Degating lines for oscillator

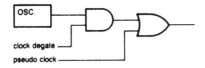

FIGURE C–4
Test points used as both inputs and outputs

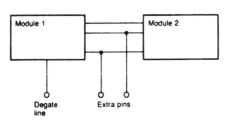

Another technique which can be used for controllability is to have a pin which, in one mode, implies system operation, and in another mode takes N inputs and gates them to a decoder. The 2^N outputs of the decoder are used to control certain nets to values which otherwise would be difficult to obtain. By so doing, the controllability of the network is enhanced.

As mentioned before, predictability is an issue which is as important as controllability and observability. Again, test points can be used here. For example, a CLEAR or PRESET function for all memory elements can be used. Thus the sequential machine can be put into a known state with very few patterns.

Another technique which falls into the category of test points and is very widely used is that of the "Bed of Nails" [Stewart, 1977] tester, Figure C–5. The Bed of Nails tester probes the underside of a board to give a larger number of points for observability and controllability. This is in addition to the normal tester contact to the board under test. The drawback of this technique is that the tester must have enough test points to be able to control and observe each one of these nails on the Bed of Nails tester. Also, there are extra loads which are placed on the nets and this can cause some drive and receive problems. Furthermore, the mechanical fixture which will hold the Bed of Nails has to be constructed, so that the normal forces on the probes are sufficient to guarantee reliable contacts. Another application for the Bed of Nails testing is to do "drive/sense nails" [Stewart, 1977] or "*in situ*" or "in-circuit" testing, which, effectively, is the technique of testing each chip on the board independently of the other chips on the board. For each chip, the appropriate nails and/or primary inputs are driven so as to prevent one chip from being driven by the other chips on the board. Once this state has been established, the isolated chip on the board can now be tested. In this case, the resolution to the failing chip is much better than edge connector tests; however, there is some exposure to incomplete testing of interconnections and care must be taken not to damage the circuit when overdriving it. Design for testability in a Bed of Nails environment must take the issues of contact reliability, multiplicity, and electrical loading into account.

Bus Architecture

An approach that has been used very successfully to attack the partitioning problem by the microcomputer designers is to use a bus structured architecture. This architecture allows access to critical buses which go to many different modules on the computer board. For example, in Figure C–6, you can see that the data bus is involved with the microprocessor module, the ROM module, the RAM module, and the I/O Controller module. If there is external access to the data bus and three of the four modules can be turned off the data bus—that is, their outputs can be put into a high-impedance state (three-state driver)—then the data bus could be used to drive

FIGURE C–5
"Bed of Nails" test

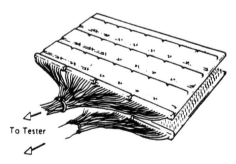

To Tester

FIGURE C–6
Bus structured microcomputer

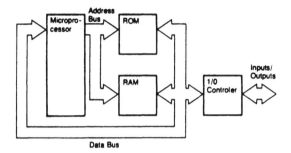

the fourth module, as if it were a primary input (or primary output) to that particular module. Similarly, with the address bus, access again must be controlled externally to the board, and thus the address bus can be very useful to controlling test patterns to the microcomputer board. These buses, in essence, partition the board in a unique way, so that testing of subunits can be accomplished. A drawback of bus-structured designs comes with faults on the bus itself. If a bus wire is stuck, any module or the bus trace itself may be the culprit. Normal testing is done by deducing the location of a fault from voltage information. Isolating a bus failure may require current measurements, which are much more difficult to do.

Signature Analysis

This technique for testing, introduced in 1977 [Nadig, 1977; White, 1978, Frohwerk, 1977], is heavily reliant on planning done in the design stage. That is why this technique falls between the Ad Hoc and the Structured Approaches for Design for Testability, since some care must be taken at the board level in order to ensure proper operation of this Signature Analysis of the board [HP-a]. Signature Analysis is well-suited to bus structure architectures, as previously mentioned and in particular, those associated with microcomputers. This will become more apparent shortly.

The integral part of the Signature Analysis approach is that of a linear feedback shift register [Peterson and Weldon, 1972]. Figure C–7 shows an example of a 3-bit linear feedback shift register. This linear feedback shift register is made up of three shift register latches. Each one is represented by a combination of an $L1$ latch and an $L2$ latch. These can be thought of as the master latch being the $L1$ latch and the slave latch being the $L2$ latch. An "A" clock clocks all the $L1$ latches, and a "B" clock clocks all the $L2$ latches, so that turning the "A" and "B" clocks on and off independently will shift the shift register 1-bit position to the right. Furthermore, this linear shift register has an EXCLUSIVE-OR gate which takes the output, $Q2$, the second bit in the shift register, and EXCLUSIVE-OR's it with the third bit in the shift register, $Q3$. The result of that EXCLUSIVE-OR is

FIGURE C–7
Counting capabilities of a linear feedback shift register

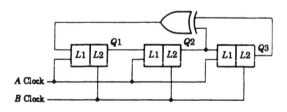

the input to the first shift register. A single clock could be used for this shift register, which is generally the case; however, this concept will be used shortly when some of the structured design approaches are discussed which use two nonoverlapping clocks. Figure C–7 shows how this linear feedback shift register will count for different initial values.

For longer shift registers, the maximal length linear feedback configurations can be obtained by consulting tables [Peterson and Weldon, 1972] to determine where to tap off the linear feedback shift register to perform the EXCLUSIVE-OR function. Of course, only EXCLUSIVE-OR blocks can be used, otherwise, the linearity would not be preserved.

The key to Signature Analysis is to design a network which can stimulate itself. A good example of such a network would be microprocessor-based boards, since they can stimulate themselves using the intelligence of the processor driven by the memory on the board.

The Signature Analysis procedure is one which has the shift register in the Signature Analysis tool, which is external to the board and not part of the board in any way, synchronized with the clocking that occurs on the board; see Figure C–8. A probe is used to probe a particular net on the board. The result of that probe is EXCLUSIVE-OR'ed into the linear feedback shift register. Of course, it is important that the linear feedback shift register be initialized to the same starting place every time, and that the clocking sequence be a fixed number, so that the tests can be repeated. The board must also have some initialization, so that its response will be repeated as well.

After a fixed number of clock periods—let's assume 50—a particular value will be stored in $Q1$, $Q2$, and $Q3$. It is not necessarily the value that would have occurred if the linear feedback shift register was just counted 50 times—Modulo 7. The value will be changed, because the values coming from the board via the probe will not necessarily be a continuous string of 1's; there will be 1's intermixed with 0's.

The place where the shift register stops on the Signature Analysis Tool—that is, the values for $Q1$, $Q2$, and $Q3$ is the Signature for that particular node for the good machine. The question is: If there were errors present at one or more points in the string of 50 observations of that particular net of the board, would the value stored in the shift register for $Q1$, $Q2$, and $Q3$ be different than the one for the good machine? It has been shown that with a 16-bit linear feedback shift register, the probability of detecting one or more errors is extremely high [Frohwerk, 1977]. In essence, the signature, or "residue," is the remainder of the data stream after division by an irreduceable polynomial. There is considerable data compression—that is, after the results of a

FIGURE C–8

Use of signature analysis tool

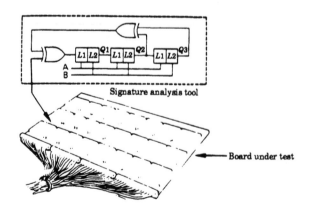

Signature analysis tool

Board under test

number of shifting operations, the test data are reduced to 16 bits, or, in the case of Figure C–8, 3 bits. Thus the result of the Signature Analysis tool is basically a Go/No-Go for the output for that particular module.

If the bad output for that module were allowed to cycle around through a number of other modules on the board and then feed back into this particular module, it would not be clear after examining all the nodes in the loop which module was defective—whether it was the module whose output was being observed, or whether it was another module upstream in the path. This gives rise to two requirements for Signature Analysis. First of all, closed-loop paths must be broken at the board level. Second, the best place to start probing with Signature Analysis is with a "kernel" of logic. In other words, on a microprocessor-based board, one would start with the outputs of the microprocessor itself and then build up from that particular point, once it has been determined that the microprocessor is good.

This breaking of closed loops is a tenet of Design for Testability and for Signature Analysis. There is a little overhead for implementing Signature Analysis. Some ROM space would be required (to stimulate the self-test), as well as extra jumpers, in order to break closed loops on the board. Once this is done, however, the test can be obtained for very little cost. The only question that remains is about the quality of the tests—that is, how good are the tests that are being generated, do they cover all the faults, etc.

Unfortunately, the logic models—for example, microprocessors—are not readily available to the board user. Even if a microprocessor logic model were available, they would not be able to do a complete fault simulation of the patterns because it would be too large. Hence, Signature Analysis may be the best that could be done for this particular board with the given inputs which the designer has. Presently, large numbers of users are currently using the Signature Analysis technique to test boards containing LSI and VLSI components.

STRUCTURED DESIGN FOR TESTABILITY

Today, with the utilization of LSI and VLSI technology, it has become apparent that even more care will have to be taken in the design stage in order to ensure testability and produceability of digital networks. This has led to rigorous and highly structured design practices. These efforts are being spearheaded not by the makers of LSI/VLSI devices but by electronics firms which possess captive IC facilities and the manufacturers of large main-frame computers.

Most structured design practices [Bottorff and Muehldorf, 1977; Ando, 1980; DasGupta, Eichelberger, and Williams, 1978; Eichelberger and Williams, 1977, 1978; Eichelberger et al. 1978; Funatsu, Wakatuski, and Arima, 1975; Koenemann, Mucha, and Zwiehoff, 1979; Stewart, 1977; Toth and Holt, 1974; Williams and Angell, 1973; Williams, 1978] are built upon the concept that if the values in all the latches can be controlled to any specific value, and if they can be observed with a very straightforward operation then the test generation, and possibly, the fault task, can be reduced to that of doing test generation and fault simulation for a combinatorial logic network. A control signal can switch the memory elements from their normal mode of operation to a mode that makes them controllable and observable.

It appears from the literature that several companies, such as IBM, Fujitsu Ltd., Sperry-Univac, and Nippon Electric Co., Ltd. [Bottorff and Muehldorf, 1977; Ando, 1980; DasGupta, Eichelberger, and Williams, 1978; Eichelberger and Williams, 1977, 1978; Eichelberger et al. 1978; Funatsu, Wakatuski, and Arima, 1975; Koenemann, Mucha, and Zwiehoff, 1979; Stewart, 1977; Toth and Holt, 1974; Williams and Angell, 1973; Williams, 1978] have been dedicating formidable amounts of resources toward Structured Design for Testability. One notes simply by scanning the literature on testing, that many of the practical concepts and tools for testing were developed by main-frame manufacturers who do not lack for processor power. It is significant, then, that these companies, with their resources, have recognized that unstructured designs lead to unacceptable testing problems. Presently, IBM has extensively documented its efforts in Structured Design for Testability, and these are reviewed first.

Level-Sensitive Scan Design (LSSD)

With the concept that the memory elements in an IC can be threaded together into a shift register, the memory elements values can be both controlled and observed. Figure C–9 shows the familiar generalized sequential circuit model modified to use a shift register. This technique enhances both controllability and observability, allowing us to augment testing by controlling inputs and internal states, and easily examining internal state behavior. An apparent disadvantage is the serialization of the test, potentially costing more time for actually running a test.

LSSD is IBM's discipline for structural design for testability. "Scan" refers to the ability to shift into or out of any state of the network. "Level-sensitive" refers to constraints on circuit excitation, logic depth, and the handling of clocked circuitry. A key element in the design is the "shift register latch" (SRL) such as can be implemented in Figure C–10. Such a circuit is immune to most anomalies in the ac characteristics of the clock, requiring only that it remain high (sample) at least long enough to stabilize the feedback loop, before being returned to the low (hold) state [Eichelberger and Williams, 1977, 1978]. The lines D and C form the normal mode memory function while lines I, A, B, and $L2$ comprise additional circuitry for the shift register function.

The shift registers are threaded by connecting I to $L2$ and operated by clocking lines A and B in two-phase fashion. Figure C–11 shows four modules threaded for shift register action. Now note in Figure C–11 that each module could be an SRL or, one level up, a board containing threaded IC's, etc. Each level of packaging requires the same four additional lines to implement the shift register scan feature. Figure C–12 depicts a general structure for an LSSD subsystem with a two-phase system clock. Additional rules concerning the gating of clocks, etc., are given by Williams and Eichelberger [1977, 1978]. Also, it is not practical to implement RAM with SRL memory, so additional procedures are required to handle embedded RAM circuitry [Eichelberger et al. 1978].

Given that an LSSD structure is achieved, what are the rewards? It turns out that the network can now be thought of as purely combinational, where tests are applied via primary inputs and shift register outputs. The testing of combinational circuits is a well understood and (barely) tractable problem. Now techniques such as the D-Algorithm [Roth, 1966] compiled code Boolean simulation [Chang, Manning, and Metze, 1970; Agrawal and Agrawal, 1972; Seshu, 1965; Seshu and Freeman, 1962], and adaptive random test generation [Parker, 1976; Schnurmann, Lindbloom,

FIGURE C–9

Classical model of a sequential network utilizing a shift register for storage

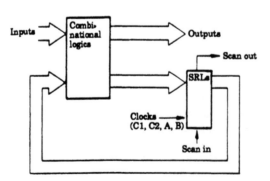

FIGURE C–10
Shift register latch (SRL): (a) symbolic representation; (b) implementation in AND-INVERT gates

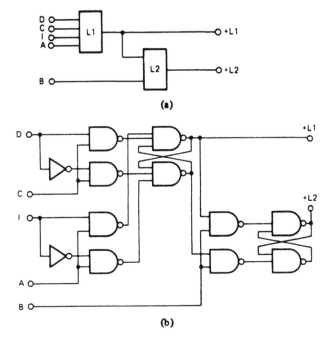

(a)

(b)

FIGURE C–11
Interconnection of SRL's on an integrated circuit and board

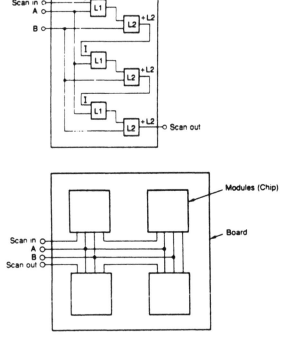

FIGURE C–12

*General structure
of an LSSD subsys-
tem with two sys-
tem clocks*

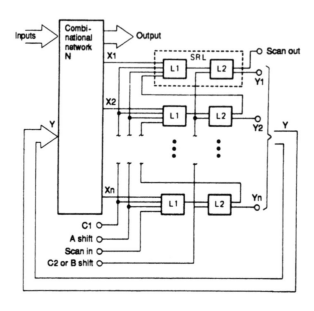

and Carpenter, 1975; Williams and Eichelberger, 1977] are again viable approaches to the testing problem. Further, as small subsystems are tested, their aggregates into larger systems are also testable by cataloging the position of each testable subsystem in the shift register chain. System tests become (ideally) simple concatenations of subsystem tests. Though ideals are rarely achieved, the potential for solving otherwise hopeless testing problems is very encouraging.

In considering the cost performance impacts, there are a number of negative impacts associated with the LSSD design philosophy. First of all, the shift register latches in the shift register are, logically, two or three times as complex as simple latches. Up to four additional primary inputs/outputs are required at each package level for control of the shift registers. External asynchronous input signals must not change more than once every clock cycle. Finally, all timing within the subsystem is controlled by externally generated clock signals.

In terms of additional complexity of the shift register hold latches, the overhead from experience has been in the range of 4 to 20 percent. The difference is due to the extent to which the system designer made use of the L2 latches for system function. It has been reported in the IBM System 38 literature that 85 percent of the L2 latches were used for system function. This drastically reduces the overhead associated with this design technique.

With respect to the primary inputs/outputs that are required to operate the shift register, this can be reduced significantly by making functional use of some of the pins. For example, the scan-out pin could be a functional output of an SRL for that particular chip. Also, overall performance of the subsystem may be degraded by the clocking requirement, but the effect should be small.

The LSSD structured design approach for Design for Testability eliminates or alleviates some of the problems in designing, manufacturing and maintaining LSI systems at a reasonable cost.

Scan Path

In 1975, a survey paper of test generation systems in Japan was presented by members of Nippon Electric Co., Ltd. [Funatsu, Wakatsuki, and Arima, 1975]. In that survey paper, a technique they described as Scan Path was presented. The Scan Path technique has the same objectives as the LSSD approach which has just been described. The Scan Path technique similarities and differences to the LSSD approach will be presented.

The memory elements that are used in the Scan Path approach are shown in Figure C–13. This memory element is called a raceless D-type flip-flop with Scan Path.

In system operation, Clock 2 is at a logic value of 1 for the entire period. This, in essence, blocks the test or scan input from affecting the values in the first latch. This D-type flip-flop really contains two latches. Also, by having Clock 2 at a logic value of 1, the values in Latch 2 are not disturbed.

Clock 1 is the sole clock in system operation for this D-type flip-flop. When Clock 1 is at a value of 0, the System Data Input can be loaded into Latch 1. As long as Clock 1 is 0 for sufficient time to latch up the data, it can then turn off. As it turns off, it then will make Latch 2 sensitive to the data output of Latch 1. As long as Clock 1 is equal to a 1 so that data can be latched up into Latch 2, reliable operation will occur. This assumes that the output of Latch 2 does not come around and feed the system data input to Latch 1 and change it during the time that the inputs to both Latch 1 and Latch 2 are active. The period of time that this can occur is related to the delay of the inverter block for Clock 1. A similar phenomenon will occur with Clock 2 and its associated inverter block. This race condition is the exposure to the use of only one system check.

This points out a significant difference between the Scan Path approach and the LSSD approach. One of the basic principles of the LSSD approach is level-sensitive operation—the ability to operate the clocks in such a fashion that no races will exist. In the LSSD approach, a separate clock is required for Latch 1 from the clock that operates Latch 2.

In terms of the scanning function, the D-type flip-flop with Scan Path has its own scan input called test input. This is clocked into the *L*1 latch by Clock 2 when Clock 2 is a 0, and the results

FIGURE C–13
Raceless D-type flip-flop with Scan Path

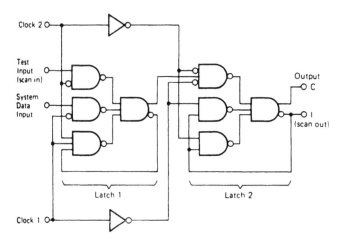

of the $L1$ latch are clocked into Latch 2 when Clock 2 is a 1. Again, this applies to master/slave operation of Latch 1 and Latch 2 with its associated race with proper attention to delays this race will not be a problem.

Another feature of the Scan Path approach is the configuration used at the logic card level. Modules on the logic card are all connected up into a serial scan path, such that for each card, there is one scan path. In addition, there are gates for selecting a particular card in a subsystem. In Figure C–14, when X and Y are both equal to 1—that is the selection mechanism—Clock 2 will then be allowed to shift data through the scan path. Any other time, Clock 2 will be blocked, and its output will be blocked. The reason for blocking the output is that a number of card outputs can then be put together; thus the blocking function will put their output to noncontrolling values, so that a particular card can have unique control of the unique test output for that system.

It has been reported by the Nippon Electric Company that they have used the Scan Path approach, plus partitioning which will be described next, for systems with 100,000 blocks or more. This was for the FLT-700 System, which is a large processor system.

The partitioning technique is one which automatically separates the combinational network into smaller subnetworks, so that the test generator can do test generation for the small subnetworks, rather than the larger networks. A partition is automatically generated by backtracing from the D-type flip-flops, through the combinational logic, until it encounters a D-type flip-flop in the backtrace (or primary input). Some care must be taken so that the partitions do not get too large.

To that end, the Nippon Electric Company approach has used a controlled D-type flip-flop to block the backtracing of certain partitions when they become too high. This is another facet of Design for Testability—that is, the introduction of extra flip-flops totally independent of function, in order to control the partitioning algorithm.

Other than the lack of the level sensitive attribute to the Scan Path approach, the technique is very similar to the LSSD approach. The introduction of the Scan Path approach was the first practical implementation of shift registers for testing which was incorported in a total system.

Scan/Set Logic

A technique similar to Scan Path and LSSD, but not exactly the same, is the Scan/Set technique put forth by Sperry-Univac [Stewart, 1977]. The basic concept of this technique is to have shift

FIGURE C–14
Configuration of
Scan Path on card

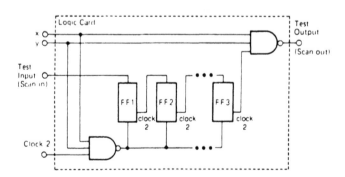

registers, as in Scan Path or in LSSD, but these shift registers are not in the data path. That is, they are not in the system data path; they are independent of all the system latches. Figure C–15 shows an example of the Scan/Set Logic, referred to as bit serial logic.

The basic concept is that the sequential network can be sampled at up to 64 points. These points can be loaded into the 64-bit shift register with a single clock. Once the 64 bits are loaded, a shifting process will occur, and the data will be scanned out through the scan-out pin. In the case of the set function, the 64 bits can be funneled into the system logic, and then the appropriate clocking structure required to load data into the system latches is required in this system logic. Furthermore, the set function could also be used to control different paths to ease the testing function.

In general, this serial Scan/Set Logic would be integrated onto the same chip that contains sequential system logic. However, some applications have been put forth where the bit serial Scan/Set Logic was off-chip, and the bit-serial Scan/Set Logic only sampled outputs or drove inputs to facilitate in-circuit testing.

Recently, Motorola has come forth with a chip which is T^2L and which has I^2L logic integrated on that same chip. This has the Scan/Set Logic bit serial shift registers built in I^2L. The T^2L portion of the chip is a gate array, and the I^2L is on the chip, whether the customer wants it or not. It is up to the customer to use the bit-serial logic if he chooses.

At this point, it should be explained that if all the latches within the system sequential network are not both scanned and set, then the test generation function is not necessarily reduced to a total combinational test generation function and fault simulation function. However, this technique will greatly reduce the task of test generation and fault simulation.

Again, the Scan/Set technique has the same objectives as Scan Path and LSSD—that is, controllability and observability. However, in terms of its implementation, it is not required that the set function set all system latches, or that the scan function scan all system latches. This design flexibility would have a reflection in the software support required to implement such a technique.

Another advantage of this technique is that the scan function can occur during system operation—that is, the sampling pulse to the 64-bit serial shift register can occur while system clocks are being applied to the system sequential logic, so that a snapshot of the sequential machine can be obtained and off-loaded without any degradation in system performance.

FIGURE C–15
Scan/Set Logic (bit-serial)

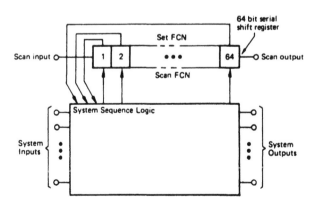

Random-Access Scan

Another technique similar to the Scan Path technique and LSSD is the Random-Access Scan technique put forth by Fujitsu [Ando, 1980]. This technique has the same objective as Scan Path and LSSD—that is, to have complete controllability and observability of all internal latches. Thus the test generation function can be reduced to that of combinational test generation and combinational fault simulation as well.

Random-Access Scan differs from the other two techniques in that shift registers are not employed. What is employed is an addressing scheme which allows each latch to be uniquely selected, so that it can be either controlled or observed. The mechanism for addressing is very similar to that of a Random-Access Memory, and hence, its name.

Figures C–16 and C–17 show the two basic latch configurations that are required for the Random-Access Scan approach. Figure C–16 is a single latch which has added to it an extra data port which is a Scan Data In port (SDI). These data are clocked into the latch by the SCK clock. The SCK clock can only affect this latch, if both the *X* and *Y* addresses are one. Furthermore, when the *X* address and *Y* address are one, then the Scan Data Out (SDO) point can be observed. System data labeled Data in Figures C–16 and C–17 are loaded into this latch by the system clock labeled *CK*.

The set/reset-type addressable latch in Figure C–17 does not have a scan clock to load data into the system latch. This latch is first cleared by the *CL* line, and the *CL* line is connected to other latches that are also set/reset-type addressable latches. This, then, places the output value *Q* to a 0 value. A preset is directed at those latches that are required to be set to a 1 for that particular test. This preset is directed by addressing each one of those latches and applying the preset pulse labeled *PR*. The output of the latch Q will then go to a 1. The observability mechanism for Scan Data Out is exactly the same as for the latch shown in Figure C–16.

FIGURE C–16
Polarity-hold-type addressable latch

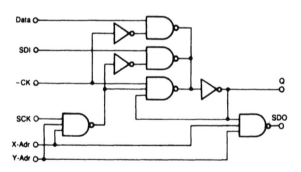

FIGURE C–17
Set/Reset type addressable latch

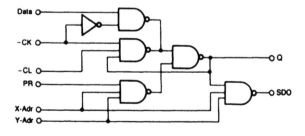

Figure C–18 gives an overall view of the system configuration of the Random-Access Scan approach. Notice that, basically there is a Y address, an X address, a decoder, the addressable storage elements, which are the memory elements or latches, and the sequential machine, system clocks, and CLEAR function. There is also an SDI which is the input for a given latch, an SDO which is the output data for that given latch, and a scan clock. There is also one logic gate necessary to create the preset function.

The Random-Access Scan technique allows the observability and controllability of all system latches. In addition, any point in the combinational network can be observed with the addition of one gate per observation point, as well as one address in the address gate, per observation point.

While the Scan Path approach and the LSSD approach require two latches for every point which needs to be observed, the overhead for Random-Access Scan is about three to four gates per storage element. In terms of primary inputs/outputs, the overhead is between 10 and 20. This pin overhead can be diminished by using the serial scan approach for the X and Y address counter, which would lead to 6 primary inputs/outputs.

SELF-TESTING AND BUILT-IN TESTS

As a natural outgrowth of the Structured Design approach for "Design for Testability," Self-Tests and Built-In Tests have been getting considerably more attention. Four techniques will be discussed, which fall into this category, BILBO, Syndrome Testing, Testing by Verifying Walsh Testing Coefficients, and Autonomous Testing. Each of these techniques will be described.

Built-In Logic Block Observation, BILBO

A technique recently presented takes the Scan Path and LSSD concept and integrates it with the Signature Analysis concept. The end result is a technique for Built-In Logic Block Observation, BILBO [Koenemann, Mucha, and Zwiehoff, 1979].

FIGURE C–18
*Random-Access
Scan network*

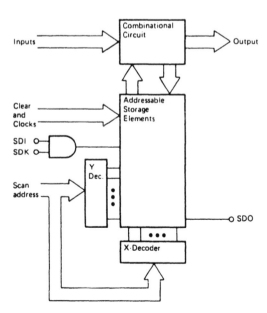

Figure C–19 gives the form of an 8-bit BILBO register. The blocks labeled L_i ($i = 1, 2, \ldots, 8$) are the system latches. B_1 and B_2 are control values for controlling the different functions that the BILBO register can perform. S_{IN} is the scan-in input to the 8-bit register, and S_{OUT} is the scan-out for the 8-bit register. Q_i ($i = 1, 2, \ldots, 8$) are the output values for the eight system latches. Z_i ($i = 1, 2, \ldots, 8$) are the inputs from the combinational logic. The structure that this network will be embedded into will be discussed shortly.

There are three primary modes of operation for this register, as well as one secondary mode of operation for this register. The first is shown in Figure C–19(b)—that is, with B_1 and B_2 equal to 11. This is a Basic System Operation mode, in which the Z_i values are loaded into the L_i, and the outputs are available on Q_i for system operation. This would be your normal register function.

When B_1B_2 equals 00, the BILBO register takes on the form of a linear shift register, as shown in Figure C–19(c). Data moves from the scan-in input to the left, through some inverters, and basically lining up the eight registers into a single scan path, until the scan-out is reached. This is similar to Scan Path and LSSD.

The third mode is when B_1B_2 equals 10. In this mode, the BILBO register takes on the attributes of a linear feedback shift register of maximal length with multiple linear inputs. This is very similar to a Signature Analysis register, except that there is more than one input. In this situation, there are eight unique inputs. Thus after a certain number of shift clocks, say, 100, there would be a unique signature left in the BILBO register for the good machine. This good machine signature could be off-loaded from the register by changing from Mode $B_1B_2 = 10$ to Mode $B_1B_2 = 00$, in which case a shift register operation would exist, and the signature then could be observed from the scan-out primary output.

The fourth function that the BILBO register can perform is B_1B_2 equal to 01, which would force a reset on the register. (This is not depicted in Figure C–19.)

The BILBO registers are used in the system operation, as shown in Figure C–20. Basically, a BILBO register with combinational logic and another BILBO register with combinational logic, as

FIGURE C–19
BILBO and its different modes: (a) general form of BILBO register; (b) $B_1B_2 = 11$ system orientation mode; (c) $B_1B_2 = 00$ linear shift register mode; (d) $B_1B_2 = 10$ signature analysis register with m multiple inputs ($Z_1, Z_2, \ldots, Z_8$)

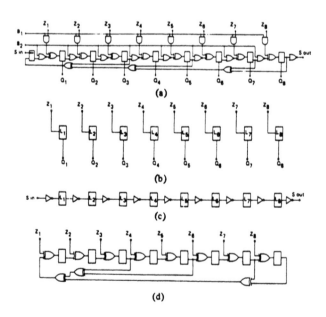

FIGURE C–20
Use of BILBO registers to test combinational Network 1

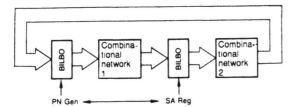

well as the output of the second combinational logic network can feed back into the input of the first BILBO register. The BILBO approach takes one other fact into account, and that is that, in general, combinational logic is highly susceptible to random patterns. Thus if the inputs to the BILBO register, $Z_1, Z_2, \ldots, Z_8$, can be controlled to fixed values, such that the BILBO register is in the maximal length linear feedback shift register mode (Signature Analysis) it will output a sequence of patterns which are very close to random patterns. Thus random patterns can be generated quite readily from this register. These sequences are called Pseudo Random Patterns (PN).

If, in the first operation, this BILBO register on the left in Figure C–20 is used as the PN generator—that is, its data inputs are held to fixed values—then the output of that BILBO register will be random patterns. This will then do a reasonable test, if sufficient numbers of patterns are applied, of the Combinational Logic Network 1. The results of this test can be stored in a Signature Analysis register approach with multiple inputs to the BILBO register on the right. After a fixed number of patterns have been applied, the signature is scanned out of the BILBO register on the right for good machine compliance. If that is successfully completed, then the roles are reversed, and the BILBO register on the right will be used as a PN sequence generator; the BILBO register on the left will then be used as a Signature Analysis register with multiple inputs from Combinational Logic Network 2; see Figure C–21. In this mode, the Combinational Logic Network 2 will have random patterns applied to its inputs and its outputs stored in the BILBO register on the far left. Thus the testing of the combinational logic networks 1 and 2 can be completed at very high speeds by only applying the shift clocks, while the two BILBO registers are in the Signature Analysis mode. At the conclusion of the tests, off-loading of patterns can occur, and determination of good machine operation can be made.

This technique solves the problem of test generation and fault simulation if the combinational networks are susceptible to random patterns. There are some known networks which are not susceptible to random patterns. They are Programmable Logic Arrays (PLA's); see Figure C–22. The reason for this is that the fan-in in PLA's is too large. If an AND gate in the search array had 20 inputs, then each random pattern would have $1/2^{20}$ probability of coming up with the correct

FIGURE C–21
Use of BILBO registers to test combinational Network 2

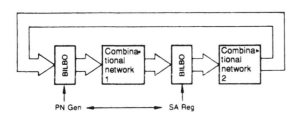

FIGURE C–22
PLA model

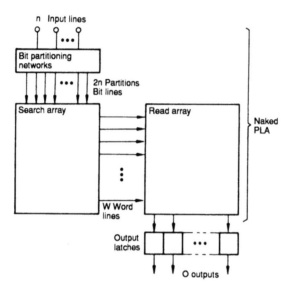

input pattern. On the other hand, random combinational logic networks with maximum fan-in of 4 can do quite well with random patterns.

The BILBO technique solves another problem and that is of test data volume. In LSSD, Scan Path, Scan/Set, or Random-Access Scan, a considerable amount of test data volume is involved with the shifting in and out. With BILBO, if 100 patterns are run between scan-outs, the test data volume may be reduced by a factor of 100. The overhead for this technique is higher than for LSSD since about two EXCLUSIVE-OR's must be used per latch position. Also, there is more delay in the system data path (one or two gate delays). If VLSI has the huge number of logic gates available then this may be a very efficient way to use them.

Syndrome Testing

Recently, a technique was shown which could be used to test a network with fairly minor changes to the network. The technique is Syndrome Testing. The technique requires that all 2^n patterns be applied to the input of the network and then the number of 1's on the output be counted [Savir, 1980, 1981].

Testing is done by comparing the number of 1's for the good machine to the number of 1's for the faulty machine. If there is a difference, the fault(s) in the faulty machine are detected (or Syndrome testable). To be more formal the Syndrome is:

Definition 1: The *Syndrome S* of a Boolean function is defined as

$$S = \frac{K}{2^n}$$

where K is the number of minterns realized by the function, and n is the number of binary input lines to the Boolean function.

Not all Boolean functions are totally Syndrome testable for all the single stuck-at-faults. Procedures are given in Savir [1980] with a minimal or near minimal number of primary inputs to make the networks Syndrome testable. In a number of "real networks" (i.e., SN74181, etc.) the number of extra primary inputs needed was at most one (< 5 percent) and not more than two gates (< 4 percent) were needed. An extension [Savir, 1981] to this work was published which showed a way of making a network Syndrome testable by adding extra inputs. This resulted in a somewhat longer test sequence. This is accomplished by holding some input constant while applying all 2^k inputs ($k < n$), then holding others constant and applying 2^l input patterns to l inputs. Whether the network is modified or not, the test data volume for a Syndrome testable design is extremely low. The general test setup is shown in Figure C–23.

The structure requires a pattern generator which applies all possible patterns once, a counter to count the 1's, and a compare network. The overhead quoted is necessary to make the OUT Syndrome testable and does not include the pattern generator, counter, or compare register.

Testing by Verifying Walsh Coefficients

A technique which is similar to Syndrome Testing, in that it requires all possible input patterns be applied to the combinational network, is testing by verifying Walsh coefficients [Susskind, 1981]. This technique only checks two of the Walsh coefficients and then makes conclusions about the network with respect to stuck-at-faults.

In order to calculate the Walsh coefficients, the logical value 0(1) is associated with the arithmetic value $-1(+1)$. There are 2^n Walsh functions. W_0 is defined to be 1, W_i is derived from all possible (arithmetic) products of the subject of independent input variables selected for that Walsh function. Table C–1 shows the Walsh function for W_2, $W_{1,3}$, then W_2F, $W_{1,3}F$, finally W_{all} and $W_{all}F$. These values are calculated for the network in Figure C–24. If the values are summed for $W_{all}F$, the Walsh coefficient C_{all} is calculated. The Walsh coefficient C_0 is just W_0F summed. This is equivalent to the Syndrome in magnitude times 2^n. If $C_{all} \neq 0$ then all stuck-at-faults on primary inputs will be detected by measuring C_{all}. If the fault is present $C_{all} = 0$. If the network has $C_{all} = 0$ it can be easily modified such that $C_{all} \neq 0$. If the network has reconvergent fan-out

FIGURE C–23
Syndrome test structure

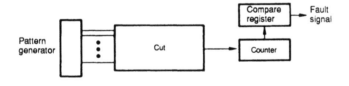

TABLE C–1
Examples of Walsh functions and Walsh coefficients

$X_1X_2X_3$	W_2	$W_{1,3}$	F	W_2F	$W_{1,3}F$	W_{ALL}	$W_{ALL}F$
0 0 0	−1	+1	0	+1	−1	+1	+1
0 0 1	−1	−1	0	+1	+1	−1	−1
0 1 0	+1	+1	0	−1	−1	−1	−1
0 1 1	+1	−1	1	+1	−1	+1	−1
1 0 0	−1	−1	0	+1	+1	−1	−1
1 0 1	−1	+1	1	−1	+1	+1	−1
1 1 0	+1	−1	1	+1	−1	+1	1
1 1 1	+1	+1	1	+1	+1	−1	+1

$C_{ALL} = 4$

FIGURE C–24
Function to be tested with Walsh coefficients

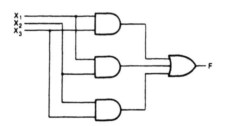

then further checks need to be made (the number of inverters in each path has a certain property); see Susskind [1981]. If these are successful, then by checking C_{all} and C_0, all the single stuck-at-faults can be detected. Some design constraints maybe needed to make sure that the network is testable by measuring C_{all} and C_0. Figure C–25 shows the network needed to determine C_{all} and C_0. The value P is the parity of the driving counter and the response counter is an up/down counter. Note, two passes must be made of the driving counter, one for C_{all} and one for C_0.

Autonomous Testing

The fourth technique which will be discussed in the area of self-test/built-in-test is Autonomous Testing [McCluskey and Bozorgui-Nesbat, 1981]. Autonomous Testing like Syndrome Testing and testing Walsh coefficients requires all possible patterns be applied to the network inputs. However, with Autonomous Testing the outputs of the network must be checked for each pattern against the value for the good machine. The result is that irrespective of the fault model Autonomous Testing will detect the faults (assuming the faulty machine does not turn into a sequential machine from a combinational machine). In order to help the network apply its own patterns and accumulate the results of the tests rather than observing every pattern for 2^n input patterns, a structure similar to the BILBO register is used. This register has some unique attributes and is shown in Figures C–26 to C–29. If a combinational network has 100 inputs, the network must be modified such that the subnetwork can be verified and, thus, the whole network will be tested.

Two approaches to partitioning are presented in the paper "Design for Autonomous Test" [McCluskey and Bozorgui-Nesbat, 1981]. The first is to use multiplexers to separate the network and the second is a Sensitized Partitioning to separate the network. Figure C–30 shows the general network with multiplexers, Figure C–31 shows the network in functional mode, and Figure C–32

FIGURE C–25
Tester for verifying C_0 and C_{all} Walsh coefficients

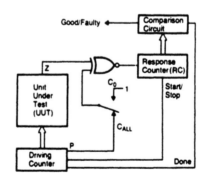

FIGURE C–26
Reconfigurable 3-bit LFSR module

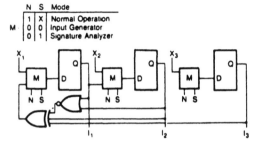

FIGURE C–27
Reconfigurable 3-bit LFSR module

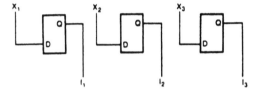

N = 1: Normal Operation

FIGURE C–28
Reconfigurable 3-bit LFSR module

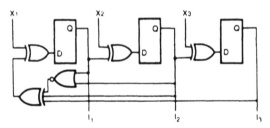

N = 0. S = 1 Signature Analyzer

FIGURE C–29
Reconfigurable 3-bit LFSR module

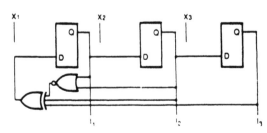

N = 0. S = 0 Input Generator

FIGURE C–30
Autonomous testing—general network

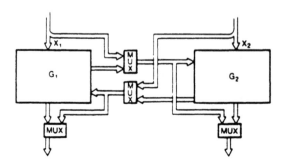

FIGURE C–31
Autonomous testing—functional mode

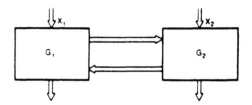

FIGURE C–32
Autonomous testing—configuration to test network G_1

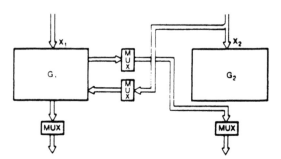

shows the network in a mode to test subnetwork G_1. This approach could involve a significant gate overhead to implement in some networks. Thus the Sensitized Partitioning approach is put forth. For example, the 74181 ALU/Function Generator is partitioned using the Sensitized Partitioning. By inspecting the network, two types of subnetworks can be partitioned out, four subnetworks N_1, one subnetwork of N_2 (Figures C–33 and C–34). By further inspection, all the L_i outputs of network N_1 can be tested by holding $S_2 = S_3 =$ low. Further, all the H_i outputs of network N_1 can be tested by holding $S_0 = S_1 =$ high, since sensitized paths exist through the subnetwork N_2. Thus far fewer than 2^n input patterns can be applied to the network to test it.

CONCLUSION

The area of Design for Testability is becoming a popular topic by necessity. Those users of LSI/VLSI which do not have their own captive IC facilities are at the mercy of the vendors for information. And, until the vendor information is drastically changed, the Ad Hoc approaches to design for testability will be the only answer.

FIGURE C–33
Autonomous test-ing with sensitized partitioning

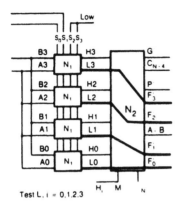

Test L, i = 0,1,2,3

FIGURE C–34
Autonomous test-ing with sensitized partitioning

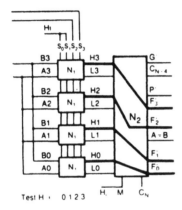

Test H i 0 1 2 3

In that segment of the industry which can afford to implement the Structured Design for Testability approach, there is considerable hope of getting quality test patterns at a very modest cost. Furthermore, many innovative techniques are appearing in the Structured Approach and probably will continue as we meander through VLSI and into more dense technologies.

There is a new opportunity arriving in the form of gate arrays that allow low volume users access to VLSI technology. If they choose, structured design disciplines can be utilized. Perhaps "Silicon Foundaries" of the future will offer a combined package of structured, testable modules and support software to automatically provide the user with finished parts AND tests.

REFERENCES

General References and Surveys. Breuer, 1976; Chang, Manning, and Metze, 1970; Friedman and Menon, 1971; Hennie, 1968; IEEE, Inc., 1972; Kovijanic, 1977; Muehldorf, 1976; Muehldorf and Savkar, 1981; Peterson and Weldon, 1972; Susskind, 1973; Williams and Parker, 1979.

Designing for Testability. HP-a; Akers, 1977; Ando, 1980; Bottorff and Muehldorf, 1977; DasGupta, Eichelberger, and Williams, 1978; HP-b; Eichelberger, Muehldorf, Walter, and Williams, 1978; Eichelberger and Williams, 1977, 1978; Funatsu, Wakatsuki, and Arima, 1975; Godoy, Franklin, and Bottorff, 1977; Hayes, 1974; Hayes and Friedman, 1973; Koenemann, Mucha, and Zwiehoff,

1979; Lippman and Donn, 1979; Nadig, 1977, 1979; Neil and Goodner, 1979; Reddy, 1972; Saliya and Reddy, 1974; Stewart, 1977; Toth and Holt, 1974; White, 1978; Williams, 1978; Williams and Angell, 1973.

Faults and Fault Modeling. Boute, 1972, 1974; Boute and McCluskey, 1971; Dias, 1975; Hayes, 1971; McCluskey and Clegg, 1971; Mei, 1970, 1974; Ogus, 1975; Parker and McCluskey, 1975; Saliya and Reddy, 1975; Schertz and Metze, 1972; Shedletsky and McCluskey, 1975, 1976; To, 1973; Wang, 1975.

Testing and Fault Location. Batni and Kime, 1976; Bisset, 1977; Czepiel, Foreman, and Prilik, 1976; Frohwerk, 1977; Grimmer, 1976; Groves, 1979; Hayes, 1975a, 1975b, 1976; Healy, 1977; Lee, 1976; Losq, 1976; Palmquist and Chapman, 1976; Parker, 1976; Shedletsky, 1975; Strini, 1978; Weller, 1977.

Testability Measures. Dejka, 1977; Goldstein, 1979; Keiner and West, 1977; Kovijanic, 1979; Stephenson and Grason, 1976.

Test Generation. Agrawal and Agrawal, 1972; Armstrong, 1966; Betancourt, 1973; Bossen and Hong, 1971; Bottorff et al., 1977; Edlred, 1959; Goel, 1980; Hsieh et al., 1977; Ku and Masson, 1975; Muehldorf, 1978; Muehldorf and Williams, 1977; Page, 1969; Papaioannou, 1977; Parker, 1973, 1976; Putzolu and Roth, 1971; Roth, 1966; Roth, Bouricius and Schneider, 1967; Schneider, 1967; Schnurmann, Lindbloom, and Carpenter, 1975; Sellers, Hsiao, and Bearnson, 1968; Wang, 1975; Williams and Eichelberger, 1977; Yau and Yang, 1975.

Simulation. Armstrong, 1972; Breuer, 1970; Chiang et al., 1974; Eichelberger, 1965; Manning and Chang, 1968; McCluskey and Bozorgui-Nesbat, 1981; Parker, 1979; Savir, 1980, 1981; Seller, Hsiao, and Bearnson, 1968; Seshu, 1965; Seshu and Freeman, 1962; Storey and Barry, 1977; Susskind, 1981; Szygenda, 1972; Szygenda, Rouse, and Thompson, 1970; Szygenda and Thompson, 1976; Ulrich and Baker, 1973, 1974; Ulrich, Baker, and Williams, 1972.

APPENDIX D

Summary of MIL-HDBK-217E Reliability Model

Experience has shown that 90 percent or more of the failure rate of a typical digital printed circuit board is accounted for by the integrated circuit chips. To a first approximation the failure rates of the printed circuit board, capacitors, and resistors can be ignored in design studies. Hence, this appendix only summarizes the MIL-HDBK-217E model for integrated circuit chips. For boards populated primarily by discrete devices, or for nonelectronic components, the reader is referred to U.S. Department of Defense [1986].

FAILURE RATE MODEL AND FACTORS

The failure rate, λ, in failures per million hours for monolithic MOS and bipolar chips takes the form of

$$\lambda = \pi_L \pi_Q (C_1 \pi_T \pi_V + C_2 \pi_E)$$

Values of each factor will be discussed in turn.

Learning Factor

The learning factor π_L has a value of 10 if the device is new, if there are major changes in the fabrication process, or if the fabrication process is being restarted after an extended interruption. Otherwise the value of π_L is 1.0.

Quality Factor

The quality factor π_Q is a function of the amount of device screening. Table D–1 lists the values of π_Q.

Temperature Acceleration Factor

The temperature acceleration factor π_T is a function of device technology, package type, case temperature, and power dissipation:

$$\pi_T = 0.1 e^{(-A[(1/(T_j + 273)) - (1/298)])}$$

where A is a function of technology and package type as given in Table D–2 and T_j is the worst-case junction temperature. T_j is given by

$$T_j = T_C + \Theta_{JC} P$$

where T_c = case temperature (°C)

Θ_{JC} = junction to case thermal resistance (°C/watt) for a device soldered onto a printed circuit board.

P = worst-case power dissipation

TABLE D–1
Quality factors

Quality Level	Screening Standard	π_Q
S	MIL-M-38510, Class S	0.25
B	MIL-M-38510, Class B	1.0
B-1	STD-883, paragraph 1.2.1	2.0
B-2	Same as B-1 with some tests waived	5.0
D	Commercial, hermetically sealed	10.0
D-1	Commercial, organic seal	20.0

TABLE D–2 *Technology and package parameter A used in calculation of π_T*

Technology	Package Type	A	Technology	Package Type	A
TTL, ECL	Hermetic	4635	Low Power Schottky TTL	Nonhermetic	6373
TTL, ECL	Nonhermetic	5214	PMOS, NMOS	Nonhermetic	8111
Schottky TTL	Hermetic	5214	CMOS	Hermetic	6373
Schottky TTL	Nonhermetic	5794	CMOS	Nonhermetic	9270
Low Power Schottky	Hermetic	5794	Linear	Hermetic	7532
TTL, PMOS, NMOS			Linear	Nonhermetic	10429

If Θ_{JC} is unknown, the values in the following table may be used:

Package Type	Number of Pins	Θ_{JC}
Hermetic DIP	≤ 22	30
Hermetic DIP	>22	25
Nonhermetic DIP	≤ 22	125
Nonhermetic DIP	>22	100

Some useful values of π_T are given in Table D–3.

Voltage Stress Factor

The voltage stress factor π_V is 1.0 for all technologies other than CMOS. π_V is also 1.0 for CMOS with $V_{DD} = 5$ volts. For supply voltage between 12 and 15.5 volts,

$$\pi_V = 0.11 e^x$$

where $x = \dfrac{0.168 V_s (T_j + 273)}{298}$

with V_s the supply voltage.

Application Environment Factor

The application environment factor π_E depends on the operational environment as indicated in Table D–4.

TABLE D–3 *Some useful values of* π_T

Junction Temperature	Low-Power TTL		CMOS		TTL	
	Hermetic	Nonhermetic	Hermetic	Nonhermetic	Hermetic	Nonhermetic
25 (°C)	0.1	0.1	0.1	0.1	0.1	0.1
40 (°C)	0.26	0.28	0.28	0.44	0.21	0.23
70 (°C)	1.3	1.7	1.7	5.9	0.77	1.0
90 (°C)	3.25	4.6	4.6	26	1.6	2.3

TABLE D–4 *Environmental factor* π_E

Environment	Example	π_E	Environment	Example	π_E
Ground, benign	Computer room	0.38	Ground, mobile	Jeep	4.2
Space flight	Satellite	0.9	Airborne, uninhabited, transport	Equipment bay of long-mission aircraft	3.0
Ground, fixed	Factory floor	2.5			
Airborne, inhabited, transport	Cockpit of long-mission aircraft	2.5	Airborne, uninhabited, fighter	Equipment bay of high-performance aircraft	9.0
Airborne, inhabited, fighter	Cockpit of high-performance aircraft	6.0	Naval, unsheltered	Engine room of a surface ship	5.7
Naval, shelter	Bridge of a surface ship	4.0	Missile, launch	Missile	13.0

Complexity Factors

Complexity factor C_1 is a function of the device complexity and the device function as given in Table D–5. Complexity factor C_2 is a function of package complexity and is also given in Table D–5. Reliability calculations and design trade-offs are tedious and time-consuming and are best handled by programs such as Lambda.

However, the user must be fully aware of the model parameters, the significance of the parameters, and the model's sensitivity to the parameters. Otherwise, the model will not produce meaningful, calibratable predictions.

REFERENCE   U.S. Department of Defense, 1986.

TABLE D–5
Complexity factors

C_1 for Logic			
Component Type	Function	Complexity up to	Value for C_1
Logic	Gates	100	0.01
		1,000	0.02
		3,000	0.04
		10,000	0.08
		30,000	0.16
PLA, PAL	Gates	100	0.06
		1,000	0.12
		5,000	0.24
Microprocessor	Data path width in bits	8	0.03
		16	0.06
		32	0.12
Linear	Transistors	100	0.01
		300	0.02
		1,000	0.04

C_1 for Memories						
Bit Complexity up to	RAM			ROM		
	MOS Dynamic	Static	Bipolar Static	MOS	Bipolar	PROM
4K	0.025	0.05	0.05	0.035	0.06	0.06
16K	0.025	0.05	0.10	0.035	0.06	0.06
64K	0.05	0.10	—	0.07	0.12	0.12
256K	0.10	0.20	—	0.14	—	0.24
1M	0.20	0.40	—	0.28	—	0.48

C_2 for Package Complexity	
Package Type	C_2
Hermetic DIPs with solder or weld seals	$2.8(10)^{-4}(N_P)^{1.08}$
Hermetic DIPs with glass seals	$9(10)^{-5}(N_P)^{1.51}$
Nonhermetic DIPs	$2(10)^{-4}(N_P)^{1.23}$
Hermetic Flatpacks	$3(10)^{-5}(N_P)^{1.82}$
Hermetic Cans	$3(10)^{-5}(N_P)^{2.01}$

Note: N_P is the number of pins on the package connected to the device substrate.

APPENDIX E

Algebraic Solutions to Markov Models

Jeffrey P. Hansen

The analytical equations for the steady-state availability can be derived directly from the Markov transition diagram [Solberg, 1975]. The unnormalized probability of state occupancy of an n state Markov model $(K_0, K_1, K_2, \ldots, K_{n-1})$ is found by enumerating all of the intrees that converge on each of the nodes in the graph. An intree is a spanning tree with the constraint that every node except one has exactly one edge leaving, and the terminal node has no edges leaving it. Intrees have the property that there is exactly one path from any node to the terminal node. For every intree, the rates for the edges in the intree are multiplied together. The unnormalized solution for that node will then be the sum of all the intrees for that node.

As an example, consider the Markov model for a duplex system with a voting element in Figure E–1. The voting element compares the outputs along with check bits provided by the two systems and selects the one with consistent check bits in the case of disagreement.

The states for the model are

0   All OK
1   One system down
2   Two systems down
3   Voting element down
4   One system and voting element down
5   Two systems and voting element down

The parameters of this model are

λ Failure rate of system
μ Repair rate of system
λ_v Failure rate of voting element
μ_v Repair rate of voting element

It is assumed for this model that there is only one repairperson, and that the repairperson will attempt to repair the voting element first if it is down. For state 0, there are four possible intrees shown in Figure E–2. Multiplying the transition rates for the arcs in these trees, the unnormalized probability for state 0 is

$$K_0 = \mu_v^3 \mu^2 + 2\mu_v^2 \mu^2 \lambda + \mu_v^2 \mu^2 \lambda + 2\mu_v \mu^2 \lambda^2 = \mu_v^3 \mu^2 + 3\mu_v^2 \mu^2 \lambda + 2\mu_v \mu^2 \lambda^2$$

By analogy, the unnormalized solutions can be found for the other nodes. They are

$$K_1 = 2\mu_v^3 \mu \lambda + 6\mu_v^2 \mu \lambda^2 + 2\mu_v^2 \mu \lambda_v \lambda + 4\mu_v \mu \lambda^3 + 2\mu_v \mu \lambda_v \lambda^2$$

$$K_2 = 2\mu_v^3 \lambda^2 + 6\mu_v^2 \lambda^3 + 4\mu_v^2 \lambda_v \lambda^2 + 4\mu_v \lambda^4 + 2\mu_v \lambda_v^2 \lambda^2 + 2\mu_v \mu \lambda_v \lambda^2 + 6\mu_v \lambda_v \lambda^3$$

$$K_3 = \mu_v^2 \mu^2 \lambda_v + \mu_v \mu^2 \lambda_v \lambda$$

$$K_4 = 2\mu_v^2 \mu \lambda_v \lambda + 2\mu_v \mu^2 \lambda_v \lambda + 2\mu_v \mu \lambda_v^2 \lambda + 4\mu_v \mu \lambda_v \lambda^2$$

FIGURE E–1
Duplex system with decision element

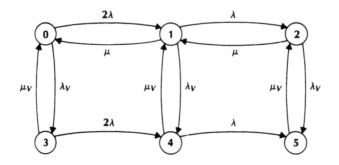

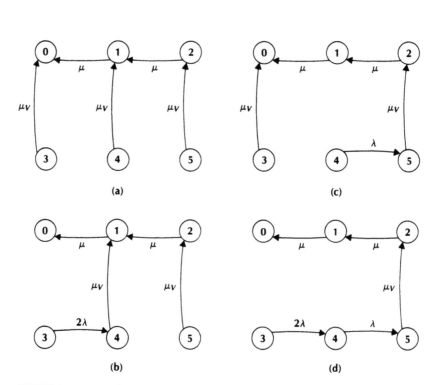

FIGURE E–2 *Intrees for state 0*

$$K_5 = 2\lambda_v^3\lambda^2 + 2\mu_v^2\lambda_v\lambda^2 + 2\mu^2\lambda_v\lambda^2 + 6\lambda_v^2\lambda^3 + 4\mu_v\lambda_v^2\lambda^2 + 2\mu_v\mu\lambda_v\lambda^2 + 6\mu_v\lambda_v\lambda^3 + 4\mu\lambda_v^2\lambda^2 + 4\mu\lambda_v\lambda^3 + 4\lambda_v\lambda^4$$

The steady-state probabilities can be found by normalizing the K_i. This is done by dividing each of the unnormalized probabilities by the sum of the unnormalized probabilities. Thus,

$$P_i = \frac{K_i}{\Sigma_j K_j}$$

**SOLUTION OF
MTTF MODELS**

To solve for MTTF [Hansen, 1989] we will define the variable X_{ji} to be the average time to go from state i to state j. In an MTTF model, we can assume there is only one trapping state since all trapping states can be merged together. If the initial state is i and the trapping state is t, then the MTTF will be X_{ti}. Now consider modifying the MTTF model to include an additional transition from t to i as shown in Figure E–3. The average time between visits of state t is X_{tt}, which will be the sum of the MTTF (X_{ti}) and the mean time to go from state t to state i ($1/\Omega$):

$$X_{tt} = X_{ti} + \frac{1}{\Omega} \tag{E.1}$$

The probability of being in a state is the average time before leaving that state divided by the average time between visits of that state:

$$P_t = \frac{1/\Omega}{X_{tt}} \tag{E.2}$$

$$X_{tt} = \frac{1}{\Omega P_t} \tag{E.3}$$

So if we substitute equation (E.3) back into (E.1), we get

$$\frac{1}{\Omega P_t} = X_{ti} + \frac{1}{\Omega} \tag{E.4}$$

$$X_{ti} = \frac{1}{\Omega P_t} - \frac{1}{\Omega} \tag{E.5}$$

Finally, taking the limit as Ω goes to infinity,

$$\text{MTTF} = X_{it} = \lim_{\Omega \to \infty} \frac{1}{\Omega P_t} - \frac{1}{\Omega} = \lim_{\Omega \to \infty} \frac{1}{\Omega P_t} \tag{E.6}$$

Thus, the MTTF for a Markov model can be derived by adding an Ω transition from the trapping state to the initial state, solving the resulting model for availability and using equation (E.6). Equation (E.6) can be rewritten using the unnormalized probabilities as

$$\text{MTTF} = \lim_{\Omega \to \infty} \frac{1}{\Omega} \frac{\Sigma_j K_j}{K_t} = \lim_{\Omega \to \infty} \frac{1/\Omega \Sigma_j K_j}{K_t} \tag{E.7}$$

FIGURE E–3
MTTF example

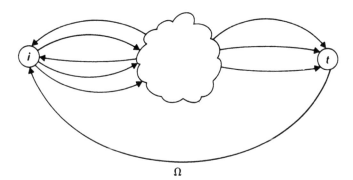

Note that none of the intrees for state t will include the Ω edge, since including that edge would violate the condition that no edges leaving a state can be used in the intree for that state. Furthermore, every intree for all of the other states will include the Ω edge since every intree must include all nodes, and the Ω node is the only edge that can be used to get to node t. Thus, it follows that as Ω goes to infinity, multiplying the unnormalized probabilities by $1/\Omega$ in the numerator of equation (E.7) will result in cancellation of the Ω term for all of the probabilities except K_t. K_t will drop out of the numerator since it contains no terms involving Ω. Cancellation of Ω from the unnormalized expression is the same as setting it to one, so we can write:

$$\text{MTTF} = \left.\frac{\sum_{j \neq t} K_j}{K_t}\right|_{\Omega=1}$$

COMPLETE SOLUTION FOR THREE- AND FOUR-STATE MODELS

This technique can be used to derive the general solution for a Markov model where each state transition is symbolically represented as λ_{ji}, where λ_{ji} is the transition rate from state i to state j. The complete solution for a three-state model is

$$K_0 = \lambda_{21}\lambda_{10} + \lambda_{20}\lambda_{12} + \lambda_{20}\lambda_{10}$$

$$K_1 = \lambda_{21}\lambda_{02} + \lambda_{21}\lambda_{01} + \lambda_{20}\lambda_{01}$$

$$K_2 = \lambda_{12}\lambda_{02} + \lambda_{12}\lambda_{01} + \lambda_{10}\lambda_{02}$$

$$P_0 = \frac{K_0}{K_0 + K_1 + K_2}$$

$$P_1 = \frac{K_1}{K_0 + K_1 + K_2}$$

$$P_2 = \frac{K_2}{K_0 + K_1 + K_2}$$

The complete solution for a four-state model is

$$K_0 = \lambda_{32}\lambda_{31}\lambda_{03} + \lambda_{32}\lambda_{21}\lambda_{03} + \lambda_{32}\lambda_{13}\lambda_{01} + \lambda_{32}\lambda_{03}\lambda_{01} + \lambda_{31}\lambda_{23}\lambda_{02} + \lambda_{31}\lambda_{12}\lambda_{03} + \lambda_{31}\lambda_{03}\lambda_{02} + \lambda_{23}\lambda_{21}\lambda_{02} + \lambda_{23}\lambda_{12}\lambda_{01} + \lambda_{23}\lambda_{02}\lambda_{01} + \lambda_{21}\lambda_{13}\lambda_{02} + \lambda_{21}\lambda_{03}\lambda_{02} + \lambda_{13}\lambda_{12}\lambda_{01} + \lambda_{13}\lambda_{02}\lambda_{01} + \lambda_{12}\lambda_{03}\lambda_{01} + \lambda_{03}\lambda_{02}\lambda_{01}$$

$$K_1 = \lambda_{32}\lambda_{30}\lambda_{13} + \lambda_{32}\lambda_{20}\lambda_{13} + \lambda_{32}\lambda_{13}\lambda_{10} + \lambda_{32}\lambda_{10}\lambda_{03} + \lambda_{30}\lambda_{23}\lambda_{12} + \lambda_{30}\lambda_{13}\lambda_{12} + \lambda_{30}\lambda_{13}\lambda_{02} + \lambda_{23}\lambda_{20}\lambda_{12} + \lambda_{23}\lambda_{12}\lambda_{10} + \lambda_{23}\lambda_{10}\lambda_{02} + \lambda_{20}\lambda_{13}\lambda_{12} + \lambda_{20}\lambda_{12}\lambda_{03} + \lambda_{13}\lambda_{12}\lambda_{10} + \lambda_{13}\lambda_{10}\lambda_{02} + \lambda_{12}\lambda_{10}\lambda_{03} + \lambda_{10}\lambda_{03}\lambda_{02}$$

$$K_2 = \lambda_{31}\lambda_{30}\lambda_{23} + \lambda_{31}\lambda_{23}\lambda_{20} + \lambda_{31}\lambda_{23}\lambda_{10} + \lambda_{31}\lambda_{20}\lambda_{03} + \lambda_{30}\lambda_{23}\lambda_{21} + \lambda_{30}\lambda_{23}\lambda_{01} + \lambda_{30}\lambda_{21}\lambda_{13} + \lambda_{23}\lambda_{21}\lambda_{20} + \lambda_{23}\lambda_{21}\lambda_{10} + \lambda_{23}\lambda_{20}\lambda_{01} + \lambda_{21}\lambda_{20}\lambda_{13} + \lambda_{21}\lambda_{20}\lambda_{03} + \lambda_{21}\lambda_{13}\lambda_{10} + \lambda_{21}\lambda_{10}\lambda_{03} + \lambda_{20}\lambda_{13}\lambda_{01} + \lambda_{20}\lambda_{03}\lambda_{01}$$

$$K_3 = \lambda_{32}\lambda_{31}\lambda_{30} + \lambda_{32}\lambda_{31}\lambda_{20} + \lambda_{32}\lambda_{31}\lambda_{10} + \lambda_{32}\lambda_{30}\lambda_{21} + \lambda_{32}\lambda_{30}\lambda_{01} + \lambda_{32}\lambda_{21}\lambda_{20} + \lambda_{32}\lambda_{21}\lambda_{10} + \lambda_{32}\lambda_{20}\lambda_{01} + \lambda_{31}\lambda_{30}\lambda_{12} + \lambda_{31}\lambda_{30}\lambda_{02} + \lambda_{31}\lambda_{20}\lambda_{12} + \lambda_{31}\lambda_{12}\lambda_{10} + \lambda_{31}\lambda_{10}\lambda_{02} + \lambda_{30}\lambda_{21}\lambda_{02} + \lambda_{30}\lambda_{12}\lambda_{01} + \lambda_{30}\lambda_{02}\lambda_{01}$$

$$P_0 = \frac{K_0}{K_0 + K_1 + K_2 + K_3}$$

$$P_1 = \frac{K_1}{K_0 + K_1 + K_2 + K_3}$$

$$P_2 = \frac{K_2}{K_0 + K_1 + K_2 + K_3}$$

$$P_3 = \frac{K_3}{K_0 + K_1 + K_2 + K_3}$$

SOLUTIONS TO COMMONLY ENCOUNTERED MARKOV MODELS

For an $(n + 1)$-state model with 1 repairperson (n modules),

$$P_k = \frac{\lambda^k \mu^{n-k} \dfrac{n!}{(n-k)!}}{\displaystyle\sum_{j=0}^{n} \lambda^j \mu^{n-j} \dfrac{n!}{(n-j)!}}$$

For an $(n + 1)$-state model with n repairperson (n modules),

$$P_k = \frac{\lambda^k \mu^{n-k} \dfrac{n!}{(n-k)!} \dfrac{n!}{k!}}{\displaystyle\sum_{j=0}^{n} \lambda^j \mu^{n-j} \dfrac{n!}{(n-j)!} \dfrac{n!}{j!}} = \frac{\lambda^k \mu^{n-k} \binom{n}{k}}{\displaystyle\sum_{j=0}^{n} \lambda^j \mu^{n-j} \binom{n}{j}} = \frac{\lambda^k \mu^{n-k} \binom{n}{k}}{(\mu + \lambda)^n}$$

The MTTF for a 1-of-n model with 1 repairperson is

$$\text{MTTF} = \frac{\displaystyle\sum_{k=0}^{n-1} \dfrac{n!}{(n-k)!} \sum_{j=k}^{n-1} \lambda^j \mu^{n-1-j}(j-k)!}{n!\lambda^n} = \frac{\displaystyle\sum_{j=0}^{n-1} \lambda^k \mu^{n-1-k} \sum_{k=0}^{j} \dfrac{n!(j-k)!}{(n-k)!}}{n!\lambda^n} = \frac{\displaystyle\sum_{j=0}^{n-1} \lambda^{n-1-j} \mu^j C_j}{n!\lambda^n}$$

where $\quad C_j = \dfrac{n! - (n-j)!(j!)}{j(j!)} = \dfrac{(n-j)!}{j}\left[\binom{n}{j} - 1\right] \quad$ for $j > 0$

$$C_0 = n![\Psi(n+1) - \Psi(1)] = n!\left(\frac{1}{1} + \frac{1}{2} + \frac{1}{3} + \cdots + \frac{1}{n}\right)$$

The MTTF for an m-of-n model with 1 repairperson is

$$\text{MTTF} = \frac{\displaystyle\sum_{k=0}^{n-m} \dfrac{n!}{(n-k)!} \sum_{j=k}^{n-m} \lambda^j \mu^{n-mj}(j-k+m-1)!}{n!\lambda^{n-m+1}}$$

$$= \frac{\displaystyle\sum_{j=0}^{n-m} \lambda^k \mu^{n-m-k} \sum_{k=0}^{j} \dfrac{n!(j-k+m-1)!}{(n-k)!}}{n!\lambda^{n-m+1}} = \frac{\displaystyle\sum_{j=0}^{n-m} \lambda^{n-m-j} \mu^j C_j}{n!\lambda^{n-m+1}}$$

where $\quad C_j = \dfrac{n!(m-1)! - n!(m-1+j)!}{j(m-1+j)!} = \dfrac{(n-j)!}{j}\left[\dfrac{\binom{n}{j}}{\binom{m-1+j}{j}} - 1\right]$ for $j > 0$

$$C_0 = n![\Psi(n+1) - \Psi(m)] = n!\left(\frac{1}{m} + \frac{1}{m+1} + \frac{1}{m+2} + \cdots + \frac{1}{n}\right)$$

Table E–1 summarizes commonly encountered availability models while Table E–2 summarizes MTTF models.

REFERENCES

Hansen, 1989; Solberg, 1975.

TABLE E–1 *Availability of commonly encountered systems*

	1 Repairperson	2 Repairpersons	3 Repairpersons
2 need 1 without coverage	$\dfrac{\mu^2 + 2\lambda\mu}{\mu^2 + 2\lambda\mu + 2\lambda^2}$	$\dfrac{2\mu^2 + 4\lambda\mu}{2\mu^2 + 4\lambda\mu + 2\lambda^2}$	
2 need 1 with coverage	$\dfrac{\mu^2 + 2\lambda\mu}{\mu^2 + 2\lambda\mu + 2\lambda^2 + 2\lambda\mu(1 - c)}$	$\dfrac{2\mu^2 + 4\lambda\mu}{2\mu^2 + 4\lambda\mu + 2\lambda^2 + 2\lambda\mu(1 - c)}$	
3 need 1	$\dfrac{\mu^3 + 3\mu^2\lambda + 6\mu\lambda^2}{\mu^3 + 3\mu^2\lambda + 6\mu\lambda^2 + 6\lambda^3}$	$\dfrac{4\mu^3 + 21\mu^2\lambda + 21\mu\lambda^2}{4\mu^3 + 21\mu^2\lambda + 21\mu\lambda^2 + 6\lambda^3}$	$\dfrac{\mu^3 + 3\mu^2\lambda + 3\mu\lambda^2}{\mu^3 + 3\mu^2\lambda + 3\mu\lambda^2 + \lambda^3}$
3 need 2	$\dfrac{\mu^3 + 3\mu^2\lambda}{\mu^3 + 3\mu^2\lambda + 6\mu\lambda^2 + 6\lambda^3}$	$\dfrac{4\mu^3 + 21\mu^2\lambda}{4\mu^3 + 21\mu^2\lambda + 21\mu\lambda^2 + 6\lambda^3}$	$\dfrac{\mu^3 + 3\mu^2\lambda}{\mu^3 + 3\mu^2\lambda + 3\mu\lambda^2 + \lambda^3}$

TABLE E–2
MTTF of commonly encountered systems

	1 Repairperson	2 Repairpersons
2 need 1 without coverage	$\dfrac{\mu + 3\lambda}{2\lambda^2}$	
2 need 1 with coverage	$\dfrac{\mu + \lambda + 2\lambda c}{2\lambda^2 + 2\mu\lambda(1 - c)}$	
3 need 1	$\dfrac{2\mu^2 + 4\mu\lambda + 11\lambda^2}{6\lambda^3}$	$\dfrac{2\mu^2 + 7\mu\lambda + 11\lambda^2}{6\lambda^3}$
3 need 2 without coverage	$\dfrac{\mu + 5\lambda}{6\lambda^2}$	
3 need 2 with coverage	$\dfrac{\mu + 2\lambda + 3\lambda c}{6\lambda^2 + 3\mu\lambda(1 - c)}$	

GLOSSARY

Acceptance Test. A test usually performed after each stage of assembly during the manufacturing process. The test focuses on the functional behavior of the system.

ARM (Availability, Reliability, and Maintainability). Used by UNIVAC to describe aspects of dependability.

Arrhenius Equation. An equation relating the chemical reaction rate with temperature. It is frequently used in accelerated temperature testing.

Availability, A(t). The instantaneous probability that the system is operational at time *t*. If the limit of this function exists as *t* goes to infinity, *A(t)* expresses the expected fraction of time the system is available to perform useful computations.

Axiomatic Models. A class of models in which software reliability is postulated to obey certain universal laws.

Bathtub Curve. A term frequently used to describe the curve that depicts failure rate as a function of time. The name is derived from the typical shape of the curve.

Boolean Difference. An algebraic-based test-generation technique.

Bridging. A fault where two or more adjacent signal lines are physically shorted together.

Circuit Level. A level in the hierarchy of digital systems composed of resistors, capacitors, inductors, and power sources.

Combinatorial Modeling. Models in which the probability of success is the sum of the probabilities of being in a "working" state. Once a module has failed, it is assumed always to yield incorrect results. Once the system enters a failed state, subsequent failures cannot return the system to a functional state.

Compensating Module Failures. Failures in a redundant system that cancel each other's effect. For example, in triplication and voting, one module can fail to stuck-at-one while the other can fail to stuck-at-zero so that the voter output follows that of the remaining good module.

Confidence Interval. A *P*-level confidence interval is a range within which the actual value of the estimated parameter would fall with probability *P* if an experiment were repeated many times.

Coverage. The probability that a system successfully recovers from a specified type of failure.

D-Algorithm. An intelligent simulation technique for generation of tests through path synthesization and propagation of a symbol D, which defines the difference between the good and faulted circuits.

Data Domain Models. A model for software reliability in which the probability of error is related to the size of the input data space exercised.

Design Diversity. The use of multiple independent teams to produce alternative designs. The system output is derived from the majority vote of the concurrently executing alternatives. The goal is to minimize design errors.

Design Maturity Test (DMT). A design maturity test estimates the mean time to failure for a new product before it is committed to volume manufacture.

Deterministic Model. A model whose variables take on a constant value.

Diagnosis. The procedure by which a faulty unit is identified. There are two basic approaches to diagnosis: specification-based diagnosis and symptom-based diagnosis.

Digital Diagnostic Center (DDC). A remote diagnostic facility for computer-to-computer communications and testing.

EREP (Error Recording Edit Program). Used by IBM to process system event logs.

Error. Manifestation of a fault within a program or data structure.

Error-Correcting Code (ECC). The systematic application of redundant information which can be used to reconstruct the original input data even in the presence of errors.

Error-Detection Mechanism (EDM). Constructs within a system designed to detect errors. A simple example would be parity.

Failure. Occurs when the delivered service deviates from the specified service. Service can be viewed from several levels of abstraction ranging from chip to system level.

Failure Mode Effect Analysis (FMEA). A procedure whereby a list of proposed failure modes is assembled and the response of the system to each failure is predicted.

Failure Rate. A function that expresses the number of failures per unit time.

Fault. An erroneous state of hardware or software resulting from failures of components, physical interference from the environment, operator error, or incorrect design.

Feedback Shift Register (FSR). A device commonly used in codes to compress information from a long string of serial data.

Field Replaceable Unit (FRU). The smallest portion of a system that can be replaced in the field by a field service engineer.

Functional Testing. Testing procedures based upon the behavior of a circuit instead of its structure.

Hybrid Redundancy. A combination of triplication and voting with standby spares. When one of the voted modules disagrees, it is replaced by one of the standby spares.

Infant Mortality. A term used to describe the early life failures of components and systems. These failures are typically caused by defects introduced during the manufacturing process.

Intermittent. Describes a fault or error that is only occasionally present because of unstable hardware or varying hardware or software states.

Level-Sensitive Scan Design (LSSD). The use of scan in/scan out shift registers for increasing the controllability/observability of sequential logic. It is used to convert sequential circuits into combinational circuits for testing.

Life-Cycle Cost (LCC). The total cost of a system throughout its life, including purchase, installation, maintenance, and operation.

Logic Level. A level in the hierarchy of digital systems composed of gates, flip-flops, registers, and operators.

Markov Model. A model in which the states of a system are represented by nodes in a graph and the probability of transitioning between states is represented by arcs. Discrete-time models require all state transitions to occur at fixed intervals, and they assign probabilities to each possible transition. Continuous-time models allow state transitions to occur at varying, random intervals, with transition rates assigned to possible transitions. For reliability models, the transition rates are the module hazard functions and repair rate functions, which are possibly modified by coverage factors. The basic assumption underlying Markov models is that the probability of a given state transition depends only on the current state.

Mean Number of Instructions to Restart (MNIR). The expected number of instructions executed from system startup until system failure.

Mean Time Between Failures (MTBF). The expected or average time between consecutive hard failures in systems with repair. It is a function of both a failure process and a repair process.

Mean Time Between Software Errors (MTBSE). Expected time between errors produced by software.

Mean Time To Crash (MTTC). The expected time to recoverable system failure.

Mean Time To Error (MTTE). The expected time to error.

Mean Time To Failure (MTTF). The expected time of the first system failure in a population of identical systems, given successful startup at time $t = 0$.

Mean Time To Repair (MTTR). The expected time to repair a system or subsystem and restore it to operation.

Mean Time To Restart (MTTS). The expected time between system reloads.

MIL-HDBK-217. Abbreviation for the "Military Standardization Handbook: Reliability Prediction of Electronic Equipment" published and periodically updated by the U.S. Department of Defense.

Mission Time. The mission time function $MT(r)$ is the time at which the system reliability falls below the level r.

M-of-N Systems. A generalization of the parallel model in which M (rather than one) of the N modules are required for the system to be functioning correctly.

N Version Programming. A software approach to design diversity. Different design teams generate independent software implements whose outputs are voted upon at runtime to produce the system output.

OLTEP (On-Line Test Executive Program). A term used by IBM to describe its diagnostic executive.

OLTS (On-Line Functional Test). IBM's on-line diagnostic exerciser.

Parametric Testing. Test used to evaluate the electrical properties of a component and compare them to specifications. This test is typically done during incoming inspection.

Path Synthesization. A test-generation technique based upon the propagation of signals to outputs.

Permanent. Describes a failure, fault, or error that is continuous and stable.

PMS Level. A level in the hierarchy of digital systems composed of input/output devices, memories, and processors. PMS is an abbreviation for the major components of this level: processors, memories, and switches.

Poisson Distribution. The probability of the occurrence of an event in an interval of time is proportional to the time interval. The probability of an event is independent of any other event, that is, the distribution is "memoryless."

Probabilistic Models. A model whose parameters are random variables.

Process Maturity Testing (PMT). A procedure to evaluate the reproducibility of the manufacturing process and the contribution of the process to system failures.

Program Level. A level in the hierarchy of digital systems composed of instruction sets and high-level programming languages.

RAMP (Reliability, Availability, and Maintainability Program). Used by Digital Equipment Corporation to describe various aspects of dependability.

RAS (Reliability, Availability, and Serviceability). Used by IBM to describe all aspects of dependability.

Reliability, R(t). The conditional probability that the system has survived the interval [0, t], given that it was operational at time $t = 0$.

Reliability Block Diagram (RBD). A parallel structure representing alternative paths for which a system is declared functional. Each path is composed of a series of components, all of which must operate correctly for the path to be considered working.

Screening. A procedure usually applied at the component level to test for and eliminate defective components.

Sequential Probability Ratio Test (SPRT). A procedure for establishing the mean time to failure of a system. Upper and lower bounds, as well as risk factors, define the degree of uncertainty acceptable in the outcome of the test.

Series/Parallel Systems. Systems in which a set of alternative paths exists, any one of which is sufficient for correct system operation. The alternative paths are represented as a parallel construct. The set of criteria that must be met for each path is represented by a serial string in which the failure of any member causes the path to fail.

Signature Analysis. A technique used in testing to compress test output information into a signature for comparison to a known result.

Specification-Based Diagnosis. The use of system design specifications to provide information on the expected behavior of a system under the application of various input patterns. Stimulus/response testing based upon the logic schematic of a circuit is a common example.

Strife Testing. A combination of stress and life testing applied to prototype systems. External stresses applied during the test help define the amount of margin in the design.

Stuck-At. A fault model usually applied at the logic level for lines, gates, and pins constrained to a single logical value.

Symptom-Based Diagnosis. The use of information generated during normal operation to diagnose the source of failure.

Test Coverage. Fraction of faults that a test detects from an assumed fault list.

Time Domain Model. Relates software reliability to the number of bugs present in the software at a given time during its development.

Transient. Describes a fault or error resulting from temporary environmental conditions.

Triple Modular Redundancy (TMR). A redundant structure in which two of three parts must function correctly for the system to function. Typically, the outputs of a TMR system feed a voter, which selects the majority.

Unidirectional. A single failure that affects multiple signal lines. The multiple signal lines that are in error are all in the same logical direction (i.e., correct zeros have been transformed into incorrect ones).

Unit Under Test (UUT). The system to which tests are applied.

Wear Out. A term describing the end of life of a system where aging is the dominant source of failure.

REFERENCES

[Abraham, 1975] Abraham, J.A. "A Combinatorial Solution to the Reliability of Interwoven Redundant Logic Networks." *IEEE Trans. Comp.* C-24 (May 1975): 578–584.

[Abraham and Fuchs, 1986] Abraham, J.A., and W.K. Fuchs. "Fault and Error Models for VLSI." *Proceedings of the IEEE* 74(5) (May 1986): 639–654.

[Abraham, Ghosh, and Ray-Chaudhuri, 1968] Abraham, C.T.; S.P. Ghosh; and D.K. Ray-Chaudhuri. "File Organization Schemes Based on Finite Geometries." *Information and Control* 12, no. 2 (February 1968): 143–163.

[Abraham and Siewiorek, 1974] Abraham, J.A., and D.P. Siewiorek. "An Algorithm for the Accurate Reliability Evaluation of Triple Modular Redundancy Networks." *IEEE Trans. Comp.* C-23 (July 1974): 682–692.

[Abramson, 1959] Abramson, N.M. "A Class of Systematic Codes for Non-Independent Errors." *IRE Trans. Info. Theory* IT-5, no. 4 (December 1959): 150–157.

[Acree, 1980] Acree, A.T., Jr. *On Mutation*. Ph.D. diss., Georgia Institute of Technology, School of Information and Computer Science, Atlanta, GA, August 1980.

[Acree et al., 1982] Acree, A.T.; T.A. Budd; R.A. DeMillo; R.J. Lipton; and F.G. Sayward. "Mutation Analysis." Technical Report GIT-ICS 79/08. Georgia Institute of Technology, Atlanta, GA, August 1982.

[Adams, Agrawal, and Siegel, 1987] Adams, G.B.; D.P. Agrawal; and J.H. Siegel. "Fault-Tolerant Multistage Interconnection Networks." *IEEE Computer* (June 1987): 14–27.

[Adrion et al., 1982] Adrion, W.R.; M.A. Branstad; and J.C. Cheriavsky. "Validation, Verification, and Testing of Computer Software." *ACM Computing Surveys* 14(2) (June 1982): 159–192.

[Adshead, Jain, and Knowles, 1972] Adshead, H.G.; G.C. Jain; and A.J. Knowles. "New Dimensions in Automatic Logic Testing and Diagnostics." In *Proceedings International Conference on Computer Aided Design*, Institute of Electrical Engineers, 1972, pp. 112–118.

[Aggarwal and Rai, 1978] Aggarwal, K.K., and S. Rai. "Symbolic Reliability Evaluation Using Logical Signal Relations." *IEEE Trans. Rel.* R-27, no. 3 (August 1978): 202–205.

[Agnew, Forbes, and Stieglitz, 1967] Agnew, P.W.; R.E. Forbes; and C.B. Stieglitz. "An Approach to Self-Repairing Computers." In *Digest 1st Annual IEEE Computer Conf.*, Chicago, 1967: 60–64.

[Agrawal and Agrawal, 1972] Agrawal, V., and P. Agrawal. "An Automatic Test Generation System for ILLIAC IV Logic Boards." *IEEE Trans. Comp.* C-21, no. 9 (September 1972): 1015–1017.

[Akers, 1977] Akers, S.B. "Partitioning for Testability." *J. Des. Automat. Fault-Tolerant Comp.* 1, no. 2, Feb. 1977.

[Albert, 1956] Albert, A.A. *Fundamental Concepts of Higher Algebra*. Chicago: University of Chicago Press, 1956.

[Allers et al., 1983] Allers, J.E.; A.H. Huizinga; J.A. Kukla; J.D. Sipes; and R.T. Yeh. "No. 5ESS™—Strategies for Reliability in a Distributed Processing Environment." In *Proceedings of the 1983 IEEE International Symposium on Fault-Tolerant Computing* (FTCS–13), Milan, Italy, June 1983, pp. 388–391.

[Almassy, 1979] Almassy, G. "Limits of Models in Reliability Engineering." In *Proc. Annual Reliability and Maintainability Symposium, 1979*, IEEE Reliability Society, 1979, pp. 364–367.

[Alonso, Hopkins, and Thaler, 1966] Alonso, R.L.; A.L. Hopkins, Jr.; and H.A. Thaler. "Design Criteria for a Spacecraft Computer." In *Proc. Seminar on Spaceborne Multiprocessors*, Boston, 1966, pp. 21–28.

[Alonso, Hopkins, and Thaler, 1967] Alonso, R.L.; A.L. Hopkins, Jr.; and H.A. Thaler. "A Multiprocessing Structure." In *Digest 1st IEEE Computer Conf.*, Chicago, 1967, pp. 56–60.

[AMD, 1979] AMD. *The AM 2900 Family Data Book*. Sunnyvale, CA, 1979.

[Anderson, 1971] Anderson, D.A. "Design of Self-Checking Digital Networks Using Code Techniques." Ph.D. diss., University of Illinois, Champaign-Urbana, 1971.

[Anderson, 1985] Anderson, T., ed. *Resilient Computing Systems*, vol. 1. New York: John Wiley and Sons, 1985.

[Anderson and Jensen, 1975] Anderson, G.A., and E.D. Jensen. "Computer Interconnection Structures: Taxonomy Characteristics and Examples." *ACM Computing Surveys* 7, no. 4 (December 1975): 197–215.

[Anderson and Knight, 1983] Anderson, T., and J.C. Knight. "A Framework for Software Fault Tolerance in Real-Time Systems." *IEEE Trans. Soft. Eng.* SE-9, no. 3 (May 1983): 355–364.

[Anderson and Lee, 1979] Anderson, T., and P.A. Lee. "The Provision of Recoverable Interfaces." In *Proceedings of 9th International Symposium on Fault-Tolerant Comput-*

ing, IEEE Computer Society, Madison, WI, 1979, pp. 87–94.

[Anderson and Lee, 1981] Anderson, T., and P.A. Lee. *Fault-Tolerance: Principles and Practice.* Englewood Cliffs, NJ: Prentice-Hall, 1981.

[Anderson, Lee, and Shrivastava, 1979] Anderson, T.; P.A. Lee; and S.K. Shrivastava. "System Fault Tolerance." In T. Anderson and B. Randell, eds., *Computing Systems Reliability: An Advanced Course.* Cambridge: Cambridge University Press, 1979, pp. 153–210.

[Anderson and Macri, 1967] Anderson, J.E., and F.J. Macri. "Multiple Redundancy Applications in a Computer." In *Proc. Annual Symp. Rel.*, Washington, DC, 1967, pp. 553–562.

[Anderson and Metze, 1973] Anderson, D.A., and G. Metze. "Design of Totally Self-Checking Check Circuits for m-out-of-n Codes." *IEEE Trans. Comp.* C-22 (March 1973): 263–269.

[Anderson et al., 1985] Anderson, T.; P.A. Barrett; D.N. Halliwell; and M.R. Moulding. "Software Fault Tolerance: An Evaluation." *IEEE Trans. Soft. Eng.* SE-11, no. 12 (December 1985).

[Anderson et al., 1987] Anderson, L.G.; C.H. Bowers; D.L. Carney; J.J. Kulzer; and W.W. Parker. "Distributed Systems Tradeoffs." In *International Switching Symposium Proceedings*, Phoenix, AZ, March 1987.

[Andrews et al., 1969] Andrews, R.J.; J.J. Driscoll; J.A. Herndon; P.C. Richards; and L.R. Roberts. "Service Features and Call Processing Plan." *Bell Sys. Tech. J.* 48, no. 8 (October 1969): 2713–2764.

[Ando, 1980] Ando, H. "Testing VLSI with Random Access Scan." In *Dig. Papers Compcon 80*, IEEE Pub. 80CH1491-0C, pp. 50–52, Feb. 1980.

[ARINC, 1964] ARINC Research Corporation. *Reliability Engineering.* Englewood Cliffs, NJ: Prentice-Hall, 1964.

[Arlat, Crouzet, and LaPrie, 1989] Arlat, J.; Y. Crouzet; and J.C. LaPrie. "Fault Injection for Dependability Validation of Fault-Tolerant Computing Systems." In *Proceedings of the 19th IEEE International Symposium on Fault-Tolerant Computers*, June 1989, Chicago, IL, pp. 348–355.

[Armstrong, 1961] Armstrong, D.B. "A General Method of Applying Error Correction to Synchronous Digital Systems." *Bell Sys. Tech. J.* 40 (March 1961): 577–593.

[Armstrong, 1966] Armstrong, D.B. "On Finding a Nearly Minimal Set of Fault Detection Tests for Combinational Logic Nets." *IEEE Trans. Electron. Comput.* EC-15, no. 1 (February 1966): 66–73.

[Armstrong, 1972] Armstrong, D.B. "A Deductive Method for Simulating Faults in Logic Circuits." *IEEE Trans. Comp.* C-22, no. 5 (May 1972): 464–471.

[Arulpragasm and Swarz, 1980] Arulpragasm, J.A., and R.S. Swarz. "A Design for Process State Preservation on Storage Unit Failure." In *Digest of 10th International Symposium on Fault-Tolerant Computing*, IEEE Computer Society, Kyoto, Japan, 1980, pp. 47–52.

[Ashjaee and Reddy, 1976] Ashjaee, and S.M. Reddy. "On Totally Self-Checking Checkers for Separable Codes." In *Proceedings of 6th International Symposium on Fault-Tolerant Computing*, IEEE Computer Society, Pittsburgh, PA, 1976, 151–156.

[Ault et al., 1964] Ault, C.F.; L.E. Gallaher; T.S. Greenwood; and D.C. Koehler. "No. 1 ESS Program Store." *Bell Sys. Tech. J.* 43 (September 1964): 2097–2146.

[Ault et al., 1977] Ault, C.F.; J.H. Brewster; T.S. Greenwood; R.E. Haglund; W.A. Read; and M.W. Rolund. "1A Processor-Memory Systems." *Bell Sys. Tech. J.* 56, no. 2 (February 1977): 181–205.

[Avizienis, 1964] Avizienis, A. "A Set of Algorithms for a Diagnosable Arithmetic Unit." Jet Propulsion Lab 34–546. Pasadena, CA: JPL Tech Reports, 1964.

[Avizienis, 1965] Avizienis, A. "A Study of the Effectiveness of Fault-Detecting Codes for Binary Arithmetic." Jet Propulsion Lab 32–711. Pasadena, CA: JPL Tech Reports, 1965.

[Avizienis, 1966a] Avizienis, A. "Codes for Fault Detection in Digital Arithmetic Processors." In W.A. Kalenich, ed., *Information Processing 1965: Proc. IFIP Congress*, vol. 2. Washington, DC: Spartan Books, 1966, p. 634.

[Avizienis, 1966b] Avizienis, A. "The Diagnosable Arithmetic Processor." In *Space Programs Summary*. Pasadena, CA: Jet Propulsion Lab, 1966, pp. 76–80.

[Avizienis, 1967a] Avizienis, A. "Concurrent Diagnosis of Arithmetic Processors." In *Digest of 1st Annual IEEE Computer Conf.*, 1967, pp. 34–37.

[Avizienis, 1967b] Avizienis, A. "Application of Codes in Digital Computer Systems." In *International Conference on Information Theory*, San Remo, Italy, 1967.

[Avizienis, 1967c] Avizienis, A. "Design of Fault-Tolerant Computers." In *FJCC, AFIPS Conf. Proc.*, vol. 31. Washington, DC: Thompson, 1967, pp. 733–743.

[Avizienis, 1968] Avizienis, A. "An Experimental Self-Repairing Computer." In A.J.H. Morrell, ed., *Information Processing 1968, Proc. IFIP Congress*, vol. 2. New York: North Holland, 1968, pp. 872–877.

[Avizienis, 1969] Avizienis, A. "Digital Fault Diagnosis by Low-Cost Arithmetical Coding Techniques." In *Proc. Purdue Centennial Year Symposium Information Processing*, vol. 1, Lafayette, IN, 1969, pp. 81–91.

[Avizienis, 1971] Avizienis, A. "Arithmetic Error Codes: Cost and Effectiveness Studies for Application in Digital

System Design." *IEEE Trans. Comp.* C-20 (November 1971): 1322–1331.

[Avizienis, 1973] Avizienis, A. "Arithmetic Algorithms for Error-Coded Operands." *IEEE Trans. Comp.* C-22 (June 1973): 566–572.

[Avizienis, 1975] Avizienis, A. "Architecture of Fault-Tolerant Computing Systems." In *Digest of 5th IEEE International Symposium on Fault-Tolerant Computing,* Paris, France, 1975, pp. 3–16.

[Avizienis, 1976] Avizienis, A. "Approaches to Computer Reliability Then and Now." In *AFIPS Conf. Proc.,* vol. 45. Montvale, NJ: AFIPS Press, 1976, pp. 401–411.

[Avizienis, 1977] Avizienis, A. "Fault-Tolerant Computing—Progress, Problems, and Prospects." In *Proceedings IFIP Congress.* New York: North Holland, 1977, pp. 405–420.

[Avizienis, 1978] Avizienis, A. "Fault-Tolerance: The Survival Attribute of Digital Systems." *Proceedings of the IEEE* 66 (October 1978): 1109–1125.

[Avizienis, 1985] Avizienis, A. "The N-Version Approach to Fault-Tolerant Software." *IEEE Trans. Soft. Eng.* SE-11(12) (December 1985): 1491–1501.

[Avizienis, 1989] Avizienis, A. "Software Fault Tolerance." *XI World Computer Congress, IFIP Congress '89,* (August 1989).

[Avizienis and Chen, 1977] Avizienis, A., and L. Chen. "On the Implementation of N-Version Programming for Software Fault-Tolerance During Execution." *Proc. COMPSAC 77* (November 1977): 149–155.

[Avizienis and Kelly, 1984] Avizienis, A., and J.P.J. Kelly. "Fault Tolerance by Design Diversity: Concepts and Experiments." *Computer* 17(8) (August 1984): 67–80.

[Avizienis and Laprie, 1986] Avizienis, A., and J.-C. Laprie. "Dependable Computing: From Concepts to Design Diversity," *Proceedings of the IEEE* 74(5) (May 1986): 629–638.

[Avizienis, Lyu, and Schutz, 1988] Avizienis, A.; M.R. Lyu; and W. Schutz. "In Search of Effective Diversity: A Six-Language Study of Fault-Tolerant Flight Control Software." In *Proceedings of the IEEE 18th International Symposium on Fault-Tolerant Computing,* Tokyo, Japan (1988), pp. 15–22.

[Avizienis and Rennels, 1972] Avizienis, A., and D.A. Rennels. "Fault-Tolerance Experiments with the JPL Star Computer." *Digest of Papers. COMPCON '72* (September 1972): 321–324.

[Avizienis et al., 1969] Avizienis, A.; F.P. Mathur; D.A. Rennels; and J.A. Rohr. "Automatic Maintenance of Aerospace Computers and Spacecraft Information and Control Systems." In *Proc. AIAA Aerosp. Comput. Syst. Conf.,* AIAA Paper 69–966, 1969.

[Avizienis et al., 1971] Avizienis, A.; G.C. Gilley; F.P. Mathur; D.A. Rennels; J.A. Rohr; and D.K. Rubin. "The STAR (Self-Testing and Repairing) Computer: An Investigation on the Theory and Practice of Fault-Tolerant Computer Design." *IEEE Trans. Comp.* C-20 (November 1971): 1312–1321.

[Avizienis et al., 1985] Avizienis, A.; G. Gunningberg; J.P.J. Kelly; R.T. Lyu; L. Strigini; P. Traverse; K.S. Tso; and U. Voges. "Software Fault Tolerance by Design Diversity; DEDIX: A Tool for Experiments." In *Proc. IFAC Workshop SAFECOMP'85,* Como, Italy (October 1985): 173–178.

[AWST, 1981] "Velocity, Altitude Regimes to Push Computer Limits," *Aviation Week & Space Technology* 6 (April 1981): 49–51.

[Ball, 1980] Ball, M.O. "Complexity of Network Reliability Computations." *Networks* 10 (1980): 153–155.

[Ball and Hardie, 1967] Ball, M.O., and F. Hardie. "Effects and Detection of Intermittent Failures in Digital Systems." IBM 67–825-2137, 1967.

[Barclay, Dossey, and Nolan, 1986] Barclay, D.K.; E.M. Dossey; and T.H. Nolan. "5ESS™ Switching System Software: Office Database Generation." *AT&T Technical Journal, 5ESS™ Switch Software* (January 1986): 115–129.

[Barker, 1953] Barker, R.H. "Group Synchronizing of Binary Digital Systems." In W. Jackson, ed., *Communication Theory,* vol. 4. New York: Academic Press, 1953, pp. 273–287.

[Barlow and Proschan, 1965] Barlow, R.E., and F. Proschan. *Mathematical Theory of Reliability.* New York: Wiley, 1965.

[Barlow and Proschan, 1975] Barlow, R.E., and F. Proschan. *Statistical Theory of Reliability and Life Testing: Probability Models.* New York: Holt, Rinehart and Winston, 1975.

[Barnes et al., 1968] Barnes, G.H.; R.M. Brown; M. Kato; D.J. Kuch; D.L. Skotnick; and R.A. Stokes. "The Illiac IV Computer." *IEEE Trans. Comp.* C-17 (August 1968): 746–757.

[Barsi and Maestrini, 1973] Barsi, F., and P. Maestrini. "Error Correcting Properties of Redundant Residue Number Systems." *IEEE Trans. Comp.* C-22 (March 1973): 307–924.

[Barsi and Maestrini, 1974] Barsi, F., and P. Mestrini. "Error Detection and Correction by Product Codes in Residue Number Systems." *IEEE Trans. Comp.* C-23 (September 1974): 915–924.

[Bartlett, 1978] Bartlett, J.F. "A 'NonStop' Operating System." In *Proc. Hawaii Int. Conf. of System Sciences,* Honolulu, HI, 1978, pp. 103–119.

[Bartlett, 1981] Bartlett, J.F. "A NonStop Kernel." *ACM 8th Symposium on Operating Systems Principles*, Pacific Grove, CA, vol. 15, no. 5 (December 1981): 22–29.

[Barton and Schmitt, 1983] Barton, M.E., and D.A. Schmitt. "Craft Interface." *Bell Sys. Tech. J.* 62. no. 1, pt. 2 (January 1983): 383–398.

[Barton et al., 1990] Barton, James H.; Edward W. Czeck; Zary Z. Segall; and Daniel P. Siewiorek. "Fault Injection Experiments Using FIAT." *IEEE Transactions on Computers, Special Issue on Fault Tolerant Computing*, vol. 39, no. 4 (April 1990).

[Bartow and McGuire, 1970] Bartow, N., and R. McGuire. "System/360 Model 85 Microdiagnostics." *SJCC AFIPS Conf. Proc.*, vol. 36. Montvale, NJ: AFIPS Press, 1970, pp. 191–197.

[Basham, 1976] Basham, G.R. "New Error-Correcting Technique for Solid-State Memories Saves Hardware." *Computer Design* 15 (October 1976): 110–113.

[Bashkow, Friets, and Karson, 1963] Bashkow, T.R.; J. Friets; and A. Karson. "A Programming System for Detection and Diagnosis of Machine Malfunctions." *IEEE Trans. Elec. Comp.* EC-12, no. 1 (February 1963): 10–17.

[Baskin, Borgerson, and Roberts, 1972] Baskin, H.B.; B.R. Borgerson; and R. Roberts. "PRIME—A Modular Architecture for Terminal Oriented Systems." In *Conf. Proc.*, vol. 40. Montvale, NJ: AFIPS Press, 1972, pp. 431–437.

[Batni and Kime, 1976] Batni, R.P., and C.R. Kime. "A Module Level Testing Approach for Combinational Networks." *IEEE Trans. Comp.* C-25, no. 6 (June 1976): 594–604.

[Bauer, Croxall, and Davis, 1985] Bauer, H.A.; L.M. Croxall; and E.A. Davis. "The 5ESS™ Switching System: System Test, First-Office Application, and Early Field Experience." *AT&T Technical Journal* 64, no. 6, pt. 2 (July–August 1985): 1503–1522.

[Bavuso, 1984] Bavuso, S.J. "A User's View of CARE III." In *Proc. 1984 Annual Reliability and Maintainability Symposium* (January 1984): 382–389.

[Bavuso et al., 1987] Bavuso, S.J.; J.B. Dugan; K.S. Trivedi; E.M. Rothmann; and W.E. Smith. "Analysis of Typical Fault-Tolerant Architectures Using HARP." *IEEE Trans. Rel.* R-36, no. 2 (March 1987): 176–185.

[Beaudry, 1978] Beaudry, M.D. "Performance Related Reliability Measures for Computing Systems." *IEEE Trans. Comp.* C-27 (June 1978): 540 547.

[Becker, 1983] Becker, J.O. (ed). "The 3B20D Processor and DMERT Operating System." *Bell Sys. Tech. J.* 62, no. 1 (January 1983) (special issue on 3B20D).

[Becker et al., 1978] Becker, J.O.; J.G. Cheoalier; R.K. Eisenhart; J.H. Forster; A.W. Fulton; and W.L. Harrod.

"1A Processor Technology and Physical Design." *Bell Sys. Tech. J.* 56 (February 1978): 207–236.

[Beh et al., 1982] Beh, C.C.; K.H. Arya; C.E. Radke; and K.E. Torku. "Do Stuck Faults Reflect Manufacturing Defects?" In *1982 IEEE Test Conference* (1982): 35–42.

[Beister, 1968] Beister, J. "On the Implementation of Failure-Tolerant Counters." *IEEE Trans. Comp.* C-17 (September 1968): 885–886.

[Bell and Newell, 1971] Bell, C.G., and A. Newell. *Computer Structures: Readings and Examples.* New York: McGraw-Hill, 1971.

[Bell and Strecker, 1976] Bell, C.G., and W.D. Strecker. "Computer Structures: What Have We Learned from the PDP-11?" *Proc. Third Ann. Symp. on Comp. Architecture.* Clearwater, FL: IEEE/ACM, 1976, pp. 1–14.

[Bell et al., 1970] Bell, C.G.; R. Cady; H. McFarland; B. Delaji; J. O'Loughlin; R. Noonan; and W. Wulf. "A New Architecture for Mini-Computers: The DEC PDP-11." In *SJCC, AFIPS Conf. Proc.* vol. 36, 1970, pp. 657–675.

[Bell et al., 1978] Bell, C.G.; A. Kotok; T.N. Hastings; and R. Hill. "The Evolution of the DECsystem 10." *Comm. ACM* 21 (January 1978): 44–63.

[Bellis, 1978] Bellis, H. "Comparing Analytical Reliability Models to Hard and Transient Failure Data." Master's thesis, Carnegie-Mellon University Department of Electrical Engineering, Pittsburgh, PA, 1978.

[Bennetts, 1972] Bennetts, R.G. "A Realistic Approach to Fault Detection Test Set Generation for Combinational Logic Circuits." *BCS Computer Journal* 15, no. 3 (1972): 238–246.

[Bennetts, 1973] Bennetts, R.G. "A Contribution to the Boolean Difference Procedure for Generating Tests for Combinational Logic Circuits." In *BCS Datafair Conf. Proc.*, vol. 2, 1973, pp. 431–436.

[Bennetts, 1974] Bennetts, R. "Automatic Test Sequence Generation for Complex Digital Networks." In *Proc. Automatic Testing, 1974 Conference*, 1974, pp. 27–36.

[Bennetts, 1975] Bennetts, R.G. "On the Analysis of Fault Trees." *IEEE Trans. Rel.* R-24 (August 1975): 175–185.

[Bennetts, 1976] Bennetts, R.G. "An Evaluation of Techniques for Designing Easily-Tested Combinational Logic Circuits." In *Proc. Automatic Testing, 1976 Conference*, 1976, pp. 94–106.

Bennetts and Lewing, 1971] Bennetts, R.G., and D.W. Lewing. "Fault Diagnosis of Digital Systems—A Review." *Computer* 4, no. 4 (July/August 1971): 12–20.

[Bennetts and Scott, 1976] Bennetts, R.B., and R.V. Scott. "Recent Developments in the Theory and Practice of Testable Logic Design." *Computer* 9, no. 6 (June 1976): 47–62.

[Bennetts et al., 1975] Bennetts, R.G.; D.C. Brittle; A.C. Prior; and J.L. Washington. "A Modular Approach to Test Sequence Generation for Large Digital Networks." *Digital Processes* 1, no. 1 (1975): 3–24.

[Berger, 1961] Berger, J.M. "A Note on Burst Error Detection Codes for Asymmetric Channels." *Information and Control* 4, no. 3 (March 1961): 68–73.

[Berger and Lawrence, 1974] Berger, R.W.; and K. Lawrence. "Estimating Weibull Parameters by Linear and Nonlinear Regression." *Technometrics*, 16, no. 4 (November 1974): 617–619.

[Berger and Mandelbrot, 1963] Berger, J.M., and B. Mandelbrot. "A New Model for Error Clustering in Telephone Circuits." *IBM J. Res. and Dev.* 7, no. 3 (July 1963): 224–236.

[Berlekamp, 1964] Berlekamp, E.R. "Note on Recurrent Codes." *IEEE Trans. Info. Theory* IT-10, no. 3 (July 1964): 257–259.

[Berlekamp, 1968] Berlekamp, E.R. *Algebraic Coding Theory.* New York: McGraw-Hill, 1968.

[Betancourt, 1973] Betancourt, R. "Derivation of Minimum Test Sets for Unate Logical Circuits." *IEEE Trans. Comp.* C-22, no. 11 (November 1973): 1264–1269.

[Beuscher et al., 1969] Beuscher, H.J.; G.E. Fessler; D.W. Huffman; P.J. Kennedy; and E. Nussbaum. "Administration and Maintenance Plan." *Bell Sys. Tech. J.* 48, no. 8 (October 1969): 2765–2815.

[Bhandari, Simon, and Siewiorek, 1990] Bhandari, Inderpal S.; Herbert A. Simon; and Daniel P. Siewiorek. "Optimal Probe Selection in Diagnostic Search." *IEEE Transactions on Systems, Man, and Cybernetics*, 1990.

[Bhargava, 1987] Bhargava, B.K. *Concurrency Control and Reliability in Distributed Systems.* New York: Van Nostrand Reinhold Company, 1987.

[Bhatt and Kinney, 1978] Bhatt, A.K., and L.L. Kinney. "A High Speed Parallel Encoder/Decoder for b-Adjacent Error-Checking Codes." In *Proc. Third USA–Japan Computer Conf,* AFIPS, 1978, pp. 203–207.

[Birdsall and Ristenblatt, 1958] Birdsall, T.G., and M.P. Ristenblatt. "Introduction to Linear Shift-Register Generated Sequences." Ann Arbor: University of Michigan Research Institute, 1958.

[Bishop et al., 1985] Bishop, P.; D. Esp; M. Barnes; P. Humphreys; G. Dahll; J. Lahti; and S. Yoshimura. "Project on Diverse Software—An Experiment in Software Reliable Software." *Proc. IFAC Workshop SAFECOMP'85* (October 1985).

[Bishop et al., 1986] Bishop, P.G.; D.G. Esp; M. Barnes; P. Humphreys; G. Dahi; and J. Lahti. "PODS—A Project on Diverse Software." *IEEE Trans. Soft. Eng.* SE-12, no. 9 (1986): 929–940.

[Bisset, 1977] Bisset, S. "Eshaustive Testing of Microprocessors and Related Devices: A Practical Solution." In *Dig. Papers, 1977 Semiconductor Test Symp.* (October 1977): 38–41.

[Bitton, 1989] Bitton, D. "Arm Scheduling in Shadowed Disks." *CompCon 1989*, IEEE Press, March 1989, pp. 132–136.

[Bitton and Gray, 1988] Bitton, D., and J. Gray. "Disk Shadowing." *Proceedings of 14th Conference on Very Large Data Bases*, September 1988, pp. 331–338.

[Black, Sundberg, and Walker, 1977] Black, C.J.; C.E. Sundberg; and W.K.S. Walker. "Development of a Spaceborne Memory with a Single Error and Erasure Correction Scheme." In *Digest of 7th International Symposium on Fault-Tolerant Computing*, IEEE Computer Society, Los Angeles, CA, 1977, pp. 50–55.

[Blahut, 1984] Blahut, R.E. *Theory and Practice of Error Control Codes.* Reading, MA: Addison-Wesley, 1983 (Reprinted with corrections 1984).

[Blodgett and Barbour, 1982] Blodgett, A.J., and D.R. Barbour. "Thermal Conduction Module: A High-Performance Multilayer Ceramic Package." *IBM J. Res. and Dev.* 26, no. 1 (January 1982): 30–37.

[BNR, 1984] Bell Northern Research. *Telesys*, vol. 1, 1984.

[Boone, Liebergot, and Sedmak, 1980] Boone, L.A.; H.L. Liebergot; and R.M. Sedmak. "Availability, Reliability, and Maintainability Aspects of the Sperry Univac 1100/60." In *Digest of 10th International Symposium on Fault-Tolerant Computing*, IEEE Computer Society, Kyoto, Japan, 1980, pp. 3–8.

[Borgerson and Freitas, 1975] Borgerson, B.R., and R.F. Freitas. "A Reliability Model for Gracefully Degrading and Standby-Sparing Systems." *IEEE Trans. Comp.* (May 1975): 517–525.

[Borgerson, Hanson, and Hartley, 1978] Borgerson, B.R.; M.L. Hanson; and P.A. Hartley. "The Evolution of the Sperry Univac 1100 Series: A History, Analysis and Projection." *Comm. ACM* 1 (January 1978): 25–43.

[Borgerson et al., 1979] Borgerson, B.R.; M.D. Godfrey; P.E. Hagerty; and T.R. Rykkem. "The Architecture of Sperry Univac 1100 Series Systems." In *Digest, Sixth Ann. Int. Symp. on Computer Architecture*. Philadelphia, PA: IEEE/ACM, 1979, pp. 137–146.

[Borr, 1981] Borr, A. "Transaction Monitoring in ENCOMPASS." In *Proceedings of 7th Conference on Very Large*

Data Bases (September 1981). Also Tandem Computers Technical Report TR 81.2, Cupertino, CA.

[Borr, 1984] Borr, A. "Robustness to Crash in a Distributed Database: A Non-Shared-Memory Multi-Processor Approach." In *Proceedings of 9th Conference on Very Large Data Bases* (September 1984). Also Tandem Computers Technical Report TR 84.2, Cupertino, CA.

[Bose and Caldwell, 1967] Bose, R.C., and J.G. Caldwell. "Synchronizable Error-Correcting Codes." *Information and Control* 10, no. 6 (June 1967): 616–630.

[Bose and Ray-Chaudhuri, 1960a] Bose, R.C., and D.K. Ray-Chaudhuri. "On a Class of Error-Correcting Binary Group Codes." *Information and Control* 3, no. 1 (March 1960): 68–79.

[Bose and Ray-Chaudhuri, 1960b] Bose, R.C., and D.K. Ray-Chaudhuri. "Further Results on Error-Correcting Binary Group Codes." *Information and Control* 3, no. 3 (September 1960): 279–290.

[Bossen, 1970] Bossen, D.C. "b-Adjacent Error Correction." *IBM J. Res. and Dev.* 14, no. 4 (July 1970): 402–408.

[Bossen, Chang, and Chen, 1978] Bossen, D.C.; L.C. Chang; and C.L. Chen. "Measurement and Generation of Error Correcting Codes for Package Failures." *IEEE Trans. Comp.* C-27 (March 1978): 201–204.

[Bossen and Hong, 1971] Bossen, D.C., and S.J. Hong. "Cause and Effect Analysis for Multiple Fault Detection in Combinational Networks." *IEEE Trans. Comp.* C-20 (November 1971): 1252–1257.

[Bossen and Hsiao, 1980] Bossen, D.C., and M.Y. Hsiao. "A System Solution to the Memory Soft Error Problem." *IBM J. Res. and Dev.* 24 (May 1980): 390–397.

[Bossen and Hsiao, 1982] Bossen, D.C., and M.Y. Hsiao. "Model for Transient and Permanent Error-Detection and Fault-Isolation Coverage." *IBM J. Res. and Dev.* 26, no. 1 (January 1982): 67–77.

[Boswell, 1972] Boswell, F.R. "Designing Testability into Complex Logic Boards." *Electronics International* 45, no. 17 (14 August 1972): 116–119.

[Bottorff et al., 1977] Bottorff, P.S., et al. "Test Generation for Large Networks." In *Proc. 14th Design Automation Conf*, IEEE Pub. 77CH1216–1C (June 1977): 479–485.

[Bottorff and Muehldorf, 1977] Bottorff, P., and E.I. Muehldorf. "Impact of LSI on Complex Digital Circuit Board Testing." *Electro 77*, New York (April 1977).

[Bouricius, Carter, and Schneider, 1969a] Bouricius, W.G.; W.C. Carter; and P.R. Schneider. "Reliability Modeling Techniques for Self-Repairing Computer Systems." In *Proc. 24th National Conference of the ACM*, ACM, 1969, pp. 295–309.

[Bouricius, Carter, and Schneider, 1969b] Bouricius, W.G.; W.C. Carter; and P.R. Schneider. "Reliability Modeling Techniques and Trade-Off Studies for Self-Repairing Computers," IBM RC 2378, 1969.

[Bouricius et al., 1971] Bouricius, W.G.; W.C. Carter; D.C. Jessep; P.R. Schneider; and A.B. Wadia. "Reliability Modeling for Fault-Tolerant Computers." *IEEE Trans. Comp.* C-20 (November 1971): 1306–1311.

[Boute, 1972] Boute, R. "Equivalence and Dominance Relations Between Output Faults in Sequential Machines." Tech. Rep. 38, SU-SEL-72-052, Stanford Univ. Stanford, CA (November 1972).

[Boute, 1974] Boute, R.T. "Optimal and Near-Optimal Checking Experiments for Output Faults in Sequential Machines." *IEEE Trans. Comput.* C-23, no. 11 (November 1974): 1207–1213.

[Boute and McCluskey, 1971] Boute, R., and E.J. McCluskey. "Fault Equivalence in Sequential Machines." In *Proc. Symp. on Computers and Automata*, Polytech. Inst., Brooklyn, April 13–15, 1971, pp. 483–507.

[Bowman et al., 1977] Bowman, P.W.; M.R. Diebman; F.M. Gaety; R.F. Kranzmann; E.H. Stredde; and R.J. Watters. "IA Processor Maintenance Software." *Bell Sys. Tech. J.* 56 (February 1977): 225–287.

[Bozorgui-Nesbat and McCluskey, 1980] Bozorgui-Nesbat, S., and E.J. McCluskey. "Structured Design for Testability to Eliminate Test Pattern Generation." In *Digest of 10th International Symposium on Fault-Tolerant Computing*, IEEE Computer Society, 1980, Kyoto, Japan, pp. 158–163.

[Brahme and Abraham, 1984] Brahme, D., and J.A. Abraham. "Functional Testing of Microprocessors." *IEEE Trans. Comput.* C-33, no. 6 (June 1984): 475–485.

[Bressler, Kraley, and Michel, 1975] Bressler, R.D.; M.F. Kraley; and A. Michel. "Pluribus: A Multiprocessor for Communications Networks." In *14th Annual ACM/NBS Technical Symp.—Computing in the Mid-70s: An Assessment*, 1975, pp. 13–19.

[Breuer, 1970] Breuer, M.A. "Functional Partitioning and Simulation of Digital Circuits." *IEEE Trans. Comp.* C-19, no. 11 (November 1970): 1038–1046.

[Breuer, 1973] Breuer, M.A. "Testing for Intermittent Faults in Digital Circuits." *IEEE Trans. Comp.* C-22 (March 1973): 241–246.

[Breuer and Friedman, 1976] Breuer, M.A., and A.D. Friedman. *Diagnosis and Reliable Design of Digital Systems.* Potomac, MD: Computer Science Press, 1976.

[Breuer and Friedman, 1980] Breuer, M.A., and A.D. Friedman. "Functional Level Primitives in Test Generation." *IEEE Trans. Comp.* C-29 (March 1980): 223–235.

[Brilliant, Knight, and Leveson, 1989] Brilliant, S.S.; J.C. Knight; and N.G. Leveson. "The Consistent Comparison Problem in Multi-Version Software." *IEEE Trans. Soft. Eng.* 15 (November 1989): 1481–1485.

[Brilliant, Knight, and Leveson, 1990] Brilliant, S.S.; J.C. Knight; and N.G. Leveson. "Analysis of Faults in an N-Version Software Experiment." *IEEE Trans. Soft. Eng.* SE-16(2) (February 1990): 238–247.

[Brinch Hansen, 1970] Brinch Hansen, P. "The Nucleus of a Multi-Programming System." *Comm. ACM* 13 (April 1970): 238–241.

[Brodsky, 1980] Brodsky, M. "Hardening RAMs Against Soft Errors." *Electronics* 53 (April 14, 1980): McGraw-Hill.

[Brown, 1960] Brown, D.T. "Error Detecting and Correcting Binary Codes for Arithmetic Operations." *IRE Trans. Elec. Comp.* EC-9, no. 3 (September 1960): 333–337.

[Brown, Tierney, and Wasserman, 1961] Brown, W.G.; J. Tierney; and R. Wasserman. "Improvement of Electronic-Computer Reliability Through the Use of Redundancy." *IRE Trans. Elec. Comp.* EC-10, no. 3 (September 1961): 407–416.

[Browne et al., 1969] Browne, T.E.; T.M. Quinn; W.N. Toy; and J.E. Yates. "No. 2 ESS Control Unit System." *Bell Sys. Tech. J.* 48, no. 2 (October 1969): 443–476.

[Bruckert and Josephson, 1985] Bruckert, W., and R. Josephson. "Designing Reliability into the VAX 8600 System." *Digital Technical Journal*, vol. 4, no. 1 (August 1985). Bedford, MA: 71–77.

[Brule, Johnson, and Kletsky, 1960] Brule, J.D.; R.A. Johnson; and E.J. Kletsky. "Diagnosis of Equipment Failures." *IRE Trans. Reliability and Quality Control* RQC-9 (April 1960): 23–24.

[Bryant, 1984] Bryant, R.E. "A Switch Level Model and Simulator for MOS Digital Circuits." *IEEE Trans. Comp.* C-33, no. 2 (February 1984): 160–177.

[Budd et al., 1980] Budd, T.A.; A. DeMillo; R.J. Lipton; and F.G. Sayward. "Theoretical and Empirical Studies on Using Program Mutation to Test the Functional Correctness of Programs." *Technical Report* GIT-ICS 80/01. Georgia Institute of Technology, Atlanta, GA (February 1980).

[Budlong et al., 1977] Budlong, A.H.; B.G. DeLiegish; I.M. Neville; J.S. Nowak; J.L. Quinn; and F.W. Wendloud. "1A Processor—Control System." *Bell Sys. Tech. J.* 56, no. 2 (February 1977): 135–179.

[Burman, 1985] Burman, M. "Aspects of a High Volume Production Online Banking System." *Proc. Int. Workshop on High Performance Transaction Systems*, Asilomar, CA, September 1985.

[Bussgang, 1965] Bussgang, J.J. "Some Properties of Binary Convolutional Code Generators." *IEEE Trans. Info. Theory* IT-11, no. 1 (January 1965): 90–100.

[Butler, 1986] Butler, R.W. "An Abstract Language for Specifying Markov Reliability Models." *IEEE Trans. Rel.* R-35, no. 5 (December 1986): 595–601.

[Butler and White, 1988] Butler, R.W., and A.L. White. "SURE Reliability Analysis, Program and Mathematics." *NASA Technical Paper* 2764 (March 1988).

[Butner and Iyer, 1980] Butner, S.E., and R.K. Iyer. "A Statistical Study of Reliability and System Load at SLAC." Center for Reliable Computing, Stanford University, 1980.

[Byrne and O'Reilly, 1985] Byrne, W.R., and G.P. O'Reilly. "The 5ESS™ Switching System: Applications Planning." *AT&T Technical Journal* 64, no. 6, pt. 2 (July–August 1985): 1315–1337.

[Cagle et al., 1964] Cagle, W.B.; R.S. Menne; R.S. Skinner; R.E. Staehler; and M.D. Underwood. "No 1 ESS Logic Circuits and Their Application to the Design of the Central Control." *Bell Sys. Tech. J.* 43, no. 5, pt. 1 (September 1964): 2055–2095.

[Carr, 1981] Carr, R.W. "Virtual Memory Management." Stanford, CA: Stanford University, 1981.

[Carr, 1985] Carr, R.W. "The Tandem Global Update Protocol." *Tandem Systems Review*, vol. 1.2, June 1985.

[Carter, 1983] Carter, W.C. "Architectural Considerations for Detecting Run-Time Errors in Programs." In *Proceedings of 13th International Symposium on Fault-Tolerant Computing*, IEEE, Milan, Italy, 1983, pp. 249–256.

[Carter, 1986] Carter, W.C. "System Validation—Putting the Pieces Together." In *7th AIAA/IEEE Digital Avionics Systems Conference*, 1986, pp. 687–694.

[Carter, Duke, and Jessep, 1971] Carter, W.C.; K.A. Duke; and D.C. Jessep. "A Simple Self-Testing Decoder Checking Circuit." *IEEE Trans. Comp.* C-20 (November 1971): 1413–1414.

[Carter, Duke, and Jessep, 1973] Carter, W.C.; K.A. Duke; and D.C. Jessep. "Lookaside Techniques for Minimum Circuit Memory Translators." *IEEE Trans. Comp.* C-22 (March 1973): 283–289.

[Carter and McCarthy, 1976] Carter, W.C., and C.E. McCarthy. "Implementation of an Experimental Fault-Tolerant Memory System." *IEEE Trans. Comp.* C-25 (June 1976): 557–568.

[Carter and Schneider, 1968] Carter, W.C., and P.R. Schneider. "Design of Dynamically Checked Computers." In *Proceedings IFIP Congress*, vol. 2. New York: North-Holland, 1968, pp. 878–883.

[Carter and Wadia, 1980] Carter, W.C., and A.B. Wadia. "Design and Analysis of Codes and Their Self-Checking Circuit Implementations for Correction and Detection of Multiple b-Adjacent Errors." In *Digest of 10th International Symposium on Fault-Tolerant Computing*, IEEE Computer Society, Kyoto, Japan, 1980, pp. 35–40.

[Carter, Wadia, and Jessep, 1972] Carter, W.C.; A.B. Wadia; and D.C. Jessep, Jr. "Computer Error Control by Testable Morphic Boolean Functions—A Way of Removing Hardcore." In *Digest of 2nd International Symposium on Fault-Tolerant Computing*, IEEE Computer Society, Boston, MA, 1972, pp. 154–159.

[Carter et al., 1964] Carter, W.C.; H.C. Montgomery; R.J. Preiss, and H.J. Reinheimer. "Design of Serviceability Features for the IBM System/360." *IBM J. Res. and Dev.* 8, no. 2 (April 1964): 115–126.

[Castillo, 1980] Castillo, X. "Workload, Performance, and Reliability of Digital Computing Systems." *Carnegie-Mellon University Technical Report*, Computer Science Department, 1980.

[Castillo, McConnel, and Siewiorek, 1982] Castillo, X.; S.R. McConnel; and D.P. Siewiorek. "Derivation and Calibration of a Transient Error Reliability Model." *IEEE Trans. Comput.* C-31, no. 7, (July 1982).

[Castillo and Siewiorek, 1980] Castillo, X., and D.P. Siewiorek. "A Performance-Reliability Model for Computing Systems." In *Digest of 10th International Symposium on Fault-Tolerant Computing*, Kyoto, Japan, 1980, pp. 187–192.

[Castillo and Siewiorek, 1981] Castillo, X., and D.P. Siewiorek. "Workload, Performance, and Reliability of Digital Computing Systems." *11th International Symposium on Fault-Tolerant Computing*, Portland, ME, 1981.

[Castillo and Siewiorek, 1982] Castillo, X., and D.P. Siewiorek. "A Workload Dependent Software Reliability Prediction Model." *12th Fault-Tolerant Computing Symposium*, Santa Monica, CA, 1982.

[Chan and Horst, 1989] Chan, Scott, and Robert Horst. "Building Parallelism into the Instruction Pipeline." In *High Performance Systems*, Tandem Computers, Inc., CMP Publications, December 1989, p. 54.

[Chandy and Ramamoorthy, 1972] Chandy, K.M., and C.V. Ramamoorthy. "Rollback and Recovery Strategies for Computer Programs." *IEEE Trans. Comp.* C-21 (June 1972): 546–556.

[Chaney, Ornstein, and Littlefield, 1972] Chaney, T.J.; S.M. Ornstein; and W.M. Littlefield. "Beware the Synchronizer. *CompCon* (1972): 317–319.

[Chang, 1965] Chang, H.Y. "An Algorithm for Selecting an Optimum Set of Diagnostic Tests." *IEEE Trans. Elec. Comp.* EC-14 (October 1965): 705–711.

[Chang, 1968] Chang, H.Y. "A Distinguishability Criterion for Selecting Efficient Diagnostic Tests." In *SJCC, AFIPS Conf. Proc.*, vol. 32. Washington, DC: Thompson, 1968, pp. 529–534.

[Chang, Manning, and Metze, 1970] Chang, H.Y.; E.G. Manning; and G. Metze. *Fault Diagnosis of Digital Systems*. New York: Wiley Interscience, 1970.

[Chang, Smith, and Walford, 1974] Chang, H.Y.; G.W. Smith, Jr.; and R.B. Walford. "LAMP: System Description." *Bell Sys. Tech. J.* 53 (October 1974): 1431–1449.

[Chen, 1972] Chen, C.L. "On Shortened Finite Geometry Codes." *Info Control* 20 (April 1972): 216–221.

[Chen, 1983a] Chen, C.L. "Error Correcting Codes with Byte Error Detection Capability." *IEEE Trans. Comp.* C-32 (July 1983): 615–621.

[Chen, 1983b] Chen, C.L. "Linear Codes for Masking Memory Defects." Presented at *IEEE International Symposium on Information Theory*, St. Jovite, Quebec, Canada, September 26–30, 1983.

[Chen, 1986a] Chen, C.L. "Error-Correcting Codes for Byte-Organized Memory Systems." *IEEE Trans. Info. Theory* (March 1986): 181–185.

[Chen, 1986b] Chen, C.L. "Byte-Oriented Error-Correcting Codes for Semiconductor Memory Systems." *IEEE Trans. Comp.* C-35 (July 1986): 646–648.

[Chen and Avizienis, 1978] Chen, L., and A. Avizienis. "N-Version Programming: A Fault-Tolerance Approach to Reliability of Software Operation." In *Digest of 8th International Symposium on Fault-Tolerant Computing*, IEEE Computer Society, Toulouse, France, 1978, pp. 3–9.

[Chen and Hsiao, 1984] Chen, C.L., and M.Y. Hsaio. "Error-Correcting Codes for Semiconductor Memory Applications: A State-of-the-Art Review." *IBM J. Res. and Dev.* 28, no. 2 (March 1984): 124–134.

[Chen and Rutledge, 1984] Chen, C.L., and R.A. Rutledge. "Fault-Tolerant Memory Simulator." *IBM J. Res. and Dev.* 28, no. 2 (March 1984): 184–195.

[Chen et al., 1990] Chen, P.; G. Gibson; R. Katz; and D. Patterson. "An Evaluation of Redundant Arrays of Disks Using an Amdahl 5890." In *Proceedings of ACM SIGMETRICS*, 1990, pp. 74–85.

[Cheung, 1980] Cheung, R.C. "A User-Oriented Software Reliability Model." *IEEE Trans. Soft. Eng.* SE-6, no. 6 (March 1980): 118–125.

[Cheung and Ramamoorthy, 1975] Cheung, R.C., and C.V. Ramamoorthy. "Optimal Measurement of Program Path

Frequencies and its Applications." In *Proc. Int. Federation Automatic Control Congress,* 1975.

[Chiang et al., 1974] Chiang, H.Y.P., et al. "Comparison of Parallel and Deductive Fault Simulation." *IEEE Trans. Comp.* C-23, no. 11 (November 1974): 1132–1138.

[Chiang and Standridge, 1975] Chiang, A.C.L., and R. Standridge. "Pattern Sensitivity on 4K RAM Devices." *Computer Design* 14, no. 2 (February 1975): 88–91.

[Chien, 1960] Chien, R.T. "A Class of Optimal Noiseless Load-Sharing Matrix Switches." *IBM J. Res. and Dev.* 4, no. 4 (October 1960): 414–417.

[Chien, 1964] Chien, R.T. "Cyclic Decoding Procedures for Bose-Chaudhuri-Hocquenghem Codes." *IEEE Trans. Info. Theory* IT-10, no. 4 (October 1964): 357–363.

[Chien and Frazer, 1966] Chien, R.T., and D. Frazer. "An Application of Coding Theory to Document Retrieval." *IEEE Trans. Info. Theory* IT-12, no. 2 (April 1966): 92–96.

[Chien, Hong, and Preparata, 1968] Chien, R.T.; S.J. Hong; and F.P. Preparata. "Some Contributions to the Theory of Arithmetic Codes." In *Proc. Hawaii Int. Conf. on Systems Sciences.* Honolulu, HI: University of Hawaii Press, 1968, pp. 460–462.

[Chillarege and Bowen, 1989] Chillarege, R., and N.S. Bowen. "Understanding Large System Failures—A Fault Injection Experiment." *Proceedings of 19th IEEE International Symposium on Fault-Tolerant Computing,* Chicago, June 1989, pp. 356–363.

[Chinal, 1977] Chinal, J.P. "High Speed Parity Prediction for Binary Adders." In *Digest of 7th International Symposium on Fault-Tolerant Computing,* IEEE Computer Society, Los Angeles, CA, 1977, p. 190.

[Chou and Abraham, 1980] Chou, T.C.K., and J.A. Abraham. "Performance/Availability Model of Shared Resource Multiprocessors." *IEEE Trans. Rel.* R-29, no. 1 (April 1980): 70–74.

[Chow, n.d.] Chow, D.K. "A Geometric Approach to Coding Theory with Application to Information Retrieval." Urbana: University of Illinois Report R-368, n.d.

[Chu, 1982] Chu, R.C. "Conduction Cooling for an LSI Package." *IBM J. Res. and Dev.* 26, no. 1 (January 1982): 45–54.

[Clune, 1984] Clune, E. "Analysis of the Fault Frequent Behavior of the FTMP Multiprocessor System." *Technical Report* CMU-CS-84-130, Carnegie-Mellon University, Pittsburgh, PA, 1984.

[Clune, Segall, and Siewiorek, 1984] Clune, E.; Z. Segall; and D. Siewiorek. "Validation of Fault-Free Behavior of a Reliable Multiprocessor System, FTMP: A Case Study." *International Conference on Automation and Computer Control,* San Diego, CA, 1984.

[Clune, Segall, and Siewiorek, 1985] Clune, E.; Z. Segall; and D. Siewiorek. "Fault-Free Behavior of Reliable Multiprocessor Systems: FTMP Experiments in AIRLAB." *NASA* CR-177967, Carnegie-Mellon University, August 1985.

[Constantine, 1958] Constantine, G., Jr. "A Load-Sharing Matrix Switch." *IBM J. Res. and Dev.* 2, no. 3 (July 1958): 204–211.

[Cook et al., 1973] Cook, R.W.; W.H. Sisson; T.F. Storey; and W.N. Toy. "Design of a Self-Checking Microprogram Control." *IEEE Trans. Comp.* C-22 (March 1973): 255–262.

[Cooper and Chow, 1976] Cooper, A.E., and W.T. Chow. "Development of On-Board Space Computer Systems." *IBM J. Res. and Dev.* 20, no. 1 (January 1976): 5–19.

[Cordi, 1984] Cordi, V.A. "4381's Error-Detection Fault-Isolation Speeds Repairs." *Computer Systems Equipment Design* (November 1984): 23–29.

[Cornell and Halstead, 1976] Cornell, L., and M.H. Halstead. "Predicting the Number of Bugs Expected in a Program Module." Purdue University CSD-TR-20r, 1976.

[Costes, Landrault, and Laprie, 1978] Costes, A.; C. Landrault; and J.C. Laprie. "Reliability and Availability Models for Maintained Systems Featuring Hardware Failures and Design Faults." *IEEE Trans. Comp.* C-27 (June 1978): 548–560.

[Costes et al., 1981] Costes, A.; J.E. Doucet; C. Landrault; and J.C. Laprie. "SURF: A Program for Dependability Evaluation of Complex Fault-Tolerant Computing Systems." In *Digest of the 11th Annual International Symposium on Fault-Tolerant Computing,* Portland, ME, June 1981, pp. 72–78.

[Courtois, 1979] Courtois, B. "Some Results About the Efficiency of Simple Mechanisms for the Detection of Microcomputer Malfunctions." In *9th International Symposium on Fault-Tolerant Computing,* Madison, WI, 1979, pp. 71–74.

[Craig, 1964] Craig, E.J. *Laplace and Fourier Transforms for Electrical Engineers.* New York: Hold, Rinehart and Winston, 1964.

[Craig, 1980] Craig, S.R. "Incoming Inspection and Test Programs." *Electronics Test* (October 1980): 58–73.

[Cristian, 1982] Cristian, F. "Exception Handling and Software Fault Tolerance." *IEEE Trans. Comp.* C-31, no. 6 (June 1982): 531–540.

[Crouzet and Decouty, 1982] Crouzet, Y., and B. Decouty. "Measurement of Fault Detection Mechanisms Efficiency: Results." In *12th International Symposium on Fault-Tolerant Computing,* Santa Monica, CA, 1982, pp. 373–376.

[Crouzet and Landrault, 1980] Crouzet, Y., and C. Landrault. "Design of Self-Checking MOS LSI Circuits, Application to a Four-Bit Microprocessor." *IEEE Trans. Comp.* C-29 (June 1980): 532–537.

[Czeck et al., 1986] Czeck, Edward W.; Frank E. Feather; Ann Marie Grizzaffi; George B. Finelli; Zary Segall; and Daniel P. Siewiorek. "Fault-Free Performance Validation of Avionic Multiprocessors." *7th Digital Avionic System Conference,* Dallas, TX, October 1986.

[Czeck et al., 1987] Czeck, E.W.; F.E. Feather; A.M. Grizzaffi, Z.Z. Segall; and D.P. Siewiorek. "Fault-Free Performance Validation of Fault-Tolerant Multiprocessors." *NASA* CR-178236, Carnegie-Mellon University (January 1987).

[Czeck et al., 1987] Czeck, E.W.; D.P. Siewiorek; and Z.Z. Segall. "Software Implemented Fault Insertion: An FTMP Example." *NASA* CR-178423, Carnegie-Mellon University (October 1987).

[Czepiel, Foreman, and Prilik, 1976] Czepiel, R.J.; S.H. Foreman; and R.J. Prilik. "System for Logic, Parametric and Analog Testing." In *Dig. Papers, 1976 Semiconductor Test Symp.* (October 1976): 54–69.

[Daly, Hopkins, and McKenna, 1973] Daly, W.M.; A.L. Hopkins, Jr.; and J.F. McKenna, Jr. "A Fault-Tolerant Clocking System." In *Digest of 3rd International Symposium on Fault-Tolerant Computing,* Palo Alto, CA, IEEE Computer Society, 1973.

[Dandapani and Reddy, 1974] Dandapani, R., and S.M. Reddy. "On the Design of Logic Networks with Redundancy and Testability Considerations." *IEEE Trans. Comp.* C-23 (November 1974): 1139–1149.

[Dandapani, Reddy, and Robinson, 1970] Dandapani, R.; S.M. Reddy; and J.P. Robinson. "An Investigation into Redundancy and Testability of Combinational Logic Networks." AD 174-157, 1970.

[Dao, 1973] Dao, T.T. "Design and Implementation of a Non-Binary Code for Byte-Organized Memory with Binary and Quaternary Logics." In *Proceedings of the 9th International Symposium on Multi-Valued Logic,* Rosemont, IL, May 1973, pp. 24–26.

[DasGupta, Eichelberger, and Williams, 1978] DasGupta, S.; E.B. Eichelberger; and T.W. Williams. "LSI Chip Design for Testability." In *Dig. Tech. Papers, 1978 Int. Solid-State Circuits Conf.,* San Francisco, CA, February 1978, pp. 216–217.

[Datamation, 1979] "The Microarchitecture of Univac's 1100/60." *Datamation* (July 1979): 173–178.

[Davidson, 1984] Davidson, S. "Fault Simulation at the Architectural Level." In *International Test Conference,* 1984, pp. 669–679.

[Davidson and Lewandowski, 1986] Davidson, S., and J.L. Lewandowski. "ESIM/AFS—A Concurrent Architectural Level Fault Simulator." In *International Test Conference,* 1986, pp. 375–383.

[Davies and Wakerly, 1978] Davies, D, and J.F. Wakerly. "Synchronization and Matching in Redundant Systems." *IEEE Trans. Comp.* C-27 (June 1978): 531–539.

[Davis et al., 1981] Davis, J.H.; J. Janik, Jr.; R.D. Royer; and B.J. Yokelson. "No. 5ESS System Architecture." In *Proceedings of the 10th International Switching Symposium,* September 1981, Montreal.

[DeAngelis and Lauro, 1976] DeAngelis, D., and J.A. Lauro. "Software Recovery in the Fault-Tolerant Spaceborne Computer." In *Digest of 6th International Symposium on Fault-Tolerant Computing,* IEEE Computer Society, Pittsburgh, PA, 1976, pp. 143–148.

[DEC, 1971] Digital Equipment Corporation. *PDP-8/e Engineering Circuit Diagrams.* Bedford, MA, 1971.

[DEC, 1972] Digital Equipment Corporation. *PDP-8/e Maintenance Manual.* DEC-8E-HR1B-D. Bedford, MA, 1972.

[DEC, 1975a] Digital Equipment Corporation. *LSI-11 PDP-11/03 User's Manual.* Bedford, MA, 1975.

[DEC, 1975b] Digital Equipment Corporation. *RXV-11 User's Manual.* Bedford, MA, 1975.

[DEC, 1975c] Digital Equipment Corporation. "A Reliability Report." Bedford, MA, 1975.

[DEC, 1977] Digital Equipment Corporation. *VAX-11/780 Architecture Handbook.* Bedford, MA, 1977.

[DEC, 1978] Digital Equipment Corporation. *TOPS-10 and TOPS-20 SYSERR Manual.* Bedford, MA 1978.

[DEC, 1979] Digital Equipment Corporation. *PDP-11 Bus Handbook.* Bedford, MA, 1979.

[Deckert et al., 1977] Deckert, J.C.; M.N. Desai; J.J. Deyst; and A.J. Willsky. "F8-DFBW Sensor Failure Identification Using Analytic Redundancy." *IEEE Trans. Autom. Contr.* AC-22, no. 5 (October 1977): 795–803.

[Decouty et al., 1980] Decouty, B.; G. Michel; and C. Wagner. "An Evaluation Tool of Fault Detection Mechanisms Efficiency." In *10th International Symposium on Fault-Tolerant Computing,* Kyoto, Japan, 1980, pp. 225–227.

[DeGroot, 1975] DeGroot, M.H. *Probability and Statistics.* Reading, MA: Addison-Wesley, 1975.

[Dejka, 1977] Dejka, W.J. "Measure of Testability in Device and System Design." In *Proceedings of 20th Midwest Symposium on Circuits Systems,* August 1977, pp. 39–52.

[DeMillo, Lipton, and Sayward, 1978] DeMillo, R.A.; R.J. Lipton; and F.G. Sayward. "Hints on Test Data Selection:

Help for the Practicing Programmer." *Computer*, vol. 11, no. 4, (April 1978): 34–43.

[Dennis, 1974] Dennis, N.G. "Ultrareliable Voter Switches, with a Bibliography of Mechanization." *Microelectronics and Reliability* (August 1974): 299–308.

[DeSousa and Mathur, 1978] DeSousa, P.T., and F.P. Mathur. "Sift-Out Modular Redundancy." *IEEE Trans. Comp.* C-27 (July 1978): 624–627.

[Deswarte et al., 1986] Deswarte, Y.; K. Alami; and O. Tedaldi. "Realization, Validation, and Operation of a Fault-Tolerant Multiprocessor: ARMURE." In *16th International Symposium on Fault-Tolerant Computing*, Vienna, Austria, 1986, pp. 8–13.

[Deyst and Hopkins] Deyst, J.J., Jr., and A.L. Hopkins, Jr. "Highly Survivable Integrated Avionics." *Astronautics and Aeronautics*.

[Dias, 1975] Dias, F.J.O. "Fault Masking in Combinational Logic Circuits." *IEEE Trans. Comp.* C-24 (May 1975): 476–482.

[Diaz, Azema, and Ayache, 1979] Diaz, M.; P. Azema; and J.M. Ayache. "Unified Design of Self-Checking and Fail-Safe Combinational Circuits and Sequential Machines." *IEEE Trans. Comp.* C-28 (March 1979): 276–281.

[Diaz, Geffroy, and Courvoisier, 1974] Diaz, M.; J.C. Geffroy; and M. Courvoisier. "On-Set Realization of Fail-Safe Sequential Machines." *IEEE Trans. Comp.* C-23 (February 1974): 133–138.

[Dickinson, Jackson, and Randa, 1964] Dickinson, M.M.; J.B. Jackson; and G.C. Randa. "Saturn V Launch Vehicle Digital Computer and Data Adapter." In *FJCC. AFIPS Conf. Proc.*, vol. 26, 1964, pp. 510–516.

[Dijkstra, 1968] Dijkstra, E.W. "The Structure of the 'THE' Multiprogramming System." *Comm ACM* 11 (1968): 341–346.

[Dolotta et al., 1976] Dolotta, T.A.; M.I. Bernstein; R.S. Dickson, Jr.; N.A. France; B.A. Rosenblatt; D.M. Smith; and T.B. Steel, Jr. *Data Processing in 1980–1985*. New York: Wiley, 1976.

[Downing, Nowak, and Tuomenoksa, 1964] Downing, R.W.; J.S. Nowak; and L.S. Tuomenoksa. "No 1 ESS Maintenance Plan." *Bell Sys. Tech. J.* 43, no. 5, pt. 1 (September 1964): 1961–2019.

[Droulette, 1971] Droulette, D.L. "Recovery through Programming System/360–System/370." In *SJCC AFIPS Conf. Proc.*, vol. 38. Montvale, NJ: AFIPS Press, 1971, pp. 467–476.

[Duane, 1964] Duane, J.T. "Learning Curve Approach to Reliability Monitoring." *IEEE Trans. Aerospace.*, vol. 2 (April 1964): 363–366.

[Dunham, 1986] Dunham, J.R. "Experiments in Software Reliability: Life-Critical Applications." *IEEE Trans. Soft. Eng.* SE-12, no. 1 (January 1986): 110–123.

[Dunham and Lauterbach, 1988] Dunham, J.R., and L.A. Lauterbach. "An Experiment in Software Reliability: Additional Analyses Using Data from Automated Replications." *NASA CR-178395* (January 1988).

[Eames and Spann, 1977] Eames, S., and A. Spann. "Life Cycle Cost Analysis Utilizing Generalized Data Elements." In *Proc. 15th Annual Spring Reliability Seminar*, IEEE Boston Section, 1977, pp. 12–39.

[Eckhardt and Lee, 1985] Eckhardt, D.E., and L.D. Lee. "A Theoretical Basis for the Analysis of Multi-Version Software Subject to Coincident Errors." *IEEE Trans. Soft. Eng.* SE-11, no. 12 (December 1985): 1511–1517.

[Eddy, 1987] Eddy, J. "Remote Support Strategy." *Tandem Systems Review* 3, no. 1 (March 1987): 12–16.

[Edlred, 1959] Edlred, R.D. "Test Routines Based on Symbolic Logic Statements." *J. Assoc. Comput. Mach.* 6, no. 1 (1959): 33–36.

[Edmond et al., 1990] Edmond, Patrick; Anurag P. Gupta; Daniel P. Siewiorek; and Audrey A. Brennan. "ASSURE: Automated Design for Dependability." *27th ACM/IEEE Design Automation Conference*, Orlando, FL, June, 1990.

[Efstathiou and Halatsis, 1983] Efstathiou, C., and C. Halatsis. "Modular Realization of Totally Self Checking Checkers for M-Out-Of-N Codes." In *Digest of the 13th International Symposium on Fault-Tolerant Computing*, IEEE Computer Society, Milan, Italy, June 1983, pp. 154–161.

[Eichelberger, 1965] Eichelberger, E.B. "Hazard Detection in Combinational and Sequential Switching Circuits." *IBM J. Res. and Dev.* (March 1965).

[Eichelberger and Williams, 1977] Eichelberger, E.B., and T.W. Williams. "A Logic Design Structure for LSI Testing." In *Proc. of 14th Design Automation Conference*, IEEE Pub. 77CH1216–1C, June 1977, pp. 462–468.

[Eichelberger and Williams, 1978] Eichelberger, E.B., and T.W. Williams. "A Logic Design Structure for LSI Testability." *J. Des. Automat. Fault-Tolerant Comput.* 2, no. 2 (May 1978): 165–178.

[Eichelberger et al., 1978] Eichelberger, E.B.; E.J. Muehldorf; R.G. Walter; and T.W. Williams. "A Logic Design Structure for Testing Internal Arrays." In *Proc. of 3rd USA–Japan Computer Conference*, San Francisco, CA, October 1978, pp. 266–272.

[Eisenbies, 1967] Eisenbies, J.L. "Conventions for Digital Data Communication Design." *IBM Syst. J.* 6, no. 4 (1967): 167–302.

[Elias, 1954] Elias, P. "Error-Free Coding." *IRE Trans. Professional Group on Information Theory* PGIT-4 (1954): 29–37.

[Elkind, 1980a] Elkind, S.A. "Fail Users Manual." Carnegie-Mellon University Department of Electrical Engineering, Pittsburgh, PA, 1980.

[Elkind, 1980b] Elkind, S.A. "Towards Automatic Design of Reliable Systems." Ph.D. Diss. proposal, Carnegie-Mellon University Department of Electrical Engineering, Pittsburgh, PA, 1980.

[Elkind and Siewiorek, 1978] Elkind, S.A., and D.P. Siewiorek. "Reliability and Performance Models for Error Correcting Memory and Register Arrays." Carnegie-Mellon University, Pittsburgh, PA, CMU-CS-78-118, 1978.

[Elkind and Siewiorek, 1980] Elkind, S.A., and D.P. Siewiorek. "Reliability and Performance of Error-Correcting Memory and Register Arrays." *IEEE Trans. Comp.* C-29 (October 1980): 920–927.

[Elmendorf, 1972] Elmendorf, W.R. "Fault-Tolerant Programming." In *Proceedings of 2nd International Symposium on Fault-Tolerant Computing*, Boston, MA, 1972, pp. 79–84.

[Elmendorf, 1980] Elmendorf, C.H. "Meeting High Standards with Extended Operating System" *Bell Labs Rec.* (March 1980): 97–103.

[Elspas and Short, 1962] Elspas, B., and R.A. Short. "A Note on Optimum Burst-Error-Correcting Codes." *IRE Trans. Info. Theory* IT-8, no. 1 (January 1962): 39–42.

[Englert et al., 1989] Englert, S.; J. Gray; and P. Shah. "A Benchmark of NonStop SQL Release 2 Demonstrating Near-Linear Speedup and Scaleup on Large Databases," Tandem TR 89.4, 1989.

[Enright, 1985] Enright, J. "DP2 Performance." *Tandem Systems Review* 1, no. 2 (June 1985): 33–43.

[Enslow, 1974] Enslow, P.H., Jr., ed. *Multiprocessors and Parallel Processing.* New York: Wiley, 1974.

[Enslow, 1977] Enslow, P.H., Jr. "Multiprocessor Organization—A Survey." ACM *Computing Surveys* 9 (March 1977): 103–129.

[Esary and Proschan, 1962] Esary, J.D., and F. Proschan. "The Reliability of Coherent Systems." In Wilcox and Mann, eds., *Redundancy Techniques for Computing Systems.* Washington, DC: Spartan Books, 1962, pp. 47–61.

[Fabre et al., 1988] Fabre, J.; Y. Deswarte; J. Laprie; and D. Powell. "Saturation: Reduced Idleness for Improved Fault-Tolerance." In *IEEE Proc. of 18th International Symposium on Fault-Tolerant Computing*, June 1988, Tokyo, Japan, pp. 200–205.

[Fano, 1963] Fano, R.M. "A Heuristic Discussion of Probabilistic Decoding." *IEEE Trans. Info. Theory* IT-9, no. 2 (January 1963): 64–74.

[Fantini, 1984] Fantini, F. "Reliability Problems with VLSI." *Microelectronics Reliability* 24(2) (1984): 275–296.

[Farmer, 1973] Farmer, D.E. "Algorithms for Designing Fault-Detection Experiments for Sequential Machines." *IEEE Trans. Comp.* C-22 (February 1973): 159–167.

[Feather, 1985] Feather, F. "Validation of a Fault Tolerant Multiprocessor: Baseline Experiments and Workload Implementation." *Technical Report* CMU-CS-85-145, Carnegie-Mellon University, Pittsburgh, PA, 1985.

[Feather, Siewiorek, and Segall, 1986a] Feather, F.; D. Siewiorek; and Z. Segall. "Fault-Free Validation of a Fault-Tolerant Multiprocessor: Baseline Experiments and Workload Implementation." *NASA* CR-178075. Carnegie-Mellon University, Pittsburgh, PA, April 1986.

[Feather, Siewiorek, and Segall, 1986b] Feather, Frank; Daniel Siewiorek; and Zary Segall. "Validation of Fault-Tolerant Multiprocessors." *6th International Conference on Distributed Computing Systems.* Cambridge, MA, May 1986.

[Ferdinand, 1974] Ferdinand, A.E. "A Theory of Systems Complexity." *Int. J. Gen. Syst.* 1 (1974): 19–33.

[Ferguson, 1987] Ferguson, F.J. *Inductive Fault Analysis of VLSI Circuits.* Ph.D. Diss., Carnegie-Mellon University, Electrical and Computer Engineering Department, Pittsburgh, PA, October 1987.

[Ferris-Prabhu, 1979] Ferris-Prabhu, A.V. "Improving Memory Reliability through Error Correction." *Computer Design* 18 (July 1979): 137–144.

[Finelli, 1987] Finelli, G.B. "Characterization of Fault Recovery through Fault Injection on FTMP." *IEEE Trans. Reliability* R-36(2) (June 1987): 164–170.

[Finelli, 1988] Finelli, G.B. "Results of Software Error-Data Experiments." *AIAA/AHS/ASEE Aircraft Design, Systems and Operations Conference*, AIAA '88, Atlanta, GA, September 1988.

[Finkelstein, 1970] Finkelstein, H.A. "An Investigation into the Extension of Redundancy Techniques." Coordinated Science Laboratory, University of Illinois R-455, Urbana, IL, 1970.

[Fire, 1959] Fire, P. "A Class of Multiple-Error-Correcting Binary Codes for Non-Independent Errors." Sylvania Reconnaissance Systems Laboratory RSL-E-2, Mountain View, CA, 1959.

[Fitzsimmons and Love, 1978] Fitzsimmons, A., and T. Love. "A Review and Evaluation of Software Science." *ACM Computing Surveys* 10 (March 1978): 3–18.

[5ESS, 1986] 5ESS Switch System Description (International Version, 1986–1B-206D/HE), AT&T.

[Fleckenstein, 1974] Fleckenstein, W.O. "Bell System ESS Family Present and Future." In *ISS Record*, Munich, Germany, 1974.

[Flehinger, 1958] Flehinger, B.J. "Reliability Improvement through Redundancy at Various Systems Levels." *IBM J. Res. and Dev.*, no. 2 (April 1958): 148–158.

[Fleischer, 1977] Fleischer, G.E. "Voyager Altitude Control Flight Software Techniques for Fault Detection/Correction." AIAA Paper No. 77–1058, presented at the Guidance and Control Conference, Hollywood, FL, August 1977.

[Floyd, 1967] Floyd, R.W. "Assigning Meanings to Programs." In J.T. Schwartz, ed., *Mathematical Aspects of Computer Science*. Providence, RI: American Mathematical Society, 1967, pp. 19–32.

[Foley, 1979] Foley, E. "The Effects of the Microelectronics Revolution on the Systems and Board Test." *Computer* 12, no. 10 (October 1979): 32–38.

[Forney, 1965] Forney, G.D. "On Decoding BCH Codes." *IEEE Trans. Info. Theory* IT-11, no. 4 (October 1965): 549–557.

[Forney, 1966] Forney, G.D. "Generalized Minimum Distance Coding." *IEEE Trans. Info. Theory* IT-12, no. 2 (April 1966): 125–131.

[Frank and Frisch, 1970] Frank, H., and I.T. Frisch. "Analysis and Design of Survivable Networks." *IEEE Trans. Comm. Tech.* COM-18 (May 1970): 501–519.

[Frank and Yau, 1966] Frank, H., and S.S. Yau. "Improving Reliability of a Sequential Machine by Error-Correcting State Assignments." *IEEE Trans. Elec. Comp.* 15 (February 1966): 111–113.

[Frechette and Tanner, 1979] Frechette, T.J., and F. Tanner. "Support Processor Analyzer Errors Caught by Latches." *Electronics* 52, no. 23 (November 1979): McGraw-Hill, 116–118.

[Freeman and Metze, 1972] Freeman, H.A., and G. Metze. "Fault Tolerant Computers Using 'Dotted Logic' Redundancy Techniques." *IEEE Trans. Comp.* C-21 (August 1972): 867–871.

[Freiman, 1962] Freiman, C.V. "Optimal Error Detection Codes for Completely Asymmetric Binary Channels." *Information and Control* 5, no. 1 (March 1962): 64–71.

[Freiman and Robinson, 1965] Freiman, C.V., and J.P. Robinson. "A Comparison of Block and Recurrent Codes for the Correction of Independent Errors." *IEEE Trans. Info. Theory* IT-11, no. 3 (July 1965): 445–449.

[Frey, 1967] Frey, A.H., Jr. "Adaptive Decoding without Feedback." In *Proc. Int. Symp. on Information Theory*, Athens, 1967.

[Frey and Benice, 1964] Frey, A.H., Jr., and R.J. Benice. "An Analysis of Retransmission Systems." *IEEE Trans. Comm. Tech.* COM-12 (December 1964): 135–146.

[Friedman, 1967] Freidman, A.D. "Fault Detection in Redundant Circuits." *IEEE Trans. Elec. Comp.* EC-16 (February 1967): 99–100.

[Friedman, 1973] Friedman, A.D. "Easily Testable Iterative Systems." *IEEE Trans. Comp.* C-22 (December 1973): 1061–1064.

[Friedman and Menon, 1971] Friedman, A.D., and P.R. Menon. *Fault Detection in Digital Circuits*. Englewood Cliffs, NJ: Prentice-Hall, 1971.

[Friedman and Menon, 1973] Friedman, A.D., and P.R. Menon. "Restricted Checking Sequences for Sequential Machines." *IEEE Trans. Comp.* C-22 (April 1973): 397–399.

[Frohwerk, 1977] Frohwerk, R.A. "Signature Analysis: A New Digital Field Service Method." *Hewlett-Packard J.* (May 1977): 2–8.

[FTSC, 1976] "The Fault-Tolerant Spaceborne Computer." In *Digest of 6th International Symposium on Fault-Tolerant Computing*, IEEE Computer Society, Pittsburgh, PA, 1976, pp. 129–147.

[Fuchs and Abraham, 1984] Fuchs, W.K., and Abraham, J.A. "A Unified Approach to Concurrent Error Detection in Highly Structured Logic Arrays." In *Digest of 14th International Symposium on Fault-Tolerant Computing*, IEEE Computer Society, Kissimmee, FL, 1984, pp. 4–9.

[Fuhrer, Shen, and Yates, 1986] Fuhrer, P.T.; M.Y. Shen; and J.E. Yates. "5ESS Switching System Software: Interactive Query and Data Update." *AT&T Technical Journal*, 5ESS™ Switch Software (January 1986): 47–59.

[Fujiwara and Kawakami, 1977] Fujiwara, E., and T. Kawakami. "Modularized b-Adjacent Error Correction." In *Digest of 7th International Symposium on Fault-Tolerant Computing*, IEEE Computer Society, Los Angeles, CA, 1977, p. 199.

[Fujiwara and Kinoshita, 1974] Fujiwara, H., and K. Kinoshita. "Design of Diagnosable Sequential Machines Utilizing Extra Outputs." *IEEE Trans. Comp.* C-23 (February 1974): 138–145.

[Fujiwara and Matsuoka, 1985] Fujiwara, E., and K. Matsuoka. "A Totally Self-Checking Generalized Prediction Checker and Its Use for Built-in Testing." In *Digest of 15th International Symposium on Fault-Tolerant Computing*, IEEE Computer Society, Ann Arbor, MI, June 1985, pp. 384–389.

[Funami and Halstead, 1975] Funami, Y., and M.H. Halstead. "A Software Physics Analysis of Akiyama's Debugging Data." Purdue University CSD-TR-144, 1975.

[Funatsu, Watatsuki, and Arima, 1975] Funatsu, S., N. Wakatsuki, and T. Arima. "Test Generation Systems in Japan." In *Proc. 12th Design Automation Symposium*, June 1975, pp. 114–122.

[Fuqua, 1987] Fuqua, N.B. "Reliability Engineering for Electronic Design." Marcel Dekker, Inc., 1987, pp. 307–310.

[Gaitanis, 1988] Gaitanis, N. "The Design of TSC Error C/D Circuits for SEC/DED Codes." *IEEE Trans. Comp.* (March 1988): 258–265.

[Galiay, Crouzet, and Vergniault, 1980] Galiay, J.; Y. Crouzet; and M. Vergniault. "Physical Versus Logical Fault Models MOS LSI Circuits: Impact on Their Testability." *IEEE Trans. Comp.* C-29(6) (June 1980): 527–531.

[Gandhi, Knoue, and Henley, 1972] Gandhi, S.L.; K. Knoue; and E.J. Henley. "Computer Aided System Reliability Analysis and Optimization." In *Proc. IFIP Working Conference on Principles of Computer-Aided Design*, Eindhoven, 1972, pp. 283–308.

[Garcia, 1988] Garcia, J. "Built-In-Self-Test for the Tandem NonStop CLX Processor." In *Digest of Papers, CompCon Spring 1988*, San Francisco, CA, 1988.

[Garner, 1958] Garner, H.L. "Generalized Parity Checking." *IRE Trans. Elec. Comp.* EC-7 (September 1958): 207–213.

[Garner, 1966] Garner, H.L. "Error Codes for Arithmetic Operations." *IEEE Trans. Elec. Comp.* EC-15 (October 1966): 763–769.

[Gavrilov, 1960] Gavrilov, M.A. "Structural Redundancy and Reliability of Relay Circuits." In *Proceedings International Federation of Automatic Control Congress*, 1960, pp. 838–844.

[Gay and Ketelsen, 1979] Gay, F.A., and M.L. Ketelsen. "Performance Evaluation for Gracefully Degrading Systems." In *Digest of 9th International Symposium on Fault-Tolerant Computing*, IEEE, Madison, WI, 1979, pp. 51–58.

[Gear, 1976] Gear, G. "Intel 2708 8K UV Erasable PROM." Intel Corporation RR-12, Santa Clara, CA, 1976, pp. 51–58.

[Geiger et al., 1979] Geiger, W.; L. Gmeiner; H. Trauboth; and U. Voges. "Program Testing Techniques for Nuclear Reactor Protection Systems." *IEEE Comp.* (August 1979).

[Geilhufe, 1979] Geilhufe, M. "Soft Errors in Semiconductor Memories." In *Digest of Papers Spring CompCon.*, IEEE Computer Society, 1979, pp. 210–216.

[Geist and Trivedi, 1983] Geist, R.M., and K.S. Trivedi. "Ultrahigh Reliability Prediction for Fault-Tolerant Computer Systems." *IEEE Trans. Comp.* C-32, no. 12 (December 1983).

[General Radio, n.d.] General Radio Co. Ltd., Systems Division. *How to Design Logic Boards for Easier Automatic Testing and Troubleshooting*, n.d.

[Genke, Harding, and Staehler, 1964] Genke, R.M.; P.A. Harding; and R.E. Staehler. "No. 1 ESS Call Store–A-AO, 2-Megabit Ferrite Sheet Memory." *Bell Sys. Tech. J.* 43, no. 5, part 1 (September 1964): 2147–2191.

[Gibson et al., 1989] Gibson, G.; L. Hellerstein; R. Karp; R. Katz; and D. Patterson. "Error Correction in Large Disk Arrays." In *Proceedings of ASPLOS III*, 1989, pp. 123–132.

[Gill, 1966] Gill, A. "On the Series-to-Parallel Transformations of Linear Sequential Circuits." *IEEE Trans. Elec. Comp.* EC-15 (February 1966): 107–108.

[Gilley, 1970] Gilley, G.C. *Automatic Maintenance of Spacecraft Systems for Long-Life Deep-Space Missions.* Ph.D. Diss., University of California, Department of Computer Science, Los Angeles, 1970.

[Gmeiner and Voges, 1979] Gmeiner, L., and U. Voges. "Software Diversity in Reactor Protection Systems: An Experiment." *Proc. IFAC Workshop*, Stuttgart, FRG, May 16–18, 1979.

[Godoy, Franklin, and Bottorff, 1977] Godoy, H.C.; G.B. Franklin; and P.S. Bottorff. "Automatic Checking of Logic Design Structure for Compliance with Testability Groundrules." In *Proc. 14th Design Automation Conf.*, IEEE Pub. 77CH1216–1C, June 1977, pp. 469–478.

[Goel, 1980] Goel, P. "Test Generation Costs Analysis and Projections." Presented at the 17th Design Automation Conf., Minneapolis, MN, 1980.

[Goethals, 1971] Goethals, J.M. "On the Golay Perfect Binary Code." *J. Comb. Theory* 11 (September 1971): 178–186.

[Goetz, 1972] Goetz, F.M. "Design for Detection: An Attempt at Complete Fault Detection of a Store." In *Digest of Papers, CompCon '72* (September 1972): 325–328.

[Goetz, 1974] Goetz, F.M. "Complementary Fault Simulation." In *Proc. 3rd Annual Texas Conf. Computing Systems*, Austin, TX, 1974.

[Golan and Hlavicka, 1983] Golan, P., and J. Hlavicka. "New Method for Parallel Decoding of Double-Error Correcting Group Codes." In *Proceedings of the 13th International Symposium on Fault-Tolerant Computing*, Milan, Italy, June 1983, pp. 338–341.

[Golay, 1949] Golay, M.J.E. "Notes on Digital Coding." In *Proceedings of the IRE* 37 (1949): 657.

[Golay, 1958] Golay, M.J.E. "Notes on the Penny-Weighing Problem, Lossless Symbol Coding with Nonprimes, etc." *IRE Trans. Info. Theory* IT-4, no. 3 (September 1958): 103–109.

[Goldberg, 1975] Goldberg, J. "New Problems in Fault-Tolerant Computing." In *Int. Digest Fifth IEEE Symposium on Fault-Tolerant Computing*, Computer Society, Paris, France, 1975.

[Goldberg, Levitt, and Short, 1966] Goldberg, J.; K.N. Levitt; and R.A. Short. "Techniques for the Realization of Ultra-Reliable Spaceborne Computers." Menlo Park, CA: Stanford Research Institute, 1966.

[Goldberg, Levitt, and Wensley, 1974] Goldberg, J.; K.N. Levitt; and J.H. Wensley. "An Organization for a Highly Reliable Memory." *IEEE Trans. Comp.* C-23 (July 1974): 693–705.

[Goldstein, 1979] Goldstein, L.H. "Controllability/Observability Analysis of Digital Circuits." *IEEE Trans. Circuits Syst.* CAS-26, no. 9 (September 1979): 685–693.

[Goyal et al., 1986] Goyal, A.; W.C. Carter; E. de Souza e Silver; S.S. Lavenberg; and K.S. Trivedi. "The System Availability Estimator." In *Digest on 16th International Symposium on Fault-Tolerant Computing*, Vienna, Austria, June 1986, pp. 84–89.

[Grason and Nagle, 1980] Grason, J., and A. Nagle. "Digital Test Generation and Design for Testability." In *Proc. 17th Annual Design Automation Conference.* IEEE/ACM, 1980, pp. 175–189.

[Gray, 1979] Gray J. "Notes on Database Operating Systems." In *Operating Systems, an Advanced Course.* Springer Verlag, 1979.

[Gray, 1985] Gray, J., "Why Do Computers Stop and What Can Be Done About It?" Tandem TR85.7, June 1985, Tandem Computers, Cupertino, CA.

[Gray, 1987] Gray, J. Private communication.

[Gray, 1990] Gray, J. "A Census of Tandem System Availability: 1985–1990." Tandem Computers TR 90.1, 1990.

[Gray and Anderton, 1985] Gray, J., and M. Anderton. "Distributed Database Systems—Four Case Studies." Tandem Computers TR 85.5.

[Gray and Siewiorek, 1991] Gray, Jim, and Daniel P. Siewiorek. "High-Availability Computer Systems." *Computer*, vol. 24, no. 9 (September 1991): 39–48.

[Griesmer, Miller, and Roth, 1962] Griesmer, J.E.; R.E. Miller; and J.P. Roth. "The Design of Digital Circuits to Eliminate Catastrophic Failures." In Wilcox and Mann, eds., *Redundancy Techniques for Computing Systems.* Washington, DC: Spartan Books, 1962, pp. 328–348.

[Grimmer, 1976] Grimmer, B.A. "Test Techniques for Circuit Boards Containing Large Memories and Microprocessors." In *Dig. Papers, 1976 Semiconductor Test Symposium*, (October 1976), pp. 16–21.

[Groves, 1979] Groves, W.A. "Rapid Digital Fault Isolation with FASTRACE." *Hewlett-Packard J.* (March 1979): 8–13.

[Grzelakowski, Campbell, and Dubman, 1983] Grzelakowski, M.E.; J.H. Campbell; and M.R. Dubman. "DMERT Operating System." *Bell Sys. Tech. J.* 62, no. 1, pt. 2 (January 1983): 303–322.

[Gudz, 1977] Gudz, R.T. "Application of the Pluribus Multiprocessor in a Distributed Data Collection and Processing Network." In *Conf. Rec. OCEANS 77*, 1977.

[Gumpertz, 1981] Gumpertz, R. *Error Detection with Memory Tags.* Ph.D. Diss., Carnegie-Mellon University, Pittsburgh, PA, December 1981.

[Gupta, Porter, and Lathrop, 1974] Gupta, A.; W.A. Porter; and J.W. Lathrop. "Defect Analysis and Yield Degradation of Integrated Circuits." *IEEE J. Solid-State Circuits* SC-9 (June 1974): 96–103.

[Gurzi, 1965] Gurzi, K.J. "Estimates for the Best Placement of Voters in a Triplicated Logic Network." *IEEE Trans. Elec. Comp.* EC-14 (October 1965): 711–717.

[Gustafson and Spacacio, 1982] Gustafson, R.N., and F.J. Sparacio. "IBM 3081 Processor Unit: Design Considerations and Design Process." *IBM J. Res. and Dev.* 26, no. 1 (January 1982): 12–21.

[Haerder and Reuter, 1983] Haerder, T., and A. Reuter. "Principles of Transaction-Oriented Database Recovery." *ACM Computing Surveys* 15.4 (December 1983).

[Hagelbarger, 1959] Hagelbarger, D.W. "Recurrent Codes: Easily Mechanized, Burst-Correcting Binary Codes." *Bell Sys. Tech. J.* 38, no. 4 (July 1959): 969–984.

[Haglund and Peterson, 1983] Haglund, R.E., and L.D. Peterson. "3B20D File Memory Systems." *Bell Sys. Tech. J.* 62, no. 1, pt. 2 (January 1983): 235–254.

[Halbert and Bose, 1984] Halbert, M.P., and S.M. Bose. "Design Approach for a VLSI Self-Checking MIL-STD-1750A Microprocessor." In *Digest of 14th International Symposium on Fault-Tolerant Computing*, IEEE Computer Society, Kissimmee, FL, 1984, pp. 254–259.

[Halstead, 1979] "Commemorative Issue in Honor of Dr. Maurice H. Halstead." Special issue of *IEEE Trans. Soft. Eng.* SE-5, no. 2 (March 1979).

[Hamming, 1950] Hamming, W.R. "Error Detecting and Error Correcting Codes." *Bell Sys. Tech. J.* 29, no. 2 (April 1950): 147–160.

[Hampel and Winder, 1971] Hampel, D., and R.O. Winder. "Threshold Logic." *IEEE Spectrum* (May 1971): 32–39.

[Hansen, 1988] Hansen, J.P. *Trend Analysis and Modeling of Uni/Multi-Processor Event Logs.* Master's thesis, Department of Electrical and Computer Engineering, Carnegie-Mellon University, Pittsburgh, PA, 1988.

[Hansen, Peterson, and Whittington, 1983] Hansen, R.C.; R.W. Peterson; and N.O. Whittington. "Fault Detection and Recovery." *Bell Sys. Tech. J.* 62, no. 1, pt. 2 (January 1983): 349–366.

[Harr, Taylor, and Ulrich, 1969] Harr, J.A.; F.F. Taylor; and W. Ulrich. "Organization of the No. 1 ESS Central Processor." *Bell Sys. Tech. J.* 48 (September 1969).

[Harrahy, 1977] Harrahy, J.J. "Assessment of Plastic, Commercial Grade IC Failure Rates Achieved in Field Operation." In *Proc. 15th Annual Spring Reliability Seminar.* IEEE Boston Section, 1977, pp. 144–172.

[Hayes, 1971] Hayes, J.P. "A NAND Model for Fault Diagnosis in Combinational Logic Networks." *IEEE Trans. Comp.* C-20 (December 1971): 1496–1506.

[Hayes, 1974] Hayes, J.P. "On Modifying Logic Networks to Improve Their Diagnosability." *IEEE Trans. Comp.* C-23 (January 1974): 56–62.

[Hayes, 1975a] Hayes, J.P. "Detection of Pattern Sensitive Faults in Random Access Memories." *IEEE Trans. Comp.* C-24, no. 2 (February 1975): 150–160.

[Hayes, 1975b] Hayes, J.P. "Testing Logic Circuits by Transition Counting." In *FTC-5, Dig. Papers, 5th International Symposium on Fault Tolerant Computing,* Paris, France, June 1975, pp. 215–219.

[Hayes, 1976] Hayes, J.P. "Rapid Count Testing for Combinational Logic Circuits." *IEEE Trans. Comp.* C-25, no. 6 (June 1976): 613–620.

[Hayes, 1985] Hayes, J.P. "Fault Modeling." *IEEE Design and Test* (April 1985): 88–95.

[Hayes and Friedman, 1973] Hayes, J.P., and A.D. Friedman. "Test Point Placement to Simplify Fault Detection." In *FTC-3, Dig. Papers, 1973 Symposium on Fault-Tolerant Computing,* June 1973, pp. 73–78.

[Hayes and Friedman, 1974] Hayes, J.P., and A.D. Friedman. "Test Point Placement to Simplify Fault Detection." *IEEE Trans. Comp.* C-23 (July 1974): 727–735.

[Healy, 1977] Healy, J.T. "Economic Realities of Testing Microprocessors." In *Dig. Papers, 1977 Semiconductor Test Symposium,* October 1977, pp. 47–52.

[Heart, 1975] Heart, F.E. "The ARPA Network." In R.L. Grimsdale and F.F. Kuo, eds., *Communication Networks: Proc. NATO Advanced Study Institute of September 1973.* Leyden: Noordhoff, 1975, pp. 19–33.

[Heart et al., 1970] Heart, F.E.; R.E. Hahn; S.M. Ornstein; W.R. Crowther; and D.C. Walden. "The Interface Message Processor for the ARPA Computer Network." In *AFIPS Conf. Proc.,* vol. 36. Montvale, NJ: AFIPS Press, 1970, pp. 551–567.

[Heart et al., 1973] Heart. F.E.; S.M. Ornstein; W.R. Crowther; and W.B. Barker. "A New Minicomputer/Multiprocessor for the ARPA Network." In *AFIPS Conf. Proc.,* vol. 42. Montvale, NJ: AFIPS Press, 1973, pp. 529–537.

[Heart et al., 1976] Heart, F.E.; S.M. Ornstein; W.R. Crowther; W.B. Barker; M.F. Kraley; R.D. Bressler; and A. Michel. "The Pluribus Multiprocessor System." In *Multiprocessor Systems: Infotech State of the Art Report.* Maidenhead, England: Infotech International Ltd., 1976, pp. 307–330.

[Hecht, 1976] Hecht, H. "Fault-Tolerant Software for Real-Time Applications." *ACM Computing Surveys* 8 (December 1976): 391–407.

[Henderson, 1961] Henderson, D.S. "Residue Class Error Checking Codes." In *Preprints Papers 16th Natl. Meet. Ass. Comput. Mach.,* ACM, 1961.

[Hennie, 1964] Hennie, F.C. "Fault Detecting Experiments for Sequential Circuits." In *Proc. 5th Annual Symposium on Switching Theory and Logic Design,* IEEE, 1964, pp. 95–110.

[Hennie, 1968] Hennie, F.C. *Finite State Models for Logical Machines.* New York: Wiley, 1968.

[Hetherington and Kusulas, 1983] Hetherington, I.K., and P. Kusulas. "3B20D Memory Systems." *Bell Sys. Tech. J.* 62, no. 1, pt. 2 (January 1983): 207–220.

[Hewlett, 1973] Hewlett-Packard. *Hewlett-Packard Journal* 25, no. 4 (January 1973).

[Hill, 1986] Hill, R. "A First Course in Coding Theory." Oxford, UK: Clarendon Press, 1986.

[Hills, 1985] Hills, A.D. "Digital Fly-by-Wire Experience." *Proc. AGARD Lecture Series* 143 (October 1985).

[Hnatek, 1975] Hnatek, E.R. "4-Kilobit Memories Present a Challenge to Testing." *Computer Design* 14, no. 5 (May 1975): 117–125.

[Hocquenghem, 1959] Hocquenghem, A. "Codes Correcteurs d'Erreurs." *Chiffres* 2 (1959): 147–156.

[Holborow, 1972] Holborow, C.E. "An Improved Bound on the Length of Checking Experiments for Sequential Machines with Counter Cycles." *IEEE Trans. Comp.* C-21 (June 1972): 597–598.

[Holcomb and North, 1985] Holcomb, D.P., and J.C. North. "An Infant Mortality and Long-Term Failure Rate Model for Electronic Equipment." *AT&T Technical Journal* 64, no. 1 (January 1985): 15–31.

[Homan et al., 1988] Homan, P.; B. Malizia; and E. Reismer. "Overview of DSM." *Tandem Systems Review,* vol. 4.3, October 1988.

[Hong and Patel, 1972] Hong, S.J., and A.M. Patel. "A General Class of Maximal Codes for Computer Applications." *IEEE Trans. Comp.* C-21 (December 1972): 1322–1331.

[Hopkins, 1970] Hopkins, A.L., Jr. "A New Standard for Information Processing Systems for Manned Space Flight." In *Proceedings IFAC 3rd Symposium Control Systems in Space*, Toulouse, France, 1970.

[Hopkins, 1971] Hopkins, A.L., Jr. "A Fault-Tolerant Information Processing Concept for Space Vehicles." *IEEE Trans. Comp.* C-20, no. 11 (November 1971): 1394–1403.

[Hopkins, 1977] Hopkins, A.L., Jr. "Design Foundations for Survivable Integrated On-Board Computation and Control." In *Proc. Joint Automatic Control Conf.*, 1977, pp. 232–237.

[Hopkins and Smith, 1975] Hopkins, A.L., Jr., and T.B. Smith, III. "The Architectural Elements of a Symmetric Fault Tolerant Multiprocessor." *IEEE Trans. Comp.* C-24 (May 1975): 498–505.

[Hopkins and Smith, 1977a] Hopkins, A.L., Jr., and T.B. Smith, III. "OSIRIS—A Distributed Fault-Tolerant Control System." In *Digest 14th IEEE Computer Society International Conf.*, IEEE, 1977.

[Hopkins and Smith, 1977b] Hopkins, A.L., Jr., and T.B. Smith, III. United States Patent No. 4,015,246 Synchronous Fault-Tolerant Multiprocessor System, March 29, 1977.

[Hopkins, Smith, and Lala, 1978] Hopkins, A.L., Jr.; T.B. Smith, III; and J.H. Lala. "FTMP—A Highly Reliable Fault-Tolerant Multiprocessor for Aircarft." *Proceedings of the IEEE* 66 (October 1978): 1221–1239.

[Horning et al., 1974] Horning, J.J.; H.C. Lauer; P.M. Milliar-Smith; and B. Randell. "Program Structure for Error Detection and Recovery." *Lecture Notes in Computer Science*, vol. 16. New York: Springer-Verlag, 1974, pp. 171–187.

[Horowitz, 1975] Horowitz, E. *Practical Strategies for Developing Large Scale Systems*. Reading, MA: Addison-Wesley, 1975.

[Horst, 1989] Horst, R. "Reliable Design of High-Speed Cache and Control Store Memories." In *Proceedings 19th International Symposium on Fault-Tolerant Computing*, Chicago, IL, June 1989, pp. 259–266.

[Horst and Chou, 1985] Horst, R., and T. Chou. "The Hardware Architecture and Linear Expansion of Tandem NonStop Systems." In *Proceedings of the 12th International Symposium on Computer Architecture*, IEEE/ACM, June 1985.

[Horst and Gray, 1989] Horst, R., and J. Gray. "Learning from Field Experience with Fault-Tolerant Systems." In *Proceedings of International Workshop on Hardware Fault Tolerance in Multiprocessors*, University of Illinois, Urbana, June 19–20, 1989, pp. 77–79.

[Horst, Harris, and Jardine, 1990] Horst, R.; R. Harris; and R. Jardine. "Multiple Instruction Issue in the NonStop Cyclone System." In *17th International Symposium on Computer Architecture*, Seattle, WA, May 28–31, 1990.

[Horst and Metz, 1984] Horst, R., and S. Metz. "A New System Manages Hundreds of Transactions/Second." *Electronics* (April 19, 1984): 147–151.

[Hotchkiss, 1979] Hotchkiss, J. "The Roles of In-Circuit and Functional Board Test in the Manufacturing Process." *Electronic Packaging and Production* 19 (January 1979): 47–66.

[Howard, 1971] Howard, R.A. *Dynamic Probabilistic Systems*. New York: Wiley, 1971.

[Howard and Nahourai, 1978] Howard, J.S., and J. Nahourai. "Improvement in LSI Production Using an Automated Parametric Test System." *Solid State Technology* 21 (July 1978).

[Howden, 1980a] Howden, W.E. "Functional Testing and Design Abstractions." *Journal of Systems and Software* 1 (1980): 307–313.

[Howden, 1980b] Howden, W.E. "Functional Program Testing." *IEEE Trans. Soft. Eng.* SE-6(2) (March 1980): 162–169.

[Howell, Gregg, and Rabins, 1977] Howell, T.H.; G.E. Gregg; and L. Rabins. "Table Lookup Direct Decoder for Double-Error Correcting BCH Codes Using a Pair of Syndromes." U.S. Patent No. 4,030,067, June 14, 1977.

[HP-a] "A Designer's Guide to Signature Analysis." Hewlett-Packard Application Note 222, Hewlett-Packard, 5301 Stevens Creek Blvd., Santa Clara, CA 95050.

[HP-b] "Designing Digital Circuits for Testability." Hewlett-Packard Application Note 210–4, Hewlett-Packard, Loveland, CO 80537.

[Hsiao, 1970] Hsiao, M.Y. "A Class of Optimal Minimum Odd-Weight-Column SEC-DED Codes." *IBM J. Res. and Dev.* 14, no. 4 (July 1970): 395–401.

[Hsiao and Bossen, 1975] Hsiao, M.Y., and D.C. Bossen. "Orthogonal Latin Square Configuration for LSI Yield and Reliability Enhancement." *IEEE Trans. Comp.* C-24 (May 1975): 512–516.

[Hsiao, Bossen, and Chien, 1970] Hsiao, M.Y.; D.C. Bossen; and R.T. Chien. "Orthogonal Latin Square Codes." *IBM J. Res. and Dev.* 14, 4 (July 1970).

[Hsiao et al., 1981] Hsiao, M.Y.; W.C. Carter; J.W. Thomas; and W.R. Stringfellow. "Reliability, Availability, and Serviceability of IBM Computer Systems: A Quarter Century of Progress." *IBM J. Res. and Dev.* 25 (September 1981): 453–465.

[Hsieh, 1971] Hsieh, E.P. "Checking Experiments for Sequential Machines." *IEEE Trans. Comp.* C-20 (October 1971): 1152–1166.

[Hsieh et al., 1977] Hsieh, E.P., et al. "Delay Test Generation." In *Proceedings 14th Design Automation Conf.*, IEEE Pub. 77CH1216–1C (June 1977): 486–491.

[Huang and Abraham, 1984] Huang, K.H., and J.A. Abraham. "Algorithm-Based Fault Tolerance for Matrix Operations." *IEEE Trans. Comp.* C-33 (June 1984): 518–528.

[Hughes, McCluskey, and Lu, 1983] Hughes, J.L.A.; E.J. McCluskey; and D.J. Lu. "Design of Totally Self-Checking Comparators with an Arbitrary Number of Inputs." In *Digest 13th International Symposium on Fault-Tolerant Computing*, IEEE Computer Society, Milan, Italy, June 1983, p. 169.

[Huffman, 1952] Huffman, D.A. "A Method for the Construction of Minimum-Redundancy Codes." In *Proceedings of the IRE* 40 (1952): 1098–1101.

[Huffman, 1956] Huffman, D.A. "The Synthesis of Linear Sequential Coding Networks." In *Information Theory*. New York: Academic Press, 1956, pp. 77–95.

[IBM] International Business Machines. *Concepts and Facilities—IBM System/360 Operating System. System Reference Library*. GC28–6535.

[IBM] International Business Machines. *Operator's Reference—IBM System/360 Operating System. System Reference Library*. GC28–6691.

[IBM] International Business Machines. *MVT Guide—IBM System/360 Operating System. System Reference Library*. GC28–6720.

[IBM] International Business Machines. *MFT Guide—IBM System/360 Operating System. System Reference Library*. GC27–6939.

[IBM] International Business Machines. *Machine Check Handler for the IBM System/370 Models 155 and 165. Systems Logic*. GY27–7198.

[IBM] International Business Machines. "IBM SDLC General Information."

[IBM] International Business Machines. *I/O Supervisor—IBM System/360 Operating System Program Logic Manuals*. GY28–6616.

[IBM] International Business Machines. *MVT Job Management—IBM System/360 Operating System. Program Logic Manuals*. GY28–6660.

[IBM] International Business Machines. *MCH for Model 65—IBM System/360 Operating System. Program Logic Manuals*. GY27–7155.

[IBM] International Business Machines. *MCH for Model 85—IBM System/360 Operating System. Program Logic Manuals*. GY27–7184.

[IBM] International Business Machines. *MVS/XA Recovery and Reconfiguration Guide*. (GC28–1160)

[IBM] International Business Machines. *MVS/XA SPL: System Macros and Facilities*. (GC28–1150)

[IBM] International Business Machines. *MVS/XA DPL: Supervisor Services and Macros*. (GC28–1150)

[IBM] International Business Machines. *3090 Processor Complex: Hardware Recovery Guide*. (SC38-0051)

[IBM] International Business Machines. *Automated Operations Using Standard S/NM Products*. (GG24–3083)

[IBM] International Business Machines. *Automated Operations Implementation Guide*. (GG24–3111)

[IBM] International Business Machines. *MPF/NetView Migration and Automation*. (GG24–3113)

[IBM] International Business Machines. *Automated System Operations for MVS/XA Systems*. (GG24–3142)

[IBM] International Business Machines. *Automated System Operations for High Availability: Concepts and Examples*. (GG66-0260)

[IBM] International Business Machines. *IBM Innovation*. (G505-0068-01)

[IBM] International Business Machines. *The IBM 3090 Family of Processors*. (G580-1005-00)

[IBM] International Business Machines. *NetView R2 General Information and Planning*. (GC30–3463)

[IEEE, 1971a] *IEEE Trans. Comp.* C-20 (1971): 536–542, 1270–1275, 1413–1414.

[IEEE, 1971b] IEEE Computer Society. *Proceedings International Symposium on Fault-Tolerant Computing*, 1971.

[IEEE, 1972a] *IEEE Trans. Comp.* C-21 (1972): 492–495, 1189–1196.

[IEEE, 1972b] IEEE Computer Society. *Digest of 2nd International Symposium on Fault-Tolerant Computing*, 1972.

[IEEE, 1972c] IEEE, Inc., *IEEE Standard Dictionary of Electrical and Electronics Terms*. New York: Wiley-Interscience, 1972.

[IEEE, 1973a] *IEEE Trans. Comp.* C-22 (1973): 239–249, 263–269, 298–306, 662–669.

[IEEE, 1973b] IEEE Computer Society. *Digest of 3rd International Symposium on Fault-Tolerant Computing*, 1973.

[IEEE, 1974a] *IEEE Trans. Comp.* C-23 (1974): 41–47, 113–118, 369–374, 494–500, 651–657, 736–739, 1100–1102, 1149–1154.

[IEEE, 1974b] IEEE Computer Society. *Digest of 4th International Symposium on Fault-Tolerant Computing*, 1974.

[IEEE, 1975] IEEE Computer Society. *Digest of 5th International Symposium on Fault-Tolerant Computing*, 1975.

[IEEE, 1977] IEEE, Boston Section. Annual Spring Reliability Seminar, April 1977.

[Ihara et al., 1978] Ihara, H.; K. Fukuoka; Y. Kubo; and S. Yokota. "Fault-Tolerant Computer System with Three Symmetric Computers." *Proceedings of the IEEE* 66 (October 1978): 1160–1177.

[Ingle and Siewiorek, 1973a] Ingle, A.D., and D.P. Siewiorek. "Extending the Error Correction Capability of Linear Codes." Carnegie-Mellon University Technical Report, Department of Computer Science, Pittsburgh, PA, 1973.

[Ingle and Siewiorek, 1973b] Ingle, A.D., and D.P. Siewiorek. "A Reliability Model for Various Switch Designs in Hybrid Redundancy." Technical Report, Carnegie-Mellon University Department of Computer Science, Pittsburgh, PA, 1973.

[Ingle and Siewiorek, 1976] Ingle, A.D., and D.P. Siewiorek. "A Reliability Model for Various Switch Designs in Hybrid Redundancy." *IEEE Trans. Comp.* C-25 (February 1976): 115–133.

[Institute of Environmental Sciences, 1981] "Environmental Stress Screening of Electronic Hardware." In *Proceedings of the Institute of Environmental Sciences*, 1981.

[Intel, 1981] "The Intel 432 System Summary." Intel Corp., Aloha, Oregon, 1981.

[Interdata, 1975] Interdata, Inc. *Model 8/32 Processor User's Manual*, 1975.

[Irland and Stagg, 1974] Irland, E.A., and U.K. Stagg. "New Developments in Suburban and Rural ESS (No. 2 and No. 3 ESS)." In *ISS Record*, Munich, Germany, 1974.

[Iyengar and Kinney, 1982] Iyengar, S.V., and L.L. Kinney. "Concurrent Testing of Flow of Control in Simple Microprogrammed Control Units." In *Digest of the 1982 International Test Conference*, paper 16.3, IEEE, 1982, pp. 469–479.

[Iyengar and Kinney, 1985] Iyengar, S.V., and L.L. Kinney. "Concurrent Fault Detection in Microprogrammed Control Units." *IEEE Trans. Comp.* C-34 (September 1985): 810–821.

[Iyer, Young, and Iyer, 1990] Iyer, R.K.; L.T. Young; and P.V. Iyer. "Automatic Recognition of Intermittent Failures: An Experimental Study of Field Data." *IEEE Trans. Comp.* 39, no. 4 (April 1990): 525–537.

[Iyer, Young, and Sridhar, 1986] Iyer, R.K.; L.T. Young; and V. Sridhar. "Recognition of Error Symptoms in Large Systems." In *Proceedings of 1986 Fall Joint Computer Conference*, Dallas, TX, November 1986.

[Jack, Kinney, and Berg, 1977] Jack, L.A.; L.L. Kinney; and R.O. Berg. "Comparison of Alternative Self-Check Techniques in Semiconductor Memories." In *Proc. Spring CompCon*, vol. 14, IEEE Computer Society, Long Beach, CA, 1977, pp. 170–173.

[Jack et al., 1975] Jack, L.A.; R.O. Berg; L.L. Kinney; and G.J. Prom. "Coverage Analysis of Self Test Techniques for Semiconductor Memories." Honeywell Corporation Technical Report, MR12399, Minneapolis, MN, 1975.

[Jelinek, 1968] Jelinek, F. *Probabilistic Information Theory: Discrete and Memoryless Models*. New York: McGraw-Hill, 1968.

[Jelinsky and Moranda, 1973] Jelinsky, Z., and P.B. Moranda. "Applications of a Probability Based Method to a Code Heading Experiment." In *Proceedings IEEE Symposium Computer Software Reliability*, IEEE, 1973, p. 78.

[Jensen, 1963] Jensen, P.A. "Quadded NOR Logic." *IEEE Trans. Rel.* R-12, no. 3 (September 1963): 22–31.

[Jensen, 1964] Jensen, P.A. "The Reliability of Redundant Multiple-Line Networks." *IEEE Trans. Rel.* R-13, no. 1 (March 1964): 23–33.

[Jewett, 1991] Jewett, D. "Integrity S2: A Fault-Tolerant UNIX Platform." In *21st International Symposium on Fault-Tolerant Computing*, Montreal, Canada, June 1991.

[Johnson, 1987] Johnson, M. "System Considerations in the Design of the AM29000." *IEEE Micro* (August 1987): 28–41.

[Johnson, 1989] Johnson, B.W. *Design and Analysis of Fault Tolerant Digital Systems*. New York: Addison-Wesley, 1989.

[Jones, 1979] Jones, C.P. "Automatic Fault Protection in the Voyager Spacecraft." Jet Propulsion Laboratory, California Institute of Technology AIAA Paper No. 79–1919, Pasadena, CA, 1979.

[Jones and Landano, 1983] Jones, C.P., and M. Landano. "The Galileo Spacecraft System Design." AIAA Paper No. 83-0097, 21st Aerospace Services Conference, Reno, Nevada, January 10, 1983.

[Joobbani and Siewiorek, 1979] Joobbani, Rostram, and D.P. Siewiorek. "Reliability Modeling of Multiprocessor Architectures," in *Proceedings of First International Conference on Distributed Computing Systems*, Huntsville, Alabama, October, 1979, pp. 384–398.

[Jouppi and Wall, 1989] Jouppi, N.P., and D.W. Wall. "Available Instruction-Level Parallelism for Superscalar and Superpipelined Machines." In *Proc. Third International Conference on Architectural Support for Programming Languages and Operating Systems*, Boston, MA, 1989.

[**Kamal, 1975**] Kamal, S. "An Approach to the Diagnosis of Intermittent Faults." *IEEE Trans. Comp.* C-24 (May 1975): 461–467.

[**Kamal and Page, 1974**] Kamal, S., and C.V. Page. "Intermittent Faults: A Model and Detection Procedure." *IEEE Trans. Comp.* C-23 (July 1974): 173–179.

[**Kane, Anderson, and McCabe, 1983**] Kane, J.R.; R.E. Anderson; and P.S. McCabe. "Overview, Architecture, and Performance of DMERT." *Bell Sys. Tech. J.* 62, no. 1, pt. 2 (January 1983): 291–302.

[**Kaneda, 1984**] Kaneda, A. "A Class of Odd-Weight-Column SEC-DED-SBD Codes for Memory System Applications." In *Digest of 14th International Symposium on Fault-Tolerant Computing*, IEEE Computer Society, Kissimmee, FL, 1984, pp. 88–93.

[**Kaneda and Fujiwara, 1980**] Kaneda, S., and E. Fujiwara. "Single Byte Error Correcting–Double Byte Error Detecting Codes for Memory Systems." In *Digest of 10th International Symposium on Fault-Tolerant Computing*, IEEE Computer Society, Kyoto, Japan, 1980, pp. 41–46.

[**Kasami, 1963**] Kasami, T. "Optimum Shortened Cyclic Codes for Burst-Error-Correction." *IEEE Trans. Info. Theory* IT-9, no. 2 (April 1963): 105–109.

[**Kasami, Lin, and Peterson, 1967**] Kasami, T.; S. Lin; and W.W. Peterson. "Some Results on Cyclic Codes which Are Invariant Under the Affine Group and Their Applications." *Info Control* 11 (November 1967): 475–496.

[**Kasami, Lin, and Peterson, 1968**] Kasami, T.; S. Lin; and W.W. Peterson. "New Generalizations of the Reed-Muller Codes—Part I: Primitive Codes." *IEEE Trans. Info. Theory* IT-14, no. 2 (March 1968): 189–199.

[**Katsuki et al., 1978**] Katsuki, D.; E.S. Elsam; W.F. Mann; E.S. Roberts; J.F. Robinson; R.S. Skowronski; and E.W. Wolf. "Pluribus—An Operational Fault-Tolerant Multiprocessor." *Proceedings of the IEEE* 66 (October 1978): 1146–1159.

[**Katzman, 1977a**] Katzman, J.A. "System Architecture for NonStop Computing. *CompCon*, 1977, p. 77–80.

[**Katzman, 1977b**] Katzman, J.A. "A Fault-Tolerant Computing System." Tandem Computers, Inc., Cupertino, CA, 1977.

[**Kautz, 1962**] Kautz, W.H. "Codes and Coding Circuitry for Automatic Error Correction within Digital System." In R.H. Wilcox and W.C. Mann, eds., *Redundancy Techniques for Computing Systems*. Washington, DC: Spartan Books, 1962, pp. 152–195.

[**Kautz, 1968**] Kautz, W.H. "Fault Testing and Diagnosis in Combination Digital Circuits." *IEEE Trans. Comp.* C-17 (April 1968): 352–366.

[**Kautz, 1971**] Kautz, W.H. "Testing Faults in Combinational Cellular Logic Arrays." In *Proceedings 8th Annual Symposium on Switching and Automata Theory*, IEEE, 1971, pp. 161–174.

[**Kautz, Levitt, and Waksman, 1968**] Kautz, W.H.; K.N. Levitt; and A. Waksman. "Cellular Interconnection Arrays." *IEEE Trans. Comp.* C-17 (May 1968): 443–451.

[**Keiner and West, 1977**] Keiner, W.L., and R.P. West. "Testability Measures." Presented at AUTOTESTCON '77, November 1977.

[**Keister, Ketchledge, and Lovell, 1960**] Keister, W.; R.W. Ketchledge; and C.A. Lovell. "Morris Electronic Telephone Exchange." *Proc. Inst. Elec. Eng.* 107, no. 20 (1960): 257–263.

[**Keister, Ketchledge, and Vaughan, 1964**] Keister, W.; R.W. Ketchledge; and H.E. Vaughan. "No. 1 ESS: System Organization and Objectives." *Bell Sys. Tech. J.* 43, no. 5, pt. 1 (September 1964): 1831–1844.

[**Keller, 1976**] Keller, T.W. "CRAY-1 Evaluation Final Report." Los Alamos Scientific Laboratory, 1976.

[**Kelly, 1982**] Kelly, J.P.J. "Specification of Fault-Tolerant Multi-Version Software: Experimental Studies of a Design Diversity Approach." CSD-820927, *UCLA Computer Science Department*, Los Angeles, CA (September 1982).

[**Kelly and Avizienis, 1983**] Kelly, J.P.J., and A. Avizienis. "A Specification-Oriented Multi-Version Software Experiment." In *Digest of 13th International Symposium on Fault-Tolerant Computing*, Milan, Italy, June 1983, pp. 120–126.

[**Kelly et al., 1988**] Kelly, J.P.J.; D.E. Eckhardt; A. Caglayan; J.C. Knight; D.F. McAllister; and M.A. Vouk. "A Large Scale Second Generation Experiment in Multi-Version Software: Description and Early Results." In *18th International Symposium on Fault-Tolerant Computing*, Tokyo, Japan, June 1988.

[**Keneda and Fujiwara, 1982**] Keneda, S., and E. Fujiwara. "Single Byte Error Correcting Double Byte Error Detecting Codes for Memory Systems." *IEEE Trans. Comp.* C-31 (July 1982): 596–602.

[**Kennedy and Quinn, 1972**] Kennedy, P.J., and T.M. Quinn. "Recovery Strategies in the No. 2 ESS." In *Digest of 2nd International Symposium on Fault-Tolerant Computing*, IEEE, Boston, MA, 1972.

[**Khakbaz and McCluskey, 1982**] Khakbaz, J., and E.J. McCluskey. "Concurrent Error Detection and Testing for Large PLA's." *IEEE Journal of Solid-State Circuits* (April 1982): 386–394.

[**Khodadad-Mostashiry, 1979**] Khodadad-Mostashiry, B. "Parity Prediction in Combination Circuits." In *Digest of*

9th International Symposium on Fault-Tolerant Computing, IEEE Computer Society, Madison, WI, 1979.

[Kim, 1984] Kim, K.H. "Software Fault Tolerance." In C.R. Vick and C.V. Ramamoorthy, eds., *Handbook of Software Engineering*. New York: Van Nostrand Reinhold, 1984, pp. 437–455.

[Kim, 1986] Kim, M.Y. "Synchronized Disk Interleaving." *IEEE Trans. Comp.* C-35, no. 11 (November 1986).

[Kime, 1970] Kime, C.R. "An Analysis Model for Digital System Diagnosis." *IEEE Trans. Comp.* C-19 (November 1970): 1063–1073.

[Kini, 1981] Kini, V. "Automatic Synthesis of Symbolic Reliability Functions for Processor-Memory-Switch Structures." Ph.D. Diss., Electrical Engineering Department, Carnegie-Mellon University, Pittsburgh, PA, 1981.

[Kini and Siewiorek, 1982] Kini, V., and D.P. Siewiorek. "Automatic Generation of Symbolic Reliability Functions for Processor-Memory-Switch Structures." *IEEE Trans. Comp.* C-31, no. 8 (August 1982): 752–770.

[Klaassen and Van Peppen, 1977a] Klaassen, K.B., and J.C.L. Van Peppen. "Majority and Similarity Voting in Analogue Redundant Systems." *Microelectronics and Reliability* (1977): 47–54.

[Klaassen and Van Peppen, 1977b] Klaassen, K.B., and J.C.L. Van Peppen. "Reliability Improvement by Redundancy Voting in Analogue Electronic Systems." *Microelectronics and Reliability* (1977): 593–600.

[Klaschka, 1969] Klaschka, T.F. "Reliability Improvement by Redundancy in Electronic Systems, II: An Efficient New Redundancy Scheme—Radial Logic." Royal Aircraft Establishment, Ministry of Technology 69045. Farnborough, U.K., 1969.

[Klaschka, 1971] Klaschka, F. "A Method for Redundancy Scheme Performance Assessment." In *Digest of 1st International Symposium on Fault Tolerant Computing*, IEEE Computer Society, Pasadena, CA, 1971, pp. 69–73.

[Klein, 1976] Klein, M.R. Microcircuit Device Reliability, Digital Detailed Data." Reliability Analysis Center RADC MDR-4, Griffiss AFB, Rome, NY, 1976.

[Kleinrock and Naylor, 1974] Kleinrock, L., and W.F. Naylor. "On Measured Behavior of the ARPA Network" *Proc. AFIPS NCC* 43 (1974): 767–778.

[Knight and Leveson, 1985] Knight, J.C., and N.G. Leveson. "Correlated Failures in Multi-Version Software." In *Proc. IFAC Workshop SAFECOMP'85* (October 1985): 159–165.

[Knight and Leveson, 1986a] Knight, J.C., and N.G. Leveson. "An Experimental Evaluation of the Assumption of Independence in Multiversion Programming." *IEEE Trans. Soft. Eng.* SE-12, no. 1 (January 1986): 96–109.

[Knight and Leveson, 1986b] Knight, J.C., and N.G. Leveson. "An Empirical Study of Failure Probabilities in Multi-Version Software." In 16th International Symposium on Fault-Tolerant Computing, Vienna, Austria, July 1986, pp. 165–170.

[Knuth, 1969] Knuth, D.E. *The Art of Computer Programming. Volume 2: Seminumerical Algorithms*. Reading, MA: Addison-Wesley, 1969.

[Kodandapani, 1974] Kodandapani, K.L. "A Note on Easily Testable Realizations for Logic Functions." *IEEE Trans. Comp.* C-23 (March 1974): 332–333.

[Koenemann, Mucha, and Zwiehoff, 1979] Koenemann, B.; J. Mucha; and G. Zwiehoff. "Built-in Logic Block Observation Techniques." In *Dig. Papers, 1979 Test Conf.*, IEEE Pub. 79CHI609–9C, October 1979, pp. 37–41.

[Kohavi and Kohavi, 1972] Kohavi, I., and Z. Kohavi. "Detection of Multiple Faults in Combinational Logic Networks." *IEEE Trans. Comp.* C-21 (June 1972): 556–558.

[Kohavi and Lavellee, 1967] Kohavi, Z., and P. Lavellee. "Design of Sequential Machines with Fault Detection Capabilities." *IEEE Trans. Comp.* C-16 (August 1967): 473–484.

[Kohavi, Rivierre, and Kohavi, 1973] Kohavi, Z.; J.A. Rivierre; and I. Kohavi. "Machine Distinguishing Experiments." *BSC Computer Journal* 16, no. 2 (1973): 141–147.

[Kole, 1980] Kole, R.S. "An Advanced Telecommunications Protocol Controller." *Fairchild Journal of Semiconductor Progress* (January/February 1980): 4–8.

[Kopetz, 1976] Kopetz, H. *Software Reliability*. New York: Springer-Verlag, Inc., 1976.

[Kovijanic, 1977] Kovijanic, P.G. "A New Look at Test Generation and Verification." In *Proceedings 14th Design Automation Conf.*, IEEE Pub. 77CH1216–1C, June 1977, pp. 58–63.

[Kovijanic, 1979] Kovijanic, P.G. "Testability Analysis." In *Dig. Papers, 1979 Test Conf.*, IEEE Pub. 79CH1509–9C, October 1979, pp. 310–316.

[Kruus, 1963] Kruus, J. "Upper Bounds for the Mean Life of Self-Repairing Systems." University of Illinois R-172, AD-418, Urbana, IL, 1963.

[Ku and Masson, 1975] Ku, C.T., and G.M. Masson. "The Boolean Difference and Multiple Fault Analysis." *IEEE Trans. Comp.* C-24, no. 7 (July 1975): 691–695.

[Kuehn, 1969] Kuehn, E. "Computer Redundancy: Design, Performance, and Future." *IEEE Trans. Rel.* R-18, no. 1 (February 1969): 3–11.

[Kulzer, 1977] Kulzer, J.J. "Systems Reliability: A Case Study of No. 4 ESS." In *System Security and Reliability*.

Maidenhead, Berkshire, England: Infotech, 1977, pp. 186–188.

[Kunshier and Mueller, 1980] Kunshier, D.J., and D.R. Mueller. "Support Processor Based System Fault Recovery." In *Proceedings of 10th International Symposium on Fault Tolerant Computing*. IEEE Computer Society, Kyoto, Japan, 1980, pp. 197–201.

[Kurlak and Chobot, 1981] Kurlak, R.P., and J.R. Chobot. "CPU Coverage Evaluation Using Automatic Fault Injection." In *4th AIAA/IEEE Digital Avionics Systems Conference*, 81–2281 (1981): 294–300.

[Kuznetsov, Kasami, and Yamamura, 1978] Kuznetsov, A.V.; T. Kasami; and S. Yamamura. "An Error Correcting Scheme for Defective Memory." *IEEE Trans. Info. Theory* IT-24 (November 1978): 712–718.

[Lai, 1979] Lai, L. K.-W. "Error-Oriented Architecture Testing." In *National Computer Conference*, June 1979, pp. 565–576.

[Lai, 1981] Lai, L.K.-W. *Functional Testing of Digital Systems*. Ph.D. Diss., Carnegie-Mellon University, Department of Computer Science, Pittsburgh, PA, December 1981. Technical report CMU-CS-81-148a.

[Lai and Siewiorek, 1983] Lai, L.K.-W., and D.P. Siewiorek. "Functional Testing of Digital Systems." In *20th Design Automation Conference*, IEEE, 1983, pp. 207–213.

[Lala, 1978] Lala, P.K. "An Adaptive Double Error Correction Scheme for Semiconductor Memory Systems." *Digital Processes* 4 (1978): 237–243.

[Lala, 1979] Lala, P.K. "Error Correction in Semiconductor Memory Systems." *Electron. Eng.* (January 1979): 49–53.

[Lala, 1983] Lala, J.H. "Fault Detection, Isolation and Reconfiguration in FTMP: Methods and Experimental Results." In *5th AIAA/IEEE Digital Avionics Systems Conference* (1983): 21.3.1–21.3.9.

[Lala and Hopkins, 1978] Lala, J.H., and A.L. Hopkins, Jr. "Survival and Dispatch Probability Models for the FTMP Computer." In *Digest of 8th International Symposium on Fault-Tolerant Computing*, IEEE Computer Society, Toulouse, France, 1978, pp. 37–43.

[Lala and Smith, 1983] Lala, J.H., and T.B. Smith III. "Development and Evaluation of a Fault-Tolerant Multi-Processor Computer. Vol. III. FTMP Test and Evaluation." *NASA CR-166073*, Charles Stark Draper Laboratories, May 1983.

[Lamport, Shostak, and Pease, 1982] Lamport, L.; R. Shostak; and M. Pease. "The Byzantine Generals Problems." *ACM Transactions on Programming Languages and Systems* 4 (1982): 382–401.

[Lampson, 1979] Lampson, B.W. "Bravo." In Xerox Corporation, *Alto User's Handbook*. Palo Alto, CA: Xerox Palo Alto Research Center, 1979.

[Landano and Easter, 1984] Landano, M.R., and R.W. Easter. "Space Station Automated Systems Testing/Verification and the Galileo Orbiter Fault Protection Design/Verification." In *Proceedings of Institute of Environmental Sciences Conference*, Los Angeles, CA, March 22, 1984.

[Landgraff and Yau, 1971] Landgraff, R.W., and S.S. Yau. "Design and Diagnosable Iterative Arrays." *IEEE Trans. Comp.* C-20 (August 1971): 867–877.

[Lapp and Powers, 1977] Lapp, S., and G. Powers. "Computer-Aided Synthesis of Fault-Trees." *IEEE Trans. Rel.* R-26, no. 1 (April 1977): 2.

[Laprie, 1975] Laprie, J.-C. "Reliability and Availability of Repairable Structures." In *Digest of 5th International Symposium on Fault-Tolerant Computing*, IEEE Computer Society, Paris, France, 1975, pp. 87–92.

[Laprie, 1984] Laprie, J.-C. "Dependability Evaluation of Software Systems in Operation." *IEEE Trans. Soft. Eng.* SE-10, no. 6 (1984): 701–714.

[Laprie, 1985] Laprie J.-C. "Dependable Computing and Fault Tolerance: Concepts and Terminology." In *Digest of 15th International Symposium on Fault-Tolerant Computing*, IEEE Computer Society, Ann Arbor, MI, 1985, pp. 2–11.

[Larman, 1983] Larman, B.T. "The Project Galileo Fault Protection System." In *Digest of 13th International Symposium on Fault-Tolerant Computing*. IEEE Computer Society, Milan, Italy, June 28–30, 1983.

[Larsen and Reed, 1972] Larsen, R.W., and I.S. Reed. "Redundancy by Coding Versus Redundancy by Replication of Failure-Tolerant Sequential Circuits." *IEEE Trans. Comp.* C-21 (February 1972): 130–137.

[Lee, 1976] Lee, E.C. "A Simple Concept in Microprocessor Testing." In *Dig. Papers, 1976 Semiconductor Test Symposium*, IEEE Pub. 76CH1179–1C, October 1976, pp. 13–15.

[Lee, Ghani, and Heron, 1980] Lee, P.A.; N. Ghani; and K. Heron. "A Recovery Cache for the PDP-11." *IEEE Trans. Comp.* C-29 (June 1980): 546–549.

[Lenoski, 1988] Lenoski, D.E. "A Highly Integrated, Fault Tolerant Minicomputer: The NonStop CLX." In *Digest of Papers, CompCon Spring 1988*, San Francisco, CA, 1988.

[Lesser and Shedletsky, 1980] Lesser, J.D., and J.J. Shedletsky. "An Experimental Delay Test Generator for LSI Logic." *IEEE Trans. Comp.* C-29 (March 1980): 235–248.

[Leveson and Harvey, 1983] Leveson, N.G., and P.R. Harvey. "Analyzing Software Safety." *IEEE Trans. Soft. Eng.* SE-9(5) (September 1983): 569–579.

[Levine and Meyers, 1976] Levine, L., and W. Meyers. "Semiconductor Memory Reliability with Error Detecting and Correcting Codes." *Computer* 9, no. 10 (October 1976): 43–50.

[Levitt, Green, and Goldberg, 1968] Levitt, K.N.; M.W. Green; and J. Goldberg. "A Study of the Data Commutation Problems in a Self-Repairable Multiprocessor." In *SJCC, AFIPS, Conf. Proc.*, vol. 32. Washington, DC: Thompson Books, 1968, pp. 515–527.

[Lewin, Purslow, and Bennetts, 1972] Lewin, D.W.; E. Purslow; and R.G. Bennetts. "Computer Assisted Logic Design—the CALD System." In *IEEE Conference Publication CAD Conference*, 1972, pp. 343–351.

[Lewis, 1963] Lewis, T.B. "Primary Processor and Data Storage Equipment for Orbiting Astronomical Observatory." *IEEE Trans. Elec. Comp.* EC-12 (December 1963): 677–686.

[Lewis, 1979] Lewis, D.W. "A Fault-Tolerant Clock Using Standby Sparing." In *Digest of 9th International Symposium on Fault-Tolerant Computing*, IEEE Computer Society, Madison, WI, 1979, pp. 33–40.

[Libson and Harvey, 1984] Libson, M.R., and H.E. Harvey. "A General-Purpose Memory Reliability Simulator." *IBM J. Res. and Dev.* 28 (1984): 196–205.

[Lilliefors, 1969] Lilliefors, H.W. "On the Kolmogorov-Smirnov Test for the Exponential Distribution with Mean Unknown." *J. Amer. Statis. Assoc.* 64 (1969): 387–389.

[Lin, 1970] Lin, S. *An Introduction to Error-Correcting Codes.* Englewood Cliffs, NJ: Prentice-Hall, 1970.

[Lin, 1988] Lin, T.-T. *Building an On-Line Diagnosis and Trend Analysis System.* Ph.D. Diss., Department of Electrical and Computer Engineering, Carnegie-Mellon University, Pittsburgh, PA, 1988.

[Lin and Costello, 1983] Lin, S., and D.J. Costello, Jr. "Error Control Coding: Fundamentals and Applications." Englewood Cliffs, NJ: Prentice-Hall, Inc., 1983.

[Lin and Siewiorek, 1986] Lin, Ting-Ting Y., and Daniel P. Siewiorek. "Toward On-Line Diagnosis and Trend Analysis." *IEEE International Conference on Computer Design: VLSI in Computers (ICCD-85)*, Port Chester, NY, October 1986.

[Lin and Siewiorek, 1990] Lin, T.-T.Y., and D.P. Siewiorek. "Error Log Analysis: Statistical Modeling and Heuristic Trend Analysis." *IEEE Transaction on Reliability* 39, no. 4 (October 1990): 419–432.

[Linger, Mills, and Witt, 1979] Linger, R.C.; H.D. Mills; and B.I. Witt. *Structured Programming: Theory and Practice.* Reading, MA: Addison-Wesley, 1979, pp. 147–212.

[Lippman and Donn, 1979] Lippman, M.D., and E.S. Donn. "Design Forethought Promotes Easier Testing of Microcomputer Boards." *Electronics* (January 18, 1979): 113–119.

[Littlewood, 1975] Littlewood, B. "A Reliability Model for Markov Structured Software." In *IEEE Conf. Reliable Software*, 1975, pp. 204–207.

[Littlewood, 1979] Littlewood, B. "How to Measure Software Reliability and How Not To." *IEEE Trans. Soft. Eng.* SE-5, no 2 (June 1979): 103–110.

[Littlewood, 1987] Littlewood, B. *Software Reliability: Achievement and Assessment.* Oxford: Blackwell Scientific Publications, 1987.

[Littlewood and Miller, 1987] Littlewood, B., and D.R. Miller. "A Conceptual Model of Multi-Version Software." In *Digest of 17th International Symposium on Fault-Tolerant Computing*, Los Angeles, CA, July 1987, pp. 150–155.

[Lloyd and Knight, 1984] Lloyd, J.R., and J.A. Knight. "The Relationship Between Electromigration-Induced Short-Circuit and Open-Circuit Failure Times in Multi-Layer VLSI Technologies." In *International Reliability Physics Symposium*, 1984, pp. 48–51.

[Locher, Pfau, and Tietz, 1986] Locher, M.R.; L.R. Pfau; and D.W. Tietz. "5ESS™ Switching System Software: Database Management System." *AT&T Technical Journal,* 5ESS™ Switch Software (January 1986): 61–79.

[Locks, 1973] Locks, M.O. *Reliability, Maintainability, and Availability Assessment.* Washington, DC: Spartan Books/Hayden Book Company, 1973.

[Long, 1969] Long, J.E. "To the Outer Planets." *Astronautics and Aeronautics* 7 (June 1969): 32–47.

[Longden, Page, and Scantlebury, 1966] Longden, M.; L.J. Page; and R.A. Scantlebury. "An Assessment of the Value of Triplicated Redundancy in Digital Systems." In *Microelectronics and Reliability*, vol. 5. Elmsford, NY: Pergamon Press, 1966, pp. 39–55.

[Losq, 1975a] Losq, J. "Influence of Fault-Detection and Switching Mechanisms on the Reliability of Stand-by Systems." In *Digest of 5th International Symposium on Fault-Tolerant Computing*, IEEE Computer Society, Paris, France, 1975, pp. 81–86.

[Losq, 1975b] Losq, J. "A Highly Efficient Redundancy Scheme: Self-Purging Redundancy." Digital Systems Laboratory, Stanford University Tech. Report No. 62. Stanford, CA, 1975.

[Losq, 1976a] Losq, J. "A Highly Efficient Redundancy Scheme: Self-Purging Redundancy." *IEEE Trans. Comp.* C-25 (June 1976): 569–578.

[Losq, 1976b] Losq, J. "Referenceless Random Testing." In *FTCS-6, Dig. Papers, 6th International Symposium on*

Fault-Tolerant Computing, Pittsburgh, PA, June 21–23, 1976, pp. 81–86.

[Losq, 1977] Losq, J. "Effects of Failures on Gracefully Degraded Systems." In *Digest of 7th International Symposium on Fault-Tolerant Computing*, IEEE Computer Society, Los Angeles, CA, 1977, pp. 29–34.

[Losq, 1978] Losq, J. "Testing for Intermittent Failures in Combinational Circuits." In *Proc. Third USA–Japan Computer Conf.*, AFIPS and IPSJ, 1978, pp. 165–170.

[Lu, 1982] Lu, D.J. "Watchdog Processors and Structural Integrity Checking." *IEEE Trans. Comp.* C-31 (July 1982): 681–685.

[Lucky, Salz, and Weldon, 1968] Lucky, R.W.; J. Salz; and E.J. Weldon, Jr. *Principles of Data Communication.* New York: McGraw-Hill, 1968.

[Lum, 1966] Lum, V.Y. "On Bose-Chaudhuri-Hocquenghem Codes Over GF(q)." University of Illinois R-306, Urbana, IL, 1966.

[Lunde, 1977] Lunde, A. "Empirical Evaluation of Instruction Set Processor Architecture." *Comm. ACM* 20, no. 3 (March 1977): 143–153.

[Lycklama and Bayer, 1978] Lycklama, H., and D.L. Bayer. "The MERT Operating System." *Bell Sys.Tech. J.* 57, no. 6, pt. 2 (July 1978): 2049–2086.

[Lynch, Wagner, and Schwartz, 1975] Lynch, W.C.; W. Wagner; and M.S. Schwartz. "Reliability Experience with Chi/OS." *IEEE Trans. Soft. Eng.* SE-1, no. 2 (June 1975): 253–257.

[Lyon, 1990] Lyon, J. "Tandem's Remote Data Facility." In *Proceedings of CompCon 90*, IEEE Press, San Francisco, CA, February 1990.

[Lyons and Vanderkulk, 1962] Lyons, R.E., and W. Vanderkulk. "The Use of Triple-Modular Redundancy to Improve Computer Reliability." *IBM J. Res. and Dev.* 6, no. 2 (April 1962): 200–209.

[McCann and Palumbo, 1988] McCann, C.M., and D.L. Palumbo. "Reliability Model Generator for Fault-Tolerant Systems." In *8th Digital Avionics Systems Conference*, San Jose, CA, October 17–20, 1988.

[McCluskey, 1985a] McCluskey, E.J. "Built-In Self-Test Techniques." *IEEE Design & Test* (April 1985): 21–28.

[McCluskey, 1985b] McCluskey, E.J. "Built-In Self-Test Structures." *IEEE Design & Test* (April 1985): 29–36.

[McCluskey and Bozorgui-Nesbat, 1981] McCluskey, E.J., and S. Bozorgui-Nesbat. "Design for Autonomous Test." *IEEE Trans. Comp.* C-30 (November 1981): 866–887.

[McCluskey and Clegg, 1971] McCluskey, E.J., and F.W. Clegg. "Fault Equivalence in Combinational Logic Networks." *IEEE Trans. Comp.* C-20 (November 1971): 1286–1293.

[McCluskey and Ogus, 1977] McCluskey, E.J., and R.C. Ogus. "Comparative Architecture of High-Availability Computer Systems." In *Proc. CompCon*, IEEE 1977, pp. 288–293.

[McConnel, 1981] McConnel, S.R. "Analysis and Modeling of Transient Errors in Digital Computers." Ph.D. Diss., Carnegie-Mellon University, Department of Electrical Engineering, Pittsburgh, PA, 1981.

[McConnel and Siewiorek, 1981] McConnel, S.R., and D.P. Siewiorek. "Synchronization and Voting." *IEEE Trans. Comp.* C-30 (February 1981): 161–164.

[McConnel, Siewiorek, and Tsao, 1979a] McConnel, S.R.; D.P. Siewiorek; and M.M. Tsao. "The Measurement and Analysis of Transient Errors in Digital Computer Systems." In *Digest of 9th International Symposium on Fault-Tolerant Computing*, IEEE Computer Society, Madison, WI, 1979, pp. 67–70.

[McConnel, Siewiorek, and Tsao, 1979b] McConnel, S.R.; D.P. Siewiorek; and M.M. Tsao. "Transient Error Data Analysis." Technical Report, Carnegie-Mellon University, Department of Computer Science, Pittsburgh, PA, 1979.

[McDonald, 1976] McDonald, J.C. "Testing for High Reliability: A Case Study." *Computer* 9, no. 2 (February 1976): 18–21.

[McDonald and McCracken, 1977] McDonald, J.C., and P.T. McCracken. "Testing for High Reliability." In *Proc. CompCon*, IEEE, 1977, pp. 190–191.

[McGough and Swern, 1981] McGough, J.G., and F. Swern. "Measurement of Fault Latency in a Digital Avionic Mini Processor." *NASA* CR-3462, Bendix Corp., October 1981.

[McGough and Swern, 1983] McGough, J.G., and F. Swern. "Measurement of Fault Latency in a Digital Avionic Mini Processor. Part II." *NASA* CR-3651, Bendix Corp., January 1983.

[McGough, Swern, and Bavuso, 1981] McGough, J.G.; F. Swern; and S.J. Bavuso. "Methodology for Measurement of Fault Latency in a Digital Avionic Miniprocessor." In *4th AIAA/IEEE Digital Avionics Systems Conference*, 81-2282, 1981, pp. 310–314.

[McGough, Swern, and Bavuso, 1983] McGough J.G.; F. Swern; and S.J. Bavuso. "New Results in Fault Latency Modeling." In *Proceeding of the IEEE EASCON Conference*, August 1983, pp. 299–306.

[McKenzie et al., 1972] McKenzie, A.A.; B.P. Cosell; J.M. McQuillan; and M.J. Thrope. "The Network Control Center for the ARPA Network." In *Proc. 1st Int. Conf. Computer Communication*, 1972, pp. 185–191.

[McKevitt, 1972] McKevitt, J.F. "Parity Fault Detection in Semiconductor Memories." *Computer Design* 11, no. 7 (July 1972): 67–73.

[McLeod, 1988] McLeod, J. "Choosing a RISC Chip: What Drives Customers?" *Electronics* (April 28, 1988): 85–86.

[McNamara, 1977] McNamara, J.E. *Technical Aspects of Data Communications.* Bedford, MA: Digital Press, 1977.

[MacWilliams and Sloan, 1978] MacWilliams, F.J., and N.J.A. Sloane. *The Theory of Error-Correcting Codes.* New York: North-Holland, 1978.

[Mahmood, Ersoz, and McCluskey, 1985] Mahmood, A.; E. Ersoz; and E.J. McCluskey. "Concurrent System-Level Error Detection Using a Watchdog Processor." In *IEEE Proceedings 15th International Test Conference,* November 1985, pp. 145–152.

[Mahmood and McCluskey, 1988] Mahmood, A., and E.J. McCluskey. "Concurrent Error Detection Using Watchdog Processors—A Survey." *IEEE Trans. Comp.* (February 1988): 160–174.

[Mahmood, McCluskey, and Lu, 1983] Mahmood, A.; E.J. McCluskey; and D.J. Lu. "Concurrent Fault Detection Using a Watchdog Processor and Assertions." In *IEEE Proceedings 13th International Test Conference,* October 1983, pp. 622–628.

[Maison, 1971] Maison, F.P. "The MECRA: A Self-Reconfigurable Computer for Highly Reliable Process." *IEEE Trans. Comp.* C-20 (November 1971): 1382–1388.

[Mak, Abraham, and Davidson, 1982] Mak, G.P.; J.A. Abraham; and E.S. Davidson. "The Design of PLAs with Concurrent Error Detection." In *Digest of 12th International Symposium on Fault-Tolerant Computing,* IEEE Computer Society, Santa Monica, CA, June 1982, pp. 303–310.

[Mandelbaum, 1972a] Mandelbaum, D. "On Error Control in Sequential Machines." *IEEE Trans. Comp.* C-21 (May 1972): 492–495.

[Mandelbaum, 1972b] Mandelbaum, D. "Error Correction in Residue Arithmetic." *IEEE Trans. Comp.* C-21 (June 1972): 538–545.

[Mandigo, 1976] Mandigo, P.D. "No. 2B ESS: New Features for a More Efficient Processor." *Bell Labs Rec.* 54, no. 11 (December 1976): 304–309.

[Mangir, 1984] Mangir, T.E. "Sources of Failures and Yield Improvement for VLSI and Restructurable Interconnects for RVLSI and WSI: Part I—Sources of Failure and Yield Improvement for VLSI." *Proceedings of the IEEE* 72, no. 6 (June 1984): 690–708.

[Mann, Ornstein, and Kraley, 1976] Mann, W.F.; S.M. Ornstein; and M.F. Kraley. "A Network-Oriented Multiprocessor Front-End Handling Many Hosts and Hundreds of Terminals." In *AFIPS Conf. Proc.,* vol. 45. Montvale, NJ: AFIPS Press, 1976, pp. 533–540.

[Manning and Chang, 1968] Manning, E., and H.Y. Chang. "Functional Technique for Efficient Digital Fault Simulation." In *IEEE Int. Conv. Dig.* (1968), p. 194.

[Marchal, 1985] Marchal, P. "Updating Functional Fault Models for Microprocessors Internal Buses." In *15th International Symposium on Fault-Tolerant Computing,* IEEE Computer Society, Ann Arbor, MI, 1985, pp. 58–64.

[Marouf and Friedman, 1977] Marouf, M.A., and A.D. Friedman. "Efficient Design of Self-Checking Checkers for m-out-of-n Codes." In *Digest of 7th International Symposium on Fault-Tolerant Computing,* IEEE Computer Society, Los Angeles, CA, 1977, pp. 134–149.

[Marouf and Friedman, 1978] Marouf, M.A., and A.D. Friedman. "Design of Self-Checking Checkers for Berger Codes." In *Digest of 8th International Symposium on Fault Tolerant Computing,* IEEE Computer Society, Toulouse, France, 1978, pp. 179–184.

[Martin, 1982] Martin, D.J. "Dissimilar Software in High Integrity Applications in Flight Controls." In *Proc. AGARD-CPP-330* (September 1982): 36.1–36.13.

[Massey, 1963] Massey, J. *Threshold Decoding.* Cambridge, MA: MIT Press, 1963.

[Massey, 1969] Massey, J.L. "Feedback Shift-Register Synthesis and BCH Decoding." *IEEE Trans. Info. Theory* IT-15 (January 1969): 122–127.

[Mathur, 1971a] Mathur, F.P. "Reliability Estimation Procedures and CARE: The Computer Aided Reliability Estimation Program." *Jet Propulsion Laboratory Quarterly Tech. Review* 1 (October 1971).

[Mathur, 1971b] Mathur, F.P. "On Reliability Modeling and Analysis of Ultra-Reliable Fault-Tolerant Digital Systems." *IEEE Trans. Comp.* C-20 (November 1971): 1376–1382.

[Mathur and Avizienis, 1970] Mathur, F.P., and A. Avizienis. "Reliability Analysis and Architecture of a Hybrid-Redundant Digital System: Generalized Triple Modular Redundancy with Self-Repair." In *SJCC, AFIPS Conf. Proc.,* vol. 36. Montvale, NJ: AFIPS Press, 1970, pp. 375–383.

[Mathur and DeSousa, 1975] Mathur, F.P., and P. DeSousa. "Reliability Modeling and Analysis of General Modular Redundant Systems." *IEEE Trans. Rel.* R-24, no. 5 (December 1975): 296–299.

[Maxion and Siewiorek, 1985] Maxion, Roy A., and Daniel P. Siewiorek. "Symptom Based Diagnosis," *IEEE International Conference on Computer Design: VLSI in Computers (ICCD-85),* Port Chester, New York, October 1985.

[Mei, 1970] Mei, K.C.Y. "Fault Dominance in Combinational Circuits." Digital Systems Lab, Stanford University Technician Note 2, Stanford, CA, 1970.

[Mei, 1974] Mei, K.C.Y. "Bridging and Stuck-At-Faults." *IEEE Trans. Comp.* C-23 (July 1974): 720–727.

[Melliar-Smith, 1977] Melliar-Smith, P.M. "Permissible Processor Loadings for Various Scheduling Algorithms." Menlo Park, CA: SRI International, 1977.

[Melsa and Cohen, 1978] Melsa, J.L., and D.L. Cohen. *Decision and Estimation Theory*. New York: McGraw-Hill, 1978.

[Menon and Friedman, 1971] Menon, P.R., and A.D. Friedman. "Fault Detection in Iterative Logic Arrays." *IEEE Trans. Comp.* C-20 (May 1971): 524–535.

[Meraud, Browaeys, and Germain, 1976] Meraud, C.; F. Browaeys; and G. Germain. "Automatic Rollback Techniques of the COPRA Computer." In *Digest of 6th International Symposium on Fault-Tolerant Computing*, IEEE Computer Society, Pittsburgh, PA, pp. 23–31.

[Meraud et al., 1979] Meraud, C.; F. Browaeys; J.P. Queille; and G. Germain. "Hardware and Software Design of the Fault-Tolerant Computer COPRA." In *Digest of 9th International Symposium on Fault-Tolerant Computing*, IEEE Computing Society, Madison, WI, p. 167.

[Meyer, 1971] Meyer, J.F. "Fault Tolerant Sequential Machines." *IEEE Trans. Comp.* C-20 (October 1971): 1167–1177.

[Meyer, 1978] Meyer, J.F. "On Evaluating the Performability of Degradable Computing Systems." In *Digest of 8th International Symposium on Fault-Tolerant Computing*, IEEE Computer Society, Toulouse, France, 1978, pp. 44–49.

[Meyer, Furchgott, and Wu, 1979] Meyer, J.F.; D.G. Furchgott; and L.T. Wu. "Performability Evaluation of the SIFT Computer." In *Digest of 9th International Symposium on Fault-Tolerant Computing*, IEEE Computer Society, Madison, WI, 1979, pp. 43–50.

[Meyer, Furchgott, and Wu, 1980] Meyer, J.F.; D.G. Furchgott; and L.T. Wu. "Performability Evaluation of the SIFT Computer." *IEEE Trans Comp.* C-29 (June 1980): 501–509.

[Meyer and Yeh, 1971] Meyer, J.F., and K. Yeh. "Diagnosable Machine Realizations of Sequential Behavior." In *Digest of 1st International Symposium on Fault-Tolerant Computing*, IEEE Computer Society, Pasadena, CA, 1971.

[Middendorf and Hausken, 1984] Middendorf, M.J., and T. Hausken. "Observed Physical Effects and Failure Analysis of EOS/ESD on MOS Devices." In *International Symposium for Testing and Failure Analysis*, October 1984, pp. 205–213.

[Mikhail, Bartoldus, and Rutledge, 1982] Mikhail, W.K.; R.W. Bartoldus; and R.A. Rutledge. "The Reliability of

Memory with Single-Error Correction." *IEEE Trans. Comp.* C-31 (June 1982): 560–564.

[Miller and Freund, 1965] Miller, I., and J. Freund. *Probability and Statistics for Engineers*. Englewood Cliffs, NJ: Prentice-Hall, 1965.

[Mine and Hatayama, 1979] Mine, H., and K. Hatayama. "Performance Evaluation of a Fault-Tolerant Computing System." In *Digest of 9th International Symposium on Fault-Tolerant Computing*, IEEE Computer Society, Madison, WI, 1979, pp. 59–62.

[Mine and Koga, 1967] Mine, H., and Y. Koga. "Basic Properties and a Construction Method for Fail-Safe Logical Systems." *IEEE Trans. Elec. Comp.* EC-16 (June 1967): 282–289.

[Misra, 1970] Misra, K.B. "An Algorithm for the Reliability Evaluation of Redundant Networks." *IEEE Trans. Rel.* R-19, no. 4 (November 1970): 146–151.

[Miyamoto, 1975] Miyamoto, I. "Software Reliability in Online Real Time Environment." In *Proc. Int. Conf. Reliable Software*, IEEE, 1975, pp. 518–527.

[Mohanly, 1973] Mohanly, S.N. "Models and Measurements for Quality Assessment of Software." *ACM Computer Surveys* 11 (September 1973): 250–275.

[Monachino, 1982] Monachino, M. "Design Verification System for Large-Scale LSI Designs." *IBM J. Res. and Dev.* 26, no. 1 (January 1982): 89–99.

[Moore and Shannon, 1956] Moore, E.F., and C.E. Shannon. "Reliable Circuits Using Less Reliable Relays." *J. Franklin Inst.* 262 (September 1956): 191–208.

[Morganti, 1978] Morganti, M. Personal communication to authors, 1978.

[Morganti, Coppadoro, and Ceru, 1978] Morganti, M.; G. Coppadoro; and S. Ceru. "UDET 7116—Common Control for PCM Telephone Exchange: Diagnostic Software Design and Availability Evaluation." In *Digest of 8th International Symposium on Fault-Tolerant Computing*, IEEE Computer Society, Toulouse, France, 1978, pp. 16–23.

[Morris, 1980] Morris, D. "ECC Chip Reduces Error Rate in Dynamic RAMS." *Computer Design* 19 (October 1980): 137–142.

[Mourad and Andrews, 1985] Mourad, S., and D. Andrews. "The Reliability of the IBM/XA Operating System." In *Digest of 15th International Symposium on Fault-Tolerant Computing*, IEEE Computer Society Press, Ann Arbor, MI, June 1985.

[Muehldorf, 1975] Muehldorf, E.I. "Fault Clustering: Modeling and Observation of Experimental LSI Chips." *IEEE J. Solid-State Circuits* SC-10 (August 1975): 237–244.

[Muehldorf, 1976] Muehldorf, E.I. "Designing LSI Logic for Testability." In *Dig. Papers, 1976 Ann. Semiconductor Test Symp.*, IEEE Pub. 76CH1179–1C, October 1976, pp. 45–49.

[Muehldorf, 1978] Muehldorf, E.I. "Test Pattern Generation As a Part of the Total Design Process." In *LSI and Boards: Dig. Papers, 1978 Ann. Semiconductor Test Symp.*, October 1978, pp. 4–7.

[Muehldorf and Savkar, 1981] Muehldorf, E.I., and A.D. Savkar. "LSI Logic Testing—An Overview." *IEEE Trans. Comp.* C-30, no. 1 (January 1981): 1–17.

[Muehldorf and Williams, 1977] Muehldorf, E.I., and T.W. Williams. "Optimized Stuck Fault Test Patterns for PLA Macros." In *Dig. Papers, 1977 Semiconductor Test Symp.*, IEEE Pub. 77CH1216–7C, October 1977, pp. 89–101.

[Mukai and Tohma, 1974] Mukai, Y., and Y. Tohma. "A Method for the Realization of Fail-Safe Asynchronous Sequential Circuits." *IEEE Trans. Comp.* C-23 (July 1974): 736–739.

[Mukhopadhyay and Schmitz, 1970] Mukhopadhyay, A., and G. Schmitz. "Minimization of EXCLUSIVE OR and LOGICAL EQUIVALENCE Switching Circuits." *IEEE Trans. Comp.* C-19 (February 1970): 132–140.

[Muller, 1954] Muller, D.E. "Application of Boolean Algebra to Switching Circuit Design and to Error Detection." *IRE Trans. Elec. Comp.* ED-3 (September 1954): 6–12.

[Muntz and Lui, 1990] Muntz, R., and J. Lui. "Performance Analysis of Disk Arrays Under Failure." In *Proceedings of the 16th Conference on Very Large Data Bases*, 1990, pp. 162–173.

[Murakami, Kinoshita, and Ozaki, 1970] Murakami, S.; K. Kinoshita; and H. Ozaki. "Sequential Machines Capable of Fault Diagnosis." *IEEE Trans. Comp.* C-19 (November 1970): 1079–1085.

[Murphy, 1964] Murphy, B.T. "Cost-Size Optima of Monolithic Integrated Circuits." *Proceedings of the IEEE* 52 (December 1964): 1537–1545.

[Murray, Hopkins, and Wensley, 1977] Murray, N.D.; A.L. Hopkins, Jr.; and J.H. Wensley. "Highly Reliable Multiprocessors." In P. Kurzhals, ed., *Integrity in Electronic Flight Control Systems*. Neuilly-sur-Seine, France: AGARD–NATO, 1977, pp. 17.1–17.16.

[Musa, 1975] Musa, J.D. "A Theory of Software Reliability and Its Applications." *IEEE Trans. Soft Eng.* SE-1, no. 3 (September 1975): 312–327.

[Musa, Iannino, and Okumoto, 1986] Musa, J.D.; A. Iannino; and K. Okumoto. *Software Reliability: Measurement, Prediction, Application.* New York: McGraw-Hill Book Company, 1986.

[Myers, 1976] Myers, G.J. *Software Reliability: Principles and Practices.* New York: John Wiley and Sons, 1976.

[Myers et al., 1977] Myers, M.N.; W.A. Route; and K.W. Yoder. "Maintenance Software." *Bell Sys. Tech. J.* 56, no. 7 (September 1977): 1139–1167.

[Nadig, 1977] Nadig, H.J. "Signature Analysis—Concepts, Examples and Guidelines." *Hewlett-Packard Journal* (May 1977): 15–21.

[Nagel and Skrivan, 1982] Nagel, P.M., and J.A. Skrivan. "Software Reliability: Repetitive Run Experimentation and Modeling." *NASA-Langley Research Center*, Hampton, VA, NASA CR-165836, February 1982.

[Nakagawa and Osaki, 1975] Nakagawa, T., and S. Osaki. "The Discrete Weibull Distribution." *IEEE Trans. Rel.* R-24, no. 5 (December 1975): 300–301.

[Namjoo, 1982] Namjoo, M. "Techniques for Concurrent Testing of VLSI Processor Operation." In *Proceedings of 12th International Symposium on Fault-Tolerant Computing*, IEEE Computer Society, Santa Monica, CA, June 1982, pp. 461–468.

[Namjoo, 1983] Namjoo, M. "Cerberus-16: An Architecture for a General Purpose Watchdog Processor." In *Digest of 13th International Symposium on Fault-Tolerant Computing*, IEEE Computer Society, Milan, Italy, June 1983, pp. 216–219.

[Nanya and Tohma, 1983] Nanya, T., and Y. Tohma. "A 3-Level Realization of Totally Self-Checking Checkers for M-Out-Of-N Codes." In *Digest of 13th International Symposium on Fault-Tolerant Computing*, IEEE Computer Society, Milan, Italy, June 1983, pp. 173–176.

[NASA, 1979a] *Validation Methods for Fault-Tolerant Avionics and Control Systems: Working Group Meeting I. NASA* Conference Publication 2114. NASA Langley Research Center, March 1979, ORI Incorporated, Compilers.

[NASA, 1979b] *Validation Methods Research for Fault-Tolerant Computer Systems: Preliminary Working Group II Report.* NASA Langley Research Center, September 1979, System and Measurements Division. Research Triangle Institute.

[Negrini, Sami, and Stefanelli, 1986] Negrini, R.; M. Sami; and R. Stefanelli. "Fault Tolerance Techniques for Array Structures Used in Supercomputing." *IEEE Computer* (February 1986): 78–87.

[Neil and Goodner, 1979] Neil, M., and R. Goodner. "Designing a Serviceman's Needs into Microprocessor Based Systems." *Electronics* (March 1979): 122–128.

[Nellen, 1985] Nellen, E. "New GUARDIAN 90 Timekeeping Facilities." *Tandem Systems Review*, vol. 1.2, June 1985.

[Nellen, 1986] Nellen, E. "Managing System Time Under GUARDIAN 90." *Tandem Systems Review,* vol. 2.1, February 1986.

[Nelson, 1973] Nelson, E.C. "A Statistical Basis for Software Reliability Assessment." TRW, 1973.

[Nelson, 1982] Nelson, R. "Effortless Error Management." *Computer Design* 21 (February 1982): 163–168.

[Neumann and Rao, 1975] Neumann, P.G., and T.R.N. Rao. "Error-Correcting Codes for Byte-Organized Arithmetic Processors." *IEEE Trans. Comp.* C-24 (March 1975): 226–232.

[Ng, 1988] Ng, S. "Some Design Issues in Disk Arrays." Technical Report RJ6590. IBM Research Division, Almaden Research Center, Almaden, CA, 1988.

[Ng and Avizienis, 1980] Ng, Y.W., and A. Avizienis. "A Unified Reliability Model for Fault-Tolerant Computers." *IEEE Trans. Comp.* C-29 (November 1980): 1002–1011.

[Nicholls, 1979] Nicholls, D.B. "Microcircuit Device Reliability, Digital Failure Rate Data." Reliability Analysis Center RADC MDR-12. Rome, NY: Griffiss AFB, 1979.

[Northcutt, 1980] Northcutt, J.D. "The Design and Implementation of Fault Insertion Capabilities for ISPS." In *18th Design Automation Conference,* IEEE, 1980, pp. 197–209.

[Nowak, 1976] Nowak, J.S. "No. 1A ESS—A New High Capacity Switching System." In *Int. Switching Symp. Record,* Japan, 1976.

[O'Brien, 1976] O'Brien, F.J. "Rollback Point Insertion Strategies." In *Digest of 6th International Fault-Tolerant Computing Symposium,* IEEE Computer Society, Pittsburgh, PA, 1976, pp. 138–142.

[Ogus, 1973] Ogus, R.C. "Fault-Tolerance of the Iterative Cell Array Switch for Hybrid Redundancy Through the Use of Failsafe Logic." Digital Systems Lab, Stanford University Departments of Electrical Engineering and Computer Science, Stanford, CA, 1973.

[Ogus, 1974] Ogus, R.C. "Fault-Tolerance of the Iterative Cell Array Switch for Hybrid Redundancy." *IEEE Trans. Comp.* C-23 (July 1974): 667–681.

[Ogus, 1975] Ogus, R.C. "The Probability of a Correct Output from a Combinational Circuit." *IEEE Trans. Comp.* C-24, no. 5 (May 1975): 534–544.

[Ohm, 1979] Ohm, V.J. "Reliability Considerations for Semiconductor Memories." In *Spring Digest of Papers,* CompCon, IEEE Computer Society, 1979, pp. 207–209.

[Oktay, Dessauer, and Horvath, 1983] Oktay, S.; B. Dessauer; and J.L. Horvath. "New Internal and External Cooling Enhancements for the Air-Cooled IBM 4381 Module."

IEEE International Conference on Computer Design, November 1983 (Special Session, not in proceedings).

[Oldham, Chien, and Tang, 1968] Oldham, I.B.; R.T. Chien; and D.T. Tang. "Error Detection and Correction in a Photo-Digital Memory System." *IBM J. Res. and Dev.* 12, no. 6 (November 1968): 422–430.

[Ornstein and Walden, 1975] Ornstein, S.M., and D.C. Walden. "The Evolution of a High Performance Modular Packet-Switch." In *Proc. Int. Conf. Communications,* vol. 1, 1975, pp. 6.17–6.21.

[Ornstein et al., 1972] Ornstein, S.M.; F.E. Heart; W.R. Crowther; S.B. Russell; H.K. Rising; and A. Michel. "The Terminal IMP for the ARPA Computer Network." *AFIPS Conf. Proc.,* vol. 40. Montvale, NJ: AFIPS Press, 1972, pp. 243–254.

[Ornstein et al., 1975] Ornstein, S.M.; W.R. Crowther; M.F. Kraley; R.D. Bressler; A. Michel; and F.E. Heart. "Pluribus—A Reliable Multiprocessor." In *AFIPS Conf. Proc.,* vol. 44. Montvale, NJ: AFIPS Press, 1975, pp. 551–559.

[Osman and Weiss, 1973] Osman, M.Y., and C.D. Weiss. "Shared Logic Realizations of Dynamically Self-Checked and Fault-Tolerant Logic." *IEEE Trans. Comp.* C-22 (March 1973): 298–306.

[Ossfeldt and Jonsson, 1980] Ossfeldt, B.E., and I. Jonsson. "Recovery and Diagnostics in the Central Control of the AXE Switching System." *IEEE Trans. Comp.* C-29 (June 1980): 482–491.

[Ozgunner, 1977] Ozgunner, F. "Design of Totally Self-Checking Asynchronous and Synchronous Sequential Machines." In *Digest of 7th International Symposium on Fault-Tolerant Computing,* IEEE Computer Society, Los Angeles, CA, 1977, pp. 124–129.

[Page, 1969] Page, M.R. "Generation of Diagnostic Tests Using Prime Implicants." Coordinated Science Lab. Rep. R-414, University of Illinois, Urbana, May 1969.

[Palmquist and Chapman, 1976] Palmquist, S., and D. Chapman. "Expanding the Boundaries of LSI Testing with an Advanced Pattern Controller." In *Dig. Papers, 1976 Semiconductor Test Symp.,* October 1976, pp. 70–75.

[Palumbo and Finelli, 1987] Palumbo, D.L., and G.B. Finelli. "A Technique for Evaluating the Application of Pin-Level Stuck-at Fault Model to VLSI." *NASA* TP-2738, Langley Research Center, September 1987.

[Papaioannou, 1977] Papaioannou, S.G. "Optimal Test Generation in Combinational Networks by Pseudo Boolean Programming." *IEEE Trans. Comp.* 26, no. 6 (June 1977): 553–560.

[Parker, 1973] Parker, K.P. "Probabilistic Test Generation," Tech. Note 18, Digital Systems Laboratory, Stanford University, Stanford, CA, January 1973.

[Parker, 1976a] Parker, K.P. "Compact Testing: Testing with Compressed Data." In *FTCS-6, Dig. Papers, 6th International Symposium on Fault-Tolerant Computing,* Pittsburgh, PA, June 21–23, 1976.

[Parker, 1976b] Parker, K.P. "Adaptive Random Test Generation." *J. Des. Automat. Fault Tolerant Comput.* 1, no. 1, October 1976, pp. 62–83.

[Parker, 1979] Parker, K.P. "Software Simulator Speeds Digital Board Test Generation." *Hewlett-Packard J.* (March 1979): 13–19.

[Parker and McCluskey, 1975] Parker, K.P., and E.J. McCluskey. "Analysis of Logic Circuits with Faults Using Input Signal Probabilities." *IEEE Trans. Comp.* C-24, no. 5 (May 1975): 573–578.

[Pascoe, 1975] Pascoe, W. "2107A/2107B N-Channel Silicon Gate MOS 4K RAMS." Santa Clara, CA: Intel Corporation RR-7, 1975.

[Patterson, Gibson, and Katz, 1988] Patterson, D.; A.G. Gibson; and R.H. Katz. "A Case for Redundant Arrays of Inexpensive Disks (RAID)." In *Proceedings of ACM SIGMOD,* 1988, pp. 109–116.

[Patterson and Metze, 1974] Patterson, W.W., and G. Metze. "A Fail-Safe Asynchronous Sequential Machine." *IEEE Trans. Comp.* C-23 (April 1974): 369–374.

[Pearson and Hartley, 1954] Pearson, E.S., and H.O. Hartley, eds. *Biometrica Tables for Statisticians,* vol. 1. Cambridge: Cambridge University Press, 1954.

[Pease, Shostak, and Lamport, 1980] Pease, M.; R. Shostak; and L. Lamport. "Reaching Agreement in the Presence of Faults." *Journal of the Association for Computing Machinery* 27, no. 2 (April 1980): 228–234.

[Peterson, 1958] Peterson, W.W. "On Checking an Adder." *IBM J. Res. and Dev.* 2, no. 2 (April 1958): 166–168.

[Peterson, 1961] Peterson, W.W. *Error-Correcting Codes.* Cambridge, MA: MIT Press, 1961.

[Peterson and Weldon, 1972] Peterson, W.W., and E.J. Weldon, Jr. *Error-Correcting Codes,* 2nd ed. Cambridge, MA: MIT Press, 1972.

[Phister, 1979] Phister, M., Jr. *Data Processing Technology and Economics.* Bedford, MA: Digital Press, 1979.

[Pierce, 1962] Pierce W.H. "Adaptive Vote-Takers Improve the Use of Redundancy." In R.H. Wilcox and W.C. Mann, eds., *Redundancy Techniques for Computing Systems.* Washington, DC: Spartan Books, 1962, pp. 229–250.

[Pierce, 1965] Pierce, W.H. *Failure Tolerant Design.* New York: Academic Press, 1965.

[Pierce, 1977] Pierce, R. "Service Economic Model Simulator." *Electro* (November 2, 1977).

[Piestrak, 1983] Piestrak, S. "Design Method of Totally Self-Checking Checkers for M-Out-Of-N Codes." In *Digest of 13th International Symposium on Fault-Tolerant Computing,* IEEE Computer Society, Milan, Italy, June 1983, pp. 162–168.

[Pittler, Powers, and Schnabel, 1982] Pittler, M.S.; D.M. Powers; and D.L. Schnabel. "System Development and Technology Aspects of the IBM 3081 Processor Complex." *IBM J. Res. and Dev.* 26, no. 1 (January 1982): 2–11.

[Platteter, 1980] Platteter, D.G. "Transparent Protection of Untestable LSI Microprocessors." In *Digest of 10th International Symposium on Fault-Tolerant Computing,* IEEE Computer Society, Kyoto, Japan, 1980, pp. 345–347.

[Poage and McCluskey, 1963] Poage, J.F., and E.I. McCluskey. "Derivation of Optimum Tests to Detect Faults in Combinational Circuits." In *Mathematical Theory of Automation.* New York: Polytechnic Press, 1963.

[Poage and McCluskey, 1964] Poage, J.F., and E.J. McCluskey. "Derivation of Optimum Tests for Sequential Machines." In *Proceedings of 5th Annual Symposium on Switching Circuits Theory and Logic Design,* 1964, pp. 95–110.

[Posa, 1980] Posa, J.G. "Memory Makers Turn to Redundancy." *Electronics* 53, McGraw-Hill (December 1980): 108–110.

[Pradhan, 1978a] Pradhan, D.K. "Asynchronous State Assignments with Unateness Properties and Fault-Secure Design." *IEEE Trans. Comp.* C-27 (May 1978): 396–404.

[Pradhan, 1978b] Pradhan, D.K. "Fault-Tolerant Asynchronous Networks Using Read-Only Memories." *IEEE Trans. Comp.* C-27 (Julyt 1978): 674–679.

[Pradhan, 1980] Pradhan, D.K. "A New Class of Error-Correcting/Detecting Codes for Fault-Tolerant Computer Applications." *IEEE Trans. Comp.* C-29 (June 1980): 471–481.

[Pradhan, 1986] Pradhan, D.K. (Ed.) *Fault-Tolerant Computing: Theory and Techniques,* vols. I and II. Englewood Cliffs, NJ: Prentice-Hall, 1986.

[Pradhan and Reddy, 1974a] Pradhan, D.K., and S.M. Reddy. "Design of Two-Level Fault-Tolerant Networks. *IEEE Trans. Comp.* C-23 (January 1974): 41–47.

[Pradhan and Reddy, 1974b] Pradhan, D.K., and S.M. Reddy. "Fault-Tolerant Asynchronous Networks." *IEEE Trans. Comp.* C-23 (January 1974): 651–658.

[Pradhan and Stiffler, 1980] Pradhan, D.K., and J.J. Stiffler. "Error-Correcting Codes and Self-Check Circuits." *Computer* 13, no. 3 (March 1980): 27–37.

[Prange, 1957] Prange, E. "Cyclic Error Correcting Codes in Two Symbols." Bedford, MA: U.S. Air Force Cambridge Research Center AFCRC-TN-58-156, 1957.

[Preparata, Metze, and Chien, 1967] Preparata, F.P.; G. Metze; and R.T. Chien. "On the Connection Assignment Problem of Diagnosable System." *IEEE Trans. Elec. Comp.* EC-16 (December 1967): 848–854.

[Punches, 1986] Punches, K. "Burn-in and Strife Testing." *Quality Progress* (May 1986): 93–94.

[Putzolu and Roth, 1971] Putzolu, G.R., and J.P. Roth. "A Heuristic Algorithm for Testing of Asynchronous Circuits." *IEEE Trans. Comp.* C-20, no. 6 (June 1971): 639–647.

[Queyssac, 1979] Queyssac, D. "Projecting VLSI's Impact on Microprocessors." *IEEE Spectrum* 16, no. 5 (1979): 38–41.

[Quinn and Goetz, 1983] Quinn, J.L., and F.M. Goetz. "Diagnostic Tests and Control Software." *Bell Sys. Tech. J.* 62, no. 1, pt. 2 (January 1983): 367–382.

[Ramamoorthy and Han, 1973] Ramamoorthy, C.V., and Y.W. Han. "Reliability Analysis of Systems with Concurrent Error Detection." University of California at Berkeley, Departments of Electrical Engineering and Computer Science, 1973.

[Ramamoorthy et al., 1981] Ramamoorthy, C.V.; Y. Mok; F. Bastani; G. Chin; and K. Suzuki. "Application of a Methodology for the Development and Validation of Reliable Process Control Software." *IEEE Trans. Soft. Eng.* SE-7, no. 6 (November 1981): 537–555.

[Ramarao and Adams, 1988] Ramarao, K.V.S., and J.C. Adams. "On the Diagnosis of Byzantine Faults." In *Proceedings of 7th Symposium on Reliable Distributed Systems*, Columbus, OH, 1988, pp. 144–153.

[Randell, 1975] Randell, B. "System Structure for Software Fault Tolerance." *IEEE Trans. Soft. Eng.* SE-1, no. 2 (June 1975): 220–232.

[Randell, Lee, and Treleaven, 1978] Randell, B.; P.A. Lee; and P.C. Treleaven. "Reliability Issues in Computing System Design. *Computing Surveys* 10, no. 2 (June 1978): 123–165.

[Rao, 1970] Rao, T.R.N. "Biresidue Error-Correcting Codes for Computer Arithmetic." *IEEE Trans. Comp.* C-19 (May 1970): 398–402.

[Rao, 1972] Rao, T.R.N. "Error Correction in Adders Using Systematic Subcodes." *IEEE Trans. Comp.* C-21 (March 1972): 254–259.

[Rao, 1974] Rao, T.R.N. *Error Coding for Arithmetic Processors.* New York: Academic Press, 1974.

[Rao and Garcia, 1971] Rao, T.R.N., and O.N. Garcia. "Cyclic and Multiresidue Codes for Arithmetic Operations." *IEEE Trans. Info. Theory* IT-17, no. 1 (January 1971): 85–91.

[Ratner, 1973] Ratner, R.S. "Computational Requirements and Technology." Menlo Park, CA: SRI International, 1973.

[Ray-Chaudhuri, 1961] Ray-Chaudhuri, D.K. "On the Construction of Minimally Redundant Reliable Systems Design." *Bell Sys. Tech. J.* 40, no. 2 (March 1961): 595–611.

[Raytheon, 1974] Raytheon Company. *Reliability Model Derivation of a Fault-Tolerant, Dual, Spare-Switching Digital Computer System.* NASA CR-132441. Sudbury, MA: 1974.

[Raytheon, 1976] Raytheon Company. *An Engineering Treatise on the CARE II Dual Mode and Coverage Models.* NASA CR-144993. Sudbury, MA: 1976.

[Reddy, 1972a] Reddy, S.M. "Easily Testable Realization for Logic Functions." *IEEE Trans. Comp.* C-21 (November 1972): 1183–1188.

[Reddy, 1972b] Reddy, S.M. "A Design Procedure for Fault-Locatable Switching Circuits." *IEEE Trans. Comp.* C-21 (December 1972): 1421–1426.

[Reddy, 1978] Reddy, S.M. "A Class of Linear Codes for Error Control in Byte-per-Card Organized Digital Systems." *IEEE Trans. Comp.* C-27 (May 1978): 455–459.

[Reddy and Banerjee, 1989] Reddy, A., and P. Banerjee. "Performance Evaluation of Multiple-Disk I/O Systems." In *Proceedings of the International Conference on Parallel Processing*, 1989, pp. 1315–1318.

[Reddy and Wilson, 1974] Reddy, S.M., and J.R. Wilson. "Easily Testable Cellular Realizations for (exactly p)-out-of-n and (p or more)-out-of-n Logic Functions." *IEEE Trans. Comp* C-23 (January 1974): 98–100.

[Reed, 1954] Reed, I.S. "A Class of Multiple-Error-Correcting Codes and the Decoding Scheme." *IRE Trans. Professional Group on Information Theory* PGIT-4 (September 1954): 38–49.

[Reed and Brimley, 1962] Reed, I.S., and D.E. Brimley. "On Increasing the Operating Life of Unattended Machines." RAND Corporation RM-3338-PR. Santa Monica, CA: 1962.

[Reed and Chiang, 1970] Reed, I.S., and A.C.L. Chiang. "Coding Techniques for Failure-Tolerant Counters." *IEEE Trans. Comp.* C-19 (November 1970): 1035–1038.

[Reed and Soloman, 1960] Reed, I.S., and G. Soloman. "Polynomial Codes over Certain Finite Fields." *Journal of the Society for Industrial and Applied Mathematics 8, no. 2 (1960): 300–304.

[Reilly, Sutton, Nasser, and Griscom, 1982] Reilly, J.; A. Sutton; R. Nasser; and R. Griscom. "Processor Controller for the IBM 3081." *IBM J. Res. and Dev.* 26, no. 1 (January 1982): 22–29.

[Reliability, 1976a] Reliability Analysis Center. *Microcircuit Device Reliability: Memory/LSI Data*, MDR-3. Rome, NY: Griffiss AFB, 1976.

[Reliability, 1976b] Reliability Analysis Center. *Microcircuit Device Reliability: Digital Detailed Data*, MDR-4. Rome, NY: Griffiss AFB, 1976.

[Reliability, 1979a] Reliability Analysis Center. *Digital Failure Rate Data*, MDR-12. Rome, NY: Griffiss AFB, 1979.

[Reliability, 1979b] Reliability Analysis Center. *Memory/LSI Data*, MDR-13. Rome, NY: Griffiss AFB, 1979.

[Rennels, 1980] Rennels, D.A. "Distributed Fault-Tolerant Computer Systems." *Computer* 13, no. 3 (March 1980): 55–65.

[Reynolds and Kinsbergen, 1975] Reynolds, C.H., and J.E. Kinsbergen. "Tracking Reliability and Availability." *Datamation* 21, no. 11 (November 1975): 106–116.

[Rhodes, 1964] Rhodes, L.J. "Effects of Failure Modes on Redundancy." In *Proc. 10th National Symp. Reliability and Quality Control*, Washington, DC, 1964, pp. 360–364.

[Richard, 1976] Richard, B. "Automatic Error Correction in Memory Systems." *Computer Design* 15 (May 1976): 179–182.

[Rickers, 1975/76] Rickers, H.C. "Microcircuit Device Reliability Memory/LSI Data." Reliability Analysis Center, RADC/RBRAC MDR-3. Rome, NY: Griffiss AFB, 1975–1976.

[Ritchie and Thompson, 1978] Ritchie, D., and K. Thompson. "The UNIX Time-Sharing System." *Bell Sys. Tech. J.* 57, no. 6, pt. 2 (July 1978): 1905–1930.

[Robach and Saucier, 1980] Robach, C., and G. Saucier. "Microprocessor Functional Testing." In *Digest of Papers of 1980 International Test Conference*, IEEE, 1980, pp. 433–443.

[Roberts, 1965] Roberts, N.H. *Mathematical Methods in Reliability Engineering*. New York: McGraw-Hill, 1965.

[Roberts and Wessler, 1970] Roberts, L.G., and B.D. Wessler. "Computer Network Development to Achieve Resource Sharing." In *AFIPS Conf. Proc.*, vol. 36. Montvale, NJ: AFIPS Press, 1970, pp. 543–549.

[Robinson, 1965] Robinson, J.P. "An Upper Bound on Minimal Distance of Convolutional Code." *IEEE Trans. Info. Theory* IT-11, no. 4 (October 1965): 567–571.

[Robinson and Roubine, 1977] Robinson, L., and O. Roubine. "SECIAL—A Specification and Assertion Language." Menlo Park, CA: SRI International, 1977.

[Robinson et al., 1976] Robinson, L.; K.N. Levitt; P.G. Neuman; and A.K. Saxena. "A Formal Methodology for the Design of Operating System Software." In R.T. Yeh, ed., *Current Trends in Programming Methodology*, vol. 1. Englewood Cliffs, NJ: Prentice-Hall, 1976, pp. 61–110.

[Rolund, Beckett, and Harms, 1983] Rolund, M.W.; J.T. Beckett; and D.A. Harms. "3B20D Central Processing Unit." *Bell Sys. Tech. J.* 62, no. 1, pt. 2 (January 1983): 191–206.

[Romano, 1977] Romano, A. *Applied Statistics for Science and Industry*. Boston: Allyn and Bacon, 1977.

[Rosenthal, 1977] Rosenthal, A. "Computing the Reliability of Complex Networks." *SIAM J. Appl. Math.* 32, no. 2 (March 1977): 384–393.

[Ross, 1972] Ross, S.M. *Introduction to Probability Models*. New York: Academic Press, 1972.

[Roth, 1966] Roth, J.P. "Diagnosis of Automata Failures: A Calculus and a Method." *IBM J. Res. and Dev.* 10, no. 4 (July 1966): 278–281.

[Roth, Bouricius, and Schneider, 1967] Roth, J.P.; W.G. Bouricius; and P.R. Schneider. "Programmed Algorithms to Compute Tests to Detect and Distinguish between Failures in Logic Circuits." *IEEE Trans. Elec. Comp.* EC-16 (October 1967): 567–580.

[Roth et al., 1967] Roth, J.P.; W.G. Bouricius; W.C. Carter; and P.R. Schneider. "Phase II of an Architectural Study for a Self-Repairing Computer." SAMSO-TR-67-106. El Segundo, CA: U.S. Air Force Space and Missile Division.

[Rubin, 1967] Rubin, D.K. "The Approximate Reliability of Triply Redundant Majority-Voted Systems." In *Digest 1st Annual IEEE Comput. Conf.*, IEEE Publications, Chicago, 1967, pp. 46–49.

[Rudolph, 1967] Rudolph, L.D. "A Class of Majority Logic Decodable Codes." *IEEE Trans. Info. Theory* IT-13, no. 12 (April 1967): 305–306.

[Russel, 1978] Russel, R.M. "The CRAY-1 Computer System." *Comm. ACM* 21 (January 1978): 63–72.

[Russel, 1980] Russel, S.C. "Incoming Inspection and Test Programs." *Electronic Test* (October 1980): 46–57.

[Russell and Kime, 1971] Russell, J.D., and C.R. Kime. "Structural Factors in the Fault Diagnosis of Combinational Networks." *IEEE Trans. Comp.* C-20 (November 1971): 1276–1285.

[Russell and Tiedeman, 1979] Russell, D.L., and M.J. Tiedeman. "Multiprocess Recovery Using Conversations." In

Digest of 9th International Symposium on Fault-Tolerant Computing, IEEE Computer Society, Madison, WI, 1979, pp. 106–110.

[Russo, 1965] Russo, R.L. "Synthesis of Error-Tolerant Counters Using Minimum Distance Three State Assignments." *IEEE Trans. Elec. Comp.* EC-14 (June 1965): 359–366.

[SAE, 1986] SAE Committee S-18A. "Fault/Tolerant Analysis for Digital Systems and Equipment." *Aerospace Recommended Practice ARP-1834.* Society of Automotive Engineers, Warrendale, PA, August 1986.

[Saglietti and Ehrenberger, 1986] Saglietti, F., and W. Ehrenberger. "Software Diversity—Some Considerations about Its Benefits and Limitations." In *Proc. IFAC Workshop Safecomp 86,* Sarlat, France, October 1986.

[Sahner and Trivedi, 1987] Sahner, R.A., and K.S. Trivedi. "Reliability Modeling Using SHARPE." *IEEE Trans. Rel.* R-36, no. 2 (June 1987): 186–193.

[Saib, 1977] Saib, S.H. "Executable Assertions—An Aid to Reliable Software." In *11th Asilomar Conference on Circuits, Systems, and Computers,* Asilomar, CA, November 1977, pp. 277–281.

[Saliya and Reddy, 1974] Saliya, K.K., and S.M. Reddy. "On Minimally Testable Logic Networks." *IEEE Trans. Comp.* C-23 (November 1974): 552–554.

[Saliya and Reddy, 1975] Saliya, K.K., and S.M. Reddy. "Fault Detecting Test Sets for Reed-Muller Canonic Networks." *IEEE Trans. Comp.* C-24 (October 1975): 995–998.

[Sanders and Meyer, 1986] Sanders, W.H., and J.F. Meyer. "METASAN: A Performability Evaluation Tool Based on Stochastic Activity Networks." In Proc. 1986 Fall Joint Comput. Conf., November 2–6, 1986, pp. 807–816.

[Satyanarayana and Prabhakar, 1978] Satyanarayana, A., and A. Prabhakar. "New Topological Formula and Rapid Algorithm for Reliability Analysis of Complex Networks." *IEEE Trans. Rel.* R-17, no. 2 (June 1978): 82–100.

[Savir, 1978] Savir, J. "Testing for Intermittent Failures in Combinational Circuits by Minimizing the Mean Testing Time for a Given Test Quality." In *Proc. Third USA–Japan Computer Conf.,* AFIPS and IPSJ, 1978, pp. 155–161.

[Savir, 1980] Savir, J. "Syndrome—Testable Design of Combinational Circuits." *IEEE Trans. Comp.* C-29 (June 1980) (corrections: November 1980): 442–451.

[Savir, 1981] Savir, J. "Syndrome Testing of 'Syndrome-Untestable' Combinational Circuits." *IEEE Trans. Comp.* C-30 (August 1981): 606–608.

[Sawin, 1975] Sawin, D.H. "Design of Reliable Synchronous Sequential Circuits." *IEEE Trans. Comp.* C-24 (May 1975): 567–570.

[Schalkwijk and Kailath, 1966] Schalkwijk, J.P., and T. Kailath. "A Coding Scheme for Additive Noise Channels with Feedback—Part I: No Bandwidth Constraint." *IEEE Trans. Info. Theory* IT-12, no. 4 (April 1966): 172–188.

[Schertz and Metze, 1972] Schertz, D.R., and G. Metze. "A New Representation for Faults in Combinational Digital Circuits." *IEEE Trans. Comp.* C-21, no. 8 (August 1972): 858–866.

[Schick and Wolverton, 1978] Schick, G.J., and R.W. Wolverton. "An Analysis of Computing Software Reliability Models." *IEEE Trans. Soft. Eng.* SE-4, no. 2 (March 1978): 104–120.

[Schmid et al., 1982] Schmid, M.; R. Trapp; A. Davidoff; and G. Masson. "Upset Exposure by Means of Abstract Verification." In *Digest of 12th International Symposium on Fault-Tolerant Computing,* IEEE Computer Society, Santa Monica, CA, June 1982, pp. 237–244.

[Schmid et al., 1983] Schmid, M.E.; R.L. Trapp; G.M. Masson; and A.E. Davidoff. "Realization and Performance of Simple Program Flow Upset Monitors." The Johns Hopkins University, 1983.

[Schneider, 1967] Schneider, P.R. "On the Necessity to Examine D-Chains in Diagnostic Test Generation—An Example." *IBM J. Res. and Dev.,* no. 11 (November 1967): 114.

[Schneider, 1974] Schneider, D. "Designing Logic Boards for Automatic Testing." *Electronics International* 47, no. 15 (July 1974).

[Schneidewind, 1975] Schneidewind, N.F. "Analysis of Error Processes in Computer Software." In *Pro. Int. Conf. Reliable Software,* IEEE, 1975, pp. 337–346.

[Schnurmann, Lindbloom, and Carpenter, 1975] Schnurmann, H.D.; E. Lindbloom; and R.G. Carpenter. "The Weighted Random Test Pattern Generation." *IEEE Trans. Comp.* C-24, no. 7 (July 1975): 695–700.

[Schriefer, Voges, and Weber, 1983] Schriefer, D.; U. Voges; and G. Weber. "Design and Construction of a Reliable Microcomputer-Based LMFBR Protection System." *International Atomic Energy Agency,* IAEA-SM-265/21, Vienna, 1983.

[Schuette and Shen, 1987] Schuette, M.A., and J.P. Shen. "Processor Control Flow Monitoring Using Signatured Instruction Streams." *IEEE Trans. Comp.* C-36(3) (March 1987): 264–276.

[Schuette et al., 1986] Schuette, M.A.; J.P. Shen; D.P. Siewiorek; and Y.X. Zhu. "Experimental Evaluation of Two Concurrent Error Detection Schemes." In *Proceedings of 16th International Symposium on Fault-Tolerant Computing,* Vienna, Austria, July 1986, pp. 138–143.

[Schulze et al., 1989] Schulze, M.; G. Gibson; R. Katz; and D. Patterson. "How Reliable Is a RAID?" In *Proceedings of COMPCON*, 1989, pp. 118–123.

[Sedmak and Liebergot, 1978] Sedmak, R.M., and H.L. Liebergot. "Fault Tolerance of a General Purpose Computer Implemented by Very Large Scale Integrating." In *Digest of 8th International Symposium on Fault-Tolerant Computing*, IEEE Computer Society, Toulouse, France, 1978, pp. 137–143.

[Sedmak and Liebergot, 1980] Sedmak, R.M., and H.L. Liebergot. "Fault Tolerance of a General Purpose Computer Implemented by Very Large Scale Integrating." *IEEE Trans. Comp.* C-29 (June 1980): 492–500.

[Segall et al., 1988] Segall, Z.; D. Vrsalovic; D. Siewiorek; D. Yaskin; J. Kownacki; J. Barton; B. Dancey; A. Robinson; and T. Lin. "FIAT-Fault Injection Based Automated Testing Environment." In *18th International Symposium on Fault-Tolerant Computing*, IEEE Computer Society, Toyko, Japan, 1988, pp. 102–107.

[Seley and Vigilante, 1964] Seley, E.L., and F.S. Vigilante. "Common Control—For an Electronic Private Branch Exchange." *IEEE Trans. Comm. Electron.* 83, no. 73 (July 1964): 321–329.

[Sellers, 1962] Sellers, E.F. "Bit Loss and Gain Correction Code." *IEEE Trans. Info. Theory* IT-8, no. 1 (January 1962): 36–38.

[Sellers, Hsiao, and Bearnson, 1968a] Sellers, E.F.; M.Y Hsiao; and L.W. Bearnson. "Analyzing Errors with the Boolean Difference." *IEEE Trans. Comp.* C-17 (July 1968): 676–683.

[Sellers, Hsiao, and Bearnson, 1968b] Sellers, E.F.; M.Y. Hsiao; and L.W. Bearnson. *Error Detecting Logic for Digital Computers*. New York: McGraw-Hill, 1968.

[Seraphim, 1982] Seraphim, D.P. "A New Set of Printed-Circuit Technologies for the IBM 3081 Processor Unit." *IBM J. Res. and Dev.* 26, no. 1 (January 1982): 37–44.

[Seshu, 1965] Seshu, S. "On an Improved Diagnosis Program." *IEEE Trans. Electron. Comput.* EC-14, no. 1 (February 1965): 76–79.

[Seshu and Freeman, 1962] Seshu, S., and D.N. Freeman. "The Diagnosis of Asynchronous Sequential Switching Systems. *IRE Trans. Elec. Comp.* EC-11, no. 8 (August 1962): 459–465.

[Shannon, 1948] Shannon, C.E. "A Mathematical Theory of Communications." *Bell Sys. Tech. J.* 27, no. 3 (July 1948): 379–423, 623–656.

[Shannon, 1959] Shannon, C.E. "Probability of Error for Optimal Codes in a Gaussian Channel." *Bell Sys. Tech. J.* 38 (May 1959): 611–656.

[Shedletsky, 1975] Shedletsky, J.J. "A Rationale for the Random Testing of Combinational Digital Circuits." In *Dig. Papers, CompCon 75 Fall Meet*, Washington, DC, September 9–11, 1975, pp. 5–9.

[Shedletsky, 1978a] Shedletsky, J.J. "Error Correction by Alternative Data Retry." *IEEE Trans. Comp.* C-27 (February 1978): 106–112.

[Shedletsky, 1978b] Shedletsky, J.J. "A Rollback Interval for Networks with an Imperfect Self Checking Property." *IEEE Trans. Comp.* C-27 (June 1978): 500–508.

[Shedletsky and McCluskey, 1975] Shedletsky, J.J., and E.J. McCluskey. "The Error Latency of a Fault in a Combinatorial, Digital Circuit." In *Digest of 5th International Symposium on Fault-Tolerant Computing*, IEEE Computer Society, Paris, France, 1975, pp. 210–314.

[Shedletsky and McCluskey, 1976] Shedletsky, J.J., and E.J. McCluskey. "The Error Latency of a Fault in a Sequential Circuit." *IEEE Trans. Comp.* C-25 (June 1976): 655–659.

[Shen and Hayes, 1980] Shen, J.P., and J.P. Hayes. "Fault Tolerance of a Class of Connecting Architecture." In *Proc. Seventh Ann. Symp. on Computer Architecture*. La Boule, France: IEEE Press, 1980, pp. 61–71.

[Shen, Maly, and Ferguson, 1985] Shen, J.P.; W. Maly; and F.J. Ferguson. "Inductive Fault Analysis of MOS Integrated Circuits." *IEEE Design and Test of Computers* 2(6) (December 1985): 13–26.

[Shen and Schuette, 1983] Shen, J.P., and M.A. Schuette. "On-Line Monitoring Using Signatured Instruction Streams." *IEEE Proc. 13th Int'l. Test Conference*, October 1983, pp. 275–282.

[Shimeall and Leveson, 1988] Shimeall, T.J., and N.G. Leveson. "An Empirical Comparison of Software Fault Tolerance and Fault Elimination." *Second Workshop on Software Testing, Verification, and Analysis*, Baniff, Canada, July 1988.

[Shin and Lee, 1986] Shin, K.G., and Y.H. Lee. "Measurement and Application of Fault Latency." *IEEE Trans. Comp.* C-35(4) (April 1986): 370–375.

[Shooman, 1968] Shooman, M.L. *Probabilistic Reliability: An Engineering Approach*. New York: McGraw-Hill, 1968.

[Shooman, 1970] Shooman, M.L. "The Equivalence of Reliability Diagrams and Fault-Tree Analysis." *IEEE Trans. Rel.* R-19, no. 2 (May 1970): 74–75.

[Shooman, 1973] Shooman, M.L. "Operational Testing and Software Reliability Estimation During Program Development." In *Record, IEEE Symposium on Computer Software Reliability*, 1973, pp. 51–57.

[Shooman, 1990] Shooman, M.L. *Probabilistic Reliability: An Engineering Approach*, Second Edition. Melbourne, FL: Robert E. Krieger, 1990.

[Short, 1968] Short, R.A. "The Attainment of Reliable Digital Systems through the Use of Redundancy: A Survey." *IEEE Computer Group News* 2 (March 1968): 2–17.

[Shostak, 1977] Shostak, R.E. "Proving the Reliability of a Fault-Tolerant Computer System." In *Proc. 14th Comput. Soc. Int. Conf.*, 1977.

[Shrivastava and Akinpelu, 1978] Shrivastava, S.K., and Akinpelu, A.A. "Fault-Tolerant Sequential Programming Using Recovery Blocks." In *Digest of 8th International Symposium on Fault-Tolerant Computing*, IEEE Computer Society, Toulouse, France, 1978, p. 207.

[Siewiorek, 1975] Siewiorek, D.P. "Reliability Modeling of Compensating Module Failures in Majority Voted Redundancy." *IEEE Trans. Comp.* C-24 (May 1975): 525–533.

[Siewiorek, 1977] Siewiorek, D.P. "Multiprocessors: Reliability Modeling and Graceful Degradation." In *Infotech State of Art Conference on System Reliability*. London: Infotech International Ltd., 1977, pp. 48–73.

[Siewiorek, 1984] Siewiorek, D.P. "Architecture of Fault-Tolerant Computers." *Computer*, vol. 17, no. 8 (August 1984): pp. 9–18.

[Siewiorek, 1990] Siewiorek, D.P. "Fault Tolerance in Commercial Computers." *Computer*, vol. 23, no. 7 (July 1990): 26–37.

[Siewiorek, 1991] Siewiorek, D.P. "Architecture of Fault-Tolerant Computers: An Historical Perspective." *Proceedings of the IEEE*, vol. 79, no. 12 (December 1991): 1710–1734.

[Siewiorek, Bell, and Newell, 1982] Siewiorek, D.P.; C.G. Bell; and A. Newell. *Computer Structures: Principles and Examples*. New York: McGraw-Hill, 1982.

[Siewiorek, Canepa, and Clark, 1976] Siewiorek, D.P.; M. Canepa; and S. Clark. "C.vmp: The Analysis, Architecture, and Implementation of a Fault Tolerant Multiprocessor." Technical Report Carnegie-Mellon University Departments of Electrical Engineering and Computer Science, Pittsburgh, PA.

[Siewiorek, Canepa, and Clark, 1977] Siewiorek, D.P.; M. Canepa; and S. Clark. "C.vmp: The Architecture and Implementation of a Fault-Tolerant Multiprocessor." In *Proceedings of 7th International Symposium on Fault-Tolerant Computing*, IEEE Computer Society, Los Angeles, CA, 1977, pp. 37–43.

[Siewiorek and Lai, 1981] Siewiorek, D.P., and Larry K.W. Lai. "Testing of Digital Systems." *Proceedings of the IEEE*, vol. 69, no. 10 (October, 1981): pp. 1321–1333.

[Siewiorek and McCluskey, 1973a] Siewiorek, D.P., and E.J. McCluskey. "Switch Complexity in Systems with Hybrid Redundancy." *IEEE Trans. Comp.* C-22 (March 1973): 276–282.

[Siewiorek and McCluskey, 1973b] Siewiorek, D.P., and E.J. McCluskey. "An Iterative Cell Switch Design for Hybrid Redundancy." *IEEE Trans. Comp.* C-22 (March 1973): 290–297.

[Siewiorek and Rennels, 1980] Siewiorek, D.P., and D. Rennels. "Workshop Report: Fault-Tolerant VLSI Design." *Computer* (December 1980): 51–53.

[Siewiorek and Swarz, 1981] Siewiorek, D.P., and R. Swarz. "Reliability and Maintainability Features in the VAX-11/750," *11th International Symposium on Fault-Tolerant Computing*, Portland, ME, June, 1981.

[Siewiorek and Swarz, 1982] Siewiorek, D.P., and R.S. Swarz. *The Theory and Practice of Reliable System Design*. Bedford, MA: Digital Press, Digital Equipment Corporation, 1982.

[Siewiorek et al., 1978a] Siewiorek, D.P.; V. Kini; H. Mashburn; S.R. McConnel; and M.M. Tsao. "A Case Study of C.mmp, Cm*, and C.vmp: Part I—Experiences with Fault Tolerance in Multiprocessor Systems." In *Proceedings of the IEEE* 66 (October 1978): 1178–1199.

[Siewiorek et al., 1978b] Siewiorek, D.P.; V. Kini; R. Joobbani; and H. Bellis. "A Case Study of C.mmp, Cm*, and C.vmp: Part II—Predicting and Calibrating Reliability of Multiprocessor Systems." In *Proceedings of the IEEE* 66 (October 1978): 1200–1220.

[Signetics, 1975] Signetics Product Reliability Report R363, June 1975, Signetics Corporation, Sunnyvale, CA.

[Sih and Hsiao, 1966] Sih, K.Y., and M.Y. Hsiao. "Cyclic Codes in Multiple Channel Parallel Systems." *IEEE Trans. Elec. Com.* EC-15 (December 1966): 927–930.

[Silberman and Spillinger, 1986] Silberman, G.M., and I. Spillinger. "The Difference Fault Model Using Functional Fault Simulation to Obtain Implementation Fault Coverage." In *International Test Conference*, 1986, pp. 332–339.

[Sklaroff, 1976] Sklaroff, J.R. "Redundancy Management Technique for Space Shuttle Computers." *IBM J. Res. and Dev.* 20, no. 1 (January 1976): 20–28.

[Slepian, 1956] Slepian, D. "A Class of Binary Signalling Alphabets." *Bell Sys. Tech. J.* 35 (January 1956): 203–234.

[Smith, 1972] Smith, D.J. *Reliability Engineering*. New York: Barnes and Noble, 1972.

[Smith, 1975] Smith, T.B., III. "A Damage- and Fault-Tolerant Input/Output Network." *IEEE Trans. Comp.* C-24 (May 1975): 506–512.

[Smith and Andrews, 1981] Smith, W.B., and F.T. Andrews. "No. 5ESS™ Overview." In *Proceedings of the 10th International Switching Symposium*, Montreal, Canada, September 1981.

[Smith and Hopkins, 1978] Smith, T.B., III, and A.L. Hopkins, Jr. "Architectural Description of a Fault-Tolerant Multiprocessor Engineering Prototype." In *Digest of 8th International Symposium on Fault-Tolerant Computing*, IEEE Computer Society, Toulouse, France, 1978, p. 194.

[Smith and Metze, 1978] Smith, J.E., and G. Metze. "Strongly Fault Secure Logic Networks." *IEEE Trans. Comp.* C-27 (June 1978): 491–499.

[Snow and Siewiorek, 1978] Snow, E., and D.P. Siewiorek. "Impact of Implementation Design Tradeoffs on Performance.: The PDP-11, A Case Study." In C.G. Bell, J.C. Mudge, and J.E. McNamara, eds., *Computer Engineering: A DEC View of Hardware Design*. Bedford, MA: Digital Press, 1978, pp. 327–364.

[Snyder, 1975] Snyder, D.L. *Random Point Processes*. New York: Wiley, 1975.

[Sohi, Franklin, and Saluja, 1989] Sohi, G.S.; M. Franklin; and K.K. Saluja. "A Study of Time-Redundant Fault Tolerance Techniques for High-Performance Pipelined Computers." In *Proceedings of 19th International Symposium on Fault-Tolerant Computing*, Chicago, IL, June 1989, pp. 436–443.

[Solberg, 1975] Solberg, J.J. "A Graph Theoretic Formula for the Steady State Distribution of Finite Markov Processes." *Management Science* 21(9) (May 1975): 1040–1048.

[Spencer and Vigilante, 1969] Spencer, A.E., and F.S. Vigilante. "No. 2 ESS—System Organization and Objectives." *Bell Sys. Tech. J.* 48 (October 1969): 2607–2618.

[Sperry, 1979] Sperry Univac Corporation. "The Microarchitecture of Univac's 1100/60." *Datamation* (July 1979): 173–178.

[Spillman, 1977] Spillman, R.J. "A Markov Model of Intermittent Faults in Digital Systems." In *Digest of 7th International Symposium on Fault-Tolerant Computing*, IEEE Computer Society, Los Angeles, CA, 1977, pp. 157–161.

[Sridhar and Thatte, 1982] Sridhar, T., and S.M. Thatte. "Concurrent Checking of Program Flow in VLSI Processors." In *Digest of the 1982 International Test Conference*, IEEE, 1982, paper 9.2, pp. 191–199.

[Srinivasan, 1971a] Srinivasan, C.V. "Codes for Error Correction in High-Speed Memory Systems, Part I: Correction of Cell Defects in Integrated Memories." *IEEE Trans. Comp.* C-20 (August 1971): 882–888.

[Srinivasan, 1971b] Srinivasan, C.V. "Codes for Error Correction in High-Speed Memory Systems, Part II: Correction of Temporary and Catastrophic Errors." *IEEE Trans. Comp.* C-20 (December 1971): 1514–1520.

[Staehler, 1977] Staehler, R.E. "1A Processor—Organizations and Objectives." *Bell Sys. Tech. J.* 56, no. 2 (February 1977): 119–134.

[Staehler and Watters, 1976] Staehler, R.E., and R.J. Watters. "1A Processor—An Ultra-Dependable Common Control." In *Int. Switching Symp. Record*, Japan, 1976.

[Stapper, 1973] Stapper, C.H. "Defect Density Distribution for LSI Yield Calculations." *IEEE Trans. Elec. Devices* ED-20 (July 1973): 655–657.

[Stephenson and Grason, 1976] Stephenson, J.E., and J. Grason. "A Testability Measure for Register Transfer Level Digital Circuits." In *Proceedings of 6th International Symposium on Fault-Tolerant Computing*, IEEE Computer Society, Pittsburgh, PA, June 1976, pp. 101–107.

[Stewart, 1977] Stewart, J.H. "Future Testing of Large LSI Circuit Cards." In *IEEE Digest of Papers, 1977 Semiconductor Test Symposium*, Cherry Hill, NJ, 1977, pp. 6–15.

[Stewart, 1978] Stewart, J.H. "Application of Scan Set for Error Detection and Diagnostics." In *IEEE Digest of Papers, 1978 Semiconductor Test Conference*, Cherry Hill, NJ, 1978, pp. 152–158.

[Stiffler, 1976] Stiffler, J.J. "Architectural Design for Near-100% Fault Coverage." In *Digest of 6th International Symposium on Fault-Tolerant Computing*, IEEE Computer Society, Pittsburgh, PA, 1976.

[Stiffler, 1978] Stiffler, J.J. "Coding for Random-Access Memories." *IEEE Trans. Comp.* C-27 (June 1978): 526–531.

[Stiffler, Bryant, and Guccione, 1979] Stiffler, J.J.; L.A. Bryant; and L. Guccione. "CARE III Final Report: Phase One." NASA Langley Research Center, NASA Contractor Report 159122. Langley, VA: 1979.

[Stiffler and Van Doren, 1979] Stiffler, J.J., and A.H. Van Doren. "FTSC—Fault Tolerant Spaceborne Computer." In *9th International Symposium on Fault-Tolerant Computing*, IEEE Computer Society, Madison, WI, 1979, p. 143.

[Stonebraker and Schloss, 1990] Stonebraker, M., and G. Schloss. "Distributed RAID—A New Multiple Copy Algorithm." In *Conference on Data Engineering*, 1990, pp. 430–437.

[Storey, 1976] Storey, T.F. "Design of a Microprogram Control for a Processor in an Electronic Switching System." *Bell Sys. Tech. J.*, no. 2 (February 1976): 183–232.

[Storey and Barry, 1977] Storey, T.M., and J.W. Barry. "Delay Test Simulation." In *Proc. 14th Design Automation Conf.*, IEEE, June 1977, pp. 491–494.

[Strecker, 1978] Strecker, W.D. "VAX-11/780—A Virtual Address Extension to the DEC PDP-11 Family." NCC AFIPS Proceedings, vol. 47. Montvale, NJ: AFIPS Press, 1978, pp. 967–980.

[Strini, 1978] Strini, V.P. "Fault Location in a Semiconductor Random Access Memory Unit." *IEEE Trans. Comp.* C-27, no. 4 (April 1978): 379–385.

[Sturges, 1926] Sturges. "The Choice of a Class Interval." *J. Amer. Statistical Association* 21 (1926): 65–66.

[Su, Koren, and Malaiya, 1978] Su, S.Y.H.; I. Koren; and Y.K. Malaiya. "A Continuous-Parameter Markov Model and Detection Procedures for Intermittent Faults." *IEEE Trans. Comp.* C-27 (June 1978): 567–570.

[Su and Lin, 1984] Su, S.Y.H., and T. Lin. "Functional Testing Techniques for Digital LSI/VLSI Devices." In *21st Design Automation Conference*, IEEE, 1984, pp. 517–528.

[Sundberg, 1978] Sundberg, C.-E.W. "Erasure and Error Decoding for Semiconductor Memories." *IEEE Trans. Comp.* C-27 (August 1978): 696–705.

[Susskind, 1972] Susskind, A.K. "Additional Applications of the Boolean Difference to Fault Detection and Diagnosis." In *Digest of 2nd International Symposium on Fault-Tolerant Computing*, IEEE Computer Society, Boston, MA, 1972, pp. 58–61.

[Susskind, 1973] Susskind, A.K. "Diagnostics for Logic Networks." *IEEE Spectrum* 10 (October 1973): 40–47.

[Susskind, 1981] Susskind, A.K. "Testing by Verifying Walsh Coefficients." In *Proc. 11th Ann. Symp. on Fault-Tolerant Computing*, Portland, ME, June 1981, pp. 206–208.

[Swan, 1977] Swan, R.J. "The Switching Structure and Addressing Architecture of an Extensible Multiprocessor: The Cm*." Ph.D. Diss., Carnegie-Mellon University, Pittsburgh, PA, 1977.

[Swan, Fuller, and Siewiorek, 1977] Swan, R.J.; S.H. Fuller; and D.P. Siewiorek. "Cm*—A Modular Multi-Microprocessor." In *AFIPS Conf. Proc.*, vol. 46. Montvale, NJ: AFIPS Press, 1977, pp. 637–644.

[Szygenda, 1972] Szygenda, S.A. "TEGAS2—Anatomy of a General Purpose Test Generation and Simulation System for Digital Logic." In *Proc. 9th Design Automation Workshop*, 1972, pp. 116–127.

[Szygenda, Rouse, and Thompson, 1970] Szygenda, S.A.; D.M. Rouse; and E.W. Thompson. "A Model for Implementation of a Universal Time Delay Simulation for Large Digital Networks." In *AFIPS Conf. Proc.*, vol. 36, 1970, pp. 207–216.

[Szygenda and Thompson, 1976] Szygenda, S.A., and E.W. Thompson. "Modeling and Digital Simulation for Design Verification Diagnosis." *IEEE Trans. Comp.* C-25, no. 12 (December 1976): 1242–1253.

[Tamir, Tremblay, and Rennels, 1988] Tamir, Y.; M. Tremblay; and D.A. Rennels. "The Implementation and Ap-plication of Micro Rollback in Fault-Tolerant VLSI Systems." In *Digest of 18th International Symposium on Fault-Tolerant Computing*, IEEE Computer Society, Tokyo, Japan, June 1988, pp. 234–239.

[Tammaru and Angell, 1967] Tammaru, E., and J.B. Angell. "Redundancy for LSI Yield Enhancement." *IEEE J. Solid-State Circuits* SC-2 (December 1967): 172–182.

[Tandem, 1976] Tandem Computers. *Tandem/16 System Description*. Cupertino, CA: 1976.

[Tandem, 1985] Tandem Computers. *Introduction to PATHWAY*. Cupertino, CA: 1985.

[Tandem, 1987] Tandem Computers. *EXPAND Reference Manual*. Cupertino, CA: 1987.

[Tandem Database Group, 1988] Tandem Database Group. "NonStop SQL, A Distributed High Performance, High Availability Implementation of SQL." In D. Gawlick, ed., *Proceedings of 2nd High Performance Transaction Processing Workshop*. New York: Springer Verlag, 1989.

Tandem Performance Group, 1988] Tandem Performance Group. "A Benchmark of NonStop SQL on the Debit-Credit Transaction." SIGMOD 88, ACM, June 1988.

[Tang, 1965] Tang, D.T. "Dual Codes Are Variable Redundancy Codes." In *IEEE International Convention Record* 13 (1965): 220–226.

[Tang and Chien, 1966] Tang, D.T., and R.T. Chien. "Cyclic Product Codes and Their Implementation." *Information and Control* 9, no. 2 (April 1966): 196–209.

[Tang and Chien, 1969] Tang, D.T., and R.T. Chien. "Coding for Error Control." *IBM Sys. J.* 8, no. 1 (1969): 48–85.

[Tao, Lala, and Hartmann, 1987] Tao, D.L.; P.K. Lala; and C.R.P. Hartmann. "Three-Level Totally Self-Checking Checker for 1-out-of-n Code." In *Digest of 17th International Symposium on Fault-Tolerant Computing*, IEEE Computer Society, Pittsburgh, PA, July 1987, pp. 108–113.

[Tasar and Tasar, 1977] Tasar, O., and V. Tasar. "A Study of Intermittent Faults in Digital Computers." In *AFIPS Conf. Proc.*, vol. 46. Montvale, NJ: AFIPS Press, 1977, pp. 807–811.

[Taylor, Morgan, and Black, 1980] Taylor, D.J.; D.E. Morgan; and J.P. Black. "Redundancy in Data Structures: Improving Software Fault Tolerance." *IEEE Trans. Soft. Eng.* SE-6, no. 6 (November 1980): 585–594.

[Tendolkar and Swann, 1982] Tendolkar, N.N., and R.L. Swann. "Automated Diagnostic Methodology for the IBM 3081 Processor Complex." *IBM J. Res. and Dev.* 26, no. 1 (January 1982): 78–88.

[Téoste, 1962] Teoste, R. "Design of a Repairable Redundant Computer." *IRE Trans. Elec. Comp.* C-11 (October 1962): 643–649.

[Teoste, 1964] Teoste, R. "Digital Circuit Redundancy." *IEEE Trans. Rel.* R-13, no. 3 (June 1964): 42–61.

[Texas, 1976] Texas Instruments. *The TTL Data Book for Design Engineers*, 2d. ed. Dallas, Texas, 1976.

[Texas, n.d.] Texas Instruments. *Preliminary Reliability Report for TI Series TMS4030, TMS4050, TMS4060 4K RAMS*. Bulletin CR-112. Dallas, TX, n.d.

[Thatte and Abraham, 1978] Thatte, S.M., and J.A. Abraham. "A Methodology for Functional Level Testing of Microprocessors." In *Digest of 8th International Symposium on Fault-Tolerant Computing*, IEEE Computer Society, Toulouse, France, 1978, pp. 90–95.

[Thatte and Abraham, 1979] Thatte, S, and J. Abraham. "Test Generation for General Microprocessor Architectures." In *9th International Symposium on Fault-Tolerant Computing*, IEEE Computer Society, Madison, WI, 1979, pp. 203–210.

[Thatte and Abraham, 1980] Thatte, S.M., and J.A. Abraham. "Test Generation for Microprocessor." *IEEE Trans. Comp.* C-29(6) (June 1980): 429–441.

[Thayer, Lipow, and Nelson, 1978] Thayer, T.A.; M. Lipow; and E.C. Nelson. *Software Reliability*. New York: North-Holland, 1978.

[Thoman, Bain, and Antle, 1969] Thoman, D.R.; L.J. Bain; and C.E. Antle. "Inferences on the Parameters of the Weibull Distribution." *Technometrics* 11, no. 3 (August 1969): 445–460.

[Thompson and Ritchie, 1974] Thompson, K., and D.M. Ritchie. "The UNIX Time-Sharing System." *Comm. ACM* 17 (July 1974): 365–375.

[Timoc et al., 1983] Timoc, C.; M. Buehler; T. Griswold; C. Pina; F. Scott; and L. Hess. "Logical Models of Physical Failures." In *International Test Conference*, 1983, pp. 546–553.

[To, 1973] To, K. "Fault Folding for Irredundant and Redundant Combinational Circuits." *IEEE Trans. Comp.* C-22, no. 11 (November 1973): 1008–1015.

[Tohma, 1974] Tohma, Y. "Design Technique of Fail-Safe Sequential Circuits Using Flip-Flops for Internal Memory." *IEEE Trans. Comp.* C-23 (November 1974): 1149–1154.

[Tohma and Aoyagi, 1968] Tohma, Y., and S. Aoyagi. "Failure-Tolerant Sequential Machines Using Past Information." *Electronics and Communications in Japan* 51-C, no. 11 (1968): 95–101. Also *IEEE Trans. Comp.* C-20 (April 1971): 392–396.

[Tohma and Aoyagi, 1971] Tohma, Y., and S. Aoyagi. "Failure-Tolerant Sequential Machines with Past Information." *IEEE Trans. Comp.* C-20 (April 1971): 392–396.

[Tohma, Ohyama, and Sakai, 1971] Tohma, Y.; Y. Ohyama; and R. Sakai. "Realization of Fail-Safe Sequential Machines Using a k-out-of-n Code." *IEEE Trans. Comp.* C-20 (November 1971): 1270–1275.

[Tokura, Kasami, and Hashimoto, 1971] Tokura, N.; T. Kasami; and A. Hashimoto. "Fail-Safe Logic Nets." *IEEE Trans. Comp.* C-20 (March 1971): 323–330.

[Tom, 1988] Tom, G. "Tandem's Subsystem Programmatic Interface." *Tandem Systems Review*, vol. 4.3, 1988.

[Tong, 1966] Tong, S.Y. "Synchronization Recovery Techniques for Binary Cyclic Codes." *Bell Sys. Tech. J.* 45 (April 1966): 561–596.

[TOPS, 1970] "TOPS Outer Planet Spacecraft." *Astronautics and Aeronautics* 8 (September 1970).

[Torng, 1972] Torng, H.C. *Switching Circuits: Theory and Logic Design*. Reading, MA: Addison-Wesley, 1972.

[Toth and Holt, 1974] Toth, A., and C. Holt. "Automated Data-Based Driven Digital Testing." *Computer* (January 1974): 13–19.

[Toy, 1978] Toy, W.N. "Fault-Tolerant Design of Local ESS Processors." *Proceedings of the IEEE* 66 (October 1978): 1126–1145.

[Toy and Gallaher, 1983] Toy, W.N., and L.E. Gallaher. "Overview and Architecture of 3B20D Processor." *Bell Sys. Tech. J.* 62, no. 1, pt. 2 (January 1983): 181–190.

[Trivedi, 1982] Trivedi, K. *Probability and Statistics with Reliability, Queuing, and Computer Science Applications*. Englewood Cliffs, NJ: Prentice-Hall, 1982.

[Trivedi and Shooman, 1975] Trivedi, A.K., and M.L. Shooman. "A Many-State Markov Model for the Estimation and Prediction of Computer Software Performance." In *Proc. Int. Conf. on Reliable Software*, IEEE Computer Society, Los Angeles, CA, 1975, pp. 208–220.

[Troisi, 1985] Troisi, J. "Introducing TMDS, Tandem's New On-line Diagnostic System." *Tandem Systems Review*, vol. 1.2 (June 1985): 98–105.

[Troy, 1977] Troy, R. "Dynamic Reconfiguration: An Algorithm and Its Efficiency Evaluation." In *Digest of 7th International Symposium on Fault-Tolerant Computing*, IEEE Computer Society, Los Angeles, CA, 1977, pp. 44–49.

[Troy, 1978] Troy, R. "Rollback Model for Interactive Processes." In *Digest of 8th International Symposium on Fault-Tolerant Computing*, IEEE Computer Society, Toulouse, France, 1978.

[Tryon, 1962] Tryon, J.G. "Quadded Logic." In R.H. Wilcox and W.C. Mann, eds., *Redundancy Techniques for Computing Systems*. Washington, DC: Spartan Books, 1962, pp. 205–228.

[Tsao, 1978] Tsao, M.M. "A Study of Transient Errors on Cm*." Master's report, Carnegie-Mellon University, 1978.

[Tsao, 1982] Tsao, M.M. "A PDP-8 Implementation AMD Bit-Sized Microprocessors." In D.P. Siewiorek; C.G. Bell; and A. Newell, *Computer Structures: Principles and Examples.* New York: McGraw-Hill, 1982, pp. 219–226.

[Tsao, 1983] Tsao, M.M. *Trend Analysis and Fault Prediction.* Ph.D. Diss., Department of Electrical and Computer Engineering, Carnegie-Mellon University, Pittsburgh, PA, 1983.

[Tsao and Siewiorek, 1983] Tsao, M., and D.P. Siewiorek. "Trend Analysis on System Error Files." *13th International Fault-Tolerant Computing Symposium,* Milan, Italy, June, 1983.

[Tsao et al., 1982] Tsao, M.; A. Wilson; R. McGarity; C.-J. Tseng; and D.P. Siewiorek. "Design of a C.fast: A Single Chip Fault-Tolerant Microprocessor." *12th Fault-Tolerant Computing Symposium,* Santa Monica, CA, June, 1982.

[Tsiang and Ulrich, 1962] Tsiang, S.H., and W. Ulrich. "Automatic Trouble Diagnosis of Complex Logic Circuits." *Bell Sys. Tech. J.* (July 1962).

[Tso and Avizienis, 1987] Tso, K., and A. Avizienis. "Community Error Recovery in N-Version Software." In *17th International Symposium on Fault-Tolerant Computing,* IEEE Computer Society, Pittsburgh, PA, July 1987, pp. 127–133.

[Tsybakov, 1975] Tsybakov, B.S. "Defects and Error Correction." *Problemy Peredachi Informatsii* 11 (1975): 21–30.

[Turin, 1965] Turin, G.L. "Signal Design for Sequential Detection Systems with Feedback." *IEEE Trans. Info. Theory* IT-11, no. 7 (July 1965): 401–408.

[Ullman, 1966] Ullman, J.D. "Near-Optional, Single-Synchronization-Error-Correcting Code." *IEEE Trans. Info. Theory* IT-12, no. 4 (October 1966): 418–425.

[Ulrich and Baker, 1973] Ulrich, E.G., and T. Baker. "The Concurrent Simulation of Nearly Identical Digital Networks." In *Proc. 10th Design Automation Workshop,* June 1973, pp. 145–150.

[Ulrich and Baker, 1974] Ulrich, E.G., and T. Baker. "Concurrent Simulation of Nearly Identical Digital Networks." *Computer* 7, no. 4 (April 1974): 39–44.

[Ulrich, Baker, and Williams, 1972] Ulrich, E.G.; T. Baker; and L.R. Williams. "Fault Test Analysis Techniques Based on Simulation." In *Proc. 9th Design Automation Workshop,* 1972, pp. 111–115.

[Uren, 1986] Uren, S. "Message System Performance Tests." *Tandem Systems Review,* vol. 3.4, December 1986.

[U.S., 1965] U.S. Department of Defense. *Military Standardization Handbook: Reliability Prediction of Electronic Equipment.* MIL-HDBK-217, 1965.

[U.S., 1974] U.S. Department of Defense. *Military Standardization Handbook: Reliability Prediction of Electronic Equipment.* MIL-HDBK-217B, 1974.

[U.S., 1976] U.S. Department of Defense. *Military Standardization Handbook: Reliability Prediction of Electronic Equipment.* MIL-STD-HDBK-217B, Notice 1, 1976.

[U.S., 1979] U.S. Department of Defense. *Military Standardization Handbook: Reliability Prediction of Electronic Equipment.* MIL-HDBK-217C, 1979.

[U.S., 1980] U.S. Department of Defense. *Military Standardization Handbook: Reliability Prediction of Electronic Equipment.* MIL-HDBK-217C, Notice 1, 1980.

[U.S., 1986a] U.S. Department of Defense. "Reliability/ Design, Thermal Applications." MIL-HDBK-251, January 19, 1978.

[U.S., 1986b] U.S. Department of Defense. "Military Standard: Reliability Testing for Engineering Development, Qualification, and Production." MIL-STD-78ID, 1986.

[Usas, 1978] Usas, A.M. "Checksum Versus Residue Codes for Multiple Error Detection." In *Digest of 8th International Symposium on Fault-Tolerant Computing,* IEEE Computer Society, Toulouse, France, p. 224.

[U.S. Patent, 1977a] U.S. Patent No. 4 015 246. "Synchronous Fault-Tolerant Multiprocessor System." Washington, DC, 1977.

[U.S. Patent, 1977b] U.S. Patent No. 4 035 766. Washington, DC, 1977.

[VAX 8600/8650, 1986] "System Description and Processor Overview, EK-KA 86S-TD-002." Bedford, MA: Digital Equipment Corporation, 1986.

[Voges, 1985] Voges, U. "Application of a Fault-Tolerant Microprocessor-Based Core-Surveillance System in a German Fast Breeder Reactor." *EPRI-Conference,* Phoenix, AZ, April 1985, pp. 9–12.

[Voges, Fetsch, and Gmeiner, 1982] Voges, U.; F. Fetsch; and L. Gmeiner. "Use of Microprocessors in a Safety-Oriented Reactor Shut-Down System." In E. Lauger and J. Moltoft, eds., *Reliability in Electrical and Electronic Components and Systems.* New York: North-Holland, 1982.

[von Alven, 1964] von Alven, W.H., ed. *Reliability Engineering.* Englewood Cliffs, NJ: Prentice-Hall, 1964.

[von Neumann, 1956] von Neumann, J. "Probabilistic Logics and the Synthesis of Reliable Organisms from Unreliable Components." In C.E. Shannon and J. McCarthy, eds., *Automata Studies*. Princeton: Princeton University Press, 1956, pp. 43–98.

[**Vouk et al., 1986**] Vouk, M., et al. "On Testing of Functionally Equivalent Components of Fault-Tolerant Software." *IEEE 10th International Computer Software and Application Conference*, 1986.

[**Wachter, 1975**] Wachter, W.J. "System Malfunction Detection and Correction." In *Digest of 5th International Symposium on Fault-Tolerant Computing*, IEEE Computer Society, Paris, France, 1975, pp. 196–201.

[**Wadsack, 1978**] Wadsack, R.L. "Fault Modeling and Logic Simulation of CMOS and MOS Integrated Circuits." *Bell Sys. Tech. J.* 57(5) (May–June 1978): 1449–1473.

[**Wakerly, 1974**] Wakerly, J. "Partially Self-Checking Circuits and Their Use in Performing Logical Operations." *IEEE Trans. Comp.* C-23 (July 1974): 658–666.

[**Wakerly, 1976**] Wakerly, J. "Microcomputer Reliability Improvement Using Triple-Modular Redundancy." In *Proceedings of the IEEE* 64 (June 1976): 889–895.

[**Wakerly, 1978**] Wakerly, J. *Error Detecting Codes, Self-Checking Circuits and Applications*. New York: North-Holland, 1978.

[**Waksman, 1968**] Waksman, A. "A Permutation Network." *J. ACM* 15, no. 1 (January 1968): 159–163.

[**Wallace and Barnes, 1984**] Wallace, J.J., and W.W. Barnes. "Designing for Ultrahigh Availability: The UNIX RTR Operating System." *Computer* 17, no. 8 (August 1984): 31–39.

[**Wang, 1975a**] Wang, D.T. "An Algorithm for the Detection of Test Sets for Combinational Logic Networks." *IEEE Trans. Comp.* C-24, no. 7 (July 1975): 742–746.

[**Wang, 1975b**] Wang, D.T. "Properties of Faults and Criticalities of Values Under Tests for Combinational Networks." *IEEE Trans. Comp.* C-24, no. 7 (July 1975): 746–750.

[**Wang and Lovelace, 1977**] Wang, S.D., and K. Lovelace. "Improvement of Memory Reliability by Single-Bit-Error Correction." *Proceedings CompCon* (Spring 1977). Long Beach, CA: IEEE Press, 1977.

[**Warner, 1974**] Warner, R.M., Jr. "Applying a Composite Model to the IC Yield Problem." *IEEE J. Solid-State Circuits* SC-9, no. 6 (June 1974): 86–95.

[**Watanabe, 1986**] Watanabe, E. (trans.). "Survey on Computer Security." *Japan Info. Dev. Corp.*, March 1986.

[**Watson and Hastings, 1966**] Watson, R.W., and C.W. Hastings. "Self-Checked Computation Using Residue Arithmetic." *Proceedings of the IEEE* 54 (December 1966): 1920–1931.

[**Weissberger, 1980**] Weissberger, A.J. "An LSI Implementation of an Intelligent CRC Computer and Programmable Character Comparator." *IEEE Trans. Comp.* C-29 (February 1980): 116–124.

[**Weldon, 1966**] Weldon, E.J. "Difference-Set Cyclic Codes." *Bell Sys. Tech. J.* 45 (September 1966): 1045–1057.

[**Weldon, 1967**] Weldon, E.J. "A Note on Synchronization Recovery with Extended Cyclic Codes." In *Proc. First Annual Princeton Conference on Information Sciences and Systems*, Princeton, NJ, 1967, p. 233.

[**Weldon, 1968**] Weldon, E.J. "New Generalizations of the Reed-Muller Codes—Part II: Nonprimitive Codes." *IEEE Trans. Info. Theory* IT-14, no. 2 (March 1968): 199–205.

[**Weller, 1977**] Weller, C.W. "An Engineering Approach to IC Test System Maintenance." In *Dig. Papers, 1977 Semiconductor Test Symp.* (October 1977): 144–145.

[**Wensley, 1972**] Wensley, J.H. "SIFT Software Implemented Fault Tolerance." In *FJCC*, AFIPS Conf. Proc., vol. 41, pp. 243–253. Montvale, NJ: AFIPS Press, 1972.

[**Wensley et al., 1973**] Wensley, J.H., et al. *Architecture*. Menlo Park, CA: SRI International, 1973.

[**Wensley et al., 1976**] Wensley, J.H.; M.W. Green; K.N. Levitt; and R.E. Shostak. "The Design, Analysis, and Verification of the SIFT Fault Tolerant System." In *Proc. 2nd Int. Conf. Software Engineering*, IEEE Computer Society, Long Beach, CA, 1976, pp. 458–469.

[**Wensley et al., 1978**] Wensley, J.H.; L. Lamport; J. Goldberg; M.W. Green; K.N. Levitt; P.M. Melliar-Smith; R.E. Shostak; and C.B. Weinstock. "SIFT: Design and Analysis of a Fault-Tolerant Computer for Aircraft Control." *Proceedings of the IEEE* 66 (October 1978): 1240–1255.

[**White, 1978**] White, H. "Signature Analysis, Enhancing the Serviceability of Microprocessor-Based Industrial Products." In *Proc. 4th IECI Annual Conf.*, IEEE Pub. 78CH1312-8, March 1978, pp. 68–76.

[**White, 1987**] White, L. "Enhancements to TMDS." *Tandem Systems Review*, vol. 3.2, June 1987.

[**Wilcox and Mann, 1962**] Wilcox, R.H., and W.C. Mann. *Redundancy Techniques for Computer Systems*. Washington, DC: Spartan Books, 1962.

[**Wilken and Shen, 1987**] Wilken, K.D., and J.P. Shen. "Embedded Signature Monitoring: Analysis and Technique." In *Proc. 1987 International Test Conference*, IEEE, paper #14.1, pp. 324–333.

[**Wilken and Shen, 1988**] Wilken, K.D., and J.P. Shen. "Continuous Signature Monitoring: Efficient Concurrent-Detection of Processor Control Errors." In *Proc. 1988 International Test Conference*, IEEE, paper #43.1, pp. 914–925.

[Wilkov, 1972] Wilkov, R. "Analysis and Design of Reliable Computer Networks." *IEEE Trans. Communication* COM-20, no. 3 (1972): 660.

[Williams, 1978] Williams, T.W. "Utilization of a Structured Design for Reliability and Serviceability." In *Dig., Government Microcircuits Applications Conf.*, Monterey, CA, November 1978, pp. 441–444.

[Williams and Angell, 1973] Williams, M.J., and J.B. Angell. "Enhancing Testability of LSI Circuits via Test Points and Additional Logic." *IEEE Trans. Comp.* C-22 (January 1973): 46–60.

[Williams and Eichelberger, 1977] Williams, T.W., and E.E. Eichelberger. "Random Patterns Within a Structured Sequential Logic Design." In *Dig. Papers, 1977 Semiconductor Test Symp.*, IEEE Pub. 77CH1261–7C, October 1977, p. 27.

[Williams and Parker, 1979] Williams, T.W., and K.P. Parker. "Testing Logic Networks and Designing for Testability." *Computer* 12, no. 10 (October 1979): 9–21.

[Williams and Parker, 1983] Williams, T.W., and K.P. Parker. "Design for Testability—A Survey." *Proceedings IEEE*, vol. 71, no. 1 (January 1983): 98–112.

[Wolf, 1969] Wolf, J.K. "Adding Two Information Symbols to Certain Non-binary BCH Codes and Some Applications." *Bell Sys. Tech. J.* 48 (1969): 2405–2424.

[E.W. Wolf, 1973] Wolf, E.W. "An Advanced Computer Communication Network." In *AIAA Computer Network Systems Conf. Record*, 1973.

[J.K. Wolf, 1973] Wolf, J.K. "A Survey of Coding Theory: 1967–1972." *IEEE Trans. Info. Theory* IT-19, no. 4 (July 1973): 381–389.

[Wolverton and Shick, 1974] Wolverton, R.W., and G.J. Shick. "Assessment of Software Reliability." TRW-SS-73-04. Los Angeles, CA: 1974.

[Wozencraft, 1957] Wozencraft, J.M. "Sequential Decoding for Reliable Communicating." Research Laboratory for Electronics, MIT TR325. Boston, MA: 1957.

[Wulf and Bell, 1972] Wulf, W.A., and C.G. Bell. "C.mmp—A Multi-Mini-Processor." In *AFIPS Conf. Proc.*, vol. 41. Montvale, NJ: AFIPS Press, 1972, pp. 765–777.

[Wyle and Burnett, 1967] Wyle, H., and G.J. Burnett. "Some Relationships Between Failure Detection Probability and Computer System Reliability. In *FJCC, AFIPS Conf. Proc.*, vol. 31. Montvale, NJ: Academic Press, 1967, pp. 745–756.

[Wyner and Ash, 1963] Wyner, A.D., and R.B. Ash. "Analysis of Recurrent Codes." *IEEE Trans. Info. Theory* IT-11, no. 3 (July 1963): 148–156.

[Yakowitz, 1977] Yakowitz, S.J. *Computational Probability and Simulation*. Reading, MA: Addison-Wesley, 1977.

[Yamato and Tama, 1978] Yamato, J.T., and T.K. Tama. "Error Correcting and Controlling System." U.S. Patent No. 4,107,652, August 15, 1978.

[Yang et al., 1985] Yang, X.Z.; G. York; W.P. Birmingham; and D.P. Siewiorek. "Fault Recovery of Triplicated Software on the Intel iAPX 432." In *Proc. 5th International Conference on Distributed Computing Systems* (May 1985): 438–443.

[Yau and Chen, 1980] Yau, S.S., and F.C. Chen. "An Approach to Concurrent Control Flow Checking." *IEEE Trans. Soft. Eng.* SE-6(2) (March 1980): 126–137.

[Yau and Yang, 1975] Yau, S.S., and S.C. Yang. "Multiple Fault Detection for Combinational Logic Circuits." *IEEE Trans. Comp.* C-24, no. 5 (May 1975): 233–242.

[York, Siewiorek, and Segall, 1983] York, Gary; D.P. Siewiorek; and Z. Segall. "Asynchronous Software Voting in NMR Computer Structures." *IEEE Third Symposium on Reliability in Distributed Software and Database Systems*, Clearwater Beach, FL, October, 1983.

[York, Siewiorek, and Zhu, 1985] York, Gary; D.P. Siewiorek; and Y.X. Zhu. "Compensating Faults in Triple Modular Redundancy." *15th Fault-Tolerant Computing Symposium*, Ann Arbor, MI, June 1985.

[Yount, 1984] Yount, L.J. "Architectural Solutions to Safety Problems of Digital Flight-Critical Systems for Commercial Transports." In *Proc. AIAA/IEEE Digital Avionics Systems Conference and Technical Display*, December 1984.

[Yourdon, 1972a] Yourdon, E. "Reliability Measurements for Third Generation Systems." In *Proceedings of the Annual Reliability and Maintainability Symposium*, IEEE Computer Society, 1972, pp. 174–182.

[Yourdan, 1972b] Yourdan, E. *Design of On-Line Computing Systems*. Englewood Cliffs, NJ: Prentice-Hall, 1972.

CREDITS (continued from copyright page)

The Galileo Case—pp. 679–690; Figures 9–4, 9–5, 9–6; Tables 9–4, 9–5: Robert W. Kocsis, *Galileo Orbiter Fault Protection System*, Jet Propulsion Laboratory, California Institute of Technology, under contract with National Aeronautics and Space Administration.

The C.vmp Case—pp. 694–709; Figures 10–1 through 10–8; Tables 10–1 through 10–5: D.P. Siewiorek, V. Kini, H. Mashburn, S. McConnel, and M. Tsao, "A Case Study of C.mmp, Cm*, and C.vmp: Part I—Experiences with Fault Tolerance in Multiprocessor Systems." In *Proceedings of the IEEE*, Vol. 66, No. 10, October 1978, pp. 1178–1199. Copyright © 1978 IEEE. Reprinted by permission.

The SIFT Case—pp. 710–735; Figures 10–9 through 10–16; Tables 10–6, 10–7, 10–8: J.H. Wensley, L. Lamport, J. Goldberg et al., "SIFT: Design and Analysis of a Fault-Tolerant Computer for Aircraft Control." In *Proceedings of the IEEE*, Vol. 66, No. 10, October 1978, pp. 1240–1255. Copyright © 1978 IEEE. Reprinted by permission.

The VAXft 310 Case—pp. 745–767; Figures 11–4 through 11–13; Tables 11–1, 11–2: W. Bruckert and T. Bissett, "The VAXft 310 Case: A Fault-Tolerant System by Digital Equipment Corporation," Digital Equipment Corporation, Marlboro, MA. Courtesy of Digital Equipment Corporation.

Appendix A: C.L. Chen and M.Y. Hsiao, "Error-Correcting Codes for Semiconductor Memory Applications: A State-of-the-Art Review," *IBM Journal of Research and Development*, Vol. 28, No. 2. Copyright 1984 by International Business Machines Corporation. Reprinted by permission.

Appendix B: Algirdas Avizienis, "Arithmetic Error Codes: Cost and Effectiveness Studies for Application in Digital System Design," *IEEE Transactions on Computers*, Vol. C-20, No. 11, pp. 1322–1331. Copyright © 1977 IEEE. Reprinted by permission.

Appendix C: Thomas W. Williams and Kenneth P. Parker, "Design for Testability—A Survey," *Proceedings IEEE*, Vol. 71, No. 1, pp. 98–112, January 1983. Copyright © 1983 IEEE. Reprinted by permission.

Appendix D: U.S. Department of Defense. From U.S. Department of Defense, *Military Standardization Handbook: Reliability Prediction of Electronic Equipment*, MLK-HDBK-271B, Washington, DC, 1976.

Appendix E: Jeffrey P. Hansen, *Trend Analysis and Modeling of Uni/Multi-Processor Event Logs*, Master's thesis, Department of Electrical and Computer Engineering, Carnegie-Mellon University, Pittsburgh, PA, 1988. (Previously unpublished work.)

INDEX